श्रीविष्णुमहापुराणम्

THE VIṢṆU MAHĀPURĀṆAM

English Translation by
MANMATHA NATH DUTT
M.A., M.R.A.S.

Introduction & Edited by
DR. PUSHPENDRA KUMAR

BOOK EASTERN EBL LINKERS

EASTERN BOOK LINKERS
DELHI

Publishers :
EASTERN BOOK LINKERS

H. O. : 5825, New Chandrawal,
Jawahar Nagar, Delhi-110007
Ph. : 23850287, 9811232913

Show Room : 4806/24, Bharat Ram Road,
Daryaganj, New Delhi-110002
Ph. : 23285413

e-mail : eblindology@gmail.com
eblinfo76@gmail.com
Website : www.eblindology.com

Second Edition : 2018

Price : ₹ 1000

ISBN : 978-81-7854-070-2

VIṢṆU MAHĀPURĀṆAṂ
By **Manmatha Nath Dutt** *Ed. by* **Dr. Pushpendra Kumar**

Printed at : **R.K. Print Service, Delhi**

INTRODUCTION

The study of Viṣṇu Purāṇa, one of the oldest Purāṇa proves that the fact is that each Mahā Purāṇa has preferences, but no exclusions, in regard to the gods. Whether we call a Purāṇa a Śaiva Purāṇa or a Vaiṣṇava Purāṇa, we find references to the *līlās* (exploits) of various gods in each of them. For the purpose of intensifying devotion to one god, it is a denial of godhood to the other gods. In the *Brahma Purāṇa*, Viṣṇu teaches Mārkaṇḍeya that he is identical with Śiva. The *Padma Purāṇa* says in express terms : 'Brahmā, Viṣṇu, and Maheśvara, though three in from, are one entity. There is no difference among the three except that of attributes. The *Vāyu Purāṇa* says that he who affirms superiority and inferiority among the gods is a ignorant fellow and that he who realizes their oneness is a man of true knowledge. The story of Atri's penance as described in the *Bhāgavata* (IV.1. 17-29) clearly proves the same truth... We find it stated in the *Viṣṇu Purāṇa* that 'The Bhagavān Viṣṇu, though one, assumes the three forms of Hiraṇyagarbha (Brahmā), Hari (Viṣṇu), and Śaṅkara (Śiva) for creation, preservation, and destruction of introduction. The Viṣṇu Purāṇas are very important Purāṇas for tracing the social development of the Ancient Hindus and given us pictures of the Real and ideal Brāhmanical society in different ages, but they do not help us in any way in understanding how far the Brāhmanical ideas were followed in practice, or how the people at large led their life. It is these Mahā Purāṇas which can be our main guides in this direction, only if we use them with proper discrimination and judgement. It should be mentioned here that the Mahā Purāṇas are not works of social history, but references to social conditions in them are often incidental and sometimes international. The Purāṇas make it clear to us that Hindu society in ancient India, unlike that of the present time, was a living one with great vital force, which could mould itself according to circumstances and absorb easily and without much ado. Not only the numerous native tribes scattered all over the country, but also hordes of castless foreigners who poured into this land during the early centuries of the Christian era.

Among other subjects of interest dealt with in the present Mahā Purāṇas is geography, which came to be introduced from early times in connection with re-creation; and many of the extant Mahā Purāṇas contain a few chapters each on this topic. According to Purāṇic tradition, the earth consisted of seven *dvīpas* or continents, namely, Jambū-dvīpa, Plakṣa-dvīpa, Sālmali-dvīpa, and Puskara-dvīpa, krauñca-dvīpa, Śāka-dvīpa, and Puṣkara-dvīpa, each of which was divided into a number of *varṣas* or subcontinents. These *dvīpas* were surrounded by seven oceans containing water having the taste respectively of salt, sugarcane-juice, wine, clarified butter, curd, milk, and good drinking water. The Jambū-dvīpa, which occupied the central position, had in its middle a golden mountain called Meru, from which a number of other mountains including the Himālaya radiated in different directions like the petals of a lotus. This *dvīpa* was divided into nine *varṣas* or subcontinents, one of which was called Bhārata-varṣa (India). The Mahā Purāṇas supply information about all the seven *dvīpas* about their measurements, their mountains and rivers, their residents, their presiding deities, the longevity and general standard of morality of the people, and other details. They give special attention to the description of Jambū-dvīpa and more particular of Bhārata-varṣa, which in early times occupied a much bigger area than at present, and which has been praised as the *karma-bhūmi* (place for work) for those who aspire after-life heaven or final liberation. Although the chapters on geography still contain, in spite of later modifications, much valuable information about the topography of the ancient world, especially of India, it is rather disappointing to find that the Purāṇic geographical tradition also, like the dynastic accounts, has been influenced considerably by mythological explanations.

The encyclopaedic character of the present Mahā Purāṇas is not universal, but is peculiar to only three of them, namely the *Matsya, Agni,* and *Garuḍa,* which, besides dealing with the usual Purāṇa topics, contain chapters on astronomy, astrology, superstitions, omens and portents, medical science, treatment of children suffering under the influence of unfavourable planets, treatment of cows, horses and elephants, knowledge of snakes, treatment of snake-bite, knowledge of precious stones, coronation and duties of kings, politics, science of war, archery, use of other arms, agriculture, gardening, metrics, grammar, lexicography, dramaturgy, poetics, music, dancing architecture, construction of images of deities, and so on. In dealing with the topics mentioned above, these Purāṇas sometimes give summaries of ancient Sanskrit works, such as the *Rāmāyaṇa, Mahābhārata, Harivaṁśa,* etc., and often plagiarize verses, or even entire chapters from other standard works, some of which have already been mentioned in connection with analysing the contents of the *Agni* and the *Garuḍa Purāṇa*. The chapters on omens and portents of the *Matsya Purāṇa* must have been based on an ancient work ascribed to Vṛddha-Garga. Thus, by turning themselves into something like encyclopaedias, the above three Mahā Purāṇas have preserved summaries and fragments of ancient works, some of which have been lost for ever.

For this new character the *Matsya Purāṇa* is undoubtedly indebted to the *Viṣṇu-dharmottara,* which was written either in southern Kashmir or in the northern most part of the Punjab sometime during the fifth century A.D., and from which the *Matsya Purāṇa* might have taken a large number of chapters, including those dealing with some of the topics mentioned above. The *Agni Purāṇa,* which as F.E. Pargiter says, followed the Matsya Purāṇa tradition as regards the Aikṣvāku genealogy, must have imitated the latter work in its new character more successfully; and the *Garuḍa Purāṇa* was clearly modelled on the *Agni.* It is not known what led the *Viṣṇu-dharmottara* to appear in such a new character. It may be that from the fourth century A.D. the Hindus began to feel keenly the necessity not only of popularizing the study of the different branches of Sanskrit learning as against the literary activities of the Buddhists, Jains and others, but also of increasing the importance of the Purāṇas as repositories of knowledge so that these might find favour with highly educated people also.

The Mahā Purāṇas as religious works have been respectfully studied for centuries, and are still read, by the people of this country, because these works have shown them the easiest way of attaining peace and perfection in life and have put forth, often in the forms of myths and stories, easy solutions of those difficult problems with, which one is sure to be confronted in one's religious and social life. As a matter of fact, the Purāṇas have rendered the greatest service in effecting the racial and religious unification of the diverse people of India. They have treated every religious faith of the soil, unless it was dogmatically atheistic, with respect and with a synthetic attitude, and accorded to it a position in the Purāṇic pantheism by explaining its deity and its principles through a reconciliation of the teachings of Sāṁkhya and Vedānta. It is the Purāṇas which have brought about unity in diversity, and taught religious toleration to the followers of different faiths by making them realize that God is one, though called by different names. It is mainly through these works that Vedic ideas and ideals of religion and society have survived up to the present day and got wide circulation among the people of India and outside. The Purāṇas are, therefore, perfectly justified when they say :

Yo vidyāccaturo vedān sāṅgopaniṣado dvijaḥ /
Na cet purāṇaṁ saṁvidyān naiva sa syād vicakṣaṇaḥ //
Itihāsa-purāṇābhyāṁ vedaṁ samupabṛṁhayet /
Bibhety alpa-śrutād vedo māṁ ayaṁ prahariṣyati //

That learned (Brāhmaṇa), who knows the four Vedas with the Aṅgas (supplementary sciences) and the Upaniṣads, should not be (regarded as) proficient unless he thoroughly knows the Purāṇa literature. He should reinforce the Vedas with the Itihāsa and the Purāṇa. The Vedas are afraid of him who is deficient in traditional knowledge (thinking) He will hurt me.

The harmony which the Purāṇas brought about in the doctrines of 'knowledge', 'action'; and 'devotion'; and in the Vedic and non-Vedic views of life and conduct, exerted its influence in all strata of Hindu society, with the result that the life of the average Hindu of the present day presents a texture into which various ideas and practices of different times and regions have been interwoven with an unparalleled symmetry. In the eyes of a non-Hindu, the Purāṇic culture and religion appear as a bundle of contradictions. Yet a Hindu finds nothing difficult or inconsistent in his ideas and practices, and leads his life with perfect ease and harmony. He is rarely found to be absolutely foreign to the truths of life and conduct his ancestors discovered for him. Even an illiterate Hindu living far away from the seats of learning, is not totally ignorant of the principles and philosophical truths taught in the Purāṇas; and as a result he has a very broad view of life and a deep sense of tolerance and accommodation, which can rarely be expected elsewhere of a person like him. This is so only because of the fact that the epics and the Purāṇas, have played a very important part in the life of the Hindus for more than two thousand years. They have brought home to the common man the wisdom of the saints of the highest order without creating any discord. The authors of these works took every individual into consideration and made such prescriptions as would benefit him in his social and religious life. In giving recognition to a man's personal worth, they slackened the rigours of the caste-system and declared, 'Being remembered, or talked of, or seen, or touched, a devotee of the Lord, even if he be a Caṇḍāla, purifies (the people) easily. They allowed greater freedom to women and śūdras in social and religious matters, with the result that these neglected members of Hindu society could have their own religious life and worship their deities themselves. The religion and philosophy professed by the Purāṇas had such a great appeal that even scholars, philosophers, or religious reformers, like Vijñāna Bhikṣu, Rāmānuja, Mādhva, Vallabha, and Jīva Gosvāmin, to mention only a few, very frequently drew upon the Purāṇas in their own works in support of their philosophical views; and this utilization led to the greater popularity of these works with all grades of Hindu population.

Sectarian excesses are sometimes found in the extant Mahā Purāṇas, but these are due to the want of proper understanding of the idea of absolute or unswerving devotion (*aikāntikī bhakti*), on which the Purāṇic religion is principally based; and it is owing to this idea that Brahmā, Viṣṇu, Śiva, and other deities, have been praised individually as the highest one in some Purāṇa or other.

Most of the present Purāṇas refer to the five characteristics which are called Pañca-lakṣaṇa in the Amarakośa. According to the definition given in the above mentioned source a Purāṇa must deal with five topics viz., Sarga (Creation), Pratisarga (recreation), Vaṁśa (Genealogies of gods and sages). Manvantarāni the Manu-period of time, i.e. great periods, each of which have a Manu as ancestor of the human race and vaṁśanucarita the history of the dynasties. But none of these Purāṇas confirm to this definition. The Purāṇas like Vāyu, Viṣṇu, Matsya and Brahmāṇḍa keep close to the Pañca-Lakṣaṇa ideal but are not in complete agreement with it. This definition does not take into account the sectarian matter which is available in the Purāṇas. This colouring of the Purāṇas took place at a later period.

The Purāṇas give great importance to matters religious and social. In these Purāṇas also, in which the five topics have been dealt with there are to be found chapters on social customs and glories of gods. Thus, the present Purāṇas have practically turned into Smṛti codes. This new form of the Purāṇas does not seem to have attained before the beginning of the Christian era. Even as early as six Century A.D. the Purāṇas began to incorporate matters on Hindu rites and customs. Medhātithi quotes in his Bhāṣya on the Manu Smṛti a number of verses from the Purāṇas. Though the majority of these verses are concerned with creation philosophy etc. a few of them relate definitely to Smṛti matters. Thus Purāṇas gradually modified their original character and turned into important codes of Hindu rites and customs by including chapters on Varṇāśrama-dharma, Ācāra, Śrāddha, Prāyaścitta, Dāna, Pūja, Vrata, Tīrtha, Pratiṣṭhā, Dīkṣā, Utssarga etc.

With a view to increase the importance of the Purāṇas in the changed social environments the re-editing could be done in three ways : viz....... (1) by adding fresh chapters to the already existing ones (2); by substituting the latter by the former and (3) by writing new works bearing old titles. All these processes being equally practised with respect to Purāṇas, some retained their earlier materials, some lost many of the earlier chapter which were replaced by others of later times, and some became totally new works. But they had a common feature in all of them came to have units belonging to different ages. It should be mentioned here that the fresh additions to the Purāṇas were not always fresh composition, but chapters and verses were often transferred from one Purāṇa to another or from the Smṛti and other works to the Purāṇas, obviously to enrich the latter. According to Ballālasena, the Linga Purāṇa took its chapter on the big donations (Mahādāna) from Matsya-Purāṇa.

In the final phase of the development of the Purāṇic literature sectarian matter came to be added to them and this was the chief distinguishing features in the case of the later ones among the eighteen Purāṇas as their names themselves suggest. Devotional and laudatory verses in praise of Śiva, Viṣṇu, Brahmā or some other deity of the Hindu pantheon constitute the kernal of sectarianism. A critical perusals of the sectarian matter as embodied in the extant Purāṇic literature clearly indicates that certain devotional writers being impelled by their love and devotion for their deity, wrote certain chapters or complete texts in adoration of their particular deity and conveniently incorporated them into the various Purāṇas. The chapters on geography, heaven and hell, various ill-omens, astronomy, astrology, music, architecture, poetics, had been incorporated in the Purāṇas.

References to the Purāṇas occur in the Milindapañho (earlier than 300 A.D.) Bühler collects many early quotation from and references to the Purāṇas and points out that the account of the future kings in the Vāyu-Purāṇa, Viṣṇu-Purāṇa, Matsya and Brahmāṇḍa-Purāṇa seems to stop with the imperial Guptas and their contemporaries. Thus the Purāṇas, at least the important ones among them, may have been finalised during the Gupta period. As for the date of the Purāṇas, Pargiter takes into account the historical data available in the Matsya, Vāyu, Brahmāṇḍa, Viṣṇu and Bhāgavata and thinks that the first compilation of the historical matter may have been made in the reign of the Andhra King Yajñaśri about the end of the 2nd C.A.D. that the first certain addition was traditions. He even charges the Brāhmaṇas for suppression of facts, regards their literature utterly unreliable and thinks that the Kṣatriya tradition embodied in the epics and the Purāṇas are very important for the reconstruction of the ancient India; for according to him, they contain genuine gems of old historical matter. Pargiter has misunderstood the very trend of ancient traditions. The times when these traditions were taking form, had not then witnessed the watertight compartments of Brāhmaṇas and the Kṣatriyas as was the case subsequently. At that period the institution of the four social order was not evolved. The process of evolution had merely started. As to the date of the Purāṇas it is very difficult to came to any definite conclusion. The earlier scholars stressing the sectarian and religions matter in the Purāṇas assign a modern date to them.

Wilson realised the difficulty of solving the problem of the date of the Purāṇas and thinks that they are works of different ages compiled under different circumstances, the precise nature of which we can but imperfectly conjecture from internal evidence and from what we know of history of religious opinion in India. He takes into account the religious matter in the Purāṇas smacking of the present popular form of Hinduism which in his opinion, took shape not earlier than 8th or 9th C.A.D., the probable date of Śaṅkarācārya and were perhaps finally established during the period when Rāmānuja (12 C.A.D), Madhvācārya (13th made in the original Bhaviṣya-Purāṇa about A.D. 260, soon after which it was incorporated in the Matsya-Purāṇa. This account was extended to the rise of the Gupta kingdom before the year 335 A.D. which augumented compilation is what the Vāyu and Brahmāṇḍa contain and the Viṣṇu and the Bhāgavata have condensed. According to Smith the Purāṇas in some shape were already authoritative in the 4th C.B.C. on the basis of a reference to Purāṇa in Kauṭilya's Arthaśāstra which directs the king to spend his afternoon in the study of Itihāsa comprising Purāṇa Itivṛtta etc.

The *Viṣṇu Purāṇa* was narrated by Parāśara to his pupil Maitreya. It is divided into six parts, each of which is subdivided into many chapters. The first, part gives an account of creation, which is attributed to Puruṣa and Prakṛti. Viṣṇu, who is Paramātman, described to create the universe so that the souls might perform their *karma* (work) and attain *mokṣa* (salvation) by means of God-realization. Creation is due to His mercy (*kṛpā*) and is His sport (*līlā*). Then follow accounts of the *avatāra* (incarnation) of Lord Viṣṇu as *varāha* (boar), of the *Svāyambhava-manvantara*, of the Prajāpatis (lords of creation), of the churning of the ocean which yielded nectar (*amṛta*). The life of Dhruva who, by his devotion of Viṣṇu, was lifted to the supreme height of the *Dhruva-maṇḍala*. Dhruva's descendants are then described. The power of faith is Viṣṇu, finds its most magnificent expression in the legend of Prahlāda. The second part describes the earth and the nether worlds, and the courses five characteristics were thought to be meant for the Upapurāṇas. In the Mahāpurāṇas genealogies of the kings and sages were discussed often fabricated and sections on holy places etc., were composed by different times and freely attached to the Purāṇas as their integral parts so that the extents of these works varied.

A perusal of the extent Purāṇic literature shows the varied nature of its contents which may be analysed as (1) Gāthā and Ākhayāna or legendary accounts (2) Vaṁśa or genealogies of the Vedic seers and the kings (3) Mythology (4) Cosmogony (5) Dharmaśāstra matter (6) popular religious beliefs and (7) miscellaneous topics. In the Purāṇas are preserved old traditions in the form of songs e.g. the songs of Yayāti, Māndhātā, Arjuna etc. The Purāṇas describe several Ākhyānas and upākhyānas of which the more important ones are those pertaining to (1) Purūravas Urvaśī; (2) Yayāti-carita, (3) Bhārgava-Paraśurāma-carita, (5) Hariścandra, (6) Vena or Pṛthucarita, (7) Dhruva-Carita (8) Prahlāda-carita, (9) Savitrī-Satyāvān-Ākhyāna, (10) Rāma-Dāśarathī-carita, (11) Kṛṣṇa-carita. The genealogies occupy a prominent place in the extent Purāṇas. Nearly all of them give there lists. These genealogical accounts include the pedigrees of the important families of the Vedic seers and the royal dynasties of both solar and lunar.

The extent Purāṇas contain a good number of mythological stories about gods, goddess and demons which represent various chronological and cultural strata. The stories of Devāsura saṅgrāma, Manu and Ilā Dakṣa-Prajāpati and his daughter, Śiva and Brahmā are important for tracing the culture evolution of the Āryans from the earliest times. The roots of most of these accounts may well be traced to earliest literature, the Brāhmaṇas and the Vedas. The mythology of the Purāṇas revolves more or less round the three important gods of Āryan family, Viṣṇu, Śiva and Śakti.

All possible material available in the domain of philosophy, mythology, superstition etc. was freely utilized in the cosmological accounts of the Purāṇas. These accounts give a very minute detail about creation. The cosmological ideas as adopted in the Purāṇas badly lack a systematic presentation. Mythology is mixed up with cosmogony.

A study of the references to Purāṇas in the Sūtra literature shows that by the 4th Century B.C. they had ceased to be merely of historical and mythological interest, they had also attained the position more or less of a social code. They had more or less, become as authoritative as a treatises on Dharmaśāstras. A perusal of the extant Purāṇas shows, that they contain so much matter which may easily be transferred to the Dharmaśāstra literature. The chapters in the present Purāṇas, dealing with Varṇāśrama-dharma. Śrāddha, Kalpa, Rājadharma and similar other topics clearly indicate that with the growth in popularity of Purāṇic literature, matter from the existent Dharmaśāstra literature came to be embodied in the Purāṇas. The writer on Dharmaśūtras literature like Aparārka, Ballālasena, Hemādri etc., regard the Purāṇas as sources of Dharma and do not fail to quote from the Bhaviṣya-Purāṇa as glosses on Manu. The third part speaks of the Manus, the Indras, the gods, the sages and the Vyāsas (compilers). The fourth one deals with the genealogies of the king of the solar and the lunar dynasty, and brings them up to the kaliyuga, among whom are included the Magadha and Andhra kings and even later dynasties. The fifth part describes the life of Kṛṣṇa. The last part is philosophical and teaches how devotion of Lord Viṣṇu is the best means to the attainment of salvation.

Consequently, the extant Purāṇas in their present forms have to be used with the greatest caution for any historical purpose. Another difficulty which confronts every reader of the Purāṇas is the want of critical editions of the these works. Not even the *Vāyu Purāṇa,* which is the most important of all the Purāṇic works, for its valuable the manuscripts of different provinces of India. It is only the intensive and comparative study of the Purāṇas based on highly critical editions which can help us to some extent in reconstructing the political history of pre-Buddhist India. But unfortunately most of the comparatively early Purāṇic works, or portions thereof, which were replaced by others of more recent dates, have been lost for ever.

The safest sources for the ancient legends of the Hindus, after the Vedas, are no doubt the two great poems, the Rāmāyaṇa and Mahābhārata. The first offers only few, but they are of a primitive character. The Mahābhārata is more fertile in fiction, but it is more miscellaneous, and much that it contains is of equivocal authenticity, and uncertain date. Still it affords many materials that are genuine, and it is evidently the great fountain from which most, if not all, of the Purāṇas have drawn; as it intimates itself, when it declares that there is no legend current in the world which has not its origin in the Mahābhārata.

A work of some extent professing to be part of the Mahābhārata may more accurately be tanked with the Paurāṇic compilations of least authenticity, and latest origin. The Harivaṁśa is chiefly occupied with the adventures of Kṛṣṇa, but, as introductory to his era, it records particulars of the creations of the world, and of the patriarchal and regal dynasties. This is done with much carelessness and inaccuracy of compilation, as I have had occasion frequently to notice in the following pages.

A comparison of the subjects of the following pages with those of the other Purāṇas will sufficiently show that of the whole series the Viṣṇu Purāṇa most closely conforms to the definition of a Pañca-lakṣaṇa Purāṇa, or one which treats of five specified topics. It comprehends them all; and although it has infused a portion of extraneous and sectorial matter, it has done so with sobriety and with judgment, and has not suffered the fervour of its religious zeal to transport it into very wide deviations from the prescribed path. The legendary tales which it has inserted are few, and are conveniently arranged, so that they do not distinct the attention of the compiler from objects of more permanent interest and importance.

The first book of the six, into which the work is divided, is occupied chiefly with the details of creation, primary (Sarga) and secondary (Pratisarga); the first explaining how the universe proceeds from Prakṛti, or eternal crude matter, the second, in what manner the forms of things are developed from the elementary substances previously evolved, or how they reappear after their temporary of the first occurs only at the end of the life of Brahmā, when not only all the gods and all other forms are annihilated, but the elements are again merged into primary substance, besides which one only spiritual being exists : the latter takes place at the end of every Kalpa, or a day of Brahmā, and affects only the forms of inferior creatures, and lower worlds, leaving the substance of the universe entire, and sages and gods unharmed. The explanation of these events involves a description of the periods of time upon which they depend, and which are accordingly detailed. Their character has been a source of very unnecessary perplexity to European writers, as they belong to a scheme of chronology wholly mythological, having no reference to any real or supposed history of the Hindus, but applicable, according to their system, to the infinite and eternal revolutions of the universe. In these notions, and in that of the co-eternity of spirit and matter, the theogony and cosmogony of the Purāṇas, as they appear in the Viṣṇu Purāṇa, belong to and illustrate systems of high antiquity, of which we have only fragmentary traces in the records of other nations.

The course of the elemental creation is in the Viṣṇu, as in other Purāṇas, taken from the Sāṁkhya philosophy, but the agency that operates upon passive matter is exhibited, in consequence of a partial adoption of the illusory theory of the Vedānta philosophy, and the prevalence of the Paurāṇic doctrine of Pantheism. However incompatible with the independent existence of Pradhāna or crude matter, and however incongruous with the separate condition of pure spirit or Puruṣa, it is declared repeatedly that Viṣṇu, as one with the supreme being, is note only spirit, but crude matter; and not only the latter, but all visible substance, and Time. He is Puruṣa, 'spirit'; Pradhāna, 'crude matter;' Vyakta, visible form; and Kāla, time. This cannot but be regarded as a departure from the primitive dogmas of the Hindus, in which the distinctness of the Deity and his works were enunciated; was explained away by the personification of attributes in action, which afterwards came to be considered as real divinities, Brahmā, Viṣṇu, and Śiva, charged severally for a given reason with the creation, preservation, and temporary annihilation of material forms. These divinities are in the following pages, consistently with the tendency of a Vaiṣṇava work, declared to be no other than Viṣṇu. In Śaiva Purāṇas they are in like manner identified with Śiva. The Purāṇas thus displaying and explaining the seeming incompatibility, of which there are traces in other ancient mythologies, between three distinct hypostasis of one superior deity, and the identification of one of other of those hypostasis with their common and separate original.

After the world has been fitted for the reception of living creatures, it is peopled by the will-engendered sons of Brahmā, the Prajāpatis or patriarchs, and their posterity. It would seem as if a primitive tradition of the descent of mankind from seven holy personages had at first prevailed, but that in the course of time it had been expanded into complicated, and not always consistent, amplification. How could these Ṛsis or patriarchs have posterity? It was necessary to provide them with wives. In order to account for their existence, the Manu Svāyambhuva and his wife Śatarupā were added to the scheme, or Brahmā becomes twofold, male and female, and daughters are then begotten, who are married to the Prajāpatis. Upon this basis various legends of Brahmā's double nature, some no doubt as old as the Vedas, have been constructed : But although they may have been derived in some degree from the authentic tradition of the origin of mankind from a single pair, yet the circumstances intended to give more interest and precision, and conduced, in apparently later times, to a coarseness of realization which was neither the letter nor spirit of the original legend. Svāyambhuva, the son of the self-born or uncreated, and his wife Śatarupā, the hundred-formed or multiform, are themselves allegories; and their female descendants, who become the wives of the Ṛsis, are Faith, Devotion, Content, Intelligence, Tradition, and the like; whilst amongst their posterity we have the different phases of the moon, and the sacrificial fires. In another creation the chief source of creatures is the patriarch Dakṣa (ability), whose daughters, Virtues or Passions or Astronomical Phenomena, are the mothers of all existing things. These legends, perplexed as they appear to be, seem to admit of allowable solution, in the conjecture that the Prajāpatis and Ṛsis were real personages, the authors of the Hindu system of social, moral, and religious obligations, and the first observers of the heavens, and teachers of astronomical science.

The royal personages of the Svāyambhuva Manvantara are but few, but they are described in the outset as governing the earth in the dawn of society, and as introducing agriculture and civilisation. How much of their story rests upon a traditional remembrance of their actions, it would be useless to conjecture, although there is no extravagance in supposing that the legends relate to a period prior to the full establishment in India of the Brāhmanical institutions. The legends of Dhruva and Prahlāda, which are intermingled with these particulars, are in all probability ancient, but they are amplified, in a strain conformable to the Vaiṣṇava purport of this Purāṇa, by doctrines and prayers asserting the identity of Viṣṇu with the supreme. It is clear that the stories do not originate with this Purāṇa. In that of Prahlāda particularly, as hereafter pointed out, circumstances essential to the completeness of the story are only alluded to, not recounted; showing indisputably the writer's having availed himself of some prior authority for his narration.

The second book opens with a continuation of the kings of the first manvantara; amongst whom, Bharata is said to have given a name to India, called after him Bhāratavarṣa. This leads to a detail of the geographical system of the Purāṇas, with mount Meru, the seven circular continents, and their surrounding oceans, to the limits of the world; all of which are mythological fictions, in which there is little reason to imagine that any topographical truths are concealed. With regard to Bhārata, or India, the case is different : the mountains and rivers which are named are readily verifiable, and the cities and nations that are particularized may also in many instances be proved to have had a real existence. The list is not a very long one in the Viṣṇu Purāṇa, and is probably abridged from some more ample detail like that which the Mahābhārata affords, and which, in the hope of supplying information with respect to a subject yet imperfectly investigated, the ancient political condition of India, have been inserted and elucidated.

The description which this book also contains of the planetary and other spheres is equally mythological, although occasionally presenting practical details and notions in which there is an approach to accuracy. The concluding legend of Bharata–in his former life the king so named, but now a brāhman, who acquires true wisdom, and thereby attains liberation–is palpably an invention of the compiler, and is peculiar to the Purāṇa.

The arrangement of the Vedas and other writings considered sacred by the Hindus, being in fact the authorities of their religious rites and belief, which is described in the beginning of the third book, is of much importance to the history of Hindu literature, and of the Hindu religion. The sage Vyāsa is here represented, not as the author, but the arranger or compiler of the Vedas, the Itihāsas, and Purāṇas. His name denotes his character, meaning the arranger of distributor; and the recurrence of many Vyāsas, many individuals, who new modelled the Hindu scriptures, has nothing in it that is improbable except the fabulous intervals by which their labours are separated. The rearranging, the refashioning, of old materials, is nothing more than the progress of time would be likely to render necessary. The last compilation is that of Kṛṣṇa Dvaipāyana, assisted by Brahmans, who were already conversant with the subjects respectively assigned to them. They were the members of a school of thought supposed by the Hindus to have flourished in a period more remote, no doubt, than the truth, but not at all unlikely have been instituted at some time prior to the accounts of India which we owe to Greek writers, and in which we see enough of the system to justify our inferring that it was then entire. That there have been other Vyāsas and other schools since that date, that Brahmans unknown of name have remodelled some of the Hindu scriptures, and especially the Purāṇas, cannot reasonably be contested, after dispassionately weighing the strong internal evidence which all of them afford of the intermixture of unauthorized and comparatively modern ingredients. But the same internal testimony furnishes proof equally decisive of the anterior existence of ancient materials; and it is there fore as idle as it is irrational to dispute the antiquity or authenticity of the greater portion of the contents of the Purāṇas, in the face of abundant positive and circumstantial evidence of the legends which they narrate, and the integrity of the institutions which they describe, at least three centuries before the Christian era. But the origin and development of their doctrines, traditions, and institutions, were not the work of a day; and the testimony that establishes their existence three centuries before Christianity, carries it back to a much more remote antiquity, to an antiquity that is probably not surpassed by any of the prevailing fictions, institutions, or belief, of the ancient world.

The remainder of the third book describes the leading institutions of the Hindus, the duties of castes, the obligations of different stages of life, and the celebration of osequial rites, in a short but primitive strain, and in harmony with the laws of Manu. It is a distinguishing feature of the Viṣṇu Purāṇa, and it is characteristic of its being the work of an earlier period than most of the Purāṇas, that it enjoins no sectarial or other acts of devotion; no Vratas, occasional self-imposed observances; no holidays, no birthdays of Kṛṣṇa, no nights dedicated to Lakṣmī; no sacrifices nor modes of worship other than those conformable to the ritual of the Vedas. It contains no Māhātmyas, or golden legends, even of the temples in which Viṣṇu is adored.

The fourth book contains all that the Hindus have of their ancient history. It is a tolerably comprehensive list of dynasties and individuals; it is a barren record of events. It can scarcely be doubted, however, that much of it is a genuine chronicle of persons, if not of occurrences. That it is discredited by palpable absurdities in regard to the longevity of the princes of the earlier dynasties must be granted, and the particulars preserved of some of them are trivial and fabulous : still there is an inartifical simplicity and consistency in the succession of persons, and a possibility and probability in some of the transactions which give to these traditions the semblance of authenticity, and render it likely that they are not altogether without foundation. At any rate, in the absence of all other sources of information, the record, such as it is, deserves not to be altogether set aside. It is not essential to its credibility or its usefulness that any exact chronological adjustment of the different reigns should be attempted. Their distribution amongst the several Yugas, undertaken by Jones or his Pandits, finds no countenance from the original texts, farther than an incidental notice of the age in which a particular monarch ruled, or the general fact that the dynasties prior to Kṛṣṇa precede the time of the great war, and the beginning of the Kali age; both which events we are not obliged, with the Hindus, to place five thousand years ago. To that age the solar dynasty of princes offers ninety-three descents, the lunar but forty-five, though they both commence at the same time. Some names may have been added to the former list, some omitted in the latter; and it seems most likely, that, notwithstanding their synchronous beginning, the prince of the lunar race were subsequent to those of the solar dynasty. They avowedly branched off from the solar line; and the legend of Sudyumna, that explains the connection, has every appearance of having been contrived for the purpose of referring it to a period more remote than the truth. Deducting however from the larger number of princes a considerable proportion, there is nothing to shock probability in supposing that the Hindu dynasties and their ramifications were spread through an interval of about twelve centuries anterior to the war of the Mahābhārata, and conjecturing that event to have happened about fourteen centuries before Christianity, thus carrying the commencement of the regal dynasties of India to about two thousand six hundred years before that date. This may or may not be too remote; but it is sufficient, in a subject where precision is impossible, to be satisfied with the general impression, that in the dynasties of kings detailed in the Purāṇas we have a record which, although it cannot fail to have suffered detriment from age, and may have been injured by careless or injudicious compilation, preserves an account, not wholly undeserving of confidence, of the establishment and succession of regular monarchies amongst the Hindus, from as early an era, and for as continuous a duration, as any in the credible annals of mankind.

The circumstances that are told of the first princes have evident relation to the colonization of India, and the gradual extension of the authority of new races over an uninhabited or uncivilized region. It is commonly admitted that the Brahmanical religion and civilization were brought into India from without. Certainly, there are tribes on the borders, and in the heart of the country, who are still not Hindus; and passages in the Rāmāyaṇa and Mahābhārata and Manu, and the uniform traditions of the people themselves, point to a period when Bengal, Orissa, and the whole of Dekhin, were inhabited by degraded or outcaste, that is, by barbarous tribes. The traditions of the Purāṇas confirm these views, but they lead no assistance to the determination of the question whence the Hindus came; whether from a central Asiatic nation, as Jones supposed, or from the Causasian mountains, the plains of Babylonia, or the borders of the Caspian, as conjectured by Klaproth, Vans Kennedy, and Schlegel. The affinities of the Sanskrit language prove a common origin of the now widely scattered nations amongst whose dialects they are traceable, and render it unquestionable that they must all have spread abroad from some centrical spot in that part of the globe first inhabited by mankind, according to the inspired record. Whether any indication of such an event be discoverable in the Vedas, remains to be determined; but it would have been obviously incompatible with the Paurāṇic system to have referred the origin of Indian princes and principalities to other than native sources. We need not therefore expect from them any information as to the foreign derivation of the Hindus.

The earliest seat of the Hindus within the confines of Hindustān was undoubtedly the eastern confines of the Punjab. The holy land of Manu and the Purāṇas lies between the Dṛṣadvatī. According to some authorities, it was the abode of Vyāsa, the compiler of the Vedas and Purāṇas; and agreeably to another, when on once occasion the Vedas had fallen into disuse, and been forgotten, the Brahmans were again instructed in them the Sārasvata, the son of Sarasvatī. One of the most distinguished of the tribes of the Brahmans is known as the Sārasvata; and the same word is employed by Colebrooke to denote that modification of Sanskrit which is termed generally Prakrit, and which in this case he supposes to have been the language of the Sārasvata nation, which occupied the banks of the river Sarasvatī. The river itself receives its appellation from Satasvatī, the goddess of learning, under whose auspices the sacred literature of the Hindus assumed shape and authority. These indications render it certain, that whatever seeds were imported from without, it was in the country adjacent to the Sarasvatī river that they were first planted, and cultivated and reared in Hindustān.

The tract of land thus assigned for the first establishment of Hinduism in India is of very circumscribed extent, and could not have been the site of any numerous tribe or nation. The traditions that evidence the early settlement of the Hindus in this quarter, ascribe to the settlers more and religious, than of a secular character, and combine with the very narrow bound of the holy land to render it possible that the earliest emigrants were the members, not of a political, so much as of a religious community; that they were a colony of priests not in the restricted sense in which we use the term, but in that in which it still applies in India, to an Agrahāra, a village or hamlet of Brahmans, who, although married, and having families, and engaging in tillage, in domestic duties, and in the conduct of secular interests affecting the community, are still supposed to devote their principal attention to sacred study and religious offices. A society of this description, with its artificers and servants, and perhaps with a body of martial followers, might have found a home in the Brahmā-vartta of Manu, the land which thence was entitled the holy, or more literally the uncivilized, unlettered aborigines the rudiments of social organization, literature, and religion; partly, in all probability, brought along with them, and partly devised and fashioned by degrees for the growing necessities of new conditions of society. Those with whom this civilization commenced would have had ample inducements to prosecute their successful work, and in the course of time the improvement which germinated on the banks of the Sarasvatī was extended beyond the borders of the Yamunā and the Ganges.

We have no satisfactory intimation of the stages by which the political organization of the people of Upper India traversed the space between the Sarasvatī and the more easterly region, where it seems to have taken a concentrated form, and whence it diverged in various directions, throughout Hindustān. The Manu of the present period, Vaivasvata, the son of the sun, is regarded as the founder of Ayodhyā; and that city continued to be the capital of the most celebrated branch of his descendants, the posterity of Ikṣvāku. The Viṣnu Purāṇa evidently intends to describe the radiation of conquest or colonization from this spot, in the accounts it gives of the dispersion of Vaivasvata's posterity : and although it is difficult to understand what could have led early settlers in India to such a site, it is not inconveniently situated as a commanding position, whence emigrations might proceed to the east, the west, and the south. This seems to have happened : a branch from the house of Ikṣvāku spread into Tirhut, constituting the Maithilā kings; and the posterity of another of Vaivasvata's sons reigned at Vaiśālī in southern Tirhut.

The most adventurous emigrations, however, took place through the lunar dynasty, which, as observed above, originates from the solar, in fact but one race and source for the whole. Leaving out of consideration the legend of Sudyumna's double transformation, the first prince of Pratiṣṭhāna, a city south from Ayodhyā, was one of Vaivasvata's children, equally with Ikṣvāku. The sons of Purūravas, the second of this branch, extended, by themselves or their posterity, in every direction : to the east of Kāśī, Magadha, Banaras, and Bihar; southwards to the Vindhya hills, and across them to Vidarbha or Berar; westwards along the Narmadā to Kuśasthali or Dwārakā in Gujarat; and in a north-westerly direction to Mathurā and Hastināpura. These movements are very distinctly discoverable amidst the circumstances narrated in the fourth book of the Viṣṇu Purāṇa, and are precisely such as might be expected from a radiation of colonies from Ayodhyā. Intimations also occur of settlements in Baṅga, Kaliṅga, and the Dakkhin; But they are brief and indistinct, and have the appearance of additions subsequent to the comprehension of those countries within the pale of Hinduism.

Besides these traces of migration and settlement, several curious circumstances, not likely to be unauthorized inventions, are hinted in these historical traditions. The distinction of castes was not fully developed prior to the colonization. Of the sons of Vaivasvata, some, as kings, were Kṣatriyas; but one, founded a tribe of Brahmans, another became a Vaiśya, and a fourth a Śūdra. It is also said of other princes, that they established the four castes amongst their subjects. There are also various notices of Brāhmanical Gotras, or families, proceeding from Kṣatriya races : and there are several indications of severe struggles between the two ruling castes, not for temporal, but for spiritual dominion, the right to teach the Vedas. This seems to be the especial purport of the inveterate hostility that prevailed between the Brahman Vasiṣṭha and the Kṣatriya Viśvāmitra, who, as the Rāmāyaṇa relates, compelled the gods to make him a Brahman also, and whose posterity became very celebrated as the Kauśika Brahmans. Other legends, again, such as Dakṣa's sacrifice, denote sectarial strife; and the legend of Paraśurāma reveals a conflict even for temporal authority between the two ruling castes. More or less weight will be attached to these conjectures, according to the temperament of different inquirers; but, fully aware of the facility with which plausible deductions may cheat the fancy, and little disposed to relax all curb upon the imagination. It is difficult to regard these legends as wholly unsubstantial fictions, or devoid of all resemblance to the realities of the past.

The Viṣṇu Purāṇa, in common with those Purāṇas which contain similar lists, specifies kings and dynasties with greater precision, and offers political and chronological particulars, to which on the score of probability there is nothing to object. In truth their general accuracy has been incontrovertibly established. Inscriptions on columns of stone, on rocks, on coins, deciphered only of late years, through the extraordinary ingenuity and perseverance of James Prinsep, have verified the names of races, and titles of princes—the Gupta and Andhra Rājās, mentioned in the Purāṇas—and have placed beyond dispute the identity of Candragupta and Sandrocottus : thus giving us a fixed point from which to compute the date of other persons and events. Thus the Viṣṇu Purāṇa specifies the interval between Candragupta and the great war to be eleven hundred years; and the occurrence of the latter little more than fourteen centuries B.C., as shown in my observations on the passage," remarkably concurs with inferences of the like date from different premises. The historical notices that follow are considerably confused, but they probably afford an accurate picture of the political distractions of India at the time when they were written; and much of the perplexity arises from the corrupt state of the manuscripts, the obscure brevity of the record, and our total want of the means of collateral illustration.

The fifth book of the Viṣṇu Purāṇa is exclusively occupied with the life of Kṛṣṇa. This is one of the distinguishing characteristics of the Purāṇa, and is one argument against its antiquity. It is possible, though not yet proved, that Kṛṣṇa as an Avatāra of Viṣṇu, is mentioned in an indisputably genuine text of the Vedas. He is conspicuously prominent in the Mahābhārata, but very contradictory described there. The part that he usually performs is that of a mere mortal, although the passages are numerous that attach divinity to his person. There are, however, no descriptions in the Mahābhārata of his juvenile frolics, of his sports in Vṛndāvan, his pastimes with the cow-boys, or even his destruction of the Asuras sent to kill him. These stories have all a modern complexion : they do not harmonize with the tone of the ancient legends, which is generally grave, and sometimes majestic : they are the creations of purile taste, and sometimes majestic : they are the creations of a puerile taste, and grovelling imagination. These chapters of the Viṣṇu Purāṇa offer some difficulties as to their originality : they are the same as those on the same subject in the Brahma Purāṇa : they are not very dissimilar to those of the Bhāgavata.

The latter has some incidents which the Viṣṇu has not, and may therefore be thought to have improved upon the prior narrative of the latter. On the other hand, abridgment is equally a proof of posteriority as amplification. The simpler style of the Viṣṇu Purāṇa is however in favour of its priority; and the miscellaneous composition of the Brahma Purāṇa renders it likely to have borrowed these chapters from the Viṣṇu. The life of Kṛṣṇa in the Hari-vaṃśa and the Brahma-vaivartta are indisputably of later date.

The last book contains an account of the dissolution of the world, in both its major and minor cataclysms; and in the particulars of the end of all things by five and water, as well as in the principle of their perpetual renovation, presents a faithful exhibition of opinions that were general in the ancient world. The metaphysical annihilation of the universe, the release of the spirit from bodily existence, offers, as already remarked, other analogies to doctrines and practices taught by Pythagoras and Plato.

The Viṣṇu Purāṇa has kept very clear of particulars from which an approximation to its date may be conjectured. No place is described of which the sacredness has any known limit, nor any work cited of probable recent composition. The Vedas, the Purāṇas, other works forming the body of Sanskrit literature, are named; and so is the Mahābhārata. Both Bauddhas and Jains are adverted to. It was therefore written before the former had disappeared; but they existed in some parts of India as late as the twelfth century at least; and it is probable that the Purāṇa was compiled before that period. The Gupta kings reigned in the fourth and fifth century; the historical record of the Purāṇa which mentions them was therefore later : and there seems little doubt that the same alludes to the first incursions of the Muhammadans, which took place in the eighth century; which brings it still lower. In describing the latter dynasties, some, if not all, of which were no doubt contemporary, they are described as reigning altogether seven hundred and ninety-six years. Why this duration should have been chosen does not appear, unless, in conjunction with the number of years which are said to have elapsed between the great war and the last of the Andhra dynasty, which preceded these different races and which amounted to two thousand three hundred and fifty, the compiler was influenced by the actual date at which he wrote. The aggregate 94 Burnet has collected the opinions of the ancient world on this subject, tracing them, as he says, "to the earliest people, and the first appearances of wisdom, after the flood." The Hindu account explains what is imperfect of contradictory in ancient tradition, as handed down from other and less carefully perpetuated sources.

It is the boast of inductive philosophy, that it draws its conclusions from the careful observation and accumulation of facts; and it is equally the business of all philosophical research to determine its facts before it ventures upon speculation. This procedure has not been observed in the investigation of the mythology and traditions of the Hindus. Impatience to generalize has availed itself greedily of whatever promised to afford materials of generalization; and the most erroneous views have been confidently advocated, because the guides to which their authors trusted were ignorant or insufficient. The information gleaned by Jones was gathered in an early season of Sanskrit study, before the field was cultivated. The documents to which Wilford trusted proved to be in grate part fabrications, and where genuine, were mixed up with so much loose and unauthenticated matter, and so overwhelmed with extravagance of speculation, that his citations need to be carefully and skilfully sifted, before they can be serviceably employed. The descriptions of Ward are too deeply tinctured by his prejudices to be implicity confided in; and they are also derived in a great measure from the oral or written communications of Bengali paṇḍits, who are not in general very deeply real in the authorities of their mythology.

With the publication of this important Purāṇa alongwith English translation from a rare book by Manmatha Nath Dutta will help the scholars and the devotees as well. I am happy to present the Viṣṇu Purāṇa recomposed by Eastern Book Linkers in the hands of the scholars. I hope that this will encourage the Purāṇic studies in India and in the world.

Pushpendra Kumar

CONTENTS

अथ प्रथमोऽंशः

Part I

अथ द्वितीयोऽंशः

Part II

अथ तृतीयोऽंशः

Part III

अथ चतुर्थोऽंशः

Part IV

अथ पञ्चमोऽंशः

Part V

॥ अथ श्रीविष्णुमहापुराणम् प्रथमोंशः॥

THE VIṢṆUMAHĀPURĀṆAM, PART - I

श्रीमते रामानुजाय नमः

अथ प्रथमेंशेः प्रथमोऽध्यायः

Part I : Section 1

नारायणं नमस्कृत्य नरं चैव नरोत्तमम्।।
देवीं सरस्वतीं व्यासं ततो जयमुदीरयेत्।। १।।

श्रीसूत उवाच

।। ॐ पराशरं मुनिवरं कृतपौर्वाह्निकक्रियम्।।
मैत्रेयः परिपप्रच्छ प्रणिपत्याभिवाद्य च।। १।।
त्वत्तो हि वेदाध्ययनमधीतमखिलं गुरो।।
धर्मशास्त्राणि सर्वाणि तथाङ्गानि यथाक्रमम्।। २।।

Om![1] Salutation unto Vāsudeva![2] O Puṇḍarīkāṣ,[3] victory unto thee! I bow unto thee, O origin of the universe! O Hṛṣikeśa,[4] O great Puruṣa, O thou the first born! That Viṣṇu,[5] who is eternal, indecayable one, who is Brahmā, the Īśvara and the Puruṣa,—who causeth the creation, the sustentation and the dissolution (of the world) consequent on the qualities[6] being agitated,—and from whom hath sprung the cosmos with Pradhāna,[7] Buddhi, etc.;—may he confer on us excellent understanding wealth[8] and emancipation! Bowing down unto Viṣṇu, lord of the universe, and saluting Brahmā and the rest, and paying reverence unto my preceptor, I will rehearse the Purāṇa that is equal to the Vedas. Saluting and paying homage unto that best of ascetics, Parāśara—son unto Vasiṣṭha's son—versed in annals and the Purāṇas,[9] accomplished in the Vedas and the branches thereof, and learned in the mysteries of the scriptures,—who had finished his first daily devotions.—Maitreya asked him, saying,—"O preceptor, I have one by one

1. This mystic monosyllable plays a prominent part in Sanskrit Scriptural literature. Composed, according to some, of the letters *a*, *u*, and *ma*. Signifying Brahmā, Creator; Viṣṇu, preserver; and Śiva, destroyer;—it expresses the three in One; and is said to possess great power spiritually—T.
2. In this translation, such epithets as, although compounded of general terms, have through usage come to mean some particular individual, have been retained untranslated, their renderings being only appended in footnotes.—*Vāsudeva* is *Vasudeva's son* , an appellation of Kṛṣṇa; which again, although the name of the most celebrated incarnation of Viṣṇu, means—*dark-blue* or *brown*—T.
3. *Puṇḍarīka-akṣa*—having *eyes* resembling the *pale lotus*—T.
4. *Hṛṣika*—organ of sense, and *ica*—*lord*. Hṛṣikeśa—sovereign of the senses,—i.e. the cause of their action and abstention—T
5. Viṣṇu means *all-pervading*—T.
6. The three cardinal qualities—goodness, passion and darkness.—T.
7. Unformed Natures is designated by several epithets-Pradhāna, Prakṛti, Avyakta (unmanifested), etc.—T.
8. Wealth is of eight, *viz*., *aṇimā*, *laghimā*, *Prāpti*, *prākamya*, *mahimā*, *ichitva*, *vachitva*, and *kāmāvachāyitā*—Anima is the power of reducing one's self to the minutest proportions; *laghimā* is that of rendering one's self exceedingly light,—*prāpti* is the power of obtaining anything that is wished; *prakamya* is irresistibility of the Will; *ichitva* is supremacy; *vasitva* is the power of bringing all under sway; and *Kāmavosayita* is the power of supressing desire.—T.
9. A Purāṇa treats of these five subjects, *viz*., (i) the creation. (2) destruction and renovation of the world, (3) royal dynasties, (4) regins of the Manus, and (5) genealogies.—T.

studied near thee all the scriptures as well as the Vedas and their branches.

तवत्प्रसादान्मुनिश्रेष्ठ मामन्ये नाकृतश्रमम्।।
वक्ष्यन्ति सर्वशास्त्रेषु प्रायशो येपि विद्विषः।। ३।।
सोहमिच्छामि धर्मज्ञ श्रोतुं त्वत्तो यथा जगत्।।
बभूव भूयश्च यथा महाभाग भविष्यति।। ४।।
यन्मयं च जगद्ब्रह्मन्यतश्चैतच्चराचरम्।
लीनमासीद्यथा यत्रा लयमेष्यति यत्र च।। ५।।
यत्प्रमाणानि भूतानि देवादीनां च संभवम्।।
समुद्रपर्वतानां च संस्थानं च यथा भुवः।। ६।।
सूर्यादीनां च संस्थानं प्रमाणं मुनिसत्तम।।
देवादीनां तथा वंशान्मनून्मन्वन्तराणि च।। ७।।

It is owing to thy grace that, O foremost of ascetics, almost all of those that are even our enemies, confess that I have studied all the branches of knowledge. O thou congnisant of righteousness, I am desirous of hearing from thee how this universe came into being, and how, O virtuous one, it shall be in the future; in what, O Brāhmaṇa, the cosmos consists; wherefrom sprang this system of mobile and immobile objects; where it lay at first and where it shall dissolve itself; as to the objects that have manifested themselves; the genesis of the gods; the establishement of seas and mountains and the earth, and that of the sun, *etc.*; and the dimensions thereof; the genealogies of the deities,—all about the Manus, and the Manvantaras.[1]

कल्पान् कल्पविभागांश्च चातुर्युगविकल्पितान्।।
कल्पांतस्य स्वरूपं च युगधर्मांश्च कृत्स्नशः।। ८।।
देवर्षिपार्थिवानां च चरितं यन्महामुने।।
वेदशाखाप्रणयनं यथावद्व्यसकर्तृकम्।। ९।।
धर्मांश्च ब्राह्मणादीनां तथा चाश्रमवासिनाम्।।

And Kalpas and Vikalpas of Kalpas[2] composed of the fourfold division into Yugas; the character of the close of Kalpas; and the entire tendencies of the Yugas; and, O mighty ascetic, the history of Devarṣis[3] and monarchs; the proper division by Vyāsa of the Vedas into different parts; and the morality concerning Brāhmaṇas and others, as well as that of householders.

श्रोतुमिच्छाम्यहं सर्वं त्वत्तो वासिष्ठनन्दन।। १०।।
ब्रह्मन्प्रसादप्रवणं कुरुष्व मयि मानसम्।।
येनाहमेतज्जानीयां त्वत्प्रसादान्महामुने।। ११।।

O son of Vasiṣṭha, I wish to hear all this realted by thee. O Brāhmaṇa, incline thy mind favourably unto me, so that, O mighty anchoret, I may know all this through thy grace."

श्रीपराशर उवाच

साधु मैत्रेय धर्मज्ञ स्मारितोस्मि पुरातनम्।।
पितुः पिता मे भगवान् वसिष्ठो यदुवाच ह।। १२।।

Parāśara said :—Excellent well; O Maitreya, O thou that art conversant with righteousness. Thou bringest into my recollection what of old my grandsire, the reverend Vasiṣṭha, had said of old.

विश्वामित्रप्रयुक्तेन रक्षसा भक्षितः पुरा।।
श्रुतस्तातस्ततः क्रोधो मैत्रेयाभून्ममातुलः।। १३।।

When I heard that my sire had been devoured by the Rākṣasa sent by Viśvāmitra, I was wrought up with an exceeding rage.

ततोऽहं रक्षसां सत्रं विनाशाय समारभम्।
भस्मीभूताश्च शतशस्तस्मिन्सत्रे निशाचराः।। १४।।

Then I set about disturbing the sacrifice of the Rākṣas; and in that sacrifice reduced to ashes night-rangers by hundreds.

ततः संक्षीयमाणेषु तेषु रक्षस्वशेषतः।।
मामुवाच महाभागो वसिष्ठो मत्पितामहः।। १५।।
अलमत्यन्तकोपेन तात मन्युमिमं जहि।।
राक्षसा नापराध्यन्ति पितुस्ते विहितं हि तत्।। १६।।

On the Rakṣas under-going extermination, the eminently pious Vasiṣṭha, my grandfather, said unto me,—'Do not indulge in excessive wrath. O child, control this passion of thine. Albeit the Rākṣasas did thus unto thy sire, yet have they not trans-gressed.

1. The regins of Manus.
2. A *kalpa* is a day and night of Brahmā, consisting of 4,320,000,000 solar sydereal years, or years of mortals, emasuring the duration of the world.—T.
3. An order of saints.

मूढानामेव भवति क्रोधो ज्ञानवतां कुतः ।।
हन्यते तात कः केन यतः स्वकृतभुक्पुमान् ।। १७ ।।

सञ्चितस्यापि महता वत्स क्लेशेन मानवैः ।।
यशसस्तपसश्चैव क्रोधो नाशकरः परः ।। १८ ।।

This ire springeth up in fools; but where is the anger of the wise? Who, my child, destroyeth whom? Persons[1] but reap their acts. O child, anger heweth away the great and immense asceticism and fame acquired with extreme toil by men.

स्वर्गापवर्गव्यासेधकारणं परमर्षयः ।।
वर्जयंति सदा क्रोधं तात मा तद्वशो भव ।। १९ ।।

अलं निशाचरैर्दग्धैर्दीनैरनपकारिभिः ।।
सत्रं ते विरमत्वेतत्क्षमासारा हि साधवः ।। २० ।।

एवं तातेन तेनाहमनुनीतो महात्मना ।।
उपसंहृतवान्सत्रं सद्यस्तद्वाक्यगौरवात् ।। २१ ।।

The prime saints ever banish anger, which retardeth heaven and emancipation. Therefore, my child, do not thou come under its sway. No need of burning the night-rangers, who have not wronged. Stop this sacrifice of thine. Pious people are composed of forgiveness.' Thus exhorted by my high-souled grandsire, I, for the sake of the dignity of his speech, stopped the sacrifice.

ततः प्रीतः स भगवान्वसिष्ठो मुनिसत्तमः ।।
संप्राप्तश्च तदा तत्र पुलस्त्यो ब्रह्मणः सुतः ।। २२ ।।

Thereat, that foremost of ascetics, the reverend Vasiṣṭha was gratified. And it came to pass that there appeared then Pulastya, son unto Brahmā.

पितामहेन दत्तार्घ्यः कृतासनपरिग्रहः ।।
मामुवाच महाभागो मैत्रेय पुलहाग्रजः ।। २३ ।।

And when my grandfather had offered him *arghya*,[2] and when he had taken his seat, O Maitreya, the exceedingly righteous elder brother of Pulaha addressed me.

पुलस्त्य उवाच

वैरे महति यद्वाक्याद्गुरोरद्याश्रिता क्षमा ।।
त्वया तस्मात्समस्तानि भवाञ्शास्त्राणि वेत्स्यति ।। २४ ।।

Pulastya said :—"As, albeit a mighty enmity existeth (between thyself and the Rākṣasas), thou hast resorted to forgiveness at the words of thy superior, thou shalt master all the branches of knowledge.

सन्ततेर्न ममोच्छेदः क्रुद्धेनापि यतः कृतः ।।
त्वया तस्मान्महाभाग ददाम्यन्यं महावरम् ।। २५ ।।

And as, although highly enraged, thou hast not cut off my sons, I, O pious one, shall confer on thee a mighty boon.

पुराणसंहिताकर्त्ता भवान्वत्स भविष्यति ।।
देवतापारमार्थ्यं च यथावद्वेत्स्यते भवान् ।। २६ ।।

Thou shalt be the author of the Purāṇa and Saṁhitā,[3] and thou shalt attain a consum-mate knowledge of the celestials.

प्रवृत्ते च निवृत्ते च कर्मण्यस्तमला मतिः ।।
मत्प्रसादादसंदिग्धा तव वत्स भविष्यति ।। २७ ।।

And through my grace, O child, thy intelligence shall be clear, and unobstructed as concerns the Present and the Past.'

ततश्च प्राह भगवान्वसिष्ठो मे पितामहः ।।
पुलस्त्येन यदुक्तं ते सर्वमेतद्भविष्यति ।। २८ ।।

Then my grandsire, the reverend Vasiṣṭha, said,—'What Pulastya hath uttered to thee, must be so.'

इतिं पूर्वं वसिष्ठेन पुलस्त्येन च धीमता ।
यदुक्तं तत्स्मृतिं याति त्वत्प्रश्नादखिलं मम ।। २९ ।।

At thy question I remember me in full of all that formerly had been said unto me by Vasiṣṭha and the intelligent Pulastya.

सोऽहं वदाभ्यशेषं ते मैत्रेय परिपृच्छते ।।
पुराणसंहितां सम्यक् तां निबोध यथातथम् ।। ३० ।।

And, O Maitreya, as thou hast asked me, I shall at length relate unto thee adequately the Purāṇa Saṁhitā.—Do thou understand that properly.

विष्णोः सकाशादुद्भूतं जगत्तत्रैव च स्थितम् ।।
स्थितिसंयमकर्ताऽसौ जगतोस्य जगच्च सः ।। ३१ ।।

1. The text has *puman*—male beings.—T.
2. An oblation of various ingredients offered by way of respect—T.
3. An arrangement of the text of Vedas into short sentences; or a compilation—T.

This universe hath sprung from Viṣṇu,—and in Him it is established. He is the cause of the creation, maintencance and destruction thereof, and He is the universe."

।। इति श्रीविष्णुपुराणे प्रथमेंशे प्रथमोऽध्यायः ।। १ ।।

अथ प्रथमेंशेः द्वितियोऽध्यायः

Part I : Section 2

श्रीपराशर उवाच

अविकाराय शुद्धाय नित्याय परमात्मने।।
सदैकरूपरूपाय विष्णवे सर्वजिष्णवे।। १।।

Parāśara said :—"I bow unto Him that is holy and eternal—the supreme Soul who is ever uniform,—even Viṣṇu, the Lord of all.

नमो हिरण्यगर्भाय हरये शंकराय च।।
वासुदेवाय ताराय सर्गस्थित्यन्तकारिणे।। २।।

I bow unto Hiranyagarbha, unto Hara and Śankara, unto Vāsudeva the saviour, even him who bringeth about creation, maintenance and destruction to everything.

एकानेकस्वरूपाय स्थूलसूक्ष्मात्मने नमः।।
अव्यक्तव्यक्तरूपाय विष्णवे मुक्तिहेतवे।। ३।।

I bow unto him that is uniform yet hath a multiplicity of forms; who is both subtle and gross;—who is manifested and unmanifested; unto Viṣṇu, the cause of salvation.

सर्गस्थितिविनाशानां जगतो यो जगन्मयः।।
मूलभूतो नमस्तस्मै विष्णवे परमात्मने।। ४।।
आधारभूतं विश्वस्याप्यणीयांसमणीयसाम्।।
प्रणम्य सर्वभूतस्थमच्युतं पुरुषोत्तमम्।। ५।।
ज्ञानस्वरूपमत्यन्तनिर्मलं परमार्थतः।।
तमेवार्थ स्वरूपेण भ्रान्तिदर्शनतः स्थितम्।। ६।।
विष्णुं ग्रसिष्णुं विश्वस्य स्थितौ सर्गे तथा प्रभुम्।।
प्रणम्य जगतामीशमजभक्षयमव्ययम्।। ७।।

I bow unto Viṣṇu, the supreme Soul, who pervadeth the universe, and who is the fundamental cause of the creation, sustenance and extinction of everything. And bowing down unto Him, who is the stay of the universe,—who is minuter than the minutest monad,—who resides in every being—unto the undeteriorating foremost Puruṣa, who is extremely pure, and constitutes knowledge of the highest kind,—who in consequence of the erroneous sight (of people) seemeth to be endowed with a shape; unto the Viṣṇu who can compass the creation, maintenance and destruction of the universe,—saluting the Lord of the world, un-born, unchangeable and undeteriorating,—

कथयामि यथापूर्वं दक्षाद्यैर्मुनिसत्तमैः।।
पृष्टः प्रोवाच भगवानब्जयोनिः पितामहः।। ८।।
तैश्चोक्तं पुरुकुत्साय भूभुजे नर्मदातटे।।
सारस्वताय तेनापि मह्यं सारस्वतेन च।। ९।।

I shall relate what formerly, asked by Dakṣa and other great ascetics, the reverend lotus sprung Great-sire said unto them, and what they rehearsed unto king Purukutsa on the banks of the Narmadā; and what he, in his turn, related to Sāraswata,—and the last unto me.

परः पराणां परमः परमात्मात्मसंस्थितः।।
रूपवर्णादिनिर्देशविशेषणविवर्जितः ।।१०।।
अपक्षयविनाशाभ्यां परिणामर्धिजन्मभिः।।
वर्जितः शक्यते वक्तुं यः सदास्तीति केवलम्।। ११।।
सर्वत्रासौ समस्तं च वसत्यत्रेति वै यतः।।
ततः स वासुदेवेति विद्वद्भिः परिपठ्यते।। १२।।

He who is Prime and Greater than the greatest, who is the supreme Soul resident in himself,—who cannot be differentiated by form, colour, *etc.*, who is without deterioration or destruction, and without birth, growth and dissolution; who can only be asserted as existing,—is called by the learned Vāsudeva, in consequence of his existing everywhere and in all objects.[1]

1. Vasudeva is named from his residing in all objects and his endowing them with splendour." *Mokṣa Dharma*.—T.

तद्ब्रह्म परमं नित्यमजमक्षयमव्ययम्।।
एकस्वरूपं तु सदा हेयाभावाच्च निर्मलम्।। १३।।

That Brahmā is prime and eternal,—without birth, change or deterioration. He is uniform, and pure in consequence of the absence of the ignoble.

तदेव सर्वमेवैतद्व्यक्ताव्यक्तास्वरूपवत्।।
तथा पुरुषरूपेण कालरूपेण च स्थितम्।। १४।।

He is all this (that is)—he is Manifested and Unmanifested;[1] and he exists as the Primal Puruṣa and Time.

परस्य ब्रह्मणो रूपं पुरुषः प्रथमं द्विज।।
व्यक्ताव्यक्ते तथैवान्ये रूपे कालस्तथापरम्।। १५।।
प्रधानपुरुषव्यक्तकालानां परमं हि यत्।।
पश्यन्ति सूरयः शुद्धं तद्विष्णोः परमं पदम्।। १६।।
प्रधानपुरुषव्यक्तकालास्तु प्रविभागाश।।
रूपाणि स्थितिसर्गान्तव्यक्तिसद्भावहेतवः।। १७।।

O twice-born one, the first form of the Primaeval Brahmā is a Male Being. His other forms are Manifested and Unmanifested, Time, and the rest.[2] The wise see that sacred state of Viṣṇu, which is superior to Pradhāna Puruṣa, Manifest and Time. The forms of Viṣṇu, first consisting of Pradhāna, Puruṣa,[3] Manifest and Time, are the causes and expressions[4] of creation, sustenance, and destruction.

व्यक्तं विष्णुस्तथाव्यक्तं पुरुषः काल एव च।।
क्रीडतो बालकस्येव चेष्टां तस्य निशामय।। १८।।

Do thou understand that *Vyakta*,[5] Viṣṇu, *Avyakta*, *Puruṣa* and Time are the exertions of Him, resembling those of a child sporting.

अव्यक्तं कारणं यत्तत्प्रधानमृषिसत्तमैः।।
प्रोच्यते प्रकृतिः सूक्ष्मा नित्यं सदसदात्मकम्।। १९।।
अक्षय्यं नान्यदाधारममेयमजरं ध्रुवम्।।
शब्दस्पर्शविहीनं तद्रूपादिभिरसंहितम्।। २०।।

That which is the Unmanifested Cause, is called subtle Nature by the foremost saints,—external, and instinct with cause and effect. It is indestructible, supportless, immeasurable, undeteriorating, real devoid of sound or touch, and without form, etc.

त्रिगुणं तज्जगद्योनिरनादिप्रभवाप्ययम्।।
तेनाग्रे सर्वमेवासीद्व्याप्तं वै प्रलयादनु।। २१।।

It hath three several modes;—and is the mother of the Universe, without beginning and is the end of all. Formerly after the universal dissolution, everything was permeated by it.

वेदवादविदो विद्वन्नियता ब्रह्मवादिनः।।
पठन्ति चैतमेवार्थं प्रधानप्रतिपादकम्।। २२।।

O Brāhmaṇa, those versed in the language of the Veda,—exercising self-control and medita-ting the Deity, read the sense expressive of Pradhāna, thus.

नाहो न रात्रिर्न नभो न भूमिर्नासीत्तमोज्योतिरभूच्च नान्यत्।।
श्रोत्रादिबुद्ध्यानुपलभ्यमेकं प्राधानिकं ब्रह्म पुमांस्त-
दासीत्।। २३।।

Day was not, nor night, nor sky, nor earth. And there was neither darkness nor yet light. And there existed then Pradhāna, Brahmā and the Puruṣa,—incapable of being apprehended by ear and the other organs, or the intellect.

विष्णोः स्वरूपात्परतोदिते द्वे रूपे प्रधानं पुरुषश्च विप्र।।
तस्यैव तेऽन्येन धृते वियुक्ते रूपांतरं तद्द्विज काल-
संज्ञम्।। २४।।

1. *Vyakta* and *Avyakta*—the names respectively of *formed* and *unformed* matter.—T.
2. According to the Sāṅkhya system, which the author follows in his cosmogony, prior to creation, the Universe existed in Nature like a mangoes tree existing latent in a mangoe-stone; and in the fullness of time, favoured by the Primeval male and Time, the evolution of all was brought about.—T.
3. Male being.—T.
4. Followers of Sāṅkhya Philosophy hold that the equilibrium of the three principles or modes, is Prakṛti—Primal nature.—T.
5. "Here let us remind our readers of the argument by which we are led to conclude that the visible system (*vyakta*) is not the whole universe, and that there must be an invisible order of things (*Avyakta* which will remain and possess energy when the present system has passed away. It is, moreover, very closely connected with the present system, inasmuch as this may be looked upon as *come into being through its means.*" The italics are mine.

As O Vipra, the prime Viṣṇu hath two forms, Pradhāna and Puruṣa, so, O twice-born one, he hath another, which is joined to him (on the occasion of creation) and severed from him during the universal dissolution; and this is called Kāla (Time).

प्रकृतौ संस्थितं व्यक्तमतीतप्रलये तु यत्।।
तस्मात्प्राकृतसंज्ञोयमुच्यते प्रतिसञ्चरः।। २५।।

During the past dissolution, in consequence of the *Vyakta* remaining nascent in Prakṛti, this circumstance in popular parlance is called Kāla.

अनादिर्भवान्कालो नान्तोस्य द्विज विद्यते।।
अव्युच्छिन्ना स्ततस्त्वेते सर्गस्थित्यन्तसंयमाः।। २६।।

O twice-born one, the revered Kāla hath no beginning and hath no end; and in it genesis, stability and dissolution are uninterrupted.

गुणसाम्ये ततस्तस्मिन्पृथक्पुंसि व्यवस्थिते।।
कालस्वरूपं तद्विष्णोर्मैत्रेय परिवर्त्तते।। २७।।

On the occasion of the universal dissolution, when Prakṛti and Puruṣa remain separate, O Maitreya, there exists the form of Viṣṇu termed Kāla.

ततस्तु तत्परं ब्रह्म परमात्मा जगन्मयः।।
सर्वगः सर्वभूतेशः सर्वात्मा परमेश्वरः।। २८।।
प्रधानपुरुषौ चापि प्रविश्यात्मेच्छया हरिः।।
क्षोभयामास संप्राप्ते सर्गकाले व्ययाव्ययौ।। २९।।

Then at the time of creation, the supreme Brahmā, the Prime spirit pervading the universe, reaching everywhere—the lord of all beings, and the soul of all—the foremost Lord, Hari, entering into Pradhāna and Puruṣa, agitated them.

यथा सन्निधिमात्रेण गन्धः क्षोभाय जायते।।
मनसो नोपकर्तृत्वात्तथाऽसौ परमेश्वरः।। ३०।।

And as odour, simply by reason of its proximity, and without any act, stirreth the mind, even so did the Supreme Lord.

स एव क्षोभको ब्रह्मन् क्षोभ्यश्च पुरुषोत्तमः।।
स संकोचविकासाभ्यां प्रधानत्वेपि च स्थितः।। ३१।।

That best of males, O Brāhmaṇa, is he that stirreth, and He it is that is stirred; he possessing in himself the three modes alike when in equilibrium and when not, entereth into Pradhāna.

विकासाणुस्वरूपैश्च ब्रह्म रूपादिभिस्तथा।।
व्यक्तस्वरूपश्च तथा विष्णुः सर्वेश्वरेश्वरः।। ३२।।

And that Lord of Lords, Viṣṇu, manifests himself in gross elements in subtle objects, and in such forms as Brahmā and others.

गुणसाम्यात्ततस्तस्मात्क्षेत्रज्ञाधिष्ठितान्मुने।।
गुणव्यञ्जनसंभूतिः सर्गकाले द्विजोत्तम।। ३३।।

And, O best of twice-born ones, on the occasion of creation, from the equipoise of the principles presided over by Kṣetrajña,[1] springs up that which manifests the principles.[2]

प्रधानतत्त्वमुद्भूतं महान्तं तत्समावृणोत्।।
सात्त्विको राजसश्चैव तामसश्च त्रिधा महान्।। ३४।।
प्रधानतत्त्वेन समं त्वचा बीजमिवावृतम्।।
वैकारिकस्तैजसश्च भूतादिश्चैव तामसः।। ३५।।

And then Pradhāna overspread Mahat; and the three kinds of Mahat pertaining respectively to goodness, passion and foulness, were enveloped by Pradhāna, even as the rind envelopeth the seed. And from the three kinds of Mahat sprang three kinds of *ahaṅkāra*,[3] (consciousness), *viz.*, *vaikārika*, *taijasa* and *bhutādi*[4]

त्रिविधोयमहंकारो महत्तत्वादजायत।।
भूतेन्द्रियाणां हेतुस्स त्रिगुणत्वान्महामुने।।
यथा प्रधानेन महान्महता स तथा वृतः।। ३६।।

And, O mighty ascetic, as *Pradhāna* had enveloped Mahat, that cause of the elements and the senses, *viz.*, *ahaṅkāra*, from its containing

1. Emanation of Divinity.
2. Or Buddhi—the intellect. This is also called Mahat—the Great one. It is the substance or essence by which the soul obtains a knowledge of external things.—T.
3. *Ahaṅkāra* is the substance or *ens* connected with thought Buddhis, in which consciousness inheres. It is the Mid-stuff of Prof. Clifford, assumed as the original ground our being i.e. of all formal being.—T.
4. Connected successively with goodness, passion and foulness.—T.

the three principles, was in its turn, enveloped by Mahat.

भूतादिस्तु विकुर्वाणः शब्दतन्मात्रकं तत।
ससर्ज शब्दतन्मात्रादाकाशं शब्दलक्षणम्।। ३७।।

Then the *bhutādi*,[1] etc., being wrought, produced the rudiments of sound, and from the latter came into being ether, having the property of sound.

शब्दमात्रं तथाकाशं भूतादिः स समावृणोत्।।
आकाशस्तु विकुर्वाणः स्पर्शमात्रं ससर्ज ह।। ३८।।
बलवानभवद्वायुस्तस्य स्पर्शो गुणो मतः।।
आकाशं शब्दमात्रं तु स्पर्शमात्रं समावृणोत्।। ३९।।

And (anon) the *bhutādi* overspread the rudiments of sound as well as the ether; and, ether being wrought, produced the rudiments of touch; and then sprang the powerful air, whose property is known to be touch. And ether furnished with nascent audibility, covered air, endowed with tangibility.

ततो वायुर्विकुर्वाणो रूपमात्रं ससर्ज्ज ह।।
ज्योतिरुत्पद्यते वायोस्तदूपगुणमुच्यते।। ४०।।

And then the air, wrought up, brought forth the rudiments of form. Light came from the air, and its property is said to be form.

स्पर्शमात्रं तु वै वायू रूपमात्रं समावृणोत्।।
ज्योतिश्चापि विकुर्वाणं रसमात्रं ससर्ज ह।। ४१।।
सम्भवन्ति ततोंभांसि रसाधाराणि तानि च।।
रसमात्राणि चाम्भांसि रूपमात्रं समावृणोत्।। ४२।।

And the rudimental air endowed with touch, enveloped the rudimental tangibility. And light, being agitated, caused the taste; and thereform sprang water, the residence of taste.

विकुर्वाणानि चाम्भांसि गन्धमात्रं ससर्जिरे।।
संघातो जायते तस्मात्तस्य गंधो गुणो मतः।। ४३।।

And the rudiments of from overspread the rudiments of taste. And water, stirred, developed the rudiments of odour; therefrom sprang hardness endued with the property of odour.

तस्मिंस्तस्मिंस्तु तन्मात्रं तेन तन्मात्रता स्मृता।। ४४।।

1. *Ahaṅkāra* relating to foulness.

The subtle condition of a property existing in diverse objects is called Tanmātrā.

तन्मात्राण्यविशेषाणि अविशेषास्ततो हि ते।। ४५।।
न शान्ता नापि घेरास्ते न मूढाश्चाविशेषिणः।।
भूततन्मात्रसर्गोयमहंकारात्तु तामसात्।। ४६।।
तेजसानीन्द्रियाण्याहुर्देवा वैकारिका दश।।
एकादशं मनश्चात्र देवा वैकारिकाः स्मृताः।। ४७।।

In consequence of the Tanmātrās not being differentiated, they are undistinguish-able : they are not agreeable or unpleasant or cause dullness,—and they are not marked by any distinguishing feature. From the conscious-ness related to darkness sprang the five rudiments and the five elements; from the consciousness relating to light sprang the organs of sense; and from the consciousness relating to goddness sprang the ten deities.[2] The mind is the eleventh (organ).[3]

त्वक् चक्षुर्नासिका जिह्वा श्रोत्रमत्र च पञ्चमम्।।
शब्दादीनामवाप्त्यर्थं बुद्धियुक्तानि वै द्विज।। ४८।।

The deities are known to have sprung from the principle of goodness. O twice-born one, the touch, the eye, the nose, the tongue, and the ear for the fifth, are designed for the perception of sound, *etc.*, and are backed by intellect.

पायूपस्थौ करौ पादौ वाक् च मैत्रेय पञ्चमी।।
विसर्गशिल्पगत्युक्ति कर्म तेषां च कथ्यते।। ४९।।

The other organs are the anus, the organs of generation, the hands, the feet, and the vocal organs for the fifth; and the functions of these are excretion, articulation, motion, and mechanic labour.

2. Cardinal Point, Wind, Sun, Pracheta [regent of water], Aśvinī Kumāra, Fire, Indra, Upendra Kṛṣṇa, Mitra, Prajāpati.—T.

3. "Mind" says Maudesley in *Physiology of mind* "used in the sense of substance or essence, and brain used in the sense of organ of mental function, are, at bottom, names of the same substance." In the system of Kapila, which the author follows, everything connected in function with sensuous objects, is as material as the objects themselves, being equally an emanation from *Prakṛti*.—T.

आकाशवायुतेजांसि सलिलं पृथिवी तथा।।
शब्दादिभिर्गुणैर्ब्रह्मन्संयुक्तान्युत्तरोत्तरैः ।।५०।।
शान्ता घोराश्च मूढाश्च विशेषास्तेन ते स्मृताः।।५१।।

Ether, air, light, water, and earth, O Brahmāna, are respectively furnished with the properties of sound etc; and in consequence of their being agreeable or otherwise, or bringing on delusion,—they are known as *Viśeṣa.*[1]

नानावीर्याः पृथग्भूतास्ततस्ते संहतिं विना।।
नाशक्नुवन्प्रजाः स्त्रष्टुमसमागम्य कृत्स्नशः।।५२।।

And endowed with distinct energies, they without combining, and being all of the interfused, could not create objects.

समेत्यान्योन्यसंयोगं परस्परसमाश्रयाः।।
एकसंघातलक्ष्याश्च संप्राप्यैक्यमशेषतः।। ५३।।

And then, coming together, and each supporting the others, they attained firmness and harmony and a uniform appearance.

पुरुषाधिष्ठितत्वाच्च प्रधानानुग्रहेण च।।
महदाद्या विशेषान्ता ह्यण्डमुत्पादयन्ति ते।। ५४।।

And in consequence of their being presided over by the Puraṣa, and favoured by Pradhāna, (who was ripe for it), those, commencing from Mahat and ending in Viśeṣa, brought forth an egg.

तत्क्रमेण विवृद्धं सज्जलबुद्बुदवत्समम्।।
भूतेभ्योण्डं महाबुद्धे महत्तदुदकेशयम्।।
प्राकृतं ब्रह्मरूपस्य विष्णोः स्थानमनुत्तमम्।।५५।।

And that egg resembling a watery bubble, fostered by the elements, attained dimensions. O thou of exceeding intelligence; and that egg formed by Prakṛti, resting on water, became the body of Viṣṇu wearing the form of Brahmā.

तत्राव्यक्तस्वरूपोऽसौ व्यक्तरूपो जगत्पतिः।।
विष्णुर्ब्रह्मस्वरूपेण स्वयमेव व्यवस्थितः।। ५६।।

And there Viṣṇu—lord of the universe—who is incapable of being perceived,—becoming manifest, remained in the form of Brahmā.[2]

1. *Specific.*
2. As Hiraṇyagarbha.—T.

मेरुरुल्बमभूत्तस्य जरायुश्च महीधराः।।
गर्भोदकं समुद्राश्च तस्यासन्सुमहात्मनः।। ५७।।
साद्रिद्वीपसमुद्राश्च सज्योतिर्लोकसंग्रह।।

And Meru became the bellows-like inner covering of that exceedingly high-souled one, and the other mountains became his outer covering; and the seas served for his water in the womb.

तस्मिन्नण्डेऽभवद्विप्र सदेवासुरमानुषः।।५८।।
वारिवह्न्यनिलाकाशैस्ततो भूतादिना बहि।।
वृतं दशगुणैरण्डं भूतादिर्महता तथा।।५९।।

And, O Vipra, in that egg sprang mountains and islands, and seas, light, and numbers of worlds, and deities, Asuras and human beings. And that egg was environed ten times successively with water, fire, air, ether, and *bhutādi* and the *bhutādi* was surrounded in the same way by *mahat.*

अव्यक्तेनावृतो ब्रह्मंस्तैः सर्वैः सहितो महान्।।
एभिरावरणैरण्डं सप्तभिः प्राकृतैर्वृतम्।।
नालिकेरफलस्यान्तर्बीजं बाह्यदलैरिव।। ६०।।

And *mahat*[3] along with all those was also covered by *avyakta.*[4] As the internal cocoanut fruit is covered by the external rind, *etc.* even so was the surrounded by the natural coverings.

जुषन् रजो गुणं तत्र स्वयं विश्वेश्वरो हरिः।।
ब्रह्मा भूत्वास्य जगतो विसृष्टौ संप्रवर्त्तते।। ६१।।

Then the lord of the universe, inspiring the principle of passion,[5] and becoming Brahmā, became engaged on creation.

सृष्टं च पात्यनुयुगं यावत्कल्पविकल्पना।।
सत्त्वभृद्भगवान्विष्णुरप्रमेयपराक्रमः ।।६२।।

And until the expiry of Kalpa,[6] the worship-

3. Lit. the Great one—so consciousness or egoism is styled.—T.
4. *Vide ante.*—T.
5. The three *guṇas*—generally translated qualities,—but more properly modes or principles—have a physical as well as a moral significance in the sacred literature of the Hindus. "They are not mere accidents of nature but are of its essence and enter into its composition." Davis' *Hindu Philosophy.*—T.
6. *Vide ante.*—T.

ful Viṣṇu of immeasurable power, instinct with the principle of goodness, sustaineth creation.

तमोद्रेकी च कल्पान्ते रुद्ररूपी जनार्दनः।।
मैत्रेयाखिलभूतानि भक्षयत्यतिदारुणः।। ६३।।

And at the end of a Kalpa, O Maitreya, Janārddana,[3] surcharged with the principle of foulness, wearing a fierce form and becoming terrific swalloweth up all.

भक्षयित्वा च भूतानि जगत्येकार्णवीकृते।।
नागपर्यङ्कशयने शेते च परमेश्वरः।। ६४।।
प्रबुद्धश्च पुनः सृष्टिं करोति ब्रह्मरूपधृक्।। ६५।।

And having swallowed up all beings, anon the cosmos becoming one ocean, the supreme Lord lieth down on the couch[4] (formed by) the serpent. And walking, he, wearing the form of Brahmā, again addresseth himself to creation.

सृष्टिस्थित्यन्तकरणीं ब्रह्मविष्णुशिवात्मिकाम्।।
स संज्ञां याति भगवानेक एव जनार्दनः।। ६६।।

And in consequence of his creating, sustaining and dissolving verily one Janārddana acquireth the appellations of Brahmā, Viṣṇu and Śiva.

स्रष्टा सृजति चात्मानं विष्णुः पाल्यं च पाति च।।
उपसंह्रियते चान्ते संहर्ता च स्वयं प्रभुः।। ६७।।

As creator, Viṣṇu createth himself, and, as sustainer, he sustaineth himself, and, finally, becoming the destroyer, the Lord himself destroyeth everything.

पृथिव्यापस्तथा तेजो वायुराकाश एव च।।
सर्वेन्द्रियान्तःकरणं पुरुषाख्यं हि यज्जगत्।। ६८।।
स एव सर्वभूतात्मा विश्वरूपो यतोऽव्ययः।।
सर्गादिकं तु तस्यैव भूतस्थमुपकारकम्।। ६९।।
स एव सृज्यः स च सर्गकर्ता स एव पात्यत्ति च पाल्यते च।।
ब्रह्माद्यवस्थाभिरशेषमूर्तिर्विष्णुर्वरिष्ठो वरदो वरेण्यः।। ७०।।

And as earth, water, light, air and ether, all the organs of sense and the heart go by the name *Puruṣa*, (Viṣṇu as being the Primal male, is the author of all these). And, as he is the lord of all beings, and, as, knowing no decay, he hath the universe for his form, even he is the creator of all, and his also are the ends attained by beings."[5]

।। इति श्रीविष्णु पुराणे प्रथमेंशे द्वितीयोऽध्यायः।। २।।

अथ प्रथमेंशेः तृतीयोऽध्यायः

Part I : Section 3

मैत्रेय उवाच

निर्गुणस्याप्रमेयस्य शुद्धस्याप्यमलात्मनः।।
कथं सर्गादिकर्तृत्वं ब्रह्मणोभ्युपगम्यते।। १।।

Maitreya said :—"How can Brahmā, who is devoid of quality and confineless and pure and unblamed of soul, possibly engage in creation, *etc.*?"

श्रीपराशर उवाच

शक्तयः सर्वभावानामचिन्त्यज्ञानगोचराः।।
यतोऽतो ब्रह्मणस्तास्तु सर्गाद्या भावशक्तयः।।
भवंति तपतां श्रेष्ठ पावकस्य यथोष्णता।। २।।

Thereat Parāśara said,—"As the powers of many an object are incomprehensible and incapable of being construed to sense, the powers of creation etc., possessed by Brahmā, like the heat of fire, are also so. O foremost of ascetics, hearken how the Professor of the eight kinds of wealth becomes engaged in creation.

3. This is an appelation of Viṣṇu, meaning, *he who* worshipped. This Purana as the *locus classicus* of the Vaiṣṇavas, recognises Viṣṇu as in one the Creator and the Destroyer, without assigning the function of destruction to Śiva.—T.
4. The hundred-hooded serpent, Śeṣa or Ananta, also conceived as a from of Viṣṇu himself.—T.
5. The acts of human beings, *etc.*, are also his property.

तन्निबोध यथा सर्गे भगवान्संप्रवर्त्तते ।।
नारायणाख्यो भगवान्ब्रह्मा लोकपितामहः ।। ३ ।।

O wise one, in consequence of the eternal reverend Viṣṇu coming into being from objects, as Brahmā the Grand-father, he is designated as produced.

उत्पन्नः प्रोच्यते विद्वन्नित्यमेवोपचारतः ।। ४ ।।
निजेन तस्य मानेन आयुर्वर्षशतं स्मृतम् ।।
तत्पराख्यं तदर्द्धं च परार्द्धमभिधीयते ।। ५ ।।

According to the measure set by him human life is known as consisting of an hundred years. This (age) is called *parā*, and the half thereof Parārdha.

कालस्वरूपं विष्णोश्च यन्मयोक्तं तवानघ ।।
तेन तस्य निबोध त्वं परिमाणोपपादनम् ।। ६ ।।
अन्येषां चैव जन्तूनां चराणामचराश्च ये ।।
भूभूभृत्सागरादीनामशेषाणां च सत्तम ।। ७ ।।

O sinless one, do thou listen to me as I mention unto thee the divisions of that which I have named unto thee as the Time-form of Viṣṇu,—in relation to Him as well as other creatures, and mobile and immobile objects, and the seas and all other things, O best of men.

काष्ठा पञ्चदशाख्याता निमेषा मुनिसत्तम ।।
काष्ठात्रिंशत्कला त्रिंशत्कला मौहूर्त्तिको विधिः ।। ८ ।।
तावत्संख्यैरहोरात्रं मुहूर्तैर्मानुषं स्मृतम् ।।
अहोरात्राणि तावन्ति मासः पक्षद्वयात्मकः ।। ९ ।।

O chief of asceteics, *Kāṣṭhā* is composed of fifteen *nimeṣas;*[1] thirty *kāṣṭhā* is composed of fifteen *nimeṣas;* thirty *kāṣṭhās* make up a *kalā;* and thirty *kalās* a *muhūrta*; and as many *muhūrtas* make up a day and a night unto human beings. As many days and nights form a month; and a month consists of two fortnights.

तैः षड्भिरयनं वर्षं द्वेऽयने दक्षिणोत्तरे ।।
अयनं दक्षिणं रात्रिर्देवानामुत्तरं दिनम् ।। १० ।।

Six months form an *ayana;* and an year is composed of two *ayaṇas*, one northern, the other southern. The outhern *ayana* is the night of the celestials, as the northern is their day.

दिव्यैर्वर्षसहस्रैस्तु कृतत्रेतादिसंज्ञितम् ।।
चतुर्युगं द्वादशभिस्तद्विभागं निबोध मे ।। ११ ।।

The period of twelve thousan years of the deities constitute the four Yugas, *viz.*, Kṛta, Tretā, and the others.[2] Do thou understand that.[3]

चत्वारि त्रीणि द्वे चैकं कृतादिषु यथाक्रमम् ।।
दिव्याब्दानां सहस्राणि युगेष्वाहुः ।। १२ ।।
तत्प्रमाणैः शतैः संध्या पूर्वा तत्राभिधीयते ।।
सन्ध्यांशश्चैव तत्तुल्यो युगस्यानंतरो हि सः ।। १३ ।।

Chronologists say that four, three, two, and one thousand divine years successively compose Kṛta and the other Yugas. An hundred divine years are said to constitute the first tuilight, as another hundred years the last, of the Yuga.

सन्ध्यासंध्यांशयोरन्तर्यः कालो मुनिसत्तम ।।
युगाख्यः स तु विज्ञेयः कृतत्रेतादिसंज्ञितः ।। १४ ।।
कृत त्रेता द्वापरश्च कलिश्चैव चतुर्युगम् ।।
प्रोच्यते तत्सहस्रं च ब्रह्मणो दिवसं मुने ।। १५ ।।
ब्रह्मणो दिवसे ब्रह्मन्मनवस्तु चतुर्दश ।।
भवन्ति परिणामं च तेषां कालकृतं शृणु ।। १६ ।।

The space that intervenes between these twilights goeth by the name of Yuga, embracing krita, Tretā and the rest. And O anchoret, a thousand of the four Yugas, krita, Trek Dwāpara and Kali, constitute one day of Brahmā. One day of Brahmā O Brāhmaṇa, compriseth four and ten reigns of the Manus.[4] Listen to the chronology thereof!

सप्तर्षयः सुराः शक्रो मनुस्तत्सूनवो नृपाः ।।
एककाले हि सृज्यन्ते संह्रियन्ते च पूर्ववत् ।। १७ ।।

The seven saints, the celestials, Śakra, Manu, and his sons—kings all of them—are

1. A *nimeṣa* is the twinkling of an eye.

2. *i.e.* Dwāpara and Kali.
3. The division of the Yugas.
4. A generic name of the Progenitors of mankind.

created at the same time and, as formerly,[1] are destroyed at the same time.

चतुर्युगाणां संख्याता साधिका ह्येकसप्ततिः ।।
मन्वन्तरं मनोः कालः सुरादीनां च सत्तम ।। १८ ।।

O excellent one, a little over seventy-one four Yugas constitute a Manvantara—the period of Manu as well as the gods.

अष्टौ शस्त सहस्राणि दिव्यया संख्यया स्मृतम् ।।
द्विपञ्चाशत्तथान्यानि सहस्राण्यधिकानि तु ।। १९ ।।
त्रिंशत्कोट्यस्तु संपूर्णाः संख्याताः संख्यया द्विज ।।
सप्तषष्टिस्तथान्यानि नियुतानि महामुने ।। २० ।।
विंशतिस्तु सहस्राणि कालेयमधिकं विना ।।
मन्वन्तरस्य संख्येयं मानुषैर्वत्सरैर्द्विज ।। २१ ।।

Manvantara takes up over eight *Lakṣas*[2] and fifty-two thousand years; and, O twice-born one, full thirty[3] *koṭis*, above sixty-seven[4] *niyutas* and about twenty thousand human years.

चतुर्दशगुणो ह्येष कालो ब्राह्ममहः स्मृतम् ।।
ब्राह्मो नैमित्तिको नाम तस्यान्ते प्रतिसञ्चरः ।। २२ ।।

Ten and fourteen such periods[5] form one day of Brahmā. Then comes on his sleep[6] and at the end thereof, the universal dissolution.

तदा हि दह्यते सर्वं त्रैलोक्यं भूर्भुवादिकम् ।।
जनं प्रयान्ति तापार्ता महर्लोकनिवासिनः ।। २३ ।।

And then all the trinue world, comprising *Bhur*, *Bhuva* and the rest, are in conflagration, and the dwellers of the regions of *Maha* exercised with the heat, resort to the regions of *Jana*.

एकार्णवे तु त्रैलोक्ये ब्रह्मा नारायणात्मकः ।।
भोगिशय्यां गतः शेते त्रैलोक्यग्रासबृंहितः ।। २४ ।।
जनस्थैर्योगिभिर्देवश्चिंत्यमानोब्जसम्भवः ।।
तत्प्रमाणां हि तां रात्रिं तदन्ते सृजते पुनः ।। २५ ।।

On the three regions being reduced to one sheet of sea, that deity, the lotus-sprung Brahmā instinct with Nārāyaṇa, contemplated by the *Yogīs*[7] of Janasthāna,—with the intention of swallowing up the three worlds,—lieth down on the bed (formed by) the serpent. And having spent the might measuring that period,[8] at the end thereof the begins anew the work of creation.

एवं तु ब्रह्मणो वर्षमेवं वर्षशतं च यत् ।।
शतं हि तस्य वर्षाणां परमायुर्महात्मनः ।। २६ ।।

This is the year of Brahmā and thus is the space of his hundred years; and the life of that high-souled one is an hundred (such) years.

एकमस्य व्यतीतं तु परार्द्धं ब्रह्मणोऽनघ ।।
तस्यान्तेभून्महाकल्पः पाद्म इत्यभिविश्रुतः ।। २७ ।।

O thou without sin, one half of Brahmā's life is spent. On the expiration thereof passeth away a Mahākalpa—which is called Pādma.

द्वितीयस्य परार्द्धस्य वर्तमानस्य वै द्विज ।।
वाराह इति कल्पोयं प्रथमः परिकीर्तितः ।। २८ ।।

O twice-born one, this is the Kalpa distinguished as Vārāha belonging to the second *Parārddha*, which is present."

श्रीमैत्रेय उवाच

।। इति श्रीविष्णुपुराणे प्रथमेंशे तृतीयोऽध्यायः ।। ३ ।।

1. I fail to perceive the sense of this, unless it meant *as they have been created afortime.*—T.
2. Lacs.
3. One million.
4. Ten millions.
5. Manvantaras.
6. Extending over as many Manvantaras.
7. Person practising a certain process entitled *Yoga*.
8. The time of creation.

अथ प्रथमेंशे: चतुर्थोऽध्याय:

Part I : Section 4

ब्रह्मा नारायणाख्योऽसौ कल्पादौ भगवान्यथा।।
ससर्ज सर्वभूतानि तदाचक्ष्व महामुने।। १।।

Maitreya said :—"O mighty ascetic, relate unto me how the reverend Brahmā whose name is Nārāyaṇa, created all beings at the commencement of the Kalpa." (Thereat)

श्रीपराशर उवाच

प्रजा: ससर्ज भगवान्ब्रह्मा नारायणात्मक:।।
प्रजापतिपतिर्देवो यथा तन्मे निशामय।। २।।

Parāśara said :—"Hear as to how that god, the lord of Prajāpati,[1] the reverend Brahmā instinct with Nārāyaṇa, created beings.

अतीतकल्पावसाने निशासुप्तोत्थित: प्रभु:।।
सत्त्वोद्रिक्तस्तथा ब्रह्मा शून्यं लोकमवैक्षत।। ३।।

On the expiration of the past Kalpa, that Master, Brahmā, surcharged with the energy of righteousness, awaking from his slumbers, saw the universe—void of all.

नारायण: परोऽचिन्त्य: परेषामपि स प्रभु:।।
ब्रह्मस्वरूपी भगवाननादि: सर्वसम्भव:।। ४।।

And the supreme, incomprehensible Nārāyaṇa—the lord of the greatest—as the worshipful Brahmā, became engaged in creation.

इमं चोदाहरन्त्यत्र लोकं नारायणं प्रति।।
ब्रह्मस्वरूपिणं देवं जगत: प्रभवाप्ययम्।। ५।।

This *śloka* is used with reference to the divine Nārāyaṇa, the creator of the universe in the form of Brahmā.

आपो नारा इति प्रोक्ता आपो वै नरसूनव:।।
अयनं तस्य ता: पूर्वं तेन नारायण: स्मृत:।। ६।।

Āpa is named *nāra*, having been created by Nara;[2] and in days of yore, (water) having been the abode of him, he hath hence been called Nārāyaṇa.

1. A divine personage sprung from Brahmā.—T.
2. A name of Viṣṇu.—T.

तोयान्त:स्थां महीं ज्ञात्वा जगत्येकार्णवीकृते।।
अनुमानात्तदुद्धारं कर्तुकाम: प्रजापति:।। ७।।

And on the universe becoming one ocean, the creator of all beings, the Lord resting on water, inferring that the earth was thus placed, set his heart on delivering her.

अकरोत्स्वतनूमन्यां कल्पादिषु यथा पुरा।।
मत्स्यकूर्मादिकां तद्वद्वाराहं वपुरास्थित:।। ८।।

And as he, on former occasions, had assumed the forms of a fish, a Tortoise *etc.*, he now assumed the form of a Boar.

वेदयज्ञमयं रूपमशेषजगत: स्थितौ।।
स्थित: स्थिरात्मा सर्वात्मा परमात्मा प्रजापति:।। ९।।

जनलोकगतैस्सिद्धैस्सनकाद्यैरभिष्टुत:।।
प्रविवेश तदा तोयमात्माधारो धराधर:।। १०।।

निरीक्ष्य तं सदा देवी पातालतलमागतम्।।
तुष्टाव प्रणता भूत्वा भक्तिनम्रा वसुन्धरा।। ११।।

And for sustaining the entire universe, the lord of creatures, impregnated with the Veda and sacrifices, of serene soul and the soul of all,— the Supreme spirit—stay of soul, and the prop of the Earth, hymned by the Siddhas inhabiting the region of Jana,— Sanaka and others,—then entered water.— And seeing him enter the nether regions, that exalted one, the Earth, bowing low in humility and reverence, began to praise him.

श्रीपृथिव्युवाच

नमस्ते पुण्डरीकाक्ष शंखचक्रगदाधर।।
मामुद्धरास्मादद्य त्वं त्वत्तोऽहं पूर्वमुत्थिता।। १२।।

And the Earth said :—'I bow unto thee, who art all being; I bow unto thee, holding the conch and the mace. Do thou resuce me from here, now, as, thou hadst formerly done.

त्वयाहमुद्धृता पूर्वं त्वन्मयाहं जनार्दन।।
तथान्यानि च भूतानि गगनादीन्यशेषत:।। १३।।

I had formerly been delivered by thee. O

Janārddana, I as well as other things, such as the sky, *etc.*, are permeated by thee.

नमस्ते परमात्मात्मन्पुरुषात्मन्नमोस्तु ते।।
प्रधानव्यक्तभूताय कालभूताय ते नमः।। १४।।

Reverence unto thee, O prime spirit, O male soul, I bow unto thee. I bow unto thee, who art *pradhāna* and *vyakta*, and who art Time.

त्वं कर्ता सर्वभूतानां त्वं पाता त्वं विनाशकृत्।।
सर्गादिषु प्रभो ब्रह्मविष्णुरुद्रात्मरूपधृक्।। १५।।

Thou, wearing the forms of Brahmā, Viṣṇu and Rudra, art the creator of all beings, and thou art the maintainer as well as the destroyer thereof.

सम्भक्षयित्वा सकलं जगत्येकार्णवीकृते।।
शेषे त्वमेव गोविंद चिन्त्यमानो मनीषिभिः।। १६।।

Having destroyed everything, thou, O Govinda,[1] on the universe having become one Ocean,—contemplated by the pious, reposest (on the serpent-couch).

भवतो यत्परं तत्त्वं तन्न जानाति कश्चन।।
अवतारेषु यद्रूपं तदर्चन्ति दिवौकसः।। १७।।

None knoweth the high mystery encompassing thee; and the deities do but adore that form in which thou incarnatest thyself.

त्वामाराध्य परं ब्रह्म याता मुक्तिं मुमुक्षवः।।
वासुदेवमनाराध्य को मोक्षं समवाप्स्यति।। १८।।

O supreme Brahmā, adoring thee, those desirous of emancipation, attain the same. Who, not worshipping Vasudeva, obtaineth liberation?

यत्किंचिन्मनसा ग्राह्यं यद्ग्राह्यं चक्षुरादिभिः।।
बुद्ध्या च यत्परिच्छेद्यं तद्रूपमखिलं तव।। १९।।

Thy entire form comprehends all that may be secured by the mind, all that may be perceived by sight and the other senses, all that may be discriminated by thought.

त्वन्मयाहं त्वदाधारा त्वत्सृष्टा त्वत्समाश्रया।।
माधवीमिति लोकोयमभिधत्ते ततो हि माम्।। २०।।

And I am supported, and created, and maintained by thee. And for this it is that people call me Mādhavi.[2]

जयाखिलज्ञानमय जय स्थूलमयाव्यय।।
जयाऽनन्त जयाव्यक्त जय व्यक्तमय प्रभो।। २१।।

Victory to thee, O thou that art all knowledge! Victory to thee, who art gross and undeteriorating! Victory to thee, O thou that art infinite! Victory to thee, thou that art the Nascent! Victory to thee, thou that art

परापरात्मन्विश्वात्मञ्जय यज्ञ पतेऽनघ।।
त्वं यज्ञस्त्वं वषट्कारस्त्वमोंकारस्त्वमग्नयः।। २२।।

Manifest. Thou, O lord! O prime of prime souls! O soul of the Universe! Victory to thee, O master of sacrifice, thou who art sinless! Thou art Sacrifice, and *Vaṣaṭkāra,*[3] and thou, *Oṁkāra*[4] and thou, Fire.

त्वं वेदास्त्वं तदाङ्गानि त्वं यज्ञपुरुषो हरे।।
सूर्यादयो ग्रहास्तारा नक्षत्राण्यखिलं जगत्।। २३।।

Thou art the Vedas, and thou the branches thereof, and thou Hari,[5] art the person presiding over sacrifice. Thou art the Sun, *etc.*, and the planets and stars, and thou the entire universe.

मूर्तामूर्तमदृश्यं च दृश्यं च पुरुषोत्तम।।
यच्चोक्तं यच्च नैवोक्तं मयात्र परमेश्वर।।
तत्सर्वं त्वं नमस्तुभ्यं भूयोभूयो नमोनमः।। २४।।

And O foremost god, thou art all that is formless and that is formed, and that is hard and, O best of male beings, all that I have mentioned and also all that I have left unmentioned. I bow down unto unto thee. I bow unto thee again and again."

श्रीपराशर उवाच

एवं संस्तूयमानस्तु पृथिव्या धरणीधरः।।
सामस्वरध्वनिः श्रीमाञ् जगर्ज पतिघर्घरम्।। २५।।

1. This term, a common appellation of Kṛṣṇa, is derived variously. *Go*—Language, [the language of the Vedas] and *vinda—who winows;* or *go—heaven* or a *cow, and* vid—to obtain,—*by whom heaven is obtained, or who obtains felicity by protecting kien.*—T.

2. Mādhava being one of the names of Kṛṣṇa, *Mādhavī* means related to *Mādhava*.—T.
3. Oblation into fire with the utterance of *Vaṣkaṭa*.—T.
4. The utterance of *Om*.—T.
5. Another appellation of Kṛṣṇa, from the root, *hri*—to take or seize. *Hari* possibly means *he that takes men's hearts.*—T.

Parāśara said :—"Thus eulogised by Earth, that graceful one, the holder thereof, began to roar in Sāma[1] accents.

ततः समुत्क्षिप्य धरां स्वदंष्ट्रया
महावराहः स्फुटपद्मलोचनः।।
रसातलादुत्पलपत्रसन्निभः समुत्थितो
नील इवाचलो महान्।। २६।।

Then heaving up the Earth with his razors from the deep, the mighty Boar, having eyes resembling blown lotuses,—and himself like unto lotus-leaves,—rose up like a gigantic dark-blue mountain.

उत्तिष्ठता तेन मुखानिलाहतं
तत्संभवाम्भो जनलोकसंश्रयान्।।
प्रक्षालयामास हि तान्महाद्युतीन्
सनन्दनादीनपकल्मषान् मुनीन्।। २७।।

And as he emerged, the troubled water dashed by the wind forced out from his mouth, surging up, splashed the highly resplendent and sinless ascetics, Sanandana and others, dwellers of the regions of Jana.

प्रयान्ति तोयानि खुराग्रविक्षत-
रसातलेऽधः कृतशब्दसन्तति।।
श्वासानिलास्ताः परितः प्रयांति
सिद्धा जने ये नियता वसन्ति।।२८।।

And on the nether regions being broken up by the hoof-impacts (of the boar), the wather began to run down with roars; and the Siddhas constantly inhabiting the regions of Jana, were moved about by the air of his breath.

उत्तिष्ठतस्तस्य जलार्द्रकुक्षे-
र्महावराहस्य महीं विगृह्य।।
विधुन्वतो वेदमयं शरीरं
रोमान्तरस्था मुनयः स्तुवन्ति।। २९।।

And the ascetics, placed in the tactual pores of the mighty bore as he rose up holding the Earth in his abdominal cavity and kept shaking his Veda-impregnated person,—experienced the highest bliss.

तं तुष्टुवुस्तोषपरीतचेतसो
लोके जने ये निवसन्ति योगिनः।।
सनन्दनाद्या ह्यतिनम्रकन्धरा
धराधरं धीरतरोद्धतेक्षणम्।। ३०।।

And *yogīs* dwelling in the regions of *Jana*, Sanandana and others, with delighted hearts, and with heads bent in humility, humned the holder of the Earth, remaining moveless, with his eyes expanded,—saying,—

जयेश्वराणां परमेश केशव
प्रभो गदाशंखधरासिचक्रधृक्।।
प्रसूतिनाशस्थितिहेतुरीश्वरस्त्वमेव
नान्यत्परमं च यत्पदम्।। ३१।।

"Victory unto thee, O foremost God of gods,—O Keśava,[2] O weilder of the conch, mace, sword and discus! The cause of creation, destruction and sustentation, save thee, supreme state there is none whatever.

पादेषु वेदास्तव यूपदंष्ट्रा
दन्तेषु यज्ञाश्चितयश्च वक्त्रे।।
हुताशजिह्वोसि तनूरुहाणि
दर्भाः प्रभो यज्ञपुमांस्त्वमेव।। ३२।।

The Vedas are thy feet, and the *yupa*,[3] thy larger tooth, and Sacrifice, thy smaller; the place of the (sacrificial fire) is thy mouth, and the fire itself thy tongue; and *darva* is thy down. O Lord, thou art the person presiding over Sacrifice.

विलोचने रात्र्यहनी महात्मन्-
सर्वाश्रयं ब्रह्मपरं शिरस्ते।।
सूक्तान्यशेषाणि सटाकलापो
घ्राणं समस्तानि हवींषि देव।। ३३।।

O mighty soul, day and night are thy eyes; and that refuge of all-the state of Brahmā himself—is thy head; the entire complement of *Sūktas*[4] composeth thy matted locks; and thy tongue is the sacrificial offerings, O god.

स्रुक्तुण्डसामस्वरधीरनाद-
प्राग्वंशकाया खिलसत्रसन्धे।।

---

1. i.e. belonging to the Sāma Veda, which used to be sung.—T.

2. An appelation of Kṛṣṇa, derived from Ka—*Brahma, and* īśa—Śiva and *va who goes*—ie., *one that goes before Brahma and Śiva*, or from *Keśa*—*hair*, and *va—who possesses—fair-haired.*—T.
3. Sacrificial stake.
4. Hymns of the Rig Veda.—T.

पूर्तेष्टधर्मश्रवणोसि देव
सनातनात्मन्भगवन्प्रसीद।। ३४।।

O thou having the (sacrificial) ladle for thy face! O thou who hast the solemn accents of Sāma for thy voice, O thou that hast the front-part of the sacrificial ground, for thy body! O thou who hast all the sacrifice for thy joints! O god, thou hast for thy ears the morality of the *Smṛtis* as well as the *Śrutis.*[1]

पदक्रमाक्रान्तभुवं भवन्तमादिस्थितं चाक्षरविश्वमूर्ते।।
विश्वस्य विद्मः परमेश्वरोऽसि प्रसीद नाथोसि परावर-
स्य।। ३५।।

Be thou propitiated! O undeteriorating one, O thou that hast the Universe for thy form, we know thee as having covered the Earth with thy paces, and that thou art the casuse and stay thereof.

दंष्ट्राग्रविन्यस्तमशेषमेतद्भूमण्डलं नाथ विभाव्यते ते।।
विगाहतः पद्मवनं विलग्नं सरोजिनीपत्रमिवोढ-
पंकम्।। ३६।।

Thou art the foremost Lord of the cosmos. Be thou gracious! Thou art the master of the mobile and the immobile. Raised on thy razor-ends, all this Earth, O Lord, seemeth like a lotus-leaf besmeared with mud on the tusk of an elephant that hath plunged into a pool of lotuses.

द्यावापृथिव्योरतुलप्रभाव यदन्तरं तद्वपुषा तवैव।।
व्याप्तं जगद्व्याप्तिसमर्थदीप्ते हिताय विश्वस्य विभो भव
त्वम्।। ३७।।

परमार्थस्त्वमेवैको नान्योस्ति जगतः पते।।
तवैष महिमा येन व्याप्तमेतच्चराचरम्।। ३८।।

O thou of unparalleled power, all the space between heaven and earth hath been covered with thy body. O thou, the universe hath been enveloped with whose splendour, O Lord, prove thou of profit to the universe.

यदेतद्दृश्यते मूर्त्तमेतज्ज्ञानात्मनास्तव।।
भ्रान्तिज्ञानेन पश्यन्ति जगद्रूपमयोगिनः।। ३९।।

1. Hindu scriptures are broadly divided into (1) *Sruti*—audition; and (2) *Smriti*—reminiscence. The former corresponds *to the Christian Revelation, and the other is tradition.*—T.

Thou art the sole highest reality,—there is none other, sovereign of the universe. And this glory in which the mobile and the immobile are enfolded,—is thine.

ज्ञानस्वरूपमखिलं जगदेतदबुद्धयः।।
अर्थस्वरूपं पश्यन्तो भ्राम्यन्ते मोहसंप्लवे।। ४०।।

O thou that art knowledge, unspiritual people, through ignorance, look upon this form of thine displayed in the world. Foolish persons, regarding this entire universe impregnated with knowledge, as real, fall into a sea of delusion.

ये तु ज्ञानविदः शुद्धचेतसस्तेऽखिलं जगत्।।
ज्ञानात्मकं प्रपश्यन्ति त्वद्रूपं परमेश्वर।। ४१।।

But O supreme lord, those that are versed in knowledge and are of pure spirit, look on this entire universe as thy form replete with knowledge.

प्रसीद सर्व सर्वात्मन्भवाय जगतामिमाम्।।
उद्धरोर्वीममेयात्मञ्छन्नो देह्यब्जलोचन।। ४२।।

O Sarva, O soul of all! Be thou gracious! For the good of this world do thou, O thou of immeasurable soul, raise the Earth up. O lotus-eyed one, confer on us what is good.

सत्त्वोद्रिक्तोऽसि भगवन् गोविंद पृथिवीमिमाम्।।
समुद्धर भवायेश शन्नो देह्यब्जलोचन।। ४३।।

Thou, O reverend one, art surcharged with the virtue of goodness. O Govinda, for the benefit (of all), O lord, raise up this Earth. O lotus-eyed one, confer on us what is good.

सर्गप्रवृत्तिर्भवतो जगतामुपकारिणी।।
भवत्वेषा नमस्तेऽस्तु शन्नो देह्यब्जलोचन।। ४४।।

Mayst thou incline thy mind to creation fraught with profit to the universe! We bow unto thee. O lotus-eyed one, confer on us what is good."

श्रीपराशर उवाच

एवं संस्तूयमानस्तु परमात्मा महीधरः।।
उज्जहार क्षितिं क्षिप्रं न्यस्तवांश्च महाम्भसि।। ४५।।

Parāśara said :—"Thus hymned by the divinities, that supreme soul, the holder of

Earth, at once lifted her up, and set her on the mighty sea.

तस्योपरि जलौघस्य महती नौरिव स्थिता।।
विततत्त्वात्तु देहस्य न मही याति संप्लवम्।। ४६।।

And, resting on the sea like a giant bark, Earth did not sink in consequence of the flatness of her frame.

ततः क्षितिं समां कृत्वा पृथिव्यां सोचिनोद्गिरीन्।।
यथाविभागं भगवाननादिः परमेश्वरः।। ४७।।

Then leveling the Earth, the worshipful supreme Lord without beginning, placed mountains on her in proper order.

प्राक्सर्गदग्धानखिलान्पर्वतान्पृथिवीतले।।
अमोघेन प्रभावेण ससर्जामोघवाञ्छितः।। ४८।।

And by his infallible power, that one of truthful purposes created on the Earth all the mountains that had been burnt on the occasion of the burning of the foregone creation.

भूविभागं ततः कृत्वा सप्तद्वीपान्यथातथम्।।
भूराद्यांश्चतुरो लोकान्पूर्ववत्समकल्पयत्।। ४९।।

And then; properly dividing the land containing seven islands, he, as formerly, created the four regions, viz., *Bhuva* and the rest.

ब्रह्मरूपधरो देवस्ततोऽसौ रजसा वृतः।।
चकार सृष्टिं भगवांश्चतुर्वक्त्रधरो हरिः।। ५०।।

And then, possessed with the principle of passion, the reverend Deity, Hari, wearing the form of Brahmā and assuming four faces, set about creation.

निमित्तमात्रमेवाऽसौ सृज्यानां सर्गकर्मणि।।
प्रधानकारणीभूता यतो वै सृज्यशक्तयः।। ५१।।

But in the matter of creation, he was an instrument merely as the force resident in the things created, was the principal Cause.

निमित्तमात्रं मुक्त्वैवं नान्यत्किंचिदपेक्षते।।
नीयते तपतां श्रेष्ठ स्वशक्त्या वस्तु वस्तुताम्।।५२।।

Being ripe for development, (objects at the time of creation) desiderate nothing more. O foremost of those practising austerities, objects attain their objectivity by virtue of their inherent force"[1]

1. This approaches wonderfully the theory of Spontaneous creation, which is accepted by the out-sand-out apostles of Modern Science.—The most uncompromising advocates of Evolution could not outdo the Hindu sage of yore, in formulating their faith in (to give a Spencerian turn to the expression) the *unknowable* force, which, *unintelligent* itself, brings about this wonderful system of things; instinct with infinite wisdom and love! Queer, however, would the classification read,—Parāśara, Darwin, Spencer, Huxley, Heckel, Tyndall, *etc.*—T.

।। इति श्रीविष्णुपुराणे प्रथमेंशे पृथिव्युद्धारश्चतुर्थोऽध्यायः।।४।।

अथ प्रथमेंशेः पञ्चमोऽध्यायः

Part I : Section 5

श्रीमैत्रेय उवाच

यथा ससर्ज देवोऽसौ देवर्षिपितृदानवान्।।
मनुष्यतिर्यग्वृक्षादीन्भूव्योमसलिलौकस।। १।।

यद्गुणं यत्स्वभावं च यद्रूपं च जगद्द्विज।।
सर्गादौ सृष्टवान्ब्रह्मा तन्ममाचक्ष्व कृत्स्नशः।। २।।

Maitreya said :—"O twice-born one, tell thou me truly how the Deity created celestials, and saints, and Pitṛs,[1] Dānavas, and men, and beasts, and trees, and those inhabiting land and water and air; as well as concerning (the respective) qualities and characters and natures (of the creatures) dwelling in Earth,—which Brahmā had created at the commencement of creation."

1. Ancestral manes.

श्रीपराशर उवाच

मैत्रेय कथयाम्येतच्छृणुष्व सुसमाहितः।।
यथा ससर्ज देवोसौ देवादीनखिलान्विभुः।। ३।।

Thereat Parāśara said—"O Maitreya, listen thou heedfully! I shall tell thee how the Lord God created all,—deities and the rest.

सृष्टिं चिंतय तस्तस्य कल्पादिषु यथा पुरा।।
अबुद्धिपूर्वकः सर्गः प्रादुर्भूतस्तमोमयः।। ४।।

As he was contemplating creation as in former Kalpas, through lack of vigilance was generated Illusion, formed of Foulness.—

तमोमोहो महामोहस्तामिस्त्रो ह्यन्धसंज्ञितः।।
अविद्या पञ्चपर्वैषा प्रादुर्भूता महात्मनः।। ५।।

Five are the kinds of illusion which spring from this high-souled one, viz., *tamas, moha mahāmoha, tāmisra* and *andhatāmisra.*[1]

पञ्चधाऽवस्थितः सर्गो ध्यायतो प्रतिबोधवान्।।
बहिरन्तोऽप्रकाशश्च संवृतात्मा नगात्मकः।। ६।।

And as (Brahmā) contemplated, were created five kinds of things, trees, *etc.*, having no sense, undeveloped internally as well as externally, and of pent-up selves.

मुख्या नगा यतः प्रोक्ता मुख्यसर्गस्ततस्त्वयम्।। ७।।

As these trees etc. were the first objects of creation, they are designated the principal creation.

तं दृष्ट्वाऽसाधकं सर्गममन्यदपरं पुनः।। ८।।

But finding these incapable of answering the end, he thought of again creating other things.

तस्याभिध्यायतः सर्गस्तिर्यक्स्त्रोतोभ्यवर्त्तत।।
यस्मात्तिर्यक्प्रवृत्तिस्स तिर्यक्स्त्रोतास्ततः स्मृतः।। ९।।

And as he was revolving creation, sprang up the *Tiryyaksrotas.*[2] Those that live in *Tiryyaksrotas.* They are beasts, *etc.*,—composed mainly of foulness, and devoid of liberal curiosity.

पश्चादयस्ते विख्यातास्तमःप्राया ह्यवेदिनः।।
उत्पथग्राहिणश्चैव तेऽज्ञाने ज्ञानमानिनः।। १०।।

Leading unrestrained lives, these, alberit devoid of knowledge deem themselves as possessing the same.

अहंकृता अहंमाना अष्टाविंशद्वधात्मकाः।।
अतः प्रकाशास्ते सर्वे आवृताश्च परस्परम्।। ११।।

Proud, and considering vastly of themselves, they are subject to eight and twenty kinds of ills.[3] And although developed internally, they cannot express themselves to each other.

तमप्यसाधक मत्वा ध्यायतोन्यस्ततोऽभवत्।।
ऊर्ध्वस्त्रोतास्तृतीयस्तु सात्त्विकोर्ध्वमवर्त्तत।। १२।।

And finding even these as insufficient for his purpose, (Brahmā) bethought him of other ways; and there came into being the third class of objects, named *Urddhasrotas,*[4] in whom the principle of goodness predominates.

ते सुखप्रीतिबहुला बहिरन्तश्च नावृताः।।
प्रकाशा बहिरन्तश्च ऊर्ध्वस्त्रोतोद्भवाः स्मृताः।। १३।।

They have great capacity for pleasure and happiness; and being developed alike externally and internally and, in consequence, more fitted to express themselves on both sides, have been designated *Urddhasrotas.*

तुष्टात्मानस्तृतीयस्तु देवसर्गस्तु स स्मृतः।।
तस्मिन्सर्गेभवत्प्रीतिर्निष्पन्ने ब्रह्मणस्तदा।। १४।।

This third creation, that of the deities—is called *Tuṣṭātman.*[5] And great was the pleasure of Brahmā on the consummation of this creation.

---

1. *Tamas* bring about love of one's own person, etc., *moha* produces a sense of authority over offspring etc. *mahāmoha* generates desire of sensual gratification, *tāmisra* causes anger on any impediment coming in the way of enjoyment and through *andhatāmisra* one is led to conserve health and the good things of life.—T.
2. Lit. the stream of beings living according to nature.—T.
3. Some of these are physical, such as leprosy, deafness, blindness, inertia, dumbness, smallnessness, impotence; some are mental and moral. It is, however, difficult for us of these times to see how beasts, etc. are more subject to these evils than human beings. The author may possibly have a meaning of his own, which in the absence of adequate commentary, we fail to arrive at.—T.
4. The stream of being, tending upwards.—T.
5. Lit. *soul-satisfying.*—T.

ततोन्यं स तदा दध्यौ साधकं सर्गमुत्तमम्।।
असाधकांस्तु ताञ्ज्ञात्वा मुख्यसर्गादिसम्भवान्।। १५।।

But, deeming these main creations as not fulfilling his purpose, he revolved within himself another excellent creation, capable of bringing about his end.

तथाभिध्यायतस्तस्य सत्याभिध्यायिनस्ततः।।
प्रादुर्बभूव चाव्यक्तादर्वाक्स्रोतास्तु साधकः।। १६।।

As that one of true resolve was thus meditating, there came forth from *avyakta* the *arvvyāksrotas* competent to accomplish his purpose.

यस्मादर्वाग्व्यवर्त्तन्त ततोर्वाक्स्रोतसस्तु ते।।
ते च प्रकाशबहुलास्तभोद्रिक्ता रजोधिकाः।। १७।।

And as these eat by swallowing down, they are called *arvvyāksrotas.* They are bountifully developed; and, albeit, possessing a share of foulness, have passion in a larger measure.

तस्मात्ते दुःखबहुला भूयोभूयश्च कारिणः।।
प्रकाशा बहिरन्तश्च मनुष्याः साधकास्तु ते।। १८।।

And it is for this that in them unhappiness preponderates, and that they act continually.[1] They are developed internally and externally,—they are human beings fulfilling the purpose (of the Creator).

इत्येते कथिताः सर्गाः षडत्र मुनिसत्तम।।
प्रथमो महतः सर्गो विज्ञेयो ब्रह्मणस्तु सः।। १९।।

तन्मात्राणां द्वितीयश्च भूतसर्गो हि स स्मृतः।।

Thus, O foremost of ascetics, have Inarrated unto thee the genesis of the six orders of creation. Brahmā first created *Mahata,* next he created *Tanmātrās,* which reckon as the second class, and are comprehended under the designation of *Bhūtasarga.*[2]

वैकारिकस्तृतीयस्तु सर्ग ऐन्द्रियकः स्मृतः।। २०।।

इत्येष प्राकृतः सर्गः सम्भूतो बुद्धिपूर्वकः।।
मुख्यसर्गश्चतुर्थस्तु मुख्या वै स्थावराः स्मृताः।। २१।।

1. The first circumstance, remarks the commentator, is owing to the presence, the next, to that of passion.—T.
2. *Lit.* the creation of the elements.

The third creation is *Vaikārika,* and is known as *aindrīya.*[3] Thus hath been the creation of Buddhi and the others, which is called *Prākṛta.*[4] And the main creation counts as the fourth, and includes the immobile objects.

तिर्यक्स्रोतास्तु यः प्रोक्तस्तैर्यग्योन्यः स उच्यते।।
तदूर्ध्वस्नोतसां षष्ठो देवसर्गस्तु संस्मृतः।। २२।।

By the name of *Tiryyaksrotas* is meant, beasts, *etc.* And the sixth creation is *Urddhasrotas,* which is known as *Devasarga.*[5]

ततोऽर्वाक्स्रोतसां सर्गः सप्तमः स तु मानुषः।। २३।।
अष्टमोऽनुग्रहः सर्गः सात्त्विकस्तामसश्च सः।।

And the seventh is *Arvvāksrotas* which is man. The eighth is the creation of *Anugrahas*[6] composed of goodness and passion.

पञ्चैते वैकृताः सर्गाः प्राकृतास्तु त्रयः स्मृताः।। २४।।
प्राकृतो वैकृतश्चैव कौमारो नवमः स्मृतः।।
इत्येते वै समाख्याता नव सर्गाः प्रजापतेः।। २५।।

Five are the *Vaikṛta*[7] acts of creation; and three are *Prākṛta.*—And they together constitute *Prākṛta* and *Vaikṛta.* And the ninth is known as Kaumāra. Thus have I described unto thee the nine acts of creation of the Lord of creatures.

प्राकृता वैकृताश्चैव जगतो मूलहेतवः।।
सृजतो जगदीशस्य किमन्यच्छ्रोतुमिच्छसि।। २६।।

The *Prākṛta* and the Vaikṛta are the radical causes of the world. What wouldst thou further hear of the Lord of the universe, engaged in creation?"

श्रीमैत्रेय उवाच
संक्षेपात्कथितः सर्गो देवादीनां मुने त्वया।।
विस्तराच्छ्रोतुमिच्छामि त्वत्ते मुनिवरोत्तम।। २७।।

Maitreya said :—"O ascetics, thou hast narrated unto me in brief the origin of gods *etc.* But, O best of the foremost anchorets, I wish to hear this at length."

3. i.e. *pertaining to the Indrīyas*—organ of sense.
4. From *Prakriti—nature.*
5. Creation of the gods.
6. An order of deities.
7. i.e. relating to the excited condition of anything.

श्रीपराशर उवाच

कर्मभिर्भाविताः पूर्वैः कुशलाः कुशलैस्तुताः।।
ख्यात्या तया ह्यनिर्मुक्ताः संहारे ह्युपसं हृताः।। २८।।

स्थावरान्ताःसुराद्यास्तु प्रजा ब्रह्मंश्चतुर्विधाः।।
ब्रह्मणः कुर्वतः सृष्टिं जज्ञिरे मानसास्तु ताः।। २९।।

Parāśara said :—"O Brāhmaṇa, on Brahmā being engaged in creation, from his mind issued the four orders of beings commencing with celestials and concluding with the immobile,—and although these are destroyed at the time of universal dissolution, they are never bereft of the mental tendencies they acquire in existence, consequent on their acts; or of the good or bad fortune resulting respectively from their fair or foul actions.[1]

ततो देवासुरपितॄन्मनुष्यांश्च चतुष्टयम्।।
सिसृक्षुरम्भांस्येतानि स्वमात्मानमयूयुजत्।। ३०।।

युक्तात्मनस्तमोमात्रा ह्युद्रिक्ताऽभूत्प्रजापतेः।।
सिसृक्षोर्जघनात्पूर्वमसुरा जज्ञिरे ततः।। ३१।।

Then desirous of creating deities, *Asuras*, ancestors and men, all going under the name of *ambha*. Brahmā began to contemplate. And as the lord of beings concentrated his soul, passion overspread him; and first from forth his hips came out *Asuras*.

उत्ससर्ज ततस्तां तु तमोमात्रात्मिकां तनुम्।।
सा तु व्यक्ता तनुस्तेन मैत्रेयाभूद्विभावरी।। ३२।।

And then (Brahmā) renounced his person surcharged with darkness; and, O Maitreya, on being renounced by him, Foulness was converted into Night.[2]

सिसृक्षुरन्यदेहस्थः प्रीतिमाप ततः सुराः।।
सत्त्वोद्रिक्ताः समुद्भूता मुखतो ब्रह्मणो द्विज।। ३३।।

And having assumed another body, he (again) became desirous of creating, and from the face of the pleased Brahmā, came forth, O twice-born one, celestials surcharged with the virtue of goodness.

त्यक्ता सापि तनुस्तेन सत्त्वप्रायमभूद्दिनम्।।
ततो हि बलिनो रात्रावसुरा देवता दिवा।। ३४।।

And body also having been resigned, the quality of righteousness was turned into Day. And therefore it is that *Asuras* are powerful by night and dieties by day.

सत्त्वमात्रात्मिकामेव ततोन्यां जगृहे तनुम्।।
पितृवन्मन्यमानस्य पितरस्तस्य जज्ञिरे।। ३५।।

And he then assumed a person, fraught with goodness; and, he being honoured as a sire, out of him sprang the ancestors,

उत्ससर्ज ततस्तां तु पितॄन्सृष्ट्वापि स प्रभुः।।
सा चोत्सृष्टाभवत्संध्या दिन नक्तान्तरस्थिता।। ३६।।

And having created the ancestors, the Lord renounced the form also. And on being renounced, the same became Twilight, remaining between day and night.

रजोमात्रात्मिकामन्यां जगृहे स तनुं ततः।।
रजोमात्रोत्कटा जाता मनुष्या द्विजसत्तम।। ३७।।

And then he assumed a person filled with the principle of passion; and, O foremost of the twice-born ones, thereat sprang men fierce, with passion entering into their composition.

तामप्याशु स तत्याज तनुं सद्यः प्रजापतिः।।
ज्योत्स्ना समभवत्सापि प्राक्सन्ध्या याऽभिधीयत।। ३८।।

And the lord of creatures speedily resigned that form also,—And it became Moonlight, which is termed *prāksandhyā*.[1]

ज्योत्स्नागमे तु बलिनो मनुष्याः पितरस्तथा।।
मैत्रेय संध्यासमये तस्मादेते भवन्ति वै।। ३९।।

And therefore it is, O Maitreya, man and the *Pitṛs*, become powerful in Moonlight and Twilight.

1. This passage is very obscure. It is not clear how acts, whether fair or foul or indifferent, can apply to immobile objects, the very statement of whose name carries with it a negation of movement. T.
2. In Sanskrit *tamas* menas *darkness*, along with the principle of foulness.

3. Meaning, *going before twilight*.

ज्योत्स्ना राज्यहनी संध्या चत्वार्येतानि वै प्रभोः ।।
ब्रह्मणस्तु शरीराणि त्रिगुणोपाश्रयाणि तु ।। ४० ।।

Moonlight, Night, Day, and Twilight,—these four, are the bodies of Brahmā, endowed with the three principles.

रजोमात्रात्मिकामेव ततोन्यां जगृहे तनुम् ।।
ततः क्षुद्ब्रह्मणो जाता जज्ञे कामस्तया ततः ।। ४१ ।।

And then he assumed another body filled with the principle of passion, and thereat sprung Hunger from Brahmā, and from Hunger, wrath.

क्षुत्क्षामानन्धकारेथ सोसृजद्भगवांस्ततः ।।
विरूपाः श्मश्रुला जातास्तेभ्यधावं स्ततः प्रभुम् ।। ४२ ।।

Then the reverend one in the dark created beings frightful and bearded, and always exercised with hunger.

मैवं भो रक्ष्यतामेष यैरुक्तं राक्षसास्तु ते ।।
ऊचुः खादाम इत्यन्ये ये ते यक्षास्तु जक्षणात् ।। ४३ ।।

And (as soon as these) were created, they rushed at the Lord. And of those that cried,—'Ho! don't do this,—save him,'—are Rākṣasas;[1] and others the said,—'We shall eat him up,'—are Yakṣas, from *Jakṣaṇa*,[2] eating.

अप्रियेण तु तान्दृष्ट्वा केशाः शीर्यन्त वेधसः ।।
हीनाश्च शिरसो भूयः समारोहन्त तच्छिरः ।। ४४ ।।

Seeing them mischieveous, the hair of the Deity fell off,—and having fallen off from his head, it again rose to his head.

सर्पणात्तेऽभवन् सर्पा हीनत्वादहयः स्मृताः ।।
ततः क्रुद्धो जगत्स्त्रष्टा क्रोधात्मानो विनिर्ममे ।।
वर्णेन कपिशेनोग्रभूतास्ते पिशिताशनाः ।। ४५ ।।

And from their movement (*sarpaṇa*), the hair became *sarpas*,[3]—and from their having fallen off, they are known as *ahis*.[4] Then the creator of the universe, waxing wroth, generated some beings of wrathful souls. Twenty-hued, they are beings subsisting on flesh.

ध्यायतोंगात्समुत्पन्ना गन्धर्वास्तस्य तत्क्षणात् ।।
पिबन्तो जज्ञिरे वाचं गन्धर्वास्तेन ते द्विज ।। ४६ ।।

And then came forth from him Gandharvas, whose office is music. O regenerate one, as these came into being, drinking in strains (of music), they are called Gandharvas.

एतानि सृष्ट्वा भगवान्ब्रह्मा तच्छक्तिचोदितः ।।
ततः स्वच्छन्दतोन्यानि वयांसि वयसोऽसृजत् ।। ४७ ।।

All these beings created the reverend Brahmā, directed by inherent force resident in these (respectively). Then he at his pleasure created another order of beings—fowls of the air.

अवयो वक्षसश्चक्रे मुखतोजाः स सृष्टवान् ।।
सृष्टवानुदराद्गाश्च पार्श्वाभ्यां च प्रजापतिः ।। ४८ ।।

And he created sheep from his breast, and goats from his mouth. And the lord of creatures created kine from his womb and flanks.

पद्भ्यां चाश्वान्समातङ्गान्रासभान्गवयान्मृगान् ।।
उष्ट्रानश्वतरांश्चैव न्यङ्कूनन्याश्च जातयः ।। ४९ ।।

And he created from his feet horses, elephants, *śarabhas*,[5] *gavayas*,[6] deer, camels, mules, *nyaṅkuṣ*[7] and other species.

ओषध्यः फलमूलिन्यो रोमभ्यस्तस्य जज्ञिरे ।।
त्रेतायुगमुखे ब्रह्मा कल्पस्यादौ द्विजोत्तम ।।
सृष्ट्वापश्चौषधीः सम्यग्युयोज स तदाध्वरे ।। ५० ।।

And from his down sprang medicinal herbs furnished with fruits and roots. And, O twice-born one, at the commencement of the *Tretā-Yuga* and on the eve of the Kalpa, Brahmā, having created the beasts and the drugs, then set them apart respectively for sacrifice.

गौरजः पुरुषो मेषश्चाश्वाश्वतरगर्दभाः ।।
एतान्ग्राम्यान्पशूनाहुरारण्यांश्च निबोध मे ।। ५१ ।।

1. From *Rakṣa—protect.*
2. From the verb *ha leave.*
3. Serpents.
4. Serpents.

5. A fabulous animal having eight legs, inhabiting the snowy mountainous regions.—T.
6. *Bos Gavus.*
7. A species of deer.

Fair complexioned males, sheep, horses, mules, and asses, were called *Grāmyā*[1] animals. And know also those that are wild.

श्वापदा द्विखुरा हस्ती वानराः पक्षिपञ्चमाः ।।
औदकाः पशवः षष्ठाः सप्तमास्तु सरीसृपाः ।। ५२ ।।

(These are) beasts of prey, the cloven-hoofed, elephants, monkeys and fifthly, birds, and, sixthly, acquatic animals, and, seventhly, reptiles.

गायत्रं च ऋचश्चैव त्रिवृत्सोमं रथन्तरम् ।।
अग्निष्टोमं च यज्ञानां निर्ममे प्रथमान्मुखात् ।। ५३ ।।

Then form his first mouth he generated the *Gāyatrī*,[2] the *Ṛcas*,[3] the *Trivatṣṭoma*[4] the *Rathantara*,[5] and the *Agniṣṭoma*[6] among sacrifices.

यजूंषि त्रैष्टुभं छन्दः स्तोमं पञ्चदशं तथा ।।
बृहत्साम तथोक्थं च दक्षिणादसृजन्मुखात् ।। ५४ ।।

Then from his sourthern mouth he created the *Yajuṣ*,[7] the *Triṣṭubha* metre, the fifteenth Stoma,[8] the *Vṛhat Sāman*,[9] and the *Uktha*.[10]

सामानि जगतीछन्दः स्तोमं सप्तदशं तथा ।।
वैरूपमतिरात्रं च पश्चिमादसृजन्मुखात् ।। ५५ ।।

And from his western mouth, he created the *Sāmas* and the *Jagati* metre, the seventeenth *Stoma*, the *Vairūpa*[11] and the *Atirātra*.[12]

एकविंशमथर्वाणमाप्तोर्यामाणमेव च ।।
अनुष्टुभं च वैराजमुत्तरादसृजन्मुखात् ।। ५६ ।।

And from his northern mouth he brought forth the twenty-first *Stoma*, the Atharva Veda, the *Aptoryāma*,[13] the *Anishtubha* metre, and the *Vairāgya* Sāma.

उच्चावचानि भूतानि गात्रेभ्यस्तस्य जज्ञिरे ।।
देवासुरपितॄन् सृष्ट्वा मनुष्यांश्च प्रजापतिः ।। ५७ ।।

ततः पुनः ससर्जादौ संकल्पस्य पितामहः ।।
यक्षान् पिशाचान्गन्धर्वान् तथैवाप्सरसां गणान् ।। ५८ ।।

नरकिन्नररक्षांसि वयः पशुमृगोरगान् ।।
अव्ययं च व्ययं चैव यदिदं स्थाणुजंगमम् ।। ५९ ।।

Thus from his person came forth and ignoble. And having created gods, *Asuras*, *Pitris*, and men, that lord of beings, the great-sire, at the commencement of the Kalpa, created Yakṣas, Piśācas,[14] Gandharvas, and numbers of Apsarās; and that lord, the reverend Brahmā, the first Cause, created Naras,[15] Kinnaras,[16] Rākṣasas, birds, beasts, deer, serpents, and mobile and immobile objects lasting or otherwise.

तत्ससर्ज तदा ब्रह्मा भगवानादिकृत्प्रभुः ।।
तेषां ये यानि कर्माणि प्राक्सृष्ट्यां प्रतिपेदिरे ।।
तान्येव ते प्रपद्यन्ते सृज्यमानाः पुनःपुनः ।। ६० ।।

And in successive creations, verily each creature is born into those acts which it used to perform in its former existence.[17]

हिंस्राहिंस्रे मृदुक्रूरे धर्माधर्मावृतानृते ।।
तद्भाविताः प्रपद्यन्ते तस्मात्तत्तस्य रोचते ।। ६१ ।।

इन्द्रियार्थेषु भूतेषु शरीरेषु च स प्रभुः ।।
नानात्वं विनियोगं च धातैवं व्यसृजत्स्वयम् ।। ६२ ।।

नाम रूपं च भूतानां कृत्यानां च प्रपञ्चनम् ।।
वेदशब्देभ्य एवादौ देवादीनां चकार सः ।। ६३ ।।

1. i.e. belonging to village.—T.
2. The most sacred hymn in all the Vedas, in praise of the Sun, as representing the Supreme sun of the spiritual Universe. J—T.
3. Hymns of the Ṛg-Veda.
4. A kind of sacrifice.
5. A division of the Sāma Veda, so named.
6. A sacrifice.
7. A division of the Vedas.
8. Song of the Sāma Veda.
9. A part of the Sāma Veda, Vṛhat means *great*.
10. A metre of the Sāma Veda.
11. Songs of the Sāma Veda.
12. A kind of Sacrifice.
13. A kind of Sacrifice.
14. Inferior spectres revelling in the morally foul and the physically filthy.—T.
15. Horse-hipped beings.
16. Horse-faced beings.
17. A profound view, in imaginative vesture, of *Heredity*. The Author imparts a comprehensiveness and sublimity to the doctrine which is unsurpassed.—T.

Some are cruel and some kind, some mild and some harsh, some virtuous and some vicious, some truthful and some false,—in consequence of their inheriting their respective natures as developed in previous births; and it is also for this that each affects a particular course of conduct (in preference to others).[1] The Diety is the lord of all objects of enjoyment, of all creatures, and all bodies; and it is the Deity who had personally divided and differentiated them.

ऋषीणां नामधेयानि यथा वेदश्रुतानि वै।।
तथा नियोगयोग्यानि ह्यन्येषामपि सोऽकरोत्।। ६४।।

And at the beginning from the Vedic Vocabulary he assigned names unto creatures, celestials and other, as well as unto sacrifices; and also fixed forms and shapes thereof. And from the auditory Veda, he assigned appellations unto the sages,—and appointed them to their respective functions.

यथर्तुष्वृतुलिंगानि नानारूपाणि पर्यये।।
दृश्यन्ते तानि तान्येव तथा भावा युगादिषु।। ६५।।

And as the signs of the seasons successively manifest themselves, the characteristics, of the *Yugas* are seen in due order.

करोत्येवंविधां सृष्टिं कल्पादौ स पुनःपुनः।।
सिसृक्षाशक्तियुक्तोसौ सृज्यशक्ति प्रचोदितः।। ६६।।

And instinct with energy arising from a desire of creation, He, actuated by the creative impulse, thus again and again bringeth about creation at the commencement of Kalpas."

।। इति श्रीविष्णुपुराणे प्रथमेंशे पञ्चमोऽध्यायः।।५।।

अथ प्रथमेंशेः षष्ठोऽध्यायः

Part I : Section 6

श्रीमैत्रेय उवाच

अर्वाक्स्रोतास्तु कथितो भवता यस्तु मानुषः।।
ब्रह्मन्विस्तरतो ब्रूहि ब्रह्मा तमसृजद्यथा।। १।।

Maitreya said :—"Thou hast called man by the term *Arvāksrotas.* But O Brāhmaṇa, tell me at length how Brahmā created him.

यथा च वर्णानसृजद्यद्गुणांश्च प्रजापतिः।।
यच्च तेषां स्मृतं कर्म विप्रादीनां तदुच्यताम्।। २।।

And tell me also how he created the orders, —and, O mighty ascetic, of their qualities; and the offices assigned to Vipras and the rest."

श्रीपराशर उवाच

सत्याभिध्यायिनः पूर्वं सिसृक्षोर्ब्रह्मणो जगत्।।
अजायन्त द्विजश्रेष्ठ सत्त्वोद्रिक्ता मुखात्प्रजाः।। ३।।
वक्षसो रजसोद्रिक्तास्तथा वै ब्रह्मणोऽभवन्।।
रजसा तमसा चैव समुद्रिक्तास्तथोरुतः।। ४।।

पद्भ्यामन्याः प्रजा ब्रह्मा ससर्ज द्विजसत्तम।।
तमः प्रधानास्ताः सर्वाश्चातुर्वर्ण्यमिदं तत।। ५।।

Parāśara said :—"O foremost of twice-born ones, when Brahmā of true intents was inspired with the desire of creating the *kosmos* from his mouth, O formost of twice-born ones, came out creatures surcharged with the principle of goodness; and from the breast of Brahmā creatures surcharged with the principle of passion; and from his thighs came out beings surcharged with both goodness and foulness; and, O best of regenerate ones, from his feet Brahmā created other beings, who were impregnated with the principle of dullness. This is the forefold division into orders.

ब्राह्मणाः क्षत्रिया वैश्याः शूद्राश्च द्विजसत्तम।।
पादोरुवक्षस्थलतो मुखतश्च समुद्गताः।। ६।।

And, O excellent Brāhmaṇa, Brāhmaṇas, Kṣatriyas, Vaiśyas and Śūdras, came from the feet, the thighs, the chest and the mouth of Brahmā.

यज्ञनिष्पत्तये सर्वमेतद्ब्रह्मा चकार वै।।
चातुर्वर्ण्यं महाभाग यज्ञसाधनमुत्तमम्।। ७।।

1. A little liberality has been indulged in translating this sentence, as the construction of original is involved and complicated.—T.

O exalted one, Brahmā brought into being these four orders capable of satisfactorily performing sacrifices, in order to the successful celebration of them.

यज्ञैराप्यायिता देवा वृष्ट्युत्सर्गेण वै प्रजा:।।
आप्याययन्ते धर्मज्ञ यज्ञा: कल्याणहेतवा:।। ८।।

O thou cognisant of righteousness, the celestials, gratified with sacrifices, in turn gratify creatures,—and therefore sacrifices conduce to welfare.

निष्पाद्यन्ते नरैस्तैस्तु स्वधर्माभिरतैस्सदा।।
विशुद्धाचरणोपेतैः सद्भिः सन्मार्गगामिभि।। ९।।

It is men engaged in observing their proper morality, of pure ways, and good, and walking the path of righteousness,—who perform sacrifices.

स्वसर्गापवर्गौ मानुष्यात्प्राप्नुवंति नरा मुने।।
यच्चाभिरुचितं स्थानां तद्यान्ति मनुजा द्विज।। १०।।

It is by virtue of having been born as human beings that men, O ascetic, can obtain heaven and emancipation; and, O twice-born one, that they can go to the wished-for regions.

प्रजास्ता ब्रह्मणा सृष्टाश्चातुर्वर्ण्यव्यवस्थिता:।।
सम्यक्छ्रद्धा: समाचारप्रवणा मुनिसत्तम।। ११।।

O foremost of ascetics, men (at the beginning) having been divided into four orders, were reverent and of excellent ways. Then they lived wherever they liked,—without any let.

यथेच्छावासनिरता: सर्वबाधाविवर्जिता:।।
शुद्धान्त:करणा: शुद्धा: कर्मानुष्ठाननिर्मला:।। १२।।

And they were pure in heart,—unpolluted; and cleansed in consequence of their observing all rites.

शुद्धे च तासां मनसि शुद्धेन्त:संस्थिते हरौ।।
शुर्द्धज्ञानं प्रपश्यन्ति बिल्वाख्यं येन तत्पदम्।। १३।।

And their minds being pure and the Pure Hari residing in their heart, they perceived that state which goeth after the name of Viṣṇu, and which is genuine knowledge.

तत: कालात्मको योऽसौ स चांश: कथितो हरे:।।
स पातयत्यघं घोरमल्पमल्पाल्पसारवत्।। १४।।

Then that portion of Hari which is fraught with Fatality, spread sin (amongst men), causing slight pleasure and an overmeasure of woe.

अधर्मबीजमुद्भूतं तमोलोभसमुद्भवम्।।
प्रजासु तासु मैत्रेय रागादिकमसाधकम्।। १५।।

O Maitreya, this, composed of anger, *etc*, springs from the seed of unrighteousness and begets delusion and covetousness,—and stands in the way of the attainment (of the *summun bonum*).

तत: सा सहजा सिद्धिस्तासां नातीव जायते।।
रसोल्लासादयश्चान्या: सिद्धयोष्टौ भवंति या:।। १६।।

And men anon could not (any more) completely attain the eight kinds of success, Rasa, Ullāsa, *etc*.

तासु क्षीणास्वशेषासु वर्द्धमाने च पातके।।
द्वंद्वाभिभवदु:खार्तास्ता भवंति तत: प्रजा:।। १७।।

And on sin progressing, and those becoming exceedingly feeble, creatures became subject to physical changes[1] and to all the miseries consequent thereon.

ततो दुर्गाणि ताश्चक्रुर्धान्वं पार्वतमौदकम्।।
कृत्रिमं च तथा दुर्गं पुरखर्वटकादिकम्।। १८।।

Then they constructed forts composed of trees, or rocks, or water; and artificial forts; and cities; and towns.

गृहाणि च यथान्यायं तेषु चक्रु: पुरादिषु।।
शीतातपादिबाधानां प्रशमाय महामते।। १९।।

And, O mightly ascetic, they only made houses in those towns, *etc.*, for shelter from cold, the sun, and other (physical discomforts).

प्रतीकारमिमं कृत्वा शीतादेस्ता: प्रजा: पुन:।।
वार्तोपायं ततश्चक्रुर्हस्तसिद्धिं च कर्मजाम्।। २०।।

Having thus provided against cold, etc,

1. *Dwvandābhihuta*—subject to duality, i.e. came under the Law of Relativity, in the sense of Professor Bain. See *Senses and Intellect*.

men then betook themselves to tasks capable of being performed with the hands, for subsistence.

व्रीहयश्च यवाश्चैव गोधूमाश्चाणवस्तिलाः।।
प्रियंगवो ह्युदाराश्च कोरदूषाः सतीनकाः।। २१।।

माषा मुद्गा मसूराश्च निष्पावाः सकुलणात्थकाः।।
आढक्यश्चणकाश्चैव शणाः सप्तदश स्मृताः।। २२।।

And *Vrīhi*,[1] barley, wheat, small seeds, sessame, *priyaṅgu*,[2] *udāra*, *kodrava*,[3] *cinaka*,[4] *māṣa*,[5] *mudga*,[6] *masūra*, *simbi*,[7] *kulaththaka*,[8] *āraki*,[9] oats, and hemp,—these seventeen kinds, O ascetic, were among the rural plants grown.

इत्येता ओषधीनां तु ग्राम्यानां जातयो मुने।।
ओषध्यो यज्ञियाश्चैव ग्राम्यारण्याश्चतुर्दश।। २३।।

व्रीहयस्सयवा माषा गोधूमाश्चाणवस्तिलाः।।
प्रियंगुसप्तमा ह्येते अष्टमास्तु कुलत्थकाः।। २४।।

And fourteen sorts are the plants intended to be used in sacrifice, divided into *grāmya*[10] and *āraṇya*,[11] *Vrīhi*, barley, *māṣa*, wheat, small seeds, *priyaṅgu*, sessame, *kulaththaka*, these eight belong to villages.

श्यामाकास्त्वथ नीवारा जर्तिलाः सगवेधुकाः।।
तथा वेणुयवाः प्रोक्तास्तथा मर्कटका मुने।। २५।।

And Syāmāka,[12] *nirāba*,[13] *jartila*,[14] *gavedhuka*, *beṇuyava*, and *markaṭaka*,[15]—(these), O ascetic, (are the plants growing wild in the woods).

ग्राम्यारण्याः स्मृता ह्येता ओषध्यस्तु चतुर्दश।।
यज्ञनिष्पत्तये यज्ञस्तथासां हेतुरुत्तमः।। २६।।

These fourteen species of plants, *grāmya* and *āraṇya*, are intended for the celebration of sacrifices, and they are very useful for the purpose.

एताश्च सह यज्ञेन प्रजानां कारणं परम्।।
परावरविदः प्राज्ञास्ततो यज्ञान्वितन्वते।। २७।।

All these plants together with sacrifices are the causes of the increase of population; and it is for this those versed in the highest signifcance of things celebrate sacrifices.

अहन्यहन्यनुष्ठानं यज्ञानां मुनिसत्तम।।
उपकारकरं पुंसां क्रियमाणा घशान्तिदम्।। २८।।

By performing sacrifices day after day, one, O foremost of ascetics, reapeth great good, and hath one's sins, committed, shorn of their rancour.

येषां तु कालसृष्टोऽसौ पापबिन्दुर्महामुने।।
चेतःसु ववृधे चक्रुस्ते न यज्ञेषु मानसम्।। २९।।

O mighty-minded one, it is those only in whose minds the drop of sin attaineth proportions, that set their face against sacrifices.

वेदवादांस्तथा वेदान्यज्ञ कर्मादिकं च यत्।।
तत्सर्वं निन्दयामासुर्यज्ञव्यासेधकारिणः।। ३०।।

These reprobating the ordinance of the Veda and the divinities presiding over sacrifices, endeavour to stand in the way of sacrifices.

प्रवृत्तिमार्गव्युच्छित्तिकारिणो वेदनिन्दकाः।।
दुरात्मानो दुराचारा बभूवुः कुटिलाशयाः।। ३१।।

And wicked wights of evil ways and crooked aims, running the Vedas down, lay the axe at the root of courses leading to progress.

संसिद्धायां तु वार्तायां प्रजाः सृष्ट्वा प्रजापतिः।।
मर्यादां स्थापयामास यथास्थानं यथागुणम्।। ३२।।
वर्णा नामाश्रमाणां च धर्माधर्मभृतां वर।।
लोकांश्च सर्ववर्णानां सम्यग्धर्मानुपालिनाम्।। ३३।।

---

1. Rice of various kinds; of which eight only are enumerated by authorities.
2. A medicinal plant, and perfume, *Panicum Italicum*.
3. A species of grain eaten by the lower people *Paspalum Kora*.
4. A sort of panic, P. *miliaceum*.
5. A sort of kidney-bean :—*phaseolus radiatus*.
6. *Phaseolus mūnga*.
7. A sort of pulse or lentil—*Eroum Hirsutum; cassia alata*.
8. *Dalichos biflorus*.
9. *Cytius cajan*.
10. From *grāma—village*.
11. From *aranya—wood*.
12. *Panicum mantacium*. Also P. coloumn.
13. *Wild sessanum*.
14. *Coix barbata*.
15. A fruit.

Having created men, the Lord, on their means of subsistence according with their respective qualities, having been settled, placed them duly in consonance with dignity; and, O best of those practising righteousness, ordained the codes of duty in respect of the orders; and their modes of life; and the regions attainable by them; concerning all the castes, observing the rules of their respective orders.

प्राजापत्यं ब्राह्मणानां स्मृतं स्थानं क्रियावताम्।।
स्थानमैन्द्रं क्षत्रियाणां संग्रामेष्वनिवर्त्तताम्।। ३४।।

And the sphere assigned to Brāhmaṇas observing the rules of their order, is that of the Creator himself. And the sphere assigned to Kṣatriyas, not turning away from fight, is that of Indra.

वैश्यानां मारुतं स्थानं स्वधर्ममनुवर्तिनाम्।।
गान्धर्वं शूद्रजातीनां परिचर्यानुवर्त्तिनाम्।। ३५।।

And Vaiśyas, following the laws of their order, attain the regions of Mārut.[1] And those belonging to the Śūdra caste that spend their lives in serving (the other orders), attain the regions of the Gandharvas.

अष्टाशीतिसहस्राणि मुनीनामूर्ध्वरेतसाम्।।
स्मृतं तेषां तु यत्स्थानं तदेव गुरुवासिनाम्।। ३६।।

Those practising the Brahmācarya injunctions attain the regions of Mārut belonging to the eight and eighty thousand ascetics that have drawn up their vital fluid.

सप्तर्षीणां तु यत्स्थानं स्मृतं तद्वैवनौकसाम्।।
प्राजापत्यं गृहस्थानां न्यासिनां ब्रह्मसंज्ञितम्।। ३७।।

And those living in the forest reap the place of the seven sages; householders repair to the regions of the creator; and medicants, to the sphere named Brahmā.

योगिनाममृतं स्थानं स्वात्मसंतोषकारिणाम्।। ३८।।

The sphere of the *yogīs* is Amṛta[2]—which is the supreme state of Viṣṇu himself.

एकान्तिनः सदा ब्रह्मध्यायिनो योगिनश्च ये।।
तेषां तु परमं स्थानं यत्तत्पश्यन्ति सूरयः।। ३९।।

Those *yogīs* that contemplate Brahmā with a single soul,—of these is that supreme state which is seen by the celestials.

गत्वागत्वा निवर्त्तन्ते चंद्रसूर्यादयौ ग्रहाः।।
अद्यापि न निवर्त्तन्ते द्वादशाक्षरचिंतकाः।। ४०।।

The sun, the moon, and the other planets, going to this region again and again, return therefrom again and again,—but to this day those that contemplate the twelve-lettered (Mantra),[3] do not have to return therefrom.

तामिस्रमन्धतामिस्रं महारौरवरौरवौ।।
असिपत्रवनं घोरं कालसूत्रमवीचिकम्।। ४१।।
विनिन्दकानां वेदस्य यज्ञव्याघातकारिणाम्।।
स्थानमेतत्समाख्यातं स्वधर्मत्यागिनश्च ये।। ४२।।

Tāmisra, Andhatāmisra, Mahāraurava, Raurava, Aśipatravana, Ghora, and the waveless Kālasūtra,—these are appointed the regions of those that revile the Vedas,—that obstruct sacrifices; and that abandon their own religion."

।। इति श्रीविष्णुमहापुराणे प्रथमेंशे षष्ठोऽध्यायः।। ६।।

अथ प्रथमेंशेः सप्तमोऽध्यायः

Part I : Section 7

श्रीपराशर उवाच

ततोभिध्यायतस्तस्य जज्ञिरे मानसाः प्रजाः।।
तच्छरीरसमुत्पन्नैः कार्यैस्तैः करणैः सह।।
क्षेत्रज्ञाः समवर्त्तन्त गात्रेभ्यस्तस्यः धीमतः।। १।।

Parāśara said :—"Then came forth unto him the mind-sprung beings, embodying causes and consequences arising from his own person.

1. i.e. the Wind-god.

2. *Ambrosia.*
2. A formula, embodying the name of Vāsudeva.

ते सर्वे समवर्त्तन्त ये मया प्रागुदाहृताः।।
देवाद्याः स्थावरान्ताश्च त्रैगुण्यविषये स्थिताः।। २।।

एवंभूतानि सृष्टानि चराणि स्थावराणि च।। ३।।

And out of the body of that intelligent one came out the souls. And thus were generated all those mobile and immobile objects beginning with the deities and concluding with the immovable,—which are established in the three several spheres,[1]—and of which I have told thee before.

यदास्य ताः प्रजाः सर्वा न व्यवर्धन्त धीमतः।।
अथान्यान्मानसान्पुत्रान्सदृशानात्मनोऽसृजत्।। ४।।
भृगुं पुलस्त्यं पुलहं क्रतुमङ्गिरसं तथा।।
मरीचिं, दक्षमत्रिं च वसिष्ठं चैव मानसान्।। ५।।

And when these beings of that intelligent one did not multiply, then he created other mind-begotten sons, resembling himself,—viz., Bhṛgu, Pulastya, Pulaha, Kratu, Aṅgiras, Marīci, Dakṣa, Atri, and the mind-sprung Vasiṣṭha.

नव ब्रह्माण इत्येते पुराणे निश्चयं गताः।। ६।।

The Purāṇa saith that these nine resemble Brahmā himself.

ख्यातिं भूमिं च संभूतिं क्षमां प्रीतिं तथैव च।।
सन्नतिं च तथैवोर्ज्जामनसूयां तथैव च।। ७।।
प्रसूतिं च ततः सृष्ट्वा ददौ तेषां महात्मनाम्।।
पत्न्यो भवध्वमित्युक्त्वा तेषामेव तु दत्तवान्।। ८।।
सनन्दनादयो ये च पूर्वसृष्टास्तु वेधसा।।
न ते लोकेष्वसज्जन्त निरपेक्षाः प्रजासु ते।। ९।।
सर्वे तेऽभ्या गतज्ञाना वीतरागा विमत्सराः।।
तेष्वेवं निरपेक्षेषु लोकसृष्टौ महात्मनः।। १०।।
ब्रह्मणोभून्महान् क्रोधस्त्रैलोक्यदहनमक्षमः।।
तस्य क्रोधात्समुद्भूतज्वालामालातिदीपितम्।।
ब्रह्मणोभूत्तदा सर्वं त्रैलोक्यमखिलं मुने।। ११।।

Those who formerly had been created by Vedas, being bereft of love and hate, had possessed of the highest knowledge, did not take to the world, or produce offspring. And these being indifferent to the increase of people, a mighty wrath took possession of Brahmā, capable of consuming the three worlds. And, O anchoret, the entire triune universe was then illuminated with the flame flowing frm the ire of Brahmā.

1. viz. the upper, middle, and nether regions.

भ्रकुटीकुटिलात्तस्यललाटात्क्रोधदीपितात्।।
समुत्पन्नस्तदा रुद्रो मध्याह्नार्कसमप्रभः।। १२।।
अर्धनारीनरवपुः प्रचण्डोऽतिशरीरवान्।।
विभजात्मानमित्युक्त्वा तं ब्रह्मान्तर्दधे ततः।। १३।।

And then from his furrowed forehead inflamed with wrath sprang Rudra, resembling the mid-day Sun; having a body, half-female,—terrific; and of a prodigious person. And saying unto him,—"Divide thou thyself."—Brahmā then vanished.

तथोक्तोसौ द्विधा स्त्रीत्वं पुरुषत्वं तथाऽकरोत्।।
विभेदपुरुषत्वं च दशधा चैकधा पुनः।। १४।।
सौम्यासौम्यैस्तदाशान्ताऽशान्तैः स्त्रीत्वं च स प्रभुः।।
विभेद बहुधा देवः स्वरूपैरसितैः सितैः।। १५।।

Thus directed, he divided himself into a male and a female. And then he divided the mle into one and ten parts; and the Lord God also divided the female into Saumya,[2] Asaumya,[3] Śānta,[4] Aśānta,[5] Sīta,[6] Asita,[7] and many other parts resembling himself.

ततो ब्रह्मात्मसंभूतं पूर्वं स्वायंभुवं प्रभुः।।
आत्मानमेव कृत वान्प्रजापाल्ये मनुं द्विज।। १६।।

Then the Lord appointed the Self-create Manu, formerly sprung from Brahmā's self, and resembling himself, to rule creature.

शतरूपां च तां नारीं तपोनिर्धूतकल्मषाम्।।
स्वायंभुवो मनुर्देवः पत्नीत्वे जगृहे प्रभुः।। १७।।

And that lord, the divine Self-create Manu, took to wife the female Śatarūpā,[8] purged of all sin through asceticism.

2. Mildness.
3. Insolence.
4. Meek.
5. Wild
6. White.
7. Dark.
8. Having an hundred forms.

तस्मात्तु पुरुषाद्देवी शतरूपा व्यजायत।।
प्रियव्रतोत्तानपादौ प्रसूत्याकूतिसंज्ञितम्।। १८।।
कन्याद्वयं च धर्मज्ञ रूपौदार्यगुणान्वितम्।।
ददौ प्रसूतिं दक्षाय आकूतिं रुचये पुरा।। १९।।

And to that person Śatarūpā bore Priyavrata and Uttānapāda; and two daughters, named Prasūti and Akuti,—endowed, O thou cognisant of righteousness, with the perfections of beauty, and nobility. And the Lord of creatures of old conferred Prasūti on Dakṣa, and Ākūti on Rucya.

प्रजापतिः स जग्राह तयोर्जज्ञे सदक्षिणः।।
पुत्रो यज्ञे महाभाग दम्पत्योर्मिथुनं ततः।। २०।।

And unto this wedded couple were born, O exceedingly righteous one, Yajña and Dakṣiṇā; and these were then united in marriage.

यज्ञस्य दक्षिणायां तु पुत्रा द्वादश जज्ञिरे।।
यामा इति सामख्याता देवाः स्वायंभुवे मनौ।। २१।।

And ten sons were borne to Yajña[1] by Dakṣiṇā.[2] At the time of the Self-create Manu, these went by the designations of *Deva* and *Yāma*.

प्रसूत्यां च तथा दक्षश्चतस्रो विंशतिस्तथा।।
ससर्ज कन्यास्तासां च सम्यङ्नामानि मे शृणु।। २२।।
श्रद्धा लक्ष्मीर्धृतिस्तुष्टिर्मेधा पुष्टिस्तथा क्रिया।।
बुद्धिर्लज्जा वपुः शांतिः सिद्धिः कीर्तिस्त्रयोदशी।। २३।।

And on Prasūti, Dakṣa begat four and twenty daughters,—whose names do thou hear, Śraddhā,[3] Lakṣmī,[4] Dhṛti,[5] Tuṣṭi[6] Puṣṭi,[7] Medhā,[8] Kriyā[9] Buddhi,[10] Lajjā,[11] Vapu[12] Śānti, Siddhi,[13] and Kṛti.[14]

1. Sacrifice.
2. Gift in sacrifice to Brāhmaṇas.
3. Veneration.
4. The goddess of wealth.
5. Patience.
6. Satisfaction.
7. Nourishment.
8. Intelligence.
9. Act.
10. Intellect.
11. Bashfulness.
12. Body.
13. Success.
14. Fame.

पत्न्यर्थं प्रतिजग्राह धर्मो दाक्षायणीः प्रभुः।।
ताभ्यः शिष्टायवीयस्य एकादश सुलोचनाः।। २४।।

The thirteen daughters of Dakṣa were wedded by the Lord Dharma.[15] The daughters remaining after these elder ones, were eleven, furnished with fair eyes,—

ख्यातिः सत्यथ संभूतिः स्मृतिः प्रीतिः क्षमा तथा।।
सन्ततिश्चानसूया च ऊर्जा स्वाहा स्वधा तथा।। २५।।

Khyāti,[16] Satī,[17] Sambhūti,[18] Smṛti,[19] Prīti[20] Kṣamā,[21] Sannati,[22] Anasūyā,[23] Urjjā,[24] Svāhā,[25] and Svadhā.

भृगुर्भवो मरीचिश्च तथा चैवांगिरा मुनिः।।
पुलस्त्यः पुलहश्चैव क्रतुश्चर्षिवरस्तथा।। २६।।
अत्रिर्वसिष्ठो वह्निश्च पितरश्च यथाक्रमम्।।
ख्यात्याद्या जगृहुः कन्या मुनयो मुनि सत्तम।। २७।।

Bhṛgu, Bhava, Marīci, Aṅgiras, Pulastya, Pulaha, Kratu, Atri, Vasiṣṭha, Vanhi, and the *pitṛs*, espoused respectively the dauthers, Khyāti and the rest, O foremost of ascetics.

श्रद्धा कामं चला दर्पं नियमं धृतिरात्मजम्।।
सन्तोषं च तथा तुष्टिर्लोभं पुष्टिरसूयत।। २८।।

And then Śraddhā brought forth Kāma;[26] and Calā,[27] Darpa;[28] and Dhṛti, Niyama[29] as her son; and Tuṣṭi,[30] Santoṣa;[31] and Puṣṭi,[32] Lobha.[33]

15. Righteousness.
16. Renown.
17. Chaste.
18. Birth.
19. Memory.
20. Gratification.
21. Forgiveness.
22. Reverence.
23. Good-natured.
24. Energy.
25. This and the last are words uttered while one is offering oblations.
26. Sexual desire.
27. Lakṣmī.
28. Pride.
29. Restraint.
30. Satisfaction.
31. Contentment.
32. Nourishment.
33. Greed.

मेधा श्रुतं क्रिया दण्डं नयं विनयमेव च।। २९।।

बोधं बुद्धिस्तथा लज्जा विनयं वपुरात्मजम्।।
व्यवसायं प्रजज्ञे वै क्षेमं शान्तिरसूयत।। ३०।।

सुखं सिद्धिर्यशः कीर्त्तिरित्येते धर्मसूनवः।।
कामाद्रतिः सुतं हर्षं धर्मपौत्रमसूयत।। ३१।।

And Medhā[1] brought forth Śrutam;[2] and Kriyā,[3] Daṇḍam[4] Naya,[5] and Vinaya;[6] and Buddhi,[7] Bodha;[8] and Lajjā, Vinaya; and Vapu,[9] Vyavasāya[10] as her son; and Śānti brought forth Kṣamā; and Siddhi, Sukha;[11] and Kīrti, Yaśas.[12] These are the offspring of Dharma Nanda bore unto Kāma, Harṣa[13]—grandson unto Dharma.

हिंसा भार्या त्वधर्मस्य ततो जज्ञे तथानृतम्।।
कन्या च निकृतिस्तामयां माया जज्ञे च वेदना।। ३२।।

Himsā[14] was the wife of Adharma;[15] and from her were born Anṛta,[16] and a daughter—Nikṛti.[17] And from these came forth Bhaya[18] and Naraka;[19] and two daughters—Māyā[20] and Vedanā.[21]

माया च वेदना चैव मिथुनं त्विदमेतयोः।।
तयोर्जज्ञेथ वै माया मृत्युं भूतापहारिणम्।। ३३।।

वेदना स्वसुतं चापि दुःखं जज्ञेऽथ रौरवात्।।
मृत्योर्व्याधिजराशोकतृष्णाक्रोधाश्च जज्ञिरे।। ३४।।

And Māyā and Bhaya gave birth to Mṛtyu[22]—that allayer of the three kinds of heat,[23] and Vedanā bore unto Raurava, a son named Duḥkha.[24] And from Mṛtyu sprang Vyādhi[25] Jwara,[26] Śoka,[27] Tṛṣṇā,[28] and Krodha.[29]

दुःखोत्तराः स्मृता ह्येते सर्वे चाधर्मलक्षणाः।।
नैषां पुत्रोस्ति वै भार्या ते सर्वे ह्यूर्ध्वरेतसः।। ३५।।

रौद्राण्येतानि रूपाणि विष्णोर्मुनिवरात्मज।।
नित्यप्रलयहेतुत्वं जगतोस्य प्रयान्ति वै।। ३६।।

These ultimately lead to misery; and all have marks of unrighteousness. They have no wives, being all of vital fluid drawn up.[30] And, O son of the Prime ascetic, these are the terrific forms of Viṣṇu; and they ever bring on the universal dissolution.

दक्षो मरीचिरत्रिश्च भृग्वाद्याश्च प्रजेश्वराः।।
जगत्यत्र महाभाग नित्यसर्गस्य हेतवः।। ३७।।

And, O exalted one, Dakṣa, Marīci, Bhṛgu, and others—lords of creatures—are always the causes of the creation of the universe.

मनवो मनुपुत्राश्च भूपा वीर्यधराश्च ये।।
सन्मार्गनिरताः शूरास्ते सर्वे स्थितिकारिणः।। ३८।।

And the Manus and their sons and kings possessed of wealth and prowess, and ever abiding by the way of righteousness,—and

1. Intellect.
2. Knowledge.
3. Action.
4. Punishment.
5. Justice.
6. Humility.
7. Intellect.
8. Apprehension.
9. Body.
10. Exertion
11. Felicity.
12. Fame.
13. Cheerfulness.
14. Malice.
15. Unrighteousness.
16. Falsehodd.
17. Wickedness.
18. Fear.
19. Hell.
20. Illusion.
21. Pain.
22. Death.
23. Tapa—lit. heat—here means the three kinds of pain,—natural, supernatural and nomenon accompanying all pain—namely, *heat in the* part *affected*. And physical pain in any part of the body is invariably found to be accompanied with *heat* at that locality.—T.
24. Misery.
25. Disease.
26. Decrepitude.
27. Grief.
28. Thirst.
29. Anger.
30. The reader will readily perceive that all this is allegorical, although the allegory is by no means on all fours. The entire fabric, it may truly be said, of Hinduisim is upreared upon an allegorical foundation; out the allegory having been missed, it has degenerated itself into a system of degrading superstition.—T.

heroic,—are the causes of the maintenance of the cosmos."

श्रीमैत्रेय उवाच

येयं नित्या स्थितिर्ब्रह्मन्नित्यसर्गस्तथेरितः ।।
नित्याभावश्च तेषां वै स्वरूपं मम कथ्यताम् ।। ३९ ।।

Maitreya said :—"O Brāhmaṇa, thou hast alluded to constant creation, constant sustenance and constant dissolution. Do thou describe unto me the characteristics of them."

श्रीपराशर उवाच

सर्गस्थितिविनाशांश्च भगवान्मधुसूदनः ।।
तैस्तैरूपैरचिंत्यात्मा करोत्यव्याहतो विभुः ।। ४० ।।

(Thereat) Parāśara said :—"That one of incomprehensible soul,—the reverend destroyer of Madhu—the Lord assuming respective shapes, effects the creation, maintenance and destruction (of the Universe).

नैमित्तिकः प्राकृतिकस्तथैवात्यन्तिको द्विज ।।
नित्यश्च सर्वभूतानां प्रलयोऽयं चतुर्द्धवधः ।। ४१ ।।

The dissolution (of beings) is of four kinds, *viz.*, O twice-born one, Naimittika, Prākṛtika Atyantika, and Nitya.

ब्राह्मो नैमित्तिकस्तत्र च्छेतेयं जगतीपतिः ।।
प्रयामि प्राकृतं चैव ब्रह्माण्डं प्रकृतौ लयम ।। ४२ ।।

When, on the expiry of his Day, Brahmā—the lord of the Universe—lieth down, takes place the dissolution called *Naimittika.* When the mundane egg dissolveth itself away in Primaeval Nature, takes place the Prākṛta dissolution.

ज्ञानादात्यन्तिकः प्रोक्तो योगिनः परमात्मनि ।।
नित्यः सदैव भूतानां यो विनाशो दिवानिशम् ।। ४३ ।।

The fusion of the *Yogīs* into the Supreme Soul through knowledge, is the Atyantika dissolution.

प्रसूतिः प्रकृतेर्या तु सा सृष्टिः प्राकृता स्मृता ।।
दैनंदिनी तथा प्रोक्ता नान्तरप्रलयादनु ।। ४४ ।।

And the constant dissolution of things taking place day and night, goeth by the name of *Nitya.*

भूतान्यनुदिने यत्र जायन्ते मुनिसत्तम ।।
नित्यसर्गो हि स प्रोक्तः पुराणार्थविचक्षणैः ।। ४५ ।।

The creation which comes of Primaeval matter, is known as Prakṛti; that which takes place at the end of a minor dissolution, is known as *Dainandini;* and, O foremost of anchorets, the constant daily creation of beings, is called Nitya by the wise versed in the import of the Purāṇas,

एवं सर्वशरीरेषु भगवान्भूतभावनः ।।
संस्थितः कुरुते विष्णुरुत्पत्तिस्थितिसंयमान् ।। ४६ ।।

Thus that origin of all beings, Viṣṇu, remaining in the bodies of all things, bringeth about creation, maintenance and destruction.

सृष्टि स्थितिविनाशानां शक्तयः सर्वदेहिषु ।।
वैष्णव्यः परिवर्त्तन्ते मैत्रेयाहर्निशं समाः ।। ४७ ।।

O Maitreya, the energies of Viṣṇu relative to creation, sustenance, and destruction, remaining in the bodies of all beings, are ever coursing on day and night.

गुणत्रयमयं ह्येतद्ब्रह्मन् शक्तित्रयं महत् ।।
योऽतियात स यात्येव परं नावर्त्तते पुनः ।। ४८ ।।

O Brāhmaṇa, he that, compounded of these mighty powers, overruleth the three principles, attaineth the Supreme state (of Viṣṇu) and hath not to come back to this scene."

।। इति श्रीविष्णुपुराणे प्रथमेंशे सप्तमोऽध्यायः ।। ७ ।।

अथ प्रथमेंशेः अष्टमोऽध्यायः

Part I : Section 8

श्रीपराशर उवाच

कथितस्तामसः सर्गो ब्रह्मणस्ते महामुने।।
रुद्रसर्गं प्रवक्ष्यामि तन्मे निगदतः शृणु।। १।।

Parāśara said :—"O mighty ascetic, I have narrated unto thee the creation of Brahmā connected with the principle of dullness. Now I shall unfold unto thee the creation called Rudra.

कल्पादावात्मनस्तुल्यं सुतं प्रध्यायतस्ततः।।
प्रादुरासीत्प्रभोरंके कुमारो नीललोहितः।। २।।

Do thou hearken as I proceed! At the outset of a Kalpa, as the Lord was rapt in thoughts about a son resembling himself, on his lap appeared one hued red-blue.

रुरोद सुस्वरं सोथ प्राद्रवद्द्विजसत्तम।।
किं त्वं रोदिषि तं ब्रह्मा रुदन्तं प्रत्युवाच ह ।। ३।।

And, O best of regenerate persons, crying in sweet tones, he went about. And as he was crying, Brahmā asked him,—'Why dost thou weep?'

नाम देहीति तं सोऽथ प्रत्युवाच प्रजापतिः।।
रुद्रस्त्वं देवनाम्नासि मारोदीर्धैर्यमावह।।
एवमुक्तः पुनः सोऽथ सप्तकृत्वो रुरोद वै।। ४।।

And thereon, he said unto the Lord of creatures,—'Let me have a name.' And (the Lord said),—'O divine one, thou art named Rudra. Do not cry. Have patience.' Thus accosted, he again cried for seven times.

ततोन्यानि ददौ तस्मै सप्त नामानि वै प्रभुः।।
स्थानानि चैषामष्टानां पत्नीः पुत्रांश्च स प्रभुः।। ५।।

And thereat the Lord gave him seven other names; and assigned six receipients thereof, as well as the six wives and sons of the latter.

भवं शर्वमथेशानं तथा पशुपतिं द्विज।।
भीममुग्रं महादेवमुवाच स पितामहः।। ६।।

Bhava, Śarva, Īśāna, Paśupati, Bhīma, Ugra, and Mahādeva,—these seven names were mentioned by the Great-father.

चक्रे नामान्यथैतानि स्थानान्येषां चकार सः।।
सूर्यो जलं मही वायुर्वह्निराकाशमेव च।।
दीक्षितो ब्राह्मणः सोम इत्येतास्तनवः क्रमात्।। ७।।

And the holders thereof were respectively the Sun, water, earth, fire, air, ether, the initiated Brāhmaṇa, and Soma.

सुवर्चला तथैवोषा विकेशी चापरा शिवा।।
स्वाहा दिशस्तथा दीक्षा रोहिणी च यथाक्रमम्।।८।।

सूर्यादीनां द्विजश्रेष्ठ रुद्राद्यैर्नामभिः सह।।
पत्न्यः स्मृता महाभाग तदपत्यानि मे शृणु।। ९।।
एषां सूतिप्रसूतिभ्यामिदमापूरितं जगत्।। १०।।

And Suvarcalā, Umā, Sukeśī, Śiva, Diśa, Dīkṣā, and Rohiṇī,—are, O best of men, the wives of the Rudras, named the Sun, etc. And hearken (unto me) reciting the names of their offspring, whose sons and grandsons have filled the universe.

शनैश्चरस्तथा शुक्रो लोहिताङ्गो मनोजवः।।
स्कन्दः सर्गोऽथ सन्तानो बुधश्चानुक्रमात्सुताः।। ११।।

Śanaiścara, Śuka, Lohitānga, Manojava, Skanda, Swaraga, Santāna and Buddha,—these are respectively the sons (of the Eight Forms).

एवंप्रकारो रुद्रोऽसौ सतीं भार्यामनिन्दिताम्।।
उपयेमे दुहितरं दक्षस्यैव प्रजापतेः।। १२।।
दक्षकोपाच्च तत्याज सा सती स्वकलेवरम्।।
हिमवद्दुहिता साऽभून्मेनायां द्विजसत्तम।। १३।।
उपयेमे पुनश्चोमामनन्यां भगवान्हरः।। १४।।

Rudra, formed thus, took to his wife Satī. And though Dakṣa's ire, Satī renounced her person. And then, O best of the born ones, she became the daughter of Himavat by name Umā. Then the reverend Bhava again Umā, who was his solely.

देवौ धातृविधातारौ भृगोः ख्यातिरसूयत।।
श्रियं च देवदेवस्य पत्नी नारायणस्य या।। १५।।

And Bhṛgu's wife, Khyāti, brought forth the gods—Dhātā and Vidhātā; as well as Śrī, who is Nārāyaṇa's spouse."

श्रीमैत्रेय उवाच

क्षीराब्धौ श्रीः समुत्पन्नाश्रूयतेऽमृतमन्थने।।
भृगोः ख्यात्यां समुत्पन्नेत्येतदाह कथं भवान्।। १६।।

Maitreya said :—"We have heard that Śrī arose from the Ocean of milk on the occasion of the churning of the deep. But why dost thous say that she was begot by Bhṛgu on Khyāti?"

श्रीपराशर उवाच

नित्यैवैषा जगन्माता विष्णोः श्रीरनपायिनी।।
यथा सर्वगतो विष्णुस्तथैवेयं द्विजोत्तम।। १७।।

Thereat Parāśara said :—"That mother of Universe—Viṣṇu's energy—is enduring and underteriorating, O foremost of the twice-born ones, even as Viṣṇu is omnipresent, so this one also.

अर्थो विष्णुरियं वाणी नीतिरेषा नयो हरिः।।
बोधो विष्णुरियं बुद्धिर्धर्मोऽसौ सत्क्रिया त्वियम्।। १८।।

Visṇu is the sense and she is the word; she is morality, Viṣṇu is justice; Viṣṇu is perception, and she the power thereof; he is merit, and she the act of piety.—

स्त्रष्टा विष्णुरियं सृष्टिः श्रीर्भूमिर्भूधरो हरिः।।
सन्तोषो भगवाल्लँक्ष्मीस्तुष्टिर्मैत्रेय शाश्वती।। १९।।

इच्छा श्रीर्भगवान्कामो यज्ञोऽसौ दक्षिणा त्वियम्।।
आज्याहुतिरसौ देवी पुरोडाशो जनार्द्दनः।। २०।।

Viṣṇu is the creator, and she the creation; Śrī is earth,—and Hari, the supporter thereof. The reverend one is contentment, and, O Maitreya, Lakṣmī is permanent peace; Śrī is desire, and the worshipful one is Kāma; he is sacrifice, and she the *dakṣiṇā;* the goddess is the first libation, and Janārddana is *Puroḍāśa;*[1]

पत्नीशाला मुने लक्ष्मीः प्राग्वंशो मधुसूदनः।।
चितिर्लक्ष्मीर्हरिर्यूप इध्मा श्रीर्भगवान्कुशः।। २१।।

O ascetic, Lakṣmī is *patniśālā,*[2] and Madhusūdana is the *prākvaṁśa*[3] (of a sacrifice); Lakṣmī is the *citti* and Hari is the *yūpa;*[4] Lakṣmī is sacrificial fuel, and the reverend one is Kuśa.

सामस्वरूपी भगवानुद्गीतिः कमलालया।।
स्वाहा लक्ष्मीर्जगन्नाथो वासुदेवो हुताशनः।। २२।।

शंकरो भगवाञ्छौरिर्गौरीलक्ष्मीर्द्विजोत्तम।।
मैत्रेय केशवः सूर्यस्तत्प्रभा कमलालया।। २३।।

The reverend one is Sāman, the Lotus-dwelling Śrī is Udgīti;[5] Lakṣmī is Svāhā, that Lord of the Universe,—Vāsudeva—is fire, the worshipful Śaurī is Śaṅkara, (the mistress of) Wealth is, O best of the twice-born one, Gaurī. O Maitreya, Keśava is the Sun, the Lotus-seated one is the splendour thereof.

विष्णुः पितृगणः पद्मा स्वधा शाश्वतपुष्टिदा।।
द्यौः श्रीः सर्वात्मको विष्णुरवकाशोतिविस्तरः।। २४।।

Viṣṇu are the paternal manes, and the Lotus-throned one is Svadhā, ever conferring gratification; Śrī is the city of the celestials.

शशांकः श्रीधरः कान्तिः श्रीस्तथैवानपायिनी।।
धृतिर्लक्ष्मीर्जगच्चेष्टा वायुः सर्वत्रगो हरिः।। २५।।

जलधिर्द्विजगोविंदस्तद्वेला श्रीर्महामुने।।
लक्ष्मीस्वरूपमिंद्राणी देवेन्द्रो मधुसूदनः।। २६।।

That soul of all—Viṣṇu—is the exceedingly spacious sky; the support of Śrī is the Moon, and Śrī is the constant resplendence thereof; Lakṣmī is Fortitude and Exertion; Hari is the aircoursing everywhere. O twice-born one, Govinda is the Ocean; and, O magnianmous Vipra, Śrī is the shore thereof. Lakṣmī is like the spouse of Indra, and the Destroyer of Madhu is the Indra of the immortals.

यमश्चक्रधरः साक्षाद्धूमोर्णा कमलालया।।
ऋद्धिः श्रीः श्रीधरो देवः स्वयमेव धनेश्वरः।। २७।।

1. Clarified butter as offered in oblations to fire with cakes of ground barley meal that have been well steeped in it.—T.

2. The room opposite to that which contains the materials for an oblation and in which the family and friends of the sacrifice assemble.
3. An oblong with quadrangular sides.
4. A sacrificial stake.
5. The hymns of the Sāma Veda.

गौरी लक्ष्मीर्महाभागा केशवो वरुणः स्वयम्।।
श्रीर्देवसेना विप्रेन्द्र देवसेनापतिर्हरिः।। २८।।

The holder of the discus is Yama himself, and the Lotus-presiding one is Dhumorṇa.[1] Śrī is Prosperity, that god—the supporter of Śrī—is the Lord himself of riches. Lakṣmī is the highly exalted Gaurī and Keśava is Varuṇa himself. Śrī is the celestial host, O foremost of Vipras, and Hari is the lord thereof.

अवष्टंभो गदापाणिः शक्तिर्लक्ष्मीर्द्विजोत्तम।।
काष्ठा लक्ष्मीर्निमेषोऽसौ मुहूर्त्तोऽसौ कला त्वियम्।। २९।।
ज्योत्स्ना लक्ष्मीः प्रदीपोऽसौ सर्वः सर्वेश्वरो हरिः।।

The mace-handed one is Avastambha, and, O best of the regenerate, Lakṣmī is Energy. Lakṣmī is Kāṣṭha,[2] and he is Nimeṣa.[3] He is *muhūrta*, and she is *kalā*; Lakṣmī is the light, and Hari, or Śarva—lord of all—is the lamp.

लताभूता जगन्माता श्रीर्विष्णुर्दुमसंज्ञितः।। ३०।।
विभावरी श्रीर्दिवसो देवचक्रगदाधरः।।

The Mother of the universe is the plant, and Viṣṇu—the spouse of Śrī—is the tree established. Śrī is Night, and that deity—the holder of the discus and mace—is Day.

वरप्रदो वरो विष्णुर्वधूः पद्मवनालया।। ३१।।
नदस्वरूपी भगवाञ्छ्रीर्नदीरूपसंस्थिता।।
ध्वजश्च पुण्डरीकाक्षः पताका कमलालया।। ३२।।

The boon-bestowing Viṣṇu is the bridegroom, and she dwelling in the lotus-grove is the Bride. The reverend One is like a male river. Puṇḍarīkakṣa is the (banner), and the Lotus-seated Śrī is the Ensign.

तृष्णा लक्ष्मीर्जगन्नाथो लोभो नारायणः परः।।
रती रागश्च मैत्रेय लक्ष्मीर्गोविंद एव च।। ३३।।
किं चातिबहुनोक्तेन संक्षेपेणेदमुच्यते।। ३४।।

Lakṣmī is Thirst, and that master of the Universe, the Great Nārāyaṇa, is Desire. And, O thou cognisant of righteousness, Lakṣmī is Thirst, and that master of the Universe, the Great Nārāyaṇa, is Desire. And, O thou cognisant of righteousness, Lakṣmī and Govinda are respectively Attachment and Love. What is the use of dilating?

देवतिर्यङ्मनुष्यादौ पुन्नामा भगवान्हरिः।।
स्त्रीनाम्नी श्रीश्च विज्ञेया नानयोर्विद्यते परम्।। ३५।।

I tell thee this in brief,—the Reverend Hari compriseth gods, men, beasts and other creatures that are termed male; and, O Maitreya, Lakṣmī compriseth all that are termed female. There exists naught that is beyond these."

।। इति श्रीविष्णुपुराणे प्रथमेंशे अष्टमोऽध्यायः।।८।।

अथ प्रथमेंशेः नवमोऽध्यायः

Part I : Section 9

श्रीपराशर उवाच

इदं च शृणु मैत्रेय यत्पृष्टोहमिह त्वया।।
श्रीसम्बन्धं मयाप्येतच्छ्रुतमासीन्मरीचितः।। १।।

Parāśara said :—"O Maitreya, listen to what I say anent thy question about Śrī, as I had heard from Marīci.

दुर्वासाः शंकरस्यांशश्चार पृथिवीमिमाम्।।
स ददर्श स्त्रजं दिव्यामृषिर्विद्याधरीकरे।। २।।
संतानकानामखिलं यस्या गंधेन वासितम्।।
अतिसेव्यमभूद्ब्रह्मन् तद्वनं वनचारिणाम्।। ३।।

That Emanation of Śaṅkara—Durvāsā—was ranging this Earth. And it came to pass that the sage saw in the hand of a Vidyādharī a celestial garland,—perfumed by which, O Brāhmaṇa, that entire forest of Santānakās[4] had become surpassingly charming to the rangers of woods.

उन्मत्तव्रतधृग्विप्रस्तां दृष्ट्वा शोभनां स्त्रजम्।।
तां ययाचे वरारोहां विद्याधरवधूं तत।। ४।।

And it came to pass that on seeing that graceful garland, that mad Vipra practising the vows, asked for the same of that bride of a Vidyādhara.

1. A division of time.
2. Wife of Yama.
3. Time taken up by the twinkling of an eye.
4. A kind of celestial tree.

याचिता तेन तन्वंगी मालां विद्याधरांगना।।
ददौ तस्मै विशालाक्षी सादरं प्रणिपत्य तम्।। ५।।

And solicited by him, that slender-framed and large-eyed spouse of a Vidyādhara, saluting him with regard made it over unto him.

तामादायात्मनो मूर्द्धिन स्त्रजमुन्मत्तरूपधृक्।।
कृत्वा स विप्रो मैत्रेय परिबभ्राम मेदिनीम् ।। ६।।

And thereat, laying the wreath on his head, that Vipra wearing the form of a maniac proceeded to roam about the earth.

स ददर्श तमायान्तमुन्मत्तैरावते स्थितम्।।
त्रैलोक्याधिपतिं देवं सह देवैः शचीपतिम्।। ७।।
तामात्मनः स शिरसः स्त्रजमुन्मत्त षट्पदाम्।।
आदायामरराजाय चिक्षेपोन्मत्तवन्मुनिः।। ८।।

And then he saw that deity—Śaci's lord—sovereign of the three regions—mounted on the mad Airāvata,—approaching along with the celestials. And the ascetic, resembling a mad man, taking from his head that garland, whose odour was maddening six-footed (black-bees), threw it on the sovereign of the celestials.

गृहीत्वाऽमरराजेन स्त्रगैरावतमूर्द्धनि।।
न्यस्ता रराज कैलासशिखरे जाह्नवी यथा।। ९।।

And thereon the king of the immortals, taking the wreath, placed it over the head of Airāvata; and thus placed, the same appeared like the Jahnavi on the peak of Kailāśa.

मदान्धकारिताक्षोसौ गन्धाकृष्टेन वारणः।।
करेणाघ्राय चिक्षेप तां स्त्रजं धरणीतले।। १०।।

And it came to pass that the elephant with his eyes blinded by the temporal exudation,—on being assiled by the odour, smelt the perfume wit his trunk (raised),—and then cast the same away to the earth.

ततश्चुक्रोध भगवान्दुर्वासा मुनि सत्तमः।।
मैत्रेय देवराजानं क्रुद्धश्चैतदुवाच ह।। ११।।

Then was wroth the reverend Durvāsā, best of anchorets; and, O Maitreya, being enraged, he spoke unto the sovereign of the celestials, saying,—

दुर्वासा उवाच
ऐश्वर्यमददुष्टात्मन्नतिस्तब्धोसि वासव।।
श्रियो धाम स्त्रजं यस्त्वं मद्दत्तां नाभिनन्दसि।। १२।।
प्रसाद इति नोक्तं ते प्रणिपातपुरःसरम्।।
हर्षोत्फुल्लकपोलेन न चापि शिरसा धृता।। १३।।
मया दत्तामि मां मालां यस्मान्न बजह्न मन्यसे।।
त्रैलोक्यश्रीरतो मूढ विनाशमुपयास्यति।। १४।।

'O thou intoxicated with wealth! O wicked of soul! O Vāsava! how art thou puffed up. But inasmuch as thou dost not regard this wreath, which is the abode of Auspicious-ness,—and as, bowing down the head, thou hast not, said,—Thy favour!—nor, with thy cheeks beaming with delight, hast thou placed it on thy head,—as, in (brief), thou dost not pay high homage to this garland given by me,—O fool, thy celestial prosperity shall depart from thee.

मां मन्यसे त्वं सदृशं नूनं शक्रेतरद्विजैः।।
अतोवमा नमास्मासु मानिना भवता कृतम्।। १५।।

Surely, O Śakra, me thou deemest like other twice-born ones; and therefore, thou thinking immensely of thyself, hast thus slighted me.

मद्दत्ता भवता यस्मात्क्षिप्ता माला महीतले।।
तस्मात्प्रणष्टलक्ष्मीकं त्रैलोक्यं ते भविष्यति।। १६।।

And as thou hast cast away the wreath given by me to the earth, therefore thy Triune world shall be reft of Auspiciousness.

यस्य सञ्जातकोपस्य भयमेति चराचरम्।।
तं त्वं मामतिगर्वेण देवराजावमन्यसे।। १७।।

Me whom when wroth the mobile and the immobile fear,—thou, O monarch of the immortals, hast insulted from thy excess of arrogance."

श्रीपराशर उवाच
महेन्द्रो वारणस्कंधादवतीर्य त्वरान्वितः।।
प्रसादयामास मुनिं दुर्वाससमकल्मषम्।। १८।।

Parāśara said :—"Thereat the great Indra, swiftly alighting from the back of his elephant, propitiated the sinless Durvāsā.

प्रसाद्यमानः स तदा प्रणिपातपुरःसरम्।।
इत्युवाच सहस्त्राक्षं दुर्वासा मुनि सत्तमः।। १९।।

And propitiated by him with his head humbled, that best of ascetics—Durvāsā—answered the thousand-eyed (Deity).

दुर्वासा उवाच

नाहं कृपालुहृदयो न च मां भजते क्षमा।।
अन्ये ते मुनयः शक्र दुर्वाससमवेहि माम्।। २०।।

Durvāsā said : —'I am not kind of heart; nor doth for-giveness find, a place in me. They, O Śakra, are other ascetics; but know me as Durvāsā.

गौतमादिभिरन्यैस्त्वं गर्वमारोपितो मुधा।।
अक्षान्तिसारसर्वस्वं दुर्वाससमवेहि माम्।। २१।।

Gautama and others have for nothing fostered thy pride. But me thou must know as Durvāsā, who is nothing if not unforgiving.

वसिष्ठाद्यैर्दयासारैस्तोत्रं कुर्वद्भिरुच्चकैः।।
गर्वं गतोसि येनैवं मामप्यद्यावमन्यसे।। २२।।

And having been hymned aloud by Vasiṣṭha and others,—overflowing with clemency, thou hast grown haughty,—and it is for this reason that thou hast grown haughty,—and it is for this reason that thou insultest even me in this way.

ज्वलज्जटाकलापस्य भृकुटीकुटिलं मुखम्।।
निरीक्ष्य कस्त्रिभुवने मम यो न गतो भयम्।। २३।।

Who is there in all these three regions that beholding the frowning face of mine furnished with flaming matted locks,—can keep off fear; forgive I will not.

नाहं क्षमिष्ये बहुना किमुक्तेन शतक्रतो।।
विडंबनामिमां भूयः करोष्यनुनयात्मिकाम्।। २४।।

What then is the use, O thou of an hundred sacrifices, of thy expending much speech. Thou again and again puttest thyself to useless trouble in thus beseeching me."

श्रीपराशर उवाच

इत्युक्त्वा प्रययौ विप्रो देवराजोपि तं पुनः।।
आरुह्यैरावतं ब्रह्मन् प्रययावमरावतीम्।। २५।।

Parāśara said :—"Having said this, the Vipra went away. And, O Brāhmaṇa, the monarch of the immortals also, mounting Airāvata, went to Amarāvatī.

ततः प्रभृति निःश्रीकं सशक्रं भुवनत्रयम्।।
मैत्रेयासीदपध्वस्तं संक्षी णौषधिवीरुधम्।। २६।।

O Maitreya, from that time the three worlds with Śakra became shorn of Auspiciousness, and the glory thereof faded; and sacrifices and medicinal herbs grew feebler.

न यज्ञाः समवर्त्तन्ते न तपस्यन्ति तापसाः।।
च दानादिधर्मेषु मनश्चक्रे तदा जनः।। २७।।

And no sacrifices are performed, and none practised asceticism; and none taketh any delight in good works, such as charity.

निःसत्त्वाः सकला लोका लोभाद्युपहतेन्द्रियाः।।
स्वल्पेपि हि बभूवुस्ते साभिलाषा द्विजोत्तम।। २८।।

And all men, void of power, came under the masterdom of the senses; and O prime of the regenerate ones, they could not restrain their hearts even in things intrinsically small.

यतः सत्त्वं ततो लक्ष्मीः सत्त्वं भूत्यनुसारि च।।
निःश्रीकाणां कुतः सत्त्वं विना तेन गुणाः कुतः।। २९।।

Where strength is, there is Prosperity, and strength ever followed Prosperity. Where is the strength of the inauspicious?

बलशौर्याद्यभावश्च पुरुषाणां गुणैर्विना।।
लघनायः समस्तस्य बलशौर्यविवर्जितः।। ३०।।
भवत्यपध्वस्तमतिर्लंघितः प्रथितः पुमान्।।

And without strength, where are virtue? And without virtues, persons cannot have power, affluence, etc. And those divorced by power and wealth, are overriden by all. And, when, overruled a person albeit possessed of fame, loseth his sense.

एवमत्यन्तनिःश्रीके त्रैलोक्ये सत्ववर्जिते।। ३१।।
दवान् प्रति बलोद्योगं चक्रुर्दैतेयदानवाः।। ३२।।

On the three worlds, shorn of Auspiciousness, being bereft of strength Daityas and Dānavas began to use force against the celestials.

लोभाभिभूता निःश्रीका दैत्याः सत्त्वविवर्जिताः।।
श्रिया विहीनैर्निःसत्वैर्देवैश्चक्रुस्ततो रणम्।। ३३।।

And the Daityas, shorn of Auspiciousness and devoid of strength, being overmastered by covetousness, entered upon hostilities with the celestials, having neither Auspiciousness nor strength.

विजितास्त्रिदशा दैत्यैरिन्द्राद्याः शरणं ययुः ।।
पितामहं महाभागं हुताशनापुरोगमाः ।। ३४ ।।

And the celestials, Indra and the rest, on being vanquished by the Daityas,—with the god of Fire at their head,—sought the protection of the exceedingly exalted Great-father.

यथावत्कथितो देवैर्ब्रह्मा प्राह ततः सुरान् ।।

And, having been addressed duly by the deities, Brahmā, then spoke unto the celestials.

परावरेशं शरणं व्रजध्वमसुरार्दनम् ।। ३५ ।।
उत्पत्तिस्थितिनाशानामहेतुं हेतुमीश्वरम् ।।
प्रजा पतिपतिं विष्णुमनन्तपराजिहतम् ।। ३६ ।।

And Brahmā said :—'Do ye seek the protection of the Supreme of supreme deities, that Lord, the Destroyer of Asuras, the cause of all,—as well as of creation, protection and destruction, the Lord of the lord of creatures—Viṣṇu; Infinite; the unvanquished.

प्रधानपुंसोरजयोः कारणं कार्यभूतयोः ।।
प्रणतार्त्तिहरं विष्णुं स वः श्रेयो विधास्यति ।। ३७ ।।

The cause of the unborn Pradhāna and Puruṣa ripe for creation; Him that taketh off the misery of the humble; even Viṣṇu. He will provide for your welfare.'

श्रीपराशर उवाच

एवमुक्त्वा सुरान्सर्वान् ब्रह्मा लोकपितामहः ।।
क्षीरोदस्योत्तरं तीरं तैरेव सहितो ययौ ।। ३८ ।।

Having spoken thus unto the assembled celestials, Brahmā—Great father of all—went along with them to the Northern shore of the Milky Ocean.

स गत्वा त्रिदशैः सर्वैः समवेतः पितामहः ।।
तुष्टाव वाग्भिरिष्टाभिः परावरपतिं हरिम् ।। ३९ ।।

And repairing thither surrounded by all the celestials, the Greatness father, with excellent speech eulogized the prime of prime and the master—Hari.

ब्रह्मोवाच

नमामि सर्वं सर्वेशमनन्तमजमव्ययम् ।।
लोकधाम धराधारमप्रकाशमभेदिनम् ।। ४० ।।
नारायणमणीयांसमशेषाणामणीयसाम् ।।
समस्तानां गरिष्ठं च भूरादीनां गरीयसाम् ।। ४१ ।।
यत्र सर्वं यतः सर्वमुत्पन्नं मत्पुरःसरम् ।।
सर्वभूतश्च यो देवः पराणामपि यः परः ।। ४२ ।।
परः परस्मात्पुरुषात्परमात्मस्वरूपधृक् ।।
योगिभिश्चिन्त्यते योऽसौ मुक्तिहेतोर्मुमुक्षुभिः ।। ४३ ।।
सत्त्वादयो न सन्तीशे यत्र च प्राकृता गुणाः ।।

And Brahmā said,—"We bow unto thee, who art All and the Lord of all,—who art infinite, unborn and unspent : who art unmanifested and without difference; Nārāyaṇa,—who art the subtlest of all subtile objects : and who art the weightiest of all things weighty on earth; He in whom and from whom are all things that have sprung into existence, commencing with *Sat* : who surpassest the Prime person; and art the Embodiment of the Supreme Spirit; who are contemplated in order to emancipation by *Yogīs* desirous of deliverence; in whom are not Goodness and the rest,—nor the attributes inhereing in Prakṛti.

स शुद्धः सर्वशुद्धेभ्यः पुमानाद्यः प्रसीदतु ।। ४४ ।।
कला काष्ठा मुहूर्त्तादिकालसूत्रस्य गोचरे ।।
यस्य शक्तिर्न शुद्धस्य स नो विष्णुः प्रसीदतु ।। ४५ ।।
प्रोच्यते परमेशो हि यः शुद्धोऽप्युपचारतः ।।
प्रसीदतु स नो विष्णुरात्मा यः सर्वदेहिनाम् ।। ४६ ।।
यः कारणं च कार्यं च कारणस्यापि कारणम् ।।
कार्यस्यापि च यः कार्यं प्रसीदतु स नो हरिः ।। ४७ ।।

May that one pure beyond all things pure—that primaeval Male be propitious (to us)! May that pure Hari, whose power is not tethered to *kalā, kāṣṭhā, nimeśa, etc.*, prove propitious (to us)! May He that is styled the Supreme Lord, who is free from all things,—that Viṣṇu who is the Soul of embodied things,—be propitious (to as)! May that Hari, who is cause as well as effect, who is the cause even of the cause,—who again is, the effect of the effect,—prove propitious to me!

कार्यकार्यस्य यत्कार्यं तत्कार्यस्यापि यः स्वयम् ।।
तत्कार्यकार्यभूतो यस्ततश्च प्रणतास्म तम् ।। ४८ ।।

We bow down unto Him who is the effect

of the effect,—and who is also is Himself the effect of that effect,—and who the effect of the effect thereof.

कारणं कारणस्यापि तस्य कारणकारणम्।।
तत्कारणानां हेतुं तं प्रणता स्म परेश्वरम्।। ४९।।

We bow unto thee who art the foremost of the celestials,—who art the cause of even the cause,—and the cause of the cause of the cause,—and the origin of all these causes combined.

भोक्तारं भोग्यभूतं च स्रष्टारं सृज्यमेव च।।
कार्यकर्तृस्वरूपं तं प्रणता स्म परं पदम्।। ५०।।
विशुद्धबोधवन्नित्यमजमक्षयमव्ययम्।।
अव्यक्तम विकारं यत्तद्विष्णोः परमं पदम्।। ५१।।
न स्थूलं न च सूक्ष्मं यन्न विशेषणगोचरम्।
तत्पदं परमं विष्णोः प्रणमाम सदाऽमलम्।। ५२।।
यस्या युतायुतांशांशे विश्वशक्तिरियं स्थिता।।
परब्रह्मस्वरूपं यत्प्रणमामस्तमव्ययम्।। ५३।।

We bow down unto that Supreme State which is the creator as well as the created,—and which is at once cause and consequence. We bow unto that Prime State of Viṣṇu which is pure cognition, which is constant, causeless, underteriorating and unspent; and which is the unmanifested and unmodified. We bow down unto that Prime and ever pure state of Viṣṇus, which is not gross and yet not subtile; which cannot be differentiated. We bow unto that undeteriorating one who is the Supreme Brahmā,—and in one of whose Ayuta[1] of Ayuta portion is this cosmic energy established.

यद्योगिनः सदोद्युक्ताः पुण्यपाक्षयेक्षयम्।।
पश्यन्ति प्रणवे चिन्त्यं तद्विष्णोः परमं पदम्।।५४।।
यन्न देवा न मुनयो न चाहं न च शङ्करः।।
जानन्ति परमेश स्य तद्विष्णोः परमं पदम्।। ५५।।
शक्तयो यस्य देवस्य ब्रह्मविष्णुशिवात्मिकाः।।
भवन्त्यभूतपूर्वस्य तद्विष्णोः परमं पदम्।। ५६।।

We bow unto that Prime State of Viṣṇu—that Supreme Deity—which is not known either to the deities, or the ascetics, or me, or Śankara himself. We bow unto that Supreme incomprehensible and indestructible State of Viṣṇu, which, on the exhaustion of their merits and demirits, the *Yogīs*, ever perserving, view, grounded in the Pranava.[2] We bow to the Prime State of that God Viṣṇu, who is without equal, and whose energy is Brahmā, Viṣṇu and Śiva.

सर्वेश सर्वभूतात्मन्सर्व सर्वाश्रयाच्युत।।
प्रसीद विष्णो भक्तानां व्रज नो दृष्टिगोचरम्।।५७।।

O Lord of all! O soul of all beings! O thou that art all! O refuge of all! O thou that never fallest off! O Viṣṇu, be thou propitious! Come thou within the ken of us who are thy devotees!"

श्रीपराशर उवाच

इत्युदीरितमाकर्ण्य ब्रह्मणस्त्रिदशास्ततः।।
प्रणम्योचुः प्रसीदेति व्रज नो दृष्टि गोचरम्।।५८।।
यन्नायं भगवान् ब्रह्मा जानाति परमं पदम्।।
तन्नताः स्म जगद्धाम तव सर्वगताच्युत।। ५९।।

Parāśara said :—Hearing this invocation of Brahmā, and then the deities, bowing down, said,—"Be propitious! Come thou within the range of our vision? O thou that art in every thing! O thou that never fallest off! O support of the Universe! we bow unto that Prime State which even the reverend Brahmā doth not know."

इत्यन्ते वचसस्तेषां देवानां ब्रह्मणस्तथा।।
ऊचुर्देवर्षयस्सर्वे बृहस्पतिपुरोगमाः।। ६०।।
आद्यो यज्ञः पुमानीड्यः पूर्वेषां यश्च पूर्वजः।।
तन्नताः स्म जगत्स्त्रष्टुः स्त्रष्टारम विशेषणम्।। ६१।।
भगवन्भूतभव्येश यज्ञमूर्त्तिधराव्यय।।
प्रसीद प्रणतानां त्वं सर्वेषां देहि दर्शनम्।। ६२।।

When the deities as well as Brahmā had ended thus, the Devarṣis,[3] headed by Bṛhaspati,[4] said,—"We bow down unto him—the creator of the cosmos devoid of difference—who is primaeval, who is the Sacrificial Person, who is worthy of being extolled, and who is

1. Ten thousand.
2. A designation of *Om*, for which see before.
3. *Lit.—Celestial saints*—an order of saints.
4. The preceptor of the deities.

prior in birth to everything. O Worshipful one! O thou that art the Lord of past and Future! O thou who hast the Universe for thy form! O underteriorating one Be propitious; and manifest thyself unto us who humble ourselves.

एष ब्रह्मा सहास्माभिः सह रुद्रैस्त्रिलोचनः।।
सर्वादित्यैः समं पूषा पावकोऽयं सहाग्निभिः।। ६३।।

This is Brahmā; and this is Trilocana in[1] company with the Rudras. And this is the Sun along with the Ādityas;[2] and this is the God of Fire with Agni.

अश्विनौ वसवश्चेमे सर्वे चैते मरुद्गणाः।।
साध्या विश्वे तथा देवा देवेंद्रश्चायमीश्वरः।। ६४।।

And these are the two Aśvinas and the Vasus; and these are the Maruts. And these are the Sādhyas, and these the Viśvas; and these the deities,—and this the Lord Indra of the celestials.

प्रणामप्रवणा नाथ दैत्यसैन्यैः पराजिताः।।
शरणं त्वामनुप्राप्ताः समस्ता देवतागणाः।। ६५।।

O Lord, all the hosts of the celestials, having been routed by the forces of the Daityas, seek shelter at thy hands, standing in humble guise."

श्रीपराशर उवाच

एवं संस्तूयमानस्तु भगवाञ्छंखचक्रधृक्।।
जगाम दर्शनं तेषां मैत्रेय परमेश्वरः।। ६६।।

Parāśara said :—O Maitreya, thus hymned (by the deities), that reverend one—the holder of the conch and discus—that supreme Lord—rendered himself visible unto them.

तं दृष्ट्वा ते तदा देवाः शंखचक्रगदाधरम्।।
अपूर्वरूपसंस्थानं तेजसां राशिमूर्जितम्।। ६७।।

प्रणम्य प्रणताः सर्वे संक्षोभ स्तिमितेक्षणाः।।
तुष्टुवुः पुण्डरीकाक्षं पितामहपुरोगमाः।। ६८।।

And seeing then that holder of the conch, discus and mace, that abode of wonderful grace,—a very mass of energy,—the deities, with the Great-father at their head, bowing down in humble guise, with their eyes quivering with agitation, began to hymn Puṇḍarīkākṣa.

देवा ऊचु

नमोनमो विशेषस्त्वं त्वं ब्रह्मा त्वं पिनाकधृक्।।
इंद्रस्त्वमग्निः पवनो वरुणः सविता यमः।। ६९।।

And the celestials said :—"Salutation! Salutation unto thee! O thou that art without! difference! Thou art Brahmā, and thou art the holder of Pināka.[3] Thou art Indra, and Agni and Pavana,[4] and Varuṇa, and the Sun, and Yama.

वसवो मरुतः साध्या विश्वेदेवगणा भवान्।।
योऽयं तवाग्रतो देव समीपं देवतागणः।।
स त्वमेव जगत्स्त्रष्टा यतः सर्वगतो भवान्।। ७०।।

And the Vasus, and the Maruts, and the Sādhyas, and the Viśva gods thou. And, O god, those deities that have come unto thee are even thyself, who art the creator of the Universe,—since thou art in everything.

त्वं यस्त्वं वषट्कारस्त्वमोङ्कारः प्रजापतिः।।
विद्या वेद्यं च सर्वात्मँस्त्वन्मयं चाखिलं जगत्।। ७१।।

Thou art sacrifice, and thou Vaṣatkāra, and thou Prajāpati. And, O soul of all, thou art knowable and unknowable; and this entire universe is permeated with thee.

त्वामार्त्ताः शरणं विष्णो प्रयाता दैत्यनिर्जिताः।।
वयं प्रसीद सर्वात्मंस्तेजसाप्याययस्व नः।। ७२।।

O Viṣṇu, worsted by the Daityas, we seek refuge of thee. O Soul of all, be propitious unto us; and do thou favour us by vouchsafing us thy energy.

तावदार्त्तिस्तथा वांछा तावन्मोहस्तथा सुखम्।।
यावन्न याति शरणं त्वामशेषाघनाशनम्।। ७३।।

So long affliction lasts, so long the desire of defeating the foe agitates the heart, as long doth stupor last and so long is misery experienced,—as one doth not throw one's self on thy protection, O thou that destroyest all sins.

1. Lit *three-eyed*—a name of Śiva.

2. Suns keeping company with the proper, who presides over them.

3. The bow, or the Trident of Śiva.

4. The Wind-god.

त्वं प्रसादं प्रसन्नात्मन् प्रपन्नानां कुरुष्व नः।।
तेजसां नाथ सर्वेषां स्वशक्त्याप्यायनं कुरु।। ७४।।

Therefore, O thou of complacent soul, do thou extend thy grace unto us. O master of all energy, do thou favour us with thy own power."

श्रीपराशर उवाच

एवं संस्तूयमानस्तु प्रणतैरमरैर्हरिः।।
प्रसन्नदृष्टिर्भगवानिदमाह स विश्वकृत्।। ७५।।

Parāśara said :—"Thus eulogised by the immortals, that creator of the cosmos—the worshipful Hari—casting a complacent glance, spoke (as follows).

तेजसो भवतां देवाः करिष्याम्युपबृंहणम्।।
वदाम्यहं यत्क्रियतां भवद्भिस्तदिदं सुराः।। ७६।।

And the auspicious reverend One said,—'Ye gods, I shall increase your power. Let the deities do as I say.

आनीय सहिता दैत्यैः क्षीराब्धौ सकलौषधीः।।
प्रक्षिप्यात्रामृतार्थं ताः सकला दैत्यदानवैः।।
मंथानं मन्दरं कृत्वा नेत्रं कृत्वा च वासुकिम्।। ७७।।

मथ्यतामममृतं देवाः सहाये मय्यवस्थिते।। ७८।।

Bring in company with the Daityas all the medicinal plants to the shore of the Ocean of milk, and making Mandara the churning-stick and Vāsuki the cord, let the deities churn (the Ocean) for ambrosia, I assisting them.

सामपूर्वं च दैतेयास्तत्र साहाय्यकर्मणि।।
सामान्यफलभोक्तारो यूयं वाच्या भविष्यथ।। ७९।।

And concluding peace with the progeny of the Daitya's, ye should enlist their services in this task; and tell them,—Ye shall in common with us reap the fruit of this undertaking.

मथ्यमाने च तत्राब्धौ यत्समुत्पत्स्यतेऽमृतम्।।
तत्पानाद्बलिनो यूयममराश्च भविष्यथ।। ८०।।

And on the sea being churned, ye should by drinking the nectar that will come up, attain access of strength and be immortal to boot.

तथा चाहं करिष्यामि ते यथा त्रिदशद्विषः।।
न प्राप्स्यन्त्यमृतं देवाः केवलं क्लेशभागिनः।। ८१।।

And, ye gods, I shall so order that the enemies of the celestials shall not get ambrosia,—but shall only undergo all the trouble."

श्रीपराशर उवाच

इत्युक्ता देवदेवेन सर्व एव तदा सुराः।।
सन्धानमसुरैः कृत्व यत्नवन्तोऽमृतेऽभवन्।। ८२।।

Parāśara said :—"Thus addressed by the god of gods, all the celestials, concluding peace with the Asuras, set about churning for ambrosia.

नानौषधीः समानीय देवदैतेयदानवाः।।
शिप्त्वा क्षीराब्धिपयसि शर दभ्रामलत्विषि।। ८३।।

मंथानं मंदरं कृत्वा नेत्रं कृत्व च वासुकिम्।।
ततो मथितुमारब्धा मैत्रेय तरसाऽमृतम्।। ८४।।

And procuring various medicinal herbs, the deities, the offspring of the Daityas, and the Dānavas,—throwing the same into the waters of the ocean of milk, resembling autumnal clouds,—and O Maitreya, making Mandara the churning-stick and Vāsuki the twine,—at once addressed themselves to churning for ambrosia.

विबुधाः सहिताः सर्वे यतः पुच्छं ततः कृताः।।
कृष्णेन वासुकेर्दैत्याः पूर्वकाये निवेशिताः।। ८५।।

And instructed by Kṛṣṇa, the gods in a body held that (part of Vāsuki's body) where the tail was, and the Daityas held by the fore-part of his body.

ते तस्य मुखनिश्वासवह्नितापहतात्विषः।।
निस्तेजसोऽसुराः सर्वे बभूवुरमितौजसः।। ८६।।

And, O thou of measureless splendour, the Asuras, smitten with the fire sprung from the breath of Vāsuki's hood, became enfeebled.

तेनैव मुखनिश्वासवायुनास्तबलाहकैः।।
पुच्छप्रदेशे वर्षद्भिस्तदा चाप्यायिताः सुराः।। ८७।।

And clouds scattered by the breath issuing from Vāsuki's mouth, showering down at his tail, the deities were enlivened.

क्षीरोदमध्ये भगवान्कूर्मरूपी स्वयं हरिः।।
मन्थनाद्रेरधिष्ठानं भ्रमतोऽभून्महामुने।। ८८।।

And, O mighty ascetic, remaining in the midst of the Milky sea in the shape of a tortoise, the revered Hari himself became the support of the churning-stick.

रूपेणान्येन देवानां मध्ये चक्रगदाधरः ।।
चकर्ष नराग राजानं दैत्यमध्येऽपरेच ।। ८९ ।।

And the holder of the discus and mace, remaining in one form in the midst of the immortals, and in another, in the midst of the Daityas,—began to pull the king of serpents.

उपर्याक्रान्तवाञ्शैलं बृहद्रूपेण केशवः ।।
तथापरेण मैत्रेय यन्न दृष्टं सुरासुरैः ।। ९० ।।

And, O Maitreya, in another gigantic form, Keśava pulled mountain upwards,—which form was seen neither of the celestials nor the Asuras.

तेजसा नागराजानं तथाप्यायितवान्हरिः ।।
अन्येन तेजसा देवानुपबृंहितवान्प्रभुः ।। ९१ ।।

And Hari obliged with energy the king of serpents; and the Lord invigorated the immortals with another energy.

मथ्यमाने ततस्तस्मिन्क्षीराब्धौ देवदानवैः ।।
हविर्धामाऽभवत्पूर्वं सुरभिः सुरपूजिता ।। ९२ ।।

And on the Milky-sea being churned by the celestials and the Asuras, first came into existence Śurabhi, worshipped of the celestials,—home of clarified butter.

जग्मुर्मुदं ततो देवा दानवाश्च महामुने ।।
व्याक्षिप्तचेतसश्चैव बभूवुस्तिमितेक्षणाः ।। ९३ ।।

And thereat both the deities and the Dānavas experienced very great delight, O great ascetic; and with their minds attracted, they steadily gazed at her.

किमेतदितिसिद्धानां दिवि चिंतयतां ततः ।।
बभूव वारुणी देवी मदाघूर्णितलोचना ।। ९४ ।।

And as the Siddhas were questioning within themselves,—'What is this?'—out came the exalted Vāruṇī, with her eyes rolling in consequence of intoxication.

कृतावर्तात्ततस्तस्मात्क्षीरोदाद्वासयञ्जगत् ।।
गन्धेन पारिजातोभूद्देवस्त्रीनन्दनस्तरुः ।। ९५ ।।

And then perfuming the universe with odur, from fourth a whirlpool of the Milky-sea arose Pārijāta—the tree in which the celestial females delight.

रूपौदार्यगुणोपेतस्था चाप्सरसां गणः ।।
क्षीरोदधेः समुत्पन्नो मैत्रेय परमाद्भुतः ।। ९६ ।।

And then, O Maitreya, from the Milky-ocean arose numbers of Apsarās, wonderful exceedingly, and furnished with grace and nobility.

ततःशीतांशुरभवज्जगृहे तं महेश्वरः ।।
जगृहुश्च विषं नागाः क्षीरोदाब्धिसमुत्थितम् ।। ९७ ।।

And then sprang the Mild-rayed one[1]; and Maheśwara appropriated him. And the serpents appropriated the poison that sprang from the Milky-sea.

ततो धन्वन्तरिर्देवः श्वेताम्बरधरस्स्वयम् ।।
बिभ्रत्कमंडलुं पूर्णममृतस्य समुत्थितः ।। ९८ ।।

And then arose the divine Dhanwantari[2]; clad in white raiment, bearing a Kamaṇḍalu[3] filled with nectar.

ततः स्वस्थमनस्कास्ते सर्वे दैतेयदानवाः ।।
बभूवुर्मुदिताः सर्वे मैत्रेय मुनिभिः सह ।। ९९ ।।

And thereat, O Maitreya, all the Daityas' sons and the Dānavas, along with the ascetics, felt delighted.

ततः स्फुरत्कान्तिमती विकासिकमले स्थिता ।।
श्रीर्देवी पयसस्तस्मादुद्भूता धृतपङ्कजा ।। १०० ।।

And then from the water arose the exalted Śrī, endowed with excellent grace,—seated on a blown lotus, and carrying also a lotus in her hand.

तां तुष्टुवुर्मुदा युक्ताः श्रीसूक्तेन महर्षयः ।। १०१ ।।

विश्वावसुमखास्तस्या गन्धर्वाः पुरतो जगुः ।।
घृताचीप्रमुखास्तत्र ननृतुश्चा प्सरोगणाः ।। १०२ ।।

And filled with delight, her hymned the

1. Himanśu name of the Moon.
2. The Esculapius of the Hindus.
3. A vessel so named.

mighty saints with the *Śrī Sūkta*[1]; and the Gandharvas, headed by Viśvavasu, began to chaunt before her. And, O Brāhmaṇa, bevies of Apsarās—Ghṛtāci and others—began to dance.

गंगाद्याः सरितस्तोयैः स्नानार्थमुपतस्थिरे ।।
दिग्गजा हेमपात्रस्थमादाय विमलं जलम् ।।
स्नापयाञ्चक्रिरे देवीं सर्वलो कमहेश्वरीम् ।। १०३ ।।

And the rivers—Gaṅgā and the rest—came with water, for bathing her. And an elephant of one of the cardinal points, taking water out of the golden vessels, bathed that goddess—the mighty Mistress of all the worlds.

क्षीरोदो रूपधृक्तस्यै मालामम्लानपंकजाम् ।।
ददौ विभूषणान्यङ्गे विश्वकर्मा चकार ह ।। १०४ ।।

And he Milky-sea, assuming a form, presented her with a wreath of unfading lotuses; and Viśvakarmā decked her person with ornaments.

दिव्यमाल्याम्बरधरा स्नाता भूषणभूषिता ।।
पश्यतां सर्वदेवानां ययौ वक्षस्थलं हरेः ।। १०५ ।।

And wearing divine garlands, and attire, bathed and adorned with ornament, she in the sight of all the celestials sought the bosom of Hari.

तया विलोकिता देवा हरिवक्षस्थलस्थया ।।
लक्ष्म्या मैत्रेय सहसा परां निर्वृतिमागताः ।। १०६ ।।

And on being gazed at by the goddess Lakṣmī remaining in Hari's bosom the celestials, O Maitreya, suddenly attained excess of delight.

उद्वेगं परमं जग्मुर्दैत्या विष्णु पराङ्मुखाः ।।
त्यक्ता लक्ष्म्या महाभाग विप्रचित्तिपुरोगमाः ।। १०७ ।।

And, O exceedingly pious one, on being overlooked by Lakṣmī, the Daityas, ever disregarding Viṣṇu—headed by Vipracittī—were wrought up with extreme anxiety.

ततस्ते जगृहुर्दैत्या धन्वन्तरिकरस्थितम् ।।
कमण्डलुं महावीर्या यत्राऽऽस्तेऽमृतमुत्तमम् ।। १०८ ।।

And then, O twice-born one, the Daityas, endowed with great prowess, possessed themselves of the Kamaṇḍalu that was in the hand of Dhanwantarī, and which contained the ambrosia.

मायया मोहयित्वा तान्विष्णुः स्त्रीरूपसंस्थितः ।।
दानवेभ्यस्तदादाय देवेभ्यः प्रददौ प्रभुः ।। १०९ ।।

And then Viṣṇu, assuming a female form, and thereby exciting their desire, secured the same, and then the Lord made it over unto the celestials.

ततः पपुः सुरगुणाः शक्राद्यास्तत्तदाऽमृतम् ।।
उद्यतायुधनिस्त्रंशा दैत्यास्तांश्च समभ्ययुः ।। ११० ।।

And then the immortals,—Śakra and the rest—quaffed off the ambrosia; and thereat the Daityas rushed against them with upraised weapons and *Nistraṁśās*[2].

पीतेऽमृते च बलिभिर्देवैर्दैत्यचमूस्तदा ।।
वध्यमाना दिशो भेजे पातालं च विवेश वै ।। १११ ।।

And having drunk ambrosia, the invigorated gods beat the Daitya-hosts, and these flew in all directions and entered the nether regions.

ततो देवा मुदा युक्ताः शंखचक्रगदाभृतम् ।।
प्रणिपत्य यथापूर्वमाशासत्तत्त्रिविष्टपम् ।। ११२ ।।

Then the deities, bowing down unto the bearer of the conch, discus and mace, as formerly, began to govern the celestial regions.

ततः प्रसन्नभाः सूर्यः प्रययौ स्वेन वर्त्मना ।।
ज्योतींषि च यथामार्गं प्रययुर्मुनिसत्तम ।। ११३ ।।

And then the glad-rayed Sun began to course in his own path; and, O best of ascetics, the luminaries also gyrated in their own orbits.

जज्वाल भगवांश्चोच्चैश्चारुदीप्तिर्विभावसुः ।।
धर्मे च सर्वभूतानां तदा मतिरजायत ।। ११४ ।।

And then the reverend Fire, crowned with a fair splendour, began to burn brightly. And, all creatures felt a regard for righteousness.

त्रैलोक्यं च श्रिया जुष्टं बभूव द्विजसत्तम ।।
शक्रश्च त्रिदशश्रेष्ठः पुनः श्रीमानजायत ।। ११५ ।।

1. A hymn of the Ṛg Veda.

2. A scimitar—a sacrificial knife.

And, O foremost of anchorets, the triune world was furnished with grace; and that chief of the celestials—Śakra—again waxed graceful.

सिंहासनगतः शक्रस्संप्राप्य त्रिदिवं पुनः।।
देवराज्ये स्थितो देवीं तुष्टावाब्जकरां ततः।। ११६।।

And Śakra, seated on his throne, receiving back the celestial regions, and established in his celestial sovereignty, began to hymn the Goddess holding a lotus in her hand.

इन्द्र उवाच

नमस्ये सर्वलोकानां जननीमब्जसम्भवाम्।।
श्रियमुन्निद्रपद्माक्षीं विष्णुवक्षस्थलस्थिताम्।। ११७।।
पद्मालयां पद्मकरां पद्मपत्रनिभेक्षणाम्।।
वंदे पद्ममुखीं देवीं पद्मनाभप्रियामहम्।। ११८।।

And Indra said,—'I salute the Lotus-sprung mother of all beings—unto Śrī having lotus-like eyes, and reposing in the bosom of Viṣṇu.

त्वं सिद्धिस्त्वं स्वधा स्वाहा सुधा त्वं लोकपावनी।।
सन्ध्या रात्रिः प्रभा भूतिर्मेधा श्रद्धा सरस्वती।। १९।।

Thou art Siddhi, and thou art nectar, and thou Svāhā and Svadhā, O purifier of the worlds. And thou art twilight and light and lustre, and affluence, and intelligence, and veneration, and Saraswati.

यज्ञविद्या महाविद्या गुह्यविद्या च शोभने।।
आत्मविद्या च देवि त्वं विमुक्तिफलदायिनी।। १२०।।

Thou art the learning of sacrifice; thou art the worship of the Universe-form (of the Most High); thou art the Occult Learning, O beauteous one; and thou art the knowledge of Brahmā, O goddess,—thou art the knowledge of Brahmā, O goddess,—and thou art the bestower of the fruit of emancipation.

आन्वीक्षिकी त्रयीवार्त्ता दण्डनीतिस्त्वमेव च।।
सौम्यासौम्यैर्जगद्रूपैस्त्वयैत्तद्देवि पूरितम्।। १२१।।

And thou art the Science of Dialectics; and thou art the Three (Vedas); and thou art the *Vārttā*; and thou art the knowledge of chastisement, *etc*. O goddess, this universe is filled with thy gentle and terrific forms.

का त्वन्या त्वामृते देवि सर्वयज्ञमयं वपुः।।
अध्यास्ते देवदेवस्य योगिचिन्त्यं गदाभृतः।। १२२।।

And, O goddess, who, save thee, can dwell in the person of that god of gods, the bearer of the mace, who is contemplated by the *yogīs*.

त्वया देवि परित्यक्तं सकलं भुवनत्रयम्।।
विनष्टप्रायमभवत्त्वयेदानीं समेधितम्।। १२३।।

O goddess, the triple world, having been renounced by thee, had come to the verge of destruction; and, through thee hath it again recovered its position.

दाराः पुत्रास्तथाऽगारसुहृद्धान्यधनादिकम्।।
भवत्येतन्महाभागे नित्यं त्वद्वीक्षणान्नृणाम्।। १२४।।

And, O exalted one, men come by wives and sons, and houses, and friends, and corn, and wealth through thy kind look.

शरीरारोग्यमैश्वर्यमरिपक्षक्षयः सुखम्।।
देवि त्वद्दृष्टिदृष्टानां पुरुषाणां न दुर्लभम्।। १२५।।

And, O goddess, freedom from bodily ailments, riches, destruction of foes, and felicity, are not difficult of attainment for those people that view thy glances.

त्वं माता सर्वलोकानां देवदेवो हरिः पिता।।
त्वयैतद्विष्णुना चाम्ब जगद्व्याप्तं चराचराम्।। १२६।।

Thou art the mother of all creatures, as that god of gods—Hari—is their father. And this universe consisting of mobile and immobile, was primaevally permeated by thee as well as Viṣṇu.

मा नः कोशं तथा गोष्ठं मा गृहं मा परिच्छदम्।।
मा शरीरं कलत्रं च त्यजेथाः सर्वपावनि।। १२७।।

And, O thou that purifiest everything, if thou forsakest (us), neither out treasures, nor our cattle, nor our houses, nor our attires, nor our bodies, nor our wives, are secure unto us.

मा पुत्रान्मा सुहृद्वर्गं मा पशून्मा विभूषणम्।।
त्यजेथा मम देवस्य विष्णोर्वक्षःस्थलालये।। १२८।।

O thou that residest in the bosom of that god, Viṣṇu, if thou forsakest me, neither sons, nor friends, nor ornaments are secure unto me.

सत्त्वेन सत्यशौचाभ्यां तथा शीलादिभिर्गुणैः।।
त्यज्यंते ते नराः सद्यः संत्यक्ता ये त्वयाऽमले।। १२९।।

O stainless one, he that is forsaken by thee, is also forsaken by goodness, truth, purity character, and other virtues.

त्वया विलोकिताः सद्यः शीलाद्यैरखिलैर्गुणैः।।
कुलैश्वर्यैश्च युज्यंते पुरुषा निर्गुणा अपि।। १३०।।

And, those that are glanced at by thee,—albeit devoid of any good quality, ever attain note, on account of character and other virtues, as well as lineage, and wealth.

स श्लाघ्यः स गुणी धन्यः स कुलीनः स बुद्धिमान्।।
स शूरः स च विक्रान्तो यस्त्वयां देवि वीक्षितः।। १३१।।

And, O goddess, he that is looked at by thee, is praiseworthy and accomplished and blessed and intelligent and high-born and heroic and possessed of prowess.

सद्यो वैगुण्यमायाति शीलाद्याः सकला गुणाः।।
पराङ्मुखी जगद्धात्री यस्य त्वं विष्णुवल्लभे।। १३२।।

And, O nurse of the Universe, O beloved of Viṣṇu, all virtues, character, *etc.* are instantly prevented in him from whom thou turnest away thy countenance.

न ते वर्णयितुं शक्ता गुणाञ्जिह्वापि वेधसः।।
प्रसीद देवि पद्माक्षि मास्मांस्त्याक्षीः कदाचन।। १३३।।

But the tongue even of the Deity is incapable of celebrating thy perfections. O lotus-eyed one, prove auspicious! Me mayest thou never renounce.

श्रीपराशर उवाच

एवं श्रीः संस्तुता सम्यक् प्राह देवी शतक्रतुम्।।
शृण्वतां सर्वदेवानां सर्वभूतस्थिता द्विज।। १३४।।

Parāśara said,—"Thus eulogised to the height, the goddess Śrī resident in all beings spoke unto Śatakratu[1] in the hearing of all the gods.

1. *Lit.*—The performer of an hundred sacrifices. It is a name of Indra.

श्रीरुवाच

परितुष्टास्मि देवेश स्तोत्रेणानेन ते हरे।।
वरं वृणीष्व यस्त्विष्टो वर दाहं तवागता।। १३५।।

And Śrī said,—"O chief of the celestials, O Hari, pleased am I with thy hymn. Do thou mention the boon thou desirest. I have come hither to confer the same on thee.

इंद्र उवाच

वरदा यदि मे देवि वरार्हो यदि वाप्यहम्।।
त्रैलोक्यं न त्वया त्याज्यमेष मेस्तु वरः परः।। १३६।।

Thereat Indra said,—'O goddess, if thou wouldst confer a boon on me, if I am worthy of one, let this be the great boon, that this triple world thou wouldst not forsake.

स्तोत्रेण यस्तथैतेन त्वां स्तोष्यंत्यब्धिसम्भवे।।
स त्वया न परित्याज्यो द्वितीयोस्तु वरो मम।। १३७।।

And let this be the second boon that him also thou wouldst not forsake, who, O ocean-sprung One, shall propitiate thee with this hymn.

श्रीरुवाच।।

त्रैलोक्यं त्रिदशश्रेष्ठ न सन्त्यक्ष्यामि वासव।।
दत्तो वरो मयायन्ते स्तोत्राराधनतुष्टया।। १३८।।

Thereat Śrī said,—'O foremost of the celestials, O Vāsava, this triple world will I not leave. I confer upon thee this boon, being pleased with thy hymn and prayer.

यश्च सायं तथा प्रातः स्तोत्रेणानेन मानवः।।
मां स्तोष्यति न तस्याहं भविष्यामि पराङ्मुखी।। १३९।।

And I shall never be displeased with him whoever shall chaunt this hymn.

श्रीपराशर उवाच

एवं ददौ वरं देवी देवराजाय वै पुरा।।
मैत्रेय श्रीर्महाभागा स्तोत्राराधनतोषिता।। १४०।।

Parāśara siad,—"O Maitreya, formerly the great goddess, Śrī, being pleased with the hymn and prayer, conferred this boon on the lord of the celestials.

भृगोः ख्यात्यां समुत्पन्ना श्रीः पूर्वमुदधेः पुनः।।
देवदानवयत्नेन प्रसूताऽमृतमन्थने।। १४१।।

In the days of yore, Śrī was begot of Bhṛgu on *Khyāti*. And she again came out of the Ocean when it was churned by the celestials.

एवं यदा जगत्स्वामी देवदेवो जनार्दनः।।
अवतारं करोत्येषा तदा श्रीस्तत्सहायिनी।। १४२।।

As the great god Janārddana[1], the lord of the Universe, goes through incarnations, so does Śrī to help Him.

पुनश्च पद्मादुत्पन्ना आदित्योभूद्यदा हरिः।।
यदा तु भार्गवो रामस्तदाभूद्धरणी त्वियम्।। १४३।।

When Hari assumed the form of a dwarf, she took birth as a lotus, and when He descended on earth as Paraśurāma, she appeared as the Earth.

राघवत्वेऽभवत्सीता रुक्मिणी कृष्णजन्मति।।
अन्येषु चावतारेषु विष्णोरेषानपायिनी।। १४४।।

At time of the incarnation of Rāma, she became Sītā, and when He was born as Kṛṣṇa, she became Rukmiṇī. And thus in all the incarnations, she assisted Viṣṇu.

देवत्वे देवदेहेयं मनुष्यत्वे च मानुषी।।
विष्णोर्देहानुरूपां वै करोत्येषाऽऽत्मनस्तुनम्।। १४५।।

When he had a celestial shape, she assumed the shape of a celestial, and when he assumed a human form, she took a human shape.

यश्चैतच्छृणुयाज्जन्म लक्ष्म्या यश्च पठेन्नरः।।
श्रियो न विच्युतिस्तस्य गृहे यावत्कुलत्रयम्।। १४६।।

She changed her body (human or celestial) according as Viṣṇu did. Śrī does not renounce the abode of him for three generations, who reads or hears of this story of her birth.

पठ्यते येषु चैवेयं गृहेषु श्रीस्तुतिर्मुने।।
अलक्ष्मीः कलहाधारा न तेष्वास्ते कदाचन।। १४७।।

O sage, never can quarrelsome *Alakṣmī*,[2] dwell in that house where this hymn of Śrī is chanted.

एतत्ते कथितं ब्रह्मन्यन्मां त्वं परिपृच्छसि।।
क्षीराब्धौ श्रीर्यथा जाता पूर्वं भृगुसुता सती।। १४८।।

O Brāhmaṇa, I have related unto thee everything of what thou didst ask me for—how Śrī formerly was born as the daughter of Bhṛgu and how she afterwards came out of the Ocean of milk.

इति सकल विभूत्यवाप्तिहेतुः
स्तुतिरियमिन्द्रमुखोद्गता हि लक्ष्म्याः।।
अनुदिनमिह पठ्यते नृभिर्यैर्वसति
न तेषु कदाचिदप्यलक्ष्मीः।। १४९।।

This eulogy of Lakṣmī, the source of all wealth, came out of the mouth of the lord of celestials. Poverty can never infest those persons on earth, who chaunt this hymn every day.

।। इति श्रीविष्णुपुराणे प्रथमेंशे नवमोऽध्यायः।। ९।।

अथ प्रथमेंशेः दशमोऽध्यायः

Part I : Section 10

श्रीमैत्रेय उवाच

कथितं मे त्वया सर्वं यत्पृष्टोसि मया मुने।।
भृगुसर्गात्प्रभृत्येष सर्गो मे कथ्यतां पुनः।। १।।

Maitreya said,—"O great sage, thou hast related unto me all I had asked thee for. Do thou now give me again an account of the family of Bhṛgu from Bhṛgu downwards.

श्रीपराशर उवाच

भृगोः ख्यात्यां समुत्पन्ना लक्ष्मीर्विष्णुपरिग्रहः।।
तथा धातृविधातारौ ख्यात्यां जातौ सुतौ भृगोः।। २।।

1. Another name of Viṣṇu.

2. The genius of ill-luck.

Parāśara said,—"Lakṣmī was born of Bhṛgu and Khyāti and became the spouse of Viṣṇu. And two more sons were born of Bhṛgu and Khyāti namely Dhātā and Vidhātā.

आयतिर्नियतिश्चैव मेरोः कन्ये महात्मनः।।
भार्ये धातृविधात्रोस्ते तयोर्जातौ सुतावुभौ।। ३।।

Two daughters, by name Āyati and Niyati were born of the high-souled Meru. And Dhātā and Vidhāta took them as their wives.

प्राणश्चैव मृकण्डुश्च मार्कण्डेयोमृकण्डुतः।।
ततो वेदशिरा जज्ञे प्राणस्यापि सुतं शृणु।। ४।।

They gave birth to two sons named Prāṇa and Mṛkaṇḍu. Of Mṛkaṇḍu again was born a son named Mārkaṇḍeya. And hear then again, a son was born of Prāṇa by name Vedaśirā.

प्राणस्य द्युतिमान्पुत्रो राजवांश्च ततोऽभवत्।।
ततो वंशो महाभाग विस्तरं भार्गवो गतः।। ५।।

Of the other sons of Prāṇa one was named Kṛtimān and the other Rājavān. And in this way did spread the family of the great Bhṛgu.

पत्नी मरीचेः संभूतिः पौर्णमासमसूयत।।
विरजाः पर्वतश्चैव तस्य पुत्रो महात्मनः।। ६।।

Mārīca's spouse Sambhuti gave birth to a son named Paurṇamāsam. And of him were born two sons named Virajā and Śarvaga.

वंशसंकीर्तने पुत्रान्वदिष्येहं ततो द्विज।।
स्मृतिश्चाङ्गिरसः पत्नी प्रसूता कन्यकास्तथा।।
सिनीवाली कुहूश्चैव राका चानुमती तथा।। ७।।

And their sons I shall mention, O twice-born one, when I shall relate the lineage at leisure. And Aṅgirā's wife Smṛti gave birth to four daughters, named Sinīvālī, Kuhū, Rākā and Anumati.

अनसूया तथैवात्रेर्जज्ञे निष्कल्मषान्सुतान्।।
सोमं दुर्वाससं चैव दत्तात्रेयं च योगिनम्।। ८।।

And by Atri, Anasūyā gave birth to three sons untouched by sin named Soma, Durvāsā and the sage Dattātreya.

प्रीत्यां पुलस्त्यभार्यायां दत्तोलिस्तत्सुतोऽभवत्।।
पूर्वजन्मति योऽगस्त्यः स्मृतः स्वायंभुवेन्तरे।। ९।।

And Pulastya's wife Preeti gave birth to a child named Dattoli, who in his former birth or in the Svayambhuva Manvantara was known as the sage Agastya.

कर्दमश्चार्वरीवांश्च सहिष्णुश्च सुतास्त्रयः।।
क्षमा तु सुषवे भार्या पुलहस्य प्रजापतेः।। १०।।

Kṣamā, the wife of the Patriarch Pulaha was the mother of three sons, Kardama, Avarian and Sahiṣṇu.

क्रतोश्च सन्ततिर्भार्या वालखिल्यानसूयत।।
षष्टिपुत्रसहस्राणि मुनीनामूर्ध्वरेतसाम्।।
अंगुष्ठपर्वमात्राणां ज्वलद्भास्करतेजसाम्।। ११।।

The wife of Kratu, Santati, brought forth the sixty thousand Bālakhilyas, pigmy sages, no bigger than a joint of the thumb, chaste, pious resplendent as the rays of the Sun.

ऊर्जायां तु वसिष्ठस्य सप्ताजायन्त वै सुताः।। १२।।

रजो गोत्रोर्द्धबाहुश्च सवनश्चानघस्तथा।।
सुतपाः शुक्र इत्येते सर्वे सप्तर्षयोऽमलाः।। १३।।

Vasiṣṭha had seven sons by his wife Urjja, Rajas, Gātra, Ūrdhabāhu, Basana, Anagha, Sūtapas and Śukra, the seven pure sages.

योऽसावन्यभिमानी स्यात् ब्रह्मणस्तनयोऽग्रजः।।
तस्मात्स्वाहा सुताँल्लेभे त्रीनुदारौजसो द्विज।। १४।।

The Agni, named Abhimāni, who is the eldest born of Brahmā, had, by Svāhā, three sons of surpassing brilliancy :—

पावकं पवमानं तु शुचिं चापि जलाशिनम्।। १५।।

Pāvaka, Pavamāna and Śuci who drinks up water.

तेषां तु सन्ततावन्ये चत्वारिंशच्च पञ्च च।।
कथ्यन्ते वह्नयश्चैते पितापुत्रत्रयं च यत्।। १६।।

एवमेकोनपञ्चाशद्वह्नयः परिकीर्तिताः।। १७।।

They had forty-five sons who (with the son of Brahmā, the Agni named Abhimānī and his three descendants) constitute the forthy-nine Fires.

पितरो ब्रह्मणा सृष्टा व्याख्याता ये मया द्विज।।
अग्निष्वात्ता बर्हिषदोऽनग्नयः साग्नयश्च ये।। १८।।

I have mentioned the progenitors (Pitras) who were created by Brahmā. Of those by Agniśwattas and Varhiṣads the former being devcid and the latter, possessed of Fires[1].

तेभ्यः स्वधा सुते जज्ञे मेनां वै धारिणीं तथा ।।
ते उभे ब्रह्मवादिन्यौ योगिन्यावप्युभे द्विज ।। १९ ।।

उत्तमज्ञानसंपन्ने सर्वैः समुदितैर्गुणैः ।। २० ।।

Svadhā had two daughters Menā and Baidhāriṇī. They were both, O twice-born one, acquainted with theological truth and given up to religious meditation, accomplished in perfect wisdom and adorned with all estimble qualities.

इत्येषा दक्षकन्यानां कथिता सत्यसंततिः ।।
श्रद्धावान्संस्मरभेतामनपत्यो न जायते ।। २१ ।।

Thus I have narrated the progeny of the dauthers of Dakṣa. He who hears it with reverence, shall never want offspring.

।। इति श्रीविष्णुपुराणे प्रथमेंशे दशमोऽध्यायः ।। १० ।।

अथ प्रथमेंशेः एकादशोऽध्यायः

Part I : Section 11

श्रीपराशर उवाच

प्रियव्रतोत्तानपादौ मनोः स्वायंभुवस्य तु ।।
द्वौ पुत्रौ तु महावीर्यौ धर्मज्ञौ कथितौ तव ।। १ ।।

Parāśara said :—I mentioned unto that the Manu Svāyambhava had two heroic and pious sons Priyavrata and and Uttānapāda.

तयोरुत्तानपादस्य सुरुच्यामुत्तमः सुतः ।।
अभीष्टायामभृद्ब्रह्मन्पितुरत्यन्तवल्लभः ।। २ ।।

O these two, O Brāhmaṇa, Uttānapāda, had, by his favourtie wife Suruci, a son, Uttama, whom he dearly loved.

सुनीतिर्नाम या राज्ञ स्तस्यासीन्महिषी द्विज ।।
स नाति प्रीतिमांस्तस्यामभूद्यस्या ध्रुवः सुतः ।। ३ ।।

O twice-born one, the king had another queen by name Sunīti, to whom he was less attached. By her he had another son Dhruva.

राजासनस्थितस्याङ्क पितुर्भ्रातरमाश्रितम् ।।
दृष्ट्वोत्तमं ध्रुवश्चक्रे तमारोढुं मनोरथम् ।। ४ ।।

Beholding his brother Uttama on the lap of his father as he was seated upon his throne, Dhruva was desirous of ascending to the same place.

प्रत्यक्षं भूपतिस्तस्याः सुरुच्या नाभ्यनन्दत ।।
प्रणयेनागतं पुत्रमुत्संगारोहणोत्सुकम् ।। ५ ।।

But as Suruci was present the king could not receive his son, approaching there delightedly and desiring to be taken on his father's knee.

सपत्नी तनयं दृष्ट्वा तमंकारोहणोत्सुकम् ।।
स्वपुत्रं च तथारूढं सुरुत्चिर्वाक्यमब्रवीतं ।। ६ ।।

Beholding the child of her *sapatnī*[2] thus anxious to be placed on his father's lap and her own son already seated there Suruci said,—

क्रियते किं वृथा वत्स महानेष मनोरथः ।।
अन्यस्त्रीगर्भजातेन ह्यसंभूयममोदरे ।। ७ ।।

"O child, why do you vainly cherish such a presumptuous desire born as thou art from a different mother and art no son of mine.

उत्तमोत्तममप्राप्यमविवेको हि वाञ्छसि ।।
सत्यं सुतस्त्वमप्यस्य किं तु न त्वं मया धृतः ।। ८ ।।

Thou art inconsiderate enough to aspire to a station which is fit for excellent Uttama. It is true thou art the son of the king but I have not given thee birth.

1. According to the commentator this distinction is derived from the Vedas. The first class or agnishwattas consists of those householders who when alive, did not offer burnt sacrifices : the second of those who presented oblations with fire.

2. The other wife of the king.

एतद्राजासनं सर्वं भूभृत्संश्रयकेतनम्।।
योग्यं ममैव पुत्रस्य किमात्मा क्लिश्यतेत्वया।। ९।।

This regal throne, the seat of the king of kings is suited to my son only; why shouldst thou trouble thyself for it.

उच्चैर्मनोरथस्तेयं मत्पुत्रस्येव किं वृथा।।
सुनीत्यामात्मनो जन्म किं त्वया नावगम्यते।। १०।।

Why does thou idly cherish such an ambition as if thou wert my son? Dost thou not know that thou art the offspring of Suniti?

श्रीपराशर उवाच

उत्सृज्य पितरं बालस्तच्छ्रुत्वा मातृभाषितम्।।
जगाम कुपितो मातुर्निजाया द्विज मंदिरम्।। ११।।

Parāśara said :—"O twice-born one, hearing the words of his step-mother, and qutting his father, the boy repaired in a passion to the apartment of his own mother.

तं दृष्ट्वा कुपितं पुत्रमीषत्प्रस्फुरिताधरम्।।
सुनीतिरंकमारोप्य मैत्रेयेदमभाषत।। १२।।

Beholding him angry and his lips trembling, Suniti took him upon her lap and said,—"O child, who is the cause of your anger?

वत्स कः कोपहेतुस्ते कश्च त्वां नाभि नन्दति।।
कोवजानाति पितरं वत्स यस्तेपराध्यति।। १३।।

Who hath not welcomed thee? Who doth not know, that by behaving ill towards thee he hath offended thy father?"

श्रीपराशर उवाच

इत्युक्तः सकलं मात्रे कथयामास तद्यथा।।
सुरुचिः प्राह भूपालप्रत्यक्षमतिगर्विता।। १४।।

Being thus addressed Dhruva repeated to his mother all that the arrogant Suruci had said to him in the presence of the king.

विनिश्वस्येति कथिते तस्मिन्पुत्रेण दुर्मना।।
श्वासक्षामेक्षणा दीना सुनीतिर्वाक्यमब्रवीत्।। १५।।

Her son having related all these sighing, she was greatly distressed. And Sunīti, rendered poorly, with her eyes dimmed, sighed and said,—

सुनीतिरुवाच

सुरुचिः सत्यमाहेदं मन्दभाग्योसि पुत्रक।।
न हि पुण्यवतां वत्स सत्नैरेव मुच्यते।। १६।।

"Suruci has rightly spoken; thine, child, is as an unfortunate fate; those who are born to fortune are not liable to the insults of their step-mothers.

नोद्वेगस्तात कर्त्तव्यः कृतं यद्भवता पुरा।।
तत्कोपहर्त्तुं शक्नोति दातुं कश्चाकृतं त्वया।। १७।।

तत्त्वया नात्र कर्त्तव्यं दुःखं तद्वाक्यसम्भवम्।। १८।।

Yet be not afflicted, my child, for who shall efface what thou hast formerly done, or shall assign to thee what thou hast left undone.

राजासनं राजच्छत्रं वराश्वावरवारणाः।।
यस्य पुण्यानि तस्यैते मत्वैतच्छाम्य पुत्रक।। १९।।

The regal throne, the umbrella of royalty, excellent horses and elephants are his whose virtues have deserved them; remember this my son and be consoled.

अन्यजन्मकृतैः पुण्यैः सुरुच्या सुरुचिर्नृपः।।
भार्येति प्रोच्यते चान्यां मद्विधा पुण्यवर्जिता।। २०।।

That the king favours Suruci is the reward of her merits in a former birth. The name of wife alone belongs to such as I, who have not equal merit.

पुण्योपचयसंपन्नस्तस्याः पुत्रस्तथोत्तमः।।
मम पुत्रस्तथा जातः स्वल्पपुण्यो ध्रुवौ भवान्।। २१।।

Her son is the progeny of accumulated piety and is born as Uttama and mine son art thou, O Dhruva, of inferior merit.

तथापि दुःखं न भवान् कर्त्तुमर्हसि पुत्रक।।
यस्य यावत्स तेनैव स्वेन तुष्यति मानवः।। २२।।

It does not behove thee, O my child, to be sorry on this account; a wise man will be satisfied with the degree which appertains to him.

यदि ते दुःखमत्यर्थं सुरुच्या वचसाभवत्।।
तत्पुण्योपचये यत्नं कुरु सर्वफलप्रदे।। २३।।

If thou art greatly hurt at the words of

Suruci, do you try to amass piety which bestows all good.

सुशीलो भव धर्मात्मा मैत्रः प्राणिहिते रतः।।
निम्नं यथापः प्रवाणाः पात्रमायान्ति सम्पदः।। २४।।

Be thou good-natured, virtuous-souled, friendly and engaged in doing good to all living creatures; for prosperity descends upon worthy persons as water flows towards low ground.

ध्रुव उवाच

अम्ब यवमिदं प्रात्थ प्रशमाय वचो मम।।
नैतद्दुर्वचसा भिन्ने हृदये मम तिष्ठति।। २५।।

Dhruva said :—"O mother, what thou hast said to console me doth not find place in my heart which has been rent asunder by harsh words.

सोहं तथा नतिष्यामि तथा सर्वोत्तमोत्तमम्।।
स्थानं प्राप्स्याम्यशेषाणां जगतामभिपूजितम्।। २६।।

I shall so exert that I may attain to the most exalted rank adored by the whole world.

सुरुचिर्दयिता राज्ञस्तस्या जातोस्मि नोदरात्।।
प्रभावं पश्य मेंब त्वं वृद्धस्यापि तवोदरे।। २७।।

I am not born of Suruci who is the favourite wife of the king. Do thou behold my prowess, O mother, who am born of and reared by thee.

उत्तमः स मम भ्राता यो गर्भेण धृतस्तया।।
स राजासनमाप्नोतु पित्रा दत्तं तथास्तु तत्।। २८।।

Let Uttama, my brother, who is not born of thee, receive the regal throne, conferred on him by my father.

नान्यदत्तमभीप्स्यामि स्थानमम्ब स्वकर्मणा।।
इच्छामि तदहं स्थानं यत्र प्राप पिता मम।। २९।।

I do not wish to have that, which is given by others, O mother I shall by my actions acquire such a position which had not been enjoyed even by my father.

श्रीपराशर उवाच

निर्जगाम गृहान्मातुरित्युक्त्वा मातरं ध्रुवः।।
पुराच्च निर्गम्य ततस्तद्बाह्योपवनं ययौ।। ३०।।

Parāśara said :—"Having addressed his mother thus, Dhruva issued out of his mother's dwelling. And quitting the city, he repaired to a neighbouring thicket.

स ददर्श मुनींस्तत्र सप्तपूर्वागतान्ध्रुवः।।
कृष्णाजिनोत्तरीयेषु विष्टरेषु समास्थितान्।। ३१।।

He beheld there seven ascetics, who had repaired there before, sitting upon the hides of the black antelope, which they had taken from off their persons, and spread over the holy *kuśa* grass.

स राजपुत्रस्तान्सर्वान्प्रणिपत्याभ्य भाषत।।
प्रश्रयावनतः सम्यगभिवादनपूर्वकम्।। ३२।।

Saluting them respectfully and bowing unto them humbly the prince said, "Do ye know me, O great ascetics, as the son of Uttānapāda, born of Suniti.

ध्रुव उवाच

उत्तानपादतनयं मां निबोधत सत्तमाः।।
जातं सुनीत्यां निर्वेदाद्युष्माकं प्राप्तमन्तिकम्।। ३३।।

Being dissatisfied with the world, I have apeared before you.

ऋषय ऊचुः

चतुःपञ्चाब्दसंभूतो बालस्त्वं नृपनन्दन।।
निर्वेदकारणां किंचित्तव नाद्यापि वर्त्तते।। ३४।।

The ṛṣis replied :—"O prince, thou art only a boy and but four or five years of age. There can be no reason why you should be dissatisfied with life.

न चिंत्यं भवतः किंचिदिध्रयते भूपतिः पिता।।
न चैवेष्ट वियोगादि तव पश्याम बालक।। ३५।।

You connot be disgusted with anxiety since thy father reigns; we cannot imagine, O boy, that you suffer the pain of separation from the object of your affections.

शरीरे न च ते व्याधिरस्माभिरुपलक्ष्यते।।
निर्वेदः किन्निमित्तस्ते कथ्यतां यदि विद्यते।। ३६।।

Nor do we see any sign of disease on your person. What is the cause of your dissatisfaction? Tell us if it is known to you.

श्रीपराशर उवाच

ततः स कथयामास सुरुच्या यदुदाहृतम्।।
तन्निशम्य ततः प्रोचुर्मुनयस्ते परस्परम्।। ३७।।

Parāśara said,—Thereupon he repeated unto them what Suruci had spoken to him. And having heard that they said to one another,—

अहो क्षात्रं परं तेजो बालस्यापि यदक्षमा।।
सपत्न्या मातुरुक्तं यद्धृदयान्नापसर्पति।। ३८।।

"Oh! How wonderful is the vehemence of Kṣatriya nature? He is a mere boy and still he cannot stoop to indignities and he has not been able to remove from his mind what his step-mother had said.

भोभोः क्षत्रियदायादः निर्वेदाद्यत्त्वयाधुना।।
कर्तुं व्यवसितं तन्नः कथ्यतां यदि रोचते।। ३९।।

O son of Kṣatriya, if it pleases thee, tell us what thou desirest to do through your dissatisfaction with the world.

यच्च कार्यं तवास्माभिः साहाय्यममितद्युते।।
तदुच्यतां विवक्षुस्त्वमस्माभिरुपलक्ष्यसे।। ४०।।

O thou of immeasurable prowess, tell us in what thou wishest to have our help? Speak freely : for we perceive that thou desirest to have something from us.

ध्रुव उवाच

नाह मर्थमभीप्सामि न राज्यं द्विजसत्तमाः।।
तत्स्थानमेकमिच्छामि भुक्तं नान्येन यत्पुरा।। ४१।।

Dhruva said,—"O ye foremost of twice-born ones, I wish not for riches, neither do I long for a kingdom. I aspire to a station which hath never been acquired by any before.

एतन्मे क्रियतां सम्यक्कथ्यतां प्राप्यते यथा।।
स्थानमग्रयं समस्तेभ्यः स्थानेभ्यो मुनिसत्तमाः।। ४२।।

O excellent sages, tell me how I may effect this and attain to that station which is the most elevated in this world.

मरीचिरुवाच

अनाराधितगोविन्दैर्नैरैः स्थानं नृपात्मज।।
न हि संप्राप्यते श्रेष्ठं तस्मादाराधयाच्युतम्।। ४३।।

Marīci said—"O Prince, none can attain to that best of stations who does not propitiate Govinda. Do thou therefore worship the undecaying.

अत्रिरुवाच

परः पराणां पुरुषो यस्य तुष्टो जनार्दनः।।
संप्राप्नोत्यक्षयं स्थानमेतत्सत्यं मयोदितम्।। ४४।।

Atri said—"He with whom is pleased the first of spirits Janārdana, gets at this imperishable dignity—I mention unto you the truth.

अङ्गिरा उवाच

यस्यान्तः सर्वमेवेदमच्युतस्याव्ययात्मनः।।
तामराधय गोविन्दं स्थानमग्र्यं यदीच्छसि।। ४५।।

Aṅgirā said,—"If thou desirest for an exalted station do thou worship Govinda in whom immutable and undecaying, all that is, exists.

पुलस्त्य उवाच

परं ब्रह्म परं धाम योऽसौ ब्रह्म तथा परम्।।
तमाराध्य हरिं याति मुक्तिमप्यति दुर्लभाम्।। ४६।।

Pulastya said,—"Worshipping the divine Hari, the Supreme Soul, the Supreme Stay and Supreme Brahmā thou mayst attain to eternal liberation, what of reaching that most exalted station.

पुलह उवाच

ऐन्द्रमिन्द्रः परं स्थानं यमाराध्य जगत्पतिम्।।
प्राप यज्ञपतिं विष्णुं तमाराधय सुव्रत।। ४७।।

Pulaha said,—Do thou adore, O pious boy, that Viṣṇu, the lord of sacrifice, and Universe, worshipping whom Indra obtained the dignity of a king of the celestials.

क्रतुरुवाच

यो यज्ञपुरुषो यज्ञो योगेशः परमः पुमान्।।
तस्मिंस्तुष्टे यदप्राप्यं किंतदस्ति जनार्दने।। ४८।।

Kratu said,—"Nothing is difficult to attain if Janārdana is pleased, who is the soul of sacrifice in sacrifices and supreme spirit in abstract contemplation.

वसिष्ठ उवाच

प्राप्नोष्याराधिते विष्णौ मनसा यद्यदिच्छति ।।
त्रैलोक्यान्तर्गतं स्थानं किमु वत्सोत्तमोत्तमम् ।। ४९ ।।

Vasiṣṭha observed :—"Anything, that a man desires, may be obtained in this world by adoring Viṣṇu what of that exalted position.

ध्रुव उवाच

आराध्यः कथितो देवो भवद्भिः प्रणतस्य मे ।।
मया तत्परितोषाय यज्जप्तव्यं तदुच्यताम् ।। ५० ।।

Dhruva said :—"You have told me, humbly bowing before, what is the deity to be adored : do ye now inform me of the prayer which is to be meditated by me to propitiate him.

यथा चाराधनं तस्य मया कार्यं महात्मनः ।।
प्रसादसुमुखास्तन्मे कथयन्तु महर्षयः ।। ५१ ।।

May the great ascetics, delightedly inform me of the prayer by which I may propitiate the God.

ऋषय ऊचुः

राजपुत्र यथा विष्णोराराधनपरैर्नरैः ।।
कार्यमाराधनं तन्नो यथावच्छ्रोतुमर्हसि ।। ५२ ।।

बाह्यार्थादखिलाच्चित्तं त्याजयेत्प्रथमं नरः ।।
तस्मिन्नेव जगद्धाम्नि ततः कुर्वीत निश्चलम् ।। ५३ ।।

The Ṛṣis said,—"O Prince, hear, we shall relate unto thee, how those, who are devoted unto Viṣṇu, shall worship Him. They shall first withdraw their minds from all exterior objects and then fix it steadily on that being in whom the world exists.

एवमेकाग्रचित्तेन तन्मयेन धृतात्मना ।।
जप्तव्यं यन्नि बोधैतत्तन्नः पार्थिवनन्दन ।। ५४ ।।

O Prince, hear from us the prayer that is to be recited by him, who has thus concentrated his thoughts on one only object, whose heart is filled with his spirit, and who has controlled himself.

हिरण्यगर्भपुरुषप्रधानव्यक्तरूपिणे ।।
ॐ नमो वासुदेवाय शुद्धज्ञानस्वरूपिणे ।। ५५ ।।

'Om, salutation to Vasudeva, who is manifest as Brahmā, Viṣṇu and Śiva, and whose form is inscrutable.

एतज्जजाप भगवान् जप्यं स्वायंभुवो मनुः ।।
पितामहस्तव पुरा तस्य तुष्टो जनार्दनः ।। ५६ ।।

This pray was offered in olden times by your grandsire, the Manu Svayambhuva, and propitiated by which, Janārdana conferred upon him prosperity, which he desired, unequalled in three worlds.

ददौ यथाभिलषितां सिद्धिं त्रैलोक्यदुर्लभाम् ।।
तथा त्वमपि गोविन्दं तोषयैतत्सदा जपन् ।। ५७ ।।

Do thou therefore try to propitiate Govinda by reciting this prayer continually.

।। इति श्रीविष्णुपुराणे प्रथमेंशे एकादशोऽध्यायः ।। ११ ।।

अथ प्रथमेंशे: द्वादशोऽध्यायः

Part I : Section 12

श्रीपराशर उवाच

निशम्यैतद शेषेण मैत्रेय नृपतेः सुतः ।।
निर्जगाम वनात्तस्मात्प्रणिपत्य स तानृषीन् ।। १ ।।

Parāśara said :—"O Maitreya, hearing these words from beginning to end, that Prince, saluting these sages, issued out of that thicket.

कृतकृत्यमिवात्मानं मन्यमानस्ततो द्विज ।।
मधुसंज्ञं महापुण्यं जगाम यमुनातटम् ।। २ ।।

पुनश्च मधुसंज्ञेन दैत्येनाधिष्ठितं यतः ।।
ततो मधुवनं नाम्ना ख्यातमत्र महीतले ।। ३ ।।

And confiding in the accomplishment of his object, O twice-born one, he repaired to the holy place on the banks of the Yamunā called Madhuvana, or the grove of Madhu, called after the name of a demon of that name who resided there and was known thus on the earth.

हत्वा च लवणं रक्षो मधुपुत्रं महाबलम्।।
शत्रुघ्नो मधुरां नाम पुरीं यत्र चकार वै।। ४।।

Slaying the highly powerful son of the Rākṣasa, Madhu-Lavaṇa, Śatrughna (the youngest son of Daśaratha), founded a city at that spot which was named Mathurā.

यत्र वै देवदेवस्य सान्निध्यं हरिमेधसः।।
सर्वपापहरे तस्मिंस्तपस्तीर्थे चकार सः।। ५।।

And Dhruva engaged in performing penance at that holy shrine the purifier of all sin, where was Mahādeva, the god of Gods meditating upon Hari.

मरीचिमुख्यैर्मुनिभिर्यथोद्दिष्टमभूत्तथा ।।
आत्मन्यशेपदेवेशं स्थितं विष्णुममन्यत।। ६।।

In accordance with instruction given by Marīci and others, he began to contemplate, Viṣṇu the sovereign of the gods, seated in himself.

अनन्यचेतसस्तस्य ध्यायतो भगवान्हरिः।।
सर्वभूतगतो विप्र सर्वभावगतोऽभवत्।। ७।।

O twice-born one, Dhruva thus contemplating him, having his mind perfectly withdrawn from all other thoughts, the Great Hari, ever existing in all creatures and natures, took possession of his heart.

मनस्यवस्थिते तस्मिन्विष्णौ मैत्रेय योगिनः।।
न शशाक धरा भारमुद्वोढुं भूतधारिणी।। ८।।

O Maitreya, Viṣṇu thus occupying the heart of that one engaged in his meditation, the earth, the supporter of elemental life, could not sustain his height.

वामपादस्थिते तस्मिन्ननानार्द्धेन मेदिनी।।
द्वितीयं च ननामार्द्धं क्षितेर्दक्षिणतः स्थिते।। ९।।

When he used to stand upoon his left foot (for praying) one half of the earth bent beneath him and when he used to stand upon his right foot the other half of the earth sank down.

पादांगुष्ठेन संपीड्य यथा स वसुधां स्थितः।।
तदा समस्ता वसुधा चचाल सह पर्वतैः।। १०।।

And when he used to stand touching the earth with his toes, the whole earth shook with its mountains and rivers, O twice-born one.

नद्यो नदाः समुद्राश्च संक्षोभं परमं ययुः।।
तत्क्षोभादमराः क्षोभं परं जग्मुर्महामुने।। ११।।

यामा नाम तदा देवा मैत्रेय परमाकुलाः।।
इन्द्रेण सह संमन्त्र्यं ध्यानभंगुं प्रचक्रमुः।। १२।।

The rivers and seas were greatly agitated thereby and even the celestials called Yāmās, being greatly alarmed, in consultation with Indra began to concert measures for interrupting the devout exercises of Dhruva.

कूष्माण्डा विविधैम्पैर्महेन्द्रेण महामुने।।
समाधिभङ्गमत्यन्तमारब्धाः कर्त्तुमातुराः।। १३।।

And, O great ascetics, the Kūṣmāṇḍas in company with Indra, assuming, various shapes actively engaged in obstructing his meditations.

सुनीतिर्नाम तन्माता सास्रा तत्पुरतः स्थिता।।
पुत्रेति करुणां वाचमाह मायामयी तदा।। १४।।

One assuming, by virtue of illusion, the shape of his mother Sunīti, stood before him, with tears in his eyes, and saying in tender accents—

पुत्रकास्मान्निवर्त्तस्व शरीरात्यवद्दारुणात्।।
निर्बन्धतो मया लब्धो बहुभिस्त्वं मनोरथैः।। १५।।

"My son, desist from this penance, that is destroying thy health. I have after many troubles gained thee and have formed many hopes in thee.

दीनामेकां परित्यक्तुमनाथां न त्वमर्हसि।।
सपत्नीवचनाद्वत्स अगतेस्त्वं गतिर्मम।। १६।।

O child, it does not behove thee to forsake me, at the words of my rival, helpless, alone and unprotected. Thou art my only refuge.

क्व च त्वं पञ्चवर्षीयः क्वचैतद्दारुणं तपः।।
निवर्ततां मनः कष्टान्निर्बन्धात्फलवर्जितात्।। १७।।

Thou art a boy of five years old. Such a hard pinance doth not become thee. Desist therefore from such fearful practices which are not productive of any beneficial result.

कालः क्रीडनकानान्ते तदान्तेऽध्ययनस्य ते।।
ततः समस्तभोगानां तदन्ते चेष्यते तपः।। १८।।

For thee this is the time of youthful pastime, then comes the season for study, then the period of worldly enjoyment and lastly that of austere devotion.

कालः क्रीडनकानां यस्तव बालस्य पुत्रक।।
तस्मिंस्त्वमिच्छसि तपः किं नाशायात्मनो रतः।।१९।।

O my boy, thou art but a child, this is the season of thy play—why hast thou then engaged in asceticism to destroy thyself?

मत्प्रीतिः परमो धर्मो वयोवस्थाक्रियाक्रमम्।।
अनुवर्त्तस्व मा मोहान्निवर्त्तास्मादधर्मतः।। २०।।

Thy chief duty consists in thy devotion to me now. Do thou engage in such works as become thy age and circumstances.

परित्यजति वत्साद्य यद्येतन्न भवांस्तपः।।
त्यक्ष्याम्यहमिह प्राणांस्ततो वै पश्यतस्तव।। २१।।

Be not guided by bewildering error and desist from such unrighteous actions. If thou dost not renounce to-day these devout austeries I shall terminate my life before thee.

श्रीपराशर उवाच

तां प्रलापवतीमेवं बाष्पाकुलविलोचनाम्।।
समाहितमना विष्णौ पश्यन्नपि न दृष्टवान्।। २२।।

Parāśara said :—But Dhruva being wholly intent upon seeing Viṣṇu did not behold his mother weeping, with her eyes bleared with tears.

वत्स वत्स सुधोराणि रक्षांस्येतानि भीषणे।।
वनेऽभ्युद्यतशस्त्राणि समायान्त्यपगम्यताम्।। २३।।

"O child! O child! fly, the hideous Rākṣasas, with uplifted weapons are coming this side of the forest.

इत्युक्त्वा प्रययौ साथ रक्षांस्याविर्बभुस्ततः।।
अभ्युद्यतोग्रशस्त्राणि ज्वालामालामकुलैर्मुखैः।।२४।।

Saying this (the illusion) disappeared. Instantly crowded there the Rākṣasas uplifting terrible arms and with countenances emitting fiery flame.

ततो नादानतीवोग्रान्राजपुत्रस्य ते पुरः।।
मुमुचुर्दीप्तशस्त्राणि भ्रामयन्तो निशाचराः।। २५।।

They began to emit hideous cries before that prince and whirl and toss their threatening weapons.

शिवाश्च शतशो नेदुः सज्वालाः कवलैर्मुखैः।।
त्रासाय तस्य बालस्य योगयुक्तस्य सर्वदा।। २६।।

Hundreds of jackals, from whose mouths gushed out flame, while they expanded them, yelled horrible cries to appal the boy wholly engrossed by meditation.

हन्यतां हन्यतामेष छिद्यतां छिद्यतामयम्।।
भक्ष्यतां भक्ष्यतां चाय मित्यूचुस्ते निशाचरा।। २७।।

Those night-rangers cried out : "Kill him, kill him, tear him to pieces; eat him up, eat him up.

ततो नानाविधान्नादान् सिंहोष्ट्रमकराननाः।।
त्रासाय राजपुत्रस्य नेदुस्ते रजनीचराः।। २८।।

And those goblins having faces of lions, and camels, and crocodiles, howled about to strike terror into the heart of the prince.

रक्षांसि तानि ते नादाः शिवास्तान्यायुधानि च।।
गोविन्दासक्तचित्तस्य ययुर्नेन्द्रियगोचरम्।। २९।।

All these (illusions of) Rākṣasas and jackals, their cries and weapons made no impression upon his senses whose mind was completely given up to the meditation of Govinda.

एकाग्रचेताः सततं विष्णुमेवात्मसंश्रयम्।।
दृष्टवान्पृथिवीनाथपुत्रो नान्यं कथञ्चन।। ३०।।

The son of the lord of earth, entirely taken up by one idea, beheld continually. Viṣṇu only seated in himself and saw no other object.

ततः सर्वासु मायासु विलीनासु पुनः सुराः।।
संक्षोभं परमं जग्मुस्तत्पराभवशङ्किताः।। ३१।।

ते समेत्य जगद्योनिमनादिनिधनं हरिम्।।
शरण्यं शरणं यातास्तपसा तस्य तापिता।। ३२।।

All these illusions being thus baffled the celestials were greatly disturbed. Being terrified at this discomfiture and afflicted by the devout austerities of the boy the celestials assembled and repaired in a body for help to Hari, who is the creator of the universe, and without beginning or end.

देवा ऊचुः

देवदेव जगन्नाथ परेश पुरुषोत्तम।।
ध्रुवस्य तपसा तप्तास्त्वां वयं शरणं गताः।। ३३।।

The celestials said :—"O lord of the celestials! O lord of the world! O great god! O supreme spirit! being afflicted by the devout austerities of Dhruva, we have come to thee to seek thy refuge.

दिने दिने कलालेशैः शशाङ्कः पूर्यते यथा।।
तथायं तपसा देव प्रयात्यृद्धिमहर्निशम्।। ३४।।

As the moon increases in his orb day by day, so, O lord, (this boy) by his devotion is approaching incessantly superhuman power.

औत्तानपादितपसा वयमित्थं जनार्दन।।
भीतास्त्वां शरणं यातास्तपसस्तं निवर्तय।। ३५।।

O Janārdana, we have been greatly alarmed by the devout auterities of the son of Uttānapāda and have taken thy refuge : do thou desist him from his devout exercises.

न विद्मः किं स शक्रत्वं सूर्य्यत्वं किमभीप्सति।।
वित्तपाम्बुपसोमानां साभिलाषः पदेषु किम्।। ३६।।

We do not know whose position he aspireth to—whether the throne of Śakra, of the sun, of the lord of wealth or that of Varuṇa the lord of water.

तदस्माकं प्रसीदेश हृदयाच्छल्यमुद्धर।।
उत्तानपादतनयं तपसः सन्निवर्त्तय।। ३७।।

O lord, be propitiated with us, remove this mace of affliction from our breast and desist the son of Uttānapāda from his devout exercises.

श्रीभगवानुवाच

नेन्द्रत्वं न च सूर्यत्वं नैवाम्बुपधनेशताम्।।
प्रार्थयत्येष यं कामं तं करोम्यखिलं सुरा।। ३८।।

The Great God (Viṣṇu) replied :—"He aspireth not to the throne of Indra, nor to the sovereignty of the solar orb or the deep, nor to the rank of the lord of riches. I shall soon confer on him, O celestials, what he desireth to have.

यात देवा यथाकामं स्वस्थानं विगतज्वराः।।
निवर्त्तयाम्यहं बालं तपस्यासक्तमानसम्।। ३९।।

Removed of your anxiety do you all proceed to your respective quarters—I shall soon desist that boy, whose mind is wholly engrossed with devout meditation.

श्रीपराशर उवाच

इत्युक्ता देवदेवेन प्रणम्य त्रिदशास्ततः।।
प्रययुः स्वानि धिष्ण्यानि शतक्रतुपुरोगमाः।। ४०।।

Parāśara said :—Being thus addressed by Viṣṇu the celestials headed by the performer of hundred sacrifices, saluting him, repaired to their respective habitations.

भगवानपि सर्वात्मा तन्मयत्वेन तोषितः।।
गत्वा ध्रुवमुवाचेदं चतुर्भुजवपुर्हरिः।। ४१।।

And that Great God, who is all things, being pleased with Dhruva's whole-minded devotedness to him, assuming his shape with four arms, approached him and said,—

श्रीभगवानुवाच

औत्तानपादे भद्रं ते तपसा परितोषतः।।
वरदोहमनुप्राप्तो वरं वरय सुव्रत।। ४२।।

"May good betide thee, O son of Uttānapāda! I am pleased with thy devout exercises. I have come here to confer boons on thee—do thou beg one, O thou of firm vows.

बाह्यार्थनिरपेक्षं ते मयि चित्तं यदा हितम्।।
तुष्टोहं भवतस्तेन तद्वृणीष्व वरं परम्।। ४३।।

Withdrawing thy mind from external objects while thou hast dedicated it to me alone—I am greatly pleased with thee; do thou therefore beg of me an excellent boon.

पराशर उवाच

श्रुत्वेत्थं गदितं तस्य देवदेवस्य बालकः।।
उन्मीलिताक्षो ददृशे ध्यानदृष्टं हरिं पुरः।। ४४।।

Parāśara said—"Hearning the words of that great God, the boy opened his eyes and beheld before him that Hari whom he had seen in his meditation.

शंखचक्रगदाशाङ्गवरासिधरमच्युतम् ।।
किरीटिनं समालोक्य जगाम शिरसा महीम्।। ४५।।

And beholding him with the conch, the discus, the mace, the bow and the scimitar in hand and crowned with a diadem, he bowed his head down to the earth.

रोमांचिताङ्गः सहसा साध्वसं परमं गतः।।
स्तवाय देवदेवस्य स चक्रे मानसं ध्रुवः।। ४६।।

With his hair standing erect and being greatly stricken with fear, Dhruva addressed himself for worshipping that great God.

किं वदामि स्तुतावस्य केनोक्तेनास्य संस्तुतिः।।
इत्याकुलमतिर्देवं तमेव शरणं ययौ।। ४७।।

Reflecting how he could offer thanks unto him, and what he could say in his praise, he was greatly perplexed with anxiety and then at last had recourse to that deity.

ध्रुव उवाच

भगवन्यदि मे तोषं तपसा परमं गतः।।
स्तोतुं तदहमिच्छामि वरमेनं प्रयच्छ मे।। ४८।।

Dhruva said,—"O great God if thou art greatly pleased with my devout exercise, do thou confer upon me this boon, that I may praise thee whenever I wish.

(ब्रह्माद्यैर्यस्य वेदज्ञैर्ज्ञायते यस्य नो गति।।
तं त्वां कथमहं देव स्तोतुं शक्नोमि बालकः।।
त्वद्भक्तिप्रवणं ह्येतत्परमेश्वर मे मनः।।
स्तोतुं प्रवृत्तं त्वत्पादौ तत्र प्रज्ञां प्रयच्छ मे)

O god, I am a boy, how shall I be able to sing thy glory, whom even the great sages like Brahmā, conversant with Vedas, have not been able to know sufficiently. My heart is filled with devotion to thee, O lord, do thou grant me the understanding of placing my praises at thy feet.

श्रीपराशर उवाच

शंखप्रांतेन गोविन्दस्तं पस्पर्श कृताञ्जलिम्।।
उत्तानपादतनयं द्विजवर्य जगत्पतिः।। ४९।।

Parāśara said,—"O foremost of twice-born ones, the lord of the earth Govinda touched with the tip of his conch, the son of Uttānapāda standing with joined palms.

अथ प्रसन्नवदनः स क्षणान्नृपनन्दनः।।
तुष्टाव प्रणतो भूत्वा भूतधातारमच्युतम्।। ५०।।

And greatly pleased, that prince, bending low his head, praised that undecaying protector of living beings.

ध्रुव उवाच

भूमिरापोनलो वायुः खं मनो बुद्धिरेव च।।
भूतादिरादि प्रकृतिर्यस्य रूपं नतोस्मि तम्।। ५१।।

Dhruva said,—"I bow unto Him whose forms are earth, water, fire, air, ether, mind, intellect, the first element, primaeval nature, and the pure, subtle-all, pervading soul that excels nature.

शुद्धः सूक्ष्मोखिलव्यापी प्रधानात्परतः पुमान्।।
यस्य रूपं नमस्तस्मै पुरुषाय गुणात्मने।। ५२।।

भूतादीनां समस्तानां गंधादीनां च शाश्वतः।।
बुध्यादीनां प्रधानस्य पुरुषस्य च यः परः।। ५३।।

Salutation unto that Puruṣa who is devoid of qualities, pure, subtle, extending all over the earth, and who is separate from Prakṛti; who is supreme over all elements, all objects of sense, intellect and who is separate even from Puruṣa.

तं ब्रह्मभूतमात्मानमशेषजगतः पतिम्।।
प्रपद्ये शरणं शुद्धं त्वद्रूपं परमेश्वर।। ५४।।

I seek refuge unto him, who is one with Brahmā, who is the soul of the whole universe, pure, and who is the foremost of all gods.

बृहत्त्वाद्बृंहणत्वाच्च यद्रूपं ब्रह्मसंज्ञितम्।।
तस्मै नमस्ते सर्वात्स्त्रन्योगिचिन्त्याऽविकारिणे।।५५।।

Salutation unto that form of thine, O thou the soul of all things, which is designated as Brahmā by virtue of his pervading and maintaining the whole Universe, which is unchangeable and meditated upon by the sages.

सहस्त्रशीर्षा पुरुषः सहस्त्राक्षः सहस्त्रपात्।।
सर्वव्यापी भुवः स्पर्शादत्यतिष्टद्दशांगुलम्।।५६।।

Thou art the great god pervading the whole universe with a thousand heads, a thousand eyes, a thousand feet and who passes ten inches beyond its contact.[1]

यद्भूतं यच्च वै भव्यं पुरुषोत्तम तद्भवान्।।
त्वत्तो विराट् स्वराट् सम्राट् त्वत्तश्चाप्यधिपूरुषः।।५७।।

Thou art that excellent Puruṣa—whatever has been and whatever is to be. Thou art the progenitor of Virāṭ[2], Swarāṭ[3], Smarāṭ[4] and Adipuruṣa.

अत्यरिच्त सोधश्च तिर्यगूर्ध्वं च वै भुवः।।
त्वत्तो विश्वमिदं जातं त्वत्तो भूतं भविष्यति।।५८।।

The lower and upper and middle parts of the earth are not without thee—the whole universe is from thee—whatever has been and whatever shall be.

त्वद्रूपधारिणश्चान्तः सर्वभूतमिदं जगत्।।
त्वत्तो यज्ञः सर्वहुतः पृषदाज्यं पशुद्वधा।। ५९।।

The whole universe is thy form and exists in thee. From thee is sacrifice derived, and all oblations and curds and ghee and animals of either class (domestic or wild).

त्वत्तो ऋोथ सामानि त्वत्तश्छन्दांसि जज्ञिरे।।
त्वत्तो यजूंष्यजायन्त त्वत्तोश्वाश्चैकतो दतः।। ६०।।

From thee the Ṛg Veda, the Sāma Veda, the metres of the Vedas and the Yajur Veda have sprung.

गावस्त्वत्तः समुद्भूतास्त्वत्तोजा अवयो मृगाः।।
त्वन्मुखाद्ब्राह्मणास्त्वत्तो बाहोः क्षत्रमजायत।।६१।।
वैश्यास्तवोरुजाः शूद्रास्तव पद्भ्यां समुद्गताः।।

Horses and cows having teeth in one jaw only have been created by thee and as well as goats, sheep and deer. Brāhmaṇas originated from thy mouth; warriors from thy arms; Vaiśyas from thy thighs and Śūdras from thy feet.

अक्ष्णोः सूर्योनिलः प्राणाच्चन्द्रमा मनसस्तव।।६२।।
प्राणोन्तः सुपिराज्जातो मुखादग्निरजायत।।
नाभितो गगनं द्यौश्च शिरसः समवर्तत।। ६३।।
दिशः श्रोत्राक्षितिः पभ्द्यां त्वत्तः सर्वमभूदिदम्।।६४।।

From thine eyes came the Sun, from thy mind the moon, from thy central veins the Vital breath, from thy mouth the fire, from thy navel the sky, from thy head the heavens, from thy ears the regions and from thy feet the earth. And from thee the whole world was derived.

न्यग्रोधः सुमहानल्पे यथा बीजे व्यवस्थितः।।
संयमे विश्वमखिलं बीजभूते तथा त्वयि।। ६५।।

As the wide-spreading Nyagrodha (Indian fig-tree) exists (before it grows up into a tree) in a small seed, so at the time of dissolution, the whole word; exists in thee as its germ.

बीजादंकुरसम्भूतो न्यग्रोधस्तु समुत्थितः।।
विस्तारं च यथा याति त्वत्तः सृष्टौ तथा जगत्।।६६।।

As the Nyagrodha, originating from its seed, spread gradually into a huge tree, so the creation originating from thee expands itself into the universe.

यथा हि कदली नान्या त्वक्पत्रादपि दृश्यते।।
एवं विश्वस्य नान्यस्त्वं त्वत्स्थायीश्वर दृश्यते।।६७।।

O lord, as nothing is visible of a plantain tree, except its bark and leaves, so nothing is seen in thee except the whole universe.

ह्लादिनी संधिनी संवित्त्वय्येका सर्वसंस्थितौ।।
ह्लादतापकरी मिश्रा त्वयि नो गुणवर्जिते।। ६८।।

The faculties of intellect that are the source of pleasure and pain exist in thee as one with all existence. But the sources of pleasure and pain, singly or blended, do not exist in thee freed as thou art from all qualities.

पृथग्भूतैकभूताय भूतभूताय ते नमः।।
प्रभूतभूतभूताय तुभ्यं भूतात्मने नमः।। ६९।।

Salutation to thee, who art the subtile rudiment, who art single when a cause, but manifold in actions.

व्यक्तं प्रधानपुरुषौ विराट् सम्राट् स्वराट् तथा।।
विभाव्यतेन्तःकरणे पुरुषेष्वक्षयो भवान् ।। ७०।।

1. Contact with the univer—meaning who is not restricted by its boundaries.
2. The material univer.
3. Brahmā the creator.
4. Manu.

Salutation to thee, who art the proximate cause of life and action and identical with the great elements.

सर्वस्मिन्नसर्वभूतस्त्वं सर्वः सर्वस्वरूपधृक्।।
सर्वं त्वत्तस्ततश्च त्वं नमः सर्वात्मनेऽस्तु ते।। ७१।।

Thou art manifest in spiritual knowledge, thou art the great Purusha, Brāhmaṇa, Brahmā and Manu. Thou art beheld by mental contemplation and imperishable.

सर्वात्मकोसि सर्वेश सर्वभूतस्थितो यतः।।
कथयामि ततः किं ते सर्वं वेत्सि हृदि स्थितम्।। ७२।।

Thou abidest in all, art element of all; thou assumest all forms; all elements are from thee and thou art the soul of all—glory unto thee as thou art the soul of all, lord of all things—the origin of all things. What shall I speak unto thee, as thou knowest every thing, being seated in all hearts?

सर्वात्मन्सर्वभूतेश सर्वसत्वसद्भव।।
सर्वभूतो भवान्वेत्ति सर्वसत्त्वमनोरथम्।। ७३।।

O thou the soul of all thing, the sovereign lord of all ereations—the source of all elements, thou knowest all creatures and their desires.

यो मे मनोरथे नाम सफलः स त्वया कृतः।।
तपश्च तप्तं सफलं यद्दृष्टोसि जगत्पते।। ७४।।

O lord, do thou satisfy my desire. O lord of earth, my devout exercises have been crowned with success to-day since I have beheld thee.

श्रीभगवानुवाच

तपसस्तत्फलं प्राप्तं दृष्टोऽहं त्वया ध्रुव।।
मद्दर्शनं हि विफलं राजपुत्र न जायते।। ७५।।

The Lord said :—"Thy devotion hath been crowned with success since thou hast beheld me, O Dhruva. The sight of me, never goes without any result, O prince.

वरं वरय तस्मात्त्वं यथाभिमतमात्मनः।।
सर्वं संपद्यते पुंसां मयि दृष्टिपथं गते।। ७६।।

Do thou ask of me a boon, whatever thou wishest for : whenever I appear before men all their desires are satisfied.

ध्रुव उचाच

भगवन्भूतभव्येश सर्वस्यास्ते भवान् हृदि।।
किमज्ञातं तव ब्रह्मन्मनसा यन्मयेक्षितम्।। ७७।।

Dhruva said :—"O lord! O sovereign of all creatures, thou dost exist in the hearts of all. How can that be unknown to thee, O lord what I am cherishing in my mind?

तथापि तुभ्यं देवेश कथयिष्यामि यन्मया।।
प्रार्थ्यते दुर्विनीतेन हृदयेनातिदुर्लभम्।। ७८।।

Yet O lord of celestials, I shall mention unto thee, the object hard to attain, which my presumptuous mind panteth after.

किं वा सर्वजगत्स्रष्टः प्रसन्ने त्वयि दुर्लभम्।।
त्वत्प्रसादफलं भुंक्ते त्रैलोक्यं मघ वानपि।। ७९।।

But what can there be which cannot be got at, if thou art pleased, O creator of the universe; for it is by thy favour, that Indra enjoyed the sovereignty of three worlds.

नैतद्राजासनं योग्यमजातस्य ममोदरात्।।
इति गर्वादवोचन्मां सपत्नीमातुरुच्चकैः।। ८०।।

"This regal throne is not for thee, since thou art not born of me. These haughty words my step-mother addressed loudly unto me.

आधारभूतं जगतः सर्वेषामुत्तमोत्तमम्।।
प्रार्थयामि प्रभो स्थानं त्वत्प्रसादादतोव्ययम्।।८१।।

By thy favour I beg of thee, O lord, an exalted station, which surpasses all others, which is the support of the universe and shall last for ever.

श्रीभगवानुवाच

यत्वया प्रार्थ्यते स्थानमेतत्प्राप्स्यति वै भवान्।।
त्वयाऽहं तोषितः पूर्वमन्यजन्मनिबालक।। ८२।।

The Lord said :—"Forsooth shalt thou attain to the station thou art soliciting for; for, O boy even in thy former birth, thou didst satisfy me (with thy austere devotion).

त्वमासीर्ब्राह्मणः पूर्वं मय्येकाग्रमतिः सदा।।
मातापित्रोश्च शुश्रूषुर्निजधर्मानुपालकः।। ८३।।

Thou wast, in thy previous existence, a

Brāhmin, devoted with all thy heart unto me, ever dutiful to thy parents and always satisfying thy duties.

कालेन गच्छता मित्रं राजपुत्रस्तवाभवत् ।।
यौवनेखिलेभोगाढ्यो दर्शनीयोज्ज्वलाकृतिः ।।८४।।

In course of time, a prince became they friend, who in his youth indulged in all sensual pleasures, who was of a beautiful appearance and bright form.

तत्सङ्गात्तस्य तामृद्धिमवलोक्यातिदुर्लभाम् ।।
भवेयं राजपुत्रोहमिति वाञ्छा त्वया कृता ।। ८५ ।।

While in his company and beholding his riches, hard to acquire, thou didst desire that you might be born as the son of a king.

ततो यथाभिलषिता प्राप्ता ते राजपुत्रता ।।
उत्तानपादस्य गृहे जातोसि ध्रुव दुर्लभे ।। ८६ ।।

It is by virtue of that desire, thou art born as a prince in the mansion of Uttānapāda, O Dhruva, which cannot be easily obtained.

अन्येषां दुर्लभं स्थानं कुले स्वायम्भुवस्य यत् ।।८७।।
तस्यैतदपरं बाल येनाहं परितोषितः ।।
मामाराध्य नरो मुक्तिमवाप्नोत्यविलम्बिताम् ।।८८ ।।
मय्यर्पितमना बाल किमु स्वर्गादिकं पदम् ।। ८९ ।।
त्रैलोक्यादधिके स्थाने सर्वताराग्रहाश्रयः ।।
भविष्यति न सन्देहो मत्प्रसादाद्भवान्ध्रुव ।। ९० ।।

The birth, in the race of Swambhuva, is considered by others, as a great boon and for this I was propitiated by thee, O boy; but now thou art not valuing it so much. The man, who worships me, obtains in no time, liberation from life : what is the abode of celestials to one, whose mind is centered in me, O boy! Thou shalt, by my favour, O Dhruva, attain to a station, which is above the three worlds and become the stay of stars and planets : there is not the least doubt about it.

सूर्यात्सोमात्तथा भौमात्सोमपुत्राद्बृहस्पतेः ।।
सितार्कतनयादीनां सर्वर्क्षाणां तथा ध्रुव ।। ९१ ।।

सप्तर्षीणामशेषाणां ये च वैमानिकाः सुराः ।।
सर्वेषामुपरि स्थानं तव दत्तं मया ध्रुव ।। ९२ ।।

I do confer upon thee, O Dhruva, a station, which is above those of the Sun, the Moon, stars, Mercury, Venus, Saturn and all other constellations; above the regions of the seven Ṛsis and the divinities who traverse the atmosphere.

केचिच्चतुर्युगं यावत्केचिन्मन्वन्तरं सुराः ।।
तिष्ठन्ति भवतो दत्ता मया वै कल्पसंस्थितिः ।। ९३ ।।

Some of the celestials live for four ages; some for the reign of a Manu; but thou shalt live the duration of a Kalpa.

सुनीति रपि ते माता त्वदासन्नातिनिर्मला ।।
विमाने तारका भूत्वा तावत्कालं निवत्स्यति ।। ९४ ।।

Thy mother, Sunīti too, metamorphosed into a clear star, shall exist by thee in the welkin for the same period.

ये च त्वां मानवाः प्रातः सायं च सुसमाहि ताः ।।
कीर्त्तयिष्यंति तेषां च महत्पुण्यं भविष्यति ।। ९५ ।।

People singing thy glory, with concentrated minds, morning and evening, shall attain to an accession of piety.

श्रीपराशर उवाच
एवं पूर्वं जगन्नाथाद्देवदेवाज्जनार्दनात् ।।
वरं प्राप्य ध्रुवः स्थान मध्यास्ते स महामते ।। ९६ ।।
स्वयं शुश्रूषणाद्धर्म्यान्मातापित्रोश्च वै तथा ।।
द्वादशाक्षरमाहत्म्यात्तपसश्च प्रभावतः ।। ९७ ।।

Parāśara said :—"O thou of a great mind, obtaining this boon, from Janārdana, the sovereign of the celestials and the lord of earth, Dhruva attained to this excellent station.

तस्याभिमानमृद्धिं च महिमानं निरीक्ष्य हि ।।
देवासुराणामाचार्यः श्लोकमत्रोशना, जगौ । ९८ ।।

Beholding the increase of his honour and glory, the preceptor of the celestials and Asuras, Uśānas, repeated these verses.

अहोस्य तपसो वीर्यमहोस्य तपसः फलम् ।।
यदेनं पुरतः कृत्वा ध्रुवं सप्तर्षयस्थिताः ।। ९९ ।।

"Oh how great is the strength to his austere devotion, and how mightly is the success thereof, since the seven Ṛsis, are preceded by him.

ध्रुवस्य जननी चेयं सुनीतिर्नाम सूनृता।।
अस्याश्च महिमानं कः शक्तो वर्णयितुं भुवि।। १००।।

This too is Dhruva's mother Sunīti, who is otherwise named Sunṛtā. Who on this earth, can recount her glory?

त्रैलोक्याश्रयतां प्राप्तं परं स्थानं स्थिरायति।।
स्थानं प्राप्ता परं धृत्वा या कुचिविवरे ध्रुवम्।। १०१।।

Giving birth to Dhruva, she hath got at a station which is the refuge of the three worlds, and which is a station eminent above all.

यश्चैतत्कीर्त्तयेन्नित्यं ध्रुवस्यारोहणं दिवि।।
सर्वपापविनिर्मुक्तः स्वर्गलोके महीयते।। १०२।।

He, who shall celebrate the translation of Dhruva into the abode of the celestials, shall be released from his sins, and be adored in heaven.

स्थानभ्रंशं न चाप्नोति दिवि वा यदि वा भुवि।।
सर्वकल्याणसंयुक्तो दीर्घकालं स जीवति।। १०३।।

He shall not lose his station, either in this world, or in heaven (after death) and shall live long, possessed of every blessing.

।। इति श्रीविष्णुपुराणे प्रथमेंशे द्वादशोऽध्यायः।। १२।।

अथ प्रथमेंशे: त्रयदशोऽध्यायः

Part I : Section 13

श्रीपराशर उवाच

ध्रुवाच्छिष्टिं च भव्यं च भव्याच्छम्भुर्व्यजायत।।
शिष्टेराधत्त सुच्छाया पूचपुत्रानकल्मषान्।। १।।
रिपुं रिपुजयं विप्रं वृकलं वृकतेजसम्।।

Parāśara said :—"By Dhruva the abode of all blessings, his spouse Śambhu gave birth to two sons, Śiṣṭi and Bhavya. Sucaya, the wife of Siṣṭi gave birth to five sons, freed from sin, by name, Ripu, Ripuñjaya, Sipra, Vṛkala, and Vṛkatejas.

रिपोराधत्त बृहती चाक्षुषं सर्वतेजसम्।। २।।
अजीजनत्पुष्करिण्यां वारुण्यां चाक्षुषो मनुम्।।
प्रजापतेरात्मजायां वीरणस्य महात्मनः।। ३।।

Of these Ripu begat upon Vṛhatī, a highly effulgent son named Cakṣuṣa, who again begot the Manu Cakṣuṣa on Puṣkariṇī of the race of Varuṇa, who was the daughter of the high-souled patriarch Araṇya.

मनोरजायन्त दशा नड्वलायां महौजसः।।
कन्यायां तपतां श्रेष्ठ वैराजस्य प्रजापतेः।। ४।।

कुरुः पुरुः शतद्युम्नस्तपस्वी सत्यवाञ्छचिः।।
अग्निष्टोमोतिरात्रश्च सुद्युम्नश्चेति ते नव।।
अभिमन्युश्च दशमो नड्वलायां महौजसः।। 5।।

O great sage, the patriarch Vairāja had a daughter named Naḍbala, on whom Manu begot ten highly effulgent sons—Uru, Pooru, Śatadyumna, Tapasher, Satyavāk, Kavī, Agniṣṭoma, Atirātra, Sudyumnya and Abhimanyu.

कुरोरजनयत्पुत्रान् षडाग्नेयी महाप्रभान्।।
अङ्ग सुमनसं ख्यातिं क्रतुमङ्गिरसं शिबिम्।। ६।।

Uru begot on his wife Agneyī six highly effulgent sons—Aṅga, Sumanas, Khyāti, Kratu, Aṅgiras and Śiva.

अङ्गात्सुनीथापत्यं वै वेनमेकमजायत।।
प्रजार्थमृषयस्तस्य ममन्थुर्दक्षिणं करम्।। ७।।

And Aṅga begot on Sunītha one son named Vena. O great sages, with a view to multiply his progeny, the Ṛṣis rubbed his right hand.

वेनस्य पाणौ मथिते सम्बभूव महामुने।।
वैन्यो नाम महीपालो यः पृथुः परिकीर्त्तितः।। ८।।
येन दुग्धा मही पूर्वं प्रजानां हितकारणात्।। ९।।

And from his arm sprang a famous king named Vainya, who was celebrated as Pṛthu for milking the earth for the advantage of his subjects.

मैत्रेय उवाच

किमर्थं मथितः पाणिर्वेनस्य परमर्षिभिः।।
यत्र जज्ञे महावीर्यः स पृथुर्मुनिसत्तम।। १०।।

Maitreya said,—"O foremost of ascetics, do thou tell me why the right hand of Vena was rubbed by the great Ṛṣis, in consequence of which the mighty and powerful Pṛthu was born.

श्रीपराशर उवाच

सुनीथा नाम या कन्या मृत्योः प्रथमतोऽभवत्।।
अङ्गस्य भार्या सा दत्ता तस्यं वेनो व्यजायत।। ११।।

Parāśara said,—"Originally a daughter was born of Mṛtya named Sunītha. Aṅga, married her. And she gave birth to Vena.

स मातामहदोषेण तेन मृत्योः सुतात्मजः।।
निसर्गादेष मैत्रेय दुष्ट एव व्यजायत।। १२।।

O Maitreya, being born from the daughter of Mṛtyu, he inherited the evil propensities of his grand father.

अभिषिक्तो यदा राज्ये स वेनः परमर्षिभिः।।
घोष यामास स तदा पृथिव्यां पृथिवीपतिः।। १३।।

When he was inaugurated by the great Ṛṣis, Vena caused it to be proclaimed everywhere that he was the lord of the earth.

न यष्टव्यं न दातव्यं न होतव्यं कथाञ्चन।।
भोक्ता यज्ञस्य कस्त्वन्योऽह्यहं यज्ञपतिः प्रभुः।। १४।।

No one would undertake any sacrifice, offer any oblation or make any gift. "I am the king the lord of sacrifice, no one is entitled to oblation except myself."

ततस्तमृषयः पूर्वं संपूज्यं पृथिवीपतिम्।।
ऊचुः सामकलं वाक्यं मैत्रेय समुपस्थिताः।। १५।।

Thereupon the Ṛṣis assembled there and worshipping the lord of earth, addressed him, O Maitreya, with sweet words.

ऋषय ऊचुः

भोभो राजन् शृणुष्व त्वं यद्वदाम महीपते।।
राज्यं देहोपकाराय प्रजानां च हितं परम्।। १६।।

The Ṛṣis said,—"O king, O lord, do thou hear, what we speak unto thee, for then thy health as well as the interest of thy subjects shall be secure.

दीर्घसत्रेण देवेशं सर्वयज्ञेश्वरं हरिम्।।
पूजयिष्याम भद्रं ते तस्यांशस्ते भविष्यति।। १७।।

We purpose to worship, for thy welfare, with protracted rites, Hari, the lord of the celestials and sacrifices.

यज्ञेन यज्ञपुरुषो विष्णुः संप्रीणितो नृप।।
अस्माभिर्भवतः कामान्सर्वानेव प्रदास्यति।। १८।।

And thou shalt also be entitled to a share in it. If, O king, with our sacrifices, the lord of sacrifices in propitaited, he shall also satisfy all thy desires.

यज्ञैर्यज्ञेश्वरो येषां राष्ट्रे संपूज्यते हरिः।।
तेषां सर्वेप्सितावाप्तिं ददाति नृप भूभृताम।। १९।।

In whose kingdom, O king, Hari, the lord of sacrifices is worshipped with sacrifices, he confers on him, the satisfaction of all his desires.

वेन उवाच

मत्तः कोऽभ्यधिकोन्योस्ति कश्चाराध्यो ममापरः।।
कोयं हरिरिति ख्यातो यो वो यज्ञेश्वरो मतः।। २०।।

Vena said—"Who is there above me that, I even, shall have to worship him. Who is that person, who is known as Hari and whom ye do all consider as the lord of sacrifices?

ब्रह्मा जनार्दनः शम्भुरिन्द्रो वायुर्यमो रविः।।
हुतभुग्वरुणो धाता पूषा भूमिर्निशाकरः।। २१।।

एते चान्ये च ये देवाः शापानुग्रहकारिणः।।
नृपस्यैते शरीरस्थाः सर्वदेवमयो नृपः।। २२।।

Brahmā, Janārdana, Śambhu, Indra, Vāyu, Yama, the Sun, Fire, Varuṇa, Dhātā, Pūṣā, (the sun) Bhūmi (earth) and the lord of earth (the moon)—these and all others who are capable of imprecating curses and conferring boons (on mankind) do all exist in the person of a king for the essence of a sovereign is all that is divine.

एवं ज्ञात्वा मयाज्ञप्तं यद्यथा क्रियतां तथा।।
न दातव्यं न रुष्टव्यं न होतव्यं च भो द्विजाः।। २३।।

O twice born ones, understanding this full

well, do ye all obey my commands—you should not make gifts or offer oblations unto any one (but me) and should not worship any body else.

भर्तृशुश्रूषणं धर्मो यथा स्त्रीणां परो मतः।।
ममाज्ञापालनं धर्मो भवतां च तथा द्विजाः।। २४।।

As to serve her own husband is the prime duty of a female, so it is incumbent upon you, O twice-born ones, to satisfy my behests only.

ऋषय ऊचुः

देह्यनुज्ञां महाराज मा धर्मो यातु संक्षयम्।।
हविषां परिणामोऽयं यदेतदखिलं जगत्।। २५।।

The Ṛsis said,—"Give us command, O great king, to undertake sacrifices, so that piety may not suffer decrease. All this world is but the outcome of oblations."[1]

श्रीपराशर उवाच

इति विज्ञाप्यमनोऽपि स वेनः परमर्षिभिः।।
यदा ददाति नानुज्ञां प्रोक्तः प्रोक्तः पुनः पुनः।। २६।।

Parāśara said,—"Being thus addressed by the great Ṛsis and requested by them often and often, Vena did not give them.

ततस्ते मुनयः सर्वे कोपामर्षसमन्विताः।।
हन्यतां हन्यतां पाप इत्यूचुस्ते परस्परम्।। २७।।

Thereupon all the ascetics, being stricken with excessive ire, cried out "kill him!—kill this vicious weight!

यो यज्ञपुरुषं विष्णुमनादिनिधनं प्रभुम्।।
विनिन्दत्यधमाचारो न स योग्यो भुवः पतिः।। २८।।

He, who vilifies our lord the sovereign of sacrifices, without beginning or end, is not worth of the sovereignty of the earth.

इत्युक्त्वा मंत्रपूतैस्तैः कुशैर्मुनिगणा नृपम्।।
निजघ्नुर्निहतं पूर्वं भगवन्निन्दनादिना।। २९।।

Saying this, the ascetics, slew that king, with the blades of Kuśa grass, consecrated by prayer, who had already been destroyed by his impiety towards God.

ततश्च मुनयो रेणुं ददृशुः सर्वतो द्विज।।
किमेतदितिः चासन्नात्पप्रच्छुस्ते जनास्तदा।। ३०।।

Thereupon those ascetics beheld dust on all sides and said to the people who were nigh, 'What is this?'!

आख्यातं च जनैस्तेषां चोरीभूतैरराजके।।
राष्ट्रे तु लोकैरारब्धं परस्वादानमातुरैः।। ३१।।

To which the people replied—"The kingdom is without a king and hence the robbers and thieves have engaged in their dishonest work of encroaching upon the property of others.

तेषामुदीर्णवेगानां चोराणां मुनिसत्तमाः।।
समुहदृश्यते रेणुः परवित्तापहारिणाम्।। ३२।।

And O great asceties, this dust has been raised by those robbers hastening to seize other's property.

ततः संमंत्र्य ते सर्वे मुनयस्तस्य भूभृतः।।
ममन्थुरूरुं पुत्रार्थमनपत्यस्य यत्नतः।। ३३।।

Thereupon consulting with each other those ascetics, intent upon creating a prince, began to rub the thing of that childless monarch.

मथ्यमानात्समुत्तस्थौ तस्योरोः पुरुषः किल।।
दग्धस्थूणाप्रतीकाशः खल्वाटास्योतिह्रस्वकः।। ३४।।

The thigh being thus rubbed, there arose a being of the conplexion of a charred stake, with flattened features and of a dwarfish sature.

किं करोमीति तान्सर्वान्स विप्रानाह चातुरः।।
निषीदेति तमूचुस्ते निषादस्तेन सोऽभवत्।। ३५।।

And he speedly addressed all the ascetics there saying, "What shall I do?" Whereto they replied—"Sit down" (Niṣada) and thence his name was Niṣada.

ततस्तत्संभवा जाता विन्ध्यशैलनिवानिसः।।
निषादा मुनिशार्दूल पापकर्मोपलक्षणाः।। ३६।।

O foremost of ascetics, from this person, sprang a race called Niṣadas who inhabit the Vindya mountain and are characterised by the exterior tokens of depravity.

1 Receiving oblations Indra pours rains by which harvest grows and upon which the world lives.—T.

तेन द्वारेण तत्पापं निष्क्रान्तं तस्य भूपतेः।।
निषादास्ते ततो जाता वेनकल्मषना शनाः।। ३७।।

By this means the wickedness of the king (Vena) was extracted and the Niṣadas was thus born destroying Vena's sons.

तस्यैव दक्षिणं हस्तं ममन्थुस्ते ततो द्विजाः।। ३८।।
मथ्यमाने च तत्राभूत्पृथुर्वैन्यः प्रतापवान्।।
दीप्यमानः स्ववपुषा साक्षादग्निरिव ज्वलन्।। ३९।।

Thereupon those twice-born ones began to rub the right hand of Vena from which sprang the highly powerful son of Vena named Pṛthu resplendent in person and burning like the fire itself.

आद्यमाजगवं नाम खात्पपात ततो धनुः।।
शराश्च दिव्या नभसः कवचं च पपात ह।। ४०।।
तस्मिन् जाते तुं भूतानि संप्रहृष्टानि सर्वशः।। ४१।।

Thereupon from the welkin fell down the original bow of Hara named Pināka, and the celestial arrow and the celestial armour. Pṛthu thus born, all the beings around were greatly delighted.

सत्पुत्रेणैव जातेन वेनोपि त्रिदिवं ययौ।।
पुन्नाम्नो नरकात् त्रातः सुतेन सुमहात्मना।। ४२।।

And at the birth of that pious son, Vena too attained to the region of celestials and was delivered by that high-souled one from the hell named *Pāt*.

तं समुद्राश्च नद्यश्च रत्नान्यादाय सर्वशः।।
तोयानि चाभिषेकार्थं सर्वाण्येवोपतस्थिरे।। ४३।।

Thereupon the seas and rivers from all sides came there with holy water and pearls and gems of diverse kinds, for his inauguration on the throne.

पितामहश्च भवान्देवैराङ्गिरसैः सह।।
स्थावराणि च भूतानि जङ्गमानि च सर्वशः।।
समागम्य तदा वैन्यमभ्यसिञ्चन्नराधिपम्।। ४४।।

The great parent of all, Brahmā, with the celestials and the descendants of Aṅgiras (the fires) and with all things, animate or inanimate, came there and performed the ceremony of consecrating the lord of people—the son of king of Vena.

हस्ते तु दक्षिणे चक्रं दृष्ट्वा तस्य पितामहः।।
विष्णोरंशं पृथुं मत्वा परितोषं परं ययौ।। ४५।।

And beholding in his right hand the mark of the discus of Viṣṇu and recognising a portion of that deity in Pṛthu the great parent attained to an excess of delight.

विष्णुचक्र करे चिह्नं सर्वेषां चक्रवर्तिनाम्।।
भवत्यव्याहतो यस्य प्रभावस्त्रिदशैरपि।। ४६।।

For all those who become the sovereign kings of the earth, have always the mark of the discus of Viṣṇu in their hands.

महता राजराज्येन पृथुर्वैन्यः प्रतापवान्।।
सोभिषिक्तो महातेजा विधिवद्धर्मकोविदैः।। ४७।।

The highly powerful Pṛthu, the son of Vena, being thus invested with a mighty dominion, his power was unimpeded even in the region of the celestials.

पित्रा पराजितास्तस्य प्रजास्तेनानुराञ्जिताः।।
अनुरागात्ततस्तस्य नाम राजेत्यजायत।। ४८।।

That highly effulgent one, being installed according to due rites, by these who were skilled in religious rites, those subjects even, who were disaffected in his father's regeme, became fully attached unto him.

आपस्तस्तंभिरे चास्य समुद्रमभियास्यतः।।
पर्वताश्च ददुर्मार्गं ध्वजभङ्गश्च नाभवत्।। ४९।।

And in consequence of his attachment unto his subjects he was known all over as "the king". The waters became solid when he traversed the deep; the mountains opened him a way and his banners were unbroken even when he passed through the forests.

अकृष्टपच्या पृथिवी सिद्ध्यन्त्यन्नानि चिंतया।।
सर्वकामदुघा गावः पुटके पुटके मधु।। ५०।।

(In his time) the earth yeilded crops without cultivation; people got their food without any thought—the king gave milk at any time and honey was stored in every flower.

तस्य वै जातमात्रस्य यज्ञे पैतामहे शुभे।।
सूतः सूत्यां समुत्पन्नः सौत्येऽहनि महामतिः।। ५१।।

At the auspecious sacrifice which was performed at the birth of Pṛthu and which was headed by the great parent—the highly intelligent Sūta was produced from the juice of the moon plant.

तस्मिन्नेव महायज्ञेजज्ञे प्राज्ञोऽथ मागधः।।
प्रोक्तौ तदा मुनिवरैस्तावुभौ सूतमागधौ।। ५२।।

And in that great sacrifice the highly intelligent Māgadha was also born. Thereupon the Ṛsis accosted Sūta and Māgadha saying :—

स्तूयतामेष नृपतिः पृथुर्वैन्यः प्रतापवान्।।
कर्मैतदनुरूपं वां पात्रं स्तोत्रस्य चापरम्।। ५३।।

Do you sing the glory of this powerful king Pṛthu, the son of Vena. This is your special function and he is the fit object of your praise,

ततस्तावूचतुद्धवप्रान्सर्वानेव कृताूजली।।
अद्य जातस्य नो कर्म ज्ञायतेस्य महीपतेः।। ५४।।

गुणा न चास्य ज्ञायन्ते न चास्य प्रथितं यशः।।
स्तोत्रं किमाश्रयं त्वस्य कार्यमस्माभिरुच्यताम्।। ५५।।

Thereupon both of them, with folded hands, spoke unto the twice-born ones saying—"This king is born to-day—his works or merits we are not cognizant of; nor his fame has spread abroad—tell us on what subject shall we base our praise?"

ऋषय ऊचुः

करिष्यत्येष सत्कर्म चक्रवर्ती महाबलः।।
गुणा भविष्या ये चास्य तैरयं स्तूयतां नृपः।। ५६।।

The Ṛsis said,—"Sing his glory mentioning the works he shall perform, becoming the emperor of the earth and the merits he shall be crowned with.

श्रीपराशर उवाच

ततः स नृपतिस्तोषं तच्छ्रुत्वा परमं ययौ।।
सद्गुणैः श्लाघ्यतामेति तस्माच्छ्लाघ्या गुणा मम।। ५७।।

Parāśara said,—"Hearing these words the king was highly gratified and reflected, saying—"Persons (in this world) are eulogised for their various actions. And surely my virtuous action shall be the theme of these bards.

तस्माद्यदद्य स्तोत्रेण गुणनिर्वर्णनं त्विमौ।।
करिष्येते करिष्यामि तदेवाहं समाहितः।। ५८।।

And whatever merits, they will related in their panegyric, I will acquire with all my attention.

यदिमौ वर्जनीयं च किंचिदत्र वदिष्यतः।।
तदहं वर्जयिष्यामीत्येवं चक्रे मतिं नृपः।। ५९।।

And whatever faults they shall recommend to be avoided I shall always shun." The king resolved thus.

अथ तौ चक्रतुः स्तोत्रं पृथोर्वैन्यस्य धीमतः।।
भविष्यैः कर्मभिः सम्यक्सुस्वरौ सूतमागधौ।। ६०।।

Thereupon Sūta and Māgadha, with sweet-voiced discourses, sang the future virtues of the intelligent Pṛthu, the son of Vena.—

सत्यवाग्दानशीलोयं सत्यसन्धो नरेश्वरः।।
ह्रीमान्मैत्रः क्षमाशीलो विक्रान्तो दुष्टशासनः।। ६१।।

धर्मज्ञश्च कृतज्ञश्च दयावान् प्रियभाषकः।।
मान्यान्मानयिता यज्वा ब्रह्मण्यः साधुसम्मतः।। ६२।।

He shall be truthful, charitable, observer of his promises, the lord of people, wise, benevolent, patient, valient and the supresser of the wicked; pious, grateful, kind, sweet-spoken; shall always respect the venerable, perform sacrifices, respect the Brāhmins and shall be always recognised by the pious.

समः शत्रौ च मित्रे च व्यवहारस्थितौ नृपः।। ६३।।

He shall cherish the good and in administering justice shall be indiffernet to friend or foe.

सूतेनोक्तान् गुणानित्थं स तदा मागधेन च।।
चकार हृदि तादृक् च कर्मणा कृतवानसौ।। ६४।।

He cherished in his mind the virtues thus celebrated by Sūta and Māgadha and practised them in his life.

ततस्तु पृथिवीपालः पालयन्पृथिवीमिमाम्।।
इयाज विविधैर्यज्ञैर्महद्भिर्भूरिदक्षिणैः।। ६५।।

·Thereupon that king governed the earth and performed many sacrifices accompanied with liberal donations.

तं प्रजाः पृथिवीनाथमुपतस्थुः क्षुधार्दिताः।।
ओषधीषु प्रणष्टासु तस्मिन्काले ह्यराजके।।
तमूचुस्ते नताः पृष्टास्तत्रागमनकारणम्।। ६६।।

One day the subjects tricken with hunger appraoched the king for all the edible plants had perished during the season of anarchy. And when asked by him the cause of thus coming they said—

प्रजा ऊचुः

अराजके नृपश्रेष्ठ धरित्र्या सकलौषधीः।।
ग्रस्तास्ततः क्षयं यान्ति प्रजाः सर्वाः प्रजेश्वर।। ६७।।

'O foremost of kings, during the period of anarchy all vegetable products were withheld and, O lord of men, many are now perishing for want of food.

त्वन्नो वृत्तिप्रदो धात्रा प्रजापालो निरूपितः।।
देहि नः क्षुत्परीतानां प्रजानां जीवनौषधीः।। ६८।।

Thou hast been appointed (by the Providence) as our lord and sustainer—grant us vegetable—the support of our lives who are dying with hunger.

श्रीपराशर उवाच

ततस्तु नपतिर्दिव्यमादाय जगवं धनुः।।
शरांश्च दिव्यान्मकुपितः सोन्वधावद्वसुन्धराम् ।। ६९।।

Parāśara said,—"Hearing this, the king, inflamed with wrath, took up his bow Pināka and his celestial arrows and issued forth to assail the Earth.

ततो ननाश त्वरिता गौर्भूत्वा च वसुन्धरा।।
सा लोकान्ब्रह्मलोकादीन्संत्रासादगमन्महीं।। ७०।।

यत्र यत्र ययौ देवी सा तदा भूतधारिणी।।
तत्र तत्रे तत्र तुसा वैन्यं ददृशेऽभ्युद्यतायुधम्।। ७१।।

And the Earth too, assuming the shape of a cow, instantly fled away. From his fear she traversed the Brahmā and all other regions—and wherever she, the supporter of elements, went, she beheld the son of Vena, with uplifted weapons.

ततस्तं प्राह वसुधा पृथुं राजपराक्रमम्।।
प्रवेपमाना तब्दाणपरित्राणपरा यणा।। ७२।।

At last trembling with terror, the earth, desirous to escape his arrows, addressed Pṛthu, the hero of resistless prowess,—

पृथिव्युवाच

स्त्रीवधे त्वं महापापं किं नरेन्द्र न पश्यसि।।
येन मां हंतमत्यर्थं प्रकरोषि नृपोद्यमम्।। ७३।।

Pṛthivi said :—"O lord of men, do thou not know that there is a great sin hanging upon the destruction of females—why dost thou then try to slay me?"

पृथुरुवाच

एकस्मिन् यत्र निधनं प्रापिते दुष्टकारिणि।।
बहूनां भवति क्षेमं तस्य पुण्यप्रदो वधः।। ७४।।

Pṛthu said,—"O thou the perpetrator of vicious deeds, when by the destruction of one malignant being the happiness of many is secured—that destruction is considered as an act of virtue.

पृथिव्युवाच

प्रजानामुपकाराय यदि मां त्वं हनिष्यसि।।
आधारः कः प्रजानां ते नृपश्रेष्ठ भविष्यति।। ७५।।

The Earth said,—"If dost thou, for the behoof of thy subjects, slay me, who shall support them, O foremost of kings?"

पृथुरुवाच

त्वां हत्वा वसुधे बाणैर्मच्छासनपराङ्मुखीम्।।
आत्म योगबलेनेमा धारयिष्याम्यहं प्रजाः।। ७६।।

Pṛthu said,—"O Earth, slaying thee with my arrows, who art beyond my control, I shall support my own men, by virtue of my own devotion.

श्रीपराशर उवाच

ततः प्रणम्य वसुधा तं भूयः प्राह पार्थिवम्।।
प्रवेपिताङ्गी परमं साध्वसं समुपागता।। ७७।।

Parāśara said,—Thereupon the earth, overcome with fear, trembled and bowing unto him, addressed that king again, saying,—

पृथिव्युवाच

उपायतः समारब्धाः सर्वे सिद्धयन्त्युपक्रमाः ।।
तस्माद्वदाम्युपायं ते तं कुरुष्व यदीच्छसि।। ७८।।

"All undertakings prove successful whenever suitable means, to accomplish them are employed. I shall now suggest thee a means, which, if pleases thee, thou mayst accept.

समस्ता या मया जीर्णा नरनाथ महौषधीः ।।
यदीच्छसि प्रदास्यामि ताः क्षीरपरिणामिनीः ।। ७९ ।।

O lord of men, the edible plants, which I had devoured before, I may return thee, if thou likest, in the shape of milk.

तस्मात्प्रजाहितार्थाय मम धर्मभृतां वर।।
तं तु वत्सं कुरुष्व त्वं क्षरेयं येन वत्सला।। ८०।।

O thou the foremost of the pious, for the behoof of thy subjects, give me a calf by which I may be able to secrete milk.

समां च कुरु सर्वत्र येन क्षीरं समंततः।।
वरौषधीबीजभूतं बीजं सर्वत्र भावये।। ८१।।

O hero, make also all places level, so that I may produce, equally around, milk which is the source of all vigitation."

श्रीपराशर उवाच

तत उत्सारयामास शैलान् शतसहस्त्रशः।।
धनुष्कोट्या पदा वैन्यस्तेन शैला विवर्द्धिताः।।८२।।

Parāśara said,—Thereupon the son of Vena with his bow and, uprooted mountains by hundreds and thousands and thenceforth all the hills are lying sacttered all around.[1]

न हि पूर्वविसर्गे वै विषमे पृथिवीतले।।
प्रविभागः पुराणां वा ग्रामाणां वा पुराऽभवत्।।८३।।

Before this the surface of the earth was irregular, and there was no bundaries of villages and cities.

न सस्यानि न गोरक्ष्यं न कृषिर्न वणिक्पथः।।
वैन्यात्प्रभृति मैत्रेय सर्वस्यैतस्य सम्भवः।। ८४।।

There was no cultivation, no pasture, no agriculture, no high way for merchants; all these originated, O Maitreya, in the reign of the son of Vena.

यत्रयत्र समं त्वस्य भूमेरासीद्द्विजोत्तम।।
तत्रतत्र प्रजाः सर्वा निवासं समरोचयत्।। ८५।।

Whatever there was level ground, the king made habitations for the subjects.

आहारः फलमूलानि प्रजानामभवत्तदा।।
कृच्छ्रेण महता सोपि प्रणष्टास्वौषधीषु वै।। ८६।।

Before his time, the fruits and roots, which were the staple food of the subjects, were procured with great difficulty for all vegetables were destroyed.

स कल्पयित्वा वत्सं तु मनुं स्वायंभुवं प्रभुम्।।
स्वपाणौ पृथिवीनाथो दुदोह पृथिवीं पृथुः।।
सस्यजातानि सर्वाणि प्रजानां हितकाम्यया।। ८७।।

Thereupon having made, the Swaymbhuva Manu, the calf, that lord of men, Pṛthu, milked the earth with his own hands.

तेनान्नेन प्रजास्तात वर्तन्तेद्यापि नित्यशः।। ८८।।

He desiring the benefit of his subjects, corns and vegitables of all kinds were produced upon which the people even now and perpetually subsist.

प्राणप्रदाता स पृथुर्यस्माद्भूमेरभूत्पिता।।
ततस्तु पृथिवीसंज्ञामवापाखिलधारिणी।। ८९।।

By conferring life on her, Pṛthu became the father of the Earth and thence she got the patronymic Pṛthivī (the daughter of Pṛthu).

ततश्च देवैर्मुनिभिर्दैत्यै रक्षोभिरद्रिभिः।।
गन्धर्वैरुरगैर्यक्षैः पितृभिस्तरुभिस्तथा।। ९०।।

तत्तत्पात्रमुपादाय तत्तद्दुग्धं मुने पयः।।
वत्सदोग्धृविशेषाश्च तेषां तद्योनयोऽभवन्।। ९१।।

Thereupon the celestials the ascetics, the demons, the Rākṣasas, the mountains, the

1. Another text reads *Vivardhita*, meaning—And they were thenceforth piled upon one another.

Gandharvas, the Uragas, the Yakṣas, the Pitṛs, and the trees, with their respective vessels, milked the earth, as much O Manu, as they required. And the milker and the calf were both peculiar to their own species.

सैषा धात्री विधात्री च धारिणी पोषणी तथा।।
सर्वस्य तु ततः पृथ्वी विष्णुपादतलोद्भवा।। ९२।।

The Earth, the mother, the nurse, the supporter and the nourisher of all creations was produced from the sole of the foot of Viṣṇu.

एवं प्रभावस्स पृथुः पुत्रो वैन्यस्य वीर्यवान्।।
जज्ञे महीपतिः पूर्वो राजाभूज्जनरञ्जनात्।। ९३।।

And Pṛthu, the son of Vena, became so very powerful, that by virtue of his pleasing the subjects he was the first man who was styled the lord of the earth.

य इदं जन्म वैन्यस्य पृथोः संकीर्त्तयेन्नरः।।
न तस्य दुष्कृतं किंचित्फलदायि प्रजायते।। ९४।।

He who shall relate the story of the birth of the son of Vena shall never suffer any retribution for his iniquitous deeds.

दुस्स्वप्नोपशमं नृणां श्रृण्वतामेतदुत्तमम्।।
पृथोर्जन्मप्रभावश्च करोति सततं नृणाम्।। ९५।।

And he who shall hear of the birth and virtues of Pṛthu shall be relieved from the affliction of evil dreams.

।। इति श्रीविष्णुपुराणे प्रथमेंशे त्रयोदशोऽध्यायः।। १३।।

अथ प्रथमेंशेः चतुर्दशोऽध्यायः

Part I : Section 14

श्रीपराशर उवाच

पृथोः पुत्रो तु धर्मज्ञौ जज्ञा तेन्तद्ध्यद्धवादिनौ।।
शिखण्डिनी हविर्धानमन्तर्धानाद्व्यजायत।। १।।

Paraśara said—From Pṛthu were born two highly powerful sons named Antradhāna and Pāli. And Antardhāna begot on Śikhaṇḍinī a son named Havirdhāna.

हविर्धानात् पडाग्नेयी धिषणाऽजनयत्सुतान्।।
प्राचीनबर्हिषं शुक्रं गयं कृष्णं वृजाजिनौ।। २।।

And Havirdhāna again begot on Dhīṣaṇa six son—named, Prācīnabarhiṣa, Śukra Gaya, Kṛṣṇa, Braja and Ajīna.

प्राचीनबर्हिर्भगवान्महानासीत्प्रजापति ।।
हविर्धानान्महाभाग येन संवधताः प्रजाः।। ३।।

Prācīnabarhiṣa was a mighty prince and patriarch by whom mankind was multiplied after the death of Havirdhāna.

प्राचीनाग्राः कुशास्तस्य पृथिव्यां विश्रुता मुने।।
प्राचीनबर्हिरभवत्ख्यातो भुवि महाबलः।। ४।।

He was called Prācīnabarhiṣa on account of his placing upon the earth (at the time of his prayer) the sacred grass pointing to the east.

समुद्रतनयायां तु कृतदारो महीपतिः।।
महतस्तमसः पारे सवर्णायां महामते।। ५।।

After a protracted devotion that lord of earth married the daughter of the ocean named Savaraṇā.

सवर्णाधत्त सामुद्री दश प्राचीनबद्धहषः।।
सर्वे प्राचेतसो नाम धनुर्वेदस्य पारगाः।। ६।।

And Prācīnabarhiṣa, begot on Savarṇā, the daughter of the Ocean ten sons, who were all called Pracetas and were all well-skilled in archery.

अपृथग्धर्मचरणास्ते तप्यन्त महत्तपः।।
दशवर्ष सहस्त्राणि समुद्रसलिलेशयाः।। ७।।

They all parctised the same religious austerities and remained immersed in the bed of the deep for ten thousand years.

श्रीमैत्रेय उवाच

यदर्थं ते महात्मानस्तपस्तेपुर्महामुने।।
प्राचेतसः समुद्राम्भस्येतदाख्यातुमर्हसि।। ८।।

Maitreya said,—Do thou, O great ascetic, tell me, why those high-soulded Pracetas practised austerities being immersed in the deep.

श्रीपराशर उवाच

पित्रा प्रचेतसः प्रोक्ताः प्रजार्थममितात्मना ।।
प्रजापतिनियुक्तेन बहुमानपुरस्सरम् ।। ९ ।।

Parāśara said,—Welcoming the high-souled Prācīnabarhiṣa, the Patriarch requested him to multiply race.

प्राचीनबर्हिरुवाच

ब्रह्मणा देवदेवेन समादिष्टोस्म्यहं सुताः ।।
प्रजाः संवर्द्धनीयास्ते मया चोक्तं तथेति तत् ।। १० ।।

And he accordingly addressed his sons, saying,—'O my son, I have been commanded by Brahmā, the god of gods to multiply mankind.

तन्मम प्रीतये पुत्राः प्रजावृद्धिमतंद्रिताः ।।
कुरुध्वं माननीया वः सम्यगाज्ञा प्रजापते ।। ११ ।।

And I too had promised obedience. Do ye therefore, my sons, diligently promote the increase of mankind. You shall all with reverence obey the commands of the Patriarch.

श्रीपराशर उवाच

ततस्ते तत्पितुः श्रुत्वा वचनं नृपनंदनाः ।।
तथेत्युक्त्वा च तं भूयः पप्रच्छुः पितरं मुने ।। १२ ।।

Parāśara said,—Hearing the words of their father those princes said, "So be it" and repeatedly addressed him.

प्रचेतस ऊचुः

येन तात प्रजावृद्धौ समर्था कर्मणा वयम् ।।
भवेम तत् समस्तं नः कर्म व्याख्यातुमर्हसि ।। १३ ।।

O Muni, saying,—"By what, O father, we shall be able to multiply mankind? It behoveth thee to mention this unto me.

पितोवाच

आराध्य वरदं विष्णुमिष्टप्राप्तिमसंशयम् ।।
समेति नान्यथा मर्त्यः किमन्यत्कथायमि वः ।। १४ ।।

The father said,—"There is no doubt that people shall meet with an accomplishment of all their desires, if they worship Viṣṇu, the conferrer of boons. There is no other alternative. What future can I tell you?

तस्मात्प्रजा विवृद्ध्यर्थं सर्वभूतप्रभुं हरिम् ।।
आराधयत गोविन्दं यदि सिद्धिमभीप्सथ ।। १५ ।।

If you wish to succeed, do you adore Govinda who is Hari, the lord of all beings, in order to bring about the increase of mankind.

धर्ममर्थं च कामं च मोक्षं चान्विच्छतां सदा ।।
आराधनीयो भगवाननादिपुरुषोत्तमः ।। १६ ।।

The excellent Puruṣa, without beginning, should be worshipped by him who wishes for virtue, wealth, enjoyment or liberation.

यस्मिन्नाराधिते सर्गं चकारादौ प्रजापतिः ।।
तारामध्याच्युतं वृद्धिः प्रजानां वो भविष्यति ।। १७ ।।

Adore him, who is imperishable and propitiating whom the great Patriarch Brahmā succeeded in creating the universe.

श्रीपराशर उवाच

इत्येवमुक्तास्ते पित्रा पुत्राः प्राचेतसो दश ।।
मग्नाः पयोधिसलिले तपस्तेपुः समाहिताः ।। १८ ।।

Parāśara said,—Being thus addressed by their father the ten Pracetas plunged into the deep and with concentrated minds, engaed in devotion.

दशवर्षसहस्राणि न्यस्तचित्ता जगत्पतौ ।।
नारायणे मुनिश्रेष्ठ सर्वलोकपरायणे ।। १९ ।।

O foremost of ascetics, with their minds wholly devoted to Nārāyaṇa, the refuge of all creatures and the lord of the universe, and withdrawing their thoughts from all other exterior objects, they remained (in the state of devotion) for ten thousand years.

तत्रैवावस्थिता देवमेकाग्रमनसो हरिम् ।।
तुष्टुवुर्यस्तुतः कामान् स्तोतुरिष्टान्प्रयच्छति ।। २० ।।

And remaining there they worshipped with concentrated minds that great God Hari, who, when propitiated, confers, on all those who praise him, whatever they desire.

श्रीमैत्रेय उवाच

स्तवं प्रचेतसो विष्णोः समुद्राम्भसि संस्थिताः ।।
चक्रुस्तन्मे मुनिश्रेष्ठ सुपुण्यं वक्तुमर्हसि ।। २१ ।।

Maitreya said,—"O foremost of ascetics, the praises addressed to Viṣṇu, by those Pracetas, lying plunged in the depths of the ocean are sacred and it behoveth thee to relate them unto me.

श्रीपराशर उवाच

शृणु मैत्रेय गोविन्दं यथापूर्वं प्रचेतसः।।
तुष्टुवुस्तन्मयीभूताः समुद्रसलिलेशयाः।। २२।।

Parāśara said—Do thou hear—(I shall recount) the praises addressed, of old, to Govinda by the Pracetas as they stood in the waters of the deep.

प्रचेतस ऊचुः

नताः स्म सर्ववचसां प्रतिष्ठा यत्र शाश्वती।।
तमाद्यन्तमशेषस्य जगतः परमं प्रभुम्।। २३।।
ज्योतिराद्यमनौपम्यमणवनन्तमपारवत्।।
योनिभूतमशेषस्य स्थावरस्य चरस्य च।। २४।।

यस्याहः प्रथमं रूपमरूपस्य तथा निशा।।
संध्या च परमेशस्य तस्मै कालात्मने नमः।। २५।।

Pracetas said,—"We bow unto him who is the eternal theme of all speech, who is the beginning of the boundless universe and the lord of it; who is the primeval light—who has not the like of him; indivisible and infinite; who is the creator of all things, mobile and immobile—salutation unto him, who is one with time, who is without form—and whose first form is the day and the second and third form are the evening and night.

भुज्यतेऽनुदिनं देवैः पितृभिश्च सुधात्मकः।।
बीजभूतं समस्तस्य तस्मै सोमात्मनेन मः।। २६।।

Salutation unto him, who is the same with the moon who is the life of all living beings, and who is the receptacle of ambrosia, drunk daily by the celestials and progenitors.

यस्तमांस्यत्ति तीव्रात्मा प्रभाभिर्भासयन्नभः।।
धर्मशीताम्भसां योनिस्तस्मै सूर्यात्मने नमः।। २७।।

Salutation unto him, who is one with the sun, who with his fierce rays, dispells darkness from the sky and who is the creator of the seasons—the summer, the winter and the rains.

काठिन्यवान् यो बिभर्ति जगद्देतदशेषतः।।
शब्दादिसंश्रयो व्यापी तस्मै भूम्यात्मने नमः।। २८।।

Salutation unto him, who is one with the earth—who, being solid, is supporting the whole universe and is the asylum of smell and all other objects of sense.

यद्योनिभूतं जगतो बीजं यत्सर्वदेहिनाम्।।
तत्तोयरूपमीशस्य नमामो हरिमेधसः।। २९।।

We bow to that form of Hari, which is water, which is the seed of all living beings and the womb of the world.

यो मुखं सर्वदेवानां हव्यभुक्कव्यभुक् तथा।।
पितृणां च नमस्तस्मै विष्णवे पावकात्मने।। ३०।।

Salutation unto Viṣṇu, who is one with Fire, who is the mouth of the celestials being the eater of the Havya and who is the mouth of the progenitors being the eater of the Kavya.

पञ्चधावस्थितो देहे यश्चेष्टां कुरुतेऽनिशम्।।
आकाशयोनिर्भगवांस्तस्मै वाय्वात्मने नमः।। ३१।।

Salutation unto him who is at one with the air, which exists as five vital airs in the body causing constant vital action and is the origin of ether.

अवकाशमशेषाणां भूतानांयः प्रयच्छति।।
अनन्तमूर्तिमाञ्छुद्धस्तस्मै व्योमात्मने नमः ।। ३२।।

Salutation unto him, who is at one with the atmosphere, who is pure, whose form and end cannot be perceived, who is shapaless and limitless and who gives seperate existence to all creatures.

समस्तेन्द्रियसर्गस्य यः सदा स्थानमुत्तमम्।।
तस्मै शब्दादिरूपाय नमः कृष्णाय वेधसे।। ३३।।

Salutation unto Kṛṣṇa, who is the creator, is perceived in the form of sensible objects and is the direction of the faculties of sense.

गृह्णाति विषयान्नित्यमिन्द्रियात्माक्षराक्षरः।।
यस्तस्मै ज्ञानमूलाय नतास्म हरिमेधसे।। ३४।।

We bow unto Hari, who is one with senses both subtle and substantial, who receives the impression of the senses, and who is the source of all knowledge.

गृहीतानिन्द्रियैरर्थानात्मने यः प्रयच्छति।।
अन्तःकरणरूपाय तस्मै विश्वात्मने नमः।। ३५।।

Salutation unto that universal soul, who as intellect carries the impressions received by the senses to the soul—

यस्मिन्ननन्ते सकलं विश्वं यस्मात्तथोद्गतम्।।
लयस्थानं च यस्तस्मै नमः प्रकृतिधर्मणे।। ३६।।

Salutation unto him who is Prakṛti—who has created the Universe, who is maintaining it and in whom it shall perish.

शुद्धः सँल्लक्ष्यते भ्रान्त्या गुणवानिव योऽगुणः।।
तमात्मरूपिणं देव नतास्म पुरुषोत्तमम्।। ३७।।

We bow unto that excellent Puruṣa, who albeit freed from all and devoid of all qualities, appears, to the creatures labouring under mistakes, and enveloped with all qualities.

अविकारमजं शुद्धं निर्गुणं यन्निरजनम्।।
नतास्म तत्परं ब्रह्म विष्णोर्यत्परमं पदम्।। ३८।।

अदीर्घह्रस्वमस्थूलणवनमश्यामलोहितम्।।
अस्नेहच्छायमतनुमसक्तमशरीरिणम्।। ३९।।

अनाका शमसंस्पर्शमगन्धमरसं च यत्।।
अचक्षुश्रोत्रमचलमवाक्पाणिममानसम्।। ४०।।

अनामगोमत्रसुखमतेजस्कमहेतुकम्।।
अभयं भ्रांतिरहितम निद्रमजरामरम्।। ४१।।

अरजोशब्दममृतमप्लुप्तं यदसंवृतम्।।
पूर्वापरेण वै यस्मिंस्तद्विष्णोः परमं पदम्।। ४२।।

Salutation unto that Brahmā, who is the ultimate condition of Viṣṇu. Who is unchangeable, without birth, pure, void of qualities and free from accidents; who is neither high nor low neither massive nor thin, has neither shape, nor colour, nor shadow, nor substance nor affection nor body; who is neither ethereal nor capable of being touched; who is neither smell nor taste; who has no eyes, ears, or motion or speech, breath or mind; who is without name, *gotra*, countenance or lustre; who is without fear or mistake; without blame, desease or death; who is free from passion, without sins, imperceptible, inactive, independent of place and time separated from all investing properties, but exercising irresistible might, and who is at one with all beings and dependant upon one.

परमेशत्वगुणवत्सर्वभूतम संश्रयम्।।
नतास्म तत्पदं विष्णोर्जिह्वादृग्गोचरं न यत्।। ४३।।

Salutation to that nature of Viṣṇu which tongue cannot describe nor eye hath seen.

श्रीपराशर उवाच

एवं प्रचेतसो विष्णुं स्तुवन्तस्तत्समाधयः।।
दशवर्षसहस्राणि तपश्चेरुर्महार्णवे।। ४४।।

Parāśara said—Thus glorifying Viṣṇu the Pracetas performed austerities for ten thousand years in the depths of the sea.

ततः प्रसन्नो भगवांस्तेषामन्तर्जले हरिः।।
ददौ दर्शनमुन्निद्रनीलोत्पलदलच्छविः।। ४५।।

Thereupon Hari, having the complexion of the full-blown lotus leaf, being pleased, appeared before them even in the midst of waters.

पतत्रि राजमारूढमवलोक्य प्रचेतसः।।
प्रणिपेतुः शिरोभिस्तं भक्तिभारावनामितैः।। ४६।।

And beholding him mounted on Garuḍa, the Pracetas bending low their heads with reverence, saluted him.

ततस्तानाह भगवान्व्रयतामीप्सतो वरः।।
प्रसाद सुमुखोहं वो वरदः समुपस्थितः।। ४७।।

Thereupon Viṣṇu addressed them, saying,—"Do you ask of me a boon. Being pleased with you I have come here to confer boons on you.

ततस्तमूचुर्वरदं प्रणिपत्य प्रचेतसः।।
यथा पित्रा समादिष्टं प्रजानां वृद्धिकारणम्।। ४८।।

Bowing unto that giver of boons, the Pracetas—asked of him the multiplication of mankind as ordered by their parents.

स चापि देवस्तं दत्वा यथाभिलषितं वरम्।।
अन्तर्धानं जगामाशु ते च निश्चक्रमुर्जलात्।। ४९।।

And granting them the wished for boon Viṣṇu disappeared instantly and Pracetas too came out of the sea.

।। इति श्रीविष्णुपुराणे प्रथमेंशे प्रचेतास्तवो नाम चतुर्दशोऽध्यायः।। १४।।

अथ प्रथमेंशेः पञ्चदशोऽध्यायः

Part I : Section 15

श्रीपराशर उवाच

तपश्चरत्सु पृथिवीं प्रचेतः सु महीरुहाः।।
अरक्ष्यमाणामावव्रुर्बभूवाथ प्रजाक्षयः।। १।।

Parāśara said,—When the Pracetas were thus engaged in devout exercises the earth was covered with huge trees and the subjects suffered decease.

नाशकन्मरुतो वातुं वृतं खमभवद्द्रुमैः।।
दशवर्षसहस्राणि न शकुश्चेष्टितुं प्रजाः।। २।।

The welkin being obstructed with the branches of trees, the wind did not blow for ten thousand years and the mankind did not labour.

तान्दृष्ट्वा जलनिष्क्रान्ताः सर्वे क्रुद्धाः प्रचेतसः।।
मुखेभ्यो वायुमग्निं च तेऽसृजन् जातमन्यव।। ३।।

And when the Pracetas came out of the water they were greatly inflamed with ire beholding the earth, and wind and flame issued out of their mouths.

उन्मूलानथ तान्वृक्षान्कृत्वा वायुरशोषयत्।।
तानग्निरदहद्धोरस्तत्राभूद्द्रुम संक्षयः।। ४।।

The wind uprooted all the trees and left them sear and dry and the fierce fire consumed and thus the earth was cleared off the forests.

द्रुमक्षयमथो दृष्ट्वा किञ्चिच्छिष्टेषु शाखिषु।।
उपगम्याब्रवीदेतान्राजा सोमः प्रजापतीन्।। ५।।

Beholding all the trees thus destroyed and only few left, their king Soma approached those princes and said,—

कोपं यच्छत राजानः शृणुध्वं च वचो मम।।
सन्धानं वः करिष्यामि सह क्षितिरुहैरहम्।। ६।।

"Renounce your ire, O princes, and hear what I say; I shall bring about peace between you and the trees.

रत्नभूता च कन्येयं वार्क्षेयी वरवर्णिनी।।
भविष्यज्जानता पूर्वं मया गोभिर्विवर्द्धिता।। ७।।

This precious and beautiful maiden, sprung from the trees, has been nourished by me with my rays who am cognizant of futurity.

मारिषा नाम नाम्नैषा वृक्षाणामिति निर्मिता।।
भार्या वोस्तु महाभागा ध्रुवं वंशविवर्द्धिनी।। ८।।

Her name is Māriṣā and she has sprung from the trees. That lucky damsel shall be your wife and the multiplier of the family of Dhruva.

युष्माकं तेजसोर्द्धेन मम चार्द्धेन तेजसः।।
अस्यामुत्पत्स्यते विद्वान्दक्षोनाम प्रजापतिः।। ९।।
मम चांशेन संयुक्तो युष्मत्तेजोमयेन वै।।
तेजसाग्निसमो भूयः प्रजाः संवर्द्धयिष्यति।। १०।।

From a half of your lustre and half of mine, the learned and the great Patriarch Dakṣa shall be begotten on her; your lustre as well as mine being conjoined in him he shall be effulgent like fire and multiply the human race.

कण्डुर्नाम मुनिः पूर्वमासीद्वेदविदां वरः।।
सुरम्ये गोमतीतीरे स तेपे परमं तपः।। ११।।

There lived in the days of yore an ascetic named Kaṇḍu—the foremost of those conversant with the Vedas. He engaged in an austere devotion on the picturesque bank of the river Gomatī.

तत्क्षोभाय सुरेन्द्रेण प्रम्लोचाख्या वराप्सराः।।
प्रयुक्ता क्षोभयामास तमृषिं सा शुचिस्मिता।। १२।।

To obstruct his devotion a highly beautiful nymph named, Pramlocā was despatched by the king of the celestials. And being thus engaged, the sweet-smiling nymph diverted the sage from the practice of his pious austerities.

क्षोभितः स तया सार्द्धं वर्षाणामधिकं शतम्।।
अतिष्ठन्मन्दरद्रोण्यां विषयासक्तमानसः।। १३।।

Being thus diverted he lived with her for a hundred and fifty years at the valley of the mount Mandara, his mind being wholly given up to worldly enjoyment.

तं सा प्राह महाभाग गन्तुमिच्छाम्यहं दिवम्।।
प्रसादसुमुखो ब्रह्मन्ननुज्ञां दातुमर्हसि।। १४।।

Once on a time the damsel said to the high-souled Ṛṣi,—"O Brāhmaṇa, I desrie to go to the abode of the celestials—do thou, with a delighted countenance, grant me the permission.

तयैवमुक्तः स मुनिस्तस्यामासक्तमानसः।।
दिनानि कतिचिद्भद्रे स्थीयतामित्यभाषत।। १५।।

Being thus addressed by her, the ascetic, solely attached to her, replied,—"O fair lady, do thou stay a few days more with me.

एवमुक्ता ततस्तेन साग्रं वर्षशतं पुनः।।
बुभुजे विषयांस्तन्वी तेन साकं महात्मना।। १६।।

Being thus requested by him that damsel of a slender person, enjoyed earthly pleasures in the company of that high-souled ascetic, for more than a hundred years.

अनुज्ञां देहि भगवन् व्रजामि त्रिदशालयम्।।
उक्तस्तथेति स पुनः स्थीयतामित्यभाषत।। १७।।

And being again accosted by her with "O lord! allow me to return to the abode of the celestials" he again requested her to stay a few days more with him.

पुनर्गते वर्षशते साधिके सा शुभानना।।
यामीत्याह दिवं ब्रह्मन्प्रणयस्मितशोभनम्।। १८।।

After the expiration of another hundred years the beautiful damsel, with a smile of love, again said,—"I shall now go to the abode of the celestials, O Brāhmaṇa.

उक्तस्तयैवं स मुनिरुपगुह्यायते क्षणाम्।।
इहास्यतां क्षणं सुभ्रु चिरकालं गमिष्यसि।। १९।।

Being thus addressed the ascetic, detaining the fair-eyed damsel, said,—"Stay a little more, thou shalt depart for a long time.

सा क्रीडमाना सुश्रोणी सह तेनर्षिणा पुनः।।
शतद्वयं किंचिदूनं वर्षाणामन्वतिष्ठत।। २०।।

Afraid of incurring an imprecation the graceful nymph lived with the ascetic for nearly two hundred years more.

गमनाय महाभाग देवराजनिवेशनम्।।
प्रोक्तः प्रोक्तस्तया तन्व्या स्थीयतामित्यभाषत।। २१।।

The high-souled sage was repeatedly asked by the nymph to allow her to repair to the abode of the lord of the celestials and she was as often desired by him to remain.

तस्य शापभयाद्भीता दाक्षिण्येन च दक्षिणा।।
प्रोक्ता प्रणयभङ्गार्त्तिवेदिनी न जहौ मुनिम्।। २२।।
तया च रमतस्तस्य परमर्षेरहर्निशम्।।
नवंनवमभूत्प्रेम मन्मथाविष्टचेतसः।। २३।।

Afraid of his curse, excelling in amiable manners and knowing full well the pain consequent upon the separation from an object of love she did not quit the ascetic, who, enjoying in her company day and night and having his mind possessed by cupid, became fully attached unto her.

एकदा तु त्वरायुक्तो निश्चक्रामोटजान्मुनिः।।
निष्क्रामन्तं च कुत्रेति गम्यते प्राह सा शुभा।। २४।।

Once while he was speedily issuing out of the cottage the nymph said to him. "Where are you going?"

इत्युक्तः स तया प्राह परिवृत्तमहः शुभे।।
सन्ध्योपास्तिं करिष्यामि क्रियालोपोन्यथा भवेत्।। २५।।

Whereto he replied, "O damsel, the day is fast approaching its close, I must perform my evening ablutions or else I shall neglect a duty.

ततः प्रहस्य सुदती तं सा प्राह महामुनिम्।।
किमद्य सर्वधर्मज्ञ परिवृत्तमहस्त्व।। २६।।

Thereupon smiling, she, delightedly, said to the sage,—"O thou conversant with all religions, why dost thou talk of to-day approaching its close?

बहूनां विप्र वर्षाणां परिवृत्तम हस्तव।।
गतमेतन्न कुरुते विस्मयं कस्य कथ्यताम्।। २७।।

It thy day, O Brāhmaṇa, the aggregate of many hundred years? Shall it not create astonishment in other? Do thou tell me.

मुनिरुवाच

प्रातस्त्वमागता भद्रे नदीतीरमिदं शुभम्।।
मया दृष्टासि तन्वङ्गि प्रविष्टासि ममाश्रमम्।। २८।।

The ascetic said,—"O fair damsel, you came to the riverside this morning—I saw you there and brought you to my hermitage.

इयं च वर्तते सन्ध्या परिणाममहर्गतम्।।
उपहासः किमर्थोयं सद्भावः कथ्यतां मम।। २९।।

The day has passed and the evening has well-nigh arrived. Tell me in sooth what the truth is". The (nymph) Pramlocā said,—

प्रम्लोचोवाच

प्रत्यूषस्यागता ब्रह्मन् सत्यमेतन्न तन्मृषा।।
नन्वस्य तस्य कालस्य गतान्यब्दशतानि ते।। ३०।।

"True it is, O Brāhmaṇa, that I came here at dawn. It is not false—but after that hundreds of years have flown away.

सोम उवाच

ततस्स साध्वसो विप्रस्तां पप्रच्छायतेक्षणाम्।।
कथ्यतां भीरु कः कालस्त्वया मे रमतः सह।। ३१।।

Thereupon, the sage, stricken with fear, asked that nymph, having expansive eyes, saying,—"Tell me how many years I have spent in enjoyment with you.

प्रम्लोचोवाच

सप्तोत्तराण्यतीतानि नववर्ष शतानि ते।।
मासाश्च षट्तथैवान्यत्समतीतं दिनत्रयम्।। ३२।।

Pramlocā said,—"You have spent nine hundred and seven years six months and three days.

ऋषिरुवाच

सत्यं भीरु वदस्येतत्परिहासोथ वा शुभे।।
दिनमेकमहं मन्ये त्वया सार्द्धमिहासितम्।। ३३।।

The ascetic again said,—"No more of laughter, O fair nymph, tell me the truth: methinks I have spent one day in your company.

प्रम्लोचोवाच

वदिष्याम्यनृतं ब्रह्मन्कथमत्र तवान्तिके।।
विशेषेणाद्य भवता पृष्टा मार्गानुवर्तिना।। ३४।।

To which Pramlocā replied : "O venerable sage why shall I speak untruth unto thee since I have been specially requested by thee to-day to speak the truth.

सोम उवाच

निशम्य तद्वचः सत्यं स मुनिर्नृपनन्दनाः।।
धिक्धिक् मामित्यतीवेत्थं निनिन्दात्मानमात्मना।। ३५।।

Soma said,—"Princes, when the sage had heard these words and thought them to be true he began to reproach himself exclaiming", O fie, fie upon me; my penance has been obstructed—

मुनिरुवाच

तपांसि मम नष्टानि हतं ब्रह्मविदां धनम्।।
हतो विवेकः केनापि योषिन्मोहाय निर्मिता।। ३६।।

The wealth of those who are cognizant of Brahmā, has been stolen; my judgement has been blinded; by whom women have been created to beguile mankind?

ऊर्मिषट्कातिगं ब्रह्म ज्ञेयमात्मजयेन मे।।
मतिरेषा हृता येन धिक् तं कामं महाग्रहम्।। ३७।।

O fie upon that passion by which my self-control has been stolen whereby I was about to attain the knowledge of Brahmā who is above the reach of those who are immersed in the six waves—namely, hunger, thirst, sorrow, stupification, decay and death.

व्रतानि वेदवेद्याप्तिकारणान्यखिलानि च।।
नरकग्राममार्गेण सङ्गेनापहृतानि मे।। ३८।।

By this evil company, which is the road to hell all my austerities, leading to the acquisition of the wisdom of the Vedas, have been obstructed.

विनिन्द्येत्थं स धर्मज्ञः स्वयमात्मानमात्मना।।
तामप्सरसमासीनामिदं वचनमब्रवीत्।। ३९।।

Having thus reviled himself the pious sage spoke to the nymph, who was near him, saying,—

गच्छ पापे यथाकामं यत्कार्यं तत्कृतं त्वया।।
देवराजस्य मत्क्षोभं कुर्वन्त्या भावचेष्टितैः।। ४०।।

"Go where dost thou wish, O vile nymph—

thou hast performed that for which thou hast been enjoyed by the lord of the celestials—thou hast obstructed my penances with thy facinations.

न त्वां करोम्यहं भस्म क्रोधतीव्रेण वह्निा।।
सतां सप्तपदं मैत्रमुषि तोहं त्वया सह।। ४१।।

I do not reduce thee to ashes with the fierce fire of my rage. Seven paces together are quite sufficent for the friendship of the pious, and thou and I have lived together for a pretty long time.

अथवा वा तव को दोषः किं वा कुप्याम्यहं तव।।
ममैव दोषो नितरां येनाहमजितेन्द्रियः।। ४२।।

Or what for is thy folly—and why should I be offended with thee—verily this is an outcome of my own folly since I have not been able to control my passions.

यया शक्रप्रियार्थिन्या कृतो मे तपसो व्ययः।।
त्वया धिक्तां महामोहमञ्जूषां सुजुगुप्सिताम्।। ४३।।

O fie on hated thee, the box of fascinations, who, to win favour with Śakra, has disturbed my devotion.

सोम उवाच

यावदित्थं स विप्रर्षिस्तां ब्रवीति सुमध्यमाम्।।
तावद्गलत्स्वेदजला साबभूवातिवेपथुः।। ४४।।

Soma said,—"While the sage spoke thus to the nymph she perspired and stood trembling.

प्रवेषमानां सततं खिन्नगात्रलतां सतीम्।।
गच्छ गच्छेति सक्रोधमुवाच मुनिसत्तमः।। ४५।।

Thereupon, the foremost of ascetics again said angrily to her, thus trembling and with drops of perspiration issuing from every pore—"Depart! Depart.

सा तु निर्भर्त्सिता तेन विनिष्क्रम्य तदाश्रमात्।।
आकाशगामिनी स्वेदं ममार्ज तरुपल्लवैः।। ४६।।

Being thus remonstrated with by that sage she issued out of the hermitage and began to wend her way by the welkin, rubbing the perspiration with the leaves of the trees.

निर्मार्जमाना गात्राणि गलत्स्वेदजलानि वै।।
वृक्षाद्वृक्षं ययौ बाला तदग्रारुणपल्लवैः।। ४७।।

She went forth from tree to tree rubbing her limbs and the perspiration with the durky shoots.

ऋषिणा यस्तदा गर्भस्तस्या देहे समाहितः।।
निर्जगाम स रोमाञ्चस्वेदरूपी तदङ्गतः।। ४८।।

And the child, she had conceived by the sage, came out from the pores of her skin, in drops of perspiration.

तं वृक्षा जगृहुर्गर्भमेकं चक्रे तु मारुतः।।
मया चाप्यायितो गोभिः स तदा ववृधे शनैः।।४९।।

The trees received those drops and the wind collected them. I protected with my rays till it increased in size gradually.

वृक्षाग्रगर्भसम्भूता मारिषाख्या वरानना।।
तां प्रदास्यन्ति वो वृक्षाः कोप एष प्रशाम्यताम्।।५०।।

Because she sprang from the drops on the tops of the trees that fair damsel was called Māriṣā; the trees will give her to thee—let your anger be appeased.

कण्डोरपत्यमेवं सा वृक्षेभ्यश्च समुद्गता।।
ममापत्यं तथा वायोः प्रम्लोचातनया च सा।।५१।।

She is Kaṇḍu's child—she was sprung from the trees—she is my offspring as well as that of the wind and she is also the daughter Pramlocā.

स चापि भगवान् कण्डुः क्षीणे तपसि सत्तमः।।
पुरुषोत्तमाख्यं मैत्रेय विष्णोरायतनं ययौ।। ५२।।

And the great sage, Kaṇḍu, on the wane of his devotion, repaired to the region of Viṣṇu called Puruṣottama, O Maitreya.

तत्रैकाग्रमतिर्भूत्वा चकाराराधनं हरेः।।
ब्रह्मपारमयं कुर्वञ्जपमेकाग्रमानसः।।
ऊर्ध्वबाहुर्महायोगी स्थित्वासौ भूपनन्दनाः।। ५३।।

And there he, O princes, devoted himself, with his whole mind to the adoration of Viṣṇu and engaged in the *Yoga*, with uplifted hands and uttering the prayers comprehending the supreme truths of the Vedas.

प्रचेतस ऊचुः

ब्रह्मपारं मुने श्रोतुमिच्छामः परमं स्तवम्।।
जपता कण्डुना देवो येनाराध्यत केशवः।। ५४।।

The Pracetasas said,—"We wish to hear of the excellent prayers of the sage, by which Kaṇḍu engaged in devotion and in the adoration of Keśava.

सोम उवाच

पारं परं विष्णुरपारपारः परः परेभ्यः परमार्थरूपी ।।
स ब्रह्मपारः परपारभूतः परः पराणामपि पारपारः ।।५५ ।।

On which Soma repeated them : —"Viṣṇu is beyond the limit of all earthly things, he is the infinite; through him we may get at the other end of the limitless deep—the earth : he is above all that is above; he is the finite truth : he is worthy of being approached by those who are conversant with the Vedas; the limit of elemental being; above the perception of the senses and the protectors (the divinities who proctect the creation).

स कारणं कारणतस्तोपि तस्यापि हेतुः परहेतुहेतुः ।।
कार्येषु चैवं सह कर्मकर्तृरूपैरशेषैरवतीह सर्वम् ।। ५६ ।।

He is the cause of cause; the casue of the cause in cause; the cause of finite cause; and in effects he, both as every object and agent, preserves the creation.

ब्रह्म प्रभुर्ब्रह्म स सर्वभूतो ब्रह्म प्रजानां पतिरच्युतोऽसौ।
ब्रह्माव्ययं नित्यमजं स विष्णुरपक्षयाद्यैरखिलै-
रसङ्गि ।।५७।।

He is Brahmā the lord; Brahmā all beings; Brahmā the creator of the human race; the undecaying, imperishable and eternal; he is spread all over the earth, unborn incapable of increase or diminution.

ब्रह्माक्षरमजं नित्यं यथाऽसौ पुरुषोत्तमः ।।
तथा रागादयो दोषाः प्रयांतु प्रशमं मम ।। ५८ ।।

Puruṣottama, is the eternal, unborn, immutable Brahmā. May he annihilate the infirmities of my nature.

सोम उवाच

एतद्ब्रह्म पराख्यं वै संस्तवं पमं जपन् ।।
अवाप परमां सिद्धिं स तमाराध्य केशवम् ।। ५९ ।।

Repeating those prayers, comprehending the essence of divine truth and propitiating Keśava the ascetic attained to the final emancipation.

(इमं स्तवं यः पठति शृणुयाद्वापि नित्यशः ।।
स कामदोषैरखिलैर्मुक्तः प्राप्नोति वाञ्छितम् ।।)
इयं च मारिषा पूर्वमासीद्या तां ब्रवीमि वः ।।
कार्यगौरवमेतस्याः कथने फलदायि वः ।। ६० ।।

I shall now describe to you what Māriṣā was in her previous birth—for a recital of her glorious acts will be of immense benefit to you.

अपुत्रा प्रागियं विष्णुं भृते भर्त्तरि सत्तमाः ।।
भूपत्नी महाभागा तोषयामास भक्तितः ।। ६१ ।।

O princes, she was in her previous birth a queen, and was left childless at her husband's death; and she therefore propitiated Viṣṇu with zealous devotion.

आराधितस्तया विष्णुः प्राह प्रत्यक्षतां गतः ।।
वरं वृणीष्वेति याभे सा च प्राहात्मवाछितम् ।। ६२ ।।

Thus pleased with her devotion Viṣṇu appeared to her in person and said,—"Do thou beg of me a boon.

भगवन्बालवैधव्याद्वृथाजन्माहमीदृशी ।।
मन्दभाग्या समुद्भूता विफला च जगत्पते ।। ६३ ।।

Whereto she replied communicating her desire,—"O lord of earth—I am a widow from my childhood—unfortunate as I am, in vain is my birth on this earth.

भवन्तु पतयः श्लाघ्या मम जन्मनि जन्मनि ।।
त्वत्प्रसादात्तथा पुत्रः प्रजापतिवसमोस्तु मे ।। ६४ ।।

कुलं शीलं वयः सत्यं दाक्षिण्यं क्षिप्र कारिता ।।
अविसंवादिता सत्वं वृद्धसेवा कृतज्ञता ।। ६५ ।।

रूपसम्पत्समायुक्ता सर्वस्य प्रियदर्शना ।।
आयोनिजा च जायेयं त्वन्प्रसादादधोक्षज ।। ६६ ।।

Do thou so favour me, that I may be blessed with a good husband in every birth and a son equal to a patriarch amongst men; I may be possessed of beauty and wealth and may be pleasing unto all—that I may be born out of the ordinary course.

सोम उवाच

तयैवमुक्तो देवेशो हृषीकेश उवाच ताम्।।
प्रणामनम्रामुत्थाप्य वरदः परमेश्वरः।। ६७।।

Hṛṣikeśa, the lord of the celestials, the giver of all boons thus prayed to, raised her from her prostrate attitude and said,—

देव उवाच

भविष्यन्ति महावीर्या एकस्मिन्नेव जन्मनि।।
प्रख्यातोदारकर्माणो भवत्याः पतयो दश।। ६८।।

In one birth you shall have ten husbands of great prowess whose fame shall spread far and wide.

पुत्रञ्च सुमहावीर्यं महाबलपराक्रमम्।।
प्रजा पतिगुणैर्युक्तं त्वमवाप्स्यसि शोभने।। ६९।।

And O fair damsel, you shall have a great son gifted with mighty prowess and all the accomplishments that are to be seen in the great Patriarch.

वंशानां तस्य कर्तृत्वं जगत्यस्मिन्भविष्यति।।
त्रैलोक्यमखिला सूतिस्तस्य चापूरयिष्ति।। ७०।।

The supremacy of his family shall be established all over the universe and the three worlds shall be filled with his descendants.

त्वं चाप्ययोनिजा साध्वी रूपौदार्यगुणान्विता।।
मनःप्रीतिकरी नृणां मत्प्रसादाद्भविष्यसि।। ७१।।

And you, by my favour, shall be of marvellous birth, chaste, endowed with grace and loveliness and delightful to men.

इत्युक्त्वान्तर्दधे देवस्तां विशालविलोचनाम्।।
सा चेयं मारिषा जाता युष्मत्पत्नी नृपात्मजाः।। ७२।।

Having thus spoken to that fair damsel, having spacious eyes, the Deity disappeared and the princess, was accordingly born as Māriṣā, who is given to you for a wife, Princes.

श्रीपराशर उवाच

ततः सोमस्य वचनाज्जगृहुस्ते प्रचेतसः।।
संहृत्य कोपं वृक्षेभ्यः पत्नीधर्मेण मारिषाम्।। ७३।।

Parāśara said :—"Thereupon renouncing their ire against the trees at the words of Soma, the Pracetas took Māriṣā the righteously to wife.

दशभ्यस्तु प्रचेतोभ्यो मारिषायां प्रजापतिः।।
जज्ञे दक्षो महाभागो यः पूर्वं ब्रह्मणोऽभवत्।। ७४।।

And the Ten Pracetas begot on Māriṣā the eminent Patriarch, Dakṣa, who had (in a former birth) been born as the son of Brahmā.

स तु दक्षो महाभागस्सृष्ट्यर्थं सुमहामते।।
पुत्रानुत्पादयामास प्रजासृष्ट्यर्थमात्मनः।। ७५।।

O thou of great mind, for the multiplication of creation and increase of his own race this eminent Dakṣa created progeny.

अवरांश्च वरांश्चैव द्विपदोथ चतुष्पदान्।।
आदेशं ब्रह्मणः कुर्वन् सृष्ट्यर्थं समुपस्थितः।। ७६।।

Obeying the mandate of Brahmā for the furtherance of creation he made moveable and immoveable things, hipeds and quadrupeds.

स सृष्ट्वा मनसा दक्षः पश्चादसृजत स्त्रियः।।
ददौ स दश धर्माय कश्यपाय त्रयोदश।।
कालस्य नयने युक्ताः सप्तविंशतिमिन्दवे।। ७७।।

Having created (that) by his will he created females out of which ten were conferred on Dharma, thirteen on Kāśyapa and twenty-seven who regulate the course of time on the Moon.

तासु देवास्तथा दैत्या नागा गावस्तथा खगाः।।
गन्धर्वाप्सर सश्चैव दानवाद्याश्च जज्ञिरे।। ७८।।

And from them were produced the gods, the demons, the snake-gods, cows, birds, singers, the spirits of evil and others.

ततः प्रभृति मैत्रेय प्रजा मैथुनसम्भवाः।।
संकल्पाद्दर्शनात्स्पर्शात्पूर्वेषामभवन् प्रजाः।।
तपोविशेषैः सिद्धानां तदात्यन्ततपस्विनाम्।। ७९।।

Thenceforth creatures were produced by sexual intercourse. O Maitreya—before that they were generated, by the will, by sight, by touch and by the influence of austerities practised by the ascetics of accomplished piety.

श्रीमैत्रेय उवाच

अङ्गुष्ठाद्दक्षिणाद्दक्षः पूर्वं जातो मया श्रुतः।।
कथं प्राचेतसो भूयः समुत्पन्नो महामुने।। ८०।।

Maitreya said :—"O great ascetic, Dakṣa, as I am informed, was born from the right thumb of Brahmā : tell how he was born again as the son of Ten Pracetas.

एष मे संशयो ब्रह्मन्सुमहान्हृदि वर्त्तते।।
यद्दौहित्रश्च सोमस्य पुनः श्वशुरतां गतः।। ८१।।

Another great doubt exists in my mind O Brahmā that how could he, who was the grandson of Soma, be also his father-in-law.

श्रीपराशर उवाच

उत्पत्तिश्च निरोधश्च नित्यो भूतेषु सर्वदा।।
ऋषयोत्र न मुह्यन्ति ये चान्ये दिव्यचक्षुषः।। ८२।।

Parāśara said :—"O thou of great piety, birth and death are constant in all creatures. Ṛṣis having divine vision do not wonder at it.

युगेयुगे भवन्त्येते दक्षाद्या मुनिसत्तम।।
पुनश्चैवं निरुद्ध्यन्ते विद्वांस्तत्र न मुह्यति।। ८३।।

Dakṣa and other eminent ascetics take birth in every age and they again cease to be : the learned are not perplexed by it.

कनिष्ठ्यं ज्यैष्ठ्यमप्येषां पूर्वं नाभूद्‌द्विजोत्तम।।
तप एव गरीयोभूत्प्रभावश्चैव कारणम्।। ८४।।

O foremost of the twice-born ones, in the days of yore there was neither senior nor junior (by age); asceticism and spiritual power were the sole causes of being considered as senior.

मैत्रेय उवाच

देवानां दानवानां च गन्धर्वोरगरक्षसाम्।।
उत्पत्तिं विस्तरेणेह मम ब्रह्मन्प्रकीर्त्तय।। ८५।।

Maitreya said :—"O Brāhmaṇa, do thou relate at length, the origin of the gods, demons, Gandharvas, serpents and goblins.

श्रीपराशर उवाच

प्रजाः सृजेति व्यादिष्टः पूर्वं दक्षः स्वयंभुवा।।
यथा ससर्ज भूतानि तथा शृणु महामुने।। ८६।।

Parāśara said :—"do thou hear, O thou of a high-mind, how commanded by Brahmā, Dakṣa created living creatures.

मानसान्येव भूतानि पूर्वं दक्षोऽसृजत्तदा।।
देवानृषीन्सगन्धर्वानसुरान्पन्नगांस्तथा।। ८७।।

At first Dakṣa created his will-born progeny—the deities, the Ṛṣis, the Gandharvas, the demons and the snake-gods.

यदास्य सृजमानस्य न व्यवर्धन्त ताः प्रजाः।।
ततः संचिन्त्य स पुनः सृष्टिहेतोः प्रजापतिः।।८८।।

When he found, O twice-born one, that his mind-born progeny did not multiply he began to meditate upon some other means of increasing the living creatures.

मैथुनेनैव धर्मेण सिसृक्षुर्विविधाः प्रजाः।।
असक्नीमावहत्कन्यां वीरणस्य प्रजापतेः।।
सुतां सुतपसा युक्तां महतीं लोकधारिणीम्।। ८९।।

Then, desirous of multiplying the race by means of sexual intercourse he married the daughter of the Patriarch Vīraṇa by name Aśikni who was devoted to austerities and the eminent supportress of the world.

अथ पुत्रसहस्राणि वैरुण्यां पञ्च वीर्यवान।।
असिक्न्यां जनयामास सर्गहेतोः प्रजापतिः।। ९०।।

And the energetic Patriarch for the multiplication of the progeny begot on Aśikni the daughter of Veerana, five thousand sons.

तान्दृष्ट्वा नारदो विप्र संविवर्द्धयिषून्प्रजा।।
संगम्य प्रियसंवादो देवर्षिरिदमब्रवीत्।। ९१।।

And beholding them desirous of multiplying the race, the divine ascetic Nārada approaching them addressed them with sweet words—Nārada said,—

हे हर्यश्वा महावीर्याः प्रजा यूयं करिष्यथ।।
ईदृश्योदृश्यते यत्नो भवतां श्रूयतामिदम्।। ९२।।

बालिशा बत यूयं वै नास्या जानीत वै भुवः।।
अन्तरूर्ध्वमधश्चैव कथं सृक्ष्यथ वै प्रजाः।। ९३।।

"O ye highly powerful Haryāśvas, it is evident that you intend multiplying the progeny—do ye hear this : you like ignorant people, do know not the middle, the height and the depth of the world : how would you propagate progeny then?

ऊर्ध्वं तिर्यगधश्चैव यदाऽप्रतिहता गतिः ।।
तदा कस्माद्भवो नान्तं सर्वे द्रक्ष्यथ बालिशाः ।। ९४ ।।

Your understanding is not hindered by interval, height or depth, why do ye not O fools, behold the end of the universe?" Parāśara said—

ते तु तद्वचनं श्रुत्वा प्रयाताः सर्वतो दिशम् ।।
अद्यापि नो निवर्तन्ते समुद्रेभ्य इवापगाः ।। ९५ ।।

"Having heard these words they repaired to various quarters and have not returned as yet as the rivers lose themselves in the ocean (and do not come back).

हर्यश्वेष्वथ नष्टेषु दक्षः प्राचेतसः पुनः ।।
वैरुण्यामथ पुत्राणां सहस्रमसृजत्प्रभुः ।। ९६ ।।

The Haryāśvas having gone away the Patriarch Dakṣa again begot thousand sons upon the daughter of Vīraṇa.

विवर्द्धयिषवस्ते तु शबलाश्वाः प्रजाः पुनः ।।
पूर्वोक्तं वचनं ब्रह्मन्नारदेनैव नोदिताः ।। ९७ ।।

And they, who were named Śabalāśvas, were desirous of multiplying mankind and they were again addressed by Nārada, Brāhmaṇa, with the words mentioned before.

अन्योन्यमूचुस्ते सर्वे सम्यगाह महामुनिः ।।
भ्रातृणां पदवी चैव गन्तव्या नात्र संशयः ।। ९८ ।।

They said to one another,—"What the Muni had said is perfectly true. We must follow the path wended by our brothers : there is not the least doubt about it.

ज्ञात्वा प्रमाणं पृथ्व्याश्च प्रजास्सृज्यामहे ततः ।। ९९ ।।
तेपि तेनैव मार्गेण प्रयाताः सर्वतोमुखम् ।।
अद्यापि न निवर्त्तन्ते समुद्रेभ्य इवापगाः ।।

And ascertaining the extent of the universe we will multiply our race : They also went to various quarters by the path (followed by their brothers) and have not returned like rivers flowing into the deep.

ततः प्रभृति वै भ्राता भ्रातुरन्वेषणे द्विज ।।
प्रयातो नश्यति तथा तन्न कार्यं विजानता ।। १०० ।।

Thenceforth, O twice-born one, a brother searching after a brother, is generally lost : the wise do not resort to such actions.

तांश्चापि नष्टान् विज्ञाय पुत्रान् दक्षः प्रजापतिः ।।
क्रोधं चक्रे महाभागो नारदं स शशाप च ।। १०१ ।।

Finding that all his sons had disappeared the eminent Patriarch Dakṣa was worked with ire and imprecated Nārada.

सर्गकामस्ततो विद्वान्स मैत्रेय प्रजापतिः ।।
षष्टिं दक्षोऽसृजत्कन्या वैरुण्यामिति नः श्रुतम् ।। १०२ ।।

We have heard, O Maitreya, that thereupon the learned Patriarch Dakṣa, desirous to multiply the race begot upon the daughter of Vīraṇa sixty daughters.

ददौ स दश धर्माय कश्यपाय त्रयोदश ।।
सप्तविंशति सोमाय चतस्रोऽरिष्टनेमिने ।। १०३ ।।

द्वे चैव बहुपुत्राय द्वे चैवाङ्गिरसे तथा ।।
द्वे कृशाश्वाय विदुषे तासां नामानि मे शृणु ।। १०४ ।।

Of whom he gave ten to Dharma, thirteen to Kāśyapa, twenty-seven to Soma, four to Ariṣṭanemi, two to Bahuputra, two to Aṅgiras and two to the learned Kṛśāśva. Do thou hear their names from me.

अरुन्धती वसुर्जामिर्लंघा भानुमरुत्वती ।।
संकल्पा च मुहूर्ता च साध्या विश्वा च तादृशी ।।
धर्मपत्न्यो दश त्वेतास्तास्वपत्यानि मे शृणु ।।
विश्वेदेवास्तु विश्वायाः साध्या साध्यानजायत ।।
मरुत्वत्यां मरुत्वन्तो, वसोश्च वसवः स्मृताः ।। १०५ ।।

Arundhati, Vasu, Yami, Lambha, Bhami Marūtvati, Saṅkalpa, Muhūrta, Sadhyā and Viśva were the ten, wives of Dharma. I will mention their offspring. Viśvadevas[1] were the sons of Viśva and the Sādhyās[2] were the sons of Sādhyā. The Maruts or Winds were the offspring of Marutvatī and the Vasus of Vasu.

भानोस्तु भानवः पुत्रा मुहूर्तायां मुहूर्तजाः ।। १०६ ।।

The Bhānus (or suns) were the sons of

1. A class of deities to whom daily offerings are to be made.
2. are the personifications of Vedic rites and prayers.

Bhānu and the deities governing the moments of Muhūrta.

लंघायाश्चैव घोषोथ नागवीथी तु जामिजा।। १०७।।

Ghoṣa was born of Lamghā and Nāgavithī[1] was born of Yāmī (night).

पृथिवीविषयं सर्वमरुन्धत्याम जायत।।
संकल्पायास्तु सर्वात्मा जज्ञे संकल्प एव हि।। १०८।।

And all the objects of the world were born of Arundhati and Saṅkalpa (pious determination) was the son of Saṅkalpa.

ये त्वनेकवसुप्राणदेवा ज्योतिःपुरोगमाः।।
वसवोष्टौ समाख्यातास्तेषां वक्ष्यामि विस्तरम्।। १०९।।

I shall mention at length the particulars of the eight Vasus who abound in effulgence and night.

आपो ध्रुवश्च सोमश्च धर्मश्चैवानिलोऽनलः।।
प्रत्यूषश्च प्रभासश्च वसवो नामभिः स्मृताः।। ११०।।

They are Āpa, Dhruva, Soma, Dharma, Anila, Anala, Pratyūṣa and Prabhāsa.

आपस्य पुत्रो वैतण्डः श्रमः शान्तोऽध्वनिस्तथा।।
ध्रुवस्य पुत्रो भगवान्कालो लोकप्रकालनः।। १११।।

The sons of Āpa were Vaitaṇḍya, Śrama (weariness) Śrānta (fatigue) and Dhur, and the son of Dhruva was the great Kāla (Time) the cherisher of the world.

सोमस्य भगवान्वर्चो वर्चस्वी येन जायते।। ११२।।

The son of Soma was Varcas (light) by whom was generated Varcasvī (radiance).

धर्मस्य पुत्रो द्रविणो हुतहव्यवहस्तथा।।
मनोहरायां शिशिरः प्राणोथ रवणस्तथा।। ११३।।

And Dharma had, by his wife Manoharā, Draviṇā, Hutatavyāvaha, Śiśira, Prāṇa and Ravaṇa.

अनिलस्य शिवा भार्या तस्याः पुत्रो मनोजवः।।
अविज्ञातगतिश्चैव द्वौ पुत्रावनिलस्य तु।। ११४।।

Anila's wife was Śiva; and he had by her two sons—Manojava (swift as thought) and Avijñātagatī (unknowable motion).

1. The milky way.

अग्निपुत्रः कुमारस्तु शरस्तम्बे व्यजायत।।
तस्य शाखो विशाखश्च नैगमेयश्च पृष्ठजाः।। ११५।।

The son of Agni—Kumāra, was born in a clump of Sāra reeds, whose sons were Śākha, Viśākha, Naigameya and Pṛṣṭhaja.

अपत्यं कृत्तिकानां तु कार्त्तिकेय इति स्मृतः।। ११६।।

The son of Kṛtikās was named Kārtikeya.

प्रत्यूषस्य विदुः पुत्रं ऋषि नाम्नाथ देवलम्।।
द्वौ पुत्रौ देवलस्यापि क्षमावन्तौ मनीषिणौ।। ११७।।

The son of Pratyūṣa was the great ascetic Devala who had two intelligent and philosophic sons.

बृहस्पतेस्तु भगिनी वरस्त्री ब्रह्मचारिणी।।
योगसिद्धा जगत्कृत्स्नमसत्ता विचरत्युत।।
प्रभासस्य तु सा भार्या वसूनामष्टमस्य तु।। ११८।।

The great ascetic Bṛhaspati had a sister who was the foremost of the females, virtuous and of accomplished asceticism. Without being attached to the world she travelled all over the world. She became the spouse of Prabhāsa the eighth Vasu.

विश्वकर्मा महाभागस्तस्यां जज्ञे प्रजापतिः।।
कर्ता शिल्पसहस्त्राणां त्रिदशानां च वार्द्धकिः।। ११९।।

Of her was born the noble Patriarch Viśvakarmā the author of a thousand arts, the architect of the celestials, the inventor of all ornaments and the foremost of the artists.

भूषणानां व सर्वेषां कर्ता शिल्पवतां वरः।।
यः सर्वेषां विमानानि देवतानां चकार ह।।
मनुष्याश्चोपजीवन्ति यस्य शिल्पं महात्मनः।। १२०।।

He constructed the chariots of all the deities; and by the skill of that high-souled one, people obtain subsistence. He had four sons whose names hear from me.

अजैकपादहिर्बुध्न्यस्त्वष्टा रुद्रश्च वीर्यवान्।।
त्वष्टुश्चाप्यात्मजः पुत्रो विश्वरूपो महातपाः।। १२१।।

They were Ajaikapāda, Ahirbudhnya, Twaṣṭṛ and Rudra and they were all wise. And the self-born son of Twaṣṭṛ was also the famous Viśvarūpa.

हरश्च बहुरूपश्च त्र्यम्बकश्चापराजितः।।
वृषाकपिश्च शम्भुश्च कपर्दी रैवतः स्मृतः।। १२२।।

मृगव्याधश्च शर्वश्च कपाली च महामुने।।
एकादशैते कथिता रुद्रास्त्रिभुवनेश्वराः।। १२३।।
शतं त्वेकं समाख्यातं रुद्राणाममितौजसाम्।।

There are eleven well-known Rudras, lords of the three worlds—Hara, Bahurūpa, Tryaṁbaka, Aparājitā, Vṛṣakapi, Śambhu, Kāpārddi, Raivata, Mṛgavyādha, Śarava and Kapāli; but there are a hundred names of the Rudras of unmitigated prowess.

काश्यपस्य तु भार्या यास्तासां नामानि मे शृणु।।
अदितिर्दितिर्दनुश्चैवारिष्टा च सुरसा खसा।। १२४।।

सुरभिर्विनता चैव ताम्रा क्रोधवशा इरा।।
कद्रुर्मुनिश्च धर्मज्ञ तदपत्यानि मे शृणु।। १२५।।

Kāśyapa married the thirteen daughters of Dakṣa namely Aditi, Diti, Danu, Arṣṭa, Śurasā, Śūrabhi, Vinātā, Tāmrā, Krodhavaśā, Iḍā, Khasā, Kadru and Muni. I will describe their progeny to you.

पूर्वमन्वन्तरे श्रेष्ठा द्वादशासन्सुरोत्तमाः।।
तुषिता नाम तेऽन्योन्यमूचुर्वैवस्वतेन्तरे।। १२६।।

उपस्थितेऽतियशसश्चाक्षुषस्यान्तरे मनोः।।
समवायीकृताः सर्वे समागम्य परस्परम्।। १२७।।

There were twelve well-known celestials in a former Manvantara, named Tuṣitas, who, on the approach of the present Manvantara and at the end of the reign of Manu Cakṣuṣa assembled and said to one another,—

आगच्छत द्रुतं देवा अदितिं संप्रविश्य वै।
मन्वन्तरे प्रसूयामस्तन्नः श्रेयो भवेदिति।। १२८।।

"O deities, let us all speedily enter into the womb of Aditi that we may be born in the next manwantara for we shall thereby be again crowned with blessings.

एवमुक्त्वा तु ते सर्वे चाक्षुषस्यान्तरे मनोः।।
मारीचात्कश्यपाज्जाता अदित्या दक्षकन्यया।। १२९।।

Having said this they at the end of the reign of Manu Cākṣuṣa were born the sons of Kāśyapa, the sons of Mārīci by Aditi the daughter of Dakṣa.

तत्र विष्णुश्चशक्रश्च जज्ञाते पुनरेव हि।।
अर्यमा चैव धाता च त्वष्टा पूषा तथैव च।। १३०।।

विवस्वान्सविता चैव मित्रो वरुण एव च।।
अंशुर्भगश्चातितेजा आदित्या द्वादश स्मृताः।। १३१।।

चाक्षुषस्यान्तरे पूर्वमासन्ये तुषिताः सुराः।।
वैवस्वतेऽन्तरे ते वै आदित्या द्वादश स्मृताः।। १३२।।

Of them were born first Viṣṇu and Śakra and the Āryamān, Dhātā, Tvaṣṭṛ, Pūṣān, Vivaswat, Sāvitrī, Mitra, Varuṇa, Aṁśu and Bhaga. These who, in the reign of Cākṣuṣa Manu were Tuṣitas, were called the twelve Ādityas in the Manvantara of Vaivasvata.

सप्तविंशति याः प्रोक्ताः सोमपत्न्योथ सुव्रताः।।
सर्वा नक्षत्रयोगिन्यस्तन्नाम्नश्चैव ताः स्मृताः।।
तासामपत्यान्यभवन्दीप्तान्यमिततेजसाम्।। १३३।।

The twenty-seven virtuous daughters of the Patriarch who were married to the Moon were all well-known as the nymphs of the lunar constellations after their names; they had children of unmitigated efflugence.

अरिष्टनेमिपत्नीनामपत्यानीह षोडश।। १३४।।

The wives of Ariṣṭanemī bore him sixteen children.

बहुपुत्रस्य विदुषश्चतस्रो विद्युतः स्मृताः।। १३५।।

The daughters of the learned Bahuputra were the four lightnings.

प्रत्यङ्गिरसजाः श्रेष्ठा ऋचो ब्रह्मर्षिसत्कृताः।। १३६।।
कृशाश्वस्य तु देवर्षेर्देवप्रहरणाः स्मृताः।। १३७।।

The excellent Paratyaṅgirasa Ṛcās were born from the wives of Aṅgiras and the celestial weapons were the children of the Ṛṣi Kṛśāśva.

एते युगसहस्रान्ते जायन्ते पुनरेव हि।।
सर्वे देवगणास्तात त्रयस्त्रिंशत्तु छन्दजाः।।
तेषामपीह सततं निरोधोत्पत्तिरुच्यते।। १३८।।

यथा सूर्यस्य मैत्रेय उदयास्तमनाविह।।
एवं देवनिकायास्ते सम्भवन्ति युगेयुगे।। १३९।।

These deities take their birth once after the expiry of a thousand *yugas;* they are thirty-three in number and their appearance and disappearance is here spoken of as birth and death and O Maitreya these divinities appear and disappear age after age as the sun sets and rises again.

दित्या पुत्रद्वयं जज्ञे कश्यपादिति नः श्रुतमः ।।
हिरण्यकशिपुश्चैव हिरण्याक्षश्च दुर्जयः ।। १४० ।।

It is said that Kāśyapa begot on Diti two sons—one was named Hiraṇyakaśipu and the other was named Hiraṇyākṣa and both of them were invincible.

सिंहिका चाभवत्कन्या विप्रचित्तेः परिग्रहः ।। १४१ ।।

She had also a daughter named Siṁhikā who was married to Vipracitta.

हिरण्यकशिपोः पुत्राश्चत्वारः प्रथितौजसः ।।
अनुह्लादश्च ह्लादश्च प्रह्लादश्चैव बुद्धिमान् ।।
संह्लादश्च महावीर्या दैत्यवंशविवर्द्धना ।। १४२ ।।

Hiraṇyakaśipu had four highly effulgent sons—named Anuhlāda, Hlāda, Prahlāda and Saṁhlāda;—they were all highly intelligent, powerful and the multiplier of the Daitya race.

तेषां मध्ये महाभाग सर्वत्र समदृग्वशी ।।
प्रह्लादः परमां भक्तिं य उवाच जनार्दने ।। १४३ ।।

O noble sage, amongst these, Prahlāda, looking impartially on all things, devoted his whole faith to Janārdana.

दैत्येन्द्रदीपितो वह्निः सर्वांगोपचितो द्विज ।।
न ददाह च यं विप्र वासुदेवे हृदि स्थिते ।। १४४ ।।

O twice-born one, the flames lighted by the king of Daityas did not consume him in whose heart Vāsudeva was present.

महार्णवान्तःसलिले स्थितस्य चलतो मही ।।
चचाल चलता यस्य पाशबद्धस्य धीमतः ।। १४५ ।।

The whole earth shook, when bound with ropes, he moved in the midst of the water of the deep.

न भिन्नं विविधैः शस्त्रैर्यस्य दैत्येन्द्रपातितैः ।।
शरीरमद्रिकठिनं सर्वत्राच्युतचेतसः ।। १४६ ।।

विपानलोज्ज्वलमुखा यस्य दैत्यप्रचोदिताः ।।
नान्ताया सर्पपतयो बभूवु रुरुतेजसः ।। १४७ ।।

Having his mind entirely engrossed by Acyuta his body firm as the rock was not assailed by the diverse weapons hurled on him by the order of the king of Daityas.

And the venomous snakes could not destroy him (even).

शैलैराक्रान्तदेहोपि यः स्मरन्पुरुषोत्तमम् ।।
तत्याज नात्मनः प्राणान् विष्णुस्मरणदंशितः ।। १४८ ।।

And he remembering the excellent Puruṣa and protected by the recollection of Viṣṇu as his armour he did not renounce his life albeit overwhelmed with rocks.

पतन्तमुच्चा दवनिर्यमुपेत्य महामतिम् ।।
दधार दैत्यपतिना क्षिप्तं स्वर्गनिवासिना ।। १४९ ।।

The earth received the high-minded (Prahlāda) when he was hurled from on high by the king of Daityas residing in Svarga.

यस्य सशोषको वायुर्देहे दैत्येन्द्रयोजितः ।।
अवाप संक्षयं सद्यश्चित्तस्थे मधुसूदने ।। १५० ।।

The slayer of Madhu being present in his mind, the wind sent into his body to wither him up, was itself destroyed.

विषाणभङ्गमुन्मत्ता मदहानिं च दिग्गजाः ।।
यस्य वक्षःस्थले प्राप्ता दैत्येन्द्रपरिणामिताः ।। १५१ ।।

Being ordered by the lord of Daityas the maddened elephants of the spheres broke their trunks and baffled their pride against his firm breast.

यस्य चोत्पादिता कृत्या दैत्यराजपुरोहितैः ।।
बभूव नान्ताय पुरा गोविन्दासक्तचेतसः ।। १५२ ।।

The rites of the priests of the Daitya monarch were useless to bring about the destruction of one who was attached to Govinda.

शम्बरस्य च मायानां सहस्त्रमतिमायिनः ।।
यस्मिन्प्रयुक्तं चक्रेण कृष्णस्य वितथीकृतम् ।। १५३ ।।

The thousand illusions of the illusive Śambara were baffled by the discus of Kṛṣṇa.

दैत्येन्द्रसूदोपहृतं यस्य हालाहलं विषम् ।।
जरयामास मतिमानविकारममत्सरी ।। १५४ ।।

The poison offered by the cooks, at the command of the king of Daityas, could not produce any change upon the intellignet (Prahlāda) void of pride, who unhestitatingly partook that.

समचेता जगत्यस्मिन्यः सर्वेष्वेव जन्तुषु।।
यथात्मनि तथान्येषां परं मैत्रगुणान्वितः।। १५५।।

He looked impartially upon the world and all creatures, was full of kindness and regarded all things equally and as identical with himself.

धर्मात्मा सत्यशौर्यादिगुणानामाकरः परः।।
उपमानमशेषाणां साधूनां य सदाभवत्।। १५६।।

He was pious and an inexhaustible mine of purity and truth and a model for all pious men.

।। इति श्रीविष्णुपुराणे प्रथमेंशे पञ्चदशोऽध्यायः।। १५।।

अथ प्रथमेंशेः षोडशोऽध्यायः

Part I : Section 16

श्रीमैत्रेय उचाच

कथितो भवता वंशो मानवानां महात्मनाम्।।
कारणं चास्य जगतो विष्णुरेव सनातनः।। १।।

चत्त्वेतद्ध्भगवानाह प्रह्लादं दैत्यसत्तमम्।।
ददाह नाग्निर्नास्त्रैश्च क्षुण्णस्तत्याज जीवितम्।। २।।

जगाम वसुधा क्षोभं यत्राब्धिसलिले स्थिते।।
पाशैर्बद्धे विचलति विक्षिप्ताङ्गैः समाहता।। ३।।

Maitreya said—"O great ascetic, you have described to me the human races and the ever-existing Viṣṇu, the cause of the world; but who was this Prahlāda the foremost of the Daityas of whom you spoke and whom fire could not burn, and who did not die even when assailed by weapons. And Prahlāda being present in the waters, in bonds, earth trembled, agitated by his movements.

शैलैराक्रान्तदेहोपि न ममार च यः पुरा।।
त्वया चातीव माहात्म्यं कथितं यस्य धीमतः।। ४।।

तस्य प्रभावमतुलं विष्णोर्भक्तिमतो मुने।।
श्रोतुमिच्छामि यस्यैतच्चरितं दीप्ततेजसः।। ५।।

And he did not die before albeit overwhelmed with rocks. Thou hast related the unlimited glory of that intellignet Prahlāda. O muni, I am desirous to hear an account of the character and unequalled might of that effulgent worshipper of Viṣṇu.

किंनिमित्तमसौ शस्त्रैर्विक्षिप्तो दितिजैर्मुने।।
किमर्थं चाब्धिसलिले विक्षिप्तो धर्मतत्परः।।

O Muni, Why was he assailed by the descendants of Diti with weapons? And why was he, ever engaged in pious observances, thrown into water?

आक्रान्तः पर्वतैः कस्माद्दष्टचैव महोरगैः।।
क्षिप्तःकिमद्रिशिखरात्किं वा पावकसञ्चये।। ७।।

For what was he overwhelmed with rocks? And why bitten by venomous snakes? Why thrown down from the mountain-top? Why cast into fire?

दिग्दन्निां दन्तभूमि स च कस्मान्निरूपितः।।
सशोषकोनिलश्चास्य प्रयुक्तः किं महासुरैः।। ८।।

And why was he made a butt for the tusks of the elephants of spheres? And why was wind sent by the mighty Asuras into his body to wither him up?

कृत्यां च दैत्यगुरवो युयुजुस्तत्र किं मुने।।
शम्बश्चापि मायानां सहस्त्रं किं प्रयुक्तवान्।। ९।।

O Muni, Why the spiritual guides of the Daityas were engaged in ceremonies for his destruction? And why did the Daitya Śambara spread thousands of illusions for his destruction?

हालाहलं विषमहो दैत्यसूदैर्महात्मनः।।
कस्माद्दत्तं विनाशाय यज्जीर्णं तेन धीमता।। १०।।

Why did the cooks of the Daitya-chief offer him poison for his destruction which was digested by that high-souled sage?

एतत्सर्वं महाभाग प्रह्लादस्य महात्मनः।।
चरितं श्रोतुमिच्छामि महामाहात्म्यसूचकम्।। ११।।

O noble Manu—I wish to hear all this—an account of the high-souled Prahlāda, full of marvellous glories.

न हि कौतूहलं तत्र यद्दैत्यैर्निहतो हि सः।।
अनन्यमनसो विष्णौ कः समर्थो निपातने।। १२।।

I am not the least surprised for the Daityas not being able to destroy him : for who can slay him whose mind is solely devoted to Viṣṇu?

तस्मिन्धर्मपरे नित्यं केशवाराधनोद्यते।।
स्ववंशप्रभवैर्दैत्यैः कृतो द्वेषोतिदुष्करः।। १३।।

Why did the Daityas, born in his race, cherish dreadful malice against him ever engaged in pious observances and in the worship of Keśava?

धर्मात्मनि महाभागे विष्णुभक्ते विमत्सरे।।
दैतेयैः प्रहृतं कस्मात्तन्ममाख्यातुमर्हसि।। १४।।

Relate to me, Why the sons of Diti offer violence to one so pious,—high-souled and ever devoted to Viṣṇu and free from sin?

प्रहरन्ति महात्मानो विपक्षा अपि नेदृशे।।
गुणैस्समन्विते साधौ किं पुनर्यः स्वपक्षजः।। १५।।

The great cannot offer violence to a person gifted with such qualities even if he be an enemy; how could his own kin (behave thus towards him)?

तदेतत्कथ्यतां सर्वं विस्तरान्मुनिपुङ्गव।।
दैत्येश्वरस्य चरितं श्रोतुमिच्छाम्यशेषतः।। १६।।

O foremost of the Muni, do thou relate all this—the character of the sovereign of Daityas. I wish to hear it at length.

।। इति श्रीविष्णुपुराणे प्रथमेंशे षोडशोऽध्यायः।। १६।।

अथ प्रथमेंशेः सप्तदशोऽध्यायः

Part I : Section 17

श्रीपराशर उवाच

मैत्रेय श्रूयतां सम्यक् चरितं तस्य धीमतः।।
प्रह्लादस्य सदोदारचरितस्य महात्मनः।। १।।

Parāśara said :—"Maitreya, hear the interesting story of the wise, high-souled and magnanimous Prahlāda.

दितेः पुत्रो महावीर्यो हिरण्यकशिपुः पुरा।।
त्रैलोक्यं वशमानिन्ये ब्रह्मणो वरदर्पितः।। २।।

In the days of yore the three worlds were brought into subjection by the valiant son of Diti—Hiraṇyakaśipu, proud of the boon conferred on him by Brahmā.

इन्द्रत्वमकरोद्दैत्यः स चासीत्सविता स्वयम्।।
वायुरग्निरपां नाथः सोमश्चाभून्महासुरः।। ३।।

That Daitya had usurped the sovereignty of Indra and exercised the functions of the sun, of air, of the lord of waters, of fire and of the moon.

धनानामधिपः सोऽभूत्सएवासीत्स्वयं यमः।।
यज्ञभागानशेषांस्तु स स्वयं बुभुजेऽसुरः।। ४।।

He himself became the lord of riches and Yama; and that Asura appropriated to himself, without reserve, all that was offered in sacrifice to the celestials.

देवाः स्वर्गं परित्यज्य तत्रासान्मुनिसत्तम।।
विचेरुरवनौ सर्वे बिभ्राणा मानुषीं तनुम्।। ५।।

O foremost of ascetics, renouncing their own region the celestials, through his fear, wandered upon the earth, disguised in mortal shapes.

जित्वा त्रिभुवनं सर्वं त्रैलोक्यैश्वर्यदर्पितः।।
उपगीयमानो गन्धर्वैर्बुभुजे विषयान्प्रियान्।। ६।।

Having conquered the three worlds, he was inflated with the pride of the riches, and being eulogised by the Gandharvas, enjoyed all wished for objects.

पानासक्तं महात्मानं हिरण्यकशिपुं तदा।।
उपासाञ्चक्रिरे सर्वे सिद्धगन्धर्वपन्नगाः।। ७।।

Thereupon all the Siddhas, Gandharvas and Pannāgas worshipped the valiant Hiraṇyakaśipu addicted to drinking.

अवादयन् जगुश्चान्ये जयशब्दं तथापरे।।
दैत्यराजस्य पुरतश्चक्रुः सिद्धा मुदान्विताः।। ८।।

The Siddhas stood delighted before the Daitya chief, some singing, some playing on musical instruments and others shouting out cries of victory.

तत्र प्रनृत्ताप्सरसि स्फाटिकाभ्रमयेऽसुरः।।
पपौ पानं मुदा युक्तः प्रासादे सुमनोहरे।। ९।।

When the Asura delightedly quaffed the inebriating cup in his picturesque crystal palace, the nymphs danced there gracefully.

तस्य पुत्रो महाभागः प्रह्लादो नाम नामतः।।
पपाठ बालपाठ्यानि गुरुगेहंगतोऽर्भकः।। १०।।

His illustrious son, by name Prahlāda, while yet a boy, residing in the dwelling of his preceptor, read such readings as are studied in early years.

एकदा तु स धर्मात्मा जगाम गुरुणा सह।।
पानासक्तस्य पुरतः पितुर्दैत्यपतेस्तदा।। ११।।

Once on a time the high-souled (Prahlāda) in the company of his preceptor appeared before his father the Daitya-chief while drinking.

पादप्रणामावनतं तमुत्थाप्य पिता सुतम्।।
हिरण्यकशिपुः प्राह प्रह्लादममितौजसम्।। १२।।

The father Hiraṇyakaśipu, raising up his son prostrate at his feet, spoke to Prahlāda of unmitigated prowess, saying,—

हिरण्यकशिपुरुवाच

पठ्यतां भवता वत्स सारभूतं सुभाषितम्।।
कालेनैतावता यत्ते सदोद्युक्तेन शिक्षितम्।। १३।।

"Repeat, boy, agreeably, the substance of what you have read during the period.

प्रह्लाद उवाच

श्रूयतां तात वक्ष्यामि सारभूतं तवाज्ञया।।
समाहितमना भूत्वा यन्मे चेतस्यवस्थि तम्।। १४।।

Prahlāda said,—"Hear, father I will repeat the substance of what I have read. Hear attentively what occupies my thoughts.

अनादिमध्यान्तमजमवृद्धिक्षयमच्युतम्।।
प्रणतोस्म्यन्तसन्तानं सर्वकारणकारणम्।। १५।।

I bow to that Great Being who is without beginning, middle or end, increase or diminution : the imperishable lord of the world, the universal cause of causes.

श्रीपराशर उवाच

एतन्निशम्य दैत्येन्द्रः सकोपो रक्तलोचनः।।
विलोक्य तद्गुरुं प्राह स्फुरिताधरपल्लवः।। १६।।

Parāśara said :—Hearing those words the lord of the Daityas, his eyes red with ire and lip swollen with indignation, looked towards the preceptor and said,—

हिरण्यकशिपुरुवाच

ब्रह्मबन्धो किमेतत्ते विपक्ष स्तुतिसंहितम्।।
असारं ग्राहितो बालो मामवज्ञाय दुर्मते।। १७।।

"O vile Brāhmaṇa, what is this? O vicious-minded, thou hast, in disrespect to me, taught my boy the worthless commendation of my foe.

गुरुरुवाच

दैत्येश्वर न कोपस्य वशमागन्तुमर्हसि।।
ममोपदेशजनितं नायं वदति ते सुतः।। १८।।

The preceptor replied,—"O sovereign of Daityas, it doth not behove thee to give way to anger; I have not taught thy son what he has uttered.

हिरण्यकशिपुरुवाच

अनुशिष्टोसि केनेदृग्वत्स प्रह्लाद कथ्यताम्।।
मयोपदिष्टं नेत्येष प्रब्रवीति गुरुस्तव।। १९।।

Hiraṇyakaśipu said,—"Prahlāda, my boy, by whom then you have been thus taught. Your preceptor says that he has not instructed you thus.

प्रह्लाद उवाच

शास्ता विष्णुरशेषस्य जगतो यो हृदि स्थितः।।
तमृते परमात्मानं तात कः केन शास्यते।। २०।।

Prahlāda replied,—"Viṣṇu, O father, is the instructor of the whole world and is present in our minds. Who else, but that Great Soul can teach us (any thing)?"

हिरण्यकशिपुरुवाच

कोयं विष्णुः सुदुर्बुद्धे यं ब्रवीषि पुनः पुनः।।
जगतामीश्वरस्येह पुरतः प्रसभ मम।। २१।।

Hiranyakaśipu said,—"O thou of vile understanding, who is this Viṣṇu, of whom thou art speaking again and again before me the valiant lord of the world?"

प्रह्लाद उवाच

न शब्दागोचरे यस्य योगिध्येयं परं पदम्।।
यतो यश्च स्वयं विश्वं स विष्णुः परमेश्वरः।। २२।।

Prahlāda said,—"He is Viṣṇu, the great God, who is being meditated upon by the devout, whose glory cannot be described in words, who is all things and from whom all things proceed.

हिरण्यकशिपुरुवाच

परमेश्वरसंज्ञोज्ञ किमन्यो मय्यवस्थिते।।
तथापि मर्तुकामस्त्वं प्रब्रवीषि पुनः पुनः।। २३।।

Hiranyakaśipu said,—"O fool, myself living, to whom else you give the tittle of supreme lord? Are you desirous of death that you are mentioning this again and again?"

प्रह्लाद उवाच

न केवलं तात मम प्रजानां
स ब्रह्मभूतो भवतश्च विष्णुः।।
धाता विधाता परमेश्वरश्च प्रसीद
कोपं कुरुषे किमर्थम्।। २४।।

Prahlāda replied,—"O father, Viṣṇu, who is Brahmā, is not only the creator, preserver and supreme lord of me only, but of all creatures as well as of thyself. Be propitiated; why art thou angry?"

हिरण्यकशिपुरुवाच

प्रविष्टः कोस्य हृदये दुर्बुद्धेरतिपापकृत्।।
येनेदृशान्यसाधूनि वदत्याविष्टमानसः।। २५।।

Hiranyakaśipu said,—"What evil spirit has entered into the breast of this silly lad, that, he, like one possessed, gives expression to such profane words.

प्रह्लाद उवाच

न केवलं मद्धृदयं स विष्णु-
राक्रम्य लोकानखिलानवस्थितः।।
स मां त्वदांदीश्च पितस्समस्तान्-
समस्तचेष्टासु युनक्ति सर्वगः।। २६।।

Prahlāda said,—"That Viṣṇu is not only present in my mind, but he pervades the whole universe; He is omnipresent and commands me, thyself and all creatures.

हिरण्यकशिपुरुवाच

निष्कास्यतामयं पापः शास्यतां च गुरोर्गृहे।।
योजितो दुर्मतिः केन विपक्षाविषयस्तुतौ।। २७।।

"Hiranyakaśipu said :—"Away with this wicked boy; take him again to the preceptor's house and govern him; perhaps he has been taught by some vicious-minded (men) to sing the glories of my foes.

श्रीपराशर उवाच

इत्युक्तोसौ तदा दैत्यैर्नीतो गुरुगृहं पुनः।।
जग्राह विद्यामनिशं गुरुशुश्रूषणोद्यतः।। २८।।

Parāśara said :—"He having said this Prahlāda was again conducted to the preceptor's house by the Daityas, where always prompt to attend upon the preceptor he received instructions constantly.

कालेतीतेति महति प्रह्लादमसुरेश्वरः।।
समाहूयाब्रवीद्गाथा काचित्पुत्रक गीयताम्।। २९।।

After a considerable time that lord of Asuras sent for Prahlāda again and said "O my boy, recite me some poetical composition."

प्रह्लाद उवाच

यतः प्रधानपुरुषौ यतश्चैतच्चराचरम्।।
कारणं सकलस्यास्य स नो विष्णुः प्रसीदतु।। ३०।।

Prahlāda said—"May that Viṣṇu be propitiated with us, from, whom matter and soul originate and all that is mobile and immobile proceeds and who is the cause of all this creation."

हिरण्यकशिपुरुवाच

दुरात्मा वध्यतामेष नानेनार्थोस्ति जीवता।।
स्वपक्षहानिकर्तृत्वाद्यः कुलाङ्गारतां गतः।। ३१।।

Hiraṇyakshipu said :—"Destroy this vicious-minded boy; there is no use of his life; he is a fraud to his own family since he has proved a traitor to his kin."

श्रीपराशर उवाच

इत्याज्ञप्तास्ततस्तेन प्रगृहीतमहायुधाः।।
उद्यतास्तस्य नाशाय दैत्याः शतसहस्रशः।। ३२।।

Parāśara said :—Being thus commanded by him, hundreds and thousands of Daityas, with huge weapons, addressed themselves for his destruction.

प्रह्लाद उवाच

विष्णुः शस्त्रेषु युष्मासु मयि चासौ व्यवस्थितः।।
दैत्यास्तेन सत्येन माक्रमन्त्वायुधानि मे।। ३३।।

Prahlāda said to the Daityas :—"Since Viṣṇu is present in your weapons as well as in mind, your weapons shall fail to hurt me."

श्रीपराशर उवाच

ततस्तैश्शतशो दैत्यैः शस्त्रौषधैराहतोपि सन्।।
नावाप वेदनामल्पामभूच्चैव पुनर्नवः।। ३४।।

Parāśara said—Thereupon hundreds of Daityas assailed Prahlāda with their weapons but he did not feel the least pain and his strength was ever renewed.

हिरण्यकशिपुरुवाच

दुर्बुद्धे विनिवर्तस्व वैरिपक्षस्तवाहतः।।
अभयं ते प्रयच्छामि मातिमूढमतिर्भव।। ३५।।

Hiraṇyakśipu said—"O you of vile understanding, refrain from glorifying my enemy; I promise you immunity, be not so foolish."

प्रह्लाद उवाच

भयं भयानामपहारिणि स्थिते
मनस्यनन्ते मम कुत्रा तिष्ठति।।
यस्मिन्स्मृते जन्मजरान्कादि-
भयानि सर्वाण्यपयान्ति तात।। ३६।।

Prahlāda replied : "No fear can overwhelm me since that immortal remover of all dangers is present in my mind, the very recollection of whom is enough to remove all perils consequent upon birth and human infirmities."

हिरण्यकशिपुरुवाच

भोभोः सर्पाः दुराचारमेनमत्यन्तदुर्मतिम्।।
विषज्वालाकुलैर्वक्त्रैः सद्यो नयतः संक्षयम्।। ३७।।

Hiraṇyakaśipu said—"O serpents, speedily bring this vicious lad to destruction with your envenomed fangs."

श्रीपराशर उचाच

इत्युक्तास्ते ततः सर्पाः कुहकास्तक्षकादयः।।
अदशन्त समस्तेषु गात्रेष्वतिविषोल्बणाः।। ३८।।

Parāśara said :—Being thus commanded by him, Kuhaka, Takṣaka, Andhaka and many other venomous serpents, bit him in every part of his body.

स त्वासक्तमतिः कृष्णे दश्यमानो महोरगैः।।
न विवेदात्मनो गात्रं तत्स्मृत्याह्लादसुस्थितः।। ३९।।

But with his mind solely devoted to Kṛṣṇa he remained in that pleasureable recollection; he could not feel anything although he was bitten by deadliest serpents.

सर्पा ऊचुः

दंष्ट्रा विशीर्णा मणयः
स्फुटन्ति फणेषु तापो हृदयेषु कंपः।।
नास्य त्वचः स्वल्पमपीह
भिन्नं प्रसाधि दैत्येश्वर कार्यमन्यत्।। ४०।।

The serpents said to the sovereign of the Daityas—"Our fangs are broken; our jewelled crests are shattered; our hoods are burning; our hearts are trembling; but the skin of this body is unheart; O king of Daityas, Resort to some other expendient."

हिरण्यकशिपुरुवाच

हे दिग्गजाः संकटदन्तमिश्रा
घ्नतैनमस्मद्रिपुपक्षभिन्नम्।।

तज्जा विनाशाय भवन्ति तस्य
यथाऽरणेः प्रज्वलितो हुताशः ।। ४१ ।।

Hiraṇyakaśipu said :—"O Elephants of the spheres, unite your tusks and slay this deserter of his own family and the supporter of our enemy : sometimes our own descendants bring about our own destruction as the fire consumes the wood from which it proceeds."

श्रीपराशर उवाच

ततः स दिग्गजैर्बालो भूभृच्छिखरसन्निभैः ।।
पातितो धरणीपृष्ठे विषाणैर्वावपीडितः ।। ४२ ।।

स्मरतस्तस्य गोविन्दमिभदन्ताः सहस्त्रशः ।।
शीर्णा वक्षस्थलं प्राप्य स प्राह पितरं ततः ।। ४३ ।।

Parāśara said :—The boy was then cast down on the earth being assailed by the tusks of those elephants of the spheres as huge as mountain peaks; but he recollecting Govinda, thousands of tusks were blunted against his breast : he then spoke to his father :

दन्ता गजानां कुलिशाग्रनिष्ठुराः शीर्णा यदेतेन बलं ममैतत् ।।
महाविपत्तापविनाशनोऽयं जनार्दनानुस्मरणानुभावः ।। ४४ ।।

"The tusks of the elephants hards a adament have been blunted. This is not on account of any strength of mine but is consequent upon my calling upon Janārdana who destroys all dangers and sins the sources of all these evils."

हिरण्यकशिपुरुवाच

ज्वाल्यतामसुरा वह्निरपसर्पत दिग्गजाः ।।
वायो समेधयाग्निं त्वं दह्यतामेष पापकृत् ।। ४५ ।।

Hiraṇyakaśipu said :—"Away, O ye elephants of the spheres. O Asuras, light out fire; O deity of the winds, blow up the fire, and let this perpetrator of endless iniquities be destroyed therein."

श्रीपराशर उवाच

महाकाष्ठचयस्थं तमसुरेन्द्रसुतं ततः ।।
प्रज्वाल्य दानवा वह्निं ददहुः स्वामिनोदिताः ।। ४६ ।।

Parāśara said :—Thereupon commanded by their master the Dānavas piled a huge heap of wood around the son of the king of Asuras and then put fire thereto burn him.

प्रह्लाद उवाच

तातैष वह्निः पवनेरितोपि
न मां दहत्यत्र समन्ततोहम् ।।
पश्यामि पद्मास्तरणास्तृतानि
शीतानि सर्वासिण दिशां मुखानि ।। ४७ ।।

Prahlāda said :—"This fire, although blown up by the wind, doth not burn me : I behold all around me the face of the quarters, cool, and the beds of lotuses."

श्रीपराशर उवाच

अथ दैत्येश्वरं प्रोचुर्भार्गवस्यात्मजा द्विजाः ।।
पुरोहिता महात्मानः साम्ना संस्तूय वाग्मिनः ।। ४८ ।।

Parāśara said :—Thereupon the twice-born ones, the sons of Bhārgava, the high-minded priests skilled in speech and the reciters of Śama Veda, eulogising him.

पुरोहिता ऊचुः

राजन्नियम्यतां कोपो बालेपि तनये निजे ।।
कोपो देवनिकायेषु तेषु ते सफलो यतः ।। ४९ ।।

Said to the sovereign of the Daityas,—"O king, subdue thy anger against this lad, thy own begotten son. Even thy ire against the celestials bore fruits.

(ततः पुरोहितैरुक्तो हिरण्यकशिपुः स्त्रकैः)
तथातथैनं बालं ते शासितारो वयं नृप ।।
यथा विपक्षनाशाय विनीतस्ते भविष्यति ।। ५० ।।

O king, we shall so bring up this boy, that he growing humble shall engage in the destruction of thy enemies.

बालत्वं सर्वदोषाणां दैत्यराजास्पदं यतः ।।
ततोत्र कोपमत्यर्थं योक्तुमर्हसि नार्भके ।। ५१ ।।

O king of daityas, since childishness is the root of all these evils, it behoveth thee to renounce thy ire against this boy.

न त्यक्ष्यति हरेः पक्षमस्माकं वचनाद्यदि ।।
ततः कृत्यां वधायास्य करिष्यामोऽनिवर्त्तिनीम् ।। ५२ ।।

If he according to our instructions, does not abandon the cause of Hari we shall then concert infallible measures to bring about his destruction."

श्रीपराशर उवाच

एवमभ्यर्थितस्तैस्तु दैत्यराजः पुरोहितैः ।।
दैत्यैर्निष्कासयामास पुत्रं पावकसञ्चयात् ।। ५३ ।।

Parāśara said :—Thereupon being thus solicited by the priests the king of Daityas had his son brought out from the flames by the Daityas.

ततो गुरुगृहे बालः स वसन्बालदानवान् ।।
अध्यापयामास मुहुरुपदेशान्तरे गुरो ।। ५४ ।।

Thence-forth residing in the house of the preceptor the boy Prahlāda, whenever he got an opportunity, gave lessons himself to the sons of the Dānavas.

प्रह्लाद उवाच

श्रूयतां परमार्थो मे दैतेया दितिजात्मजाः ।।
न चान्यथैतन्मन्तव्यं नात्र लोभादिकारणम् ।। ५५ ।।

Prahlāda said,—O sons of the descendants of Diti, hear from me the supreme truth : do not take my instruction otherwise for there is no touch of covetousness.

जन्म बाल्यं ततः सर्वो जन्तुः प्राप्नोति यौवनम् ।।
अव्याहतैव भवति ततोनुदिवसं जरा ।। ५६ ।।

ततश्च मृत्युमभ्येति जन्तुर्दैत्येश्वरात्मजाः ।।
प्रत्यक्षं दृश्यते चैतदस्माकं भवतां तथा ।। ५७ ।।

All creatures are born first, then they attain to infancy and youth and then succeed gradually the inevitable decay; and then they meet with death, O sons of the Daitya-chiefs. This myself and you all have witnessed.

मृतस्य च पुनर्जन्म भवत्येतच्च नान्यथा ।।
आगमोऽयं तथा यच्च नोपादानं विनोद्भवः ।। ५८ ।।

He who is dead is born again—this cannot be gain said; the sacred texts warrant it. Birth is consequent upon the virtue and vice of pristine actions.

गर्भवासादि यावत्तु पुनर्जन्मोपपादनम् ।।
सम स्तावस्थकं तावद्दुःखमेवावगम्यताम् ।। ५९ ।।

क्षुत्तृष्णोपशमं तद्वच्छीताद्युपशमं सुखम् ।।
मन्यते बालबुद्धित्वाद्दुःखमेव हि तत्पुनः ।। ६० ।।

अत्यन्तस्तिमिताङ्गानां व्यायामेन सुखैषिणाम् ।।
भ्रान्तिज्ञानावृताक्षाणां दुःखमेव सुखायते ।। ६१ ।।

All conditions from conception to re-birth are tinged with pain. The simpleton, in his childishness, thinks that the alleviation of hunger, thirst cold and the like is identified with pleasure; but in sooth that is pain; for exercise gives delight to those whose limbs are incapable of motion and suffering affords pleasure to those whose understanding is blinded with delusion.

क्व शरीरमशेषाणां श्लेष्मादीनां महाचयः ।।
क्व कान्तिशोभासौन्दर्यरमणीयादयो गुणाः ।। ६२ ।।

Where is this vile body which is a compound of phlegm and other humours and where are its beauty, grace, loveliness ad other qualities?

मांसासृक्पूयविण्मूत्रस्नायुमज्जास्थिसंहतौ ।।
देहे चेत्प्रीतिमान् मूढो भविता नरकेप्यसौ ।। ६३ ।।

The foolish wight will take delight even in hell, who is fond of this body composed of flesh, blood, matter, ordure, urnie, membrane, marrow, and bones.

अग्नेः शीतेन तोयस्य तृषा भक्तस्य च क्षुधा ।।
क्रियते सुखकर्तृत्वं तद्विलोमस्य चेतरैः ।। ६४ ।।

The agreeableness of fire is produced by cold; of water by thirst; of food by hunger; and thus all other things are rendered agreeable by their contraries.

करोति हे दैत्यसुता यावन्मात्रं परिग्रहम् ।।
तावन्मात्रं स एवास्य दुःखं चेतसि यच्छति ।। ६५ ।।

O children of Daityas, he, who will take to a wife will introduce so much of pain into his bosom.

यावतः कुरुते जन्तुः सम्बन्धान्मनसः प्रियान् ।।
तावन्तोस्य निखन्यन्ते हृदये शोकशङ्कवः ।। ६६ ।।

The more a man will create dear relations, the more deeply will be implanted the thorns of anxiety in his heart.

यद्यद्गृहे तन्मनसि यत्र तत्रावतिष्ठतः।।
नाशदाहोपकरणं तस्य तत्रैव तिष्ठति।। ६७।।

He, who has got large possessions in his house, is troubled, wherever he goes, with the anxiety that they may be lost or burnt or stolen.

जन्मन्यत्र महद्दुःखं म्रियमाणस्य चापि तत्।।
यातनासु यमस्योग्रं गर्भसंक्रमणेषु च।। ६८।।

Then there is a great pain in being born : the dying are afflicted by the tortures of Death and again by the pain of passing into the womb.

गर्भेषु सुखलेशोपि भवद्भिरनुमीयते।।
यदि तत्कथ्यतामेवं सर्वं दुःखमयं जगत्।। ६९।।

Fancy, there is not the least pleasure in the embryo state; you must then admit that the world is full of miseries.

तदेवमतिदुःखानामास्पदेत्र भवार्णवे।।
भवतां कथ्यते सत्यं विष्णुरेकः परायणः।। ७०।।

Verily I speak unto you, that in this ocean of the world infested with many miseries Viṣṇu is your only stay.

मा जानीत वयं बाला देही देहेषु शाश्वतः।।
जरायौवनजन्माद्या धर्मा देहस्य नात्मनः।। ७१।।

Do not consider yourselves as mere boys and therefore ignorant of it for the spirit embodied in your bodies is eternal. Birth, youth and decay are the properties of the body not of the soul.

बालोहं तावदिच्छातो यतिष्ये श्रेयसे युवा।।
युवाहं वार्द्धके प्राप्ते करिष्याम्यात्मनो हितम्।। ७२।।

I am now a child—when I shall be young I shall exert myself for my behoof; I am yet a youth and when I shall grow old I shall work for the benefit of my soul.

वृद्धोऽहं मम कार्याणि समस्तानि न गोचरे।।
किं करिष्यामि मंदात्मा समर्थेन न यत्कृतम्।। ७३।।

I am old now—all my senses have failed my and I cannot exert myself. What shall I do now, vicious-minded as I am?

एवं दुराशया क्षिप्तमानसः पुरुषः सदा।।
श्रेयसोऽभिमुखं याति न कदाचित्पिपासितः।। ७४।।

I did not do anything when I was capable of doing it. Thus, men, although thirsting after knowledge, having their minds distracted by vain hopes, do not attain to beatitude.

बाल्ये क्रीडनकासक्ता यौवने विषयोन्मुखाः।।
अज्ञ नयन्त्यशक्तया च वार्द्धकं समुपस्थितम्।। ७५।।

The ignorant, addicted to sport in boyhood, to worldly things in youth, find, when they become incapable, that old age is come upon them.

तस्माद्बाल्ये विवेकात्मा यतेत श्रेयसे सदा।।
बाल्ययौवनवृद्धाद्यैर्देहभावैरसंयुतः।। ७६।।

Therefore let the soul even in childhood exert itself for its welfare independent of the conditions of infancy, youth or age.

तदेतद्वो मयाख्यातं यदि जानीत नानृतम्।।
तदस्मत्प्रीतये विष्णुः स्मर्यतां बन्धमुक्तिदः।। ७७।।

This is then what I speak unto you. If you think that it is not ture, do you, for my satisfaction, think of Viṣṇu the liberator from all bondage.

प्रयासः स्मरणे कोस्य स्मृतो यच्छति शोभनम्।।
पापक्षयश्च भवति स्मरतां तमहर्निशम्।। ७८।।

What trouble is there in calling him to mind? When remembered he bestows prosperity upon people.

सर्वभूतस्थिते तस्मिन्मतिर्मैत्री दिवानिशम्।।
भवतां जायतामेवं सर्वक्लेशान्प्रहास्यथ।। ७९।।

And if you recollect Him day and night there will be an end of all sins. Let your mind be fixed on Him day and night who is present in all beings and you shall laugh at every trouble.

तापत्रयेणाभिहतं यदेतदखिलं जगत्।।
तदा शोच्येषु भूतेषु द्वेषं प्राज्ञः करोति कः।। ८०।।

The whole world is subject to a triple[1]

---

1. The three kinds of affliction referred to in the Sāṅkhya Philosophy. internal, bodily or mental affliction. External, such as injuries received from men or animals. Superhuman—such as miseries inflicted by gods, or through some supernatural agency.

affliction. What wise man would cherish hatered against beings who are all objects of compassion?

अथ भद्राणि भूतानि हीनशक्तिरहं परम्।।
मुदं तदापि कुर्वीत हानिर्द्वेषफलं यतः।। ८१।।

If others are crowned with prosperity and I am incapable of enjoy the same why should I be malignant against those who are more prosperous than myself? I should rather be glad for their happiness for the suppression of malice is itself a reward.

बद्धवैराणि भूतानि द्वेषं कुर्वन्ति चेत्ततः।।
सुशोच्यान्यतिमोहेन व्याप्तानीति मनीषिणाम्।। ८२।।

Even those who cherish malice against foes are considered as objects of pity by the wise, as being overwhelmed with delusion.

एते भिन्नदृशां दैत्या विकल्पाः कथिता मया।।
कृत्वाभ्युपगमं तत्र संक्षेपः श्रूयतां मम।। ८३।।

O Daityas, admitting the distinction between myself and all other creatures, I have described to you the various reasons for repressing hate. Hear briefly the duties of those who approach the Deity.

विस्तारः सर्वभूतस्य विष्णोः सर्वमिदं जगत्।।
द्रष्टव्यमात्मवत्तस्मादभेदेन विचक्षणैः।। ८४।।

This whole world is the manifestation of Viṣṇu who is identified with all beings. The wise therefore do not regard any difference between themselves and all other creatures.

समुत्सृज्यासुरं भावं तस्माद्यूयं यथा वयम्।।
तथा यत्नं करिष्यामो यथा प्राप्स्याम निर्वृतिम्।। ८५।।

या नाग्निना न चार्केण नेन्दुना न च वायुना।।
पजन्यवरुणाभ्यां वा न सिद्धैर्न च राक्षसैः।। ८६।।

न यक्षैर्न च दैत्येन्द्रैर्नोरगैर्न च किन्नरैः।।
न मनुष्यैर्न पशुभिर्दोषैर्नैवात्मसम्भवैः।। ८७।।

ज्वराक्षिरोगातीसारप्लीहगुल्मादिकैस्तथा।।
द्वेषेर्ष्यामत्सराद्यैर्वा रागलोभादिभिः क्षयम्।। ८८।।

Let us therefore renounce the angry passions of our race and so exert ourselves that we may obtain that perfect beatitude which is beyond the power of the deities, of fire, of the sun, of the moon, of wind, of Indra, of the regent of the sea, of the Siddhas, of the Rākṣasas, of the Daitya-chief, of the serpents, of Kinnaras, of men, or beasts or human weaknesses and which is uninterrupted by various deseases such as fever, eye-desease etc., by hatred, malice, passion or desire.

न चान्यैर्नीयते कैश्चिन्नित्या यात्यन्तनिर्मला।।
तामाप्नोत्यमलेन्यस्य केशवे हृदयं नरः।। ८९।।

The beatitude, which can not be destroyed by others which is pure and eternal, can be enjoyed by him, who fixes his mind on Keśava.

असारसंसारविवर्तनेषु मा यात तोषं प्रसभं ब्रवीमि।।
सर्वत्र दैत्यास्समतामुपैत समत्वमाराधनमच्युतस्य।। ९०।।

Verily I speak unto you, that you shall attain no satisfaction through various revolutions of this world. O Daityas, regard all creatures with impartiality—this is the adoration of the undecaying (Viṣṇu).

तस्मिन्प्रसन्ने किमिहास्त्यलभ्यं
धर्मार्थकामैरलमल्पकास्ते।।
समाश्रिताद्ब्रह्मतरोरनन्तान्निः
संशयं प्राप्स्यथ वै महत्फलम्।। ९१।।

He being propitiated what cannot be attained—wealth, pleasure, virtues are things of the little significance. Do ye resort to the exhaustless tree of true wisdom and undoubtedly you shall reap precious fruits therefrom.

।। इति श्रीविष्णुपुराणे प्रथमेंशे प्रह्लादनुचरितं नाम सप्तदशोऽध्यायः।। १७।।

अथ प्रथमेंशेः अष्टदशोऽध्यायः

Part I : Section 18

श्रीपराशर उवाच

तस्यैतां दावनवाश्रेष्टां दृष्ट्वा दैत्यपतेर्भयात्।।
आचचख्युः स चोवाच सूदानाहूय सत्वरः।। १।।

Parāśara said :—Having observed the conduct of Prahlāda, the Dānavas, out of fear, reported it to the king.

हिरण्यकशिपुरुवाच

हे सूदा मम पुत्रोसावन्येषामपि दुर्मतिः।।
कुमार्गदेशिको दुष्टो हन्यतामविलम्बितम्।। २।।

Hiraṇyakaśipu sent for his cooks and said —"O cooks—my vile and wicked son is teaching others his impious doctrines.

हालाहलं विषं तस्य सर्वभक्षेषु दीयताम्।।
अविज्ञातमसौ पापो हन्यतां मा विचार्यताम्।। ३।।

Do ye slay him without his knowledge by mixing up deadly poison with all his viands. Do not hesitate to destroy that wretch"

श्रीपराशर उवाच

ते तथैव ततश्चक्रुः प्रह्लादाय महात्मने।।
विषदानं यथाज्ञाप्तं पित्रा तस्य महात्मनः।। ४।।

Parāśara said :—Thereupon they offered poison to the high, souled Prahlāda as they were commanded by his sire.

हालाहलं विषं घोरमनन्तोच्चारणेन सः।।
अभिमन्त्र्य सहान्नेन मैत्रेय बुभुजे तदा।। ५।।

O Maitreya, repeating the name of the imperishable and mixing that poison with his food he ate it up.

अविकारं स तद्भुक्त्वा प्रह्लादः स्वस्थमानसः।।
अनन्तख्यातिनिर्वीर्यंजरयामास तद्विषम्।। ६।।

Prahlāda did not suffer any harm either in body or in mind for the very name of the endless baffled the power of the poison.

ततः सूदा भयत्रस्ता जीर्णं दृष्ट्वा महद्विषम्।।
दैत्येश्वरमुपागम्य प्रणिपत्येदमब्रुवन्।। ७।।

Beholding that deadly poison digested by him, they stricken with fear approached the king of Daityas.

सूदा ऊचुः

दैत्यराज विषं दत्तमस्माभिरतिभीषणम्।।
जीर्णं तेन सहान्नेन प्रह्लादेन सुतेन ते।। ८।।

They said : "O king of Daityas, deadliest poison was offered by us but it was digested with food by thy son Prahlāda."

हिरण्यकशिपुरुवाच

त्वर्यतां त्वर्यतां हे हे सद्यो दैत्यपुरोहिताः।।
कृत्यां तस्य विनाशाय उत्पा दयत मा चिरम्।। ९।।

Hiraṇyakaśipu said,—"Hasten, hasten, O ye priests of the Daityas : do ye speedily perform the rites that will bring about his destruction."

श्रीपराशर उवाच

सकाशमागम्य ततः प्रह्लादस्य पुरोहिताः।।
सामपूर्वमथोचुस्ते प्रह्लादं विनयान्वितम्।। १०।।

Parāśara said :—Thereupon the priests approaching Prahlāda and beholding him lowly consoled him.

पुरोहिता ऊचुः

जातस्त्रैलोक्यविख्यात आयुष्मन्ब्रह्मणः कुले।।
दैत्यराजस्य तनयो हिरण्यकशिपोर्भवान्।। ११।।

Purohita said,—"Thou hast been born in the family of Brahmā celebrated in the three worlds and thou art the son of Hiraṇyakaśipu the king of Daityas.

किं देवैः किमनन्तेन किमन्येन तवाश्रयः।।
पिता ते सर्वलोकानां त्वं तथैव भविष्यसि।। १२।।

Why dost thou depend upon the gods? Thy father is the refuge of all people :—thou dost also become the same.

तस्मात्परित्यजैनां त्वं विपक्षस्तवसंहिताम्।।
श्लाघ्यः पिता समस्तानां गुरुणां परमो गुरुः।। १३।।

Do thou ronounce eulogising the enemy of thy family : know that a father is the most venerable of all preceptors."

प्रह्लाद उवाच

एवमेतन्महाभाः श्लाघ्यमेतन्महाकुलम् ।।
मरीचेः सकलेप्यस्मिन् त्रैलोक्ये नान्यथा वदेत् ।। १४ ।।

Prahlāda said—"O illustrious Brāhmins, that ye have said is true—the family of Marīci is celebrated in the three worlds—this cannot be gainsaid.

पिता च मम सर्वस्मिञ्जगत्युत्कृष्टचेष्टितः ।।
एतदप्यवगच्छामि सत्यमत्रापि नानृतम् ।। १५ ।।

My father has attained to the foremost place in the world by his actions—I have known this to be true—there is not the least shadow of untruth.

गुरूणामपि सर्वेषां पिता परमको गुरुः ।।
यदुक्तं भ्रान्तिस्तत्रापि स्वल्पापि हि न विद्यते ।। १६ ।।

That a father is the most venerable of all preceptors—I do not find the least mistake in this assertion.

पिता गुरुर्न सन्देहः पूजनीयः प्रयत्नतः ।।
तत्रापि नापराध्यामी त्येवं मनसि मे स्थितम् ।। १७ ।।

Forsooth, father is a venerable preceptor and is to be respected with all care. Methinks I have not committed any offence in this respect.

यत्त्वेतत्किमनन्तेनेत्युक्तं युष्माभिरीदृशम् ।।
को ब्रवीति यथान्याय्यं किं तु नैतद्वचोर्थवत् ।। १८ ।।

You have said, Why do you seek shelter of the eternal?" I do not know how far this statement is sound and reasonable."

इत्युक्त्वा सोऽभवन्मौनी तेषां गौरवयंत्रितः ।।
प्रहस्य च पुनः प्राह किमनन्तेन साध्विति ।। १९ ।।

Having said this Prahlāda remained speechless for some time to uphold their dignity. And again smiling he said :

साधु भोः किमनन्तेन साधु भो गुरुवो मम ।।
श्रूयतां यदनन्तेन यदि खेदं न यास्यथ ।। २० ।।

"Why do you seek shelter of the eternal" was it fair for you to accost me thus? What need of the eternal? Most admirable, most worthy of you, O my preceptors. If it does not pain you, hear what need there is of the eternal.

धर्मार्थकाममोक्षाश्च पुरुषार्था उदाहृताः ।।
चतुष्टयमिदं यस्मात्तस्मात्किं किमिदं वच ।। २१ ।।

Virtue, desire, wealth and emancipation are the fourfold objects of men. Is it vain to adore him who is the source of these four objects? Why do ye speak in vain?

मरीचिमिश्रैर्दक्षाद्यैस्तथैवान्यैरनन्ततः ।।
धर्मः प्राप्तस्तथा चान्यैरर्थः कामस्तथाऽपरैः ।। २२ ।।

Mārīcī and other ascetics, the Patriarch Dakṣa and other eminent men attained to virtue and others and obtained the enjoyment of their desires.

तन्तत्त्ववेदिनो भूत्वा ज्ञानध्यानसमाधिभिः ।।
अवापुर्मुक्तिमपरे पुरुषा ध्वस्तबंधनाः ।। २३ ।।

Others, through true wisdom and holy contemplation, have come to know his essence, and being freed from the bondage of the world have obtained emancipation.

सम्पदैश्वर्यमाहात्म्यज्ञानसन्ततिकर्मणाम् ।।
विमुक्तेश्चैकतो लभ्यं मूलमाराधनं हरेः ।। २४ ।।

The adoration of Hari, attainable by unity, is the root of all wealth, dignity, glory, wisdom, progeny, piety and emancipation.

यतो धर्मार्थकामाख्यं मुक्तिश्चापि फलं द्विजाः ।।
तेनापि किंकिमित्येवमनन्तेन किमुच्यते ।। २५ ।।

O twice-born one, virtue, wealth, desire and final emancipation (all) proceed from him (and still you say) what need is of the eternal?

किं चापि बहुनोक्तेन भवन्तो गुरवो मम ।।
वदन्तु साधु वासाधु विवेकोस्माकमल्पकः ।। २६ ।।

बहुनात्र किमुक्तेन स एव जगतः पतिः ।।
स कर्त्ता च विकर्त्ता च संहर्ता च हृदि स्थितः ।। २७ ।।

स भोक्ता भोज्यमप्येवं स एव जगदीश्वरः ।।
भवद्भिरेतत्क्षंतव्यं बाल्यादुक्तं तु यन्मया ।। २८ ।।

What is the use of speaking more, you are

all my preceptors—speak ye good or evil, limited is my understanding."

पुरोहिता ऊचुः

दह्यमानस्त्वमस्माभिरग्निना बाल रक्षितः।।
भूयो न वक्ष्यसीत्येवं नैव ज्ञातोस्यबुद्धिमान्।। २९।।

The priests said—"O boy thou wert about to be consumed by fire, but we saved you thinking that you would not give vent to such words again.

यदास्मद्वचनान्मोहग्राहं न त्यक्षते भवान्।।
ततः कृत्यां विनाशाय तव सृक्ष्याम दुर्मते।। ३०।।

We know how foolish you are. If you, at our words, do not remove this hallucination we shall, O vicious-minded one, perform rites for your destruction."

प्रह्लाद उवाच

कः केन हन्यते जन्तुर्जन्तुः कः केन रक्ष्यते।।
हन्ति रक्षति चैवात्मा ह्यसत्साधु समाचरन्।। ३१।।

Prahlāda said—"Who slayeth what living creature—who preserveth what living creature?

कर्मणा जायते सर्वं कर्मैव गतिसाधनम्।।
तस्मात्सर्वप्रयत्नेन साधुकर्म समाचरेत्।। ३२।।

Every one is his own destroyer or preserver accordingly as he follows evil or good."

श्रीपराशर उवाच

इत्युक्तास्तेन ते क्रुद्धा दैत्यराजपुरोहिताः।।
मकृत्यामुत्पादयामासुर्ज्वालामालोज्ज्वलाकृतिम्।। ३३।।

Parāśara said :—Being thus addressed, the priests of the Daitya-chief were excited with rage, and instantly, by virtue of their magical powers, created a female form enveloped with fiery flame.

अतिभीमा समागम्य पादन्यासक्षतक्षितिः।।
शूलेन साधु संक्रुद्ध तं जघानाशु वक्षसि।। ३४।।

That highly dreadful figure, under whose tread earth trembled, greatly wroth, struck him instantly on his breast with a dart.

तत्तस्य हृदयं प्राप्य शूलं बालस्य दीप्तिमत्।।
जगाम खण्डितं भूमौ तत्रापि शतधा गतम्।। ३५।।

That fiery dart reaching speedily the breast of the boy fell on the ground broken into hundred pieces.

यत्रानपायी भगवान् हृद्यास्ते हरिरीश्वरः।।
भङ्गौ भवति वज्रस्य तत्र शूलस्य का कथा।। ३६।।

Even a thunder-bolt is shattered against the breast of him in whose heart the imperishable Hari resides—what to speak of a dart?

अपापे तत्र पापैश्च पातिता दैत्यायाजकैः।।
तानेव सा जघानाशु कृत्या नाशं जगाम च।। ३७।।

The magic, which was directed by the vicious priests against the guileless (Prahlāda), then fell upon them and slew them all.

कृत्यया दह्यमानांस्तान्विलोक्य स महामतिः।।
त्राहि कृष्णेत्यनन्तेति वदन्नभ्यवपद्यत।। ३८।।

And beholding them thus consumed by fire noble Prahlāda exclaiming, "Save, O Kṛṣṇa, o Eternal" approached them

प्रह्लाद उवाच

सर्वव्यापिन् जगद्रूप जगत्स्त्रष्टर्जनार्दन।।
पाहि विप्रानिमानस्माद्दुःसहान्मंत्रपावकात्।। ३९।।

Prahlāda said—"O thou who art manifest in the universe, O thou spread all over the universe, O thou the creator of the universe, O Janārdana! do thou save these Brāhmaṇas from the unbearable flame set up by their magical incantations.

यथा सर्वेषु भूतेषु सर्वव्यापी जगद्गुरुः।।
विष्णुरेव तथा सर्वे जीवन्त्वेते पुरोहिताः।। ४०।।

As the omnipresent Viṣṇu, the preceptor of the world, is present in all creatures, let these priests regain their life.

यथा सर्वगतं विष्णुं मन्यमानोनपायिनम्।।
चिन्तयाम्यरिपक्षेपि जीवन्त्वेते पुरोहिताः।। ४१।।

Viṣṇu being present everywhere, as I did not consider fire as my enemy let the priests be restored to life.

ये हन्तुमागता दत्तं यैर्विषं यैर्हुताशनः।।
यैर्दिग्गजैरहं क्षुण्णो दष्टः सर्पैश्च यैरपि।। ४२।।

I regarded with a friendly attitude all those who came to slay me, those who offerd me poison, those who kindled fire, the elephants of the skies and serpents by whom I was bitten.

तेष्वहं मित्रभावेन समः पापोस्मि न क्वचित्।।
यथा तेनाद्य सत्येन जीवन्त्वसुरयाजकाः।। ४३।।

And I never entertained malice against them; if this be true let the priests of Asuras be restored to life."

श्रीपराशर उवाच

इत्युक्तास्तेन ते सर्वे संस्पृष्टाश्च निरामयाः।।
समुत्तस्थुर्द्विजा भूयस्तमूचुः प्रश्रयान्वितम्।। ४४।।

Parāśara said :—He having said this they all, touched, rose up unhurt, and spoke to Prahlāda who was humble,—

पुरोहिता ऊचुः

दीर्घायुरप्रतिहतो बलवीर्यसमन्वितः।।
पुत्रपौत्रधनैश्वर्यैर्युक्तो वत्स भवोत्तमः।। ४५।।

Purohita said :—"O boy, O foremost of all, be thou crowned with a long life, unaunted strength and prowess."

श्रीपराशर उवाच

इत्युक्त्वा तं ततो गत्वा यथावृत्तं पुरोहिताः।।
दैत्यराजाय सकलमाचचख्युर्महामुने।। ४६।।

Parāśara said :—O great Muni, having said this, the priests repaired to the king of Daityas and related to him everything.

।। इति श्रीविष्णुपुराणे प्रथमेंशे प्रह्लादचरितेऽष्टादशोऽध्यायः।।१८।।

अथ प्रथमेंशेः एकोनविंशतितमोऽध्यायः

Part I : Section 19

श्रीपराशर उवाच

हिरण्यकशिपुः श्रुत्वा तां कृत्यां वितथीकृताम्।।
आहूय पुत्रं पप्रच्छ प्रभावस्यास्य कारणम्।। १।।

Parāśara said :—When Hiraṇyakaśipu had heard that the magical charms (of the priests) had been baffled he sent for his son and asked him of the secret of his prowess,—

हिरण्यकशिपुरुवाच

प्रह्लाद सुप्रभावोसि किमेतत्ते विचेष्टितम्।।
एतन्मंत्रादिजनितमुताहो सहजं तव।। २।।

Hiraṇyakaśipu said :—Prahlāda, thou art gifted with extraordinary prowess—is it the result of your self-exercise or the outcome of magical powers or thou art, from birth, gifted with it?"

श्रीपराशर उवाच

एवं पृष्टस्तदा पित्रा प्रह्लादोऽसुरबालकः।।
प्रणिपत्य पितुः पादाविदं वचनमब्रवीत्।। ३।।

Parāśara said :—Being thus interrogated by his father the Asura boy Prahlāda bowed down to his father's feet and said,—

न मंत्रादिकृतं तात न च नैसद्गिको मम।।
प्रभाव एष सामान्यो यस्य यस्याच्युतो हृदि।। ४।।

This is not the outcome of magical powers, O father—nor is it natural with me. This is trifling to him in whose mind resides the undecaying.

अन्येषां यो न पापानि चिन्तयत्यात्मनो यथा।।
तस्य पापागमस्तात हेत्वभावान्न विद्यते।। ५।।

He who does not cherish malice against others, O father, and regards all like his own self, is not visited by any affliction inasmuch as the cause does not exist.

कर्मणा मनसा वाचा परपीडां करोति यः।।
तद्बीजं जन्म फलति प्रभूतं तस्य चाशुभम्।। ६।।

He who tortures others in act, thought or speech, sows the seed of numberless miseries.

सोहं न पापमिच्छामि न करोमि वदामि वा।।
चिन्तयन्सर्वभूतस्थमात्मन्यपि च केशवम्।। ७।।

I wish no evil to any; neither do nor speak it; I always meditate, in me, upon Keśava who is existent in all beings.

शारीरं मानसं दुःखं दैवं भूतभवं तथा।।
सर्वत्र शुभचित्तस्य तस्य मे जायते कुतः।। ८।।

Why should miseries, physical or mental, or those inflicted by elements, or the gods, affect me, whose soul is purified?

एवं सर्वेषु भूतेषु भक्तिरव्यभिचारिणी।।
कर्तव्या पण्डितैर्ज्ञात्वा सर्वभूतमयं हरिम्।। ९।।

Considering that Hari exists in all beings the learned should assiduously love all creatures."

श्रीपराशर उवाच

इति श्रुत्वा स दैत्येन्द्रः प्रासादशिखरे स्थितः।।
क्रोधान्धकारितमुखः प्राह दैतेयकिंकरान्।। १०।।

Parāśara said :—Having heard this the Daitya-king, seated on the summit of his palace, having his face darkened with ire.

हिरण्यकशिपुरुवाच

दुरात्मा क्षिप्यतामस्मात्प्रासादाच्छतयोजनात्।।
गिरिपृष्ठे पतत्वस्मिन् शिलाभिन्नङ्गसंहितः।। ११।।

Hiraṇyakaśipu said :—I said to his attendants—"Throw this vicious-souled one, from this palace which is hundred *yojanas* in height, down upon the tops of the mountains, so that his body may be crushed into pieces against the rocks."

ततस्तं चिक्षुपुः सर्वे बालं दैतेयदानवाः।।
पपात सोप्यधः क्षिप्तो हृदयेनोद्वहद्धरिम्।। १२।।

Thereupon all these Daityas and Dānavas hurled that boy down: and he fell down cherishing Hari in his mind.

पतमानं जगद्धात्री जगद्धातरि केशवे।।
भक्तियुक्तं दधारैनमुपसंगम्य मेदिनी।। १३।।

And Earth, the upholder of the world, approaching, received him falling who was devoted to Keśava the protector of the world.

ततो विलोक्य तं स्वस्थमविशिर्णास्थिपञ्जरम्।।
हिरण्यकशिपुः प्राह शम्बरं मायिनां वरम्।। १४।।

Thereupon beholding him unhurt and having no bone fractured, Hiraṇyakaśipu said to Śambara the foremost of those conversant with charms :—

हिरण्यकशिपुरुवाच

नास्माभिः शक्यते हन्तुमसौ दुर्बुद्धिबालकः।।
मायां वेत्ति भवांस्तस्मान्माययैनं निषूदय।। १५।।

"We have not been able to slay this vicious-minded lad : thou art congnisant of various charms : do thou slay him."

शम्बर उवाच

सूदयाम्येव दैत्येन्द्र पश्य मायाबलं मम।।
सहस्रमत्र मायानां पश्य कोटिशतं तथा।। १६।।

Śambara said :—"Instantly shall I slay him, O king of Daityas : do thou behold my power of illusion which can invent thousands and myriads of artifices."

श्रीपराशर उवाच

ततः स ससृजे मायां प्रह्लादे शम्बरोऽसुरः।।
विनाशमिच्छन्दुर्बुद्धिः सर्वत्र समदर्शनि।। १७।।

Parāśara said :—Thereupon that silly Asura Śambara, desirous of destroying the boy, practised his magical charms against Prahlāda, looking upon all creatures with an impartial eye.

समाहितमतिर्भूत्वा शम्बरेपि विमत्सरः।।
मैत्रेय सोपि प्रह्लादः सस्मार मधुसूदनम्।। १८।।

With a heart tranquil and void of malice even against Śamvara, O Maitreya, Prahlāda engaged in the meditation of the destroyer of Madhu.

श्रीपराशर उवाच

ततो भगवता तस्य रक्षार्थं चक्रमुत्तमम्।।
आजगाम समाज्ञप्तं ज्वालामालि सुदर्शनम्।। १९।।

Parāśara said :—Thereupon to protect him the excellent and flaming discus Sudarśana was despatched by the Great God.

तेन मायासहस्रं तच्छम्बरस्याशुगामिना।।
बालस्य रक्षता देहमेकैकं चारिशोधितम्।। २०।।

Thereupon thousands of Śambara's illusions were baffled by the quick-coursing discus for the protection of that boy.

संशोषकं तथा वायुं दैत्येन्द्रस्त्विदमब्रवीत्।।
शीघ्रमेष ममादेशाद्दुरात्मा नीयतां क्षयम्।। २१।।

Thereupon the Daitya-king spoke to the withering wind saying,—"Do thou, speedily, at my command, bring this vicious-minded boy to destruction."

तथेत्युक्त्वा तु सोप्येनं विवेश पवनो लघु।।
शीतोतिरूक्षः शोषाय तद्देहस्यातिदुः सहः।। २२।।

Saying "So be it" the wind immediately penetrated into his body—cold, cutting and insufferable, for his destruction.

तेनाविष्टमथात्मानं स बुद्ध्वा दैत्यबालकः।।
हृदयेन महात्मानं दधार धरणीधरम्।। २३।।

Perceiving that wind had entered into his body the Daitya boy again meditated, in his mind, upon the great upholder of the earth.

हृदयस्थस्ततस्तस्य तं वायुमति भीषणम्।।
पपौ जनार्दनः क्रुद्धः स ययौ पवनः क्षयम्।। २४।।

And Janārdana, present in his mind, wroth, drank up that dreadful wind. And the wind thus met with its own destruction.

क्षीणासु सर्वमायासु पवने च क्षयं गते।।
जगाम सोपि भवनं गुरोरेव महामतिः।। २५।।

All the magical charms being thus baffled, the wind being thus annihilated, the high-minded Prahlāda again repaired to the abode of his preceptor.

अहन्यहन्यथाचार्यो नीतिं राज्यफलप्रदाम्।।
ग्राहयामास तं बालं राज्ञामुशनसा कृताम्।। २६।।

And the preceptor instructed that boy daily in the science of polity essentially necessary for the administration of the government and invented by Uṣanas for the behoof of kings.

गृहीतनीतिशास्त्रं तं विनीतं च यदा गुरुः।।
मेने तदैनं तत्पित्रे कथयामास शिक्षितम्।। २७।।

When the preceptor found him well-versed in all political sciences and humble, he then communicated it to his father, saying,—

आचार्य उवाच

गृहीतनीतिशास्त्रस्ते पुत्रो दैत्यपते कृतः।।
प्रह्लादस्तत्त्वतो वेत्ति भार्गवेण यदीरितम्।। २८।।

"O lord of Daityas, thy son Prahlāda has become conversant with the principles of government as laid down by the descendant of Bhṛgu."

हिरण्यकशिपुरुवाच

मित्रेषु वर्तेत कथमरिवर्गेषु भूपतिः।।
प्रह्लाद त्रिषु लोकेषु मध्यस्थेषु कथं चरेत्।। २९।।

Thereat Hiraṇyakaśipu said to his son,—"Prahlāda, how should a king conduct himself towards friends or foes and what steps he should take at the three periods (*i.e.* advance, retrogression and peace)?

कथं मंत्रि ष्वमात्येषु बाह्येष्वाभ्यंतरेषु च।।
चारेषु पौरवर्गेषु शङ्कितेष्वितरेषु च।। ३०।।

How should he behave towards his ministers, courtiers, the state and household officers, his emissaries, his subjects, those of doubtful allegiance and his open enemies?

कृत्याकृत्यविधानञ्च दुर्गाटविकसाधनम्।।
प्रह्लाद कथ्यतां सम्यक् तथा कण्टकशोधनम्।। ३१।।

एतच्चान्यच्च सकलमधीतं भवता यथा।।
तथा मे कथ्यतां ज्ञातुं तवेच्छामि मनोगतम्।। ३२।।

With whom should he make alliance; with whom enter into war; what sort of fortress he should build; how forest and mountain tribes should be removed : all this and all other things you have read, do thou relate to me : I wish to hear thy mind."

श्रीपराशर उवाच

प्रणिपत्य पितुः पादौ तदा प्रश्रयभूषणः।।
प्रह्लादः प्राह दैत्येन्द्रं कृताञ्जलिपुटस्तथा।। ३३।।

Parāśara said :—Thereupon bowing to the feet of his father, Prahlāda, who had humility as his ornament, said, with folded palms, to that Daitya-king.

प्रह्लाद उवाच

ममो पदिष्टं सकलं गुरुणा नात्र संशयः।।
गृहीतन्तु मया किन्तु न सदेतन्मतम्मम।। ३४।।

Prahlāda said :— "Forsooth I have been instructed in all these by my preceptor and I have learnt them; but I do not approve of all of them.

साम चोपप्रदानं च भेददण्डो तथापरौ।।
उपायाः कथिताः सर्वे मित्रादीनां च साधने।। ३५।।

For the subjection of friends and foes four expedients have been prescribed by all—namely—conciliation, gift, punishment and sowing dissension.

तानेवाहं न पश्यामि मित्रादीस्तात मा क्रुधः।।
साध्याभावे महाबाहो साधनैः किं प्रयोजनम्।। ३६।।

But O father, be not angry, I know neither friends nor enemies. O thou of mighty arms where there is nothing to be effected what is the use of resorting to the means for effecting it?

सर्वभूतात्मके तात जगन्नाथे जगन्मये।।
परमात्मनि गोविन्दे मित्रामित्रकथा कुतः।। ३७।।

O father, it is useless to talk of friend or foe in Govinda, who is identical with all beings, manifest all over the universe, the lord of it and the Great Soul.

त्वय्यस्ति भगवान् विष्णुर्मयि चान्यत्र चास्ति सः।।
यतस्ततोयं मित्रं मे शत्रुश्चेति पृथक्कुतः।। ३८।।

The Great Viṣṇu exists in thee, in me as well as in all other creatures; and then what is the use of making such distinction as he is friend and he is foe !

तदेभिरलमत्यर्थं दुष्टारम्भोक्तिविस्तरैः।।
अविद्यान्तर्गतैर्यत्नः कर्त्तव्यस्तात शोभने।। ३९।।

It is useless therefore to cultivate such tedious and unprofitable sciences which contain but false knowledge.

विद्याबुद्धिरविद्यायामज्ञानान्तात जायते।।
बालोग्निं किं न खद्योतमसुरेश्वर मन्यते।। ४०।।

It is but proper, O father, to engage in the cultivation of the knowledge of self. O father, the idea that ignorance is knowledge arises from ignorance only. A boy, O lord of Asuras, regards the fire-fly as fire.

तत्कर्म यन्न बन्धाय सा विद्या या विमुक्तये।।
आयासायापरं कर्म विद्यान्या शिल्पनैपुणम्।। ४१।।

That is (proper) action that liberates us from the bondage of the world and that is (true) knowledge that leads us to the path of emancipation; all other actions lead but to weariness and all other knowledge is turned only into cleverness of an artist.

तदेतदवगम्याहमसारं सारमुत्तमम्।।
निशामय महाभाग प्रणिपत्य ब्रवीमि ते।। ४२।।

Considering all this knowledge as useless I shall relate to thee respectfully what is really profitable; do thou, O great king, hear it.

न चिन्तयति को राज्यं को धनं नाभिवाञ्छति।।
तथापि भाव्यमेवैतदुभयं प्राप्यते नरैः।। ४३।।

Who does not think of a kingdom? Who does not desire for riches? But all these are acquirable by the piety accumulated in a pristine birth—so the pious obtain them both.

सर्व एव महाभाग महत्त्वं प्रति सोद्यमाः।।
तथापि पुंसां भाग्यानि नोद्यमा भूतिहेतवः।। ४४।।

O great king, all men desire to be great—but this greatness is not acquired by exertion, it is the destiny that confers it upon men.

जडानामविवेकानामशूराणामपि प्रभो।।
भोग्यभोज्यानि राज्यानि सन्त्यनीतिमतामपि।। ४५।।

O lord, kingdoms are acquired by fate, even by the stupid, the ignorant, the cowardly and those who are ignorant, the cowardly and those who are ignorant of the science of government.

तस्माद्यतेत पुण्येषु य इच्छेन्महतीं श्रियम्।।
यतितव्यं समत्वे च निर्वाणमपि चेच्छता।। ४६।।

Therefore, he, who longs for greatness, should try to acquire piety. He, who desires for final beautitude, should try to regard all people with an impartial eye.

देवा मनुष्याः पशवः पक्षिवृक्षसरीसृपाः।।
रूपमेतदनन्तस्य विष्णोर्भिन्नमिव स्थितम्।। ४७।।

Gods, men, animals, birds, reptiles, all are but diverse manifestations of the eternal Viṣṇu and exist in a separate state.

एतद्विजानता सर्वं जगत्स्थावरजङ्गमम्।।
दृष्टव्यमात्मवद्विष्णुर्यतोयं विश्वरूपधृक्।। ४८।।

By him, who knows this, the whole world, moveable and immoveable, is considered as at one with him—all proceeding alike from Viṣṇu assuming the universal form.

एवं ज्ञाते स भगवाननादिः परमेश्वरः।।
प्रसीदत्यच्युतस्तस्मिन्प्रसन्ने क्लेशसंक्षयः।। ४९।।

When a man obtains this knowledge, the undecaying and eternal Viṣṇu—the remover of all afflictions, is propitiated with him."

श्रीपराशर उवाच

एतच्छ्रुत्वा तु कोपेन समुत्थाय वरासनात्।।
हिरण्यकशिपुः पुत्रं पदा वक्षस्यताडयत्।। ५०।।

Parāśara said :—Having heard this and got up from the excellent seat, in great rage, Hiraṇyakaśipu spurned his son on the breast with this foot.

उवाच च स कोपेन सामर्षः प्रज्वलन्निव।।
निष्पिष्य पाणिना पाणिं हन्तुकामो जगद्यथा।।५१।।

And burning in ire and wringing his hands as if bent upon destroying the whole universe, he exclaimed

हिरण्यकशिपुरुवाच

हे विप्रचिते हे राहो हे बलैष महार्णवे।।
नागपाशैर्दृढैर्बद्ध्वा क्षिप्यतां मा विलंब्यताम्।।५२।।

अन्यथा सकला लोकास्तथा दैतेयदानवाः।।
अनुयास्यन्ति मूढस्य मतमस्य दुरात्मनः।। ५३।।

Hiraṇyakaśipu said :—"Ho Vipracitta! Ho Rāhu! Ho Vāli binding this boy with serpents, do ye throw him unto the deep : delay not or else the Daityas, the Dānavas and all other people shall be initated into doctrines of this stupid and vicious boy.

बहुशो वारितोस्माभिरयं पापस्तथाप्यरेः।।
स्तुतिं करोति दुष्टानां वध एवोपकारकः।। ५४।।

We have prevented him many a time and off and still he persists in chanting the glories of our foe : it is proper to destroy the wicked boy at once."

पराशर उवाच

ततस्ते सत्वरा दैत्या बद्ध्वा तं नाग बन्धनैः।।
भर्तुराज्ञां पुरस्कृत्य चिक्षिपुः सलिलार्णवे।। ५५।।

Parāśara said :—Thereupon obeying the mandate of their master the Daityas speedily bound him with ropes and threw him into the water.

ततश्चचाल चलता प्रह्लादेन महार्णवः।।
उद्वेलोभूत्परं क्षोभमुपेत्य च समन्ततः।। ५६।।

Thereupon with Prahlāda triembled the mighty deep; and being agitated throughout, it rose in mighty waves.

भूर्लोकमखिलं दृष्ट्वा प्लाव्यमानं महाम्भसा।।
हिरण्यकशिपुर्दैत्यानिदमाह महामते।। ५७।।

Beholding the earth about to be submerged by the great ocean, Hiraṇyakaśipu again said to the Daityas,—

हिरण्यकशिपुरुवाच

दैतेयाः सकलैः शैलैरत्रैव वरुणालये।।
निश्छिद्रैः सर्वशः सर्वैश्चीयतामेष दुर्मतिः।। ५८।।

"O ye descendants of Diti! Do ye bury this wicked boy in the deep with rocks.

नाग्निर्दहति नैवायं शस्त्रैश्छिन्नो न चोरगैः।।
क्षयं नीतो न वातेन न विषेण न कृत्यया।। ५९।।

Fire did not burn him; the weapons did not hurt him : the serpents could not bite him; nor the withering blast, poison, and the magical incantations bring about his destruction.

न मायाभिर्न चैवोच्चात्पातितो न च दिग्गजैः।।
बालोतिदुष्टचित्तोयं नानेना र्थोस्ति जीवता।। ६०।।

He baffled the illustion (of Śambara), fell unhurt from the loftiest mountains, foiled the elephants of the skies. He is a wicked boy and his life is a perpetual source of miseries.

तदेष तोयमध्ये तु समाक्रान्तो महीधरैः।।
तिष्ठत्वब्दसहस्रान्तं प्राणान्हास्यति दुर्मतिः।। ६१।।

Let him be buried down with rocks into the deep. If the remains in that wise for a thousand years he may lose his life."

ततो दैत्या दानवाश्च पर्वतैस्तं महोदधौ।।
आक्रम्य चयनं चक्रुर्योजनानि सहस्त्रशः।। ६२।।

Thereupon the Daityas and Dānavas. Attacking Prahlāda in the mighty deep with rocks, covered thousands of *yojanas* therewith.

स चितः पर्वतैरन्तः समुद्रस्य महामतिः।।
तुष्टावाह्निक वेलायामेकाग्रमतिरच्युतम्।। ६३।।

And lying at the bed of the deep covered with rocks, the high-minded Prahlāda, offered thus; with undisturbed mind, his daily praise to the undecaying,—

प्रह्लाद उवाच

नमस्ते पुण्डरीकाक्ष नमस्ते पुरुषोत्तम।।
नमस्ते सर्वलोकात्मन्नमस्ते तिग्मचक्रिणे।। ६४।।

"Salutation unto thee, O Puṇḍarīkākṣa, salutation unto thee, O thou excellent Puruṣas! Salutation unto thee, O thou the soul of all worlds! Salutation unto thee, O thou the welder of sharp discus!

नमो ब्रह्मण्यदेवाय गोब्राह्मणहिताय च।।
जगद्धिताय कृष्णाय गोविन्दाय नमोनमः।। ६५।।

Salutation unto the best of Brāhmaṇas! to the friend of Brāhmaṇas and of kine! to Kṛṣṇa, the benefactor of the world and salutation to Govinda!

ब्रह्मत्वे सृजते विश्वं स्थितौ पालयते पुनः।।
रुद्ररूपाय कल्पान्ते नमस्तुभ्यं त्रिमूर्तये।। ६६।।

Salutation to him, who as Brahmā creates the universe and who, being existent all over, preserves it. Salutation to thee, who dost at the end of Kalpa assume the from of Rudra, and who art tri-form.

देवा यक्षाः सुराः सिद्धा नागा गन्धर्वकिन्नराः।।
पिशाचा राक्षसाश्चैव मनुष्याः पशवस्तथा।। ६७।।

पक्षिणस्थावराश्चैव पिपीलिकसरीसृपाः।।
भूम्यापोग्निर्नभोवायुः शब्दः स्पर्शस्तथा रसः।। ६८।।

रूपं गन्धो मनो बुद्धिरात्मा कालस्तथा गुणाः।।
एतेषां परमार्थश्च सर्वमेतत्त्वमच्युत।। ६९।।

Thou art, Acyuta, the cause of gods, Yakṣas, Asuras, Siddhas, serpents, choristers, dancers, goblins, demons, men, beasts, birds, insects, reptiles, plants, and stones, earth, fire wanter, sky, wind, sound, touch, taste, colour, flavour, mind, intellect, soul, time, and the properties of nature; and these are all manifestations of thine.

विद्याविद्ये भवान्सत्यमसत्यं त्वं विषामृते।।
प्रवृत्तं च निवृत्तं च कर्म वेदोदितं भवान्।। ७०।।

Thou art knowledge and ignorance, thou art truth and untruth; thou art poison and nectar; thou art the performance and continauance of acts and thou art the actions laid down in the Vedas.

समस्तकर्मभोक्ता च कर्मोपकरणानि च।।
त्वमेव विष्णो सर्वाणि सर्वकर्मफलं च यत्।। ७१।।

Thou art the enjoyer of the fruits of all actions and the means for effecting them. Thou, Viṣṇu, who art all, art the fruit of all acts of piety.

मय्यन्यत्र तथान्येषु भूतेषु भुवनेषु च।।
तवैवाव्याप्तिरैश्वर्यगुणसंसूचिकी प्रभो।। ७२।।

Thou art in me, in others and spread all over the vast universe. Thy universal manifestation indicates might and goodness.

त्वां योगिनश्चिंतयन्ति त्वां यजंति च याजकाः।।
हव्यकव्यभुगेकस्त्वं पितृदेवस्वरूपधृक्।। ७३।।

O lord, The ascetics meditate upon thee, the priests offer sacrifice to thee. Thou, idenetical with progenitors and celestials, receivest burnt-offerings and oblations.

रूपं महत्ते स्थितमत्र विश्वं ततश्च सूक्ष्मं जगदेतदीश।।
रूपाणि सर्वाणि च भूतभेदास्तेष्वन्तरात्माख्यमतीव सूक्ष्मम्।। ७४।।

The universe is a huge manifestation of thine; the world is lesser than that, O lord; and lesser than that are all the subtile elements and elementary being and thy subtlest form is the subtile prinipie within them that is called soul.

तस्माच्च सूक्ष्मादिविशेषणानामगोचरे यत्परमात्मरूपम्।।
किमप्यचिन्त्यं तव रूपमस्ति तस्मै: नमस्ते पुरुषोत्तमाय।।
७५।।

Thou hast in thee a supreme soul, better than this soul and beyond the perception of all subtile elements and which cannot be conceived. Glory be to that Puruṣottam form of thine.

सर्वभूतेषु सर्वात्मन्या शक्तिरपरा तव।।
गुणाश्रया नमस्तस्यै शाश्वतायै सुरेश्वर।। ७६।।

And salutation be to that imperishable form of thine, O lord of gods, which is the soul of all creatures, another manifestation of thy might and which is the refuge of all qualities.

यातीतगोचरा वाचां मनसां चाविशेषणा।।
ज्ञानिज्ञानपरिच्छेद्या तां वन्दे स्वेश्वरीं पराम्।। ७७।।

I bow unto that supreme goddess who is beyond the perception of senses, the description of the tongue and mind and who is to be distinguished only by the wisdom of the truly wise.

ॐ नमो वासुदेवाय तस्मै भगवते सदा।।
व्यतिरिक्तं न यस्यास्ति व्यतिरिक्तोखिलस्य यः।।७८।।

Salutation unto the Great God Vāsudeva, who is not separate from any thing and at the same time separate from all.

नमस्तस्मै नमस्तस्मै नमस्तस्मै महात्मने।।
नाम रूपं न यस्यैको योस्तित्वेनोपलभ्यते।। ७९।।

Salutation again and again to that Great Spirit who has neither name nor form and whose existence can only be perceived.

यस्यावताररूपाणि समर्चन्ति दिवौकसः।।
अपश्यन्तः परं रूपं नमस्तस्मै महात्मने।। ८०।।

Salutation unto that Great Spirit, whose incarnate forms on earth the deities adore, being unable to behold his true form.

योन्तस्तिष्ठन्नशेषस्य पश्यतीशः शुभाशुभम्।।
तं सर्वसाक्षिणं विश्वं नमस्ये परमेश्वरम्।। ८१।।

Salutation unto that Great God Viṣṇu, the witness of all, who being present in all minds, beholds the good and evil of all.

नमोस्तु विष्णवे तस्मै यस्या भिन्नमिदं जगत्।।
ध्येयः स जगतामाद्यः स प्रसीदतु मेऽव्ययः।। ८२।।

Salutation unto that Viṣṇu, from whom this world is not distinct. May He, who is the object of the world's meditation, its beginning, and who is undecaying, be propitiated with me.

यत्रोतमेतत्प्रोतं च विश्वमक्षरमव्ययम्।।
आधारभूतः सर्वस्य स प्रसीदतु मे हरिः।। ८३।।

May that Hari have compassion upon me, who is the stay of all, in whom the universe is wapred and woven and who is imperishable and undecaying.

ॐ नमो विष्णवे तस्मै नमस्तस्मै पुनः पुनः।।
यत्र सर्वं यतः सर्वं यः सर्वं सर्वसंश्रयः।। ८४।।

Salutation again and again unto Viṣṇu, in who all things exist, from whom all things proceed and who is the supporter of all.

सर्वगत्वादनन्तस्य स एवाहमवस्थितः।।
मत्तः सर्वमहं सर्वं मयि सर्वं सनातने।। ८५।।

Salutation to him who also am I, and who is everywhere and through whom all things are from me. I am all things and all things are from me who am eternal.

अहमेवाक्षयो नित्यः परमात्मात्मसंश्रयः।।
ब्रह्मसंज्ञोऽहमेवाग्रे तथान्ते च परः पुमान्।। ८६।।

I am undecaying eternal, the asylum of the supreme spirit. Brahmā is my appellation that is at the beginning and end of all things."

।। इति श्रीविष्णुपुराणे प्रथमेंशे एकोनविंशतितमोऽध्यायः।। १९।।

अथ प्रथमेंशे: विंशोऽध्याय:
Part I : Section 20

श्रीपराशर उवाच

एवं संचिन्तयन्विष्णुमभेदेनात्मनो द्विज।।
तन्मयत्वमवाप्यग्र्यं मेने चात्मानमच्युतम्।। १।।

Parāśara said :—"O twice-born! Thus meditating upon Viṣṇu as identical with himself he attained to that unification, which is desired by all and regarded him as the undecaying divinity.

विसस्मार तथात्मानं नान्यत्किञ्चिदजानत्।।
अहमेवा व्ययोऽनन्तः परमात्मेत्यचिन्तयत्।। २।।

He forgot his individuality and was not conscious of anything. And he thought that he himself was the endless, undecaying supreme soul.

तस्य तद्भावनायोगात्क्षीणपापस्य वै क्रमात्।।
शुद्धेन्तःकरणे विष्णुस्तस्थौ ज्ञानमयोच्युतः।। ३।।

And on account of this efficient notion of identity, the undecaying Viṣṇu, whose essence is wisdom, appeared in his mind which was wholly purified from sin.

योगप्रभावात्प्रह्लादे जाते विष्णुमयेऽसुरे।।
चलत्युरगबन्धैस्तैर्मैत्रेय त्रुटितं क्षणात्।। ४।।

When the Asura Prahlāda had become indentified with Viṣṇu by virtue of contemplation all the bonds were at once severed, as soonas he shook.

भ्रान्तग्राहगणः सोर्मिर्ययौ क्षोभं महार्णवः।।
चचाल च मही सर्वा सशैलवनकानना।। ५।।

The mighty deep rose up in waves and the monsters therein were terrified. And the earth trembled with all her mountains and forests.

स च तं शैलसंघातं दैत्यैर्न्यस्तमथोपरि।।
उत्क्षिप्य तस्मात्सलिलान्निश्चक्राम महामतिः।। ६।।

And throwing aside the pile of rocks that were placed by the Daityas on his breast, the high-minded Prahlāda came out of waters.

दृष्ट्वा च स जगद्भूयो गगनाद्युपलक्षणम्।।
प्रह्लादोस्मीति सस्मार पुनरात्मानमात्मनि।। ७।।

And beholding the outer world, earth and heaven, he remembered who he was and knew himself to be Prahlāda.

तुष्टाव च पुनर्धीमाननादिं पुरुषोत्तमम्।।
एकाग्रमतिरव्यग्रो यतवाक्कायमानसः।। ८।।

And again the wise boy, with his mind solely devoted to him and controlling his mind and speech, sang the glory of that excellent Puruṣa who is without beginning.

प्रह्लाद उवाच

ॐ नमः परमार्थाय स्थूल सूक्ष्मक्षराक्षर।।
व्यक्ताव्यक्तकलातीत सकलेश निरञ्जन।। ९।।

Prahlāda said,—"Salutation unto thee who art the true wisdom, who art subtle and substantial, mutable and immutable, perceptible and unperceptible, who art with form and without it, indescribable and describable.

गुणाञ्जन गुणाधार निर्गुणात्मन् गुणस्थित।।
मूर्त्तामूर्तमहामूर्ते सूक्ष्ममूर्ते स्फुटास्फुट।। १०।।

करालसौम्यरूपात्मन्विद्याऽविद्यामयाच्युत।।
सदसद्रूपसद्भाव सदसद्भावभावन।। ११।।

नित्यानित्यप्रपञ्चात्मन्निष्प्रञ्चामलाश्रित।।
एकानेक नमस्तुभ्यं वासुदेवादिकारण।। १२।।

Thou art the asylum of all attributes; thou art without qualities and with them; thou art with shape and without it; thou art minute and vast; visible and invisible; thou art hideousness and beauty; O undecaying Hari! thou art wisdom and ignorance. Thou art cause and effect; existence and non-existence; thou dost comprise all that is good and evil; thou art the substance of all perishable and imperishable elements and the refuge of all undeveloped rudiments. Salutation unto thee who art both one and many, Vāsudeva and the first cause of all.

यः स्थूलसूक्ष्मः प्रकटः प्रकाशो यः सर्वभूतो न च सर्वभूतः।।
विश्वं यतश्चैतदविश्वहेतो नमोस्तु तस्मै पुरुषोत्तमाय।। १३।।

Salutation unto that excellent Puruṣa, who is both large and small, manifest and hidden, who is present in all beings and not, and from whom proceeds the universe although distinct from unviersal cause."

पराशर उवाच

तस्य तच्चेतसो देवः स्तुतिमित्थं प्रकुर्वतः।।
आविर्बभूव भगवान् पीताम्बरधरो हरिः।। १४।।

Parāśara said :—While with his mind thus devoted to Viṣṇu robes suddenly appeared before him.

ससम्भ्रमस्तमालोक्य समुत्थायाकुलाक्षरम्।।
नमोस्तु विष्णोवेत्येतद्व्याजहारासकृद्द्विज।। १५।।

Beholding him, he respectfully rose and with hestitating speech exclaimed repeatedly "Glory unto Viṣṇu" and said,—

प्रह्लाद उवाच

देव प्रपन्नार्त्तिहर प्रसादं कुरु केशव।।
अवलोकनदानेन भूयो मां पावयाच्युत।। १६।।

'O thou who removest the affliction of thy followers, O Keśava, do thou be propitious unto me. Do thou again purify me, O eternal god, with thy sight."

श्रीभगवानुवाच

कुर्वतस्ते प्रसन्नोऽहं भक्तिमव्यभिचारिणीम्।।
यथाभिलषितो मत्तः प्रह्लाद व्रीयतां वरः।। १७।।

The Deity replied,—"I am propitiated with thee for thy unshaken devotion unto me. Ask of me, Prahlāda, whatever thou wishest."

प्रह्लाद उवाच

नाथ योनि सहस्त्रेषु येषु येषु व्रजाम्यहम्।।
तेषु तेष्वच्युताभक्तिरच्युतास्तु सदा त्वयि।। १८।।

Prahlāda said,—"My faith in thee may never suffer decrease in all the thousand births through which I may be doomed to pass.

या प्रीतिरविवेकानां विषयेष्वनपायिनी।।
त्वामनुस्मरतः सा मे हृदयान्मापसर्पतु।। १९।।

May my devotion unto thee be as firm as the attachment cherished by the ignorant people towards all worldly objects."

श्रीभगवानुवाच

मयि भक्तिस्तवास्त्येव भूयोप्यवं भविष्यति।।
वरस्तु मत्तः प्रह्लाद व्रीयतां यस्तवेप्सितः।। २०।।

The Deity replied,—"Thou hast already devotion unto me—and it shall ever be the same; but do thou beg of me a boon, O Prahlāda, whatever thou wishest."

प्रह्लाद उवाच

मयि द्वेषानुबन्धोभूत्संस्तुतावुद्यते तव।।
मत्पितुस्तत्कृतं पापं देव यस्य प्रणश्यतु।। २१।।

Prahlāda said,—"My father has treated me malignantly for proclaiming thy praises. O lord, do thou remove the sin he hath thus committed.

शस्त्राणि पातितन्यंगे क्षिप्तो यच्चाग्निसंहतौ।।
दंशितश्चोरगैर्दत्त यद्विषं मम भोजने।। २२।।

बद्धा समुद्रे यत्क्षिप्तो यच्चितोऽस्मि शिलोच्चयैः।।
अन्यानि चाप्यसाधूनि यानि पित्रा कृतानि मे।। २३।।

He assailed me with weapons—he had me thrown into fire, bitten by the serpents, had poison mixed up with my viands, had me cast into the deep in bonds, and buried down with rocks and many other ills he had wrought against me out of malice for being devoted unto thee.

त्वयि भक्तिमतो द्वेषादघं तत्संभवं च यत्।।
त्वत्प्रसादात्प्रभो सद्यस्तेन मुच्यतु मे पिता।। २४।।

May my father, O lord, by thy mercy, be speedily relieved of the sin he hath thus committed."

श्रीभगवानुवाच

प्रह्लाद सर्वमेतत्ते मत्प्रसादाद्भविष्यति।।
अन्यच्च ते वरं दद्मि व्रीयतामसुरात्मज।। २५।।

The Deity replied,—Prahlāda, all this shall be accomplished by my mercy. I wish to confer upon thee another boon, O son of Asura, do thou beg it."

प्रह्लाद उवाच

कृतकृत्योस्मि भगवन्वरेणानेन यत्त्वयि।।
भवित्री त्वत्प्रसादेन भक्तिरव्यभिचारिणी।। २६।।

Prahlāda said,—"All my desires, O lord, have been fulfilled by the boon thou hast confered upon me, that my faith in thee mya never suffer derease.

धर्मार्थकामैः किं तस्य मुक्तिस्तस्य करे स्थिता।।
समस्तजगतां मूले यस्य भक्तिः स्थिरा त्वयि।। २७।।

What to speak of wealth, virtue or desire, even emancipation is in his hands who has firm devotion in thee, the root of the universal world."

श्रीभगवानुवाच

यथा ते निश्चलं चेतो मयि भक्तिसमन्वितम्।।
तथा त्वं मत्प्रसादेन निर्वाणम्परमाप्स्यसि।। २८।।

The Deity said,—"As unshaken is thy devotion unto me thou shalt by my mercy obtain final emancipation from existence."

श्रीपराशर उवाच

इत्युक्त्वन्तर्दधे विष्णुस्तस्य मैत्रेय पश्यतः।।
स चापि पुनरागम्य ववन्दे चरणौ पितुः।। २९।।

Parāśara said :—Having said this Viṣṇu disappeared from his sight, O Maitreya and Prahlāda again went to his father and bowed down before him.

तं पिता मूर्ध्न्युपाघ्राय परिष्वज्य च पीडितम्।।
जीवसीत्याह वत्सेति बाष्पार्द्रनयनो द्विज।। ३०।।

Having smelt his forehead, embraced him and shed tears, the father said, "Dost thou live my child?

प्रीतिमांश्चाऽभवत्तस्मिन्ननुतापी महासुरः।।
गुरुपित्रोश्चकारैवं शुश्रूषां सोपि धर्मवित्।। ३१।।

The Great Asura treated him with kindness and repented for his past actions. And Prahlāda conversánt with piety, attended diligently upon his father and preceptor.

पितर्युपरतिं नीते नरसिंह स्वरूपिणा।।
विष्णुना सोपि दैत्यानां मैत्रेयाभूत्पतिस्ततः।। ३२।।

After his father had been slain by Viṣṇu in the form of the man-lion, he became, O Maitreya, the sovereign of the Daityas.

ततो राज्यद्युतिं प्राप्य कर्मशुद्धिकरीं द्विज।।
पुत्रपौत्रांश्च सुबहूनवाप्यैश्वर्यमेव च।। ३३।।

And obtaining the splendours of royalty on account of piety, he came by immense wealth and was blessed with a numerous progeny.

क्षीणाधिकारः स यदा पुण्यपापविवर्जितः।।
तदा स भगवद्ध्यानात्परं निर्वाणमाप्तवान्!।। ३४।।

At the expiration of the regal power and freed from the consequences of moral merit or demerit, he obtained, by virtue of his meditation of the deity final emancipation from future births.

एवं प्रभावो दैत्योसौ मैत्रेयासीन्महामतिः।।
प्रह्लादो भगवद्भक्तो यं त्वं मामनुपृच्छसि।। ३५।।

So powerful was the wise Daitya Prahlāda devoted to Viṣṇu, O Maitreya, about whom you asked me.

यस्त्वेतच्चरितं तस्य प्रह्लादस्य महात्मनः।।
शृणोति तस्य पापानि सद्यो गच्छन्ति संक्षयम्।। ३६।।

Whoever listens to the story of Prahlāda, is speedily freed from all sins.

अहोरात्रकृतं पापं प्रह्लादचरितं नरः।।
शृण्वन् पठंश्च मैत्रेय व्यपोहति न संशयः।। ३७।।

Forsooth a man is released from the iniquities he commits day and night by once hearing or reading the history of Prahlāda.

पौर्णमास्याममावास्यामष्टम्यामथ वा पठन्।।
द्वादश्यां वा तदाप्नोति गोप्रदानफलं द्विज।। ३८।।

The reading of this history, on the day of full-mon, of new-moon or in the eighth and twelveth days of the lunar half month, shall offer fruit tantamount to the gift of a cow, O twice-born one.

प्रह्लादं सकलापत्सु यथा रक्षितवान्हरिः।।
तथा रक्षति यस्तस्य शृणोति चरितं सदा।। ३९।।

As Hari protected Prahlāda in all his calamities so he shall protect him who constantly listens to his history.

।। इति श्रीविष्णुपुराणे प्रथमेंशे विंशोऽध्यायः।। २०।।

अथ प्रथमेंशे: एकविंशोऽध्याय:

Part I : Section 21

श्रीपराशर उवाच

प्रह्लादपुत्र आयुष्माञ्छिबिर्बाष्कल एव च।।
विरोचनस्तु प्राह्लादर्बिलिर्जज्ञे विरोचनात्।। १।।
बले: पुत्रशतं त्वासीद्बाणज्येष्ठं महामुने।।

Parāśara said :—The sons of Prahlāda were Ayuṣmān Śivi and Vāṣkala. The son of Prahlāda were Ayuṣmān Śivi and Vāṣkala. The son of Prahlāda was named Virocana, whose son was Bali who had a hundred sons of whom Vāna was the eldest, O great Muni.

हिरण्याक्षसुताश्चासन्सर्व एव महाबला:।। २।।
झर्झर: शकुनिश्चैव भूतसन्तापनस्तथा।।
महानाभो महाबाहु: कालनाभस्तथापर:।। ३।।
अभवन्दनुपुत्राश्च द्विमूर्द्धा शंबरस्तथा।।
अयोमुख: शंकुशिरा: कपिल: शंकरस्तथा।। ४।।
एकचक्रो महाबाहुस्तारकश्च महाबल:।।
स्वर्भानुर्वृषपर्वा च पुलोम च महाबल:।। ५।।
एते दनो: सुता: ख्याता विप्रचित्तिश्च वीर्यवान्।। ६।।

All the sons of Hiraṇyākṣa were also gifted with great prowess—Jharjhara, Śakuni, Bhūtasantāpana, Mahānābha, Mahābāhu and Kālanābhan[1]. Danu had many sons—Dwimūrddha, Śaṅkara, Ayomukha, Śaṅku-śiras, Kapila, Śambara, Ekacakra, Mahābāhu, the mighty Tāraka, Swarbhānu, Vṛṣaparvan, Pulomon and the mighty Viprachitti : these the powerful and renowned sons Danu.

स्वर्भानोस्तु प्रभा कन्या शर्मिष्ठा वार्षपर्वणी।।
उपदानी हयशिरा: प्रख्याता वरकन्यका:।। ७।।

Swarbhānu had a daughter named Prabhā and Sarmiṣṭhā was the daughter of Vṛṣaparvan who had two other dauthers named Upadānavī and Hayaśirā.

वैश्वानरसुते चोभे पुलोमा कालका तथा।।
उभे सुते महाभागे मारीचेस्तु परिग्रह:।। ८।।

1. There is another reading which has been translated by Wilson. "The mighty-armed and Valiant Tāraka.

ताभ्यां पुत्रसहस्राणि षष्टिर्दानवसत्तमा:।।
पौलोमा: कालकेयाश्च मारीचतनया: स्मृता:।। ९।।
ततोऽपरेमहावीर्या दारुणा स्त्वतिनिर्घृणा:।।

The two daughters of Vaiśvānara were named Pulomā and Kālikā who were both married to Kaśyapa and bore him sixty thousand celebrated Dānavas called Paulomas and Ḳālakañjas, who were mighty, dreadful and cruel.

सिंहिकायामथोतपन्ना विप्रचित्ते: सुतास्तथा।। १०।।
त्र्यंश: शल्यश्च बलवान् नभश्चैव महाबल:।।
वातापी नमुचिश्चैव इल्वल: खसृमस्तथा।। ११।।
अन्धको नरकश्चैव कालनाभस्तथैव च।।
स्वर्भानुश्च महावीर्यो वक्त्रयोधी महासुर:।। १२।।

Viprachitti begot on Siṁhikā several sons named—Vyānśa, Śalya the strong, Nābha the powerful, Vātāpi, Namuci, Ilvala, Khaśrima, Añjaka, Naraka, Kālanābha, the Valiant, Svarbhānu and the mighty Vaktrayodhi.

एते वै दानवा: श्रेष्ठा दनुवंशविवर्द्धना:।।
एतेषां पुत्रपौत्राश्च शतोशोऽथ सहस्रश:।। १३।।

These were the most eminent Dānavas who multiplied the race of Danu. Their children and grand children were by hundreds and thousands.

प्रह्लादस्य तु दैत्यस्य निवात कवचा: कुले।।
समुत्पन्ना: सुमहता तपसा भावितात्मन:।। १४।।

In the family of the Daitya Prahlāda, the Nivāta Kavacas were born, who were greatly purified by rigid austerities.

षट् सुता: सुमहासत्त्वास्ताम्राया: परिकीर्त्तिता:।।
शुकी श्येनी च भासी च सुग्रीवी शुचिगृद्ध्रका।। १५।।

Six daughters, gifted with great energy were born to, Tāmra—named Śukī, Śyenī, Bhāsī, Sugrīvī, Śucī, and Gṛdhṛkā.

शुकी शुकानजनयदुलूकप्रत्युलूकिकान्।।
श्येनी श्येनांस्तथा भासी भासान्गृद्धांश्च गृद्ध्रयपि।। १६।।

शुच्यौदकान्पक्षिगणान्सुग्रीवी तु व्यजायत।।
अश्वानुष्ट्रान्गर्दभांश्च ताम्रावंशः प्रकीर्त्तितः।। १७।।

Śukī gave birth to parrots, owls, and crows, Śyenī to hawks, Bhāsī to kites; Gṛdhrika to vultures, Śucī to water-fowl; Sugrīvī to horses, camels and asses. These were the offsprings of Tāmra.

विनतायास्तु द्वौ पुत्रौ विरतौ गरुडारुणौ।।
सुपर्णः पततां श्रेष्ठो दारुणः पन्नगाशनः।। १८।।

Vānati had two well-known sons, named Garuḍa and Varuṇa; the former also called Suparṇa was the lord of the feathered tribes and the dreadful enemy of the serpents.

सुरसायां सहस्त्रं तु सर्पाणाममितौजसाम्।।
अनेकशिरसां ब्रह्मन् खेचराणां महात्मनाम्।। १९।।

The offsprings of Śurasā were a thousand powerful many-headed serpents coursing the welkin.

काद्रवेयास्तु बलिनः सहस्त्रममितौजसः।।
सुपर्णवशगा ब्रह्मन् जज्ञिरे नैकमस्तकाः।। २०।।

Kadrū had also a thousand powerful sons of unmitigated prowess—all subject to Garuḍa and many-headed.

तेषां प्रधानभूतास्तु शेषवासुकितक्षकाः।।
शंखश्वेतो महापद्मः कम्बलाश्वतरौ तथा।। २१।।
एलापुत्रस्तथा नागः कर्कोटकधनञ्जयौ।।
एते चान्ये च बहवो दन्दशूका विषोल्बणाः।। २२।।
गणं क्रोणवशं विद्धि तस्याः सर्वे च दंष्ट्रिणः।।
स्थलजाः पक्षिणोब्जाश्च दारुणाः पिशिताशनाः।। २३।।

The most celebrated amongst them were, Śeṣa, Vāsuki, Takṣaka, Śaṅkha, Sweta, Mahāpadma, Kambala, Aśvatara, Elapatra, Nāga, Karkkoṭa, Dhanañjaya, and many other deadly and poisonous serpents.

क्रोधात्तु पिशाचांश्च जनयामास महाबलान्।।
गास्तु वै जनयामास सुरभीर्महिषीस्तथा।। २४।।

Krodas gave birth to highly powerful monsters and Śūravī gave birth to cows and buffaloes.

इरावृक्षलतावल्लीस्तृणजातीश्च सर्वशः।। २४।।
स्वसा तु यक्षरक्षांसि मुनिरप्सरसस्तथा।।
अरिष्टा तु महासत्त्वान् गन्धर्वान्समजीजनत्।।२५।।

Irā was the mother of trees an creeping plants and shrubs and every kind of grass : Khāsa of the Rākṣasas and Yakṣas : Muni of Apsarās and Arṣṭha of the celebrated Gandharvas.

एते कश्यपदायादाः कीर्त्तिताः स्थाणुजङ्गमाः।।
तेषां पुत्राश्च पौत्राश्च शतशोथ सहस्त्रशः।। २६।।

These were the offsprings of Kāśyapa whether moveable or stationary; their children and grand children multiplied by hundreds and thousands.

एष मन्वन्तरे सर्गो ब्रह्मन्स्वरोचिषे स्मृतः।। २७।।

Such was the creation, O Brahmā in the Svarocisa (or the second) Manvantara.

वैवस्वते च महति वारुणे वितते कृतौ।।
जुह्वानस्य ब्रह्मणो वै प्रजासर्ग इहोच्यते।। २८।।

In the present or Vaisvaswata Manvantara Brahmā being engaged in sacrifices undertaken by Varuṇa I shall describe to you the manner in which in which the progeny multiplied.

पूर्वं यत्र तु सप्तर्षीनुत्पन्नान्सप्तमानसान्।।
पुत्रत्वे कल्पयामास स्वयमेव पितामहः।।

The great Patriarch begot as his sons the seven Ṛṣis, who were in the days of yore, engendered by his mind.

गन्धर्वभोगिदेवानां दानवानां च सत्तम।। २९।।

दितिर्विनष्टपुत्रा वै तोषयामास काश्यपम्।।
तया चाराधितःसम्यक्काश्यपस्तपतां वरः।। ३०।।
वरेण च्छन्दयामास सा च वव्रे ततो वरम्।।
पुत्रमिन्द्रवधार्थाय समर्थममितौजसम्।। ३१।।

O best of ascetics, when there was a quarrel amongst the Gandharvas, serpents, Dānavas and gods, Diti, having lost all her children, propitiated Kāśyapa. Being perfectly adored by her, Kāśyapa, the foremost of the ascetics, promised her a boon and Diti prayed for it in th shape of a valiant son capable of destroying Indra.

स च तस्मै वरं प्रादाद्भार्यायै मुनिसत्तमः।।
दत्त्वा च वरमत्युग्रं कश्यपस्तामुवाच ह।। ३२।।

O excellent Muni, he granted his spouse that boon. And having granted her that boon Kaśyapa said—

शक्रं पुत्रो निहन्ता ते यदि गर्भं शरच्छतम्।।
समाहितातिप्रयता शौचिनी धारयिष्यसि।। ३३।।

"You shall give birth to a son who shall destroy Śakra, if with pious thoughts and a pure body, you carry the babe in your womb for a hundred years."

इत्येवमुक्त्वा तां देवीं संगतः कश्यपो मुनिः।।
दधार सा च तं गर्भं सम्यक्छौचसमन्विता।। ३४।।

Having said this the ascetic Kaśyapa remained with her and she conceived being perfectly pure.

गर्भमात्मवधार्थाय ज्ञात्वा तं मघवानपि।।
शुश्रूषुस्तामथागच्छद्विनयादमराधिपः।। ३५।।

Knowing that this conception was for its own destruction, Indra the lord of immortals, came to her and attended upon her with humility.

तस्याश्चैवान्तरप्रेप्सुरतिष्ठत्पाकशासनः ।।
ऊने वर्षशते चास्या ददर्शान्तरमात्मना।। ३६।।
अकृत्वा पादयोः शौचं दितिः शयनमाविशत्।।

And the slayer of Pāka wanted there to thwart her intention. At last in the last year of the century he found out an opportunity. Diti, without washing her feet, went to bed.

निद्रां चाहारयामास तस्याः कुक्षिं प्रविश्य सः।। ३७।।

वज्रपाणिर्महागर्भं चिच्छेदाथ स सप्तधा।।
सम्पीड्यमानो वज्रेण स रुरोदातिदारुणम्।। ३८।।
मा रोदीरिति तं शक्रः पुनः पुनरभाषत।।

And when she was asleep the wielder of the thunder-bolt entered into her womb and severed the embryo into seven pieces. The child, thus severed, cried out bitterly in the womb but Śakra again and again said "Do not cry."

सोऽभवत्सप्तधा गर्भस्तमिंद्रः कुपितः पुनः।। ३९।।

एकैकं सप्तधा चक्रे वज्रेणारिविदारिणा।।
मरुतो नाम देवास्ते बभूवुरतिवेगिनः।। ४०।।

The embryo was thus cut into seven portions, and Indra, wroth again, cut each portion into seven pieces with his thunder-bolt. From these originated the swift-coursing deities called Maruts (winds).

यदुक्तं वै भगवता तेनैव मरुतोऽभवन्।।
देवा एकोनपञ्चाशत्सहाया वज्रपाणिनः।। ४१।।

They got this name from the words with which Indra had addressed the embryo (Ma—rooda—do not cry) and became forty-nine divinities, the assistants of the wielder of the thunder bolt.

।। इति श्रीविष्णुपुराणे प्रथमेंशे एकविंशोऽध्यायः।। २१।।

अथ प्रथमेंशेः द्वाविंशोऽध्यायः

Part I : Section 22

श्रीपराशर उवाच

यदाभिषिक्तः स पृथुः पूर्वं राज्ये महर्षिभिः।।
ततः क्रमेण राज्यानि ददौ लोकपितामहः।। १।।

Parāśara said :—When Pṛthu was installed on the throne by the great Ṛṣis the great Patriarch by and by conferred kingdoms upon other kings.

नक्षत्रग्रहविप्राणां वीरुधां चाप्यशेषतः।।
सोमं राज्ये दधद्ब्रह्मा यज्ञानां तपसामपि।। २।।

He bestowed upon the moon the sovereignty of stars, plantes, twice-born ones, grass, creeping plants sacrifices and penances.

राज्ञां वैश्रवणं राज्ये जलानां वरुणं तथा।।
आदित्यानां पतिं विष्णुं वसूनामथ पावकम्।। ३।।

Vaiśravaṇa was made king over kings, and Varuṇa was made lord of waters. Viṣṇu was made the king of Ādityas and Pāvaka of Vasus.

प्रजापतीनां दक्षं तु वासवं मरुतामपि।।
दैत्यानां दानवानां च प्रह्लादमधिपं ददौ।। ४।।

Dakṣa was made the lord of Patriarchs and Vāsava of Maruts. And he conferred the sovereignty of Daityas and Dānavas upon Prahlāda.

पितृणां धर्मराजानं यमं राज्येऽभ्यषेचयत्।।
ऐरावतं गजेंद्राणामशेषाणां पतिं ददौ।। ५।।

And Yama, the king of justice, was made the king of the manes (Pitṛs). Airāvata was made the king of many elephants.

पतत्रिणां तु गुरुडं देवानामपि वासवम्।।
उच्चैःश्रवसमश्वानां वृषभं तु गवामपि।। ६।।

Garuḍa of birds, Vāsava of the celestials. Ucaiśravas was made the king of horses and Vṛṣabha of kine.

मृगाणां चैव सर्वेषां राज्ये सिंहं ददौ प्रभुः।।
शेषं तु दन्दशूकानामकरोत्पतिमव्ययः।। ७।।

Śeṣa became the king of serpents, the lion, the monarch of the beasts and the holy fig-tree the king of the trees.

हिमालयं स्थावरणां मुनीनां कपिलं मुनिम्।।
नखिनां दंष्ट्रिणां चैव मृगाणां व्याघ्रमीश्वरम्।। ८।।

वनस्पतीनां राजानं प्लक्षमेवाभ्यषेचयत्।।
एवमेवान्यजातीनां प्राधान्येनाकरोत्प्रभून।। ९।।

एवं विभज्य राज्यानि दिशां पालाननन्तरम्।।
प्रजापतिपतिर्ब्रह्मा स्थापयामास सर्वतः।। १०।।
पूर्वस्यां दिशि राजानं वैराजस्य प्रजापतेः।।
दिशापालं सुधन्वानं सुतं वै सोऽभ्यषेचयत्।। ११।।

दक्षिणस्यां दिशि तथा कर्दमस्य प्रजापतेः।।
पुत्रं शंखपदं नाम राजानं सोऽभ्यषेचयत्।। १२।।

पश्चिमस्यां दिशि तथा रजसः पुत्रमच्युतम्।।
केतुमन्तं महात्मानं राजानं सोऽभ्यषेचयत्।। १३।।

तथा हिरण्यरोमाणं पर्जन्यस्य प्रजापतेः।।
उदीच्यां दिशि दुर्द्धर्षं राजानमभ्यषेचयत्।। १४।।

Having thus divided the kingdom the great Patriarch Brahmā appointed divinities to protect the different quarters: he made Sudhanwan, the son of the patriarch Virāja, the protector of the east; Śaṅkhapāda, the son of the patriarch Kardama, of the south; the immortal Ketumat, the son of Rajas, protector of the west and Hiraṇyaroman the son of the patriarch Parjanya, protector of the north.

तैरियं पृथिवी सर्वा सप्तद्वीपा सपत्तना।।
यथाप्रदेशमद्यापि धर्मतः परिपाल्यते।। १५।।

By these the whole earth, with its even islands and cities, was righteously governed, each confining himself to his own limit.

एते सर्वे प्रवृत्तस्य स्थितौ विष्णोर्महात्मनः।।
विभूतिभूता राजानो ये चान्ये मुनिसत्तम।। १६।।

All these and others appointed to govern the creation are but portions of the Great Viṣṇu, O foremost of Munis.

ये भविष्यन्ति ये भूताः सर्वे भूतेश्वरा द्विज।।
ते सर्वे सर्वभूतस्य विष्णोरंशा द्विजोत्तम।। १७।।

All the kings who have been and who shall be, O foremost of twice-born ones, are the portions of Viṣṇu.

ये तु देवाधिपतयो ये च दैत्याधिपास्तथा।।
दानवानां च ये नाथा ये नाथाः पिशिताशिनाम्।। १८।।

पशूनां ये च पतयः पतयो ये च पक्षिणाम्।।
मनुष्याणां च सर्पाणां नागानामधिपाश्च ये।। १९।।

वृक्षाणां पर्वतानां च ग्रहाणां चापि येऽधिपाः।।
अतीता वर्त्तमानाश्च ये भविष्यन्ति चापरे।।
ते सर्वे सर्वभूतस्य विष्णोरंशसमुद्भवाः।। २०।।

The lords of celestials, the kings of the Daityas, the sovereigns of the Dānavas, the rulers of the demons, the kings of the beasts, birds, men, serpents, Nāgas, the best of trees, of mountains, of planets—those that were, those that are, and those that shall be, are but portions of Viṣṇu who is identical with the universe.

न हि पालनसामर्थ्यमृते सर्वेश्वरं हरिम्।।
स्थितं स्थितौ महाप्राज्ञ भवत्यन्यस्य कस्यचित्।। २१।।

None else is capable of protecting the world, but Hari, the lord of all. O greatly wise ascetic, the essence of the universal creation exists in him and none else.

सृजत्येष जगत्सृष्टौ स्थितौ पाति सनातनः।।
हन्ति चैवान्तकत्वेन रजःसत्त्वादिसंश्रयः।। २२।।

The eternal Viṣṇu invested respectively with the qualities of foulness, goodness, and darkness, creates the universe, preserves it and destroys it.

चतुर्विभागः संसृष्टौ चतुर्धा संस्थितः स्थितौ।।
प्रलयं च करोत्यन्ते चतुर्भेदो जनार्दनः।। २३।।

By a four-fold manifestation of himself he creates the world and in the same way preserves and destroys it.

एकेनांशेन ब्रह्मासौ भवत्यव्यक्तमूर्त्तिमान्।।
मरीचिमिश्राः पतयः प्रजानां चान्यभागशः।। २४।।

कालस्तृतीयस्तस्यांशः सर्वभूतानि चापरः।।
इत्थं चतुर्द्धा संसृष्टौ वर्त्ततेसौ रजोगुणः।। २५।।

In one manifestation as Brahmā, the inivisbile (Viṣṇu) assumes a visible shape; in his second manifestation he appears as the patriarch Marīci and others; Kāla is the third manifestation and all other beings constitute his fourth manifestation. Thus he becomes four-fold in his creation invested with the quality of goodness.

एकांशेनास्थितो विष्णुः करोति प्रतिपालनम्।।
मन्वादिरूपश्चान्येन कालरूपोऽपरेण च।। २६।।

The Deity in one portion as Viṣṇu, preserves the creation; in his second portion he assumes the shape of Manu and others; in his third portion he assumes the sahpe of time, and in his fourth portion he assumes the shape of all beings.

सर्वभूतेषु चान्येन संस्थितः कुरुते स्थितिम्।।
सत्त्वं गुणं समाश्रित्य जगतः पुरुषोत्तमः।। २७।।

And thus invested with the quality of goodness, the excellent Puruṣa preserves the universe.

आश्रित्य तमसो वृत्तिमन्तकाले तथा पुनः।।
रुद्रस्वरूपो भगवानेकांशेन भवत्यजः।। २८।।

And invested with the quality of darkness at the end of creation the un-born Deity, in one portion, assumes the form of Rudra.

अग्न्यन्तकादिरूपेण भागेनान्येन वर्त्तते।।
कालस्वरूपो भागो यस्सर्वभूतानि चापरः।। २९।।

In another portion he assumes the shape of fire—in another he assumes the shape of time, and in his fourth portion he assumes the shape of all beings.

विनाशं कुर्वतस्तस्य चतुर्द्धैवं महात्मनः।।
विभागकल्पना ब्रह्मन् कथ्यते सार्वकालिकी।। ३०।।

And thus in his four-fold form he is the destroyer of the universe. This is the four-fold division of the Deity, O Brāhmaṇa, at all seasons.

ब्रह्मा दक्षादयः कालस्तथैवाखिलजन्तवः।।
विभूतयो हरेरेता जगतः सृष्टिहेतवः।। ३१।।

Brahmā, Dakṣa, time and all beings, are the energies of the Great Hari, which are the causes of creation.

विष्णुर्मन्वादयः कालः सर्वभूतानि च द्विज।।
स्थितेर्निमित्तभूतस्य विष्णो रेता विभूतयः।। ३२।।

Viṣṇu, Manu, time and all beings are energies, O twice-born one, of Viṣṇu, which are causes of preservation.

रुद्रः कालान्तकाद्याश्च समस्ताश्चैव जन्तवः।।
चतुर्धा प्रलयायैता जनार्दनविभूतयः।। ३३।।

Rudra, Āntaka, time and all other creatures are the energies of Janārdana that are intended for universal dissolution.

जगदादौ तथा मध्ये सृष्टिराप्रलया द्विज।।
धात्रा मरीचिमिश्रैश्च क्रियते जन्तुभिस्तथा।। ३४।।

In the beginning of the creation, till the hour of dissolution, Brahmā, the patriarchs and all other animals, are engaged with the work of creation.

ब्रह्मा सृजत्यादिकाले मरीचिप्रमुखास्ततः।।
उत्पादयन्त्यपत्यानि जन्तवश्च प्रतिक्षणम्।। ३५।।

At first Brahmā created the universe, then Marīci and others were engaged in multiplying the race and then the other animals multiply it every moment.

कालेन न विना ब्रह्मा सृष्टिनिष्पादको द्विज।।
न प्रजापतयः सर्वे न चैवाऽखिलजन्तवः।। ३६।।

O twice-born one, Brahmā cannot create the universe unless the proper time comes, and Marīci and other partriarchs as well as other animals, independent of time, cannot help the creation.

एवमेव विभागोयं स्थितावप्युपदिश्यति।।
चतुर्धा तस्य देवस्य मैत्रेय प्रलये तथा।। ३७।।

Thus at the time of creation as well as that of dissolution the four-fold divisions of the Great Deity are equally essential, O Maitreya.

यत्किञ्चित्सृज्यते येन सत्त्वजातेन वै द्विज।।
तस्य सृज्यस्य सम्भूतौ तत्सर्वं वै हरेस्तनुः।। ३८।।

Whatever is generated by any living being, O twice-born one—the agenet is considered as a portion of Hari.

हंति यावच्च यत्किञ्चित्सत्त्वं स्थावरजङ्गमम्।।
जनार्दनस्य तद्रौद्रं मैत्रेयान्तकरं वपुः।। ३९।।

And whatever destroys and living being, moveable or immoveable, is cosidered as the destroying portion of Janārdana as Rudra.

एवमेष जगत्स्नष्टा जगत्पाता तथा जगत्।।
जगद्भक्षयिता देवः समस्तस्य जनार्दनः।। ४०।।

In this wise Janārdana is the creator, preserver and destroyer of the universe.

सृष्टिस्थित्यन्तकालेषु त्रिधैवं संप्रवर्तते।।
गुणप्रवृत्या परमं पदं तस्यागुणं महत्।। ४१।।

And assuming three qualities he is three-fold—in creation, preservation and destruction—but his true form is void of these qualities.

तच्च ज्ञानमयं व्यापि स्वसंवेद्यमनौपमम्।।
चतुष्प्रकारं तदपि स्वरूपं परमात्मनः।। ४२।।

And the four-fold manifestation of the Deity comprises true wisdom, pervades the universe, and does not admit of any similitude.

श्रीमैत्रेय उवाच

चतुःप्रकारतां तस्य ब्रह्मभूतस्य हे मुने।।
ममाचक्ष्व यथान्यायं यदुक्तं परमं पदम्।। ४३।।

Maitreya said :—"Describe to me, in sooth, O Muni, how could the supreme condition of the Deity admit of four varieties?"

श्रीपराशर उवाच

मैत्रेय कारणं प्रोक्तं साधनं सर्ववस्तुषु।।
साध्यं च वस्त्वभिमतं यत्साधयितुमात्मनः।। ४४।।

Parāśara said :—O Maitreya, that which is called the cause of a thing is the means of accomplishing it; and what is the desire of the soul to accomplish is the thing accomplished.

योगिनो मुक्तिकामस्य प्राणायामादिसाधनम्।।
साध्यं च परमं ब्रह्म पुनर्नावर्त्तते यतः।। ४५।।

The suspension of breath and the like operations, of the Yogī who is intent upon obtaining final emancipation, are his means and the end is the supreme Brahmā from whom he does not return to the world.

साधनालम्बनं ज्ञानं मुक्तये योगिनां हि यत्।।
स भेदः प्रथमस्तस्य ब्रह्मभूतस्य वै मुने।। ४६।।

O Muni, the means, adopted for liberation by the ascetic, is the discriminative knowledge and this is the first variety of the condition of Brahmā.

यूञ्जतः क्लेशमुक्तयर्थं साध्यं यद्ब्रह्म योगिनः।।
तदालम्बनविज्ञानं द्वितीयोंशो महामुने।। ४७।।

O great Muni, the second portion is the knowledge that is to be obtained by the ascetics for liberation from suffering.

उभयोस्त्वविभागेन साध्यसाधनयोर्हि यत्।।
विज्ञानमद्वैतमयं तद्भगोभान्यो मयोदितः।। ४८।।

By the third sort, they arrive at the knowledge of the identity of the end and the means and the rejection of the idea of duality.

ज्ञानत्रयस्य वै तस्य विशेषो यो महामुने।।
तन्निराकरणद्वारा दर्शितात्मस्वरूपवत्।। ४९।।

निर्व्यापारमनाख्येयं व्याप्तिमात्रमनूपमम्।।
आत्मसम्बोधविषयं सत्तामात्रमलक्षणम्।। ५०।।

प्रशान्तमभयं शुद्धं दुर्द्धवभाव्यमसंश्रयम्।।
विष्णो र्ज्ञानमयस्योक्तं तज्ज्ञानं ब्रह्मसंज्ञितम्।। ५१।।

The last sort is the removal of whatever differences may have been formed regarding the three first varieties of knowledge and the necessary contemplation of the true essence of soul. The highest condition Viṣṇu, who is identical with wisdom, is the knowledge of the truth. This knowledge requires no exercise, is not to be taught, is spread all over, admitṣ of no exercise, is not to be taught, is spread all over, admits of no comparison with anything, which does not require any other thing to explain it, which is itself existent and does not require any explanation, which is calm, fearless and pure, which is not the subject of reasoning and does not require any support. And this knowledge is the excellent condition of Viṣṇu.

तत्र ज्ञाननिरोधेन योगिनो यान्ति ये लयम्।।
संसारकर्षणोप्तौ ते यान्ति निर्बीजतां द्विज।। ५२।।

O twice-born one, these ascetics, who, by the destruction of ignorance, emerge themselves in this knowledge of Brahmā, lose the semenial property and do not germinate in the field of worldly existence.[1]

एवंप्रकारममलं नित्यं व्यापकमक्षयम्।।
समस्तहेयरहितं विष्णवाख्यं परमं पदम्।। ५३।।

That which is the excellent condition of Viṣṇu is pure, eternal, universal, undecaying and uniform.

तद्ब्रह्म परमं योगी यतो नावर्त्तते पुनः।।
श्रयत्यपुण्योपरमे क्षीणक्लेशेऽतिनिर्मले।। ५४।।

And the ascetic who obtains this supreme condition of Brahmā is not required to be born again, for he is freed from the distinction of virtue and vice and suffering.

द्वे रूपे ब्रह्मणस्तस्य मूर्त्तं चामूर्तमेव च।।
क्षराक्षरस्वरूपे ते सर्वभूतेष्ववस्थिते।। ५५।।

There are two states of Brahmā—one with shape and the other without it—one perishable and the other imperishable.

अक्षरं तत्परं ब्रह्म क्षरं सर्वमिदं जगत्।।
एकदेशस्थितस्याग्नेर्ज्योत्स्ना विस्तारिणी यथा।।
परस्य ब्रह्मणः शक्तिस्तथेदमखिलं जगत्।। ५६।।

These two states and manifest everywhere. As the blaze of fire, at one place, spreads light and heat all around so this vast universe is nothing but the manifestation of the energy of the undecaying and eternal Brahmā.

तत्राप्यासन्नदूरत्वाद्बहुत्वस्वल्पतामयः।।
ज्योत्स्नाभेदोस्ति तच्छक्तेस्तद्वन्मैत्रेय विद्यते।। ५७।।

And as the light and heat are stronger or feebler proportionate to the distance of the spot, so the energy of Brahmā is more or less manifest in beings as they are more or less remote from him.

ब्रह्मविष्णुशिवा ब्रह्मन्प्रधाना ब्रह्मशक्तयः।।
ततश्च देवा मैत्रेय न्यूना दक्षादयस्ततः।। ५८।।

O Brāhmaṇ, Brahmā, Viṣṇu and Śiva are the most powerful energies of Brahmā : next to them, O Maitreya, are the inferior celestials—

ततो मनुष्याः पशवो मृगपक्षिसरीसृपाः।।
न्यूनान्यूनतराश्चैव वृक्षगुल्मादयस्तथा।। ५९।।

Next to them, men, beasts, birds and serpents and then the trees and plants each growing feebler proportionate to their distance from the Supreme God.

तदेतदक्षरं नित्यं जगन्मुनिवराखिलम्।।
आविर्भावतिरोभावजन्मनाशविकल्पवत्।। ६०।।

In this way, the world, although eternal and indestructable, appears and disappears as if being subject to birth and death.

सर्वशक्ति मयो विष्णुः स्वरूपं ब्रह्मणः परम्।।
मूर्त्तं यद्योगिभिः पूर्वं योगारम्भेषु चिन्त्यते।। ६१।।

1. i.e., Those who obtain this highest knowledge regarding the condition of Brahmā are freed future births i.e. they are not required any more to go through the cycle of births.

The all-powerful Viṣṇu is but the manifestation of Brahmā. He being invested with form, the *Yogīs* worship him at the very commencement.

सालम्बनो महायोगः सबीजो यत्र संस्थितः।।
मनस्यव्याहते सम्यग्युञ्जतां जायते मुने।। ६२।।

And the great ascetics, with their minds unagitated, in whose minds exists great spirit of devotion with the object to be meditated upon and along with the means for effecting it, endeavour to bring about mystic union with him.

स परः परशक्तीनां ब्रह्मणः समनन्तरम्।।
मूर्त्तं ब्रह्म महाभाग सर्वब्रह्ममयो हरिः।। ६३।।

O great Muni, Hari is the most powerful of all the energies of Brahmā, because he is the most immediate. And he is an embodiment of Brahmā because he is composed entirely of his essence.

यत्र सर्वमिदं प्रोतमोतं चैवाखिलं जगत्।।
ततो जगज्जगत्यस्मिन्स जगच्चाखिलं मुने।। ६४।।

In him the whole universe is interwoven—from him and in him is the universe, O Muni.

क्षराक्षरमयो विष्णुर्बिभर्त्त्यखिलमीश्वरः।।
पुरुषाव्याकृतमयं भूषणास्त्रस्वरूपवत्।। ६५।।

Viṣṇu, the lord of the universe containing all that is destructable and indestructable, holds the creation material and spiritual with his ornaments and weapons."

श्रीमैत्रेय उवाच

भूषणास्त्रस्वरूपस्थं यच्चैतदखिलं जगत्।।
बिभर्त्ति भगवान्विष्णु स्तन्ममाख्यातुमर्हसि।। ६६।।

Maitreya said :—Do thou relate to me how does the great God Viṣṇu hold the universe with his ornaments and weapons.

श्रीपराशर उवाच

नमस्कृत्वाप्रमेयाय विष्णवे प्रभविष्णवे।।
कथयामि यथाख्यातं वसिष्ठेन ममा भवत्।। ६७।।

Parāśara said :—Having bowed down unto the mighty and indescribable Viṣṇu I shall relate to you what was formerly described by Vasiṣṭha.

आत्मानमस्य जगतो निर्लेपमगुणामलम्।।
बिभर्त्ति कौस्तुभमणिस्वरूपं भगवान्हरिः।। ६८।।

The Great Hari holds the pure soul of the world uncontaminated and divested of qualities like the Kaustava gem.

श्रीवत्ससंस्थानधर मनन्ते न समाश्रितम्।।
प्रधानं बुद्धिरप्यास्ते गदारूपेण माधवे।। ६९।।

The undecaying holds *Prakṛti* as Śrīvatsa mark and intellect exists in Mādhava in the shape of his mace.

भूतादिमिंद्रियादिं च द्विधाहङ्कारमीश्वरः।।
बिभद्धत्त शंखरूपेण शार्ङ्गरूपेण च स्थितम्।। ७०।।

The lord holds the two-folded divisions of egotism namely into elements and organs of sense in the shape of his conch-shell and bow.

चलत्स्वरूपमत्यन्तं जवेनान्तारितानिलम्।।
चक्रस्वरूपं च मनो धत्ते विष्णुकरे स्थितम्।। ७१।।

He holds in his hand, in the shape of discus, mind which is the strength of all and excels wind in its flight.

पञ्चरूपा तु या माला वैजयन्ती गदाभृतः।।
सा भूतहेतुसंघाता भूतमाला च वै द्विज।। ७२।।

The necklace, of the holder of mace, namely Vaijayantī, contains five precious gems (pearl, ruby, emerald, sapphire and diamond) being the emblems of the five elemental rudiments.

यानीन्द्रियाण्यशेषाणि बुद्धिकर्मात्मकानि वै।।
शररूपाण्यशेषाणि तानि धत्ते जनार्द्दनः।। ७३।।

Janārdana holds the faculties of action and preception in the shape of numerous shafts.

बिभर्त्ति यच्चासिरत्लमच्युतोत्यन्तनिर्मलम्।।
विद्यामय तु तज्ज्ञानमविद्या कोशसंस्थितम्।। ७४।।

The holy wisdom is the bright sword of Acyuta concealed sometimes in the scabbard of ignorance.

इत्थं पुमान्प्रधानं च बुद्ध्यहङ्कारमेव च।।
भूतानि च हृषीकेशे मनः सर्वेन्द्रियाणि च।।
विद्याविद्ये च मैत्रेय सर्वमेतत्समाश्रितम्।। ७५।।

In this wise, O Maitreya, Hṛṣikeśa is the refuge of soul, nature, intellect, egotism, the elements, the senses, mind, ignorance and wisdom.

अस्त्रभूषणमसंस्थानस्वरूपं रूपवर्जितः।।
बिभर्त्ति मायारूपोसौ श्रेयसे प्राणिनां हरिः।। ७६।।

And although Hari is without any shape, yet, he, for the behoof of mankind, in his dillusive form, embodies the elements of the world as his weapons and ornaments.

सविकारं प्रधानं च पुमांश्चैवाखिलं जगत्।।
बिभर्त्ति पुण्डरीकाक्षस्तदेवं परमेश्वरः।। ७७।।

Then the lotus-eyed deity, the lord of the universe, holds the nature and the universe.

या विद्या या तथाविद्या यत्सद्यच्चासदव्ययम्।।
तत्सर्वं सर्वभूतेशे मैत्रेय मधुसूदने।। ७८।।

O Maitreya, true wisdom, ignorance, all that is transient, all that is everlasting, exist in the slayer of Madhu, the lord of all creatures.

कलाकाष्ठानिमेषादिदिनर्त्वयनहायनैः।।
कालस्वरूपो भगवानपापो हरिरव्ययः।। ७९।।

The time with its division of seconds, minutes, days, months, seasons, and years, is but the manifestation of the Great Hari.

भूर्लोकोथक भुवर्लोकस्वर्लोको मुनिसत्तम।।
महर्जनस्तपः सत्यं सप्त लोका इमे विभुः।। ८०।।

O Great Muni, the seven worlds, the earth, the sky, the heaven, the world of Patriarchs, of sages, of saints, of truth are but diverse manifestations of his.

लोकात्ममूर्त्तिः सर्वेषां पूर्वेषामपि पूर्वजः।।
आधारः सर्वविद्यानां स्वयमेव हरिः स्थितः।। ८१।।

His form is the whole universe; he is first born before all the first-born. He is the refuge of all being; he is himself self-sustained; his various forms are celestials, men and animals.

देवमानुषपश्वादिस्वरूपैर्बहुभिः स्थितः।।
ततः सर्वेश्वरोऽनन्तो भूतमूर्त्तिरमूर्त्तिमान्।। ८२।।

Therefore he is the supreme lord of all; eternal; he has a visible shape and is without it.

ऋचो यजूंषि सामानि तथैवाथर्वणानि वै।।
इतिहासोपवेदाश्च वेदान्तेषु तथोक्तयः।। ८३।।

He is known in the Vedānta as the Ṛc, Yajuṣ, Sāma and and Atharva Vedas, history and sacred science.

वेदांगानि समस्तानि मन्वा दिगदितानि च।।
शास्त्राण्यशेषाण्याख्यानान्यनुवाकाश्च ये क्वचित्।। ८४।।
काव्यालापाश्च ये केचिद्गीतकान्यखिलानि च।।
शब्दमूर्ति धरस्यैतद्वपुर्विष्णोर्महात्मनः।। ८५।।

The Vedas with their manifold divisions, the institutes of Manu and the writings of other law-givers, sacred lores and their translations, poems and all that is said or sung are bodily forms of that Great Viṣṇu in the shape of sound.

यानि मूर्तान्यमूर्तानि यान्यत्रान्यत्र वा क्वचित्।।
सन्ति वै वस्तुजातानि तानि सर्वाणि तद्वपुः।। ८६।।

All kinds of things with or without form—here or elsewhere are the body of Viṣṇu.

अहं हरिः सर्वमिदं जानर्दनो नान्यत्ततः कारणकार्यजातम्।।
ईदृङ्मनो यस्य न तस्य भूयो भवोद्भवा द्वन्द्वगदा
भवन्ति।। ८७।।

I am Hari; all this is Janārdana; cause and effect proceed from none else but him. He, who is cognizant of these truths, shall never be subject to the afflictions of worldly existence.

इत्येष तेंशः प्रथमः पुराणस्यास्य वै द्विज।।
यथावत्कथितो यस्मिन्धृते पापैः प्रमुच्यते।। ८८।।

Thus, O twice-born one, the first portion of the Purāṇa, has been related to you, hearing which one may be freed from sins.

कार्त्तिक्यां पुष्कर स्नाने द्वादशाब्देन यत्फलम्।।
तदस्य श्रवणात्सव मैत्रेयाप्नोति मानवः।। ८९।।

The man, who hears this, obtains the fruit of bathing in the Puṣkara[1] lake for twelve years in the month of *Kārtik.*

1. This lake is still to be seen near Ajmere.

देवर्षिपितृगन्धर्वयक्षादीनां च सम्भवम्।।
भवन्ति शृण्वतः पुंसो देवाद्या वरदा मुने।। ९०।।

O Muni, the celestials confer upon him, who hears this Purāṇa, the dignity of a divine sage, of a patriarch, or of a spirit of a heaven.

।। इति श्रीविष्णुमहापुराणे प्रथमेंशे द्वाविंशोऽध्यायः।। २२।।

।। इति श्रीपराशरमुनिविरचिते श्रीविष्णुपरत्वनिर्णायके
श्रीमति विष्णुमहापुराणे प्रथमांशः समाप्तः।।

।। अथ श्रीविष्णुमहापुराणे द्वितीयोंशः ।।

THE VIṢṆUMAHĀPURĀṆAM, PART - II

।। श्रीमते रामानुजाय नमः ।।

अथ द्वितीयेंशेः प्रथमोऽध्यायः

Part II : Section 1

मैत्रेय उवाच

भगवन्सम्यगाख्यातं ममैतदखिलं त्वया ।।
जगतः सर्गसम्बन्धि यत्पृष्टोसि गुरो मया ।। १ ।।

Maitreya said :—O venerable Sir, O preceptor, you have fully described unto me all that I asked you regarding the creation of the universe.

योयमंशो जगत्सृष्टिसम्बन्धो गदितस्त्वया ।।
तत्राहं श्रोतुमिच्छामि भूयोपि मुनिसत्तम ।। २ ।।

But there is a portion of this subject, O foremost of ascetics, which I desire to hear again.

प्रियव्रतोत्तानपादौ सुतौ स्वयम्भुवस्य यौ ।।
तयोरुत्तानपादस्य ध्रुवः पुत्रस्त्वयोदितः ।। ३ ।।

Priyavrata and Uttānapāda were the two sons of Swayambhuva Manu and you related to me the story of Dhruva, the son of Uttānapāda.

प्रियव्रतस्य नैवोक्ता भवता द्विज सन्ततिः ।।
तामहं श्रोतुमिच्छामि प्रसन्नो वक्तुमर्हसि ।। ४ ।।

But, O twice-born one, you did not mention the progeny of Priyavrata and I wish to hear from you an account of his family.

श्रीपराशर उवाच

कर्दमस्यात्मजां कन्यामुपयेमे प्रियव्रतः ।।
सम्राट् कुक्षी च तत्कन्ये दशपुत्रास्तथाऽपरे ।। ५ ।।

महाप्रज्ञा महावीर्या विनी ता दयिताः पितुः ।।
प्रियव्रतसुताः ख्यातास्तेषां नामानि मे शृणु ।। ६ ।।

आग्नीध्रश्चाग्निबाहुश्च वपुष्मान्द्युतिमांस्तथा ।।
मेधा मेधातिथिर्भव्यः सवनः पुत्र एव च ।। ७ ।।

Parāśara said :—Priyavrata married Kanyā[1], the daughter of Kardama, and had by her two daughters anmed Samrāṭ and Kukṣī and ten sons, wise, valiant, humble obedient to their father; named Agnidhra, Agnivāhu, Vapuṣmat, Dyutimat, Medhā, Bhavya, Śavalā, Putra.

ज्योतिष्मान्दशमस्तेषां सत्यनामा सुतोऽभवत् ।।
प्रियव्रतस्य पुत्रास्ते प्रख्याता बलवीर्यतः ।। ८ ।।

And the tenth of them was Jyotiṣmān; and the significance of this name was made good by him. All the sons of Priyavrata were celebrated for strength and prowess.

मेधाग्निबाहुपुत्रास्तु त्रयो योगपरायणाः ।।
जातिस्मरा महाभागा न राज्याय मनो दधुः ।। ९ ।।

Of these three, Medhā, Agnivāhu and Putra, were given up to religious devotion. And those high-souled ones remembering the actions of their pristine births, did not wish for kingdom.

निर्मलाः सर्वकालन्तु समस्तार्थेषु वै मुने ।।
चक्रुः क्रियां यथान्यायमफलाकांक्षिणो हि ते ।। १० ।।

And they deligently and in due time practised the rites of austerities, wholly disinterested and expecting no reward.

प्रियव्रतो ददौ तेषां सप्तानां मुनिसत्तम ।।
सप्तद्वीपानि मैत्रेय विभज्य सुमहात्मनाम् ।। ११ ।।

O Maitreya, O foremost of Munis, Pryavrata conferred the seven islands upon his seven illustrious sons.

---

1. Mārkaṇḍeya and Vāyu Purāṇas having Kāmya as the name of the daughter of Kardama, Wilson has adopted this name.

जम्बूद्वीपं महाभाग सोग्नीध्राय ददौ पिता।।
मेधातिथेस्तथा प्रादात्प्लक्षद्वीपं तथापरम्।। १२।।

शाल्मले च वपुष्मन्तं नरेन्द्रमभिषिक्तवान्।।
ज्योतिष्मन्तं कुशद्वीपे राजानं कृतवान्प्रभुः।। १३।।

द्युतिमंतं च राजानं क्रौञ्चद्वीपे समादिशत्।।
शाकद्वीपेश्वरं चापि भव्यं चक्रे प्रियव्रतः।। १४।।

पुष्कराधिपतिं चक्रे सवनं चापि स प्रभुः।।

The father conferred upon Agnidhra the sovereignty of Jambūdvīpa; to Medhātithi he gave Plakṣadvīpa : he made Vapuṣmat the sovereign over the Dvīpa of Śālmali : and appointed Jyotiṣmat, king of Kuśadvīpa : he made Dutimat the king of Krauñcadvīpa, Bhavya the king of Śakadvīpa and Savala the sovereign of the Dvīpa of Puṣkara.

जम्बूद्वीपेश्वरो यस्तु आग्नीध्रो मुनिसत्तम।। १५।।

तस्य पुत्रा बभूवुस्ते प्रजापतिसमा नव।।
नाभिः किंपुरुषश्चैव हरिवर्ष इलावृतः।। १६।।

रम्यो हिरण्वान्षष्ठश्च कुरुभद्राश्व एव च।।
केतुमालस्तथैवान्यः साधुचेष्टोऽभवन्नृ सः।। १७।।

O foremost of Munis, Agnidhra, the king of Jambūdvīpa had nine sons, all equal to the patriarchs in prowess.—Nābhi, Kimpuruṣa, Harivarṣa, Ilāvṛta, Ramya, Hiraṇvat, Kuru, Bhadrāśva and Ketumāla, who was a prince ever devoted to the practice of piety.

जम्बूद्वीपवि भागांश्च तेषां विप्र निशामय।।
पित्रा दत्तं हिमांह्व तु वर्षं नाभेस्तु दक्षिणम्।। १८।।

Hear next, O Brāhmaṇa, from me how he divided Jambūdvīpa amongst his sons. He conferred on Nābhi the country called Hima, south of Himavān or snowy mountains.

हेमकूटं तथा वर्षं ददौ किंपुरुषाय सः।।
तृतीयं नैषधं वर्षं हरिवर्षाय दत्तवान्।। १९।।

And he gave to Kimpuruṣa the country of Himakūṭa and to Harivarṣa the country of Niṣada.

इलावृताय प्रददौ मेरुर्यत्र तु मध्यमः।।
नीलाचलाश्रितं वर्षं रम्याय प्रददौ पिता।। २०।।

And he bestowed upon Ilāvṛta the country in the çentre of which mount Meru is situated. And he conferred upon Kāmya the countries lying between it and the Nīla mountain.

श्वेतं पदुत्तरं तस्मात्पित्रा दत्तं हिरण्वते।। २१।।

He gave to Hirāvat the country lying to the north of it.

तदुत्तरं शृङ्गवतो वर्षं तत्कुरवे ददौ।।
मेरोः पूर्वेण यद्वर्षं भद्राश्वाय प्रदत्तवान्।। २२।।

गन्धमाधनवर्षं तु केतुमालाय दत्तवान्।।
इत्येतानि ददौ तेभ्यः पुत्रेभ्यः स नरेश्वरः।। २३।।

He gave to Kuru the country bounded by Śrīṅgavat. He gave to Bhadrāśva the countries situate on the east of Meru and he gave to Ketumāla Gandhamādana which was situate on the west of it. Thus that lord of men, conferred the various portions of his kingdom, upon his sons.

वर्षेष्वेतेषु तान्पुत्रानभिषिच्य स भूमिपः।।
सालग्रामं महापुण्यं मैत्रेय तपसे ययौ।। २४।।

And having installed his sons as kings of diverse regions that lord of earth retired to the holy place of pilgrimage Śālagrāma and engaged in penance, O Maitreya.

यानि किंपुरुषादीनि वर्षाण्यष्टौ महामुने।।
तेषां स्वाभाविकी सिद्धिः सुखप्राया ह्ययत्नतः।। २५।।

O great Muni, the eight countries, Kimpuruṣa and others are places of perfect enjoyment and spontaneous happiness.

विपर्ययो न तेष्वस्ति जरामृत्युभयं न च।।
धर्माधर्मौ न तेष्वास्तां नोत्तमाधममध्यमाः।। २६।।

In those countries there is no viccissitude of circumstances, no fear of decrepitude or death, no distinction of virtue and vice, better or worse.

न तेष्वस्ति युगावस्था क्षेत्रेष्वष्टसु सर्वदा।।
हिमाह्वयं तु वै वर्षं नाभेरासीन्महात्मनः।।
तस्यर्षभोऽभवत्पुत्रो मेरुदेव्यां महाद्युतिः।। २७।।

ऋषभाद्भरतो जज्ञे ज्येष्ठः पुत्रशतस्य सः।।

Nor in these eight countries are to be seen the effects wrought by the cycle of ages. The high-souled Nābhi, who had obtained the country of Nimahwa as his kingdom, had by his queen Meru, the highly effulgent son

Ṛṣabha; and who had again a hundred sons, the eldest of whom was Bharata.

कृत्वा राज्यं स्वधर्मेण तथेष्ट्वा विविधान्मखान्।। २८।।
अभिषिच्य सुतं वीरं भरतं पृथिवीपतिः।।
तपसे स महाभागः पुलहस्याश्रमं ययौ।। २९।।
वानप्रस्थविधानेन तत्रापि कृतनिश्चयः।।
तपस्तेपे यथान्यायमियाज स महीपतिः।। ३०।।

Having ruled over the kingdom piously and performed many sacrifices the illustrious Ṛṣabha installed his eldest son Bharata as the lord of the earth and went to the hermitage of Pulastya, being bent upon practising religious penance according to the prescribed rites of an anchoret.

तपसा कर्षितोत्यर्थं कृशो धमनिसन्ततः।।
नग्नो वीटां मुखे कृत्वा वीराध्वानं ततो गतः।। ३१।।

He practised religious austerities duly until he was so reduced as to be but a collection of skin and fibres. Thereupon putting a pebble in his mouth he went naked to the great road.

ततश्च भारतं वर्षमेतल्लोकेषु गीयते।।
भरताय यतः पित्रा दत्तं प्रातिष्ठता वनम्।। ३२।।

And from then the country was handed over to Bharata by his father on retiring to woods and it was called Bhārata.

सुमतिर्भरतस्याभूत्पुत्रः परमधार्मिकः।।
कृत्वा सम्यग्ददौ तस्मै राज्यमिष्टमखं पिता।। ३३।।
पुत्रसंक्रामितश्रीस्तु भरतः स महीपतिः।।

Bharata had a highly pious son named Sumati. Having ruled the kingdom for some time, the king Bharata, who was fond of sacrifices, conferred it upon his son and invested him with all royal splendours.

योगाभ्यासरतः प्राणान्सालग्रामेऽत्यजन्मुने।। ३४।।
अजायत च विप्रोसौ योगिनां प्रवरे कुले।।
मैत्रेय तस्य चरितं कथयिष्यामि ते पुनः।। ३५।।

O Muni, having engaged in austere practices, he renounced his life at the holy place of Śālagrāma. He was again born in a distinguished family of ascetics, which I shall describe to you later on.

सुमतेस्तेजसस्तस्मादिन्द्रद्युम्नो व्यजायत।।
परमेष्ठी ततस्तस्मात्प्रतिहारस्तदन्वयः।। ३६।।
प्रतिहर्तेति विख्यात उत्पन्नस्तस्य चात्मजः।।
भवस्तस्मादथोद्गीथः प्रास्ताविस्तत्सुतो विभुः।। ३७।।

From the illustrious Sumati was born Indradyumna : his son was Pratihāra, who had an illustrious son named Pratiharttā; his son was Bhava who begot Udgītha, who, begot Prāstara, whose son was Vibhu (Pṛthu).

पृथुस्ततस्ततो नक्तो नक्तस्यापि गयः सुतः।।
नरो गयस्य तनयस्तत्पुत्रोभूद्विराट् ततः।। ३८।।

Pṛthu's son was Nakta, whose son was Gaya, whose son was Nara, whose son was Virāṭ.

तस्य पुत्रो महावीर्यो धीमांस्तस्मादजायत।।
महान्तस्तत्सुतश्चाभून्मनस्युस्तस्य चात्मजः।। ३९।।
त्वष्टा त्वष्टुश्च विरजो रजस्तस्याप्यभूत्सुतः।।
शतजिदजसस्तस्य जज्ञे पुत्रशतं मुने।। ४०।।
विष्वग्ज्योतिप्रधानास्ते यैरिमा वर्द्धिताः प्रजाः।।

Virāṭ's son was the brave Dhimat who begot Maharta, whose son was Manasyu, whose son was Tvaṣṭṛ, whose son was Virāja, whose son was Raja, whose son was Satyajit, who had a hundred sons, of whom Viśvagyotiṣ was the eldest.

तैरिदं भारतं वर्षं नवभेदमलंकृतम्।। ४१।।
तेषां वंशप्रसूतैश्च भुक्तेयं भारती पुरा।।
कृतत्रेतादि सर्गेण युगाख्यामेकसप्ततिम्।। ४२।।

Under the rule of these princes Bhāratvarṣa was divided into nine parts and their progeny successively ruled the country for seventy-one cycles.

एष स्वायंभुवः सर्गो येनेदं पूरितं जगत्।।
वाराहे तु मुने कल्पे पूर्वमन्वन्तराधिपः।। ४३।।

O Muni, this was the progeny of Swaymabhuva Manu, by whom the earth was peopled, who was the lord of the first Manwantara in the Kalpa of Varāha.

।। इति श्रीविष्णुपुराणे द्वितीयेंशे प्रथमोऽध्यायः।। १।।

अथ द्वितीयेंशेः द्वितीयोऽध्यायः
Part II : Section 2

श्रीमैत्रेय उवाच

कथितो भवता ब्रह्मन्सर्गः स्वायम्भुवश्च मे।।
श्रोतुमिच्छाम्यहं त्वत्तः सकलं मंडलं भुवः।। १।।

Maitreya said :—O Brāhmaṇa, you have related to me the progeny of Swayambhuva, I wish to hear from you an account of the earth.

यावन्तः सागरा द्वीपा स्तथा वर्षाणि पर्वताः।।
वनानि सरितः पुर्यो देवादीनां तथा मुने।। २।।

यत्प्रमाणमिदं सर्वं यदाधारं यदात्मकम्।।
संस्थानमस्य च मुने यथावद्वक्तुमर्हसि।। ३।।

It behoveth thee, O Muni to relate to me how many oceans there are, how many islands, how many kingdoms, how many mountains, forests, rivers, cities of the gods; its size, its contents, its nature and its form.

श्रीपराशर उवाच

मैत्रेय श्रूयतामेतत्संक्षेपाद्ददतो मम।।
नास्य वर्षशतेनापि वक्तुं शक्यो हि विस्तरः।। ४।।

Parāśara said :—Do thou hear from me, O Maitreya, a brief account : I cannot give you a detailed account even in a century.

जम्बूप्लक्षाह्वयौ द्वीपौ शाल्मलिश्चापरो द्विज।।
कुशः क्रौञ्चस्तथा शाकः पुष्करश्चैव सप्तमः।। ५।।

एते द्वीपाः समुद्रैस्तु सप्तसप्तभिरावृताः।।
लवणेक्षुसुरासर्पिर्दधिदुग्धजलैः समम्।। ६।।

O twice-born one, the earth consists of seven islands namely Jambū, Plakṣa, Śālmali, Kuśa, Krauñca, Śāka and Puṣkara : and they are severally girt by seven great seas : the sea of salt water (Lavaṇa), of sugar-cane juice (Ikṣu), of wine (Surā) of clarified butter (Sarpi), of curds (Dadhi), of milk (Dugdha) and of fresh water (Jala).

जम्बूद्वीपः समस्तानामेतेषां मध्यसंस्थितः।।
तस्यापि मेरुर्मैत्रेय मध्ये कनकपर्वतः।। ७।।

चतुराशीतिसाहस्त्रो योजनैरस्य चोच्छ्रयः।। ८।।

Jambūdvīpa is situated in the centre of all these and in the centre of that island is situate the golden mount Meru, which is eighty-four thousand *yojanas* in height and sixteen thousand deep into the earth.

प्रविष्टः षोडशाधस्ताद्द्वात्रिंशन्मूर्ध्नि विस्तृतः।।
मूले षोडशसाहस्त्रो विस्तारस्तस्य सर्वशः।। ९।।

The diameter, at its top, is thirty-two thousand *yojanas* and at the bae sixteen thousand.

भूपद्मस्यास्य शैलोसौ कर्णिकाकारसंस्थितः।। १०।।

And this mountain is like the seed-cup of the lotus of the earth.

हिमवान्हेमकूटश्च निषधश्चास्य दक्षिणे।।
नीलः श्वेतश्च शृंगी च उत्तरे वर्षपर्वताः।। ११।।

On the south Sumeru are the mountains Himavat, Hemakūṭa and Niṣadha and on its north are the boundary mountains Nīla, Śweta and Śṛnghī.

लक्षप्रमाणौ द्वौ मध्यौ दशहीनास्तथापरे।।
सहस्त्रद्वितयोच्छ्रायास्तावद्विस्तारिणश्च ते।। १२।।

The two mountain ranges situtate in the centre are a hundred thousand lesser in extent. They are two thousand *yojanas* in height and breadth.

भारतं प्रथमं वर्षं ततः किंपुरुषं स्मृतम्।।
हरिवर्षं तथैवान्यन्मेरोर्दक्षिणतो द्विज।। १३।।

O twice-born one, the first country on the south of Sumeru is Bhārata, then Kimpuruṣa and then Harivarṣa.

रम्यकं चोत्तरं वर्षं तस्यैवानु हिरण्मयम्।।
उत्तराः कुरवश्चैव यथा वै भारतं तथा। १४।।

North of Meru is Rāmyaka, next to that is Hiraṇmaya and beyond the latter is Uttarakuru following the same direction as Bhārata.

नवसाहस्त्रमेकैकमेतेषां द्विजसत्तम।।
इलावृतं च तन्मध्ये सौवर्णो मेरुरुच्छ्रितः।। १५।।

And each of these Varṣas, O foremost of the twice-born ones, is extended over a nine thousand *Yojanas*.

मेरोश्चतुर्दिशं तत्तु नवसाविस्तृतम्।।
इलावृतं महाभाग चत्वारश्चात्र पर्वताः।। १६।।

Ilāvṛta is also of the same size and the golden mount Meru is situate in the cenetre, and the country extends nine thousand *Yojanas* in each direction from the four sides of the mountain.

विष्कंभारचिता मेरोर्योजनायुतमुच्छ्रिताः।।
नवैः सरोभिश्च समं दिक्ष्वेते केशवाचलाः।। १७।।

For fortifying the mount Meru four mountains were created as buttresses, each ten thousand *Yojans* in elevation.

पूर्वेण मन्दरो नाम दक्षिणे गन्धमादनः।।
विपुलः पश्चिमे पार्श्वे सुपार्श्वश्चोत्तरे स्मृतः।। १८।।

The one situate on the east is called Mandāra, the one on the south is called Gandhamādana, that on the west is called Vipula and that on the south Supārśva.

कदम्बस्तेषु जम्बूश्च पिप्पलो वट एव च।।
एकादशशतायामाः पादपा गिरिकेतवः।। १९।।

And on each of these stands severally a Kadamba tree, a Jambū tree, a Pīpal and a Vaṭa. And all these trees were eleven thousand *Yojanas* in height, standing as if like the banners of the mountains.

जम्बूद्वीपस्य सा जम्बूर्नामहेतुर्महामुने।।
महागजप्रमाणानि जम्ब्वास्तस्याः फलानि वै।।
पतन्ति भूभृतः पृष्ठे शीर्यमाणानि सर्वतः।। २०।।

O great Muni, because a Jambū-tree stands on that mountain that insular continent is called Jambū-dvīpa. And that tree produces Jambū-fruits like so many huge elephants. And those huge fruits are crushed into pieces as soon as they fall on the mountain.

रसेन तेषां प्रख्याता तत्र जाम्बूनदीति वै।।
सरित्प्रवर्त्तते चापि पीयते तन्निवासिभिः।। २१।।

न स्वेदो न च दौर्गन्ध्यं न जरा नेन्द्रियक्षयः।।
तत्पानात्स्वच्छमनसां जनानां तत्र जायते।। २२।।

And out of the juice of those fruits has come out the river Jambū. And the inhabitants, who drink the water of the river, do not experience perspiration, bad smell and are not subject to infirmities of age and organic decay.

तीरमृत्तद्रसं प्राप्य सुखवायुविशोषिता।।
जाम्बूनदाख्यं भवति सुवर्णं सिद्धभूषणम्।। २३।।

The soil, on the banks of that river, receiving the juice of these fruits and dried up by pleasant breeze, is turned into gold called Jambūnada out of which the ornament of the Siddhas are made.

भद्राश्वं पूर्वतो मेरोः केतुमालं च पश्चिमे।।
वर्षे द्वे तु मुनिश्रेष्ठ तयोर्मध्यमिलावृतः।। २४।।

वनं चैत्ररथं पूर्वे दक्षिणे गन्धमादनम्।।
वैभ्राजं पश्चिमे तद्वदुत्तरे नन्दनं स्मृतम्।। २५।।

Bhadrāśva is situate on the east of Meru and Ketumāla on the west. And in the middle of these two Varṣas, O foremost of Munis, is situate Ilāvṛta, on the east is the Caitrarath forest on the south Gandhamādana, on the west Vaibhrāju and on the north the forest called Nandana.

अरुणोदं महाभद्रमसितोदं समानसम्।।
सरांस्येतानि चत्वारि देवभोग्यानि सर्वदा।। २६।।

On the four sides of Meru there are four tanks the water of which is parteaken of by the celestials namely Aruṇoda, Mahābhadra, Sitoda and Mānasa.

शीताम्भश्च कुमुन्दश्च कुररी माल्यवांस्तथा।।
वैकंकप्रमुखा मेरोः पूर्वतः केसराचलाः।। २७।।

There are some mountain ranges like the filaments from the root of the lotus on the east of Meru—namely Sitānta Mukunda, Kurāri, Mālyavān and Vaikānta.

त्रिकूटः शिशिरश्चैव पतंगो रुचकस्तथा।।
निषदाद्या दक्षिणतस्यस्य केसरपर्वताः।। २८।।

शिखिवासाः सवैडूर्यः कपिलो गन्धमादनः।।
जारुधिप्रमुखास्तद्वत्पश्चिमे केसराचलाः।। २९।।

मेरोरनन्तरांगेषु जठरादिष्ववस्थिताः।।
शंखकूटोथ ऋषभो हंसो नागस्तथा परः।।
कालञ्जाद्याश्च तथा उत्तरे केसराचलाः।। ३०।।

And on the south Trikuṭa, Śiśirā, Pataṅga, Rucaka and Niṣadha, on the west Śikhivāsas, Vaiḍūrya, Kapila, Gandhamādana and Jārudho, and on the north Śaṅkhakūṭa, Ṛṣabha, Nāga, Hansa and Kālañjara. These and others extend from the heart of the Meru.

चतुर्दशसहस्त्रणि योजनानां महापुरी।।
मेरोरुपरि मैत्रेय ब्रह्मणः प्रथिता दिवि।। ३१।।

On the top of mount Meru, O Maitreya, there is a vast city, named after Brahmā, extending for fourteen thousand *Yojanas*, and celebrated in the region of the celestials.

तस्यास्समन्ततश्चाष्टौ दिशासु विदिशासु च।।
इंद्रादिलोकपालानां प्रख्याताः प्रवराः पुरः।। ३२।।

And around it in the various quarters and intermediate quarters are situate the magnificent cities of Indra and other deities presiding over various quarters.

विष्णुपादविनिष्क्रान्ता प्लावयित्वेन्दुमण्डलम्।।
समन्ताद्ब्रह्मणः पुर्यां गङ्गा पतति वै दिवः।। ३३।।

Originating from the foot of Viṣṇu, and watering the region of the moon, the Ganges falls from the heaven into the city of Brahmā.

सा तत्र पतिता दिक्षु चतुर्द्धा प्रतिपद्यते।।
सीता चालकनन्दा च चक्षुर्भद्रा च वै क्रमात्।। ३४।।

Falling there she has divided herself into four branches namely Sītā, Alakakandā, Cakṣu and Vadrā.

पूर्वेण शैलाच्छीता तु शैलं यात्यन्तरिक्षगा।।
ततश्च पूर्ववर्षेण भद्राश्वेनैति सार्णवम्।। ३५।।

Taking her course towards the east and going from one mountain to another, in the welkin Sītā, watering Vadrāśva has fallen into the ocean.

तथैवालकनन्दापि दक्षिणेनैत्य भारतम्।।
प्रयाति सागरं भूत्वा सप्तभेदा महामुने।। ३६।।

The Alakakandā flows southwards to the country of Bhārata and dividing herself into seven branches on the way, falls into the ocean, O great Muni.

चक्षुश्चं पश्चिमगिरीनतीत्य सकलास्ततः।।
पश्चिमं केतुमालाख्यं वर्षं गत्वैति सागरम्।। ३७।।

And Cakṣu crossing over all the western mountains and passing through the country of Ketumāla falls into the ocean.

भद्रा तथोत्तरगिरीनुत्तरांश्च तथा कुरून्।।
अतीत्योत्तरमम्भोधिं समभ्येति महामुने।। ३८।।

And Bhadrā, traversing the northern mountains and pasing through the country of Uttarakuru, falls into the northern ocean, O great Muni.

आनीलनिषधायामौ माल्यवद्गन्धमादनौ।।
तयोर्मध्यगतो मेरुः कर्णिकाकारसंस्थितः।। ३९।।

Meru is thus sitatued between the mountains Nīla and Niṣada (on the north and south) and between Mālyavān and Gandhamādana (on the west and east) and it lies there like the peri-carp of a lotus.

भारताः केतुमालाश्च भद्राश्वाः कुरवस्तथा।।
पत्राणि लोकपद्मस्य मर्यादाशैलबाह्यतः।। ४०।।

And the countries of Bhārata, Ketumāla Bhadrāśva and Kuru, lying outside the mountains, are like petals of the lotus of the world.

जठरो हेमकूटश्च मर्यादापर्वतावुभौ।।
तौ दक्षिणोत्तरायामावानीलनिषधायतौ।। ४१।।

Jaṭhara and Devakūṭa are two mountainous ranges extending northwards and southward and connecting the mountain Nīla and Niṣada.

गन्धमादनकैलासौ पूर्ववच्चायतावुभौ।।
अशीति योजनायामावर्णवान्तव्यवस्थितौ।। ४२।।

The two mountains Gandhamādana and Kailāśa extend towards the east and west for eight *Yojonas* from sea to sea.

निर्षेधः परियात्रश्च मर्यादापर्वतावुभौ।।
मेरोः पश्चिदिग्भागे यथा पूर्वे तथा स्थितौ।। ४३।।

Like the two mountains on the east the two ranges Niṣada and Paripātra are situated on the western side of Meru.

त्रिशृङ्गो जारुधिश्चैव उत्तरौ वर्षपर्वतौ।।
पूर्वपश्चायतावेतावर्णवान्तर्व्यवस्थितौ ।।४४।।

The two mountins Triśṛṅga and Jārudhi are sitauted on the north of Meru and they extend east and west from one sea to another.

इत्येते मुनिवर्योक्ता मर्यादापर्वतास्तव।।
जठराद्याः स्थिता मेरोस्तेषां द्वौद्वौ चतुर्दिशम्।।
मेराश्चतुर्दिशं ये तु प्रोक्ताः केसरपर्वताः।। ४५।।

Thus I have described to you the eight mountains, mentioned by the ascetics as bounding the mount Meru, and sitaute in pairs on four sides.

शीतान्ताद्या मुने तेषामतीव हि मनोरमाः।।
शैलानामन्तरे द्रोण्यः सिद्धचारणसेविताः।। ४६।।
सुरम्याणि तथा तासु काननानि पुराणि च।।
लक्ष्मीविष्ण्वग्निसूर्यादिदेवानां मुनिसत्तम।।
तास्वायतनवर्याणि जुष्टानि वरकिन्नरैः।। ४७।।

Sitānta and others which have been described to you as filament mountains are extremely charming. The vallies situate in the bosom of those mountains are frequented by Siddhas and Cāraṇas and there are many picturesque cities and forests, containing the palaces of Viṣṇu, Lakṣmī, Agni, Sūrya and other deities and inhabitated by the celestials.

गन्धर्वयक्षरक्षांसि तथा दैतेयदानवाः।।
क्रीडन्ति तासु रम्यासु शैलद्रोणीष्वहर्निशम्।। ४८।।

And in those pleasant vales Gandharvas, Yakṣas, Rākṣasas, Daityas and Dānavas sport day and night.

भौमा ह्येते स्मृताः स्वर्गा धर्मिणामालया मुने।।
नैतेषु पापकर्माणो यान्ति जन्मशतैरपि।। ४९।।

These are the abodes of the pious, O Muni and are called the regions of paradise on earth where the vicious, even after a hundred births, do not arrive.

भद्राश्वे भगवान्विष्णुरास्ते हयशिरा द्विज।।
वराहः केतुमाले तु भारते कूर्मरूपधृक्।। ५०।।

In the country of Bhadrāśva, O twice-born one, Viṣṇu resides in his horse-headed form, in Ketumāla as the boar and in Bhārata as the tortoise.

मत्स्यरूपश्च गोविंदः कुरुष्वास्ते जनार्दनः।।
विश्वरूपेण सर्वत्र सर्वः सर्वत्रगो हरिः।। ५१।।

And in Kuru Janārdana resides as the fish and Hari, the lord of all and everything, resides everywhere in his universal form.

सर्वस्याधारभूतोसौ मैत्रेयास्तेखिलात्मकः।। ५२।।

And, O Maitreya, he, the soul of the world, is the supporter of all things.

यानि किंपुरुषादीनि वर्षाण्यष्टौ महामुने।।
न तेषु शोको नायासो नोद्वेगः क्षुयादिकम्।। ५३।।

O great Muni, in the eight countries of Kimpuruṣa and others there is neither grief, exhaustion, anxiety nor hunger.

स्वस्थाः प्रजा निरातङ्कास्सर्वदुःखविवर्जिताः।।
दश द्वादशवर्षाणां सहस्राणि स्थिरायुषः।। ५४।।

All the subjects are healthy devoid of any fear, freed from all afflictions and live for ten or twelve thousand years.

न तेषु वर्षते देवो भौमान्यम्भांसि तेषु वै।।
कृतत्रेतादिकं नैव तेषु स्थानेषु कल्पना।। ५५।।

Indra does not send rain there and people live upon the water of the earth and there is no distinction of Satya, Tretā and other successive cycles.

सर्वेष्वेतेषु वर्षेषु सप्तसप्तकुलाचलाः।।
नद्यश्च शतशस्तेभ्यः प्रसूता या द्विजोत्तम।। ५६।।

In each of these countries there are seven principal mountainous ranges from which hundreds of rivers take their rise, O foremost of twice-born ones.

।। इति श्रीविष्णुमहापुराणे द्वितीयेंशे द्वितीयोऽध्यायः।। २।।

अथ द्वितीयेंशे: तृतीयोऽध्याय:
Part II : Section 3

श्रीपराशर उवाच
उत्तरं यत्समुद्रस्य हिमाद्रेश्चैव दक्षिणम्।।
वर्षं तद्भारतं नाम भारती यत्र सन्ततिः।। १।।

Parāśara said :—The country that is situate on the ocean and south of the Himālya is called Bhārata where reside the descendants of Bharata.

नवयोजनसाहस्त्रो विस्तारोस्य महामुने।।
कर्म भूमिरियं स्वर्गमपवर्गं च गच्छताम्।। २।।

The extent of this land is nine thousand *Yojanas*, and is the field of action, on account of which men go to heaven or obtain final emancipation.

महेन्द्रो मलयः सह्यः शुक्तिमानृक्षपर्वतः।।
विंध्यश्च पारियात्रश्च सप्तात्र कुलपर्वताः।। ३।।

The seven principal mountain ranges in Bhārata are Mahendra, Malaya, Sahya. Sūktimat, Ṛkṣa, Vindhya and Pāripātra.

अतः संप्राप्यते सवर्गो मुक्तिमस्मात्प्रयान्ति वै।।
तिर्यक्त्वं नरकं चापि यान्त्यतः पुरुषा मुने।। ४।।

From this land people attain to heaven or final emancipation or some hence, O Muni, fall into hell or pass into the condition of brutes.

इतः स्वर्गश्च मोक्षश्च मध्यं चान्तश्च गम्यते।।
न खल्वन्यत्र मर्त्यानां कर्मभूमौ विधीयते।। ५।।

From here people obtain heaven, liberation, or the state in mid-air, or the state in the regions under the earth for no other portion of world is the arena of actions.

भारतस्यास्य वर्षस्य नवभदान्निशामय।।
इद्रद्वीपः कसेरुश्च ताम्रपर्णो गभस्तिमान्।। ६।।
नागद्वीपस्तथा साम्यौ गन्धर्वस्त्वथा चारुणः।।
अयं तु नवमस्तेषां द्वीपः सागरसंवृतः।। ७।।
योजनानां सहस्त्रं तु द्वीपोयं दक्षिणोत्तरात्।।

Do thou again hear of the nine divisions of the country of Bhārata. They are Indra-dvīpa, Kasermut, Tāmraparṇa, Galehastimat, Nāga-dvīpa, Saumya, Gandharva and Varuṇa. The last is encircled by the sea and is a thousand *Yojanas* in extent from nort to south.

पूर्वे किराता यस्यान्ते पश्चिमे यवनाः स्थिताः।। ८।।
ब्राह्मणाः क्षत्रिया वैश्या मध्ये शूद्राश्च भागशः।।
इज्यायुधवणिज्याद्यैर्वर्तयन्तो व्यवस्थिताः।। ९।।

On the east of Bhārata live the Kirātas, and on the west Yavanas in the centre live Brāhmaṇas, Kṣtriyas, Vaiśyas, and Śūdras engaged severally in sacrifice, arms, trade and service.

शतदूचन्द्रभागाद्या हिमवत्पादनिर्गताः।।
वेदस्मृतिमुखाद्याश्च पारियात्रोद्भवा मुने।। १०।।
नर्मदा सुरसाद्याश्च नद्यो विन्ध्याद्रिनिर्गताः।।

The rivers Śatadru, Candrabhāgā and others have taken their rise from the Himālaya. Vedasmṛti and others have taken their rise from the Vindya range.

तापीपयोष्णीनिर्विन्ध्या प्रमुखा ऋक्षसंभवाः।। ११।।
गोदावरी भीमरथी कृष्णवेण्यादिकास्तथा।।
सह्यपादोद्भवा नद्यः स्मृताः पापभयापहाः।। १२।।

Tāpī, Payośinī, Nirbindhyā and others have taken their rise from Ṛkṣa; Godāverī, Bhīmarathī, Kṛṣṇavenī and others have taken their rise from Sahya mountain. And all these remove the dread of sin.

कृतमाला ताम्रपर्णीप्रमुखा मलयोद्भवाः।।
त्रिसामा चर्षिकुल्याद्या महेन्द्रप्रभवाः स्मृताः।। १३।।
ऋषिकुल्याकुमाराद्याः शुक्तिमत्पादसम्भवाः।।
आसां नद्य उपानद्यः सन्त्यन्याश्च सहस्त्रशः।। १४।।

Kṛtamāla, Tamraparṇī and others flow from the Malaya hills; Trisama, Ṛṣikulya and others from the Mahendra; and the Ṛsikulya, Kumārī and others from the Śūktimat mountains. There are thousands of rivers like these and the tributaries thereof.

तास्विमे कुरुपाञ्चाला मध्यदेशादयो जनाः ।।
पूर्वदेशादिकाश्चैव कामरूपनिवासिनः ।। १५ ।।

पुंड्राः कलिङ्गा मगधा दक्षिणाद्याश्च सर्वशः ।।
तथापरांताः सौराष्ट्राः शूराभीरास्तर्थार्बुदाः ।। १६ ।।

कारूषा मालवाश्चैव पारिपात्र निवासिनः ।।
सौवीराः सैन्धवा हूणाः साल्वाः कोसलवासिनः ।। १७ ।।

माद्रारामास्तथाम्बष्ठाः पारसीकादयस्तथा ।।
आसां पिबन्ति सलिलं वसन्ति सहिताः सदा ।।
समीपतो महाभाग हृष्टपुष्टजनाकुलाः ।। १८ ।।

The Kurus and Pāñcālas in the middle districts, the inhabitants of Kāmarūpa in the east, the Puṇḍras, Kaliṅgas, Māgadhas, and other southern nations, the Saurāṣṭras, Suras, Bhiras, Arbudas in the west, the Karūṣās and Mālavas dwelling along the Pāripātra mountains, the Sauvīras, the Saindhavas the Hūṇas, the Sālvas the inhabitants of Śakala, the Madras, the Rāmas, the Ambāṣṭhas and the Parīṣakas and others drink the waters of these rivers and live on their banks happy and prosperous.

चत्वारि भारत वर्षे युगान्यत्र महामुने ।।
कृतं त्रेता द्वापरञ्च कलिश्चान्यत्र न क्वचित् ।। १९ ।।

There are four Yugas or ages in the Bhāratavarṣa, O Great Muni, namely the Kṛta, the Tretā, the Dwāpara, and Kali—there is no such cycle of ages in any other land.

तपस्तप्यन्ति मुनयो जुह्वते चात्र यज्वनः ।।
दानानि चात्र दीयन्ते परलोकार्थमादरात् ।। २० ।।

Here the ascetics are engaged in penances, the devout offer sacrifices, and the people distribute gifts for the sake of another world.

पुरुषैर्यज्ञपुरुषो जम्बूद्वीपे सदेज्यते ।।
यज्ञैर्यज्ञमयो विष्णुरन्यद्वीपेषु चान्यथा ।। २१ ।।

In Jambū-Dvīpa, Viṣṇu, all sacrifice, in the shape of sacrificial male, is worshipped by people with sacrifices—there is altogether a different practice in other lands.

अत्रापि भारतं श्रेष्ठं जम्बूद्वीपे महामुने ।।
यतो हि कर्मभूरेषा ह्यतोन्या भोगभूमयः ।। २२ ।।

O Great Muni, Bhārata therefore is the best of all the divisions of Jambū-dvīpa, for it is the land of actions and all other divisions are places of enjoyment.

अत्र जन्मसहस्राणां सहस्रैरपि सत्तम ।।
कदाचिल्लभते जन्मुर्मानुष्यं पुण्यसञ्चयात् ।। २३ ।।

O sage, it is after many thousand births, and by the accumulation of piety, that living beings are sometimes born in Bhāratavarṣa as men.

गायन्ति देवाः किल गीतकानि धन्यास्तु ते भारत भूमिभागे ।।
स्वर्गापवर्गास्पदमार्गभूते भवन्ति भूयः पुरुषाः सुरत्वात् ।।
२४ ।।

The celestials themselves have chanted "Blessed are those who are born in Bhāratvarṣa as men even from the condition of the celestials for this is a land which leads to Paradise and final liberation.

कर्माण्यसंकल्पिततत्फलानि संन्यस्य विष्णौ परमात्म भूते ।।
अवाप्य तां कर्ममहीमनन्ते तस्मिल्लयं ये त्वमलाः
प्रयान्ति ।। २५ ।।

And all actions, that are performed by men, born in this land and freed from sins, careless of the marited rewards, are consigned by them to the eternal Viṣṇu, the Great soul and then they emerge in him.

जानीम नैतत्क्व वयं विलीने स्वर्गप्रदे कर्मणि देहबन्धम् ।।
प्राप्स्याम धन्याः खलु ते मनष्या ये भारते नेंद्रियविप्रहीनाः ।।
२६ ।।

We do not know when the actions, that have secured for us heaven, shall bear fruits and when we shall be born again. But "Blessed are those who are born in Bhāratavarṣa with perfect faculties."

नववर्षं तु मैत्रेय जम्बूद्वीपमिदं मया ।।
लक्षयोजनविस्तारं संक्षेपात्कथितं तव ।। २७ ।।

जम्बूद्वीपं समावृत्य लक्षयोजनविस्तरः ।।
मैत्रेय वलयाकारः स्थितः क्षरोदधिर्बहिः ।। २८ ।।

O Maitreya, I have, thus in short, described to you the nine divisions of Jambū-dvīpa which extend over a hundred thousand *Yojanas* and which is girt, as if by a bracelet, by the ocean of salt water which is similar in dimensions.

।। इति श्रीविष्णु महापुराणे द्वितीयेंशे तृतीयोऽध्यायः ।। ३ ।।

अथ द्वितीयेंशेः चतुर्थोऽध्यायः
Part II : Section 4

श्रीपराशर उवाच

क्षारोदेन यथा द्वीपो जम्बूसंज्ञोऽभिवेष्टितः।।
संवेष्ट्य क्षारमुदधिं प्लक्षद्वीपस्तथा स्थितः।। १।।

Parāśara said :—As Jambū-dvīpa is encircled all around by the ocean of salt water like a bracelet, so that ocean is also girt by the insular continent Plakṣa.

जम्बूद्वीपस्य विस्तारः शतसाहस्त्रसम्मितः।।
स एवं द्विगुणो ब्रह्मन् प्लक्षद्वीप उदाहृतः।। २।।

The extnet of Jambū-dvīpa is a hundred thousand *Yojanas;* and it is said, O Brāhmaṇa, that the extent of Plakṣa-dvīpa is twice as much.

सप्त मेधातिथेः पुत्राः प्लक्षद्वीपेश्वरस्य वै।।
ज्येष्ठः शान्तहयो नाम शिशिरस्तदनन्तरः।। ३।।

सुखोदयास्तथानन्दः शिवः क्षेमक एव च।।
ध्रुवश्च सप्तमस्तेषां प्लक्षद्वीपेश्वरा हि ते।। ४।।

Medhātithi, the king of Plakṣa-dvīpa, had seven sons, Śāntabhaya, Śiśira, Sukhodaya, Ananda, Śiva, Kṣemaka and Dhruva. And all these seven became kings of Plakṣā-dvīpa.

पूर्वं शान्तहयं वर्षं शिशिरं च सुखं तथा।।
आनन्दं च शिवं चैव क्षेमकं ध्रुवमेव च।। ५।।

The seven divisions were named after them—Śantābhayavarṣa, Śiśira-varṣa, Sukhanda-varṣa, Ānanda-varṣa Śiva-varṣa, Kṣemaka-varṣa, and Dhruva-varṣa.

मर्यादाकारकास्तेषां तथान्ये वर्षपर्वताः।।
सप्तैव तेषां नामानि शृणुष्व मुनिसत्तम।। ६।।

गोमेदश्चैव चन्द्रश्च नारदो दुन्दुभिस्तथा।।
सोमकः सुमनाश्चैव वैभ्राजश्चैव सप्तमः।। ७।।

These seven varṣas had seven mountain-ranges as their boundaries. Do thou hear, from me, the names of these mountains, O foremost of Munis,—Gomeda, Candra, Nārada, Dundubhi, Somaka, Sumanas, and Vaibhrāja.

वर्षाचलेषु रम्येषु वर्षेष्वेतेषु चानघाः।।
वसंति देवगन्धर्वसहिताः सततं प्रजाः।। ८।।

In all these picturesque mountians the sinless inhabitants dwell perpetually along with the celestials and Gandharvas.

तेषु पुण्या जनपदाश्चिराच्च म्रियते जनः।।
नाधयो व्याधयो वापि सर्वकालसुखं हि तत्।। ९।।

There are holy villages where people live for a long time, freed from care and pain and enjoying uninterrupted happiness.

तेषां नद्यस्तु सप्तैव वर्षाणां च समुद्रगाः।।
नामतस्ताः प्रवक्ष्यामि श्रुताः पापं हरंति याः।। १०।।

And in those divisions there are seven rivers all flowing into the ocean—I shall relate their names, hearing which all sins shall be removed.

अनुतप्ता शिखी चैव विपाशा त्रिदिवाक्लमः।।
अमृता सुकृता चैव सप्तैतास्तत्र निम्नगाः।। ११।।

They are Anutaptā, Śikhi, Vipāśā, Tridivā, Kramu, Amṛtā and Sukṛtā seven in number.

एते शैलास्तथा नद्यः प्रधानां कथितास्तव।।
क्षुद्रशैलास्तथा नद्यस्तत्र सन्ति सहस्त्रशः।।
ताः पिबन्ति सहाहृष्टा नदीर्जनपदास्तु ते।। १२।।

These are the principal rivers and mountains of Plakṣadvīpa, which I have described to you; but there are thousands of others of inferior size.

अपसर्पिणी न तेषां वै न चैवात्सर्पिणी द्विज।।
न त्वेवास्ति युगावस्था तेषु स्थानेषु सप्तसु।। १३।।

त्रेतायुगसमः कालः सर्वदैव महामते।।
प्लक्षद्वीपादिषु ब्रह्मञ् शाकद्वीपान्तिकेषु वै।। १४।।

Those, who partake of the waters of these rivers, always live happy and contented; there is neither the increase nor decrease of the population; the revolution of the four ages is not known there; O thou of great mind, the time there is uniformly of the character of Tretā Yuga.

पञ्च वर्षसहस्राणि जना जीवन्त्यनामयाः।।
धर्मः पञ्चस्वथैतेषु वर्णाश्रमविभागशः।। १५।।

In all these Dvīpas, O Brāhmaṇa, people live peacefully for five thousand years, and religious rites are severally performed by diverse castes and divisions of the people.

वर्णाश्च तत्र चत्वारस्तान्निबोध वदामि ते।। १६।।

There are four castes which I shall relate to you.

आर्यकाः कुरराश्चैव विदिश्या भाविनश्च ते।।
विप्रक्षत्रियवैश्यास्ते शूद्राश्च मुनिसत्तम।। १७।।

They are Āryaka, Kuru, Vivasa and Bhavi corresponding respectively with Brāhmaṇas, Kṣatriyas, Vaiśyas and Śūdras, O foremost of Munis.

जम्बूवृक्षप्रमाणस्तु तन्मध्ये सुमहांस्तरुः।।
प्लक्षस्तन्नामसंज्ञोयं प्लक्षद्वीपो द्विजोत्तम।। १८।।

As there is a huge Jambū-tree in the Jambū-dvīpa s there is a large fig-tree in this insular continent and this Dvīpa is called Plakṣa after the name of that tree, O foremost of twice-born ones.

इज्यते तत्र भगवांस्तैर्वर्णैरार्यकादिभिः।।
सोमरूपी जगत्स्त्रष्टा सर्वः सर्वेश्वरो हरिः।। १९।।

Hari, the all, the lord of all, the creator of the universe, is worshipped in the form of the moon by the Āryakas and other caste people.

प्लक्षद्वीपप्रमाणेन प्लक्षद्वीपः समावृतः।।
तथैवेक्षुरसोदेन परिवेषानुकारिणा।। २०।।

Plakṣa-dvīpa is girt, as if by a disc, by the sea of molasses which is equal to the island in extent.

इत्येवं तव मैत्रेय प्लक्षद्वीप उदाहृतः।।
संक्षेपेण मया भूयः शाल्मलं मे निशामय।। २१।।

I have thus given to you, O Maitreya, in a brief compass, a description of the island called Plakṣa; I shall now describe the island Śālmali; do thou hear it.

शाल्मलस्येश्वरोः वीरो वपुष्मांस्तत्सुताञ्छृणु।।
तेषां तु नामसं ज्ञानि सप्तवर्षाणि तानि वै।। २२।।

The heroic Vapuẓmat is the soverign of the Śālmali-dvīpa; do thou hear the names of his seven sons who gave names to the seven divisions of this insular continent.

श्वेतोथ हरितश्चैव जीमूतो रोहितस्तथा।।
वैद्युतो मानसश्चैव सुप्रभश्च महामुने।। २३।।

They were Śveta, Hārīta, Jīmūta, Rohita, Vaidyuta, Mānasa, and Suprabha.

शाल्मलेन समुद्रोसौ द्वीपेनेक्षुरसोदकः।।
विस्तारद्विगुणेनाथ सर्वतः संवृतः स्थितः।। २४।।

The sea of molasses is girt by this insular continent on all sides, which is twice in extent.

तत्रापि पर्वताः सप्त विज्ञेया रत्नयोनयः।।
वर्षाभिव्यञ्जका ये तु तथा सप्त च निम्नगाः।। २५।।

There are seven mountain ranges containing precious jems and dividing the Dvīpa and there are seven rivers.

कुमुदश्चोन्नतश्चैव तृतीयश्च बलाहकः।।
द्रोणो यत्र महौषध्यः स चतुर्थो महीधरः।। २६।।
कङ्कस्तु पञ्चमः षष्ठो महिषः सप्तमस्तथा।।
ककुद्मान्पर्वतवरः सरिन्नामानि मे शृणु।। २७।।

They are Kumuda, Unnata, Valāhaka, Droṇa, abounding in medicinal herbs, Kaṅka, Mahīṣa and Kakkudwat.

योनितोया वितृष्णा च चन्द्रा मुक्ता विमोचनी।।
निवृत्तिः सप्तमी तासां स्मृतास्ताः पापशान्तिदाः।। २८।।

The principal rivers are Yauni, Toyā, Vitṛṣṇa, Candra, Sukla, Vimochani and Nivṛtti; the waters of all these remove sins.

श्वेतञ्च हरतिं चैव वैद्युतं मानसं तथा।।
जीमूतं रोहिजतं चैव सुप्रभं चापि शोभ नम्।।
सप्तैतानि तु वर्षाणि चातुर्वर्ण्ययुतानि वै।। २९।।

All the varṣas namely Śweta, Hārīta, Vaidyuta, Mānasa, Jimūta and Suprava are very charming. All these varṣas are peopled by men of four castes.

शाल्मले ये तु वर्णाश्च वसन्त्येते महामुने।।
कपिलाश्चारुणाः पीताः कृष्णाश्चैव पृथक् पृथक्।। ३०।।

ब्राह्मणाः क्षत्रिया वैश्याः शूद्राश्चैव यजन्तितम्।।
भगवन्तं समस्तस्य विष्णुमात्मानमव्ययम्।।
वायुभूतं मखश्रेष्ठैर्यज्वनो यज्ञसंस्थितिम्।। ३१।।

The four castes, O great Muni, who reside in Śālmali-dvīpa, are severally known as Kapilas, Aruṇas, Pitas and Rohitas (or twany, purple, yellow and red) corresponding to Brāhmaṇas, Kṣatriyas, Vaiśyas and Śūdras, who all perform sacrifices and worship the Great undecaying Viṣṇu, the soul of all things, in the form of Vāyu (wind) with pious rites.

देवानामत्र सान्निध्यमतीव सुमनोहरे।।
शाल्मलिः सुमहान्वृक्षो नाम्ना निर्वृतिकारकः।। ३२।।

The people there enjoy frequent association with the celestials. There is a huge Śalmali (silk-cotton) tree in this insular continent, which gives its name and affords delight to gods.

एष द्वीपः समुद्रेण सुरोदेन समावृतः।।
विस्ताराच्छाल्मलस्यैव समेन तु समन्ततः।। ३३।।

This Dvīpa is encircled on all sides by the Ocean named Suroda, which is equal to the island in extent.

सुरोदकः परिवृतः कुशद्वीपेन सर्वतः।।
शाल्मलस्य तु विस्ताराद्द्विगुणेन समन्ततः।। ३४।।

This ocean Suroda is again girt on all sides by the Kuśa-dvīpa which is twice the Śālmali island in extent.

ज्योतिष्मतः कुशद्वीपे सप्त पुत्राञ्छृणुष्व तान्।। ३५।।

The king Jyotiṣmat in Kuśa-dvīpa had seven sons; do thou hear their names.

उद्भिदो वेणुमांश्चैव वैरथो लम्बनो धृतिः।।
प्रभाकरोतिकपिलस्तन्नामा वर्षपद्धतिः।। ३६।

They are Udbhida, Veṇuman, Swairatha, Lavaṇa, Dhṛti, Prabhākara and Kapita after whom the seven varṣas were severally named.

तस्मिन्वसन्ति मनुजाः सह दैतेयदानवैः।।
तथैव देवगन्धर्वयक्षकिंपुरुषादयः।। ३७।।

There live men along with the Daityas, Dānavas, gods, Gandharvas, Yakṣas, and Kimpuruṣas.

वर्णास्तत्रापि चत्वारो निजानुष्ठानतत्पराः।।
दमिनः शुष्मिणः स्नेहा मन्देहाश्च महामुने।। ३८।।
ब्राह्मणाः क्षत्रिया वैश्याः शूद्राश्चानुक्रमोदिताः।। ३९।।

The four castes devoted to the performance of their respective duties are called Damis, Suṣmis, Snehas, and Mandehas corresponding, in order to Brāhmaṇas, Kṣatriyas, Vaiśyas and Śūdras.

यथोक्तकर्मकर्तृत्वात्स्वाधिकारक्षयाय ते।।
तत्रैव तं कुशद्वीपे ब्रह्मरूपं जनार्दनम्।।
यजन्तः क्षपयन्त्युग्रमधिकारफलप्रदम्।। ४०।।

They worsip Janārdana in the form of Brahmā, in the Kuśa-dvīpa according to the rites laid down in the Śāstras for the protection of their kingdom and setting aside actions which lead to temporal rewards.

विद्रुमो हेमशैलश्च द्युतिमान् पुष्पवांस्तथा।।
कुशेशयो हरिश्चैव सप्तमो मन्दराचलः।। ४१।।
वर्षाचलास्तु सप्तैते तत्र द्वीपे महामुने।।
नद्यश्च सप्त तासां तु शृणु नामान्यनुक्रमात्।। ४२।।

There are seven mountain ranges (in this island) namely : Vidruma, Hemaśaila, Dyutimat, Puṣpavan, Kuśeṣaya, Havi and Mandarācala, O great Muni. There are seven rivers—the names of which I shall relate in order, do thou hear them.

धूतपापा शिवा चैव पवित्रा सम्मतिस्तथा।।
विद्युदम्भा मही चान्या सर्वपाप हरास्त्विमाः।। ४३।।

They are Dhūtapāpa, Śiva, Pavitra, Sanmati, Vidyudambha and Mahī. They all remove sins.

अन्याः सहस्त्रशस्तत्र क्षुद्रनद्यस्तथाचलाः।।
कुशद्वीपे कुशस्तम्बः संज्ञया तस्य तत्स्मृतम्।। ४४।।

Besides there are thousands of small rivers and mountains. There is a huge clump of Kuśa-grass and the island is named after that.

तत्प्रमाणेन स द्वीपो घृतोदेन समावृतः।।
घृतोदश्च समुद्रो वै क्रौञ्चद्वीपेन संवृतः।। ४५।।

It is girt by the Ghṛta sea (the ocean of butter) of the same dimension as this insular continent.

क्रौञ्चद्वीपो महाभाग श्रूयताञ्चपरो महान्।।
कुशद्वीपस्य विस्तारा द्द्विगुणो यस्य विस्तरः।। ४६।।

The sea of Ghṛta is encircled by Krauñca-dvīpa which is twice as large as Kuśa-dvīpa.

क्रौञ्चद्वीपे द्युतिमतः पुत्रास्तस्य महात्मनः।।
तन्नामानि च वर्षाणि तेषां चक्रे महीपतिः।। ४७।।

Dyutiman was the sovereign of this island. The high-souled king named the seven varṣas after his seven sons.

कुशलो मल्लगश्चोष्णः पीवरोथान्धकारकः।।
मुनिश्च दुन्दुभिश्चैव सप्तैते तत्सुता मुने।। ४८।।

तत्रापि देवगन्धर्वसेविताः सुमनोहराः।।
वर्षाचला महाबुद्धे तेषां नामानि मे शृणु।। ४९।।

They were Kuśala, Mallaga, Uṣna, Pīvara Andhakāraka, Muni and Dundubhī, O Muni. There are seven boundary mountains highly picturesque and resorted to by the celestials and Gandharvas, O thou of great understanding; do thou hear their names from me.

क्रौञ्चचश्च वामनश्चैव तृतीयश्चान्धकारकः।।
चतुर्थो रत्नशैलश्च स्वाहिनी हयसन्निभः।। ५०।।

दिवावृत्पञ्चमश्चात्र तथान्यः पुण्डरीकवान्।।
दुन्दुभिश्च महाशैलो द्विगुणास्ते परस्परम्।।
द्वीपाद्वीपेषु ये शैला यथा द्वीपानि ते तथा।। ५१।।

They are Krauñca, Vāmana, Andhakāraka, Devarita, Puṇḍarīkavan, Dundubhī, and Mahāśaila—each of which is double the preceding one in height as each dvīpa is twice as extensive as the one before it.

वर्षेष्वेतेषु रम्येषु तथा शैलवरेषु च।।
निवसंति निरातङ्का सह देवगणैः प्रजाः।। ५२।।

पुष्कराः पुष्कला धन्यास्तितिख्याश्च महायुगं।।
ब्राह्मणाः क्षत्रिया वैश्याः शूद्राश्चानुक्रमोदिताः।। ५३।।

In these charming mountains, people reside, freed from fear, along with the celestials. In this island, O great Muni, the Brāhmaṇas, Kṣatriyas, Vaiśyas and Śūdras are respectively called Puṣkara, Puṣkala, Dhānya and Tiṣpa.

नदीमैत्रेय ते तत्र याः पिबन्ति शृणुष्व ताः।।
सप्तप्रधानाः शतशस्तत्रान्याः क्षुद्र निम्नगाः।। ५४।।

Do thou, O Maitreya, hear the names of the rivers, the waters whereof are drunk by those men. There are seven principal rivers and hundreds of small rivers.

गौरी कुमुद्वती चैव सन्ध्या रात्रिर्मनोजवा।।
क्षान्तिश्च पुण्डरीका च सप्तैता वर्षनिम्नगाः।। ५५।।

The seven principal rivers are Gaurī, Kumudvatī, Sandhyā Rātrī, Mānojavā, Kṣānti and Puṇḍarīkā.

तत्रापि विष्णुर्भग वान्पुष्कराद्यैर्जनार्दनः।।
यागै रुद्रस्वरूपश्च इज्यते यज्ञसन्निधौ।। ५६।।

In this island the four caste people worship the great Janārdana in the form of Rudra with various sacrifices.

क्रौञ्चद्वीपः समुद्रेण दधिमण्डोदकेन च।।
आवृतः सर्वतः क्रौञ्चद्वीपतुल्येन मानतः।। ५७।।
दधिमण्डोदकश्चापि शाकद्वीपेन संवृतः।।
क्रौञ्चद्वीपस्य विस्ताराद्द्विगुणेन महामुने।। ५८।।

Krauñca is girt by the sea of curds of a similar dimension and that again is encircled by Śāka-dvīpa, which is twice as much in extent, O great Muni.

शाकद्वीपेश्वरस्यापि भव्यस्य सुमहात्मनः।।
सप्तैव तनयास्तेषां ददौ वर्षाणि सप्त सः।। ५९।।

The high-souled Bhavya, the king of Śāka-dvīpa had seven sons upon whom he severally conferred the seven portions.

जलदश्च कुमारश्च सुकुमारो मरीचकः।।
कुसुमोदश्च मौदाकिः सप्तमश्च महादुमः।। ६०।।

They are Jalada, Kumāra, Sukumāra, Marīcaka, Kusumoda, Mandāki and Mahā-druma.

तत्संज्ञान्येव तत्रापि सप्त वर्षाण्यनुक्रमात्।।
तत्रापि पर्वताः सप्त वर्षविच्छेदकारिणः।। ६१।।

The seven varṣas were named in order after the seven princes. There are seven boundary mountains.

पूर्वस्तत्रोदयगिरिर्जलाधारस्तथापरः ।।
तथा रैवतकः श्यामस्तथैवास्तगिरिद्धद्वज।।
आम्बिकेयस्तथा रम्यः केसरी पर्वतोत्तमः।। ६२।।

Of these one situate on the east is Udayagirī and others are named Jatādhāra, Raivatak, Śyāmā Aṣṭagirī, Ancikeya and Kesarī. They are all charming all excellent mountains.

शाकस्तत्र महावृक्षः सिद्धगन्धर्वसेवितः।।
यत्रत्यवातसंस्पार्शादाह्लादो जायते परः।। ६३।।

There is a large Śāka (Teak) tree, frequented by the Siddhas and Gandharvas; and the wind produced by its fluttering leaves, spreads joy.

तत्र पुण्या जनपदाश्चातुर्वर्ण्यसमन्विताः।।
नद्यश्चात्र महापुण्याः सर्वपापभयापहाः।। ६४।।

The holy lands of this insular continent were inhabited by people of four castes. There are seven sacred rivers which remove all sins—

सुकुमारी कुमारी च नलिनी धेनुका च या।।
इक्षुश्च वेणुका चैव गभस्ती सप्तमी तथा।। ६५।।

They are Sukumārī, Kamārī, Nalinī, Dhenukā; Ikṣu, Beṇukā and Gabhaṣṭi.

अन्याश्च शतशस्तत्र क्षुद्रनद्यो महामुने।।
महीधरास्तथा सन्ति शतशोथ सहस्त्रशः।। ६६।।

Besides these seven rivers there are numerous rivulets. There are hundreds and thousands of mountains.

ताः पिबन्ति मुदायुक्ता जलदादिषु ये स्थिताः।।
वर्षेषु ते जनपदाः स्वर्गादभ्येत्य मेदिनीम्।। ६७।।

People residing in Jalada varṣa pertake of the waters of these rivers. They seem to have come down from heaven to earth.

धर्महानिर्न तेष्वस्ति न संघर्षः परस्परम्।।
मर्यादाव्युत्क्रमो नापि तेषु देशेषु सप्तसु।। ६८।।

In those divisions there is no decrease of virtue; there is no quarrel and there is no deviation from honesty.

वंगाश्च मागधाश्चैव मानसा मन्दगास्तथा।।
वंगा ब्राह्मणभूयिष्ठा मागधाः क्षत्रियास्तथा।।
वैश्यास्तु मानसास्तेषां शूद्रास्तेषां तु मन्दगाः।। ६९।।

The four castes, Nṛga, Māgadha, Mānasa had Mandaga correspond respectively to Brāhmaṇas, Kṣatriyas, Vaiśyas and Śūdras.

शाकद्वीपे तु तौर्विष्णुः सूर्यरूपधरोमुने।।
यथोक्तैरिज्यते सम्यक्कर्मभिर्नियतात्मभिः।। ७०।।

They worship Viṣṇu, in the form of the sun, having controlled their minds with diverse pious observances.

शाकद्वीपस्तु मैत्रेय क्षीरोदेन समावृतः।।
शाकद्वीपप्रमाणेन वलयेनेव वेष्टितः।। ७१।।

Śāka-dvīpa, O Maitreya, is girt by the sea of milk on all sides, as by a bracelet, which is of the same dimension as the contient.

क्षीराब्धिः सर्वतो ब्रह्मन्पुष्कराख्येन वेष्टितः।।
द्वीपेन शाकद्वीपात्तु द्विगुणेन समन्ततः।। ७२।।

The sea of milk, O Brāhmaṇa, is again encircled on all sides by the insular contient of Puṣkara, which is twice the extent of Sāka-dvīpa.

पुष्करे सवनस्यापि महावीरोऽभवत्सुतः।।
धातुकिश्च तयोस्तत्र द्वे वर्षे नामचिह्निते।।
महावीरं तथैवान्यद्धातुकीखण्डसं ज्ञितम्।। ७३।।

The king Savala of Puṣkara had two sons; one was named Mahāvīra and the other Dhātukī; and the two varṣas were named after them.

एकश्चात्र महाभाग प्रख्यातो वर्षपर्वतः।।
मानसोत्तरसंज्ञो वै मध्यतो वलयाकृतिः।। ७४।।

O great sage, there is only one mighty range of mountains, named Mānosattara, which runs in a circular direction like an armlet.

योजनानां सहस्त्राणि ऊर्ध्वं पञ्चशदुच्छ्रितः।।
तावदेव च विस्तीर्णः सर्वतः परिमण्डलः।। ७५।।

पुष्करद्वीपवलयं मध्येन विभजन्निव।।

It is fifty thousand *Yojanas* in height and the same in breadth, circular on all sides, and divides the island in the middle, as if like a bracelet into two divisions.

स्थितोसौ तेन विछिन्नं जातं तद्वर्षकद्वयम्।। ७६।।

वलयाकारमेकैकं तयोर्वर्षं तथा गिरिः।। ७७।।

And being divided into two portions by that mountain they are also of a circular form.

दशवर्षसहस्राणि तत्र जीवन्ति मानवाः ।।
निरामया विशोकाश्च रागद्वेषा दिवर्जिताः ।। ७८ ।।

There the people live for ten thousand years, freed from desease, sorrow, anger and jealousy.

अधमोत्तमौ न तेष्वास्तां न वध्यवधकौ द्विज ।।
नेर्ष्यासूया भयं द्वेषो दोषो लोभादिको न च ।। ७९ ।।

There is neither virtue nor vice, killer nor slain : their is no jealousy, envy fear, hatred, malice, nor any moral delinquency.

महापीतं बहिर्वर्षं धातकीखण्डमन्ततः ।।
मानसोत्तरशैलस्य देवदैत्यादिसेवितम् ।। ८० ।।

The varṣa situate on the outside of Mānosattara is called Mahāvīra and the one situated inside is called Dhātakī : they are both frequented the celestials and Dānavas.

सत्यानृतेन तत्रास्तां द्वीपे पुष्करसंज्ञिते ।।
न तत्र नद्यः शैला वा द्वीपे वर्षद्वयान्विते ।। ८१ ।।

And in that island of Puṣakara there is neither truth nor falsehood. And in that insular continent divided into two portions there is no other mountain nor river.

तुल्यवेषास्तु मनुजा देवास्तत्रैकरूपिणः ।। ८२ ।।

All men and celestials here have the same form and dress.

वर्णाश्रमाचारहीनं धर्माचरणवर्जितम् ।।
त्रयीवार्ता दण्डनीतिशुश्रूषारहितञ्च यत् ।। ८३ ।।

There is no distinction of caste or order; they do not perform rites and the three Vedas, Purāṇas, ethics, polity and the laws of service are unknown there.

वर्षद्वयं तु मैत्रेय भौमः स्वर्गोयमुत्तमः ।।
सर्वर्तुसुखदः कालो जरारोगादिवर्जितः ।।
धातकीखण्डसंज्ञेथ महावीरे च वै मुने ।। ८४ ।।

These two portions, O Maitreya, might be denominated as parardise on earth. In these two varṣas of Dhātakī and Māhāvira, where time affords delight to the inhabitants who are freed from sickness and decay.

न्यग्रोधः पुष्करद्वीपे ब्रह्मणः स्थानमुत्तमम् ।।
तस्मिन्निवसति ब्रह्मा पूज्यमानः सुरासुरैः ।। ८५ ।।

There is a Nyagrodha-tree (Fisucus-indiaca) on this insular continent which is a favourite resort of Brahmā and where he lives worshipped by he celestials and Asuras.

स्वादूदकेनोदधिना पुष्करः परिवेष्टितः ।।
समेन पुष्करस्यैव विस्तारान्मण्डलं तथा ।। ८६ ।।

Puṣkara is encircled by Svāduka ocean (sea of fresh water) which is of equal extent with the island.

एवं द्वीपाः समुद्रैश्च सप्तसप्तभिरावृताः ।।
द्वीपश्चैव समुद्रश्च समानौ द्विगुणौ परौ ।। ८७ ।।

In this way the seven insular continents are encircled by seven seas and each ocean and island is twice the dimension of that which precedes it.

पयांसि सर्वदा सर्वसमुद्रेषु समानि वै ।।
न्यूनातिरिक्तता तेषां कदाचिन्नैव जायते ।। ८८ ।।

The water, in all these oceans, remains the same at all seasons and never increases or diminishes.

स्थालीस्थमग्निसंयोगादुद्रेकिसलिले यथा ।।
तर्थेदुवृद्धौ सलिलमंभोधौ मुनिसत्तम ।। ८९ ।।

Like the water in a caldron, which expands in consequence of heat, the waters of the oceans swell with the increase of the moon, O foremost of Munis.

अन्यूनानतिरिक्ताश्च वर्धंत्यापो ह्रसंति च ।।
उदयास्तमनेष्विंदोः पक्षयोः शुक्लकृष्णयोः ।। ९० ।।

Except in the light and dark fortnights the waters neither increase nor decrease.

दशोत्तराणि पञ्चैव ह्यंगुलानां शतानि वै ।।
अपां वृद्धिक्षयौ दृष्टौ सामुद्रीणां महामुने ।। ९१ ।।

O great Muni, the rise and fall of the waters is five hundred and ten inches.

भोजनं पुष्करद्वीपे तत्र स्वयमुपस्थितम् ।।
षड्रसं भुञ्जते विप्र प्रजाः सर्वाः सदैव हि ।। ९२ ।।

In this island of Puṣkara, O Brahman, foods are produced spontaneously and people there enjoy viands of various flavours.

स्वादूदकस्य परितो दृश्यते लोकसंस्थितिः ।।
द्विगुणा काञ्चनी भूमिः सर्वजंतुविवर्जिता ।। १३ ।।

Beyond the sea of fresh water, there is the land of gold which is twice its extent where no living beings dwell.

लोकालोकस्ततश्शैलो योजनायुतविस्तृतः ।।
उच्छ्रयेणापि तावन्ति सहस्राण्यचलो हि सः ।। १४ ।।

Beyond that is the mountain Lokāloka which is a ten thousand *Yojanas* in height and as many in breadth.

ततस्तमः समावृत्य तं शैलं सर्वतः स्थितम् ।।
तमश्चाण्डकटाहेन समन्तात्परिवेष्टितम् ।। १५ ।।

The other side of the mountain is enshrouded with perpetual darkness which again is encircled by the shell of egg.

पञ्चाशत्कोटिविस्तारा सेयमुर्वी महामुने ।।
सहैवांडकटाहेन सद्वीपाब्धिमहीधरा ।। १६ ।।

Such, O Maitreya, is the earth with all its continents, mountains and oceans and exterior shell. The extent of the earth is five hundred millions.

सेयं धात्री विधात्री च सर्वभूतगुणाधिका ।।
आधारभूता सर्वेषां मैत्रेय जगतामिति ।। १७ ।।

It is the mother and nurse of beings, the foremost of all elements and the stay of all the worlds.

।। इति श्रीविष्णुमहापुराणे द्वितीयेंशे चतुर्थोऽध्यायः ।। ४ ।।

अथ द्वितीयेंशेः पञ्चमोऽध्यायः

Part II : Section 5

श्रीपराशर उवाच

विस्तार एष कथितः पृथिव्या भवतो मया ।।
सप्ततिस्तु सहस्राणि द्विजोच्छ्रयोपि कथ्यते ।। १ ।।

Parāśara said :—The extent of the earth has been related to you by me. I have also said, O twice-born one, that the depth belew the surface is seventy thousand *Yojanas.*

दशसाहस्रमेकैकं पातालं मुनिसत्तम ।।
अतलं वितलं चैव नितलं च गभस्तिमत् ।।
महाख्यं सुतलं चाग्र्यं पातालं चापि सप्तमम् ।। २ ।।

O foremost of Munis, each of the seven regions of Pātāla, extends over ten thousand *Yojanas.* They are seven in number—namely Atala, Vitala, Nitala, Gavaṣṭimat, Mahātala, Sūtala and Pātāla.

शुक्लाकृष्णारुणाः पीताः शर्कराः शैलकाञ्चनाः ।।
भूमयो यत्र मैत्रेय वरप्रासादमंडिताः ।। ३ ।।

Thus soil is severally white, black, purple, yellow, sandy, stony and of gold.

तेषु दानवदैतेया यक्षाश्च शतशस्तथा ।।
निवसन्ति महानागजा तयश्च महामुने ।। ४ ।।

They are adorned with numberless palaces in which reside Dānavas, Daityas, Yakṣas and serpents by hundreds, O great Muni.

स्वर्लोकादपि रम्याणि पातालानीति नारदः ।।
प्राह स्वर्गसदां मध्ये पातालाभ्यागतो दिवि ।। ५ ।।

Once on a time Nārada, after coming back to heaven from these regions, declared amonst the gods that Pātāla was much more charming than heaven.

आह्लादकारिणः शुभ्रा मणयो यत्र सुप्रभाः ।।
नागाभरणभूषासु पातालं केन तत्समम् ।। ६ ।।

He exclaimed "What can be compared with Pātāla where Nāgas are adorned with beautiful and brilliant and pleasure-diffusing gems?

दैत्यदानवकन्याभिरितश्चेतश्च शोभिते ।।
पाताले कस्य न प्रीतिर्विमुक्तस्यापि जायते ।। ७ ।।

This region is embellished with the daughters of Daityas and Dānavas. Who does not find delight in Pātāla? Even those who have retired from the world find delight therein.

दिवार्करश्मयो यत्र प्रभां तन्वन्ति नातपम्।।
शशिरश्मिर्न शीताय निशि द्योताय केवलम्।। ८।।

By day, the rays of the sun diffuse joy and not heat; by night the moon diffuses illumination and not cold.

भक्ष्यभोज्यमहापानमुदितैरपि भोगिभिः।।
यत्र न ज्ञायते कालो गतोषि दनु जादिभिः।। ९।।

There the sons of Danu, always happy in the enjoyment of sweet foods and good wines, do not know how the time glides away.

वनानि नद्यो रम्याणि सरांसि कमलाकराः।।
पुंस्कोकिलाभिलापाश्च मनोज्ञान्यम्बराणि च।। १०।।

There are many charming forests, rivers and ponds abounding in lotuses and the skies are resonant with the Koil's song.

भूषणान्यतिशुभ्राणि गन्धाढ्यं चानुलेपनम्।।
वीणावेणुमृदंगानां स्वनैरापूरितानि च।। ११।।

एतान्यन्यानि चोदारभाग्यभोग्यानि दानवैः।।
दैत्योरगैश्च भुज्यन्ते पातालान्तरगोचरैः।। १२।।

Charming ornaments, fragrant perfumes, ungents, the sweet music of the lute, pipe and tabor are always enjoyed by the Daityas, Dānavas and serpents who dwell in the regions of Pātāla.

पातालानामधश्चास्ते विष्णोर्या तामरी तनुः।।
शेषाख्या यद्गुणान्वक्तुं न शक्ता दैत्यदानवाः।। १३।।

Below the regions of Pātāla there is a form of Viṣṇu called Śeṣa[1] which is the outcome of the quality of darkness. The Daityas and Dānavas are incapable of counting the glories of this Deity.

योनन्तः पठ्यते सिद्धैर्दैवो देवर्षिपूजितः।।
स सहस्रशिरा व्यक्तस्वस्तिकामलभूषणः।। १४।।

This is called Ananta by the ascetics of accomplished peity and is worshipped by the celestials and great sages. He has a thousand heads which are adorned with mystic lines.

फणामणिसहस्रेण यः स विद्योतयन्दिशः।।
सर्वान्करोति निर्वीर्यान् हिताय जगतोऽसुरान्।। १५।।

For the behoof of the world he illuminates all the quarters with the jewels on his thousand fangs and all the Asuras are disabled thereby.

मदाघूर्णितनेत्रोसौ यः सदैवैककुण्डलः।।
किरीटी स्रग्धरो भाति साग्निः श्वेत इवाचलः ।।१६।।

His eye rolls perpetually in consequence of inebriation; he has an excellent Kuṇḍala, a diadem on his head and a wreath upon each brow. He shines brilliantly like white mountain topped with flame.

नीलवासा मदोत्सिक्तः श्वेतहारोपशोभितः।।
साभ्रगङ्गाप्रवाहोसौ कैलासाद्रिरिवापरः।। १७।।

He always wears a purple raiment, is always drunk and adorned with a white neclace and appears like another Kailāśa with sable clouds and the Ganges flowing.

लाङ्गलासक्तहस्ताग्रो बिभ्रन्मुसलमुत्तमम्।।
उपास्यते स्वयं कान्त्या यो वारुण्या च मूर्त्तया।। १८।।

In one hand he holds a plough and in the other a mace. And he is being worshipped by the Goddess of wealth incarnate and Vāruṇī (the goodness of wine).

कल्पान्ते यस्य वक्त्रेभ्यो विषानलशिखोज्ज्वलः।।
संकर्षणात्मको रुद्रो निष्क्रम्यात्ति जगत्त्रयम्।। १९।।

At the time of great dissolution proceeds from his mouth the venomed fire in the form of Rudra, which devours the three worlds.

स बिभ्रच्छेखरीभूतमशेषं क्षितिमण्डलम्।।
आस्ते पातालमूलस्थः शेषोऽशेषसुरार्चितः।। २०।।

This Śeṣa form of the great God worshipped by celestials, is in Pātāla, bearing the entire world on his head like a diadem.

तस्य वीर्यं प्रभावश्च स्वरूपं रूपमेव च।।
न हि वर्णयितुं शक्यं ज्ञातुं च त्रिदशैरपि।। २१।।

1.

Even the celestials are not capable of describing or knowing his strength, prowess, form and nature.

यस्यैषा सकला पृथ्वी फणामणिशिखारुणा ।।
आस्ते कुसुममालेव कस्तद्वीर्यं वदिष्यति ।। २२ ।।

Who can describe his prowess who holds the entire earth like a garland of flowers tinged with purple dye by the brilliance of jems on his crests?

यदा विजृम्भतेनन्तो मदाघूर्णितलोचनः ।।
तदा चलति भूरेषा साब्धितोया सकानना ।। २३ ।।

गन्धर्वाप्सरसः सिद्धाः किन्नरोरगचारणाः ।।
नान्तं गुणानां गच्छन्ति तेनानन्तोयमव्ययः ।। २४ ।।

When this Ananta, with his eyes rolling with intoxication, yawns the entire earth with its oceans, rivers and forests trembles; the Gandharvas, the Apsarās, Siddhas, Kinnaras, serpents and Cāraṇas have not been able to find out the end of the qualities of his Being without end and hence he is called Ananta.

यस्य नागवधूहस्तैर्लेपितं हरिचन्दनम् ।।
मुहुः श्वासानिलापास्तं याति दिक्क्षोदवासताम् ।। २५ ।।

The sandal paste, which is ground by the wives of the Nāgas, is spread around by his breath and scatters fragrance all over the quarters.

यमाराध्य पुराणर्षिर्गर्गो ज्योतींषि तत्त्वतः ।।
ज्ञातवान्सकलं चैव निमित्तपठितं फलम् ।। २६ ।।

Having worshipped him the ancient sage Garga obtained from him a knowledge of astronomy, of the planets and of the good and evil presaged by the aspects of the heavens.

तेनेयं नागवर्येण शिरसा विधृता मही ।।
बिभर्ति मालां लोकानां सदेवासुरमानुषाम् ।। २७ ।।

The earth is supported by that Great Serpent, upon his head; and the earth again holds the garland of spheres along with men, celestials and Asuras.

।। इति श्रीविष्णु महापुराणे द्वितीयेंशे पञ्चमोऽध्यायः ।।५।।

अथ द्वितीयेंशेः षष्ठोऽध्यायः

Part II : Section 6

पराशर उवाच

ततश्च नरका विप्र भुवोधः सलिलस्य च ।।
पापिनो येषु पात्यन्ते ताञ्छृणुष्व महामुने ।। १ ।।

Parāśara said :—O Brāhmaṇa, there are some hells below the earth and the waters into which sinners falls. I shall give you an account, O great Muni.

रौरवः सूकरो रोधस्तालो विशसनस्तथा ।।
महाज्वालस्तप्तकुम्भो लवणोथ विलोहितः ।। २ ।।

रुधिराम्भो वैतरणिः क्रिमिशः क्रिमिभोजनः ।।
असिपत्रवनं कृष्णो लालाभक्षश्च दारुणः ।। ३ ।।

तथा पूयवहः पापो वह्निज्वालो ह्यधःशिराः ।।
सन्दंशः कालसूत्रश्च तमश्चाऽवीचिरेव च ।। ४ ।।

श्वभोजनोथाप्रतिष्ठाश्चाप्रचिश्च तथा परः ।।
इत्येवमादयश्चान्ये नरका भृशदारुणाः ।। ५ ।।

The names of the various hells are : Raurava, Śukara, Rodha, Tāla, Viśāsana, Mahājwālā, Taptakumbha, Lavaṇa, Vimohana, Rudhirāndha, Vaitaraṇī, Kṛmiṣā, Kṛmibhojana, Aśipatravana, Kṛṣna, Lālābhakṣa, Dāruṇā, Puyavāha, Pāpa, Vahnijwālā, Adhośiras, Sandansa, Kālasūtra, Tāmas, Avīcī, Swabhojana, Apratiṣtha, and another Avīcī.

यमस्य विषये घोराः शस्त्राग्निभयदायिनः ।।
पतन्ति येषु पुरुषाः पापकर्मरतास्तु ये ।। ६ ।।

These are the dreadful hells constituting the various provinces of the kingdom of Yama dreadful with his instruments of torture, into which are hurled down those persons, who are addicted to sinful actions.

कूटसाक्षी तथाऽसम्यक्पक्षपातेन यो वदेत् ।।
यश्चान्यदनृतं वक्ति स नरो याति रौरवम् ।। ७ ।।

Those who give false evidence, those who act as mediators through partiality, those who speak untruth, are thrown into the Raurava (dreadful) hell.

भ्रूणहा पुरहन्ता च गोघ्नश्च मुनिसत्तम।।
यान्ति ते नरकं रोधं यश्चौच्छ्वासनिरोधकः।। ८।।

He, who causes abortion, devastates a town, kills a cow, or strangles a man to death goes to the Rodha hell (or that of obstruction).

सुरापो ब्रह्महा हर्ता सुवर्णस्य च सूकरे।।
प्रयांति नरके यश्च तैः संसर्गमुपैति वै।। ९।।

He who drinks intoxicating liquors, destroys a Brāhmaṇa, steals gold or associates with them who perpetrate these crimes, goes to the Śukara (swine) hell.

राजन्यवैश्यहन्ता च तथैव गुरुतल्पगः।।
तप्तकुण्डे स्वसृगामी हन्ति राजभटांश्च यः।। १०।।

He, who murders Kṣatriya or a Vaiśya or commits adultery with the wife of his preceptor, is despatched to the Tālā (padlock) hell. And one, who holds incestuous intercourse with his sister or slays royal emissary, goes to Taptakumbha (heated jar) hell.

साध्वीविक्रयकृद्‌बंधणपालः केसरिविक्रयी।।
तप्तलोहे पतन्त्येते यश्च भक्तं परित्यजेत्।। ११।।

One, who sells his chaste wife, the jailor, one who deals in horses and forsakes his followers, is sent to Taptalohā (red-hot iron) hell.

स्नुषां सुतां चापि गत्वा महाज्वाले निपात्यते।।
अवमन्ता गुरूणां यो यश्चाक्रोष्टा नराधमः।। १२।।

One who commits incest with a daughter-in-law and daughter is sent into Mahajwālā hell.

वेददूषयिता यश्च वेदविक्रयिकश्च यः।।
अगम्यगामी यश्च स्यात्ते यान्ति लवणं द्विज।। १३।।

That vile of a man who disrespects his spiritual guide or his betters, who reviles the Vedas or sells them and who associates with women to whom they should not go, is sent into Lavaṇa hell.

चोरो विलोहे पतति मर्यादादूषकस्तथा।। १४।।

A thief and a hater of prescribed rites fall into Vimohana hell.

देवद्विजपितृद्वेष्टां रत्नदूषयिता च यः।।
स याति क्रिमिभक्षे वै क्रिमिशे च दुरिष्टकृत्।। १५।।

He who disrespects his father, the Brāhmaṇas and the gods, or one who spoils gems, falls into the Krimibhokṣa hell. He, who practises magic rites to injure others, falls into Kṛmiśa hell.

पितृदेवातिथींस्त्यक्त्वापर्यश्नति नराधमः।।
लालाभक्षे स यात्युग्रे शरकर्त्ता च वेधके।। १६।।

That vile of a man who takes his meals before offering food to the gods, to the manes and guests is despatched into Lālābhakṣa hell (where saliva is given for food). One who makes arrows is sent into Vidhaka hell.

करोति कर्णिनो यश्च यश्च खड्‌गादिकृन्नरः।।
प्रयान्त्येते विशसने नरके भृशदारुणे।। १७।।

He, who makes lances, swords and other weapons, is sent into the dreadful hell of Viṣaśana (murderous).

असत्प्रतिगृहीता तु नरके यात्यधोमुखे।।
अयाज्ययाजकश्चैव तथा नक्षत्रसूचकः।। १८।।

He who takes bribes is sent into Adhomukha hell (in which head is inverted) as well as he who offers sacrifices to improper objects and predicts the movements of stars and planets.

वेगी पूयवहे चैको याति मिष्टान्नभुङ्गरः।। १९।।

लाक्षामांसरसानां च तिलानां लवणस्य च।।
विक्रेता ब्राह्मणो याति तमेव नरकं द्विज।। २०।।

मार्जारकुक्कुटच्छागश्ववराहविहंगमान्।।
पोषयन्नरकं याति तमेव द्विजसत्तम।। २१।।

One who eats alone sweetmeats, a Brāhmaṇa who deals in lac, flesh, liquors, sesamum, or salt, one who commits violence, and those who rear up cats, cocks, goats, dogs, hogs and birds are despatched into hell Puyavāha (or where matter flows).

रङ्गोपजीवी कैवर्त्तः कुण्डाशी गरदस्तथा।।
सूची माहिषकश्चैव पर्वकारी च यो द्विजः।। २२।।

अगारदाही मित्रघ्नः शाकुनिर्ग्रामयाजकः।।
रुधिरान्धे पतन्त्येते सोमं विक्रीणते च ये।। २३।।

The Brāhmaṇa who leads the life of an actor, fisherman, who depends upon a person born in adultery, who is a prisoner, an informer, one who lives by his wife's immoral habits, who looks to secular affairs on Parva days, who is an incendiary, a faithless friend, a soothsayer, who vends birds, performs religious rites for the rustics, who sells the juice of some trees is thrown into Rudhirāndha hell (whose wells are blood).

मखहा ग्रामहन्ता च याति वैतरणीं नरः।। २४।।

He, who spoils honey or devastates a village, is sent into Vaitaraṇī hell.

रेतःपातादिकर्त्तारो मर्यादाभेदिनो हि ये।।
ते कृष्णे यान्त्यशौचाश्च कुहकाजीविनश्च ये।। २५।।

He, who causes impotence tresspasses upon others' lands, is impure and lives on magic rites, is sent into the Kṛṣṇa hell (black).

असिपत्रवनं याति वनच्छेदी वृथैव यः।।
औरभ्रिको मृगव्याधो वह्निज्वाले पतन्ति वै।। २६।।
यान्त्येते द्विज तत्रैव ये चापाकेषु वह्निदाः।। २७।।

He who uselessly cuts down trees goes to Asipatravana hell. Those who tend on sheep, those who give haunt deer and those who fire to unbaked vessels are sent to Vahnijwālā hell or of fiery flame.

व्रतानां लोपको यश्च स्वाश्रमाद्विच्युतश्च यः।।
सन्दंशयातनामध्ये पततस्तावुभावपि।। २८।।

One, who violates his own vow or trangresses the rules of his own order, goes into the Sandanśana (or the hell of pincers).

दिवा स्वप्ने च स्कन्दन्ते ये नरा ब्रह्मचारिणः।।
पुत्रैरध्यापिता ये च ते पतन्ति श्वभोजने।। २९।।

The religious student who sleeps in the day and becomes defiled and those who receive instruction from their children go to the hell called Śvabhojana (where they feed upon dogs).

एते चान्ये च नरकाः शतशोथ सहस्रशः।।
येषु दुष्कृतकर्माणः पच्यन्ते यातनागताः।। ३०।।

Besides these there are hundreds and thousands of other hells, where persons, perpetrating diverse iniquities, are visited with various punishments.

यथैव पापान्येतानि तथान्यानि सहस्रशः।।
भुज्यन्ते तानि पुरुषैर्नरकान्तगोचरैः।। ३१।।

There are thousands of hells like the numberless crimes committed by men, in which they are punished according to the nature of their offences.

वर्णाश्रमविरुद्धं च कर्म कुर्वन्ति ये नराः।।
कर्मणा मनसा वाचा निरयेषु पतन्ति ते।। ३२।।

And those who swerve from the obligation laid upon them by their caste or order, in thought, word or deed are thrown into these hells.

अधःशिरोभिर्दृश्यन्ते नारकैर्दिवि देवताः।।
देवाश्चाधोमुखान्सर्वानधः पश्यन्ति नारकान्।। ३३।।

The celestials are seen by those who are thrown into these hells, with their own heads inverted and the celestials also behold the inhabitants of hell with their heads downwards.

स्थावराः क्रिमयोब्जाश्च पक्षिणः पशवो नराः।।
धार्मिकास्त्रिदशास्तद्वन्मोक्षिणश्च यथाक्रमम्।। ३४।।

After undergoing the sufferings of hell the sinners go through the various stages of existence, namely :—inanimate things, the acquatic animals, birds, animals, men, pious men, gods and liberated spirits.

सहस्रभागप्रथमा द्वितीयानुक्रमास्तथा।।
सर्वे ह्येते महाभाग यावन्मुक्तिसमाश्रयाः।। ३५।।

O great sage, each of these stages is in succession a thousand degrees superior to that which precedes it. People go through these stages until they obtain emancipation.

यावन्तो जन्तवः स्वर्गे तावन्तो नरकौकसः।।
पापकृद्याति नरकं प्रायश्चित्तपराङ्मुखः।। ३६।।

There are as many inhabitants in hell as are in heaven : those who commit sin and do not make an expiation of guilt proceed to hell.

पापानामनुरूपाणि प्रायश्चित्तानि यद्यथा।।
तथा तथैव संस्मृत्य प्रोक्तानि परमर्षिभिः।। ३७।।

Becoming acts of expiation for every short of inquity have been laid down by the great sages.

पापे गुरूणि गुरुणि स्वल्पान्यल्पे च तद्विदः।।
प्रायश्चित्तानि मैत्रेय जगुः स्वायंभुवादयः।। ३८।।

O Maitreya, Swayambhuva and others have dictated severe penances for great crimes, and light ones for ordinary offences.

प्रायश्चित्तान्यशेषाणि तपःकर्मात्मकानि वै।।
यानि तेषामशेषाणां कृष्णानुस्मरणम्परम्।। ३९।।

Amongst the numerous arduous penances laid down by them, the remembrance of Hari is the foremost.

कृते पापेऽनुतापो वै यस्य पुंसः प्रजायते।।
प्रायश्चित्तं तु तस्यैकं हरिसंस्मरणं परम्।। ४०।।

For them, who are penitent after having committed many iniquities, the greatest penance is the remembrance of Hari.

प्रातर्निशि तथा सन्ध्यामध्याह्नादिषु संस्मरन्।।
नारायणमवाप्नोति सद्यः पापक्षयन्नरः।। ४१।।

If a man meditates upon Hari either in the morning, at sunset, midday or at night he is released from all sins.

विष्णुसंस्मरणात्क्षीणसमस्तक्लेशसञ्चयः।।
मुक्तिं प्रयाति स्वर्गाप्तिस्तस्य विघ्नोनुमीयते।। ४२।।

By meditating upon Viṣṇu he is released from the heap of worldly afflictions. He obtains final emancipation considering even heaven as impediment.

वासुदेवे मनो यस्य जपहोमार्चनादिषु।।
तस्यान्तरायो मैत्रेय देवेंद्रत्वादिकं फलम्।। ४३।।

He, whose mind is devoted to Vāsudeva in prayer, burnt offering or adoration, considers, O Maitreya, even the dignity of Indra as an obstacle to the acquirement of final liberation.

क्व नाकपृष्ठगमनं पुनरावृत्तिलक्षणम्।।
क्व जपा वासुदेवेति मुक्तिबीजमनुत्तमम्।। ४४।।

What is the use of going to heaven whence it is necessary to come back to earth? And how different is the meditation of Vāsudeva which leads to final liberation.

तस्मादहर्निशं विष्णु संस्मरन्पुरुषो मुने।।
न याति नरकं मर्त्यः संक्षीणाखिलपातकः।। ४५।।

Therefore, O Muni, the man, who meditats upon Viṣṇu day and night, is released from all sins and does not go to Naraka after death.

मनः प्रीतिकरः स्वर्गो नरकस्तद्विपर्ययः।।
नरकस्वर्गसंज्ञे वै पापपुण्ये द्विजोत्तम।। ४६।।

O foremost of twice-born ones, that which gives delight to mind is heaven, and that which gives pain is hell, hence vice is denominated as hell and virtue as heaven.

वस्त्वेकमेव दुःखाय सुखायेर्ष्यागमाय च।।
कोपाय च यतस्तस्माद्वस्तु वस्त्वात्मकं कुतः।। ४७।।

The self-same thing some times gives delight, sometimes produces pains, sometimes excites jealousy and sometimes anger.

तदेव प्रीतये भूत्वा पुनर्दुःखा य जायते।।
तदेव कोपाय यतः प्रसादाय च जायते।। ४८।।

Therefore every thing (in this world) is the source of miseries.[1] The same thing at one time brings on anger and again conduces to our delight.

तस्माद्दुःखात्मकं नास्ति न च किंचित्सुखात्मकम्।।
मनसः परिणामोयं सुखदुःखादिलक्षणः।। ४९।।

Therefore nothing in itself is either pleasurable or painful; pleasure pain and the like merely denominate the various states of the mind.

1. There is another reading *Vāstu Vastatmakan Kūṭa* : which when translated stands as "Whence they an it be considered as essentially the same with the either."

ज्ञानमेव परं ब्रह्म ज्ञानं बन्धाय चेष्यते।।
ज्ञानात्मकमिदं विश्वं न ज्ञानाद्विद्यते परम्।। ५०।।

विद्याविद्येति मैत्रेय ज्ञानमेवोपधारय।। ५१।।

Therefore true wisdom consists only in the knowledge of Brahmā, which brings on confinement to the world. True wisdom pervades through the whole universe and there is the existence of no other thing but this; ignorance and knowledge are therefore comprised in true wisdom, O Maitreya.

एवमेतन्मकयाख्यातं भवतो मण्डलं भुवः।।
पातालानि च सर्वाणि तथैव नरका द्विज।। ५२।।

समुद्राः पर्वताश्चैव द्वीपा वर्षाणि निम्नगाः।।
संक्षेपात्सर्वमाख्यातं किं भूयः श्रोतुमिच्छसि।।५३।।

O twice-born one, I have thus described to you the entire earth, all the divisions of the region under the earth and the hells, the oceans, the mountains, the insular continents, and the rivers. I have described all to you in short, what again do you hear?

।। इति श्रीविष्णुमहापुराणे द्वितीयेंशे षष्ठोऽध्यायः।। ६।।

अथ द्वितीयेंशे: सप्तमोऽध्यायः

Part II : Section 7

मैत्रेय उवाच

कथितं भूतलं ब्रह्मन्ममैतदखिलं त्वया।।
भुवर्लोकादिकाँल्लोकाञ्छ्रोतुमिच्छाम्यहं मुने।। १।।

तथैव ग्रहसंस्थानं प्रमाणानि यथा तथा।।
समाचक्ष्व महाभाग तन्मह्यं परिपृच्छते।। २।।

Maitreya said :—The entire earth has been described to me by you. O Brāhmaṇa, I wish to hear now, O Muni, an account of the regions above the world, the Bhuvar-loka, the situation and dimension of the heavenly bodies. Do you relate them to me, O great sage.

श्रीपराशर उवाच

रविचन्द्रमसोर्यावन्मयूखैरवभास्यते ।।
ससमुद्रसरिच्छैला तावती पृथिवी स्मृता।। ३।।

Parāśara said—The terrestrial sphere (or Bhurloka) comprising the oceans, rivers and mountains extends as far as it is illuminated by the rays of the sun and the moon.

यावत्प्रमाणा पृथिवी विस्तारपरिमण्डलात्।।
नभस्तावत्प्रमाणं वै व्यासमण्डलो द्विज।। ४।।

The atmospheric sphere (or the Bhuvar-loka), of the same extent both in diameter and circumference, spreads upwards, O twice-born one, as far as the heaven.

भूमेर्योजनलक्षे तु सौरं मैत्रेय मण्डलम्।।
लक्षाद्दिवाकरस्यापि मण्डलं शशिनः स्थितम्।।५।।

The solar region is situated a hundred thousand Yojanas from the earth; and the region of the moon is situated at an equal distance from the sun.

पूर्णे शतसहस्रे तु योजनानां निशाकरात्।।
नक्षत्र मण्डलं कृत्स्नमुपरिष्टात्प्रकाशते।। ६।।

About the same distance above the moon is sitauted the orbit of all the lunar constellations.

द्वे लक्षे चोत्तरे ब्रह्मन् बुधो नक्षत्रमण्डलात्।।
तावत्प्रमाणभागे तु बुधस्याप्युशनाः स्थितः।। ७।।

And two hundred thousand Yojanas, upwards, O Brāhmaṇa, is situated the region of the planet Buddha (Mercury).

अङ्गारकोपि शुक्रस्य तत्प्रमाणे व्यवस्थितः।।
लक्षद्वये तु भौमस्य स्थितो देवपुरोहितः।। ८।।

And at the same distance above that is situate the planet Śukra (Venus). And at the same distance above that is Aṅgāraka (Mars). And at the same distance above that is the priest of gods (Bṛhaspati or Jupiter).

सौरिर्बृहस्पतेश्चोर्ध्वे द्विलक्षे समवस्थितः।।
सप्तर्षिमण्डलं तस्माल्लक्षमेकं द्विजोत्तम।। ९।।

ऋषिभ्यस्तु सहस्राणां शतादूर्ध्वं व्यवस्थितः ।।
मेढीभूतः समस्तस्य ज्योतिश्चक्रस्य वै ध्रुवः ।। १० ।।

And Śani (Saturn) is two hundred and fifty thousand Yojanas above Jupiter. O foremost of twice-born ones, one hundred thousand leagues above that is the region of seven Ṛṣis. And at a similar distance above that is Dhruva (the pole-star) the axis of the circle of planets.

त्रैलोक्यमेतत्कथितमुत्सेधेन महामुने ।।
इज्याफलस्य भूरेषा इज्या चात्र प्रतिष्ठिता ।। ११ ।।

Thus I have described to you, O great Muni, the elevation of three spheres, which constitute the region of the fruits of works. And the land of works is also here namely Bhārata.

ध्रुवादूर्ध्वं महर्लोको यत्र ते कल्प वासिनः ।।
एकयोजनकोटिस्तु यत्र ते कल्पवासिनः ।। १२ ।।

At a distance of one Koṭi Yojanas above Dhruva is Maharloha (the region of saints) the inhabitants of which live for a Kalpa (or a day of Brahmā).

द्वे कोटी तु जनो लोको यत्र ते ब्रह्मणः सुताः ।।
सनन्दनाद्याः प्रथिता मैत्रेयामलचेतसः ।। १३ ।।

And at a distance of two Koṭi Yojanas above that is Janaloka where reside the pure-minded sons of Brahmā, Sananda and others, of whom I had described to you before, O Maitreya.

चतुर्गुणात्तरे चोर्ध्वं जनलोकात्तपः स्थितः ।।
वैराजा यत्र ते देवाः स्थिता दाहविवर्जिताः ।। १४ ।।

And at a distance of eight Koṭi Yojanas is Tapa-loka where reside the celestials named *Baibhrājas*, unconsumable by fire.

षड्गुणेन तपोलोकात्सत्यलोको विराजते ।।
अपुनर्मारका यत्र ब्रह्मलोको हि संस्मृतः ।। १५ ।।

At six times the distance from Tapaloka is situated Satya-loka, where-in the inhabitants do not know death and which is otherwise named Brahmā-loka.

पादगम्यन्तु यत्किञ्चिद्वस्त्वस्ति पृथिवीमयम् ।।
स भूर्लोकः समाख्यातो विस्तरोस्य मयोदितः ।। १६ ।।

Wherever earthly object exists which may be trodden by feet, that makes up Bhur-loka whose dimensions I have already described to you.

भूमिसूर्यान्तरं यच्च सिद्धादिमुनि सेवितम् ।।
भुवर्लोकस्तु सोप्युक्तो द्वितीयो मुनिसत्तम् ।। १७ ।।

The region that extends from the earth to the sun is called Bhur-loka, inhabited by the Siddhas, Munis and others and which is called the second sphere, O foremost of sages.

ध्रुवसूर्यान्तरं यच्च नियुतानि चतुर्दश ।।
स्वर्लोकः सोपि गदितो लोकसं स्थानचिन्तकैः ।। १८ ।।

The distance, between the Sun and Dhruva which extends over fourteen hundred thousands leagues, is called Swar-loka by those who are conversant with the position of planets.

त्रैलोक्यमेतत्कृतकं मैत्रेय परिपठ्यते ।।
जनस्तपस्तथा सत्यमिति चाकृतकं त्रयम् ।। १९ ।।

These three spheres are called transitory, O Maitreya and three, Jana, Tapa and Satya, are termed durable.

कृतकाकृतयोर्मध्ये महर्लोक इति स्मृतः ।।
शून्यो भवति कल्पान्ते योत्यन्तं न विनश्यति ।। २० ।।

And Mahar-loka, which is situated between these two, partakes of the nature of the both and though it becomes devoid of all beings at the end of Kalpa it is not finally destroyed.

एते सप्त मया लोका मैत्रेय कथितास्तव ।।
पातालानि च सप्तैव ब्रह्माण्डस्यैष विस्तरः ।। २१ ।।

I have thus described to you. O Maitreya, the seven Lokas, and the seven Pātālas constituting the extent of the whole world.

एतदण्डकटाहेन तिर्यक् चोध्वमधस्तथा ।।
कपित्थस्य यथा बीजं सर्वतो वै समावृतम् ।। २२ ।।

As the seed is covered by its rind so the world is girt on every side and above and below by the shell of the egg of Brahmā.

दशोत्तरेण पयसा मैत्रेयांडं च तद्वृतम् ।।
सर्वोम्बुपरिधानोसौ वह्निना वेष्टितो बहिः ।। २३ ।।

And this shell again, O Maitreya, is

encircled by water which extends over space equal to ten times the earth. And the waters again are encompassed on the outer surface by fire.

वह्निश्च वायुना वायुर्मैत्रेय नभसा वृतः।।
भूतादिना नभः सोपि महता परिवेष्टितः।।
दशोत्तराण्यशेषाणि मैत्रेयैतानि सप्त वै।। २४।।

And this fire is encompassed by the air, and the air by the sky, the sky by the origin of the elements and that again by the intellect, O Maitreya. And each of these seven extends ten times the breadth of one it encircles, O Maitreya.

महान्तं च समावृत्य प्रधानं समवस्थितम्।।
अनन्तस्य न तस्यान्तः संख्यानं चापि विद्यते।। २५।।

And the last is encircled by the Chief-Principle. This supreme nature has no end and cannot be measured.

तदनन्तमसंख्यातप्रमाणं चापि वै यतः।।
हेतुभूतमशेषस्य प्रकृतिः सा परा मुने।। २६।।
अंडानां तु सहस्राणां सहस्राण्ययुतानि च।।
ईदृशानां तथा तत्र कोटिकोटिशतानि च।। २७।।

It is therefore called endless, immeasurable and the cause of all existing things. This Prakṛti, O Muni, is the source of the endless universe and of thousand, ten thousands and millions and thousands of millions of mundane eggs.

दारुण्यग्निर्यथा तैलं तिले तद्वत्पुमानपि।।
प्रधानेऽवस्थितो व्यापी चेतनात्मात्मवेदनः।। २८।।

As fire exists in wood, oil exists in sessamun, so the self-conscious, all-spreading and self-irraviating soul exists in this Pradhāna.

प्रधानं च पुमांश्चैव सर्वभूतात्मभूतया।।
विष्णुशक्त्या महाबुद्धे वृतौ संश्रयधर्मिणौ।। २९।।

O thou of great intellect, this nature and soul exist as dependants and are encompassed by the energy of Viṣṇu, which is the soul of the universe.

तयोः सैव पृथग्भावकारणं संश्रयस्य च।।
क्षोभकारणभूता च सर्गकाले महामते।। ३०।।

O thou of great mind, this energy of Viṣṇu separates them at the time of dissolution and unites them at the time of creation. And this at the beginning of creation is the cause of this agitation.

यथा सक्तं जले वातो बिभर्त्ति कणिकाशतम्।।
शक्तिः सापि तथा विष्णोः प्रधानपुरुषात्मकम्।। ३१।।

As the wind agitates the surface of water in a hundred bubbles so this energy of Viṣṇu which is at one with the nature and soul influences the universe.[1]

यथा च पादयोर्मूलस्कन्धशाखादिसंयुतः।।
आदिबीजात्प्रभवति बीजान्यन्यानि वै ततः।। ३२।।

प्रभवन्ति ततस्तेभ्यः सम्भवन्त्यपरे द्रुमाः।।
तेपि तल्लक्षणद्रव्यकारणानुगता मुने।। ३३।।

एवमव्याकृतात्पूर्वं जायन्ते महदादयः।।
विशेषान्तास्ततस्तेभ्यः संभवंत्यसुरादयः।।
तैभ्यश्च पुत्रास्तेषां च पुत्राणामपरे सुताः।। ३४।।

As a tree, containing root, stem and branches, originates from an original seed and produces other seeds, from which grow other trees, similar in kind to the first, so from Pradhāna germinate intellect and other rudiments of things—from them grow grosser elements—from them Asuras and others and who again are followed by sons and sons of sons.

बीजाद्वृक्षप्ररोहेण यथा नापचयस्तरोः।।
भूतानां भूतसर्गेण नैवास्त्यपचयस्तथा।। ३५।।

As the first tree is not spoiled when another grows out of it so there is no waste of beings by the creation of others.

सन्निधानाद्यथाकाशकालाद्याः कारणं तरोः।।
तथैवापरिणामेन विश्वस्य भगवान्हरिः।। ३६।।

As space, time and the like are the cause of the tree so the divine Hari is the cause of the developments of the universe.

व्रीहिबीजे यथा मूलं नालं पत्राङ्कुरौ तथा।।
काण्डकोषस्तु पुष्पं च क्षीरं तद्वच्च तण्डुलाः।। ३७।।

1. There is another reading *Pradhāna puruṣottam* qualifying the universe i.e. universe consisting of inert nature and soul.

तुषाः कणाश्च सन्तो वै यान्त्याविर्भावमात्मनः।।
प्ररोहहेतुसामग्र्यमासाद्य मुनिसत्तम।। ३८।।
तथा कर्मस्वनेकेषु देवाद्याः समवस्थिताः।।
विष्णुशक्तिं समतासाद्य प्ररोहमुपयान्ति वै।। ३९।।

As all the portions of the plant remaining in the seed of rice, or the root, the culm, the leaf, the short, the steam, the bud, the fruit, the milk, the grain, the chaff, the ear, grow up when they come in contact with those things which help their growth (earth and water), so the celestials, men and other beings, remaining in the states to which they are destined in consequence of their good or bad actions, appear in their full growth by virtue of the energy of Viṣṇu.

स च विष्णुः परं ब्रह्म यतः सर्वमिदं जगत्।।
जगच्च यो यत्र चेदं यस्मिंश्च लयमेष्यति।। ४०।।

He is Viṣṇu, the great Brahmā, from whom the creation of the unvierse has proceeded, who is the world, in whom the world exists and in whom it will be dissovled.

तद्ब्रह्म तत्परं धाम सदसत्परमं पदम्।।
यस्य सर्वमभेदेन यतश्चैतच्चराचरम्।। ४१।।

He is Brahmā, the excellent abode, the excellent state, the essence of all that is visible and invisible, from whom proceeds, the creation, animate and inanimate.

स एव मूलप्रकृतिर्व्यक्तरूपी जगच्च सः।।
तस्मिन्नेव लयं सर्वं याति तत्र च तिष्ठति।। ४२।।

He is the primary nature, manifestation of the universe, in whom all beings exist and in whom all beings will finally immerge.

क्रत्ता क्रियाणां स च इज्यते
कतुः स एवतत्कर्मफलं च तस्य।।
स्त्रुगादियत्साधनमप्यशेषं
हरेर्न किञ्चिद्व्यतिरिक्तमस्ति।। ४३।।

He is the performer of all devotional rites, he is the sacrifice; he is the fruit that it confers and he is the tools by which it is celebrated. There is no other thing but Hari.

।। इति श्रीविष्णुमहापुराणे द्वितीयेंशे सप्तमोऽध्यायः।।७।।

अथ द्वितीयेंशेः अष्टमोऽध्यायः

Part II : Section 8

श्रीपराशर उवाच

व्याख्यातमेतद्ब्रह्माण्डसंस्थानं तव सुव्रत।।
ततः प्रमाणसंस्थाने सूर्यादीनां शृणुष्व मे।। १।।

Parāśara said :—I have described to you the system of the universe in general : I shall now describe the sitautions and dimensions of the sun and other luminaries.

योजनानां सहस्त्राणि भास्करस्य रथो नव।।
ईषादण्डस्तथैवास्य द्विगुणो मुनिसत्तम्।। २।।

सार्धकोटिस्तथा सप्त नियुतान्यधिकानि वै।।
योजनानां तु तस्या क्षस्तत्र चक्रं प्रतिष्ठितम्।। ३।।

त्रिनाभिमति पञ्चारे षण्णेमिन्यक्षयात्मके।।
संवत्सरमये कृत्स्नं कालचक्रं प्रतिष्ठितम्।। ४।।

O foremost of Munis, the chariot of the sun is nine thousand leagues in length and the pole is of twice that size; the axle is more than fifteen millions and seven hundred thousand *yoyanas* long[1], on which a wheel is placed with three naves, five spokes and six peripheries. It is undecaying and continues for the year and consequently all the cycles of the time are placed herein.

हयाश्च सप्तच्छदांसि तेषां नामानि मे शृणु।।
गायत्री च बृहत्युष्णिग्जगती त्रिष्टुभेव च।। ५।।

चत्वारिंशत्सहस्त्राणिद्वितीयोऽक्षो विवस्वतः।।
पञ्चान्यानि तु सार्धानि स्यन्दनस्य महामते।। ६।।

1. The three naves are the three portions of the day namely, morning, noon and night; the five spokes are the five cyclic years and the six peripheries are the six seasons.

अक्षप्रमाणमुभयोः प्रमाणं तद्युगार्द्धयो।।
ह्रस्वो क्षस्तद्युगार्द्धेन ध्रुवाधारो रथस्य वै।।
द्वितीयेक्षे तु तच्चक्रं संस्थितं मानसाचले।। ७।।

The second axle of his chariot is forty five thousand, five hundred leagues long. O thou of great mind, the two halves of the yoke are respectively as long as two axles. The short axle and the short yoke are supported by pole star : the end of the longer axle to which is fixed the wheel is situate on Mānasā mountain. The seven steeds which draw the sun's car are the metres of the Vedas Gāyatrī, Vṛhatī, Uṣṇiḥ, Yayātī, Triṣṭubh, Anushtubh and Paṅkti.

मानसोत्तरशैलस्यः पूर्वतो वासवी पुरी।।
दक्षिणे तु यम स्यान्याप्रतीच्यां वरुणस्य च।।
उत्तरेण च सोमस्य तासां नामानि मे शृणु।। ८।।

The city of Vāsava is situated on the eastern side of the Mānosottara mountain, on its shouthern side is the city of wealth, on its western side is the city of Varuṇa and on the northern side is the city of Soma. I shall relate the names of those cities; do thou hear them.

वस्वौकसारा शक्रस्य याम्या संयमनी तथा।।
पुरी सुखा जलेशस्य सोमस्य च विभावरी।। ९।।

The city of Śakra is named Vasvoksārā, that of Yama is called Samyamanī; that of Varuṇa is named Mukhyā and that of Soma Vibhāvarī.

काष्ठां गतो दक्षिणतः क्षिप्तेषुरिव सर्पति।।
मैत्रेय भगवान्भानुर्ज्योतिषां चक्रसंयुतः।। १०।।

अहोरात्रव्यवस्थानकारणं भगवान्रविः।।
देवयानः परः पन्था योगिनां क्लेशसंक्षये।। ११।।

O Maitreya, the glorious sun moves speedily like a dart on his southern course attended by the constellations of the Zodiac : He creates day and night and is the divine path of the sages who have got over the worldly afflictions.

दिवसस्य रविर्मध्ये सर्वकालं व्यवस्थितः।।
सर्वद्वीपेषु मैत्रेय निशार्द्धस्य च सन्मुखः।। १२।।

उदयास्तमने चैव सर्वकालं तु सम्मुखे।।
विदिशासु त्वशेषासु तथा ब्रह्मन् दिशासु च।। १३।।

O Maitreya, while in one insular continent the sun shines in midday, in the opposite Dvīpas it will be midnight; rising and setting thus take place at all seasons and are always opposed in the different cardinal and intermediate points of horizon.

यैर्यत्र दृश्यते भास्वान्स तेषामुदयः स्मृतः।।
तिरोभावं च यत्रैति तत्रैवास्तमनं रवेः।। १४।।

Wherever the sun is visible he is said to rise there and wherever he dissappears from view he is said to be set.

नैवास्तमनमर्कस्य नोदयः सर्वदा सतः।।
उदयास्तमनाख्यं हि दर्शनादर्शनं रवेः।। १५।।

In south, their is neither rising nor setting of the sun; for he always exists; the appearance and disappearance of the sun are merely called rising and setting.

शक्रादीनां पुरे तिष्ठन् स्पृशत्येष पुरत्रयम्।।
विकोणौ द्वौ विकोणस्थस्त्रीन् कोणान्द्वे पुरे तथा।। १६।।

When the sun is in the cities of Śakra and others, the three cities and two intermidiate points are illuminated; and when he is in an intermediate point he extends light to the two cities and three intermediate points.

उदितो वर्द्धमानाभिराध्याह्नात्तपन्रविः।।
ततः परं ह्रसन्तीभिर्गोभिरस्तं नियच्छति।। १७।।

From the time of his rising till midday the rays of the sun gradually increase; and from then he moves towards setting with his diminishing rays.

उदयास्तमनाभ्यां च स्मृते पूर्वापरे दिशौ।।
यावत्पुरस्तात्तपति तावत्पृष्ठे च पार्श्वयोः।। १८।।

ऋतेऽमरगिरेर्मेरोरुपरि ब्रह्मणः सभाम्।।
येये मरीचयोर्कस्य प्रयान्ति ब्रह्मणः सभाम्।।
तेते निरस्तास्तद्भासा प्रतीपमुपयान्ति वै।। १९।।

By the rising and the setting of the sun the east and west quartars are acertained. As far as the sun shines in front so far he shines behind, and thus on both the sides illuminating all the places except the court of Brahmā which is situate on the summit of Meru—the mountain of the celestials. When the rays of the sun reach the court of Brahmā they are repelled and driven back by the radiance which prevails there.

तस्माद्दिश्युत्तरस्यां वै दिवारात्रिः सदैव हि।।
सर्वेषां द्वीपवर्षाणां मेरुरुत्तरतो यतः।। २०।।

Consequently there is the alternation of day and night in the northern quarter in as much as all the insular continents are situated on the north of Meru.

प्रभा विवस्वतो रात्रावस्तं गच्छति भास्करे।।
विशत्यग्निमतो रात्रो वह्निर्दूरात्प्रकाशते।। २१।।

The radiance of the sun, after its setting, is deposited in fire and hence fire is visible even at a greater distance in night.

वह्नेः प्रभा तथा भानुर्दिनेष्वाविशति द्विज।।
अतीव वह्निसंयोगादतः सूर्यः प्रकाशते।। २२।।

During day the rays of fire enter into the sun by virtue of which the sun becomes more brilliant.

तेजसी भास्करराग्नेये प्रकाशोष्णस्वरूपिणी।।
परस्परानुप्रवेशादाप्यायेते दिवानिशम्।। २३।।

Elemental light and heat, proceeding respectively from the sun and fire and mixing with each other, prevail in diverse degrees both by day and night.

दक्षिणोत्तरभूम्यर्द्धे समुत्तिष्ठति भास्करे।।
अहोरात्रं विशत्यम्भस्तमः प्राकाश्यशीलवत्।। २४।।
आताम्रा हि भवत्यापो दिवानक्तप्रवेशनात्।।
दिनं विशति चैवांभो भास्करेस्तमुपेयुषि।।
तस्माच्छुक्ला भवन्त्यापो नक्तमह्नः प्रवेशनात्।। २५।।

When the sun prevails either in the northern or southern hemisphere day or night goes into waters according as they are attacked by darkness or light; it is for this reason that waters appear dark by day because night is within them and white by night because when the sun is set the light of the day enters therein.

एवं पुष्करमध्येन यदा याति दिवाकरः।।
त्रिंशद्भागस्तु मेदिन्यास्तदा मौहूर्त्तिकी गतिः।। २६।।
कुलाल चक्रपर्यन्ते भ्रमन्नेष दिवाकरः।।
करोत्यहस्तथा रात्रिं विमुञ्चन्मेदिनीं द्विजः।। २७।।

When the sun goes to Puṣkara Dvīpa, a thirtieth part of the circumference of the globe, his course is equal in time to one Muhūrtta; and whirling round like the circumference of the wheel of a potter the alternately spreads day and night on the surface of the earth.

अयनस्योत्तरस्यादौ मकरं याति भास्करः।।
ततः कुम्भं च मीनं च राशे राश्यंतरं द्विज।। २८।।

At the begining of his northern course the sun passes to Capricornus, thence to Aquarieas, thence to Pisces, successively passing from one sign of the Zodiac to another.

त्रिष्वेतेष्वथ भुक्तेषु ततो वैषुवत्तीं गतिम्।।
प्रयाति सविता कुर्वन्नहोरात्रं ततः समम्।। २९।।

After he has gone through them the sun gets at the vernal equinox when he makes the day and night of equal duration.

ततो रात्रिः क्षयं याति वर्द्धतेऽनुदिनं दिनम्।। ३०।।

ततश्च मिथुनस्यान्ते परां काष्ठामुपागतः।।
राशिं कर्कटकं प्राप्य कुरुते दक्षिणायनम्।। ३१।।

From then the length of the night decreases and the day grows longer until the sun reaches the end of Gemini when he follows a different course and entering Cancer begins his declension to the south.

कुलालचक्रपर्यंतो यथाशीघ्रं प्रवर्त्तते।।
दक्षिणप्रक्रमे सूर्यस्तथा शीघ्रं प्रवर्त्तते।। ३२।।

The sun moves quickly on his southern course like the circumference of a potter's wheel revolving respectively.

अतिवेगितया कालं वायुवेगबलाच्चरन्।।
तस्मात्प्रकृष्टां भूमिं तु कालेनाल्पेन गच्छति।। ३३।।

He glides along his course with the velocity of the wind and traverses a great distance in a short time.

सूर्यो द्वादशभिः शैघ्र्यान्मुहूर्त्तै दक्षिणायने।।
त्रयोदशार्द्धमृक्षाणामह्ना तु चरति द्विज।।
मुहूर्त्तैस्तावदृक्षाणि नक्तमष्टादशैश्चरन्।। ३४।।

In twelve Muhūrttas it goes through thirteen lunar asterisms and a half during the day, and during the night, it goes through the same distance only in eighteen Muhūrttas.

कुलालचक्रमध्यस्थो यथा मन्दं प्रसर्पति ।।
तथोदगयने सूर्यः सर्पते मन्दविक्रमः ।। ३५ ।।

तस्माद्दीर्घेण कालेन भूमिमल्पां तु गच्छति ।।
अष्टादशमुहूर्तं यदुत्तरायणापश्चिमम् ।। ३६ ।।

अहर्भवति तच्चापि चरते मन्दविक्रमः ।। ३७ ।।

त्रयोदशार्द्धमह्ना तु ऋक्षाणां चरते रविः ।।
मुहूर्तैस्तावदृक्षाणि रात्रौ द्वादशभिश्चरन् ।। ३८ ।।

As the centre of the potter's wheel revolves more slowly than the circumference so the sun in his northern course revolves with less rapidity and passes over a less space of the earth in a longer time, until at the end of his northern route the day is again eighteen Muhūrttas long and the night twelve the sun passing through them by day and night respectively in those periods.

अतो मन्दतरं नाभ्यां चक्रं भ्रमति वै यथा ।।
मृत्पिण्ड इव मध्यस्थो ध्रुवो भ्रमति वै तथा ।। ३९ ।।

कुलालचक्रनाभिस्तु यथा तत्रैव वर्तते ।।
ध्रुवस्तथा हि मैत्रेय तत्रैव परिवर्तते ।। ४० ।।

As the lump of the clay on the centre of the potter's wheel revolves most slowly, so the polar star, which is the centre of the Zodiacal wheel, moves very slowly and always remains in the centre like the clay.

उभयोः काष्ठयोर्मध्ये भ्रमतो मण्डलानि तु ।।
दिवा नक्तं च सूर्यस्य मन्दा शीघ्रा च वै गतिः ।। ४१ ।।

The relative length of the day or night is dependant upon the greater or less motion with which the sun revolves through the degrees between the two points of horizon.

मन्दाह्नि यस्मिन्नयने शीघ्रा नक्तं तदा गतिः ।।
शीघ्रा निशि यदा चास्य तदा मंदा दिवा गतिः ।। ४२ ।।

During the midday when his diurnal course is quickest his nocturnal is slowest and when he moves quickly by night he moves slowly by day.

एक प्रमाणमेवैष मार्गं याति दिवाकरः ।।
अहोरात्रेण यो भुंक्ते समस्ता राशयो द्विज ।। ४३ ।।

षडेव राशीन् यो भुंक्ते रात्रावन्यांश्च षड् दिवा ।। ४४ ।।

The length of his journey in both the cases is the same; for during the day and night he travels through all the signs of the Zodiac or six by night and six by day.

राशिप्रमाणजनिता दीर्घह्रस्वात्मता दिने ।।
तथा निशायां राशीनां प्रमाणैर्लघुदीर्घता ।। ४५ ।।

The length and shortness of the day are measured by the extent of the sings; and the duration of day and night is measured by the period which the sun takes to pass through them.

दिनादेर्दीर्घह्रस्वत्वं तद्भोगेनैव जायते ।।
उत्तरे प्रक्रमे शीघ्रा निशि मंदा गतिर्दिवा ।। ४६ ।।

दक्षिणे त्वयने चैव विपरीतां विवस्वतः ।। ४७ ।।

When he declines towards the north the sun moves quickest by night and slowest by day and when he declines towards the south the case is thoroughly the reverse.

उषा रात्रिः समाख्याताव्युष्टिश्चाप्युच्यते दिनम् ।।
प्रोच्यते च तथा संध्या उषाव्युष्ट्योर्यदन्तरम् ।। ४८ ।।

The night is called Uṣā and the day is called Vyuṣṭa and the intervening time between them is called Sandhyā.

संध्याकाले च संप्राप्ते रौद्रे परमदारुणे ।।
मन्देहा राक्षसा घोराः सूर्यमिच्छन्ति खादितुम् ।। ४९ ।।

When the dreadful Sandhyā sets in, the awful Rākṣasas named Mandehas attempt to devour the sun.

प्रजापतिकृतः शापस्तेषां मैत्रेय रक्षसाम् ।।
अक्षयत्वं शरीराणां मरणं च दिने दिने ।। ५० ।।

O Maitreya, the Patriarch Brahmā imprecated this curse upon them that they should perish by day and revive at other times.

ततः सूर्यस्य तैर्युद्धं भवत्यत्यन्तदारुणम् ।।
ततो द्विजोत्तमा स्तोयं संक्षिपन्ति महामुने ।। ५१ ।।

ॐकारब्रह्मसंयुक्तं गायत्र्या चाभिमन्त्रितम्।।
तेन दह्यन्ति ते पापा वज्रीभूतेन वारिणा।। ५२।।

For this reason a fierce contest takes place daily between them and the sun. At this time, O great Muni, the pious Brāhmins scatter water purified by the mystical Oṁkāra and consecrated by the Gāyatrī[1] and by means of this water as by a thunder-bolt the dreadful Rākṣasas are destroyed.

अग्निहोत्रे हूयते या समन्त्रा प्रथमाहुतिः।।
सूर्योज्योतिः सहस्रांशुः समा दीप्यति भास्करः।।५३।।

While during the course of morning rites the first oblation of offered with solemn invocations, the sun, having thousand rays, appears with unclouded splendour.

ओंकारो भगवान्विष्णुस्त्रिधामा वचसां पतिः।।
तदुच्चारणतस्ते तु विनाशं यांति राक्षसाः।। ५४।।

Oṁkāra is the glorious Viṣṇu, the essence of the three Vedas, the lord of speech; and by its mention the Rākṣasas are slain.

वैष्णवोंशः परः सूर्यो योन्तर्ज्योतिरसंप्लवम्।।
अभियायक ॐकारस्तस्य तत्प्रेरकं परम्।। ५५।।

The sun is a principal portion of Viṣṇu and light is his immutable essence, the manifestation of which is made by the mystic syllable Om.

तेन संप्रेरितं ज्योतिरोंकारेणाथ दीप्तिमत्।।
दहत्यशेषरक्षांसि मन्देहाख्यान्यघानि वै।। ५६।।

Light, spread by the utterance of Omkāra, becomes radiant and burns up completely the Rākṣasas denominated as Mandehas.

तस्मान्नोल्लंघनं कार्यं संध्योपासनकर्मणः।।
स हन्ति सूर्यं सन्ध्याया नोपास्तिं कुरुते तु यः।।५७।।

Therefore one should not be dilatory in the performance of Sandhyā sacrifice; for he, who neglects it, is guitly of the murder of the sun.

ततः प्रयाति भगवान्ब्राह्मणैरभिरक्षितः।।
बालखिल्यादिभिश्चैवस जगतः पालनोद्यतः।।५८।।

Being thus protected by the Brāhmaṇas called Bālakhilyas the sun proceeds to protect the world.

काष्ठा निमेषा दश पञ्च
चैव त्रिंशच्च काष्ठा गणयेत्कलां च।।
त्रिंशत्कलश्चैव भवेन्मुहूर्तस्तै-
स्त्रिंशता रात्र्यहनी समेते।। ५९।।

ह्रासवृद्धी त्वहर्भागैर्दिवसानां यथाक्रमम्।।
सन्ध्यामुहूर्त्तमात्रा वै ह्रासवृद्धौ समा स्मृता।। ६०।।

Fifteen Nimeshas (twinkling of the eye) make a Kāṣṭhā; thirty Kāṣṭhs make one Kalā; thirty Kalās a Muhūrtta and thirty Muhūrttas a day and night; the divisions of the day become longer or shorter in the way explained before. But as regards increase or decrease Sandhyā is always the same for it is only one Muhūrtta.

रेखाप्रभृत्यथादित्ये त्रिमुहूर्त्तगते रवौ।।
प्रातः स्मृतस्ततः कालो भागश्चाह्नः स पञ्चमः।। ६१।।

From the time when half of the sun's orb is visible to the expiration of three Muhūrttas the interval is called Prātar (morning) forming a fifth portion of the day.

तस्मात्प्रातस्तनात्कालात्त्रिमुहूर्त्तस्तु सङ्गवः।।
मध्याह्नस्त्रिमुहूर्त्तस्तु तस्मात्कालात्तु सङ्गवात्।। ६२।।

तस्मान्माध्याह्निकात्कालादपराह्ण इति स्मृतः।।
त्रय एव मुहूर्त्तास्तु कालभागः स्मृतो बुधैः।। ६३।।

अपराह्णे व्यतीते तु कालः सायह्न एव च।।
दशपञ्च मुहूर्तं वै मुहूर्तास्त्रय एव च।। ६४।।

The next portion or three Muhūrttas from morning is called Sangava (forenoon); the three next Muhūrttas make the midday; the three next Muhūttas constitute the afternoon; the three next Muhūttas make the evening; and thus the fifteen Muhūrttas of the day are divided into five portions of three each.

दशपञ्च मुहूर्तं वै अहर्वैषुवतं स्मृतम्।। ६५।।

वर्द्धते ह्रसते चैवाप्ययने दक्षिणोत्तरे।।
अहस्तु ग्रसते रात्रिं रात्रिर्ग्रसति वासरम्।। ६६।।

But the day comprises fifteen Muhūrttas only at the equinoxes and increases and

1. It is a Vedic verse in the shape of a short prayer to the sun.

diminishes in number as the sun declines towards the north or the south, when the day encroaches upon the night and the night upon the day.

शरद्वसन्तयोर्मध्ये विषुवं तु विभाव्यते।।
तुलामेषगते भानौ समरात्रिदिनं तु तत्।। ६७।।

The equinoxes take place during the spring and autumn when the sun enters the signs of Aries and Libra.

कर्कटावस्थिते भानौ दक्षिणायनमुच्यते।।
उत्तरायणमप्युक्तं मकरस्थे दिवाकरे।। ६८।।

When the sun enters Capricorn his progress towards the north begins and when he enters Cancer his progress towards the south commences.

त्रिंशन्मुहूर्तं कथितमहोरात्रं तु यन्मया।।
तानि पञ्चदश ब्रह्मन् पक्ष इत्यभिधीयते।। ६९।।

मासः पक्षद्वयेनोक्तो द्वौ मासौ चार्कजावृतुः।।
ऋतुत्रयं चाप्ययनं द्वेऽयने वर्षसंज्ञिते।। ७०।।

Fifteen day of thirty Muhūrttas each are called Pakṣa (fortnight); two fortnights make one month and two months a solar season and three seasons make one Ayana (a northern or southern declination) and two Ayanas make one year.

संवत्सरादयः पञ्च चतुर्मासविकल्पिताः।।
निश्चयः सर्वकालस्य युगमित्यभिधीयते।। ७१।।

Years are made up of four kinds of months[1] and five years make one Yuga or cycle.

संवत्सरस्तु प्रथमो द्वितीयः परिवत्सरः।।
इद्वत्सरस्तृतीयस्तु चतुर्थश्चानुवत्सरः।।
वत्सरः पञ्चमश्चात्र कालोयं युगसंज्ञितः।। ७२।।

The years are respectively called Samvatsara, Parivatsara, Anuvatsara and Vatsara. This is the time called a Yuga.

1. (a) The *Saura* containing the sun's passage through a sign of zodiac; (b) Candra containing thirty lunations; (c) Savana containing thirty days of sunrise and sunset; (d) Nakṣatra or the moon's revolution through the twenty-eight lunar mansions.

यः श्वेतस्योत्तरः शैलः शृङ्गवानिति विश्रुतः।।
त्रीणि तस्य तु शृंगाणि मैरयं शृंगवान्स्मृतः।। ७३।।

दक्षिणं चोत्तरं चेव मध्यं वैषुवतं तथा।

The mountain that is situate in the north of Bhāratvarṣa is called Śṛṅgavān for its having three principal horns or peaks, one to the north, one to the south and one is the centre.

शरद्वसंतयोर्मध्ये तद्भानुः प्रतिपद्यते।।
मेषादौ च तुलादौ च मैत्रेय विषुवं स्मृतम्।। ७४।।

तदा तुल्यमहोरात्रं करोति तिमिरापहः।।
दशपञ्च मुहूर्तं वै तदेतदुभयं स्मृतम्।। ७५।।

The last is called equinoctial for the sun goes there in the middle of the two seasons of spring and autumn, arriving at the equinoctical points in the first degrees of Aries and Libra and making day and night of equal duration of fifteen Muhūrttas each.

प्रथमे कृत्तिकाभागे यदा भास्वांस्तदा शशी।।
विशाखानां चतुर्थेशे मुने तिष्ठत्यसंशयम्।। ७६।।

विशाखानां यदा सूर्यश्चरत्यंशं तृतीयकम्।।
तदा चन्द्रं विजानीयात्कृत्तिकाशिरसि स्थितम्।।७७।।

तदैव विषुवाख्योऽयं कालः पुण्योऽभिधीयते।।

When the sun is in the first degree of Kīrti and the moon in the fourth of Viśākhā or when the sun is in the third degree of Viśākhā and the moon is in the head of Kṛtikā that equinoctial season is holy and is called the Mahāviṣubha.

तदा दानादि देयानि देवेभ्यः प्रयतात्मभिः।। ७८।।

ब्राह्मणेभ्यः पितृभ्यश्च मुखमेतत्तु दानजम्।।

At this time devout persons should make offering to the celestials and the manes and gifts to the Brāhmaṇas, for such gifts produce happiness.

दत्तदानस्तु विषुवे कृतकृत्योभिजायते।। ७९।।
अहोरात्रार्द्धमासो तु कलाः काष्ठाः क्षणास्तथा।।
पौर्णमासी तथा ज्ञेया अमावास्या तथैव च।।
सिनीवाली कुहूश्चैव एका चानुमतिस्तथा।। ८०।।

Liberality at the equinoxes is always fruitful to the donor, and day and night seconds, minutes and hours, intercalary months, the day at full moon (Paurṇamāsī); the day of conjunction, when the moon rises invisible, the day, when it is first seen, the day when it first disappears, the day when the moon is quite round and the day when one digit.is deficient are the seasons when gifts prove meritorious.

तपस्तपस्यौ मधुमाधवौ च शुक्रः शुचिश्चायनमुत्तरं स्यात्।।
नभोनभस्यौ च इषस्तथोर्जस्सहःसहस्याविति दक्षिणं तत्
।।८१।।

The sun declines towards the north in the months of Tapas, Tapasyā, Madhu, Mādhava, Śukra and Sūci and declines towards the south in the months of Nabhas, Nabhasya, Īśa, Urja, Sahas, Sahasya.

लोका लोकश्च यशशैलः प्रागुक्तो भवतो मया।।
लोकपालास्तु चत्वारस्तत्र तिष्ठन्ति सुव्रताः।।८२।।

There live four devout protectors of the world on the mount Lokāloka of which I had mentioned to you formerly.

सुधामा शङ्खपाच्चैव कर्दमस्यात्मजौ द्विज।।
हिरण्यरोमा चैवान्यश्चतुर्थः केतुमानपि।। ८३।।

These are severally named Sudhāman, Śaṅkhapād—the two sons of Kardama, Hiraṇyaroman and Ketumat.

निर्द्वन्द्वा निरभीमाना निस्तन्द्रा निष्परिग्रहाः।।
लोकपालाः स्थिता ह्येते लोका लोके चतुर्दिशम्।।८४।।

These four protectors of the world live around the mountain Lokāloka. They are devoid of malice, haughtiness, are active and have not taken to wives.

उत्तरं पदगस्त्यस्य अजवीथ्याश्च दक्षिणम्।।
पितृयानः स वै पन्था वैश्वानरपथाद्बहिः।। ८५।।

On the north of Agastya, and south of Ajabīthī (the line of the Goat) and outside the Vaiśvānarapath is situate the road of the Pitṛs.

तत्रासते महात्मान ऋषयो येऽग्निहोत्रिणः।।
भूतारम्भकृतं ब्रह्म शंसन्तो ऋत्विगुद्यताः।।
प्रारभन्ते तु ये लोकास्तेषां पन्थाः स दक्षिणः।।८६।।

There live the great Ṛṣis who offer oblations to the fire. They read those portions of the Vedas which contain injunctions for the multiplication of the progeny.

चलितं ते पुनर्ब्रह्म स्थापयन्ति युगेयुगे।।
सन्तत्या तपसा चैव मर्यादाभिः श्रुतेन च।। ८७।।

They perform the duties of ministrant priests and at the end of yugas they make new rules of conduct and re-establish the interrupted ritual of the Vedas. And after their death they proceed by the southern course.

जायमानास्तु पूर्वे च पश्चिमानां गृहेषु वै।।
पश्चिमाश्चैव पूर्वेषां जायन्ते निधनेष्विह।। ८८।।
एवमावर्त्तमानास्ते तिष्ठन्ति नियतव्रताः।।
सवितुर्दक्षिणं मार्गं श्रिता ह्याचन्द्रतारकम्।। ८९।।

Mutually descending from each other in successive births, progenitor coming from descendant and descendant from progenitor, they repeatedly appear in different houses and races along with their prosterity, austere practices and established rites, residing to the south of the solar orb as long as the moon and stars endure.

नागवीथ्युत्तरं यच्च सप्तर्षिभ्यश्च दक्षिणम्।।
उत्तरः सवितुः पंथा देवयानश्च स स्मृतः।। ९०।।

The path of the celestials is situate on the north of the solar sphere of the Nāgavīthī and south of the seven Ṛṣis.

तत्र ते वासिनः सिद्धा विमला ब्रह्मचारिणः।।
सन्ततिं ते जुगुप्संति तस्मान्मृत्युद्धजतश्च तैः।। ९१।।

There reside the Siddhas of subdued senses, continent and pure, not desirous of having offspring and consequently victorious over death.

अष्टाशीतिसहस्त्राणि मुनीनामूर्ध्वरेतसाम्।।
उदक्पन्थानमर्यम्णः स्थिता ह्याभूतसंप्लवम्।। ९२।।

Eighty-eight thousand of these continent acetics live in the regions north of the Sun till the time of dissolution.

ते संप्रयोगाल्लोभस्य मैथुनस्य च वर्जनात्।।
इच्छाद्वेषाप्रवृत्त्या च भूतारम्भवि वर्जनात्।। ९३।।

They are freed from covetousness and concupiscence, love and hatred and are not engaged in the work of procreation.

पुनश्च कामासंयोगाच्छब्दादेर्दोषदर्शनात्।।
इत्येभिः कारणैः शुद्धास्तेमृतत्वं हि भेजिरे।। ९४।।

They always detect the deficiency of the properties of elementary matter and being freed from these desires they do not meet with any obstacle in the way of asceticism.

आभूतसंप्लवं स्थानममृतत्वं विभाव्यते।।
त्रैलोक्यस्थितिकालोयमपुनर्मार उच्यते।। ९५।।

For these reasons they are highly pure and have attained to immortality. By immortality is meant existence to the end of the Kalpa : living as long as three regions exist is exemption from death.

ब्रह्महत्याश्वमेधाभ्यां पापपुण्यकृतो विधिः।।
आभूतसंप्लवान्तन्तु फलमुक्तं तयोर्द्विज।। ९६।।
यावन्मात्रे प्रदेशे तु मैत्रेयावस्थितो ध्रुवः।।

The consequences of the acts of impiety or piety such as Brāhmaṇicide and Aśvamedha last until the end of a Kalpa when all within the interval between Dhruva and the earth is destroyed.

क्षयमायाति तावत्तु भूमेराभूतसंप्लवात्।। ९७।।
ऊर्ध्वोत्तरमृषिभ्यस्तु ध्रुवो यत्र व्यवस्थितः।।
एतद्विष्णुपदं दिव्यं तृतीयं व्योम्नि भासुरम्।। ९८।।
निर्धूतदोषपङ्कानां यतीनां संयतात्मनाम्।।
स्थानं तत्परमं विप्र पुण्यपापपरिक्षये।। ९९।।

The region between the seven Ṛṣis and Dhruva, the third region of the sky is the excellent celestial path of Viṣṇu and is the splendid abode, O twice-born one, of the ascetics, who have controlled their senses and are freed from sins and in whom virtue and vice are annihilated.

अपुण्यपुण्योपरमे क्षीणाशेषाप्तिहेतवः।।
यत्र गत्वा न शोचन्ति तद्विष्णोः परपं पदम्।। १००।।

Those in whom virtue and vice are annihilated and who are freed from the consequences of piety or iniquity go to this excellent place of Viṣṇu where they never suffer sorrow.

धर्मध्रुवाद्यास्तिष्ठन्ति यत्र ते लोकसाक्षिणः।।
तत्साष्र्ट्योत्पन्नयोगर्धिस्तद्विष्णोः परमं पदम्।। १०१।।

There live Dharma, Dhruva and other spectators of the world radiant with the superhuman faculties of Viṣṇu obtained by virtue, of religious meditation.

यत्रोतमेतत्प्रोतं च यद्भूतं सचराचरम्।।
भाव्यं च विश्वं मैत्रेय तद्विष्णोः परमं पदम्।। १०२।।

With this excellent place of Viṣṇu, O Maitreya, are interwoven all that is and all that ever shall be, animate or inanimate.

दिवीव चक्षुराततं योगिनां तन्मयात्मनाम्।।
विवेकज्ञानदृष्टं च तद्विष्णोः परमं पदम्।। १०३।।

The seat of Viṣṇu is being meditated upon by the wisdom of Yogīs at one with supreme light as the radiant eye of heaven.

यस्मिन्प्रतिषिठतो भास्वान्मेढीभूतः स्वयं ध्रुवः।।
ध्रुवे च सर्वज्योतींषि ज्योतिष्वम्भोमुचो द्विज।। १०४।।

In this portion the splendid Dhruva is stationed as the pivot of atmosphere. On Dhruva are placed the seven great planets and on them depend the clouds.

मेघेषु संगता वृष्टिर्वृष्टेः सृष्टेश्च पोषणम्।।
आप्यायनं च सर्वेषां देवादीनां महामुने।। १०५।।

O great Muni, from clouds, proceed the rains; from them the water which is the nutriment and delight of all the celestials and the rest.

ततश्चाज्याहुतिद्वारा पोषितास्ते हविर्भुजः।।
वृष्टेः कारणतां यांति भूतानां स्थितये पुनः।। १०६।।

The celestials who receive oblations, being pleased by burnt offerings, cause the rain to fall for the support of created beings.

एवमेतत्पदं विष्णोस्तृतीयममलात्मकम्।।
आधारभूतं लोकानां त्रयाणां वृष्टिकारणम्।। १०७।।

This holy seat of Viṣṇu is the stay of the three worlds as it is the source of the rain.

ततः प्रभवति ब्रह्मन्सर्वपापहरा सरित्।।
गंगा देवांगनांगानामनुलेपनपिञ्जरा।। १०८।।

वामपादाम्बुजांगुष्ठनखस्रोतोविनिर्गताम्।।
विष्णोर्बिभर्त्ति यां भक्तया शिरसाहर्निशं ध्रुवः।। १०९।।

From this region, O Brāhmaṇa, proceeds the river Ganges, that removes all sins, embrowned with the unguents of the nymphs of heaven. She issues from the nail of the great toe of Viṣṇu's left foot. Dhruva, with devotion, holds her on his crown day and night.

ततः सप्तर्षयो यस्याः प्राणायामपरायणाः।।
तिष्ठन्ति वीचिमालाभिरुह्यमानजटाजले।। ११०।।

And thence the seven Ṛṣis practise their devout austerities in her water wreathing their braided locks with her waves.

वार्योघैः संततैर्यस्याः प्लावितं शशिमण्डलम्।।
भूयोधिकतरां कांतिं वहत्येतदुह क्षये।। १११।।

The orb of the moon, surrounded by her accumulated current, increased in lustre by her contact.

मेरुपृष्ठे पतत्युच्चैर्निष्क्रांता शशिमण्डलात्।।
जगतः पावनार्थाय प्रयाति च चतुर्दिशम्।। ११२।।

Having issued from the moon she falls on the mount Sumeru and thence to purify the world, flows to the four quarters of the earth.

सीता चाल कनन्दा च चक्षुर्भद्रा च संस्थिता।।
एकैव या चतुर्भेदा दिग्भेदगतिलक्षणा।। ११३।।

Sītā, Alakanandā, Cakṣu and Bhadrā are only the four divisions of one river and are named so after the regions towards which it proceeds.

भेदं चालकनन्दाख्यं यस्याः शर्वोपि दक्षिणाम्।।
दधार शिरसा प्रीत्या वर्षाणामधिकं शतम्।। ११४।।

Alakanandā, which flows towards the south, was borne delightedly on his head by Mahādeva for more than a hundred years.

शम्भोर्जटाकलापाच्च विनिष्क्रान्तास्थिशर्कराः।।
प्लावयित्वा दिवं निन्ये या पापान्सगरात्मजान्।। ११५।।

And having issued from the braided locks of Śambhu and washed the sins of the sinful sons of Sagara it raised them to heaven.

स्नातस्य सलिले यस्याः सद्यः पापं प्रणश्यति।।
अपूर्वपुण्यप्राप्तिश्च सद्यो मैत्रेय जायते।। ११६।।

O Maitreya, the iniquities of any man, who bathes in this river, are instantly removed and they obtain unprecedented virtue.

दत्ताः पितृभ्यो यत्रापस्तनयैः श्रद्धयान्वितैः।।
समाशतं प्रयच्छंति तृप्तिं मैत्रेय दुर्लभाम्।। ११७।।

And its water, if offered reverentially for three years by the sons to their manes, gives them rare gratification.

यस्यामिष्ट्वा महायज्ञैर्यज्ञेशं पुरुषोत्तमम्।।
द्विजभूपाः परां सिद्धिमवारपुर्दिवि चेह च।। ११८।।

Having worshipped the excellent Puruṣa, the lord of sacrifices, with sacrifices in this river, many, born in the race of twice-born ones, obtain whatever they desire either here or in heaven.

स्नानाद्विधूतपापाश्च यज्जलैर्यतयस्तथा।।
केशबासक्तमनसः प्रांप्ता निर्वाणमुत्तमम्।। ११९।।

Saints, who are purified by bathing in the waters of this river, and whose minds are devoted to Keśava, obtain final liberation.

श्रुताऽभिलषिता दृष्टा स्पृष्टा पीताऽवगाहिता।।
या पावयति भूतानि कीर्तिता च दिनेदिने।। १२०।।

The sacred river, when heard of, desired, seen, touched, bathed in, or hymned, day by day purifies all beings.

गगागंगेति यैर्नाम योजनाना शतष्वपि।।
स्थितैरुच्चारितं हन्ति पापं जन्मत्रयार्जितम्।। १२१।।

And those who living even at a distance of hundred *yojanas* exclaim "Gaṅgā and Gaṅgā" are relieved of the sins committed during the three previous existences.

यतः सा पावनायालं त्रयाणां जगतामपि।।
समुद्भूता परं तत्तु तृतीयं भगवत्पदम्।। १२२।।

The place, from which this river has issued for the purification of the three worlds, is the third division of the celestial region—the seat of Viṣṇu.

।। इति श्रीविष्णुमहापुराणे द्वितीयेंशेऽष्टमोऽध्यायः।।८।।

अथ द्वितीयेंशेः नवमोऽध्यायः
Part II : Section 9

श्रीपराशर उवाच

तारामयं भगवतः शिशुमाराकृति प्रभोः।।
दिवि रूपं हरेर्यत्तु तस्य पुच्छे स्थितो ध्रुवः।। १।।

Parāśara said :—The form of the glorious Hari containing the constellations, in the shape of a porpoise in the tail of which is attached Dhruva, is seen in heaven.

सैष भ्रमन् भ्रामयति चन्द्रादित्यादिकान् ग्रहान्।।
भ्रमन्तमनु तं यान्ति नक्षत्राणि च चक्रवत्।। २।।

सूर्याचन्द्रमसो तारा नक्षत्राणि ग्रहैः सह।।
वातानीकमयैर्बन्धैर्ध्रुवे बद्धानि तानि वै।। ३।।

As Dhruva revolves, it makes the moon, the sun and stars to revolve also, and all the planets follow in its circular path; for the sun, moon and all the luminaries are in sooth tied to the polar star by aerial cords.

शिशुमाराकृति प्रोक्तं यद्रूपं ज्योतिषां दिवि।।
नारायणोऽयनं धाम्नां तस्याधारः स्वयं हृदि।। ४।।

The porpoise figure of the celestial sphere, which has been described by me to you, is upheld by Nārāyaṇa, who himself, the source of all radiance, is seated in its heart.

उत्तानपादपुत्रस्तु तमाराध्य जगत्पतिम्।।
स तारा शिशुमारस्य ध्रुवः पुच्छे व्यव स्थितः।।५।।

And having worshipped the lord of people, Dhruva, the son of Uttānapāda shines in the tail of the steller porpoise.

आधारः शिशुमारस्य सर्वाध्यक्षो जनार्दनः।।
ध्रुवस्य शिशुमारस्तु ध्रुवे भानुर्व्यवस्थितः।। ६।।

Janārdana, the lord of all, is the supporter of this porpoise-shaped sphere—and this sphere is the supporter of Dhruva; and by Dhruva the sun is upheld.

तदाधारं जगच्चेदं सदेवासुरमानुषम्।। ७।।

O Brāhmaṇa, I shall describe how this earth is upheld by the sun; do thou listen to it attentively.

येन विप्र विधानेन तन्ममैकमनाः शृणु।।
विवस्वानष्टभिर्मासैरादायापो रसात्मिकाः।।
वर्षत्यम्बु ततश्चान्नमन्नादप्यखिलं जगत्।। ८।।

During eight months of the year the sun attracts the waters of the earth, and during the remaining four months he pours them upon the earth : from rain grows corn and by corn the whole world is upheld.

विवस्वानंशुभिस्तीक्ष्णैरादाय जगतो जलम्।।
सोमं पुष्णात्यथेन्दुश्च वायुनाडीमयैर्दिवि।।
नालैर्विक्षिपतेऽभ्रेषु धूमाग्न्यनिलमूर्तिषु।। ९।।

The sun absorbs the moisture of the earth by means of his scorching rays and nuourishes the moon thereby. And the moon through tubes of air distributes them to the clouds which are made of smoke, fire and wind.

न भ्रश्यन्ति यतस्तेभ्यो जलान्यभ्राणि तान्यतः।।
अभ्रस्थाः प्रपतंत्यापो वायुना समुदीरिताः।।
संस्कारं कालजनितं मैत्रेयासाद्य निर्मलाः।। १०।।

The clouds are called Abhras because their contents are not dispersed. The waters in the clouds, being driven by the wind, and freed from impurities by the sweetening process of the time, descend (upon earth), O Maitreya.

सरित्समुद्रभौमास्तु तथापः प्राणिसम्भवाः।।
चतुष्प्रकारा भगवानादत्ते सविता मुने।। ११।।

The glorious sun, O Maitreya, exhales moisture from four sources, namely—seas, rivers, the earth and the living creatures.

आकाशगंगासलिलं तथादायगभस्तिमान्।।
अनभ्रगतमेवोर्व्यां सद्यः क्षिपति रश्मिभिः।। १२।।

तस्य संस्पर्शनिर्धूतपापपंको द्विजोत्तम।।
न याति नरकं मर्त्यो दिव्यं स्नानं हि तत्स्मृतम्।। १३।।

He immediately pours down on earth, without turning it into cloud, the water that he absorbs from the Gaṅgā of the skeis, and people who are touched by this water are freed from all iniquities and are not constrained to see hell. This is called celestial ablution.

दृष्टसूर्यं हि यद्वारि पतत्यभ्रैर्विना दिवः ।।
आकाशगंगासलिलं तद्गोभिः क्षिप्यते रवेः ।। १४ ।।

When the sun comes in view and the water comes down from the sky without cloud then the waters of the Gaṅgā in the skies are sprinkled by the rays of the sun.

कृत्तिकादिषु ऋक्षेषु विषमेषु च यद्दिवः ।।
दृष्टार्कपतितं ज्ञेयं तद्गांगं दिग्गजोज्झितम् ।। १५ ।।

And the water that falls from the sky when the sun is in the mansion of Kṛttikā and the other asterisms counted by odd numbers, the water of the Gaṅgā is scattered by the elephants of the spheres.

युग्मर्क्षेषु च यत्तोयं पतत्यर्कोज्झितं दिवः ।।
तत्सूर्यरश्मिभिः सर्वं समादाय निरस्यते ।। १६ ।।

The water, that falls from the bright and cloudless sky when the sun is in the mansion of Rohiṇī and other even asterisms, is distributed by his own beams.

उभयं पुण्यमत्यर्थं नृणां पापभयापहम् ।।
आकाशगंगासलिलं दिव्यं स्नानं महामुने ।। १७ ।।

O twice-born one, both the waters are holy and they wash away the sins of the people : it is the water of the Gaṅgā in the skies and is termed celestial ablution.

यत्तु मेघैः समुत्सृष्टं वारि तत्प्राणिनां द्विज ।।
पुष्णात्यौषधयः सर्वा जीवनायामृतं हि तत् ।। १८ ।।

The water that the clouds distribute upon earth is in fact, the ambrosia of living beings : for it sustains the plants which are the support of their existence.

तेन वृद्धिं परां नीतः सकलश्चौषधीगणः ।।
साधकः फलपाकान्तः प्रजानां द्विज जायते ।। १९ ।।

By this water all vegetables grow and are matured and become the means of bringing about the well being of mankind, seen and unseen.

तेन यज्ञान्यथाप्रोक्तान्मानवाः शास्त्रचक्षुषः ।।
कुर्वन्त्यहरहस्तैश्च देवानाप्याययन्ति ते ।। २० ।।

Those men, who have got holy scriptures as their eyes, perform sacrifices with them and give gratification to the celestials.

एवं यज्ञाश्च वेदाश्च वर्णाश्च द्विजपूर्वकाः ।।
सर्वे देवनिकायाश्च सर्वे भूतगणाश्च ये ।। २१ ।।

In this wise all sacrifices, all celestials, Brāhmaṇas and other castes, all infernal creatures, all animals and the whole world are supported by the rains which produce food.

वृष्ट्या धृतमिदं सर्वमन्नं निष्पाद्यते यया ।।
सापि निष्पाद्यते वृष्टिः सवित्रा मुनिसत्तम ।। २२ ।।

O great Muni, this rain, which is the source of manifold blessings, proceeds from the sun.

आधारभूतः सवितुर्ध्रुवो मुनिवरोत्तम ।।
ध्रुवस्य शिशुमारोऽसौ सोपि नारायणात्मकः ।। २३ ।।
हृदि नारायणस्तस्य शिशुमारस्य संस्थितः ।।
बिभर्त्ता सर्वभूतानामादिभूतः सनातनः ।। २४ ।।

And the sun, O foremost of Munis, is upheld by Dhruva, which is again supported by the porpoise-shaped sphere which is at one with Nārāyaṇa; for the ever-existing glorious Nārāyaṇa, the supporter of the universe and the primary deity, is seated in the heart of the porpoise-shaped steller sphere.

।। इति श्रीविष्णुमहापुराणे द्वितीयेंशे नवमोऽध्यायः ।। ९ ।।

अथ द्वितीयेंशे: दशमोऽध्याय:
Part II : Section 10

श्रीपराशर उवाच

त्र्यशीतिमण्डलशतं काष्ठयोरन्तरं द्वयो:।।
आरोहणावरोहाभ्यां भानोरब्देन या गति:।। १।।

Parāśara said :—Between the extreme northern and southern points the sun has to travel in a year one hundred and eighty degrees, ascending and descending.

स रथोधिष्ठितो देवैरादित्यै ऋषिभिस्तथा।।
गन्धर्वैरप्सरोभिश्च ग्रामणीसर्पराक्षसै:।। २।।

His car is guided by divine Ādityas, Ṛṣis, Gandharvas, Apsarās, Yakṣas, serpents, and Rākṣasas.

धाता क्रतुस्थला चैव पुलस्त्यो वासुकिस्तथा।।
रथभृद्ग्रामणीर्हेतिस्तुम्बुरुश्चैव सप्तम:।। ३।।

एते वसन्ति वै चैत्रे मधुमासे सदैव हि।।
मैत्रेय स्यन्दने भानो: सप्तमासाधिकारिण:।। ४।।

The Aditya Dhātrī, the sage Pulastya, the Gandharva Tumburu, the nymph Kratuṣṭalā, the Yakṣa Rathakṛt, the serpent Vāsuki and the Rākṣasas Heti, live in the sun's car as its seven guardians, in the month of Madhu or Caitra.

अर्यमा पुलहश्चैव रथौजा: पुञ्जिकस्थला।।
प्रहेति: कच्छवीरश्च नारदश्च रथे रवे:।। ५।।

In the month of Vaiśākha or Mādhava the seven are Āryamat, Pulaha, Nārada, Puñjikā-ṣṭhali Rathaujas, Kacchvīrā and Praheti.

माधवे निवसन्त्येते शुचिसंज्ञे निबोध मे।। ६।।

मित्रोत्रिस्तक्षको रक्ष: पौरुषेयोथ मेनका।।
हाहा रथस्वनश्चैव मैत्रेयैते वसन्ति वै।। ७।।

In the month of Suci or Jyeṣṭha they are Mitra, Atri, Hāhā Menā, Rathaśwana, Takṣaka, and Pauruṣeya.

वरुणो वसिष्ठो रम्भा च सहजन्या हुहूरथ:।।
रथचित्रस्तथा शुक्रे वसन्त्याषाढसंज्ञके।। ८।।

In the month of Śukra or Āṣāḍha they are Varuṇa, Vasiṣṭha, Huhū, Sahajanyā, Rathacitra, Nāga and Budha.

इन्द्रो विश्ववासु: स्रोता एलापुत्रस्तथांगिरा:।।
प्रम्लोचा च नभस्येते सप्तिश्चार्के वसन्ति वै।। ९।।

In the month of Nabhas or Śrāvaṇa they are Indra, Aṅgiras, Viśwāvasu, Pramlocā, Śrotas and Elaputra.

विवस्वानुग्रसेनश्च भृगुरापूरणस्तथा।।
अनुम्लोचा शंखपालो व्याघ्रो भाद्रपदे तथा।। १०।।

In the month of Bhādrapada they are Vivaswat, Bhṛgu, Ugrasena, Anumlocā, Apūraṇa, Śaṅkhapāla and Vyāghra.

पूषा च सुरुचिर्वातो गौतमोथ धनञ्जय:।।
सुषेणोऽन्यो घृताची च वसन्त्याश्वयुजे रवौ।। ११।।

In the month of Aświna they are Pūṣān, Gautama, Suruci, Ghṛtaci, Śuṣeṇa, Dhanañjaya and Vāta.

विश्वावसुर्भरद्वाज: पर्जन्यैरावतौ तथा।।
विश्वाची सेनजिच्चापि कार्त्तिके च वसन्ति वै।। १२।।

In the month of Kārtik they are Parjanya, Bhāradwāja, (another) Viśwāvasu, Viśwāci, Senajit, Airāvata and Cāpa.

अंश: काश्यपतार्क्ष्यास्तु महापद्मस्तथोर्वशी।।
चित्रसेनस्तथा विद्युन्मार्गशीर्षेधिकारिण:।। १३।।

In Agrahāyaṇa or Mārgaśirṣa they are Aṅsu, Kāśyapa Citrasena, Urvaśī Tārkṣya, Mahāpadma and Vidyut.

क्रतुर्भगस्तथोर्णायु: स्फूर्ज: कार्कोटकस्तथा।।
अरिष्टनेमिश्चैवान्या पूर्वचित्तिर्वराप्सरा:।। १४।।

पौषमासे वसन्त्येते सप्त भास्करमण्डले।।
लोकप्रकाशनार्थाय विप्रवर्याधिकारिण:।। १५।।

In the month of Pauṣa, Bhaga, Kratu, Urṇayu, Pūrvachitti, Arṣṭanemi, Karkoṭaka, and Sphurja are seven who live in the sun's orbit and distribute light throughout the universe.

त्वष्टाथ जमदग्निश्च कम्बलोथ तिलोत्तमा।।
ब्रह्मोपेतोथ ऋतजिद्धृतराष्ट्रोथ सप्तमः।। १६।।
माघमासे वसन्त्येते सप्त मैत्रेय भास्करे।।

In the month of Māgha the seven are, Tvaṣṭṛ, Jāmadagni, Dhṛtarāṣṭra, Tillottamā, Ṛtajit, Kambala, and Brahmapeta.

श्रूयतां चापरे सूर्ये फाल्गुने निवसन्ति ये।। १७।।
विष्णुरश्वतरो रम्भा सूर्यवर्चाश्च सत्यजित्।।
विश्वामित्रस्तथा रक्षो यज्ञोपेतो महामुने।। १८।।

In the month of Phālguṇa those living in the sun are Viṣṇu, Viśvāmitra, Sūryavarcās, Rambhā, Satyajit, Aśwatara and Yajñāpeta.

मासेष्वेतेषु मैत्रेय वसन्त्येते तु सप्तकाः।।
सवितुर्मण्डले ब्रह्मन्विष्णुशक्त्युपबृंहिताः।। १९।।

In this wise, O Maitreya, a group of seen celestial beings supported by the energy of Viṣṇu lives, during the several months, in the orb of the sun.

स्तुवन्ति मुनयः सूर्यं गंधर्वैर्गीयते पुरः।।
नृत्यन्त्यप्सरसो यान्ति सूर्यस्यानुनिशाचराः।। २०।।
वहन्ति पन्नगा यक्षैः क्रियतेऽभीषुसंग्रहः।। २१।।
वालखिल्यास्तथैवैनं परिवार्य समासते।। २२।।

The sage chants his glory, the Gandharva sings and the nymph dances before him; the night-rangers attend upon his steps; the serpent harnesses his horses and the Yakṣa trims the reins and the Bālakhilyas surround his chariot.

सोयं सप्तगणः सूर्यमण्डले मुनिसत्तम।।
हिमोष्णवारिवृष्टीनां हेतुः स्वसमयं गतः।। २३।।

O foremost of Munis, these seven groups, residing in the suns, orb at their respective seasons, become the instrumentals in the distribution of cold, heat and rain.

।। इति श्रीविष्णुमहापुराणे द्वितीयेंशे दशमोऽध्यायः।।१०।।

अथ द्वितीयेंशेः एकादशोऽध्यायः

Part II : Section 11

मैत्रेय उवाच

यदेतद्भगवानाह गणः सप्तविधो रवेः।।
मण्डले हिमतापादेः कारणं तन्मया श्रुतम्।। १।।

Maitreya said :—I have heard as described by you, O holy preceptor, the seven groups of beings who are present in the sun's orb and are the agents in the distribution of heat and cold.

व्यापारश्चापि कथितो गन्धर्वोरगरक्षसाम्।।
ऋषीणां वालखिल्यानां तथैवाप्सरसां गुरो।। २।।
यक्षाणां च रथे भानोर्विष्णुशक्तिधृतात्मनाम्।।
किं चादित्यस्य यत्कर्म तन्नात्रोक्तं त्वया मुने।। ३।।

You have also described the individual functions of the Gandharvas, serpents, Rākṣasas, sages, Bālakhilyas Apsvarās and Yakṣas who, supported by the enrgy of Viṣṇu, remain as guardians in the sun's car but you have not described the function of the sun himself.

यदि सप्तगणो वारि हिममुष्णं च वर्षति।।
तत्किमत्र रवेर्येन वृष्टिः सूर्यादितीर्यते।। ४।।

If the seven beings stationed in the sun's ear are the agents in the distribution of heat, cold and rain, how can it also be true, as mentioned by you before, that rain proceeds from the sun?

विवस्वानुदितो मध्ये यात्यस्तमिति किं जनः।।
ब्रवीत्येतत्समं कर्म यदि सप्तगणस्य तत्।। ५।।

If the act of the collective seven be same then why the people say that the sun rises, reaches the meridian or sets?

पराशर उवाच

मैत्रेय श्रूयतामेतद्यद्भवान्परिपृच्छति।।
यथा सप्तगणोप्येकः प्राधान्येनाधिको रविः।। ६।।

Parāśara said :—O Maitreya, hear what you have asked me. The sun, though at one with seven beings in his orbit, is separate from them being their head.

सर्वशक्तिः परा विष्णो ऋग्यजुःसामसंज्ञिता।।
सैषा त्रयी तपत्यंहो जगतश्च हिनस्ति या।। ७।।

The whole and great energy of Viṣṇu, which is called the three Vedas,—Ṛc Yajuṣ and Sāman lightens the whole universe and destroys its iniquity.

सैष विष्णुः स्थितः स्थित्यां जगतः पालनोद्यतः।।
ऋग्यजुः सामभूतोन्तः सवितुर्द्विज तिष्ठति।। ८।।

This energy exists as Viṣṇu for the preservation of the universe and abiding as the three Vedas within the sun.

मासिमासि रविर्योयस्तत्र तत्र हि सा परा।।
त्रयीमयी विष्णुशक्तिरवस्थानं करोति वै।। ९।।

And wherever in every month the sun exists there is the Viṣṇu-energy composed of the three Vedas.

ऋचस्तुवन्ति पूर्वाह्णे मध्याह्नेथ यजूंषि वै।।
बृहद्रथन्तरादीनि सामान्यह्नःक्षये रविम्।। १०।।

The Ṛcas shine in the morning, the hymns of Yajuṣ at noon and Vṛhad-rathontạra and other portions of the Sāman in the afternoon.

अंगमेषा त्रयी विष्णो ऋग्यजुःसामसंज्ञिता।।
विष्णुशक्तिरवस्थानं सदादित्ये करोति सा।। ११।।

This threefold manifestation of Viṣṇu designated under the three Vedas is the energy of Viṣṇu that influences the divine positions of the sun.

न केवलं रवेः शक्तिर्वैष्णवी सा त्रयीमयी।।
ब्रह्माथ पुरुषो रुद्रस्त्रयमेतत्त्रयीमयम्।। १२।।

The energy of Viṣṇu does not exist only in the rob of the sun but is also manifest in Brahmā, Viṣṇu and Rudra.

सर्गादौ ऋङ्मयो ब्रह्मा स्थितौ विष्णुर्यजुर्मयः।।
रुद्रः साममयोन्ताय तस्मात्तस्याशुचिर्ध्वनिः।। १३।।

At the time of creation it is Brahmā consisting of the Ṛg-Veda;—in the work of preservation it is Viṣṇu composed of the Yajur-Veda;—and in the work of destruction it is Rudra formed of the Sāma-Veda, the utterance of which is therefore inauspicious.

एवं सा सात्त्विकी शक्तिर्वैष्णवी या त्रयीमयी।।
आत्मसप्तगणस्थं तं भास्वंतमधितिष्ठति।। १४।।

In this way the energy of Viṣṇu composed of the three Vedas exists in the sun encircled by the seven beings.

तया चाधिष्ठितः सोपि जाज्वलीति स्वरश्मिभिः।।
तमः समस्तजगतां नाशं नयति चाखिलम्।। १५।।

And the glorious sun becomes radiant by that energy of Viṣṇu and destroys the entire darkness of the universe.

स्तुवन्ति चैनं मुनयो गन्धर्वैर्गीयते पुरः।।
नृत्यन्त्योऽप्सरसो यान्ति तस्य चानु निशाचराः।। १६।।

वहन्ति पन्नगा यक्षैः क्रियतेऽभीषुसंग्रहः।।
वालखिल्यास्तथैवैनं परिवार्य समासते।। १७।।

The sages chant his glories, the Gandharvas sing and the nymphs dance before him; the Rākṣasas follow his steps, the serpents harness his steeds and the Yakṣas trim his reins and the Bālakhilyas are seated around him.

नोदेता नास्तमेता च क्दाचिच्छक्तिरूपधृक्।।
विष्णुर्विष्णोः पृथक् तस्य गणास्सप्तविधोऽप्ययम्।। १८।।

The seven beings in the sun's orb rise and set every month, but Viṣṇu, in the shape of his energy, never rises nor sets and is at once the sevenfold sun and distinct from it.

स्तम्भस्थदर्पणस्येव योऽयमासन्नतां गतः।।
छायादर्शनसंयोगं स तं प्राप्नोत्यथात्मनः।। १९।।

एवं सा वैष्णवी शक्तिर्नैवापैति ततो द्विज।।
मासानुमासं भास्वन्तमध्यास्ते तत्र संस्थितम्।। २०।।

As a man, nearing a mirror kept on a stand, observe in it his own image so the energy of Viṣṇu is never disjoined but remains month by month in the sun which he there placed.

पितृदेवमनुष्यादीन्स सदाप्याययन्प्रभुः।।
परिवर्तत्यहोरात्रकारणं सविता द्विज।। २१।।

The sovereign sun gratifying the manes,

gods and men, revolves being the instrument of day and night.

सूर्यरश्मिसुषुम्णायस्तर्पितस्तेन चन्द्रमाः।।
कृष्णपक्षेमरैः शश्वत्पीयते वै सुधामयः।। २२।।

The moon is cherished by the Suṣumnā ray of the sun. And in the dark fortnight of the month the ambrosia of its substance is drunk by the celestials.

पीतं तं द्विकलं सोमं कृष्णपक्षक्षये द्विज।।
पिबन्ति पितरस्तेषां भास्करात्तर्पणं तथा।। २३।।

And at the last day of the half month the two remaining digits are drunk by the manes; then the celestials and the progenitors are nourished by the sun.

आदत्ते रश्मिभिर्यंतु क्षितिसंस्थं रसं रविः।।
तमुत्सृजति भूतानां पुष्ट्यर्थं सस्यवृद्धये।। २४।।

तेन प्रीणात्यशेषाणि भूतानि भगवान्नाविः।।
पितृदेवमनुष्यादीनेवमाप्याययत्यसौ।। २५।।

The moisture, which the sun attracts from the earth he again distributes for the nourishment of animals and plants and thus the sun is the source of subsistance to every living being—gods, manes, mankind and the rest.

पक्षतृप्तिं तु देवानां पितृणां चैव मासिकीम्।।
शश्वत्तृप्तिं च मर्त्यानां मैत्रेयार्कः प्रयच्छति।। २६।।

The sun gratifies the celestials for a fortnight, the progenitors once a month, and men and other animals every day.

।। इति श्रीविष्णुमहापुराणे द्वितीयेंशे एकादशोऽध्यायः।। ११।।

अथ द्वितीयेंशेः द्वादशोऽध्यायः

Part II : Section 12

श्रीपराशर उवाच

रथस्त्रिचक्रः सोमस्य कुन्दाभास्तस्य वाजिनः।।
वामदक्षिणतो युक्ता दश तेन चरत्यसौ।। १।।

Parāśara said :—The car of the moon has three wheels and is drawn by ten white as the Jasmine—five on the right half and five on the left.

वीथ्याश्रयाणि ऋक्षाणि ध्रुवाधारेण वेगिना।।
ह्रासवृद्धिक्रमस्तस्य रश्मीनां सवितुर्यथा।। २।।

The asterisms upheld by Dhruva move before the sun. And the cords that fasten the moon are tightened or relaxed in the same manner like those of the sun.

अर्कस्येव हि तस्याश्वाः सकृद्युक्ता वहन्ति ते।।
कल्पमेकं मुनिश्रेष्ठ वारिगर्भसमुद्भवाः।। ३।।

O foremost of Munis, like the steeds of the sun, the horses of the moon, sprung from the waters, drag its car for a whole Kalpa.

क्षीणं पीतं सुरै सोममाप्याययति दीप्तिमान्।।
मैत्रेयैककलं सन्तं रश्मिनैकेन भास्करः।। ४।।

O Maitreya, when the moon is reduced, having its rays drank up by the celestials, to a single Kalā, the radiant sun supplied it with a single ray.

क्रमेण येन पीतोऽसौ देवैस्तेन निशाकरम्।।
आप्याययत्यनुदिनं भास्करो वारितस्करः।। ५।।

And as the moon is gradually exhusted by the celestials it is replenished in the same way every day with his rays by the sun, the plunderer of waters.

संभृतं चार्धमासेन तत्सोमस्थं सुधामृतम्।।
पिबन्ति देवा मैत्रेय सुधाहारा यतोऽमराः।। ६।।

Thus, O Maitreya, when in the half month the ambrosia is deposited in the moon, the celestials drink it for it constitutes their food.

त्रयस्त्रिंशत्सहस्राणि त्रयस्त्रिंशच्छतानि च।।
त्रयस्त्रिंशत्तथा देवाः पिबन्ति क्षणदाकरम्।। ७।।

Thirty-six thousand three hundred and thirty three divinities drink the ambrosia of the moon.

कलाद्वयावशिष्टस्तु प्रविष्टः सूर्यमण्डलम्।।
अमाख्यरश्मौ वसति अमावास्या ततः स्मृता:।।८।।

When two Kalās remain the moon enters the orbit of the sun and lives in the ray called Amā and the period is accordingly called Amāvasyā.

अप्तु तस्मिन्नहोरात्रे पूर्वं विशति चंद्रमाः।।
ततो वीरुत्सु वसति प्रयात्यर्कं ततः क्रमात्।। ९।।

During this period the moon is first immersed for a day and night in the water; thence it enters the branches and shoots of the trees and thence it proceeds to the sun.

छिनत्ति वीरुधो यस्तु वीरुत्संस्थे निशाकरे।।
पत्रं वा पातयत्येकं ब्रह्महत्यां स विन्दति।। १०।।

Hence any person, who cuts off a branch or casts down a leaf when the moon is in the trees is guilty of the crime consequent upon he destruction of a Brāhmin.

सोमं पञ्चदशे भागे किंचिच्छिष्टे कलात्मके।।
अपराह्णो पितृगणा जघन्यं पर्युपासते।।११।।

पिबन्ति द्विकलाकारं शिष्टा तस्य कला तु या।।
सुधामृतमयी पुण्या तामिन्दोः पितरो मुने।। १२।।

When the remainder of the moon contains but a fifteenth portion the manes near it in the afternoon and drink the last but sacred Kalā which is composed of ambrosia and contained in the two digits.

निस्सृतं तदमावास्यां गभस्तिभ्यः सुधामृतम्।।
मासं तृप्तिवाप्याग्र्यां पितरः सन्ति निर्वृताः।।
सौम्या बर्हिषदश्चैव अग्निष्वात्ताश्च ते त्रिधा।।१३।।

The nectar that comes from the rays of the moon on the day of conjunction is drunk by the progenitors—and they remain satisfied thereby for a month. The progenitors are divided into three classes;—Saumyas, Varhiṣadas, and Agniṣvātta.

एवं देवान् सिते पक्षे कृष्णपक्षे तथा पितॄन्।।
वीरुधश्चामृतमयैः शीतैरप्परमाणुभिः।। १४।।

In this wise, the moon, with its cooling rays, nourishes the celestials in the light fortnight and Pitṛs in the dark fortnight.

वीरुधौषधिनिष्पत्या मनुष्यपशुकीटकान्।।
आप्याययति शीतांशुः प्राकाश्यामह्लादनेन तु।।१५।।

It nourishes the plants with its cool nectary aqueous atoms. And through the development of those plants it sustains men, animals and insects and satisfies them with its radiance.

वाय्वग्निद्रव्यसंभूतो रथश्चन्द्रसुतस्य च।।
पिशंगैस्तुरगैर्युक्तः सोष्टाभिर्वायुवेगिभिः।।१६।।

The chariot of Budha, the son of the moon, is made of the wind and fire and is drawn by eight bay hosres gifted with the velocity of the wind.

सवरूथः सानुकर्षो युक्तो भूसंभवैर्हयैः।।
सोपासंगपताकस्तु शुक्रस्यापि रथो महान्।। १७।।

The huge car of Śukra (Venus) is carried by earth-bone horses, equipped with a protecting fender and a floor, armed with arrows and adorned with a pennon.

अष्टाश्वः काञ्चनः श्रीमान्भौमस्यापि रथो महान्।।
पद्मरागारुणैरश्वैः संयुक्तो वह्निसम्भवैः।। १८।।

The magnificient car of Bhauma (Mars) is made of gold, of an octagonal shape, drawn by eight steeds of a ruby red originated from fire.

अष्टाभिः पांडुरैर्युक्तो वाजिभिः काञ्चनो रथः।।
तस्मिंस्तिष्ठति वर्षान्ते राशौराशौ बृहस्पतिः।।१९।।

Bṛhaspati (Jupiter) in a golden car drawn by eight pale-coloured steeds, travels, at the end of the year, from one sign to another.

आकाशसम्भवैरश्वैः शबलैः स्यन्दनं युतम्।।
तमारुह्य शनैर्याति मन्दगामी शनैश्चरः।। २०।।

The slow-paced Śani (Saturn) travels in a car drawn by piebald horses.

स्वर्भानोस्तुरगा ह्यष्टौ भृंगाभा धूसरं रथम्।।
सकृद्युक्तास्तु मैत्रेय वहन्त्यविरतं सदा।। २१।।

O Maitreya, the chariot of Rāhu are drawn by eight black horses, which once harnessed are attached to it for ever.

आदित्यान्निस्सृतो राहुः सोमं गच्छति पर्वसु।।
आदित्यमेति सोमाच्च पुनः सौरेषु पर्वसु।। २२।।

At the time of lunar and solar eclipses the

Rāhu travels from the sun to the moon and comes back again from the moon to the sun.

तथा केतुरथस्याश्वा अप्यष्टौ वातरंहसः ।।
पलालधूमवर्णाभा लाक्षा रसनिभारुणाः ।। २३ ।।

The car of Ketu is drawn by eight horses having fleetness of the wind and of the dusky red colour of lac or of the smoke of burning straw.

एते मया ग्रहाणां वै तवाख्याता रथा नव ।।
सर्वे ध्रुवे महाभाग प्रबद्धा वायुरश्मिभिः ।। २४ ।।

I have thus described to you, O Maitreya, the chariots of the nine planets all of which are fastened to Dhruva by aerial cords.

ग्रहर्क्षताराधिष्ण्यानि ध्रुवे बद्धान्यशेषतः ।।
भ्रमन्त्युचितचारेण मैत्रेयानिलरश्मिभिः ।। २५ ।।

To Dhruva are attached the orbs of all the planets, asterisms and stars. And they all move in their respective orbits being kept in their place by their respective bands of air.

यावन्त्यश्चैव तारास्ता तावन्तो वातरश्मयः ।।
सर्वे ध्रुवे निबद्धास्ते भ्रमन्तो भ्रामयन्ति तम् ।। २६ ।।

As many are the stars so many are the aerial cords by which they are fastened to Dhruva. As thy turn round they cuase the pole-star to revolve.

तैलपीडा यथा चक्रं भ्रमन्तो भ्रामयन्ति वै ।।
तथा भ्रमन्ति ज्योतींषि वातविद्धानि सर्वशः ।। २७ ।।

As the oilman goes round the spindle and makes it revolve, so the planets revovle suspended by the aerial cords which are also whirling round a centre.

अलातचक्रवद्यान्ति वातचक्रेरितानि तु ।।
यस्माज्योतींषि वहति प्रवहस्तेन स स्मृतः ।। २८ ।।

The air is called Pravāha because it bears along the planets like a disc of fire driven by the aerial wheel.

शिशुमारस्तु यः प्रोक्तः स ध्रुवो यत्र तिष्ठति ।।
सन्निवेशं च तस्यापि शृणुष्व मुनिसत्तम ।। २९ ।।

I have related to you, O foremost of Munis, that Dhruva is fitted to the tail of the celestial porpoise : I shall now describe in detail the constituent parts; hear them as they are of great efficacy.

यदह्ना कुरुते पापं तं दृष्ट्वा निशि मुच्यते ।।
यावन्त्यश्चैव तारास्ताः शिशुमाराश्रिता दिवि ।।
तावन्त्येव तु वर्षाणि जीवत्यभ्यधिकानि च ।। ३० ।।

People are feed from the sins committed by them during the day when they behold the celestial porpoise in the night. And those who behold it live as many years as there are stars in it, in the sky or even more.

उत्तानपादस्तस्याधो विज्ञेयो ह्युत्तरो हनुः ।।
यज्ञोऽधरश्च विज्ञेयो धर्मो मूर्द्धानमाश्रितः ।। ३१ ।।

Uttānapāda is the upper jaw and sacrifice the lower jaw of that celestial porpoise.

हृदि नारायणश्चास्ते अश्विनौ पूर्वपादयोः ।।
वरुणश्चार्यमा चैव पश्चिमे तस्य सक्थिनी ।। ३२ ।।

Dhruva is situated on its brow and Nārāyaṇa in its heart. The Aśvins are its two fore-feet and Varuṇa and Āryamat are its two hinder legs.

शिश्नः संवत्सरस्तस्य मित्रोऽपानं समाश्रितः ।। ३३ ।।

Samvatsara is its sexual organ and Mitra is its organ of excretion.

पुच्छेऽग्निश्च महेन्द्रश्च कश्यपोथ ततो ध्रुवः ।।
तारका शिशुमारस्य नास्तमेति चतुष्टयम् ।। ३४ ।।

Agni, Mahendra Kāśyapa and Dhruva are successively placed in its tail : which four stars in this constelation never set.

इत्येष सन्निवेशोऽयं पृथिव्या ज्योतिषां तथा ।।
द्वीपानामुदधीनां च पर्वतानां च कीर्तितः ।। ३५ ।।

वर्षाणां च नदीनां च ये च तेषु वसन्ति वै ।।
तेषां स्वरूपमाख्यातं संक्षेपः श्रूयतां पुनः ।। ३६ ।।

I have thus related to you the situation of the earth and the stars. I had already described to you the Varṣas and rivers and the animals living there. I shall again describe them in short : hear them.

यदम्बु वैष्णवः कायस्ततो विप्र वसुन्धरा।।
पद्माकारा समुद्भूता पर्वताब्ध्यादिसंयुता।। ३७।।

From the waters which constitute the person of Viṣṇu originated the lotus-shaped earth with its seas and mountains.

ज्योतींषि विष्णुर्भुवनानि
विष्णुर्वनानि विष्णुर्गिरयो दिशश्च।।
नद्यः समुद्राश्च स एव सर्वं
यदस्ति यन्नास्ति च विप्रवर्य।। ३८।।

The stars are Viṣṇu, the words are Viṣṇu : forests, mountains, regions, streams, seas are Viṣṇu—all that is, all that shall be—all that is not are Viṣṇu.

ज्ञानस्वरूपो भगवान्यतोसावशेषमूर्त्तिर्न तु वस्तुभूतः।।
ततो हि शैलाब्धिधरादिभेदाञ्जानीहि विज्ञानविजृम्भितानि।।
३९।।

The glorious Viṣṇu is identical with knowledge. He has got endless forms but is not a substance. All the mountains, oceans and the various divisions of the earth you must consider to be the illusions of the apprehension.

यदा तु शुद्धं निजरूपि सर्वं कर्मक्षये ज्ञानमपास्तदोषम्।।
तदा हि संकल्पतरोः फलानि भवन्ति नो वस्तुषु वस्तुभेदाः।।
४०।।

When knowledge is pure, real universal independent of actions, freed from defect then the varieties of substance, which are the fruits of the tree of desire, cease to exist in matter.

वस्त्वस्ति किं कुत्रचिदादिमध्यपर्यन्तहीनं सततैकरूपम्।।
यच्चान्यथात्वं द्विज याति भूयो न तत्तथा तत्र कुतो हि
तत्त्वम्।। ४१।।

What is substance? What thing is that whcih has got no beginning, no middle and no end? And which is of one uniform nature? How can that object be called real which is subject to change and which reassumes no more its original character?

मही घटत्वं घटतः कपालिका
कपालिकाचूर्णरजस्ततोऽणुः।।
जनैः स्वकर्मस्तिमितात्मनिश्चयै-
रालक्ष्यते ब्रूहि किमत्र वस्तु।। ४२।।

The earth is seen as a jar; the jar is divided into two halves which are again broken into pieces : they again become dust and the dust is again reduced into atoms. Is this reality? And although it is considered so by man it is because his self-knowledge is obstructed by his own acts.

तस्मान्न विज्ञानमृतेस्ति
किंचित्क्वचित्कदाचिद्द्विज वस्तुजातम्।।
विज्ञानमेकं निजकर्मभेद-
विभिन्नचित्तैर्बहुधाभ्युपेतम्।। ४३।।

Therefore, O Brāhmaṇ, there is nothing anywhere, or anything real at any time save discriminative knowledge. On account of the diversity of their actions, people, having diverse temperaments, consider that one knowledge as manifold.

ज्ञानं विशुद्धं विमलं विशोकमशेषलोभादिनिरस्तसङ्गम्।।
एकं सदैकं परमः परेशः स वासुदेवो न यतोन्यदस्ति।।
४४।।

Knowledge perfect and pure, freed from pains and renouncing attachments towards all these which cause affliction—knowledge, single and eternal is the supreme Vāsudeva, besides whom there is nothing.

सद्भाव एवं भवतो मयोक्तो ज्ञानं यथा सत्यमसत्यमन्यत्।।
एतत्तु यत्संव्यवहारभूतं तत्रापि चोक्तं भुवनाश्रितं ते।। ४५।।

I have thus communicated to you the truth—the knowledge which is truth; and all that differs from it is false. That which is seen by the knowledge is but illusion of a temporal and wordly nature.

यज्ञः पशुर्वह्निरशेषऋत्विक्सोमः सुराः स्वर्गमयश्च कामः।।
इत्यादिकर्माश्रितमार्गदृष्टं भूरादिभोगाश्च फलानि तेषाम्।।
४६।।

I have also described to you the sacrifice, the victim, the fire, the priests, the acid, juce, the celestials, the desire for heaven, the path followed by acts of devotion and the worlds that path followed by acts of devotion and the worlds that are their outcome.

यच्चैतद्भुवनगतं मया तवोक्तं
सर्वत्र व्रजति हि तत्र कर्मवश्यः ।।
ज्ञात्वैवं ध्रुवमचलं सदैकरूपं
तत्कुर्याद्विशति हि येन वासुदेवम् ।। ४७ ।।

In this universe which I have described to you, only those people travel who are subject to the influece of actions. But he, who knows Vāsudeva to be eternal, immutable, and of one unchanging, universal form, should so perform them that he may enter into the deity.

।। इति श्रीविष्णुमहापुराणे द्वितीयेंशे द्वादशोऽध्यायः ।। १२ ।।

अथ द्वितीयेंशेः त्रयोदशोऽध्यायः

Part II : Section 13

मैत्रेय उवाच

भगवन्सम्यगाख्यातं यत्पृष्टोसि मया किल ।।
भूसमुद्रादिसरितां संस्थानं ग्रहसंस्थितिः ।। १ ।।
विष्णवाधारं यथा चैतत्त्रैलोक्यं समवस्थितम् ।।
परमार्थस्तु ते प्रोक्तो यथाज्ञानं प्रधानतः ।। २ ।।

Maitreya said :—"O respected Sir, all that I ask of you, has been perfectly related by you, namely the situation of the earth, seas, mountains, rivers, and planets, the system of the three worlds of which Viṣṇu is the support; you have also related that the holy knowledge is pre-eminent.

यवेतद्भगवानाह भरतस्य महीपतेः ।।
श्रोतुमिच्छामि चरितं तन्ममाख्यातुमर्हसि ।। ३ ।।

You said that you would relate the story of Bhārata, the lord of the earth : it becomes you now to relate that.

भरतः स महीपालः सालग्रामेऽवसत्किल ।।
योगयुक्तः समाधाय वासुदेवे सदा मनः ।। ४ ।।

Bhārata, the protector of the earth, lived at the holy pilgrimage of Śālagrām. And he was engaged in devotion with his mind ever attached to Vāsudeva.

पुण्यदेशप्रभावेन ध्यायतश्च सदा हरिम् ।।
कथं तु नाऽभवन्मुक्तिर्यदभूत्स द्विजः पुनः ।। ५ ।।

Living at a sacred place he was always devoted to Hari : Why then he failed to obtain final liberation, O twice-born one?

विप्रत्वे च कृतं तेन यद्भूयः सुमहात्मना ।।
भरतेन मुनिश्रेष्ठ तत्सर्वं वक्तुमर्हसि ।। ६ ।।

And why was he born again as a Brāhmin, O foremost of Munis? It becomes you to relate this."

श्रीपराशर उवाच

सालग्रामे महाभागो भगवन्न्यस्तमानसः ।।
स उवास चिरं कालं मैत्रेय पृथिवीपतिः ।। ७ ।।

Parāśara said :—The illustrious lord of the earth, O Maitreya, lived for a long time at Śālagrām having his mind wholly devoted to the glorious God.

अहिंसादिष्वशेषेषु गुणेषु गुणिनां वरः ।।
अवाप परमां काष्ठां मनसश्चापि संयमे ।। ८ ।।

And having been considered, on account of his kindness and other virtues, the foremost of the virtuous, he secured in the highest degree, the entire control over his mind.

यज्ञेशाच्युत गोविन्द माधवानन्त केशव ।।
कृष्ण विष्णो हृषीकेश वासुदेव नमोस्तु ते ।। ९ ।।

The Rājā was ever repeating the names Yajñeśa, Acyuta, Govinda, Mādhava, Ananta, Keṣava, Kṛṣṇa, Viṣṇu, Hṛṣikeśa.

इति राजाह भरतो हरेर्नामानि केवलम् ।।
नान्यज्जगाद मैत्रेय किंचित्स्वप्नान्तरेपि च ।।
एतत्पदन्तदर्थं च विना नान्यदचिंतयत् ।। १० ।।

And nothing else than this did he utter even in his dreams : nor did he meditate upon anything, but those names and their significance.

समित्पुष्पकुशादानं चक्रे देवक्रियाकृते ।।
नान्यानि चक्रे कर्माणि निस्सङ्गो योगतापसः ।। ११ ।।

He accepted fuel, flowers and holy grass for the worship of the deity and did he celebrate no other religious observance being entirely given to disinterested abstract devotion.

जगाम सोभिषेकार्थमेकदा तु महानदीम्।।
सस्नौ तत्र तदा चक्रे स्नानस्यानन्तरक्रियाः।। १२।।

One day he went to the river Mahānadī for the purpose of ablution. And having bathed there he engaged in after ceremonies.

अथाजगाम तत्तीरं जलं पातुं पिपासिता।।
आसन्नप्रसवा ब्रह्मन्नेकैव हरिणी वनात्।। १३।।

Whilst thus engaged there came to the same spot a doe big with young who had come out of the forest to drink of the stream.

ततः समभवत्तत्र पीतप्राये जले तथा।।
सिंहस्य नादः सुमहान्सर्वप्राणिभयंकरः।। १४।।

Whilst the doe was drinking there was audible a dreadful uproar of a lion capable of striking terror into all creatures.

ततः सा सहसा त्रासादाप्लुता निम्नगातटम्।।
अत्युच्चारोहणेनास्या नद्यां गर्भःपपात ह।। १५।।

Thereupon, the doe, greatly terrified, jumped out of the water on the banks; on account of this great leap her fawn was suddenly brought forth and fell into the river.

तमूह्यमानं वेगेन वीचिमालापरिप्लुतम्।।
जग्राह स नृपो गर्भात्पतितं मृगपोतकम्।। १६।।

And beholding it carried away by the stream the king suddenly caught hold of the young one and saved it from being drowned.

गर्भप्रच्युतिदोषेण प्रोत्तुङ्गाक्रमणेन च।।
मैत्रेय सापि हरिणी पपात च ममार च।। १७।।

The injury which the doe had received on account of the violent exertion proved fatal. She lay down and died.

हरिणीं तां विलोक्याथ विपन्नां नृपतापसः।।
मृगपोतं समादाय निजमाश्रममागतः।। १८।।

Having observed this the royal ascetic took the fawn in his arms and came back to the hermitage.

चकारानुदिनं चासौ मृगपोतस्य वै नृपः।।
पोषणं पुष्यमाणश्च स तेन ववृधे मुने।। १९।।

There he fed it and nursed it every day : and under his fostering care it throve and grew up.

चचाराश्रमपर्यन्ते तृणानि गहनेषु सः।।
दूरं गत्वा च शार्दूलत्रासादभ्यcraft्याययौ पुनः।। २०।।

It frolicked about the hermitage and grazed upon the grass in its neighbourhood. And sometimes afraid of a tiger it used to come to the ascetic.

प्रातर्गत्वातिदूरं च सायमायात्यथाश्रमम्।।
पुनश्च भरतस्याभूदाश्रमस्योटजाऽजिरे।। २१।।

In this wise the young one sometimes wandered far away in the morning and came back to the hermitage in the evening and frolicked in the leafy bower of Bhārata.

तस्य तस्मिन्मृगे दूरसमीपपरिवर्तिनि।।
आसीच्चेतः समासक्तं न ययावन्यतो द्विज।। २२।।

His mind, O twice-born one, was thus attached to that animal, playing either in the neighbourhood or at some distance and he was unable to think of anything else.

विमुक्तराज्यतनयः प्रोज्झिताशेषबान्धवः।।
ममत्वं स चकारोच्चैस्तस्मिन्हरिणबालके।। २३।।

And the king, although he had severed all bonds of attachments to wards his friends, his kingdom, his son and wife, grew inordinately attached to this fawn.

किं वृकैर्भक्षितो व्याघ्रैः किं सिंहेन निपातितः।।
चिरायमाणे निष्क्रान्ते तस्यासीदिति मानसम्।। २४।।

When absent for an unusually long time he would think that it had been carried away by wolves, devoured by a tiger or slain by a lion.

एषा वसुमती तस्य खुराग्रक्षतकर्बुरा।। २५।।

He used to cry out,—The earth is embrowned with the prints of its hoops.

प्रीतये मम जातोसौ क्व ममैणकबालकः।।
विषाणाग्रेण मद्बाहुं कण्डूयनपरो हि सः।।
क्षेमेणाभ्यागतोरण्यादपि मां सुखयिष्यति।। २६।।

What has become of the fawn that was born for my delight? How happy I should become if he had come back from the forest. I felt his budding antlers rubbing against my arm.

एते लूनशिखास्तस्य दशनैरचिरोद्गतैः।।
कुशाः काशा विराजन्ते बटवः सामागा इव।। २७।।

These tufts, of sacred grass, the heads of which have been nibbed by his new teeth, look like pious lads chanting the Sāma-Veda.

इत्थं चिरगते तस्मिन्स चक्रे मानसं मुनिः।।
प्रीतिप्रसन्नवदनः पार्श्वस्थे चाभवन्मृगे।। २८।।

Whenever this fawn used to absent itself for a long time from the hermitage the ascetic would think thus. And he was delighted and his countenance grew animated whenever it neared him.

समाधिभङ्गस्तस्यासीत्तन्मयत्वादृतात्मनः।।
सन्त्यक्तराज्यभोगर्द्धिस्वजन स्यापि भूपतेः।। २९।।

His mind being thus engrossed by the fawn his abstraction was interrupted although he had renounced family, wealth and kingdom.

चपलं चपले तस्मिन्दूरगं दूरगामिनि।।
मृगपोतेऽभवच्चित्तं स्थैर्यवत्तस्य भूपतेः।। ३०।।

His mind became unsettled with the wanderings of the fawn. Whenever it wandered away to a great distance the king's mind followed it and when it was silent his mind became settled.

कालेन गच्छता सोऽथ कालं चक्रे महीपतिः।।
पितेव सास्त्रं पुत्रेण मृगपोतेन वीक्षितः।। ३१।।

Thus in the course of time the king became subject to its influences and was watched by the deer with tearful eyes like a son mourning for the father.

मृगमेव तदाद्राक्षीत्त्यजन्प्राणानसावपि।।
तन्मयत्वेन मैत्रेय नान्यात्किंचिदचिन्तयत्।। ३२।।

And the king, when he died, saw the young fawn only before him; and having his mind engrossed by him, O Maitreya, he did not see anything else.

ततश्च तत्कालकृतां भावनां प्राप्य तादृशीम्।।
जम्बूमार्गे महारण्ये जातो जातिस्मरो मृगः।। ३३।।

On account of such feeling at such an hour he was born again in Jambūmarga forest as a deer with the faculty of recollecting his former life.

जातिस्मरत्वादुद्विग्नः संसारस्य द्विजोत्तम।।
विहाय मातरं भूयः सालग्राममुपाययौ।। ३४।।

Cherishing a distaste for the world on account of this recollection he left his mother and again repaired to holy place of Śalagrām.

शुष्कैस्तृणैस्तथा पर्णैः स कुर्वन्नात्मपोषणम्।।
मृगत्वहेतुभूतस्य कर्मणो निष्कृतिं ययौ।। ३५।।

Living there upon dry grass and leaves he expatiated the acts which had led to his being born in such a condition : and upon his death he was born as a Brāhmin still retaining the recollection of his former life.

तत्र चोत्सृष्टदेहोसौ जज्ञे जातिस्मरो द्विजः।।
सदाचारवतां शुद्धे योगिनां प्रवरे कुले।। ३६।।

He was born in a devout and illustrious family of ascetics who rigidly observed devotional practices.

सर्वविज्ञानसंपन्नः सर्वशास्त्रार्थतत्त्ववित्।।
अपश्यत्स च मैत्रेय आत्मानं प्रकृतेः परम्।। ३७।।

Having been gifted with true knowledge and acquainted with the spirit of all sacred writings he observed soul as contradistinguished from Prakṛti (matter).

आत्मनोऽधिगतज्ञानो देवादीनि महामुने।।
सर्वभूतान्यभेदेन स ददर्श तदात्मनः।। ३८।।

And acquainted with the knowledge of self he observed the celestial and all other beings as the same.

न पपाठ गुरुप्रोक्तं कृतोपनयनः श्रुतिम्।।
न ददर्श च कर्माणि शास्त्राणि जगृहे न च।। ३९।।

When he was invested with the Brāhminical thread he did not read the Vedas with a preceptor, did not perform the ceremonies nor did he read the scriptures.

उक्तोपि बहुशः किंचिज्जडवाक्यमभाषत।।
तदप्यसंस्कारगुणं ग्राम्यवाक्योक्तिसंश्रितम्।। ४०।।

And requested again and again he replied incoherently in ungrammatical and unpolished speech.

अपध्वस्तवपुः सोपि मलिनाम्बरधृग्द्विजः।।
क्लिन्नदन्तान्तरः सर्वैः परिभूतः स नागरैः।। ४१।।

His body was unclean and he used to wear dirty clothes. Saliva dribbled from his mouth and he was treated with hatred by the people.

सम्माननापरां हानिं योगर्द्धेः कुरुते यतः।।
जनेनावमतो योगी योगसिद्धिं च विन्दति।। ४२।।

Undue respect from the people obstructs abstruction and hence the ascetics, disregarded by people, attain to the consummation of their asceticism.

तस्माच्चरेत वै योगी सतां धर्ममदूषयन्।।
जना यथा वमन्येरन्गच्छेयुर्नैवसङ्गतिम्।। ४३।।

Without polluting the way treaded by the saints the ascetics should so behave that the ordinary folk might hate them and not come in their company.

हिरण्यगर्भवचनं विचिन्त्येत्थं महामतिः।।
आत्मानं दर्शयामास जडोन्मत्ताकृतिं जने।। ४४।।

Having thus thought of this saying (Bhārata) gifted with high intellect assumed the appearance of a crazy idiot in the eyes of the people.

भुंक्ते कुल्माषवाट्यादिशाकं वन्यं फलं कणान्।।
यद्यदाप्नोति सुबहु तदत्ते कालसंयमम्।। ४५।।

He used to live on raw pulse, potherbs, wild fruit and grains of corn and whatever came in his way as a part of necessary but temporary infliction.

पितर्युपरते सोऽथ भ्रातृभ्रातृव्यबान्धवैः।।
कारितः क्षेत्रकर्मादिकदन्नाहारपोषितः।।४६।।

On the death of his father he was set to work in the field by his brothers and nephews and fed by them with wretched food.

समाक्षपीनावयवो जडकारी च कर्मणि।।
सर्वलोकोपकरणं बभूवाहारचेतनः।।४७।।

He was firm and stout like a bull and used to act like a simpleton and people used to make him work and give him food only as his wages.

तं तादृशमसंस्कारं विप्राकृतिविचेष्टितम्।।
क्षत्तासौवीर राजस्य काल्यै पशुमकल्पयत्।। ४८।।

रात्रौ तं समलंकृत्य वैशसस्य विधानतः।।
अधिष्ठितं महाकाली ज्ञात्वा योगेश्वरं तथा।। ४९।।

ततः खड्गं समादाय निशितं निशि सा तथा।।
क्षत्तारं क्रूरकर्माणमच्छिनत्कंठमूलतः।।
स्वपार्षदयुता देवी पपौ रुधिरमुल्बणम्।।५०।।

ततस्सौवीरराजस्य प्रयातस्य महात्मनः।।
विष्टिकर्त्ताथ मन्येत विष्टियोग्योयमित्यपि।।५१।।

तं तादृशं महात्मानं भस्मच्छन्नमिवानलम्।।
क्षत्ता सौवीरराजस्य विष्टियोग्यममन्यत।। ५२।।

स राजा शिबिकारूढो गंतुं कृतमतिर्द्विज।।
बभूवेक्षुमतीतीरे कपिलर्षेर्वराश्रमम्।।५३।।

श्रेयः किमत्र संसारे दुःखप्राये नृणामिति।।
प्रष्टुं तं मोक्षधर्मज्ञं कपिलाख्यं महामुनिम्।। ५४।।

Once on a time the gate-keeper of the king of Sauvīra, regarding him as an idle uneducated Brāhmin, considered him a worthy person to work without pay and took him into his master's service to assist in carrying the palanquin. One day O Brāhmaṇa, the king wished to go in palanquin to the hermitage of the great sage Kapila, situated on the banks of the river Ikṣumatī, to consult the sage, who was conversant with the virtues leading to liberation, what as most desirable in a world abounding with care and sorrow.

उवाह शिबिकां तस्य क्षत्तुर्वचनचोदितः।।
नृणां विष्टिगृहीतानामन्येषां सोपि मध्यगः।। ५५।।

And he was one of those, who had, at the order of the head servant, been compelled to carry the palanquin gratituously.

गृहीतो विष्टिना विप्रः सर्वज्ञानैकभाजनम्।।
जातिस्मरोसौ पापस्य क्षयकाम उवाह ताम्।। ५६।।

And that Brāhmaṇa, gifted with the only universal knowledge and recollecting former birth, although compelled to do this, bore the burden as the means of expatiating the sins for which he was desirous to atone.

ययौ जडमतिः सोथ मृगमात्रावलोकनम्।।
कुर्वन्मतिमतां श्रेष्ठस्तदन्ये त्वरितं ययुः।। ५७।।

While the other bearers proceeded with alacrity, he, fixing his eyes upon the pole, moved tardily.

विलोक्य नृपतिः सोथ विषमां शिबिकागतिम्।।
किमेतदित्याह समं गम्यतां शिबिका वहाः।। ५८।।

पुनस्तथैव शिबिकां विलोक्य विषमां हि सः।।
नृपः किमेतदित्याह भवद्भिर्गम्यतेन्यथा।। ५९।।

And perceiving the palanquin carried unevenly the king exclaimed 'Ho bearers! what is this? Keep equal space.' Still it went on unsteadily and the king again cried out. 'What is this? How irregularly are you going?'

भूपतेर्वदतस्तस्य श्रुत्वेत्थं बहुशो वचः।।
शिबिकावाहकाः प्रोचुरयं यातीत्यसत्वरम्।। ६०।।

When this had again and again taken place the palanquin bearers at last replied to the king, 'It is this man who lags in his space.'

राजोवाच

किं श्रान्तोस्यल्पमध्वानं त्वयोढा शिबिका मम।।
किमाया ससहो न त्वं पीवानसि निरीक्ष्यसे।। ६१।।

'How is this' said the king to the Brāhmin, 'Are you exhausted? You have carried your burden only a little way. Are you unable to bear exhaustion? But you look very robust.'

ब्राह्मण उवाच

नाहं पीवा न चैवोढा शिबिका भवतो मया।।
न श्रान्तोस्मि न चायासो सोढव्योस्ति महीपते।। ६२।।

To which the Brāhmin replied—'It is not I, O king, who am robust, nor is it I who carry your palanquin. I am not exhausted, O king! nor am I capable of fatigue.'

राजो वाच

प्रत्यक्षं दृश्यसे पीवानद्यापि शिबिका त्वयि।।
श्रमश्च भारोद्वहने भवत्येव हि देहिनाम्।। ६३।।

The king said :—'I distinctly perceive that you are stout and the palanquin is carried by you, and a heavey burden is wearisome to all persons.'

ब्राह्मण उवाच

प्रत्यक्षं भवता भूप यद्दृष्टं मम तद्वद।।
बलवानबलश्चेति वाच्यं पश्चाद्विशेषणम्।। ६४।।

The Brāhmin said :—'Tell me first what you have distinctly seen of me and then you may distinguish my properties as strong or weak.

त्वयोढा शिबिका चेति त्वय्यद्यापि च संस्थिता।।
मिथ्यैतदत्र तु भवाञ्छृणोतु वचनं मम।। ६५।।

The statement, that you behold the palanquin borne by me or placed on me, is unreal. Listen, O king, to my arguments about it.

भूमौ पादयुगं त्वास्ते जङ्घे पादद्वये स्थिते।।
ऊर्वोर्जङ्घाद्वयावस्थौ तदाधारं तथोदरम्।। ६६।।

वक्षस्थलं तथा बाहू स्कन्धौ चोदरसंस्थितौ।।
स्कन्धाश्रितेयं शिबिका मम भरोत्र किं कृतः।। ६७।।

Both the feet are placed on the ground : the legs are supported by the feet; the thigs rest upon theh legs; and the belly rests upon the things; the chest is supported by the belly and the arms and shoulders are supported by the chest; the palanquin is carried by the shoulders and then how can it be considered as my burden?

शिबिकायां स्थितं चेदं वपुस्त्वदुपलक्षितम्।।
तत्र त्वमहमप्यत्र प्रोच्यते चेदमन्यथो।। ६८।।

This body which is seated in the palanquin is known as 'thou' thence what is elsewhere called this is here distinguished as thou and I.

अहं त्वं च तथान्ये च भूतैरुह्याम पार्थिव।।
गुणप्रवाहपतितो भूतवर्गोपि यात्ययम्।। ६९।।

I and thou and others are made of elements and elements, influenced by qualities, assume a bodily shape.

कर्मवश्या गुणाश्चैते सत्त्वाद्याः पृथिवीपते।।
अविद्यासंचितं कर्म तच्चाशेषेषु जन्तुषु।। ७०।।

Qualities depend on acts, and acts perpetrated in ignorance influence the condition of all beings.

आत्मा शुद्धोक्षरः शान्तो निर्गुणः प्रकृतेः परः।।
प्रवृद्ध्यपचयौ नास्य एकस्याखिलजन्तुषु।। ७१।।

The soul is pure, imperishable, tranquial, devoid of qualities, distinct from nature and is without increase or diminution; and if it is freed from increase or diminution then with what property you say to me, 'I see that you are robust?

यदा नोपचयस्तस्य न चैवापचयो नृप।।
तदा पीवानसीतीत्थं कया युक्तया त्वयेरितम्।।७२।।

भूपादजंघाकट्यूरुजठरादिषु संस्थिते।।

If the palanquin is placed on the body, the body on the feet, the feet on the ground, then the burden is carried as much by you as by me. Why are not others, O king, feeling the burden of this palanquin.

शिबिकेयं यथा स्कन्धे तथा भारः समस्त्वया।।७३।।

तथान्यैर्जन्तुभिर्भूप शिबिकोढा न केवलम्।।
शैलद्रुमगृहोत्थोपि पृथिवी संभवोपि वा।। ७४।।

If I am exhausted with a burden that is being carried on another's shoulder, then why with the weight of this palanquin, people may be worn out with the weight of mountains, trees, houses and even of the earth.

यदा पुंसः पृथग्भावः प्राकृतैः कारणैर्नृप।।
सौढव्यस्तु तदायासः कथं वा नृपते मया।। ७५।।

When the nature of men is different, either in its essence or its cause, then it may be said that fatigue is to be undergone by me.

मद्द्रव्या शिबिका चेयं तद्द्रव्यो भूतसंग्रहः।।
भवतो मेऽखिलस्यास्य ममत्वेनोपबृंहितः।। ७६।।

The material, with which the palanquin is made, is the substance of you and me and of all others being a collection of elements collected by individuality.'

श्रीपराशर उवाच

एवमुक्त्वाभवन्मौनी स वहञ्छिबिकां द्विज।।
सोपि राजावतीर्योर्व्यां तत्पादौ जगृहे त्वरन्।। ७७।।

Parāśara said :—Having said this the Brāhmaṇa became silent and went on carrying the palanquin; the king too speedily got down from it and touched his feet.

राजोवाच

भोभो विसृज्य शिबिकां प्रसादं कुरु मे द्विजः।।
कथ्यतां को भवानत्र जाल्मरूपधरः स्थितः।।७८।।

यो भवान्यन्निमित्तं वा यदागमनकारणम्।।
तत्सर्वं कथ्यतां विद्वन्मह्यं शुश्रूषवे त्वया।। ७९।।

The king said :—O Brāhmaṇa, leave off the palanquin and be propitiated with me. Tell me who art thou under the disguise of a fool?

ब्राह्मण उवाच

श्रूयतां सोहमित्येतद्वक्तुं भूप न शक्यते।।
उपभोगनिमित्तं च सर्वत्रागमन क्रिया।। ८०।।

The Brāhmaṇa replied 'Hear me, king. Who I am it is not possible to say; I go anywhere for receiving the fruits of good and bad luck.

सुखदुःखोपभोगौ तु तौ देहाद्युपपादकौ।।
धर्माधर्मोद्भवौ भोक्तुं जन्तुर्देहादिमृच्छति।। ८१।।

The body is produced for the enjoyment of pleasure and endurance of pain. Pleasure and pain originate from virtue and vice; therefore the soul assumes bodily shape for enjoying pleasure and enduring pain cosequent upon virtue and vice.

सर्वस्यैव हि भूपाल जन्तोः सर्वत्र कारणम्।।
धर्माधर्मौ यतः कस्मात्कारणं पृच्छ्‍ते त्वया।। ८२।।

The universal cause of all living creatures is virtue or vice, why therefore enquire after the cause of my coming to this earth.'

राजोवाच

धर्माधर्मौ न सन्देहस्सर्वकार्येषु कारणम्।।
उपभोग निमित्तं च देहाद्देहान्तरागमः।। ८३।।

यस्त्वेतद्भवता प्रोक्तं सोहमित्येतदात्मनः।।
वक्तुं न शक्यते श्रोतुं तन्ममेच्छा प्रवर्तते।। ८४।।

The King said :—"That virtue and vice are the causes of all actions and that people migrate into various bodies for receiving their consequences, there is not the least doubt about it; but as regards what you have said that it is not possible for you to say who you are, it is a matter which I wish to have explained.

योस्ति सोहमिति ब्रह्मन्कथं वक्तुं न शक्यते।।
आत्मन्येष न दोषाय शब्दोहमिति यो द्विज।। ८५।।

O Brāhmaṇa, how cannot a man declare himself to be that which he (really) is : there can be no harm to one's self from applying to it the world 'I'.

ब्राह्मण उवाच

शब्दोहमिति दोषाय नात्यमन्येष तथैव तत्।।
अनात्मन्यात्मविज्ञानं शब्दो वा भ्रान्तिलक्षणः।।८६।।

The Brāhmaṇa said :—To use the word 'I' undoubtedly is detrimental; but it is not improperly used if it is applied merely to the soul. But the term is erroneous in as much as it conceives that to be the self or soul which is not self or soul.

जिह्वा ब्रवीत्यहमिति दन्तोष्ठौ तालुके नृप।।
एतेनाहं यतः सर्वे वाङ्निष्पादनहेतवः।।८७।।

The tongue articulates the word 'I' assisted by the lips, the teeth and the palate; and these are the origin of the expression, as they are the causes of the production of speech.

किं हेतुभिर्वदत्येषा वागेवाहमिति स्वयम्।।
अतः पीवानसीत्येतद्वक्तुमित्थं न युज्यते।। ८८।।

If by these instruments speech can utter the word 'I' it is not at all proper to say that speech itself is 'I'.

पिण्डः पृथग्यतः पुंसः शिरःपाण्यादिलक्षणः।।
ततोहमिति कुत्रैतां संज्ञां राजन्करोम्यहम्।। ८९।।

O king, the body of a man having hands, feet and other limbs is composed of various parts : to what part shall we apply the word 'I'?

यद्यन्योस्ति परः कोपि मत्तः पार्थिवसत्तम।
तदैषोहमयं चान्यो वक्तुमेवमपीष्यते।। ९०।।
यदा समस्तादेहेषु पुमानेको व्यवस्थितः।।
तदा हि को भवान्सोहमित्येतद्विफलं वचः।। ९१।।

If another being had existed in this body quite different from me, then it may be said, O king, that *this* is I, *that* is the other; while one soul inhabits the whole body, then such questions as "Who are you? Who am I?" are useless.

त्वं राजा शिबिका चेयमिमे वाहाः पुरःसराः।।
अयं च भवतो लोको न सदेतन्नृपोच्यते।। ९२।।

Thou art a monarch : this is a palanquin : these are the bearers : these are thy followers : yet it is untrue that these are thine.

वृक्षाद्दारु ततश्चेयं शिबिका त्वदधिष्ठिता।।
किं वृक्षसंज्ञा वास्याः स्याद्दारुसंज्ञाथ वा नृप।।९३।।

This palanquin, in which thou art seated, is made of timber got from trees. Then tell me, what name, tree, timber or palanquin, shall be applied to it, O king.

वृक्षारूढो महाराजो नायं वदति ते जनः।।
न च दारुणि सर्वस्त्वां ब्रवीति शिबिकागतम्।।९४।।

The people shall not say that their monarch is seated on a tree or on a timber but they shall say that he is in the palanquin.

शिबिकादारुसंघातो रचनास्थितिसंस्थितः।।
अन्विष्यतां नृपश्रेष्ठ तद्भेदे शिबिका त्वया।। ९५।।

The artificial assemblage of the pieces of timber is called the palanquin : judge yourself, therefore, O king, in what the palanquin differs from the wood.

एवं छत्रशलाकानां पृथग्भावे विमृश्यताम्।।
क्व यातं छत्रमित्येतन्यास्त्वयि तथा मयि।। ९६।।

Again consider the sticks of the umbrella, in their separate state. What then is the umbrella? Apply this argument to thee and to me.

पुमांस्त्रीगौरजो वाजी कुञ्जरो विहगस्तरुः।।
देहेषु लोकसंज्ञेयं विज्ञेया कर्महेतुषु।। ९७।।

A man, a woman, a cow, a goat, a horse, an elephant, a bird, a tree, are names given to various bodies, which they assume on account of their primitive actions.

पुमान्न देवो न नरो न पशुर्न च पादपः।।
शरीराकृतिभेदास्तु भूपैते कर्मयोनयः।। ९८।।

Man is neither a god, nor a man, nor a beast, nor a tree : these are the various shapes which he assumes on account of his acts.

वस्तु राजेति यल्लोके यच्च राजभटात्मकम्।।
तथान्यच्च नृपेत्थं तन्न सत्संकल्पनामयम्।। ९९।।

O king, our name is Vasurāja and another name is Rājabhaṭa—besides you have got various other names—but none of these names is real and is nothing but the work of imagination.

यत्तु कालान्तरेणापि नान्यां संज्ञामुपैति वै।।
परिणामादिसंभूतां तद्वस्तु नृप तच्च किम्।। १००।।

And what thing is there in the world, O king, which being subject to changes, does not in the course of time, go by different names?

त्वं राजा सर्वलोकस्य पितुः पुत्रो रिपो रिपुः।।
पत्न्याः पतिः पिता सूनोः किं त्वां भूप वदाम्यहम्।। १०१।।

You are called the king of the world, the son of your father, the enemy of your foes, the husband of your wife, the father of your children, what name the shall I apply to you?

त्वं किमेतच्छिरः किं नु ग्रीवा तव तथादरम्।।
किमु पादादिकं त्वं वा तवैतत्किं महीपते।। १०२।।

What is your situation? Are you the head or the belly? Or are they yours? Are you the feet or are they yours?

समस्तावयवेभ्यस्त्वं पृथगभूय व्यवस्थितः।।
कोऽहमित्यत्र निपुणो भूत्वा चिन्तय पद्धथव।। १०३।।

You are, O king, separate in nature from the members of your body. Then considering properly, do you think who I am.

एवं व्यवस्थिते तत्त्वे मयाहमिति भाषितुम्।।
पृथक्करणनिष्पाद्यं शक्यते नृपते कथम्।। १०४।।

And since the truth has been got at, how is it possible for me to recognize the distinction and to apply to my individual the expression 'I'."

।। इति श्रीविष्णुमहापुराणे द्वितीयेंशे त्रयोदशोऽध्यायः।।१३।।

अथ द्वितीयेंशेः चतुर्दशोऽध्यायः

Part II : Section 14

श्रीपराशर उवाच

निशम्य तस्येति वचः परमार्थसमन्वितम्।।
प्रश्रयावनतो भूत्वा तमाह नृपतिर्द्विजम्।। १।।

Parāśara said :—Having heard his words pregnant with the true essence of things the king humbly said to the twice-born one.

राजोवाच

भगवन्यत्त्वया प्रोक्तं परमार्थमयं वचः।।
श्रुते तस्मिन्भ्रमन्तीव मनसो मम वृत्तयः।। २।।

King said :—'What you have said, O revered sir, is undoubtedly the truth—but in hearing this my mind has been greatly worked up.

एतद्विवेकविज्ञानं यदशेषेषु जन्तुषु।।
भवता दर्शितं विप्र तत्परं प्रकृतेर्महत्।। ३।।

What you have shown, O twice-born one, in various creatures to be understanding and discriminative knowledge, is very grand and distinct from plastic nature.

नाहं वहामि शिबिकां शिबिका न मयि स्थिता।।
शरीरमन्यदस्मत्तो येनेयं शिबिका धृता।। ४।।

I have not carried the palanquin nor is it placed on my shoulders. The body, which has carried the palanquin, is different from me.

गुणप्रवृत्त्या भूतानां प्रवृत्तिः कर्मचोदिता।।
प्रवर्त्तते गुणा ह्येते किं ममेति त्वयोदितम्।। ५।।

The three qualities influence the actions of the animals and these three qualities are again influenced by destiny.

एतस्मिन्परमार्थज्ञ मम श्रोत्रपथं गते।।
मनो विह्वलतामेति परमार्थार्थितां गतम्।। ६।।

This reaching my ears, O thou conversant with profound truth, my mind has been greatly disturbed for knowing that real and holy truth.

पूर्वमेव महाभागं कपिलर्षिमहं द्विज:।।
प्रष्टुमभ्युद्यतो गत्वा श्रेय: किं त्वत्र शंस मे।। ७।।

O twice-born, I had already addressed myself for going to the great ascetic Kapila, to learn of him what in this life is the most desirable object.

तदन्तरे च भवता यदेतद्वाक्यमीरितम्।।
तेनैव परमार्थार्थं त्वयि चेत: प्रधावति।। ८।।

But what, you have said in the interim, has attracted my mind towards you for being acquainted with the profound truth.

कपिलर्षिर्भगवत: सर्वभूतस्य वै द्विज।।
विष्णोरंशो जगन्मोहनाशायोर्वीमुपागत:।। ९।।

O Brāhmin, the great ascetic Kapila is a portion of the glorious Viṣṇu, who is at one with all elements.

स एव भगवान्नूनमस्माकं हितकाम्यया।।
प्रत्यक्षतामत्र गतो यथैतद्भवतोच्यते।। १०।।

He is born on earth to remove the illusions of the world. But what you has said convinces me that the great Kapalia, for my well-being, has appeared within my vision.

तन्मह्यं प्रणताय त्वं यच्छ्रेय: परमं द्विज।।
तद्वदाखिल विज्ञानजलवीच्युदधिर्भवान्।। ११।।

To me, who am thus asking, O twice-born one, explain what is the best of things, for you are an ocean overflowing with the waters of the divine wisdom.'

ब्राह्मण उवाच

भूप पृच्छसि किं श्रेय: परमार्थं नु पृच्छसि।।
श्रेयांस्यपरमार्थानि अंशेषाणि च भूपते।। १२।।

The Brāhmaṇa said—'You ask me, O lord of earth, what is the best of all things, not the great end of life. There are many things which are best in the world and there are many truths of life.

देवताराधनं कृत्वा धनसम्पदमिच्छति।।
पुत्रानिच्छति राज्यं च श्रेयस्तस्यैव तन्नृप।। १३।।

O king, some worshipping the gods desire for wealth, prosperity, children or kingdom : these are the best things in their estimation.

कर्म यज्ञात्मकं श्रेय: फलं तत्प्राप्तिलक्षणम्।।
श्रेय: प्रधानं च फले तदेवानभिसंहिते।। १४।।

A sacrifice that gives heavenly pleasures is also the best. That, which gives best rewards though not asked for, is also the best.

आत्मा ध्येय: सदा भूप योगयुक्तैस्तथा परम्।।
श्रेयस्तस्यैव संयोग: श्रेयो य: परमात्मन:।। १५।।

To him, who with concentration meditates upon the great soul, union with it is the best.

श्रेयांस्येवमनेकानि शतशोथ सहस्रश:।।
सन्त्यत्र परमार्थस्तु न त्वेते श्रूयतां च मे।। १६।।

Thus there are hundreds and thousands of best things but these are not profound truths. Hear, I shall describe to you what is the profound truth.

धर्माय त्यज्यते किंतु परमार्थो धनं यदि।।
व्ययश्च क्रियते कस्मात्कामप्राप्त्युपलक्षण:।। १७।।

If wealth is the end of life then why do people spend it for the acquisition of piety and for acquiring desired-for objects?

पुत्रश्चेत्परमार्थ: स्यात्सोप्यन्यस्य नरेश्वर:।।
परमार्थभूत: सोन्यस्य परमार्थो हि तत्पिता।। १८।।

O lord of men, if son is the end of life then the father of that son is another's end of life and he again is another's.

एवं न परमार्थोस्ति जगत्यस्मिञ्चराचरे।।
परमार्थो हि कार्याणि कारणानामशेषत:।। १९।।

If then every action becomes the end of every cause then there exists no supreme or final truth in this world.

राज्यादिप्राप्तिरत्रोका परमार्थतया यदि।।
परमार्था भवन्त्यत्र न भवंति च वै तत:।। २०।।

And if the acquirement of sovereignty be

characterized as the great end of life then finite ends would sometimes be and some times cease to be.

ऋग्यजुः-सामनिष्पाद्यं यज्ञकर्म मतं तव।।
परमार्थभूतं तत्रापि श्रूयतां गदतो मम्।। २१।।

If you consider the rites laid down by Ṛk, Yajur and Sāma Vedas as the ends of life, hear what I have got to say on that head.

यत्तु निष्पाद्यते कार्यं मृदा कारणभूतया।।
तत्कारणानुगमनाज्ज्ञायते नृप मृण्मयम्।। २२।।

Anything, that is the outcome of the instrumentity of earth, partakes of its character and consists of clay.

एवं विनाशिभिर्द्रव्यैः समिदाज्यकुशादिभिः।।
निष्पाद्यते क्रिया या तु सा भवित्री विनाशिनी।। २३।।

So any act, that is performed by such perishable things as fuel, clarified butter and Kuśa grass, must be in nature perishable.

अनाशी परमार्थश्च प्राज्ञैरभ्युपगम्यते।।
तत्तु नाशि न सन्देहो नाशिद्रव्योपपादितम्।। २४।।

तदेवाफलदं कर्म परमार्थो मतस्तव।।
मुक्तिसाधनभूतत्वात्परमार्थो न साधनम्।। २५।।

ध्यानं चैवात्मनो भूप परमार्थार्थशब्दितम्।।
भेदकारि परेभ्यस्तु परमार्थो न भेदवान्।। २६।।

The great end of life must be considered by wise men as eternal and it would be transient if it were accomplished through transitory things. If you consider that which gives no reward to be the true end of life then that which brings on final liberation is not the true end of life.

परमात्मात्मनोर्योगः परमार्थ इतीष्यते।।
मिथ्यैतदन्यद्द्रव्यं हि नैति तद्द्रव्यतां यतः।। २७।।

If the union of the individual soul with the Great soul is considered as the supreme end of life then this becomes false : for one substance cannot become substantially another.

तस्माच्छ्रेयांस्यशेषाणि नृपैतानि न संशयः।।
परमार्थस्तु भूपाल संक्षेपाच्छ्रयतां मम।। २८।।

Thus there are undoubtedly very many best things in this world : hear from me, in short O king, the true end of life.

एको व्यापी समः शुद्धो निर्गुणः प्रकृतेः परः।।
जन्मवृद्ध्यादिरहित आत्मा सर्वगतोव्ययः।। २९।।

परज्ञानमयो सद्भिर्नामजात्यादिभिर्विभुः।।
न योगवान्न युक्तोभून्नैव पार्थिव योक्ष्यते।। ३०।।

It is soul, one, all-pervading, uniform, perfect supreme over nature, freed from birth, growth and destruction, omnipresent undecaying, made up of true knowledge, independent and not connected with unreal things, with name, species and the rest and in time, present, past and future.

तस्यात्मपरदेहेषु सतोप्येकमयं हि यत्।।
विज्ञानं परमार्थोसौ द्वैतिनोऽतथ्यदर्शनः।। ३१।।

The spirit, which is essentially one in one's own and in all other bodies, is the true wisdom of one who knows the unity and the true principles of things.

वेणुरन्ध्रप्रभेदेन भेदः षड्जादिसंज्ञितः।।
अभेदव्यापिनोवायोस्तथास्य परमात्मनः।। ३२।।

As air spreading all over the world going through the perforation of a flute is distinguished as the notes of the scale so the (true) nature of the great spirit is one though it assumes various forms consequent upon the fruits of actions.

एकस्वरूपभेदश्च बाह्यकर्मावृतिप्रजः।।
देवादिभेदेपध्वस्ते नास्त्येवावरणे हि सः।। ३३।।

When the difference, between the various froms, such as that of god and man, is destroyed then the distinction of things ceaes."

।। इति श्रीविष्णुमहापुराणे द्वितीयेंशे चतुर्दशोऽध्यायः।। १४।।

अथ द्वितीयेंशे: पञ्चदशोऽध्याय:
Part II : Section 15

श्रीपराशर उवाच

इत्युक्ते मौनिनं भूयश्चिन्तयानं महीपतिम्।।
प्रत्युवाचाथ विप्रोसावद्वैतान्तर्गतां कथाम्।। १।।

Parāśara said :—Having heard those words the king became speechless and engaged in meditation and the Brāhmin told a tale illustrating the principles of unity.

ब्राह्मण उवाच

श्रूयतां नृपशार्दूल यद्गीतमृभुणा पुरा।।
अवबोधं जनयता निदाघस्य महात्मन:।। २।।

The Brāhmin said—"Hear O great king what in the days of yore Ṛbhu said for the instruction of illustrious Nidagha.

ऋभुर्नामाऽभवत्पुत्रो ब्रह्मण: परमेष्ठिन:।।
विज्ञाततत्त्वसद्भावो निसर्गादेव भूपते।। ३।।

The great patriarch Brahmā had a son by name Ṛbhu, who was by nature, king, conversant with true wisdom.

तस्य शिष्यो निदाघोभूत्पुलस्त्यतनय: पुरा।।
प्रादादशेषविज्ञानं स तस्मै परया मुदा।। ४।।

A son of Pulastya by name Nidagha became his disciple and (Ṛbhu) greatly delighted gave him various instructions.

अवाप्तज्ञानतंत्रस्य न तस्याद्वैतवासना।।
स ऋभुस्तर्कयामास निदाघस्य नरेश्वर।। ५।।

O lord of men, he being thus instructed, Ṛbhu did not doubt of his being fully confirmed in the doctrines of unity.

देविकायास्तटे वीरनगरं नाम वै पुरम्।।
समृद्धमतिरम्यं च पुलस्त्येन निवेशितम्।। ६।।

The residence of Pulastya was at Vīranagara, a big, beautiful city, situated on the banks of the river Devika.

रम्योपवनपर्यन्ते स तस्मिन्पाद्धथ वोत्तम।।
निदाघो नाम योगज्ञ ऋभुशिष्योवसत्पुरा।। ७।।

And there lived in a beautiful grove near this river, Nidāgha, the desciple of Ṛbhu, acquainted with all devotional practices.

दिव्ये वर्षसहस्रे तु समतीतेस्य तत्पुरम्।।
जगाम स ऋभु: शिष्यं निदाघमवलोकक:।। ८।।

स तस्य वैश्वदेवान्ते द्वारालोकनगोचरे।।
स्थितस्तेन गृहीतार्घ्यो निजवेश्म प्रवेशित:।। ९।।

After thousand divine years Ṛbhu went to the city of Pulastya to see his pupil who stood at the gate after the completion of the sacrifice to Viśvadevas. He was beheld by his pupil who came there specially to offer him Arghya, (the usual present) and led him into the house.

प्रक्षालितांघ्रिपाणिं च कृता सनपरिग्रहम्।।
उवाच स द्विजश्रेष्ठो भुज्यतामिति सादरम्।। १०।।

And when his hands and feet were washed and he was seated Nidāgha requested him respectfully to eat.

ऋभुरुवाच

भो विप्रवर्य भोक्तव्यं यदन्नं भवतो गृहे।।
तत्कथ्यतां कदन्नेषु न प्रीति: सततं मम।। ११।।

Ṛbhu said—'O foremost of Brāhmins, tell me what food is there in your house? I do not like wretched food.'

निदाघ उवाच

सक्तुयावकवाट्यानामपूपानां च मे गृहे।।
यद्रोचते द्विजश्रेष्ठ तत्वं भुंक्ष्व यथेच्छया।। १२।।

Nidāgha siad—'There are cakes, of meal, rice, barley and pulse in my house. Eat, O revernend Sir, whatever pleases you best.'

ऋभुरुवाच

कदन्नानि द्विजैतानि मृष्टमन्नं प्रयच्छ मे।।
संयावपायसादीनि द्रप्सफाणितवन्ति च।। १३।।

Ṛbhu :—O twice-born one, these are wretched viands. Give me sweet meats. Give me rice boiled with sugar wheaten cakes and milk with curd and molasses.'

निदाघ उवाच

हेहे शालिनि मद्गेहे यत्किंचिदतिशोभनम्।।
भक्ष्योपसाधनं मृष्टं तेनास्यान्नं प्रसाधय।। १४।।

Nidāgha said—'O dame, quickly prepare whatever is most excellent and sweet in my house and satisfy him therewith.'

ब्राह्मण उवाच

इत्युक्ता तेन सा पत्नी मृष्टमन्नं द्विजस्य यत्।।
प्रसाधितवती तद्वै भर्तुर्वचनगौरवात्।। १५।।

Having been thus addressed the wife of Nidāgha in consonance with her husband's behest prepared sweet food and placed it before the Brāhmin.

तं भुक्तवन्तमिच्छातो मृष्टमन्नं महामुनिम्।।
निदाघः प्राह भूपाल प्रश्रयावनतः स्थितः।। १६।।

And, O king, he then, spoke humbly to the great Muni, who was delightedly eating the meal.

निदाघ उवाच

अपि ते परमा तृप्तिरुत्पन्ना तुष्टिरेव च।।
अपि ते मानसं स्वस्थमाहारेण कृतं द्विज।। १७।।

Nidāgha—'Have you been greatly delighted with this meal, O twice-born one? Has your mind obtained contentment?

क्वनिवासो भवान्विप्र क्व च गन्तुं समुद्यतः।।
आगम्यते च भवता यतस्तच्च द्विजोच्यताम्।। १८।।

Where is your residence, O Brāhmin and where are you going? And tell me, whence art thou coming, O twice-born one?

ऋभुरुवाच

क्षुद्यस्य तस्य भुक्तेन्ने तृप्तिर्ब्राह्मण जायते।।
न मे क्षुन्नाभवत्तृप्तिः कस्मान्मां परिपृच्छसि।। १९।।

Ṛbhu said :—'O twice-born one, he, who has got appetite, is pleased with his meals. I have got no appetite and hence have got no satisfaction : why do you question me in vain?

वह्निना पार्थिवे धातौ क्षपिते क्षुत्समुद्भवः।।
भवत्यम्भसि च क्षीणे नृणां तृडपि जायते।। २०।।

Hunger is created, when by fire the earthly element is dried : and thirst is produced when the moisture of the body is absorbed by internal heat.

क्षुत्तृष्णे देहधर्माख्ये न ममैते यतो द्विज।।
ततःक्षुत्सम्भवाभावात्तृप्तिरस्त्येव मे सदा।। २१।।

These are the two functions of the body, O twice-born one, not mine—I am satisfied with that by which they are removed.

मनसः स्वस्थता तुष्टिश्चित्तधर्माविमौ द्विज।।
चेतसो यस्य तत्पृच्छ पुमानेभिर्न युज्यते।। २२।।

And pleasure and contentment are the faculties of the mind, O twice-born one : ask those men about it whose minds are affected by them.

क्व निवासस्तवेत्युक्तं क्व गन्तासि च यत्त्वया।।
कुतश्चागम्यते तत्र त्रितयेपि निबोध मे।। २३।।

As regards your three other questions—Where I dwell, wither I go and whence I come, hear my reply.

पुमान्सर्वगतो व्यापी आकाशवदयं यतः।।
कुतः कुत्र क्व गन्तासीत्ये तदप्यर्थवत्कथम्।। २४।।

Man goes everywhere and penetrates everywhere like the ether. Then is it rational to ask "Where is thy residence? Whence are you coming?

सोहं गन्ता न चागन्ता नैकदेशनिकेतनः।।
त्वं चान्ये च न च त्वं च नान्ये नैवाहमप्यहम्।। २५।।

And where will you go? I am not coming from anywhere. I shall not go anywhere and I do not live in one place.

मृष्टं न मृष्टमप्येषा जिज्ञासा में कृता तव।।
किं वक्ष्यसीति तत्रापि श्रूयतां द्विजसत्तम।। २६।।

किमस्वाद्वथ वा मृष्टं भुञ्जतोस्ति द्विजोत्तम।।
मृष्टमेव यथा मृष्टं तदेवोद्वेगकारकम्।। २७।।

अमृष्टं जायते मृष्टं मृष्टादुद्विजते जनः।।
आदिमध्यावसानेषु किमन्नं रुचिकारकम्।। २८।।

Such is the case with you and other men. What people see of you is not real *you*; what people, see of other men are not real *they*, and what people see of me is not real *I*. I made distinction between the sweetened and not sweetened food only to hear of your opinion about that : do thou hear my explanation about this, O twice-born one. Is there anything really sweet and not sweet to him who takes meals? That which is considered sweet is no longer so when it causes the sense of repletion, and that which is not sweet, becomes so when a man considers it as such.

मृण्मयं हि गृहं यद्वन्मृदा लिप्तं स्थिरं भवेत्।।
पार्थिवोयं तथा देहः पार्थिवैः परमाणुभिः।। २९।।

What food is there which is equally delightful from the first to the middle and last? As a house built of clay is strengthened by fresh plaster so this earthly body is maintained by earthly atoms.

यवगोधूममुद्गादि घृतं तैलं पयो दधि।।
गुडं फलादीनि तथा पार्थिवाः परमाणवः।। ३०।।

And barley, wheat, pulse, butter, oil, milk, curds, treacle, fruits and the like are made of earthly atoms.

तदेतद्भवता ज्ञात्वा मृष्टामृष्टविचारि यत्।।
तन्मनस्समतालम्बि कार्यं साम्यं हि मुक्तये।। ३१।।

You have now understood what is sweet and what is not; do you so act that you may be impressed with notion of identity which leads to final liberation."

ब्राह्मण उवाच

इत्याकर्ण्य वचस्तस्य परमार्थाश्रितं नृप।।
प्रणिपत्य महाभागो निदाघो वाक्यमब्रवीत्।। ३२।।

Having heard those words explaining the true end of life, the illustrious Nidāgha humbly bowed to him said—"Be then propitiated with me, O twice-born one.

प्रसीद मद्धितार्थाय कथ्यतां यत्त्वमागतः।।
नष्टो मोहस्तवाकर्ण्य वचांस्येतानि मे द्विज।। ३३।।

Thou hast come here for my welfare. Tell me whence thou hast come? Hearing thy words the infatuation of my mind is removed."

ऋभुरुवाच

ऋभुरस्मि तवाचार्यः प्रज्ञादानाय ते द्विज।।
इहागतोहं यास्यामि परमार्थस्तवोदितः।। ३४।।

Ṛbhu said :—"O twice-born one, I am thy preceptor Ṛbhu. I have come here to confer upon thee the true knowledge. Now I depart; for you have been acquainted with the true end of life.

एवमेकमिदं विद्धि न भेदि सकलं जगत्।।
वासुदेवाभिधेयस्य स्वरूपं परमात्मनः।। ३५।।

Consider again this universe to be one undivided nature of the supreme spirit Vāsudeva."

ब्राह्मण उवाच

तथेत्युक्त्वा निदाघेन प्रणिपातपुरःसरम्।।
पूजितः परया भक्त्या इच्छातः प्रययावृभुः।। ३६।।

Brāhmaṇa said :—Having said 'so be it' Nidāgha reverentially bowed to and worshipped him. And Ṛbhu too repaired to his wished for quarter.

।। इति श्रीविष्णुमहापुराणे द्वितीयेंशे पञ्चदशोऽध्यायः।। १५।।

अथ द्वितीयेंशे: षोडशोऽध्याय:

Part II : Section 16

ब्राह्मण उवाच

ऋभुर्वर्षसहस्रे तु समतीते नरेश्वर।।
निदाघज्ञानदानाय तदेव नगरं ययौ।। १।।

Brāhmaṇa said—After the expiration of another thousand years Ṛbhu again repaired to that city for conferring knowledge upon him.

नगरस्य बहि: सोथ निदाघं ददृशे मुनि:।।
महाबलपरीवारं पुरं विशति पार्थिवे।। २।।

The ascetic beheld Nidāgha at the outside of the city when the king was about to enter it with a huge army and a host of relations.

दूरे स्थितं महाभागं जनसम्मर्दवर्जकम्।।
क्षुत्क्षामकण्ठमायान्तमरण्यात्ससमित्कुशम्।। ३।।

He saw his illustrious pupil standing at a distance avoiding the crowd—his throat was parched with hunger and thirst consequent upon carrying thicket fuel and holy grass.

दृष्ट्वा निदाघं स ऋभुरुपगम्याभिवाद्य च।।
उवाच कस्मादेकान्ते स्थीयते भवता द्विज।। ४।।

Beholding Nidāgha and saluting him Ṛbhu said—'Why are you standing aloof, O twice-born one?'

निदाघ उवाच

भो विप्र जनसंमर्दो महानेष नरेश्वर:।।
प्रविविक्षु: पुरं रम्यं तेनात्र स्थीयते मया।। ५।।

Nidāgha said :—"There is a great rush of people for the lord of men is entering this huge and picturesque city : I am staying to avoid the crowd."

ऋभुरुवाच

नराधिपोत्र कतम: कतमश्चेतरो जन:।।
कथ्यतां मे द्विजश्रेष्ठ त्वमभिज्ञो मतो मम।। ६।।

Ṛbhu said :—"O foremost of twice-born one, who is the king amongst these? And who are his attendents. Methinks you know all these. Tell me."

निदाघ उवाच

योयं गजेन्द्रमुन्मत्तमद्रि शृंगसमुच्छ्रितम्।।
अधिरूढो नरेंद्रोऽयं परिलोकस्तथेतर:।। ७।।

Nidāgha said :—"He, who is seated on the infuriated elephant, huge as a mountain, is the king : and all others are his attendents."

ऋभुरुवाच

एतौ हि गजराजानौ युगपद्दर्शितौ मम।।
भवता न विशेषणे पृथक्चिह्नोपलक्षणौ।। ८।।

Ṛbhu said :—"You have simultaneously pointed out to me both the king and the elephant, but you have not particularly said, who is the king and which is the elephant.

तत्कथ्यतां महाभाग विशेषो भवतानयो:।।
ज्ञातुमिच्छाम्यहं कोत्र गज: को वा नराधिप:।। ९।।

Therefore O illustrious one, tell me in particular, who is the king and which is the elephant; I am anxious to know it."

निदाघ उवाच

गजो योयमथो ब्रह्मन्नुपर्यस्यैष भूपति:।।
वाह्यवाहकसम्बन्धं को न जानाति वै द्विज।। १०।।

Nidāgha said :—"That which is under is the elephant and one who is above is the king. Who is not aware, O twice-born one, of the relation between that which bears and that which is borne?"

ऋभुरुवाच

जानाम्यहं यथा ब्रह्मंस्तथा मामवबोधय।।
अध:शब्दनिगद्यं हि किं चोर्ध्वमभिधीयते।। ११।।

Ṛbhu said :—"Explain to me in the way in which I can understand it. What is meant by the word *underneath* and what is meant by the word *above*?"

ब्राह्मण उवाच

इत्युक्त: सहसारुह्य निदाघ: प्राह तमृभुम्।।
श्रूयतां कथयाम्येष यन्मां त्वं परिपृच्छसि।। १२।।

Brāhmaṇa said :—As soon as he had said this Nidāgha jumped upon Ṛbhu and said—"Hear what you have asked of me.

उपर्यहं यथा राजा त्वमधः कुञ्जरो यथा।।
अवबोधाय ते ब्रह्मन्दृष्टान्तो दर्शितो मया।। १३।।

I am above like the king, you are underneath like the elephant. I show this example, O Brāhmaṇa, for your better information."

ऋभुरुवाच

त्वं राजेव द्विजश्रेष्ठ स्थितोहं गजवद्यदि।।
तदेतत्त्वं समाचक्ष्व कतमस्त्वमहं तथा।। १४।।

Ṛbhu said :—"O foremost of Brāhmins, it seems that you are as if the king and I am the elephant and tell me now which of us two is *you* and which is *I*."

ब्राह्मण उवाच

इत्यचुक्तः सत्वरं तस्य प्रगृह्यचरणावुभौ।।
निदाघस्त्वाह भगवानाचार्यस्त्वमृभुर्ध्रुवम्।। १५।।

Brāhmaṇa said :—Ṛbhu having said this Nidāgha, speedily got down and falling at his feet said—"Sure thou art my saintly preceptor Ṛbhu.

नान्यस्याद्वैतसंस्कारसंस्कृतं मानसं तथा।।
यथाचार्यस्य तेन त्वां मन्ये प्राप्तमहं गुरुम्।। १६।।

The mind of no other person is so much acquainted with the principles of unity as that of the mind of my preceptor. Therefore I know that thou art he."

ऋभुरुवाच

तवोपदेशदानाय पूर्वशु श्रूषणादृतः।।
गुरुस्नेहादृभुर्नाम निदाघ समुपागतः।। १७।।

Ṛbhu said :—"O Nidagha, I am you preceptor Ṛbhu. Pleased with the attention which you had shown to me before, I have come here to give you instructions O you gifted with a high mind.

तदेतदुपदिष्टं ते संक्षेपेण महामते।।
परमार्थसारभूतं यत्तदद्वैतमशेषतः।। १८।।

I have briefly described to you the divine truth, the essence of which is the none-quality of all."

ब्राह्मण उवाच

एवमुक्त्वा ययौ विद्वान्निदाघं स ऋभुर्गुरुः।।
निदाघोप्युपदेशेन तेनाद्वैतपरोभवत्।। १९।।

Having said this the learned Ṛbhu went away. Nidāgha, too by his instructions, was impressed with belief in unity.

सर्वभूतान्यभेदेन ददृशे स तदात्मनः।।
यथा ब्रह्मपरो मुक्तिमवाप परमां द्विजः।। २०।।

He began to observe all beings in no way distinct from him. And being devoted Brahmā he obtained final liberation.

तथा त्वमपि धर्मज्ञ तुल्योत्मरिपुबांधवः।।
भव सर्गगतं जानन्नात्मानमवनीपते।। २१।।

"Therefore, O king, O thou, conversant with duty, do thou, consider thyself as one with all beings, regarding equally friend or foe.

सितनीलादिभेदेन यथैकं दृश्यते नभः।।
भ्रान्तदृष्टिभिरात्मापि तथैकः सन्पृथक्पृथक्।। २२।।

As the same sky looks apparently as white or blue so Soul, which is in reality one, appers diversified to erroneous vision.

एकः समस्तं यदिहास्ति किंचित्तदच्युतो नास्ति परं ततोन्यत्।।
सोहं स च त्वं स च सर्वमेतदात्मस्वरूपं त्यज भेदमोहम्।। २३।।

That, which exists in the universe, is one which is Acyuta. There is nothing distinct from Him. He is I : He is thou : He is all : This universe is His form. Give up therefore the misconceived notion of distinction."

श्रीपराशर उवाच

इतीरितस्तेन स राजवर्यस्तत्याज भेदं परमार्थदृष्टिः।।
स चापि जातिस्मरणाप्तबोधस्तत्रैव जन्मन्यपवर्गमाप।।
२४।।

Parāśara said :—The Brāhmin having uttered this the king became cognizant of the true end of life. He renounced all idea of distinction and the Brāhmin, who, on account of the recollection of former lives, had obtained perfect knowledge, now acquired liberation from future births.

इति भरतनरेन्द्रसारवृत्तं कथयति
यश्च शृणोति भक्तियुक्तः ।।
स विमलमतिरेति नात्म मोहं
भवति च संसरणेषु मुक्तियोग्यः ।। २५ ।।

He, who will reverentially hear this story of Bhārata or narrate it, will have his mind illuminated and will not mistake the nature of individuality. And he who remembers it even shall be considered an object of reverence.

।। इति श्रीविष्णुमहापुराणे द्वितीयेंशे षोडशोऽध्यायः ।। १६ ।।

।। इति श्रीविष्णुमहापुराणे द्वितीयोंशः समाप्तः ।।

।। अथ श्रीविष्णुमहापुराणे तृतीयोंशः ।।

THE VIṢṆUMAHĀPURĀṆAM, PART - III

।। श्रीमते रामानुजाय नमः ।।

अथ तृतीयेंशे: प्रथमोऽध्यायः

Part III Section 1

मैत्रेय उवाच

कथिता गुरुणा सम्यग्मूसमुद्रादिसंस्थितिः ।।
सूर्यादीनां च संस्थानं ज्योतिषां चातिविस्तरात् ।। १ ।।

देवादीनां तथा सृष्टिर्ऋषीणां चापि वर्णिता ।।
चातुर्वर्ण्यस्य चोत्पत्तिस्तिर्यग्योनिगतस्य च ।। २ ।।

ध्रुवप्रह्लादचरितं विस्तराच्च त्वयोदितम् ।।
मन्वंतराण्यशेषाणि श्रोतुमिच्छाम्यनुक्रमात् ।। ३ ।।

Maitreya said :—The situation of the earth and of seas the system of the sun and the other planets, the creation of the celestials and the rest and of the Ṛsis, the origin of the four castes and of the brute creation and the stories of Dhruva and Prahlāda have been fully described by thee, my preceptor.

मन्वंतराधिपांश्चैव शक्रदेवपुरोगमान् ।।
भवतां कथितानेताञ्छ्रोतुमिच्छाम्यहं गुरो ।। ४ ।।

Do thou describe to me, O Venerable Sir, all the Manvantaras and all the presiding dieties with Śakra as their chief. I wish to hear this from you.

श्रीपराशर उवाच

अतीतानागतानीह यानि मन्वंतराणि वै ।।
तान्यहं भवतः सम्यक्कथयामि यथा क्रमम् ।। ५ ।।

Parāśara said :—"I shall serially describe to you all the Manvantaras that had passed away and all that shall take place.

स्वायंभुवो मनुः पूर्वं परः स्वारोचिषस्तथा ।।
उत्तमस्तामसश्चैव रैवतश्चाक्षुषस्तथा ।। ६ ।।

षडेते मनवोतीतास्सांप्रतं तु रवेस्सुतः ।।
वैवस्वतोयं यस्त्वेतत्सप्तमं वर्त्ततेंतरम् ।। ७ ।।

The first Manu was Svayambhuva. Then came Svārocisa then Auttami, then Tāmasa, then Raivata, then Cākṣusa; these six Manus have passed away. Vaivasvata, the son of the sun now presides over the seventh Manwantara, which is the present period.

स्वायंभुवं तु कथितं कल्पादावंतरं मया ।।
देवास्सप्तर्षयश्चैव यथावत्कथिता मया ।। ८ ।।

The era of Svayambhuva Manu, which took place in the beginning of Kalpa together with the celestials, saints and other personages, has been related by me.

अत ऊर्ध्वं प्रवक्ष्यामि मनोस्स्वरोचिषस्य तु ।।
मन्वंतराधिपान्सम्यग्देवर्षींस्तत्सुतांस्तथा ।। ९ ।।

I will now describe to you the period of Svārocisa Manu together with the presiding deities, saints and his sons.

पारावतास्सतुषिता देवास्स्वारोचिषेंतरे ।।
विपश्चित्तत्र देवेंद्रो मैत्रेयासीन्महाबलः ।। १० ।।

ऊर्जस्तंभस्तथा प्राणो वातोर्थ पृषभस्तथा ।।
निरयश्च परीवांश्च तत्र सप्तर्षयोऽभवन् ।। ११ ।।

चैत्रकिंपुरुषाद्याश्च सुतास्स्वारोचिषस्य तु ।।
द्वितीयमेतद्व्याख्यातमंतरं शृणु चोत्तमम् ।। १२ ।।

There flourished two classes of celestials in the Manvantara of Svārocisa named Pārāvatas and Tuṣitas—and the king of the celestials was the powerful Vipaścit; the seven Ṛsis were Urja, Stambha, Prāṇa, Dattoli, Ṛsabha, Niścara, Arvarivat; and the sons of the Manu were, Caitra, Kimpurusa and others. I have thus described to you the second Manvantara.

तृतीयेप्यंतरे ब्रह्मन्नुत्तमो नाम यो मनुः।।
सुशांतिर्नाम देवेंद्रो मैत्रेयासीत्सुताञ्छृणु।। १३।।

सुधामानस्तथा सत्या जपाश्चाथ प्रतर्दनाः।।
वशवर्तिश्च पञ्चैते गणा द्वादशकास्स्मृताः।। १४।।

In the third Manvantara of Uttami, Suśānti was the king of the celestials, who were severally denominated as the Sudhāmas, Satyas, Śivas, Pradersanas and Vasavartis and each of these order cosisted of twelve deities.

वसिष्ठतनया ह्येते सप्त सप्तर्षयोभवन्।।
अजः परशुदीप्ताद्ब्यास्तथोत्तममनोस्सुताः।। १५।।

The seven sons of Vasiṣṭha were the seven celestial saints and Aja, Parasu, Divya and others were the sons of the Manu.

तामसस्यांतरे देवास्सुपारा हरयस्तथा।।
सत्याश्च सुधियश्चैव सप्तविंशतिका गणाः।। १६।।

In the reign of Tāmasa the fourth Manu, the Surupas, Haris, Satyas and Sudhis were the orders of the celestials each consisting of twenty-seven.

शिबिरिंद्रस्तथा चासीच्छतयज्ञोपलक्षणः।।
सप्तर्ष यश्च ये तेषां तेषां नामानि मे शृणु।। १७।।

ज्योतिर्धामा पृथुः कात्यश्चैत्रोग्निर्धनकस्तथा।।
पीवरश्चर्षयो ह्येते सप्त तत्रापि चांतरे।। १८।।

Śivī was their king who was named Satakratu by his performance of hundred sacrifices; the seven Ṛṣis were Jyotirdhāmā, Pṛthu, Kāvya, Caitra, Agni, Dhanaka and Pivara.

नरः ख्यातिः केतुरूपो जानुजंघादयस्तथा।।
पुत्रास्तु तामसस्यासन्राजानस्सुमहाबलाः।। १९।।

The sons of Tāmasa were the powerful kings Nara, Khyāti, Sāntahaya, Jānujaṅghā and others.

पञ्चमे वापि मैत्रेय रैवतो नाम नामतः।।
मनुर्विभुश्च तत्रेंद्रो देवांश्चात्रांतरे शृणु।। २०।।

अमिताभा भूतरया बैकुंठास्सुप्तमेधसः।।
एते देवगणस्तत्र चतुर्दश चतुर्दश।। २१।।

In the fifth Manvantara Raivata was the Manu : Indra was their king and the celestials were Amitābhas, Abhutarajasas, Vaikuṇṭhas, and Sumedhasas each consisting of fourteen divinities.

हिरण्यरोमा वेदश्रिरूर्ध्वबाहुस्तथावरः।।
वेदबाहुस्सुधामा च पर्जन्यश्च महामुनिः।।
एते सप्तर्षयो विप्र तत्रासन्नैवतेंतरे।। २२।।

The seven Ṛṣis were Hiraṇyaromā, Vedasrī, Urddhabāhu, Vedabāhu, Sudhāman, Parjanya and Mahāmuni.

बलबंधुश्च संभाव्यस्सत्यकाद्याश्च तत्सुताः।।
नरेन्द्राश्च महावीर्य्यां बभूवुर्मुनिसत्तम।। २३।।

The sons of Raivata were Balabandhu, Susamhavya, Satyaka and other brave kings.

स्वारोचिषश्चोत्तमश्च तामसो रैवतस्तथा।।
प्रियव्रतान्वया ह्येते चत्वारो मनवस्स्मृताः।। २४।।

विष्णुमाराध्य तपसा स राजर्षिः प्रियव्रतः।।
मन्वंतराधिपानेताल्लँब्धवानात्मवंशजान्।। २५।।

These four Manus, Svārociṣas, Uttami, Tāmasa and Raivata were born in the race of Pryavrata who propitiated Viṣṇu by his devotions and obtained in consequence thereof these rulers of Manvantara as his son.

षष्ठे मन्वंतरे चासीच्चाक्षुषाख्यस्तथा मनुः।।
मनोजवस्तथैवेंद्रो देवानापि निबोध मे।। २६।।

आप्याः प्रसूता भव्याश्च पृथुकाश्च दिवौकसः।।
महानुभावा लेखाश्च पञ्चैते ह्यष्टका गणाः।। २७।।

सुमेधा विरजाश्चैव हविष्मानुत्तमो मधुः।।
अतिनामा सहिष्णुश्च सप्तासन्निति चर्षयः।। २८।।

ऊरुः पूरुश्शतद्युम्नप्रमुखास्सुमहाबलाः।।
चाक्षुषस्य मनोः पुत्राः पृथिवीपतयोऽभवन्।। २९।।

In the sixth Manvantara Cākṣuṣa was the Manu, when Manojava became the king of the celestials who were grouped as Adyas, Prastutas, Bhavyas, Pṛthugas, and the high-minded Lekhas each consisting of eight divinities; the seven Ṛṣis were Sumedhas, Virajas, Haviṣmat, Uttama, Madhu, Abhinaman and Sahiṣṇu. The sons of Cakṣuṣa were the mighty Uru, Puru, Śatadyumna and other kings of the earth.

विवस्वतस्सुतो विप्र श्राद्धदेवो महाद्युतिः।।
मनुस्संवर्त्तते धीमान् सांप्रतं सप्तमेंतरे।। ३०।।

O twice-born one, the Manu, who reigns in

the present period is the wise and illustrious lord of obsequies the offspring of the sun.

आदित्यवसुरुद्राद्या देवाश्चात्र महामुने।।
पुरंदरस्तथैवात्र मैत्रेय त्रिदशेश्वरः।। ३१।।

The celestials are the Ādityas, Vasus and Rudras. Their king is Purandara.

वशिष्ठः काश्यपोथात्रिर्जमदग्निस्सगौतमः।।
विश्वामित्रभरद्वाजौ सप्त सप्तर्षयोऽभवन्।। ३२।।

Vasiṣtha, Kāśyapa, Atri, Jamadagni, Gautama, Viśvāmitra and Bhāradwāja are the seven Ṛsis.

इक्ष्वाकुश्च नृगश्चैव धृष्टः शर्य्यातिरेव च।।
नरिष्यंतश्च विख्यातो नाभागोरिष्ट एव च।। ३३।।

करूषश्च पृषध्रश्च सुमहाँल्लोकविश्रुतः।।
मनोर्वैवस्वतस्यैते नव पुत्राः सुधाद्धमकाः।। ३४।।

And the nine pious sons of Vaivasvata Manu are the kings Ikṣavāku, Nabhaga, Dhṛṣṭa, Sanyati, Nariṣyanta, Nabhanidiṣṭa, Karuṣa, Pṛsadhra and the well known Vasumat.

विष्णुशक्तिरनौपम्या सत्वोद्रिक्ता स्थितौ स्थिता।।
मन्वंतरेश्वशेषेषु देवत्वेनाधितिष्ठति।। ३५।।

The incomparable energy, of Viṣṇu at one with the quality of goodness and preserving all created things, rules over all the Manvantaras in the shape of divinity.

अंशेन तस्या जज्ञेऽसौ यज्ञस्वा यंभुवेंतरे।।
आकूत्यां मानसो देव उत्पन्नः प्रथमेंतरे।। ३६।।

From a part of that divinity Yajña was born in the Swāyambhuva Manvantara the will-begotten child of Akuti.

ततः पुनः स वै देवः प्राप्ते स्वारोचिषेंतरे।।
तुषितायां समुत्पन्नो ह्याजिषस्तुषितैः सह।। ३७।।

And at the arrival of the Manvantara of Svārocisa the irrepressible Yajña was born as Ajita along with Tuṣitas the sons of Tuṣitā.

औत्तमेप्यंतरे देवस्तुषितस्तु पुनस्स वै।।
सत्यायामभवत्सत्यः सत्यैस्सह सुरोत्तमैः।। ३८।।

And at the advent of the Manvantara of Auttama, Tushitas were born as the excellent Satyas, of Satya.

तामसस्यांतरे चैव संप्राप्ते पुनरेव हि।।
हर्य्यायां हरिभिस्सार्द्धं हरिरेव बभूव ह।। ३९।।

In the Manvantara of Tāmasa, Satya became Hari along with the Haris, the children of Hari.

रैवतेप्यंतरे देवस्संभूत्यां मानसो हरिः।।
संभूतो रैवतैस्सार्द्धं देवैर्देववरो हरिः।। ४०।।

And in the Raivata Manvantara of Śambhūti the excellent Hari was born as Manasa along with the celestials called Abhutarajasas.

चाक्षुषे चांतरे देवो वैकुण्ठः पुरुषोत्तमः।।
विकुण्ठायामसौ जज्ञे वैकुंठैर्दैवतैः सह।। ४१।।

In the next Manvantara Viṣṇu was born of Vikuṇṭī, as Vaikuṇṭha along with the celestials called Vaikuṇṭhas.

मन्वंतरेत्र संप्राप्ते तथा वैवस्वते द्विज।।
वामनः काश्यपाद्विष्णुरदित्यां संबभूव ह।। ४२।।

In the present period Viṣṇu was again born as Vāmana the son of Kāśyapa by Aditi.

त्रिभिः क्रमैरिमाँल्लोकाञ्जित्वा येन महात्मना।।
पुरंदराय त्रैलोक्यं दत्तं निहतकंटकम्।। ४३।।

With three paces he conquered the worlds and having released them from all disturbances he gave them to Purandara.

इत्येतास्तनवस्तस्य सप्तमन्वंतरेषु वै।।
सप्तस्वेवाभवन्विप्र याभिः संवर्द्धिताः प्रजाः।।४४।।

By these seven persons, in the various Manvantaras, the created beings have been preserved.

यस्माद्विष्टमिदं विश्वं यस्य शक्त्या महात्मनः।।
तस्मात्स प्रोच्यते विष्णुर्विशेर्धातोः प्रवेशनात्।। ४५।।

सर्वे च देवा मनवस्समस्तास्सप्तर्षयो ये मनुसूनवश्च।।
इन्द्रश्च योऽयं त्रिदशेशभूतो विष्णोरशेषास्तु विभूतयस्ताः।।
४६।।

He is called Viṣṇu because his energy pervades the whole world from the root *Vis* to 'enter' or 'pervade :' and all the celestials, the Manus, the kings of the gods are but the impersonations of the power of Viṣṇu.

।।इति श्रीविष्णुमहापुराणे तृतीयेंशे प्रथमोऽध्यायः।। १।।

अथ तृतीयेंशे: द्वितीयोऽध्याय:
Part III : Section 2

मैत्रेय उवाच

प्रोक्ता न्येतानि भवता सप्त मन्वंतराणि वै।।
भविष्याण्यपि विप्रर्षे ममाख्यातुं त्वमर्हसि।। १।।

Maitreya said :—O foremost of Brāhmins, you have described to me the seven Manvantaras that have passed away. It behoves you to describe now the Manvantaras that shall take place in future.

श्रीपराशर उवाच

सूर्य्यस्य पत्नी संज्ञाभूत्तनया विश्वकर्मण:।।
मनुर्यमो यमी चैव तदपत्यानि वै मुने।। २।।

Parāśara said :—Sañjñā, the daughter of Viśvakarman, was the wife of the sun, and bore him three children, the manu Vaivasvata, Yama and the goddess Yamī.

असहंती तु सा भर्तुस्तेजश्छायां युयोज वै।।
भर्त्तृशुश्रूषणेरण्य स्वयं च तपसे ययौ।। ३।।

Being unable to endure the fevours of her husband, she engaged Chāyā in his attendance and repaired to the forest to practise devout austerities.

संज्ञेयमित्यथार्कश्च छायायामात्मजत्रयम्।।
शनैश्चर मनुं चान्यं तपतीं चाप्यजीजनत्।। ४।।

Considering that Chāyā as Sañjñā, he got upon her three other children—Sanaiścara (Saturn) another Manu Sāvarṇī and a daughter Tapati.

छायासंज्ञा ददौ शापं यमाय कुपिता यदा।।
तदान्येयमसौ बुद्धिरित्यासीद्यमसूर्य्ययो:।। ५।।

ततो विवस्वानाख्यातां तयैवारण्यसंस्थिताम्।।
समाधिदृष्ट्या ददृशे तामश्वां तपसि स्थिताम्।। ६।।

Once on a time being offended with Yama, the son of Sañjñā, Chāyā imprecated a curse upon him and gave out to Yama and the sun that she was not in reality Sañjñā the mother of the former. (Having heard this) the sun, by his meditation saw her as a mare in the region of Uttara Kuru.

वाजिरूपधर: सोथ तस्यां देवावथाश्विनौ।।
जनयामास रेवंतं रेतसोंते च भास्कर:।। ७।।

Thereupon assuming the shape of a horse the sun begot upon Sañjñā three other children the two Aśvins, and Revanta and brought her back to his own house.

आनिन्ये च पुन: संज्ञां स्वस्थानं भगवान्रवि:।।
तेजसश्शमनं चास्य विश्वकर्मा चकार ह।। ८।।

To deminish his fervours Viśvakarman placed him on his lathe and reduced some of his effulgence; to the eighth portion, for more than which was insperable.

भ्रममारोप्य सूर्य्यं तु तस्य तेजोनि शातनम्।।
कृतवानष्टमं भागं स व्यशातयदव्ययम्।। ९।।

यत्तस्माद्वैष्णवं तेजश्शातितं विश्वकर्मणा।।
जाज्वल्यमानमपतत्तद्भूमौ मुनिस त्तम।। १०।।

त्वष्टैव तेजसा तेन विष्णौश्चक्रमकल्पयत्।।
त्रिशूलं चैव शर्वस्य शिबिकां धनदस्य च।। ११।।

शक्तिं गुहस्य देवानामन्येषां च यदायुधम्।।
तत्सर्वं तेजसा तेन विश्वकर्मा व्यवर्द्धयत्।। १२।।

The portions of the divine Vaiṣṇava effulgence that were in the sun being field off by Viśvakarman, fell down shining on the earth and the artist constructed of them the discus of Viṣṇu—the trident of Śiva, the weapon of the god of wealth, the lance of Kārtikeya, and the weapons of the other celestials : all these Viśvakarman made from the additional rays of the sun.

छायासंज्ञासुतो योसौ द्वितीय: कथितो मनु:।।
पूर्वजस्यासवर्णोसौ सावर्णिस्तेन कथ्यते।। १३।।

The son of Chāyā, who was also called a Manu, was Sāvarṇī on account of his belonging to the same caste as his elder brother the Manu Vaivasvata.

तस्य मन्वंतरं ह्येतत्सावर्णिकमथाष्टमम्।।
तच्छृणुष्व महाभाग भविष्यत्कथयामि ते।। १४।।

He rules over the coming or eighth Manvantara, the details whereof and of those following I shall now describe.

सावद्धणस्तु मनुर्योसौ मैत्रेय भविता ततः।।
सुतपाश्चामिताभाश्च मुख्याश्चापि तथा सुराः।। १५।।

In the era when Sāvarṇī shall be the Manu the orders of the celestials will be Sūtapas, Amitābhas and Mukṣyas, each consisting of twenty-one divinities.

तेषां गणाश्च देवानामेकैको विंशकः स्मृतः।।
सप्तर्षीनपि वक्ष्यामि भविष्यान्मुनिसत्तम।। १६।।

दीप्तिमान् गालवो रामः कृपो द्रोणिस्तथा परः।।
मत्पुत्रश्च तथा व्यास ऋष्यशृंगश्च सप्तमः।। १७।।

The seven Ṛṣis will be Dīptimat, Gālava, Rāma, Kṛpa, Drauṇī : my son Vyāsa will be the sixth and the seventh will be Ṛṣyaśṛṅga.

विष्णु प्रसादादनघः पातालंतरगोचरः।।
विरोचनसुतस्तेषां बलिरिंद्रो भविष्यति।। १८।।

The chief of the celestials will be Bali—the innocent son of Virocona who, on account of Viṣṇu's favour, is the king of a portion of Pātāla.

विरजाश्चोर्वरीवांश्च निर्मोकाद्यास्तथापरे।।
सावर्णेस्तु मनोः पुत्रा भविष्यंति नेरश्वराः।। १९।।

The sons of Sāvarṇī will be Virajās, Arvarivas, Nirmoha and others.

नवमो दक्षसावर्णिर्भविष्यति मुने मनुः।। २०।।

O Maitreya, Dakṣa-Sāvarṇī will be the ninth Manu.

पारा मरीचिगर्भाश्च सुधर्माणस्तथा त्रिधा।।
भविष्यंति तथा देवा ह्येकैको द्वादशो गणः।। २१।।

The Pārās, Marīcigarbhas and Sudharmas will be the three orders of the celestials each consisting of twelve divinities.

तेषामिंद्रो महावीर्य्यो भविष्यत्यद्भुतो द्विज।। २२।।

Indra Adbhuta will be their mighty king.

सवनो द्युतिमान् भव्यो वसुर्मेधातिथिस्तथा।।
ज्योतिष्मान् सप्तमः सत्यस्तत्रैते च महर्षयः।। २३।।

Savana Dyutimut, Bhavya, Vasu Medhātithī, Jyotiṣmān and Satya, will be the seven Ṛṣis.

धृतकेतुर्दीप्तिकेतुः पञ्चहस्तनिरामयौ।।
पृथुश्रवाद्याश्च तथा दक्षसावर्णिकात्मजाः।। २४।।

Dhṛtaketu, Dṛptiketu, Pañcaśāsta, Nirmaya, Pṛthusrava and others will be sons of the Manu.

दशमो ब्रह्मसावर्णिर्भविष्यति मुने मनुः।।
सुधामानो विशुद्धाश्च शतसंख्यास्तथा सुराः।। २५।।

तेषामिंद्रश्च भविता शांतिर्नाम महाबलः।।
सप्तर्षयो भविष्यंति ये तथा ताञ्छृणुष्व ह।। २६।।

In the tenth period Brahmā-Sāvarṇī will be the Manu; the celestials will be the Sudhamas, Viruddhas and Śatasāṅkhyas : their king will be the powerful Śānti.

हविष्मान्सुकृतस्सत्यस्तपोमूर्त्तिस्तथापरः।।
नाभागोऽप्रतिमौजाश्च सत्यकेतुस्तथैव च।। २७।।

सुक्षेत्रश्चोत्तमौजाश्च भूरिषेणादयो दश।।
ब्रह्मसावर्णिपुत्रास्तु रक्षिष्यंति वसुंधराम्।। २८।।

The Ṛṣis will be Haviṣmān, Sukṛti, Satya, Apammurtti, Nabhāga, Apratimaujas and Satyaketu and the ten sons of the Manu will be Sukṣetra, Uttamaujās, Hariṣeṇa and others.

एकादशश्च भविता धर्मसावर्णिको मनुः।। २९।।

विहंगमाः कामगमा निर्वाणा ऋषयस्तथा।।
गणास्त्वेते तदा मुख्या देवानां च भविष्यताम्।।
एकैकस्त्रिंशकस्तेषां गणश्चेंद्रश्च वै पृषा।। ३०।।

In the eleventh period Dharma-Sāvarṇī will be the Manu and the leading celestials will be Vihaṅgamas, Kāmāgamas and Nirmanaratis each consisting of thirty; Vrisha will be their king.

निःस्वरश्चाग्नितेजाश्च वपुष्मान्घृणिरारुणिः।।
हविष्माननघश्चैव भाव्याः सप्तर्षयस्तथा।। ३१।।

The Ṛṣis will be Niścara, Agnitejas, Vapuṣman, Viṣṇu, Āruṇī. Haviṣman and Aṅgha.

सर्वत्रगस्सुधर्मा च देवानीकादयस्तथा।।
भविष्यंति मनोस्तस्य तनयाः पृथवीश्वराः।। ३२।।

Savarga, Śarvadharma, Devanika and others—the kings of the earth—will be the sons of the Manu.

रुद्रपुत्रस्तु सावर्णिर्भविता द्वादशो मनुः।।
ऋतुधामा च तत्रेंद्रो भविता शृणु मे सुरान्।। ३३।।

In the twelfth period Savarṇī, the son of Rudra, will be the Manu. Ṛtudhama will be the king of the gods who will the Manu.

हरिता रोहिता देवास्तथा सुमनसो द्विज।।
सुकर्माणः सुरापाश्च दशकाः पञ्च वै गणाः।। ३४।।

Ṛtudhama will be the king of the gods who will be Haritās Lohitās, Sumanasas, and Śukarmas, each consisting of fifteen divinities.

तपस्वी सुतपाश्चैव तपोमूर्त्तिस्तपोतपो-
धृतिर्द्युतिश्चान्यः सप्तमस्तु तपोधनः।।
सप्तर्षयस्त्विमे तस्य पुत्रानपि निबोध मे।। ३५।।

The Ṛṣis will be Tapasvī, Sutapas, Tapomūrttī, Taporatī, Tapodhṛti, Tapodyuti and Tapodhana.

देववानुपदेवश्च देवश्रेष्ठादयस्तथा।।
मनोस्तस्य महावीर्य्या भविष्यंति महानृपाः।। ३६।।

And the Manu's sons will be Devavān, Upadeva, Devareṣṭa and others—who will be the powerful kings of the earth.

त्रयोदशो रुचिर्नामा भविष्यति मुने मनुः।। ३७।।

In the thirteenth period Rauchya will be the Manu.

सुत्रामाणः सुकर्माणः सुधर्माणस्तथामराः।।
त्रयस्त्रिंशद्विभेदास्ते देवानां यत्र वै गणाः।। ३८।।
दिवस्पतिर्महावीर्य्यस्तेषामिंद्रो भविष्यति।। ३९।।

The gods will be the Sudhmanas, Sudharmans and Śukarmans each consisting of thirty-three. Their king will be Divaspati.

निर्मोहस्तत्त्वदर्शी च निष्प्रकंप्यो निरुत्सुकः।।
धृतिमानव्ययश्चान्यस्सप्तमस्सुतपा मुनिः।।
सप्तर्षयस्त्वमी तस्य पुत्रानपि निबोध मे।। ४०।।

The Ṛṣis will be Nirmoha, Tatwadersin, Niṣprakampa, Nirutsuka, Dhṛtimat, Avyaya, and Sutpas.

चित्रसेनविचित्राद्या भविष्यंति महीक्षितः।। ४१।।

The sons of the Manu will be Citrasena, Vicitra, and others who will be the kings of the earth.

भौमश्चतुर्दशश्चाप मैत्रेय भविता मनुः।।
शुचिरिंद्रः सुरगणास्तत्र पञ्च शृणुष्व तान्।। ४२।।
चाक्षुषाश्च पवित्राश्च कनिष्ठा भ्राजिकास्तथा।।
वाचावृद्धाश्च वै देवास्सप्तर्षीनपि मे शृणु।। ४३।।
अग्निबाहुः शुचिः शुक्रो मागधोग्नीध्र एव च।।
युक्तस्तथा जितश्चान्यो मनुपुत्रानतः शृणु।। ४४।।

At the fourteenth period Bhautya will be the Manu and Suci will be the king of the celestials who will be the Cakṣuṣas, Pavitras, Kaniṣṭhas, Bhājiras and Vavṛddhas, The seven Ṛṣis will be Agnibāhu, Śuci, Śukra Māgadha, Gṛghra, Yukta and Ajita.

ऊरुगंभीरबुद्ध्याद्या मनोस्तस्य सुता नृपाः।।
कथिता मुनिशार्दूल पालयिष्यंति ये महीम्।। ४५।।

Uru, Gabhira, Bradhna and other will be sons of Manu who will be the kings of the earth.

चतुर्युगाते वेदानां जायते किल विप्लवः।।
प्रवर्त्तयंति तानेत्या भुवं सप्तर्षयो दिवः।। ४६।।

At the end of every four Yugas the Vedas disappear. And the seven Ṛṣis descending on the earth again establish them.

कृतेकृते स्मृतेद्धवप्र प्रणेता जायते मनुः।।
देवा यज्ञभुजस्ते तु यावन्मन्वंतरं तु तत्।। ४७।।

In every Kṛta age the presiding Manu becomes the legislator and during the Manwantara the celestials of the various classes receive sacrifices.

भवंति ये मनोः पुत्रा यावन्मन्वंतरं तु तैः।।
तदन्वयोद्भवैश्चैव तावद्भूः परिपाल्यते।। ४८।।

And those born in the race of Manus lord over the earth for that period.

मनुस्सप्तर्षयो देवा भूपालाश्च मनोः सुताः।।
मन्वंतरे भवंत्येते शक्रश्चैवाधिकारिणः।। ४९।।
चतुर्दशभिरेतैस्तु गतैर्मन्वंतरैर्द्विज।।
सहस्त्रयुगपर्य्यंतः कल्पो निश्शेष उच्यते।। ५०।।

In every Manvantara, the Manu, the seven Ṛṣis, the king of the gods and the sons of the Manu rule over the earth.

तावत्प्रमाणा च निशा ततो भवति सत्तम।।
ब्रह्म रूपधरश्शेते शेषाहावंबुसंप्लवे।। ५१।।

In this wise, O Brāhmin, fourteen Manvantaras constitute a Kalpa. And it is succeeded by a night of similar duration.

त्रैलोक्यमखिलं ग्रस्त्वा भगवानादिकृद्विभुः।।
स्वमायासंस्थितो विप्र सर्वभूतो जनार्दनः।। ५२।।

And the glorious Janārdana, wearing form of Brahmā, the essence of all things, the lord of all, the creator of all, involved in his own illusions and having swallowed up three shperes, sleeps upon the serpent Śeṣa in the midst of the ocean.

ततः प्रबुद्धो भगवान् यथा पूर्वं तथा पुनः।।
सृष्टिं करोत्यव्ययात्मा कल्पेकल्पे रजोगुणः।।५३।।

And awaking after sleep the undecaying Hari, resorting to the quality of foulness, creates all things as they were before.

मनवो भूभुजस्सेंद्रा देवास्सप्तर्षयस्तथा।।
सात्त्विकोंशः स्थितिकरो जगतो द्विजसत्तम।।५४।।

And by virtue of part of his essence which is identical with the quality of goodness he, as the Manus, the celestials, their chiefs, kings, as well as the seven Ṛṣis, preserves the universe.

चतुर्युगेप्यसौ विष्णुः स्थितिव्यापारलक्षणः।।
युगव्यवस्थां कुरुते तथा मैत्रेय तच्छृणु।।५५।।

I will now explain to you, O Maitreya, how Viṣṇu, who is regarded as Providence all through the four ages, preserved (the universe).

कृते युगे परं ज्ञानं कपिलादिस्वरूपधृक्।।
ददाति सर्वभूतात्मा सर्वभूतहिते रतः।। ५६।।

In the Kṛta Yuga, He, for the behoof of all creatures, was born as the great ascetic Kapila and imparted to them true wisdom.

चक्रवर्त्तिस्वरूपेण त्रेतायामपि स प्रभुः।।
दुष्टानां निग्रहं कुर्वन्परिपाति जगत्त्रयम्।। ५७।।

In the Tretā Yuga he was born as the Lord Paramount and repressed the wicked and protected the three worlds.

वेदमेकं चतुर्भेदं कृत्वा शाखाशतैर्विभुः।।
करोति बहुलं भूयो वेदव्यासस्वरूपधृक्।। ५८।।

In the Dwāpara Yuga He was born as Vyāsa and divided the Vedas into four divisions which were again divided into various branches; which were again divided into diverse sections.

वेदांस्तु द्वापरे व्यस्य कलेरंते पुनर्हरिः।।
कल्किस्वरूपी दुर्वृत्तान्मार्गे स्थापयति प्रभुः।।५९।।

And at the end of Kali the fourth Yuga, He shall be born as Kalki and shall lead again the wicked to the paths of piety.

एवमेतज्जगत्सर्वं शश्वत्पाति करोति च।।
हंति चांतेष्वनंतात्मा नास्त्यस्माद्व्यतिरेकि यत्।।६०।।

Thus the endless Viṣṇu creates, preserves and destroys the universe. And there is none else but Him.

भूतं भव्यं भविष्यं च सर्वभूतान्महात्मनः।।
तदत्रान्यत्र वा विप्र सद्भावः कथितस्तव।। ६१।।

I have thus described to you, O Brāhmaṇa, the real nature of that Great Being who is at one with all things, and besides whom there is nothing else, nor has there been, nor will there be either here or elsewhere.

मन्वंतराण्यशेषाणि कथितानि मया तव।।
मन्वंतराधिपांश्चैव किमन्यत्कथयामि ते।। ६२।।

I have also described to you all the Manvantaras with their presiding deities. What else do you wish to hear?"

।। इति श्रीविष्णुमहापुराणे तृतीयेंशे द्वितीयोऽध्यायः।। २।।

अथ तृतीयेंशेः तृतीयोऽध्यायः
Part III : Section 3

मैत्रेय उवाच

ज्ञातमेतन्मया त्वत्तो यथा सर्वमिदं जगत्।।
विष्णुर्विष्णौ विष्णुतश्च न परं विद्यते ततः।। १।।

Maitreya said :—I had been informed before by you that this universe is but the manifestation of Viṣṇu, that it exists in Him and that there is nothing else distinct from Him.

एतत्तु श्रोतुमिच्छामि व्यस्ता वेदा महात्मना।।
वेदव्यासस्वरूपेण यथा तेन युगेयुगे।। २।।

I wish now to hear how the illustrious Veda-vyāsa divided the Vedas into various sections in diverse Yugas.

यस्मिन्यस्मिन्युगे व्यासो यो य आसीन्महामुने।।
तंतमाचक्ष्व भगवच्छाखाभेदांश्च मे वद।। ३।।

Describe to me, O great Muni, who were the Vyāsas in different eras, and what were the various divisions of the Vedas?

श्रीपराशर उवाच

वेदद्रुमस्य मैत्रेय शाखाभेदास्सहस्रशः।।
न शक्तो विस्तराद्वक्तुं संक्षेपेण शृणुष्व तम्।। ४।।

Parāśara said :—O Maitreya,—The great tree of Vedas has a thousand branches. It is impossible for me to describe them at length. Listen, I shall, however, describe them in short.

द्वापरेद्वापरे विष्णुर्व्यासरूपी महामुने।।
वेदमेकं सुबहुंधा कुरुते जगतो हितः।। ५।।

O great Muni, the glorious Viṣṇu, in the form of Vyāsa, at every Dwāpara Yuga, for the benefit of mankind, divided the Vedas into various branches.

वीर्यं तेजो बलं चाल्पं मनुष्याणामवेक्ष्य च।।
हिताय सर्वभूतानां वेदभेदान्करोति सः।। ६।।

Beholding the diminution of the prowess and energy of mankind, He, for their behoof, divided the Vedas into various divisions.

ययासौ कुरुते तन्वा वेदमेकं पृथक् प्रभुः।।
वेदव्यासाभिधाना तु सा च मूर्तिर्मधुद्विषं।। ७।।

The form, in which the glorious Viṣṇu divides the Vedas, is named Veda-vyāsa.

यस्मिन्मन्वंतरे व्यासा येये स्युस्तान्निबोध मे।।
यथा च भेदश्शाखानं व्यासेन क्रियते मुने।। ८।।

Listen, I shall now describe to you, O Muni, who were the Vyāsas in their respective periods and how they divided the Vedas.

अष्टाविंशतिकृत्वो वै वेदो व्यस्तो महर्षिभिः।।
वैवस्वतेंतरे तस्मिन्द्वापरेषु पुनःपुनः।। ९।।

वेदव्यासा व्यतीता ये ह्यष्टाविंशति सत्तम।।
चतुर्धा यैः कृतो वेदो द्वापरेषु पुनःपुनः।। १०।।

In the Vaisvaswata Manvantara in the Dwāpara age, the Ṛṣis divided the Vedas twenty-eight times and accordingly twenty-eight Vyāsas have passed away who divided the Vedas in their respective periods into four.

द्वापरे प्रथमे व्यस्तस्स्वयं वेदः स्वयंभुवा।।
द्वितीये द्वापरे चैव वेदव्यासः प्रजापतिः।। ११।।

तृतीये चोशना व्यासश्चतुर्थे च बृहस्पतिः।।
सविता पञ्चमे व्यासः षष्ठे मृत्युस्स्मृतः प्रभुः।। १२।।

सप्तमे च तथैवेंद्रो वसिष्ठश्चाष्टमे स्मृतः।।
सारस्वतश्च नवमे त्रिधामा दशमे स्मृतः।। १३।।

एकादशे तु त्रिशिखो भरद्वाजस्ततः परः।।
त्रयोदशे चांतरिक्षो वर्णी चापि चतुर्दशे।। १४।।

त्र्यारुणः पञ्चदशे षोडशे तु धनञ्जयः।।
ऋतुञ्जयः सप्तदशे तदूर्ध्वं च जयस्स्मृतः।। १५।।

ततो व्यासो भरद्वाजो भरद्वाजाच्च गौतमः।।
गौतमादुत्तरो व्यासो हर्य्यात्मा योभिधीयते।। १६।।

अथ हर्य्यात्मनोंते च स्मृतो वाजश्रवा मुनिः।।
सोमशुष्कायणस्तस्मात्तृणबिंदुरिति स्मृतः।। १७।।

ऋक्षोभूद्भर्गवस्तस्माद्वाल्मीकिर्योभिधीयते।।
तस्मादस्मत्पिता शक्तिर्व्यासस्तस्मादहं मुने।। १८।।

जातुकर्णोभवन्मत्तः कृष्णद्वैपायनस्ततः।।
अष्टाविंशतिरित्येते वेदव्यासाः पुरातनाः।। १९।।

एको वेदश्चतुर्द्धा तु तैः कृतो द्वापरादिषु।। २०।।

In the Dwāpara age the distribution was made by Svayambhuva (Brahmā) himself; in the second period Veda-vyāsa was the Manu; in the third, Uṣanas; in the fourth, Vṛhaspati : in the fifth, Savitri; in the sixth, Mṛtyu; in the seventh, Indra; in the eight, Vasiṣṭha; in the ninth, Sāraswata; in the tenth, Tridhāman; in the eleventh, Trivreṣan; in the twelfth, Bhāradwāja; in the thirteenth, Antarikṣa; in the fourteenth, Vapra; in the fifteenth, Trayyaruṇa; in the sixteenth, Dhanañjaya; in the seventeenth, Kṛtañjaya; in the eighteenth, Ṛṇa; in the nineteenth, Bhāradwāja; in the twentieth, Gautama; in the twenty-first, Uttama, also called Haryātmā; in the twenty-second, Vena, who is otherwise named Rājaśravas; in the twenty-third, Somasuṣmāpana, also Tṛṇa-Vindu; in the twenty-fourth, Ṛkṣa, the descendant of Bhṛgu, who is known by the name Vālmīki; in the twenty-fifth my father Śakti was the Vyāsa; I was the Vyāsa of the twenty-sixth period; and was succeeded by Jaratkāru; the Vyāsa, in the twenty-eighth period, was Kṛṣṇa Dwaipāyana. These are the twenty-eight elder Vyāsa who divided the Vedas into four in the preceding Dwāpara ages.

भविष्ये द्वापरे चापि द्रौणिर्व्यासो भविष्यति।।
व्यतीते मम पुत्रेस्मिन् कृष्णद्वैपायने मुने।। २१।।

In the next Dwāpara, Drauṇī, the son of Droṇa, will be the Vyāsa when my son the Muni Kṛṣṇa Dwaipāyana, who is the actual Vyāsa, shall cease to be.

ध्रुवमे काक्षरं ब्रह्म ओमित्येव व्यवस्थितम्।।
बृहत्वाद्बंहणत्वाच्च तद्ब्रह्मेत्यभिधीयते।। २२।।

The syllable Oṁ is defined to be the eternal monosyllabic Brahmā. The word Brahmā is derived from the root Vṛha *to increase* because it is infinite and because it is the cause by which the Vedas developed.

प्रणवावस्थितं नित्यं भूर्भुवस्स्वरितीर्य्यते।।
ऋग्यजुस्सामाथर्वाणो यत्तस्मै ब्रह्मणे नमः।। २३।।

The regions, Bhur, Bhuva and Swa exist in bhrama, who is Oṁ. Glory to Brahmā, who is known as Oṁ and who is at one with Ṛk, Yajur, and Sāma.

जगतः प्रलयोत्पत्त्योर्यत्तत्कारणसंज्ञितम्।।
महतः परमं गुह्यं तस्मै सुब्रह्मणे नमः।। २४।।

अगाधापारमक्षय्यं जगत्संमोहनालयम्।।
स्वप्रकाशप्रवृत्तिभ्यां पुरुषार्थप्रयोजनम्।। २५।।

Salutation unto Brahmā who is the cause of creation and destruction, who is the great and mysterious cause of the intellectual principle (Mahat), who is devoid of limit in time and space and is freed from diminution and decay, from whom proceeds worldly illusion and in whom exists the end of soul through the qualities of goodness and foulness.

सांख्यज्ञानवतां निष्ठा गतिश्शमदमात्मनाम्।।
यत्तदव्यक्तममृतं प्रवृत्तिर्ब्रह्म शाश्वतम्।। २६।।

प्रधानमात्मयोनिश्च गुहासंस्थं च शब्द्यते।।
अविभागं तथा शुक्रमक्षयं बहुधात्मकम्।। २७।।

He is the refuge of those who are acquainted with the Sāṅkhya philosophy and those who have mastered their thoughts and passions. He is the invisible and imperishable Brahmā, assuming various forms but invariable in substance and the chief self-create principle.

परमब्रह्मणे तस्मै नित्यमेव नमोनमः।।
यद्रूपं वासुदेवस्य परमात्मस्वरूपिणः।। २८।।

He lightens the recesses of heart, is indivisible, radiant, undecaying and multiform. Salutation unto this supreme Brahmā, ever and ever—this form of Vāsudeva who is at one with the supreme spirit.

एकद्ब्रह्म त्रिधा भेदमभेदमपि स प्रभुः।।
सर्वभेदेष्वभेदोसौभिद्यते भिन्नबुद्धिभिः।। २९।।

This Brahmā, although diversified as threefold, is identical, is the lord of all, exists as one in all creatures, and is perceived as many on account of their diversity of understanding.

सऋङ्मयस्सामभयः सर्वात्मा सा यजुर्मयः।।
ऋग्यजुस्सामसारात्मा स एवात्मा शरीरिणाम्।। ३०।।

He, composed of Ṛk, Sāma and Yajur Vedas, is at the same time their essence as He is the soul of all embodied spirits. He, though at one with the Vedas, creates them and divides them into various branches.

स भिद्यते वेदमयस्स्ववेदं
करोति भेदैर्बहुभिस्सशाखम्।।

शाखाप्रणेता स समस्तशाखा-
ज्ञानस्वरूपो भगवानसंगः।। ३१।।

He is the author of these divisions—He is those branches. He is the author of these divisions—He is those branches collectively; for that eternal lord is the essence of true knowledge.

।। इति श्रीविष्णुमहापुराणे तृतीयेंशे तृतीयोऽध्यायः।। ३।।

अथ तृतीयेंशेः चतुर्थोऽध्यायः

Part III : Section 4

श्रीपराशर उवाच

आद्यो वेदश्चतुष्पादः कृतः साहस्त्रसम्भितः।।
ततो दशगुणः कृत्स्नो यज्ञोयं सर्वकामधुक्।। १।।

Parāśara said :—The original Veda, divided into four branches, consists of one hundred thousand Stanzas—and from it originated sacrifice of ten kinds—the fulfiller of all desires.

ततोत्र मत्सुतो व्यासो अष्टाविंशतिमेंतरे।।
वेदमेकं चतुष्पादं चातुर्द्धा व्यभजत्प्रभुः।। २।।

In the twenty-eighth Dwāpara era, my son Vyāsa divided the Veda into four branches.

यथा च तेन वै व्यस्ता वेदब्यासेन धीमता।।
वेदास्तथा समस्तैस्तैर्व्यस्ता व्यस्तैस्तथा मया।। ३।।

As the Veda was divided by the intelligent Veda-Vyāsa, so it was divided at various other periods by myself and other Vyāsas.

तदनेनैव वेदानां शाखाभेदान्द्विजोत्तम।।
चतुर्युगेषु पठितान्समस्तेष्ववधारय।। ४।।

In this way, O foremost of twice-born ones, the Veda is divided into various branches and the people of the four Yugas perform sacrifices.

कृष्णद्वैपायनं व्यासं विद्धि नारायणं प्रभुम्।।
को ह्यन्यो भुवि मैत्रेय महाभारतकृद्भवेत।। ५।।

O Maitreya, know this Kṛṣṇa Dwaipāyana Vyāsa, as the Nārāyaṇa, for who else on this earth could have composed the Mahābhārata?

तेन व्यस्ता यथा वेदा मत्पुत्रेण महात्मना।।
द्वापरे ह्यत्र मैत्रेय तस्मिञ्छृणु यथातथम्।। ६।।

How in the Dwāpara age the Veda was divided by my high-souled son, I shall describe, O Maitreya, : do thou hear it.

ब्रह्मणा चोदितो व्यासो वेदान्व्यस्तुं प्रचक्रमे।।
अथ शिष्यान्प्रजग्राह चतुरो वेदपारगान्।। ७।।

When Vyāsa was engaged by Brahmā in the work of arranging the Vedas, he took four persons, proficient in those works, as his disciples.

ऋग्वेदपाठकं पैलं जग्राह स महामुनिः।।
वैशंपायननामानं यजुर्वेदस्य चाग्रहीत्।। ८।।

He appointed Paila reader of the Ṛc; Vaiśampāyana of Yajuṣ; and Jaiminī of the Sāma Veda.

जैमिनिं सामवेदस्य तथैवाथर्ववेदवित्।।
सुमंतुस्तस्य शिष्योभूद्वेदव्यासस्य धीमतः।। ९।।

And Sumantu, who was acquainted with the Atharva-Veda, was also the disciple of the learned Vyāsa.

रोमहर्षणनामनं महाबुद्धिं महामुनिः।।
सूतं जग्राह शिष्यं स इतिहासपुराणयोः।। १०।।

He also took Sūta, who was named Lomaharṣaṇa, as his desciple in history and Purāṇas.

एक आसीद्यजुर्वेदस्तं चतुर्द्धा व्यकल्पयत्।।
चातुर्होत्रमभूत्तस्मिंस्तेन यज्ञमथाकरोत्।। ११।।

There was but one Yajur Veda, which he divided into four parts—from which originated the sacrificial rite that is performed by the four orders of priests.

आध्वर्यवं यजुर्भिस्तु ऋग्भिर्होत्रं तथा मुनिः।।
औद्गात्रं सामभिश्चक्रे ब्रह्मत्वं चाप्यथर्वभिः।। १२।।

ततस्स ऋचु उद्धृत्य ऋग्वेदं कृतवान्मुनिः।।
यजूंषि च यजुर्वेदं सामवेदं च सामभिः।। १३।।

राज्ञां चाथर्ववेदेन सर्वकर्माणि च प्रभुः।।
कारयामास मैत्रेय ब्रह्मत्वं च यथास्थिति।। १४।।

In this, the Muni enjoined the Adhwaryu to recite the prayers of Yajuns; the Hotri to sing the hymn of (Ṛk-Veda); the Udgātri to sing the hymns of Sāma-Veda and the Brāhmaṇa to utter the formulae of the Atharva-Veda. He then compiled the Ṛg-Veda with the collection of these hymns (Ṛcas); the Yajur-Veda with the prayers and directions named Yajuṣ; and Sāma-Veda, with those called Sāma; and with the Atharvas he laid down the function of the Brāhmaṇa and the rules for the performance of all the ceremonies by kings.

सोऽयमेको यथा वेदस्तरुस्तेन पृथक्कृतः।।
चतुर्धाथ ततो जातं वेदपादपकाननम्।। १५।।

In this way the huge Veda tree was divided into four stems, which soon spread out into an extensive forest.

बिभेद प्रथमं विप्र पैलो ऋग्वेदपादपम्।।
इन्द्रप्रमितये प्रादाद्बष्कलाय च संहिते।। १६।।

O Brāhmin, Paila first divided the Ṛg-Veda and gave the two Saṁhitās to Indra-Pramati and to Bhāṣkali.

चतुर्धा स बिभेदाथ बाष्कलोपि च संहिताम्।।
बोधादिभ्यो ददौ ताश्च शिष्येभ्यस्समहामुनिः।। १७।।

बोध्याग्निमाढकौ तद्वद्याज्ञवल्क्यपराशरौ।।
प्रतिशाखास्तु शाखायास्तस्यास्ते जगृहुर्मुने।। १८।।

Bhāṣkali again divided his Saṁhitā into four and handed them over to his disciples baudhya, Agnimathara, Yājñavalkya, and Parāśara; and they studied these secondary branches from the original O Muni.

इंद्रप्रमितिरेकां तु संहितां स्वसुतं ततः।।
मांडुकेयं महात्मानं मैत्रेयाध्यापयत्तदा।। १९।।
तस्य शिष्यप्रशिष्येभ्यः पुत्रशिष्यक्रमाद्ययौ।। २०।।

Indra-Pramati, O Maitreya, gave his Saṁhitā to his magnanimous son Māṇḍukeya, which thence descended through successive generations and disciples.

वेदमित्रस्तु शाकल्यः संहितां तामधीतवान्।।
चकार संहिताः पञ्च शिष्येभ्यः प्रददौ च ताः।। २१।।

तस्य शिष्यास्तु ये पञ्च तेषां नामानि मे शृणु।।
मुद्गलो गोमुखश्चैव वात्स्यश्शालीय एव च।।
शरीरः पञ्चमश्चासीन्मैत्रेय सुमहामतिः।। २२।।

Vedamitra, otherwise called Śākalya, read the same Saṁhitā and divided it into five Saṁhitās which he gave to his disciples named severally Mudgala, Goswalu, Vāsya, Sāliya and Śiśira.

संहितात्रितयं चक्रे शाकपूर्णस्तथेतरः।।
निरुक्तमकरोत्तद्वच्चतुर्थं मुनिसत्तम।। २३।।

Sākapūrni made a different classification of the original Saṁhitā into three and added a Nirukta (glossary) constituting a fourth.

क्रौञ्चो वैतालिकस्तद्वद्बलाकश्च महामुनिः।।
निरुक्तश्च चतुर्थोभूद्वेदवेदांगपारगः।। २४।।

And he gave these three Saṁhitās to his three pupils, Krauñca, Vaitalaki, and Valaka. And the glossary was given to the fourth who was named Niruktakṛt and who was versed in the Vedas and their various branches.

इत्येतः प्रतिशाखाभ्यो ह्यनुशाखा द्विजोत्तम।।
बाष्कलश्चापरास्तिस्त्रस्संहिताः कृतवान्द्विज।।
शिष्यः कालायनिर्गार्ग्यस्तृतीयश्च कथाजपः।। २५।।

In this way, O foremost of twice-born ones, Vedas, their divisions and sub-divisions sprang up. Baṣkalī composed three other Saṁhitās which he gave to his three pupils Kalyaṇī, Gārgya, and Kathajava.

इत्येता बह्वृचाः प्रोक्ताः संहिता यैः प्रवर्त्तिताः।। २६।।

These are they by whom various Saṁhitās have been composed.

।। इति श्रीविष्णुमहापुराणे तृतीयेंशे चतुर्थोऽध्यायः।। ४।।

अथ तृतीयेंशेः पञ्चमोऽध्यायः

Part III : Section 5

श्रीपराशर उवाच

यजुर्वेदतरोश्शाखास्सप्तविंशन्महामुनिः।।
वैशंपायननामासौ व्यासशिष्यश्चकार वै।। १।।
शिष्येभ्यः प्रददौ ताश्च जगृहुस्तेष्यनुक्रमात्।। २।।
याज्ञवल्क्यस्तु तत्राभूद्ब्रह्मरातसुतो द्विज।।

Parāśara said :—The high-minded disciple of Vyāsa. Vaiśaṁpāyana made out twenty-seven branches of the tree Yajur-Veda and gave them to as many disciples, of whom Yājña-valkya, the son of Brahmarata was famous for piety and obedience to his preceptor.

शिष्यः परमधर्मज्ञौ गुरुवृत्तिपरस्सदा।। ३।।

ऋषिर्योद्य महामेरोः समाजे नागमिष्यति।।
तस्य वै सप्तरात्रात्तु ब्रह्महत्त्या भविष्यति।। ४।।

पूर्वमेवं मुनिगणैस्समयो यः कृतो द्विज।।
वैशंपायन एकस्तु तं व्यतिक्रांतवांस्तदा।। ५।।

Formerly at one time the Munis had entered into a covenant that any one of them, who at a ceretain time, did not join a council held on mount Meru, should perpetrate the crime of Brāhmiṇicide within a period of seven nights. Vaiśaṁpāyana alone was not present at the appointed hour and so broke the engagement.

स्वस्त्रीयं बालकं सोथ पदा स्पृष्टमताडयत्।। ६।।

And he accidently slew the child of his sister by a kick of his foot.

शिष्यानाह स भोः शिष्या ब्रह्महत्त्यापहं व्रतम्।।
चरध्वं मतकृते सर्वे न विचार्य्यमिदं तथा।। ७।।

Thereupon he said to his disciples—"O my disciples, do ye engage in such ceremonies as will remove the sin consequent upon the destruction of a Brāhmin on my behalf. You need not hesitate in this."

अथाह याज्ञवल्क्यस्तु किमेभिर्भगवन्द्विजैः।।
क्लेशितैरल्पतेजोभिश्चरिष्येहमिदं व्रतम्।। ८।।

Thereupon Yājñavalkya said—"What is the use of troubling these miserable and inefficient Brāhmaṇas? I shall alone perfom this penance."

ततः क्रुद्धो गुरुः प्राह याज्ञवल्क्यं महामुनिम्।।
मुच्यतां यत्त्वयाधीतं मत्तो विप्रावमानक।। ९।।

Thereupon the high-minded preceptor, enraged, said to him—"O thou who hast insulted these Brāhmins, relinquish all thou hast learnt from me.

निस्तेजसो वसदस्येनान्यत्त्वं ब्राह्मणपुंगवान्।।
तेन शिष्येण नार्थोस्ति ममाज्ञाभंगकारिणा।। १०।।

Dost thou say that these Brāhmins are inefficient? What is the use of a disciple who disobeys my commands."

याज्ञवल्क्यस्ततः प्राह भक्तयैतत्ते मयोदितम्।।
ममाप्यलं त्वयाधीतं यन्मया तदिदं द्विज।। ११।।

Whereto Yājñavalkya replied—"I spoke this out of my devotion to thee. It is more than enough—do thou take, O twice-born one, what I have learnt from thee."

श्रीपराशर उवाच

इत्युक्तो रुधिराक्तानि सरूपाणि यजूंषि सः।।
छर्दयित्वा ददौ तस्मै ययौ स स्वेच्छया मुनिः।। १२।।

Having said this, he ejected from his stomach the texts of Yajuṣ stained in blood. He then went away.

यजूंष्यथ विसृष्टानि याज्ञवल्क्येन वै द्विज।।
जगृहुस्तित्तिरा भूत्वा तैत्तिरीयास्तु ते ततः।। १३।।

ब्रह्महत्यावृतं चीर्णं गुरुणा चोदितैस्तु तैः।।
चाक्रुराध्वर्यवं ते तु चरणान्मुनिसत्तम।। १४।।

The other pupils of Vaiśaṁpāyana transforming themselves into partridges (Tittirī) picked up the texts which he had ejected, which, in consequence thereof, were called Taittrīya and the pupils were named the Caraka professors, of the Yajuṣ, from *Cāraṇa*—'going through.'

1. That is performing the expiatory rites for their master.

याज्ञवल्क्योपि मैत्रेय प्राणायामपरायणः ।।
तुष्टाव प्रयतस्सूर्यं यजूंष्यभिलषंस्ततः ।। १५ ।।

Yājñavalkya too, O Maitreya, who was accomplished in Devout practices engaged in propitiating the sun, being desirous of recovering the texts of the Yajuṣ.

याज्ञवल्क्य उवाच

नमस्सवित्रे द्वाराय मुक्तेरमिततेजसे ।।
ऋग्यजुस्सामभूताय त्रयीधाम्ने च ते नमः ।। १६ ।।

Yājñavalkya said :—Salutation unto the sun who is the gate of final emancipation, the spring of bright radiance, the three-fold source of splendour as the Ṛg, the Yajur and the Sāma-Vedas.

नमोग्नीषोमभूताय जगतः कारणात्मने ।।
भास्कराय परं तेजस्सौषुम्णरुचिबिभ्रते ।। १७ ।।

Salutation unto him, who is the *Agniṣome*[1] sacrifice, the casue of the universe and who is charged with radiant heat and the Suṣumna ray.

कलाकाष्ठानिमेषादिकालज्ञानात्मरूपिणे ।।
ध्येयाय विष्णुरूपाय परमाक्षररूपिणे ।। १८ ।।

Salutation unto him, who is identical with the idea of time and all its divisions of hours, minutes and seconds, who is the visible form of Viṣṇu, as the impersonation of the mystic Oṁ.

बिभर्त्ति यस्सुरगणानाप्यायेंदुं स्वरश्मिभिः ।।
स्वयधामृतेन च पितृंस्तस्मै तृप्त्यात्मने नमः ।। १९ ।।

हिमांबुधर्मवृष्टीनां कर्त्ता भर्त्ता च यः प्रभुः ।।
तस्मै त्रिकालरूपाय नमस्सूर्याय वेधसे ।। २० ।।

अपहंति तमो यश्च जगतोस्य जगत्पतिः ।।
तस्य धामधरो देवो नमस्तस्मै विवस्वते ।। २१ ।।

Salutation unto him, who is gratification, who nourishes the moon with his rays and feeds the manes and the gods with nectar and ambrosia; salutation unto the sun, who in the form of three seasons distributes and absorbs the water in the time of the rains, of cold and heat salutation unto Vaivasvata, who, alone as the lord of the world, dispels darkness and who is clothed with the quality of goodness.

सत्कर्मयोग्यो न जनो नैवापः शुद्धिकारणम् ।।
यस्मिन्ननुदिते तस्मै नमो देवाय भास्वते ।। २२ ।।

स्पृष्टो यदंशुभिर्लोकः क्रियायोग्यो हि जायते ।।
पवित्रकारणात्माय तस्मै शुद्धात्मने नः ।। २३ ।।

Salutation unto him, until whose rising people cannot perform religious ceremonies, water does not purify and who is the source of all religious rites.

नमः सवित्रे सूर्य्याय भास्कराय विवस्वते ।।
आदित्यायादिभूताय देवादीनां नमो नमः ।। २४ ।।

Salutation unto him who is the centre and source of purification. Glory to Savitrī, to Sūrya, to Bhāskara, Vaivasvata, to Āditya to the first-born of the celestials and demons.

हिरण्मयं रथं यस्य केतवोमृतवाजिनः ।।
वहंति भुवनालोकचक्षुषं तं नमाम्यहम् ।। २५ ।।

Salutation unto him who is the eye of the universe borne in a golden car whose banners scatter ambrosia.

श्रीपराशर उवाच

इत्येवसदिभिस्तेन स्तूयमानस्मा वै रविः ।।
वाजिरूपधरः प्राह व्रीयतामिति वाञ्छितम् ।। २६ ।।

Parāśara said :—being thus eulogised by Yājñavalkya the sun assumed the form of a horse and said—"Ask of me what you desire."

याज्ञवल्क्यस्तदा प्राह प्रणिपत्य दिवाकरम् ।।
यजूंषि तानि मे देहि यानि संति न मे गुरौ ।। २७ ।।

Having bowed unto him Yājñavalkya said—"Confer upon me a knowledge of those texts of Yajuṣ which even my preceptor does not know."

श्रीपराशर उवाच

एवमुक्तो ददौ तस्मै यजूंषि भगवान्रविः ।।
अयातयामसंज्ञानि यानि वेत्ति न तद्गुरुः ।। २८ ।।

Parāśara said :—Being thus addressed, the

1. There is another reading *Agniṣoma* Bhūtaya which professor Wilson has adopted i.e. who as fire and the moon.

sun gave to him the texts of Yajuṣ called Ayatayama which Vaiśaṁpāyana even did not know.

यजूंषि यैरधीतानि तानि विप्रैर्द्विजोत्तम।।
वाजिनस्ते समाख्याताः सूर्योप्यश्वोभवद्यतः।। २९।।

Because these texts were imparted by the sun in the form of a horse, the Brāhmins who study this portion are called Vajis (horses).

शाखाभेदास्तु तेषां वै दश पञ्च च वाजिनाम्।।
काण्वाद्यास्सुमहाभागा याज्ञवल्क्याः प्रकीर्त्तिताः।। ३०।।

Fifteen branches of this school originated from Kaṇva and other pupils of Yājñawalkya.

।। इति श्रीविष्णु महापुराणे तृतीयेंशे पञ्चमोऽध्यायः।। ६।।

अथ तृतीयेंशेः षष्ठोऽध्यायः

Part III : Section 6

श्रीपराशर उवाच

सामवेदतरोश्शाखा व्यासशिष्यस्स जैमिनिः।।
क्रमेण येन मैत्रेय बिभेद श्रृणु तन्मम।। १।।

Parāśara said :—Hear O Maitreya, how Jaiminī, the pupil of Vyāsa, divided the branches of Sāma-Veda.

सुमंतुस्तस्य पुत्रोभूत्सुत्वानश्चाभवत्सुतः।।
अधीतवंतौ चैकैकां संहितां तौ महामती।। २।।

The son of Jaiminī was Sumanta whose son was Śukarman. They both studied the same Saṁhitā under Jaiminī.

सहस्त्रसंहिताभेदं सुकर्मा तत्सुतस्ततः।।
चकार तं च तच्छिष्यौ जगृहाते महाव्रतौ।। ३।।

हिरण्यनाभः कौसल्यः पौष्यिंजिश्च द्विजोत्तम।।
उदीच्यास्सामगाः शिष्यास्तस्य पञ्चशतं स्मृताः।।४।।

The latter composed Sahasra Saṁhitā which he gave to his two pupils named Hiraṇyanābha, otherwise named Kauśalyā and Pauṣyinijī. Fifteen pupils of the latter composed as many Saṁhitās and they were called the northern chanters of Sāman.

हिरण्यनाभात्तावत्यस्संहिता यैर्द्विजोत्तमैः।।
गृहीतास्तेपि चोच्यंते पंडितैः प्राच्यसामगाः।। ५।।

लोकाक्षिर्नौधमिश्चैव कक्षीवाँल्लांगलिस्तथा।।
पौष्यिंजिशिष्यास्तद्भेदैस्संहिता बहुलीकृताः।। ६।।

Hiraṇyanābha had as many desciples who were called the eastern chanters of Sāman. Lokākṣmī, Kuṭhami, Kuśidi and Laṅgali were the pupils of Pauṣyinjī; and by them and their desciples, many other branches were made.

हिरण्यनाभशिष्यस्तु चतुर्विंशतिसंहिताः।।
प्रोवाच कृतनामासौ शिष्येभ्यश्च महामुनिः।। ७।।

There was another learned disciple of Hiraṇyanābha by name Kṛti who gave twenty-four Saṁhitās to as many pupils; who again divided Sāma-Veda into various branches.

तैश्चापि सामवेदोसौ शाखाभिर्बहुलीकृतः।।
अथर्वणामथो वक्ष्ये संहितानां समुच्चयम्।।
अथर्ववेदं स मुनिस्सुमंतुरमितद्युतिः।। ८।।
शिष्यमध्यापयामास कबंधं सोपि तं द्विधा।।
कृत्वा तु देवदर्शाय तथा पथ्याय दत्तवान्।। ९।।

I will now give you an account of the various branches of Atharva-Veda. The highly illustrious ascetic Sumanta taught this Veda to his pupil Kabandha who divided it into two and gave them to Devadarśa and Pathya.

देवदर्शस्य शिष्यास्तु मेधोब्रह्मबलिस्तथा।।
शौल्कायनिः पिप्पलादस्तथान्यो द्विजसत्तम्।। १०।।

The disciples of Devadarśa were Medha, Brāhmabali, Śaulkāyani, and Pippalāda.

पथ्यस्यापि त्रयश्शिष्याः कृता यौद्विज संहिताः।।
जाबालिः कुमुदादिश्च तृतीयश्शौनको द्विज।। ११।।

Pathya had three disciples, Jājalī, Kumudādi and Śaunaka to whom were severally given three Saṁhitās.

शौनकस्तु द्विधा कृत्वा ददावेकां तु बभ्रवे।।
द्वितीयां संहितां प्रदात्सैंधवाय च संज्ञिने।। १२।।

सैंधवान्मुंजिकेशश्च द्वेधाभिन्नास्त्रिधा पुनः।।
नक्षत्रकल्पो वेदानां संहितानां तथैव च।। १३।।

चतुर्थस्स्यादांगिरसश्शांतिकल्पश्च पञ्चमः।।
श्रेष्ठास्त्वथर्वणामेते संहितानां विकल्पकाः।। १४।।

Śaunaka divided his Saṁhitā into two and gave them to his disciples Babhru and Saindhavāyan and from them originated two schools the Saindhavas and Muñjakesas. The Saṁhitās of the Atharva-Veda are divided into five Kalpas or ceremonials; namely Nakṣatra Kalpa or rules for worshipping the planets; the Vaitāna Kalpa or rules for oblations; the Saṁhitā Kalpa or rules for sacrifices; the Aṅgirasa Kalpa or incantations and prayers for the destruction of enemies; the Śānti Kalpa—or prayers for averting evil.

आख्यानैश्चाप्युपाख्यानैर्गाथाभिः कल्पशुद्धिभिः।।
पुराणसंहितां चक्रे पुराणार्थविशारदः।। १५।।

The glorious Veda-Vyāsa, conversant with the knoweldge of Purāṇas, composed a Paurāṇik Saṁhitā consisting of historical and legendary traditions, prayers and hymns and sacred chronology.

प्रख्यातो व्यासशिष्योभूत्सूतो वै रोमहर्षणः।।
पुराणसंहितां तस्मै ददौ व्यासो महामतिः।। १६।।

He had a distinguished pupil Sūta, who was otherwise named Romaharṣaṇa, to whom he gave the Purāṇas.

सुमतिश्चाग्निवार्चाश्च मित्रायुश्शांसपायनः।।
अकृतव्रणसावर्णिष्षट्शिष्यास्तस्य चाभवन्।। १७।।

काश्यपः संहिताकर्त्ता सावणिशांसपयानः।।
रोमहर्षणिका चान्या तिसृणां मूलसंहिता।। १८।।

Sūta had six disciples, Sumati, Agnivarcas, Mitrayu, Sānsapāyana, Akṛtavraṇa, who is otherwise called Kāśyapa and Sāvarṇī.

The last three composed three principal Saṁhitās and Romaharṣaṇa himself compiled a fourth, which is named (after him) Romaharṣaṇika.

चतुष्टयेन भेदेन संहितानामिदं मुने।। १९।।

The substance of these four Saṁhitās is embodied in this Viṣṇu-Purāṇa.

आद्यं सर्वपुराणानां पुराणं ब्राह्ममुच्यते।।
अष्टादश पुराणानि पुराणज्ञाः प्रचक्षते।। २०।।

ब्राह्मं पाद्मं वैष्णवं च शैवं भागवतं तथा।।
तथाऽन्यं नारदीयं च मार्कंण्डेयं च सप्तमम्।। २१।।

आग्नेयमष्टमं चैव भविष्यन्नवमं स्मृतम्।।
दशमं ब्रह्मवैवर्त्तं लैंगमेकादशं स्मृतम्।। २२।।

वाराहं द्वादशं चैव स्कांदं चात्र त्रयोदशम्।।
चतुर्दशं वामनं च कौर्मं पञ्चदशं तथा।।
मात्स्यं च गारुडं चैव ब्राह्मंडं च ततः परम्।।
महापुराणान्येतानि ह्यष्टादश महामुने।। २३।।

Brāhma is the first of all the Purāṇas. Those, who are conversant with the knowledge of Purāṇas, enumerate, them as eighteen—Brāhma, Padma, Vaiṣṇava, Śaiva, Bhāgavata, Nāradīya, Mārkaṇḍeya, Agenya, Bhaviṣyat, Brahmā Vaivartta, Liṅga, Varāha, Skanda, Vāmana, Kūrama, Matsya, Gāruḍa, Brāhmaṇḍa.

तथा चोप पुराणानि मुनिभिः कथितानि च।।
सर्गश्च प्रतिसर्गश्च वंशमन्वंतराणि च।।
सर्वेष्वेतेषु कथ्यंते वंशानुचरितं च यत्।। २४।।

The creation of the universe and its successive generations, the genealogies of patriarchs and kings, the Manvantaras, and the royal dynasties are described in the Purāṇas.

यदेतत्तव मैत्रेय पुराणं कथ्यते मया।।
एतद्वैष्णवसंज्ञं वै पाद्मस्यसमनंतरम्।। २५।।

The Purāṇa, which I have described to you, O Maitreya, is Vaiṣṇava and is next to Padma.

सर्गे च प्रतिसर्गे च वंशमन्वंतरादिषु।।
कथ्यते भगवान्विष्णुरशोषेष्विव सत्तम।। २६।।

And in every part, in the creation of universe and the successive generations, in the description of the genealogies of the patriarchs it has declared the glory of the great Viṣṇu.

अंगानि वेदाश्चत्वारो मीमांसान्यायविस्तरः।।
पुराणं धर्मशास्त्रं च विद्या ह्येताश्चतुर्दश।। २७।।

There are fourteen principal kinds of knowledge—namely, the four Vedas, the six Aṅgas[1], the Mīmāṁsā (theology), Nyāya (logic), Dharma (the institutes of law) and the Purāṇas.

आयुर्वेदो धनुर्वेदो गांधर्वश्चैव ते त्रयः।।
अर्थशास्त्रं चतुर्थं तु विद्या ह्यष्टादशैव ताः।। २८।।

And they are enumerated as eighteen with the addition of these four—Ayur-Veda, medical science taught by Dhanwantarī; Dhanur-Veda, the science of archery, taught by Bhṛgu; Ghāndharva-Veda, the art of music, dancing etc. of which the Muni Bharata was the author; and the Artha Śāstram or the science of Government, taught by Bṛhaspati.

ज्ञेया ब्रह्मर्षयः पूर्वं तेभ्यो देवर्षयः पुनः।।
राजर्षयः पुनस्तेभ्य ऋषिप्रकृतयस्त्रयः।। २९।।

There are three orders of Ṛṣis—the royal Ṛṣis or princes who have devoted themselves to devotion as Viśvāmitra; divine Ṛṣis or demi-gods, as Nārada; and Brahmā Ṛṣis, who are the sons of Brahmā as Vasiṣṭha and others.

इति शाखास्समाख्याताश्शाखाभेदास्तथैव च।।
कर्त्तारश्चैव शाखानां भेदहेतुस्तथोदितः।। ३०।।

I have thus realted to you the various branches of the Vedas and their sub-divisions, the persons by whom they made and the object with which they were ushured into existence.

सर्व मन्वंतरेष्वेवं शाखाभेदास्समाः स्मृताः।। ३१।।

Such was the division in all the Manwantaras.

प्राजापत्या श्रुतिर्नित्या तद्विकल्पास्त्विमे द्विज।। ३२।।

The primitive Veda, which was instituted by Brahmā at the beginning of Kalpa, is eternal; these branches are but its modification.

एतत्ते कथितं सर्वं यत्पृष्टोहमिह त्वया।।
मैत्रेय वेदसंबंधः किमन्यत्कथयामि ते।। ३३।।

I have thus related to you, Maitreya, the Vedas which you desired to hear. What else do you wish to hear now?

।। इति श्रीविष्णुमहापुराणे तृतीयेंशे षष्ठोऽध्यायः।। ६।।

अथ तृतीयेंशेः सप्तमोऽध्यायः

Part III : Section 7

मैत्रेय उवाच
यथा वत्कथितं सर्वं यत्पृष्टोसि मया गुरो।।
श्रोतुमिच्छाम्यहं त्वेकं तद्भवान्प्रब्रवीतु मे।। १।।

Maitreya said :—O twice-born one, you have related to me what I have asked of you.

सप्तद्वीपानि पातालविधयश्च महामुने।।
सप्तलोकश्च येंतस्था ब्रह्मांडस्यास्य सर्वतः।। २।।

स्थूलैः सूक्ष्मैस्तथा सूक्ष्मसूक्ष्मात्सूक्ष्मतरैस्स्मृता।।
स्थूलात्स्थूलतरैश्चैव सर्वं प्राणिभिरावृतम्।। ३।।

I wish to hear one thing more from you : Relate that to me. o great Muni, this egg of Brahmā, consisting seven zones, seven subterrestiaf regions, and seven spheres, abounds in living creatures, large or small, smaller and smallest, larger and largest.

अंगुलस्याष्टभागोपि न सोस्ति मुनिसत्तम।।
वसंति प्राणिनो यत्र कर्म बंधनिबंधना।। ४।।
सर्वे चैते वशं यांति यमस्य भगवन् किल।।
आयुषोंते तथा यांति यातनास्तत्प्रचोदिताः।। ५।।

And there is not the eighth part of an inch where they do not dwell. And all these are bound by chains of acts and at the end of existence are subject to the power of Yama by whom they are doomed to dreadful punishments. And being freed from those inflictions they are born as celestials, men and the like.

1. These are the subsidiary portion of the Vedas—namely (a) Śikṣā, rules for reciting prayers (b) Kalpa, ritual (c) *Vyākaraṇa*, (grammar) (d) *Nirukta*, glossary (e) *Chandas*, metre (f) *Jyotiṣ*, astronomy.

यातनाभ्यः परिभ्रष्टा देवाद्यास्वथ योनिषु।।
जंतवः परिवर्त्तंते शास्त्राणामेष निर्णयः।। ६।।

सोहमिच्छामि तच्छ्रोतुं यमस्य वशवद्धत्तनः।।
न भवंति नरा येन तत्कर्म कथयस्व मे।। ७।।

And those living creatures, as Śāstras inform us, perpetually revolve. I wish to hear from you, performing what pure actions people are freed from subjection to Yama.

श्रीपराशर उवाच

अयमेव मुने प्रश्नो नकुलेन महात्मना।।
पृष्टः पितामहः प्राह भीष्मो यत्तच्छृणुष्व मे।। ८।।

Parāśara said :—O Muni, hear from me what his grandfather Bhīṣma said when this question was put to him by the high-souled Nakula.

भीष्म उवाच

पुरा ममागतो वत्स सखा कालिंगको द्विजः।।
स मामुवाच प्रष्टो वै मया जातिस्मरो मुनिः।। ९।।

Bhīṣma said :—O my son, there came on a certain time, a friend of mine, a Brāhmin from Kaliṅga country, to visit me.

तेनाख्यातमिदं सर्वमित्थं चैतद्भविष्यति।।
तथा च तदभूद्वत्स यथोक्तं तेन धीमता।। १०।।

He told me that he had put this question to an ascetic who had the recollection of his previous births.

स पृष्टश्च मया भूयः श्रद्दधानेन वै द्विजः।।
यद्यदाह न तदृष्टमन्यथा हि मया क्वचित्।। ११।।

To which the Muni replied 'What is now shall be (the same) in future'. What was said by that intelligent sage proved to be true. When that twice-born one was again accosted by me with due reverence, he said that he had never found otherwise what had been related to him.

एकदा तु मया पृष्टमेतद्यद्भवतोदितम्।।
प्राह कालिंगको विप्रस्स्मृत्वा तस्य मुनेर्वचः।। १२।।

जातिस्मरेण कथितो रहस्यः परमो मम।।
यमकिंकरयोर्योभूत्संवादस्तं ब्रवीमि ते।। १३।।

Once I put to him the same question which you have asked. And he, remembering the words of the Brāhmin who retained the recollection of his former births, said—"I shall reveal to you the mystery that was revealed to me by the Brāhmin retaining the recollection of his former births and I shall describe to you a dialogue that took place between Yama and one of his ministers."

कालिंग उवाच

स्वपुरुषमभिवीक्ष्य पाशहस्तं वदति यमः किल तस्य कर्णमूले।।
परिहर मधुसूदनप्रपन्नान्प्रभुरहमन्यनृणामवैष्णवानाम् ।।१४।।

The Brāhmin of Kaliṅga said—"Beholding his own emissary with a noose in hand approach, the Yama said to his ears 'Never bring here any one who has obtained the shelter the shelter of the slayer of Madhu; for I am the lord of all spirits but not of the spirits of those who are devoted Viṣṇu.

अहममरवरार्चितेन धात्रा यम
इति लोकहिताहिते नियुक्तः।।
हरिगुरुवशगोस्मि न स्वतंत्रः
प्रभवति संयमने ममापि विष्णुः।। १५।।

I was appointed by Brahmā, honoured by the immortals, to sit in judgement upon the good and bad conduct of mankind. Hari is my lord; I am not independent, for he can mete out punishment to me.

कंट कमुकुटकर्णिकादिभेदैः
कनकमभेदमपीष्यते यथैकम्।।
सुरपशुमनुजादिकल्पनाभि-
र्हरिरखिलाभिरुदीर्यते तथैकः।। १६।।

As gold, though (in reality) it is one substance, appears diversified as bracelets, tiaras and earrings, so Hari, though He is one appears many as gods, animals and man.

क्षितितलपरमाणवोनिलांते
पुनरुपयांति यथैकतां धरित्र्याः।।
सुरपशुमनुजादयस्तथांते
गुणकलुषेण सनातनेन तेन।। १७।।

As the drops of water, raised by wind from the earth, sink again into the earth when the wind disappears, so gods, man and animals created by the agitation of qualities are reunited with the eternal with the end of disturbance.

हरिममरवरार्चितांघ्रिपद्मं प्रणमति
यः परमार्थतो हि मर्त्यः।।
तमपगतसमस्तपापबंधं व्रज
परिहृत्य यथाग्निमाज्यसिक्तम्।। १८।।

He, who reverentially bows unto Hari, whose lotus-feet are being meditated upon by the celestials, is freed from all iniquities. Do you avoid such a man who is freed from all sinful bonds like unto fire fed with clarified butter."

इति यमवचनं निशम्य पाशी
यम पुरुषस्तमुवाच धर्मराजम्।।
कथय मम विभो समस्तधातुर्भवति
हरेः खलुः यादृशोस्य भक्तः।। १९।।

Having heard these words of Yama, his messenger, with noose in hand, said "Tell me, O Lord, how am I to distinguish the worshipper of Hari, who is the Lord of all beings?"

यम उवाच

न चलित निज वर्णधर्मतो
यस्सममतिरात्मसुहृद्विपक्षपक्षे।।
न हरित न च हंति किंचिदुच्चैः
स्थितमनसं तमवेहि विष्णुभक्तम्।। २०।।

Yama said—"Consider him as the worshipper of Viṣṇu who never swerves from the duties asigned to his caste, who regards with an impartial eye his own self, his friends and enemies, does not steal nor injure any body and whose mind is freed from all passions.

कलिकलुषमलेन यस्य नाऽऽत्मा
विमलमतेमलिनीकृतस्तमेनम्।।
मनसि कृतजनार्दनं मनुष्यं
सततमवेहि हरेरतीव भक्तम।। २१।।

Know him to be a follower of Hari, whose heart is not sullied by iniquities of Kali who meditate Janārdana in his mind freed from illusions.

कनकमपि रहस्यवेक्ष्य बुद्ध्या
तृणमिव यस्समवैति वै परस्वम्।।
भवति च भगवत्यनन्यचेताः
पुरुषवरं तमवेहि विष्णुभक्तम्।। २२।।

Consider that excellent man to be a worshipper of Viṣṇu, who, looking upon good in secret, holds that which is another's wealth as grass and devotes all his thoughts to the Lord.

स्फटिकगिरिशिलामलः क्व
विष्णुर्मनसि नृणां क्व च त्सरादिदोषः।।
न हि तुहिनमयूखरश्मिपुञ्जे
भवति हुताशनदीप्तिजः प्रतापः।। २३।।

There is Viṣṇu as mountain of clear crystal : for how can he live in the hearts of those men sullied with malice and envy? The glowing heat of fire does not exist in the cluster of the cooling rays of the moon.

विमलमतिरमत्सरः प्रशांतश्शुचिचतिखिलसत्त्वमित्रभूतः।।
प्रियहितवचनोऽस्तमानमायो वसति सदा हृदि तस्य
वासुदेवः।। २४।।

Vāsudeva always resides in his heart whose mind is pure, free from malice, quiet, who has a pure character, is a friend to all, speaking wisely and kindly, humble and sincere.

वसति हृदि सनातने च तस्मिन्-
भवति पुमाञ्जगतोस्य सौम्यरूपः।।
क्षितिरसमतिरम्यमात्मनोंतः
कथयति चारुतयैव सालपोतः।। २५।।

The eternal Viṣṇu residing in his heart a man appears lovely to all, as a beautiful young Sāl-tree declares that there is the excellent juice inside it.

यमनियमविधूत कल्मषाणामनुदिनमच्युतसक्तमानसानाम्।।
अपगतमदमानमत्सारणां त्यज भट दूरतरेण मानवानाम्।।
२६।।

Depart, O my emissary, speedily from those men, whose sins have been washed away by self-control and moral descipline, whose minds are always devoted to the undecaying and who are freed from avarice, unkindness and malice.

ह्विद यदि भगवाननादि रास्ते हरिररिशंखगदाधरोव्ययात्मा।।
तदघविघातकर्त्तृभिन्नं भवति कथं सति चांधकारमर्के।।
२७।।

If the divine Hari, who is without beginning or end and is armed with a sword, conch and mace, lives in the heart of a man he is freed from all sins; for how can darkness exist in the sun?

हरति परधनं निहंति जंतून्वदति
तथा नृतनिष्ठुराणि यश्च।।
अशुभजनितदुर्मदस्य पुंसः
कलुषमतेर्हृदि तस्य नास्त्यनंतः।। २८।।

He, who pilfers another's wealth, slays animals, speaks untrue and cruel words, whose mind is impure and is addicted to impious actions, does not get the Endless in his heart.

न सहति परसंपदं विनिंदां कलुषमतिः कुरुते सतामसाधुः।।
न यजति न ददाति यश्च संतं मनसि न तस्य
जनार्दनोऽधमस्य।। २९।।

Janārdana does not reside in the heart of that vile wight who cannot bear the prosperity of another, who vilifies the vious, does not perform sacrifice and does not make gifts to the pious.

परमसुहृदि बांधवे कलत्रे सुततनयापितृमातृभृत्यवर्गे।।
शठमतिरुपयाति योर्थतृष्णां तमधमचेष्टमवेहि नास्य
भक्तम्।। ३०।।

Consider not that person, engaged in vile actions as the worshipper of Viṣṇu, who by foul means, earns wealth for his dear friend, wife, son, daughter, father, mother or servants.

अशुभमतिरसत्प्रवृत्ति सक्तस्सततमनार्य्यकुशीलसंगमत्तः।।
अनुदिनकृतपापबंधयुक्तः पुरुषपशुर्न हि वासुदेवभक्तः।।
३१।।

That beast of a man is not a follower of Vāsudeva whose mind is addicted to foul actions, who is always engaged in vile actions, who lives for a long time in evil company and who always endeavours to drown himself in sins.

सकलमिदमहं च वासुदेवः परमपुमान्परमेश्वरस्य एकः।।
इति मतिरचलाभवत्यनंते हृदयगते व्रजतान्विहाय दूरात्।।
३२।।

Do you stand aloof from those persons in whose hearts resides Ananta from him, who by his pure understanding conceives the supreme male and ruler Vāsudeva as one with his devotees and the whole world.

कमलनयन वासुदेव विष्णो
धरणिधराच्युत शंख चक्रपाणे।।
भवशरणमितिरयंति ये वै
त्यज भट दूरतरेण तानपापान्।। ३३।।
वसति मनसि यस्य सोव्ययात्मा
पुरुषवरस्य न तस्य दृष्टि पाते।।
तव गतिरथ वा ममास्ति
चक्रप्रतिहतवीर्यबलस्य सोन्यलोक्यः।। ३४।।

Do you depart from those, O my emissary, who are freed from sins and who always invoke the lotus-eyed Vāsudeva, Viṣṇu, the upholder of the earth, the immortal weilder of the discus and the shell, the refuge of the world do not approach him in whose heart dwells the imperishable soul for he is protected against my power by the discus of his deity and he is bound for the heaven of Viṣṇu."

कालिङ्ग उवाच

इति निजभटशासनाय देवो
रवितनयस्स किलाह धर्मराजः।।
मम कथितमिदं च तेन तुभ्यं
कुरुवर सम्यगिदं मयापि चोक्तम्।। ३५।।

The Brāhmin of Kaliṅga said—O foremost of Kurus, these were the instructions given by the king of justice, the son of the sun, to his servant. Taht servant communicated those instructions to me and I have in turn related them to you.

श्रीभीष्म उवाच

नकुलैतन्ममाख्यातं पूर्वं तेन द्विजन्मना।।
कलिङ्गदेशादभ्येत्य प्रीतेन सुमहात्मना।। ३६।।

Bhīṣma said :—This was communicated to me, O Nakula, by the Brāhmin, hailing from Kaliṅga.

मयाप्येतद्यथान्यायं सभ्यग्वत्स तवोदितम्।।
यथा विष्णुमृतेनान्यत्त्राणं संसारसागरे।। ३७।।

And I have duly related that to you, O my son, and thus there is no protection in the ocean of the world but Viṣṇu.

किंकराः पाशदंडाश्च न यमो न च यातनाः।।
समर्थास्तस्य यस्यात्मा केशिवालंबनस्सदा।। ३८।।

They whose minds are always devoted to Keśava, have no fear from death, his servant, his rod, his noose and his tortures.

श्रीपराशर उवाच

एतन्मुने समाख्यातं गीतं वैवस्वतेन यत्।।
त्वत्प्रश्नानुगतं सम्यक्किमन्यच्छ्रोतुमिच्छसि।। ३९।।

Parāśara said :—O Muni I have thus described to you what you desired me to say and what was related by the son of Vivaswat. What else do you wish to hear?

।। इति श्रीविष्णुमहापुराणे तृतीयेंशे सप्तमोऽध्यायः।। ७।।

अथ तृतीयेंशेः अष्टमोऽध्यायः

Part III : Section 8

मैत्रेय उवाच

भगवन्भगवान्देवः संसारबिजिगीषुभिः।।
समाख्याहि जगन्नाथो विष्णुराराध्यते यथा।। १।।

Maitreya said :—O reverend sir, tell me how should they worship the glorious Viṣṇu, the lord of the earth, who desire to get at the other end of the ocean of the world.

आराधिताच्च गोविंदादाराधनपरैर्नरैः।।
यत्प्राप्यते फलं श्रोतुं तच्चेच्छामि महामुने।। २।।

I wish to hear from you, O great Muni, what fruits can be obtained by worshipping the glorious Viṣṇu.

श्रीपराशर उवाच

यत्पृच्छति भवानेतत्सगरेण महात्मना।।
और्वः प्राह यथा पृष्टस्तन्मे निगदतश्शृणु।। ३।।

Parāśara said :—The question you have put to me, was put to Aurva by the high-souled Sagara. Do you hear from me what he said (on this).

सगरः प्रणिपत्त्यैनमौर्वं पप्रच्छ भार्गवम्।।
विष्णोराराधनोपायसंबंधं मुनिसत्तम।। ४।।
फलं चाराधिते विष्णौ यत्पुंसामभिजायते।।
स चाह पृष्टो यत्नेन तस्मं तन्मेखिलं शृणु।। ५।।

Having bowed to Aurva born in the race of Bhṛgu, Sagara said—"O foremost of Munis, tell me the mode of worshipping Viṣṇu, and the fruits that a man can obtain by worshipping him." Hear from me, O Maitreya, all that he said when thus questioned (by Sagara).

और्व उवाच

भौमं मनोरथं स्वर्गं स्वर्गे रम्यं च यत्पदम्।।
प्राप्नोत्याराधिते विष्णौ निर्वाणमपि चौत्तमम्।। ६।।

Aurva said :—Viṣṇu being worshipped, a man obtains the consummation of all earthly desires and attains to the regions of the celestials and of Brahmā and even final liberation.

यद्यदिच्छति यावच्च फलमाराधितेऽच्युते।।
तत्तदाप्नोति राजेंद्र भूरि स्वल्पमथापि वा।। ७।।

O king of kings, whatever a man desires, either small, or great, he gets by the worship of Acyuta. O king of earth, you have asked me how Viṣṇu can be worshipped.

यत्तु पृच्छसि भूपाल कथामाराध्यते हरिः।।
तदहं सकलं तुभ्यं कथयामि निबोध मे।। ८।।

Hear I shall relate all that to you. He is the true worshipper of Viṣṇu who observes duly the duties of the four castes and rules of four *Āśramas.*

वर्णाश्रमाचारवता पुरुषेण परः पुमान्।।
विष्णुराराध्यते पंथा नान्यस्तत्तोषकारकः।। ९।।

यजन्मयज्ञान्यजत्येनं जपंत्येनं जपन्नृप।।
निघ्नन्नन्यान्हिनस्त्येनं सर्वभूतो यतो हरिः।। १०।।

There is no other means of satisfying Viṣṇu. He who offers sacrifices, sacrifices to him : he who recites prayers, prays to him; he who injures living beings injures him; for, Hari is identical with all living beings.

तस्मात्सदाचारवता पुरुषेण जनार्दनः।।
आराध्यस्तु स्ववर्णोक्तधर्मानुष्ठानकारिणा।। ११।।

Therefore, he, who observes duly the duties of his caste, is said to worship the glorious Janārdana.

ब्राह्मणः क्षत्रियो वैश्यः शूद्रश्च पृथिवीपते।।
स्वधर्मतत्परो विष्णुमाराधयति नान्यथा।। १२।।

O lord of earth, the Brāhmaṇa, the Kṣatriya, the Vaiśya, the Śūdra by attending to the duties prescribed by his caste, best worships Viṣṇu.

परापवादं पैशुन्यमनृतं च न भाषते।।
अन्योद्वेगकरं वापि तोष्यते तेन केशवः।। १३।।

He, who does not vilify another either in his presence, or in his absence, who does not speak untruth, does not injure others, pleases Keśava the best.

परदारपरद्रव्यपरहिंसासु यो रतिम्।।
न करोति पुमान्भूप तोष्यते तेन केशवः।। १४।।

Keśava is best pleased with him, O king, who does not covet another's wife, wealth and who does not bear ill feeling towards any.

न ताडयति नो हंति प्राणिनो न च हिंसकः।
यो मनुष्यो मनुष्येंद्र तोष्यते तेन केशवः।। १५।।

O lord of men, Keśava is pleased with him who neither beats nor slays any animate or inanimate thing.

देवद्विजगुरूणां च शुश्रूषासु सदोद्यतः।।
तोष्यते तेन गोविंदः पुरुषेण नरेश्वर।। १६।।

O lord of men, Govinda is pleased with that man who is ever intent upon serving the gods, the Brāhmaṇas and his spiritual preceptor.

यथात्मनि च पुत्रे च सर्वभूतेषु यत्तथा।।
हितकामो हरिस्तेन सर्वदा तोष्यते सुखम्।। १७।।

Hari is always satisfied with him who is ever anxious for the welfare of all creatures, his children and his own soul.

यस्य रागादिदोषेण न दुष्टं नृप मानसम्।।
विशुद्धचेतसा विष्णुस्तोष्यते तेन सर्वदा।। १८।।

Viṣṇu is always pleased with that pure-minded man whose mind is not sullied with anger and other passions.

वर्णाश्रमेषु ये धर्माश्शास्त्रोक्ता मुनिसत्तम।।
तेषु तिष्ठन्नरो विष्णुमा राधयति नान्यथा।। १९।।

He best worships Viṣṇu, O king, who observes the duties laid down by scripture for every caste and condition of life; there is no other mode."

सगर उवाच

तदहं श्रोतुमिच्छामि वर्णधर्मानशेषतः।।
तथैवाश्रमधर्मांश्च द्विजवर्य्य ब्रवीहि तान्।। २०।।

Sagara said :—O foremost of twice-born ones, I wish to hear of the duties of caste and condition. Relate them to me.

और्व उवाच

ब्राह्मणक्षत्रियविशां शूद्राणां च यथाक्रमम्।।
त्वमेकाग्रमतिर्भूत्वा शृणु धर्मान्मयोदितान्।। २१।।

Aurva said :—Hear attentively from me in order the duties of the Brāhmaṇa, the Kṣatriya, the Vaiśya and the Śūdra.

दानं दद्याद्यजेद्देवान्यज्ञै स्स्वाध्यायतत्परः।।
नित्योदकी भवेद्विप्रः कुर्याच्चाग्निपरिग्रहम्।। २२।।

The duties of the Brāhmins consist in making gifts, worshipping the celestials with sacrifices, studying the Vedas, performing oblations and libations with water and preserving the sacred fire.

वृत्त्यर्थं याजयेच्चान्यानन्यानध्यापयेत्तथा।।
कुर्य्यात्प्रतिग्रहादानं शुक्लार्थान्न्यायतो द्विजः।। २३।।

For maintenance, he may offer sacrifices for others, teach others and may accept liberal presents in a becoming manner.

सर्वभूतहितं कुर्य्यान्नाहितं कस्यचिद्द्विजः।
मैत्री समस्तभूतेषु ब्राह्मणस्योत्तमं धनम्।। २४।।

He must advance the well-being of all and do injury to none—for the greatest wealth of a

Brāhmaṇa consists in cherishing kind feelings towards all.

ग्राव्णि रत्ने च पारक्ये समबुद्धिर्भवेद्द्विजः ।।
ऋतावभिगमः पत्न्यां शस्यते चास्य पार्थिव ।। २५ ।।

He must consider with an equal eye, the jewel and stone belonging to another. He should at proper seasons beget offspring on his wife, O king of earth.

दानानि दद्यादिच्छातो द्विजेभ्यः क्षत्रियोपि वा ।।
यजेच्च विविधैर्यज्ञैरधीयीत च पार्थिवः ।। २६ ।।

The duties of the Kṣatriyas consist in making gifts to the Brāhmins at pleasure, in worshipping Viṣṇu with various sacrifices and receiving instructions from the preceptor.

शस्त्राजीवो महीरक्षा प्रवरा तस्य जीविका ।।
तत्रापि प्रथमः कल्पः पृथिवीपरिपालनम् ।। २७ ।।

His principal sources of maintenance are arms and protection of the earth. But his greatest duty consists in guarding the earth.

धरित्रीपालनेनैव कृतकृत्या नराधिपाः ।।
भवंति नृपतेरंशा यतो यज्ञादिकर्मणाम् ।। २८ ।।

By protecting the earth a king attains his objects; for he gets a share of the merit of all sacrifices.

दृष्टानां शासनाद्राजा शिष्टानं परिपालनात् ।।
प्राप्नोत्यभिमताँल्लोकान्वर्णसंस्थां करोति यः ।। २९ ।।

If a king, by maintaining the order of caste, represses the wicked, supports the pious he proceeds to whatever region he desires.

पाशुपाल्यं च वाणिज्यं कृषिं च मनुजेश्वर ।।
वैश्याय जीविकां ब्रह्मा ददौ लोकपितामहः ।। ३० ।।

तस्याप्यध्ययनं यज्ञो दानं धर्मश्च शस्यते ।।
नित्यनैमित्तिकादीनामनुष्ठानं च कर्मणाम् ।। ३१ ।।

द्विजातिसंश्रितं कर्म तादर्थ्यं तेन पोषणम् ।।
क्रयविक्रयजैर्वापि धनैः कारूद्भवेन वा ।। ३२ ।।

O lord of men, the great Patriarch Brahmā, has assigned to the Vaiśyas, for their maintenance, the feeding of the cattle, commerce and agriculture. Study, sacrifice and gift are also within the duties of the Vaiśyas : besides these they may also observe the other fixed and occasional rites.

शूद्रस्य सन्न तिश्शौचं सेवा स्वामिन्यमायया ।।
अमंत्रयज्ञो ह्यस्तेयं तत्संगो विप्ररक्षणम् ।। ३३ ।।

दानं च दद्याच्छूद्रोपि पाकयज्ञैर्यजेत च ।।
पित्र्यादिकं च तत्सर्वं शूद्रः कुर्वीत तेन वै ।। ३४ ।।

भृत्यादिभरणार्थाय सर्वेषां च परिग्रहः ।।
ऋतुकालेभिगमनं स्वदारेषु महीपते ।। ३५ ।।

The Śūdra must maintain himself by attending upon the three castes, or by the profits of trade, or the earnings of mechanical labour. He may also make gifts, offer the sacrifices in which food is presented and he may also make obsequial offerings.

दया समस्तभूतेषु तितिक्षा नातिमानिता ।।
सत्यं शौचमनायासो मंगलं प्रियवादिता ।। ३६ ।।

मैत्र्यस्पृहा तथा तद्वदकार्पण्यं नरेश्वर ।।
अनसूया च सामान्यवर्णानां कथिता गुणाः ।। ३७ ।।

आश्रमाणां च सर्वेषामेते सामान्यलक्षणाः ।।
गुणांस्तथावद्धर्मांश्च विप्रादीनामिमाञ्छृणु ।। ३८ ।।

Besides these, the four castes have got other duties namely—the acquisition of wealth for the support of servants, co-habitation with their wives for the sake of children, kindness towards all creatures, patience, humility, truth, purity, contentment, decorum of manners, gentleness of speech, friendliness, freedom from envy or avarice and the habit of vilifying. These also constitute the duties of every condition of life.

क्षात्रं कर्म द्विजस्योक्तं वैश्यं कर्म तथा पदि ।।
राजन्यस्य च वैश्योक्तं शूद्रकर्म न चैतयोः ।। ३९ ।।

सामर्थ्ये सति तत्त्याज्यमुभाभ्यामपि पार्थिव ।।
तदेवापदि कर्त्तव्यं न कुर्यात्कर्मसंकरम् ।। ४० ।।

In cases of emergency a Brāhmin may follow the occupations of a Kṣatriya or Vaiśya; the Kṣatriya may adopt those of Vaiśya and the Vaiśya those of Kṣatriya : but the last two should never adopt the functions of the Śūdra if they could avoid them.

इत्येते कथिता राजन्वर्णधर्मा मया तव।।
धर्मानाश्रमिणां सम्यग्ब्रुवतो मे निशामय।। ४१।।

And if that be not possible they must at any rate avoid the functions of the mined caste. I will now describe to you, O king, the duties of the several *Āśramas*.

।। इति श्रीविष्णुमहापुराणे तृतीयेंशेऽष्टमोध्यायः।।८।।

अथ तृतीयेंशेः नवमोऽध्यायः

Part III : Section 9

और्व उवाच

बालः कृतोपनयनो वेदाहरणतत्परः।।
गुरुगेहे वसेद्भूप ब्रह्मचारी समाहितः।। १।।

Aurva said :—O king, when a youth is invested with the sacred thread, he must reside in the house of his preceptor and study the Vedas with a concentrated mind, and leading a life of continence.

शौचाचारव्रतं तत्र कार्य्यं शुश्रूषणं गुरोः।।
व्रतानि चरता ग्राह्यो वेदश्च कृतबुद्धिना।। २।।

He must, with pure practices, wait upon his spiritual preceptor and with the performance of religious rites acquire the Veda.

उभे संध्ये रविं भूप तथैवाग्निं समाहितः।।
उपतिष्ठेत्तदा कुर्य्याद्गुरोरप्यभिवादनम्।। ३।।

He must, O king, with concentration, worship both in the morning and evening, the fire and the sun and after that he must bow to his spiritual guide.

स्थिते तिष्ठेदव्रजेद्याते नीचैरासीत चासति।।
शिष्यो गुरोर्नृपश्रेष्ठ प्रतिकूलं न सञ्चरेत्।। ४।।

O king, he must stand when his preceptor is standing, he must move when he is walking and he must sit beneath him when he is seated; he must never sit nor walk, nor stand when his teacher does the otherwise.

तेनै वोक्तं पठेद्वेदं नान्यचित्तः पुरस्थितः।।
अनुज्ञातश्च भिक्षान्नमश्नीयाद्गुरुणा ततः।। ५।।

Whatever portion of the Vedas he shall be taught by his preceptor, he must read that with undivided mind before him. He must beg when permitted by his teacher and eat the food thus collected.

अवगाहेदपः पूर्वमाचार्य्येणावगाहितः।।
समिज्जलादिकं चास्य काल्यं काल्यमुपानयेत्।।६।।

He must bathe in the water which has been first used by his preceptor and every morning he must bring for him fuel, water or anything that he may require.

गृहीतग्राह्यवेदश्च ततोनुज्ञामवाप्य च।।
गार्हस्थ्यमाविशेत्प्राज्ञो निष्पन्नगुरुनिष्कृतिः।। ७।।

विधिनावाप्तदारस्तु धनं प्राप्य स्वकर्मणा।।
गृहस्थकार्य्यमखिलं कुर्य्याद्भूपाल शक्तितः।। ८।।

Having thus completed his studies, he must receive dismissal from his preceptor and then enter into the order of the householder; and taking to himself withlawful ceremonies, house, wife and wealth, he must discharge to the best of his power the duties of his life.

निवापेन पितॄनर्चन्यज्ञैर्देवांस्तथातिथीन्।।
अन्नैर्मुनींश्च स्वाध्यायैरपत्येन प्रजापतिम्।। ९।।

भूनि बलिभिश्चैव वात्सल्येनाखिलं जगत्।।
प्राप्नोति लोकान्पुरुषो निजकर्मसमाद्धजतान्।। १०।।

He must satisfy the manes with cakes, the celestials with sacrifices, the guests with hospitality, the ṛṣis with holy study, the Patriarch with progeny, the spirits with oblations and all the worlds with truthful words. By thus discharging his duties a householder may attain to heaven.

भिक्षाभुजश्च ये केचित्परिव्राड्ब्रह्मचारिणः।।
तेप्यत्रैव प्रतिष्ठंते गार्हस्थ्यं तेन वै परम्।। ११।।

A householder is a refuge to those who depend upon alms for their maintenance and those who lead an intinerant life of self denial : thus the condition of the householder is the best of all.

वेदाहरणकार्य्याय तीर्थस्नानाय च प्रभो।।
अटंति वसुधां विप्राः पृथिवीदर्शनाय च।। १२।।

अनिकेता ह्यनाहारा यत्र सायंगृहाश्च ये।।
तेषां गृहस्थः सर्वेषां प्रतिष्ठा योनिरेव च।। १३।।

O lord, the Brāhmins travel all over the earth either for studying the Vedas or for beholding the holy places; many of them are houseless and without food and live for the night at the house at which they arrive in the evening. The householder is always a refuge to these people.

तेषां स्वागतदानादिवक्तव्यं मधुरं नृप।।
गृहागतानां दद्याच्च शयनासनभोजनम्।। १४।।

O king, it is his duty to welcome them and address them kindly and to provide them, whenever they come to his house, with a bed, a seat and food.

अतिथिर्यस्य भग्नाशो गृहात्प्रतिनिवर्त्तते।।
स दत्वा दुष्कृतं तस्मै पुण्यमादाय गच्छति।। १५।।

If a guest goes back disappointed from a house he leaves behind his iniquities and takes away the accumulated piety of the householder.

अवज्ञानमहंकारो दंभश्चैव गृह सतः।।
परितापोपघातौ च पारुष्यं च न शस्यते।। १६।।

यस्तु सम्यक्करोत्येवं गृहस्थः परमं विधिम्।।
सर्वबंधविनिर्मुक्तो लोकानाप्नोत्यनुत्तमान्।। १७।।

In the house of a good man, contumely, arrogance, hypocrisy, repining, contradiction and violence are strictly prohibited : and the householder, who performs the principal duty of hospitality, is freed from all chains and attains to better stations after death.

वयःपरिणतो राजन्कृतकृत्यो गृहाश्रमी।।
पुत्रेषु भार्यां निक्षिप्य वनं गच्छेत्सहैव वा।। १८।।

O king, having performed all these duties, when a householder is stricken in years, he must proceed to woods, eigther with his wife, or leaving her to the chrage of his son.

पर्णमूलफलाहारः केशश्मश्रुजटाधरः।।
भूमिशायी भवेत्तत्र मुनिस्सर्वातिथिर्नृप ।। १९।।

He must live there upon leaves, roots and fruits; allow his hair and beard to grow, and braid the former upon his brows and sleep upon the ground.

चर्मकाशकुशैः कुर्य्यात्परिधानोत्तरीयके।।
तद्वत्त्रिषवणं स्नानं शस्तमस्य नरेश्वर।। २०।।

His dress must be made of skin or of Kāśa and Kuśa grasses. He must bathe thrice a day, offer oblations to the celestials and to fire and treat all his guests with hospitality.

देवताभ्यर्चनं होमस्सर्वाभ्यागतपूजनम्।।
भिक्षाबलिप्रदानं च शस्तमस्य नरेश्वर।। २१।।

वन्यस्नेहेन गात्राणामभ्यंगश्चास्य शस्यते।।
तपश्च तस्य राजेंद्र शीतोष्णादिसहिष्णुता।। २२।।

He must beg alms and give food to all creatures. He must annoint himself with such unguents as are found in the forest and while carrying on his devout practices he must endure heat and cold.

यस्त्वेतां नियतश्चर्यां वानप्रस्थश्चरेन्मुनिः।
स दहत्यग्निवद्दोषाञ्जयेल्लोकांश्च शाश्वतान्।। २३।।

He, who leading the life of a hermit, follows these rules, destroys like fire all imperfections, and attains to the region of Brāhmaṇa.

चतुर्थश्चाश्रमो भिक्षोः प्रोच्यते यो मनीषिभिः।।
तस्य स्वरूपं गदतो मम श्रोतुं नृपार्हसि।। २४।।

The fourth condition of life, O king, is called by the sages, that of a mendicant. I shall relate the characteristics thereof : do thou hear.

पुत्रद्रव्यकलत्रेषु त्यक्तस्नेहो नराधिप।।
चतुर्थमाश्रमस्थानं गच्छेन्निर्धूतमत्सरः।। २५।।

O lord of men, having relinquished all attachments for wife, children and other earthly objects, men leading the life of a hermit, must enter into the fourth stage of life.

त्रैवर्गिकांस्त्यजेत्सर्वानारंभानवनीपते ।।
मित्रादिषु समो मैत्रस्समस्तेष्वेव जंतुषु।। २६ ।।

He must forego the three objects of life, namely pleasure, wealth and virtue either secular or religious. And regarding all with an equal eye, he must be friend to all living beings.

जरायुजांडजादीनां वाङ्मनःकायकर्मभिः ।।
युक्तः कुर्वीत न द्रोहं सर्वसंगांश्च वर्जयेत्।। २७ ।।

And being devoted, he must not injure any living creature, human or brute, either in act, word, or thought and renounce all attachments.

एकरात्रस्थितिर्ग्रामे पञ्चरात्रस्थितिः पुरे ।।
तथा तिष्ठेद्यथाप्रीतिर्द्वेषो वा नास्य जायते।। २८ ।।

He must not live more tahn one night in a village and more than five nights in a city. He must live in all those places where good feeling and not animosity is created in mind.

प्राणयात्रानिमित्तं च व्यंगारे भुक्तवज्जने।।
काले प्रशस्तवर्णानां भिक्षार्थं पर्यटेद्गुहान्।। २९ ।।

He must, for his maintenance, beg for alms at the hosues o0f the three first castes at the time when fires have been put out and peoples have eaten.

कामः क्रोधस्तथा दर्पमोहलोभादयश्च ये।।
तांस्तु सर्वान्परित्यज्य परिव्राणिनर्ममो भवेत्।। ३० ।।

The itinerant beggar must not call anything his own and must suppress desire, anger, covetousness, pride and folly.

अभयं सर्वभूतेभ्यो दत्वा यश्चरते मुनिः ।।
तस्यापि सर्वभूतेभ्यो न भयं विद्यते क्वचित्।। ३१ ।।

The ascetic, who gives no cause of fear to any living creatuare, does not apprehend any danger from them.

कृत्वाग्निहोत्रं स्वशरीरसंस्थं
शारीरमग्निं स्वमुखे जुहोति।।
विप्रस्तु भैक्ष्योपहितैर्हविर्भि-
श्चिताग्निकानां व्रजति स्म लोकान्।। ३२ ।।

The Brāhmin, who, having placed the sacrificial fire in his own body, feeds that flame with the butter that is procured by alms, through the altar of his mouth, goes to his own proper abode.

मोक्षाश्रमं यश्चरते यथोक्तं शुचिस्सुखं कल्पितबुद्धियुक्तः ।।
अनिंधनं ज्योतिरिव प्रशांतस्स ब्रह्मलोकं श्रयते द्विजातिः ।।
३३ ।।

But the Brahman who longs for final emancipation, who has got a pure heart, and whose mind is perfected by self-investigation, goes to the region of Brāhmaṇa, which is quiet and is as bright as the flameless smoke.

।। इति श्रीविष्णु महापुराणे तृतीयेंशे नवमोऽध्यायः ।। ९ ।।

अथ तृतीयेंशेः दशमोऽध्यायः

Part III Section 10

सगर उवाच

कथितं चातुराश्रम्यं चातुर्वर्ण्यक्रियास्तथा।।
पुंसः क्रियामहं श्रोतुमिच्छामि द्विजसत्तम।। १ ।।

Sagara said :—O foremost of twice-born ones, you have described to me the duties of the four orders and four castes.

नित्यनैमित्तिकाः काम्याः क्रियाः पुंसामशेषतः ।।
समाख्याहि भृगुश्रेष्ठ सर्वज्ञो ह्यसि मे मतः।। २ ।।

I wish to hear from you the religious observances of men. Methinks you know every thing, O foremost of Vṛgus, tell me all about these observances, either invariable occasional or voluntary.

और्व उवाच

यदेतयुक्तं भवता नित्यनैमित्तिकाश्रयम्।।
तदहं कथयिष्यांमि शृणुष्वैकमना मम।। ३ ।।

Whereto Aurva replied, "I shall describe to you all you have asked, the invariable and occasional ceremonies of men : do you hear, O king.

जातस्य जातकर्मादिक्रियाकांडमशेषतः।।
पुत्रस्य कुर्वीत पिता श्राद्धं चाभ्युदयात्मकम्।। ४।।

As soon as a son is born his father should perform the ceremonies consequent upon the birth of a child and all other initiatory ceremonies as well as a Śrāddha which is the source of prosperity.

युग्मांस्तु प्राङ्मुखान्विप्रान्भोजयेन्मनुजेश्वर।।
यथा तृप्तिस्तथा कुर्य्याद्दैवं पित्र्यं द्विजन्मनाम्।। ५।।

He must feed two Brāhminis, seated with their faces to the east and according to his means must offer sacrifices to the celestials and the progenitors, O lord of earth.

दध्ना युक्तैस्सबदरैर्मिश्रान्पिंडान्मुदा युतः।।
नांदीमुखेभ्यस्तीर्थेन दद्याद्दैवेन पार्थिव।। ६।।

He must delightedly offer to the manes, balls of meat mixed with curds, barley and jujubes with the four part of his finger.

प्राजापत्येन वा सर्वमुपचारं प्रदक्षिणम्।।
कुर्वीत तत्तथाशेषवृद्धिकालेषु भूपते।। ७।।

On every occasion of prosperity, he must perform this with all offerings and go through circumambulations.

ततश्च नाम कुर्वीत पितैव दशमेहनि।।
देवपूर्वं नराख्यं हि शर्मवर्मादिसंयुतम्।। ८।।

Upon the tenth day after birth the father should give a name to the child, the first term of which shall be the name of a god and the second of a man as Śarman or Varman.

शर्मेति ब्राह्मणस्योक्तं वर्मेति क्षत्रसंश्रयम्।।
गुप्तदासात्मकं नाम प्रशस्तं वैश्यशूद्रयोः।। ९।।

The former is the proper designation of a Brāhmin, and the second of a Kṣatriya. And the Vaiśyas and Śūdras should have the designation of Gupta and Dāsa.

नार्थहीनं न चाशस्तं नापशब्दयुतं तथा।।
नामंगल्यं जुगुप्साकं नाम कुर्यात्समाक्षरम्।। १०।।

A name should not be devoid of any meaning, should not be indecent, absurd, inauspicious nor dreadful.

नातिदीर्घं नातिह्रस्वं नातिगुर्वक्षरान्वितम्।।
सुखोच्चार्यं तु तन्नाम कुर्याद्यत्प्रणवाक्षरम्।। ११।।

It should contain an even number of syllables; it should not be too long nor too short, nor too full of long vowels, but contain a due proportion of short vowels and be easily articulated.

ततोऽनंतरसंस्कारसंस्कृतो गुरुवेश्मनि।।
यथोक्तविधिमाश्रित्य कुर्य्याद्विद्यापरिग्रहम्।। १२।।

After going through these initiatory ceremonies and being purified the youth should acquire knowledge from his preceptor.

गृहीतविद्यो गुरवे दत्त्वा च गुरुदक्षिणाम्।।
गार्हस्थ्यमिच्छन्भूपाल कुर्य्याद्दारपरिग्रहम्।। १३।।

And having acquired knowledge from the preceptor and given him presents, O king, he should, desirous of entering the order of householders, marry.

ब्रह्मचर्येण वा कालं कुर्यात्संकल्पपूर्वकम्।।
गुरोश्शुश्रूषणं कुर्यात्तत्पुत्रादेरथापि वा।। १४।।
वैखानसो वापि भवेत्परिव्राडथ वेच्छया।।
पूर्वसंकल्पितं यादृक् तादृक्कुर्यान्नराधिप।। १५।।

If he desires to continue his life as a student, he should, taking that vow, engage in the service of his preceptor and his descendant or he may, according to his premediated inclination, O king, at once become a hermit or adopt the order of the religious mendicant.

वर्षैरेकगुणां भार्य्यामुद्वहेत्त्रिगुणस्स्वयम्।।
नाति केशामकेशां वा नातिकृष्णां न पिंगलाम्।। १६।।

He must marry a maiden, who is of a third of his age, one who has not too much of hair, but is not without any, one who is not very black nor yellow complexioned and who is nor from birth a cripple or deformed.

निसर्गतोधिकांगां व न्यूनांगामपि नोद्वहेत्।।
नाविशुद्धां सरोमां वाकुलजां वापि रोगिणीम्।। १७।।

न दुष्टां दुष्टवाक्यां वा व्यंगिनीं पितृमातृतः।।
न श्मश्रुव्यञ्जनवतीं न चैव पुरुषाकृतिम्।। १८।।

न घर्घरस्वरां क्षामां तथा काकस्वरां न च।।
नानिबंधेक्षणां तद्वद्वृत्तक्षीं नोद्वहेद्बुधः।। १९।।

यस्याश्च रोमशे जंघे गुल्फौ यस्यास्तथोन्नतौ।।
गंडयोः कूपरौ यस्या हसंत्यास्तां न चोद्वहेत्।। २०।।

He must not marry a girl, who is vicious or unhealthy, born of a low family, or suffering from any disease; one who may have been badly trained, one who talks improperly, one who inherited some disease from father or mother; one who has a beard and has got a masculine appearance; one who speaks thick or thin or croaks like a craven, who has got eyes without eye lashes, or sufficiently covered with them; one who has got legs covered with hairs, thick ankles; one, who has dimples in her cheeks when laughing.

नातिरूक्षच्छविं पांडुकरजामरुणेक्षणाम्।।
आपीन हस्तपादां च नकन्यामुद्वहेब्दुधः।। २१।।

The learned should not marry a girl who has not got a tender countenance, who has got white nails, and who has got red eyes.

न वामनां नातिदीर्घां नोद्वहेत्संहतभ्रुवम्।।
न चातिच्छिद्रदशनां न करालमुखीं नरः।। २२।।

The wise and prudent should not marry one whose hands and legs are heavy, who is a dwarf, or who is very tall or one whose eye-brows meet, or whose teeth are far apart and resemble tusks.

पञ्चमीं मातृपक्षाच्च पितृपक्षाच्च सप्तमीम्।।
गृहस्थश्चोद्वहेत्कन्यां न्यायेन विधिना नृप।। २३।।

O king, a householder should marry a girl who is at least five degrees distant in descent from his mother and seven degrees from his father.

ब्राह्मौ दैवस्तथैवार्षः प्राजापत्यस्तथासुरः।।
गांधर्वराक्षसौ चान्यौ पैशाचश्चाष्टमो मतः।। २४।।

There are eight forms of marriage—namely, Brāhma, Daiva, the Arṣa, Prājāpatya, Asura, Gāndharva, Rākṣasa and Paiśāca and the last is the worst.

एतेषां यस्य यो धर्मो वर्णस्योक्तो महर्षिभिः।।
कुर्वीत दारग्रहणं तेनान्यं परिवर्जयेत्।। २५।।

And every one should marry according to the mode enjoined to his caste by the sages and should never marry according to the Paiśāca mode.

सधर्मचारिणीं प्राप्य गार्हस्थ्यं सहितस्तया।।
समुद्वहेद्ददात्येतत्सम्यगूढं महाफलम्।। २६।।

Thus entering the order of householders, if a man takes a wife observing the same religious and civil obligations and perform all the ceremonies of his orders in her company, he derives great benefit from such a wife."

।। इति श्रीविष्णुमहापुराणे तृतीयेंशे दशमोऽध्यायः।। १०।।

अथ तृतीयेंशेः एकादशोऽध्यायः

Part III : Section 11

सगर उवाच

गृहस्थस्य सदाचारं श्रोतुमिच्छाभ्यहं मुने।।
लोकादस्मात्परस्माच्च यमातिष्ठन्न हीयते।। १।।

Sagara said :—"O Muni, I wish to hear from you of such religious observances, performing which a householder does not meet with the wane of piety either in this world or in the next."

और्व उवाच

श्रूयतां पृथिवीपाल सदाचारस्य लक्षणम्।।
सदाचारवता पुंसा जितौ लोकावुभावपि।। २।।

Aurva said :—"Hear, O lord earth, an account of all those religious observances celebrating which a man conquers both this and the next world.

साधवः क्षीणदोषास्तु सच्छब्दः साधुवाचकः।।
तेषामाचरणं यस्तु सदाचारस्स उच्यते।। ३।।

The term *sat* means *Sādhu*; and they are called *Sādhus* or saints who are freed from all blemishes. And their practices are called Sadācāras.

सप्तर्षयोथ मनवः प्रजानां पतयस्तथा।।
सदाचारस्य वक्तारः कर्तारश्च महीपते।। ४।।

O lord of earth, the seven Ṛṣis, the Manus and the Patriarchs are those who have laid down and observed those practices.

ब्राह्मे मुहूर्त्ते चोत्थाय मनसा मतिमान्नृप।।
प्रबुद्धश्चिन्तयेद्धर्ममर्थं चाप्यविरोधिनम्।। ५।।

Let the wise, O king, get up at Brahmā Muhūrtta[1], when the mind is at rest meditate upon virtue and wealth not in compatible with the former.

अपीडया तयोः काममुभयोरपि चिंतयेत्।।
दृष्टादृष्टविनाशाय त्रिवर्गे समदर्शिना।। ६।।

He should also meditate upon desire not conflicting with the other two. And he must equally meditate upon the three ends of life for the purpose of counteracting the unseen consequences of good or best acts.

परित्यजेदर्थकामौ धर्मपीडाकरौ नृप।।
धर्ममप्यसुखोदर्कं लोकविद्विष्टमेव च।। ७।।

He should renounce, O king, such wealth and desire as stand in the way of virtue, and he should abstain from such religious acts as give uneasiness, and as are not compatible with the rules of society.

ततः काल्यं समुत्थाय कुर्य्यान्मूत्रं नरेश्वर।। ८।।
नैर्ऋत्यामिषुविक्षेपमतीत्याभ्यधिकं भुवः।।
दूरादावसथान्मूत्रं पुरीषं च विसर्जयेत्।। ९।।

O lord of men, having got up from bed early in the morning, he must offer adoration to the sun and then proceeding to the South-East quarter at a distance of a bow-shot or more, or somewhere remote from the village he must void the impurities of nature.

1. The third Muhūrtta about two hours before sunrise.

पादावनेजनोच्छिष्टे प्रक्षिपेन्न गृहांगणे।। १०।।

A man should not void the impurities of nature either in the courtyard of his house or in any place where is the print of a man's foot.

आत्मच्छायां तरुच्छायां गोसूर्य्याग्न्यनिलांस्तथा।।
गुरुद्विजादींस्तु बुधो नाधिमेहेत्कदाचन।। ११।।

The wise should not pass urine either on his own shadow, nor on the shadow of a tree, nor on a cow, nor against the sun nor on fire, nor against the wind, nor on spiritual preceptor, nor men of the first three castes.

न कृष्टे सस्यमध्ये वा गोव्रजे जनसंसदि।।
न वर्त्मनि न नद्यादितीर्थेषु पुरुषर्षभ।। १२।।
नाप्सु नैवांभसस्तीरे श्मशाने न समाचरेत्।।
उत्सर्गं वै पुरीषस्य मूत्रस्य च विसर्जनम्।। १३।।

Nor he should pass excrement in a ploughed field, or a pasturage, or in the company of men, or on a high road, or in rivers and the like which are holy, or on the bank of a river or in a cremation ground.

उदङ्मुखो दिवामूत्रं विपरीतमुखो निशि।।
कुर्वीतानापदि प्रज्ञो मूत्रोत्सर्गं च पार्थिव।। १४।।

O king, the wise should pass urine with his face towards the north during the day and towards the south during the night.

तृणैरास्तीर्य्य वसुधां वस्त्रप्रावृतमस्तकः।।
तिष्ठेन्नातिचिरं तत्र नैव किंचिदुदीरयेत्।। १५।।

While passing excrement he should spread grass on the earth and cover his head with cloth and should not wait there long, and should not speak during that time.

वल्मीकमूषिकोद्धृतां मृदं नांतर्जला तथा।।
शौचावशिष्टां गेहाच्च नादद्याल्लेपसंभवाम्।। १६।।
अणुप्राण्युपपन्नां च हलोत्खातां च पार्थिव।।
परित्यजेन्मृदो ह्येतास्सकलाश्शौचकर्मणि।। १७।।
एका लिंगे गुदे तिस्रो दश वामकरे नृप।।
हस्तद्वये चय सप्त स्युर्मृदश्शौचोपपादिकाः।। १८।।

To clean his hand he should not take earth from an ant-hill, nor a rat-hole, nor from water, nor from what has been left after being used for that purpose, nor from what has been thrown up by insects, or turned over by the plough. He must avoid all these kinds of earth for the purpose of cleanliness; he should use bandful after passing urine, three handfuls after passing excrement, ten handfuls are to be rubbed over the left hand and seven on both hands.

अच्छेनागंधलेपेन जलेनाबुद्बुदेन च।।
आचामेच्चमृदं भूयस्तथा दद्यात्समाहितः।। १९।।
निष्पादितांघ्रिशौचस्तु पादावभ्युक्ष्य तैः पुनः।।

He should then rince his mouth with pure water which is neither fetid, nor frothy nor full of bubbles. After that, he should, being composed, use earth to cleanse his feet, washing them well with water.

त्रिःपिबेत्सलिलं तेन तथा द्विः परिमार्जयेत्।। २०।।
शिर्षण्यानि ततः खानि मूर्द्धानं च समालभेत्।।
बाहू नाभिं च तोयेन हृदयं चापि संस्पृशेत्।। २१।।
स्वाचांतस्तु ततः कुर्यात्पुमान्केशप्रसाधनम्।।
आदर्शाञ्जनमांगल्यं दूर्वाद्यालंभनानि च।। २२।।

He must then drink water thrice and wash his face twice with it and then touch with his head, the cavities of the eys, ear and nostrils, the forehead, navel and he heart. Having finally washed his mouth the must clean and arrange his hairs and must decorate his body, before a looking glass with unguents, garlands and perfumes.

ततस्ववर्णधर्मेण वृत्त्यर्थं च धनार्जनम्।।
कुर्वीत श्रद्धासंपन्नो यजेच्च पृथिवीपते।। २३।।

He, then according to the practice of his caste, should earn money for maintenance and should worship the deities with firm faith.

सोमसंस्था हविस्संस्थाः पाकसंस्थास्तु संस्थिताः।।
धने यतो मनुष्याणां यतेतातो धनार्जने।। २४।।

Sacrifices with acid juice, those with clarified butter and those with offerings of food, may be performed with wealth; therefore men should endeavour much to acquire wealth.

नदीनदतटाकेषु देवखातजलेषु च।।
नित्यक्रियार्थं स्नायीत गीरिप्रस्रवणेषु च।। २५।।
कूपेषूद्धततोयेन स्नानं कुर्वीत वा भुवि।।
गृहेषूद्धततोयेन ह्यथवा भुव्यसंभवे।। २६।।

For performing daily devotional rites a man should bathe in the water of a river, a natural channel, or a mountain torrent or he should bathe on a dry ground with the water drawn from well or he should bring that water to his house if he had any objection to bathing on the spot.

शुचिवस्त्रधरः स्नातो देवर्षिपितृतर्पणम्।।
तेषामेव हि तीर्थेन कुर्वीत सुसमाहितः।। २७।।

Bathed and clad in clean clothes, he should, with concentrated mind offer oblations to the manes and Ṛsis with that water.

त्रिरपः प्रीणनार्थाय देवानामपवर्जयेत्।।
ऋषीणां च यथान्यायं सकृच्चापि प्रजापतेः।। २८।।

He should offer water thrice for the satisfaction of the celestials, thrice for the satisfaction of the Ṛsis and once for the patriarchs.

पितृणां प्रीणनार्थाय तदपः पृथिवीपते।।
पितामहेभ्यश्च तथा प्रीणयेत्प्रपितामहान्।। २९।।
मातामहाय तत्पित्रे तत्पित्रे च समाहितः।।
दद्यात्पैत्रेण तीर्थेन काम्यं चान्यच्छृणुष्व मे।। ३०।।
मात्रे स्वमात्रे तन्मात्रे गुरुपत्न्ये तथा नृप।।
गुरूणां मातुलानां च स्निग्धमित्राय भूंभुजे।। ३१।।

He should make three libations for the satisfaction of the manes. He should, with the part of the hand sacred to the manes, offer water to his paternal grand father, great grand father, maternal grand father, great grand father and his father, and according to his pleasure to his own mother and his mother's mother and grand mother, to the wife of his preceptor, to his preceptor, his maternal uncle, and other relations, to a dear friend and to the king.

इदं चापि जपेदंबु दद्यादात्मेच्छया नृप।।
उपकाराय भूतानां कृतदेवादितर्पणम्।। ३२।।

देवासुरास्तथा यक्षा नागगंधर्वराक्षसाः।।
पिशाचा गुह्यकास्सिद्धाः कूष्मांडाः पशवः खगाः।। ३३।।

जलेचरा भूनिलया वाय्वाहाराश्च जंतवः।।
तृप्तिमेतेन यांत्याशु मद्दत्तेनांबुनाऽखिलाः।। ३४।।

He should then, O king, offer water to the celestials for the benefit of all animals, reciting the prayer. "May the celestials, demons, Yakṣas, serpents, Rākṣasas, Gandharvas, Piśācas, Guhyakas, Siddhas, Kūṣmāṇḍas, trees, birds, fish, all that in habit the waters or the earth, or the air, be propitiated by the water I have offered to them.

नरकेषु समस्तेषु यातनासु च संस्थिताः।।
तेषामाप्यायनायैतद्दीयते सलिलं मया।। ३५।।

This water is presented by me for the mitigation of the sufferings of all those who have been put to hell.

ये बांधवाबांधवा ये येन्यजन्मनि बांधवाः।।
ते तृप्तिमखिला यांतु ये चास्मत्तोभिवांछति।। ३६।।

Let them be propitiated with this water who are my friends, who are not my friends, who were my friends in my former birth and all those who expect water from me.

यत्र क्वचनसंस्थानां क्षुत्तृष्णोपहतात्मनाम्।।
इदमाप्यायनायास्तु मया दत्तं तिलोदकम्।। ३७।।

May this water and sesamum offered by me remove the hunger and thirst of all those who are suffering therefrom wherever they may live."

काम्योदकप्रदानं ते मयैतत्कथितं नृप।।
यद्दत्त्वा प्रीणयत्येतन्मनुष्यस्सकलं जगत्।।
जगदाप्यायनोद्भूतं पुण्यमाप्नोति चानघ।। ३८।।

दत्त्वा काम्योदकं सम्यगेतेभ्यः श्राद्धयान्वितः।।
आचम्य च ततो दद्यात्सूर्याय सलिलाञ्जलिम्।। ३९।।

The offerings, of water, O king, in the manner I have described, give satisfaction to all the world. Having offered water duly and reverentially to all the sinless man obtains the piety that comes from satisfying the world. Having rinsed his mouth he must offer water to the sun touching his forehead with folded hands and reciting the following prayer—

नमो विवस्वते ब्रह्मभास्वते विष्णुतेजसे।।
जगत्सवित्रे शुचये सवित्रे कर्मसाक्षिणे।। ४०।।

"Salutation to the radiant Vaivaswat—the effulgence of Viṣṇu; to the pure illuminator of the universe; to Sāvitrī, the giver of fruits for all actions."

ततो गृहाऽर्चनं कुर्यादभीष्टसुरपूजनम्।।
जलाभिषेकैः पुष्पैश्च धूपाद्यैश्च निवेदनम्।। ४१।।

He must then go through the family worship, offering water, flowers, and incence to the tutelary deity.

अपूर्वमग्निहोत्रं च कुर्यात्प्राग्ब्रह्मणे नृप।। ४२।।

प्रजापतिं समुद्दिश्य दद्यादाहुतिमादरात्।।
गृहेभ्यः काश्यपायाथ ततोनुमतये क्रमात्।। ४३।।

तच्छेषं मणिके पृथ्वीपर्जन्येभ्यः क्षिपेत्ततः।।
द्वारे धातुर्विधातुश्च मध्ये च ब्रह्मणे क्षिपेत्।। ४४।।

He must then offer oblations to fire, first invoking Brahmā then Prajāpati. He must then offer water to Guhya, Kāśyapa and Anumatī in succession and then offer the remainder to the earth, to wather and to rain in a pitcher at hand. O foremost of men, he must offer water to Dhātrī Vidhātrī at the doors of his house and to Brahmā in the middle of it.

गृहस्य पुरुषव्याघ्र दिग्देवानपि मे शृणु।। ४५।।

Hear from me how he should then worship the deities presiding over the various quarters.

इंद्राय धर्मराजाय वरुणाय तथेंदवे।।
प्राच्यादिषु बुधो दद्याद्धुतशेषात्मकं बलिम्।। ४६।।

He should offer the Bali containing the remaining portions of the oblations to Indra, Yama, Varuṇa and Soma on the four sides of his house.

प्रागुत्तरे च दिग्भागे धन्वंतरिबलिं बुधः।।
निर्वपेद्वैश्वदेवं च कर्म कुर्यादतः परम्।। ४७।।

वायव्यां वायवे दिक्षु समस्तासु यथादिशम्।।
ब्रह्मणे चांतरिक्षाय भानवे च क्षिपेद्बलिम्।। ४८।।
विश्वेदेवान्विश्वभूतानष्टौ विश्वपतीन्पितॄन्।।
यक्षाणां च समुद्दिश्य बलिं दद्यान्नरेश्वर।। ४९।।

And in the north-east quarter the wise should offer it to Dhanvantarī; then he should offer the remaining portion to Viśvadevas, then in the north-east to wind then in all directions to the cardinal points, to Brahmā, to the atmosphere, and to the sun, to all the celestials, to all beings, to the lords of beings, to the manes, and to Yakṣas.

ततोन्यदन्नमादाय भूमिभागे शुचौ बुधः।।
दद्यादशेषभूतेभ्यस्स्वेच्छया सुसमाहितः।। ५०।।

Thereupon taking other rice the learned should cast it on a clean spot of ground as an offering to all beings and with a collected mind should repeat the following prayer—

देवा मनुष्याः पशवो भवति
सिद्धास्सयक्षोरगदैत्यसंघाः।।
प्रेताः पिशाचास्तरवस्स मस्ता
ये चान्नमिच्छंति मयात्र दत्तम्।। ५१।।
पिपीलिकाः कीटपतंगकाद्या
बुभुक्षिताः कर्मनिबंधबद्धाः।।
प्रयांति ते तृप्तिमिदं मयान्नं
तेभ्यो विसृष्टं सुखिनो भवंतु।। ५२।।

"May celestials, men, animals, birds, saints. Yakṣas, serpents, demons, ghosts, goblins, trees and all those who desire food from me; may ants, worms, moths and other insects who are hungry and chained in acts, obtain satisfaction from food offered by me and enjoy bliss.

येषां न माता न पिता न बंधुर्नैवान्नसिद्धिर्न तथान्नमस्ति।।
तत्तृप्तयेऽन्नं भुवि दत्तमेव ते यांतु तृप्तिं मुदिता भवंतु।।
५३।।

I offer this food on the ground for them who have got no mother, no father, no friends, no food, nor the means for preparing it.

भूतानि सर्वाणि तथान्नमेतदहं च विष्णुर्न यतोन्यदस्ति।।
तस्मादहं भूतनिकायभूतन्नं प्रयच्छामि भवाय तेषाम्।।५४।।

May they be satisfied with the food offered for their satisfaction. All these animals, this food and myself are at one with Viṣṇu—for there exists nothing but Viṣṇu; I am not different from all beings, and therefore for their sustenance I offer this food.

चतुर्दशो भूतगणो य एष तत्र स्थिता येऽखिलभूसंघाः।।
तृप्त्यर्थमन्नं हि मया निसृष्टं तेषामिदं ते मुदिता भवंतु।।
५५।।

May all beings, that belong to the fourteen orders of existent things, be satisfied and delighted with the food offered by me."

इत्युच्चार्य्य नरो दद्यादन्नं श्रद्धा समन्वितः।।
भुवि सर्वोपकाराय गृही सर्वाश्रयो यतः।। ५६।।

Having repeated this prayer the householder should devoutly throw the food on the ground for the benefit of all beings; for the householder is thence the supporter of them all.

श्वचंडालविहंगानां भुवि दद्यान्नरेश्वर।।
ये चान्ये पतिताः केचिदपुत्राः संति मानवाः।।५७।।
ततो गोदोहमात्रं वै कालं तिष्ठेद्गृहांगणे।।
अतिथिग्रहणार्थाय तदूर्ध्वं तु यथेच्छया।। ५८।।

He should also disperse food on the ground for dogs, outcasts, birds and all mean and degraded persons. Thereupon to receive guests the householder should wait in the countryard of his house as long as it takes to milch a cow or for a longer period if he pleases.

अतिथिं तत्र संप्राप्तं पूजयेत्स्वागतादिना।।
तथासनप्रदानेन पादप्रक्षालनेन च।।५९।।
श्रद्धया चान्नदानेन प्रियप्रश्नोत्तरेण च।।
गच्छतश्चानुयानेन प्रीतिमुत्पादयेद्गृही।।६०।।

If a guest comes he must be recieved with all hospitality; he must be offered a seat, his feat are to be washed, food should be respectfully given to him, he must be spoken to with all kindness and civility and when he goes away, the firendly wishes of the host must accompany him.

अज्ञातकुलनामानमन्यदेशादुपागतम्।।
पूजयेदतिथिं सम्यङ्नैकग्रामनिवासिनम्।। ६१।।

The householder should pay attention to that guest who comes from another place and whose lineage is not known.

अकिंचनमसं बंधमज्ञातकुलशीलिनम्।।
असंपूज्यातिथिं भुक्त्वा भोक्तुकामं व्रजत्यधः।। ६२।।

He should not make him a guest who is an inhabitant of the same village. He who feeds himself, neglecting a guest, who is por, who is not his relation, who comes from another place and is desirous of eating, goes to hell.

स्वाध्यायगोत्राचरणमपृष्ट्वा च तथा कुलम्।।
हिरण्यगर्भबुद्ध्या तं मन्येताभ्यागतं गृही।। ६३।।

The householder should receive his guest regarding him as the golden embryo[1] without inquiring his studies, his schools, his practices or his race.

पित्रर्थं चापरं विप्रमेकमप्याशयेन्नृप।।
तद्देश्यं विदिताचारसंभूतिं पाञ्चयज्ञिकम्।। ६४।।

A householder, O king, at the Śrāddha ceremony of his father, should feed another Brāhmin, who is of the same village, whose pedigree and practices are known and who performs the five sacramental rites.

अन्नाग्रं च समुद्धृत्य हंतकारोपकल्पितम्।।
निर्वापभूतं भूपाल श्रोत्रियायोपपादयेत्।। ६५।।

He should also present to a Brāhmin, who is well versed in the Vedas, four handfuls of food, set apart, with the exclamation Hanta.

दद्याच्च भिक्षात्रितयं परिव्राड्ब्रह्मचारिणाम्।।
इच्छया च बुधो दद्याद्विभवे सत्यवारितम्।। ६६।।

If he has got means left after making these three sorts of gifts, the learned should, according to this pleasure, make gifts to a mendicant and a religious student.

इत्येतेतिथयः प्रोक्ताः प्रागुक्ता भिक्षवश्च ये।।
चतुरः पूजयित्वैतान्नृप पापात्प्रमुच्यते।। ६७।।

1. The mundane egg floating on the water at creation, of that metal, or of similar colour from which the deity issued according to some legends; i.e. he should treat him with all reverence.

These three, with the addition of the mendicant described before, are to be considered as guests; and he, who treats these four sorts of persons with hospitality, is freed of the debt due to his fellow beings.

अतिथिर्यस्य भग्नाशो गृहात्प्रतिनिवर्त्तते।।
स तस्मै दुष्कृतं दत्त्वा पुण्यमादाय गच्छति।। ६८।।

The guest, who goes elsewhere disappointed from any house, transfers his own sins to the owner of the house and takes away the house-holder's merits.

धाता प्रजापतिः शक्रो वह्निर्वसुगणोऽर्यया।।
प्रविश्यातिथिमेते वै भुञ्जंतेन्नं नरेश्वर।। ६९।।

Brahmā, Prajāpati, Indra fire, the Vasus, the sun are present in the person of a guest and share the food that is offered to him.

तस्मादतिथिपूजायां यतेत सततं नरः।।
स केवलमघं भुंक्ते ह्यतिथिं विना।। ७०।।

Therefore a man should assiduously satisfy the duties of hospitality; for a man, who eats his food without giving any to his guest, feeds only upon his own sin.

ततः स्ववासिनीं दुःखीं गुर्विणीं वृद्धबालकान्।।
भोजयेत्संस्कृतान्नेन प्रथमं चरमं गृही।। ७१।।

Thereupon the householder must satisfy with well-seasoned food the damsel living in her father's house, those who are ill, the pregnant woman, the aged and the infants of the house and then he should eat himself.

अभुक्तवत्सु चैतेषु भुञ्जन्भुंक्ते स दृष्कृतम्।।
मृतश्च गत्वा नरकं श्लेष्मभुग्जायते नरः।। ७२।।

The householder, who eats his food without feeding these, feeds upon his own iniquitey and after his death is condemned in hell to feed upon phlegm.

अस्नाताशी मलं भुंक्ते ह्यजपी पूयशोणितम्।।
असंस्कृतान्नभुङ्मूत्रं बालादिप्रथमं शकृत्।। ७३।।
अहोमी च कृमीन्भुंक्ते अदत्त्वा विषमाश्नुते।। ७४।।

He, who eats, without performing ablutions, feeds upon filth; he, who eats without repeating his prayers, feeds upon matter and blood; he, who eats unconsecrated food, drinks urine; and he, who eats before the infants and the aged are fed, is doomed in hell to live upon ordure.

तस्माच्छृणुष्व राजेंद्र यथा भुञ्जीत वै गृही।।
भुञ्जतश्च यथा पुंसः पापबंधो न जायते।। ७५।।

इह चारोग्यविपुलं बलबुद्धिस्तथा नृप।।
भवत्यरिष्टशांतिश्च वैरिपक्षाभिचारिणः।। ७६।।

O foremost of kings, I shall now describe, do you hear, how a householder should eat for which he would not be sullied with iniquity, his perpetual health and increased vigour would be secured and all evils and hostilities would be averted.

स्नातो यथावत्कृत्वा च देवर्षिपितृतर्पणम्।।
प्रशस्तरत्नपाणिस्तु भुञ्जीत प्रयतो गृही।। ७७।।

कृते जपे हुते वह्नौ शुद्धवस्त्रधरो नृप।।
दत्वाऽतिथिभ्यो विप्रेभ्यो गुरुभ्यस्संश्रिताय च।।
पुण्यगंधश्शस्तमाल्यधारी चैव नरेश्वर।। ७८।।

Having bathed and offered duly libations to the celestials, Ṛṣis and manes and adorned his hand with precious jewels, having recited introductory prayers, offered oblations with fire, food to guests, to Brāhmaṇas, to his elders and to his family, the householder should take his meal, wearing unsullied cloth, excellent garlands and sprinkled with perfumes.

नैकवस्त्रधरो नार्द्रपाणिपादो महीपते।।
विशुद्धवदनः प्रीतो भुञ्जीत न विदिङ्मुखः।। ७९।।

He must not eat, O lord of men, with a single garment on, nor with wet hands and feet.

प्राङ्मुखोदङ्मुखो वापि न चैवान्यमना नरः।।
अन्नं प्रशस्तं पथ्यं च प्रोक्षितं प्रोक्षणोदकैः।। ८०।।

न कुत्सिताहृतं नैव जुगुप्सापदसंस्कृतम्।।
दत्त्वा तु भक्तं शिष्येभ्यः क्षुधितेभ्यस्तथा गृही।। ८१।।

He must not eat with his face directed to any intermidiate point of horizon, but facing the east or the north; and with a smiling countenance, happy and attentive, let him take good and wholesome food boiled with clean water, procured from no mean person, nor by improper means nor improperly cooked.

प्रशस्तशुद्धपात्रे तु भुञ्जीताकुपितो द्विजः।। ८२।।

Having given a part to his hungry campanions he should take food without reproach from a clean, handsome vessels which must not be placed upon a low stool or bed.

नासंदिसंस्थिते पात्रे नादेशे च नरेश्वर।।
नाकाले नातिसंकीर्णे दत्त्वाग्रं च नरोग्नये।। ८३।।

मंत्राभिमंत्रितं शस्तं न च पर्युषितं नृप।।
अन्यत्र फलमूलेभ्यश्शुष्कशाखादिकात्तथा।। ८४।।

He must not take his food in an unbecoming place or out of season or in an unsuitable mood, giving the first morsel to fire His food, O king, must be consecrated with suitable texts, must be good and must not be stale except in the case of fruit or meat. Nor it should be made of dry vegetable substances other than jujubes or preparation of molasses.

तद्वद्धारीतकेभ्यश्च गुडभक्ष्येभ्य एव च।।
भुञ्जीतोद्धृतसा राणि न कदापि नरेश्वर।। ८५।।

And a man should never eat that of which the juices have been extrancted.

न शेषं पुरुषोश्नीयादन्यत्र जगतीपते।।
मध्वंबुदधिसर्पिभ्यस्सक्तुभ्यश्च विवेकवान्।। ८६।।

Nor a man should so eat as nothing will be left of his meal except in the case of flour, cakes, honey, water, curds and butter.

अश्नीयात्तन्मयो भूत्वा पूर्वं तु मधुरं रसम्।।
लवणाम्लौ तथा मध्ये कटुतिक्तादिकांस्ततः।। ८७।।

He should with a devoted mind first taste that which has good flavour; in the middle he should take salt and sour things and in the end he should take those which are pungent and bitter.

प्राग्द्रवं पुरुषोश्नीयान्मध्ये कठिनभो जनः।।
अंते पुनर्द्रवाशी तु बलारोग्ये न मुञ्चति।। ८८।।

The person, who begins his food with fluid things, takes solid food in the middle and finishes with fluid things, will ever be strong and healthy.

अनिंद्यं भक्षयेदित्थं वाग्यतोन्नमकुत्सयन्।।
पञ्चग्रासं महामौनं प्राणाद्याप्या यनं हि तत्।। ८९।।

In this wise he should take such food as is not prohibited, should be silent at the time of eating and should take five handfuls for the nutriment of the vital principle.

भुक्त्वा सम्यगथाचम्य प्राङ्मुखोदङ्मुखोपि वा।।
यथावत्पुनराचामेत्पाणी प्रक्षाल्य मूलतः।। ९०।।

स्वस्थः प्रशांतचित्तस्तु कृतासनपरिग्रहः।।
अभीष्टदेवतानां तु कुर्वीत स्मरणं नरः।। ९१।।

अग्निराप्याययेद्धातुं पार्थिवं पवनेरितः।।
दत्तावकाशं नभसा जरयत्यस्तु मे सुखम्।। ९२।।

After he has taken his food, he should, facing the east or the north, rinse his mouth, and having washed his hands up to the wrist he should again sip water. Then with a satisfied and calm mind he should take his seat, meditate upon his tutelary deity and pray "May fire excited by air cause this food to digest in the space afforded by the etherial atmosphere, convert this into the earthly elements of this body and give me satisfaction.

अन्नं बलाय मे भूमेरपामग्न्यनिलस्य च।।
भवत्येतत्परिणतं ममास्त्यब्याहतं सुखम्।। ९३।।

प्राणापानसमानानामुदानव्यानयोस्तथा।।
अन्नं पुष्टि करं चास्तु ममाप्यव्याहतं सुखम्।। ९४।।

May this food, when assimilated, contribute to the vigour of the earth, water, fire, and air (Prāṇa, Apāna, Samāna, Udāna, Vyāna) of my body and afford unmixed satisfaction.

अगस्तिरग्निर्वडवानलश्च भुक्तं मयान्नं जरयत्वशेषम्।।
सुखं च मे तत्परिणामसंभवं यच्छंत्वरोगं मम चास्तु देहे।।
९५।।

May Agasti, Agni and submarine fire bring about the digestion of the food I have taken and may I enjoy happiness consequent thereupon and may my body be freed from all ills.

विष्णुस्समस्तेंद्रियदेहदेही वृथा न भूतो भगवान्यथैकः।।
सत्येन तेनात्तमशेषमन्नमारोग्यतां मे परिणाममेतु।। ९६।।

May Viṣṇu, who is the chief principle of all senses, of all bodies and souls, be propitiated with my faith and may cause such assimilation of the food I have eaten as may invigorate my health.

विष्णुरत्ता तथैवान्नं परिणामश्च वै तथा।।
सत्येन तेन मद्भुक्तं जीर्यत्यन्नमिदं तथा।। ९७।।

Verily Viṣnu is the eater, the food and the nourishment, may the food, I have taken, through this faith, be digested."

इत्युच्चार्य्य स्वहस्तेन परिमृज्य तथोदरम्।।
अनायासप्रदायीनि कुर्य्यात्कर्माण्यतंद्रितः।। ९८।।

Having recited this prayer he should rub his stomach with his hand, and renouncing idleness should engage in such action as can easily he performed.

सच्छास्त्रादिविनोदेन सन्मार्गादविरोधिना।।
दिनं नयेत्ततस्संध्यामुपतिष्ठेत्समाहितः।। ९९।।

दिनांतसंध्यां सूर्येण पूर्वामृक्षैर्युतां बुधः।।
उपतिष्ठेद्यथान्याय्यं सम्यगाचम्य पार्थिव।। १००।।

He should spend the day in the reading of sacred writings and in such amusements as are authorized by the righteous and when the Sandhyā sets in he must engage is devotion O king, he must perform the morning rites before the stars have disappeared and perform the evening rites before the sun has quite set.

सर्वकालमुपस्थानं संध्ययोः पार्थिवेष्यते।।
अन्यत्र सूतकाशौचविभ्रमातुरभीतितः।। १०१।।

The morning and evening rites should never be neglected except at seasons of impurity, anxiety, sickness or alarm.

सूर्येणाभ्युदितो यश्च त्यक्तः सूर्येण वा स्वपन्।।
अन्यत्रातुरभावात्तु प्रायश्चित्ती भवेन्नरः।। १०२।।

He, who but for illness lies on bed at the hours of sunrise and sunset, is guilty of iniquity.

तस्मादनुदिते सूर्य्ये समुत्थाय महीपते।।
उपतिष्ठेन्नरस्संध्यामस्वपंश्च दिनांतजाम्।। १०३।।

Therefore a man should rise before the sun in the morning and sleep not until after he has set.

उपतिष्ठंति वै संध्यां ये न पूर्वां न पश्चिमाम्।।
व्रजंति ते दुरात्मानस्तथामिस्त्रं नरकं नृप।। १०४।।

Those, who sinfully neglect the performance of both the morning and evening rites, go to the hell of darkness after death.

पुनः पाकमुपादाय सायमप्यवनीपते।।
वैश्वदेवनिमित्तं वै पत्न्या-सार्द्धं बलिं हरेत्।। १०५।।

And having prepared food in the evening, the wife, of the householder with a view to obtain the fruit of the Viśvadeva rite, should give food, without offering any prayers, to outcasts or unclean persons.

तत्रापि श्वपचादिभ्यस्तथैवान्नविसर्जनम्।। १०६।।
अतिथिं चागतं तत्र स्वशक्त्या पूजयेद्बुधः।।
पादशौचास नप्रह्वस्वागतोक्त्या च पूजनम्।।
ततश्चान्नप्रदानेन शयनेन च पार्थिव।। १०७।।

The householder, as his means allow, should again show hospitality to any guest who may come receiving him with the salutation of evening and offering him water to wash his feet, a seat, a supper and a bed.

दिवातिथौ तु विमुखे गते यत्पातकं नृप।।
तदेवाष्टगुणं पुंसस्सूर्य्योढे विमुखे गते।। १०८।।

The sin, consequent upon not receiving hospitably a guest who comes after sunset, is eight times greater than that of turning away one who comes during the day.

तस्मात्स्वशक्त्या राजेंद्र सूर्य्योढमतिथिं नरः।।
पूजयेत्पूजिते तस्मिन्पूजितास्सर्वदेवताः।। १०९।।

A person should therefore particularly show respect to him who seeks refuge after sunset, for the respect, given to his satisfaction, will afford pleasure to all the celestials.

अन्नशाकांबुदानेन स्वशक्त्वाया पूजयेत्पुमान्।।
शयनप्रस्तरमहीप्रदानैरथवापि तम्।। ११०।।

The householder should, therefore, as his means permit him, give a guest food, potherbs, water, a bed, a mat, or if he cannot give any thing more, ground only on which to lie.

कृतपादादिशौचस्तु भुक्त्वा सायं ततो गृही।।
गच्छेच्छटयामस्फुटितामपि दारुमयीं नृप।। १११।।
नाविशालां न वै भुग्नां नासमां मलिनां न च।।
न च जंतुमयींशय्यामधितिष्ठेदनास्तृताम्।। ११२।।

Having taken his evening meal and washed his feet a householder should take rest. His bed must be complete and made of wood, it must have ample space, must not be cracked nor uneven, nor dirty nor infested by insects and must have a bedding.

प्राच्यां दिशि शिरश्शस्तं याम्यायामथ वा नृप।।
सदैव स्वपतः पुंसौ विपरीतं तु रोगदम्।। ११३।।

The householder must sleep with his head either to the east or to the south; any other position is unhealthy.

ऋतावुपगमश्शस्तस्स्वपत्न्यामवनीपते ।।
पुन्नमर्क्षे शुभे काले ज्येष्ठायुग्मासु रात्रिषु।। ११४।।
नाद्यूनां तु स्त्रियं गच्छेन्नातुरां न रजस्वलाम्।।
नानिष्टां न प्रकुपितां न त्रस्तां न च गद्धभणीम्।। ११५।।

In proper time, under the influence of an auspicious planet and in an auspicious moment he should go to his wife if she is not unbathed, sick, unwell, unwilling, angry, pregnant, hungry or over-fed.

नादक्षिणां नान्यकामां नाकामां नान्ययोषितम्।।
क्षुत्क्षामां नातिभुक्तां वा स्वयं चैभिर्गुणैर्युतः।। ११६।।

He should also be free from all these imperfections and should be neatly dressed and adorned and excited by tenderness and affection.

स्नातस्स्त्रग्गंधधृक्प्रीतो नाध्मातः क्षुधितोपि वा।।
सकामस्सानुरागश्च व्यवायं पुरुषो व्रजेत्।। ११७।।

Having bathed, wearing garlands, using perfumes, delighted and animated by desire he should go to his wife—not being hungry and excited with anxiety.

चतुर्दश्यष्टमी चैव तथामाचाथ पूर्णिमा।।
पर्वाण्येतानि राजेंद्र रविसंक्रांतिरेव च।। ११८।।

There are certain days on which the use of unguents, flesh and women is prohibited as the eighth and fourteeth lunar days, new-moon and full-moon and the entrance of the sun into a new sign.

तैलस्त्रीमांससंभोगी सर्वेष्वेतेषु वै पुमान्।।
विण्मूत्रभोजनं नाम प्रयाति नरकं मृतः।। ११९।।

On these occasions the wise should control their appetites and engage in the worship of the celestials as laid down in scripture, in meditation and prayer.

अशेषपर्वस्वेतेषु तस्मात्संयमिभिर्बुधैः।।
भाव्यं सच्छास्त्रदेवेज्याध्यानजप्यपरैर्नरैः।। १२०।।

And he, who acts otherwise, will be doomed to a hell where he will be constrained to live upon ordure.

नान्ययोनावयोनौ वा नोपयुक्तौषधस्तथा।।
द्विजदेवगुरूणां च व्यवायी नाश्रमे भवेत्।। १२१।।

A man should not excite his desires by medicines nor satisfy them with unnatural objects or in public or holy places.

चैत्यचत्वरतीरेषु नैव गोष्ठे चतुष्पथे।।
नैव श्मशानोपवने सलिलेषु महीपते।। १२२।।

A man should not go to a woman under a huge tree, in the courtyard, in a place of pilgrimage, in pasturage, where four streets meet in a cremation ground, in a garden or in the waters.

प्रोक्तपर्वस्वशेषेषु नैव भूपाल संध्ययोः।।
गच्छेद्व्यवायं मनसा न मूत्रोच्चारपीडितः।। १२३।।

On all these occasions mentioned before in the morning or in the evening or being unclean the wise should not cohabit with women.

पर्वस्वभिगमोनिन्द्यो दिवा पापप्रदो नृप।।
भुवि रोगावहो नृणामप्रशस्तो जलाशये।। १२४।।

If a man goes to a woman during the Parva he loses wealth, if during the day he is visited with sin, if he cohabits with a woman on ground he loses his fame.

परदारान्न गच्छेत मनसापि कथञ्चन।।
किमु वाचास्थिबंधोपि नास्ति तेषु व्यवायिनाम्।। १२५।।

A man should not think voluptuously of another's wife, nor should he speak to her for that purpose; for such a weight will be born in his next life as a creeping insect.

मृतो नरकमभ्येति हीयते त्रापि चायुषः।।
परदाररतिः पुंसामिह चामुत्र भीतिदा।। १२६।।

The cohabitation with another's wife is a source of fear to him both in this life and in the next—for in this he loses his longivity and in the next he is doomed to hell.

इति मत्वा स्वादरेषु ऋतुमत्सु बुधो व्रजेत्।।
यथोक्तदोषहीनेषु सकामेष्वनृतावपि।। १२७।।

Considering all these things a man should approach his own wife in proper season or even at other times.

।। इति श्रीविष्णुमहापुराणे तृतीयेंशे एकादशोऽध्यायः।। ११।।

अथ तृतीयेंशेः द्वादशोऽध्यायः

Part III : Section 12

और्व उवाच

देवगोब्राह्मणान्सिद्धन्वृद्धाचार्यां स्तथार्चयेत्।।
द्विकालं च नमेत्संध्यामग्नीनुपचरेत्तथा।। १।।

Aurva said :—The householder should venerate, gods, king, Brāhmaṇas, saints, aged persons and holy preceptors.

सदानुपहते वस्त्रे प्रशस्ताश्च महौषधीः।।
गारुडानि च रत्नानि बिभृयात्प्रयतो नरः।। २।।

प्रस्निग्धामलकेशश्च सुगंधश्चारुवेषधृक्।।
सितास्सुमनसो हृद्या बिभृयाच्च नरस्सदा।। ३।।

He should also observe duly the two Sandhyās and offer oblations to fire. He should use untorn garments, delicate herbs and flowers, wear emeralds and other precious stones, keep his hair neat and clean, perfume his body with delicious unguents and should always go out handsomely dressed and decorated with garlands and white flowers.

किंचित्परस्वं न हरेन्नाल्पमप्यप्रियं वदेत्।।
प्रियं च नानृतं ब्रूयान्नान्यदोषानुदीरयेत्।। ४।।

He should not misappropriate another's property nor should treat him unkindly. He should always speak amiably and the truth and should not speak out publicly another's faults.

नान्यस्त्रियं तथा वैरं रोचयेत्पुरुषर्षभ।।
न दुष्टं यानमारोहेत्कूलच्छायां न संश्रयेत्।। ५।।

O foremost of men, he should not envy another's prosperity—nor should he create enmity with another; he should not use a broken conveyance, nor should he sit under the shadow of a tree on the banks of a river.

विद्विष्टपतितोन्मत्तबहुवैरादिकीटकैः।।
वर्द्धकीबंधकीभर्त्तुः क्षुद्रानृतकथैस्सह।। ६।।
तथातिव्ययशीलेश्च परिवादरतैश्शठैः।।
बुधो मैत्रीं न कुर्वीत नैकः पंथानमाश्रयेत्।। ७।।

The wise should not make friends with, nor should they wend the same way with, one who is hated, who is a sinner or a drunkard, who has many enemies, or who is lousy with a harlot or her gallant, with a pauper or a liar, with a prodigal, a slanderer or a knave.

नावगाहेज्जलौघस्य वेगमग्रे नरेश्वर।।
प्रदीप्तं वेश्म न विशेन्नारोहेच्छिखरं तरोः।। ८।।
न कुर्य्याद्दंतसंघर्षं कुष्णियाच्च न नासिकाम्।।
नासंवृतमुखी जृभेच्छ्वासकासौ विसर्जयेत्।। ९।।
नोच्चैर्हसेत्सशब्दं च न मुञ्चेत्पवनं बुधः।।
नखान्न खादयेच्छिंद्यान्न तृणं न महीं लिखेत्।। १०।।
न श्मश्रु भक्षयेल्लोष्टं न मृद्नीयाद्विचक्षणः।।
ज्योतींष्यमेध्यशस्तानि नाभिवीक्षेत च प्रभो।। ११।।

A man should not bathe in river when it is ebb-tide, should not enter a house when it is on fire nor climb to the top of a tree; nor (when in the company of others) clean his teeth, nor blow his nose nor grape without covering his mouth, nor clean his throat, nor cough, nor laugh loudly, nor emit wind with noise, nor bite his nails, nor cut grass, nor cratch ground, nor put his beard into his mouth, nor crumble a clod of clay, nor look upon the planets when he is unclean.

नग्नां परस्त्रियं चैव सूर्य्यं चास्तमयोदये।।
न हुंकुर्याच्छवं गंधं शवगंधो हि सोमजः।। १२।।

He should not see another's wife when she is naked nor see the sun at the time of its rising or setting. He should not express disgust at a dead body for the odour of it is the produce of the moon.

चतुष्पथं चैत्यतरुं श्मशानोपवनानि च।।
दुष्टस्त्रीसन्निकर्षं च वर्जयेन्निशि सर्वदा।। १३।।

He should avoid, during the night, the place where four roads meet, the village tree, the forest adjacent to a cremation ground and a loose woman.

पूज्यदेवद्विजज्योतिश्छायां नातिक्रमेद् बुधः।।
नैकश्शून्याटवीं गच्छेत्तथा शून्यगृहे वसेत्।। १४।।

The wise should not pass across the shadow of a venerable person, of an image of a deity, of a flag and of a heavenly luminary. He should not travel alone in a forest nor sleep alone in an empty house.

केशास्थिकंटकामेध्यबलिभस्मतुषांस्तथा।।
स्नानार्द्रधरणीं चैव दूरतः परिवर्जयेत्।। १५।।

He should live at a distance from hair, bones, thorn, filth, remnants of offerings, ashes, chaff, and earth wet with water in which another has bathed.

नानार्यानाश्रयेत्कांश्चिन्न जिह्मं रोचयेद्बुदुधः।।
उपसर्पेन्न वै व्यालं चिरं तिष्ठेन्न वोत्थितः।। १६।।

He should not seek the shelter of a degraded weight and should renounce the company of wily persons.

अतीव जागर स्वप्ने तद्वत्स्थानासने बुधः।।
न सेवेत तथा शय्यां व्यायामं च नरेश्वर।। १७।।

He should not appraoch voracious animals and should not lie down on bed long after sleep is broken. He should not, for a too long time, lie down on bed, sleep, keep up nights, sit and take exercise.

दंष्ट्रिणशशृंगिणश्चैव प्राज्ञो दूरेण वर्जयेत्।।
अवश्यायं च राजेंद्र पुरोवातातपौ तथा।। १८।।

The wise should avoid, even at a distance, animals with tusks and horns and exposure to frost, wind and sunshine.

न स्नायान्न स्वपेन्नग्नो न चैवोपस्पृशेद्बुधः।।
मुक्तकेशश्च नाचामेद्देवाद्यर्चां च वर्जयेत्।। १९।।

A man should neither bathe, nor sleep nor rinse his mouth when he is naked; he should not wash his mouth nor perform any sacred rite with his waistband loosened.

होमदेवार्चनाद्यासु क्रियास्वाचमने तथा।।
नैकवस्त्रः प्रवर्त्तेत द्विजपादावनेजने।। २०।।

Nor he should, with one piece of cloth on, offer oblations to fire, sacrifice to the celestials, wash his mouth, salute a Brāhmaṇa or utter a prayer.

नासमञ्जसशीलैस्तु सहासीत कथञ्चन।।
सद्वृत्तसन्निकर्षो हि क्षणार्द्धमपि शस्यते।। २१।।

He should not associate with evil companions—the intercourse for half an instant, with the pious is desirable.

विरोधं नोत्तमर्गच्छेन्नाधमैश्च सदा बुधः।।
विवाहश्च विवादश्च तुल्यशीलैर्नृपेष्यते।। २२।।

The wise should not quarrel with men inferior or superior to them; dispute and marriage with equals are always desirable.

नारभेत कलिं प्राज्ञश्शुष्कवैरं च वर्जयेत्।।
अप्यल्पहानिस्सोढव्या वैरेणार्थागमं त्यजेत्।। २३।।

The wise should never enter into dispute and should always avoid useless enmity. It is better to suffer a trifling loss but he should not acquire wealth by hostility.

स्नातो नांगानि संमार्जेत्स्नानशाट्या न पाणिना।।
न च निर्धूनयेत्केशान्नाचामेच्चैव चोत्थितः।। २४।।

When bathed he should not wipe his limbs with the cloth he has put on nor with his hands; he should not shake his hair nor rinse his mouth before he has risen.

पादेन नाक्रमेत्पादं न पूज्याभिमुखं नयेत्।।
नोच्चासनं गुरोरग्रे भजेताविनयान्वितः।। २५।।

He should not put one foot upon another nor spread out his foot before his elders but should modestly sit in a posture called Vīrāsana *i.e.*, on his knees.

अपसव्यं न गच्छेच्च देवागारचतुष्पथान्।।
मांगल्यपूज्यांश्च तथा विपरीतान्न दक्षिणम्।। २६।।

He should not go round a temple upon his left hand nor circumambulate any venerable object in the reverse direction.

सोमार्काग्न्यंबुवायूनां पूज्यानां च न संमुखम्।।
कुर्यान्निष्ठीवविण्मूत्रसमुत्सर्गं च पंडितः।। २७।।

The wise should not spit nor void impurities before the moon, fire, the sun, water, wind, or any respectable person.

तिष्ठन्न मूत्र येत्तद्वत्पथिष्वपि न मूत्रयेत्।।
श्लेष्मविण्मूत्ररक्तानि सर्वदैव न लंघयेत्।। २८।।

Nor should he pass urine standing or upon a public way; he should not pass over phlegm, ordure, urine or blood; nor should he spit forth the mucus of the throat at the time of eating, offering sacrifices or oblations or reciting prayers or before a respectable person.

श्लेष्मशिंघाणिकोत्सर्गो नान्नकाले प्रशस्यते।।
बलिमंगल जप्यादौ न होमे न महाजने।। २९।।

A man should not treat women disrespectfully nor should he place too much confidence in them.

योषितो नावमन्येत न चासां विश्वसेद्बुधः।।
न चैवेर्ष्या भवेत्तासु न धिक्कुर्यात्कदाचन।। ३०।।

He should not deal with them impatiently nor should he give them supremacy in important matters.

मंगल्यपूर्वरत्नाज्यपूज्याननभिवाद्य च।।
न निष्क्रमेद्गुहात्प्राज्ञसदाचारपरो नरः।। ३१।।

O king, wise persons, ever treading the path of morality, should not issue out of his house without saluting the chaplets, flowers, jewels, clarified butter and venerable persons.

चतुष्पथान्नमस्कुर्यात्काले होमपरो भवेत्।।
दीनभ्युद्धरेत्साधूनुपासीत बहुश्रुतान्।। ३२।।

He should salute the places where four roads meet, perform sacrifices at proper season, relieve the poor and venerate the learned and good-natured.

देवर्षिपूजकस्सम्यक्पितृपिंडोदकप्रदः ।।
सत्कर्त्ता चातिथीनां यः स लोकानुत्तमान्व्रजेत्।। ३३।।

He who worships the celestials and saints, gives cakes and water to the manes, and performs hospitality, attains to exalted stations after death.

हितं मितं प्रियं काले वश्यात्मा योभिभाषते।।
स याति लोकानाह्लादहेतुभूतान्नृपाक्षयान्।। ३४।।

He who speaks wisely, moderately and compassionately proceeds to the regions which are the perpetual sources of bliss.

धीमान्ह्रीमान्क्षमायुक्तो ह्यास्तिको विनयान्वितः।।
विद्याभिजनवृद्धानां याति लोकाननुत्तमान्।। ३५।।

He who is intelligent, bashful, forgiving, god-fearing and humble, proceeds to the region which is attainable by the learned and those born in a pious race.

अकालगर्जितादौ च पर्वस्वाशौ चकादिषु।।
अनध्यायं बुधः कुर्यादुपरागादिके तथा।। ३६।।

The wise should not read the Vedas on the Parva days, on impure seasons, upon untimely thunder and the occurence of eclipses.

समं नयति यः क्रुद्धान्सर्वबंधुरमत्सरी।।
भीताश्वासनकृत्साधुस्स्वर्गस्तस्याल्पकं फलम्।। ३७।।

The attainment of heaven is a trifling thing to him who allays the anger of the angry, who is friend to all and freed from malice, and who removes the fear of the pious.

वर्षातपादिषु च्छत्री दंडी रात्र्यटवीषु च।।
शरीरत्राणकामो वै सोपानत्कस्सदा व्रजेत्।। ३८।।

A man should use an umbrella to protect him, against the sun and rain; he should carry a rod when he goes by night or through a forest and he should use shoes if he wishes to save his body from being hurt.

नोर्ध्वं न तिर्यग्दूरं वा न पश्यन्पर्यटेद्बुधः।।
युगमात्रं महीपृष्ठं नरो गच्छेद्विलोकयन्।। ३९।।

As he proceeds he should not look up nor about him, nor afar off but keep his eyes upon the ground to the extent of a couple of yards.

दोषहेतूनशेषांश्च वश्यात्मा यो निरस्यति।।
तस्य धर्मार्थकामानां हानिर्नाल्पापि जायते।। ४०।।

He, who, having controlled himself, puts a stop to the sources of all these imperfections, meets with no obstacle in the acquisition of piety, wealth and desire.

सदाचाररतः प्राज्ञो विद्याविनयशिक्षितः।।
पापेप्यपापः परुषे ह्यभिधत्ते प्रियाणि यः।।
मैत्रीद्रवांतःकरण स्तस्य मुक्तिः करे स्थिता।। ४१।।

Final emancipation is in his grasp, who is sinless towards them who commit mischief by him, who speaks amicably to them who use harsh words and whose soul melts with the benevolence.

ये कामक्रोधलोभानां वीतरागा न गोचरे।।
सदाचारस्थितास्तेषामनुभावैर्धृता मही।। ४२।।

The earth is upheld by the truthfulness of those who have controlled their passions, and who, always following pious observances, are not sullied by desire, covetousness and anger.

तस्मात्सत्यंवदेत्प्राज्ञो यत्परप्रीतिकारणम्।।
सत्यं यत्परदुःखाय तदा मौनपरो भवेत्।। ४३।।

A man should therefore speak truth when it is agreeable and he should be silent when that truth would give pain.

प्रियमुक्तं हितं नैतदिति मत्वा न तद्वदेत्।।
श्रेयस्तत्र हितं वाच्यं यद्यप्यत्यंतमप्रियम्।। ४४।।

He should avoid agreeable words when they are detrimental and unreasonable, for it is always better to speak those disagreeable words which would produce salutary effect, although it would give offence.

प्राणिनामुपकाराय यथैवेह परत्र च।।
कर्मणा मनसा वाचा तदेव मतिमान्वदेत्।। ४५।।

A prudent man should always cultivate that, in act, thought and speech, which conduces to the well-being of all living creatures both in this world and the next."

।। इति श्रीविष्णुमहापुराणे तृतीयेंशे द्वादशोऽध्यायः।।१२।।

अथ तृतीयेंशेः त्रयोदशोऽध्यायः

Part III : Section 13

और्व उवाच
सचैलस्य पितुः स्नानं जाते पुत्रे विधीयते।।
जातकर्म तदा कुर्याच्छ्राद्धमभ्युदये च यत्।। १।।

Aurva said :—A father, without changing his cloth, should bathe when a son is born; he should then go through the ceremonies consequent upon the birth and perform the Śrāddha which should always be celebrated upon occasions of prosperity.

युग्मान्देवांश्च पित्र्यांश्च सम्यक्सव्यक्रमाद्द्विजान्।।
पूजयेद्भोजयेच्चैव तन्मना नान्यमानसः।। २।।

With a composed mind and thinking on nothing else, he should worhip both the celestials and the manes and reverentially go round keeping Brāhmaṇas on his left hand and offer them food.

दध्यक्षतैस्सबदरैः प्राङ्मुखोदङ्मुखोपि वा।।
देवतीर्थेन वै पिंडान्दद्यात्कायेन वा नृप।। ३।।

And standing with his face directed to the east, he should, with the portions of the hand sacred to the celestials and Prajāpati, offer balls of food with curds, unbruised grain and jujubes.

नांदीमुखः पितृगणस्तेन श्राद्धेन पार्थिव।।
प्रीयते तत्तु कर्तव्यं पुरुषैस्सर्ववृद्धिषु।। ४।।

He should perform on every accession of prosperity the Śrāddha ceremony, by which the manes called Nāndimukhas are propitiated.

कन्यापुत्रविवाहेषु प्रवेशेषु च वेश्मनः।।
नामकर्मणि बालानं चूडाकर्मादिके तथा।। ५।।
सीमंतोन्नयने चैव पुत्रादिमुखदर्शने।।
नांदीमुखे पितृगणं पूजयेत्प्रयतो गृही।। ६।।

On the occasion of the marriage of a son or daughter on entering a new house, on giving a name to a child on performing his tonsure and other purification rites at the binding of the mother's hair during gestation, on first, seeing the face of a son and on similar other occasions a householder should deligently worship the manes so named.

पितृपूजाक्रमः प्रोक्तो वृद्धावेष सनातनः।।
श्रूयतामवनीपाल प्रेम कर्म क्रियाविधिः।। ७।।

I have described to you, O king, the mode of worshipping the manes, as laid down by ancient sages; hear, I shall now describe the rules for the performance of obsequial rites.

प्रेतदेहं शुभैः स्त्रानैस्स्नापितं स्नग्विभूषितम्।।
दग्ध्वा ग्रामादबहिः स्नात्वा सचैलस्सलिलाशये।।८।।
यत्र तत्र स्थितायैतद मुकायेति वादिनः।।
दक्षिणाभिमुखा दद्युर्बांधवास्सलिलाञ्जलीन्।। ९।।

"Having washed the dead body with sacred water, adorned it with garlands and reduced it to ashes outside the village, the relatives having bathed with their clothes on, should stand with their faces to the south and offer libations to the dead, addressing him by name and saying.

प्रविष्टाश्च समं गोभिर्ग्रामं नक्षत्रदर्शने।।
कटकर्म ततः कुर्याद्भूमौ प्रस्तरशायिनः।। १०।।

"Whatever thou mayst be." (And if it burnt during the day), they should return to the village along with the cattle coming from pastrue, and when stars appears, should go to rest, sleeping on mats spread upon the earth.

दातव्योनुदिनं पिंडः प्रेताय भुवि पार्थिव।।
दिवा च भक्तं भोक्तव्यममांसं मनुजर्षभ।। ११।।

(And as long as the morning lasts) ever day a ball of food should be placed on the ground as an offering to the dead and they should take rice without flesh.

दिनानि तानि चेच्छतः कर्त्तव्यं विप्रभोजनम्।।
प्रेता यांति तथा तृप्तिं बंधुवर्गेण भुंजता।। १२।।

And as long as the mourner wishes he should feed the Brāhmaṇas for the soul of the dead derives pleasure in as much as his kinsmen are satisfied with their entertainment.

प्रथमेह्नि तृतीये च सप्तमे नवमे तथा।।
वस्त्रत्यागबहिस्स्नाने कृत्वा दद्यात्तिलोदकम्।।१३।।

(After the death of a person) on the first day, or the third, or seventh or ninth, his relatives should chanage their clothes and bathe out of doors and offer a libation of water with sesamum-seeds.

चतुर्थेह्नि च कर्त्तव्यं तस्यास्थिचयनं नृप।।
तदूर्ध्वमंगसंस्पर्शस्सपिंडानामपीष्यते।।१४।।

On the fourth day the bones and ashes should be collected; after which the body, of one connected with the dead by offerings of funeral cakes, shold be touched without thereby incurring impurity.

योग्यास्सर्वक्रियाणां तु समानसलिलास्तथा।।
अनुलेपनपुष्पादिभोगादन्यत्र पार्थिव।। १५।।

And those who are related by presentation of water are qualified for any business.

शय्यासनोपभोगश्च सपिंडानामपीष्यते।।
भस्मास्थि चयनादूर्ध्वं संयोगो न तु योषिताम्।।१६।।

The former class of kinsmen are allowed to use beds but still they are prohibited from using arguments and flowers and must observe continence after ashes and bones have been collected.

बाले देशांतरस्थे च पतिते च मुनौ मृते।।
सद्यश्शौचं तथेच्छातो जलाग्न्युद्बंधनादिषु।।१७।।

When a child is dead, or one who is abroad, or one who is degraded, or one who is a spiritual guide, or when one commits suicide, or when one destroys himself by water, fire or by hanging, the period of uncleanliness is over as soon as the news is received.

मृतबंधोर्दशाहानि कुलस्यान्नं न भुज्यते।।
दानं प्रतिग्रहो होमः स्वाध्यायश्च निवर्त्तते।। १८।।

The food of a family, in which a relation is dead, should not be taken for ten days. During the period of uncleanliness, gits, acceptance, sacrifice and the study of sacred writtings should be suspended.

विप्रस्येतद्द्वादशाहं राजन्यस्याप्यशौचकम्।।
अर्द्धमासं तु वैश्यस्य मासं शूद्रस्य शुद्धये।। १९।।

The term of uncleanliness for a Brāhmin is ten days; for a Kṣatriya twelve days; for a Vaiśya fifteen days and for a Śūdra a whole month.

अयुजो भोजयेत्कामं द्विजानंते ततो दिने।।
दद्याद्दर्भेषु पिंडं च प्रेतायोच्छिष्टसन्निधौ।। २०।।

On the first day after the period of impurity is over, the nearest relative of the dead should feed Brāhmins at this pleasure, but in uneven number and should offer to the dead a ball of rice upon holy grass placed near the remaining portion of the food that has been consumed.

वार्य्यायुधप्रतोदास्तु दंडश्च द्विजभोजनात्।।
स्प्रष्टव्योनंतरं वर्णैः शुद्धेरंते ततः क्रमात्।। २१।।

After the Brāhmaṇas have been fed, the mourner, according to his caste, should touch water, an weapon of goad or a staff—for he is purified by such contact.

ततस्सवर्ण धर्मा ये विप्रादीनामुदाहृताः।।
तान्कुर्वीत पुमाञ्जीवेन्निजधर्मार्जनैस्तथा।। २२।।

He should then resume the duties assigned to this caste and maintain his livelihood by the acquisition of wealth.

मृताहनि च कर्त्तव्यमेकोद्दिष्टमतः परम्।।
आह्वानादि क्रिया दैवनियोगरहितेन यत्।। २३।।

He should then perform the Śrāddha of his deceased relative on the day of his death in each month (for a year).

एकोर्घ्यस्तत्र दातव्यस्तथैवैकपवित्रकम्।।
प्रेताय पिंडो दातव्यो भुक्तवत्सु द्विजातिषु।। २४।।

And then feeding the Brāhmins in an uneven number he should offer balls to the deceased.

प्रश्नश्च तत्राभिरतिर्यजमानद्विजन्मनाम्।।
अक्षय्यममुकस्येति वक्तव्यं विरतौ तथा।। २५।।

The Brāhmins should then be accosted by the sacrificer if they are satisfied and after they have declared their satisfaction he should relate the prayer, "May this ever satisfy such a one."

एकोद्दिष्टमयो धर्म इत्थमावत्सरात्स्मृतः।।
सपिंडीकरणं तस्मिन्काले राजेंद्र तच्छृणु।। २६।।

The Śrāddha, which is called Ekoddiṣṭha, should be performed monthly for one year after the death of a person.

एकोद्दिष्टविधानेने कार्यं तदपि पार्थिव।।
संवत्सरेथ षष्ठे वा मासे वा द्वादशेह्नि तत्।। २७।।

And at the expiry of one year the ceremony called Sapiṇḍana should be observed. Hear, O king (I shall describe) how shall that be celegrated.

तिलगंधोदकैर्युक्तं तत्र पात्रचतुष्टयम्।। २८।।

This ceremony should be celebrated in the same way as monthly obsequies—only four vessels should be placed with water perfumes and sesamum.

पात्रं प्रेतस्य तत्रैकं पैत्रं पात्रत्रयं तथा।।
सेचयेत्पितृपात्रेषु प्रेतपात्रं ततस्त्रिषु।। २९।।

O king, (of these four) one should be dedicated to the deceased and three to the manes, and the contents of the former should be transferred to the latter three.

ततः पितृत्वमापन्ने तस्मिन्प्रेते महीपते।।
श्राद्धधर्मैरशषस्तु तत्पूर्वानर्चयेत्पितॄन्।। ३०।।

After the deceased has been included in the list of manes, O king of earth, the ancestors should be again worshipped with all the ceremonies of the Śrāddha.

पुत्रः पौत्रः प्रपौत्रो वा भ्राता वा भ्रातृसंततिः।।
सपिंड संततिर्वापि क्रियार्हो नृप जायते।। ३१।।

The persons connected by the offering of cake, who are competent to celebrate the obsequial ceremonies, are the son, grandson, great grandson, a kinsman of the dead, the descendants of a brother or the prosperity of one connected by funeral offerings.

तेषामभावे सर्वेषां समानोदकसंततिः।।
मातृपक्षसपिंडेन संबंधा ये जलेन वा।। ३२।।

And when all these relations are wanting, the ceremony may be performed by those allied by the offerings of water only or those allied by offerings of cakes or water to maternal ancestors.

कुल द्वयेपि चोच्छिन्ने स्त्रीभिः कार्याः क्रिया नृप।।
पितृमातृसपिंडैस्तु समानसलिलैस्तथा।। ३३।।

When males, both in the maternal and paternal families, are extinct, the funeral obsequies may be performed by women or by those who are connected with the deceased in social and religious institutions or by him who inherits his property.

संघातांतर्गतैर्वापि कार्याः प्रेतस्य च क्रियाः।।
उत्सन्नबंधुरिक्थाद्वा कारयेदवनीपतिः।। ३४।।

And even when friends and those, who will inherit his property, are wanting the king may have, his obsequial rites, initiative intermediate and subsiquent, celebrated.

पूर्वाः क्रिया मध्यमाश्च तथा चैवोत्तराः क्रियाः।।
त्रिप्रकाराः क्रियास्सर्वास्तासां भेदं शृणुष्व मे।। ३५।।

Hear, I shall now describe the difference of these three classes of rites. The first are those which are performed after the burning of the dead body until the touching of water, weapons etc.

आदाहाद्यादशाहाश्च स्पर्शाद्यंतास्तु याः क्रियाः।।
ताः पूर्वा मध्यमा मासि मास्येकोद्दिष्टसंज्ञिताः।। ३६।।

प्रेते पितृ त्वमापन्ने सपिंडीकरणादनु।।
क्रियंते याः क्रियाः पित्र्याः प्रोच्यंते ता नृपोत्तराः।। ३७।।

The Śrāddhas, called Ekoddiṣtha which are

performed every month, are called intermediate rites; and the ceremonies, which follow Sapiṇḍakaraṇa when the deceased becomes one of his ancestors, are called subsequent rites—from this time the ceremonies becomes general and ancestral.

पितृमातृसपिंडैस्तु समानसलिलैस्तथा ।।
संघातांतर्गतैर्वापि राज्ञा तद्धनहारिणा ।। ३८ ।।

The initiative ceremonies should be performed by the relative of the father or mother whether allied by the offering of the cake or of water by the companions of the dead man or by the king who inherits his property.

पूर्वाः क्रियाश्च कर्त्तव्याः पुत्राद्यैरेव चोत्तराः ।।
दौहित्रैर्वा नृपश्रेष्ठ कार्य्यास्तत्तनयैस्तथा ।। ३९ ।।

Both the intermediate and subsequent rites should be celebrated by sons and other relations, and by daughter's sons and their sons.

मृताहनि च कर्त्तव्यास्त्रीणामप्युत्तराः क्रियाः ।।
प्रतिसंवत्सरं राजन्नेकोद्दिष्टविधानतः ।। ४० ।।

In every year, O king, the obsequial ceremonis should be performed either by males or females, in the same way as the ceremonies of month by obsequies are enjoined.

तस्मादुत्तरसंज्ञायाः क्रियास्ताः शृणु पार्थिव ।।
यथायथा च कर्त्तव्या विधिना येन चानघ ।। ४१ ।।

Hear O king, I shall now describe, at what seasons and in what manner those ceremonies are to be performed."

।। इति श्रीविष्णुमहापुराणे तृतीयेंशे त्रयोदशोऽध्यायः ।। १३ ।।

अथ तृतीयेंशेः चतुर्दशोऽध्यायः
Part III : Section 14

और्व उवाच

ब्रह्मेंद्ररुद्रनासत्यसूर्याग्निवसुमारुतान् ।।
विश्वेदेवान्पितृगणान्वयांसि मनुजान्पशून् ।। १ ।।

सरीसृपानृषिगणान्यच्चान्यद्भूत संज्ञितम् ।।
श्राद्धं श्रद्धान्वितः कुर्वन्प्रीणयत्यखिलं जगत् ।। २ ।।

Aurva said :—"When a man celebrates reverentially the Śrāddha of his ancestors, Brahmā, Indra, Rudra, two Aśvins, the sun, fire, Vasus, Maruts, Viśvadevas, Ṛsis, birds, men, beasts, reptiles, manes and all other creatures, become propitiated.

मासिमास्यसिते पक्षे पञ्चदश्यां नरेश्वर ।।
तथापष्टकासु कुर्वीत काम्यान्कालाञ्छृणुष्व मे ।। ३ ।।

This should be performed, O king, every month, on the fifteenth day of the dark fortnight, or on the eighth day of the same period in some months or at particular seasons.

श्राद्धार्हमागतं द्रव्यं विशिष्टमथ वा द्विजम् ।।
श्राद्धं कुर्वीत विज्ञाय व्यतीपातेऽयने तथा ।। ४ ।।

Hear, I shall now explain them. A householder should celebrate it when will find all requisites ready, when a learned Brāhmin has come to the house for which ancestral ceremonies are appropriate.

विषुवे चापि संप्राप्ते ग्रहणे शशि सूर्ययोः ।।
समस्तेष्वेव भूपाल राशिष्वर्के च गच्छति ।। ५ ।।

नक्षत्रग्रहपीडासु दुष्टस्वप्नावलोकने ।।
इच्छाश्राद्धानि कुर्वीत नवसस्यागमे तथा ।। ६ ।।

He should voluntarily offer sacrifice upon any atmospheric portent, at the equinoctial and solstitial periods, at eclipses of the sun and moon, on the sun's entrance into a Zodiacal sign, upon unpropitious aspects of the planets and asterisms, on dreaming unlucky dreams and on eating the grain of the year's harvest.

अमवस्या यदा मैत्रविशाखास्वातियोगिनी ।।
श्राद्धैः पितृगणस्तृप्तिं तथाप्नोत्यष्टवार्षिकीम् ।। ७ ।।

अमवाया यदा पुष्ये रौद्रेथर्क्षे पुनर्वसौ ।।
द्वादशाब्दं तदा तृप्तिं प्रयांति पितरोर्चिताः ।। ८ ।।

The manes obtain satisfaction for eight

years from ancestral offerings upon the day of the new moon when the star of the conjunction is Anurādhā, Viśākhā or Swāti and for twelve years when it is Puṣya, Ārdrā or Punarvasu.

वासवाजैकपादर्क्षे पितृणां तृप्तिमिच्छताम्।।
वारुणे वाप्यमावास्या देवानामपि दुर्लभा।। ९।।

नवस्वृक्षेष्वमावास्या यदैतेष्ववनीपते।।
तदा हि तृप्तिदं श्राद्धं पितृणां शृणु चापरम्।। १०।।

गीतं सनत्कुमारेण यथैलाय महात्मने।।
पृच्छते पितृभक्ताय प्रश्रयावनताय च।। ११।।

He, who desries to satisfy the celestials or the manes, very seldom gets an opportunity on a day of new moon when the stars are those of Dhaniṣtha, Pūrvabhādrapadā or Śatabhiṣā. Hear also the description of another class of Śrāddhas which give special delight to the manes as explained by Sanatkumāra the sons of Brahmā, to the noble Purūravas when brimful with faith and devotion to the manes he asked how he might please them.

सनत्कुमार उवाच

वैशाखमासस्य च या तृतीया नवम्यसौ कार्तिकशुक्लपक्षे।।
नभस्यमासस्य च कृष्णपक्षे त्रयोदशी पञ्चदशी च माघे।।
१२।।

एता युगाद्याः कथिताः। पुराणेष्वनंतपुण्यास्तिथयश्चतस्नः।।
उपप्लवे चंद्रमसो रवेश्च त्रिष्वष्टकास्वप्ययनद्वये च।। १३।।

Sanatakumāra said :—The third lunar day of the month of Vaiśākhā (April, May) and the ninth of Kārtika (October) November) in the light fornight; the thirteenth of Nabha (July, August) and the fifteenth of Māgha (January, February) in the dark fornight are called by the sages of yore the anniversaries of the first day of Yuga and are regarded as most sacred.

पानीयमप्यत्र तिलैर्विमिश्रं दद्यात्पितृभ्यः प्रयतो मनुष्यः।।
श्राद्धं कृतं तेन समासहस्त्रं रहस्यमेतत्पितरो वदंति।। १४।।

माघेऽसिते पञ्चदशी कदाचिदुपैति योगं यादि वारुणेन।।
ऋक्षेण कालस्स परः पितृणां न ह्यल्पपुण्यैर्नृप लभ्यतेसौ।।
१५।।

काले धनिष्ठ्र यदि नाम तस्मिन्भवेत्तु भूपाल तदा पितृभ्यः।।
दत्तं जलान्नं प्रददाति तृप्तिं वर्षायुतं तत्कुलजैर्मनुष्यैः।।
१६।।

तत्रैव चेद्भाद्रपदानुपूर्वाः काले यथावत्क्रियते पितृभ्यः।।
श्राद्धं परां तृप्तिमुपैति तेन युगं सहस्त्रं पितरस्स्वपंति।।
१७।।

On these days water mixed with sesamum-seed should be duly offered to the progenitors as well as on every lunar and solar eclipse; on the eight lunataions of the dark fortnights of Agrahāyaṇa, Māgha and Phālguṇa on the two days beginning the solistices when the mights and days alternately begin to diminish; on the days which are the anniversaries of the beginning of Manvantaras; when the sun is in the path of the goat and on all these occasions when meteors appear. A Śrāddha, performed on these occasions, gives pleasure to the manes for a thousand years; and this is the secret which they have given. The fifteenth day, of the dark fortnight in the month of Māgha when united with the conjunction of the asterism over which Varuṇa rules, is also a sacred season when offerings particularly afford delight to the manes. When the asterism Dhaniṣṭhā is united with the day of new moon, food and water, offered by members of respectable families, satisfy the manes for ten thousand years. And on the day of new moon when Ārdrā is in the ascendant they rest satisfied by offerings for a whole age.

गंगां शतदूं यमुनां विपाशां सरस्वतीं नैमिशगोमतीं वा।।
तत्रावगाह्यार्चनमादरेण कृत्वा पितृणां दुरितानि हंति।। १८।।

He, who after having offered food and libations to the manes bathes in the Ganges, Satlaj, Vipāśa Sarasvatī or the Gomatī at Naimiṣa, is freed from all sins.

गायंति चैतत्पितरः कदानु हर्षादमी तृप्तिमवाप्य भूयः।।
माघासितांते शुभतीर्थतोयैर्यास्याम तृप्तिं तनयादिदत्तैः।।
१९।।

The manes also sing—"After having obtained gratification for a twelve month we shall derive further satisfaction by libations offered by oŭr descendants at some place of pilgrimage at the end of the dark fortnight of Māgha.

चित्तं च वित्तं च नृणां विशुद्धं
शस्तं च कालः कथितो विधिश्च।।
पात्रं यथोक्तं परमा च भक्ति-
र्नृणां प्रयच्छंत्यभिवाञ्छितानि।। २०।।

(The songs of Pitṛs) confer upon men purity of mind, prosperity, prosperous seasons, perfect rites and firm faith and all other things which they desire.

पितृगीतान्तथैवात्र श्लोकां स्ताञ्छृणु पार्थिव।।
श्रुत्वा तथैव भवता भाव्यं तत्रादृतात्मना।। २१।।

Hear, O king, I shall repeat some verses as sung by the manes, hearing which, you will follows them with a controlled mind.

अपि धन्यः कुले जायादस्माकं मतिमान्नरः।।
अकुर्वन्वित्तशाठ्यं यः पिंडान्नो निर्वपिष्यति।। २२।।

"That wise man who does not shrink from spending his wealth and presents us with cakes shall be born in an illustirous family.

रत्नं वस्त्रं महायानं सर्वभोगादिकं वसु।।
विभवे सति विप्रेभ्यो योस्मानुद्दिश्य दास्यति।। २३।।

He should, if he is rich, give to Brāhmaṇas in our honour, jewels, cloths, land, conveyances, wealth and various other eatables.

अन्नैन वा यथाशक्त्या कालेस्मिन्भक्तिनम्रधीः।।
भोजयिष्यति विप्राग्र्यांस्तन्मात्रविभवो नरः।। २४।।

If he has not got so much wealth he should feed with faith and humility excellent Brāhmaṇas according to his means.

असमर्थोन्नदानस्य धान्यमामं स्वशक्तितः।।
प्रदास्यति द्विजाग्रेभ्यः स्वल्पाल्यां वापि दक्षिणाम्।। २५।।

If he cannot afford to give them food even he should according to his might, present them with unboiled grain or with some gifts however trifling they may be.

तत्राप्यसामर्थ्ययुतः कराग्राग्रस्थितांस्तिलान्।।
प्रणम्य द्विजमुख्याय कस्मैचिद्भूप दास्यति।। २६।।

Should he utterly unable even to do this, O king, he must give to some excellent Brāhmin, bowing before him sesamum-seeds, adhering to the lips of his fingers.

तिलैस्सप्ताष्टभिर्वापि समवेतं जलाञ्जलिम्।।
भक्तिनम्रस्समुद्दिश्य भुव्यस्माकं प्रदास्यति।। २७।।

Or he should sprinkle water mixed with seven or eight sesamum-seeds to us upon the ground; or he should gather, as he may, fodder for a day and gie it to a cow, by which he will, if firm in faith, give us satisfaction.

यतः कुतश्चित्संप्राप्य गोभ्यो वापि गवाह्निकम्।।
अभावे प्रीणयन्नस्माञ्छ्रद्धायुक्तः प्रदास्यति।। २८।।

सर्वाभावे वनं गत्वा कक्षमूलप्रदर्शकः।।
सूर्यादिलोकापालानामिदमुच्चैर्वदिष्यति।। २९।।

And if it is impossible for him to go through any of these he should go to a forest raise up his arms to the sun and other planets and say aloud—"I have no money, nor property nor grain nor any thing whatever which I may give as an offering to my ancestors.

न मेऽस्ति वित्तं न धनं च
नान्यच्छ्राद्धोपयोग्यं स्वपितृन्नतोस्मि।।
तृप्यंतु भक्त्या पितरो मयैतो
कृतो भुजौ वर्त्मनि मारुतस्य ।। ३०।।

So I reverentially bow unto my ancestors; may they be propitiated with my devotion only—I throw up my arms in the air."

और्व उवाच

इत्येतत्पितृभिर्गीतं भावाभावप्रयोजनम्।।
यः करोति कृतं तेन श्राद्धं भवति पार्थिव।। ३१।।

These are the words of the progenitors. O king, he who endeavours to satisfy their desires, performs the ancestral rite called Śrāddha.

।। इति श्रीविष्णुमहापुराणे तृतीयेंशे चतुर्दशोऽध्यायः।। १४।।

अथ तृतीयेंशेः पञ्चदशोऽध्यायः
Part III : Section 15

और्व उवाच

ब्राह्मणान्भोजयेच्छ्राद्धे यद्गुणांस्तान्निबोध मे।। १।।

Aurva said :—Hear, O king, what description of Brāhmaṇa should be fed at ancestral ceremonies.

त्रिणाचिकेतस्त्रिमधुस्त्रिसुपर्णष्षडंगवित्।।
वेदविच्छ्रोत्रियो योगी तथा वै ज्येष्ठसामगः।। २।।

ऋत्विक्स्वस्त्रेयदौहित्रजामातृश्चशुरास्तथा।।
मातुलोथ तपोनिष्ठः पञ्चाग्न्यभिरतस्तथा।।
शिष्यास्संबंधिनश्चैव मातापितृरतश्च यः।। ३।।

He must be Triṇaciketa, Trimadhu and Trisuparṇa[1]; or one who is versed in the six supplementary sciences of the Vedas; one who is well acquainted with the Vedas; one who practises the duties laid down in the Vedas[2], one who is, Yogī[3], one who is *Jyeṣtha Samaga*[4]; an officiating priest, a sister's son, a daughter's son, a son-in-law, a father-in-law, a maternal uncle, an ascetic, a Brāhmaṇa who keeps up the five fires, a pupil, kinsman; one who respects is parents.

एतान्नियोजयेच्छ्राद्धे पूर्वोक्तान्प्रथमे नृपे।।
ब्राह्मणान्पितृतुष्ट्यर्थमनुकल्पेष्वनंतरान्।। ४।।

O king, a man should employ the Brāhmaṇas first mentioned in the performance of the the Śrāddha ceremony of his ancestors; and in the subsidiary rites performed to please his manes he should engage the others.

मित्रध्रुक्कुनखी क्लीबश्श्यावदंतस्तथा द्विजः।।
कन्या दूषयितावह्निवेदोज्झस्सोमविक्रयी।। ५।।

अभिशस्तस्तथा स्तेनः पिशुनो ग्रामयाजकः।।
भृतकाध्यापकस्तद्वद्भृतकाध्यापितश्च यः।। ६।।

परपूर्वापतिश्चैव मातापित्रोस्तथोज्झकः।।
वृषलीसूतिपोष्टा च वृषलीपतिरेव च।। ७।।

तथा देवलकश्चैव श्राद्धे नार्हति केतनम्।। ८।।

He should not invite at a Śrāddha ceremony a false friend, one who has got ugly nails, one who is eunuch, one who has got black teeth, a ravisher, Brāhmaṇa who neglects the service of fire and secred duty, a vender of Soma plant, a man accused of any crime, a thief, a calumniator, a Brāhmaṇa who performs the religious ceremonies for degraded persons, one who gives instructions to his servants in sacred writings; or one who is instructed in it by his servant, the husband of a woman who has been formerly betrothed to another, a man who has neglected his parents, the protector of a Śūdra, the husband of a Śūdra woman, and a Brāhmaṇa who worships idols.

प्रथमेह्नि बुधश्शस्ताञ्छ्रोत्रियादीन्निमंत्रयेत्।।
कथयेच्च तथैवैषां नियोगान्पितृदैविकान्।। ९।।

On the day of the Srāddha a waise man should invite eminent teachers of Vedas and other Brāhmins, and according to their instructions he must settle what is to be dedicated to the celestials and what to the manes.

ततः क्रोधव्यवायादीनायासं तैर्द्विजैस्सह।।
यजमानो न कुर्वीत दोषस्तत्र महानयम्।। १०।।

And in the company of the Brāhmins he should abstain from anger, continence and hard work.

श्राद्धे नियुक्तो भुक्त्वा वा भोजयित्वा नियुज्य च।।
व्यवायी रेतसो गर्त्ते मज्जयत्यात्मनः पितॄन्।। ११।।

---

1. The Brāhmaṇas here are classed into Triṇaciketa, Trimadhu and Trisuparṇa. The first is so called from reciting three Anuvākas of the Kāṭhaka Branch of the Yajur-Veda, beginning with the term *Triṇaciketa*, etc.; the second from three Anuvākas of the Same Veda beginning *Madhuvata;* and the third from a similar portion commencing *Brahmavan namami.*
2. There is some difference between *Veda vit* and *Śrotriya*—The first studies the Vedas only and the second practises the rites thereof.
3. Yogī is one who practises strictest penances.
4. A chantet of the principal Sāma-Veda. Portions of it contained in the Araṇyaka are called the Jyeṣtha 'elder' or principal Sāman.

He, who having eaten himself in a Śrāddha and fed Brāhmaṇas and appointed them to their sacred offices, is guilty of incontinence, thereby dooms his progenitors to shameful suffering.

तस्मात्प्रथममत्रोक्तं द्विजाग्र्याणां निमंत्रणम्।।
अनिमंत्र्य द्विजानेवमागतान्भोजयेद्यतीन्।। १२।।

Therefore on the day before the Śrāddha, eminent Brāhmaṇas should be invited. If a Brāhmaṇa, who has controlled his senses, comes to the house uninvited he should also be entertained with food.

पादशौचादिना गेहमागतान्पूजयेद्द्विजान्।। १३।।

पवित्रपाणिराचांतानासनेषूपवेशयेत्।।
पितृणामयुजो युग्मान्देवानामिच्छया द्विजान्।। १४।।

देवानामेकमेकं वा पितृणां च नियोजयेत्।। १५।।

The Brāhmins are to be respectfully received with water for their feet and after they have rinsed their mouths and washed their hands they should be offered seats. An uneven number of Brāhmins for the manes and an even number for the gods, as many as he can, should be employed; or one only on each occasion.

तथा मातामहश्राद्धं वैश्वदेवसमन्वितम्।।
कुर्वीत भक्तिसंपन्न स्तत्र वा वैश्वदैविकम्।। १६।।

Thus the householder, with faith, should offer oblations to the maternal grand father along with the worship of Viśvadevas or he should perform the Viśvadevas[1] ceremony.

प्राङ्मुखान्भोजयेद्विप्रान्देवनामुभयात्मकान्।।
पितॄन् पितामहानां च भोजयेच्चाप्युदङ्मुखान्।। १७।।

He should feed the Brāhmins, who are for the gods and maternal ancestors with their faces to the east. And there who are for the paternal ancestors and ancestors in general should be fed with their faces to the north.

पृथक्तयोः केचिदाहुः श्राद्धस्य करणं नृप।।
एकत्रैकेन पाकेन वदंत्यन्ये महर्षयः।। १८।।

Some say, O king, that seperate Śrāddha should be performed for these two classes of ancestors and others hold that they should both be entertained with the same food.

विष्टरार्थं कुशं दत्त्वा संपूज्यार्घ्यं विधानतः।।
कुर्या दावाहनं प्राज्ञो देवानां तदनुज्ञया।। १९।।

The wise should spread Kuśa grass for the seats of the Brāhmaṇas and then worship them with libations; and having received permission from them he should then invoke the deities.

यवांबुना च देवानां दद्यादर्घ्यं विधानवित्।।
स्नग्गंधधूपदीपांश्च तेभ्यो दद्याद्यथाविधि।। २०।।

Then the man who is acquainted with the ritual should offer a libation to the gods with water and barley and then flowers, perfumes and incense.

पितृणामपसव्यं तत्सर्वमेवोपकल्पयेत्।।
अनुज्ञां च ततः प्राप्य दत्तवा दर्भान्द्विधाकृतान्।। २१।।

मंत्रपूर्वं पितृणां तु कुर्याच्चावाहनं बुधः।।
तिलांबुना चापसव्यं दद्यादर्घ्यादिकं नृप।। २२।।

Then he should offer libations to the manes placed upon his left; and having first provided seats of Kuśa grass, he, with the permission of the Brāhmaṇas, should invoke with the usual prayers, the manes to the ceremony, offering libation on his left hand of water and sesamum.

काले तत्रातिथिं प्राप्तमन्नकामं नृपाध्वगम्।।
ब्राह्मणैरभ्यनुज्ञातः कामं तमपि भोजयेत्।। २३।।
योगिनो विविधै रूपैर्नराणामुपकारिणः।।
भ्रमंति पृथिवीमेतामविज्ञातस्वरूपिणः।। २४।।

If any guest arives at the time who is desirous of eating or who is passing along the road he should worship him with the permission of Brāhmaṇas; for the saints, for the behoof of mankind, travel over the earth disguised in various shapes and forms.

तस्मादभ्यर्चयेत्प्राप्तं श्राद्धकालेऽतिथिं बुधः।।
श्राद्धक्रियाफलं हंति नरेंद्रापूजितोऽतिथिः।। २५।।

It is for this reason, O king, that the wise worship a person who comes at such an hour—and if a guest is neglected—the fruits of an ancestral offering are baffled.

1. It is a ceremony which comprehends offerings to both paternal and maternal ancestors or ancestors in general.

जुहुयाद्व्यञ्जनक्षारवर्जमन्नं ततोऽनले।।
अनुज्ञातो द्विजैस्तैस्तु त्रिकृत्वः पुरुषर्षभ।। २६।।

With the permission of the Brāhmaṇas assisting in the ceremony the householder should offer food without salt and seasoning to fire three several times, exclaiming first.

अग्नये कव्यवाहाय स्वधेत्यादौ नृपाहुतिः।।
सोमाय वै पितृमते दातव्या तदनंतरम्।। २७।।
वैवस्वताय चैवान्या तृतीया दीयते ततः।।
हुता वशिष्टमल्पान्नं विप्रपात्रेषु निर्वपेत्।। २८।।

"To fire, the conveyance of oblations; to the progenitors Swāhā." Next addressing the oblations to Soma, the lord of the progenitors and giving the third to Vaivaswat. He should then place the residue in the dishes of the ancestors.

ततोन्नं मृष्टमत्यर्थमभीष्टमतिसंस्कृतम्।।
दत्त्वा जुषध्वमिच्छातो वाच्यमेतदनिष्ठुरम्।। २९।।

He should then offer to Brāhmaṇas choice viands well dressed and seasoned and profuse and request them most gently to partake of it at their pleasure.

भोक्तव्यं तैश्च तच्चित्तैर्मौनिभिस्सुमुखैः सुखम्।।
अक्रुद्ध्यता चात्वरता देयं तेनापि भक्तितः।। ३०।।

The Brāhmaṇas should attentively, in silence and with smiling faces eat that food. The sacrificer not hungrily, nor in hate but with devout faith should offer that food.

रक्षोघ्नमंत्रपठनं भूमेरास्तरणं तिलैः।।
कृत्वाध्येयास्स्वपितरस्त एव द्विजसत्तमाः।। ३१।।

Thereupon repeating the prayers that slay Rākṣas and scattering sesamum-seeds on the ground he should regard these eminent Brāhmaṇas as his ancestors and addressed them (saying).

पिता पितामहश्चैव तथैव प्रपितामहः।।
मम तृप्तिं प्रयांत्वद्य विप्रदेहेषु संस्थिताः।। ३२।।

"May my father, grand father and great grand father enter the persons of these Brāhmaṇas and be propitiated with (my offerings).

पिता पितामहश्चैव तथैव प्रपितामहः।।
मम तृप्तिं प्रयान्त्वद्य होमाप्यायितमूर्तयः।। ३३।।

May my father, grand father and great grand father derive satisfaction from these oblations to fire.

पिता पितामहश्चैव तथैव प्रपितामहः।।
तृप्तिं प्रयांतु पिंडेन मया दत्तेन भूतले।। ३४।।

May my father grand father, great grand father derive gratification from the balls of food placed by me upon the ground.

पिता पितामहश्चैव तथैव प्रपितामहः।।
तृप्तिं प्रयांतु मे भक्त्या मयैतत्समुदाहृतम्।। ३५।।

May my father, grand father, great grand father be propitiated with what I have offered them, this day, in faith.

मातामहस्तृप्तिमुपैतु तस्य तथा पिता तस्य पिता ततोन्यः।।
विश्वे च देवाः परमां प्रयांतु तृप्तिं प्रणश्यंतु च यातुधानाः।।
३६।।

May my maternal grand father, his father and his father derive gratification from my offerings. May all the celestials derive satisfaction and evil beings die.

यज्ञेश्वरो हव्य समस्तकव्यो भोक्ताव्ययात्मा हरिरीश्वरोत्र।।
तत्संनिधानादपयांतु सद्यो रक्षांस्यशेषाण्यसुराश्च सर्वे।। ३७।।

May the imperishable Hari the lord of sacrifice accept the oblation offerered to the manes or to the celestials and may all malignant spirits and enemies of the celestials depart from the ceremony."

तृप्तेष्वेतेषु विकिरेदन्नं विप्रेषु भूतले।।
दद्यादाचमनार्थाय तेभ्यो वारि सकृत्सकृत्।। ३८।।

When the Brāhmaṇas have been entertained with food to their satisfaction he should scatter a portion of the food on the ground and present them individually with water to rinse their mouths.

सुतृप्तैस्तैरनुज्ञातस्सर्वेणान्नेन भूतले।।
सतिलेन ततः पिंडान्सम्यग्दद्यात्समाहितः।। ३९।।

And then obtaining their permission he should place upon the ground, balls made up of boiled rice and condiments along with sesamum-seeds.

पितृतीर्थेन सलिलं तथैव सलिलाञ्जलिम्।।
मातामहेभ्यस्तेनैव पिंडांस्तीर्थेन निर्वपेत्।। ४०।।

He should then offer libation along with sesamum-seeds with the part of the hand sacred to the manes; and with the same part of the hand he should offer cakes to his maternal ancestors. He should diligently make gifts on all these occasions in lonely places, naturally picturesque and by the side of streams.

दक्षिणाग्रेषु दर्भेषु पुष्पधूपादिपूजितम्।।
स्वपित्रे प्रथमं पिंडं दद्यादुच्छिष्टसन्निधौ।। ४१।।

पितामहाय चैवान्यं तत्पित्रे च तथापरम्।।
दर्भमूले लेपभुजः प्रीणयेल्लेपघर्षणैः।। ४२।।

Upon Kuśa grass the tips of which are directed to the south and lying near the remants of meats the householder should present the first ball of food consecrated with flowers and incense to his father; second to his grand father and the third to his great grand father; and then wiping his hands with the roots of Kuśa grass he should satisfy them who are contented with the wipings thereof.

पिंडैर्मातामहांस्तद्वद्गंधमाल्यादिसंयुतैः।।
पूजयित्वा द्विजाग्र्याणां दद्याच्चाचमनं ततः।।४३।।

Then having satisfied the maternal ancestors with balls of food consecrated with incense and flowers he should offer water to the principal Brāhmaṇas to rinse their mouths.

पितृभ्यः प्रथमं भक्त्यातन्मनस्को नरेश्वर।।
सुस्वधेत्याशिषा युक्तां दद्याच्छक्त्या च दक्षिणाम्।।४४।।

दत्त्वा च दक्षिणां तेभ्यो वाचयेद्वैश्वदैविकान्।।
प्रीयंतामिह ये विश्वेदेवास्तेन इतीरयेत्।। ४५।।

And then giving presents to the Brāhmaṇas with attention and piety according to his means soliciting their benedictions accompanied with the exclamation "Swadhā" and having distributed those presents to the Brāhmaṇas he should address the gods saying "May the Viśvadevas be propitiated' and receive the reply thereto from the Brāhmaṇas.

तथेति योक्ते तैर्विप्रैः प्रार्थनीयास्तथाशिपः।।
पश्चाद्विसर्जयेद्देवान्पूर्वं पैत्र्यान्महीपते।। ४६।।

The Brāhmaṇas having said 'So be it,' and granted him blessings he should first send away his paternal ancestors and then the celestials.

माता महानामप्येवं सह देवैः क्रमः स्मृतः।।
भोजयेच्च स्वशक्तया च दाने तद्वद्विसर्जने।। ४७।।

The same order as regards food, gift and dismissal should be observed with the maternal ancestors and the gods.

आपादशौचनात्पूर्वं कुर्याद्देवद्विजन्मसु।।
विसर्जनं तु प्रथमं पैत्रं मातामहेषु वै।। ४८।।

Beginning with the washing of the feet and ending with the dismissal of the god and Brāhmaṇas all the ceremonies should be first performed for paternal ancestors and then for maternal ancestors.

विसर्जयेत्प्रीतिवचस्सम्मान्याभ्यर्थितास्ततः।।
निवर्त्तेताभ्यनुज्ञात आद्वारंताननुव्रजेत्।। ४९।।

Thereupon he should dismiss the Brāhmaṇas with sweet words and reverence, follow them to the gate and then come back with their permission.

ततस्तु वैश्वदेवाख्यं कुर्यान्नित्यक्रियां बुधः।।
भुञ्जीयाच्च समं पूज्य भृत्यबंधुभिरात्मनः।। ५०।।

The wise will then perform the invariable ceremony called the worship of Viśvadevas and then with a controlled mind he should take his meals in the company of revered persons, friends and servants.

एवं श्राद्धं बुधः कुर्यात्पैत्र्यं मातामहं तथा।।
श्राद्धैराप्यायिता दद्युस्सर्वान्कामान्पितामहाः।।५१।।

The learned should then celebrate the ancestral ceremony—for the ancestors being propitiated all his desires are fulfilled.

त्रीणि श्राद्धे पवित्राणि दौहित्रः कुतपस्तिलाः।।
रजतस्य कथा दानं तथा संकीर्त्तनादिकम्।। ५२।।

The things are specially considered sacred at obserquies namely a daughter's son, a Nepal blanket and sesamum-seeds; the gift or naming or seeing of silver is also auspicious.

वर्ज्यानि कुर्वता श्राद्धं क्रोधोध्वगमनं त्वरा।।
भोक्तुरप्यत्र राजेंद्र त्रयमेतन्न शस्यते।। ५३।।

O king, the person performing a Śrāddha ceremony should abstain from anger, walking about and hurry and those who take their meals at the Śrāddha should also avoid them.

विश्वेदेवास्सपितरस्तथा मातामहा नृप।।
कुलं चाप्यायते पुंसां सर्वं श्राद्धं प्रकुर्वताम्।। ५४।।

O king Viśvadevas, paternal ancestors, and maternal ancestors are pleased with him who performs these obsequial rites.

सोमाधारः पितृगणो योगाधारश्च चंद्रमाः।।
श्राद्धे योगिनियोगस्तु तस्माद्भूपाल शस्यते।। ५५।।

O king, the moon is the supporter of the manes and he is sustained by acts of austere devotion. Hence one, who practises austerities, should be appointed at the performance of a Śrāddha.

सहस्रस्यापि विप्राणां योगी चेत्पुरतःस्थितः।।
सर्वान्भोक्तृंस्तारयति यजमानं तथा नृप।। ५६।।

O king, if there is one Yogī is the midst of a thousand Brāhmaṇas, he liberates both the sacrificer and all those who take their meals there.

।। इति श्रीविष्णुमहापुराणे तृतीयेंशे पञ्चदशोऽध्यायः।। १५।।

अथ तृतीयेंशेः षोडशोऽध्यायः

Part III : Section 16

और्व उवाच

हविष्यमत्स्यमांसैस्तु शशस्य नकुलस्य च।।
सौकरच्छागलैणेयरौरवैर्गवयेन च।। १।।

Aurva said :—Ancestors are gratified for a month with Haviṣya[1], fish, or the flesh of the hare, of birds, of the hog, the goat, the antelope, the deer, the gayal, or the sheep, or with the milk of the cow[2] and various preparations thereupon.

औरभ्रगव्यैश्च तथा मासवृद्ध्या पितामहाः।।
प्रयांति तृप्तिं मांसैस्तु नित्यं वार्ध्रीणसामिषै।। २।।

They are perpetually pleased with flesh in general and with that of the long-eared white goat in particular.

खड्गमांसमतीवात्र काल शाकं तथा मधु।।
शस्तानि कर्मण्यत्यंततृप्तिदानि नरेश्वर।। ३।।

1. *Haviṣya i.e.* offerings made of rice or other grains with clarified butter.
2. The expression *Gavya* literally means all that is derived from cow. But it being associated with flesh readers may mistake it for the flesh of cow. Though the sacrifice of a cow or calf formed part of the ancient Śrāddha it is prescribed in the present age. So it must mean here milk or any preparation of it.

The flesh of the rhinoceros, the Kālaśāka, potherb and honey, give special satisfaction to those who are adored at the obsequial ceremonies.

गयामुपैत्य यः श्राद्धं करोति पृथिवीपते।।
सफलं तस्य तज्जन्म जायते पितृतुष्टिदम्।। ४।।

Blessed is he, and the king who performs at the due time the Śrāddha ceremony of his ancestors at Gayā and that affords special delight to his ancestors.

प्रशान्तिकास्सनीवाराश्श्यामाका द्विविधास्तथा।।
वन्यौषधीप्रधानास्तु श्राद्धार्हाः पुरुषर्षभ।। ५।।

यवाः प्रियंगवो मुद्गा गोधूमा व्रीहयस्तिलाः।।
निष्पावाः कोविदाराश्च सर्षपाश्चात्र शोभनाः।। ६।।

Grains that spring up spontaneously, wild-rice, white and black Panic forest vegetables, barely, wheat-rice, sesamum, various kinds of pulse and mustard are considered specially fit for ancestral offerings.

अमृताग्रयण यच्च धान्यजातं नरेश्वर।।
गजमाषानणूंश्चैव मसुरांश्च विसर्जयेत्।। ७।।

अलाबुं गृञ्जनं चैव पलांडुं पिंडमूलकसू।।
गांधारककरंवादिलवणान्यौषराणि च।। ८।।

आरक्ताश्चैव निर्यासाः प्रत्यक्षलवणानि च।।
वर्ज्यान्येतानि वै श्राद्धे यच्च वाचा न शस्यते।। ९।।

O king, a householder should not offer any kind of grain that is not rendered sacred by religious rites nor the pulse called Rājamāṣa, nor millet, nor lentils, nor gourds, nor garlick, nor onions, nor nightshade, nor camel's thron, nor salt, nor the efflorescence of salt deserts, nor red vegetable extracts, nor any thing that looks like salt, nor any thing that is hated by people.

नक्ताहृतमनुच्छिन्नं तृप्यते न च यत्र गौः।।
दुर्गंधिफेनिलं चांबु श्राद्धयोग्यं न पार्थिव।। १०।।

He should not offer that water at a Śrāddha that has been brought by night, or has been left off, or is so little as cannot satisfy a cow, or smells badly or is covered with froth.

क्षीरमेकशफानां यदौष्ट्रमाविकमेव च।।
मार्गं च माहिषं चैव वर्जयेच्छ्राद्धकर्मणिः।। ११।।

He should not offer milk of animals with undivided hoof, of a camel, a ewe, a deer, or a buffalo.

षंडापविद्धचंडालपापिपाषंडरोगिभिः।।
कृकवाकुश्वाननग्नवानरग्रामसूकरैः ।। १२।।
उदक्यासूतिकाशौचमृतहारैश्च वीक्षिते।।
श्राद्धे सुरा न पितरो भुञ्जंते पुरुषर्षभ।। १३।।

Neither the celestials nor the manes will partake of the food if a Śrāddha is looked at by a eunuch, a foundling, an outcast, a heretic, a drunken man, or one diseased, a cock, a naked ascetic, a monkey, a village hag, by a woman in her courses or pregnant, by an unclean person, or by a carrier of corpses.

तस्मात्परिश्रिते कुर्याच्छ्राद्धं श्रद्धासमन्वितः।।
उर्व्यां च तिलविक्षेपाद्यातुधानान्निवारयेत्।। १४।।

The ceremony should be celebrated on a plot of ground carefully enclosed. The performer should scatter sesamum on the ground and drive away evil spirits.

नखादिना चोपपन्नं केशकीटादिभिर्नृप।।
न चैवाभिषवैर्मिश्रमन्नं पर्युषितं तथा।। १५।।

He should not offer food that is fetid, or spoiled by hairs or insects, or mixed with acid gruel, or stale.

श्रद्धासमन्वितैर्दत्तं पितृभ्यो नामगोत्रतः।।
यदाहारास्तु ते जातास्तदाहारत्वमेति तत्।। १६।।

Whatever pure food is offered to the manes, with faith and mentioning their names and race, gives them nourishment.

श्रूयते चापि पितृभिर्गीता गाथा महीपते।।
इक्ष्वाकोर्मनुपुत्रस्य कलापोपवने पुरा।। १७।।

O king, in the days of yore, in the forest of Kalāpa the Pitṛs said to Ikṣvāku, the son of Manu.

अपि नस्ते भविष्यंति कुले सन्मार्गशीलिनः।।
गयामुपेत्य ये पिंडान्दास्यंत्यस्माकमादरात्।। १८।।

"Those, who shall respectfully offer to us cakes at Gayā, shall follow a righteous path.

अपि नस्स कुले जापाद्यो नो दद्यात्त्रयोदशीम्।।
पायसं मधुसर्पिभ्यो वर्षासु च मघासु च।। १९।।
गौरीं वाष्पुद्वहेत्कन्यां नीलं वा वृषमुत्सृजेत्।।
यजेत वाश्वमेधेन विधिवद्दक्षिणावता।। २०।।

May he be born in our family, who shall give us on the thirteenth of Bhādrapada and Māgha milk, honey and clarified butter, who shall marry a maiden, shall liberate a black bull and shall liberate a horse sacrifice accompanied with liberal presents.

।। इति श्रीविष्णुमहापुराणे तृतीयेंशे षोडशोऽध्यायः।। १६।।

अथ तृतीयेंशे: सप्तदशोऽध्याय:
Part III : Section 17

श्रीपराशर उवाच

इत्याह भगवानौर्वस्सगराय महात्मने।।
सदाचारं पुरा सम्यङ् मैत्रेय परिपृच्छते।। १।।

मयाप्येतदशेषेण कथितं भवतो द्विज।।
समुल्लंघ्य सदाचारं कश्चिन्नाप्नोति शोभनम्।। २।।

Parāśara said :—In the days of yore the glorious Aurva, when accosted by the illustrious king Sagara, said thus regarding the usages to be practised by mankind. I have described to you all those observances which no one should violate.

श्रीमैत्रेय उवाच

षंडापविद्धप्रमुखा विदिता भगवन्मया।।
उदक्याद्याश्च मे सम्यङ् नग्नमिच्छामि वेदितुम।। ३।।

को नग्न: किं समाचारो नग्नसंज्ञां नरो लभेत्।।
नग्नस्वरूपमिच्छामि यथावत्कथितं त्वया।।
श्रोतुं धर्मभृतां श्रेष्ठ न ह्यस्त्यविदितं तव।। ४।।

Maitreya said :—O venerable Sir, I know all those who are called Ṣaṇḍa[1], Apabidha[2] and Udakī[3] but I wish to know who is called Nagna; doing what he is called so, and what is the character of such a person to whom you have referred.

श्रीपराशर उवाच

ऋग्यजुस्सामसंज्ञेयं त्रयी वर्णावृतिर्द्विज।।
एतामुज्झति यो मोहात्स नग्न: पातकी द्विज:।। ५।।

Parāśara said :—The Ṛg, Yajur and Sāma Vedas are the three-fold covering of the several castes and the sinful wight who throws off this is called nacked or apostate.

त्रयी समस्तवर्णानां द्विजसंवरणं यत:।।
नग्नो भवत्युज्झितायां यतस्तस्यां न संशय:।। ६।।

The three Vedas constitute the dress of all men and when people neglect them they are left bare.

इदं च श्रूयतामन्यद्यद्भीष्माय महात्मने।।
कथयामास धर्मज्ञो वसिष्ठोऽस्मत्पितामह:।। ७।।

Hear, what my grand father the pious Vasiṣṭha said about this to the noble Bhīṣma.

मयापि तस्य गदतश्श्रुतमेतन्महात्मन:।।
नग्नसंबंधि मैत्रेय यत्पृष्टोहमिह त्वया।। ८।।

O Maitreya I heard what my grand-father said about this.

देवासुरमभूद्युद्धं द्विव्यमब्दशतं पुरा।।
तस्मिन्पराजिता देवा दैत्यैर्ह्लादपुरोगमै:।। ९।।

There took place in the days of yore a battle between the gods and demons for the period of a divine year in which the gods were defeated by the demons under the command of Hrāda.

क्षीरोदस्योत्तरं कूलं गत्वा तप्यन्त वै तप:।।
विष्णोराराधनार्थाय जुगश्चेमं स्तवं तदा।। १०।।

The celestials, who were defeated, fled away to the northern shore of the milky ocean, where being engaged in devout practices, they thus prayed to Viṣṇu—

देवा ऊचु:

आराधनाय लोकानां विष्णोरीशस्य यां गिरम्।।
वक्ष्यामो भगवानद्य तया विष्णु: प्रसीदतु।। ११।।

"May the glorious Viṣṇu, who is without beginning, the lord of all beings, be propitiated with the words that we are going to address to him.

यतो भूतान्यशेषाणि प्रसूतानि महात्मन:।।
यस्मिंश्च लयमेष्यंति कस्तं स्तोतुमिहेश्वर:।। १२।।

Who can sing the glories of that great God from whom have originated all beings and in whom they cease to exist?

1. Eunuch.
2. One ejected from the society.
3. A woman in her course.

तथाप्यरातिविध्वंसध्वस्तवीर्य्या भयार्थिनः।।
त्वां स्तोष्यामस्तवोक्तीनां याथार्थ्यं नैव गोचरे।। १३।।

Though thy true greatness is not within the reach of words still we have been engaged in glorifying thee being discomfitted by our enemies.

त्वमुर्वी सलिलं वह्निर्वायुराकाशमेव च।।
समस्तमंतःकरणं प्रधानं तत्परः पुमान्।। १४।।

Thou art earth, water, fire, air, ether, mind, Prakṛti and Puruṣa.

एकं तवैतद्भूतात्मन्मूर्त्तमूर्त्तमयं वपुः।।
आब्रह्मस्तंबपर्यंतं स्थानकालविभेदवत्।। १५।।

O thou art one with all souls, thy form, visible or unvisible, pervades all from Brahmā to a stock diversified by time and place.

तत्रेशं तव यत्पूर्वं त्वन्नाभिकमलोद्भवम्।।
रूपं विश्वोपकाराय तस्मै ब्रह्मात्मने नमः।। १६।।

Salutation to thee, who art Brahmā originated from the lotus springing from thy navel for the purpose of creation.

शक्रार्करुद्रवस्वश्विमरुत्सोमादिभेदवत्।।
वयमेकं स्वरूपं ते तस्मै देवात्मने नमः।। १७।।

Salutation to thee who art Indra, the sun, Rudra, the Vasus, fire, the winds and even also ourselves.

दंभप्रायमसंबोधि तितिक्षादमवर्जितम्।।
यद्रूपं तव गोविंद तस्मै दैत्यात्मने नमः।। १८।।

Salutation to thee, O Govinda, who art at one with all demons, who are the creature of arrogance and want of discrimination uncontrolled by patience and self-control.

नातिज्ञानवहा यस्मिन्नाड्यस्तिमिततेजसि।।
शब्दादिलोभि यस्तस्मै तुभ्यं यक्षात्मने नमः।।१९।।

Salutation to thee who art at one with the Yakṣas, whose minds have no idea of perfect knowledge and who are accordingly of umitigated prowess and whose nature is charmed with sounds.

क्रौर्यं मायामयं घोरं यच्च रूपं तवासितम्।।
निशाचरात्मने तस्मै नमस्ते पुरुषोत्तम।।२०।।

Salutation to thee, O foremost of Puruṣas, who are at one with all night-rangers, originated from the quality of darkness, fierce, fraudulent and cruel.

स्वर्गस्थधर्मिसद्धर्मफलोपकरणं तव।।
धर्माख्यं च तथा रूपं नमस्तस्मै जनार्द्दन।। २१।।

Salutation to thee, O Janārddana, who art that virtue that gives rewards for the virtuous actions of those who live in heaven.

हर्षप्रायमसंसर्गि गतिमद्गमनादिषु।।
सिद्धाख्यं तव तद्रूपं तस्मै सिद्धात्मने नमः।। २२।।

Salutation to thee who arat at one with the saints of accomplished piety, who are always contented and who traverse unobstructed all permeable elements.

अतितिक्षायनं क्रूरमुपभोगसहं हरे।।
द्विजिहं तव यद्रूपं तस्मै नागात्मने नमः।। २३।।

Salutation to thee who art at one with the serpents, double tongued, impulsive, cruel, not satisfied with enjoyment and having immense wealth.

अवबोधि च यच्छांतमदोषमपकल्मषम्।।
ऋषिरूपात्मने तस्मै विश्वरूपाय ते नमः।। २४।।

Salutation to thee who art at one with the Ṛsis who are freed from sins and imperfections and at one with wisdom and tranquility.

भक्षयत्यथ कल्पांते भूतानि यदवारितम्।।
त्वद्रूपं पुंडरीकाक्ष तस्मै कालात्मने नमः।। २५।।

Salutation to thee, O thou having lotus-eyes, who art at one with time that devours, without any compunction, all created beings at the end of Kalpa.

संभक्ष्य सर्वभूतानि देवादीन्यविशेषतः।।
नृत्यत्यंते च यद्रूपं तस्मै रुद्रात्मने नमः।। २६।।

Salutation to thee who art at one with Rudra, who dances with delight after devouring all beings—gods and men.

प्रवृत्त्या रजसो यच्च कर्मणां करणात्मकम्।।
जनार्दन नमस्तस्मै त्वद्रूपाय नरात्मने।। २७।।

Salutation to thee, Janārddana, who art at one with men, who, actuated by the quality of foulness, engage in actions.

अष्टाविंशद्वधोपेतं यद्रूपं तामसं तव।।
उन्मार्गगामि सर्वात्मंस्तस्मै वश्यात्मने नमः।। २८।।

Salutation to thee who art at one with brute animals—the spirit that leads to perversity, which proceeds from the quality of darkness and is encumbered with twenty-eight kinds of obstruction.

यज्ञांगभूतं यद्रूपं जगतः स्थितिसाधनम्।।
वृक्षादिभेदैष्षड्भेदि तस्मै मुख्यात्मने नमः।। २९।।

Salutation to thee who art that chief spirit that appears diversified in the vegetable world and which are the substance of sacrifice is the agent of accomplishing the perfection of the universe.

निर्यङ्मनुष्यदेवादिव्योमशब्दादिकं च यत्।।
रूपं तवादेः सर्वस्य तस्मै सर्वात्मने नमः।। ३०।।

Salutation to thee who art identical with every thing and whose first form is the objects of perception and heaven and animals and men and celestials.

प्रधानबुद्ध्यादिमयादशेषाद्यदन्यदस्मात्परमं परात्मन्।।
रूपं तवाद्यं यद्नन्यतुल्यं तस्मै नमः कारणकारणाय।। ३१।।

Salutation to that form of thine, which is the cause of causes and which is distinct from and superior to the endless universe composed of intelligence, matter, and the like and with which nothing can be compared.

शुक्लादिदीर्घादिघनादिहीनमगोचरं यच्च विशेषणानाम्।।
शुद्धातिशुद्धं परमर्षिदृश्यं रूपाय तस्मै भगवन्नताः स्मः।।
३२।।

Salutation to thee, O great God, who hast neither colour nor extent nor dimensity and which is beyond all qualities and whose essence, purest of the pure, can be conceived only by sages.

यन्नः शरीरेषु यदन्यदेहेष्वशेषवस्तुष्वजमक्षयं यत्।।
तस्माच्च नान्यद्व्यतिरिक्तमस्ति ब्रह्मस्वरूपाय नताः स्म तस्मै।। ३३।।

Salutation to the Brahmā form of thine, who pervades in our bodies, who exists in all objects, who is without birth or decay and distinct from whom nothing exists.

सकलमिदमजस्य यस्य रूपं परमपदात्मवतस्सनातनस्य।।
तमनिधनमशेषबीजभूतं प्रभुममलं प्रणतास्म वासुदेवम्।।
३४।।

Salutation to thee, Vāsudeva, the supreme lord of all, who is unsullied, the root of all thigns, freed from dissolution, unborn, eternal, who in essence is the supreme condition of spirit and in substance the whole of the universe."

श्रीपराशर उवाच

स्तोत्रस्य चावसाने ते ददृशुः परमेश्वरम्।।
शंखचक्रगदापाणिं गरुडस्थं सुरा हरिम्।। ३५।।

Having thus recited the prayer the celestials beheld Hair the supreme lord of all, seated on Garuḍa, armed with the shell, the discus, and the mace.

तमूचुस्सकला देवाः प्रणिपातपुरस्सरम्।।
प्रसीद नाथ दैत्येभ्य स्त्राहि नश्शरणार्थिनः।। ३६।।

And having placed themselves before him they addressed him and said "Have pity upon us, O lord, and save us, who have come to thee for help, from the Daityas.

त्रैलोक्ययज्ञभागाश्च दैत्यैर्ह्रादपुरोगमैः।।
हृता नो ब्रह्मणोप्याज्ञामुल्लंघ्य परमेश्वर।। ३७।।

O supreme lord, transgressing the commands of Brahmā, the demons headed by Hrāda, have taken possession of the three worlds and appropriated the offerings which are our portion.

यद्यप्यशेषभूतस्य वयं ते च तवांशजाः।।
तथाप्यविद्याभेदेन भिन्नं पश्यामहे जगत्।। ३८।।

Though thou art at one with the endless creation and we are a portion of thyself, we, impressed by illusions, behold all things of the universe as distinct.

स्ववर्णधर्माभिरता वेदमार्गानुसारिणः।।
न शक्यास्तेरयो हंतुमस्माभिस्तपसावृताः।। ३९।।

Our enemies are engaged in the duties of their respective orders, follow the paths laid down by sacred writings and practise religious penances so we cannot lay them.

तमुपायमशेषात्मन्नस्माकं दातुमर्हसि।।
येन तानसुरान्हंतुं भवेम भगवान्क्षमाः।। ४०।।

O thou of immeasurable wisdom, do thou so instruct us that we may root out the enemies of the celestials."

श्रीपराशर उवाच

इत्युक्तो भगवांस्तेभ्यो मायामोहं शरीरतः।।
समुत्पाद्य ददौ विष्णुः प्राह चेदं सुरोत्तमान्।। ४१।।

When the glorious Viṣṇu heard their prayers he emitted from his person an illusory form which he gave to the celestials and said.

मायामोहोयमखिलान्दैत्यां स्तान्मोहयिष्यति।।
ततो वध्या भविष्यंति वेदमार्गबहिष्कृताः।। ४२।।
स्थितौ स्थितस्य मे वध्या यावंतः परिपंथिनः।।
ब्रह्मणो ह्यधिकारस्य देवा दैत्यादिकाः सुराः।। ४३।।

"This illusory form shall so deceive the Daityas, that being led astray from the path of the Vedas, they shall be slain; for all gods, demons and others, who shall transgress the authority of the Veda, shall perish by my prowess which I exercise for the preservation of the universe.

तद्गच्छत न भीः कार्या मायोहोयमग्रतः।।
गच्छन्नद्योपकाराय भवतां भविता सुराः।। ४४।।

श्रीपराशर उवाच

इत्युक्ताः प्रणिपत्यैनं ययुर्देवा यथागतम्।।
मायामोहोपि तैस्सार्द्धं ययौ यत्र महासुराः।। ४५।।

Go then; be not affraid; this illusory form shall go before you. O celestials, it shall be of great service to you, this day."

।। इति श्रीविष्णुमहापुराणे तृतीयेंशे सप्तदशोऽध्यायः।। १७।।

अथ तृतीयेंशेः अष्टादशोऽध्यायः
Part III : Section 18

श्रीपराशर उवाच

तपस्यभिरतान्सोथ मायामोहो महासुरान्।।
मैत्रेय ददृशे गत्वा नर्मदातीरसंश्रितान्।। १।।

Parāśara said :—"O Maitreya, having proceeded to the Daityas the illusory form beheld them engaged in austere penances on the banks of the river Narmadā.

ततो दिगंबरो मुंडो बर्हिपिच्छधरो द्विज।।
मायामोहोऽसुरान् श्लक्ष्णमिदं वचनमब्रवीत्।। २।।

And approaching them in the guise of a naked mendicant, with his head-shaven and carrying a bunch of peacock's, feathers he addressed them gently

मायामोह उवाच

हे दैत्यपतयो ब्रूत यदर्थं तप्यते तपः।।
ऐहिकार्थश्च पारत्र्यं तपसः फलमिच्छथ।। ३।।

The deceptive figure said :—"O lords of Daitya race—why do you practice these devout penances? Do you expect rewards in this world or in the next?

असुरा ऊचुः

पारत्र्यफललाभाय तपश्चर्या महामते।।
अस्माभिरियमारब्धा किं वा तेऽत्र विवक्षितम्।। ४।।

The Asuras said :—"O thou of great mind, we have been engaged in these penances with a view to reap fruits in the next world. Do thou tell us if thou hast got anything to say on this."

मायामोह उवाच

कुरुध्वं मम वाक्यानि यदि मुक्तिमभीप्सथ।।
अर्हध्वमेनं धर्मं च मुक्तिद्वारसंवृतम्।। ५।।

The deceptive figure said :— "If you are desirous of final emancipation hear my words, for you will obtain the revelation which is the door to final happiness.

धर्मो विमुक्तेरर्होयं नैतस्मादपरो वरः।।
अत्रैव संस्थिताः स्वर्गं विमुक्तिं वा गमिष्यथ।। ६।।

The instructions, superior to which there is nothing, I will give you, are the secret path to final emancipation. If you follow them you shall either obtain heaven or exemption from future births.

अर्हध्व! धर्ममेतं च सर्वे यूयं महाबलाः।। ७।।

O ye gifted with mighty strength, you are worthy of these instructions."

श्रीपराशर उवाच

एवंप्रकारैर्बहुभिर्युक्तिदर्शनचर्चितैः ।।
मायामोहेन ते दैत्या वेदमार्गादपा कृताः।। ८।।
धर्मायैतदधर्माय सदेतन्न सदित्यपि।।
विमुक्तये त्विदं नैतद्विमुक्तिं संप्रयच्छति।। ९।।
परमार्थोयमत्यर्थं परमार्थो न चाप्ययम्।।
कार्यमेतदकार्यं च नैतदेवं स्फुटं त्विदम्।। १०।।
दिग्वाससामयं धर्मो धर्मोयं बहुवाससाम्।। ११।।

Parāśara said :—There did the illusory figure mislead the Daityas from the teachings of the Vedas by various persuations and many spacious arguments, teaching that the same-thing might be for the sake of virtue and of vice; might be and might not be; might or might not lead to final emancipation; might be the supreme object and not the supreme object; might be effect and not be effect; might be manifest and not be manifest; might be the duty of those who go naked and who go richly dressed.

इत्यनेकांतवादं च मायामोहेन नैकधा।।
तेन दर्शयता दैतयास्स्वधर्मं त्याजिता द्विज।। १२।।

And thus were the Daityas led astray from the path of their duties by the continued teachings of their illusory teacher, keeping up the equal truth of contradictory teachings.

अर्हतैतं महाधर्मं मायामोहेन ते यतः।।
प्रोक्तास्तमाश्रिता धर्ममर्हतास्तेन तेऽभवन्।। १३।।

And those were called Arhatas from the phrase he had employed of "Ye are worthy (Arhata) of this great teaching" that is of the false teachings which he induced them to follow.

त्रयीधर्मसमुत्सर्गं मायामोहेन तेऽसुराः।।
कारितास्तन्मया ह्यासंस्ततोन्ये तत्प्रचोदिताः।। १४।।

Thus did the illusory figure lead away the Asuras from the teachings of the Vedas. And being impressed by those teachings the Asuras initiated others in all those doctrines.

तैरप्यन्ये परे तैश्च तैरप्यन्ये परे च तैः।।
अल्पैरहोभिस्संत्यक्ता तैर्दैत्यैः प्रायशस्त्रयी।। १५।।

They in their turn became teachers of the same false doctrines to each other, they were all led away from the teaching of the Vedas.

पुनश्च रक्तांबरधृङ् मायामोहो जितेंद्रियः।।
अन्यानाहासुरान् गत्वा मृद्वल्पमधुराक्षरम्।। १६।।
स्वर्गार्थं यदि वो वांछा निर्वाणार्थमथासुराः।।
तदलं पशुघातादिदुष्टधर्मैर्द्धनबोधत्।। १७।।

Then putting on garments of red colour, with collyrium in his eyes, the illusory figure again addressed others of the same family in sweet and mild accents—"O ye demons, gifted with strength, if ye wish for heaven or final rest desist from the sinful massacre of animal and hear from me what you should do.

विज्ञानमयमेवैतदशेषमवगच्छत ।।
बुध्यध्वं मे वचः सम्यग्बुधैरेवमिहोदितम्।। १८।।

The whole universe is composed of discriminative knowledge; understand my words well for they have been uttered by the wise.

जगदेतदनाधारं भ्रांतिज्ञानार्थतत्परम्।।
रागादिदुष्टमत्यर्थं भ्राम्यते भवसंकटे।। १९।।

The world is without stay and is perpetually revolving in the straits of existence being engaged in the pursuit of erroneous knowledge and sullied by passion and others.

एवं बुध्यत बुध्यध्वं बुध्यतैवमितीरयन्।।
मायामोहः स दैत्येयान्धर्ममत्याज्ञन्निजम्।। २०।।

Parāśara said :—In this wise exclaiming to

them "Know (Budhyadwam) and they saying (Budhyate), it is known," those Daityas were led away from their own religion.

नानाप्रकारवचनं स तेषां युक्तियोजनम्।।
तथातथा त्रयीधर्मं तत्यजुस्ते यथायथा।। २१।।

They thus renounced their respective duties being impressed by the reasonings and argumetns of that illusory figure.

तेप्यन्येषां तथैवोचुरन्यैरन्ये तथोदिताः।।
मैत्रेय तत्यजुर्धर्मं वेदस्मृत्युदितं परम्।। २२।।

O Maitreya, they impressed, pursuaded others to do the same and thus the heresy spread and many abandoned the practices laid down by the Vedas and Smṛtis.

अन्यानप्यन्यपाषंडप्रकारैर्बहुभिद्द्विज।।
दैतेयान्मोहयामास मायामोहोतिमोहकृत्।। २३।।

O twice-born one, with various other erroneous teachings, the illsory figure converted many other Daityas.

स्वल्पेनैव हि कालेन मायामोहेन तेऽसुराः।।
मोहितास्तत्यजुस्सर्वां त्रयीमार्गाश्रितां कथाम्।। २४।।

Being thus deluded, the Asuras, in no time, abandoned the doctrines and rites laid down by the three Vedas.

केचिद्विनिंदां वेदानां देवानामपरे द्विज।।
यज्ञकर्मकलापस्य तथान्ये च द्विजन्मनाम्।। २५।।

Some of them, O twice-born one, spoke ill of the Vedas and others villified the celestials. Some spoke against the Vedic rites and sacrifices and others calumniated the Brāhmaṇas.

नैतद्युक्तिसहं वाक्यं हिंसाधर्माय चेष्यते।।
हवींष्यनलदग्धानि फलायेत्यर्भकोदितम्।। २६।।

"The precepts" they preached "that lead to the sacrifice of animals, are highly culpable. To say that throwing clarified butter in fire produces rewards is simply childishness.

यज्ञैरनेकैर्देवत्वमवाप्येंद्रेण भुज्यते।।
शम्यादि यदि चेत्काष्ठं तद्वरं पत्रभुक्पशुः।। २७।।

If any one, after having obtained god head by multiplied ceremonies, is fed along with Indra upon the wood used as fuel in holy fire, he is lower than a brute which feeds upon leaves.

निहतस्य पशोर्यज्ञे स्वर्गप्राप्तिर्यदीष्यते।।
स्वपिता यजमानेन किन्नु तस्मान्न हन्यते।। २८।।

If a beast, being sacrificed, attains to heaven, why does not the sacrificer slay his father in a sacrifice?

तृप्तये जायते पुंसो भुक्तमन्येन चेततः।।
कुर्याच्छ्राद्धं श्रमायान्नं न वहेषुः प्रवासिनः।। २९।।

If a dead person is satisfied if another is fed at a Śrāddha then why does not the food offered by his son reach him who resides at a distance?

जनश्रद्धेयमित्येतदवगम्य ततोत्र वः।।
उपेक्षा श्रेयसे वाक्यं रोचतां यन्मयेरितम्।। ३०।।

All these words therefore depend upon individual respect so it is better for you to neglect them and appreciated mine.

न ह्याप्तवादा नभसो निपतंति महीं सुराः।।
युक्तिमद्वचनं ग्राह्यं मयान्यैश्च भवद्विधैः।। ३१।।

The words of authority, O mighty Asuras, do not fall from heaven; reasonable words only are to be acknowledged by me and persons like yourselves."

श्रीपराशर उवाच

मायामोहेन ते दैत्याः प्रकारैर्बहुभिस्तथा।।
वृथापिता यथा नैषां त्रयी कश्चिदरोचयत्।। ३२।।

Parāśara said :—By these and similar reasonings the Daityas were led away and none of them any longer acknowledged the authority of the Vedas.

इत्थमुन्मार्गयातेषु तेषु दैत्येषु तेऽमराः।।
उद्योगं परमं कृत्वा युद्धाय समुपस्थिताः।। ३३।।

After the Daityas have thus been led astray, the gods, with careful preparations, addressed themselves for fight. And there again began a terrible encounter between the gods and demons.

ततो दैवासुरं युद्धं पुनरेवाभवद्द्विज।।
हताश्च तेऽसुरा देवैः सन्मार्गपरिपंथिनः।। ३४।।

And the demons were now defeated and slain by the gods who had adhered to the righteous path.

स्वधर्मकवचं तेषामभूद्यत्प्रथमं द्विज।।
तेन रक्षाऽभवत्पूर्वं निशुर्नष्टे च तत्र ते।। ३५।।

Formerly the Daityas were protected by the armour of their own religion and they were now slain for the desertion of that armour of religion.

ततो मैत्रेय तन्मार्गवर्त्तिनो येभवञ्जनाः।।
नग्नास्ते तैर्यतस्त्यक्तं त्रयीसंवरणं तथा।।
कृताश्च तेऽसुरा देवैर्नाना वेदविनिन्दकाः।। ३६।।

For that time, O Maitreya, those, have followed the religion preached by the illusory figure, are called nacked for they following a wrong track have thrown off the garment of the Vedas.

ब्रह्मचारीगृहस्थश्च वानप्रस्थस्तथाश्रमी।।
परिव्राड् वा चतुर्थोत्र पञ्चमो नोपपद्यते।। ३७।।

There are four orders of men, namely; the religious student, the householder, the hermit and the mendicant; there is no fifth order.

वस्तु संत्यज्य गार्हस्थ्यं वानप्रस्थो न जायते।।
परिव्राट् चापि मैत्रेय स नग्नः पापकृन्नरः।। ३८।।

The sinful man, who after relinquishing the order of the householder, does not become either a hermit or a mendicant, is said to be naked.

नित्यानां कर्मणां विप्र यस्य हानिरहर्निशम्।।
अकुर्वन्विहितं कर्म शक्तः पतति तद्दिने।। ३९।।

प्रायश्चित्तेन महता शुद्धिमाप्नोत्यनापदि।।
पक्षं नित्यक्रियाहानेः कर्त्ता मैत्रेय मानवः।। ४०।।

The man, who, although able, does neglect his parmanent observances for one day, commits sin for one day; and if he neglects them, not being in trouble, for a fortinight he can be purified only by arduous expiation.

संवत्सरं क्रियाहानिर्यस्य पुंसोभिजायते।।
तस्यावलोकनात्सूर्यो निरीक्ष्यस्साधुभिस्सदा।। ४१।।

स्पृष्टे स्नानं सचेलस्य शुद्धेर्हेतुर्महामते।।
पुंसो भवति तस्योक्ता न शुद्धिः पापकर्मणः।। ४२।।

The virtuous must see the sun after looking upon a person who has neglected his permanent observances for a year; if they have touched him they must bathe with their clothes on—but that vicious one has no individual expeation for himself.

देवर्षिपितृभूतानि यस्य विप्रस्य वेश्मनि।।
प्रयांत्यनर्चितान्यत्र लोके तस्मान्न पापकृत्।। ४३।।

There is no sinner on earth, more culpable, than one in whose house celestials, progenitors and spirits are left to sigh unworshipped.

संभाषणानुप्रश्नादि सहास्यं चैव कुर्वतः।।
जायते तुल्यता तस्य तेनैव द्विज वत्सरात्।। ४४।।

No man should associate, in residence, sitting or society with him on whose person or in whose house the gods, progenitors and spirits sigh.

देवादिनिश्वासहतं शरीरं यस्य वेश्म च।।
न तेन संकरं कुर्याद्गृहासनपरिच्छदैः।। ४५।।

Conversation, exchange of civilities or association with a man is equally reprehensible who for a year has not observed pious observances.

अथ भुंक्ते गृहे तस्य करोत्यास्यां तथासने।।
शेते चाप्येकशयने स सद्यस्तत्समो भवेत्।। ४६।।

And the man, who eats in the house of such a man, or sits down with him or sleep on the same couch with him, becomes instantly in the same way culpable.

देवतापितृभूतानि तथानभ्यर्च्य योऽतिथीन्।।
भुंक्ते स पातकं भुंक्ते निष्कृतिस्तस्य नेष्यते।। ४७।।

He who eats himself without satisfying the gods, manes, spirits and guests feeds upon his own iniquity and there is no salvation for such a person.

ब्राह्मणाद्यास्तु ये वर्णास्स्वधर्मादन्यतोमुखाः।।
यांति ते नग्नसंज्ञां तु हीनकर्मस्ववस्थिताः।। ४८।।

The Brāhmaṇas and men of other castes

who neglect their respective duties or take up a degraded profession are said to be naked.

चतुर्णां। यत्र वर्णानां मैत्रेयात्यंत संकरः।।
तत्रास्या साधुवृत्तीनामुपघाताय जायते।। ४९।।

To live in a place where there is an intermixture of four castes is deterimental to the character of the righteous.

अनभ्यर्च्य ऋषीन्देवान्पितृभूतातिथींस्तथा।।
यो भुंक्ते तस्य सँल्लापात्पतंति नरके नराः।। ५०।।

Those who converse with him who eats without offering a portion to the gods, the sages, the manes, spirits and guests, are doomed to hell.

तस्मादेतान्नरो नग्नांस्त्रयीसंत्यागदूषितान्।।
सर्वदा वर्जयेत्प्राज्ञ आलापस्पर्शनादिषु।। ५१।।

A wise man should not therefore talk with or come in contact with these heretics who are rendered impure for renouncing the three Vedas.

श्रद्धावद्भिः कृतं यत्नाद्देवान्पितृपितामहान्।।
न प्रीणयति तच्छ्राद्धं यद्येभिरवीलोकितम्।। ५२।।

A Śrāddha ceremoney, although performed with great care and devotion, if looked upon by these heretics does not please the gods or progenitors.

श्रूयते च पुराख्यातो राजा शतधनुर्भुवि।।
पत्नी च शैव्या तस्याभूदतिधर्मपरायणा।। ५३।।

As described, there was in the days of yore a king named Śatadhanu whose wife Saivya was a woman of great piety.

पतिव्रता महाभागा सत्यशौचदयान्विता।।
सर्वलक्षणसंपन्ना विनयेन नयेन च।।५४।।

She was faithful to her husband, kind, sicnere, pure, and gifted with every female accomplishment, humility and discretion.

स तु राजा तया सार्द्धं देवदेवं जनार्द्दनम्।।
आराधयायामास विभुं परमेण समाधिना।।५५।।

The king, with his wife, worshipped with great devotion Janārddana the lord of gods.

होमैर्जपैस्तथा दानैरुपवासैश्च भक्तितः।।
पूजाभिश्चानु दिवसं तन्मना नान्यमानसः।। ५६।।

He daily worshipped Him with wholemindedness, oblations to fire, prayers, gifts and fasting.

एकदा तु समं स्नातौ तौ तु भार्यापती जले।।
भागीरथ्यास्समुत्तीर्णौ कार्त्तिक्यां समुपोषितौ।।
पाषंडिनमपश्येतामायांतं सम्मुखं द्विज।। ५७।।

चापाचार्यस्य तस्यासौ सखा राज्ञो महात्मनः।।
अतस्तद्गौरवात्तेन सखाभावमथाकरोत्।।५८।।

न तु सा वाग्यता देवी तस्य पत्नी पतिव्रता।।
उपोषितास्मीति रविं तस्मिन्दृष्टे ददर्श च।। ५९।।

One day when they had fasten on the full moon of Kārtika and had bathed in the Bhagirathi, they saw as they came up from the river, a heretic to approach them who was the friend of the king's military preceptor. The king, out of his respect for the preceptor, entered into conversation with him but his devoted wife Saivya did not utter a single word. And thinking that she was fasting she turned from him and looked towards the sun.

समागस्य यथान्यायं दंपती तो यथाविधि।।
विष्णोः पूजादिकं सर्वं कृतवंतौ द्विजोत्तम।। ६०।।

Having arrived at home, the husband and wife as usual perfromed the worship of Viṣṇu.

कालेन गच्छता राजा ममारासौ सपत्नजित्।।
अन्वारुरोह तं देवी चितास्थं भूपतिं पतिम्।। ६१।।

After a time the king, who had defeated all his enemies, died and the queen ascended the funeral pile of her husband.

स तु तेनापचारेण श्वा जज्ञे वसुधाधिपः।।
उपोषितेन पाषंडसँल्लापो यत्कृतोऽभवत्।। ६२।।

On account of the sin committed by Śatadhanu for speaking to a heretic while fasting he was born again as a dog.

सा तु जातिस्मरा जज्ञे काशीराजसुता शुभा।।
सर्वविज्ञानसंपूर्णा सर्वलक्षणपूजिता।। ६३।।

His wife was born as the daughter of the

king of Kāśī having a knowledge of her former birth, versed in every science and gifted with every virtue.

तां पिता दातुकामोभूद्वराय विनिवारितः।।
तयैव तन्व्याविरतो विवाहारंभतो नृपः।। ६४।।

Her father was anxious to marry her with a good husband, but she always opposed and the king was prevented from celebrating the nuptials.

ततस्सा दिव्यया दृष्ट्या दृष्ट्वा श्वानं निजं पतिम्।।
विदिशाख्यं पुरं गत्वा तदवस्थं ददर्श तम्।। ६५।।

The daughter of the king of Kāśī, by the knowledge of her pristine birth, saw that her husband was born as a dog in the city of Viśidhā.

तं दृष्ट्वैव महाभागं श्वभूतं तु पतिं तदा।।
ददौ तस्मै वराहारं सत्कारप्रवणं शुभा।। ६६।।

And having gone there she saw her husband in that plight. And knowing that animal to be her husband she placed upon his neck the bridal garland going through the marriage rites and prayers.

भुञ्जन्दत्तं तया सोन्नमतिमृष्टमभीप्सितम्।।
स्वजाति ललितं कुर्वन्बहु चाटु चकार वै।। ६७।।

And being pleased with the excellent food offered, the animal expressed his joy after the manner of his species.

अतीव व्रीडिता बाला कुर्वता चाटु तेन सा।।
प्रणामपूर्वमाहेदं दयितं तं कुयोनिजम्।। ६८।।

He thus sporting as a dog, she was greatly ashamed and bowing unto her husband„ born as a dog, she said :—

स्मर्यतां तन्महाराज दाक्षिण्यललितं त्वया।।
येन श्वयोनिमापन्नो मम चाटुकरो भवान्।। ६९।।

"O king, remember the civilities shown by you (towards your preceptor's friend) for which thou hast been born as a dog and art fawning upon me.

पाषंडिनं समाभाष्य तीर्थस्नानादनंतरम्।।
प्राप्तोसि कुत्सितां योनिं किन्न स्मरसि तत्प्रभो।।७०।।

Dost thou not remember, O My lord, that by conversing with a heretic after bathing in sacred river, thou hast been born as a dog?"

श्रीपराशर उवाच

तयैवं स्मारिते तस्मिन्पूर्वजातिकृते तदा।।
दध्यौ चिरमथा वाप निर्वेदमतिदुर्लभम्।। ७१।।

Parāśara said :—Being thus reminded the king called to his memory his former condition and was wrapt in meditation and felt humiliation.

निर्विण्णचित्तस्स ततो निर्गम्य नगराद्बहिः।।
मरुत्प्रपतनं कृत्वा सार्गालीं योनिमागतः।। ७२।।

With a broken heart he went away from the city and falling dead in a desert he was again born as a jackal.

सापि द्वितीये संप्राप्ते वीक्ष्य दिव्येन चक्षुषा।।
ज्ञात्वा सृगालं तं द्रष्टुं ययौ कोलाहलं गिरिम्।। ७३।।

In the following year the princess, again by her knowledge, perceived that he was born as a jackal and went to the mount Kolāhala to find him out.

तत्रापि दृष्ट्वा तं प्राह सार्गालीं योनिमागतम्।।
भर्त्तारमपि चार्वंगी तनया पृथिवीक्षितः।। ७४।।

Finding him there the beautiful daughter of the king thus spoke to her lord born as a jackal—

अपि स्मरसि राजेंद्र श्वयोनिस्थस्य यन्मया।।
प्रोक्तं ते पूर्वचरितं पाषंडालापसंश्रयम्।। ७५।।

"O king, dost thou not remember thy conversation with the heretic which I called to thy memory, when thou wast a dog?

पुनस्त योक्तं स ज्ञात्वा सत्यं सत्यवतां वरः।।
कानने स निराहारस्तत्याज स्वं कलेवरम्।। ७६।।

Thus accosted the king perceived what the princess had said was ture. Thereupon he abstained from eating and died.

भूयस्ततो वृको जज्ञे गत्वा तं निर्जने वने।।
स्मारयामास भर्त्तारं पूर्ववृत्तमनिंदिता।। ७७।।

न त्वं वृको महाभाग राजा शतधनुर्भवान्।।
श्वा भूत्वा त्वं सृगालोऽभूर्वृकत्वं सांप्रतं गतः।।७८।।

He was then born as a wolf but his wife repairing to a lonely forest again called back to the recollection of her husband his former state "O noble lord, thou art not a wolf but the king Śatadhanu. Thou wast born as a dog, then as a jackal and thou hast been born as a wolf."

स्मारितेन यथा व्यक्तस्तेनात्मा गृध्रतां गतः।।
अपापा सा पुनश्चैनं बोधयामास भामिनी।। ७९।।

Parāśara said :—Upon thus recollecting his former state the king renounced the life and was born again as a vulture.

नरेंद्र स्मर्यतामात्मा ह्यलं ते गृध्रचेष्टया।।
पाषंडालापजातोऽयं दोषो यद्गृध्रतां गतः।। ८०।।

His loving queen again found him in that state and called back to his memory his former condition.

ततः काकत्वमापन्नं समनंतरजन्मति।।
उवाच तन्वी भर्त्तारमुपलभ्यात्मयोगतः।। ८१।।

"O king" she cried out, "remember thy true self—do thou renounce this ugly form to which thou hast been condemned by the sin consequent upon thy conversing with a heretic."

अशेषभूभृतः पूर्वं वश्या यस्मै बलिं ददुः।।
स त्वं काकत्वमापन्नो जातोद्य बलिभुक् प्रभो।।८२।।

एवमेव बकत्वेपि स्मारितस्स पुरातनम्।।
तत्त्याज भूपतिः प्राणान्मयूरत्वमवाप च।। ८३।।

The king was next born as a crow and the princess making him out by virtue of her knowledge of the pristine birth thus spoke to her lord "O lord , thou art now being born as a crow eating the tributary grain, to whom, in a previous birth, all other kings paid tribute." Being thus reminded of his former birth the king renounced the body and was born again as a peacock.

मयूरत्वे ततस्सा वै चकारानुगतिं शुभा।।
दत्तैः प्रतिक्षणं भोज्यैर्बाला तज्जातिभोजनैः।।८४।।

Thereupon the beautiful princess began to pet him and feed him with such food as is agreeable to the peacocks.

ततस्तु जनको राजा वाजिमेधं महाक्रतुम्।।
चकार तस्यावभृथे स्नापयामास तं तदा।।८५।।

Thereupon the king, Janaka, undertook the celebration of a mighty horse sacrifice. In the ablutions with which it ended the princess caused his peacock to be bathed, bathing also herself.

सस्नौ स्वयं च तन्वंगी स्मारयामास चापि तम्।।
यथासौ श्वसृगालादियोनिं जग्राह पार्थिवः।। ८६।।

She then reminded Śatadhanu how he had been successively born as various animals.

स्मृतजन्मक्रमस्सोथ तत्त्याज स्वकलेवरम्।।
जज्ञे स जनकस्यैव पुत्रोसौ सुमहात्मनः।।८७।।

One recollecting this he renounced his life. He was then born as the son of the high-souled king Janaka.

ततस्सा पितरं तन्वी विवाहार्थमचोदयत्।।
स चापि कार यामास तस्या राजा स्वयंवरम्।।८८।।

Then the princess, having a slender person, expressed her desire to her father to be wedded.

स्वयंवरे कृते सा तं संप्राप्तं पतिमात्मनः।।
वरयामास भूयोपि भर्त्तृभावेन भामिनी।।८९।।

Her father too announced for a Swayamvara. When all had assembled at that meeting that chaste damsel found out her (former) lord and again elected him as her husband.

बुभुजे च तया सार्द्धं संभोगान्नृपनंदनः।।
पितर्युपरते राज्यं विदेहेषु चकार सः।।९०।।

The prince lived happily with her and on the death of her father ruled over the country of Videha.

इयाज यज्ञान्सुबहून्ददौ दानानि चार्थिनाम्।।
पुत्रानुत्पादयामास युयुधे च सहारिभिः।।९१।।

He celebrated many sacrifices and distributed many gifts and begot sons and defeated many enemies in war.

राज्यं भुक्त्वा यथान्यायं पालयित्वा वसुंधराम्।।
तत्त्याज स प्रियान्प्राणान्संग्रामे धर्मतो नृपः।। ९२।।

Having ruled duly and cherished the earth that king renounced his life in battle as became the warrior caste.

ततश्चितास्थं तं भूयो भर्त्तारं सा शुभेक्षणा।।
अन्वारुरोह विधिवद्यथापूर्वं मुदान्विता।। ९३।।

The princess again followed him in death and in agreement with sacred precepts once more mounted cheerfully his funeral pyre.

ततोऽवाप तया सार्द्धं राजपुत्र्या स पार्थिवः।।
ऐंद्रानतीत्य वै लोकाँल्लोकान्प्राप तदाक्षयान्।। ९४।।
स्वर्गाक्षयत्वमतुलं दांपत्यमतिदुर्लभम्।।
प्राप्तं पुण्यफलं प्राप्य संशुद्धिं तां द्विजोत्तम्।। ९५।।

Thereupon the king, with the princess, attained to the regions beyond the region of Indra, where all desires are for ever satisfied, obtaining eternal and unequalled bliss in heaven, the consummate happiness that is the reward of conjugal fidelity which is hardly attained.

एष पाषंडसंभाषाद्दोषः प्रोक्तो मया द्विज।।
तथाश्वमेधावभृथस्नानमाहात्म्यमेव च।। ९६।।

I have thus describle to you, O Maitreya, the sin consequent upon conversing with a heretic and effects of bathing after the solemn sacrifice of a horse.

तस्मात्पाषंडिभिः पापैरालापस्पर्शनं त्यजेत्।।
विशेषतः क्रियाकाले यज्ञादौ चापि दीक्षितः।। ९७।।

A man should therefore carefully avoid the conversation or coming in contact with a heretic especially at seasons of devotion and when engaged in the performance of the religious rites before a sacrifice.

क्रियाहानिर्गृहे यस्य मासमेकं प्राजयते।।
तस्यावलोकनात्सूर्यं पश्येत मतिमान्नरः।। ९८।।

The prudent should look at the sun after seeing a person in whose house domestic ceremonies have been neglected for a mouth.

किं पुनर्यैस्तु संत्यक्ता त्रयी सर्वात्मना द्विज।।
पाषंडभिजिभिः पापैर्वेदवादविरोधिभिः।। ९९।।

And there is the greatest need of expiation if they meet persons who live upon other's rice and who have wholly abandoned the Vedas and who dispute the doctrines of sacred writings.

सहालापस्तु संसर्गः सहास्या चातिपापिनी।।
पाषंडिभिर्दुराचारैस्तस्मात्तं परिवर्जयेत्।। १००।।

पाषंडिनो विकर्मस्थान्बैडालव्रतिकाञ्छठान्।।
हैतुकान्बकवृत्तींश्च वाङ्मात्रेणापि नार्चयेत्।। १०१।।

A man should not even talk withheretics, those who do forbidden acts, pretended saints, scoundrels, sceptics and hypocretes; communication with such sinful wretches ever at a distance, all association with schismatics pollutes a man; a man should therefore carefully avoid them.

दूरतस्तैस्तु संपर्कस्त्याज्यश्चाप्यतिपापिभिः।।
पाषंडिभिर्दुराचारैस्तस्मात्तान्परिवर्जयेत्।। १०२।।

एते नग्नास्तवाख्याता दृष्ट्वा श्राद्धोपघातकाः।।
येषां संभाषणात्पुंसा दिनपुण्यं प्रणश्यति।। १०३।।

These are the persons, O Maitreya, called naked, the meaning of which term you wanted me to explain. If they witness a Śrāddha ceremony that becomes fruitless—communication with whom spoils the piety of one day.

एते पाषंडिनः पापा न ह्येतानालपेद्बुधः।।
पुण्यं नश्यति संभाषादेतेषां तद्दिनोद्भवम्।। १०४।।

These are the heretics with whom the wise should not converse—and speaking to whom destroys the virtue he might have obtained on that day.

पुंसां जटाधरणमौंड्यवतां वृथैव
मोघाशिनामखिलशौचनिराकृतानम्।।
तोयप्रदानपितृपिंडबहिष्कृतानां
संभाषणादपि नरा नरकं प्रयांति।। १०५।।

Men fall into hell if they converse with them who uselessly asume the twisted hair and shaven head, who eat without offering food to gods, spirits and guest and those who do not offer cakes and libation of water to their manes.

।।इति श्रीविष्णुमहापुराणे तृतीयेंशेऽष्टादशोऽध्यायः।। १८।।

।। श्रीविष्णुमहापुराणे तृतीयांशस्समाप्तः।।

।। अथ श्रीविष्णुमहापुराणे चतुर्थोंशः ।।

THE VIṢṆUMAHĀPURĀṆAM, PART - IV

।। श्रीमते रामानुजाय नमः ।।

अथ चतुर्थेंशेः प्रथमोऽध्यायः

Part IV : Section 1

मैत्रेय उवाच

भगवन्यन्नरैः कार्य्यं। साधुकर्मण्यवस्थितैः।।
तन्मह्यं गुरुणाख्यातं नित्यनैमित्तिकात्मकम्।। १।।

Maitreya said :—O venerable sir, you have described to me the permanent and occasional observances to be observed by those pious individuals who are diligent in their devotions.

वर्णधर्मास्तथाख्याता धर्मा ये चाश्रमेषु च।।
श्रोतुमिच्छाम्यहं वंशं राज्ञां तद्ब्रूहि मे गुरौ।। २।।

You have also described to me the duties which appertain to several castes and several orders of men. I wish you to relate to me now the dynasties of the kings who have ruled over the earth.

श्रीपराशर उवाच

मैत्रेय श्रूयतामयमनकयज्वशूरवीरधीर-
भूपालालंकृतो ब्रह्मादिर्मानवो वंशः।। ३।।

Parāśara said :—Hear O Maitreya, I shall describe to you the family of Manu beginning with Brahmā and comprising a number of pious, high-minded and heroic princes.

तदस्य वंशास्यानुपूर्वीमशेषवंश
पापप्रणाशनाय मैत्रेयैतां कथां शृणु।। ४।।

It is said, that never does his family become extinct, who daily calls to his mind the family of Manu springing from Brahmā. Hear, therefore, O Maitreya, an account of the origin of his family, hearing which all sins shall be removed.

तद्यथा सकलजगतामादिरनादिभूतस्स ऋग्यजु-
स्सामादिमयो भगवान् विष्णुस्तस्य ब्रह्मणो मूर्त्तं रूपं
हिरण्यगर्भो ब्रह्मांडभूतो ब्रह्मा भगवान् प्राग्बभूव।।५।।

From the mundane egg originated Brahmā, who was Hiraṇyagarbha, the form of that supreme Brahmā which consists of Viṣṇu as identical with Ṛg, Yajur and Sāma Vedas—the first, uncreated cause of all worlds.

ब्रह्मणश्च दक्षिणांगुष्ठजन्मा दक्षप्रजापतिः
दक्षस्याप्यदितिरदितेर्विवस्वान् विव स्वतो मनुः।। ६।।

From the right thumb of Brahmā originated the Patriarch Dakṣa whose daughter was Aditi, who was the mother of the sun.

मनोरिक्ष्वाकुनृगधृष्टशर्यातिनरिष्यंतप्रांशुना-
भागदिष्टकरूषपृषध्राख्या दश पुत्रा बभूवुः।। ७।।

From the sun sprang Manu whose sons were Ikṣavāku, Nṛga, Dvṛṣṭa, Śaryāti, Nariśyanta, Prānśu, Nabhāga, Nediṣta Kāruṣa, and Pṛṣadhra.

इष्टिं च मित्रावरुणयोर्मनुः पुत्रकामश्चकार।। ८।।

तत्र तावदह्वते होतुरपचारादिला नाम कन्या बभूव।। ९।।

Being desirous of having offspring formerly Manu celebrated a sacrifice in honour of Mitra and Varuṇa; but the ceremony being unsuccessful on account of some irregularity from the presiding priest a daughter Ilā was born.

सेव च मित्रावरुणयोः प्रसादात्सुद्युम्नो
नाम मनोः पुत्रो मैत्रेय आसीत्।। १०।।

But by the mercy of the two deities however, her sex was changed and she became a man under the name of Sudyumna.

पुनश्चेश्वरकोपात्स्त्री सती सा तु सोमसूनो-
र्बुधस्याश्रमसमीपे बभ्राम।। ११।।

And he again became a woman under an imprecation (from Śiva) near the hermitage of Budha, the son of the moon.

सानुरागाच्च तस्यां बुधः पुरूरवसमात्मजमुत्यादया-
मास।। १२।।

One day while she was walking near the hermitage of Budha, he became attached to her and begot on her a son named Purūravas.

जातेपि तस्मिन्नमिततेजोभिः परमर्षिभिरिष्टिमय
ऋङ्मयो यजुर्मयस्साममयोथर्वणमयस्सर्ववेदमयो
मनोमयो ज्ञानमयो न किंचिन्मयोन्नमयो भगवान्
यज्ञपुरुषस्वरूपी सुद्युम्नस्य पुंस्त्वमभिलषद्भिर्यथाव
दिष्टस्तत्प्रसादादिला पुनरपि सुद्युम्नोऽभवत्।। १३।।

तस्याप्युत्कलगयविनतास्त्रयः पुत्रा बभूवुः।। १४।।

After his birth, the noble Ṛṣis, desiring to restore Sudyumna to his sex, prayed to the glorious Viṣṇu who is the essence of the four Vedas, of mind, of every thing and of nothing and who is the sacrificed male. By his mercy Ilā once more became Sudymna, in which character he had three sons, Utkala, Gaya and Vinatā.

सुद्युम्नस्तु स्त्रीपूर्वकत्वाद्रा ज्यभागं न लेभे।। १५।।

On account of his having been formerly born a female he did not receive any portion of his paternal kingdom.

तत्पित्रा तु वसिष्ठवचनात्प्रतिष्ठानं नाम नगरं
सुद्युम्नाय दत्तं तच्चासौ पुरूरवसे प्रादात्।। १६।।

His father however at the request of Vasiṣṭha conferred upon him the city of Pratiṣṭhā, and he gave it to Purūravas.

तदन्वयाश्च क्षत्त्रियास्सर्वे दिक्ष्वभवन्।।
प्रषध्रस्तु मनुपुत्रो गुरुगोवधाच्छूद्रत्वमगमत्।। १७।।

Of the other sons of Manu, Pṛṣadhra, on account of the sin consequent upon slaying a cow, was degraded to the condition of a Śūdra.

मनोः पुत्रः करूषः करूषात्कारूषाः क्षत्रिया
महाबलपराक्रमा बभूवुः।। १८।।

From Kāruṣa sprang the heroic persons named Kāruṣas.

दिष्टपुत्रस्तु नाभागो वैश्यतामगमत्तस्माद्बलंधनः
पुत्रोभवत्।। १९।।

बलंधनाद्वत्सप्रीतिरुदारकीर्त्तिः।। २०।।

वत्सप्रीतेः प्रांशुरभवत्।। २१।।

प्रजापतिश्च प्रांशोरेकोऽभवत्।। २२।।

ततश्च खनित्रः।। २३।।

तस्माच्चक्षुषः।। २४।।

चक्षुषाच्चातिबलपराक्रमो विंशोभवत्।। २५।।

ततो विविंशकः।। २६।।

तस्माच्च खनिनेत्रः।। २७।।

ततश्चातिविभूतिः।। २८।।

अतिविभूतेरतिबलपराक्रमः करंधमः पुत्रोभवत्।। २९।।

तस्मादप्यविक्षित्।। ३०।।

अविक्षितोप्यतिबलपराक्रमः पुत्रो मरुत्ते
नामाऽभवत्।।

यस्येमावद्यापि श्लोकौ गीयेते।। ३१।।

मरुत्तस्य यथा यज्ञस्तथा कस्यभवद्भुवि।।
सर्वं हिरण्मयं यस्य यज्ञवस्त्वतिशोभनम्।। ३२।।

The son of Nediṣtha, named Nabhāga became a Vaiśya; his son was Bhālandana, whose son was the well-known Vātsaprī; his son was Prānśu, whose son was Prajanī, whose son was Khanitra, whose son was the brave Cakṣuṣa, whose son was Viṁśa, whose son was Vivinśatī, whose son was Khaninetra, whose son was the powerful, rich, and heroic Karandhama, whose son was Avikṣit, whose son was the powerful Marutta, regarding whom this celebrated verse is recited—"Who else on this earth has been able to celebrate a sacrifice like one celebrated by Marutta? All the implements and utensils were made of gold.

अमाद्यदिंद्रस्सोमेन दक्षिणा भिर्द्विजातयः।।
मरुतः परिवेष्टारस्सदस्याश्च दिवौकसः।। ३३।।

Indra was intoxicated with the drinking of Soma juice and all the Brāhmaṇas were greatly pleased on having liberal presents. In his sacrifice the winds were the guards and the other celestials were the courtiers.

स मरुत्तश्चक्रवर्त्ती नरिष्यंतनामानं पुत्रमवाप।। ३४।।

तस्माच्च दमः।। ३५।।

दमस्य पुत्रो राजवर्धनो जज्ञे।।

राजवर्द्धनात्सुवृद्धिः।। ३७।।

सुवृद्धेः केवलः।। ३८।।

केवलात्सुधृतिरभूत्।। ३९।।

ततश्च नरः।। ४०।।

तस्माच्चंद्रः।। ४१।।

ततः केवलोभूत्।। ४२।।

केवलाद्बंधुमान्।। ४३।।

बंधुमतो वेगवान्।। ४४।।

वेगवतो बुधः।। ४५।।

ततश्च तृण बिंदुः।। ४६।।

तस्याप्येका कन्या इलविलानाम।। ४७।।

Marutta was a lord paramount; he had a son named Nariśyanta; his son was Dama; his son was Rāyavarddana; his son was Suddhṛti; his son was Nara; his son was Kevala; his son was Bandhumat; his son was Vegavat; his son was Budha; his son was Tṛṇavandu, who had a daughter under name of Ilāvila.

ततश्चालंबुसानाम वराप्सरातृणबिंदुं भेजे।। ४८।।

तस्यामप्यस्य विशालो जज्ञे यः पुरीं विशालां निर्ममे।।
४९।।

Being enermoured of Tṛṇavindu, the nymph Alambuṣā bore him a son named Viśāla by whom by whom the city Vaiśāli was founded.

हे चंद्रश्च विशालस्य पुत्रोभवत्।। ५०।।

ततश्चंद्रः।। ५१।।

तत्तनयो धूम्राक्षः।। ५२।।

तस्यापि सृञ्जयोऽभूत्।। ५३।।

सृञ्जयात्सहदेवः।। ५४।।

ततश्च कृशाश्वो नाम पुत्रोभवत्।। ५५।।

सोमदत्तः कृशाश्वाज्जज्ञे योश्वमेधानां शतमाजहार।।५६।।

तत्पुत्रो जनमेजयः।। ५७।।

जनमेजयात्सुमतिः।। ५८।।

Vinatā had a son whose name was Hemacandra; his son was Sucandra; his son was Dhūmrāśva; his son was Śrīñjaya; his son was Sahadeva; his son was Kṛṣāśva; his son was Somadatta, who performed ten times the sacrifice of a horse; his son was Janamejaya, whose son was Sunati.

एते वैशालिका भूभृतः।।५९।।

श्लोकोप्यत्र गीयते।। ६०।।

तृणबिंदोः प्रसादेन सर्वे वैशालिका नृपाः।।
दीर्घायुषो महात्मानो वीर्यवंतोतिधार्मिकाः।। ६१।।

These kings are known as Vaiśālas of them it is said—"By the mercy of Tṛṇavindhu all the kings of Vaiśāli were longlived, magnanimous and just brave."

शर्यातेः कन्या सुकन्यानामाभवत् यामुपयेमे च्यवनः।।
६२।।

Śaryāti had a daughter named Sukanyā. Cyavana married her.

आनर्त्तनामा परमधार्मिकश्शर्यातिपुत्रोभवत्।। ६३।।

आनर्त्तस्यापि रेवतनामा पुत्रो जज्ञे योसावानर्त्तविषयं
बुभुजे पुरीं च कुशस्थलीमध्युवास।। ६४।।

He had a pious son named Anartta, who had a son called Revata who governed the country called after the name of his father Anartta and lived at the capital called Kuśasthalī.

रेवतस्यापि रैवतः पुत्रः ककुद्मिनामा
धर्मात्मा भ्रातृशतस्य ज्येष्ठोऽभवत्।। ६५।।

The son of this king was Raivata or Kakudmin, the eldest of a hundred brethern.

तस्य रेवतीनाम कन्याभवत्।। ६६।।

He had a daughter named Revatī.

स तामादाय कस्येयमर्हतीति भगवंतमब्ज-
योनिं प्रष्टुं ब्रह्मलोकं जगाम।। ६७।।

He repaired with her to the region of Brahmā to consult with the god springing from lotus upon whom to confer her.

तावच्च ब्रह्मणोंतिके हाहाहूहूसंज्ञाभ्यां
गंधर्वाभ्यामतितानं नाम दिव्यं गांधर्वमगीयत।। ६८।।

When he reached there the Gandharvas, Hāhā and Hūhū, were singing before Brahmā and Raivata waited there till they had finished.

तच्च त्रिमार्गपरिवृत्तैरनेकयुगपरिवृत्तिं
तिष्ठन्नपि रैवतश्शृण्वन्मुहूर्त्तमिव मेने।। ६९।।

And the ages passed away during the performances seemed to him as a moment.

गीतावसाने च भगवंतमब्जयोनिं प्रणम्य रैवतः
कन्यायोग्यं वरमपृच्छत्।। ७०।।

When they had finished singing Raivata laid himself low before Brahmā and asked him about a fit bridegroom.

ततश्चासौ भगवानकथयत् कथय योभिमतस्ते वर
इति।। ७१।।

Brahmā said—"Whom should you wish for a son-in-law?"

पुनश्च प्रणम्य भगवते तस्मै
यथाभिमतानात्मनस्स वरान् कथयामास।।
क एषां भगवातोभिमत इति
यस्मै कन्यामिमां प्रयच्छामीति।। ७२।।

And bowing again Raivata mentioned to him various persons whom he liked.

ततः किंचिदवनतशिरास्ससस्मितं भगवानब्जयोनिराह।।
७३।।

य एते भवतोभिता नैतेषां सांप्रतं
पुत्रपौत्रापत्यापत्यसंततिरस्त्यवनीतले।। ७४।।

Nodding his head and smiling graciously Brahmā said to him—"Of those whom you have mentioned there is no trace of their family on earth.

बहूनि तवात्रेव गांधर्वं शृण्वतश्चतुर्यगान्यतीतानि।। ७५।।
सांप्रतं महीतलेष्टाविंशतितममनोश्चतुर्युगमतीतप्रायं वर्तते।।
७६।।

Many ages have passed away whilst you were listening to the songs of Gandharvas. Now the twenty-eighth graeat age of the present Manu is well-nigh gone.

आसन्नो हि कलिः।। ७७।।

Kali is fast appraoching.

अन्यस्मै कन्यारत्नमिदं भवतैकाकिनाभिमताय देयम्।।
७८।।

भवतोपि पुत्रमित्रकलत्रमंत्रिभृत्यबंधुबल-
कोशादयस्समस्ताः कालेनैतेनात्यंतमतीताः।। ७९।।

You alone give away this jewel of a daughter to some body; all thy friends ministers, servants, wife, kinsmen, armies, wealth have along since been taken away by the hand of Time."

ततः पुनरप्युत्पन्नसाध्वसो राजा भगवंतं प्रणम्य
पप्रच्छ।। ८०।।

भगवन्नेवमवस्थिते मयेयं कस्मै देयेति।। ८१।।

ततस्स भगवान् किंचिदवनम्रकंधरः
कृताञ्जलिर्भूत्वा सर्वलोकगुरुरंभोजयोनिराह।। ८२।।

That king, being terrified again, said, bowing, to Brahmā "O lord, such being the circumstance, upon whom shall I confer this daughter?" Thereupon nodding, the preceptor of the seven worlds—the god, whose throne is lotus, said to the king, standing humbly before—

ब्रह्मोवाच

न ह्यादिमध्यांतमजस्य यस्य विद्मो वयं सर्वमयस्य धातुः।।
न च स्वरूपं न परं स्वभावं न चैव सारं परमेश्वरस्य।।
८३।।

"The being, whose beginning, middle or end we donot know, who exists in all, who is the creator, whose real and infinite nature and essence we do not know is (Viṣṇu).

कलामुहूर्त्तादिमयश्च कालो न यद्विभूतेः परिणामहेतुः।।
अजन्मनाशस्य सदैकमूर्त्तेरनामरूपस्य सनातनस्य।। ८४।।

His power cannot be measured by time, consisting of moments and hours and years; he has no birth or death—all objects are his form—he is eternal—he has no forms or name.

यस्य प्रसादादहमच्युतस्य मूर्त्तिः प्रजासृष्टिकरोंतकारी।।
क्रोधाच्च रुद्रः स्थितिहेतुभूतो यस्माच्च मध्ये पुरुषः।।
परस्मात्।। ८५।।

By the mercy of that imperishable being I am the agent of creation—Rudra is the agent of destruction and Viṣṇu is the agent of preservation.

तद्रूपमास्थाय सृजत्यजोयः
स्थितौ च योऽसौ पुरुषस्वषरूपी।।
रुद्रस्वरूपेण च योत्ति विश्वं
धत्ते तथानंतवपुस्समस्तम्।। ८६।।

He, assuming my form creates the universe; in his own essence he provides for its duration; in the form of Rudra he devours all things; and with the body of Ananta he upholds them.

पाकाय योग्नित्वमुपति लोकान्बिभर्त्ति पृथ्वीवपुरव्ययात्मा।।
शक्रादिरूपी परिपाति विश्वमर्केंदुरूपश्च तमो हिनस्ति।।
८७।।

In the person of Indra and other celestials he protects mankind and as the sun and moon he dispells darkness. Assuming the nature of fire he bestows warmth and maturity, and in that of earth he nourishes all beings.

करोति चेष्टाश्श्वसनस्वरूपी
लोकस्य तृप्तिं च जलान्नरूपी।।
ददाति विश्वस्थितिसंस्थितस्तु
सर्वावकाशं च नभस्स्वरूपी।। ८८।।

In the shape of air he give activity, in the shape of water he gives satisfaction and in the shape of sky he provides space for all objects.

यस्सृज्यते सर्गकृदात्मनैव यः
पाल्यते पालयिता च देवः।।
विश्वात्मकस्संह्रयतेंतकारी पृथक्
त्रयस्यास्य च योव्ययात्मा।। ८९।।

He, being creator, creates himself; he, being preserver, preserves himself; he, being destroyer, destroys his own universal form. He is imperishable; there is nothing distinct from him.

यस्मिञ्जगद्यो जगदेतदाद्यो यं चाश्रितोस्मिूजगति स्वयंभूः।।
स सर्वभूतप्रभावो धरित्र्यां स्वांशेन विष्णुर्नृप तेऽवतीर्णः।।
९०।।

In him is the world; he is the world; and he, the primeval self-born, is again present in the world. O king, the glorious Viṣṇu has incarnated a portion of himself on earth.

कुशस्थली या तव भूव रम्या पुरी पुराभूदमरावतीव।।
सा द्वारका संप्रति तत्र चास्ते स केशवांशो बलदेवनामा।।
९१।।

O king, your picturesque city Kuśasthalī, like the city of Indra, is now called Dwārakā. There reigns a portion of Keśava in the person of Beladeva.

तस्मै त्वमेनां तनयां नरेंद्र प्रयच्छ मायामनुजाय जायाम्।।
श्लाघ्यो वेरोसौ तनया तवेयं स्त्रीरत्नभूता सदृशो हि योगः।।
९२।।

O king, confer this daughter of thine upon him, who appears under the guise of a man. He is an excellent bridegroom for this gem of a daughter and she is a fit bride."

श्रीपराशर उवाच

इतीरितोसौ कमलोद्भवेन भुवं समासाद्य पतिः प्रजानाम्।।
ददर्श ह्रवान् पुरुषान् विरूपानल्पौजसस्स्वल्प
विवेकवीर्यान्।। ९३।।

Parāśara said :—Being thus advised by the deity springing from lotus, the king returned to earth and beheld mankind, greatly reduced in size and vigour and weakened in intellect.

कुशस्थलीं तां च पुरीमुपेत्य दृष्ट्वान्यरूपां प्रददौ स कन्याम्।।
सीरायुधाय स्फटिकाचलाभवक्षस्थलायातुलधीर्नरेंद्रः।।
९४।।

Thereupon that king, having incomparable wisdom, repairing to his own city Kuśasthalī which he saw greatly changed, gave his daughter to Baladeva whose breast was as fair and radiant as crystal.

उच्चप्रमाणामिति तामवेक्ष्य स्वलांगलाग्रेण च तालकेतुः।।
विनम्रयामास ततश्च सापि बभूव सद्यो वनिता यथान्या।।
९५।।

And beholding that damsel of excessive

height the king, whose banner is a palm tree, shortened her with the end of his ploughshare. Being thus shortened she became like other women.

तां रेवतीं रैवतभूपकन्यां सीरायुधोऽसौ विधिनोपयेमे।।
दत्त्वाथ कन्यां स नृपो जगाम हेमालयं वै तपसे धृतात्मा।।
१६।।

Balarāma thus married duly Revatī, the daughter of Raivata. And the king, too giving away daughter, retired to the mountain Himālaya and engaged in penances with a subdued mind.

।। इति श्रीविष्णुमहापुराणे चतुर्थेंशे प्रथमोऽध्यायः।। १।।

अथ चतुर्थेंशेः द्वितीयोऽध्यायः

Part IV : Section 2

श्रीपराशर उवाच

यावच्च ब्रह्मलोकात्स ककुद्मी रैवतो नाभ्येति तावत्पुण्यजनसंज्ञा राक्षसास्तामस्य पुरीं कुशस्थलीं निजघ्नुः।। १।।

Whilst Kakudmin Raivata was absent in the region of Brahmā, Rākṣasas named Puṇyajanas devastated his capital Kuśasthalī.

तच्चास्य भ्रातृशतं पुण्यजनत्रासाद्दिशो भेजे।। २।।

तदन्वयाश्च क्षत्रियास्सर्वदिक्ष्वभवन्।। ३।।

His hundred brothers, afraid of the enemies, fled in different directions and their descendant the Kṣatriyas settled all over the country.

वृष्टस्यापि वार्ष्टकं क्षत्रमभवत्।। ४।।

नाभागस्यात्मजो नाभागसंज्ञोभवत्।। ५।।

तस्याप्यंबरीषः।। ६।।

अंबरीषस्यापि विरूपोभवत्।। ७।।

विरूपात्पृषदश्वो जज्ञे।। ८।।

ततश्च रथीतरः।। ९।।

अत्रायं श्लोकः

एते क्षत्रप्रसूता वै पुनश्चांगिरसातः स्मृताः।।
रथीतराणां प्रवराः क्षत्रोपेता द्विजातयः।।इति।। १०।।

From Vṛstha originated the Kṣatriya race of Vārṣṭaka; the son of Nabhāga was Nābhaga; his son was Ambarīṣa; his son was Virūpa; his son was Prishadāśva; his son was Rathitara, of whom it is said—"these princes of Rathitara family, although Kṣatriyas by birth were called Aṅgirasas or sons of Aṅgirā and were Brāhmaṇas and Kṣatriyas.

क्षुतवतश्च मनोरिक्ष्वाकुः पुत्रो जज्ञे घ्राणतः।। ११।।

As Manu was sneezing Ikṣavāku was born from his nostril.

तस्य पुत्रशतप्रधाना विकुक्षिनिमिदंडाख्यास्त्रयः पुत्रा बभूवुः।। १२।।

He had a hundred sons of whom the three well-known were Vikukṣī, Nimī and Daṇḍa.

शकुनिप्रमुखः पंश्चाशत्पुत्राः उत्तरापथरक्षितारो बभुवुः।।
१३।।

These and fifty under Śakuni were the rulers of the north.

चत्वारिंशदष्टौ च दक्षिणापथभूपालाः।। १४।।

Forty-eight were the rulers of the south.

स चेक्ष्वाकुरष्टकायाश्श्राद्धमुत्पाद्य श्राद्धार्हं मांसमानयेति विकुक्षिमाज्ञापयामास।। १५।।

Being engaged in the celebration of an ancestral rite upon Aṣṭaka day Ikṣavāku ordered Vikukṣī to bring him flesh suitable for the offering.

स तथेति गृहीताज्ञो विधृतशरासनो
वनमभ्येत्यानेकशो मृगान् हत्वा
श्रांतोतिक्षुत्परीतो विकुक्षिरेकं शशमभक्षयत्।।
शेषं च मांसमानीय पित्रे निवेदयामास।। १६।।

The prince, therefore, went into woods and slew many a deer and other wild animals for the purpose. Being exhausted with hunting he was hungry; accordingly he sat down and ate a hare.

इक्ष्वाकुकुलाचार्यो वशिष्ठस्तत्प्रोक्षणाय चोदितः प्राह।। अलमनेनामेध्येनामिषेण दुरात्मना तव पुत्रेणैतन्मांसमुपहतं यतोऽनेन शशो भक्षितः।। १७।।

And being refreshed he carried the rest of the game to his father. Vasiṣtha, the family preist of Ikṣavākus, was invited to consecrate the food; but he said that it was impure on account of Vikukṣa's having eaten a hare from amongst it.

ततश्चासौ विकुक्षिर्गुरुणैवमुक्तश्शशादसंज्ञामवाप पित्रा च परित्यक्तः।। १८।।

Being thus informed by his spiritual preceptor the father abandoned his son who, in consequence thereof, received the epithet Śaśāda (hare-eater).

पितर्युपरते चासाव खिलामेतां पृथ्वीं धर्मतश्शशास।। १९।।

On the demise of his father he piously ruled over the earth.

शशादस्य तस्य पुरञ्जयोनाम पुत्रोभवत्।। २०।।

A son, Purañjaya by name, was born to him.

तस्येदं चान्यत्।। २१।।

पुरा हि त्रेतायां देवा सुरयुद्धमतिभीष्णमभवत्।। २२।।

There took place a dreadful conflict in the Tretā yuga between the gods and demons in which the former were defeated.

तत्र चातिबलिभिरसुरैरमराः पराजितास्ते भगवंतं विष्णुमाराधयाञ्चक्रुः।। २३।।

They accordingly repaired to Viṣṇu for help and propitiated him by their adorations.

प्रसन्नश्च देवानामनादिनिधनोखिलजगत्परायणो नारायणः प्राह।। २४।।

Being propitiated the primeval deity, the eternal ruler of the universe, Nārāyaṇa said to them—

ज्ञातमेतन्मया युष्माभिर्यदभिलषितं तदर्थमिदं श्रूयताम्।। २५।।

"What you have desired is known to me. Hear how your desires shall be fulfilled.

पुरञ्जयो नाम राजर्षेश्शशादस्य तनयः क्षत्रियवरो यस्तस्य शरीरेहमंशेन स्वयमेवावतीर्य तानशेषान-सुरान्निहनिष्यामि तद्भवद्भिः पुरञ्जयोऽसुरवधार्थमुद्योगं कार्यतामिति।। २६।।

There is a foremost Kṣatriya king named Purañjaya, son of the royal saint Śaśāda. Infusing a portion of myself into his body I shall descend on earth and slay all the demons. Do you so endeavour that Purañjaya might engage in the work of the destruction of Asuras."

एतच्च श्रुत्वा प्रणम्य भगवंतं विष्णुममराः पुरञ्जय-सकाशमाजग्मुरूचुश्चैनम्।। २७।।

Hearing those words the celestials bowed unto the glorious Viṣṇu and went to Parañjaya and addressed him, saying,

भोभोः क्षत्रियवर्यास्माभिरभ्यर्थितेन भवतास्माकम-रातिवधोद्यतानां कर्तव्यं साहाय्यमिच्छामः तद्भवतास्माकमभ्यागतानां प्रणयभंगो न कार्य इत्युक्तः पुरञ्जयः प्राह्।। २८।।

"O foremost of Kṣatriyas, we have come to thee to secure thy help in the destruction of our enemies in which we have been engaged. It will not behove thee to neglect our friendship who have come here."

त्रैलोक्यनाथो योयं युष्माकमिंद्रः शतक्रतुरस्य यद्यहं स्कंधाधिरूढो युष्माकमरातिभिस्सह योत्स्ये तदहं भवतां सहायः स्याम्।। २९।।

इत्याकर्ण्य समस्तदेवैरिंद्रेण च बाढमित्येवं समन्विच्छितम्।। ३०।।

Being thus addressed Purañjaya said—"If Indra, the lord of the three worlds, the king of you all, who is known as the performer of hundred sacrifices, agrees to carry me upon his shoulders, I shall then fight with your enemies and help you." The celestials and Indra immediately said "so be it."

ततश्च शतक्रतोर्वृषरूपधारिणः ककुदि स्थितोऽतिरोष-समन्वितो भगवतश्चराचरगुरोरच्युतस्य तेजसाप्यायितो देवासुरसंग्रामे समस्तानेवासुरान्निजघान।। ३१।।

Thereupon Śatakratu assumed the shape of a bull and the king mounted upon his shoulder. And being invigorated by the power of the undecaying God, the lord of all moveable and immoveable things, he slew all the Asuras in the batle between the gods and demons.

यतश्च वृषभककुदि स्थितेन राज्ञा दैतेयबलं निषूदितमतश्चासौ ककुत्स्थसंज्ञामवाप।। ३२।।

And in consequence of his destroying the Asura army whilst seated upon the hump of the bull he obtained the appellation Kakutstha.

ककुत्स्थस्याप्यनेनाः पुत्रोऽभवत्।। ३३।।

पृथुरनेनसः।। ३४।।

पृथोर्विष्टराश्वः।। ३५।।

तस्यापि चांद्रो युवनाश्वः।। ३६।।

चांद्रस्य तस्य युवनाश्वस्य शावस्तः यः पुरीं शावस्तीं निवेशयामास।। ३७।।

The son of Kakutstha was Anenas, whose son was Pṛthu, whose son was Viśvagaśva, whose son was Arda, whose son was Yuvanāśva, whose son was Śavasta, by shom the city of Śāvasti was founded.

शावस्तस्य बृहदश्वः।। ३८।।

तस्यापि कुवलयाश्वः।। ३९।।

The son of Śavasta was Bṛhadaśva whose son was Kuvalayāśva.

योसावुदकस्य महर्षेरपकारिणं दुंदुनामानमसुरं वैष्णवेन तेजसाप्यायितः पुत्रसह स्त्रैरेकविंशद्भिः परिवृतो जवान दुंदुमारसंज्ञामवाप।। ४०।।

This prince, invigorated by the energy of Viṣṇu, slew the Asura Dhundhu, who had disturbed the pious sage Uttanka, and he was accordingly named Dhundhumāra (slayer of Dhundhu).

तस्य च तन्यास्तमस्ता एव दुंदुमुखनिश्वासागिना विप्लुष्टा विनेशुः।। ४१।।

Whilst fighting with the demon he was attended by his twenty one thousand sons, who all, with the exception of three, were consumed by the fiery breath of Dhundhu.

दृढाश्वचंद्राश्वकपिलाश्वाश्च त्रयः केवलं शेषिताः।। ४२।।

वृढाश्वाद्धर्यश्वः।। ४३।।

तस्माच्च निकुंभः।। ४४।।

निकुंभस्यामिताश्वः।। ४५।।

ततश्च कृशाश्वः।। ४६।।

तस्माच्च प्रसेनजित्।। ४७।।

प्रसेनजितो युवनाश्वोभवत्।। ४८।।

These three were Dhṛḍhāśva, Candrāśva and Kapilāśva. The son of Dhṛḍhāśva was Baryāśva, whose son was Nikumbha, whose son was Sanhatśva, whose was Kṛśāśva, whose son was Prasenajit, whose son was another Yuvanāśva.

तस्य चापुत्रस्यातिनिर्वेदान्मुनीनामाश्रममंडले निवसतो दयालुभिर्मुनिभिरपत्योत्पादनायेष्टिः कृता।। ४९।।

Being aggrieved in consequence of having no son he lived in the hermitage of saints. And being worked up with compassion of sages engaged in the performance of a religious ceremony for this offspring.

तस्यां च मध्यरात्रौ निवृत्तायां मंत्रपूतजलपूर्णं कलशं वेदिमध्ये निवेश्य ते मुनयः सुषुपुः।। ५०।।

सुप्तेषु तेषु अतीव तृट्परीतस्य भूपालस्तमाश्रमं विवेश।। ५१।।

When half the night had passed away they finished the ceremony and having placed a vessel of consecrated water upon the altar they slept.

सुप्तांश्च तानृषीन्नैवोत्थापयामास।। ५२।।

When they had slept the king, distressed with thirst, entered the cottage and did not like to disturb the Ṛsis.

तच्च कलशमपरिमेयमाहात्म्यमंत्रपूतं पपौ।। ५३।।

He then drank the water in the vessel consecrated and rendered efficacious by sacred texts.

प्रबुद्धाश्च ऋषयः पप्रच्छुः केनैतं मंत्रपूतं वारि पीतम्।।५४।।

When the Ṛṣis got up in the morning, they said—"Who has drunk this consecrated water?

अत्र हि राज्ञो युवनाश्वस्य पत्नी महाबलपराक्रमं पुत्रं जनयिष्यति।।

इत्याकर्ण्य स राजा अजानता मया पीतमित्याह।।५५।।

Drinking this the wife of the king Yuvanāśva would have given birth to a valiant son." Hearing this the king said—"I have unknowingly drunk this water."

गर्भश्च युवनाश्वस्योदरे अभवत् क्रमेण च ववृधे।।५६।।

प्राप्तसमयश्च दक्षिणांगुष्ठेन कुक्षिमवनिपतेर्निर्भिद्य निश्चक्राम।।५७।।

Accordingly a child was conceived in the belly of Yuvanāśva; it grew and in proper time it ripped open the right side of the king and was born.

स चासौ राजा ममार।।५८।।

But the king did not die.

जातो नामैष कं धास्यतीति ते मुनयः प्रोचुः।।५९।।

अथागत्य देवराजोब्रवीत् मामयं धास्यतीति।।६०।।

The son being born the Ṛṣis said—"Who will be its nurse." There appeared the king of the celestials and said He shall have me for his nurse (mamayan dhāsyati)."

ततो मांधातृनामा सोभवत्।।

वक्त्रे चास्य प्रदेशिनी न्यस्ता देवेंद्रेण न्यस्तातां पपौ।।६१।।

तां चामृतस्राविणीमास्वाद्याह्नैव स व्यवर्द्धत।।६२।।

He was thence called Māndhātā, Indra put his fore-finger into the mouth of the infant, who sucked it and drew it from heavenly nectar.

ततस्तु मांधाता चक्रवर्त्ती सप्तद्वीपां महीं बुभुजे।।६३।।

And he grew up and became a powerful king and brought the seven continents into his subjection.

तत्रायं श्लोकः।।६४।।

यावत्सूर्य उदेत्यस्तं यावच्च प्रतितिष्ठति।।
सर्वं तद्यौवनाश्वस्य मांधातुः क्षेत्रमुच्यते।।६५।।

It is said of him "From the rising of the setting sun all that is lighted by his rays is the land of Māndhātā the son of Yuvanāśva.

मांधाता शतबिंदोर्दुहितरं बिंदुमतीमुपयेमे।।६६।।

पुरुकुत्समंबरीषं मुचुकुंदं च तस्यां पुत्रत्रयमुत्पादयामास।।६७।।

पञ्चाशद्दुहितरस्तस्यामेव तस्य नृपतेर्बभूवः।।६८।।

Māndhātā married, Vindumati, the daughter of Śaśāvindu and begot on her three sons Purukutsa, Ambarīṣa and Mucukunda; he had also fifty daughters.

एकस्मिन्नंतरे बह्वृचश्च सौभरिर्नाम महर्षिरंतर्जले द्वादशाब्दं कालमुवास।।६९।।

An ascetic, named Śaubharī, versed in Ṛg-Veda lived in the waters for twelve years.

तत्र चांतर्जले संमदो नामातिबहु प्रजोतिमात्रप्रमाणो मीनाधिपतिरासीत्।।७०।।

There lived a huge fish, who was the sovereign, named Sammada. He had a numerous progeny.

तस्य च पुत्रपौत्रदौहित्राः पृष्ठतोऽग्रतः पार्श्वयोः पक्ष-पुच्छशिरसां चोपरि भ्रमंतस्तेनैव सदाहर्निशमतिनिर्वृत्ता रेमिरे।।७१।।

His children and grand children used to sport around him in all directions and he lived happily amongst them, playing with them day night before the ascetic.

स चापत्यस्पर्शोपचीयमानप्रहर्षप्रकर्षो बहुप्रकारं तस्य ऋषेः पश्यतस्तैरात्मजपुत्रपौत्रदौहित्रादिभिः सहानुदिनं सुतरां रेमे।।७२।।

Being disturbed in his devotions that ascetic, in the waters, beholding the sport of the king of fish with his children and grand children, thought within himself—

अथांतर्जलावस्थितस्सौभरिरेकाग्रतस्समाधिमपहायानुदिनं तस्य मत्स्यस्यात्मजपुत्रपौत्रदौहित्रादिभिस्सहातिरम-णीयतामवेक्ष्याचिंतयत्।।७३।।

"Blessed is the being, who, although born in a degraded state, is sporting with his children and grand children.

अहो धन्योयमीदृशमनभिमतं योन्यंतरमवाप्यैभि-
रात्मजपुत्रपौत्रदौहित्रादिभिस्सह रममाणोतीवास्माकं
स्पृहामुत्पादयति।। ७४।।

This has created envy in me and I wish to sport with my children and grand children."

वयमप्येवं पुत्रादिभिस्सह ललितं रमिष्याम
इत्येवमभिकांक्षन् स तस्मादंतर्जलान्निष्क्रम्य संतानाय
निवेष्टुकामः कन्यार्थं मांधातारं राजानमगच्छत्।।७५।।

Having thus made up his mind the ascetic speedily came up from the water and being desirous of becoming a householder went to Māndhātā to demand one of his daughters as his wife.

आगमनश्रवणसमनन्तरं चोत्थाय तेन राज्ञा
सम्यगर्घ्यादिना संपूजितः कृतासनपरिग्रहः
सौभरिरुवाच राजानम्।। ७६।।

Thereupon hearing of the arrival of the sage the king rose up from his seat and worshipped him with libation. Having taken a seat Śaubharī said to the king—

सौभरि रुवाच

निवेष्टुकामोऽस्मिनरेंद्र कन्यां
प्रयच्छ मे मा प्रणयं विभांक्षीः।।
न ह्यर्थिनः कार्यवशादुपेताः
ककुत्स्थवंशे विमुखाः प्रयांति।। ७७।।

"I have made up my mind to marry. Do you, O king, give me one of your daughters as a wife. Don't disappoint my love. If any one comes to the race of Kakutstha with a desire he does not go back disappointed.

अन्येपि संत्येव नृपाः पृथिव्यां मांधातरेषां तनयाः प्रसूताः।।
किं त्वर्थिनामर्थितदानदीक्षाकृतव्रतश्लाघ्यमिदं कुलं ते।।
७८।।

O king, there are many other sovereigns on this earth who have got daughters; but thy family is renowned above all in granting liberal gifts to them who come with that purpose.

शतार्धसंख्यास्तव संति कन्यास्तासां ममैकां नृपते प्रयच्छ।।
यत्प्रार्थनाभंगभयाद्बिभेमि तस्मादहं राजवरातिदुःखात्।।
७९।।

O king, you have got fifty daughters—confer one of them upon me so that I may be relieved from the anxiety I feel in consequence of the fear that my request may not be granted."

श्रीपराशर उवाच

इति ऋषिवचनमाकर्ण्य स राजा जराजर्जरितदेह-
मृषिपालोक्य प्रत्याख्यानकातरस्तस्माच्च शापभीतो
बिभ्यत्किंचिदधोमुखश्चिरं दध्यौ च।। ८०।।

Parāśara said—Hearing the words of the sage and beholding his body worn out with infirmities (he did not like to satisfy his desire)—but afraid of an imprecation he was much disturbed in mind and lowering his head thought for some time.

सौभरिरुवाच

नरेंद्र कस्मात्समुपैषि चिंतामसह्यमुक्तं न मयात्र किंचित्।।
यावश्यदेया तनया तयैव कृतार्थता नो यदि किं न लब्धा।।
८१।।

The Ṛsi said—"What are you meditating upon, O king? I have not asked for any such thing which you cannot give.

श्रीपराशर उवाच

अथ तस्य भगवतश्शापभीतस्सप्रश्रयस्तमुवाचासौ
राजा।।८२।।

Your daughter must be given to some body. But if you fulfil my desires what is there that cannot be obtained by you?" Thereupon the king; afraid of his displeasure, said—

राजोवाच

भगवन् अस्मत्कुलस्थितिरियं य एव कन्याभिरुचितो-
ऽभिजनवान्वरस्तस्मै कन्या प्रदीयते भगवद्याञ्च
चास्मन्मनोरथानामप्यतिगोचरवर्त्तिनी कथमप्येषा
सञ्जाता तदेवमुपस्थिते न विद्मः किं कुर्म
इत्येतन्मयाऽचिंत्यत इत्यभिहिते च तेन भूभुजा
मुनिरचिंतयत्।। ८३।।

"O illustrious sir, such is the practice in our family, that daughters must be given to such fitting persons as they shall themselves select. I did never expect that such a request would come from you—I do not know why such a desire has taken place in your mind.

अयमन्योऽस्मत्प्रत्याख्यानोपायो वृद्धोयमनभिमतः स्त्रीणां किमुत कन्यकानामित्यमुना संचिंत्यैभित-दहितमेवमस्तु तथा करिष्यामीति संचिंत्य मांधातारमुवाच।। ८४।।

This has created perplexity in me and I am at a loss what to do." Hearing that the sage thought within himself—"This is merely an indirect way of not yielding to my request. I am an old man, having no attractions for women and his daughters will not accept me. Whatever it may be, I shall to that." Thinking thus, the sage said to Māndhātā—

यद्येवं तदादिश्यतामस्माकं प्रवेशाय।।
कंन्यांतःपुरं वर्षवरो यदि कन्यैव काचिन्मामभिलषति तदाहं दारसंग्रहं परिष्यामि अन्यथा चेत्तदलमस्माक-मेतेनातीतकालारंभणेनेत्युक्त्वा विरराम।। ८५।।

ततश्च मांधात्रा मुनिशापशं कितेन कन्यांतःपुर-वर्षधरस्समाज्ञप्तः।। ८६।।

"If such be the custom of your family—give orders that I may be admitted into the interior of your palace. If any one of your daughters selects me I shall take her as my wife—if none of them be willing, I shall desist from such an attempt considering that I am too old for it." Having said this the sage was silent.

तेन सह कन्यांतःपुरं प्रविशन्नेव भगवानखिलसिद्ध-गंधर्वेभ्योतिशयेन कमनीयं रूपमकरोत्।। ८७।।

प्रवेश्य च तमृषिमंतःपुरे वर्षधरस्ताः कन्याः प्राह।।
८८।।

Being afraid of the imprecation of the sage, the king ordered the eunuch to conduct him to the inner apartment. As he entered, he assumed a form of beauty far exceeding that of men or gods. Addressing the princesses his guide said to them—

भवतीनां जनयिता महाराजस्समाज्ञापयति।। ८९।।

"Your father, young ladies, sends this pious sage to you who wanted of him a bride.

अयमस्मान् ब्रह्मर्षिः कन्यार्थं समभ्यागतः।। ९०।।

And the king has promised that he will give her to him who will select him."

मया चास्य प्रतिज्ञातं यद्यस्मत्कन्या या काचिद्भगवंतं वरयति तत्कन्याच्छंदे नाहं परिपंथानं करिष्यामी-त्याकर्ण्य सर्वा एव ताः कन्याः सानुरागाः सप्रमदाः करेणव इव मृगयूथपतिं तमृषिमहमहमिकया वरयांबभूवुरूचुश्च।। ९१।।

Hearing these words the princesses were all excited with desire and passion, and like a troop of female elephants encircling the lord of the herd, they all contended to have him as their husband.

अलं भगिन्योहमिमं वृणोमि वृणोम्यहं नैष तवानुरूपः।।
ममैष भर्त्त विधिनैव सृष्टस्सृष्टाहमस्योपशमं प्रयाहि।।
९२।।

They said to one another—"Away away, sister, I shall take him as my husband. He has already been selected by me; he is not a meet bridegroom for you. He has been purposely created by Brahmā for me as I have been created to become his wife.

वृतो मयायं प्रथमं मयायं गृहं विशन्नेव विहन्यसे किम्।।
मया मयेतिक्षितिपात्मजानां तदर्थमत्यर्थकलिर्बभूव।। ९३।।

As soon as he entered the house I selected him as my husband; why do you prevent him from becoming so?" Thus there arose a conflict amongst the daughters of the king, each contending that I have selected him as my husband.

यदा मुनिस्ता भिरतीवहार्दाद्वृतस्स कन्याभिरनिंद्यकीर्तिः।।
तदा स कन्याधिकृतो नृपाय यथावदाचष्ट विनम्रमूर्त्तिः।।
९४।।

Whose that blameless sage was thus selected by all the princess of the eunuch went to the king and with down cast loose reported to him what had taken place.

श्रीपराशर उवाच

तदवगमात्किकिमेतत्कथमेतत्कि किं करोमि किं मयाभिहितमित्याकुलमतिरनिच्छन्नपि कथमपि राजानुमेने।। ९५।।

Having received the information, the king, perplexed the more thought—"What is all this! What I am to do now! What is it that have said and then with extreme reluctance gave away all his daughter to the sage.

कृतानुरूपविवाहश्च महर्षिस्सकला एव ताः कन्यास्वमाश्रममनयत्।। ९६।।

Thus the wished or marriage of the great sage was accomplished and I took aways all the princesses to his hermitage.

तत्र चाऽशेषशिल्पकल्पप्रणेतारं धातारमिवान्यं विश्वकर्माणमाहूय सकलकन्यानामेकैकस्याः प्रोत्फुल्लपंकजाः कूजत्कलहंसकारंडवादिविहंगमा-भिरामजलाशयास्सोपधानाः सावकाशास्साधुशय्या-परिच्छदाः प्रासादाः क्रियंतामित्यादिदेश।। ९७।।

तच्च तथैवानुष्ठितमशेषशिल्पविशेषाचार्यस्त्वष्टा दर्शितवान्।। ९८।।

Thereupon he ordered Viśvakarmā like second Brahmā, the invariour of art, to construct separate palaces for each of his wives, to furnish each palace with elegant couches and seats and furniture and to attach to them spacious yard, groves with reservoirs of water where the wild duck and swan should sport amidst beds of lotuses. Thereupon the celestial architect carried out the orders of the sage.

ततः परमर्षिणा सौभरिणाज्ञप्तस्तेषु गृहेष्व-निवार्यानंदकुंदमहानिधिरासाञ्चक्रे।। ९९।।

And at the behest of the great sage, Śaubharī, the divine and inexhaustible treasure Nanda lived there permanently.

ततोऽनवरतेन भक्ष्यभोज्यलेह्याद्युपभोगैरागतानुगत-भृत्यादीनहर्निशमशेषगृहेषु ताः क्षितीशदुहितरो भोजयामासु।। १००।।

Thereupon the princesses entertained there day and night all their guests and dependant with richest and choicest viands.

एकदा तु दुहितृस्नेहाकृष्टहृदयस्स महीपति-रतिदुःखितास्ता उत सुखिता वा इति विचिंत्य तस्य महर्षेराश्रमेसमीपमुपेत्य स्फुरदंशुमालाललामां स्फटिकमयप्रासादामालामतिरम्योपवनजलाशयां ददर्श।। १०१।।

Once on a time the king, attracted by his affection for the daughters, went to the hermitage of the great ascetic to learn whether his daughters were in poverty or happiness. Repairing there he beheld a number of crystal palaces, brilliant as the rays of the sun and picturesque gardens and tanks.

प्रविश्य चैकं प्रासादामात्मजां परिष्वज्य कृतासन-परिग्रहः प्रवृद्धस्नेहनयनांबुगर्भनयनोब्रवीत्।। १०२।।

Entering one of the palaces and embracing his daughter, the king said to her with tears of affection and delight in his eyes—

अप्यत्र वत्से भवत्यास्सुखमुत किंचिदसुखमपि ते महर्षिस्स्नेहवानुत न स्मर्यतेस्मद्गृहवास इत्युक्ता तं तनया पितरमाह।। १०३।।

"Dear child, tell me how are you here. Are you happy here or not? Does the great sage treat you kindly? Do you remember thy early home"? Being thus addressed the daughter said to her father—

तातातिरमणीयः प्रासादोत्रातिमनोज्ञमुपवनमेते कलवाक्यविहंगमाभिरुताः प्रोत्फुल्लपद्माकर जलाशयाः मनोनुकूलभक्ष्यभोज्यानुलेपन-वस्त्रभूषणादिभोगो मृदूनि शयनासनानि सर्वसंपत्समेतं मे गार्हस्थ्यम्।। १०४।।

"O father, this palace is picturesque surrounded by charming gardens with birds emitting sweet notes, and tanks abounding in full-blown lotuses. I have got here rich vainds, fragrant unguents, precious ornaments, costly clothes, sift beds and every other thing that wealth can give.

तथापि केन वा जन्मभूमिर्न स्मर्यते।। १०५।।

But still they, why should I not remember my early home.

त्वत्प्रसादादिदमशेषमतिशोभनम्।। १०६।।

By thy favour I have obtained all these begs.

किं त्वेकं ममैतद्दुःखकारणं यदस्मद्गृहान्महर्षि-

रयम्मद्भर्त्ता न निष्क्रामति ममैव केवलमतिप्रीत्या सीमपपरिवर्त्तिनीनामन्यासामस्मद्भगिनीनाम्।। १०७।।

But there is one source of my grief—my husband never thus out of my house. He is solely attached to me and is all this at my side; he never goes to my sisters; for this my sister are sorry; this is the only cause of my uneasiness."

एवं च मम सोर्दर्योतिदुःखिता इत्येवमतिदुःख-कारणमित्युक्तस्तया द्वितीयं प्रासादमुपेत्य स्वतनयां परिष्वज्योपविष्टस्तथैव पृष्टवान्।। १०८।।

Taking thus addressed he went to the second palace and embracing his daughter and taking his seat he put the same question.

तयापि च सर्वमेतत्तत्प्रासादाद्युपभोगसुखं भृशमाख्यातं ममैव केवलमतिप्रीत्या पार्श्वपरिवर्त्तिनीनामन्या-सामस्मद्भगिनीनामित्येवमादि श्रुत्वा समस्तप्रसादादेषु राजा प्रविवेश तनयां तनयां तथैवापृच्छत्।। १०९।।

The same account of the enjoyment of palaces and other things was given by her; she also made the same complain that the sage was solely attached to her and paid no attention to her sisters.

सर्वाभिश्च ताभिस्तथैवाभिहितः परितोषविस्मयनि-र्भरविवशहृदयो भगवंतं सौभरिमेकांतावस्थितमुपेत्य कृतपूजोब्रवीत्।। ११०।।

Hearing this the king went round all the palaces, put the same question to all his daughters and received the same reply. Having his heart filled with satisfaction and wonder he repaired to the glorious Śaubharī who was alone and reverentially said to him—

दृष्टस्ते भगवन् सुमहानेष सिद्धिप्रभावो नैवंविधमन्यस्य कस्यचिदस्माभिर्विभूति भिर्विलसितमुपलक्षितं यदेतद्भगवतस्तपसः फलमित्यभिपूज्य तमृषिं तत्रैव तेन ऋषिवर्येण सह किंचित्कालमभिमतोपभोगान् बुभुजे स्वपुरं च जगाम।। १११।।

"O illustrious sage, marvellous is thy power—I have never seen this in any other person. Oh great is the reward of thy austere penances." Having bowed unto the sage and been welcomed by him with great reverence the king lived with him for some time and enjoying the pleasures of the place returned to his capital.

कालेन गच्छता तस्य तासु राजतनयासु पुत्रशतं सार्धमभवत्।। ११२।।

As time went on the daughters of Māndhātā bore to Śaubharī one hundred and fifty sons.

अनुदिनानुरूढस्नेहप्रसरश्च स तत्रातीव ममताकृष्ट-हृदयोऽभवत्।। ११३।।

Gradually he became more and more attached to his children and his mind was wholly ongrossed with selfish thoughts.

अप्येतेऽस्मत्पुत्राः कलभाषिणः पद्भ्यां गच्छेयुः अप्येते यौवनिनो भवेयुः अपि कृतदारानेतान् पश्येयमप्येषां पुत्रा भवेयुः अप्येतत्पुत्रान्पुत्र-समन्वितान्पश्यामीत्यादिमनोरथाननुदिनं कालसंपत्ति-प्रवृद्धानुपेक्ष्यैतच्चिंतयामास।। ११४।।

अहो मे मोहस्या तिविस्तारः।। ११५।।

He always used to think—'When will these sons of mine speak to me in sweet accents? When will they learn to walk? When will they attain to youth? When shall I see them wedded? When shall I behold them with their sons?" With these anticipations, he spent some time and at last thought "What exceeding folly is mine!

मनोरथानां न समाप्तिरस्ति वर्षायुतेनाप्यथ वापि लक्षैः।।
पूर्णेषुपूर्णेषु मनोरथानामुत्पत्तयस्संति पुनर्नवानाम्।। ११६।।

There is no end of desires even in ten thousand or a hundred thousand years. With one desire gratified another springs up. I have seen my infants walk—

पद्भ्यां गता यौवनिनश्च जाता दारैश्च संयोगमिताः प्रसूताः।।
दृष्टाः सुतास्तत्तनयप्रसूतिं द्रष्टुं पुनर्वांच्छति मेंऽतरात्मा।। ११७।।

I have seen their youth, their manhood, their marriage, their children, still my desires are not gratified and mind longs after seeing the descendants of their descendants.

द्रक्ष्यामि तेषामिति चेत्प्रसूतिं मनोरथो मे भविता ततोन्यः ।।
पूर्णेपि तत्राप्यपरस्य जन्म निवार्यते केन मनोरथस्य ।।
११८ ।।

When I shall see them another desire will spring up. When that is satisfied another wish will be engendered.

आमृत्युतो नैव मनोरथानामंतोस्ति विज्ञातमिदं मयाद्य ।।
मनोरथासक्तिपरस्य चित्तं न जायते वै परमार्थसंगि ।। ११९ ।।

How can the growth of desires be prevented? I have now learnt that there is no end of desires till death. His mind can never be devoted to the supreme spirit who is a perpetual slave of desires.

स मे समाधिर्जलवासमित्रमत्स्यस्य संगात्सहसैव नष्टः ।।
परिग्रहस्संगकृतो मयायं परिग्रहोत्था च ममातिलिप्सा ।।
१२० ।।

My devotions, whilst I was in the waters, were thwarted by my attachment to my friend, the fish. The outcome of that connection was my marriage and the result of that marriage is the cycle of worldly desires.

दुःखं यदैवैकशरीरजन्म शतार्द्धसंख्याकमिदं प्रसूतम् ।।
परिग्रहेण क्षितिपात्मजानां सुतैरनेकैर्बहुलीकृतं ।। १२१ ।।

Birth with one body is a source of many ills. By my marriage with the princess I have got one hundred and fifty sons so my miseries have been multiplied to that extent.

सुतात्मजैस्तत्तनयैश्च भूयो भूयश्च तेषां च परिग्रहेण ।।
विस्तारमेष्यत्यतिदुःख हेतुः परिग्रहो वै ममताभिधानः ।।
१२२ ।।

And they will be infinitely multiplied by their children, by their wives and their progeny—thus a married life is a source of individual anxiety.

चीर्णं तपो यत्तु जलाश्रयेण तस्यर्द्धिरेषा तपसोंतरायः ।।
मत्स्यस्य संगादभवच्च यो मे सुतादिरागो मुषितोस्मि तेन ।।
१२३ ।।

My devotions, which I practised in the waters, have been thwarted by my worldly wealth and I have been beguiled by the desire for the progeny which was created in me by the association with Sammada.

निस्संगता मुक्तिपदं यतीनां संगादशेषाः प्रभवंति दोषाः ।।
आरूढयोगो विनिपात्यतेधस्संगेन योगी किमुताल्पबुदिः ।।
१२४ ।।

अहं चरिष्यामि तदात्मनोर्थे परिग्रहग्राहगृहीतबुद्धिः ।।
यदा हि भूयः परिहीनदोषो जनस्य दुःखैर्भविता न दुःखी ।।
१२५ ।।

For the ascetics separation from the world is the only way to liberation; association with others is a source of many evils. Even the most accomplished ascetic is degraded by worldly attachments what to speak of those whose observances are incomplete. Though my intellect has been possessed by the desire of married life still I shall exert myself for the salvation of my soul so that freed from human infirmities I may be released from human suffering.

सर्वस्य धातारम चिंत्यरूपमणोरणीयांसमतिप्रमाणम् ।।
सितासितं चेश्वरमीश्वराणामाराधयिष्ये तपसैव विष्णुम् ।।
१२६ ।।

For that purpose by austere penances I shall propitiate Viṣṇu, the creator of the universe whose form cannot be ascertained, who is smaller than the smallest, larger than the largest, the source of darkness and light—the king of gods.

तस्मिन्नशेषौजसि सर्वरूपिण्यव्यक्तविस्पष्टतनावनंते ।।
ममाचलं चित्तमपेतदोषं सदास्तु विष्णावभवाय भूयः ।।
१२७ ।।

May my mind, freed from sins, be devoted to his body which is both descrete and indiscrete substance, boundlessly mighty, at one with the universe so that I may not be born again.

समस्तभूतादमलादनंतात्सर्वेश्वरादन्यदनादिमध्यात् ।।
यस्मान्न किंचित्तमहं गुरूणां परं गुरुं संश्रयमेमि विष्णुम् ।।
१२८ ।।

I seek the refuge of that Viṣṇu, who is the teacher of teachers, who is identical with all beings, the pure eternal lord of all, without beginning, middle or endand besides whom there exists nothing.

श्रीपराशर उवाच

इत्यात्मानमात्मनैवाभिधायासौ सौभरिरप हाय पुत्रगृहासनपरिग्रहादिकमशेषमर्थजातं सकल-भार्यासमन्वितो वनं प्रविवेश।। १२९।।

Parāśara said :—Having thus thought within himself Śaubarī renounced his children, his home, his splendour and wealth and repaired with his wives to the forest.

तत्राप्यनुदिनं वैखानसनिष्पाद्यमशेषक्रियाकलापं निष्पाद्य क्षपितसकलपापः परिपक्वमनोवृत्तिरात्म-न्यग्नीन्समारोप्य भिक्षुरभवत्।। १३०।।

Having daily performed there the observances of the ascetics called performed there the observances of the ascetics called Vaikhānasas (or ascetics having families) he cleansed himself from all iniquities. When his mind was ripe and freed from passions he concentrated in his spirit the sacramental fires and became a religious mendicant.

भगवत्यासज्याखिलं कर्मकलापं हित्वानं तमजमनादिनिधनमविकारमरणादिधर्ममवाप परमनन्तं परवतामच्युतं पदम्।। १३१।।

Then having made over all his actions to the glorious god he attained to the condition of Acyuta which is above change, the vicissitudes of birth, transmigration or death.

इत्येतन्मांधातृदुहितृसंबंधादाख्यातम्।। १३२।।

यश्चैतत्सौभरिचरितमनुस्मरति पठति पाठयति शृणोति श्रावयति धरत्यवधारयति लिखति लेखयति शिक्षयत्यध्यापयत्युपदिशति वा तस्य षट् जन्मानि दुस्संततिरद्धर्मो वाङ्मनसोरसन्मार्गाचरणशेषहेतुषु वा ममत्वं न भवति।। १३३।।

Whoever shall read, hear, remember, or understand this story of Śaubarī and his marriage with the daughters of Māndhātā, shall never, for eight successive births, be addicated to evil thoughts nor shall he be subject to selfishness.

।। इति श्रीविष्णुमहापुराणे चतुर्थेंशे द्वितीयोऽध्यायः।। २।।

अथ चतुर्थेंशेः तृतीयोऽध्यायः

Part IV : Section 3

अतश्च मांधातुः पुत्रसंततिरभिधीयते।। १।।

I shall now describe to you the progeny of Māndhātā.

अंबरीषस्य मांधातृतनयस्य युवनाश्वः पुत्रोऽभूत्।। २।।

तस्माद्धारीतः यतोंगिरसो हारीताः।। ३।।

The son of Ambarīṣa, the son of Māndhāta, was Yuvanāśva; his son was Harita from whom sprang Aṅgirāsa Hāritas.

रसातले मौनेया नाम गंधर्वा बभूवुष्षट्कोटिसंख्यातास्तैरशेषाणि नागकुलान्यपहृतप्रधानरत्नाधि-पत्यान्यक्रियंत।। ४।।

In the regions below the earth, the Gandharvas named Mauneyas, six million in number, had defeated the snake-gods, usurped their kingdom and stolen away all their precious jewels.

तैश्च गंधर्ववीर्यावभूतैरुरगेश्वरैस्तूयमानो भगवान-शेषदेवेश आस्ते तच्छ्रवणोन्मीलितोन्निद्रपुंडरीकनयनो जलशयनो निद्रावसानप्रबुद्धः प्रणिपत्याभिहितः।।

भगवन्नस्माकमेतेभ्यो गंधर्वेभ्यो भयमुत्पन्नं कथमुप-शममेष्यतीति।। ५।।

Defeated by the Gandharvas the serpent chiefs addressed the lord of celestials, sleeping on the surface of the ocean of milk as he awoke from his sleep; and the blossoms of this lotus eyes opened as he listened to their hymns.

आह च भगवाननादिनिधनपुरुषोत्तमो योसौ यौवनाश्वस्य मांधातुः पुरुकुत्सनामा पुत्रस्तमह-

मनुप्रविश्य तान शेषान् दुष्टगंधर्वानुंपशमं नयिष्या-
मीति।। ६।।

तदाकर्ण्य भगवते जलशायिने कृतप्रमाणाः
पुनर्नागलोकमागताः पन्नगाधिपतयो नर्मदां च
पुरुकुत्सानयनाय चोदयामासुः।। ७।।

सा चैनं रसातलं नीतवती।। ८।।

They all bowing said—"How shall we be relieved from the fear of these Gandharvas?" Where to the glorious god replied—"I shall enter into the person of Purukutsa, the son of Māndhātā, the son of Yuvanāśva and slay all the Gandharvas." On hearing these words the snake-gods bowed and went away and returning to their country sent Narmadā to secure the help of Purukutsa.

रसातलगतश्चासौ भगवत्तेजसाप्यायितात्म-
वीर्य्यस्सकलगंधर्वान्निजघान।। ९।।

पुनश्च स्वपुरमाजगाम।। १०।।

Accordingly Narmadā went to Purukutsa and led him to the regions below the earth, where, being, being filled with the energy of Viṣṇu he slew all the Gandharvas. He then returned to his own house.

सकलपन्नगाधिप तयश्च नर्मदायै वरं ददुः।।
यत्तेनुस्मरणसमवेतं नामग्रहणं करिष्यति न तस्य
सर्पविषभयं भविष्यतीति।। ११।।

And the snake-gods conferred upon Narmadā a boon that whosoever should think of her, mention her name, should never have any fear from the snakes.

अत्र च श्लोकः।। १२।।
नर्मदायै नमः प्रातर्नर्मदायै नमो निशि।।
नमोस्तु नर्मदे तुभ्यं त्राहि मां विषसर्पतः।। १३।।

This is the invocation : "Salutation unto Narmadā in the morning; salutation unto Narmadā at night, salutation to thee O Narmadā, save me from this serpent's poison."

इत्युच्चार्याहर्निशमधकारप्रवेशे वा सर्पैर्न दश्यते न
चापि कृतानुस्मरणभुजो विषमति भुक्तमुपघाताय
भवति।। १४।।

पुरुकुत्साय संततिविच्छेदो न भविष्यतीत्युरगपतयो
वरं ददुः।। १५।।

Whoever shall repeat this day and night shall not be bitten by a serpent in the dark or in entering a room. Nor shall he, who shall remember this, suffer from poison, when he eats even food mixed with it. They also conferred a boon on Purukutsa that none in this family shall be bitten.

पुरुकुत्सो नर्मदायां त्रसद्दस्युमजीजनत्।। १६।।

त्रसद्दस्युतस्संभूतोऽनरण्यः यं रावणोदिग्विजये
जघान।। १७।।

Purukutsa begot on Narmadā a son, named Traśadasya, whose son was Sambhūta, whose son was Anarañja, who was killed by Rāvaṇa when he traversed the country for conquests.

अनरण्यस्य पृषदश्वः पृषदश्वस्य हर्यश्वः पुत्रोऽभवत्।। १८।।

तस्य च हस्तः पुत्रोऽभवत्।। १९।।

ततश्च सुमनास्तस्यापि त्रिधन्वा त्रिधन्वनस्त्रय्यारुणिः।।
२०।।

त्रय्यारुणेस्सत्यव्रतः योऽसौ त्रिशंकुसंज्ञामवाप।। २१।।

स चंडालतामुपगतश्च।। २२।।

Anarañja's son was Pṛṣadāśva; his son was Haryyāśva; his son was Sumanas; his son was Tridhanwan; his son was Trayyaruṇa; his son was Satyavrata who received the name of Triśaṅku and was degraded to the state of a Caṇḍāla or outcast.

द्वादशवार्षिक्यामनावृष्ट्यां विश्वामित्रकलत्रापत्य-
पोषणार्थं चंडालप्रतिग्रहपरिहरणाय च जाह्नवीती-
रन्यग्रोधे मृगमांसमनुदिनं बबंध।। २३।।

Once on a time there was a famine for twelve years. He used to suspend flesh upon a fig-tree on the banks of the Ganges for the wife and children of Viśvāmitra—he did not give it with his own hands for he might not accept the present of a Caṇḍāla.

स तु परितुष्टेन विश्वामित्रेण सशरीरस्स्वर्गमारोपितः।। २४।।

For this Viśvāmitra was highly pleased and took him in his living body to heaven.

त्रिशंकोर्हरिश्चंद्रस्तस्माच्च रोहताश्वस्ततश्च हरितो हरितस्य चञ्चुश्चञ्चोर्विजयवसुदेवौ रुरुको विजयादुरुकस्य वृकः।। २५।।

ततो वृकस्य बाहुः योऽसौ हैहयतालजंघादिभिः पराजितोंतर्वत्न्या महिष्या सह वनं प्रविवेश।। २६।।

The son of Triśaṅku was Hariścandra, whose son was Rohitāśva, whose son was Harita, whose son was Cuñcu, who had two sons named Vijaya and Sudeva. Ruruka was the son of Vijaya and his son was Vṛka whose son was Bahu. This king was defeated by the tribes of Haihayas and Tālajaṅghās and his country was devastated by them for which he fled into woods with his wives.

तस्याश्च सपत्न्या गर्भस्तंभनाय गरो दत्तः।। २७।।

तेनास्या गर्भस्सप्तवर्षाणि जठर एव तस्थौ।। २८।।

One of those was pregnant and the rival queen being jealous gave her poison to prevent her delivery and the child was confined in the womb for seven years.

स च बाहुर्वृद्धभावादौर्वाश्रमसमीपे ममार।। २९।।

And Bāhu, being striken in years, died near the hermitage of the sage Aurva.

सा तस्य भार्या चितां कृत्वा तमारोप्यानुमरण-कृतनिश्चऽभूत।। ३०।।

अथैतामतीतानागतवर्त्तमानकालत्रयवेदी भगवानौ-र्वस्स्वाश्रमान्निर्गत्याब्रवीत्।। ३१।।

अलमलमनेनासद्ग्राहेणाखिलभूमिंडलपतिरतिवीर्यपराक्रमो नैकयज्ञकृदरातिपक्षक्षयकर्त्ता तवोदरे चक्रवर्त्ती तिष्ठति।। ३२।।

नैवमतिसाहसाध्यवसायिनी भवती भवेत्युक्ता सा तस्मादनुमरणनिर्बंधाद्विरराम।। ३३।।

Having constructed the funeral pile the queen was about to ascend it when the sage Aurva, who was congnisant of past, present and future came out of the cottage and prevented her saying—"Hold, hold! This is sinful; there is in thy womb a heroic king—the sovereign of many kingdoms, the offerer of many sacrifices, the slayer of his enemies and a lord paramount.

तेनैव च भगवता स्वाश्रममानीता।। ३४।।

Do not commit such an unrighteous act." Being addressed thus the queen gave up her intention.

तत्र कतिपयदिनाभ्यंतरे च सहैव तेन गरेणातितेजस्वी बालको जज्ञे।। ३५।।

The sage then took her to his own cottage and after some time she gave birth to a valiant son—and with him the poison came out.

तस्यौर्वो जातकर्मादिक्रिया निष्पाद्य सगर इति नाम चकार।। ३६।।

And after performing ceremonies consequent upon birth, Aurva gave him, for that, the name of Sagara (from *sa* with and *gara*, poison).

कृतोपनयनं चैनमौर्वो वेदशास्त्राण्यस्त्रं चाग्नेयं भार्गवाख्यमध्यापयामास।। ३७।।

He then invested him with the sacred cord, tought him the Vedas and the use of all weapons and especially those of fire called after Bhārgava.

उत्पन्नबुद्धिश्च मातरमब्रवीत्।। ३८।।

When Sagara grew up he one day asked his mother, saying—

अंब कथयात्र वयं क्व तातोस्माकमित्येवमादिपृच्छंतं माता सर्वमेवावोचत्।। ३९।।

ततश्च पितृराज्यापहरणादमर्षितो हैहयतालजंघादिवधाय प्रतिज्ञामकरोत्।। ४०।।

प्रायशश्च हैहयतालजंघाञ्जघान।। ४१।।

"O mother why are we living here? Who is my father? Where is he?" Being thus questioned his mother related to him everything. Hearing this he was greatly enraged and promised to recover his father's kingdom and destroy the Haihayas and Tālajaṅghās by whom it had been devastated.

शकयवनकांभोजपारदपप्लवाः हन्यमानास्तत्कुलगुरुं वसिष्ठं शरणं जग्मुः।। ४२।।

अथैनान्वसिष्ठो जीवन्मृतकान् कृत्वा सगरमाह।। ४३।।

वत्सालमेभिर्जीवन्मृतकैरनुमृतैः।। ४४।।

When he grew up he destroyed all the Haihayas and would have also destroyed the Śakas the Yavanas, Kambojas, Paradas, and Pahnavas, had they not solicited the protection of Vasiṣṭha, the family priest of Sagara. Vasiṣṭha, making them deprived of their power, although living, thus said to Sagara—"O my child, these are already dead. What is the use of pursuing them?

एते च मयैव त्वत्प्रतिज्ञापरिपालनाय निजधर्म-
द्विजसंगपरित्यांग कारिताः ।। ४५ ।।

तथेतिं तद्गुरुवचनमभिनंद्य तेषां वेषान्यत्वमकारयत् ।। ४६ ।।

To keep up your vow I have made them renounce their own religion and the company of twice-born ones." Sagara reverentially obeyed the request of his spiritual guide and imposed upon them peculiar distinguishing marks.

यवनान्मुंडितशिरसोर्द्धमुंडिताञ्छकान् प्रलंबकेशान्
पारदान् पप्लवाञ्श्मश्रुधरान् निस्स्वाध्यायवषट्कारा-
नेतानन्यांश्च क्षत्रियांश्चकार ।। ४७ ।।

He made the Yavanas shape their heads entirely and the Śakas partially. The Pāradas wore their long hair and the Pahnavas allowed their beards to grow according to his command. He withdrew from these and other Kṣatriya races the privilege of offering oblations to fire and studying the Vedas.

एते चात्मधर्मपरित्यागाद्ब्राह्मणैः परित्यक्ता म्लेच्छतां ययुः ।।
४८ ।।

And being thus deprived from the performance of religious rites and having been abandoned by the Brāhmins they all became Mlecchas.

सगरोपि स्वमधिष्ठानमागम्य अस्खलितचक्र-
स्सप्तद्वीपवतीमिमामुर्वी प्रशशास ।। ४९ ।।

Having thus recovered his kingdom Sagara ruled over the earth having seven continents with undisputed sway.

।। इति श्रीविष्णुमहापुराणे चतुर्थेंशे तृतीयोऽध्यायः ।। ३ ।।

अथ चतुर्थेंशेः चतुर्थोऽध्यायः

Part IV Section 4

श्रीपराशर उवाच

काश्यपदुहिता सुमतिर्विदर्भराजतनया केशिनी च द्वे
भार्ये सगरस्यास्ताम् ।। १ ।।

Parāśara said :—Sagara had two wives Sumati, the daughter of Kaśyapa and Keśinī, the daughter of king Vidarbha.

ताभ्यां चापत्यार्थमौर्वः परमेण समाधिनाराधितो
वरमदात् ।। २ ।।

एका वंशकरमेकं पुत्रमपरा षष्टिं पुत्रसहस्त्राणां
जनयिष्यतीति यस्या यदभिमतं तदि च्छया
गृह्यतामित्युक्ते केशिन्येकं वरयामास ।। ३ ।।

सुमतिः पुत्रसहस्त्राणि षष्टिं वव्रे ।। ४ ।।

Having no offspring the king earnestly solicited the help of the sage Aurva who conferred upon him a boon that one wife should bear him a son who would keep up the race and the other sixty thousand sons; but he allowed them to make their election.

तथेत्युक्ते अल्पैरहोभिः केशिनी पुत्रमेकमसमञ्ज-
सनामानं वंशकरमसूत ।। ५ ।।

काश्यपतनयायास्तु सुमत्याः षष्टिं पुत्र-
सहस्त्राण्यभवन् ।। ६ ।।

Keśinī chose to have one son and the other chose to have sixty thousand. Within a few days Keśinī gave birth to a son named Asamañjas who upheld the family and Sumati the daughter of Vinatā gave birth to a sixty thousand sons.

तस्मादसमञ्जसादंशुमान्नाम कुमारो जज्ञे ।। ७ ।।

स त्वसमञ्जसो बालो बाल्यादेवासद्वृत्तोभूत्।। ८।।

Asamañjas had a son whose name was Aṅśumat. Asamañjas was very wicked from his boyhood.

पिता चास्याचिंतयदयमतीतबाल्यः सुबुद्धिमान् भविष्यतीति।। ९।।

His father hoped that with manhood he would reform his conduct.

अथ तत्रापि च वयस्यतीते असच्चरितमेनं पिता तत्याज।। १०।।

But he continued same even with age so his father renounced him.

तान्यपि षष्टिः पुत्रसहस्राण्यसमञ्जसचरितमेवानुचक्रुः।। ११।।

The sixty thousand sons of Sagara followed the example of their brother Asamañjas.

ततश्चासमञ्जसचरितानुकारिभिस्सागरैरपध्वस्तयज्ञैसन्मार्गे जगति देवास्सकलविद्यामयमसंस्पृष्टमशेषदोषै-र्भगवतः पुरुषोत्तमस्यांशभूतं कपिलं प्रणम्य तदर्थमूचुः।। १२।।

भगवन्नेभिस्सगरतनयैरसमञ्ज सचरितमनुगम्यते।। १३।।

कथमेभिरसद्वृत्तमनुसरद्भिर्जगद्भविष्यतीति।। १४।।

अत्यार्त्त जगत्परित्राणाय च भगवतोत्र शरीरग्रहण-मित्याकर्ण्य भगवानाहाल्पैरेवैदिनैर्विनंक्ष्यन्तीति।। १५।।

The sons of Sagara having thus trodden the paths of virture and piety in the world the celestials went to the ascetic Kapila, who was free from guilt, versed in learning and in whom was a portion of Viṣṇu. Having bowed unto him they said—"These sons of Sagara have followed the conduct of Asamañjas. If they continue so how will the world be upheld? Thou art incarnate for the protection of the world." Hearing this Kapila said—"They shall soon be destroyed."

अत्रांतरे च सगरो हयमेधमारभत।। १६।।

Thereupon Sagara undertook the celebration of a horse sacrifice.

तस्य च पुत्रैरधिष्ठितमस्याश्वं कोप्यपहृत्य भुवो बिलं प्रविवेश।। १७।।

They were all engaged to look after the horse. Nevertheless some one stole the horse and carried it to the region below the earth.

ततस्तत्तनयाश्चाश्वखुरगतिनिर्वंधेनावनीमेकैको योजनं चख्नुः।। १८।।

He then ordered them to search out the steed. Then following the impressions of its hoops with preseverance they dug downwards each for a league.

पाताले चाश्वं परिभ्रमंतं तमवनीपतितनयास्ते ददृशुः।। १९।।

And coming to the region beneath they saw the horse walking freely.

नातिदूरेऽवस्थितं च भगवंतमपघने शरत्कालेर्कमिव तेजोभिरवनतमूर्द्धमधश्चाशेषदिशश्चोभासयमानं हयहर्त्तारं कपिलर्षिमपश्यन्।। २०।।

They saw at a distance Kapila, illuminating with the radiance of his person all the quarters, up and down like unto the autumnal sun freed from clouds.

ततश्चोद्यतायुधा दुरात्मनोऽयमस्मदपकारी यज्ञविघ्न-कारी हन्यतां हयहर्त्त हन्यतामित्यवोचन्नभ्यधावंश्च।। २१।।

Then with uplifted weapons they rushed towards him, saying—"Slay him, slay him; this villain has spoiled our sacrifice; he has stolen our horse."

ततस्तेनापि भगवता किंचिदीषत्परिवर्त्तितलोचनेन-ावलोकितास्स्वशरीरसमुत्थेनाऽग्निना दह्यमाना विनेशुः।। २२।।

Then turning his eyes a little Kapila looked towards them and with the sacred flame that came out of his body, the sons of Sagara were in no time reduced to ashes.

सगरोप्यवगम्याश्वानुसारि तत्पुत्रबलमशेषं परमर्षिणा कपिलेन तेजसा दग्धं ततोंशुमंतमसमञ्जसपुत्रमश्वा-नयनाययुयोज।। २३।।

When Sagara came to know that all his

sons, whom he had sent in quest of the horse, had been destroyed by the might of the sage Kapila he sent Asamañjas's son to bring the animal.

स तु सगरतनयखातामार्गेण कपिलमुपगम्य भक्तिनम्रस्तदा तुष्टाव।। २४।।

अथैनं भगवानाह।। २५।।

गच्छैनं पितामहायाश्वं प्रापय वरं वृणीष्व च पुत्रक पौत्राश्च ते स्वर्गाद्गंगां भुवमानेष्यन्त इति।। २६।।

Aṁśumat, proceeding by the path which Sagara's sons had dug, arrived where Kapila was and reverentially bowing unto him so pleased him that he said—"Go my son and gave over the horse to your grandfather; ask of me a boon; thy grand-son shall bring down the river of heaven on earth."

अथांशमानपि स्वर्यातानां ब्रह्मदंडहतानामस्मत्पितृणामस्वर्गयोग्यानां स्वर्गप्राप्तिकरं वरमस्माकं प्रयच्छेति प्रत्याह।। २७।।

Aṅśumat begged of the glorious Ṛṣi a boon that his uncles, who had died on account of his displeasure although unworthy of it, might be raised to heaven.

तदाकर्ण्य तं च भगवानाह उक्तमेवैतन्मयाद्य पौत्रस्ते त्रिदिवाद्गंगां भुवमानयिष्यतीति।। २८।।

The Ṛṣi said—"I have told you that your grandson shall bring down the Ganges upon earth.

तदंभसा च संस्पृष्टेष्वस्थिभस्मसु एते च स्वर्गमारोक्ष्यन्ति।। २९।।

When the ashes and bones of Sagara's sons shall be washed by her waters they shall be raised to heaven.

भगवद्विष्णुपादांगुष्ठनिर्गतस्य हि जलस्यैतन्माहात्म्यम्।। ३०।।

Such is the glory of the stream that issues from the toe of Viṣṇu that they all, who bathe in it intentionally or accidentally, go to heaven.

यन्न केवलमभिसंधिपूर्वकं स्नानाद्युपभोगेषूपकारकमनभिसंधितमप्यस्यां प्रेतप्राणस्यास्थिचर्मस्नायुकेशाद्युपस्पृष्टं शरीरजमपि पतितं सद्यश्शरीरिणं स्वर्गं नयतीत्युक्तः प्रणम्य भवगतेऽश्वमादाय पितामहयज्ञमाजगाम।। ३१।।

Even those shall go to heaven whose bones, skin, fibres, hair or any other part shall be left after death upon the earth which is contiguous to the Ganges." Thereupon reverentially bowing unto the sage and taking the steed, he went where his grandfather was celebrating the sacrifice.

सगरोप्यश्वमासाद्य तं यज्ञं समापयामास।। ३२।।

सागरं चात्मजप्रीत्या पुत्रत्वे कल्पितवान्।। ३३।।

On receiving back the horse Sagara completed the sacrifice and in memory of his sons he gave the name of Sagara[1] to the chasm which they had dug.

तस्यांशुमतो दिलीपः पुत्रोभवत्।। ३४।।

दिलीपस्य भगीरथः योऽसौ गंगां स्वर्गादिहानीय भागीरथीसंज्ञां चकार।। ३५।।

The son of Aṁśumat was Dilīpa; his son was Bhagīratha who brought down the Ganges on earth, whence she is called Bhāgīrathī.

भगीरथात्सुहोत्रस्सुहोत्राच्छ्रुतः तस्यापि नाभागः ततोंबरीषः तत्पुत्रस्सिंधुद्वीपः सिंधुद्वीपादयुतायुः।। ३६।।

तत्पुत्रश्च ऋतुपर्णः योऽसौ नलसहायोक्षहृदयज्ञोभूत्।। ३७।।

ऋतुपर्णपुत्रस्सर्वकामः।। ३८।।

तत्तनयस्सुदासः।। ३९।।

सुदासात्सौदासो मित्र सहनामा।। ४०।।

The son of Bhagīratha was Śruta, whose son was Nabhāga, whose son was Ambarīṣa, whose son was Sindhudvīpa, whose son was Ayutāśva, whose son was Ṛtuparṇa, the friend of

1. Sagara is still the name of the Bay of Bengal at the mouth of the Ganges which is held in great reverence by the Hindus. There is an island there of the same where there is a pilgrimage of Kapila where still now takes place an annual fair.

Nala, well-skilled in dice; the son of Ṛtuparṇa was Sarvakāma, whose son was Sudāsa whose son was Saudāsa named also Mitrasaha.

स चाटव्यां मृगयार्थी पर्यटन् व्याघ्रद्वयमपश्यत्।। ४१।।

ताभ्यां तद्वनमपमृगं कृतं मत्वैकं तयोर्बाणेन जघान।। ४२।।

Once going out on hunting, the Saudāsa met with a couple of tigers who had cleared the forest of the deer. He killed of these tigers with an arrow.

म्रियमाणश्चासावतिभीषणाकृतिरतिकरालवदनो राक्षसोऽभूत्।। ४३।।

At the time of dying the form of the animal was changed and it assumed that of a dreadful and hideous fiend.

द्वितीयोपि प्रतिक्रियां ते करिष्यामीत्युक्त्वांतर्धानं जगाम।। ४४।।

And the second disappeared saying—"I shall take vangeance upon you."

कालेन गच्छता सौदासो यज्ञमयजत्।। ४५।।

परिनिष्ठितयज्ञे आचार्ये वसिष्ठे निष्क्रांते तद्रक्षो वसिष्ठरूपमास्थाय यज्ञावसाने मम नरमांसभोजनं देयमिति तत्संस्क्रियतां क्षणादागमिष्यामीत्युक्त्वा-निष्क्रांतः।। ४६।।

भूयश्च सूदवेषं कृत्वा राजाज्ञया मानुषं मांसं संस्कृत्य राज्ञे न्यवेद यत्।। ४७।।

असावपि हिरण्यपात्रे मांसमादाय वसिष्ठागमन-प्रतीक्षकोऽभवत्।। ४८।।

आगताय वसिष्ठाय निवेदितवान्।। ४९।।

स चाप्यचिंतयदहोस्य राज्ञो दौश्शीलयं येनैतन्मांस-मस्माकं प्रयच्छति किमेतद्द्रव्यजातमिति ध्यानपरोभवत्।।५०।।

After some time Saudāsa celebrated a sacrifice which was conducted by Vasiṣṭha. At the end of the ceremony Vasiṣṭha went out when the Rākṣa assuming the shape of Vasiṣṭha said—"The sacrifice is finished to-day. You must give me flesh to eat; I shall just now come back." Having said this he went away and transforming himself into the shape of the cook prepared some human flesh. Saudāsa placing it on a dish of gold, waited for Vasiṣṭha. As soon as the sage came back the king offered to him the dish. Thereat the sage thought—"Alas! what improper conduct on the part of the king that he is offering me flesh!"

अपश्यच्च तन्मांसं मानुषम्।। ५१।।

Then by virtue of his meditation he came to know that it was human flesh.

अतः क्रोधकलुषीकृतचेता राजनि शापमुत्ससर्ज।।५२।।

यस्मादभोज्यमेतदस्मद्विधानां तपस्विनामवगच्छन्नपि भवान्मह्यं ददाति तस्मात्तवैवात्र लोलुपता भविष्यतीति।। ५३।।

Being worked up with ire accordingly he imprecated the king—"Since you have offered, though you know it, to such holy men as we are what should not be eaten, henceforth, your appetite shall be excited by similar food."

अनंतरं च तेनापि भगवतैवाभिहितोस्मीत्युक्ते किं किं मयाभिहितमिति मुनिः पुनरपि समाधौ तस्थौ।।५४।।

The king said—"It was yourself who commanded this food to be prepared." Vasiṣṭha said—"By me, how could that have been."

समाधिविज्ञानावगतार्थश्चानुग्रहं तस्मै चकार नात्यंतिकमेतद्द्वादशाब्दं तव भोजनं भविष्यतीति।।
५५।।

And being engaged in meditation again he found out the whole truth. Being pleased with the king he said—"The food to which I have doomed you shall not be your sustenance for ever; it shall be only so for twelve years."

असावपि प्रतिगृह्योदकाञ्जलिं मुनिशापप्रदानायोद्यतो भगवन्नयमस्मद्गुरुर्नार्हस्येनं कुलदेवताभूतमाचार्यं शप्तुमिति मदयंत्या स्वपत्न्या प्रसादितस्सस्यांबुद-रक्षणार्थं तच्छापांवु नोर्व्यां न चाकाशे चिक्षेप किं तु तेनैव स्वपदौ सिषेच।। ५६।।

And the king, taking water in his palms addressed himself for cursing the sage but gave up his intention, being reminded by his queen Madayanti that it ill became him to imprecate a curse upon a holy teacher who was the guardian divinity of the family. Unwilling to throw the water upon the earth lest it should wither up the grain for it was filled with malediction and being equally unwilling to throw it up into the air lest it should blast the clouds and dry up their contents, he threw it upon his own feet.

तेन च क्रोधाश्रितेनां बुना दग्धच्छायौ तत्पादौ
कल्माषतामुपगतौ ततस्स कल्माषपादसंज्ञामवाप।।
५७।।

Scalded by the heat which was in the water on account of his angry imprecation the feet of the king became spotted black and white and he therefore obtained the name of Kalmaṣapāda (i.e. having spotted feet).

वसिष्ठशापाच्च षष्ठेषष्ठे काले राक्षसस्वभाव-
मेत्याटव्यां पर्यटन्ननेकशो मानुषानभक्षयत्।। ५८।।

On account of Vasiṣtha's curse the king used to become a cannibal every third night and travelling through the forests devoured many men.

एकदा तु कंचिन्मुनिमृतुकाले भार्यासंगतं ददर्श।। ५९।।

Once on a time he saw pious sage engaged in dalliance with his wife.

तयोश्च तमतिभीषणं राक्षस स्वरूपमवलोक्य
त्रासाद्दंपत्योः प्रधावितयोर्ब्राह्मणं जग्राह।। ६०।।

And beholding that terrible Rākṣasa form they fled away in fear but he got hold of the husband whilst they escaping.

ततस्सा ब्राह्मणी बहुशस्तमभियाचितवती।। ६१।।

प्रसीदेक्ष्वाकुकुल तिलकभूतस्त्वं महाराजो मित्रसहो
न राक्षसः।। ६२।।

Thereupon the wife of the Brāhmaṇa begged of him her husband again and again—"Thou art the great king Mitrasaha, the pride of the Ikṣvāku race—not the Rākṣasa.

नार्हसि स्त्रीधर्मसंखाभिज्ञो मय्यकृतार्थायामस्मद्भर्त्तारं
हंतुमित्येवं बहुप्रकारं तस्यां विलपंत्यां व्याघ्रः
पशुमिवाऽरण्येऽभिमतं तं ब्राह्मणमभक्षयत्।। ६३।।

It is not proper for thee who knowest the nature of women, to carry off my husband and devour him." In vain deed she lament in many ways; he devoured the Brāhmaṇa as a tiger devours a deer.

ततश्चातिकोपसमन्विता ब्राह्मणी तं राजानं शशाप।। ६४।।

यस्मादेवं मय्यतृप्तायां त्वयायं मत्पतिर्भक्षितः
तस्मात्त्वमपि कामोपभोगप्रवृत्तेंतं प्राप्स्यसीति।। ६५।।

Being worked up with ire the Brāhmaṇa's wife addressed the king and said—"Since you have devoured my husband before I was satiated in his company, you shall die as soon as you shall associate with your queen."

शप्त्वा चैव साग्निं प्रविवेश।। ६६।।

Having thus cursed him she entered the flames.

ततस्तस्य द्वादशाब्दपर्यये विमुक्तशापस्य स्त्रीविषया-
भिलाषिणो मदयंती तं स्मारयामास।। ६७।।

After the expiration of twelve years when he was freed of the curse, he, being desirous of dallying with his wife, thought of Madayanti who reminded him of the curse of Brāhmaṇī.

ततः परमसौ स्त्रीभोगं तत्याज।। ६८।।

He, therefore, abstained from conjugal intercourse.

वसिष्ठश्चापुत्रेण राज्ञा पुत्रार्थमभ्यर्थितो मदयंत्यां
गर्भाधानं चकार।। ६९।।

Being childless he solicited the help of Vasiṣtha and Madayanti became pregnant.

यदा च सप्तवर्षाण्यसौ गर्भेण जज्ञे ततस्तं गर्भमश्मना
सा देवी जघान।। ७०।।

पुत्रश्चाजायत।। ७१।।

तस्य चाश्मक इत्यचेव नामाभवत्।। ७२।।

The child was not born for seven years, and the queen devided the womb with a sharp stone and a son was born who was named Aśmaka.

अश्मस्य मूलको नाम पुत्रोऽभवत्।। ७३।।

The son of Aśmaka was Mūlaka.

योसौ निःक्षत्रे क्ष्मामतलेस्मिन् क्रियमाणे स्त्रीभि-
र्विवस्त्राभिः परिवार्य रक्षितः ततस्तं नारीकवच-
मुदाहरंति ।। ७४ ।।

When the Kṣatriyas were rooted out from the earth, he was consealed by a number of women, hence he was called Nārīkavaca (having woman for armour).

मूलकाद्दशरथस्तस्मादिलिविलस्ततश्च विश्वमहः ।। ७५ ।।

तस्माच्च खट्वांगः योसौ देवासुरसंग्रामे देवैरभ्यर्थितो-
ऽसुराञ्जघान ।। ७६ ।।

The son of Mūlaka was Daśaratha; his son was Ilāvila; his son was Viśvasaha; his son was Khaṭvāṅga, called also Dilīpa, who, being invited by the gods in a war with the Asuras, destroyed a number of them.

स्वर्गे च कृतप्रियैर्देवैर्वरग्रहणाय चोदितः प्राह ।। ७७ ।।

Being pleased thereby the celestials asked him to pray for a boon.

यद्यवश्यं वरो ग्राह्यः तन्ममायुः कथ्यतामिति ।। ७८ ।।

Dilīpa said—"If you press me to accept a boon tell me what is the duration of my life."

अनंतरं च तैरुक्तं मुहूर्त्तमेकं प्रमाणं तवायुरित्युक्तोथा-
स्खलितगनि विमानेन लघिमादिगुणो मर्त्यलोकमा-
गम्येदमाह ।। ७९ ।।

The god said "The length of your life is but an hour." Thereupon Khaṭvāṅga, who was gifted with great, velocity, came down, in his easy-coursing car to the world of mortals.

यथा न ब्राह्मणेभ्यस्सकाशादात्मापि मे प्रियतरः न च
स्वधर्मोल्लंघनं मया कदाचिदप्यनुष्ठितं न च सकल-
देवमानुषपशुपक्षिवृक्षादिकेष्वच्युतव्यतिरेकवती
दृष्टिर्ममाभूत् तथा तमेवं मुनिजनानुस्मृतं भगवंतम-
स्खलितगतिः प्रापयेयमित्यशेषदेवगुरौ भगवत्य-
निर्देश्यवपुषि सत्तमात्रात्मन्यात्मानं परमात्मनि
वासुदेवाख्ये युयोज तत्रैव च लयमवाप ।। ८० ।।

Having reached there, he prayed and said—"If my soul has never been dearer to me than the sacred Brāhmaṇas; if I have never deviated from the satisfaction of duty; if I have never looked upon gods, men, animals, vegetables, and all created things as different from the imperishable, may I then attain unswervingly to that divine being, upon whom the holy sages meditate." Having thus spoken he was united with that supreme being—Vāsudeva who is the preceptor of all the gods, who is abstract existence and whose form cannot be described. Thus he was united with Vāsudeva and obtained absorption.

अत्रापि श्रूयते श्लोको गीतस्सप्तर्षिभिः पुरा ।।
खट्वांगेन समो नान्यः कश्चिदुर्व्यां भविष्यति ।। ८१ ।।

A stanza was cited by the seven ṛṣis in the days of yore—"There shall be no king on earth like Khaṭvāṅga.

येन स्वर्गादिहागम्य मुहूर्तं प्राप्य जीवितम् ।।
त्रयोतिसंधिता लोका बुद्ध्या सत्येन चैव हि ।। ८२ ।।

He came from heaven, dwelt an hour on eath, and became united three worlds by means of his liberality and knowledge of truth."

खट्वांगाद्दीर्घबाहुः पुत्रोऽभवत् ।। ८३ ।।

ततो रघुरभवत् ।। ८४ ।।

तस्मादप्यजः ।। ८५ ।।

अजाद्दशरथः ।। ८६ ।।

The son of Khaṭvāṅga was Dīrghabāhu, whose son was Raghu, whose son was Aja, whose son was Daśaratha.

तस्यापि भगवानब्जनाभो जगतः स्थित्यर्थमात्मांशेन
रामलक्ष्मणभरतशत्रुघ्नरूपेण चतुर्द्धा पुत्रत्वमायासीत् ।।
८७ ।।

The glorious god, from whose navel the lotus springs, was born for the protection of the world, as the four sons of Daśaratha—namely Rāma, Lakṣmaṇa, Bharata and Śatrughna.

रामोपि बाल एव विश्वामित्रयागरक्षणाय गच्छंस्ताटकां
जघान ।। ८८ ।।

While a boy Rāma was taken by Viśvāmitra to protect his sacrifice and slew Taḍakā.

यज्ञे च मारीचमिषुवाताहतं समुद्रे चिक्षेप ।। ८९ ।।

In the sacrifice, Mārīca was slain and thrown away.

सुबाहुप्रमुखांश्च क्षयमनयत् ।। ९० ।।

Suvāhu and others were also slain by him.

दर्शनमात्रेणाहल्यामपापां चकार ।। ९१ ।।

जनकगृहे च माहेश्वरं चापमनायासेन बभञ्ज ।। ९२ ।।

सीतामयोनिजां जनकराजतनयां वीर्यशुल्कां लेभे ।। ९३ ।।

He removed the iniquity of Ahlayā by merely looking upon her. Arriving at the palace of Janaka he easily broke the bow of Maheśvara, and received Sītā, self-born daughter of the king Janaka as the meed for his prowess.

सकलक्षत्त्रियक्षयकारिणमशेषहैहयकुलधूमकेतुभूतं च परशुराममपास्तवीर्यबलावलेपं चकार ।। ९४ ।।

He humbled the pride of Paraśurāma—the Ketu of the Haihaya race and the slayer of all Kṣatriyas.

पितृवचनाच्चागणितराज्याभिलाषो भ्रातृभार्यासमेतो वनं प्रविवेश ।। ९५ ।।

विराधखरदूषणादीन् कबंधवालिनौ च निजघान ।। ९६ ।।

At the behest of his sire and not being sorry for the loss of kingdom he went to woods accompanied by his brother Lakṣmaṇa and his wife, where he destroyed in battle Viradha, Khara, Dūṣaṇa and other Rākṣasas, the headless demon Kavandha and Vali the king of monkeys.

बद्ध्वा चांभोनिधिमशेषराक्षसकुलक्षयं कृत्वा दशाननापाहृतां भार्यां तद्वधादपहृतकलंकामप्यनलप्रवेशशुद्धामशेषदेवसंघैस्तूयमानशीलां जनकराजकन्यामध्योध्यामानिन्ये ।। ९७ ।।

ततश्चाभिषेकमंगलं मैत्रेय वर्षशतेनापि वक्तुं न शक्यते संक्षेपेण श्रूयताम् ।। ९८ ।।

लक्ष्मणभरतशत्रुघ्नविभीषणसुग्रीवांगदजाम्बवद्धनुमत्प्रभृतिभिस्समुत्फुल्लवदनैश्छत्रचामरादियुतैः सेव्यमानो दाशरथिर्ब्रह्मेंद्राग्नियमनिर्ऋति वरुणवायुकुबेरेशानप्रभृतिभिस्सर्वामरैर्वसिष्ठवामदेववाल्मीकिमार्कण्डेयविश्वामित्रभरद्वाजागस्त्यप्रभृतिभिर्मुनिवरैः ऋग्यजुस्सामाथर्वैस्संस्तूयमा नो नृत्यगीतवाद्याद्यखिललोकमंगलवाद्यैर्वीणावेणुमृदंगभेरीपटहशंखकाहलगोमुखप्रभृतिभिस्सुनादैस्समस्तभूभृतां मध्ये सकललोकरक्षार्थं यथोचितमभिषिक्तो दाशरथिः कोसलेंद्रो रघुकुलतिलको जानकीप्रियो भ्रातृत्रयप्रियस्सिंहासनगत एकादशाब्दसहस्त्रं राज्यमकरोत् ।। ९९ ।।

Having constructed a bridge across the deep and slain all the Rākṣasas, he brought back his spouse Sītā who had been carried away by the Ten-necked Rāvaṇa. Having purified her by the fiery ordeal, and accordingly her virtue chanted by the celestials, he returned with her to Ayodhyā.

भरतोपि गंधर्वविषयसाधनाय गच्छन् संग्रामे गंधर्वकोटिस्तिस्रो जघान ।। १०० ।।

शत्रुघ्नेनाप्यमितबलपराक्रमो मधुपुत्रो लवणो नाम राक्षसो निहतो मथुरा च निवेशिता ।। १०१ ।।

Having slain a number of Gandharvas, Bharata became the master of their country and having slain the Rākṣasa chief Lavaṇa, the son of Madhu, Śatrughna took possession of their capital Mathurā.

इत्येवमाद्यतिबलपराक्रमविक्रमणैरतिदुष्टसंहारिणोशेषस्य जगतो निष्पादितस्थितयो रामलक्ष्मण भरतशत्रुघ्नाः पुनरपि दिवमारूढाः ।। १०२ ।।

येऽपि तेषु भगवदंशेष्वनुरागिणः कोसलनगरजानपदास्तेपि तन्मनसस्तत्सालोक्यतामवापुः ।। १०३ ।।

Having thus by their unequalled might and strength saved the world from the grasp of the wicked, Rāma, Lakṣmaṇa, Bharata and Śatrughna went back to heaven and were followed by those inhabitants of Kośala who were one-mindedly devoted to those incarnate portions of Viṣṇu.

अतिदुष्टसंहारिणो रामस्य कुशलवौ द्वौ पुत्रौ लक्ष्मणस्यांगदचंद्रकेतु तक्षपुष्कलौ भरतस्य सुबाहुशूरसेनौ शत्रुघ्नस्य ।। १०४ ।।

Rāma had two sons one was named Kuśa and the other Lava. Lakṣmaṇa too had two sons by the name of Aṅgada and Candraketu. The sons of Bharata were Takṣa and Puṣkara.

Subāhu and Śūrasena were the sons of Śatrughna.

कुशस्यातिथिरतिथेरपि निषधः पुत्रोऽभूत्।। १०५।।

निषधस्याप्यनलस्तस्मादपि नभाः नभसः पुंडरीकस्तत्तनयः क्षेमधन्वा तस्य च देवानीकस्तस्याप्यहीनकोऽहीनकस्यापि रुरुस्तस्य च पारियात्रकः पारियात्राद्देवलो देवलाद्वच्चलः तस्याप्युत्कः उत्काच्च वज्रनाभस्त स्माच्छंखणस्तस्माद्युषिताश्वस्ततश्च विश्वसहो जज्ञे।। १०६।।

तस्माद्धिरण्यनाभः यो महायोगीश्वराज्जैमिनेश्शिष्यद्याज्ञवल्क्याद्योगमवाय।। १०७।।

The son of Kuśa was Atithi, whose son was Niṣadha, whose son was Nala, whose son was Nabhas, whose son was Puṇarīka, whose son was Kṣemadhanwan, whose son was Devanika, whose son was Ahinagu, whose son was Paripatra, whose son was Dala, whose son was Cala, whose son was Uktha, whose son was Vajranābha, whose son was Śānkhanātha, whose son was Abhyuthitāśva, whose son was Viśvasaha whose son was Hiraṇyanābha, who was a pupil of the great ascetic Jaiminī and imparted spiritual knowledge upon Yajñavalkya.

हिरण्यनाभस्य पुत्रः पुष्यस्तस्माद् ध्रुवसंधिस्ततस्सुदर्शनस्तस्मादग्निवर्णस्ततश्शीघ्रगस्तस्मादपि मरुः पुत्रोऽभवत्।। १०८।।

योसौ योगमास्थायाद्यापि कलापग्राममाश्रित्य तिष्ठति।। १०९।।

आगामियुगे सूर्यवंशक्षत्रव्रत आवर्त्तयिता भविष्यति।। ११०।।

The son of this pious king was Puṣya whose son was Dhruva Sandhi, whose son was Sudarśana, whose son was Agnivarṇa, whose son was Śighra, whose son was Maru, who by virtue of his power of devotion, is till living in the village called Kalāpa and who in future will be the restorer of the Kṣatriya race in the solar dynasty.

तस्यात्मजः प्रशुश्रुकस्तस्यापि सुसंधिस्ततश्चाप्यमर्षस्तस्य च सहस्वांस्ततश्च विश्वभवः।। १११।।

तस्य बृहद्बलः योर्जुनतनयेनाभिमन्युना भारतयुद्धे क्षयमनीयतम्।। ११२।।

Maru's son was Prasuśruta, whose son was Susandhi, whose son was Amarśa, whose son was Mahaśvat, whose son was Viśrutavat, whose son was Bṛhadbala, who was slain in the great war by Abhimanyu, the son of Arjuna.

एते इक्ष्वाकुभूपाला प्राधान्येन मयेरिताः।।
एतेया चरित श्रृण्वन् सर्वपापैः प्रमुच्यते।। ११३।।

These are the most illustrious kings is the race of Ikṣvāku. Whoever hears of the account of them will be freed from all sins.

।। इति श्रीविष्णुमहापुराणे चतुर्थेशे चतुर्थोऽध्यायः।। ४।।

अथ चतुर्थेशेः पञ्चमोऽध्यायः

Part IV : Section 5

श्रीपराशर उवाच

इक्ष्वाकुतनयो योसौ निमिर्नाम्ना सहस्त्रं वत्सरं सत्रमारेभे।। १।।
वसिष्ठं च होतारं वरयामास।। २।।

Parāśara said :—The son of Ikṣavāku, by name Nimī, instituted a sacrifice for a thousand years and appointed Vasiṣtha as the presiding priest.

तमाह विसष्ठोहमिंद्रेण पंचवर्षशतयागार्थ प्रथमं वृतः।। ३।।

तनंतरं प्रतिपाल्यतामागतस्तवापि ऋत्विक् भविष्यामीत्युक्ते स पृथिवीपतिर्न किंचिदुक्तवान्।। ४।।

Vasiṣtha said to him—"I have been already appointed by Indra for presiding at a sacrifice for five hundred years. Wait for some time, I shall come and officiate as a priest at your sacrifice." Being thus addressed the king did not answer.

वसिष्ठोप्यनेन समन्विच्छितमित्यमरपतेर्यागमकरोत्।।
५।।

And Vasiṣṭha went away supposing that he had agreed.

सोपि तत्काल एवा न्यैगौतमादिभिर्यागमकरोत्।। ६।।

Nimī in the meantime engaged Gautama and other ascetics and conducted the sacrifice.

समाप्ते चामरपतेर्यागे त्वरया वसिष्ठोनिमियज्ञं करिष्यामीत्याजगाम।। ७।।

तत्कर्मकर्तृत्वं च गौतमस्य दृष्ट्वा स्वपते तस्मै राज्ञे मां प्रत्याख्यायैव तदनेन गौतमाय कर्मांतरं समर्पितं यस्मात्तस्मादयं विदेहो भवष्यितीति शापं ददौ।।८।।

After the sacrifice of the king of celestials had been finished, Vasiṣṭha hurried on to celebrate Nimī's sacrifice and found that it was being conducted under the superintendence of Gautama.

प्रबुद्धश्चासाववनिपतिरपि प्राह।। ९।।

यस्मान्मामसंभाष्याज्ञानत एव शयानस्य शापोत्सर्गमसौ दुष्टगुरुश्चकार तस्मा त्तस्यापि देहः पतिष्यतीति शापं दत्त्वा देहमत्यजत्।। १०।।

Vasiṣṭha then imprecated a curse upon the king who was asleep, saying "Since the king, not informing me, has entrusted Gautama with the charge of the sacrifice, he shall cease to exist in a corporeal form. When Nimī got up he came to know what had happened and in return imprecated a curse upon his unjust preceptor that he should also cease to exist in a corporeal form as the punishment of uttering a curse upon him without previously communicating with him. Nimī then gave up his bodily form.

तच्छापाच्च मित्रावरुणयोस्तेजसि वसिष्ठस्य चेतः प्रविष्टम्।। ११।।

उर्वशीदर्शनादुद्भूतबीजप्रपातयोस्तयोस्सकाशाद्वसिष्ठो देहमपरं लेभे।। १२।।

The spirit of Vasiṣṭha, also renouncing his body, was united with the spirits of Mitra and Varuṇa for some time, when at last on account of their lustful desire for the nymph Urvaśī he was born again in a different body.

निमेरपि तच्छरीरमतिमनोहरगंधतैलादिभिरुपसंस्क्रियमाणं नैव क्लेदादिकं दोषमवाप सद्यो मृत इव तस्थौ।।
१३।।

Nimī's body continued to be as handsome and being emblamed with fragrant oils and resins it was not decomposed and remained like the corpse of one just dead.

यज्ञ समाप्तौ भगग्रहणाय देवानागतानृत्विज ऊचुः। यजमानाय वरो दीयतामिति।। १४।।

When the gods arrived there to receive their portion on the completion of the sacrifice the priests requested them to confer blessings upon the celebrator of the sacrifice.

देवैश्च छंदितोसौ निमिराह।। १५।।

भगवंतोखिलसंसारदुःखहंतारः।। १६।।

And being ordered by the celestials for the same Nimī said— "O celestials, you remove all ills from the world.

न ह्येतादृगन्यद्दुःखमस्ति यच्छरीरात्मनोर्वियोगे भवति।।
१७।।

There is not in the world a greater cause of distress than the separation of soul and body.

तदहमिच्छामि सकललोकलोचनेषु वस्तुं न पुनश्शरीरग्रहणं कर्तुमित्येवमुक्तैर्देवैरसावशेषभूतानां नेत्रेष्ववतारितः।। १८।।

ततो भूतान्युन्मेषनिरमेषं चक्रुः।। १९।।

I therefore wish to dwell in the eyes of all beings and not to take up a corporeal form any more." The celestials agreed to this and Nimī was placed by them in the eyes of all living beings and therefore their eye-lids are ever opening and shutting.

अपुत्रस्य च तस्य भूभुजः शरीरमराजकभीरवो मुनयोऽरण्या ममंथुः।। २०।।

As Nimī had no son the sages were afraid that the earth would have no ruler.

तत्र च कुमारो जज्ञे।। २१।।

जननाज्जनकसंज्ञां चावाप।। २२।।

So they churned the body of the king and a son was born who was named Janaka.

अभूद्विदेहोस्य पितेति वैदेहः मथनान्मिथिरिति।। २३।।

As his father had no body Janaka was also called Videha. He also received the name of Mithi for having been produced by *manthana* or agitation.

तस्योदावसुः पुत्रोऽभवत्।। २४।।

उदावसनोर्नंदिवर्द्धनस्ततस्सुकेतुः तस्माद्देवरातस्ततश्च बृहदुक्थः तस्य च महावीर्यस्तस्यापि सुधृतिः।। २५।।

ततश्च धृष्टकेतुरजायत।। २६।।

धृष्टकेतोर्हर्यश्वस्तस्य च मनुः मनोः प्रतिकः तस्मात्कृतरथस्तस्य देवमीढः तस्य च विबुधः विबुधस्य महाधृतिस्ततश्च कृतरातः ततो महारोमा तस्य स्वर्णरोमा तत्पुत्रो ह्रस्वरोमा ह्रस्वरोम्णस्सीर-ध्वजोऽभवत्।। २७।।

The son of Janaka as Udāvasu, whose son was Nandivarddhana, whose son was Suketu, whose son was Devarata, whose son was Bṛhaduktha, whose son was Mahāvīrya, whose son was Satyadhṛṣṭi, whose son was Dhṛṣṭaketu, whose son was Haryāśva, whose son was Maru, whose son was Pratibandhaka whose son was Kṛsaratha, whose son was Kṛta, whose son was Vibudha, whose son was Mahādhṛti, whose son was Kṛtirāta, whose son was Mahadhṛti, whose son was Suvarṇaroman, whose son was Haraswaroman, whose son was Sīradhvaja.

तस्य पुत्रार्थं यजनभुवं कृषतः सीरे सीता दुहिता समुत्पन्ना।। २८।।

Sīradhvaja ploughing the field, to make it ready for a sacrifice which he undertook in order to obtain progeny, there sprang up in the furrow a damsel who became his daughter Sītā.

सीरध्वजस्य भ्राता सांकाश्यधिपतिः कुशध्वज-नामासीत्।। २९।।

The brother of Sīradhvaja was Kuśadhvaja who was king of Kāśī.

सीरध्वजस्यापत्यं भानुमान् भानुमतश्शतद्युम्नः तस्य तु शुचिः तस्माच्चोर्जनामा पुत्रो जज्ञे।। ३०।।

तस्यापि शतध्वजः ततः कृतिः कृतेरञ्जनः तत्पुत्रः कुरुजित् ततोऽरिष्टनेमिः तस्माच्छ्रुतायुः श्रुतायुषः सुपार्श्वः तस्मात्सृञ्जयः ततः क्षेमावी क्षेमाविनोऽनेनाः तस्माद्भौमरथः तस्य सत्यरथः तस्मादुपगुः उपगोरुपगुप्तः तत्पुत्रः स्वागतस्तस्य च स्वानंदः तस्माच्च सुवर्चाः तस्य च सुपार्श्वः तस्यापि सुभाषः तस्य सुश्रुतः तस्मात्सुश्रुताज्जयः तस्य पुत्रो विजयः विजयस्य ऋतः ऋतात्सुनयः सुनयाद्वीतहव्यः तस्माद्धृतिः धृतेर्बहुलाश्वः तस्य पुत्रः कृतिः।। ३१।।

कृतौ संतिष्ठत्ययं जनकवंशः।। ३२।।

His son was named Bhānumat whose son was Śatadhyuna, whose son was Suci, whose son was Urjjavaha, whose son was Satyadhvaja, whose son was Kuni, whose son was Anyana, whose son was Retujit, whose son was Arṣṭanemi, whose son was Śrutayaś, whose son was Sañjaya, whose son was Kṣemarī, whose son was Anenas, whose son was Minaratha, whose son was Satyaratha, whose son was Upagu, whose son was Śruta, whose son was Śaśvata, whose son was Sudhanwan, whose son was Subhāsa, whose son was Suśruta, whose son was Jaya, whose son was Ṛta, whose son was Sunaya, whose son was Vitahadya whose son was Dhṛti, whose son was Bahalāśva, whose son was Kṛti with whom ended the family of Janaka.

इत्येते मैथिलाः।। ३३।।

प्रायेणैते आत्मविद्याश्रयिणो भूपालो भवंति।। ३४।।

These are the kings of Mithilā who shall be principally well-versed in spiritual knowledge.

।। इति श्रीविष्णुमहापुराणे चतर्थंशे पञ्चमोऽध्यायः।।५।।

अथ चतुर्थेंशे: षष्ठोऽध्याय:

Part IV : Section 6

मैत्रेय उवाच

सूर्यस्य वंश्या भगवन्कथिता भवता मम।।
सोमस्याप्यखिलान्वश्याञ्छ्रोतुमिच्छामि पार्थिवान्।। १ ।।

कीर्त्यते स्थिरकीर्त्तीनां येषामद्यापि संततिः।।
प्रसादसुमुखस्तान्मे ब्रह्मन्नाख्यातुमर्हसि।। २।।

Maitreya said :—O revered sir, you have described to me the solar dynasty but I wish to hear now of the kings of the lunar dynasty, who are still well-known for their glorious deeds. It behoves you to relate it gladly to me.

श्रीपराशर उवाच

श्रूयतां मुनिशार्दूल वंशः प्रतिथतेजसः।।
सोमस्यानुक्रमात्ख्याता यत्रोर्वीपतयोऽभवन्।। ३।।

Parāśara said :—O foremost of Munis, hear from, me, a description of the illustrious family of the moon which has produced many well-known kings of the earth.

अयं हि वंशोतिबलपराक्रमद्युतिशीलचेष्टावद्भि-
रतिगुणान्वितैर्नहुषययातिकार्तवीर्यार्जुनादिभिर्भूपालै-
रलंकृतः तमहं कथयामि श्रूयताम्।। ४।।

This family is adorned with many gifted with regal qualities of strength, valour, magnificence, prudence and energy such as Nahuṣa, Yayāti, Kārtavīrya, Arjuna and others. Hear I shall describe this family to you.

अखिलजगत्स्रष्टुर्भगवतो नारायणस्य नाभिसरोज-
समुद्भवाब्जयोनेर्ब्रह्मणः पुत्रोऽत्रिः।।५।।

Atri was the son of Brahmā, the creator of the universe, who originated from the lotus that grew from the navel of Nārāyaṇa.

अत्रेस्सोमः।। ६।।

तं च भगवानब्जयोनिः अशेषौषधीद्विजनक्षत्राणा-
माधिपत्येऽभ्यषेचयत्।। ७।।

The son of Atri was Soma whom Brahmā made the king of planets, Brāhmaṇas and of the stars.

स च राजसूयमकरोत्।। ८।।

तत्प्रभावादत्युत्कृष्टाधिपत्याधिष्ठातृत्वाच्चैनं मद
आविवेश।। ९।।

Some celebrated a Rājasūya sacrifice and on account of the glory derived therefrom and the vast sovereignty which he had acquired he grew haughty and licentious.

मदावलेपाच्च सकलदेवगुरोर्बृहस्पतेस्तारां नाम पत्नीं
जहार।। १०।।

He carried off Tārā, the wife of Bṛhaspati, the preceptor of gods.

बहुशश्च बृहस्पतिचोदितेन भगवता ब्रह्मणा चोद्यमान-
सकलैश्च देवर्षिभिर्याचमानोपि न मुमोच।। ११।।

Soma did not give up Bṛhaspati's wife though he was again and again requested by him, commanded by Brahmā and remonstrated by the holy sages.

तस्य चंद्रस्य च बृहस्तपेर्द्वेषादुशना पार्ष्णिग्राहोभूत्।। १२।।

अंगिरसश्च सकाशादुपलब्धविद्यो भगवान्रुद्रो बृहस्पतेः
सहाय्यमकरोत्।। १३।।

यतश्चोशना ततो जंभकुंभाद्याः समस्ता एव दैत्यदानव-
निकाया महान्तमुद्यमं चक्रुः।। १४।।

बृहस्पतेरपि सकलदेवसैन्ययुतः सहायः शक्रोऽऽभवत्।।
१५।।

Uṣanas, who was an enemy of Bṛhaspati, took the side of Soma. Rudra, who was pupil of Aṅgiras, the father of Bṛhaspati, assisted his fellow student. Because their preceptor Uṣanas joined Soma, Jambha, Kujambha, all the Daityas, Dānavas and other enemies of the celestials came to his help. Indra and all other celestials assisted Bṛhaspati.

एवं च तयोरतीवोग्रसंग्रामस्तारानिमित्तस्तारकामयो
नामाभूत्।। १६।।

Thus there took place a terrible combat which being on account of Tāraka was called Tārakamaya or Tāraka war.

ततश्च समस्तशस्त्राण्यसुरेषु रुद्रपुरोगमा देवा देवेषु चाशेषदानवा मुमुचुः ।। १७ ।।

In this the celestials led by Rudra hurled their weapons upon the Asuras and the Asuras equally overwhelmed the gods with weapons.

एवं देवासुराहवसंक्षोभक्षुब्धहृदयमशेषमेव जगद्ब्रह्माणं शरणं जगाम ।। १८ ।।

Thus in the conflict between the gods and demons the universe, greatly overwhelmed, sought protection of Brahmā.

ततश्च भगवानब्जयोनिरप्युशनसं शंकरमसुरान्देवांश्च निवार्य बृहस्पतये तारामदापयत् ।। १९ ।।

Thereupon the glorious God asked Uṣanas with the demons and Rudra with the celestials to desist from fighting and give back Tārā to Bṛhaspati.

तां चांतःप्रसवामवलोक्य बृहस्पतिरप्याह ।। २० ।।

नैष मम क्षेत्रे भवत्याऽन्यस्य सुतो धार्यस्समुत्सृजैन-मलमलमतिधाष्टर्येनेति ।। २१ ।।

Finding that she was pregnant Bṛhaspati desired her no longer to keep her burden and in satifaction of his orders she was delivered of a son whom she kept in the clump of long Muñja grass.

सा च तेनैवमुक्तातिपतिव्रता भर्तृवचनांतरं तमिषीका-स्तंबे गर्भमुत्ससर्ज ।। २२ ।।

And the child as soon as it was born proved its character of divinity by its radiance.

स चोत्सृष्टमात्र एवातितेजसा देवानां तेजांस्याचिक्षेप ।। २३ ।।

बृहस्पतिमिंदुं च तस्य कुमारस्यातिचारुतया साभिलाषौ दृष्ट्वा देवास्समुत्पन्नसंदेहास्तारां पप्रच्छुः ।। २४ ।।

सत्यं कथयास्माकमिति सुभगे सोमस्याथ वा बृहस्पतेरयं पुत्र इति ।। २५ ।।

Beholding both Bṛhaspati and Soma fascinated by the beauty of the child the celestials, to know whose son it was, asked Tārā, saying 'O damsel whose son is he? Is he Bṛhaspati's or Soma's."

एवं तैरुक्ता सा तारा ह्रिया किंचिन्नोवाच ।। २६ ।।

Being thus addressed Tārā was ashamed and did not answer.

बहुशोप्यभिहिता यदाऽसौ देवेभ्यो नाचचक्षे ततस्स कुमारस्तां शप्तुमुद्यतः प्राह ।। २७ ।।

Though she was repeatedly asked by the celestials she was still mute and the child, being enraged, was about to curse her, saying—

दुष्टेंबकस्मान्मम तातं नाख्यासि ।। २८ ।।

अद्यैव ते व्यलीकलज्जावत्यास्तथा शास्तिमहं करोमि ।। २९ ।।

यथा च नैवद्याप्यतिमंथरवचना भविष्यसीति ।। ३० ।।

अथाह भगवान् पितामहः तं कुमारं सन्निवार्य स्वयम-पृच्छत्तां ताराम् ।। ३१ ।।

कथय वत्से कस्यायमात्मजः सोमस्य वा बृहस्पतेर्वा इत्युक्ता लज्जमानाह सोमस्येति ।। ३२ ।।

"Unless, O vile woman, you immediately speak out, who is my father, I shall so punish you for your useless shame that no woman in future shall speak the truth" Brahmā again interfered and pacifying the child said, addressing Tārā "Tell me my daughter, is this the child of Bṛhaspati or of Soma? "Of Soma", said Tārā flushing.

ततः प्रस्फुरदुच्छ्वासितामलकपोकांतिर्भगवानुडुपतिः कुमारमालिंग्य साधु साधु वत्स प्राज्ञोसीति बुध इति तस्य च नाम चक्रे ।। ३३ ।।

Thereupon the countenance of the king of constellations became bright and expanded with joy. He at once embraced his son and said—"Well done my boy, forsooth thou art wise." And accordingly the joy boy was named Budha.

तदाख्यातमेवैतत् स च यथेलायामात्मजं पुरूरवस-मुत्पादयामास ।। ३४ ।।

I have already described how Budha begot Purūravas on Ilā.

पुरूरवास्त्वतिदानशीलोऽतियज्वातितेजस्वी यं सत्यवादिनमतिरूपस्विनं मनस्विनं मित्रावरुण-

शापान्मानुषे लोके मया वस्तव्यमिति कृतमतिरुर्वशी
ददर्श ।। ३५ ।।

Purūravas was a prince famous for liberatily devotion, magnificence, love of truth and beauty. Having incured the curse of the Mitra and Varuṇa Urvaśī made up her mind to live in the land of mortals and descending there saw Purūravas.

दृष्टमात्रे च तस्मिन्नपहाय मानमशेषमपास्य
स्वर्गसुखाभिलाषं तन्मनस्का भूत्वा तमेवोपतस्थे ।।
३६ ।।

As soon as she saw him she forgot all reserve and not caring for the comforts to heaven became greatly attached to him.

सोऽपि च तामतिशयितसकललोक स्त्रीकांतिसौ-
कुमार्यलावण्यगतिविलासहासादिगुणामवलोक्य
तदायत्तचित्तवृत्तिर्बभूव ।। ३७ ।।

And finding her far superior to all other females in beauty, elegance, symmetry, and delicacy, Purūravas was equally enamoured of her.

उभयमपि तन्मनस्कमनन्यदृष्टि परित्यक्तसमस्तान्य-
प्रयोजनमभूत् ।। ३८ ।।

Both the man and the woman were equally attached to each other and thought no more of any other object.

राजा तु प्रागल्भ्यात्तामाह ।। ३९ ।।

The king then boldly said—

सुभ्रु त्वामहमभिकामोऽस्मि प्रसीदाऽनुरागमुद्वहेत्युक्ता
लज्जावखंडितमुर्वशी तं प्राह ।। ४० ।।

"Fair woman, I love you; have pity on me and return my affection." Urvaśī turning her face a little through modesty said—

भवत्वेवं यदि मे समयपरिपालनं भवान्
करोतीत्याख्याते पुनरपि तामाह ।। ४१ ।।

"I will do so, if you satisfy the conditions I propose to you."

आख्याहि मे समयमिति ।। ४२ ।।

अथ पृष्टा पुनरप्यब्रवीत् ।। ४३ ।।

शयनसमीपे ममोरणकद्वयं पुत्रभूतं नापनेयम् ।। ४४ ।।

भवांश्च मया न नग्नो दृष्टव्यः ।। ४५ ।।

घृतमात्रं च ममाहार इति ।। ४६ ।।

"What are they"? asked the king "speak them out". "I have two rams" said the nymph "which I love like my children; they must be kept by my bed-side and shall not be allowed to be carried away. You must not be seen by me undressed and clarified butter alone shall be my food."

एवमेवेति भूपतिरप्याह ।। ४७ ।।

The king readily agreed to these terms.

तया सह स चावनिपतिरलकायां चैत्ररथादिव-
नेष्वमलपद्म खंडेषु मानसादिसरस्स्वतिरमणीयेषु
रममाण एकषष्टिवर्षाण्यनुदिनप्रवर्द्धमानप्रमोदो-
ऽनयत् ।। ४८ ।।

After this Purūravas and Urvaśī lived together for sixty one thousand years in Alakā, sporting amidst the groves and lakes of Caitraratha abounding in lotuses and the other forests.

उर्वशी चव तदुपभोगात्प्रतिदिनप्रवर्द्धमानानुरागा
अमरलोकवासेऽपि न स्पृहां चकार ।। ४९ ।।

By these enjoyments Urvaśī's attachment increased every day and she forgot all desire for residing in the region of immortals.

विना चोर्वश्या सुरलोकोऽप्सरसां सिद्धगंधर्वाणां च
नातिरमणीयोऽभवत् ।। ५० ।।

In the absence of Urvaśī heaven appeared devoid of beauty to the celestials, nymph genii and quiristers.

ततश्चोर्वशी पुरूरवसोस्समयविद्विश्वावसुर्गंधर्वसमवेतो
निशि शयनाभ्याशादेकमुरणकं जहार ।। ५१ ।।

तस्याकाशे नीयमानस्योर्वशी शब्दमश्रृणोत् ।। ५२ ।।

एवमुवाच च ममानाथायाः पुत्रः केनापह्रियते कं
शरणमुपयामीति ।। ५३ ।।

Knowing the engagement that Urvaśī had contracted with the king, Viśvasvasu was appointed by the Gandharvas to bring about its dissolution. And coming by night to the room where they were sleeping he carried off one of the rams : Urvaśī got up by its cries and exclaimed—'Ah me! who has stolen one of my children : Had I got a husband this would not have taken place. To whom shall I go for help?"

तदाकर्ण्य राजा मां नग्नं देवी वीक्ष्यतीति न ययौ ।। ५४ ।।

The king heard the lamentations but could not go lest he might he seen undressed.

अथान्यमप्युरणकमादाय गंधर्वा ययुः ।। ५५ ।।

The Gandharvas then took away another ram.

तस्याप्यपह्रियमाणस्याकर्ण्य शब्दमाकाशे पुनरप्यनाथास्म्यहमभर्तृका कापुरुषा श्रयेत्यार्त्तराविणी बभूव ।। ५६ ।।

Again hearing the sound of its being stolen away in the sky she lamented saying—"Alas I have got no husband. I have taken the shelter of a dastardly person."

राजाप्यमर्षवशादंधकारमेतदिति खड्गमादाय दुष्टदुष्ट हतोसीति व्याहरन्नभ्यधावत् ।। ५७ ।।

Thinking "it is darkness" the king took up a dagger and pursued them, saying—"stop, O wicked I shall soon slay you."

तावच्च गंधर्वैरप्यतीवोज्ज्वला विद्युज्जनिता ।। ५८ ।।

तत्प्रभया चोर्वशी राजानमपगतांबरं दृष्ट्वापवृत्तसमया तत्क्षणादेवापक्रान्ता ।। ५९ ।।

Immediately the Gandharvas created a flash of brilliant lightning in the room and the king was seen undressed by Urvaśī. The contract was broken and she instantly disappeared.

परित्यज्य तावप्युरणकौ गंधर्वास्सुरलोकमुपगताः ।। ६० ।।

And leaving behind the rams the Gandharvas too went to the region of the celestials.

राजापि च तौ मेषावादायातिहृष्टमनाः स्वशयनमायातो नोर्वशीं ददर्श ।। ६१ ।।

तां चापश्यन् व्यपगतांबर एवोन्मत्तरूपो बभ्राम ।। ६२ ।।

Taking the rams, the king, delighted came back to his bed-room but found no Urvaśī. Not finding her he wandered naked all over the world like a maniac.

कुरुक्षेत्रे चांभोजसरस्यन्याभिश्चतसृभिरप्यसरोभिस्समवेतामुर्वशीं ददर्श ।। ६३ ।।

At length arriving at Kurukṣetra he saw Urvaśī sporting with four other nymphs in a lake abounding in lotuses.

ततश्चोन्मत्तरूपो जाये हि तिष्ठ मनसि घोरं तिष्ठ वचसि कपटिके तिष्ठेत्येवमनेकप्रकारं सूक्तमवोचत् ।। ६४ ।।

Like a mad man the king neared him and exclaimed—"O my wife, wait, speak with me, O thou of an iron heart."

आह चोर्वशी ।। ६५ ।।

महारा जालमनेनाविवेकचेष्टितेन ।। ६६ ।।

Urvaśī replied—"O great king useless is this inconsiderate attempt.

अंतर्वत्न्यहमब्दांते भवताऽत्रागंतव्यं कुमारस्ते भविष्यति एकां च निशामहं त्वया सह वत्स्यामीत्युक्तः प्रहृष्टस्स्वपुरं जगाम ।। ६७ ।।

I am now pregnant, go away just now and come here again after a year when I shall give you a son and remain with you for one night." Being thus solaced Purūravas came back to his capital.

तासां चाप्यसरसामूर्वशी कथयामास ।। ६८ ।।

Urvaśī then said to her mates.

अयं स पुरुषोत्कृष्टो येनाहमेतावंतं कालमनुरागाकृष्टमानसा सहोषितेति ।। ६९ ।।

"This king is the excellent man being drawn by whose attachment I lived for such a long time."

एवमुक्तास्ताश्चाप्सरस ऊचुः ।। ७० ।।

Hearing this the other nymphs said.

साधुसाध्वस्य रूपमप्यनेन सहास्माकमपि सर्वकालमास्या भवेदिति ।। ७१ ।।

"Great is his beauty; we too with him could live happily for ever."

अब्दे च पूर्णे स राजा तत्राजगाम।। ७२।।

कुमारं चायुषमस्मै चोर्वशी ददौ।। ७३।।

After the expiration of a year the king again came to that place and Urvaśī gave him a son by the name of Āyuṣ.

दत्त्वा चैकां निशां तेन राज्ञा सहोषित्वा पञ्च पुत्रोत्पत्तये गर्भमवाप।। ७४।।

Living with him for one night she again became pregnant to bear to him five sons.

उवाच चैनं राजानमस्मत्प्रीत्या महाराजाय सर्व एव गंधर्वा वरदास्संवृत्ताः व्रियतां च वर इति।। ७५।।

She then said to the king—"O king all the Gandharvas, on account of their regard for me, are ready to confer upon thee a boon. Do thou pray for it."

आह च राजा।। ७६।।

विजितसकलारातिरविहतेंद्रियसामर्थ्यो बंधुमान-मितबलकोशोऽस्मि नान्यदस्माकमुर्वशीसा-लोक्यात्प्राप्तव्यमस्ति तदहमनया सहोर्वश्या कालं नेतुमभिलषामीत्युक्ते गंधर्वा राज्ञेऽग्निस्थालीं ददुः।। ७७।।

ऊचुश्चैनमग्निमाम्नायानुसारी भूत्वा त्रिधा कृत्वोर्वशीसलोकतामनोरथमुद्दिश्य सम्यग्यजेथाः ततोऽवश्यमभिलषितमवाप्स्यतीत्युक्तस्तामग्नि-स्थालीमादाय जगाम।। ७८।।

The king said—"I have slain all my enemies—my faculties are all very powerful; I have friends, relations, armies and treasures; so there is nothing which I want but living with my Urvaśī in the same region. So I wish to live with her always." After he had spoken this the Gandharvas brought to him a vessel with fire adn said,—"Take this fire and according to the precepts of the Vedas divide it into three parts : then offer oblation to it for Urvaśī and your desires shall thus be gratified." The Gandharvas having said this, the king took the vessel and went away.

अंतरटव्यामचिंतयत् अहो मेऽतीव मूढता किमहमकरवम्।। ७९।।

वह्निस्थाली मयैषानीता नोर्वशीति।। ८०।।

Then coming to a forest he thought—"Oh, what stupid I am; I have brought this vessel but not Urvaśī."

अथैनामटव्यामेवाग्निस्थालीं तत्याज स्वपुरं च जगाम।। ८१।।

Then leaving the vessel there he came back to his capital.

व्यतीतेऽर्द्धरात्रे विनिद्रश्चाचिंतयत्।। ८२।।

ममोर्वशीसालोक्यप्राप्त्यर्थमग्निस्थाली गंधर्वैर्दत्त सा च मयाटव्यां परित्यक्ता।। ८३।।

When half the night had passed he awoke and thought—"The Gandharvas conferred upon me this vessel of fire to enable me to live with Urvaśī. I have left that in the forest.

तदहं तत्र तदाहरणाय यास्यामीत्युत्थाय तत्राप्युपगतो नाग्निस्थालीमपश्यत्।। ८४।।

I shall go there to bring it." Having said this he went there but did not find the vessel.

शमीगर्भं चाश्वत्थमग्निस्थालीस्थाने दृष्ट्वाऽचिंतयत्।। ८५।।

मयात्राग्निस्थाली निक्षिप्ता सा चाश्वत्थशमी-गर्भोऽभूत्।। ८६।।

तदेनमेवाहमग्निरूपमादाय स्वपुरमभिगम्यारणीं कृत्वा तदुत्पन्नाग्नेरुपास्तिं करिष्यामीति।। ८७।।

Then beholding a young Aśwattha tree growing out of a Śamī plant he argued within himself—"I left here a vessel of fire and I now see a young Aśvattha tree growing out of a Śamī plant. I shall take type of fire to my capital and having created fire by their attrition I will worship it."

एवमेव स्वपुरमभिगम्यारणिं चकार।। ८८।।

तत्प्रमाणं चांगुलैः कुर्वन् गायत्रीमपठत्।। ८९।।

Having thus made up his mind he took the plants to his city and made their wood for attrition with pieces of as many inches long as there are syllables in the Gāyatrī.

पठतश्चाक्षरसंख्यान्येवांगुलान्यरण्यभवत्।। १०।।

He recited that holy verse and rubbed together sticks of as many inches as he recited syllables in the Gāyatrī.

तत्राग्निं निर्मथ्याग्नित्रयमाम्नायानुसारी भूत्वा जुहाव।। ११।।

उर्वशीसालोक्यं फलमभिसंधितवान्।। १२।।

Having created fire therefrom he divided it into three portions according to the precepts of the Vedas and offered oblations to it with the view of obtaining re-union with Urvaśī.

तेनैव चाग्निविधिना बहुविधान् यज्ञानिष्ट्वा गांधर्वलोकान वाप्योर्वश्या सहावियोगमवाप।। १३।।

Having performed many sacrifices with this fire he attained to the region of the Gandharvas and suffered no more separation from his beloved Urvaśī.

एकोऽग्निरादावभवत् एकेन त्वत्र मन्वंतरे त्रेधा प्रवर्तिताः।। १४।।

Thus fire, that was at first one, was made three-fold in the present Manwantara by the son of Ilā.

।। इति श्रीविष्णुमहापुराणे चतुर्थेशे षष्ठोऽध्यायः।। ६।।

अथ चतुर्थेशेः सप्तमोऽध्यायः

Part IV : Section 7

श्रीपराशर उवाच

तस्याप्यायुर्धीमानमावसुर्विश्वावसुःश्रुतायुश्शतायु-
रयुतायुरितिसंज्ञाः षट् पुत्रा अभवन्।। १।।

Purūravas has six son—Dhīmat, Amāvasu, Viśvavasu, Śatāyuṣ, and Śrutayuṣ.

तथामावसोर्भीमनामा पुत्रोऽभवत्।। २।।

भीमस्य काञ्चनः काञ्चनात्सुहोत्रः तस्यापि जह्नुः।। ३।।

The son of Amāvasu was Bhīma, whose son was Kāñcana, whose son was Suhotra, whose name was Jāhnu.

योऽसौ यज्ञवाटमखिलं गंगांभसा प्लावितमवलोक्य
क्रोधसंरक्तलोचनो भगवंतं यज्ञपुरुषमात्मनि परमेण
समाधिना समारोप्याखिलमेव गंगामपिबत्।। ४।।

Whilst celebrating a sacrifice this king beheld the whole of the place over-flowed with the waters of the Gaṅgā. Being offended therefore with his eyes red with anger he united the spirit of sacrifice with himself and by the power of his devotion drunk up the river.

अथैनं देवर्षयः प्रसादयामासुः।। ५।।

दुहितृत्वे चास्य गंगामनयन्।। ६।।

Thereupon the celestials and the sages pleased him and got back Gaṅgā in the capacity of his daughter.[1]

जह्नोश्च सुमंतुर्नाम पुत्रोऽभवत्।। ७।।

तस्याप्यजकस्ततो बलाकाश्वस्तस्मात्कुशस्तस्यापि
कुशांबकुशनाभाधूर्त्तरजसो वसुश्चेति चत्वारः पुत्रा
बभूवुः।। ८।।

The son of Jāhnu was Sumanta, whose son was Ajaka, whose son was Valākāśva, whose son was Kuśa, who had four sons, Kuśamba Kuśanābha, Amurttaya and Amāvasu.

तेषां कुशांबः शक्रतुल्यो मे पुत्रो भवेदिति तपश्चकार।। ९।।

Kusambha engaged in devout penances with the object of having a son equal to Indra.

तं चोग्रतपसमवलोक्य मा भवत्वन्योऽस्मत्तुल्यो वीर्य
इत्यात्मनैवास्येंद्रः पुत्रत्वमगच्छत्।। १०।।

Beholding the intensity of his devotions, Indra himself took birth as his son lest of his devotions, Indra himself took birth as his son lest a prince equally powerful like him might be born.

1. For this the Gaṅgā is called Jāhnavī *i.e.* issuing from Jāhnu.

स गाधिर्नाम पुत्रः कौशिकोऽभवत्।। ११।।

गाधिश्च सत्यवतीं कन्यामजनयत्।। १२।।

He was accordingly born as Gādhī had a son named Kauśika and a daughter called Satyāvatī.

तां च भार्गवः ऋचीको वव्रे।। १३।।

Ṛcika, one of the descendants of Bhṛgu, wanted her in marriage.

गाधिरप्यतिरोषणायातिवृद्धाय ब्राह्मणाय दातुमनिच्छ-
न्नेकतश्श्यामकर्णानामिंदुवर्चसामनिलरहंसामश्वानां
सहस्रं कन्याशुल्कमयाचत।। १४।।

The king was reluctant to give his daughter in marriage to a peevish old Brāhmin and wanted from him as the bridal present a thousand fleet steeds whose colour should be white with one black ear.

तेनाप्यृषिणा वरुणसकाशादुपलभ्याश्वतीर्थोत्पन्नं
तादृशमश्वसहस्रं दत्तम्।। १५।।

ततस्तामृचीकः कन्यामुपयेमे।। १६।।

ऋचीकश्च तस्याश्चरुमपत्यार्थं चकार।। १७।।

Having propitiated Varuṇa, the god of ocean, Ṛcika obtained from him, at the holy place called Avatīrtha a thousand horses. And giving them to the king he married his daughter.

तत्प्रसादितश्च तन्मात्रे क्षत्रवरपुत्रोत्पत्तये चरुमपरं
साधयामास।। १८।।

एष चरुर्भवत्सा अयमपरश्चरुस्त्वन्मात्रा सभ्यगुपयोज्य
इत्युक्त्वा वनं जगाम्।। १९।।

In order to have a son he prepared a dish of rice, barely and pulse with butter and milk for his wife to eat. And being requested by her he made a similar mixture for her mother, by partaking of which she should give birth to a martial prince. Keeping both the dishes with his wife and giving her instructions which was intended for her and which for her mother, the sage went to the forest.

उपयोगकाले च तां माता सत्यवतीमाह।। २०।।

पुत्रि सर्व एवात्मपुत्रमतिगुणमभिलषतिनात्मजाया-
भ्रातृगुणेष्वतीवादृतो भवतीति।। २१।।

At the time of taking the food her mother said to Satyavatī—"Daughter, every one wants to have a son gifted with great qualities—and no body wishes to be excelled by the qualities of his mother's brother.

अतोर्हसि ममात्मीयं चरुं दातुं मदीयं चरुमात्मानो-
पयोक्तुम्।। २२।।

मत्पुत्रेण हि सकलभूमंडलपरिपालनं कार्यं कियद्वा
ब्राह्मणस्य बलवीर्यसंपदेत्युक्ता सा स्वचरुं मात्रे
दत्तवती।। २३।।

It is therefore desirable for you to give me the food which your husband has set apart for you and to partake of that intended for me; for my son shall be the sovereign of the world. What is the use of wealth, strength and prowess for a Brāhmin." Being thus addressed Satyavatī gave her own food to her mother.

अथ वनादागत्य सत्यवतीमृषिरपश्यत्।। २४।।

आह चैनामतिपापे किमिदमकार्यं भवत्या कृतम्
अतिरौद्रं ते वपुर्लक्ष्यते।। २५।।

नूनं त्वया त्वन्मातृसात्कृतश्चरुरुपयुक्तो न युक्तमेतत्।।
२६।।

When the sage came back from the forest and saw Satyavatī he said to her—"Sinful woman, what hast thou done? Your body appears as very fearful to me. Surely thou hast taken the food which was intended for thy mother. Thou hast committed a wrong.

मया हि तत्र चरौ सकलैश्वर्यवीर्यशौर्यबलसंपदारोपिता
त्वदीयचरावप्यखिलशांतिज्ञानतितिक्षादिब्राह्मण-
गुणसंपत्।। २७।।

That food I had consecrated with the properties of power, strength and heroism; where as your food was consecrated with the qualities of a Brāhmaṇa—gentleness, knowledge and resignation.

तच्च विपरीतं कुर्वंत्यास्तवातिरौद्रास्त्रधारणपालननिष्ठः
क्षत्रियाचारः पुत्रो भविष्यति तस्याश्चोपशमरुचि-
र्ब्राह्मणाचार इत्याकर्ण्यैव सा तस्य पादौ जग्राह।। २८।।

As you have exchanged messes your son shall follow a warriors's propensities and use weapons, and fight and slay; your mother's son shall be born with the desires of a Brāhmin and shall be devoted to peace and piety." Hearing this Satyavatī fell at her husband's feet and said—

प्रणिपत्य चैनमाह।। २९।।

भगवन्मयैतदज्ञानादनुष्ठितं प्रसादं मे कुरु मैवंविधः पुत्रो भवतु काममेवंविधः पौत्रो भवत्वित्युक्ते मुनिरप्याह।। ३०।।

If this is inevitably let my grandson be such, not my son." Being thus addressed the sage said—

एवमस्त्विति।। ३१।।

"So be it."

अनंतरं च सा जमदग्निमजीजनत् ।। ३२।।

तन्माता च विश्वामित्रं जनयामास।। ३३।।

Thereupon she gave birth Jamadagni and her mother brought forth Viśvāmitra.

सत्यवत्यपि कौशिकी नाम नद्यभवत्।। ३४।। जदग्निरिक्ष्वाकुवंशेद्भवस्य रेणोतस्तनयां रेणुकाःमुपयेमे।। ३५।।

तस्यां चाशेषक्षत्रहंतारं परशुरामसंज्ञं भगवतस्सकल-लोकगुरोर्नारायणस्यांशं जमदग्निरजीजनत्।। ३६।।

Satyavatī afterwards became the Kauśikī river, Jamadagni married Reṇukā the daughter of Reṇu, born in the race of Ikṣvāku and begot on her a son, Paraśurāma the destroyer of the Kṣatriya race, who was a portion of Nārāyaṇa, the preceptor of the universe.

विश्वामित्रपुत्रस्तु भार्गव एव शुनश्शेपो देवैर्दत्तः ततश्च देवरातनामाऽभवत्।। ३७।।

Sunaḥśepa was conferred upon Viśvāmitra by the celestials as his son, who became known as Devarāta.

ततश्चान्ये मधुश्छंदोधनञ्जयकृतदेवाष्टककच्छप-हरिराख्या विश्वामित्रपुत्रा बभूवुः।। ३८।।

Viśvāmitra had other sons—Madhucchanda, Yaya, Kṛtadeva. Devāṣṭaka, Kacchapa and Harītaka.

तेषां च बहूनि कौशिकगोत्राणि ऋष्यंतरेषु विवाह्यान्यभवन्।। ३९।।

These founded many families, all of whom were known by the name of Kauśikas, and inter-married with the families of various Ṛṣis.

।। इति श्रीविष्णुमहापुराणे चतुर्थेंशे सप्तमोऽध्यायः।। ७।।

अथ चतुर्थेंशेः अष्टमोऽध्यायः

Part IV : Section 8

श्रीपराशर उवाच

पुरूरवसो ज्येष्ठः पुत्रोयस्त्वायुर्नामा स राहोर्दुहितर-मुपयेमे।। १।।

तस्यां च पञ्च पुत्रानुत्पादयामास।। २।।

नहुषक्षत्रवृद्धरंभरजिसंज्ञास्तथैवानेनाः पञ्चमः पुत्रोऽभूत्।। ३।।

Parāśara said :—Ayuṣ, the eldest son of Purūravas, married the daughter of Rāhu upon whom he begot five sons, Nahuṣa, Kṣatravṛdha, Rambha, Raji and Anenas.

क्षत्रवृद्धात्सुहोत्रः पुत्रोऽभवत्।। ४।।

काश्यपकाशगृत्समदास्त्रयस्तस्य पुत्रा बभूवुः।। ५।।

The son of Kṣatravṛdha was Suhotra, who had three sons, Kāśyapa, Kāśa and Ghṛtsamada.

गृत्समदस्य शौनकश्चातुर्वर्ण्यप्रवर्त्तयिताऽभूत्।। ६।।

The son of Ghṛtasamada was Śaunaka who first instituted the distinction of the four castes.

काश्यस्य काशेयः काशीराजः तस्माद्राष्ट्रः राष्ट्रस्य दीर्घतपाः पुत्रोऽभवत्।। ७।।

धन्वंतरिस्तु दीर्घतपसः पुत्रोऽभवत्।। ८।।

स हि संसिद्धकार्यकरणस्सकलसंभूतिष्वशेषज्ञानविदा भगवता नारायणेन चातीत संभूतौ तस्मै वरो दत्तः।। ९।।

काशीराजगोत्रेऽवतीर्य त्वमष्टधा सम्यगायुर्वेदं करिष्यसि यज्ञभागभुग्भविष्यसीति।। १०।।

The son of Kaśa was Kāśīrāja, whose son was Dīrghatamas, whose son was Dhanwantarī, who was not subject to human infirmities and who had been master of universal knowledge in every birth. In his past life Nārāyaṇa had conferred upon him the boon that he should be, in his next life, born in the race of Kṣatriya, should be the author of the eight fold system of medical science and should be entitled to a share of offerings made to the celestials.

तस्य च धन्वंतरेः पुत्रः केतुमान् केतुमतो भीमरथः तस्यापि दिवोदासः तस्यापि प्रतर्दनः।। ११।।

स च भद्रश्रेण्यवंशविनाशनादशेषशत्रवोनेनजिता इति शत्रुजिदभवत्।। १२।।

तेन च प्रीतिमतात्मपुत्रो वत्सवत्सेत्यभिहितो वत्सोऽभवत्।। १३।।

सत्यपरतया ऋतध्वजसंज्ञामवाप।। १४।।

ततश्च कुवलयनामानमश्वं लेभे ततः कुवलयाश्व इत्यस्यां पृथिव्यां प्रथितः।। १५।।

The son of Dhanwantarī, was Keśumat, whose son was Bhīmaratha, whose son was Devadāsa, whose son was Pratardana, so called from destroying the race of Bhadraśreṇya, He had various other names—as Śatrujit.

The victor of enemies' on account of his having defeated all his enemies Vatsa or 'child' for his father used to call him often times by that name; Ṛtadhvaja 'whose emblem was truth' for he was a great observer of truth; and Kuvalayāśva for he had a horse called Kuvalaya.

तस्य च वत्सस्य पुत्रोऽलर्कनामाभवत् यस्यायमद्यापि श्लोको गीयते।। १६।।

षष्टिवर्षसहस्राणि षष्टिवर्षशतानि च।।
अलर्कादपरो नान्यो बुभुजे मेदिनीं युवा।। १७।।

His son was Alarka of whom this verse is recited in the present day—"For sixty thousand and sixty hundred years no other youthful king exept Alarka governed the earth."

तस्याप्यलर्कस्य सन्नतिनामाऽभवदात्मजः।। १८।।

सन्नतेः सुनीथः तस्यापि सुकेतुः तस्माच्च धर्मकेतुर्जज्ञे।। १९।।

ततश्च सत्यकेतुः तस्माद्विभुः तत्तनयस्सुविभुः ततश्च सुकुमारस्तस्यापि दृष्टकेतुः ततश्च वीतिहोत्रः तस्माद्भार्गः भार्गस्य भार्गभूमिः ततश्चातुर्वर्ण्यप्रवृत्ति-रित्येते काश्यपभूभृतः कथिताः।। २०।।

The son of Alarka was Santati, whose son was Sunītha, whose son was Suketu, whose son was Dharmaketu, whose son was Satyaketu, whose son was Vibhu, whose son was Suvibhu, whose son was Sukumāra, whose son was Dhṛṣṭaketu, whose son was Vainahotra, whose son was Bhārga, whose son was Bhārgabhūmi, who laid down the rules of the four castes.

रजेस्तु संततिः श्रूयताम्।। २१।।

These are the desendants of Kaśa. We shall now enumerate the desendants of Raji.

।। इति श्रीविष्णुमहापुराणे चतुर्थेंशेऽष्टमोऽध्यायः।। ८।।

अथ चतुर्थेंशे: नवमोऽध्याय:
Part IV : Section 9

श्रीपराशर उवाच

रजेस्तु पञ्च पुत्रशतान्यतुलबलपराक्रमसाराण्यासन्।। १।।

Raji had five hundred sons who were all gifted with great power and heroism.

देवसुरसंग्रामारंभे च परस्परवधेप्सवो देवाश्चासुराश्च
ब्राह्माणमुपेत्य पप्रच्छुः।। २।।

भगवन्नस्माकमत्र विरोधे कतमः पक्षो जेता
भविष्यतीति ।। ३।।

Once on a time there arose a conflict between the gods and the demons, and they, all desirous of slaying the other party, inquired of Brahmā, saying "O glorious god, which of the parties shall be victorious?

अथाह भगवान।। ४।।

येषामर्थे रजिरात्मात्तायुधो योत्स्यति तत्पक्षो जेतेति।। ५।।

The deity said—"That for which Raji shall take up arms."

अथ दैत्यैरुपेत्य रजिरात्मसाहाय्यदानायाभ्यर्थितः
प्राह।। ६।।

योत्स्येऽहं भवतामर्थे यद्यहममरजयाद्भवतामिंद्रो
भविष्यामीत्याकर्ण्यैतत्तैरभिहितम्।।७।।

न वयमन्यथा वदिष्यामोऽन्यथा करिष्यामो-
ऽस्माकमिंद्रः प्रह्लादस्तदर्थमेवायमुद्यम इत्युक्त्वा
गतेष्वसुरेषु देवैरप्यसाववनिपतिरेवमेवोक्तस्तेनापि च
तथैवोक्ते दैवैरिंद्रस्त्वं भविष्यसीति समन्विच्छितम्।।
८।।

The Daityas immediately went to Raji to secure his help, which he agreed to give if they would make him their king after defeating the celestials." Hearing this the Asuras said—"We cannot say one thing and do the otherwise. Prahlāda is our king and for him we wage war." Having said this they went away and the celestials came to him for the same purpose. Raji proposed to them the same conditions and the gods agreed and said. "We shall make you our Indra."

रजिनापि देवसैन्यसहायेनानेकैर्महास्त्रैस्तद शेषमहासुर-
बलं निषूदितम्।। ९।।

अथ जितारिपक्षश्च देवेंद्रो रजिचरणयुगलमात्मनः
शिरसा निपीड्याह।। १०।।

भयत्राणादन्नदानाद्भवान स्मत्पिताऽशेषलोकाना-
मुत्तमोत्तमो भवान् यस्याहं पुत्रस्त्रिलोकेंद्रः।। ११।।

Thereupon Raji assisted the army of the celestials and by his various weapons destroyed the Asuras. When all the enemies were defeated, Indra the king of the celestials placed Raji's feet on his crown and said, "Thou art our father since thou hast released us from fear; thou art the supreme lord of all the worlds, because, I, who am the lord of the three worlds, have acknowledge thee as my father."

स चापि राजा प्रहस्याह।। १२।।

एवमस्त्वेवमस्त्वनतिक्रमणीया हि वैरिपक्षादप्यनेक-
विधचाटुवाक्यगर्भा प्रणतिरित्युक्त्वा स्वपुरं जगाम।।
१३।।

शतक्रतुरपींद्रत्वं चकार।। १४।।

The king smiling said—"So be it. Even if the enemies admit humiliation by flattering speeches that cannot be resisted." Saying this he repaired to his own city. Śatakratu too continued to rule as Indra.

स्वर्याते तु रजौ नारदर्षिचोदिता रजिपुत्राश्शतक्रतु-
मात्मपितृपुत्रं समाचारादाज्यं याचितवन्तः।। १५।।

A few days after the king went to heaven, and his sons, being incited by the sage Nārada, demanded the rank of Indra as there hereditary right.

अप्रदानेन च विजित्येन्द्रमतिबलिनः स्वयमिंद्रत्वं
चक्रुः।। १६।।

When he refused to give them the station the highly powerful princes reduced him to submission and usurped his rank.

ततश्च बहुतिथे काले ह्यतीते बृहस्पतिमेकान्ते दृष्ट्वा अपहृतत्रैलोक्ययज्ञभागः शतक्रतुरुवाच।। १७।।

बदरीफलमात्रमप्यर्हसि ममाप्यायनाय पुरोडाशखंडं दातुमित्युक्तो बृहस्पतिरुवाच।। १८।।

When some time had passed, Indra, deprived of his share in the sacrifices of three worlds, spoke to Bṛhaspati in a retired place—"Give me a little of the sacrificial butter not bigger even than a jujube for I am in want of sustenance."

यद्येवं त्वयाहं पूर्वमेव चोदितस्स्यां तन्मया त्वदर्थं किमकर्त्तव्यमित्यल्पैरेवाहोभिस्त्वां निजं पदं प्रापयिष्यामीत्यभिधाय तेषामनुदिनमाभियचारकं बुद्धिमोहाय शक्रस्य तेजोभिवृद्धये जुहाव।। १९।।

Bṛhaspati said :—"Had you applied to me before I could have done anything for you; however I will now try to gain back for you your position." Saying this he undertook the celebration of a sacrifice for increasing the power of Indra and bringing about the downfall of Raji's sons by leading them astray.

ते चापि तेन बुद्धिमोहेनाभिभूयमाना ब्रह्मद्विषो धर्मत्यागिनो वेदवादपराङ्मुखा बभूवुः।। २०।।

ततस्तानपेतधर्माचारानिंद्रो जघान।। २१।।

पुरोहिताप्यायिततेजाश्च शक्रो दिवमाक्रमत्।। २२।।

When their understanding was bewildered the princes became haters of the Brāhmins, negligent of their duties and regardless of the teachings of the Vedas; when they became devoid of religion and morality, Indra slew they became devoid of religion and morality, Indra slew them and gained back his sovereignty by the help of the priest of gods.

एतदिंद्रस्य स्वपदच्यवनादारोहणं श्रुत्वा पुरुषः स्वपदभ्रंशं दौरात्म्यं च नाप्नोति।। २३।।

Whoever shall hear of Indra's acquirement of the position, shall always keep his proper place and shall not be guilty of iniquity.

रंभस्त्वनपत्योऽभवत्।। २४।।

Rambha, the third son of Ayuṣ, had no offspring.

क्षत्रवृद्धसुतः प्रतिक्षत्रोऽभवत्।। २५।।

तत्पुत्रः सञ्जयः तस्यापि जयः तस्यापि विजयः तस्माच्च जज्ञे कृतः।। २६।।

तस्य च हर्यधनः हर्यधनसुतस्सहदेवः तस्माददी नस्तस्य जयत्सेनः ततश्च संकृतिः तत्पुत्रः क्षत्रधर्मा इत्येते क्षत्रवृद्धस्य वंश्याः।। २७।।

Kṣatravṛddha had a son named Pratikṣatrā, whose son was Sañjaya, whose son was Vijaya, whose son was Yajñakṛt, whose son was Harśavarddhana, whose son was Sahadeva, whose son was Adina, whose son was Jayasena, whose son was Saṅkṛti, whose son was Kṣatradharma. These were the progeny of Kṣātravṛddha.

ततो नहुषवंशं प्रवक्ष्यामि।। २८।।

I will now enumerate those of Nahuṣa.

।। इति श्रीविष्णुमहापुराणे चतुर्थेंशे नवमोऽध्यायः।। ९।।

अथ चतुर्थेंशेः दशमोऽध्यायः

Part IV : Section 10

श्रीपराशर उवाच

यतिययातिसंयात्यायातिवियातिकृतिसंज्ञा नहुषस्य षट् पुत्रा महाबलपराक्रमा बभूवः।। १।।

Parāśara said :—Nahuṣa had six brave sons namely, Yāti, Yayāti, Saṁyāti, Āyāti, Viyāti and Kṛti.

यतिस्तु राज्यं नैच्छत्।। २।।

ययातिस्तु भूभृदभवत्।। ३।।

Yāti declined the throne and therefore Yayāti succeeded.

उशनसश्च दुहितरं देवयानीं वार्षपर्वणीं च शर्मिष्ठामुपयेमे।। ४।।

He had two wives, Devayānī, the daughter of Uṣanas, and Śarmiṣṭhā, the daughter of Vṛṣaparvan.

अत्रानुवंशश्लोको भवति।।५।।

His genealogy is thus recited—

यदुं च दुर्वसुं चैव देवयानी व्यजायत।।
दुह्युं चानुं च पूरुं च शर्मिष्ठा वार्षपर्वणी।। ६।।

"Devayānī gave birth to two sons, Yadu and Tarvasu. Śarmiṣṭhā, the daughter of Vṛṣaparvan, gave birth to three sons, Druhya, Anu and Puru.

काव्यशापाच्च कालेनैव ययातिर्जरामवाप।। ७।।

Owing to a course of Uṣanas Yayāti became untimely old and decripit.

प्रसन्नशुक्रवपचनाच्च स्वजरां संक्रामयितुं ज्येष्ठं पुत्रं यदुमुवाच।। ८।।

Having propitiated his father-in-law however he got the permission to transer his old age to any one who would agree to take it. He first called his eldest son Yadu and then said,—

वत्स त्वन्मातामहशापादियमकालेनैव जरा ममोपस्थिता तामहं तस्यैवानुग्रहाद्भवतस्सञ्चारयामि।। ९।।

Your maternal grand-father has caused this untime decripitude of mine. By his permission I may transfer it to you for a thousand years.

एकं वर्षसहस्त्रमतृप्तोऽस्मि विषयेषु त्वद्वयसा विषयानहं भोक्तुमिच्छामि।। १०।।

नात्र भवता प्रत्याख्यानं कर्त्तव्यमित्युक्तस्स यदुर्नैच्छत्तां जरामादातुम्।। ११।।

तं च पिता शशाप त्वत्प्रसूतिर्न राज्यार्हा भविष्यतीति।। १२।।

अनंतरं च दुर्वसुं दुह्यमनुं च पृथिवीपतिर्जराग्रहणार्थं स्वयौवनप्रदानाय चाभ्यर्थयामास।। १३।।

तैरप्येकैकेन प्रत्याख्यातास्ताञ्छशाप।। १४।।

I am not still satisfied with worldly enjoyments and wish to enjoy through your youth. Do not refuse compliance with my request." Being thus addressed he did not agree to take the decay upon him for which the king imprecated a curse, saying—"No one in your prosterity shall be the king." He then successively requested Druhya, Tuvasu and Aṇu to give him their youth. They all refused and were accordingly, cursed by the king.

अथ शर्मिष्ठातनयमशेषकनीयांसं पूरुं तथैवाह।। १५।।

स चातिप्रवणमतिः सबहुमानं पितरं प्रणम्य महाप्रसादोयमस्माकमित्युदारमभिधाय जरां जग्राह।। १६।।

स्वकीयं च यौवनं स्वपित्रे ददौ।। १७।।

Lastly he called his youngest son Puru—the son of Śarmiṣṭhā and requested him for the same. That youth, of ripe understanding, at once agreed and bowing unto his father said—"I have been highly honoured." He then took upon himself his father's infirmities and gave him his youth in exchange.

सोऽपि पौरवं यौवनमासाद्य धर्माविरोधेन यथाकामं यथाकालोपपन्नं यथोत्साहं विषयांश्चचार।। १८।।

सम्यक् च प्रजापालनमकरोत्।। १९।।

Being thus gifted with renewed youth Yayāti governed the kingdom for the good of his people enjoying such pleasures as were suited to his age and strength and were in consonance with piety.

विश्वाच्या देवयान्या च सहोपभोगं भुक्त्वा कामानामंतं प्राप्स्यामीत्यनुदिनं तन्मनस्को बभूव।। २०।।

He enjoyed in the company of a nymph Viśvaci day and night thinking that there would be an end of all desires.

अनुदिनं चोपभोगतः कामानतिरम्यान्मेने।। २१।।

ततश्चैनमगायत।। २२।।

By continued enjoyment all things began to appear more pleasant to him and he then said—

श्लो०

न जातु कामः कामानामुपभोगेन शाम्यति।।
हविषा कृष्णवत्मव भूय एवाभिवर्द्धते।। २३।।

"Desire is never satiated by enjoyment as fire, fed with oil, becomes the more intense.

यत्पृथिव्यां व्रीहियवं हिरण्यं पशवः स्त्रियः।।
एकस्यापि न पर्याप्तं तस्मात्तृष्णां परित्यजेत्।। २४।।

No one is satisfied with rice, barley, gold, cattle or women; therefore renounce excessive desire.

यदा न कुरुते भावं सर्वभूतेषु पापकम्।।
समदृष्टेस्तदा पुंसः सर्वास्सुखमया दिशः।। २५।।

Whene a man does not cherish any sinful feeling towards creatures and looks on all with an equal eye—he then finds everything full of pleasure and delight.

या दुस्त्यजा दुर्मतिभिर्या न जीर्यति जीर्यतः।।
तां तृष्णां संत्यजेत्प्राज्ञस्सुखेनैवाभिपूर्यते।। २६।।

The wise become happy by renouncing that desire which the feeble minded cannot abandon and which grows not old with the aged.

जीर्यन्ति जीर्यतः केशा दंता जीर्यंति जीर्यतः।।
धनाशा जीविताशा च जीर्यतोऽपि न जीर्यतः।। २७।।

With age the hair becomes gray, the teeth fall off but the love of wealth and life is never gratified.

पूर्णं वर्षसहस्रं मे विषयासक्तचेतसः।।
तथा प्यनुदिनं तृष्णा मम तेषूपजायते।। २८।।

A thousand years have expired and still my mind is attached to worldly enjoyments : my desires are excited every day by new objects. I shall therefore renounce all enjoyments of sense and devote myself to the culture of spiritual truth.

तस्मादेतामहं त्यक्त्वा ब्रह्मण्याधाय मानसम्।।
निर्द्वंद्वो निर्ममो भूत्वा चरिष्यामि मृगैस्सह।। २९।।

And renouncing all attachments and not influenced by the alternatives of pleasure and pain I shall roam in the forest with the deer.

श्रीपराशर उवाच

पूरोस्सकाशादादाय जरां दत्त्वा च यौवनम्।।
राज्येभिषिच्य पूरुं च प्रययौ तपसे वनम्।। ३०।।

Having thus made up his mind Yayāti returned the youth to Puru and took up his own decrepitude. He then made his youngest son the sovereign and went to Tapovana (the wood of penance).

दिशि दक्षिणपूर्वस्यां दुर्वसुं च समादिशत्।।
प्रतीच्यां च तथा द्रुह्युं दक्षिणायां ततो यदुम्।। ३१।।

उदीच्यां च तथैवानुं कृत्वा मंडलिनो नृपान्।।
सर्वपृथ्वीपतिं पूरुं सोभिषिच्य वनं ययौ।। ३२।।

He appointed as viceroy—Turvasu of the south-east districts, Druhya of the west, Yadu of the south and Anu of the north—and made Puru the supreme monarch of the earth.

।। इति श्रीविष्णुमहापुराणे चतुर्थेंशे दशमोऽध्यायः।। १०।।

अथ चतुर्थेंशेः एकादशोऽध्यायः
Part IV : Section 11

श्रीपराशर उवाच

अतः परं ययातेः प्रथमपुत्रस्य यदोर्वंशमहं कथयामि।।
१।।

यत्राशेषलोकनिवासो मनुष्यसिद्धगंधर्वयक्षराक्षस-
गुह्यककिंपुरुषाप्सरोरगविहगदैत्यदानवादित्य-
रुद्रवस्वश्विमरुद्देवर्षिभिर्मुमुक्षुभिर्धर्मार्थकाम-
मोक्षार्थिभिश्च तत्तत्फललाभाय सदाभिष्टुतो-
ऽपरिच्छेद्यमाहात्म्यांशेन भगवाननादिनिधनो
विष्णुरवततार।। २।।

अत्र श्लोकः।। ३।।

यदोर्वंशं नरः श्रुत्वा सर्वपापैः प्रमुच्यते।।
यत्रावतीर्णं कृष्णाख्यं परं ब्रह्मनराकृति।। ४।।

Parāśara said :—I will first enumerate to you the descendants of Yadu, the eldest son of

Yayāti—one of whom was an incarnate portion of Viṣṇu—of whom glory cannot be described though chanted for ever to confer the fruit of all their desires—whether for virtue, wealth, pleasure or final emancipation—upon all created beings, upon men, saints, Gandharvas, spirits of evil, nymphs, centaurs, serpents, birds, demons, gods, sages, Brāhmaṇas and ascetics. Whoever shall hear of the descendants of Yadu shall be freed from all iniquities, for the supreme spirit—devoid of any form—Viṣṇu was incarnate in this family.

सहस्त्रजित्क्रोष्टुनलनहुषसंज्ञाश्चत्वारो यदुपुत्रा बभूवुः।।५।।

Yadu had four sons Sahasrajit, Kroṣṭi, Nala and Raghu.

सहस्त्रजित्पुत्रश्शतजित्।।६।।

तस्य हैहयहेहयवेणु हयास्त्रयःपुत्रा बभूवुः।।७।।

Sasajit was the son of the eldest brother and had three sons—Haihaya, Veṇu and Haya.

हैहयपुत्रो धर्मः तस्यापि धर्मनेत्रः ततः कुंतिः कुंतेः सहजित्।।८।।

तत्तनयो महिष्मान् योऽसौ माहिष्मतीं पुरीं निर्वापयामास।।९।।

तस्माद्भद्रश्रेण्यस्ततो दुर्दमस्तस्माद्धनकः धनकस्य कृतवीर्यकृताग्निकृतधर्मकृतौजसश्चत्वारः पुत्रा बभूवुः।।१०।।

The son of Haihaya was Dharmanetra, whose son was Kunti, whose son was Sahanji, Dharmanetra, whose son was Kunti, whose son was Sahanji, whose son was Mahiṣmat, whose son was Bhadraśoṇa, whose son was Dardama, whose son was Dhanaka, who had four sons, Kṛtavīryya, Kṛtāgni, Kṛtavarman and Kṛtauyyas.

कृतवीर्यादर्जुनस्सप्तद्वीपाधिपतिर्बाहुसहस्त्रो जज्ञे।।११।।

Kṛtavīryya's son was Arjuna, who was the king of the seven insular continents and the master of a thousand arms.

योऽसौ भगवदंशमत्रिकुलप्रसूतं दत्तात्रेयाख्यमाराध्य बाहुसहस्त्रमधर्मसेवानिवारणं स्वधर्म सेवित्वं रणे पृथिवीजयं धर्मतश्चानुपालनमरातिभ्योऽपराजय-मखिलजगत्प्रख्यातपुरुषाच्च मृत्युमित्येतान्वरान-भिलषितवाँल्लेभे च।।१२।।

तेनेयमशेषद्वीपवती पृथिवी सम्यक्परिपालिता।।१३।।

दशयज्ञसहस्त्राण्यसावयजत्।।१४।।

तस्य च श्लोकोऽद्यापि गीयते।।१५।।

न नूनं कार्त्तवीर्यस्य गतिं यास्यंति पार्थिवाः।।
यज्ञैर्दानैस्तपोभिर्वा प्रश्रयेण श्रुतेन च।।१६।।

अनष्टद्रव्यता च तस्य राज्येऽभवत्।।१७।।

This king propitiated the sage Dattātreya, the descendant of Atri who was an incanate portion Viṣṇu and obtained from him these boons—a thousand arms, acting always justly, governing the world with justice, protecting it impartially, victory over his enemies and death by the hands of a person renowned in the three worlds. By these means he governed the earth powerfully and justly celebrated ten thousnd sacrifices. Of him this verse is said—"The kings of the earth shall never equal him in sacrifices, liberality, in devotion in good manners and in self-control.

एवं च पञ्चाशीतिवर्षसहस्त्राण्यव्याहतारोग्य-श्रीबलपराक्रमो राज्यमकरोत्।।१८।।

In his reign nothing was lost or injured, so he governed the whole earth with undecayed health, prosperity, power and strength for eighty-five thousand years.

माहिष्मत्यां दिग्विजयाभ्यागतो नर्मदाजलावगाहन-क्रीडातिपानमदाकुलेनयायत्नेनैव तेनाशेषदेवदैत्य-गंधर्वेशजयोद्भूतमदावलेपोपि रावणः पशुरिव बद्धा स्वनगरैकांते स्थापितः।।१९।।

यश्च पञ्चा शीतिवर्षसहस्त्रोपलक्षणकालावसाने भगवन्नारायणांशेन परशुरामेणोपसंहृतः।। २०।।

Arriving at the city of Mahiṣmati, on his tour of conquests whilst its king was sporting in the waters of Narmadā excited with wine, Rāvaṇa, proud for defeating the gods, demons, Gandharvas, and their king, was taken prisoner by Kārtavīryya and confined like a tame beast in a corner in his capital. At the end of a long reign Kārtavīryya was slain by Paraśurāma who was an incarnate portion of Viṣṇu.

तस्य च पुत्रशतप्रधानाः पञ्चपुत्रा बभूवुः शूरशूरसेन वृषसेनमधुजयध्वजसंज्ञाः ।। २१ ।।

The king had hundred sons of which five were principal, namely Śūra, Śūrasena, Vṛṣaṇa, Madhu, and Jayadhvaja.

जयध्वजात्तालजंघः पुत्रोभवत् ।। २२ ।।

तालजंघस्य तालजंघाख्यं पुत्रशतमासीत् ।। २३ ।।

The son of the last was Tālajaṅghā who had a hundred sons named after him Tālajaṅghās.

एषां ज्येष्ठो वीतिहोत्रस्तथान्यो भरतः ।। २४ ।।

भरताद्वृषः ।। २५ ।।

The eldest of these was Vitihotrā, another was Bharata who had two sons—Vṛṣa and Sujati.

वृषस्य पुत्रो मधुरभवत् ।। २६ ।।

तस्यापि वृष्णिप्रमुखं पुत्रशतमासीत् ।। २७ ।।

यतो वृष्णिसंज्ञामेतद्गोत्रमवाप ।। २८ ।।

The sons of Vṛṣa was Madhu; he had a hundred sons, the chief of whom was Vṛṣṇa and from him the family obtained the name of Vṛṣṇī.

मधुसंज्ञाहेतुश्च मधुरभवत् ।। २९ ।।

यादवाश्च यदुनामोपलक्षणादिति ।। ३० ।।

From the name of their father Madhu they were called Mādhavas and from the name of their common ancestor Yadu they were all called Yādavas.

।। इति श्रीविष्णुमहापुराणे चतुर्थेंशे एकादशोऽध्यायः ।। ११ ।।

अथ चतुर्थेंशेः द्वादशोऽध्यायः

Part IV : Section 12

श्रीपराशर उवाच

क्रोष्टोस्तु यदुपुत्रस्यात्मजो ध्वजिनीवान् ।। १ ।।

ततश्च स्वातिः ततो रुशंकुः रुशंकोश्चित्ररथः ।। २ ।।

तत्तनयश्शशिबिंदुः चतुर्दशमहारत्नेशश्चक्रवर्त्यभवत् ।। ३ ।।

Parāśara said :—Kroṣṭṛ, the son of Yadu, had a son named Vṛjinvat, whose son was Suci, whose son was Kuśadra, whose son was Citraratha, whose son was Śaśavindu, who was the master of the fourteen great gems.

तस्य च शतसहस्रं पत्नी नामभवत् ।। ४ ।।

दशलक्षसंख्याश्च पुत्राः ।। ६ ।।

He had a hundred thousand wives and a million of sons.

तेषां च पृथुश्रवाः पृथुकर्मा पृथुकीर्तिः पृथुयशाः पृथुजयः पृथुदानः षट्पुत्राः प्रधानाः ।। ६ ।।

पृथुश्रवसश्च पुत्रः पृथुतमः ।। ७ ।।

The most famous of them were Pṛthuyaśas, Pṛthukarman, Pṛthujaya, Pṛthukīrtti, Pṛthudaha and Pṛthuśravas.

तस्मादुशना यो वाजिमेधानां शतमाजहार ।। ८ ।।

तस्य च शितपुर्नाम पुत्रोऽभवत् ।। ९ ।।

तस्यापि रुक्मकवचस्ततः परवृत् ।। १० ।।

तस्य परावृतो रुक्मेषुपृथुज्यामघवलितहरितसंज्ञास्तस्य पञ्चात्मजा बभूवुः ।। ११ ।।

The son of the last of these six was Tamas, whose son was Uṣanas who performed a hundred horse sacrifices. His son was Siteyus, whose son was Rukmakavaca, whose son was Paradṛt, who had five sons, Rukmeśu, Pṛthurukman, Jyamagha, Pahta, and Harita.

तस्यायमद्यापि ज्यामघस्य श्लोको गीयते ।। १२ ।।

In the present period the following verse is recited of Jyamagha—

भार्यावश्यास्तु ये केचिद्भविष्यंत्यथ वा मृताः ।।
तेषां तु ज्यामघः श्रेष्ठश्शैव्यापतिरभून्नृपः ।। १३ ।।

"Of all the husbands obedient to their

wives, who have been or who will be, the most famous is the king Jayamagha, who was the husband of Saivya."

अपुत्रा तस्य सा पत्नी शैव्या नाम तथाप्यसौ ।।
अपत्यकामोऽपि भयान्नान्यां भार्यामविंदत ।। १४ ।।

Saivya was barren—but Jayamagha was so much afraid of her that he could not take any other wife.

स त्वेकदा प्रभूतरथतुरगगजसम्मर्दाति दारुणे महाहवे युद्ध्यमानः सकलमेवारिचक्रमजयत् ।। १५ ।।

तच्चारिचक्रमपास्तपुत्रकलत्रबंधुबलकोशं स्वमधिष्ठानं परित्यज्य दिशः प्रतिविद्रुतम् ।। १६ ।।

तस्मिंश्च विद्रुतेतित्रासलोलायतलोचनयुगलं त्राहित्राहि मां तातांब भ्रातरित्याकुलविलापविधुरं स राजकन्यारत्नमद्राक्षीत् ।। १७ ।।

तद्दर्शनाच्च तस्यामनुरागानुगतांतरात्मा स नृपोऽचिंतयत् ।। १८ ।।

साध्विदं ममापत्यरहितस्य वंध्याभर्तुः सांप्रतं विधिनापत्यकारणं कन्यारत्नमुपपादितम् ।। १९ ।।

तदेतत्समुद्वहामीति ।। २० ।।

Once on a time after a hard fighting with horse and elephants the king defeated a powerful enemy who, leaving behind his wife, children, relations, army, treasure and kingdom, fled. When the enemy had fled Jayamagha saw a beautiful princess, exclaim-ing. "Save father, save me, brother" while her expansive eyes rolled wildly with fear. The king was much attracted by her beauty and cherished love for her and said to himself—"This is accidental; I have no children and am the husband of a barren lady. This maiden has fallen in my hands to keep up my family.

अथ वैनां स्यंदनमारोप्य स्वमधिष्ठानं नयामि ।। २१ ।।

तयैव देव्या शैव्ययाऽहमनुज्ञातस्समुद्वहामीति ।। २२ ।।

I will marry her. But I must take her in my car to my palace, where I must have the permission of my queen for the marriage."

अथैनां रथमारोप्य स्वनगरमगच्छत् ।। २३ ।।

So he took the princess into his car and went back to his capital.

विजयिनं च राजानमशेषपौरभृत्सपरिजनामत्यसमेता शैव्या द्रष्टुमधिष्ठानद्वारमागता ।। २४ ।।

To welcome the return of the victorious king, Saivya came to the palace gate with the ministers, courtiers and the citizens.

सा चावलोक्य राज्ञः सव्यपार्श्ववर्त्तिनीं कन्यामीषदुद्भूतामर्षस्फुरदधरपल्लवा राजानमवोचत् ।। २५ ।।

अतिचपलचित्तात्र स्यंदने केयमारोपितेति ।। २६ ।।

असावप्यनालोचितोत्तरवचनोतिभयात्तामाह स्नुषा ममेयमिति ।। २७ ।।

अथैनं शैव्योवाच ।। २८ ।।

श्लो०

नाहं प्रसूता पुत्रेण नान्या पत्न्यभवत्तव ।।
स्नुषासंबंधता ह्येषा कतमेन सुतेन ते ।। २९ ।।

And beholding a damsel on the left hand of the king Saivya with her lips swollen and trembling in jealousy said to the king—"Who is this fickle girl that is sitting with you in the chariot?" The king was not prepared with a reply and maid answer, all on a sudden through fear of his queen—"This is my daughter-in-law? I have never had a son" said Saivya "and you have no other children; of what son of yours then is this girl the wife?"

श्रीपराशर उवाच

इत्यात्मेर्ष्याकोपकलुषितवचनमुषितविवेको भयाद्दुरुक्तपरिहारार्थमिदमवनीपतिराह ।। ३० ।।

Parāśara said :—The king bewildered by the jealousy and anger which the words of Saivya displayed, gave this answer to avoid further contention.

यस्ते जनिष्यत्यात्मजस्तस्येयमनागतस्यैव भार्यानिरूपितेत्याकर्ण्योद्भूतमृदुहासा तथेत्याह ।। ३१ ।।

प्रविवेश च राज्ञा सहाधिष्ठानम् ।। ३२ ।।

अनंतरं चातिशुद्धलग्नहोरांशकावयवोक्तकृतपुत्रजन्मलाभगुणाद्वयसः परिणाममुपगतापि शैव्या स्वल्पैरेवाहोभिर्गर्भमवाप ।। ३३ ।।

कालेन च कुमारमजीजनत्।। ३४।।

The king said,—"She is the young bride of the future son whom thou shalt give birth." Hearing this Saivya gently smiled and said "so be it" and the king entered into his great palace. This conversation regarding the birth of a son having taken place in a auspicious conjunction, aspect, and season, the queen, although she was greatly advanced in years, became pregnant and bore a son.

तस्य च विदर्भ इति पिता नाम चक्रे।। ३५।।

स च तां स्नुषामपयेमे।। ३६।।

His father named him Vidarbha and married him to the damsel he had brought home.

तस्यां चाऽसौ क्रथकैशिकसंज्ञौ पुत्रावजनयत्।। ३७।।

पुनश्च तृतीयं रोमपादसंज्ञं पुत्रमजीजनद्यो नारदाद-
वाप्तज्ञानवान्भविष्यतीति।। ३८।।

रोम पादाद्बभ्रुः बभ्रोर्धृतिः धृतेः कैशिकः
कैशिकस्यापि चेदिः पुत्रोऽभवत् यस्य संततौ चैद्या
भूपालाः।। ३९।।

He had three sons, Kratha, Kaiśika and Romapāda. The son of Romapāda was Dhṛti. The son of Kaiśika was Cedī whose children were the Caidya kings.

क्रथस्य स्नुषापुत्रस्य कुंतिरभवत्।। ४०।।

कुंतेर्धृष्टिः धृष्टेर्निधृतिः निधृतेर्दशार्हस्ततश्च व्योमः
तस्यापि जीमूतः ततश्च विकृतिः ततश्च भीमरथः
तस्मान्नवरथः तस्यापि दशरथः ततश्च शकुनिः तत्तनयः
करंभिः करंभेर्देवरातोऽभवत्।। ४१।।

तस्माद्देवक्षत्रः तस्यापि मधुः मधोः कुमारवंशः
कुमारवंशादनुः अनोः पुरुमित्रः पृथिवीपतिरभवत्।।
४२।।

ततश्चांशुस्तस्माच्च सत्वतः।। ४३।।

सत्वतादेते सात्वताः।। ४४।।

The son of Kratha was Kunti, whose son was Vṛṣnī, whose son was Nirvṛti, whose son was Dasārha, whose son Vyoman, whose son was Jimūta, whose son was Vikṛti, whose son was Bhīmaratha whose son was Navaratha, whose son was Daśaratha, whose son was Śakuni, whose son was Karambhī, whose son was Devarata, whose son Devakṣtra, whose son was Madhu, whose son Anavarathu, whose son was Kuruvatsa, whose son son was Anaratha, whose son was Puruhotra, whose son was Aṁśu, whose son was Satvata, from whom the princes of this family were called Sātvatas.

इत्येतां ज्यामघस्य संततिं सम्यक्छ्रद्धासमन्वितः श्रुत्वा
पुमान् मैत्रेय स्वपापैः प्रमुच्यते।। ४५।।

This was the progeny of of Jyamagha. He, who will hear of the account, will be freed from sins.

।। इति श्रीविष्णुमहापुराणे चतुर्थेंशे द्वादशोऽध्यायः।। १२।।

अथ चतुर्थेंशेः त्रयोदशोऽध्यायः

Part IV : Section 13

श्रीपराशर उवाच

भजनभजमानदिव्यांधकदेववृधमहाभोजवृष्णि-
संज्ञास्सत्वतस्य पुत्रा बभूवुः।। १।।

Parāśara said :—The sons of Satwata were Bhajina Bhajamāna, Divya, Andhaka, Devavṛddha, Mahābhoja and Vṛṣṇī.

भजमानस्य निमिकृकणवृष्णयस्तथान्ये द्वैमात्राः
शतजित्सहस्रजिदयुतजित्संज्ञास्त्रयः।। २।।

Bhajamāna had three sons, Nimī, Kṛkaṇa, and Vṛṣṇī by one wife and as many by another, Satajit, Sahasrajit and Ayutajit.

देवावृधस्यापि बभ्रुः पुत्रोऽभवत्।। ३।।

तयोश्चायं श्लोको गीयते।। ४।।

The son of Devavṛdha was Babhru of whom this verse is recited—

यथैव शृणुमो दूरात्संपश्यामस्तथांतिकात्।।
बभ्रुः श्रेष्ठो मनुष्याणां देवैर्देवावृधस्समः।। ५।।
पुरुषाः षट् च षष्टिश्च सहस्राणि तथाऽष्ट ये।।
तेऽमृतत्वमनुप्राप्ता बभ्रोर्देवावृधादपि।। ६।।

"We hear, when we are at a distance and we see when we are near that Babhru is the foremost of men and Devavṛddha is equal to the celestials; sixty six persons who were the disciples of one and six thousand and eight who were disciples of the other obtained immortality."

महाभोजस्त्वतिधर्मात्मा तस्यान्वये भोजाः
मृत्तिकावरपुरनिवासिनो मार्त्तिकावरा बभूवुः।।७।।

Mahābhoja was a virtuous king his descendants were the Bhojas, the kings of Mirttikāvat, thence denominated Mirttikāvāttas.

वृष्णेः सुमित्रो युधाजिच्च पुत्रावभूताम्।। ८।।

Vṛṣnī had two sons Sumitra and Yudhajit; from the former Anāmitṛa and Sin; were born.

ततश्चानमित्रतथानमित्रान्निघ्नः।। ९।।

निघ्नस्य प्रसेनसत्राजितौ।। १०।।

तस्य च सत्राजितो भगवानादित्यः सखाऽभवत्।। ११।।

The son of Anamitra was Nighna who had two sons Prasena and Satrājit. The god Āditya or the sun was the friend of the latter.

एकदा त्वंभोनिधितीरसंश्रयः सूर्यं सत्राजित्तुष्टाव
तन्मनस्कतया च भास्वानभिष्टूयमानोऽग्रतस्तस्थौ।।
१२।।

Once on a time arriving at the banks of the ocean, Satrājit began to hymn the praises of the sun, with his mind solely devoted to him, upon which the deity appeared and stood before him.

ततस्त्वस्पष्टमूर्त्तिधरं चैनमालोक्य सत्राजित्सूर्यमाह।। १३।।

Seeing him in an indistinct shape he said to the Sun—"I see thee in this sky as a globe of fire—I behold thee just now in the same shape and do not perceive any distinction as a matter of favour."

यथैव व्योम्नि वह्निपिंडोपमं त्वामहमपश्यं
तथैवाद्याग्रतो गतमप्य? भगवता किंचिन्न प्रसादीकृतं
विशेषमुपलक्षयामीत्येवमुक्ते भगवता सूर्येण
निजकंठादुन्मुच्य स्यमंतकं नाम महामणिवरम-
वतार्यैकान्ते न्यस्तम्।। १४।।

ततस्तमाताम्रोज्ज्वलं ह्रस्ववपुषमीषदापिंगल-
नयनमादित्यमद्राक्षीत्।। १५।।

Being thus addressed the distinction as a matter of favour." Being thus addressed the divine sun took the jewel called Śyamantaka from off his neck and placed it at a distance and Satrājit saw him of a dwarfish from, with a body like burnished copper and with slightly reddish eyes.

कृतप्रणिपातस्तवादिकं च सत्राजितमाह भगवाना-
दित्यस्सहस्रदीधितिः वरमस्मत्तेभिमतं वृणीष्वेति।।
१६।।

While he bowed unto him the divine Sun said to Satrājit—"I wish to confer upon thee a boon; do thou pray for it."

स च तदेव मणिरत्नमयाचत।। १७।।

He then wanted that jewel.

स चापि तस्मै तद्दत्वा दीधितिपतिर्वियति
स्वधिष्ण्यमारुरोह।। १८।।

The sun gave it to him and then resumed his place in the sky.

सत्राजितोऽप्यमलमणिरत्नसनाथकंठतया सूर्य इव
तेजोभिरशेषदिगंतराण्युद्भासयन् द्वारकां विवेश ।।
१९।।

Satrājit placed that precious gem round his neck and lighting up all the quarters with his radiance like the sun entered the city of Dwārakā.

द्वारकावासी जनस्तु तमायांतमवेक्ष्य भगवंतमादिपुरुषं
पुरुषोत्तममवनिभारावतरणायांशेन मानुषरूपधारिणं
प्रणिपत्याह।। २०।।

Beholding him approach the inhabitant of Dwārakā went to that excellent Puruṣa, without beginning, who, to carry the burden of the world, assumed a mortal form, and said—

भगवन् भवंतं द्रष्टुं नूनमयमादित्य आयातीत्युक्तो भगवानुवाच।। २१।।

"O lord, forsooth, the divine sun is coming to visit you." But Kṛṣṇa smiled and said.

भगवान्नायमादित्यः सत्राजितोऽयमादित्यदत्तस्य-मंतकाख्यं महामणिरत्नं बिभ्रदत्रोपयाति।। २२।।

तदेनं विस्रब्धाः पश्यतेत्युक्तास्ते तथैव ददृशुः।। २३।।

"It is not the sun but Satrājit. He is coming here with the Śyamantaka gem conferred upon him by the sun. You all see him with a fearless heart." Hearing this the inhabitants of Dwārakā repaired to thier respective habitations.

स च तं स्यमंतकमणिमात्मनिवेशने चक्रे।। २४।।

प्रतिदिनं तन्मणिरत्नमष्टौ कनकभारान्स्रवति।। २५।।

तत्प्रभावाच्च सकलस्यैव राष्ट्रस्योपसर्गानावृष्टि-व्यालाग्नितो यद्दुर्भिक्षादिभयं न भवति।। २६।।

Satrājit too having gone to his house placed that jewel which gave daily eight loads of gold and through its uncommon power removed all fear of portents, wild beasts, fire, robbers and famine.

अच्युतोऽपि तद्दिव्यं रत्नमुग्रसेनस्य भूपतेर्योग्यमेतदिति लिप्सां चक्रे।। २७।।

गोत्रभेदभयाच्छक्तोपि न जहार।। २८।।

Kṛṣṇa thought that the gem was worthy of the king Ugrasena and desired to take it but did not do so lest it might cause some disturbance in the family.

सत्राजिदप्यच्युतो मामेतद्याचयिष्यतीत्यवगम्य रत्नलोभाद्भ्रात्रे प्रसेनाय तद्रत्नमदात्।। २९।।

तच्च शुचिना ध्रियमाणमशेषमेव सुवर्णस्रवादिकं गुणजातमुत्पादयति अन्यथा धारयंतमेव हंतीत्य-जानन्नसावपि प्रसेनस्तेन कंठसक्तेन स्यमंतकेनाश्व-मारुह्याटव्यां मृगयामगच्छत्।। ३०।।

Understanding that Kṛṣṇa would ask of him the jewel Satrājit transferred it to his brother Prasena. It was the peculiar virtue of that gem, that if worn with all purity it would yield gold and prosperity of the kingdom but if worn by a man of bad character it would bring on his death. Prasena having taken the jewel and placed it round his neck mounted his horse and went to the forest to hunt.

तत्र च सिंहाद्वधमवाप।। ३१।।

While thus hunting he was killed by a lion.

साश्वं च तं निहत्य सिंहोप्यमलमणिरत्नमास्याग्रेणादांय गंतुमभ्युद्यतः ऋक्षाधिपतिना जांबवता दृष्टो घाति तश्च।। ३२।।

The lion taking the jewel in his mouth was about to go when was seen and killed by Jāmbavat the king of the bears, who taking the jewel went to his cave and gave it to his son Sukumāra to play with.

जांबवानप्यमलमणिरत्नमादाय स्वबिलं प्रविवेश।। ३३।।

सुकुमारसंज्ञाय बालकाय च क्रीडनकमकरोत्।। ३४।।

When sometime had passed and Prasena did not come, the Yādavas began to whisper, one to another, "This must be Kṛṣṇa's doing; being willing to get the jewel and not obtaining it he has committed the murder to get this into his possession."

अनागच्छति तस्मिन्प्रसेने कृष्णो मणिरत्नमभिलषित-वान्स च प्राप्तवान्नूनमेतदस्य कर्मेत्यखिल एव यदुलोकः परस्परं कर्णाकर्ण्याऽकथयत्।। ३५।।

विदितलोकापवादवृत्तांतश्च भगवान् सर्वयदुसैन्य-परिवारपरिवृतः प्रसेनाश्वपदवीमनुससार।। ३६।।

When these calamities reached the ears of Kṛṣṇa he gathered some members of the Yadu family and in their company followed the course of Prasena by the impressions of his horse's hoops.

ददर्श चाश्वसमवेतं प्रसेनं सिंहेन विनिहतम्।। ३७।।

अखिलजनमध्ये सिंहपददर्शनकृतपरिशुद्धिः सिंहपदमनुससार।। ३८।।

ऋक्षपतिनिहतं च सिंहमप्यल्पे भूमिभागे दृष्ट्वा ततश्च तद्रत्नगौरवादृक्षस्यापि पदान्यनुययौ।। ३९।।

And having found it by this way that he and his horse had been destroyed by the lion he was acquitted by all people of any share in the death. Desirous of getting back the jewel, he thence followed the foot-marks of the lion and at no great distance came to the place where the lion had been killed by the bear.

गिरितटे च सकलमेव तद्यदुसैन्यमवस्थाप्य तत्पदानुसारी ऋक्षबिलं प्रविवेश।। ४०।।

Pursuing the foot-prints of the latter he arrived at the foot of a mountain where having kept the Yādavas he pursued the course.

अन्तःप्रविष्टश्च धात्र्याः सुकुमारकमुल्लालयन्त्या वाणीं शुश्राव।। ४१।।

And following the impressions of the feet he found out a cavern and before he entered it he heard the nurse of Sukumāra saying to him.

श्लो०

सिंहः प्रसेनमवधीत्सिंहो जाम्बवता हतः।।
सुकुमारकमा रोदीस्तव ह्येष स्यमंतकः।। ४२।।

"The lion killed Prasena; the lion has been killed by Jāmbavat : weep not Sukumāra the Syamantaka is your own."

इत्याकर्ण्योपलब्धस्यमंतकोंतःप्रविष्टः कुमार-क्रीडनकीकृतं च धात्र्या हस्ते तेजोभिर्जाज्वल्यमानं स्यमंतकं ददर्श।। ४३।।

Having thus ascertained the truth Kṛṣṇa entered into the cavern and espied the jewel in the hands of the nurse who was giving it as a plaything to Sukumāra.

तं च स्यमंतकाभिलषितचक्षुषमपूर्वपुरुषमागतं समवेक्ष्य धात्री त्राहित्राहीति व्याजहार।। ४४।।

The nurse in no time found out his approach and seeing his eyes eagerly fixed upon the jewel called aloud for help.

तदार्त्तरवश्रवणानंतरं चामर्षपूर्णहृदयः स जांबवाना-जगाम।। ४५।।

तयोश्च परस्परमुद्धतामर्षयोर्युद्धमेकविंशतिदि-नान्यभवत्।। ४६।।

Hearing her cries, Jāmbavat, worked up with anger, came to that place and an encounter took place between him and the Acyuta which continued for twenty-one days.

ते च यदुसैनिकास्तत्र सप्ताष्टदिनानि तन्निष्क्रांति-मुदीक्षमाणास्तस्थुः।। ४७।।

अनिष्क्रमणे च मधुरिपुरसाववश्यमत्र बिलेऽत्यंतं नाशमवाप्तो भविष्यत्यन्यथा तस्य जीवतः कथमेतावंति दिनानि शत्रुजये व्याक्षेपो भविष्यतीति कृताध्यवसाया द्वारकामागम्य हतः कृष्ण इति कथयामासुः।। ४८।।

The Yādavas who followed Kṛṣṇa waited there for seven or eight days expecting his return but as the slayer of Madhu did not come they arrived at the conclusion that he must have been destroyed in the cave. "It could not have taken so many days" they thought "to defeat a foe." They therefore went away, and came back to Dwārakā and announced that Kṛṣṇa had been killed.

तद्बांधवाश्च तत्कालोचितमखिलमुत्तरक्रियाकलापं चक्रुः।। ४९।।

His relatives too performed ceremonies necessary for the occasion.

ततश्चास्य युद्ध्यमानस्यातिश्रद्धादत्तविशिष्टोप-पात्रयुक्तान्नतोयादिना श्रीकृष्णस्य बलप्राणपुष्टिरभूत्।। ५०।।

Food and water offered reverentially to worthy persons tended to support his life and invigorate his strength in the conflict in which he was engaged.

इतरस्यानुदिनमतिगुरुपुरुषभेद्यमानस्य अतिनिष्ठुर-प्रहारपातपीडिताखिलावयवस्य निराहारतया बलहानिरभूत्।। ५१।।

While his enemy being exhausted by daily combat with a powerful enemy, bruised in every limb by heavy blows and enfeebled by want of food became unable to resist him.

निर्जितश्च भगवता जांबवान्प्रणिपत्य व्याजहार।। ५२।।

सुरासुरगंधर्वयक्षराक्षसादिभिरप्यखिलैर्भवान्न जेतुं शक्यः किमुतावनिगोचरैरल्पवीर्यैर्नरैर्नरावयवभूतैश्च तिर्यग्योन्यनुसृतिभिः किं पुनरस्मद्विधैरवश्यं भवता-

ऽस्मत्स्वामिना रामेणेव नारायणस्य सकलजगत्-
परायणस्यांशेन भगवता भवितव्यमित्युक्तस्तस्मै
भगवानखिलावनिभारावतरणार्थमवतरणमाचचक्षे ।।
५३ ।।

Being thus defeated by his powerful enemy Jāmbavat prostrated himself before him and said "O mighty being, thou art, for sooth invincible, by the spirits of heaven, earth or hell, thou canst not be defeated by man and powerless creatures in a human shape—what to speak of such as we are—who are of brute origin. Methinks thou art a portion of my lord Nārāyaṇa the protector of the universe." Being thus addressed by the lord of bears Kṛṣṇa explained to him fully that he had incarnated himself to take upon himself the burden of the earth.

प्रीत्यभिव्यंजितकरतलस्पर्शनेन चैनमपगतयुद्धखेदं
चकार ।। ५४ ।।

And delightedly touching him with his palms he relieved him of the pain which he had suffered from the fight.

स च प्रणिपत्य पुनरप्येनं प्रसाद्य जांबवतीं नाम कन्यां
गृहागतायार्घ्यभूतां ग्राहयामास ।। ५५ ।।

Jāmbavat again laid himself low before Kṛṣṇa and presented to him his daughter Jāmbavati as a suitable offering to a guest.

स्यमंतकमणिरत्नमपि प्रणिपत्य तस्मै प्रददौ ।। ५६ ।।

He also handed over to him the Śyamantaka jewel.

अच्युतोप्यतिप्रणतात्तस्मादग्राह्यमपि तन्मणिरत्न-
मात्मसंशोधनाय जग्राह ।। ५७ ।।

Although it was not becoming to accept a present from such an individual still he took the gem with a view to clear his reputation.

सह जांबवत्या स द्वारकामाजगाम ।। ५८ ।।

He then came back with his Bride Jāmbavatī to Dwārakā.

भगवदागमनोद्भूतहर्षोत्कर्षस्य द्वारकावासिनजनस्य
कृष्णावलोकनात्तत्क्षणमेवातिपरिणतवयसोपि
नवयौवनमिवाभवत् ।। ५९ ।।

दिष्ट्यादिष्ट्येति सकलयादवाः स्त्रियश्च
सभाजयामासुः ।। ६० ।।

When the inhabitants of Dwārakā was Kṛṣṇa come back alive they were filled with joy so that even those who were greatly filled with joy so that even those who were greatly stricken in years were filled with youthful strength; and all the members of the Yadu family, men and women, gathered round Anakadundubhi, father of the hero and congratulated him.

भगवानपि यथानुभूतमशेषं यादवसमाजे
यथावदाचचक्षे ।। ६१ ।।

स्यमंतकं च सत्राजिताय दत्वा मिथ्याभिशस्तिपरि-
शुद्धिमवाप ।। ६२ ।।

जांबवतीं चांतःपुरे निवेशयामास ।। ६३ ।।

Kṛṣṇa described to the assembled Yādavas all that had taken place exactly and giving back the Śyamantaka jewel to Satrājit was cleared off the charge of murder. He then conducted Jāmbavatī to the inner apartments.

सत्राजितोपि मयास्याभूतमलिनमारोपितमिति
जातसंत्रासात्स्वसुतां सत्यभामां भगवते भार्यार्थं ददौ ।।
६४ ।।

When Satrājit thought that he had been the instrumental of the false charge against Kṛṣṇa he was terrified and to satisfy him he gave in marriage with him his daughter Satyabhāmā.

तां चाक्रूरकृतवर्मशतधन्वप्रमुखा यादवाः
प्राग्वरयाम्बभूवुः ।। ६५ ।।

ततस्तत्प्रदानादवज्ञातमेवात्मानं मन्यमानाः सत्राजिते
वैरानुबंधं चक्रुः ।। ६६ ।।

She had evre been sought in marriage by many illustrious members of the Yadu family as Akrūra, Kṛtavarman, and Śatadhanwan, who were greatly worked up with anger on account of her being married to another, and formed a common cause of enmity against Satrājit.

अक्रूरकृतवर्मप्रमुखाश्च शतधन्वानमूचुः ।। ६७ ।।

अयमतीव दुरात्मा सत्राजितो योऽस्माभिर्भवता च

प्रार्थितोऽप्यात्मजामस्मान् भवंतं चाविगणय्य कृष्णाय दत्तवान्।। ६८।।

तदलमनेन जीवता घातयित्वैनं तन्महारत्नं स्यमंतकाख्यं त्वया किं न गृह्यते वयमभ्युपपत्स्यामो यद्यच्युतस्त्वोपरि वैरानुबंधं करिष्यतीत्येव-मुक्तस्तथेत्यसावप्याह।। ६९।।

The most leading man amongst them with Akrūra and Kṛtavarman said to Śatadhanwan—"By given her daughter to Kṛṣṇa this caitiff Satrājit had insulted you and us grossly who wanted her : why do you not kill him and take the jewel? Should Acyuta on that account enter into conflict with you we will take your part." Having secured this promise Śatadhanwan undertook to destroy Satrājit.

जतुगृहदग्धानां पांडुतनयानां विदितपरमार्थोऽपि भगवान् दुर्योधनप्रयत्नशैथिल्यकरणार्थं पार्थानुकूल्य-करणाय वारणावतं गतः।। ७०।।

When the intelligence reached Kṛṣṇa that the Pāṇḍavas had been burned in the house of wax, he, who was acquainted with the real truth, immediately started for Baraṇāvata to allay the enmity of Duryodhana and perform the necessary duties of his relationship.

गते च तस्मिन् सुप्तमेव सत्राजितं शतधन्वा जघान मणिरत्नं चाददात्।। ७१।।

Taking advantage of his absence Śatadhanwan killed Satrājit while asleep and secured the jewel for himself.

पितृवधामर्षपूर्णा च सत्यभामा शीघ्रं स्यंदनमारूढा वारणावतं गत्वा भगवतेऽहं प्रतिपादितेत्यक्षांतिमता शतधन्वनाऽस्मत्पिता व्यापादितः तच्च स्यमंतक-मणिरत्नमपहृतं यस्यावभासनेनापहृत तिमिरं त्रैलोक्यं भविष्यति।। ७२।।

तदियं त्वदीयापह्रासना तदालोच्य यदत्र युक्तं तत्क्रियतामिति कृष्णमाह।। ७३।।

When Satyabhāmā came to know this, she, highly angered on accout of her father's murder, at once ascended the chariot, went to Baraṇāvat and told her husband how Satrājit had been killed Śatadhanwan in anger on account of her being married to another, and how the jewel had been taken away by him. And she requested him to take immediate steps to avenge such a henious crime.

तया चैवमुक्तः परितुष्टांतःकरणोऽपि कृष्णः सत्यभामाममर्षताम्रनयनः प्राह।। ७४।।

Being thus informed Kṛṣṇa, though pleased at heart, said to Satyabhāmā, assuming an indignant look—"This is an inslut to me! I shall never brook it.

सत्ये सत्यं ममैवैषापहासना नाहमेतां तस्य दुरात्मनस्सहिष्ये।। ७५।।

न ह्यनुल्लंघ्य परपादपं तत्कृतनीडाश्रयिणो विहंगमा वध्यंते तदलममुनास्मत्पुरतः शोकप्रेरितवाक्य-परिकरेणेत्युक्त्वा द्वारकामभ्येत्यैकांते बलदेवं वासुदेवः प्राह।। ७६।।

One cannot destroy the birds that have built their nests on a tree without assailing it. Remove excessive grief therefore; you need not lament to excite my wrath." Immediately coming back to Dwārakā Kṛṣṇa took Baladeva apart and said to him."

मृगयागतं प्रसेनमटव्यां मृगपतिर्जघान।। ७७।।

सत्राजितोऽप्यधुना शतधन्वना निधनं प्रापितः।। ७८।।

A lion slew Prasena while hunting in the forests; and now Satrājit has been killed by Śatadhanwan.

तदुभयविनाशात्तन्मणिरत्नमावाभ्यां सामान्यं भविष्यति।। ७९।।

तदुत्तिष्ठारुह्यतां रथः शतधन्वनिधनायोद्यमं कुर्वित्य भिहितस्तथेति समन्विच्छितवान्।। ८०।।

As both these are gone, the jewel which belonged to them, is now our common right. Up then, ascend your car and destroy Śatadhanwan."

कृतोद्यमौ च तावुभावुपलभ्य शतधन्वा कृतवर्माण-मुपेत्य पार्ष्णिपूरणकर्मनिमित्तमचोद यत्।। ८१।।

Being thus excited by his brother, Balarāma engaged in the work; but Śatadhanwan being aware of their hostile intention went to Kṛtavarman and prayed for his help.

आह चैनं कृतवर्मा।। ८२।।

नाऽहं बलदेववासुदेवाभ्यां सह विरोधायाल-
मित्युक्तश्चाक्रूरमचोदयत्।। ८३।।

असावप्याह।। ८४।।

Kṛtavarman did not agree saying that he was not able to fight with both Kṛṣṇa and Baladeva. Being disappointed he again solicited Akrūra for help who said—

न हि कश्चिद्भगवता पादप्रहारपरिकंपितजगत्त्रयेण
सुररिपुवनितावैधव्यकारिणा प्रबलरिपुचक्राप्रतिहत-
चक्रेण चक्रिणा मदमुदितनयनावलोकनाखिल-
निशातनेनातिगुरुवैरिवारणापकर्षणाविकृतमहि-
मोरुसीरेण सीरिणा च सह सकलजगद्वंद्यानामम-
रवराणामपि योद्धुं समर्थः।। ८५।।

किमुताहं तदन्यश्शरणभिलष्यतामित्युक्तश्शतधनुराह।।
८६।।

"You must go to some body else for help. How should I be able to defend you? Even none, amongst the celestials whose glories are chanted throughout the universe, is capable of fighting with the holder of the discus, trodden by whose foot the three worlds tremble, whose hand makes the wives of the Asuras widows, whose weapons—no army, however powerful can resist; no one is able to fight with the wielder of ploughshare, who by his very looks, nullifies the prowess of his enemies, whose eyes roll with the joys of wine, and whose huge ploughshare manifests his prowess by destroying the most powerful enemies."

यद्यस्मत्परित्राणासमर्थं भवानात्मानमधिगच्छति
तदयमस्मत्तस्तावन्मणिः संगृह्य रक्ष्यतामिति।। ८७।।

एवमुक्तः सोऽप्याह।। ८८।।

यद्यंत्यायामप्यवस्थायां न कस्मैचिद्भवान् कथयिष्यति
तदहमेतं ग्रहीष्यामीति।। ८९।।

Whereto Śatadhanwan replied—"While such is the case and you are unable assist me, you may at least help me by keeping this jewel in your possession." "I can keep it" Akrūra said "if you promise that even in the last extremity you won't give out that the jewel is in my possession."

तथेत्युक्ते चाक्रूरस्तन्मणिरत्नं जग्राह।। ९०।।

Śatadhanwan agreed to this and Akrūra took the jewel.

शतधनुरप्य तुलवेगां शतयोजनवाहिनीं
वडवामारुह्यापक्रांतः।। ९१।।

And mounting a fleet mare that could run hundred leagues a day Śatadhanwan fled from Dwārakā.

शैव्यसुग्रीवमेघपुष्पबलाहकाश्वचतुष्टययुक्तरथस्थितौ
बलदेववासुदेवौ तमनुप्रयातौ।। ९२।।

When this intelligence reached Kṛṣṇa, he made ready his four horses, Śarvya, Sugrīva, Meghapuṣpa, and Balahaka, set them to his car and accompanied by Balarāma, started in his pursuit.

सा च वडवा शतयोजनप्रमाणमार्गमतीता पुनरपि
वाह्यमाना मिथिलावनोद्देशे प्राणानुत्ससर्ज।। ९३।।

The mare went on speedily and finished her hundred leagues but when she reached the country of Mithilā, her strength was exhausted and she dropped down and died.

शतधनुरपि तां परित्यज्य पदातिरेवाद्रवत्।। ९४।।

कृष्णोपि बलभद्रमाह।। ९५।।

Having got down, Śatadhanwan continued his flight on foot. When the pursuers came to the place where the mare had died Kṛṣṇa said to Balarāma—

तावदत्र स्यंदने भवता स्थेयमहमेनमधमाचारं पदातिरेव
पदातिमनुगम्य यावद्घातयामि अत्र हि भूभागे
दृष्टदोषास्सभया अतो नैतेश्वा भवतेमं भूमिभाग-
मुल्लंघनीयाः।। ९६।।

"Do you remain in car; I shall follow the villain on foot and kill him; the ground here is bad; and the horses will not be able to carry the car accross it."

तथेत्युक्त्वा बलदेवो रथ एव तस्थौ ।। ९७।।

कृष्णोपि द्विक्रोशमात्रं भूमिभागमनुसृत्य दूरस्थितस्यैव
चक्रं क्षिप्त्वा शतधनुषश्शिरश्चिच्छेद।। ९८।।

Accordingly Balarāma remained in the car and Kṛṣṇa followed Śatadhanwan on foot.

When he had pursued him for two Kos he discharged his discus and although Śatadhanwan was at a considerable distance the weapon dissevered his head.

तच्छरीरांबरादिषु च बहुप्रकारमन्विच्छन्नपि स्यमंतकमणिं नावाप पदा तदोपगम्य बलभद्रमाह।। ९९।।

He then searched his person and clothes very attentively but did not find the jewel. Then coming back he said to Balarāma—

वृथैवास्माभिः शतधनुर्घातितः न प्राप्तमखिलजगत्सारभूतं तन्महारत्नं स्यमंतकाख्यमित्याकर्ण्योद्भूतकोपो बलदेवो वासुदेवमाह।। १००।।

"I have for nothing destroyed Śatadhanwan—for I have not found on his person the precious gem—the quintessence of all worlds." When Balarāma heard this, he was excited with anger and said to Vāsudeva—

धिक्त्वां यस्त्वमेवमर्थलिप्सुरेतच्च ते भ्रातृत्वान्मया क्षांतं तदयं पंथास्स्वेच्छया गम्यतां न मे द्वारकया न त्वया न चाशेषबंधुभिः कार्य्यमलमलमेभिर्ममाग्रतोऽलीकशपथैरित्याक्षिप्य तत्कथां कथंचित्प्रसाद्यमानोपि न तस्थौ।। १०१।।

"Shame upon you—so greedy of wealth. I don't acknowledge you as my brother. Here his my path. Go wherever you like, I have done with Dwārakā, with you with all our house. It is useless for you to try to decieve me with these perjuries." Having remonstrated with his brother thus, who in vain tried to please him.

स विदेहपुरीं प्रविवेश।। १०२।।

जनकराजश्चार्घ्यपूर्वकमेनं गृहं प्रवेशयामास।। १०३।।

स तत्रैव च तस्थौ।। १०४।।

Balarāma went to the city of Videha, where Janaka recived him hospitably and there he remained.

वासुदेवोऽपि द्वारकामाजगाम।। १०५।।

Vāsudeva came back to Dwārakā.

यावच्च जनकराजगृहे बलभद्रोऽवतस्थे तावद्धार्त्तराष्ट्रो दुर्योधनस्तत्सकाशाद्गदाशिक्षामशिक्षयत्।। १०६।।

While Balarāma stayed in the house of Janaka, Duryodhana, the son of Dhṛtarāṣṭra learnt from him the art of fighting with the mace.

वर्षत्रयांते च बभ्रूग्रसेनप्रभृतिभिर्यादवैर्न तद्रत्नं कृष्णेनाऽपहृतमिति कृतावगतिभिर्विदेहनगरीं गत्वा बलदेवस्संप्रत्याय्य द्वारकामानीतः।। १०७।।

In this way three years passed away. Babru, Ugrasena and other Yādavas then repaired to the city of Videha and convinced Balarāma that Kṛṣṇa has stolen the jewel. They then brought him to Dwārakā.

अक्रूरोप्युत्तममणिसमुद्भूतसुवर्णेन भगवद्ध्यानपरोऽनवरतं यज्ञानियाज।। १०८।।

Akrūra too, to utilize the gold produced by the jewel, continually engaged in the celebration of sacrifices.

सवनगतौ हि क्षत्रियवैशै निघ्नन्ब्र ह्महा भवतीत्येवंप्रकारं दीक्षाकवचं प्रविष्ट एव तस्थौ।। १०९।।

Considering that the murderer, of a Kṣatriya or Vaiśya engeaged in religious duties, is the slayer of Brāhmin, Akrūra spent sixty-two years being protected by the armour of devotion.

द्विषष्टिवर्षाण्येवं तन्मणिप्रभावात्तत्रोपसर्गदुर्भिक्षमारिकामरणादिकं नाभूत्।। ११०।।

And by virtue of that gem there was no dearth, nor pestilence in the whole country.

अथाक्रूरपक्षीयैर्भोजैश्शत्रुघ्ने सात्वतस्य प्रपौत्रे व्यापादिते भोजैस्सहाक्रूरो द्वारकामपहायापक्रान्तः।। १११।।

At the end of that period, Śatrughna, the great grandson of Satvata was killed by Bhojas. As they were connected with Akrūra he accompanied them in their flight from Dwārakā.

तदपक्रांतिदिनादारभ्य तत्रोपसर्गदुर्भिक्षव्यालानावृष्टिमारिकाद्युपद्रवा बभूवुः।। ११२।।

From the time of his departure various calamities, portents, snakes, dearth plague and the like began to take place.

अथ यादवा बलभद्रोग्रसेनसमवेता मंत्रममंत्रयन्।।
११३।।

भगवानुरगारिकेतनः किमिदमेकदैव प्रचुरोपद्रवागमन-
मेतदालोच्यतामित्युक्तेंधकनामा यदुवृद्धः प्राह।।
११४।।

Thereupon the illustrious Kṛṣṇa called together Baladeva, Ugrasena and other Yādavas and consulted with them to ascertain why so many prodigies should have taken place at the same time. On this Andhaka one of the elders of the Yadu family spoke—

अस्याक्रूरस्य पितृश्वफल्को यत्र यत्राभूत्तत्रतत्र
दुर्भिक्षमारिकानावृष्ट्यादिकं नाभूत्।। ११५।।

"Wherever Swaphalka the father of Akrūra lived, there famine, plague, dearth and other visitations were unknown.

काशीराजस्य विषये त्वनावृष्ट्या च श्वफल्को नीतः
ततश्च तत्क्षणाद्देवो ववर्ष।। ११६।।

काशीराजपत्न्याश्च गर्भे कन्यारत्नं पूर्वमासीत्।। ११७।।

सा च कन्या पूर्णेपि प्रसूतिकाले नैव निश्चक्राम।।
११८।।

Once when there was want of rain in the kingdom Kāśīrāja, conceived and was big with a child but when the time of delivery came the child did not come out of the womb.

एवं च तस्य गर्भस्य द्वादशवर्षाण्यनिष्क्रामतो ययुः ।।११९।।

Twelve years went away and still the girl was unborn.

काशीराजश्च तामात्मजां गर्भस्थामाह।। १२०।।

पुत्रि कस्मान्न जायसे निष्क्रम्य तामास्यं ते द्रष्टुमिच्छामि
एतां च मातरं किमिति चिरं क्लेशयिष्यसीत्युक्ता
गर्भस्थैव व्याजहार।। १२१।।

Then the Kāśīrāja spoke to the child, saying "Daughter, why is your birth thus delayed? Come out; I wish to see you; why do you inflict this continued suffering upon your mother?" Thus addressed the infant said—

तात यद्येकैकां गां दिनेदिने ब्राह्मणाय प्रयच्छसि
तदहमन्यैस्त्रिभिर्वर्षैरस्माद्गर्भात्ततोऽवश्यं निष्क्रमिष्या-
मीत्येद्वचनमाकर्ण्य राजा दिनेदिने ब्राह्मणाय गां
प्रादात्।। १२२।।

सापि तावता कालेन जाता।। १२३।।

"O father, if you will present a cow daily to the Brāhmaṇas I shall be born at the end of three years." Accordingly the king presented a cow every day to the Brāhmaṇas and at the end of three years the girl came out of the womb.

ततस्तस्याः पिता गांदिनीति नाम चकार।। १२४।।

तां च गांदिनीं कन्यां श्वफल्कायोपकारिणे
गृहमागतायार्घ्यभूतां प्रादात्।। १२५।।

Her father called her Gāndinī and he afterwards gave her to Svaphalka when he came to his palace to help him. Gāndinī as long as she lived, gave a cow to the Brāhmaṇas every day.

तस्यामयमक्रूरः श्वफल्काज्जज्ञे।। १२६।।

Akrūra was her son by Swaphalka.

तस्यैवंगुणमिथुनादुत्पत्तिः।। १२७।।

And he is thus born from a combination of extraordinary excellence.

तत्कथमस्मिन्नपक्रान्ते अत्र दुर्भिक्षमारिकाद्युपद्रवा न
भविष्यंति।। १२८।।

When such a person is absent from us it is likely that famine, pestilence and prodigies should take place.

तदयमत्रानीयतामलमतिगुणवत्यपराधान्वेषणेनेति
यदुवृद्धस्यांधकस्यैतद्वचनमाकर्ण्य केशवोग्रसेन-
बलभद्रपुरोगमैर्यदुभिः कृतापराधतितिक्षुभिरभयं दत्वा
श्वफल्कपुत्रः स्वपुरमानीतः।। १२९।।

Let him then be requested to come back; the weak points of men of excellence, should not be too severely criticized." In accordance with the advice of Andhaka the elder, the Yādavas sent a mission headed by Keśava, Ugrasena and Balabhadra, to assure Akrūra that no notice of his fault would be taken.

तत्र चागतमात्र एव तस्य स्यमंतकमणेः प्रभावादना-
वृष्टिमारिकादुर्भिक्षव्यालाद्युपद्रवोपशमा बभूवुः।।
१३०।।

And having convinced him that he would expect no danger they brought him back to Dwārakā. As soon as he arrived on account of the virtue of the jewel, the plague, dearth, famine and every other calamity and portent disappeared.

कृष्णश्चिंतयामास।। १३१।।

स्वल्पमेतत्का रणं यदयं गांदिन्यां श्वफल्केनाक्रूरो जनितः।। १३२।।

सुमहांश्चायमनावृष्टिदुर्भिक्षमारिकाद्युपद्रवप्रतिषेधकारी प्रभावः।। १३३।।

Seeing this Kṛṣṇa thought that the birth of Akrūra from Gāndinī and Swaphalka could not bring about such an effect and he must have some other more powerful virtue to arrest pestilence and famine.

तन्नूनमस्य सकाशे स महामणिः स्यमंतकाख्यस्तिष्ठति।। १३४।।

तस्य ह्येवंविधाः प्रभावाः श्रूयन्ते।। १३५।।

"Certainly" thought he within himself "the great Śyamantaka jewel must be in his keeping, for these, as I have heard, are the properties of the jewel.

अयमपि च यज्ञादनंतरमन्यत्क्रत्वंतरं तस्यानंतरमन्यद्यज्ञांतरं चाजस्त्रमविच्छिन्नं यजतीति।। १३६।।

Akrūra too has been performing many sacrifices; his own means are not sufficient for the purpose, undoubtedly he has got the jewel in his possession."

अनल्पोपादानं चास्यासंशयमत्राऽसौ मणिवरस्तिष्ठतीति कृताध्यवसायोऽन्यत्प्रयोजनमुद्दिश्य सकलयादवसमाजमात्मगृह एवाचीकरत्।। १३७।।

तत्र चोपविष्टेष्वखिलेषु यदुषु पूर्वं प्रयोजनमुपन्यस्य पर्यवसिते च तस्मिन् प्रसंगांतरपरिहासकथामक्रूरेण कृत्वा जनार्दनस्तमक्रूरमाह।। १३८।।

Having arrived at this conclusion, he called together all the Yādavas at his house under the plea of celebrating some feast. After they had taken their seats and the object of the meeting had been explained to them and the business finished Kṛṣṇa began to converse with Akrūra and after laughing and joking, said to him—

दानपते जानीम एव वयं यथा शतधन्वना तदिदमखिलजगत्सारभूतं स्यमंतकं रत्नं भवतः समर्पितं तदशेषराष्ट्रोपकारकं भवत्सकाशे तिष्ठति तिष्ठतु सर्व एव वयं तत्प्रभावफलभुजः किं त्वेष बलभद्रोऽस्मानाशंकितवांस्तदस्मत्प्रीतये दर्शयस्वेत्यभिधाय जोषं स्थिते भगवति वासुदेवेसरत्नस्सोचिंतयत्।। १३९।।

"Kinsman, you are a prince in your liberality and we know very well that the valuable gem which was stolen by Śudhanwan was given to you and is now in your possession, to the great benefit of this kingdom. So let it remain; we all derive advantage from its virtues. But Bhalabhadra suspects that I have it and therefore, out of kindness to me shew it to the assembly."

किमत्रानुष्ठेयमन्यथा चेद्ब्रवीम्यहं तत्केवलांबरतिरोधानमन्विष्यंतो रत्नमेते द्रक्ष्यंति अतिविरोधो न क्षम इति संचिंत्य तमखिलजगत्कारणभूतं नारायणमाहाक्रूरः।। १४०।।

When Akrūra, who had the jewel in his possession, was thus taxed he hesitated what he should do. He thought—"If I deny that I have the jewel, they will search my person and find the gem hidden amongst my clothes. I cannot submit myself to a search." Thinking thus Akrūra said to Nārāyaṇa, the cause of the universe.

भगवन्ममैतत्स्यमंतरत्नं शतधनुषा समर्पितमपगते च तस्मिन्नद्य श्वः परश्वो वा भगवान् याचयिष्यतीति कृतमतिरतिकृच्छ्रेणैतावंतं कालमधारयम्।। १४१।।

"It is true, Śyamantaka jewel was given to my care by Śatadhanwan when he left this place. I expected every day that you should ask me for it and with great inconvenience to myself I have retained it.

तस्य च धारणशेक्लेनाहमशेषोपभोगेष्वसंगिमानसो न वेद्मि स्वसुखकलामपि।। १४२।।

The care of this has put me to so much

anxiety that I have not been able to enjoy any pleasure or a moment's rest.

एतावन्मात्रमप्यशेषराष्ट्रोपकारी धारयितुं न शक्नोति
भवान्मन्यत इत्यात्मना न चोदितवान्।। १४३।।

तदिदं स्यमंतकरत्नं गृह्यतामिच्छया यस्याभिमतं तस्य
समर्प्यताम्।। १४४।।

Being afraid lest you might think, that I am unfit to keep this jewel which is the source of welfare to the kingdom I did not mention to you that it is in my possession.

ततः स्वोदरवस्त्रनिगोपितमतिलघुकनकसमुद्गकगतं
प्रकटी कृतवान्।। १४५।।

Now take it yourself and give its charge to any body you like."

ततश्च निष्क्राम्य स्यमंतकमणिं तस्मिन्यदुकुलसमाजे
मुमोच।। १४६।।

Having said this Akrūra got out of his clothes a small gold box and took from it the jewel.

मुक्तमात्रे च तस्मिन्नतिकान्त्या तदखिलमास्थान-
मुद्योतितम्।। १४७।।

When it was shown to the assembled Yādavas the room in which they sat, was illuminated with its radiance,

अथाहाक्रूरः स एष मणिः शतधन्वनास्माकं समर्पितः
यस्यायं स एनं गृह्णतु इति।। १४८।।

"This" said Akrūra "is the Śyamantaka jewel which was left to my care by Śatadhanwan. Let him to whom it belongs now take it."

तमालोक्य सर्वयादवानां साधुसाध्विति विस्मितमनसां
वाचोऽश्रूयंत।। १४९।।

When the Yādavas saw the jewel they were filled with surprise and loudly expressed their joy.

तामालोक्यातीव बलभद्रो ममायमच्युतेनैव
सामान्यस्समन्विच्छित इति कृतस्पृहोऽभूत्।। १५०।।
ममैवायं पितृधनमित्यतीव च सत्यभामापि
स्पृहयांचकार।। १५१।।

Balabhadra immediately claimed the jewel as his property jointly with Acyuta as was formerly settled; whereas Satyabhāmā wanted it as her rightful property for it belonged to her father.

बलसत्यावलोकनात्कृष्णोप्यत्मानं गोचक्रांतरा-
वस्थितमिव मेने।। १५२।।

सकलयादवसमक्षं चाक्रूरमाह।। १५३।।

Between these two Kṛṣṇa considered himself as an ox between the two wheels of a cart, and thus said to Akrūra in the presence of the Yādavas—

एतद्धि मणिरत्नमात्मसंशोधनाय एतेषां यदूनां मया
दर्शितम् एतच्च मम बलभद्रस्य च सामान्यं पितृधनं
चैतत्सत्यभामाय नान्यस्यैतत्।। १५४।।

"This jewel has been shown to you all in order to clear my reputation; it is the joint-property of Balabhadra and myself and is the paternal property of Satyabhāmā.

एतच्च सर्वकालं शुचिना ब्रह्मचर्यादिगुणवता
ध्रियमाणमशेषराष्ट्रस्योपकारकमशुचिना ध्रियमाण-
माधारमेव हंति।। १५५।।

But as a source of advantage to the kingdom this jewel must be consigned to the charge of one who leads a life of perpetual continence; if worn by a impure man it will prove the cause of his death.

अतोहमस्य षोडशस्त्रीसहस्त्रपरिग्रहादसमर्थो धारणे
कथमे तत्सत्यभामा स्वीकरोति।। १५६।।

As I have sixteen thousand wives I am not qualified to use it. It is not probable that Satyabhāmā would agree to the conditions, satisfying which she may possess it.

आर्यबलभद्रेणापि मदिरापानाद्यशेषोपभोगपरित्यागः
कार्यः।। १५७।।

तदलं यदुलोकोयं बलभद्रः अहं च सत्या च त्वां
दानपते प्रार्थयामः।। १५८।।

तद्भवानेव धारयितुं समर्थः।। १५९।।

त्वद्धतं चास्य राष्ट्रस्योपकारकं तद्भवानशेषराष्ट्र-

निमित्तमेतत्पूर्ववद्धारयत्वन्यन्न वक्तव्यमित्युक्तो दानपतिस्तथेत्याह जग्राह च तन्महारत्नम्।। १६०।।

And as regards Balabhadra, he is greatly addicted to wine and sensual pleasures. We are therefore all out of question. All the Yādavas, Balabhadra, Satyabhāmā and myself request you, most libderal Akrūra, to keep this jewel in your possession, as you have done up to this time for the general behoof; for you are qualified to keep it and in your hands it has proved beneficial to the country. You must comply with your request."

ततःप्रभृत्यक्रूरः प्रकटेनैव तेनातिजाज्वल्य-मानेनात्मकंठावसक्तेनादित्य इवांशुमाली चचार।।
१६१।।

Thus requested Akrūra took the jewel and thenceforth wore it publicly round his neck where it shone with dazzling radiance and he moved about like the sun wearing a garland of light.

इत्येतद्भगवतो मिथ्याभिशस्तिक्षालनं यः स्मरति न तस्य कदाचिदल्पापि मिथ्याभिशस्तिर्भवति अव्याहताखिलेंद्रियश्चाखिलपापमोक्षमवाप्नोति।।
१६२।।

He, who remembers the vindication of Kṛṣṇa's character from false charges, shall never be subject to any false charge in the least degree and living in the full display of senses, shall be freed from every sin.

।। इति श्रीविष्णुमहापुराणे चतुर्थेंशे त्रयोदशोऽध्यायः।। १३।।

अथ चतुर्थेंशेः चतुर्दशोऽध्यायः

Part IV : Section 14

श्रीपराशर उवाच

अनमित्रस्य पुत्रः शिनिर्नामाऽभवत्।। १।।

तस्यापि सत्यकः सत्यकात्सात्यकिर्युयुधानापरनाम्रा।।
२।।

तस्मादपि सञ्जयः तत्पुत्रश्च कुणिः कुणेर्युगंधरः।। ३।।

Parāśara said :—The younger brother of Anāmitra was Sini, whose son was Satyaka, whose son was Yuyudhana, otherwise known as Sātyaki, whose son was Asanga, whose son was Yuni, whose son was Yugandhara.

इत्येते शैनेयाः।। ४।।

These princes were named Śaineyas.

अनमित्रस्यान्वये वृष्णिः तस्मात् श्वफल्कः तत्प्रभाव कथित एव।। ५।।

श्वफल्कस्यान्यः कनीयांश्चित्रकोनाम भ्राता।। ६।।

Vṛṣṇī was born in the race of Anmitra, whose son was Swaphalka the purity of whose character has been described; the younger brother of Swaphalka was named Citraka.

श्वफल्कादक्रूरो गांदिन्यामभवत्।। ७।।

तथोपमद्गुः।। ८।।

उपमद्गो मृदामृदविश्वारिमेजयगिरिक्षत्रोपक्षत्र-शतघ्नारिमर्दनधर्मदृग्दृष्टधर्मगंधमोजवाहप्रति-वाहाख्याः पुत्रास्सुताराख्या कन्या च।। ९।।

Swaphalka had by Gāndinī, besides Akrūra, Upamadgu, Midura, Sarimejaya, Giri, Kṣatrapa, Kṣatra, Śatrughna. Arimarddana, Dharmadhrīs, Dhīṣṭasarman, Gandha, Mojavaha and Prativaha. He had also a daughter, named Sutārā.

देववानु पदेवश्चाक्रूरपुत्रौ।। १०।।

Devavat and Upadeva were the sons of Akrūra.

पृथुविपृथुप्रमुखाश्चित्रकस्य पुत्रा बहवो बभूवुः।। ११।।

कुकुरभजमानशुचिकंबलबर्हिषाख्यास्तथांधकस्य चत्वारः पुत्राः।। १२।।

The sons of Citrika were Pṛtha and Viprtha and many others. Andhaka had four sons, Lukkūra, Bhojamana, Suci, Kambalavarhiṣ.

कुकुराद्धृष्टः तस्माच्च कपोतरोमा ततश्च विलोमा तस्मादपि तुंबुरुसखोऽभवदनुसंज्ञश्च।। १३।।

अनोरानकदुंदुभिः ततश्चाभिजित् अभिजितः पुनर्वसुः।। १४।।

तस्याप्याहुकः आहुकी च कन्या।। १५।।

The son of Kukkura was Viṣṭa, whose son was Kapotaroman, whose son was Viloman, whose son was Bhava, who was otherwise named Candanodakadundubhi; he was a friend of the Gandharva Tumburu; his son was Abhijit, whose son was Punarvasu, whose son was Āhuka; he had also a daughter called Āhukī.

आहुकस्य देवकोग्रसेनौ द्वौ पुत्रौ।। १६।।

The sons of Āhuka were Devaka and Ugrasena.

देववानुपदेवः सहदेवो देवरक्षिता च देवकस्य चत्वारः पुत्राः।। १७।।

तेषां वृकदेवोपदेवा देवरक्षिता श्रीदेवा शांतिदेवा सहदेवा देवकी च सप्त भगिन्यः।। १८।।

ताश्च सर्वा वसुदेव उपयेमे।। १९।।

The former had four sons Devavat, Upadeva, Sudeva and Devarakṣita and seven daughters—Vṛkadevā, Upadevā, Devarakṣitā, Śrīdevā, Śantidevā, Sahadevā and Devakī; and all the daughters were married to Vasudeva.

उग्रसेनस्यापि कंसन्यग्रोधसुनामानकाह्वशंकुसुभूमि-राष्टपालयुद्धतुष्टिसुतुष्टिमत्संज्ञाः पुत्रा बभूवुः।। २०।।

कंसाकंसवतीसुतनूराष्ट्रपलिकाह्वाश्चोग्रसेनस्य तनूजाः कन्याः।। २१।।

The sons of Ugrasena were Kansa, Nyagrodha, Sunaman, Kaṅka, Śaṅku, Subhūmi, Rāṣṭrapāla, Yuddhamuṣṭhī and Yuṣṭimat and her daughters were Kansā, Kauśāvatī, Sūtanā, Rāṣṭrapālī and Kaṅkī.

भजमानाच्च विदूरथः पुत्रोऽभवत्।। २२।।

विदूरथाच्छूरः शूराच्छमी शमिनः प्रतिक्षत्रः तस्मात्स्वयंभोजः ततश्च हृदिकः।। २३।।

The son of Bhajamāna was Viduratha, whose son was Śūra, whose son was Sāmin, whose son was Pratikṣatra, whose son was Swayambhoja, whose son was Hṛdeka, who had Kṛtavarma, Śatadhana, Devamiduśa and others.

तस्यापि कृतवर्मशतधनुर्दवार्हदेवगर्भाद्याः पुत्रा बभूवुः।। २४।।

देवगर्भस्यापि शूरः।। २५।।

शूरस्यापि मारिषा नाम पत्न्यभवत्।। २६।।

तस्यां चासौ दशपुत्रानजनयद्वसुदेवपूर्वान्।। २७।।

वसुदेवस्य जातमात्रस्यैव तद्गृहे भगवदंशा-वतारमव्याहतदृष्ट्या पश्यद्भिर्देवैर्दिव्यानकदुंदुभयो वादिताः।। २८।।

ततश्चासावानकदुंदुभिसंज्ञामवाप।। २९।।

Śūra, the son of Devamidhuśa, was married to Mariṣā and had by her ten sons. When Vasudeva, who was one these sons, was born, the celestials, to whom future is known, foresaw that the divine being would be born in his race and they therefore joyously sounded the celestial drums and accordingly Vasudeva was named Anakadundubhi.

तस्य च देवभागदेवश्रवाष्टककुच्चक्रवत्सधारक-सृञ्जयश्यामशमिकगंडूषसंज्ञा नव भ्रातरोऽभवन्।। ३०।।

पृथा श्रुतदेवा श्रुतकीर्त्तिः श्रुतश्रवा राजाधिदेवी च वसुदेवादीनां पञ्च भगिन्योऽभवन्।। ३१।।

शूरस्य कुंतिर्नाम सखाऽभवत्।। ३२।।

तस्मै चापुत्राय पृथामात्मजां विधिना शूरो दत्तवान्।। ३३।।

His brothers were Devabhaga, Devaśravas, Andhṛṣṭi, Karundhaka, Vatsabalaka, Śriñjaya, Śyāma, Śamika and Ganduṣa. They had five sisters who were named Pṛthā, Śrutadevā, Śrutakirtī Śrutāśravā and Rājādhidevī. Śūra had a friend named Kuntibhoja who had no son. And to him he presented duly his daughter Pṛthā.

तां च पांडुरुवाह।। ३४।।

तस्यां च धर्मानिलेंद्रैर्युधिष्ठरभीमसेनार्जुनाख्यास्त्रयः पुत्रास्समुत्पादिताः ।। ३५ ।।

She was married to Pāṇḍu and bore him Yudhiṣṭhira, Bhīma and Arjuna who were in reality the sons of the deities Dharma, Vāyu and Indra.

पूर्वमेवानूढायाश्च भगवता भास्वता कानीनः कर्णो नाम पुत्रोऽजन्यत ।। ३६ ।।

And whilst she was a maiden she had a son named Karṇa begotten by the divine sun.

तस्याश्च सपत्नी माद्री नामाभूत् ।। ३७ ।।

तस्यां च नासत्यदस्राभ्यां नकुलसहदेवौ पांडोः पुत्रौ जनितौ ।। ३८ ।।

Pāṇḍu had another wife named Mādrī who had by the twin sons of Āditya, Nāsatya and Dasra, two sons, Nakula and Sahadeva.

श्रुतदेवां तु वृद्धधर्मा नाम कारूश उपयेमे ।। ३९ ।।

तस्यां च दंतवक्रो नाम महासुरो जज्ञे ।। ४० ।।

A Kārusa prince by name Vṛddhaśarman married Śrutadevā and begot on her a dreadful Asura named Dantavaktra.

श्रुतकीर्त्तिमपि केकयराजा उपयेमे ।। ४१ ।।

तस्यां च संतर्दनादयः कैकेयाः पञ्च पुत्रा बभूवुः ।। ४२ ।।

राजाधिदेव्यामावंत्यौ विंदानुविंदौ जज्ञाते ।। ४३ ।।

Dhṛṣṭaketu king of Kaikeya, married Śrutakīrtī and had by her Santarddana and four others sons known as the five Kaikeyas. Jayasena, king of Avanti married Rājādhidevī and had two sons, Vinda and Anvinda.

श्रुतश्रवसमपि चेदिराजो दमघोषनामोपयेमे ।। ४४ ।।

तस्यां च शिशुपालमुत्पादयामास ।। ४५ ।।

Damaghoṣa, the king of Cedi, married Śrutāśravā and begot on her a son named Śiśupāla.

स वा पूर्वमप्युदारविक्रमो दैत्यानामदिपुरुषो हिरण्यकशिपुरभवत् ।। ४६ ।।

यश्च भगवता सकललोकगुरुणा नारसिंहेन घातितः ।। ४७ ।।

This prince in his pristine birth, was the wicked and valiant king of the Daityas, Hiraṇyakaśipu, who was killed by the divine guardian of creation.

पुनरपि अक्षयवीर्यशौर्य्यसंपत्पराक्रमगुणस्समाक्रांत-सकलत्रैलोकेश्वरप्रभावो दशाननो नामाभूत् ।। ४८ ।।

He was in another birth was born as the ten-headed Rāvaṇa, whose unequalled, strength, prowess and power were overcome by Rāma, the lord of the three worlds.

बहुकालोपभुक्तभगवत्सकाशावाप्तशरीरपातोद्भवपुण्यफलो भगवता राघवरूपिणा सोऽपि निधनमुपपादितः ।। ४९ ।।

पुनश्चेदिराजस्य दमघोषस्यात्मजश्शिशुपालनामा-ऽभवत् ।। ५० ।।

Having been destroyed by the deity in the shape of Rāghava, he was exempted from an embodied state for a long time as reward of his virtues but had now been born once more as Śiśupāla the son of Damaghoṣa, king of Cedi.

शिशुपालत्वेपि भगवतो भूभारावतारणायावतीर्णांशस्य पुंडरीकनयनाख्यस्योपरि द्वेषानुबंधमतितराञ्चकार ।। ५१ ।।

भगवता च स निधनमुपानीतस्तत्रैव परमात्मभूते मनस एकाग्रतया सायुज्यमवाप ।। ५२ ।।

भगवान् यदि प्रसन्नो यथाभिलषितं ददाति तथा अप्रसन्नोपि निघ्नन् दिव्यमनुपमं स्थानं प्रयच्छति ।। ५३ ।।

In this character he began to show greatest hostility towards Kṛṣṇa an incarnate portion of the glorious Puṇḍarīkākṣa to carry the burden of the world. He was killed by the great God. And on account of his thoughts being entirely devoted him Śiśupāla was united with him after death; for the lord giveth to those with whom he is propitiated what they desire and he confers a heavenly and exalted station even upon those whom he destroys in displeasure.

।। इति श्रीविष्णुमहापुराणे चतुर्थेंशे चतुर्दशोऽध्यायः ।। १४ ।।

अथ चतुर्थेंशे: पञ्चदशोऽध्याय:
Part IV : Section 15

मैत्रेय उवाच

हिरण्यकशिपुत्वे च रावणत्वे च विष्णुना।।
अवाप निहतो भोगानप्राप्यानमरैरपि।। १।।

Maitreya said :—Being killed by Viṣṇu as Hiraṇyakaśipu and Rāvaṇa he obtained enjoyments which are not attainable even by the immortals.

न लयं तत्र तेनैव निहत: स कथं पुन:।।
संप्राप्त: शिशुपालत्वे शाश्वते हरौ।। २।।

Why did they not obtain absorption albeit slain by Viṣṇu? And why as Śiśupāla were they absorbed into the eternal Hari?

एतदिच्छाम्यहं श्रोतुं सर्वधर्मभृतां वर।।
कौतूहलपरेणैतत्पृष्टो मे वक्तुमर्हसि।। ३।।

O foremost of those conversant with religion, I wish to hear of all these; I am greatly striken with curiosity; do thou relate them.

श्रीपराशर उवाच

दैत्येश्वरस्य वधायाखिललोकोत्पत्तिस्थिति-
विनाशकारिणा पूर्वं तनुग्रहणं कुर्वता नृसिंह
रूपमाविष्कृतम्।। ४।।

तत्र च हिरण्यकशिपोर्विष्णुरयमित्येन्न मनस्यभूत्।।
५।।

Parāśara said :—When the creator, preserver and destroyer of the universe killed Hiraṇyakaśipu, the king of Daityas, he assumed the figure of a lion and man, he was not aware that his slayer was Viṣṇu.

निरतिशयपुण्यसमुद्भूतमेतत्सत्त्वजातमिति ।। ६।।

He thought this wonderful figure was but the creation of his accumulated piety.

रजोद्रेकप्रेरितैकाग्रमतिस्तद्भावनायोगात्ततोवाप्तवधहैतुकीं
निरतिशयामेवाखिलत्रैलोक्याधिक्यकारिणीं दशाननत्वे
भोगसंपदमवाप।।७।।

And the quality of passion being predominant in his mind he obtained destruction from man-lion. And in consequence of his death at the hands of Viṣṇu he obtained sovereignty over three worlds and immense riches and enjoyments as Daśāsana.

न तु स तस्मिन्ननादिनिधने परब्रह्मभूते
भगवत्यनालंबिनि कृते मनसस्तल्लयमवाप।। ८।।

He was not absorved into the supreme spirit wholly devoted to that object.

एवं दशाननत्वेप्यनंगपराधीनतया जानकीसमासक्त-
चेतसा भगवता दाशरथिरूपधारिणा हतस्य
तदूपदर्शनमेवासीत् नायमच्युत इत्यासक्तिर्विपद्यतोंत:-
करणे मानुषबुद्धिरेव केवलमस्याभूत्।। ९।।

Daśāsana, thus being entirely subject to love and being entirely taken up by thoughts of Jānakī, could not perceive that the son of Daśaratha whom he saw, was in fact the divine Acyuta.

पुनरप्यच्युतविनिपात मात्रफलमखिलभूमंडलश्लाघ्य-
चेदिराजकुले जन्म अव्याहतैश्वर्य्यं शिशुपाल-
त्वेप्यवाप।। १०।।

At the time of his death he was impressed with the idea that his enemy was a mortal and therefore the fruit he obtained from being slain by Viṣṇu was his birth in the illustrious family of the kings Cedi and the possession of extensive dominions. And he was known as Śiśupāla.

तत्र त्वखिलानामेव स भगवन्नाम्नां त्वंकार
कारणमभवत्।। ११।।

ततश्च तत्कालकृतानां तेषामशेषाणामेवाच्युतनाम्ना-
मनवरतमनेकजन्मसु वर्द्धितविद्वेषानुबंधिचित्तो
विनिंदनसंतर्जना दिषूच्चारणमकरोत्।। १२।।

तच्च रूपमुत्फुल्लपद्मदलामलाक्षिमत्युज्ज्वलपीत-
वस्त्रधार्यमलकिरीटकेयूरहारकटकादिशोभित-
मुदारचतुर्बाहुशंखचक्रगदाधरमतिप्ररूढवैरानुभावाद-
टनभोजनस्नानासनशयनादिष्वशेषावस्थान्तरेषु
नान्यत्रोपययावस्य चेतस:।। १३।।

In this birth many circumstances occured by which he was constrained to utter the name of the great God and on all these occasions the enmity, that had accumulated through successive births, influenced his mind.

And always speaking disrespectfully of Acyuta he repeated all his names. Whether walking, eating, sitting, or sleeping his enmity was never at rest and Kṛṣṇa was always present to his mind in his ordinary form, having eyes like lotus-petals, clad and bright yellow raiment, adorned with a garland, with bracelets on his arms and writs and a diadem on his crown; having four stalwart arms bearing the conch, the discus, the mace and the lotus.

ततस्तमेवाक्रोशेषूच्चारयंस्तमेव हृदयेन धारयन्नात्मवधाय यावद्भगवद्धस्तचक्रांशुमालोज्ज्वलमक्षयतेजस्स्वरूपं ब्रह्मभूतमपगतद्वेषादिदोषं भगवंतमद्राक्षीत्।। १४।।

Uttering his names always although in malediction Kṛṣṇa was always present in his mind, and while infliction his death Śiśupāla saw him radiant with shining weapons and in his true Brahmā form void of passion and enmity.

तावच्च भगवच्चक्रेणाशु व्यापादितस्तत्स्मरणदग्धाखिलाघसञ्चयो भगवतांतमुपनीतस्ततस्मिन्नेव लयमुपययौ।। १५।।

Being slain by the discus of Viṣṇu at this moment all his sins were removed by his divine enemy and he was united with him by whose might he was destroyed.

एतत्तवाखिलं मयाभिहितम्।। १६।।

I have thus related to you everything.

अयं हि भगवान् कीर्त्तितश्च संस्मृतश्च द्वेषानुबंधेनपि अखिलसुरासुरादिदुर्ल्लभं फलं प्रयच्छति किमुत सम्यग्भक्तिमतामिति।। १७।।

He, who names or remembers the glorious Viṣṇu even in the enmity obtains Final emancipation which is not atainable by the gods or demons. It is useless to say that he, who reverentially names or remembers him, obtains final liberation.

वसुदेवस्य त्वानकदुंदुभेः पौरवीरोहिणीमदिराभद्रादेवकीप्रमुखा बह्व्यः पत्न्योऽभवन्।। १८।।

Vasudeva, otherwise named Aṅkadundubhi, and Rohiṇī, Pauravī, Bhadrā, Madirā, Devakī and several other wives.

बलभद्रशठसारणदुर्मदादीन्पुत्रान्रोहिण्यामानकदुंदुभिरुत्पादयामास।। १९।।

His sons by Rohiṇī were Balabhadra, Sāraṇa, Saru, Durmada, and others.

बलदेवोपि रेवत्यां विशठोल्मुकौ पुत्रावजनयत्।। २०।।

Balabhadra married Revatī and had by her Viśaṭha and Ulmaka.

सार्ष्टिमार्ष्टिशिशुसत्यसत्य धृतिप्रमुखाः सारणात्मजाः।। २१।।

The sons of Sāraṇa wre Marṣṭi, Marṣṭimat, Śiśu, Satyadhṛti, and others.

भद्राश्वभद्रबाहुदुर्दमभूताद्याः रोहिण्याः कुलजाः।। २२।।

Bhadrāśva, Bhadrabāhu, Durgama, Bhūta and others were born in the race of Rohiṇī.

नंदोपनंकृतकाद्या मदिरायास्तनयाः।। २३।।

भद्रायाश्चोपनिधिगदाद्याः।। २४।।

The son of Vasudeva by Madirā were Nanda, Upananda, Kṛtaka and others.

वैशाल्यां च कौशिक्योकनेवाजनयत्।। २५।।

आनकदुंदुभेर्देवक्यामपि कीर्त्तिमत्सुषेणोदायुभद्रसेनऋजदासभद्रदेवाख्याः षट् पुत्रा जज्ञिरे।। २६।।

तांश्च सर्वानेव कंसोघातितवान्।। २७।।

By his wife Vaiśālī he had one son named Kauśika. Devakī before him six sons Kṛtimat, Suśeṇa, Udāyin, Bhadrasena, Ṛjudāsa and Bhadradeha all of whom were killed by Kansa.

अनंतरं च सप्तमं गर्भमर्द्धरात्रे भगवत्प्रहिता योगनिद्रा रोहिण्या जठरमाकृष्य नीतवती।। २८।।

कर्षणाच्चासावपि संकर्षणाख्यामगमत्।। २९।।

When Devakī was again big with a child the seventh time, Yoganidrā (the sleep of devotion), despatched by Viṣṇu, extricated the embro from maternal womb at the mid-night and transferred it to that of Rohiṇī; and from having been thus taken away, the child (who was Balarāma) received the name of Saṅkarṣaṇa.

ततश्च सकलजगन्महातरुमूलभूतो भूतभविष्यादादि-
सकलसुरासुरमुनिजनमनसामप्यगोचरोऽब्जभव-
प्रमुखैरनलमुखैःप्रणम्यावनिभारहरणाय प्रसादितो
भगवाननादिमध्यनिधनो देवकीगर्भमवततार
वासुदेवः।। ३०।।

Being desirous of relieving the world of the burden, the divine Viṣṇu, the source of the vast universe, beyond the understanding of all gods, demons sages, and men, past, present or future, worshipped of Brahmā and all the celestials, who is without beginning, middle or end, descended into the womb of Devakī and was born as her son Vasudeva.

तत्प्रसादविवर्द्धमानोरुमहिमा च योगनिद्रा
नंदगोपपत्न्या यशोदाया गर्भमधितिष्ठितवती।। ३१।।

Yaganidrā, always proud to satisfy his orders, removed the embryo to Yośodā the wife of Nanda, the cow-herd.

सुप्रसन्नादित्यचंद्रादिग्रहमव्यालादिभयं स्वस्थमान-
समखिलमेवैतज्जगदपास्ताधर्ममभवत्तस्मिंश्च
पुंडरीकनयने जायमाने।। ३२।।

At this birth the earth was relieved of all sins; the sun, moon and planets shone with unclouded brilliance; all fear of evil portents was removed and universal happiness prevailed.

जातेन च तेनाखिलमेवैतत्सन्मार्गवर्त्ति जगदक्रियत।। ३३।।

And from the time of his birth people were led into the righteous path.

भगवतोप्यत्र मर्त्यलोकेऽवतीर्णस्य षोडशसहस्राण्ये-
कोत्तरशताधिकानि भार्याणमभवन्।। ३४।।

तासां च रुक्मिणी सत्यभामा जांबवती चारुहासिनी-
प्रमुखा ह्यष्टौ पत्न्यः प्रधाना बभूवुः।। ३५।।

Whilst this powerful being lived in the land of mortals he had sixteen thousand and one hundred wives of whom the Principal were Rukmiṇī, Satyabhāmā, Jāmbavatī, Jalhāsinī and four others.

तासु चाष्टावयुतानि लक्षं च पुत्राणां भगवान-
खिलमूर्तिरनादिमानजनयत्।। ३६।।

तेषां च प्रद्युम्नचारुदेष्ण्यसांबादयः त्रयोदश प्रधानाः।।
३७।।

The divine Kṛṣṇà, the universal form without beginning, begot on all these wives a hundred and eighty thousand sons, of whom thirteen were most celebrated, Pradyumna, Cārudeśaṇa, Sāmba and others.

प्रद्युम्नोपि रुक्मिणस्तनयां रुक्मवतीं नामोपयेमे।।
३८।।

तस्यामनिरुद्धौ जज्ञे।। ३९।।

Pradyumna, married Rukmāvatī, the daughter of Rukmiṇī and had by her Aniruddha.

अनिरुद्धोऽपि रुक्मिण एव पौत्रीं सुभद्रां नामोपयेमे।। ४०।।

तस्यामस्य वज्रो जज्ञे।। ४१।।

Aniruddha married Subhadrā, the grand daughter of the same Rukmiṇī and she bore him a son named Vajra.

वज्रस्य प्रतिबाहुः तस्यापि सुचारुः।। ४२।।

The son of Vajra and Pratibāhu and his son was Sucāru.

एवमनेकशतसहस्रपुरुषसंख्यस्य यदुकुलस्य पुत्रसंख्या
वर्षशतैरपि वक्तुं न शक्यते।। ४३।।

In this way the members of the Yadu family increased and were many hundreds of thousands of them so that it would be impossible to repeat their names in hundreds of years.

यतो हि श्लोकाविमावत्र चरितार्थौ।। ४४।।

Two verses regarding them are recited.

तिस्रः कोट्यस्सहस्राणामष्टाशीति शतानि च।।
कुमाराणां गृहाचार्याश्चापयोगेषु ये रताः।। ४५।।

"The domestic teachers of the boys in the use of arms numbered three crores and eighty lacs.

संख्यानं यादवानां कः करिष्यति महात्मनाम्।।
यत्रायुतानामयुतलक्षेणास्ते सदाहुकः।। ४६।।

Who shall enumerate the powerful members of the Yādava family who were tens of ten thousands and hundreds of hundred thousands in number?

देवासुरे हता ये तु दैतेयास्सुमहाबलाः ।।
उत्पन्नास्ते मनुष्येषु जनोपद्रवकारिणः ।। ४७ ।।

Those powerful Daityas, who were slain by them in the encounter between the gods and demons, were born again on earth as men, as tytants and oppressors.

तेषामुत्सादनार्थाय भुवि देवा यदोः कुले ।।
अवतीर्णाः कुलशतं यत्रैकाभ्यधिकं द्विज ।। ४८ ।।

With a view to arrests their violence the gods also descended to the land of mortals and became members of the hundred and one branches of family of Yadu.

विष्णुस्तेषां प्रमाणे च प्रभुत्वे च व्यवस्थितः ।।
निदेशस्थायिन स्तस्यववृधुस्सर्वयादवाः ।। ४९ ।।

Viṣṇu was their teacher and ruler and all the members were obedient to his commands.

इति प्रसूतिं वृष्णीनां यश्श्रृणोति नरः सदा ।।
स सर्वैः पातकैर्मुक्तो विष्णुलोकं प्रपद्यते ।। ५० ।।

Whoever hears often times of this account of the origin of the heroes of the race of Vṛṣṇī shall be freed from all iniquities and shall attain to the region of Viṣṇu.

।। इति श्रीविष्णुमहापुराणे चतुर्थेंशे पञ्चदशोऽध्यायः ।। १५ ।।

अथ चतुर्थेंशेः षोडशोऽध्यायः

Part IV : Section 16

श्रीपराशर उवाच

इत्येष समासतस्ते यदोर्वंशः कथितः ।। १ ।।

अथ दुर्वसोर्वंशमवधारय ।। २ ।।

Parāśara said :—I shall breifly give you an account of the descendants of Turvasu.

दुर्वसोर्वह्निरात्मजः वह्नेभार्गः भार्गाद्भानुः ततश्च
त्रयीसानुः तस्माच्च करंदमः तस्यापि मरुत्तः ।। ३ ।।

The son of Turvasa was Tahni, whose son was Gobhānu, whoṣe son was Traisamba, whose son was Karandhama, whose son was Marutta.

सोनपत्योभवत् ।। ४ ।।

ततश्च पौरवं दुष्यंतं पुत्रमकल्पयत् ।। ५ ।।

एवं ययातिशापात्तद्वंशः पौरवमेव वंशं समाश्रित-
वान् ।। ६ ।।

Marutta had no issue and he therefore adopted Duṣyanta of the race of Puru by which the line of Turvasa merged into that of Puru. This was brought about by the curse imprecated on his son by Yayāti.

।। इति श्रीविष्णुमहापुराण चतुर्थेंशे षोडशोऽध्यायः ।। १६ ।।

अथ चतुर्थेंशे: सप्तदशोऽध्याय:

Part IV : Section 17

श्रीपराशर उवाच

दुह्योस्तु तनयो बभ्रु:।। १।।

बभ्रोस्सेतु:।। २।।

सेतुपुत्र आरब्धनामा।। ३।।

आरब्धस्यात्मजो गांधार: गांधारस्य धर्म: धर्मात् घृत:
घृतात् दुर्दम: तत: प्रचेता।। ४।।

प्रचेतस: पुत्रश्शतधर्म: बहुलानां म्लेच्छानामुदीच्या-
नामाधिपत्यमरोत्।। ५।।

Parāśara said :—The son of Druhya was Babhru, whose son was Setu, whose son was Aradwat, whose son was Gāndhāra, whose son was Dharma, whose son was Dhṛta, whose soon was Duryaman, whose son was Pracetās, who had a hundred sons and they were the princes of the lawless Mlecchas or barbarians of the north.

।। इति श्रीविष्णुमहापुराणे चतुर्थेंशे सप्तदशोऽध्याय:।। १७।।

अथ चतुर्थेंशे: अष्टादशोऽध्याय:

Part IV : Section 18

श्रीपराशर उवाच

ययातेश्चतुर्थपुत्रस्यानोस्सभानलचक्षु:परमेषुसंज्ञास्त्रय:
पुत्रा बभूवु:।। १।।

Parāśara said :—Aṇu, the fourth son of Yayāti, had three sons, Sabhanāra, Cākṣuṣa and Paramekṣu.

सभानलपुत्र: कालानल:।। २।।

कालानलात्सृञ्जय:।। ३।।

सृञ्जयात् पुरञ्जय:।। ४।।

पुरञ्जयाज्जनमेजय:।।५।।

तस्मान्महाशाल:।। ६।।

तस्माच्च महामना:।। ७।।

तस्मादुशीनरतितीक्षू द्वौ पुत्रावुत्पन्नौ ।।८।।

The son of the first was Kālānara, whose son was Śṛñjaya, whose son was Purañjaya, whose son was Janamenjaya, whose son was Mahāśāla, whose son was Mahāmānas, who had two sons, Uśīnara and Titikṣu.

उशीनरस्यापि शिबिनृगनवकृमि वर्माख्या: पञ्च पुत्रा
बभूवु:।। ९।।

Uśīnara had five sons, Śivi, Tṛṇa, Gara, Kṛmī, Darvan.

पृषदर्भसुवीरकेकयमद्रकाश्चत्वारश्शिबिपुत्रा:।। १०।।

Śivi had four sons Vṛṣadarva, Survīra, Kaikeya and Madra.

तितीक्षोरपि रुशद्रथ: पुत्रोऽभूत्।। ११।।

तस्यापि हेम: हेमस्यापि सुतपा: सुतपसश्च बलि:।।
१२।।

यस्य क्षेत्रे दीर्घतमसांगवंगकलिंगसुह्मपौंड्राख्यं वालेयं
क्षत्रमजन्यत।। १३।।

तन्नामसंततिसंज्ञाश्च पञ्चविषया: बभूवु:।। १४।।

Titikṣu had one son Uṣadratha, whose son was Hema, whose son was Sūtapas, whose was Bali, on whose spouse five sons were begotten by Dīrghatamas—namely Aṅga, Baṅga, Kaliṅga, Sauhma and Puṇḍra and their progeny and the countries they inhabited were known by the same names.

अंगादनपानस्ततो दिविरथस्तस्माद्धर्म रथ:।। १५।।

ततश्चित्ररथ: रोमपादसंज्ञ:।। १६।।

यस्य दशरथो मित्रं जज्ञे।। १७।।

यस्याजपुत्रो दशरथश्शांतां नाम कन्यामनपत्यस्य दुहितृत्वे युयोज।। १८।।

The son of Aṅga was Pāra, whose son was Divaratha, whose son was Dharmaratha, whose son was Citraratha, whose son was Romapāda also called Daśaratha, to whom on account of his having no offspring, Daśaratha, the son of Aja gave his daughter Śāntā to be adopted.

रोमापादाच्चतुरंगः तस्मात्पृथुलाक्षः।। १९।।

ततश्चंपः यश्चंपां निवेशयामास।। २०।।

चंपस्य हर्यंगो नामात्मजोऽभूत्।। २१।।

After this Romapāda had a son named Caturaṅga, whose son was Pṛthulakṣa, whose son was Campā who founded the city of Campā.

हंगाद्भद्ररथः भद्ररथाद्बृहद्रथः बृहद्रथाद्बृहत्कर्मा बृहत्कर्मणश्च बृहद्भानुस्तस्माच्च बृहन्मनाः बृहन्मनसो जयद्रथः।। २२।।

जयद्रथो ब्रह्मक्षत्रांतरालसंभूत्यां पत्न्यां विजयं नाम पुत्रमजीजनत्।। २३।।

The son of Campā was Haryyaṅga, whose son was Bhadraratha, who had two sons, Vṛhatkarman and Bṛhadratha. The son of the former was Bṛhadbhānu, whose son was Vṛhanmānas, whose son was Jayadratha, who by a wife, who was the daughter of a Kṣatriya father and Brāhmaṇa mother, had a son named Vijaya.

विजयश्च धृतिं पुत्रमवाप।। २४।।

तस्यापि धृतव्रतः पुत्रोऽभूत्।। २५।।

धृतव्रतात्सत्यकर्मा।। २६।।

सत्यकर्मणस्त्वतिरथः।। २७।।

यो गंगांगतो मञ्जूषागतं पृथापविद्धं कर्णं पुत्रमवाप।। २८।।

Vijaya had a son whose name was Dhṛti, whose son was Dṛtavrata, whose son was Satyakarman, whose son was Ādiratha who found a son in a basket on the banks of the Ganges. This was Karṇa, the son of Pṛthā in her maidenhood.

कर्णाद्वृषसेनः इत्येतदंता अंगवंश्याः।। २९।।

Karṇa's son was Vṛṣasen. These were the Aṅga kings.

अतश्च पूरुवंशं श्रोतुमर्हसि।। ३०।।

I shall now describe to you the descendants of Puru.

इति श्रीविष्णुमहापुराणे चतुर्थांशेऽष्टादशोऽध्यायः।। १८।।

अथ चतुर्थेंशेः एकोनविंशोऽध्यायः

Part IV : Section 19

श्रीपराशर उवाच

पूरोर्जनमेजयस्तस्यापि प्रचिन्वान् प्रचिन्वतः प्रवीरः प्रवीरान्मनस्युर्मनस्योश्चाभयदः तस्यापि सुद्युस्सुद्यो र्बहुगतः तस्यापि संयातिस्संयातेरहंयातिः ततो रौद्राश्वः।। १।।

ऋतेषुकक्षेषुस्थंडिलेषुकृतेषुजलेषुधर्मेषुधृतेषु-स्थलेषुसन्नतेषुवनेषुनामानो रौद्राश्वस्य दश पुत्रा बभूवुः।। २।।

Parāśara said :—The son of Puru was Janamenjaya, whose son was Prācīnvat, whose son was Pravīra, whose son was Manasyu, whose son was Bhayāda, whose son was Sudyumna, whose son was Bahugava, whose son was Saṁyāti, whose son was Ahamyati, whose son was Raudrāśva, who had ten sons, Ṛteyu, Kakṣeyu, Sthāṇḍiteyu, Ghṛteyu, Jaleyu, Sthaleyu, Santaleyu, Dhaneyu, Vaneyu, and Vrateyu.

ऋतेषोरंतिनारः पुत्रोऽभूत्।। ३।।

सुमतिमप्रतिरथं ध्रुवं चाप्यंतिनारः पुत्रानवाप।। ४।।

The son of Ṛteyu was Rantināra, whose sons were Tansu, Apratīrtha and Dhruva.

अप्रतिरथस्य कण्वः पुत्रोऽभूत्।।५।।

तस्यापि मेधातिथिः।। ६।।

यतः कण्वायना द्विजा बभूवुः।। ७।।

अप्रतिरथस्यापरः पुत्रोऽभूदैलीनः।। ८।।

The son of the second of these was Kaṇva, whose son was Medhātithī, from whom the Kaṇvanyana Brāhmaṇas were sprung. Anila was the son Tansu, who had four sons of whom Duṣyanta was the elder.

ऐलीनस्य दुष्यंताद्याश्चत्वारः पुत्रा बभूवुः।। ९।।

दुष्यंताच्चक्रवर्त्ती भरतोऽभूत्।। १०।।

यन्नामहेतुर्देवैश्श्लोको गीयते।। ११।।

The son of Duṣyanta was the Emperor Bharata, regarding whom a verse is recited by the celestials.

माता भस्त्रा पितुः पुत्रो येन जातः स एव सः।।
भरस्व पुत्रं दुष्यंतमावमंस्थाश्शकुंतलाम्।। १२।।

रेतोधाः पुत्रो नयति नरदेव यमक्षयात्।।
त्वं चास्य धाता गर्भस्य सत्यमाह शकुंतला।। १३।।

"The mother is merely the receptable; it is the father by whom a son is begotten. Rear up thy son, Duṣyanta, treat not Śakuntalā with disrespect. Sons, who are born from the loins of their father, save their manes from hell. Thou art the father of this boy; Śakuntalā has spoken the truth."

भरतस्य पत्नित्रये नव पुत्रा बभूवुः।। १४।।

नैते ममानुरूपा इत्यभिहितास्तन्मातरः परित्याग-
भयात्तत्पुत्राञ्जघ्नुः।। १५।।

Bharata begot on his wives nine sons, beholding whom he said that they were not after him. The queens, being afraid lest he might desert them, destroyed those sons.

ततोस्य वितथे पुत्रजन्मनि पुत्रार्थिनो मरुत्सोमयाजिनो
दीर्घतमसः पाष्ण्यर्पास्तद्बृहस्पतिवीर्यादुतथ्यपत्न्यां
ममतायां समुत्पन्नो भरद्वाजाख्यः पुत्रो मरुद्भिर्दत्तः।।
१६।।

The birth of sons being thus useless the king celebrated a sacrifice in honour of Marutas. They gave him Bharadwāja, the son of Bṛhaspati by Mamatā, the wife of Utathya, expelled untimely by the kick of his half brother Dīrghatamas.

तस्यापि नामनिर्वचनश्लोकः पठ्यते।। १७।।

मूढे भर द्वाजमिमं भरद्वाजं बृहस्पते।।
यातौ यदुक्त्वा पितरौ भरद्वाजस्ततस्त्वयम्।। इति।। १८।।

The following verse expalins the meaning of the name—"Silly woman" said Bṛhaspati "cherish" this child of two fathers (Bhara-dwajam) "No, Bṛhaspati" replied Mamatā "you take care of him."

भरद्वाजस्स तस्य वितथे पुत्रजन्मनि मरुद्भिर्दत्तः ततो
वितथसंज्ञामवाप।। १९।।

So saying they both left him and from these expressions the boy was named Bharadwāja.

वितथस्यापि मन्युः पुत्रोऽभवत्।। २०।।

बृहत्क्षत्रमहावीर्यनगरगर्गा अभवन्मन्युपुत्राः।। २१।।

He was also called Vitatha for both the sons of Bharata proved fruitless. The son of Vitatha was Bhavanmanya, who had many sons, the principals among whom were Bṛhatkṣatra, Mahāvīryya, Nara and Garga.

नगरस्य संकृतिस्संकृतेर्गुरुप्रीतिरंतिदेवौ।। २२।।

गर्गाच्छिनिः ततश्च गार्ग्याश्शैन्याः क्षत्रोपेता द्विजातयो
बभूवुः।। २३।।

The son of Nara was Saṅkṛti, whose sons were Ruciradhi and Rantideva. The son of Garga was Sini and their progeny were respectively called Gārgyas and Śainyas; although Kṣatriyas by birth they became Brāhmaṇas.

महावीर्याच्च दुरुक्षयो नाम पुत्रोऽभवत्।। २४।।

तस्य त्रय्यारुणिः पुष्करिणः कपिश्च पुत्रत्रयमभूत्।।
२५।।

तच्च पुत्रत्रितयमपि पश्चाद्विप्रतामुपजगाम।। २६।।

The son of Mahāvīrya was Urukṣaya, who had three sons Trayyāruṇa, Puṣkarin and Kapi, the last of whor' became a Brāhmaṇa.

बृहत्क्षत्रस्य सुहोत्रः।। २७।।

सुहोत्राद्धस्ती य इदं हस्तिनपुरमावासयामास।। २८।।

The son of Bṛhatkṣatra was Suhotra, whose son was Hastin, who founded the city of Hastināpur.

अजमीढद्विजमीढपुरुमीढास्त्रयो हस्तिनस्तनयाः।। २९।।

The sons of Hastin were Ajamīḍha, Dvijamīḍha, Purumīḍha.

अजमीढात्कण्वः।। ३०।।

कण्वान्मेधातिथिः।। ३१।।

यतः कण्वायना द्विजाः।। ३२।।

अजमीढस्यान्यः पुत्रो बृहदिषुः।। ३३।।

बृहदिषोर्बृहद्धनुर्बृहद्धनुषश्च बृहत्कर्मा ततश्च जयद्रथस्तस्मादपि विश्वजित्।। ३४।।

ततश्च सेनजित्।। ३५।।

रुचिराश्वकाश्यदृढहनुवत्सहनुसंज्ञास्सेनजितः पुत्राः।। ३६।।

One son of Ajamīḍha was Kaṇva, whose son was Medhātithī; his other son was Bṛhadiṣu, whose son was Bṛhadvasu, whose son was Bṛhatkarman, whose son was Jayadratha, whose son was Viśvajit, whose son was Senajit, whose sons were Rucirāśva, Kasya, Dṛḍhadhanuṣa and Vasahana.

रुचिराश्वपुत्रः पृथुसेनः पृथुसेनात्पारः।। ३७।।

पारान्नीलः।। ३८।।

तस्यैकशतं पुत्राणाम्।। ३९।।

तेषां प्रधानः कांपिल्याधिपतिस्समरः।। ४०।।

समरस्यापि पारसुपारसदश्वास्त्रयः पुत्राः।। ४१।।

The son of Rucirāśva was Pṛthusena, whose son was Pāra, whose son was Nipa, who had a hundred sons, of whom the chief Samara was the king of Kāpilya. Samara had three sons Para, Sampara Sadāśva.

सुपारात्पृथुः पृथोस्सुकृतेर्विभ्राजः।। ४२।।

तस्माच्चाणुहः।। ४३।।

यश्शुकदुहितरं कीर्त्तिं नामोपयेमे।। ४४।।

अणुहाद्ब्रह्मदत्तः।। ४५।।

ततश्च विष्वक्सेनस्तस्मादुदक्सेनः।। ४६।।

भल्लाभस्तस्य चात्मजः।। ४७।।

The son of Para was Pṛtha, whose son was Sukṛti, whose son was Vibhrata, whose son was Anuha, who married Kṛtvī, the daughter of Śuka and had by her Brahmādatta, whose son was Viśvaksena, whose son was Udaksena and whose son was Bhallata.

द्विजमीढस्य तु यवीनरसंज्ञः पुत्रः।। ४८।।

तस्यापि धृतिमांस्तस्माच्च सत्यधृतिस्ततश्च दृढनेमिस्तस्माच्च सुपार्श्वस्ततस्सुमतिस्ततश्च सन्नतिमान्।। ४९।।

सन्नतिमतः कृतः पुत्रोऽभूत्।। ५०।।

यं हिरण्यनाभो योगमध्यापयामास।। ५१।।

यश्चतुर्विंशतिप्राच्यसामगानां संहिताश्चकार।। ५२।।

The son of Dvimīḍha was Yavinara, whose son was Dhṛtimat, whose son was Satyadhṛti, whose son was Dṛḍhanemi, whose son was Supārśva, whose son was Sumati, whose son was Sannatimat, whose son was Kṛta, who was taught by Hiraṇyanābha, the philosophy of Yoga and who compiled the twenty-four Saṁhitās for the use of the eastern Brāhmaṇas studying the Sāma Veda.

कृताच्चोग्रायुधः।। ५३।।

येन प्राचुर्येण नीपक्षयः कृतः।। ५४।।

The son of Kṛta was Ugrayudhas, who by his power destroyed the Nipa race of Kṣatriyas.

उग्रायुधात्क्षेम्यः क्षेम्यात्सुधीरस्तस्मादिपुञ्जयः तस्माच्च बहुरथ इत्येते पौरवाः।। ५५।।

His son was Kṣemya, whose son was Sudhīra, whose son was Nṛpañjaya, whose son was Baharatha. These were all called Pauravas.

अजमीढस्य नलिनी नाम पत्नी तस्यां नीलसंज्ञः पुत्रोऽभवत्।। ५६।।

तस्मादपि शांतिः शांतेस्सुशांति स्सुशांतेः पुरञ्जयः तस्माच्च ऋक्षः।। ५७।।

ततश्च हर्यश्वः ।। ५८ ।।

तस्मान्मुद्गलसृञ्जयबृहदिषुयवीनरकांपिल्यसंज्ञाः पञ्चानामेव तेषां विषयाणां रक्षणायालमेते मत्पुत्रा इति पित्राभिहिताः पाञ्चालाः ।। ५९ ।।

Ajamīḍha espoused Nilinī and by her had a son called Nīla, whose son was Śānti, whose son was Suśānti, whose son was Purujanu, whose son was Cakṣu, whose son was Harryāśva, who had five sons, Mudgala, Śṛñjaya, Bṛhadiṣu, Pravīra and Kāmpilya. Their father said—"These five sons of mine are capable of prtecting the countries" and hence they were called Pāñcālas—(*i.e.*, Pāñca—*five* and alam—*able*).

मुद्गलाच्च मौद्गल्याः क्षत्रोपेता द्विजातयो बभूवुः ।। ६० ।।

From Mudgala sprang the Maudgalya Brāhmaṇas.

मुद्गलाद्धर्यश्वः ।। ६१ ।।

हर्यश्वाद्दिवोदासोऽहल्या च मिथुनमभूत् ।। ६२ ।।

He had also a son called Bahwāśva, who had two children, twins, a son and daughter—Divodāsa and Ahalyā.

शरद्वतश्चाहल्यायां शतानंदोऽभवत् ।। ६३ ।।

शतानंदात्सत्यधृतिर्धनुर्वेदान्तगो जज्ञे ।। ६४ ।।

The son of Saradwat or Gautama by Ahalyā was Śatānanda, whose son was Satyadhṛti, who was well versed in military science.

सत्यधृतेर्वराप्सरसमुर्वशीं दृष्ट्वा रेतस्कन्नं शरस्तंबे पपात ।। ६५ ।।

तच्च द्विधागतमपत्यद्वयं कुमारः कन्या चाभवत् ।। ६६ ।।

Being enamoured of the nymph Urvaśī, Satyadṛti begot on her two children, a boy and a daughter.

तौ च मृगयामुपयातश्शंतनुर्दृष्ट्वा कृपया जग्राह ।। ६७ ।।

The king Śāntanu, a-hunting, found their children in a clump of long Śara grass and feeling pity for them took them and reared them up.

ततः कुमारः कृपः कन्या चाश्वत्थाम्नो जननी कृपी द्रोणाचार्यस्य पत्न्य भवत् ।। ६८ ।।

As they were brought up through *Kṛpā*, pity, they were called Kṛpa and Kṛpī. The latter became the wife of Droṇa and the mother of Aśvatthāman.

दिवोदासस्य पुत्रो मित्रायुः ।। ६९ ।।

मित्रायोश्च्यवनो नाम राजा ।। ७० ।।

च्यवनात्सुदासः सुदासात्सौदासः सौदासात्सहदेवस्तस्यापि सोमकः ।। ७१ ।।

सोमकाज्जंतुः पुत्रशतज्येष्ठोऽभवत् ।। ७२ ।।

तेषां यवीयान् पृषतः पृषताद्द्रुपदस्तस्माच्च धृष्टद्युम्नस्ततो धृष्टकेतुः ।। ७३ ।।

The son of Divodāsa was Mitrāyu, whose son was Cyavanna, whose son was Sudāsa, whose son was Saudāsa, also called Sahadeva, whose son was Somaka, who had a hundred sons of whom the eldest was Jantu and the youngest was Pṛṣta. The son of Pṛṣta was Drupada, whose son was Dhṛṣṭadyumna, whose son was Dṛṣṭaketu.

अजमीढस्यान्यो ऋक्षनामा पुत्रोऽभवत् ।। ७४ ।।

तस्य संवरणः ।। ७५ ।।

संवरणात्कुरुः ।। ७६ ।।

य इदं धर्मक्षेत्रं कुरु क्षेत्रं चकार ।। ७७ ।।

Another son of Ajamīḍha was called Ṛkṣa, whose son was Samvarāna, whose son was Kuru, who gave his name to the holy district Kurukṣetra.

सुधनुर्जह्नुपरीक्षित्प्रमुखाः कुरोः पुत्राः बभूवुः ।। ७८ ।।

His sons were Sudhanuṣ, Jāhnu, Parīkṣit, and many others.

सुधनुषः पुत्रस्सुहोत्रस्तस्माच्च्यवनः च्यवनात् कृतकः ।। ७९ ।।

ततश्चोपरिचरो वसुः ।। ८० ।।

बृहद्रथप्रत्यग्रकुशांबकुचेलमात्स्यप्रमुखाः वसोः पुत्रास्सप्ताजायंत ।। ८१ ।।

The son of Sudanuṣ was Suhotra, whose son was Cyavana, whose son was Kṛtaka, whose son was Uparicara the Vasu, who had seven children Bṛhadratha, Pratyagra, Kuśambha, Mavella, Matyasa and others.

बृहद्रथात्कुशाग्रः कुशाग्राद्वृषभः वृषभात् पुष्पवान्
तस्मात्सत्यहितः तस्मात्सुधन्वा तस्य च जतुः ।।८२।।

The son of Bṛhadratha was Kuśagra, whose son was Ṛṣabha, whose son was Puṣpavat, whose son was Satyadhṛta, whose son was Sudhanwan, whose son was Jantu.

बृंहद्रथाच्चान्यश्शकलद्वयजन्मा जरया संधितो
जरासंधनामा ।।८३।।

Bṛhadratha had another son. He was born in two parts which were joined together by a female fined named Jarā and accordingly he was named Jarāsandha.

तस्मात्सहदेवस्सहदेवात्सोमपस्ततश्च श्रुतिश्रवाः ।। ८४।।

His son was Sahadeva, whose son was Somāpi, whose son was Śrutaśravas.

इत्येते मया मागधा भूपालाः कथिताः ।। ८५ ।।

These were the kings of Magadha.

।। इति श्रीविष्णुमहापुराणे चतुर्थेंशे एकोनविंशोऽध्यायः ।। १९ ।।

अथ चतुर्थेंशे: विंशोऽध्यायः
Part IV Section 20

श्रीपराशर उवाच

परीक्षितश्च जनमेजयश्रुतसेनोग्रसेनभीमसेनाश्चत्वारः
पुत्राः ।। १ ।।

Parāśara said :—Parīkṣit had four sons—Janamejaya, Śrutasena, Ugrasena and Bhīmasena.

जह्नोस्तु सुरथोनामात्मजो बभूव ।। २ ।।

तस्यापि विदूरथः ।। ३ ।।

तस्मात्सार्वभौमस्सार्वभौमाज्जयत्सेनस्तस्मादाराधित-
स्ततश्चायुतायुरयुतायोरक्रोधनः ।।४।।

तस्माद्देवातिथिः ।। ५ ।।

ततश्च ऋक्षोऽन्योभवत् ।। ६ ।।

ऋक्षाद्भीमसेनस्ततश्च दिलीपः ।। ७ ।।

दिलीपात् प्रतीपः ।। ८ ।।

तस्यापि देवापिशंतनुबाह्लीकसंज्ञास्त्रयः पुत्रा बभूवुः ।।
९ ।।

The son of Jahnu was Sūratha, whose son was Viduratha, whose son was Śarvabhauma, whose son was Jayasena Aravin, whose son was Ayutayus, whose son was Akrodhana; one of his sons was Devatithī and another was called Ṛkṣa, whose son was Dilīpa, whose son was Pratipa, who had three sons, Devāpi, Śāntanu, and Bāhlika.

देवापिर्बाल एवारण्यं विवेश ।। १० ।।

शंतनुस्तु महीपालोऽभूत् ।। ११ ।।

The first took to a forest life in childhood and Śāntanu became the king.

अयं च तस्य श्लोकाः पृथिव्यां गीयते ।। १२ ।।

यंयं कराभ्यां स्पृशति ।। जीर्णं यौवनमेति सः ।।
शांतिं चाप्नोति येनाग्र्यां कर्मणा तेन शंतनुः ।। १३ ।।

Regarding him this verse is recited throughout the earth—"Śāntanu is his name because if he places his hands upon an old man he restores him to youth and by him men obtain tranquility."

तस्य च शंतनो राष्ट्रे द्वादशवर्षाणि देवो न ववर्ष ।। १४ ।।

In Śāntanu's kingdom there was not rain for twelve years.

ततश्चाशेषराष्ट्रविनाशमवेक्ष्याऽसौ राजा ब्राह्मणानपृच्छत्
कस्मादस्माकं राष्ट्रे देवो न वर्षति को ममापराध इति ।।
१५ ।।

ततश्च तमूचुर्ब्राह्मणाः ।। १६ ।।

When he perceived that the whole kingdom was about to be devastated he called together all the Brāhmaṇas and said to them—

अग्रजस्य ते हीयमवनिस्त्वया संभुज्यते अतः परिवेत्ता त्वमित्युक्तस्स राजा पुनस्तानपृच्छत्।। १७।।

किं मयात्र विधेयमिति ।। १८।।

"Why does not the God pour rains in my kingdom? What fault have I committed?" They told him that he was as it were a younger brother married before an elder for he was governing the kingdom which was the rightful property of his elder brother.

ततस्ते पुनरप्यूचुः।। १९।।

यावद्देवापिर्न पतनादिभिर्दोषैरभिभूयते तावदेतत्तस्याहं राज्यम्।। २०।।

तदलमेतैन तु तस्मै दीयतामित्युक्त तस्य मंत्रि-प्रवरेणाश्मराविणा तत्रारण्ये तपस्विनो वेदवाद-विरोधवक्तारः प्रयुक्ताः।। २१।।

तैरस्याप्यतिऋजुमतेर्महीपतिपुत्रस्य बुद्धिर्वेदवाद-विरोधमार्गानुसारिण्यक्रियत।। २२।।

"What then am I to do?" said the king. The Brāhmaṇas replied—"As long as the Brāhmaṇas shall not be displeased with Devāpi on account of his deviating from the path of righteousnes the kingdom is his; you should therefore give it over to him." When the minister of the king Amarisarin heard this he collected a number of ascetics who taught doctrines opposed to those of the Vedas and sent them into the forest. They met Devāpi, perverted the understanding of the simple-minded prince and led him to cherish heretical notions.

राजा च शंतनुर्द्विजवचनोत्पन्नपरिदेवनशोकस्तान् ब्राह्मणानग्रतः कृत्वाऽग्रजस्य प्रदानायारण्यं जगाम।। २३।।

Being informed of his offence by the Brāhmaṇas, Śāntanu was greatly pained. Accordingly he sent them before him into the forest and then went there himself to restore the kingdom to his elder brother.

तदाश्रममुपगताश्च तमवनतमवनीपतिपुत्रं देवापि-मुपतस्थुः।। २४।।

ते ब्राह्मणा वेदवादानुबंधीनि वचांसि राज्यमग्रजेन कर्त्तव्यमित्यिर्थवंति तमूचुः।। २५।।

When the Brāhmaṇas reached the hermitage of Devāpi they informed him, that, according to the doctrines of the Vedas, succession to a kingdom was the right of the elder brother.

असावपि देवापिर्वेदवादविरोधयुक्तिदू षितमनेकप्रकारं तानाह।। २६।।

ततस्ते ब्राह्मणाश्शंतनुमूचुः।। २७।।

But he discussed with them and set forth various arguments which were opposed to the teachings of the Vedas. When the Brāhmaṇas heard this they looked towards Śāntanu and said

आगच्छ हे राजन्नलमत्रातिनिर्बेधेन प्रशान्त एवासावना वृष्टिदोषः पतितयोयमनादिकालमभिहितवेदवचन-दूषणोच्चारणात्।। २८।।

"Come here king you need not give yourself further trouble in this matter. The dearth is gone, this man has fallen from his condition for he has uttered disrespectful words to the authority of the eternal uncreated Veda.

पतिते चाग्रजे नैव ते परिवेतृत्वं भवतीत्युक्तश्शंतनु-स्स्वपुरामागम्य राज्यमकरोत्।। २९।।

वेदवादविरोधवचनोच्चारणदूषिते च तस्मिन्देवापौ तिष्ठत्यपि ज्येष्ठभ्रातर्यखिलसस्यनिष्पत्तये ववर्ष भगवान्पर्जन्यः।। ३०।।

When the elder brother goes down to a degraded state there is no sin consequent upon prior espousals of his junior." Thereupon Śāntanu came back to his capital and governed the kingdom as before; his elder brother was degraded for declaring doctrines opposed to the Vedas. Indra poured down abundnat rain, which was followed by rich harvests.

बाह्लीकात्सोमदत्तः पुत्रोऽभूत्।। ३१।।

सोमदत्तस्यापि भूरिभूरिश्रवशल्यसंज्ञास्त्रयः पुत्र बभूवुः।। ३२।।

The son of Bahlīka was Somadatta, who had three sons, Bhūri, Bhūriśravas and Śala.

शंतनो रप्यमरनद्यां जाह्नव्यामुदारकीर्तिरशेषशास्त्रार्थ
विद्भिष्मः पुत्रोऽभूत।। ३३।।

The son of Śāntanu was the well known and the learned Bhīṣma, who was born to him by the holy Gaṅgā.

सत्यवत्यां च चित्रांगदविचित्रवीर्यौ द्वौ
पुत्रावुत्पादयामास शंतनुः।। ३४।।

He had by his wife Satyāvatī two sons, Citrāṅgada and Vicitravīrya.

चित्रांगदस्तु बाल एव चित्रांगदेनैव गंधर्वेणाहवे
निहतः।। ३५।।

Citrāṅgada, in his youth was slain in an encounter with a Gandharva called Citrāṅgada.

विचित्रवीर्योऽपि काशीराजतनये अंबांवालिके
उपयेमे।। ३६।।

तदुपभोगातिखेदाच्च यक्ष्मणा गृहीतः स
पञ्चत्वमगमत्।। ३७।।

Vicitravīrya married Ambā and Ambālikā, the daughters of the king of Kāśī, and enjoying too much connubial pleasures was attacked with consumption and died.

सत्यवतीनियोगाच्च मत्पुत्रः कृष्णद्वैपायनो मातुर्वचन-
मनतिक्रमणीयमिति कृत्वा विचित्रवीर्यक्षेत्रे धृतराष्ट्र-
पांडुतत्प्रहितभुजिष्यायां विदुरं चोत्पादयामास।। ३८।।

धृतराष्ट्रोपि गांधार्यां दुर्योधनदुश्शासनप्रधानं पुत्रशत-
मुत्पादयामास।। ३९।।

By command of Satyāvatī, my son Kṛṣṇa-Dvaipāyana, who was always obedient to his mother, begot upon the widows of his brother, the princes Dhṛtarāṣṭra and Pāṇḍu and upon a female servant Vidura. Dṛtarāṣṭra had Duryodhana, Duśśāsana and others to the extent of a hundred.

पांडोरप्यरण्ये मृगयायामृषिशापोपहतप्रजाजनन-
सामर्थ्यस्य धर्मवायुशक्रैर्युधिष्ठिरभीमसेनार्जुनाः कुंत्यां
नकुलसहदेवौ चाश्विभ्यां माद्र्यां पञ्चपुत्रा-
स्समुत्पादिताः।। ४०।।

Having incurred the imprecation of a deer whose mate he had slain in a chase, Pāṇḍu was prevented from proceating children. Accordingly his wife Kunti bore to him three sons who were begotten by the deities, Dharma, Vāyu and Indra—namely Yudhiṣṭhira, Bhīma and Arjuna. His wife Mādrī had two sons by the sons of Aśvins—namely Nakula and Sahadeva.

तेषां च द्रौपद्यां पञ्चैव पुत्रा बभूवुः।। ४१।।

These each had a son by Draupadī.

युधिष्ठिरात्प्रतिविंध्यः भीमसेनाच्छुतसेनः
श्रुतकीर्त्तिरर्जुनाच्छुतानीको नकुलाच्छुतकर्मा
सहदेवात्।। ४२।।

The son of Yudhiṣṭhira was Prativindhya; of Bhīma, Śrutasoma; of Arjuna, Śrutakīrtī; of Nakula, Śatanīka; and of Sahadeva, Śrutakarman.

अन्ये च पांडवानामात्मजास्तद्यथा।। ४३।।

The Pāṇḍavas had also other sons.

यौधेयी युधिष्ठिराद्देवकं पुत्रमवाप।। ४४।।

हिडिंबा घटोत्कचं भीमसेनात्पुत्रं लेभे।। ४५।।

काशी च भीमसेनादेव सर्वगं सुतमवाप।। ४६।।

सहदेवाच्च विजयी सुहोत्रं पुत्रमवाप।। ४७।।

रेणुमत्यां च नकुलोपि निरमित्रमजीजनत्।। ४८।।

By his wife Yaudheyī Yudhiṣṭhira had Devaka; Bhīma had by Hiḍimbā, Ghaṭotkaca, and had another by his wife Kāśī, Śarvatraga. Sahadeva had by Vijaya, Suhotra and Niramitra was the son of Nakula by Reṇutmati.

अर्जुनस्याप्युलूप्यां नागकन्यायामिरावान्नाम पुत्रो-
ऽभवत्।। ४९।।

मणिपुरपतिपुत्र्यां पुत्रिकाधर्मेण बभ्रुवाहनं नाम
पुत्रमर्जुनोऽजनयत्।। ५०।।

सुभद्रायां चार्भकत्वेपि योसावतिबलपराक्रमस्समस्ता-
रातिरथजेता सोऽभिमन्युरजायत।। ५१।।

Arjuna had Irāvat by the serpent nymph Ulūpī—by the dauther of the king of Maṇipur he had Babruvāhana, who was adopted by his maternal grand father, by his wife Subhadrā, Abhimanyu, who even in his boy-hood was famous for valour and strength and crushed the enemies' cars in fight.

अभिमन्योरुत्तरायां परिक्षीणेषु कुरुष्वश्वत्थामप्रयुक्त-
ब्रह्मास्त्रेण गर्भ एव भस्मीकृतो भगवतस्सकलसुरा-
सुरवंदितचरणयुगलस्यात्मेच्छया कारणमानुषरूप-
धारिणोनुभावात्पुनर्जीवितमवाप्य परीक्षिज्जज्ञे ।। ५२ ।।

योऽयं सांप्रतमेतद्भूमंडलमखंडितायतिधर्मेण पालय-
तीति ।। ५३ ।।

The son of Abhimanyu by his wife Uttarā was Parīkṣit, who after the destruction of all the Kurus, was killed in his mother's womb by the weapons hurled by Aśvatthāma. But by the mercy of Kṛṣṇa at whose feet bow all the gods and demons and who for his own pleasure had assumed human shape he was restored to life. This Parīkṣit now governs the earth with undisputed sway.

।। इति श्रीविष्णुमहापुराणे चतुर्थेशे विंशोऽध्यायः ।। २० ।।

अथ चतुर्थेशे: एकविंशोऽध्याय:

Part IV : Section 21

श्रीपराशर उवाच

अतः परं भविष्यानहं भूपालान्कीर्त्तयिष्यामि ।। १ ।।

Parāśara said :—I shall now give you an account of the future kings.

योऽयं सांप्रतमवनीपतिः परीक्षित्तस्यापि जनमेजय-
श्रुतसेनोग्रसेन भीमसेनाश्चत्वारः पुत्रा भविष्यंति ।। २ ।।

He, who is the sovereign now, shall have four sons, namely Janamejaya, Śrutasena, Ugrasena, and Bhīmasena.

जनमेजयस्यापि शतानीको भविष्यति ।। ३ ।।

The son of Janamejaya shall be Śatānīka.

योऽसौ याज्ञवल्क्याद्वेदमधीत्य कृपा दस्त्राण्यवाप्य
विषमविषयविरक्तचित्तवृत्तिश्च शौनकोपदेशादात्म-
ज्ञानप्रवीणः परं निर्वाणमवाप्स्यति ।। ४ ।।

He shall study the Vedas from Yajñavalkya, learn the use of weapons from Kṛpa and then disassociate himself from worldly affairs. And then receiving instructions regarding the knowledge of self from Śaunaka he shall attain final liberation.

शतानीकादश्वमेधदत्तो भविता ।। ५ ।।

तस्मादप्यधिसीमकृष्णः ।। ६ ।।

अधिसीमकृष्णान्निचक्नुः ।। ७ ।।

यो गंगयापहृते हस्तिनपुरे कौशांब्यां निवत्स्यति ।। ८ ।।

From Śatānīka shall be born Aśvamedhadatta, whose son shall be Adhisīmakṛṣna and whose son shall be Nicakṣu who shall reside in Kuśambī, when Hastināpur, shall be at the bed of the Ganges.

तस्याप्युष्णः पुत्रो भविताः ।। ९ ।।

उष्णाद्विचित्ररथः ।। १० ।।

ततः शुचिरथः ।। ११ ।।

तस्माद्वृष्णिमांस्ततस्सुषेणस्तस्यापि सुनीथ-
स्सुनीथान्नृपचक्षुस्तस्मादपि सुखिबलस्तस्य च
पारिप्लवस्ततश्च सुनयस्तस्यापि मेधावी ।। १२ ।।

मेधाविनो रिपुञ्जयस्ततोर्वस्तस्माच्च तिग्मस्तस्माद्-
बृहद्रथः बृहद्रथाद्वसुदासः ।। १३ ।।

ततोऽपरश्शतानीकः ।। १४ ।।

तस्माच्चोदयन उदयनद्विहीनरस्ततश्चदंडपाणिस्ततो
निमित्तः ।।१५ ।।

तस्माच्च क्षेमकः ।। १६ ।।

Nichakshu's son shall be Uśna, whose son shall be Citraratha, whose son shall be Śuciratha, whose son shall be Bṛṣṇimān, whose son shall be Suṣeṇa, whose son shall be Sunītha, whose son shall be Ṛca, whose son shall be Nṛcakṣu, whose son shall be Sukhabala, whose son shall be Pariplava, whose son shall be Śūnaya, whose son shall be Medhāvī, whose son shall be Nṛpañjaya, whose son shall be

Mṛdu, whose son shall be Tṛgma, whose son shall be Trihadratha, whose son shall be Vasudāna, whose son shall be the second Śatānīka, whose son shall be Udayana, whose son shall be Ahīnara, whose son shall be Khaṇḍapāṇī, whose son shall be Nīramitra, whose son shall be Kṣemaka.

अत्रायं श्लोकः ।। १७ ।।

ब्रह्मक्षत्रस्य यो यो निर्वंशो देवर्षिसत्कृतः ।।
क्षेमकं प्राप्य राजानं संस्थानं प्राप्यते कलौ ।। इति ।। १८ ।।

The following verse is recited of Kṣemaka —"The family of Kuru, that has produced many Brāhmaṇas and Kṣatriyas, that has been ornamented by many a royal saint, shall end with Kṣemaka in the Kali Yuga."

।। इति श्रीविष्णुमहापुराणे चतुर्थेंशे एकविंशोऽध्यायः ।। २१ ।।

अथ चतुर्थेंशेः द्वाविंशोऽध्यायः

Part IV : Section 22

श्रीपराशर उवाच

अतश्चेक्ष्वाकवो भविष्याः पार्थिवाः कथ्यन्ते ।। १ ।।

Parāśara said :—I shall now engage in giving you an account of the future kings of the Ikṣavāku race.

बृहद्बलस्य पुत्रो बृहत्क्षणः ।। २ ।।

तस्मादुरुक्षयस्तस्माच्च वत्सव्यूहस्ततश्च प्रतिव्योम-
स्तस्मादपि दिवाकरः ।। ३ ।।

तस्मात्सहदेवः सहदेवाद्बृहदश्वस्तत्सूनुर्भानुरथस्तस्य
च प्रतीताश्वस्तस्यापि सुप्रतीकस्ततश्च मरुदेवस्ततः
सुनक्षत्रस्तस्मात्किन्नरः ।। ४ ।।

किन्नरादंतरिक्षस्तस्मात्सुपर्णस्ततश्चामित्रजित् ।। ५ ।।

ततश्च बृहद्भ्राजस्तस्यापि धर्मी धर्मिणः कृतञ्जयः ।। ६ ।।

कृतञ्जयाद्रणञ्जयः ।। ७ ।।

रणञ्जयात्सञ्जयस्तस्माच्छाक्यश्छाक्याच्छुद्धोदनस्तस्मा-
द्राहुलस्ततः प्रसेनजित् ।। ८ ।।

ततश्च क्षुद्रकस्ततश्च कुंडकस्तस्मादपि सुरथः ।। ९ ।।

तत्पुत्रश्च सुमित्रः ।। १० ।।

The son of Bṛhadvala shall be Vṛhatkṣa̐ṇa, whose son shall be Gurukṣepa, whose son shall be Vatsa, whose son shall be Vatsabhūha, whose son shall be Pratibhyoma, whose son shall be Divākara, whose son shall be Sahadeva, whose son shall be Vṛadāśva, whose son shall be Bhānuratha, whose son shall be Supratīka, whose son shall be Marudeva, whose son shall be Sunakṣatra, whose son shall be Kinnara, whose son shall be Antarikṣa, whose son shall be Suvarṇa, whose son shall be Amitrajit, whose son shall be Bṛhadwāja whose son shall be Dharma, whose son shall be Kṛtañjaya, whose son shall be Raṇañjaya, whose son shall be Sañjaya, whose son shall be Śākya, whose son shall be Krudhodana, whose son shall be Rātula, whose son shall be Prasenajit, whose son shall be Kṣrudraka, whose son shall be Kundaka, whose son shall be Śūratha, whose son shall be the second Sumitra.

इत्येते चेक्ष्वाकवो बृहब्दलान्वयाः ।। ११ ।।

These kings of the Ikṣvāku family are the descendants of Bṛhadvala.

अत्रानुवंशश्लोकः ।। १२ ।।

इक्ष्वाकूणामयं वंशस्सुमित्रांतो भविष्यति ।।
यतस्तं प्राप्य राजानं संस्थां प्राप्स्यति वै कलौ ।। १३ ।।

There is a verse often recited regarding this race—"The family of Ikṣavāku shall extend up to Sumitra; with this king the family shall end in the Kali Yuga."

।। इति श्रीमहाविष्णुपुराणे चतुर्थेंशे द्वाविंशोऽध्यायः ।। २२ ।।

अथ चतुर्थेंशे: त्रयोविंशोऽध्याय:
Part IV : Section 23

श्रीपराशर उवाच

मागधानां बार्हद्रथानां भावि नामनुक्रमं कथयिष्यामि।। १।।

Parāśara said :—I shall now describe to you the future kings of Magadha sprung from Bṛhadratha.

अत्र हि वंशे महाबलपराक्रमा जरासंधप्रधाना बभूवु:।। २।।

In this race were born Jarāsandha and other powerful kings.

जरासंधस्य पुत्र: सहदेव:।। ३।।

सहदेवात्सोमापिस्तस्यानुश्रुतश्रवास्तस्याप्ययुतायुस्ततश्च निरमित्रस्तत्तनयस्सुनेत्रस्तस्मादपि बृहत्कर्मा।। ४।।

ततश्च सेनजित्ततश्च श्रुतञ्जयस्ततो विप्रस्तस्य च पुत्रश्शुचिनामा भविष्यति।। ६।।

तस्यापि क्षेम्यस्ततश्च सुव्रतस्सुव्रताद्धर्मस्ततस्सुश्रवा:।। ६।।

ततो दृढसेन:।। ७।।

तस्मात्सुबल:।। ८।।

सुबलात्सुनीतो भविता।। ९।।

ततस्सत्यजित्।। १०।।

तस्माद्विश्वजित्।। ११।।

तस्यापि रिपुञ्जय:।। १२।।

The son of Jarāsandha shall be Sahadeva, whose son shall be Somāpi, whose son shall be Śrutavan, whose son shall be Ayutayu, whose son shall be Niramitra, whose son shall be Sukṣatra, whose son shall be Vṛhatkarman, whose son shall be Senajit, whose son shall be Śrutañjaya, whose son shall be Vipra, whose son shall be Śuci, whose son shall be Kṣemya, whose son shall be Suvrata, whose son shall be Dharma, whose son shall be Suśrama, whose son shall be Dṛdasena, whose son shall be Sumati, whose son shall be Subala, whose son shall be Satyajit, and whose son shall be Ṛpuñjaya.

इत्येते बार्हद्रथा भूपतयो वर्षसहस्रमेकं भविष्यंति।। १३।।

The kings of the race of Bṛhadratha shall reign for a thousand years.

इति श्रीविष्णुमहापुराणे चतुर्थेंशे त्रयोविंशोऽध्याय:।। २३।।

अथ चतुर्थेंशे: चतुर्विंशोऽध्याय:
Part IV : Section 24

श्रीपराशर उवाच

योऽयं रिपुञ्जयो नाम बार्हद्रथोंत्य: तस्यामात्यो मुनिको नाम भविष्यति।। १।।

Parāśara siad :—Ṛpuñjaya, the last king of the race of Bṛhadratha, shall have minister by the name of Sunika.

स चैनं स्वामिनं हत्वा स्वपुत्रं प्रद्योतनामानमभिषेक्ष्यति।। २।।

Slaying his Master he shall place his own son Prodyuta on the throne.

तस्यापि बलाकनामा पुत्रो भविता।। ३।।

ततश्च विशाखयूप:।। ४।।

तत्पुत्रो जनक:।। ६।।

तस्य च नंदिवर्द्धन:।। ६।।

ततो नंदी।। ७।।

He shall have a son by the name of Balāka, whose son shall be Visākayupa, whose son shall be Janaka, whose son shall be Nandīvardana whose Nandī.

इत्येतेष्टत्रिंशदुत्तरमष्टशतं पञ्च प्रद्योताः पृथिवीं भोक्ष्यन्ति।। ८।।

These five kings of the family of Prodyuta shall govern the earth for hundred and thirty eight years.

ततश्च शिशुनाभः।। ९।।

Thereupon Śiśunābha (shall become the king).

तत्पुत्रः काकवर्णो भविता।। १०।।

तस्य च पुत्रः क्षेमधर्मा।। ११।।

तस्यापि क्षतौजाः।। १२।।

तत्पुत्रो विधिसारः।। १३।।

ततश्चाजातशत्रुः।। १४।।

तस्मादर्भकः।। १५।।

तस्माच्चोदयनः।। १६।।

तस्मादपि नंदिवर्द्धनः।। १७।।

ततो महानंदी।। १८।।

His son shall be Kākavarṛa, whose son shall be Kṣemadharman, whose son shall be Kṣatraujas whose son shall be Vidhisāra, whose son shall be Ajātaśatru, whose son shall be Dārvaka, whose son shall be Udhayāśva, whose son shall be Nandivardana, whose son shall be Mahānandī.

इत्येते शैशनाभा भूपालास्त्रीणि वर्षशतानि द्विषष्ट्यधिकानि भविष्यंति।। १९।।

These ten kings of the family of Śiśunāga shall lord over the earth for three hundred and sixty-two years.

महानंदि नस्ततशशूद्रागर्भोद्भवोतिलुब्धोतिबलो महापद्मनामा नंदः परशुराम इवापरोऽखिलक्षत्रांतकारी भविष्यति।। २०।।

Mahānandī shall beget a son on a Śūdra woman by name, Mahāpadmānanda, who shall be very avaricious and shall extirpate all the Kṣatriyas like Paraśurāma.

ततःप्रभृति शूद्रा भूपाला भविष्यंति।। २१।।

From that time Śūdra kings shall govern the earth.

स चैकच्छत्रामनुल्लंघितशासनो महापद्मः पृथिवीं भोक्ष्यते।। २२।।

And this Mahāpadma shall enjoy the earth as lord Paramount, and his commands shall no where be disobeyed.

तस्याप्यष्टौ सुतास्सुमाल्याद्या भवितारः।। २३।।

He shall have eight sons—Sumalya and others.

तस्य महापद्मस्यानुपृथिवीं भोक्ष्यंति।। २४।।

महापद्मपुत्राश्चैकं वर्षशतमवनीपतयो भविष्यंति।। २५।।

Mahāpadma and his eight sons shall reign for a hundred years.

ततश्च नवचैतान्नंदान् कौटिल्यो ब्राह्मणस्समुद्धरिष्यति।। २६।।

Thereupon a Brāhmaṇa, by name Kauṭilya shall root out Nanda and his sons.

तेषामभावे मौर्य्याः पृथिवीं भोक्ष्यंति।। २७।।

After the family of Nanda, Mauryas shall lord over the earth.

कौटिल्य एव चंद्रगुप्तमुत्पन्नं राज्येऽभिषेक्ष्यति।। २८।।

This Kauṭilya shall instal the Maurya king Candra-Gupta on the throne.

तस्यापि पुत्रो बिंदुसारो भविष्यति।। २९।।

तस्याप्यशोकवर्द्धनस्ततस्सुयशास्ततश्च दशरथस्ततश्च संयुतस्ततशशालिशूकस्तस्मात्सोमशर्मा तस्यापि सोमशर्मणश्शतधन्वा।। ३०।।

तस्यानुबृहद्रथनामा भविता।। ३१।।

He shall have a son by name Vindusāra, whose son shall be Aśokavardhana, whose son shall be Sujasas, whose son shall be Daśaratha, whose son shall be Saṅgata, whose son shall be Sāliśūka, whose son shall be Bṛhadratha.

एवमेते मौर्य्या दश भूपतयो भविष्यंति अब्दशतं सप्तत्रिंशदुत्तरम्।। ३२।।

These Maurya kings shall reign for hundred and seventy-three years.

तेषामंते पृथिवीं दश शुंगा भोक्ष्यंति।। ३३।।

After them the Śuṅgas will enjoy the earth.

पुष्यमित्रस्सेनापतिस्स्वामिनं हत्वा राज्यं करिष्यति तस्यात्मजोऽग्निमित्रः।। ३४।।

तस्मात्सुज्येष्ठस्ततो वसुमित्रस्तस्मादप्युदंकस्ततः पुलिंदकस्ततो घोषवसुस्तस्मादपि वज्रमित्रस्ततो भागवतः।। ३५।।

तस्माद्देवभूतिः।। ३६।।

Thereupon slaying his own master the Commander-in-chief Puṣpamitra shall establish himself on the throne. His son shall be Agnimitra, whose son shall be Sujyeṣṭha whose son shall be Vasumitra, whose son shall be Ardraka, whose son shall be Pulindaka, whose son shall be Ghosavasu, whose son shall be Vajramitra, whose son shall be Bhāgavata, whose son shall be Devabhūti.

इत्येते शुंगा द्वादशोत्तरं वर्षशतं पृथिवीं भोक्ष्यंति।। ३७।।

These ten Śuṅga kings shall reign for one hundred and twelve years.

ततः कण्वानेषा भूर्यास्यति।। ३८।।

Thereafter the Kaṇva kings shall lord over the earth.

देवभूतिं तु शुंगराजानं व्यसनिनं तस्यैवामात्यः कण्वो वसुदेवनामा तं निहत्य स्वयमवनीं भोक्ष्यति।। ३९।।

Slaying his own master, the Śuṅga king Devabhūti who shall be addicted to gambling, the minister Vasudeva shall place himself on the throne.

तस्य पुत्रो भूमित्रस्तस्यापि नारायणः।। ४०।।

नारायणात्मजस्सुशर्मा।। ४१।।

His son shall be Bhūmimitra, whose son shall be Nārāyaṇa, whose son shall be Suśarmā.

एते काण्वायनाश्चत्वारः पञ्चचत्वारिंशद्वर्षाणि भूपतयो भविष्यंति।। ४२।।

These four Kaṇva kings shall reign for forty-five years.

सुशर्माणं तु काण्वं तद्भृत्यो बलिपुच्छकनामा हत्वांध्रजातीयो वसुधां भोक्ष्यति।। ४३।।

A servant by name Sipraka of the race of Andra shall slay Suśarma, the last Kaṇva king and by force place himself on the throne.

ततश्च कृष्णनामा तद्भ्राता पृथिवी पतिर्भविष्यति।। ४४।।

तस्यापि पुत्रः शांतकर्णिस्तस्यापि पूर्णोत्संग-स्तत्पुत्रश्शातकर्णिस्तस्माच्च लम्बोदरस्तस्माच्च पिलकस्ततो मेघस्वातिस्ततः पटुमान्।। ४५।।

ततश्चारिष्टकर्मा ततो हालाहलः।। ४६।।

हालाहलात्पललकस्ततः पुलिंदसेनस्ततः सुंदरस्ततश्शातकर्णिस्तश्शिवस्वातिस्ततश्च गोमति-पुत्रस्ततपुत्रोऽलिमान्।। ४७।।

तस्यापि शांतकर्णिस्ततः शिवश्रितस्तश्च शिवस्कंध-स्तस्मादपि यज्ञश्रीस्ततो द्वियज्ञस्तस्माच्चंद्रश्रीः।। ४८।।

तस्मात्पुलोमापिहि।। ४९।।

Thereafter his brother Kṛṣṇa shall govern the earth. Kṛṣṇa's son shall be Pūrṇotsaṅga, whose son shall be Lambodara, whose son shall be Durlaka, whose son shall be Meghaswāti, whose son shall be Paruman, whose son shall be Arṣṭakarman, whose son shall be Hālāhala, whose son shall be Pathalaka, whose son shall be Prabillasen, whose son shall be the Beautiful Śātakarṇī, whose son shall be Śivaswāti, whose son shall be Gomatiputra, whose son shall be Patimari, whose son shall be Śivaśrīśatakarma, whose son shall be Sivaskandha, whose son shall be Yajñaśrī, whose son shall be Vijaya, whose son shall be Candraśrī, whose son shall be Pulomarci.

एवमेते त्रिंशच्चत्वार्यब्दशतानि षट्पञ्चाशदधिकानि पृथिवीं भोक्ष्यंति।।५०।।

These thirty illustrious Andhra kings will govern the earth for four hundred and fifty years.

आंध्रभृत्यास्सप्ताभीरप्रभृतयो दशगर्दभिनश्च भूभुजो भविष्यंति।।५१।।

ततष्षोडश भूपतयो भवितारः।।५२।।

Thereafter seven kings of the Avira race,

sixteen kings of Gardavilā race and sixteen Śaka kings shall respectively govern the earth.

ततश्चाष्टौ यवनाश्चतुर्दश तुरुष्कारा मुडाश्च त्रयोदश एकादश मौना एते वै पृथिवीपतयः पृथिवीं दशवर्षशतानि नवत्यधिकानि भोक्ष्यंति।। ५३।।

ततश्च मौना एकादश भूपतयोऽब्दशतानि त्रीणि पृथिवीं भोक्ष्यंति।।५४।।

Thereupon eight Yavana kings, fourteen Tukhara kings, thirteen Muṇḍa kings, and eighteen Manu kings shall rule the earth for thirteen hundred and ninety-nine years. Thereafter eleven Paura kings shall govern the earth for three hundred years.

तेषूत्सन्नेषु कैंकिला यवना भूपतयो भविष्यंत्यमूर्द्धाभिषिक्ताः।।५५।।

When the Pauras shall spread all over the earth the Yavanas of Kailakila shall become kings.

तेषामपत्यं विंध्य शक्तिस्ततः पुरञ्जयस्तस्माद्रामचंद्रस्तस्माद्धर्मवर्मा ततो वंगस्ततोभून्नंदनस्ततस्सुनंदी तद्भ्राता नंदियशाश्शुक्रः प्रवीर एते वर्षशतं षड्वर्षाणि भूपतयो भविष्यंति।।५६।।

And amonst them one Vindhyaśakti shall be the lord Paramount. His son shall be Purañjaya, whose son shall be Rāmacandra, whose son shall be Dharma, whose son shall be Varaṅga, whose son shall be Kṛtamaṇḍana, whose son shall be Śaśinandī, whose son shall be Nandiyasā, whose son shall be Śiśkaka, whose son shall be Pravira. These nine kings shall reign for hundred and sixty years.

ततस्तत्पुत्रास्त्रयोदशैते बाह्लिकाश्च त्रयः।।५७।।

ततः पुष्पमित्राः पटुमित्रास्त्रयोदशैकलाश्च सप्तांध्राः।। ५८।।

ततश्च कोसलायां तु नव चैव भूपतयो भविष्यंति।। ५९।।

नैषधास्तु त एव।। ६०।।

Thereafter thirteen kings of this family, three of Bāhlikā, Puṣpamitra, Patupmitra and Padmamitra, the nine kings of Saptakośala and then again nine kings of the country of Niṣdha shall respectively flourish.

मगधायां तु विश्वस्फटिक संज्ञोऽन्यान्वर्णान्करिष्यति।। ६१।।

One king of the city of Magadha by name Viśvasphaṭika shall create many a new mixed caste.

कैवर्त्तबटुपुलिंदब्राह्मणान्राज्ये स्थापयिष्यति।। ६२।।

He will root out the Kṣatriya or martial race and elevate fishermen, barbarians and Brāhmaṇas and other castes to power.

उत्साद्याखिलक्षत्रजातिं नव नागाः पद्मवत्यां नाम पुर्यामनुगंगाप्रयागं गयाद्गुप्तांश्च मागधा भोक्ष्यंति।। ६३।।

The nine Nāgas will reign in Padmāvatī, Kāntipurī and Mathurā; and the Guptas of Magadha along the Ganges to Prayāga.

कोशलांध्रपुंड्रताम्रलिप्तसमतटपुरीं च देवरक्षितो रक्षिता।। ६४।।

A king by name Devarakṣita will reign in a city on the sea shore over the Kośalas, Puṇḍras and Tāmraliptas.

कलिंगमाहिषमहेंद्रभौमान् गुहा भोक्ष्यंति।। ६५।।

The Guhas will occupy Kaliṅga, Māhihaka and the mountains of Mahendra.

नैषधनैमिषककालकोशकाञ्जनपदान्मणिधान्यकवंशा भोक्ष्यंति।। ६६।।

The race of Maṇidhanu will occupy the countires of Niṣādas, Naimiṣikas and Kalatyas.

त्रैराज्यमुषिकजनपदान्कनकाह्वयो भोक्ष्यति।। ६७।।

The people called Kanakas will occupy the Amazon county and that called Muṣika.

सौराष्ट्रावंत्यशूद्राभीरान्नर्मदामरुभूविषयांश्च व्रात्यद्विजाभीरशूद्राद्या भोक्ष्यंति।। ६८।।

सिंधुतटदाविकोर्वीचंद्रभागाकाश्मीरविषयांश्च व्रात्यम्लेच्छशूद्रादयो भोक्ष्यंति।। ६९।।

People of the degraded three tribes and Abhiras and Śūdras will occupy Saurāṣṭra, Avanti Śūra Arbuda and Marubhūmi.

And Śūdras, outcastes and barbarians will occupy the banks of the Jadus, Darvika, the Candrabhāgā and Kashmir.

एते च तुल्यकालास्सर्वे पृथिव्यां भूभुजो भविष्यंति ।। ७० ।।

These and all the contemporary kings will be of churlish spirit; violent temper and always addicated to falsehood and wickedness.

अल्पप्रसादा बृहत्कोपास्सार्वकाल मनृताधर्मरुचयः स्त्रीबालगोवधकर्त्तारः परस्वादानरुचयोल्प-सारास्तमिस्त्रप्राया उदितास्तमितप्राया अल्पायुषो महेच्छा ह्यल्पधर्मा लुब्धाश्च भविष्यन्ति ।। ७१ ।।

They will destroy women, children and cows; they will seize upon the property of their subjects, will be of limited power; they will rapidly rise and fall; the duration of their life will be very short; they will form high expectations and acquire very little piety.

तैश्च विमिश्रा जनपदास्तच्छीलानुवर्त्तिनो राजाश्रयशुष्मिणो म्लेच्छाचाराश्च विपर्ययेण वर्त्तमानाः प्रजाः क्षपयिष्यंति ।। ७२ ।।

The people of the countires, they will rule over, will imbibe the same nature. And the barbarians being powerful under royal patronage will destroy the subjects.

ततश्चानुदिनमल्पाल्पह्रासव्यवच्छेदाद्धर्मार्थयोर्जगतस्संक्षयो भविष्यति ।। ७३ ।।

Wealth and virtue will decrease day by day until the whose world will be depraved.

ततश्चार्थ एवाभिजनहेतुः ।। ७४ ।।

बलमेवाशेषधर्महेतुः ।। ७५ ।।

अभिरुचिरेव दांपत्यसंबंधहेतुः ।। ७६ ।।

स्त्रीत्वमेवोपभोगहेतुः ।। ७७ ।।

अनृतमेव व्यवहारजयहेतुः ।। ७८ ।।

उन्नतांबुतैव पृथिवीहेतुः ।। ७९ ।।

ब्रह्मसूत्रमेव विप्रत्वहेतुः ।। ८० ।।

रत्नधातुतैव श्लाघ्यताहेतुः ।। ८१ ।।

लिंगधारणमेवाश्रमहेतुः ।। ८२ ।।

अन्यायमेव वृत्तिहेतुः ।। ८३ ।।

दौर्बल्यमेवाबृत्तिहेतुः ।। ८४ ।।

अभयप्रगल्भोच्चारणमेव पांडित्यहेतुः ।। ८५ ।।

अनाढ्यतैव साधुत्वहेतुः ।। ८६ ।।

स्नानमेव प्रसाधनहेतुः ।। ८७ ।।

दानमेव धर्महेतुः ।। ८८ ।।

स्वीकरणमेव विवाहहेतुः ।। ८९ ।।

सद्वेषधार्येव पात्रम् ।। ९० ।।

दूरायतननोदकमेव तीर्थहेतुः ।। ९१ ।।

कपटवेषधारणमेव महत्त्वहेतुः ।। ९२ ।।

Wealth will be the test of pedigree and virtue; passion will be the only tie of marriage; falsehood will be the only means of success in litigation; and women will be marely the objects of sensual gratification. Earth will be respected for its mineral treasures sacrificial thread will be the only test of a Brāhmaṇa; external marks will constitute the only distinction of orders and wickedness will be the only ıncans of livelihood. Weakness will be the cause of dependance menace will be the cause of learning : gifts only will constitute virtue; wealth will be the only sign of honesty; simple ablution will be purification; mutual consent will be the marriage; a man wearing good clothes will be considered honest and water at a distance will be considered a holy spring.

इत्येवमनेकदोषोत्तरे तु भूमंडले सर्ववर्णेष्वेवं योयो बलवान्सस भूपतिर्भविष्यति ।। ९३ ।।

When the world will be thus sunk in faults, he, who will be the strongest amidst those castes, shall be the king.

एवं चातिलुब्धकराजासहाश्शैलानामंतरद्रोणीः प्रजास्संश्रयिष्यंति ।। ९४ ।।

मधुशाकमूलफलपत्रपुष्पाद्याहाराश्च भविष्यंति ।। ९५ ।।

तरुवल्कलपर्णचीरप्रावरणाश्चातिबहुप्रजाश्शीतवातातप-वर्षसहाश्च भविष्यंति ।। ९६ ।।

They will grow avaricious and the subjects, unable to bear the burden of various taxes, will take refuge amongst the valley of the mountains and will be glad to feed upon wild honey, herbs, roots, fruits, flowers and leaves : their only covering will be the bark of trees and they will be exposed to the cold and wind and sun and rain.

न च कश्चित्त्रयोविंशतिवर्षाणि जीविष्यति अनवरतं
चात्र कलियुगे क्षयमायात्यखिले एवैष जनः ।। ९७ ।।

No man shall live more than three and twenty years. Thus in the end of the Kali Yuga most of human-kind will be annihilated.

श्रौतस्मार्त्ते च धर्मे विप्लवमत्यंतमुपगते क्षीणप्राये च कलावशेषजगत्स्रष्टुश्चराचरगुरोरादिमध्यांतरहितस्य ब्रह्ममयस्यात्मरूपिणो भगवतो वासुदेवस्यां-शश्शंबलग्रामप्रधानाब्राह्मणस्य विष्णुयशसो गृहेष्टगुणर्द्धि समन्वितः कल्किरूपीजगत्यत्रावतीर्य सकलम्लेच्छदस्युदुष्टाचरणचेतसामशेषाणामपरिच्छिन्न-शक्तिमाहात्म्यः क्षयं करिष्यति ।।

स्वधर्मेषु चाखिलमेव संस्थापयिष्यति ।। ९८ ।।

Thus when the ceremonies of the Vedas and the institutes of law shall nearly have ceased, and the end of the Kali Yuga will approach, a portion of that divine being, who is the creator of the whole universe, preceptor of the mobile and immobile, who is the beginning and end of all, who is at one with all, who is identical with Brahmā and all created beings, shall incarnated himself on earth. He will be born in the family of Viṣṇuyaśas, an eminent Brāhmaṇa of Sambhala village as Kalki gifted with the eight superhuman faculties. By his irrepressible power he will slay all the Mlecchas and thieves and all those who are addicted to sins. His greatness and mighty shall be unobstructed.

अनंतरं चाशेषकलेरवसाने निशावसाने विबुद्धानामिव तेषामेव जनपदानाममलस्फटिकदलशुद्धा मतयो भविष्यंति ।। ९९ ।।

He shall again establish virtue on earth and when the Kali Yuga will completely close, the remaining people shall be awakened and their minds shall be as pure as crystal.

तेषां च बीजभूतानामशेषमनुष्याणां परिणतानामपि तत्कालकृतापत्यप्रसूतिर्भविष्यति ।। १०० ।।

The people thus purified shall be the seeds of human beings and shall procreate a progeny who shall follow the laws of Kṛta-age. A verse is recited regarding this—

तानि च तदपत्यानि कृतयुगानुसारीण्येव भविष्यंति ।।
१०१ ।।

"When the sun, moon, and the lunar asterism Tṛṣya and the planet Jupiter are in mansion the Kṛta age shall come back.

अत्रोच्यते

यथा चंद्रश्च सूर्यश्च तथा तिष्यो बृहस्पतिः ।।
एकराशौ समेष्यंति तदा भवति वै कृतम् ।। १०२ ।।

अतीता वर्त्तमानाश्च तथैवानागताश्च ये ।।
एते वंशेषु भूपालाः कथिता मुनिसत्तम ।। १०३ ।।

Thus, O great sage, I have enumerated all the kings of the solar and lunar dynesties—those who are hast and those who are present and those who shall be.

यावत्परीक्षितो जन्म यावन्नंदाभिषेचनम् ।।
एतद्वर्षसहस्रं तु ज्ञेयं पञ्चाशदुत्तरम् ।। १०४ ।।

From the birth of the king Parīkṣit and up to the installation of king Nanda it is to be known that 1065 years have passed.

सप्तर्षीणां तु यौ पूर्वौ दृश्येते ह्युदितौ दिवि ।।
तयोस्तु मध्ये नक्षत्रं दृश्यते यत्समं निशि ।। १०५ ।।

तेन सप्तर्षयो युक्तास्तिष्ठंत्यब्दशतं नृणाम् ।।

When the two first stars of the seven Ṛṣis rise in the heavens and some lunar asterism is seen at night at an equal distance then the seven Ṛṣis continue stationary in that conjunction for a hundreds years of men.

ते तु परीक्षिते काले मघास्वासन्द्विजोत्तम ।। १०६ ।।

तदा प्रवृत्तश्च कलिर्द्वादशाब्दशतात्मकः ।। १०७ ।।

At the birth of the king Parīkṣit they were in Māgha and the Kali Yuga then began which consists of twelve hundred divine years.

यदैव भगवान्विष्णोरंशो यातो दिवं द्विज।।
वसुदेवकुलोद्भूतस्तदैवात्रागतः कलिः।। १०८।।

When the portion, of Viṣṇu born in the race of Yadu went back to heaven the Kali Yuga set in.

यावत्सपादपद्माभ्यां पस्पर्शेमां वसुंधराम्।।
तावत्पृथ्वीपरिष्वंगे समर्थो नाभवत्कलिः।। १०९।।

But as long as he touched with his lotus feet the earth the Kali Yuga could not effect it.

गते सनातनस्यांशे विष्णोस्तत्र भुवो दिवम्।।
तत्याज सानुजो राज्यं धर्मपुत्रो युधिष्ठिरः।। ११०।।

As soon as the incarnation of the eternal Viṣṇu has departed, Yudhiṣṭhira the son of Dharma and his brothers renounced the kingdom.

विपरीतानि दृष्ट्वा च निमित्तानि हि पांडवः।।
याते कृष्णे चकाराऽथ सोऽभिषेकं परीक्षितः।। १११।।

Seeing evil omens, on the departure of Kṛṣṇa the son of Pāṇḍava installed Parīkṣit on the throne.

प्रयास्यंति यदा चैते पूर्वाषाढां महर्षयः।।
तदा नंदात्प्रभृत्येष गतिवृद्धिं गमिष्यति।। ११२।।

When seven Ṛṣis will be in Parvaśadha, then Nanda will begin to reign and thenceforth the influence of Kali will increase.

यस्मिन् कृष्णो दिवं यातस्तस्मिन्नेव तदाहनि।।
प्रतिपन्नं कलियुगं तस्य संख्यां निबोध मे।। ११३।।

त्रीणि लक्षाणि वर्षाणां द्विज मानुष्यसंख्यया।।
षष्टिश्चैव सहस्राणि भविष्यत्येष वै कलिः।। ११४।।

शतानि तानि दिव्यानां सप्त पञ्च च संख्यया।।
निश्शेषेण गते तस्मिन्भविष्यति पुनः कृतम्।। ११५।।

The day of Kṛṣṇas' departure from the earth will be the first of the Kali Yuga, the duration of which you shall learn from me. It will continue for 360, 800 years of men. After twelve hundred divine years the Kṛta-age shall come back.

ब्राह्मणाः क्षत्त्रिया वैशश्शूद्राश्च द्विजसत्तम।।
युगेयुगे महात्मानः समतीतास्सहस्रशः।। ११६।।

Thus, O foremost of twice-born ones, thousands of eminent Brāhmaṇas, Kṣatriyas, Vaiśyas, and Śūdras have passed away.

बहुत्वान्नामधेयानां परिसंख्या कुलेकुले।।
पौनरुक्त्याद्धि साम्याच्च न मया परिकीर्त्तिता।। १७।।

It will be tautology and useless to mention the names and numbers of them born in various families. I therefore refrain from doing so.

देवापिः पौरवो राजा पुरुश्चेक्षाकुवंशजः।।
महायोगबलोपेतौ कलापग्रामसंश्रितौ।। ११८।।

The king Devāpi of the Puru race and Maru of the Ikṣvāku race, by virtue of their great asceticism, are residing in the village of Kalāpa.

कृते युगे त्विहागम्य क्षत्त्रप्रावर्त्तकौ हि तौ।।
भविष्यतो मनोर्वंशबीजभूतौ व्यवस्थितौ।। ११९।।

When the Kṛta-age shall set in they will come to the city and give origin to the Kṣatriya dynasties.

एतेन क्रमयोगेन मनुपुत्रैर्वसुंधरा।।
कृतत्रेता द्वापराणि युगानि त्रीणि भुज्यते।। १२०।।

In this wise the earth is occupied through every series of the first three ages, Kṛta, Tretā and Dwāpara by the descendants of Manu.

कलौ ते बीजभूता वै केचित्तिष्ठंति वै मुने।।
यथैव देवापिपुरू सांप्रतं समाधिष्ठितौ।। १२१।।

As Devāpi and Maru are still living son one of them remains in the Kali Yuga to serve as the seed of the renewed generations.

एष तूद्देशतो वंशस्तवोक्तो भूभुजां मया।।
निखिलो गदितुं शक्यो नैष वर्षशतैरपि।। १२२।।

I have thus related to you briefly the families of the various kings. To relate them at length would be impossible in a hundred lives.

एते चान्ये च भूपाला यैरत्र क्षितिमंडले।।
कृतं ममत्वं मोहांधैर्नित्यं हेयकलेवरे।। १२३।।

The kings mentioned above and others, who assuming trail bodies have ruled over the ever-during world, and being binded by illusions have indulged the feeling—

कथं ममेयमचला मत्पुत्रस्य कथं मही।।
मद्वंशस्येतिचिंतार्त्ता जग्मुरंतमिमे नृपाः।। १२४।।

"This earth is mine—it is my son's—it belongs to my dynasty," have gone away.

तेभ्यः पूर्वतराश्चान्ये तेभ्यस्तेभ्यस्तथा परे।।
भविष्याश्चैव यास्यंति तेषामन्ये च येऽप्यनु।। १२५।।

Those who reigned before them, those who succeeded them, those who will be kings in future, have ceased and shall cease to be.

विलोक्यात्मजयोद्योगं यात्राव्यग्रान्नराधिपान्।।
पुष्पप्रहासैश्शरदि हसंतीव वसुंधरा।। १२६।।

The earth, with her autumnal flowers, as if smiles, beholding the king eager for conquest and fightings.

मैत्रेय पृथिवीगीताञ्छ्लोकांश्चात्र निबोध मे।।
यानाह धर्मध्वजिने जनकायासितो मुनिः।। १२७।।

Hear, O Maitreya, I shall now recite some verses that were chanted by Earth and which the Muni Asita communicated to Janaka, whose banner was virtue,

पृथिव्युवाच

कथमेष नरेंद्राणां मोहो बुद्धिमतामपि।।
येन केन सधर्माणोप्यतिविश्वस्तचेतसः।। १२८।।

"How greatly are the princes, although reasonable, mistaken, that they consider themselves immortal when they themselves are but foam upon the wave.

पूर्वमात्मजयं कृत्वा जेतुमिच्छंति मंत्रिणः।।
ततो भृत्यांश्च पौरांश्च जिगीषंते तथा रिपून्।। १२९।।

Before they have subdued themselves they endeavour to reduce their ministers, their servant, their subjects to subjection; they then attempt to defeat their enemies.

क्रमेणानेन जेष्यामो वयं पृथ्वीं ससागराम्।।
इत्यासक्तधियो मृत्युं न पश्यंत्यविदूरगम्।। १३०।।

They say 'We shall by and by subdue the sea-girt earth?' Their minds being thus always taken up with those thoughts, they cannot perceive the near approach of death.

समुद्रावरणं याति भूमंडलमथो वशम्।।
कियदात्मजयस्यैतन्मुक्तिरात्मजये फलम्।। १३१।।

The subjugation of the sea-girt earth is not so very difficult for him who has subdued him; for the final liberation is another fruit of self-control.

उत्सृज्य पूर्वजा याता यां नादाय गतः पिता।।
तां मामतीव मूढत्वाज्जेतुमिच्छंति पार्थिवाः।। १३२।।

It is through ignorance that the kings wish to possess me whom their predecessors have been constrained to leave and whom their fathers have not kept.

मत्कृते पितृपुत्राणां भ्रातॄणां चापि विग्रहः।।
जायतेत्यंतमोहेन ममत्वादृतचेतसाम्।। १३३।।

Deceived by the selfish love of power fathers fight with sons and brothers with brothers for occupying me.

पृथ्वी ममेयं सकला ममैषा मदन्वयस्यापि च शाश्वती यम्।।
योयो मृतेऽन्यत्र बभूव राजा कुबुद्धिरा सीदिति तस्यतस्य।।
।।१३४।।

दृष्ट्वा ममत्वादृतचित्तमेकं विहाय मां मृत्युवशं व्रजंतम्।।
तस्यानु यस्तस्य कथं ममत्वं हृद्यास्पदं मत्प्रभवं करोति।।
१३५।।

All the kings who reigned on this earth and who are now dead foolishly thought—'All this earth is mine—every thing is mine, it will be in my house for ever for he is dead.' How is it possible that such vain desires should be cherished by his descendants, who have seen their progenitor, on account of the thirst of dominion, compelled to desert me, whom he called his own and tread the path of dissolution.

पृथ्वी ममैषाऽऽशु परित्यजैनां वदंति ये दूतमुखैस्स्वशत्रून्।।
नराधिपास्तेषु ममातिहासः पुनश्च मूढेषु दयाऽभ्युपैति।।
१३६।।

When I hear a king communicating to another through his ambassador, 'This earth is mine—you give up all your claims for it." I laugh at first but that laughter is soon turned into pity for the infatuated fool."

श्रीपराशर उवाच

इत्येते धरणीगीताश्श्लोका मैत्रेय यैश्श्रुताः।।
ममत्वं विलयं याति तपत्यर्के यथा हिमम्।। १३७।।

Parāśara said :—These were the verses, Maitreya, which Earth chanted, hearing which ambition melts away like snow before the sun.

इत्येष कथितः सम्यङ्मनोर्वंशो मया तव।।
यत्र स्थितिप्रवृत्तस्य विष्णोरंशांशका नृपाः।। १३८।।

I have now given you a complete account of the descendants of Manu amongst whom many were endowed with a portion of Viṣṇu engaged in the preservation of the universe.

शृणोति य इमं भक्त्या मनोर्वंशमनुक्रमात्।।
तस्य पापमशेषं वै प्रणश्यत्यमलात्मनः।। १३९।।

He, who hears reverentially from the beginning to the end, of the account of this family of Manu, gets his heart purified and all this sins are removed.

धनधान्यर्द्धिमतुलां प्राप्नोत्यव्याहतेंद्रियः।।
श्रुत्वैवमखिलं वंशं प्रशस्तं शशिसूर्ययोः।। १४०।।

Hearing of the description of the illustrious solar and lunar dynasties, people, with their faculties perfect, shall live in unequelled affluence, plenty and prosperity.

इक्ष्वाकुजह्नुमांधातृसगराविक्षितान्रघून्।।
ययातिनहुषाद्यांश्च ज्ञात्वा निष्ठामुपागतान्।। १४१।।

महाबलान्महावीर्याननन्तधनसञ्चयान्।।
कृतान्कालेन बलिना कथाशेषान्नराधिपान्।। १४२।।

श्रुत्वा न पुत्रदारादौ गृहक्षेत्रादिके तथा।।
द्रव्यादौ वा कृतप्रज्ञो ममत्वं कुरुते नरः।। १४३।।

He who has heard of the races of Ikṣvāku, Jāhnu, Māndhātā, Sagara, Abikṣeta, Raghu, Yayāti, and Nahuṣa, who have all perished and of other wealthy kings gifted with great strength and power, who have been subdued by still more powerful time and are now only tale, will learn wisdom and forbear to call either children, or wife, or house or lands or wealth his own.

तप्तं तपो यैः पुरुषप्रवीरैरुद्बाहुभिर्वर्षगणाननेकान्।।
इष्ट्वा सुयज्ञैर्बलिनोतिवीर्याः कृतानुकालेन कथावशेषाः।।
१४४।।

Those heroic men, who have performed penances for many years with uplifted hands, those who have celebrated many sacrifices, have been left by time as subjects of narration.

पृथुस्समस्तान्विचचार लोकान-
तप्तं तपो यैः यो विजितारि चक्रः।।
स कालवाताभिहतः प्रणष्टः
क्षिप्तं यथा शाल्मलितूलमग्नौ।। १४५।।

That Pṛthu, even, whose discus dissevered many an enemy, who unobstructed travelled all over the regions, has been destroyed by the last of time like the light down of the Simal tree.

यः कार्त्तवीर्यो बुभुजे समस्तान्द्वीपान्समाक्रम्यहतारिचक्रः।।
कथाप्रसंगेष्वभिधीयमानस्य एव संकल्पविकल्पहेतुः।।
१४६।।

Even Kārtavīryya, who defeated numberless enemies and conquered the seven Zones of the earth, exists now only as the topic of a theme, a subject for affirmation or contradiction.

दशाननाविक्षतराघवाणामैश्वर्यमुद्भासितदिङ्मुखानाम्।।
भस्मापि शिष्टं न कथं क्षणेन भ्रूभंगपातेन धिगंतकस्य।।
१४७।।

The riches of the kings of Daśānana, Rāghava, Abikoluta and others, which dazzled all the quarters, have all been reduced to ashes by the very frown of time. Oh! fie upon such weath.

कथाशरीरत्वमवाप यद्वै मांधातृनामा भुवि चक्रवर्त्ती।।
श्रुत्वापि तत्को हि करोति साधुर्ममत्वमात्मन्यपि मंदचेताः।।
१४८।।

The lord paramount of the earth, by the name of Māndhātā now exists only in name. And what pious man, hearing this story, will be so foolish as to cherish the desire of possession in his soul?

भगीरथाद्यास्सगरं ककुत्स्थो दशननो राघवलक्ष्मणो च।।
युधिष्ठिराद्याश्च बभूवुरेते सत्यं न मिथ्या क्व नु ते न
विद्मः।। १४९।।

Bhagīratha, Sagara, Kākutstha, Daśānana Rāma, Lakṣmaṇa, Yudhiṣṭhira and others have been. Is it so?

ये सांप्रतं ये च नृपा भविष्याः प्रोक्ता मया विप्रवरोग्रवीयाः ।।
एते तथाऽन्ये च तथाभिधेयाः सर्वे भविष्यंति यथैव पूर्वे ।।
१५० ।।

Have they really existed? Where are they now? We know not! The kings, who are now reigning, who shall be kings in future, and those whose names have not been specified, shall all remain only in names like their predecessors.

एत द्विदित्वा न नरेण कार्यं ममत्वमात्मन्यपि पंडितेन ।।
तिष्ठंतु तावत्तनयात्मजायाः क्षेत्रादयो ये च शरीरिणोऽन्ये ।।
१५१ ।।

The wise man, congnizant of this, will not cherish attachment even for his own self—what to speak of children, lands and properties.

।। इति श्रीविष्णुमहापुराणे चतुर्थेंशे चतुर्विंशोध्यायः ।। २४ ।।

।। श्रीविष्णुमहापुराणे चतुर्थांशः समाप्तः ।।

।। अथ श्रीविष्णुमहापुराणे पञ्चमोंशः ।।

THE VIṢṆUMAHĀPURĀṆAM, PART - V

।। श्रीमते रामानुजाय नमः ।।

अथ पञ्चमेंशेः प्रथमोऽध्यायः

Part V : Section 1

मैत्रेय उवाच

नृपाणां कथितस्सर्वो भवता वंशविस्तरः ।।
वंशानुचरितं चैव यथावदनुवर्णितम् ।। १ ।।

Maitreya said :—You have described to me at length the origin and spread of the families of kings.

अंशावतारो ब्रह्मषे योऽयं यदुकुलोद्भवः ।।
विष्णोस्तं विस्तरेणाहं श्रोतुमिच्छामि तत्त्वतः ।। २ ।।

I wish to hear in particular, O venerable saint, why Viṣṇu incarnated a portion of himself in the family of Yadus.

चकार यानि कर्माणि भगवान्पुरुषोत्तमः ।।
अंशांशेनावतीर्योर्व्यां तत्र तानि मुने वद ।। ३ ।।

Tell me, O Muni, what actions did the illustrious and excellent Puruṣa perform in his descent upon the earth.

श्रीपराशर उवाच

मैत्रेय श्रूयतामेतद्यत्पृष्टोऽहमिह त्वया ।।
विष्णोरंशांशसंभूतिचरितं जगतो हितम् ।। ४ ।।

Parāśara said :—I shall relate to you, O Maitreya, what you have requested me to do—the birth, of a portion of Viṣṇu and the benefits which his actions conferred upon the world.

देवकस्य सुतां पूर्वं वसुदेवो महामुने ।।
उपयेमे महाभागां देवकीं देवतोपमाम् ।। ५ ।।

O great Muni, Vasudeva espoused the illustrious god-like Devakī, the daughter of Devaka.

कंसस्तयोर्वररथं चोदयामास सारथिः ।।
वसुदेवस्य देवक्या संयोगे भोजनंदनः ।। ६ ।।

After their marriage, Kansa, the increaser of the race of Bhoja, drove their car as their charioteer.

अथांतरिक्षे वागुच्चैः कंसमाभाष्य सादरम् ।।
मेघगंभीरनिर्घोषं समाभाष्येदमब्रवीत् ।। ७ ।।

A voice was heard in the sky, loud and deep as thunder, which addressing Kansa, said—

यामेतां बहसे मूढ सह भर्त्रा रथे स्थिताम् ।।
अस्यास्तवाष्टमो गर्भः प्राणानपहरिष्यति ।। ८ ।।

"O foolish, the eighth child of this damsel, whom thou art carrying in the car, along with her husband, shall destroy thy life."

श्रीपराशर उवाच

इत्याकर्ण्य समुत्पाट्य खड्गं कंसो महाबलः ।।
देवकीं हंतुमारब्धो वसुदेवोऽब्रवीदिदम् ।। ९ ।।

Parāśara said :—Hearing this the highly powerful Kansa uplifted his sword and was about to slay Devakī when Vasudeva said—

न हंतव्या महाभाग देवकी भवताऽनघ ।।
समर्पयिष्ये सकलान्गर्भानस्योदरोद्भवान् ।। १० ।।

"O thou having long arms, Devakī should not be slain by thee; I shall hand over to thee every child that she shall bring forth."

श्रीपराशर उवाच

तथेत्याह ततः कंसो वसुदेवं द्विजोत्तम ।।
न घातयामास च तां देवकीं सत्यगौरवात् ।। ११ ।।

Parāśara said :—O foremost of twice-born ones, saying 'so be it' Kansa obeyed Vasudeva's request and out of respect for him did not slay Devakī.

एतस्मिन्नेव काले तु भूरिभारावपीडिता।।
जगाम धरणी मेरौ समाजं त्रिदिवौकसाम्।। १२।।

स ब्रह्मकान्सुरान्सर्वान्प्रणिपत्याऽथ मेदिनी।।
कथयामास तत्सर्वं खेदात्करुणभाषिणी।। १३।।

In the meantime, Earth, oppressed by her heavy load, repaired to an assembly of celestials on Mount Meru and addressing them, with Brahmā, at their head, described in piteous accents all her distresses.

भूमिरुवाच
अग्निस्सुवर्णस्य गुरुर्गवां सूर्यः परो गुरुः।।
ममाप्यखिललोकानां गुरुर्नारायणो गुरुः।। १४।।

प्रजापतिपतिर्ब्रह्मा पूर्वेषामपि पूर्वजः।।
कलाकाष्ठानिमेषात्मा कालश्चाव्यक्तमूर्त्तिमान्।। १५।।

Bhūmi said :—"Agni" said Earth "is the progenitor of gold; Sūrya, the rays of light; the Supreme Nārāyaṇa, is my guide and the guide of all spheres; He is Brahmā, the lord of the lord of patriarchs, the eldest of the eldest born, one identical with minutes and hours and time having form though indiscrete.

तदंशभूतस्सर्वेषां समूहो वस्सुरोत्तमाः।। १६।।

O celestials, you are all but a portion of Him.

आदित्या मरुतस्साध्या रुद्रा वस्वश्विवह्नयः।।
पितरो ये च लोकानां स्त्रष्टारोऽत्रिपुरोगमाः।। १७।।

एते तस्याप्रमेयस्य विष्णो रूपं महात्मनः।। १८।।

The Sun, the winds, the saints, the Rudras, the Vasus, the Aśvins, fire, patriarchs of whom Attri is the first, are all but the forms of the mighty and inscrutable Viṣṇu.

यक्षराक्षसदैतेयपिशाचोरगदानवाः ।।
गंधर्वाप्सरसश्चैव रूपं विष्णोर्महात्मनः।। १९।।

The Yakṣas, the Rākṣasas, the Daityas, Piśācas, Uragas, Dānavas, Gandharvas, and Apsarās are all but the forms of the glorious Viṣṇu.

ग्रहर्क्षतारकाचित्रगगनाग्निजलानिलाः।।
अहं च विषयाश्चैव सर्वं विष्णुमयं जगत्।। २०।।

The sky painted with stars, fire, water, wind, myself, and this manifest universe are all identical with Viṣṇu.

तथा चानेकरूपस्य यस्य रूपाण्य हर्निशम्।।
बाध्यवाधकर्ता यांति कल्लोला इव सागरे।। २१।।

Still the diverse forms of that manifold being encounter and succeed one another night and day like the waves of the sea.

तत्सांप्रतममी दैत्याः कालनेमिपुरोगमाः।।
मर्त्त्यलोकं समाक्रम्य बाधन्तेऽहर्निशं प्रजाः।। २२।।

Amongst them Kālanemi and other Dānavas have occupied the regions under the earth and been distressing the subjects continually.

कालनेमिर्हतो योऽसौ विष्णुना प्रभविष्णुना।।
उग्रसेनसुताः कंसस्संभूतस्स महासुरः।। २३।।

The mighty Viṣṇu destroyed the Daitya Kālanemi and he has now been born as Kansa, the son of Ugrasena.

अरिष्टो धेनुकः केशी प्रलंबो नरकस्तथा।।
सुंदोऽसुरस्तथात्युग्रो बाणश्चापि बलेस्सुतः।। २४।।

तथान्ये च महावीर्या नृपाणां भवनेषु ये।।
समुत्पन्ना दुरात्मान स्तान्न संख्यातुमुत्सहे।। २५।।

The Asuras, Ariṣṭa, Dhenuka, Keśī, Pralamba, Nāraka, Sunda, Atyugravana, and the son of Bali and other highly powerful ones born in various royal families, cannot be counted.

अक्षोहिण्योत्र बहुला दिव्यमूर्त्तिधरास्सुराः।।
महाबलानां दृप्तानां दैत्येन्द्राणां ममोपरि।। २६।।

O celestials, many Akṣauhiṇī hosts of powerful Daityas—the chiefs of their race, assuming beautiful shapes, are now treading upon me.

तद्भूरिभारपीडार्त्ता न शक्नोम्यमरेश्वराः।।
बिभर्त्तुमात्मानमहमिति विज्ञापयामि वः।। २७।।

क्रियतां तन्महाभागा मम भारावतारणम्।।
यथा रसातलं नाहं गच्छेयमतिविह्वला।। २८।।

I am unable, being oppressed by this load, to support myself; I have therefore come to you for help, O celestial chiefs, O illustrious deities, it becomes you to relieve me of this burden lest helpless I sink into the nethermost abyss."

पराशर उवाच

इत्याकर्ण्य धरावाक्यशेषैस्त्रिदशेश्वरैः ।।
भुवो भारावतारार्थं ब्रह्मा प्राह प्रचोदितः ।। २९ ।।

Parāśara said :—Hearing these words of earth, Brahmā at their request, explained to them how her burden might be lightened.

ब्रह्मोवाच

यथाह वसुधा सर्वं सत्यमेव दिवौकसः ।।
अहं भवो भवंतश्च सर्वे नारायणात्मकाः ।। ३० ।।
विभूतयश्च यास्तस्य तासामेव परस्परम् ।।
आधिक्यन्यूनताबाध्यबाधकत्वेन वर्त्तते ।। ३१ ।।

"Deities" said Brahmā "all that earth has said is true. Myself, Śiva and you all are but a portion of Nārāyaṇa; the impresonations of his power are for ever mutually fluctuating; and excess or diminution is indicated by the predominance of the strong and the depression of the weak.

तदागच्छत गच्छामः क्षीराब्धेस्तटमुत्तमम् ।।
तत्राराध्य हरिं तस्मै सर्वं विज्ञापयाम वै ।। ३२ ।।

Come, therefore, let us go to the northern shore of the milky sea and having glorified Hari, report to him what we have heard.

सर्वथैव जगत्यर्थे स सर्वात्मा जगन्मयः ।।
सत्त्वांशेनावतीर्योर्व्यां धर्मस्य कुरुते स्थितिम् ।। ३३ ।।

He, who is the soul of all and at one with the universe, descends, for the preservation of Earth in a small portion of his essence, to establish righteousness below."

श्रीपराशर उवाच

इत्युक्त्वा प्रययौ तत्र सह देवैः पितामहः ।।
समाहितमनाश्चैवं तुष्टाव गरुडध्वजम् ।। ३४ ।।

Accordingly Brahmā, accompanied by the celestials went to the milky ocean and with minds devoted to him, praised him, whose emblem is Garuḍa.

ब्रह्मोवाच

द्वे विद्ये त्वमनाम्नायपरा चैवापरा तथा ।।
त एव भवतो रूपे मूर्त्तामूर्त्तात्मिके प्रभो ।। ३५ ।।

Brahmā said :—"O lord, thou art distinct from the Vedas, thy double nature is two-fold wisdom, superior and inferior, and thou art the essential end of both.

द्वे ब्रह्मणी त्वणीयोतिस्थूलात्मन्सर्व सर्ववित् ।।
शब्दब्रह्मपरं चैव ब्रह्म ब्रह्ममयस्य यत् ।। ३६ ।।

Thou, alike possessed and devoid of form, art the two-fold Brahma; smallest of the least and largest of the large; all and knowing all things; that spirit which is language, that spirit which is Supreme; that which is Brahmā and of which Brahmā is composed.

ऋग्वेदस्त्वं यजुर्वेदस्सामवेदस्त्वथर्वणः ।।
शिक्षा कल्पो निरुक्तं च च्छंदो ज्योतिषमेव च ।। ३७ ।।

इतिहासपुराणे च तथा व्याकरणं प्रभो ।।
मीमांसा न्यायशास्त्रं च धर्मशास्त्राण्यधोक्षज ।। ३८ ।।

Thou art the Ṛk, the Yajuṣ, the Sāman and the Atharvan Vedas. Thou art accentuation, ritual, signification, metre and astronomy; history tradition, grammar, theology, logic and law and art inscrutable.

आत्माऽऽत्मदेहगुणवद्विचाराचारि यद्वचः ।।
तदप्याद्यपते नान्यदध्यात्मात्मस्वरूपवत् ।। ३९ ।।

त्वमव्यक्तमनिर्देश्यमचिंत्यानाम वर्णवत् ।।
अपाणिपादरूपं च शुद्धं नित्यं परात्परम् ।। ४० ।।

Thou art the doctrine that seeks to find out the distinctions between soul and life and body and matter endowed with qualifications and that doctrine is nothing else but thy nature inherent in and presiding over it.

शृणोष्यकर्णः परिपश्यसि त्वमचक्षुरूपी बहुरूपरूपः ।।
अपादहस्तो जवनो ग्रहीता त्वं वेत्सि सर्वं न च सर्ववेद्यः ।।
४१ ।।

Thou art imperceptible, indescribable,

inconceivable,—without name, or colour, or hands or feet, pure, eternal and infinite.

अणोरणीयां समसत्स्वरूपं त्वां पश्यतो ज्ञाननिवृत्तिरग्र्या ।।
धीरस्य धीरस्य बिभर्ति नान्यद्वरेण्यरूपात्परतः परात्मन् ।।
४२ ।।

Thou hearest without ears and seest without eyes. Thou art one and manifold. Thou movest without feet and holdest without hands.

त्वं विश्वनाभिर्भुव नस्य गोप्ता सर्वाणि भूतानि तवांतराणि ।।
यद्भूतभव्यं यदणोरणीयः पुमांस्त्वमेकः प्रकृतेः परस्तात् ।।
४३ ।।

Thou knowest all but art not by all to be known. He who observes thee as the most subtile of atoms, not substantially existent, puts an end to ignorance and the final liberation is the need of that wise man whose understanding cherishes nothing but thee in the form of supreme delight.

एकश्चतुर्द्धा भगवान्हुताशो वर्चोविभूतिं जगतो ददासि ।।
त्वं विश्वतश्चक्षुरनंतमूर्त्ते त्रेधा पदं त्वं निदधासि धातः ।।४४ ।।

Thou art the common centre of all, the protector of the universe and all beings exist in thee. Thou art all that has been or will be. Thou art the atom of atoms; thou art spirit, thou only art separate from primeval nature. Thou, as the lord of fire, in four manifestation, givest light and fertility to Earth. Thou art the eye of all and assumer of many shapes and without any hinderance travellest the three regions of the universe.

यथाग्निरेको बहुधा समिध्यते विकारभेदैरविकाररूपः ।।
तथा भवान्सर्वगतैकरूपी रूपाण्यशेषाण्यनुपुष्यतीश ।।४५ ।।

As fire, though one, is variously lighted and though unchangeable in its essence, is modified in many ways, so thou, lord, who art omnipresent, takest upon thee all modifications, that exist.

एकं तवाग्र्यं परमं पदं यत्पश्यंति त्वां सूरयो ज्ञानदृश्यम् ।।
त्वत्तो नान्यत्किंचिदस्ति स्वरूपं यद्वा भूतं यच्च भव्यं
परात्मन् ।। ४६ ।।

Thou art one supreme; thou art that supreme and eternal state which the wise behold with the eye of knowledge.

व्यक्ताव्यक्तस्वरूपस्त्वं समष्टिव्यष्टिरूपवान् ।।
सर्वज्ञस्सर्ववित्सर्वशक्तिज्ञानबलर्द्धिमान् ।। ४७ ।।
अन्यूनश्चाप्यवृद्धिश्च स्वाधीनो नादिमान्वशी ।।
क्लमतंद्री भयक्रोधकामादिभिरसंयुतः ।। ४८ ।।

There is nothing else but thou, O lord, nothing else has been or will be. Thou art both discrete and indiscrete, universal and individual, omniscient, all-seeing, omnipotent, possessed of all wisdom and strength and power. Thou art subject, neither to increase nor decrease.

निरवद्यः परः प्राप्तेर्निरधिष्ठोऽक्षरः क्रमः ।।
सर्वेश्वरः पराधारो धाम्नां धामात्कोऽक्षयः ।। ४९ ।।

Thou art independent and without beginning. Thou art subjugator of all. Thou art not subject to weariness, sloth, fear, anger or desire. Thou art free from sin, supreme merciful, uniform, undecaying, lord over all, the support of all, the fountain of light, and imperishable.

सकलावरणातीतनिरालंबनभावन ।।
महाविभूतिसंस्थान नमस्ते पुरुषोत्तम ।। ५० ।।

Salutation unto thee, univested by material envelopes, unexposed to sensible imagining, aggregate of elemental substance, spirit supreme.

नाकारणात्कारणाद्वा कारणाकारणान्न च ।।
शरीरग्रहणं वापि धर्मत्राणाय केवलम् ।। ५१ ।।

Thou assumest a shape, O pervader of the universe, not as the consequence of virtue of vice nor from any mixture of the two, but for the sole object of upholding righteousness in the universe."

श्रीपराशर उवाच

इत्येवं संस्तवं श्रुत्वा मनसा भगवानजः ।।
ब्रह्माणमाह प्रीतेन विश्वरूपं प्रकाशयन् ।। ५२ ।।

Parāśara said :—Having heard these euloguims, the unborn universal Hari, pleased, said to Brahmā—

श्रीभगवानुवाच

भोभो ब्रह्मंस्त्वया मत्तस्सह देवैर्यदिष्यते।।
तदुच्यतामशेषं च सिद्धमेवावधार्यताम्।। ५३।।

"Tell me, Brahmā, what you and the celestials desire—and consider that as already gratified."

श्रीपराशर उवाच

ततो ब्रह्मा हरेर्दिव्यं विश्वरूप मवेक्ष्य तत्।।
तुष्टाव भूयो देवेषु साध्वसावनतात्मसु।। ५४।।

Beholding that divine and universal form of Hari, Brahmā again prostrated himself and began to chant his glories—

ब्रह्मोवाच

नमो नमस्तेस्तु सहस्रकृत्वस्सहस्रबाहो बहुवक्त्रपाद।।
नमो नमस्ते जगतः प्रवृत्तिविनाशसंस्थानकराप्रमेय।।५५।।

"Salutation unto thee, again and again, O thou having thousand forms, having thousand arms, many faces and many feet.

सूक्ष्मातिसूक्ष्मातिबृहत्प्रमाण गरीयसामप्यतिगौरवात्मन्।।
प्रधानबुद्धींद्रियवत्प्रधानमूलात्परात्मन्भगवन्प्रसीद।।५६।।

Salutation unto thee, the illimitable author of creation, destruction and preservation and the inscrutable. Be propitiated with us, O god, O great soul, most subtile of the subtile, most vast of the great; O thou, who art nature, intellect and consciousness and who art other spirit even than the spiritual root of those principles.

एषा मही देव महीप्रसूतैर्महासुरैः पीडितशैलबंधा।।
परायणं त्वां जगतामुपैति भारावतारार्थमपार सार।।५७।।

एते वयं वृत्ररिपुस्तथायं नासत्यदस्रौ वरुणस्तथैव।।
इमे च रुद्रा वसवस्ससूर्यास्समीरणाग्निप्रमुखास्तथान्ये।।
५८।।

सुरास्समस्तास्सुरनाथकार्यमेभिर्मया यच्च तदीश सर्वम्।।
आज्ञापयाज्ञां परिपालयंतस्तवैव तिष्ठाम सदास्तदोषाः।।
५९।।

O lord, this earth, oppressed by powerful Asuras and shaken to her very foundation, comes to thee, the upholder of the universe, to be relieved of her burden. Myself, Indra, the Aśvins, Varuṇa, Yama, the Rudras the Vasus, the sun, the winds, fire and all other deities are prepared to do whatever thou shalt and desire us to do. Do thou, who art perfect, O king of the celestials, give thy orders to thy servants, we are ready."

श्रीपराशर उवाच

एवं संस्तूयमानस्तु भगवान्परमेश्वरः।।
उज्जहारात्मनः केशौ सितकृष्णौ महामुने।। ६०।।

Parāśara said :—When Brahmā had said this, the supreme deity plucked off two hairs, one white and one black and said to the celestials—

उवाच च सुरानेतौ मत्केशौ वसुधातले।।
अवतीर्य भुवो भारक्लेशहानिं करिष्यतः।। ६१।।

"These my hairs shall go down upon earth and shall relieve her of the burden of her distress.

सुराश्च सकलास्स्वांशैरवतीर्य महीतले।।
कुर्वंतु युद्धमुन्मत्तैः पूर्वोत्पन्नैर्महासुरैः।। ६२।।

Let all the deities, in their own portions, descend upon earth and fight with the proud Asuras who are there assembled and every one of them shall be slain.

ततः क्षयम शेषास्ते दैतेया धरणीतले।।
प्रयास्यंति न संदेहो मद्दृक्पातविचूर्णिताः।। ६३।।
वसुदेवस्य या पत्नी देवकी देवतोपमा।।
तत्रायमष्टमो गर्भो मत्केशो भविता सुराः।। ६४।।

अवतीर्य च तत्रायं कंसं घातयिता भुवि।।
कालनेमिं समुद्भूतमित्युक्त्वांतर्दधे हरिः।। ६५।।

अदृश्याय ततस्तस्मै प्रणिपत्य महामुने।।
मेरुपृष्ठं सुरा जग्मुरवतेरुश्च भूतले।। ६६।।

Doubt not this—they shall be destroyed by the withering glance of my eyes. This, my black hair, shall be impersonated in the eighth conception of the goddess-like Devakī, the wife of Vasudeva and shall destroy Kansa, who is the demon Kālanemi." Having said this, Hari disappeared and the celestials, bowing to him, though invisible, went back to the summit of the mount Meru from where they came down on earth.

कंसाय चाष्टमो गर्भो देवक्या धरणीधरः।।
भविष्यतीत्याचचक्षे भगवान्नारदो मुनिः।। ६७।।

Thereupon the illustrious Muni Nārada said that, the supporter of the earth, Viṣṇu, would be the eighth child of Devakī.

कंसोऽपि तदुपश्रुत्य नारदात्कुपितस्ततः।।
देवकीं वसुदेवं च गृहे गुप्तावधारयत्।। ६८।।

Hearing this from Nārada, Kansa greatly excited with wrath, kept Vasudeva and Devakī in secret confinement.

वसुदेवेन कंसाय तेनैवोक्तं यथा पुरा।।
तथैव वसुदेवोपि पुत्रमर्पितवान्द्विज।। ६९।।

According to his promise Vasudeva delivered to Kansa each infant as soon as it was born.

हिरण्यकशिपोः पुत्राष्षड्गर्भा इति विश्रुताः।।
विष्णुप्रयुक्तास्तान्निद्राक्रमाद्गर्भानयोजयत्।। ७०।।

योगनिद्रा महामाया वैष्णवी मोहितं यया।।
अविद्यया जगत्सर्वं तामाह भगवान्हरिः।। ७१।।

It is said these, to the number of six, were the children of the demon Hiraṇya-Kaśipu, introduced into the womb of Devakī by Yoganidrā, at the behest of Viṣṇu, who was his illusory energy and by whom the whole world is beguiled, and who is known as utter ignorance.

श्रीभगवानुवाच

निद्रे गच्छ ममादेशात्पातालतलसंश्रयान्।।
एकैकत्वेन षड्गर्भान्देवकीजठरं नय।। ७२।।

The great god said to her—"Go, Nidrā, to the nether regions and by my command introduce their six princes to the womb of Devakī.

हतेषु तेषु कंसेन शेषाख्योंशस्ततो मम।।
अंशांशेनोदरे तस्यास्सप्तमः संभविष्यति।। ७३।।

When these shall be destroyed by Kansa, the seventh conception shall be a portion of Śeṣa, who is a portion of me.

गोकुले वसुदेवस्य भार्यान्या रोहिणी स्थिता।।
तस्यास्स संभूतिसमं देवि नेयस्त्वयोदरम्।। ७४।।

There is another wife of Vasudeva in Gokula named Rohiṇī and this you shall transfer to her, before the time of birth.

सप्तामो भोजराजस्य भयाद्रोधोपरोधतः।।
देवक्याः पतितो गर्भ इति लोको वदिष्यति।। ७५।।

The rumour shall be that Devakī miscarries through the anxiety of imprisonment and dread of the king of Bhojas.

गर्भसंकर्षणात्सोऽथ लोके संकर्षणेति वै।।
संज्ञामवाप्स्यते वीरश्श्वेताद्रिशिखरोपमः।। ७६।।

And on account of his being extracted from his mother's womb, the child shall be designated Saṅkarṣaṇa and he shall be like the peak of the white mountain in bulk and complexion.

ततोऽहं संभविष्यामि देवकीजठरे शुभे।।
भर्गं त्वया यशोदाया गंतव्यमविलंबितम्।। ७७।।

I shall myself then descend in the eighth auspicious conception of Devakī and you shall immediately enter into the womb of Yaśodā.

प्रावृट्काले च नभसि कृष्णाष्टम्यामहं निशि।।
उत्पत्स्यामि नवम्यां तु प्रसूतिं त्वमवाप्स्यसि।। ७८।।

In the night of the eighth lunation of the dark half of the month of Nabhas in the season of the rains, I shall be born. You will be born on the ninth.

यशोदाशयने मां तु देवक्यास्त्वामनिंदिते।।
मच्छक्तिप्रेरितमतिर्वसुदेवो नयिष्यति।। ७९।।

कंसश्च त्वामुपादाय देवि शैलशिलातले।।
प्रक्षेप्स्यत्यंतरिक्षे च संस्थानं त्वमवाप्स्यसि।। ८०।।

ततस्त्वां शतदृक्छक्रः प्रणम्य मम गौरवात्।।
प्रणिपातानतशिरा भगिनीत्वे ग्रहीष्यति।। ८१।।

Being aided by my energy Vasudeva shall carry me to the bed of Yaśodā and you to that of Devakī. When Kansa shall dash you against a stone, O worshipful dame, you shall attain to the sky and then the thousand-eyed Indra, out of reverence for me, shall bow unto you and shall accept you as his sister.

त्वं च शुंभनिशुंभादीन्हत्वा दैत्यान्सहस्रशः।।
स्थानैरनेकैः पृथिवीमशेषां मंडयिष्यसि।। ८२।।

Having destroyed Śumbha and Niśumbha and thousands of other Daityas you shall sanctify the earth in many places.

त्वं भूतिः सन्नतिः क्षांतिः कांतिर्द्यौः पृथिवी धृतिः।।
लज्जा पुष्टी रुषा या तु काचिदन्या त्वमेव सा।। ८३।।

You are wealth, progeny, fame, patience, heaven and earth, fortitude, modesty, nutrition, dawn and every other female (form or virtue).

ये त्वामार्य्येति दुर्गेति वेदगर्भांबिकेति च।।
भद्रेति भद्रकालीति क्षेमदा भाग्यदेति च।। ८४।।

Those, who shall reverentially invoke you, morning and evening, and praise and call you Āryā, Durgā, Vedagarbhā, Ambikā, Bhadrā, Bhadrakālikā, Kṣemī or Kṣemankarī, shall receive, by my grace, whatever they desire.

प्रातश्चैवापराह्णे च स्तोष्यंत्यानम्रमूर्त्तयः।।
तेषां हि प्रार्थितं सर्वं मत्प्रसादाद्भविष्यति।। ८५।।

And pleased with their offerings of wine and flesh and various other kinds you shall gratify the prayers of mankind.

सुरामांसोपहारैश्च भक्ष्यभोज्यैश्च पूजिता।।
नृणामशेषकामांस्त्वं प्रसन्ना संप्रदास्यसि।। ८६।।

ते सर्वे सर्वदा भद्रे मत्प्रसादादसंशयम्।।
असंदिग्धा भविष्यंति गच्छ देवि यथो दितम्।।

By my favour all men shall have perstual faith in you. Assured of this, go, goddess, and satisfy my orders!"

।। इति श्रीविष्णुमहापुराणो पञ्चमेंशे प्रथमोऽध्यायः।। १।।

अथ पञ्चमेंशेः द्वितीयोऽध्यायः

Part V : Section 2

श्रीपराशर उवाच

यथोक्तं सा जगद्धात्रा देवदेवेन वै तथा।।
षड्गर्भगर्भविन्यासं चक्रे चान्यस्य कर्षणम्।। १।।

Parāśara said :—Being thus ordered by the gods, Jagadhātrī (the nurse of the universe) transferred six embryos into the womb of Devakī.

सप्तमे रोहिणीं गर्भे प्राप्ते गर्भं ततो हरिः।।
लोकत्रयोपकाराय देवक्याः प्रविवेश ह।। २।।

And the seventh conception was conveyed into the womb of Rohiṇī after which Hari, for the behoof of the three worlds, entered into the womb of Devakī.

योगनिद्रा यशोदायास्तस्मिन्नेव तथा दिने।।
संभूता जठरे तद्वद्यथोक्तं परमेष्ठिना।। ३।।

And as commanded by the great god, Yoganidrā, on that very day entered into the womb of Yaśodā.

ततो ग्रहगणस्सम्यक्प्रचचार दिवि द्विज।।
विष्णोरंशे भुवं याते ऋतवश्चाबभुश्शुभाः।। ४।।

The portion of Viṣṇu having descended on earth, the planets moved in auspicious order and the seasons became regular and genial.

न सेहे देवकीं द्रष्टुं कश्चिदप्यतितेजसा।।
जाज्वल्यमानां तां दृष्ट्वा मनांसि क्षोभमाययुः।। ५।।

No body could gaze upon Devakī, invested with light—and beholding her thus dazzling, the minds of the people were disturbed.

अदृष्टा पुरुषैस्त्रीभिर्देवकीं देवतागणाः।।
बिभ्राणां पुषा विष्णुं तुष्टुवुस्तामहर्निशम्।। ६।।

The celestials, invisible to men and women alike, chanted the praises of Devakī, day and night, from the time that Viṣṇu entered into her person.

देवता ऊचुः

प्रकृतिस्त्वं परा सूक्ष्मो ब्रह्म गर्भाऽभवत्पुरा।।
ततो वाणी जगद्धातुर्वेदगर्भासि शोभने।। ७।।

सृज्यस्वरूपगर्भासि सृष्टिभूता सनातने।।
बीजभूता तु सर्वस्य यज्ञभूता भवस्त्रयी।। ८।।

They said—"Thou art that Prakṛti infinite and subtile, which formerly bore Brahmā in its womb. O nurse of the universe, thou art his words—from thee have sprung the Vedas, O fair damsel, O thou existing perpetually, thou art the very creation and in thy womb is the Sun : thou art the seed of all—thou art the parent of the tri-form Sacrifice.

फलगर्भा त्वमेवेज्या वह्निगर्भा तथारणिः।।
अदितिर्देवगर्भा त्वं दैत्यगर्भा तथा दितिः।। ९।।

Thou art Sacrifice whence all fruit proceeds—thou art wood whose attrition creates fire. As Aditi thou art the mother of the celestials, as Diti thou art the mother of the Daityas their foes.

ज्योत्स्ना वासरगर्भा त्वं ज्ञानगर्भासि सन्नतिः।।
नयगर्भा परा नीतिर्लज्जा त्वं प्रश्रयोद्वहा।। १०।।

Thou art light which creates day—thou art humility—the mother of true wisdom; thou art royal policy the mother of order—thou art modesty the mother of affection.

कामगर्भा तथेच्छा त्वं तुष्टिः संतोषगर्भिणी।।
मेधा च बोधगर्भासि धैर्यगर्भोद्वहा धृतिः।। ११।।
ग्रहर्क्षतारकागर्भा द्यौरस्याखिलहैतुकी।।
एता विभूतयो देवि तथान्याश्च सहस्रशः।। १२।।
तथा संख्या जगद्धात्री सांप्रतं जठरे तव।।
समुद्राद्रिनदीद्वीपवनपत्तनभूषणा ।।
ग्रामखर्वटखेटाढ्या समस्ता पृथिवी शुभे।। १३।।
समस्तवह्नयोंऽभांसि सकलाश्च समीरणाः।।
महोरगास्तथा यक्षा राक्षसाः प्रेतगुह्यकाः।। १४।।
ग्रहर्क्षतारकाचित्रविमानशत संकुलम्।।
अवकाशमशेषस्य यद्ददाति नभस्थलम्।। १५।।
भूलोकश्च भुवर्लोकस्स्वर्लोकोऽथ महर्जनः।।
तपश्च ब्रह्मलोकश्च ब्रह्मांडमखिलं शुभे।। १६।।
तदंतरे स्थिता देवा दैत्यगंधर्वचारणाः।।
महोरगास्तथा यक्षा राक्षसाः प्रेतगुह्यकाः।। १७।।
मनुष्याः पशवश्चान्ये ये च जीवा यशस्विनि।।
तैरंतस्थैरनंतोऽसौ सर्वगः सर्वभावनः।। १८।।
रूपकर्मस्वरूपाणि न परिच्छेदगोचरे।
यस्याखिलप्रमाणानि स विष्णुर्गर्भगस्तव।। १९।।

Thou art desire from whom love is produced—thou art contentment from which resignation is produced, thou art intelligence, the mother of knowledge, thou art patience the parent of fortitude; thou art heavens whose children are stars, and from thee proceeds all that exists. These and thousand others are thy mighty faculties, O goddess : and numberless are the contents of thy womb, O mother of the universe. That Viṣṇu, whose real form, nature, name, dimensions are above human conception, is in thy womb, with whom are identical the whole earth, embellished with oceans, rivers, continents, cities, villages, hamlets, towns; all the fires, waters, winds, the stars, asterisms and planets, the sky abounding in variegated cars of the celestials and ether that provides space for all substance; the spheres of earth, sky and heaven; of saints, sages; ascetics and of Brahmā; the white egg of Brahmā, with all its populations of Gods, demons, spirits, snake-gods, friends, demons, ghosts and imps, men and animals, and whatever creatures have life.

त्वं स्वाहा त्वं स्वधा विद्या स्वधा त्वं ज्योतिरंबरे।।
त्वं सर्वलोकरक्षार्थमवतीर्णा महीतले।। २०।।

Thou art Swāhā, thou art Swadhā, thou art wisdom, ambrosia, light and heaven.

प्रसीद देवि सर्वस्य जगतश्शं शुभे कुरु।।
प्रीत्या तं धारयेशानं धृतं येनाखिलं जगत्।। २१।।

Thou hast descended upon earth for the preservation of the unvierse, have pity upon us, O goddess, and do good unto the world. Be proud of bearing that deity by whom the universe is upheld."

।। इति श्रीविष्णुमहापुराणे पञ्चमेंशे द्वितीयोऽध्यायः।। २।।

अथ पञ्चमेंशे: तृतीयोऽध्याय:

Part V : Section 3

श्रीपराशर उवाच

एवं संस्तूयमाना सा देवैर्देवमधारयत्।।
गर्भेण पुंडरीकाक्षं जगतस्त्राणकारणम्।। १।।

Parāśara said :—Being thus eulogised by the celestials, Devakī conceived in her womb the lotus-eyed deity—the saviour of the universe.

ततोऽखिलजगत्पद्मबोधायाच्युतभानुना।।
देवकीपूर्वसंध्यायामाविर्भूतं महात्मना।। २।।

The sun of Acyuta rose in the dawn of Devakī, to cause the lotus-petal of the unvierse to expand.

तज्जन्मदिनमत्यर्थमाह्लाद्यमलदिङ्मुखम्।।
बभूव सर्वलोकस्य कौमुदी शशिनो यथा।। ३।।

On the day of his birth, all the quarters were lighted up with joy and it gave delight to all people like unto the rays of the moon.

संतस्संतोषमधिकं प्रशमं चंडमारुता:।।
प्रसादं निम्नगा याता जायमाने जनार्दने।। ४।।

The pious obtained new delight; the strong wind were pacified and the river flowed silently when Janārdana was about to be born.

सिंधवो निजशब्देन वाद्यं चक्रुर्मनोहरम्।।
जगुर्गंधर्वपतयो ननृतुश्चाऽप्सरोगणा:।।५।।

The oceans made music with their murmurings, The Gandharvas began to sing and the Apsarās began to dance.

ससृजु: पुष्पवर्षाणि देवा भुव्यंतरिक्षगा:।।
जज्वलुश्चाग्नयश्शांता जायमाने जनार्दने।। ६।।

At the time of Janārdana's birth the celestials, stationed in the sky, began to pour flowers and the holy fires glowed with a mild flame.

मंदं जगर्जुर्जलदा: पुष्पवृष्टिमुचो द्विज।।
अर्द्धरात्रेऽखिलाधारे जायमाने जनार्दने।। ७।।

At midnight, when the supporter of all was about to be born, the clouds began to emit low sounds and pour down rain of flowers.

फुल्लेंदीवरपत्राभं चतुर्बाहुमुदीक्ष्यतम्।।
श्रीवत्सवक्षसं जातं तुष्टावानकदुंदुभि:।। ८।।

अभिष्टूय च तं वाग्भि: प्रसन्नाभिर्महामति:।।
विज्ञापयामास तदा कंसाद्भीतो द्विजोत्तम।। ९।।

As soon as Anakadundhubhi saw the child, looking like full-blown lotus-petals, having four arms and the mystic marks Śrīvatsa on his breast; he began to chant his glories in terms of love and respect and represented the fears he entertained of Kansa.

वसुदेव उवाच

जातोसि देवदेवेश शंखचक्रगदाधरम्।।
दिव्यरूपमिदं देव प्रसादेनोपसंहर।। १०।।

Vasudeva said, "I have known thee, O sovereign lord of the celestials, O thou the holder of conch, discus and mace.

अद्यैव देव कंसोयं कुरुते मम घातनम्।।
अवतीर्ण इति ज्ञात्वा त्वमस्मिन्मम मंदिरे।। ११।।

Be pleased to withhold this thy celestials form, for Kansa will surely destroy me when he will know that thou hast descended in my dwelling."

देवक्युवाच

योऽनंतरूपोऽखिलविश्वरूपो गर्भेपि लोकान्वपुषा बिभर्त्ति।।
प्रसीदतामेषस देवदेवो यो माययाऽविष्कृतबालरूप:।।
१२।।

उपसंहर सर्वात्मन्रूपमेतच्चतुर्भुजम्।।
जानातु माऽवतारं ते कंसोयं दितिजन्मज:।। १३।।

Devakī said—"God of gods, who art identical with all things, in whose person all the religions of the world exist and who, by illusion, hast assumed the condition of an infant, have pity on me, withhold thy four-armed shape. Let not Kansa, the wicked son of Diti, know of this birth."

श्रीभगवानुवाच

स्तुतोऽहं यत्त्वया पूर्वं पुत्रार्थिन्या दतद्य ते।।
सफलं देवि सञ्जातं जातोऽहं यत्तवोदरात्।। १४।।

To this Bhāgavat replied—"O worshipful dame, I was worshipped by thee before to be born as thy son. Thy prayers have now been granted and I am now born as thy son."

श्रीपराशर उवाच

इत्युक्त्वा भगवांस्तूष्णीं बभूव मुनिसत्तम।।
वसुदेवोपि तं रात्रावादाय प्रययौ बहिः।। १५।।

So saying he was silent and Vasudeva, taking the babe, went out the same night.

मोहिताश्चाभवंस्तत्र रक्षिणो योगनिद्रया।।
मथुराद्वारपालाश्च व्रजत्यानकदुंदुभौ।। १६।।

The guards and gate-keepers of Mathurā were all charmed by Yoganidrā and none of them obstructed the passage of Anaka-dundhubhi.

वर्षतां जलदानां च तोयमत्युल्बणं निशि।।
संवृत्यानुययौ शेषः फणैरानकदुंदुभिम्।। १७।।

It was raining heavily at that time and the many-headed serpent Śeṣa followed Vasudeva spreading his hoods above their heads.

यमुनां चातिगंभीरां नानावर्त्तशताकुलाम्।।
वसुदेवो वहन्विष्णुं जानुमात्रवहां ययौ।। १८।।

And when he, with the child in his arms, crossed the Yamunā, deep as it was and dangerous with numerous whirlpools, the waters were silent and rose not above his knee.

कंसस्य करदानाय तत्रैवाभ्यागतांस्तटे।।
नेदादीन्गोपवृद्धांश्च यमुनाया ददर्श सः।। १९।।

On the bank he saw Nanda and others who had come there to bring tribute to Kansa, but they did not see him.

तस्मिन्काले यशोदापि मोहिता योगनिद्रया।।
तामेव कन्यां मैत्रेय प्रसूता मोहिते जने।। २०।।

वसुदेवोपि विन्यस्य बालमादाय दारिकाम्।।
यशोदाशयनात्तूर्णमाजगामामितद्युतिः ।। २१।।

At that time Yaśodā was also influenced by Yoganidrā, whom she had given birth as her daughter and whom the wise Vasudeva took up, placing his son in her palace by the side of the mother. He then speedily came back home.

ददृशे च प्रबुद्धा सा यशोदा जातमात्मजम्।।
नीलोत्पलदलश्यामं ततोत्यर्थं मुदं ययौ।। २२।।

When Yaśodā awoke, she found she had bee delivered of a boy as black as the dark lotus-leaves; and she was greatly delighted.

आदाय वसुदेवोऽपि दारिकां निजमंदिरे।।
देवकीशयने न्यस्य यथापूर्वमतिष्ठत।। २३।।

Vasudeva, taking the female child of Yaśodā, reached his house unperceived and placed the child in the bed of Devakī. He then remained as usual.

ततो बालध्वनिं श्रुत्वा रक्षिणस्सहसोत्थिताः।।
कंसायावेदयामासुर्देवकीप्रसवं द्विज।। २४।।

The guards were awakened by the cry of the new-born babe and starting up they informed Kansa that Devakī had given birth to a child.

कंसस्तूर्णमुपेत्यैनां ततो जग्राह बालिकाम्।।
मुञ्चमुञ्चेति देवक्या सन्नकंठ्या निवारितः।। २५।।

Kansa immediately went to the house of Vasudeva where he got hold of the infant. Devakī faintingly prevented him, crying out again and again—"Do not destroy it! Do not destroy it."

चिक्षेप च शिलापृष्ठे सा क्षिप्ता वियति स्थिता।।
अवाप रूपं सुमहत्सायुधाष्टमहाभुजम्।। २६।।

Kansa dashed it against a stone; it at once went up to the sky and expanded into a gigantic figure, having eight arms each bearing a formidable weapon.

प्रजहास तथैवोच्चैः कंसं च रुषिताऽब्रवीत्।।
किं मया क्षिप्तया कंस जातो यस्त्वां वधिष्यति।। २७।।

This terrible figure laughed and said to Kansa. "What benefit, have you derived, O Kansa, by hurling me to the ground?

सर्वस्वभूतो देवानामासीन्मृत्युः पुरा स ते।।
तदेतत्संप्रधार्याशु क्रियतां हिमात्मनः।। २८।।

He is born, who shall destroy thee, the mighty one amongst the celestials, who was formerly the destroyer. Considering this do thou accomplish what shall tend to thy welfare."

इत्युक्त्वा प्रययौ देवी दिव्यस्त्रग्गंधभूषणा।।
पश्यतो भोजराजस्य स्तुता सिद्धैर्विहायसा।। २९।।

Having said this, the goddess, decorated with heavenly unguents and garlands, and glorified by the spirits of the air, disappeared from the sight of the king of the Bhojas.

।। इति श्रीविष्णुमहापुराणे पञ्चमेंशे तृतीयोऽध्यायः।। ३।।

अथ पञ्चमेंशे: चतुर्थोऽध्यायः

Part V : Section 4

श्रीपराशर उवाच

कंसस्ततोद्विग्नमनाः प्राह सर्वान्महासुरान्।।
प्रलंबकेशिप्रमुखानाहूयासुरपुंगवान्।। १।।

Parāśara said :—Kansa, greatly disturbed in mind, called together all the leading Asuras, Pralamba, Keśin and others and said to them—

कंस उवाच

हे प्रलंब महाबाहो केशिन् धेनुक पूतने।।
अरिष्टाद्यास्तथैवाऽन्ये श्रूयतां वचनं मम।। २।।

"O ye, leading Asuras, Pralamba, Dhenuka, Pūtanā, Ariṣṭa and all others, hear my words.

मां हंतुममरैर्यत्नः कृतः किल दुरात्मभिः।।
मद्वीर्यतापितान्वीरो न त्वेतान्गणयाम्यहम्।। ३।।

O heroes, the wicked celestials, troubled by my power, have been trying to destroy me—but I do not much care for them.

किमिंद्रेणाल्पवीर्येण किं हरेणैकचारिणा।।
हरिणा वापि किं साध्यं छिद्रेष्वसुरघातिना।। ४।।

Save murdering the Asuras by fraud, what can the weak Indra and the ascetic Hara or Hari do?

किमादित्यैः किं वसुभिरल्पवीर्यैः किमग्निभिः।।
किं वान्यैरमरैः सर्वैर्मद्बहुबलनिर्जितैः।।५।।

What have we to fear from the Ādityas, the Vasus, the Agnis or any other of the immortals who have all been defeated by my resistless arms?

किं न दृष्टोमरपतिर्मया संयुगमेत्य सः।।
पृष्ठेनैव वहन्बाणानपगच्छन्नवक्षसा।। ६।।

Have you not seen the king of the celestials, when he had come out into the conflict, quickly fly from the field receiving my arrows upon his back, not bravely upon his breast?

मद्राष्ट्रे वारिता वृष्टिर्यदा शक्रेण किं तदा।।
मद्बाणभिन्नैर्जलदैरापो मुक्ता यथेप्सिताः।। ७।।

When Indra withheld rains from my kingdom, were not the clouds compelled by my arrows to pour water as much as was required?

किमुर्व्यामवनीपाला मद्बाहुबलभीरवः।।
ते सर्वे सन्नतिं याता जरासंधमृते गुरुम्।। ८।।

Are not all the kings of the earth afraid of my prowess and subject to my orders, save my father Jarāsandha?

अमरेषु ममावज्ञा जायते दैत्यपुंगवाः।।
हास्यं मे जायते वीरास्तेषु यत्नपरेष्वपि।। ९।।

O ye leading and heroic Daityas, I have already got hatred towarads the celestials—it has created my laughter that they have been trying to slay me.

तथापि खलु दुष्टानां तेषामप्यधिकं मया।।
अपकाराय दैत्येन्द्रा यतनीयं दुरात्मनाम्।। १०।।

And it is my fixed determination to inflict still deepr degradation upon those vicious and wicked-minded celestials.

तद्ये यशस्विनः केचित्पृथिव्यां ये च यज्वनः।।
कार्यो देवापकाराय तेषां सर्वात्मना वधः।। ११।।

Let us therefore kill every man who is known for liberality (in making gifts to gods and Brāhmaṇas) and let every man, who is celebrate for performing sacrifices, be slain; and thus the celestials shall be deprived of the means they live upon.

उत्पन्नश्चापि मे मृत्युर्भूतपूर्वस्स वै किल।।
इत्येद्दारिका प्राह देवकीगर्भसंभवा।। १२।।

The goddess, who has taken her birth as the child of Devakī, has said to me that he is again born who destroyed me in one of my previous birth.

तस्माद्बालेषु च परो यत्नः कार्यों महीतले।।
यत्रोद्रिक्तं बलं बाले स हन्तव्यः प्रयत्नतः।। १३।।

Let us vigorously find out all young children upon earth and let every boy in whom there are signs of unusual vigour, be killed mercilessly."

इत्याज्ञाप्यासुरान्कंसः प्रविश्याशु गृहं ततः।।
मुमोच वसुदेवं च देवकीं च निरोधतः।। १४।।

Having passed these orders Kansa went to his palace and liberated Vasudeva and Devakī from their captivity.

कंस उवाच

युवयोर्घातिता गर्भा वृथैवैते मयाऽधुना।।
कोप्यन्य एव नाशाय मम गर्भस्समुद्यतः।। १५।।

He said to them—"In vain have I killed all your children, for he, who is distined to kill me, has escaped. It is useless to regret the past.

तदलं परितापेन नूनं तद्भाविनो हि ते।।
अर्भका युवयोर्दोषाच्चायुषो यद्वियोजिताः।। १६।।

The children, who shall be born to you, after this, may enjoy life till its natural close; no one shall cut it short."

श्रीपराशर उवाच

इत्याश्वास्य विमुक्त्वा च कंसस्तौ परिशंकितः।।
अंतर्गृहं द्विजश्रेष्ठ प्रविवेश ततः स्वकम्।। १७।।

Parāśara said :—Having thus consoled them, Kansa, greatly terrified for himself, went into the inner apartments of his palace.

।। इति श्रीविष्णुमहापुराणे पञ्चमेंशे चतुर्थोऽध्यायः।। ४।।

अथ पञ्चमेंशेः पञ्चमोऽध्यायः

Part V : Section 5

श्रीपराशर उवाच

विमुक्तो वसुदेवोऽपि नंदस्य शकटं गतः।।
प्रहृष्टं दृष्टवान्नंदं पुत्रो जातो ममेति वै।। १।।

,Parāśara said :—When Vasudeva was freed, he went to the waggon of Nanda and found him greatly delighted that a son was born to him.

वसुदेवोपि तं प्राह दिष्ट्यादिष्ट्येति सादरम्।।
वार्द्धकेऽपि समुत्पन्नस्तनयोऽयं तवाधुना।। २।।

He then kindly said to him. "It is a blessing that you have got a son in your old age.

दत्तो हि वार्षिकस्सर्वो भवद्भिर्नृपतेः करः।।
यदर्थमागतास्तस्मान्ना? स्थेयं महाधनैः।। ३।।

Have you given your annual tribute to the king? If you have finished your work, you should not wait here for you are men of property.

यदर्थमागताः कार्यं तन्निष्पन्नं किमस्यते।।
भवद्भिर्गम्यतां नंद तच्छीघ्रं निजगोकुलम्।। ४।।

Why do you wait here since the work that has brought you, is finished? Go therefore, speedily, O Nanda, to your Gokula.

ममापि बालकस्तत्र रोहिणी प्रभवो हि यः।।
स रक्षणीयो भवता यथायं तनयो निजः।। ५।।

I have also got a son there, born of Rohiṇī, and he should be brought up by you as this your own son."

इत्युक्ताः प्रययुर्गोपा नंदगोपपुरोगमाः।।
शकटारोपितैर्भांडैः करं दत्त्वा महाबलाः।। ६।।

Parāśara said :—Thus having paid their dues to the king and placed their goods in their waggons, Nanda other cow-herds went to their village.

वसतां गोकुले तेषां पूतना बालघातिनी।।
सुप्तं कृष्णमुपादाय रात्रौ तस्मै स्तनं ददौ।। ७।।

And while they were thus living in Gokula, Pūtanā the child-killer, taking up Kṛṣṇa, asleep in night, gave him her breast to suck.

यस्मै यस्मै स्तनं रात्रौ पूतना संप्रयच्छति।।
तस्यतस्य क्षणेनांगं बालकस्योपहन्यते।। ८।।

And whatever child is suckled by Pūtanā in night, dies instantly having its limbs wearied and exhausted.

कृष्णस्तु तत्स्तनं गाढं कराभ्यामतिपीडितम्।।
गृहीत्वा प्राणसहितं पपौ क्रोधसमन्वितः।। ९।।

सातिमुक्तमहारावा विच्छिन्नस्नायुबंधना।।
पपात पूतना भूमौ म्रियमाणातिभीषणा।। १०।।

But laying hold of the breast with two hands, Kṛṣṇa sucked it with such violence that he drained it of the life and the terrible Pūtanā, roaring aloud and giving way in every point, fell on the ground dead.

तन्नादश्रुतिसंत्रस्ताः प्रबुद्धास्ते व्रजौकसः।।
ददृशुः पूतनोत्संगे कृष्णं तां च निपातिताम्।। ११।।

Hearing those cries, the inhabitants of Vraja, terrified, got up and saw Pūtanā lying on the earth with Kṛṣṇa in her arms.

आदाय कृष्णं संत्रस्ता यशोदापि द्विजोत्तम।।
गोपुच्छभ्रामणेनाथ बालदोषमपाकरोत्।। १२।।

गोकरीषमुपादाय नंदगोपोपि मस्तके।।
कृष्णस्य प्रददो रक्षां कुर्वंश्चैतदुदीरयन्।। १३।।

Snatching up Kṛṣṇa, Yaśodā waved over him a cow tail-brush to guard him from harm, whilst Nanda placed dried cow-dung powdered upon his head; he gave him also an amulet, saying at the same time—

नंदगोप उवाच

रक्षतु त्वामशेषाणां भूतानां प्रभवो हरिः।।
यस्य नाभिसमुद्भूतपंकजादभवज्जगत्।। १४।।

"May Hari the lord of creation, he, from the lotus of whose navel the world was produced and on the tip of whose tusks the globe was upraised from waters, protect thee.

येन दंष्ट्राग्रविधृता धारणत्यवनिर्जगत्।।
वराहरूपधृग्देवस्स त्वां रक्षतु केशवः।। १५।।

May that Keśava, who assumed the form of a boar, protect thee.

नखांकुरविनिर्भिन्नवैरिवक्षस्थलो विभुः।।
नृसिंहरूपी सर्वत्र रक्षतु त्वां जनार्दनः।। १६।।

May that Keśava, who, as the man-lion, rent with his sharp nails, the bosom of his foe, save thee.

वामनो रक्षतु सदा भवंतं यः क्षणादभूत्।।
त्रिविक्रमः क्रमाक्रांतत्रैलोक्यः स्फुरदायुधः।। १७।।

May that Keśava, who appearing first as the dwarf, traversed with all his power with three paces, the three regions of the universe, constantly protect thee.

शिरस्ते पातु गोविंदः कंठं रक्षतु केशवः।।
गुह्यं च जठरं विष्णुर्जंघे पादौ जनार्दनः।। १८।।

मुखं बाहू प्रबाहू च मनः सर्वेंद्रियाणि च।।
रक्षत्वव्याहतैश्वर्यस्तव नारायणोऽव्ययः।। १९।।

May Govinda guard thy belly, Janārddana thy legs and feet, the eternal and irresistible Nārāyaṇa thy face, thine arms, thy mind and thy faculties of sense.

शार्ङ्गचक्रगदापाणेश्शंखनादहताः क्षयम्।।
गच्छंतु प्रेतकूष्मांडराक्षसा ये तवाहिताः।। २०।।

May all ghosts, goblins and malignant spirits, that shall be engaged in thy mischief, be destroyed by the bow, the discus, the mace, the sword of Viṣṇu and the by echo of his conch shell.

त्वां पातु दिक्षु बैकुण्ठो विदिक्षु मधुसूदनः।।
हृषीकेशोंऽबरे भूमौ रक्षतु त्वां महीधरः।। २१।।

May Vaikuṇṭha guard thee in thy cardinal points and Madhusūdana in the intermediate ones. May Hṛṣikeśa defend thee in the sky and Mahīdhara upon earth."

श्रीपराशर उवाच

एवं कृतस्वस्त्ययनो नंदगोपेन बालकः।।
शायितश्शकटस्याधो बालपर्यंकिकातले।। २२।।

Having recited these prayers to avert all evil, Nanda caused the child to sleep in his bed underneath the waggon.

ते च गोपा महद्दृष्ट्वा पूतनायाः कलेवरम्।।
मृतायाः परमं त्रासं विस्मयं च तदा ययुः।। २३।।

Seeing the huge carcass of Pūtanā the cow-herds were filled with surprise and fear.

।। इति श्रीविष्णुमहापुराणे पञ्चमेंशे पञ्चमोऽध्यायः।।५।।

अथ पञ्चमेंशेः षष्ठोऽध्यायः
Part V : Section 6

श्रीपराशर उवाच

कदाचिच्छकटस्याधश्शयानो मधुसूदनः।।
चिक्षेप चरणावूर्ध्वं स्तन्यार्थी प्ररुरोद ह।। १।।

तस्य पादप्रहारेण शकटं परिवर्त्तितम्।।
विध्वस्तकुंभभांडं तद्विपरीतं पपात वै।। २।।

Parāśara said :—Once on a time the slayer of Madhu was asleep underneath the waggon, he cried for the breast and kicking up his feet he overturned the vehicle and all the pots and pans were upset and broken.

ततो हाहाकृतः सर्वो गोपगोपीजनो द्विज।।
आजगामाथ ददृशे बालमुत्तानशायिनम्।। ३।।

Hearing the noise the wives of the cow-herds came exclaiming—"Ah! Ah!" and there they found the child sleeping on his back.

गोपाः केनेति केनेदं शकटं परिवर्त्तितम्।।
तत्रैव बालकाः प्रोचुर्बालेनानेन पातितम्।। ४।।

"Who could have overturned the waggon?" exclaimed the cow-herds. "That child," said some of the boys who saw the circumstance.

रुदता दृष्टमस्माभिः पादविक्षेपपातितम्।।
शकटं परिवृत्तं वै नैतदन्यस्य चेष्टितम्।। ५।।

"We saw him," said the boys, "crying and kicking the waggon and so the waggon was upset; no one else had anything to do with it."

ततः पुनरतीवासन्गोपा विस्मयचेतसः।।
नंदगोपोपि जग्राह बालमत्यंतविस्मितः।। ६।।

यशोदा शकटारूढभग्नभांडकपालिका।।
शकटं चार्चयामास दधिपुष्पफलाक्षतैः।। ७।।

The cow-herds were therefore greatly surprised and not knowing what to do Nanda at once took up the boy and Yaśodā offered worship to the broken pieces of pots and to the waggon, with curds, flowers, fruits and unbruised grain.

गर्गश्च गोकुले तत्र वसुदेवप्रचोदितः।।
प्रच्छन्न एव गोपानां संस्कारानकरोत्तयोः।। ८।।

Being commissioned by Vasudeva, Garga performed the initiatory rites of the two boys secretly in Vraja.

ज्येष्ठं च राममित्याह कृष्णं चैव तथाऽवरम्।।
गर्गो मतिमतां श्रेष्ठो नाम कुर्वन्महामतिः।। ९।।

The eldest was named Rāma and the other Kṛṣṇa by the wise Garga, the foremost of the intelligent.

स्वल्पे नैव तु कालेन रंगिणौ तौ तदा व्रजे।।
घृष्टजानुकरौ विप्र बभूवतुरुभावपि।। १०।।

करीषभस्मदिग्धांगौ भ्रममाणावितस्ततः।।

In a short time they began to crawl about the ground, supporting themselves on their hands and knees and creeping everywhere, often amidst ashes and filth.

न निवारयितुं सेहे यशोदा तौ न रोहिणी।। ११।।
गोवाटमध्ये क्रीडंतौ वत्सवाटं गतौ पुनः।।
तदहर्जातगोवत्सपुच्छाकर्षणतत्परौ।। १२।।

Neither Rohiṇī nor Yaśodā was able to prevent them from getting into the cow-pens or amongst the calves, where they amused themselves by pulling their tales.

यदा यशोदा तौ बालावेकस्थानचराबुभौ।।
शशाक नो वारयिंतु क्रीडंतावतिचञ्चलौ।। १३।।

When Yaśodā could not prevent the two boys, who always rambled together, from playing naughtily, she became angry and taking up a stick remonstrated with Kṛṣṇa having eyes like lotus-petals.

दाम्ना मध्ये ततो बद्धा बबंध तमुलूखले।।
कृष्णमक्लिष्टकर्माणमाह चेदममर्षिता।। १४।।

Fastening a cord round his waist she tied him to the wooden mortar and being angry, she said to him—

यदि शक्नोषि गच्छ त्वमतिचञ्चलचेष्टित।।
इत्युक्त्वाथ निजं कर्म सा चकार कुटुंबिनी।। १५।।

"Now you wicked boy, get away from here, if you can." Having said this, she went about her domestic affairs.

व्यग्रायामथ तस्यां स कर्षमाण उलूखलम्।।
यमलार्जुनमध्येन जगाम कमलेक्षणः।। १६।।

As soon as she had gone, the lotus-eyed Kṛṣṇa, trying to extricate himself, pulled the mortar after him to the space between the two Arjuna trees that grew near together.

कर्षता वृक्षयोर्मध्ये तिर्यग्गतमुलूखलम्।।
भग्नावुत्तुंगशाखाग्रौ तेन तौ यमलार्जुनौ।। १७।।

Being dragged there the mortar became wedged between the two trees, and Kṛṣṇa having pulled it, the two huge trees covered with many leaves, were uprooted.

ततः कटकटाशब्दसमाकर्णनतत्परः।।
आजगाम व्रजजनो ददर्श च महाद्रुमौ।। १८।।
नवोद्गताल्पदंतांशुसितहासं च बालकम्।।
तयोर्मध्यगतं दाम्ना बद्धं गाढं तथोदरे।। १९।।

Hearing the cracking noise the inhabitants of Vraja came to see what was the matter and there they beheld the two huge trees with broken branches and stems lying on the ground with the child fixed between them, with a rope round his belly, laughing and chewing his white teeth, just budded.

ततश्च दामोदरतां स ययौ दामबंधनात्।। २०।।

It is from this that Kṛṣṇa is called Dāmodara from the binding of *dāma* (rope) round his *udara* (belly).

गोपवृद्धास्ततः सर्वे नंदगोपपुरोगमाः।।
मंत्रयामासुरुद्विग्ना महोत्पातातिभीरवः।। २१।।

The elders among the cow-herds, with Nanda at their head, looked upon these circumstances with alarm, considering them as inauspicious signs.

स्थानेनेह न नः कार्यं व्रजामोन्महावनम्।।
उत्पाता बहवो ह्यत्र दृश्यंते नाशहेतवः।। २२।।

They said—"We cannot remain in this place—let us go to some other part of the forest.

पूतनाया विनाशश्च शकटस्य विपर्ययः।।
विना वातादिदोषेण द्रुमयोः पतनं तथा।। २३।।

Here many evil omens threaten us with destruction—the death of Pūtanā, the upsetting of the waggon and the fall of the trees without their being uprooted by the wind.

वृंदावनमितस्स्थानात्तस्माद्गच्छाम मा चिरम्।।
यावद्भौममहोत्पातदोषो नाभिभवेद्व्रजम्।। २४।।

Let us go away from here without any delay and go to Vṛndāvana, where evil omens may no longer disturb us."

इति कृत्वा मतिं सर्वे गमने ते व्रजौकसः।।
ऊचुस्स्वं स्वं कुलं शीघ्रं गम्यतां मा विलंबथ।। २५।।

Having thus made up their minds, the inhabitants of Vraja communicated their intention to their families and desired them to go without delay.

ततः क्षणेन प्रययुः शकटैर्गोधनैस्तथा।।
यूथशो वत्सपालाश्च कालयंतो व्रजौकसः।। २६।।

द्रव्यावयवनिर्द्धूतं क्षणमात्रेण तत्तथा।।
काकभाससमाकीर्णं व्रजस्थानमभूद्द्विज।। २७।।

Accordingly they started with their waggons and their, cattle, deriving before them their bulls and cows and calves; they threw away the fragments of their household stores and in no time Vraja was overspread with flights of crows.

वृंदावनं भगवता कृष्णेना क्लिष्टकर्मणा।।
शुभेन मनसा ध्यातं गवां सिद्धिमभीप्सता।। २८।।

ततस्तत्रातिरूक्षेपि धर्मकाले द्विजोत्तम।।
प्रावृट्काल इवोद्भूतं नवशष्पं समंततः।। २९।।

Vṛndāvana was selected by Kṛṣṇa, who was above the influence of actions, for the sake of providing for the nourishment of the kine, for there in the hottest season the new grass springs up as profusely as the rains.

स समावासितः सर्वो व्रजो वृंदावने ततः।।
शकटावाटपर्यंतश्चंद्रार्द्धाकारसंस्थितः।। ३०।।

Having gone to Vṛndāvana from Vraja, the inhabitants of the latter drew up their waggons in the form of a crescent.

वत्सपालौ च संवृत्तौ रामदामोदरौ ततः।।
एक स्थानस्थितौ गोष्ठे चेरतुर्बाललीलया।। ३१।।

As the two boys Rāma and Dāmodara grew up, they lived always together in the same place and engaged in the same boyish sports.

बर्हिपत्रकृतापीडौ वन्यपुष्पावतंसका।।
गोपवेणुकृतातोद्यपत्रवाद्यकृतस्वनौ ।।३२।।

काकपक्षधरौ बालौ कुमाराविव पावकी।।
हसंतौ न रमंतौ च चेरतुः स्म महावनम्।। ३३।।

They made themselves crests of the peacocks' plumes and garlands of forest flowers and musical instruments of reeds and leaves or played upon the pipes used by cowherds; their hair was arranged like the wings of the crow, and they looked like two young princes and portions of the god of war.

क्वचिद्धहन्तावन्योन्यं क्रीडमानौ तथा परैः।।
गोपपुत्रैस्समं वत्सांश्चारयंतौ विचेरतुः।। ३४।।

They were robust, and walked about always laughing and playing sometimes with each other, sometimes with other boys; driving, along with other young cow-herds, the calves to the pasture.

कालेन गच्छता तौ तु सप्तवर्षौ महाव्रजे।।
सर्वस्य जगतः पालौ वत्सपालौ बभूवतुः।। ३५।।

Thus the two protectors of the universe were keepers of cattle until they became seven years old in the cow-pens of Vṛndāvana.

प्रावृट्कालस्ततोतीव मेघौघस्थगितांबरः।।
बभूव वारिधाराभिरैक्यं कुर्वन्दिशामिव।। ३६।।

प्ररूढनवशष्पाढ्या शक्रगोपाचिता मही।।
तथा मारकतीवासीत्पद्मरागविभूषिता।। ३७।।

ऊहुरुन्मार्गवाहीनि निम्नगांभांसि सर्वतः।।
मनांसि दुर्विनीतानां प्राप्य लक्ष्मीं नवामिव।। ३८।।

Then began the rainy season when the atmosphere was full of clouds and the quarters of the horizon were blended into one by the driving showers. The water of the rivers rose and overflowed their banks, and spread beyond all limits like the mind of the weak and wicked transported beyond restraint by sudden prosperity.

न रेजेंतरितश्चंद्रो निर्मालो मलिनैर्धनैः।।
सद्वादिवादो मूर्खाणां प्रगल्भाभिरिवोक्तिभिः।। ३९।।

The pure radiance of the moon was obscured by heavy vapours as the teachings of the sacred writings are darkened by the arrogant scoffs of the unbelievers.

निर्गुणेनापि चापेन शक्रस्य गगने पदम्।।
अवाप्यताविवेकस्य नृपस्यैव परिग्रहे।। ४०।।

The bow of Indra held its place unstrung in the sky like a worthless person elevated to honour by an indiscreet king.

मेघपृष्ठे बलाकानां रराज विमला ततिः।।
दुर्वृत्ते वृत्तचेष्टेव कुलीनस्यातिशोभना।। ४१।।

White line of strokes appeared upon the back of the clouds in such contrast as the bright conduct of a man of respectability opposes to the conduct of a scoundrel.

न ब बंधांबरे स्थैर्यं विद्युदत्यंतचञ्चला।।
मैत्रीव प्रवरे पुंसि दुर्जनेन प्रयोजिता।। ४२।।

The ever-fickle lightning, being newly allied with the sky, was like the friendship of a profligate for a man of substance.

मार्गा बभूवुरस्पष्टास्तृणशष्पचयावृताः।।
अर्थांतर मनुप्राप्ताः प्रजडानामिवोक्तयः।।४३।।

Overgrown by the spreading grain, the paths became difficult of being traced like the words of the ignorant carrying no definite meaning.

उन्मत्तशिखिसारंगे तस्मिन्काले महावने।।
कृष्णरामौ मुदायुक्तौ गोपालैश्चेरतुस्सह।। ४४।।

Kṛṣṇa and Rāma, delighted, began to live in the forest in that beautiful season maddening the peacocks and bees.

क्वचिद्गोभिस्समं रम्यं गेयतानरतावुभौ।।
चेरतुः क्वचिदत्यर्थं शीतवृक्षलताश्रितौ।। ४५।।

Sometimes they sang and danced with the cow-herds and sometimes sat under the cool shade of a huge tree for rest.

क्वचित्कदंबस्त्रक्चित्रौ मयूरस्त्रग्विराजितौ।।
विलिप्तौ क्वचिदासातां विविधैर्गिरिधातुभिः।।४६।।

पर्णशय्यासु संसुप्तौ क्वचिन्निद्रांतरैषिणौ।।
क्वचिद्गर्जति जीमूते हाहाकाररवाकुलौ।। ४७।।

गायतामन्य गोपानां प्रशंसापरमौ क्वचित्।।
मयूरकेकानुगतौ गोपवेणुप्रवादकौ।।४८।।

Sometimes they beautified themselves with garlands of Kadamba flowers and again with garlands of peacocks' feathers; sometimes they painted themselves with the minerals of the mountain; sometimes they slept on beds of leaves and sometimes they rejoiced with the infants of the cow-herds, hearing the muttering of the clouds; sometimes they praised the songs of the boys, sometimes mimicked the cry of the peacocks and sometimes played on pipes.

इति नानाविधैर्भावैरुत्तमप्रीतिसंयुतौ।।
क्रीडंतौ तौ वने तस्मिश्चेरतुस्तुष्टमानसौ।।४९।।

Thus greatly attached to each other and participating in various emotions and sports, Rāma and Kṛṣṇa delightedly resided in the forest.

विकाले च समं गोभिर्गोपवृंदसमन्वितौ।।
विहृत्याथ यथायोगं व्रजमेत्य महाबलौ।। ५०।।

And every evening they used to come back home like two cow-boys along with the cows and cow-herds.

गोपैस्समानैस्सहितौ क्रीडंतावमराविव।।
एवं तावूषतुस्तत्र रामकृष्णौ महाद्युति।।५१।।

And coming home in the evening, the two deities heartily engaged in sports giving delight to the sons of the cow-herds.

।। इति श्रीविष्णुमहापुराणे पञ्चमेंशे षष्ठोऽध्यायः।।६।।

अथ पञ्चमेंशेः सप्तमोऽध्यायः

Part V : Section 7

श्रीपराशर उवाच

एकदा तु विना रामं कृष्णो वृंदावनं ययौ।।
विचचार वृतो गोपैर्वन्यपुष्पस्त्रगुज्ज्वलः।। १।।

Parāśara said :—Once on a time Kṛṣṇa went to Vṛndāvana, without Balarāma; and there, adorned with garlands of wild flowers, roamed he, encircled by the cow-herds.

स जगामाथ कालिंदीं लोल कल्लोलशालिनीम्।।
तीरसंलग्नफेनौघैर्हसंतीमिव सर्वतः ।।२।।

He then repaired to the banks of Kālindī, Undulating and sparkling with foam and as if smiling when the waves dashed against the banks.

तस्याश्चातिमहाभीमं विषाग्निश्रितवारिणम्।।
ह्रदं कालीयनागस्य ददर्शातिविभीषणम्।। ३।।

There he saw the pool with the dreadful serpent Kālīya, boiling with the fires of poison.

विषाग्नि प्रसरता दग्धतीरमहीरुहम्।।
वाताहतांबुविक्षेपस्पर्शदग्धविहंगमम् ।।४।।

By the touch of that, poison the huge trees on the banks were withered and being touched by the waters raised by the wind the birds were scorched.

तमतीव महारौद्रं मृत्युवक्त्रमिवापरम्।।
विलोक्य चिंतयामास भगवान्मधुपत्यः।। ५।।

Beholding that dreadful serpent, like the second mouth of death, the illustrious Slayer of Madhu thought—

अस्मिन्वसति दुष्टात्मा कालीयोऽसौ विषायुधः।।
यो मया निर्जितस्त्यक्त्वा दुष्टो गच्छेत्पयोनिधिम्।। ६।।

"Forsooth, the wicked and poisonous serpent Kālīya lives here, who, being defeated by me, was constrained to leave the ocean whose waters were defiled.

तेनेयं दूषितां सर्वा यमुना सागरंगमा।।
न नरैर्गोधनैश्चापि तृषार्त्तैरुपभुज्यते।।७।।

By him the waters of the Yamunā, flowing to the ocean, have been poisoned, and the thirsty cows and cow-herds cannot satisfy their thirst.

तदस्य नागराजस्य कर्त्तव्यो निग्रहो मया।।
निस्त्रासास्तु सुखं येन चरेयुर्व्रजवासिनः।। ८।।

I must slay this serpent, so that the inhabitants of Vraja may live here happily freed from fear.

एतदर्थं तु लोकेस्मिन्नवतारः कृतो मया।।
यदेषामुत्पथस्थानां कार्या शांतिर्दुरात्मनाम्।। ९।।

I have descended upon the land of mortals to chastise the wicked, led astray into vicious paths.

तदेतं नातिदूरस्थं कदंबमुरुशाखिनम्।।
अधिरुह्य पतिष्यामि ह्रदेऽस्मिन्ननिलाशिनः।। १०।।

I shall therefore climb up the neighbouring Kadamba tree and jump down into the pool."

श्रीपराशर उवाच

इत्थं विचिंत्य बद्धा च गाढं परिकरं ततः।।
निपपात ह्रदे तत्र नागराजस्य वेगतः।। ११।।

Parāśara said :—Having thus though within himself he bound his clothes tightly about him and jumped boldly into the pool of the serpent-king.

तेनातिपतता तत्र क्षोभितस्स महाह्रदः।।
अत्यर्थं दूरजातांस्तु समसिञ्चन्महीरुहान्।। १२।।
ते हि दुष्टविषज्वालातप्तांबुपवनोक्षिताः।।
जज्वलुः पादपास्सद्यो ज्वालाव्याप्तदिगंतराः।।१३।।

The huge lake was agitated as soon as he fell into it, and the waves raised thereby began to sprinkle the distant trees, which being touched by the water and wind, thus poisoned, were immediately set on fire, and the whole horizon was ablaze.

आस्फोटयामास तदा कृष्णो नागह्रदे भुजम्।।
तच्छब्दश्रवणाच्चाशु नागराजोऽभ्युपागमत्।। १४।।
आताम्रनयनः कोपाद्विषज्वालाकुलैर्मुखैः।।

Having dived into the lake, Kṛṣṇa struck his arms defiantly. Hearing that noise the serpent-king immediately issued out—whose eyes were coppery and hoods were flaming with deadly venom.

वृतो महाविषैश्चान्यैरुरगैरनिलाशनैः ।।१५।।
नागपत्न्यश्च शतशो हारिहारोपशोभिताः।।
प्रकंपिततनुक्षेपचलत्कुंतलकांतयः ।।१६।।

He was encircled by many other powerful and poisonous snakes living upon air and hundreds of serpent-nymphs adorned with rich ornaments, whose carrings glittered with brilliance as the wearers moved along.

ततः प्रवेष्टितस्सर्पैस्स कृष्णो भोगबंधनैः।।
ददंशुस्तेऽपि तं कृष्णं विषज्वालाकुलैर्मुखैः।। १७।।

Coiling themselves around Kṛṣṇa, they all bit him with teeth from which fiery poison came out..

तं तत्र पतितं दृष्ट्वा सर्पभोगैर्निपीडितम्।।
गोपा व्रजमुपागम्य चुक्रुशुः शोकलालसाः।। १८।।

Beholding him in the lake thus surrounded by serpents, his companions immediately went to Vraja bewailing aloud his fate.

गोपा ऊचुः

एष मोहं गतः कृष्णो मग्नौ वै कालियह्रदे।।
भक्ष्यते नागराजेन तमागच्छत पश्यत।। १९।।

"Kṛṣṇa has foolishly jumped into the lake of the serpent Kālīya, and is being devoured by that serpent-king; do ye come and behold him."

तच्छ्रुत्वा तत्र ते गोपा वज्रपा तोपमं वचः।।
गोप्यश्च त्वरिता जग्मुर्यशोदाप्रमुखा ह्रदम्।। २०।।

Hearing those words, resembling fall of thunder, the cow-herds and their wives headed by Yaśodā, proceeded speedily towards the lake.

हाहा क्वासाविति जनो गोपीनामतिविह्वलः।।
यशोदया समं भ्रान्तो द्रुतप्रस्खलितं ययौ।। २१।।

"Alas where is Kṛṣṇa gone" cried the wives of the cow-herds greatly bewildered; and Yaśodā, terrified, with faltering steps, proceeded quickly.

नंदगोपश्च गोपाश्च रामश्चाद्भुतविक्रमः।।
त्वरितं यमुनां जग्मुः कृष्णदर्शनलालसाः।। २२।।

ददृशुश्चापि ते तत्र सर्पराजवशंगतम्।।
निष्प्रयत्नीकृतं कृष्णं सर्पभोगविवेष्टितम्।। २३।।

Rāma, gifted with great, prowess, Nanda and other cow-herds being anxious to see Kṛṣṇa, arrived quickly at the bank of the Yamunā and beheld him surrounded by snakes, possessed by the serpent-king and motionless.

नंदगोपोपि निश्चेष्टो न्यस्य पुत्रमुखे दृशम्।।
यशोदा च महाभागा बभूव मुनिसत्तम्।। २४।।

O foremost of Munis, looking at the countenance of their son, the cow-herd Nanda and the noble Yaśodā became stupefied.

गोप्यस्त्वन्या रुदंत्यश्च ददृशुः शोककातराः।।
प्रोचुश्च केशवं प्रीत्या भयकातर्यगद्गदम्।। २५।।

गोप्य ऊचुः

And the wives of the other cow-herds stricken with grief and weeping, saw him; and with words expressive of fear and affliction, they, out of love towards Keśava, said—

सर्वा यशोदया सार्द्धं विशामोत्र महाह्रदम्।।
सर्पराजस्य नो गंतुमस्माभिर्युज्यते व्रजम्।। २६।।

"We shall all with Yaśodā enter this huge lake of the serpent-king; we shall not be able to go back to Vraja.

दिवसः को विना सूर्यं विना चंद्रेण का निशा।।
विना वृषेण का गावो विना कृष्णेन को व्रजः।। २७।।

What is day without the sun, night without the moon, cow without a bull and Vraja without Kṛṣṇa?

विनाकृता न यास्यामः कृष्णेनानेन गोकुलम्।।
अरम्यं नातिसेव्यं च वारिहीनं यथा सरः।। २८।।

Without Kṛṣṇa we shall not return to Vraja, like unto a pond without water, in his absence, nor shall we roam in the forest.

यत्र नेंदीवरश्यामकायकांतिरयं हरिः।।
तेनापि मातुर्वासेन रतिरस्तीति विस्मयः।। २९।।

We do not like to live there, even if it be the house of our mothers, where there is not Hari, having the countenance like lotus-petals.

उत्फुल्लपंकजदलस्पष्टकांतिविलोचनम्।।
अपश्यंतो हरिं दीनाः कथं गोष्ठे भविष्यथ।। ३०।।

अत्यंत मधुरालापहृताशेषमनोरथम्।।
न विना पुंडरीकाक्षं यास्यामो नंदगोकुलम्।। ३१।।

How shall we live sorrowfully without beholding Hari in pasture having eyes resembling full-blown lotus-petals? We shall not go back to the house of Nanda in Gokula without the lotus-eyed Kṛṣṇa, who with his pleasant conversation has stolen all our hearts.

भोगेनावेष्टितस्यापि सर्पराजस्य पश्यत।।
स्मितशोभिमुखं गोप्यः कृष्णस्यास्मद्विलोकने।। ३२।।

O ye cow-herds! behold, Kṛṣṇa is still casting smiling looks upon us, although he is encircled by snakes engaged by the serpent-king.

श्रीपराशर उवाच

इति गोपीवचः श्रुत्वा रौहिणेयो महाबलः।।
गोपांश्च त्रासविधुरान्विलोक्य स्तिमितेक्षणान्।। ३३।।

Parāśara said :—Hearing those wards of the wives of the cow-herds and beholding the cow-herds stricken with fear the highly-powerful son of Rohiṇī looked settled (for some time).

नंदं च दीनमत्यर्थं न्यस्तदृष्टिं सुतानने ।।
मूर्च्छाकुलां यशोदां च कृष्णमहात्मसंज्ञया ।। ३४।।

And then seeing Nanda, with fixed looks towards Kṛṣṇa and Yaśodā almost in a swoon, he began to chant by signs the glories of Kṛṣṇa—

किमिदं देवदेवेश भावोऽयं मानुषस्त्वया ।।
व्यज्यतेत्यंतमात्मानं किमनंतं न वेत्सि यत् ।। ३५ ।।

"O god of gods, why art thou displaying these human characteristics? Dost thou not perceive thyself at one with one without end?

त्वमेव जगतो नाभिरराणामिव संश्रयः ।।
कर्त्तापहर्त्ता पाता च त्रैलोक्यं त्वं त्रयीमयः ।। ३६ ।।

सेंद्रैरुद्राग्निवसुभिरादित्यैर्मरुदश्विभिः ।।
चिंत्यसे त्वमचिंत्यात्मन् समस्तैश्चैव योगिभिः ।। ३७।।

जगत्यर्थं जगन्नाथ भारावतरणेच्छया ।।
अवतीर्णोऽसि मर्त्येषु तवांशश्चाहमग्रजः ।। ३८ ।।

मनुष्यलीलां भगवन् भजता भवता सुराः ।।
विडम्बयन्तस्त्वल्लीलां सर्व एव सहासते ।। ३९ ।।

Thou art the centre of creations, as the nave is of the spokes of a wheel. A portion of thee, I have even also born, as thy eldest brother. To share in the sports as men, the celestials have all descended under a like disguise.

अवतार्य भवान्पूर्वं गोकुले तु सुरांगनाः ।।
क्रीडार्थमात्मनः पश्चादवतीर्णोऽसि शाश्वत ।। ४० ।।

Having made all the goddesses descend in Gokula for thy sport, thou hast afterwards descended, although thou art existing perpetually.

अत्रावतीर्णयोः कृष्णगोपा एव हि बांधवाः ।।
गोप्यश्च सीदतः कस्मादेतान्बंधूरनुपेक्षसे ।। ४१ ।।

Wherefore Kṛṣṇa dost thou neglect these celestials who, as cow-herds, are thy friends and kin—and these sorrowing females, who also are thy relations?

दर्शितो मानुषो भावो दर्शितं बालचापलम् ।।
तदयं दम्यतां कृष्ण दुष्टात्मा दशनायुधः ।। ४२ ।।

Thou hast assumed the character of man : thou hast displayed the tricks of childhood. Now let this dreadful snake although armed with poisoned fangs, be vanquished (by thee)."

श्रीपराशर उवाच

इति संस्मारितः कृष्णः स्मितभिन्नोष्ठसंपुटः ।।
आस्फोट्य मोचयामास स्वदेहं भोगिबंधनात् ।। ४३ ।।

Parāśara said :—Being thus reminded of his real character by Rāma, Kṛṣṇa smiled gently and immediately freed himself from the coils of the snakes.

आनम्य चापि हस्ताभ्यामुभाभ्यां मध्यमं शिरः ।।
आरुह्याभुग्नशिरसः प्रणनर्त्तोरुविक्रमः ।। ४४ ।।

And catching with both his hands the middle hood of the serpent-king, that highly powerful (Kṛṣṇa) bent it down and set his foot upon the hitherto-unbended hood, and danced upon it victoriously.

प्राणाः फणेऽभवंश्चास्य कृष्णस्यांघ्रिनिकुट्टनैः ।।
यत्रोन्नतिं च कुरुते ननामास्य ततश्शिरः ।। ४५ ।।

And the hood of the serpent was bruised by the treading of Kṛṣṇa's feet, and wherever the snake attempted to raise his head, it was again trodden down.

मूर्च्छामुपाययौ भ्रांत्या नागः कृष्णस्य रेचकैः ।।
दंडपातनिपातेन ववाम रुधिरं बहु ।। ४६ ।।

Trampled upon by the feet of Kṛṣṇa as thy changed position in the dance, the snakes fainted and vomitted froth much blood.

तं विभुग्नशिरोग्रीवमास्येभ्यस्स्रुतशोणितम् ।।
विलोक्य करुणं जग्मुस्तत्पत्न्यो मधुसूदनम् ।। ४७ ।।

Seeing the head and neck of their king thus bruised and blood flowing from this mouth, the females of the snake-king implored the mercy of the slayer of Madhu.

नागपत्न्य ऊचुः

ज्ञातोऽसि देवदेवेश सर्वज्ञस्त्वमनुत्तमः ।।
परं ज्योतिरचिंत्यं यत्तदंशः परमेश्वरः ।। ४८ ।।

The females of the serpent-king said—"We have recognized thee, O god of gods, O Supreme lord of all. Thou art a portion of that supreme light and the mighty lord.

न समर्थाः सुरास्स्तोतुं यमनन्यभवं विभुम्।।
स्वरूपवर्णनं तस्य कथं योषित्करिष्यति।। ४९।।

Thou art the self-existent lord and even the celestials are unable to praise thee worthily, and how can the females truly chant thy glories?

यस्याऽखिलमहीर्व्योमजलाग्निपवनात्मकम्।।

How can we sing his glories whose portions are earth, sky, water, fire and air?

ब्रह्मांडमल्पकाल्पांशः स्तोष्यामस्तं कथं वयम्।।५०।।

यमतो न विदुर्नित्यं यत्स्वरूपं हि योगिनः।।
परमार्थमणोरल्पं स्थूलात्स्थूलं नताः स्म तम्।।५१।।

न यस्य जन्मने धाता यस्य चांताय नांतकः।।
स्थितिकर्त्ता न चान्योस्ति यस्य तस्मै नमस्सदा।।५२।।

Even the holy ascetics have in vain sought to know thy real essence. We bow to that form, which is the most subtiles of atoms, the largest of the large; to him whose birth is without a creator, whose end knows no destroyer and who alone is the cause of duration.

कोपः स्वल्पोऽपि ते नास्ति स्थितिपालनमेव ते।।
कारणं कालिय स्यास्य दमने श्रूयतां वचः।।५३।।

There is no anger in thee, thou protected the world and hence this punishment of Kālīya. Hear us.

स्त्रियोनुकंप्यास्साधूनां मूढा दीनाश्च जंतवः।।
यतस्ततोस्य दीनस्य क्षम्यतां क्षमतांवर।। ५४।।

The virtuous should pity women; and creatures are pitied even by the fools; let therefore the foremost of the forgiving have comparison upon this poor creature.

समस्त जगदाधारो भवानल्पबलः फणी।।
त्वत्पादपीडितो जह्यान्मुहूर्त्तार्द्धेन जीवितम्।। ५५।।

Thou art the upholder of the universe and this snake is gifted with but little strength, if and oppressed by thee, he shall in no time give up his life.

पन्नगोल्पवीर्योऽयं क्व भवान्भुवनाश्रयः।।
प्रीतिद्वेषौ समोत्कृष्टगोचरौ भवतोऽव्यय।। ५६।।

ततः कुरु जगत्स्वामिन्प्रसादमवसीदतः।।
प्राणांस्त्यजति नागोऽयं भर्तृभिक्षा प्रदीयताम्।।५७।।

भुवनेश जगन्नाथ महापुरुषपूर्वज।।
प्राणांस्त्यजति नागोऽयं भर्तृभिक्षां प्रयच्छ नः।।५८।।

वेदांतवेद्य देवेश दुष्टदैत्यनिरबर्हण।।
प्राणांस्त्यजति नागोऽयं भर्तृभिक्षा प्रदीयताम्।।५९।।

There is a vast difference between this poor serpent of limited strength and thyself in whom the world reposes. Friendship and enmity are felt towards equals and superiors and not for those who are infinitely inferior to us. This unfortunate snake is about to die,—give us therefore, as a matter of charity, our husband!"

श्रीपराशर उवाच

इत्युक्ते ताभिराश्वस्य क्लांतदेहोपि पन्नगः।।
प्रसीद देवदेवेति प्राह वाक्यं शनैः शनैः।। ६०।।

Parāśara said :—When the wives of the serpent-king had said this, he, too, although wearied, repeated feebly his prayers for clemency.

कालिय उवाच

तवाष्टगुणमैश्वर्यं नाथ स्वाभाविकं परम्।।
निरस्तातिशयं यस्य तस्य स्तोष्यामि किन्न्वहम्।। ६१।।

"Pardon me" he said—"O god of gods, how shall I address thee, who art possessed, through thine own strength and essence, of the eight great faculties and art in energy unmatched?

त्वं परस्त्वं परस्याद्यः परं त्वत्तः परात्मक।।
परस्मात्परमो यस्त्वं तस्य स्तोष्यामि किन्न्वहम्।। ६२।।

Thou art the Supreme, the originator of the supreme; thou art the supreme spirit and from thee, the Supreme proceeds : thou art beyond all finite objects : how can I sing thy glories?

यस्माद्ब्रह्मा च रुद्रश्च चंद्रेंद्रमरुदश्विनः।।
वसवश्च सहादित्यैस्तस्य स्तोष्यमि किन्त्वहम्।। ६३।।

एकावयवसूक्ष्मांशो यस्यैतदखिलं जगत्।।
कल्पनावयवस्यांशस्तस्य स्तोष्यामि किन्न्वहम्।। ६४।।

सदसद्रूपिणो यस्य ब्रह्माद्यास्त्रिदशेश्वराः।।
परमार्थं न जानंति तस्य स्तोष्यमि किन्त्वहम्।। ६५।।

ब्रह्माद्यैरर्चिते यस्तु गंधपुष्पानुलेपनैः।।
नंदनादिसमुद्भूतैस्सोर्च्यते वा कथं मया।। ६६।।

How can I chant his greatness from whom have sprung Brahmā, Rudra, Candra, Indra, the Maruts, the Aśvins, the Vasus and the Ādityas—of whom but, a small portion is the whole universe, which is destined to represent his essence and whose, nature, primitive or derived is beyond the conception of Brahmā and other immortals. How can I approached him who is worshipped by the celestials with incense and flowers culled from the groves of Nandana?

यस्यावताररूपाणि देवराजस्सदार्च्चति।।
न वेत्ति परमं रूपं सोऽर्च्यते वा कथं मया।। ६७।।

How can I adore him whose incarnate portion are being worshipped even by the king of celestials and whose real nature he is not conscious of?

विषयेभ्यस्समावृत्त्य सर्वाक्षाणि च योगिनः।।
यमर्चयंति ध्यानेन सोऽर्च्यते वा कथं मया।। ६८।।

हृदि संकल्प्य यद्रूपं ध्यानेनार्चंति योगिनः।।
भावपुष्पादिना नाथः सोर्च्यते वा कथं मया।। ६९।।

How can I approach him, whom the sages, having their minds withdrawn from external objects, worship in thought and enshrining whose image in their hearts present to it the flowers of sanctity?

सोऽहं ते देवदेवेश नार्चनादौ स्तुतौ न च।।
सामर्थ्यवान् कृपामात्रमनोवृत्तिः प्रसीद मे।। ७०।।

I am quite unable, O god of gods, to worship thee or sing the glories—by thy mercy only, be thou propitiated with me.

सर्पजातिरियं क्रूरा यस्यां जातोस्मि केशव।।
तत्स्वभावोऽयमत्रास्ति नापराधो ममाच्युत।। ७१।।

O Keśava, the serpents are by nature, crooked. I am born in that race, so I am also wily, which is the characteristic of my own race, so I am not to blame in this, O Acyuta.

सृज्यते भवता सर्वं तथा संह्रीयते जगत्।।
जातिरूपस्वभावाश्च सृज्यंते सृजता त्वया।। ७२।।

Every thing has created by thee and every thing is being destroyed by thee—and the species, form and nature of all thing in the world, are thy work.

यथाहं भवता सृष्टो जात्यारूपेण चेश्वर।।
स्वभावेन च साधुत्वं तथेदं चेष्टितं मया।। ७३।।

Even such and I as thou hast created me in kind, in form and in nature. Such am I and such are my actions.

यद्यन्यथा प्रवर्त्तेयं देवदेव ततो मयि।।
न्याऽयो दण्डनिपातो वै तवैव वचनं यथा।। ७४।।

Should I act differently then indeed should I deserve punishment; so thou hast destined.

तथाप्यज्ञे जगत्स्वामिन्दंडं पातितवान्मयि।।
स श्लाघ्योयं परो दंडस्त्वत्तो मे नान्यतो वरः।। ७५।।

And that I have been punished by thee, is indeed a blessing—for punishment from thee alone is a favour.

हतवीर्यो हतविषो दमितोऽहं त्वयाऽच्युत।।
जीवितं दीयतामेकमाज्ञापय करोमि किम्।। ७६।।

Behold I am now divested of strength and poison—deprived of both by thee. Save my life—I ask no more. Order me what shall I do." Being thus addressed by Kālīya.

श्रीभगवानुवाच

नात्र स्थेयं त्वया सर्प कदाचिद्यमुनाजले।।
सपुत्रपरिवारस्त्वं समुद्रसलिलं व्रज।। ७७।।
मत्पदानि च ते सर्प दृष्ट्वा मूर्द्धनि सागरे।।
गरुडः पन्नगरिपुस्त्वयि न प्रहरिष्यति।। ७८।।

Kṛṣṇa said—"You must not wait here any more; go immediately, with your family and followers, to the sea. Garuḍa, the enemy of the serpents, will not injure thee if he sees the impressions of my feet upon your hood."

श्रीपराशर उवाच

इत्युक्त्वा सर्पराजं तं मुमोच भगवान्हरिः।।
प्रणम्य सोपि कृष्णाय जगाम पयसां निधिम्।। ७९।।

पश्यतां सर्वभूतानां सभृत्यसुतबांधवः।।
समस्तभार्यासहितः परित्यज्य स्वकं ह्रदम्।। ८०।।

Parāśara said :—Having said this, Hari liberated the serpent-king, who, respectfully bowing to his victor, went to the ocean accompanied by all his wives, servants and children, leaving the sight of all and the pool he had lived in.

गते सर्पे परिष्वज्य मृतं पुनरिवागतम्।।
गोपा मूर्द्धनि हार्देन सिषिचुर्नेत्रजैर्जलैः।। ८१।।

When the snake had departed, the cowherds received back Govinda as one risen from dead and embraced him and bathed his forehead with tears of joy.

कृष्णमक्लिष्टकर्माणमन्ये विस्मितचेतस।।
तुष्टुवुर्मुदिता गोपा दृष्ट्वा शिवजलां नदीम्।। ८२।।

Others, considering the water of the river pure, were filled with surprise, and chanted the glory of Kṛṣṇa, who is above the influence of actions.

गीयमानः स गोपीभिश्चरितैस्साधुचेष्टितैः।।
संस्तूयमानो गोपैश्च कृष्णौ व्रजमुपागमत्।। ८३।।

Being thus glorified by his illustrious exploits and eulogized by the cow-herds and their wives, Kṛṣṇa came back to Vraja.

।। इति श्रीविष्णुमहापुराणे पञ्चमेंशे सप्तमोऽध्यायः।। ७।।

अथ पञ्चमेंशेः अष्टमोऽध्यायः

Part V : Section 8

श्रीपराशर उवाच

गाः पालयंतौ च पुनः सहितौ बलकेशवौ।।
भ्रममाणौ वने तस्मिन्रम्यं तालवनं गतौ।। १।।

Parāśara said :—Thereupon again driving their cattle, Keśava and Balarāma rambled together in the forest, and on one occasion went to a pleasing grove of palms.

तत्तु तालवनं दिव्यं धेनुको नाम दानवः।।
मृगमांसकृताहारः सदाध्यास्ते खराकृतिः।। २।।

There lived in that pleasing grove a demon named Dhenuka, resembling an ass in appearance and living upon the flesh of deer.

तत्तु तालवनं पक्वफलसंपत्समन्वितम्।।
दृष्ट्वा स्पृहान्विता गोपा फलादानेऽब्रुवन्वचः।। ३।।

Beholding the fruits there ripe, the cowherds, being anxious to take them, said—

गोपा ऊचुः

हे राम हे कृष्ण सदा धेनु केनैष रक्ष्यते।।
भूप्रदेशो यतस्तस्मात्पक्वानीमानि संति वै।। ४।।

फलानि पश्य तालानां गंधामोदितदिंशि वै।।
वयमेतान्यभीप्सामः पात्यंतां यदि रोचते।। ५।।

"O Rāma! O Kṛṣṇa! Dhenuka always lives here and therefore the trees are loaded with ripe fruits the smell of which perfumes the air. We wish to eat some. Will you throw some down?"

श्रीपराशर उवाच

इति गोपकुमाराणां श्रुत्वा संकर्षणो वचः।।
एतत्कर्त्तव्यमित्युक्त्वा पातयामास तानि वै।।
कृष्णश्च पातयामास भुवितानि फलानि वै।। ६।।

Hearing those words, Kṛṣṇa and Saṅkarṣaṇa brought down some fruits on the ground.

फलानां पततां शब्दमाकर्ण्य सुदुरासदः।।
आजगाम स दुष्टात्मा कोपाद्दैतेयगर्दभः।। ७।।

Hearing the sound of the falling fruits, the dreadful and malignant demons Dhenuka, having the countenance of an ass, arrived there speedily, and being angry began to kick Rāma on the breast with his hinder heels.

पद्भ्यामुभाभ्यां स तदा पश्चिमाभ्यां बलं बली।।
जघानोरसि ताभ्यां च स च तेनाभ्यगृह्यत्।। ८।।

गृहीत्वा भ्रामयामास सोंऽबरे गतजीवितम्।।
तस्मिन्नेव स चिक्षेप वेगेन तृणराजनि।। ९।।

ततः फलान्यनेकानि तालाग्रान्निपतन्खरः ।।
पृथिव्यां पातयामास महावातो घनानिव ।। १० ।।

Catching him by his both hind legs, Rāma however hurled him round till he died; then he threw up the dead body to the top of the palm tree from the branches of which it struck down enough fruits like rain drops poured down on earth by the wind.

अन्यानथ सजातीयानागतान्दैत्यगर्दभान् ।।
कृष्णश्चिक्षेप तालाग्रे बलभद्रश्च लीलया ।। ११ ।।
क्षणेनालंकृता पृथ्वी पक्वैस्तालफलैस्तदा ।।
दैत्य गर्दभदेहैश्च मैत्रेय शुशुभेऽधिकम् ।। १२ ।।

The relatives of Dhenuka came running to his help, and Kṛṣṇa and Rāma did the same thing with them until the trees were filled with dead asses and the ground was covered with ripe fruits.

ततो गावो निराबाधास्तस्मिंस्तालवने द्विज ।।
नवशष्पं सुखं चेरुर्यन्न भुक्तमभूत्पुरा ।। १३ ।।

Thenceforth the cattle grazed unobstructed in the palm groves and cropped the new pasturage where they had never gone before.

।। इति श्रीविष्णुमहापुराणे पञ्चमेंशेऽष्टमोऽध्यायः ।। ८ ।।

अथ पञ्चमेंशेः नवमोऽध्यायः

Part V : Section 9

श्रीपराशर उवाच

तस्मिन्नासभदैतेये सानुगे विनिपातिते ।।
सौम्यं तद्गोपगोपीनां रम्यं तालवनं जभौ ।। १ ।।

Parāśara said :—That demon, in the form of an ass, and all his relatives, being slain, the cow-herds and their wives began to roam at pleasure in that picturesque grove of palms.

ततस्तौ जातहर्षौ तु वसुदेवसुतावुभौ ।।
हत्वा धेनुकदैतेयं भांडीरवटमागतौ ।। २ ।।

Having slain that friend Dhenuka, the two sons of Vasudeva, greatly delighted, repaired to the Bhāṇḍira fig-tree.

क्ष्वेलमानौ प्रगायंतौ विचिन्वंतौ च पादपान् ।।
चारयंतौ च गा दूरे व्याहरंतौ च नामभिः ।। ३ ।।
निर्योगपाशस्कंधौ तौ वनमालाविभूषितौ ।।
शुशुभाते महात्मानौ बालश्रृंगाविवर्षभौ ।। ४ ।।

They began to roam about shouting and singing and collecting fruits and flowers from the trees—sometimes driving the cattle to a distant pasture, sometimes calling them by their names, sometimes carrying the foot-ropes of the kine upon their shoulds, sometimes decorating themselves with garlands of forest flowers, they appeared like two young bulls when the horns first appear.

सुवर्णाञ्जनचूर्णाभ्यां तौ तदा रूषितांबरौ ।।
महेंद्रायुधसंयुक्तौ श्वेतकृष्णाविवांबुदौ ।। ५ ।।

Dressed, the one in yellow and and the other in able garments, they appeared like two clouds one white and one black, surmounted by the bow of Indra.

चेरतुर्लोकसिद्धाभिः क्रीडाभिरितरेतरम् ।।
समस्तलोकनाथानां नाथभूतौ भुवं गतौ ।। ६ ।।

The two brothers, although lords of the universe, having descended upon earth, began to sport mutaully with frolics beneficial to the world.

मनुष्यधर्माभिरतौ मानयंतौ मनुष्यताम् ।।
तज्जातिगुणयुक्ताभिः क्रीडाभिश्चेरतुर्वनम् ।। ७ ।।

Adopting human duties and assuming human character and engaged in human sports, they stayed about in the forest.

ततस्त्वांदोलिकाभिश्च नियुद्धैश्च महाबलौ ।।
व्यायामं चक्रतुस्तत्र क्षेपणीयैस्तथाश्मभिः ।। ८ ।।

And these two highly powerful (brothers) engaged in exercise, in swinging upon the boughs of trees or in boxing and wresting and hurling stones.

तल्लिप्सुरसुरस्तत्रह्युभयो रममाणयोः।।
आजगाम प्रलंबाख्यो गोपवेषतिरोहितः।। ९।।

Having seen Kṛṣṇa and Balarāma thus sporting, the Asura Pralamba, on one occasion with a view to carry them away stealthily arrived there assuming, the guise of a cowherd.

सोऽवगाहत निश्शंकस्तेषां मध्यममानुषः।।
मानुषं वपुरा स्थाय प्रलंबो दानवोत्तमः।। १०।।

And that foremost of demons, assuming a human shape, mixed with them, unsuspected.

तयोश्छिद्रांतरप्रेप्सुरविषह्यममन्यत ।।
कृष्णं ततो रौहिणेयं हंतुं चक्रे मनोरथम्।। ११।।

Then seeking their faults he found Kṛṣṇa irrepressible and made up his mind accordingly to slay the son of Rohiṇī.

हरिणाक्रीडनं नाम बालक्रीडनकं ततः।।
प्रकुर्वन्तो हि ते सर्वे द्वौद्वौ युगपदुत्थितौ।। १२।।

The boys commenced playing at the game of leaping like deer, two, and two together.

श्रीदाम्ना सह गोविंदः प्रलंबेन तथा बलः।।
गोपालैरपरैश्चान्ये गोपालाः पुप्लुवुस्ततः।। १३।।

Govinda was matched with Śrīdāmā and Balarāma with Pralamba; the other boys were coupled with one another and went leaping away.

श्रीदामानं ततः कृष्णः प्रलंबं रोहिणीसुतः।।
जितवान्कृष्णपक्षीयैर्गोपैरन्ये पराजिताः।। १४।।

Kṛṣṇa beat his companion and Balarāma his, and the boys who were on Kṛṣṇa's side, were also victorious.

ते वाहयंतस्त्वन्योन्यं भांडीरं वटमेत्य वै।।
पुनर्निववृतुस्सर्वे येये तत्र पराजिताः।। १५।।

The boys who were defeated, carrying the victorious boys on their shoulders went to the Bhaṇḍīra fig and then came back to the starting-place.

संकर्षणं तु स्कंधेन शीघ्रमुत्क्षिप्य दानवः।।
नभस्स्थलं जगामाशु सचंद्र इव वारिदः।। १६।।

And placing Saṅkarṣaṇa speedily on his shoulders the demon Pralamba did not tary there and ran away like unto cloud with the moon.

असहन्रौहिणेयस्य स भारं दानवोत्तमः।।
ववृधे स महाकायः प्रावृषीव बलाहकः।। १७।।

Being unable to carry the weight of Rohiṇī's son that foremost of friends began to increase in bulk like unto a cloud in the rainy season.

संकर्षणस्तु तं दृष्ट्वा दग्धशैलोपमाकृतिम्।।
स्त्रग्दामलंबाभरणं मकुटाटोपमस्तकम्।। १८।।
रौद्रं शकटचक्राक्षं पादन्यास चलत्क्षितिम्।।
अभीतमनसा तेन राक्षसा रोहिणीसुतः।।
ह्रियमाणस्ततः कृष्णमिदं वचनमब्रवीत्।। १९।।

Beholding him like a scorched mountain, his head crowned with a diadem and his neck hung round with garlands, having eyes as large as cart wheels, a fearful form and shaking the earth with his thread, Balarāma called out, as he was carried away,

कृष्णकृष्ण ह्रियाम्येष पर्वतोदग्रमूर्त्तिना।।
केनापि पश्य दैत्येन गोपालच्छद्मरूपिणा।। २०।।
यदत्र सांप्रतं कार्यं मया मधुनिषूदन।।
तत्कथ्यतां प्रयात्येष दुरात्मातित्वरान्वितः।। २१।।

"Kṛṣṇa, Kṛṣṇa! I am carried off by some demon, disguised as a cow-herd and huge as a mountain! what shall I do? Tell me Madhusūdana, the villian runs away speedily."

श्रीपराशर उवाच

तमाह रामं गोविंदस्स्मितभिन्नोष्ठसंपुटः।।
महात्मा रौहिणेयस्य बलवीर्यप्रमाणवित्।। २२।।

Parāśara said :—The high-souled Kṛṣṇa, cognisant of the prowess and strength of the son of Rohiṇī, opened his mouth, smiling and said—

श्रीकृष्ण उवाच

किमयं मानुषो भावो व्यक्तमेवावलंब्यते।।
सर्वात्मन् सर्वगृह्यानां गुह्यगुह्यात्मना त्वया।। २३।।

स्मराशेषजगद्बीजकारणं कारणाग्रज।।
आत्मानमेकं तद्वच्च जगत्येकार्णवे च यत्।। २४।।

"O thou the soul of all, the cause of all cause and all that is alone when the world the destroyed, why art thou assuming clearly the character of a man?

किं न वेत्सि यथाहं च त्वं चैकं कारणं भुवः।।
भारावतारणार्थाय मर्त्यलोकमुपागतौ।। २५।।

Dost thou not know that you and are alike the origin of the world and have come to relieve it of its load?

नभश्शिरस्तेंबुवहाश्च केशाः पादो क्षितिर्वक्त्रमनंतवह्निः।।
सोमो मनस्ते श्वसितं समीरणो दिशश्चतस्त्रोऽव्यय बाहवस्ते।।
२६।।

The sky is thy head; the waters are thy person; earth is thy feet; eternal fire is thy mouth; the moon is thy mind; the wind is thy breath; the four regions are thy arms and hands.

सहस्त्रवक्त्रो भगवान्महात्मा सहस्त्रहस्तांघ्रिशरीरभेदः।।
सहस्त्रपद्मोद्भवयोनिराद्यस्सहस्त्रशस्त्वां मुनयो गृणंति।।
२७।।

O high-souled and highly-powerful lord, thou hast a thousand heads, a thousand hands and feet and bodies. Thou art the beginning of all creation—Brahmā, sprung from lotus—and the sages have praised thee in these terms for a thousand times.

दिव्यं हि रूपं तव वेत्ति नान्यो देवैरशेषैरवताररूपम्।।
तदर्च्यते वेत्सि न किं यदंते त्वय्येव विश्वं लयमभ्युपैति।।
२८।।

No one else knoweth thy divine person. The celestials worship only thy incarnate person. Dost thou not know that in the end the whole world will disappear in thee?

त्वया धृतेयं धरणी बिभर्त्ति चराचरं विश्वमनंतमूर्त्ते।।
कृतादिभेदैरज कालरूपो निमेषपूर्वो जगदेतदत्सि।। २९।।

O thou of endless forms, thou art upholding all creation, mobile and immobile. Thou, being indentical with time with its division of hours and minutes, devourest the world.

अत्तं यथा वाडववह्निनांबु हिमस्वरूपं परिगृह्य कास्तम्।।
हिमाचले भानुमतोंशुसंगाज्जलत्वमभ्येति पुनस्तदेव।।
३०।।

एवं त्वया संहरणेऽत्तमेतज्जगत्समस्तं त्वदधीनकं पुनः।।
तवैव सर्गाय समुद्यतस्य जगत्त्वमभ्येत्यसुकल्पमीश।।
३१।।

As the waters of the sea, when swallowed up by submarine fire, are transferred into winds and thrown in the form of snow upon Himācala, where coming in contact with the rays of the sun, re-assume the watery nature, so this world, devoured by thee at the time of dissolution, is again created by thee at the end of a Kalpa through thy creative energy.

भवानहं च विश्वात्मन्नेकमेव च कारणाम्।।
जगतोस्य जगत्यर्थे भेदेनावां व्यवस्थितौ।। ३२।।

Thou and I, soul of the universe, are but one and the same cause of the creation of earth, although for its protection we exist as distinct individuals.

तत्स्मर्यताममेयात्मंस्त्वयात्मा जहि दानवम्।।
मानुष्यमेवावलंब्य बंधूनां क्रियतां हितम्।। ३३।।

Bringing to thy memory, who thou art, O being of illimitable prowess, destroy thyself the demon. Suspending a while your human character, do what is right."

श्रीपराशर उवाच

इति संस्मारितो विप्र कृष्णेन सुमहात्मना।।
विहस्य पीडयामास प्रलंबं बलवान्बलः।। ३४।।

मुष्टिना सोहनन्मूर्ध्नि कोपसं रक्तलोचनः।।

Thus reminded by the noble Kṛṣṇa, the powerful Balarāma laughed and crushed Pralamba with his knees striking him simultaneously on the head and face with his fists so as to beat out both his eyes.

तेन चास्य प्रहारेण बहिर्याते विलोचने।। ३५।।

स निष्कासितमस्तिष्को मुखाच्छोणितमुद्वमन्।।
निपपात महीपृष्ठे दत्यवर्यो ममार च।। ३६।।

Vomitting blood from his mouth and having his brain forced through the skull, the demon fell upon the ground and died.

प्रलंबं निहतं दृष्ट्वा बलेनाद्भुताकर्मणा।।
प्रहृष्टास्तुष्टुवुर्गोपास्साधुसाध्विति चाब्रुवन्।। ३७।।

Seeing Pralamba slain the cow-herds were surprised and rejoiced and exclaimed "Well done!" and praised Balarāma.

संस्तूयमानो गोपैस्तु रामो दैत्ये निपातिते।।
प्रलंबे सह कृष्णेन पुनर्गाकुलमाययौ।। ३८।।

Thus praised by his play-mates and accompanied by Kṛṣṇa, Balarāma, after the death of the demon Pralamba, came back to Gokula.

।। इति श्रीविष्णुमहापुराणे पञ्चमेंशे नवमोऽध्यायः।। ९।।

अथ पञ्चमेंशेः दशमोऽध्यायः

Part V Section 10

श्रीपराशर उवाच

तयोर्विहरतोरेवं रामकेशवयोर्व्रजे।।
प्रावृड् व्यतीता विकसत्सरोजा चाभवच्छरत्।। १।।

Parāśara said :—Whilst Kṛṣṇa and Rāma were thus sporting in Vraja the rainy season ended—the autumn appeared and the lotuses became full-blown.

अवापुस्तापमत्यर्थं शफर्यः पल्वलोदके।।
पुत्रक्षेत्रादिसक्तेन ममत्वेन यथा गृही।। २।।

The Safari fish in their watery burrows, were oppressed by the heat like a man by his selfish desires, who is attached to his family.

मयूरा मौनमातस्थुः परित्यक्तमदा वने।।
असारतां परिज्ञाय संसारस्येव योगिनः।। ३।।

The peacocks, renouncing all amusements, became silent like the ascetics withdrawing themselves from worldly enjoyments considering their unreality.

उत्सृज्य जलसर्वस्वं विमलास्सितमूर्त्तयः।।
तत्यजुश्चांबरं मेघा गृहं विज्ञानिनो यथा।। ४।।

The clouds of shining whiteness, exhausted of their watery wealth, deserted the sky like the wise who have acquired wisdom, departing from their home.

शरत्सूर्यांशुतप्तानि ययुश्शोषं सरांसि च।।
बह्वालंबममत्वेन हृदयानीव देहिनाम्।। ५।।

Evaporated by the rays of the autumnal sun, the lakes were dried up, like the hearts of men withered by the contact of selfishness.

कुमुदैश्शरदंभांसि योग्यतालक्षणं ययुः।।
अवबोधैर्मनांसीव समत्वममलात्मनाम्।। ६।।

The silent water of the autumn were beautified by white water-lilies, like the minds of the pure by the perception of truth.

तारकाविमले व्योम्नि रराजाखंडमंडलः।।
चंद्रश्चरमदेहात्मो योगी साधुकुले यथा।। ७।।

The moon shone with undiminished brilliance in the sky crested with star like the saint, who has reached the last stage of bodily existence in the company of the pious.

शनकैश्शनकैस्तीरं तत्यजुश्च जलाशयाः।।
ममत्वं क्षेत्रपुत्रादिरूढमुच्चैर्यथा बुधाः।। ८।।

The rivers and lakes slowly went far off from their banks as the wise by degrees shrink from the selfish attachment that connects them with their wife and children.

पूर्वं त्यक्तैस्सरोंभोभिर्हंसा योगं पुनर्ययुः।।
क्लेशैः कुयोगिनो शेषैरंतरायहता इव।। ९।।

The swans again began to frequent those lakes which they had abandoned before like false ascetics whose devotions had abandoned before like false ascetics whose devotions are interrupted and they are again stricken with numberless afflictions.

निभृतो भवदत्यर्थं समुद्रस्स्तिमितोदकः।।
क्रमावाप्तमहायोगो निश्चलात्मा यथा यतिः।। १०।।

The ocean, with silent waters, became perfectly calm like the accomplished saint who has gone through rigid penances and has acquired undisturbed tranquility of spirit.

सर्वत्रातिप्रसन्नानि सलिलानि तथाऽभवन्।।
ज्ञाते सर्वगते विष्णौ मनांसीव सुमेधसाम्।। ११।।

Everywhere the waters are as clear and pure as the minds of the wise who behold Viṣṇu in all things.

बभूव निर्मलं व्योम शरदा ध्वस्ततोयदम्।।
योगाग्निदग्धक्लेशौघं योगिनामिव मानसम्।। १२।।

The autumnal sky was perfectly free from clouds like the heart of the ascetic, whose cares have been devoured by the fire of devotion.

सूर्यांशुजनितं तापं निन्ये तारापतिः शमम्।।
अहंमानोद्भवं दुःखं विवेकः सुमहानिव।। १३।।

The moon allayed the fervours of the sun as discrimination removes the pain consequent upon egotism.

नभसोब्दं भुवः पंकं कालुष्यं चांभसश्शरत्।।
इंद्रियाणींद्रियार्थेभ्यः प्रत्याहार इवाहरत्।। १४।।

The autumn removed the clouds from the sky; the muddiness of the earth and the discoloration of the waters, as abstraction draws away the senses from the objects of perception.

प्राणायाम इवांभोभिस्सरसां कृतपूरकैः।।
अभ्यस्यतेऽनुदिवसं रेचकाकुंभकादिभिः।। १५।।

The water of the lake, by becoming full, stationary and again declined, performed as if the exercise of inspiring, suppressing and expiring the vital air.

विमलांबरनक्षत्रे काले चाभ्यागते व्रजे।।
ददर्शेंद्रो महारंभायोद्यतांस्तान्व्रजौकसः।। १६।।

At this season, when the heavens were clear and bright with stars, Kṛṣṇa, once repairing to Vraja, saw the inhabitants engaged in the celebration of a sacrifice in honour of Śakra.

कृष्णस्तानुत्सुकान्दृष्ट्वा गोपानुत्सवलालसान्।।
कौतूहलादिदं वाक्यं प्राह वृद्धान्महामतिः।। १७।।

Beholding all the cow-herds busily and anxiously engaged in making preparation, Kṛṣṇa, gifted with high intellect, as if, out of curiosity asked the elders, saying—

कोऽयं शक्रमहो नाम येन वो हर्ष आगतः।।
प्राह तं नंदगोपश्च पृच्छंमतिसादरम्।। १८।।

"What festival of Śakra is this, in which you are taking so much delight?" To him thus asking, the cow-herd thus lovingly said—

नंदगोप उवाच

मेघानां पयसां चेशो देवराजश्शतक्रतुः।।
तेन सञ्चोदिता मेघा वर्षंत्यंबुमयं रसम्।। १९।।
तद्वृष्टिजनितं सस्यं वयमन्ये च देहिनः।।
वर्त्तयामोपयुञ्जानास्तर्पयामश्च देवताः।। २०।।

"Śatakratu (performer of hundred sacrifices), the king of the celestials, is the lord of the clouds and waters; ordered by him the clouds pour down water on earth, by which the grain is produced, on which we and other embodied beings live and by which we please the gods.

क्षीरवत्य इमा गावो वत्सवत्यश्च निर्वृताः।।
तेन संवर्द्धितैस्स्यैस्तुष्टाः पुष्टा भवंति वै।। २१।।

By this too these cows bear calves and give milk and are happy and well-nourished.

नासस्या नातृणा भूमिर्न बुभुक्षार्दितो जनः।।
दृश्यते यत्र दृश्यंते वृष्टिमंतो बलाहकाः।। २२।।

Wherever the clouds pour waters, the earth is neither barren of corn, nor bare of verdure, nor is man stricken with hunger.

भौममे तत्पयो दुग्धं गोभिः सूर्यस्य वारिदैः।।
पार्जन्यस्सर्वलोकस्योद्भवाय भुवि वर्षति।। २३।।

Having drunk the milk of the earth by means of the rays of the sun, Indra, the giver of water, pours it again on earth for the sustenance of all the worlds.

तस्मात्प्रावृषि राजानस्सर्वे शक्रं मुदा युताः।।
मखैस्सुरेशमर्चन्ति वयमन्ये च मानवाः।। २४।।

For this reason all sovereign princes offer,

with delight, sacrifices to Indra at the end of the rainy reason, and so also do we and so do the other people."

श्रीपराशर उवाच

नंदगोपस्य वचनं श्रुत्वेत्थं शक्रपूजने।।
रोषाय त्रिदशेंद्रस्य प्राह दामोदरस्तदा।। २५।।

Parāśara said :—Having heard the words of the cow-herd Nanda regarding the worship of Śakra, Dāmodara, to excite the anger of the lord of celestials, said—

न वयं कृषिकर्त्तारो वाणिज्याजीवनो न च।।
गावोस्मद्दैवतं तात वयं वनचरा यतः।। २६।।

"We, father, are neither cultivators of the soil, nor merchants—we are sojourners in the forests and cows are our gods.

आन्विक्षिकी त्रयी वार्त्ता दंडनीतिस्तथा परा।।
विद्या चतुष्टयं चैतद्वार्त्तामात्रं शृणुष्व मे।। २७।।

There are four divisions of knowledge—logical spiritual, practical, and political. Hear from me, what is the practical science.

कृषिर्वणिज्या तद्वच्च तृतीयं पशुपालनम्।।
विद्या ह्येका महाभाग वार्त्ता वृत्तित्रयाश्रया।। २८।।

Agriculture, commerce and tending of cattle—the knowledge of these three professions, O noble Sire, is the practical science.

कर्षकाणां कृषिर्वृत्तिः पण्यं विपणिजीविनाम्।।
अस्माकं गौः परावृत्तिर्वार्त्ताभेदैरियं त्रिभिः।। २९।।

Agriculture is the means of subsistence to the cultivators, buying and selling to the traders, and tending of cattle is our subsistence.

विद्यया यो यया युक्तस्तस्य सा दैवतं महत्।।
सैव पूज्यार्चनीया च सैव तस्योपकारिका।। ३०।।

The practical science has thus been divided into three branches. The object, that is cultivated by any one, should be to him, his chief deity—he must worship that, for that is his benefactor.

यो यस्य फलमश्नन्वै पूजयत्यपरं नरः।।
इह च प्रेत्य चैवासौ न तदाप्नोति शोभनम्।। ३१।।

O father, the man who worships another's deity, receiving the fruit from his own, does not obtain a prosperous sitaution either in this world or in the next.

कृष्यांता प्रथिता सीमा सीमांतं च पुनर्वनम्।।
वनांता गिरयस्सर्वे ते चास्माकं परा गतिः।। ३२।।

Where the land is no longer cultivated there are limits assigned, beyond which begins the forest; the forests are bounded by the hills and so far do our limits extend.

न द्वारबंधा वरणा न गृहक्षेत्रिणस्तथा।।
सुखिनस्त्वखिले लोके यथा वै चक्रचारिणः।। ३३।।

We are not confined within doors or walls, we have neither fields nor homes; we wander about happily wherever we like in our waggons[1].

श्रूयंते गिरयश्चैव वनेस्मिन्कामरूपिणः।।
तत्तद्रूपं समास्थाय रमंते स्वेषु सानुषु।। ३४।।

We have heard that the spirits of these mountains, assuming whatever shapes they like, walk in the woods upon their own precipices.

यदा चैते प्रबाध्यंते तेषां ये काननौकसः।।
तदा सिंहादिरूपैस्तान्घातयंति महीधराः।। ३५।।

If they are displeased with those who inhabit the forests, then transforming themselves to lions and beasts of prey, they will like the offenders.

गिरियज्ञस्त्वयं तस्माद्गोयज्ञश्च प्रवर्त्त्यताम्।।
किमस्माकं महेंद्रेण गावश्शैलाश्च देवताः।। ३६।।

We are thus bound to worship the mountains and offer sacrifices to cattle. What have we to do with Indra?

मंत्रयज्ञपरा विप्रास्सीरयज्ञाश्च कर्षकाः।।
गिरिगोयज्ञशीलाश्च वयमद्रिवनाश्रयाः।। ३७।।

Cattle and mountains are our gods.

1. The word in the text is *cakracarina*—it means also those ascetics, who make, wherever they arrive in the evening, their homes.

Brāhmaṇas offer worship with prayer; cultivators of the earth worship their land-marks; but we, who tend our cattle in the forests and mountains, should worship them and our kine.

तस्माद्गोवर्द्धनश्शैलो भवद्भिर्विविधार्हणैः।।
अर्च्यतां पूज्यतां मेध्यान्पशून्हत्या विधानतः।। ३८।।

Let prayer and offerings be then made to the mountain Govardhana and let us duly kill a victim.

सर्वघोषस्य संदोहो गृह्यतां मा विचार्यताम्।।
भोज्यंतां तेन वै विप्रास्तथा ये चाभिवांछकाः।। ३९।।

Let milk be collected from all stations and let us feed Brāhmaṇas and all others who wish to partake of it—no need of any judgment about it.

तत्रार्चिते कृते होमे भोजितेषु द्विजातिषु।।
शरत्पुष्पकृतापीडाः परिगच्छंतु गोगणाः।। ४०।।

When the oblations have been presented and the Brāhmaṇas have been fed let the cowherds circumambulate the cows decorated with garlands of autumnal flowers.

एतन्मम मतं गोपास्संप्रीत्या क्रियते यदि।।
ततः कृता भवेत्प्रीतिर्गवामद्रेस्तथा मम।। ४१।।

If the cow-herds pay attention to these suggestions, they will secure the favour of the mountain of the cattle and also mind."

श्रीपराशर उवाच

इति तस्य वचः श्रुत्वा नंदाद्यास्ते व्रजौकसः।।
प्रीत्युत्फुल्लमुखा गोपास्साधुसाध्वित्यथाब्रुवन्।। ४२।।

When Nanda and other cow-herds heard the speech of Kṛṣṇa, their faces were brillient with joy and they said that he had spoken well.

शोभनं ते मतं वत्स यदेतद्भवतोदितम्।।
तत्करिष्यामहे सर्वं गिरियज्ञः प्रवर्त्त्यताम्।। ४३।।

"You have judged alright, child" exclaimed they "we will do exactly as you have said and offer worship to the mountain."

तथा च कृतवंतस्ते गिरियज्ञं व्रजौकसः।।
दधिपायसमांसाद्यैर्ददुश्शैलबलिं ततः।। ४४।।
द्विजांश्च भोजयामासुश्शतशोऽथ सहस्रशः।। ४५।।
गावश्शैलं ततश्चक्रुरर्चितास्ताः प्रदक्षिणम्।।
वृषभाश्चातिनर्दंतस्सतोया जलदा इव।। ४६।।

Accordingly the inhabitants of Vraja worshiped the mountain presenting to it curds and milk and flesh; and they fed hundreds and thousands of Brāhmaṇas and many other guests who came to the ceremony even as Kṛṣṇa had directed; and when they had made heir offerings they circumambulated the cows and the bulls that cried as loud as roaring clouds.

गिरिमूर्द्धनि कृष्णोऽपि शैलोहमिति मूर्त्तिमान्।।
बुभुजेन्नं बहुतरं गोपवर्याहृतं द्विज।। ४७।।
स्वेनैव कृष्णो रूपेण गोपैस्सह गिरेश्शिरः।।
अधिरुह्यार्चयामास द्वितीयामात्मनस्तनुम्।। ४८।।

Upon the summit of Govaradhana Kṛṣṇa stood and said "I am the mountain" and partook of the food presented by the cow-herds; whilst in his own form as Kṛṣṇa, he ascended the hill with other cow-herds and worshipped his other self.

अंतर्द्धानं गते तस्मिन्गोपा लब्ध्वा ततो वरान्।।
कृत्वा गिरिमखं गोष्ठं निजमभ्याययुः पुनः।। ४९।।

Having promised them many blessings the mountain-person of Kṛṣṇa disappeared, and the ceremony being finished the cow-herds returned to their homes.

।। इति श्रीविष्णुमहापुराणे पञ्चमेंशे दशमोऽध्यायः।। १०।।

अथ पञ्चमेंशे: एकादशोऽध्याय:

Part V : Section 11

श्रीपराशर उवाच

मखे प्रतिहते शक्रो मैत्रेयातिरुषान्वित:।।
संवर्त्तकं नाम गणं तोयदानामथाऽब्रवीत्।। १।।

Parāśara said :—Being thus disappointed of offerings in the sacrifice, O Maitreya, Śakra, greatly angry, addressed the attendant clouds called Samvarttaka saying—

भोभो मेघा निशाम्यैतद्वचनं गदतो मम।।
आज्ञानंतरमेवाशु क्रियतामविचारितम्।। २।।

"O ye clouds! hear what I say and do ye speedily execute without any judgment my behests.

नंदगोपस्सुदुर्बुद्धिर्गोपैरन्यैस्सहायवान्।।
कृष्णाश्रयं बलाध्यातो मखभमंगमचीकरत्।। ३।।

The foolish cow-herd Nanda and his companions, relying upon the protection of Krsna have withheld the usual offerings to us.

आजीवो या: परस्तेषां गावस्तस्य च कारणम्।।
तागावो वृष्टिपातेन पीड्यन्तां वचनान्मम।। ४।।

Now therefore, distress the cattle, with wind and rain at my command, that are their subsistance and whence their occupation is derived.

अहमप्यद्रिश्रृंगाभं तुंगमारुह्य बारणम।।
साहाय्यं व: करिष्यामि वाय्वम्बूत्सर्गयोजितम्।।५।।

Ascending my elephant, huge as a mountain summit, I will give you assistance in strengthening the tempest."

श्रीपराशर उवाच

इत्याज्ञप्तास्ततस्तेन मुमुचुस्ते बलाहका:।।
वातवर्षं महाभीममभावाय गवां द्विज।। ६।।

Parāśaras said :—O twice-born one, being thus commanded by the celestials-chief, the cloud came down in a fearful storm of rain and wind to destroy the cattle.

तत: क्षणेन पृथिवी ककुभोंबरमेव च।।
एकं धारामहासारपूरेणनाभवन्मुने।। ७।।

In a moment, the earth the points of the horizon and the sky were all blended into one by the heavy and incessant showers.

विद्युल्लताकषाघातत्रस्तैरिव घनैर्घनम्।।
नादापूरितदिक्चक्रैर्धारासारमपात्यत।। ८।।

Being afraid of the lightning's scourage, the clouds filled the quarters with their muttering and pouring down uninterpted torrents.

अंधकारीकृते लोके वर्षद्भिरनिशं घनै:।।
अधश्चोर्ध्वं च तिर्यक् च जगदाप्यमिवाभवत्।। ९।।

The clouds pouring down waters day and night, the earth was filled with darkness; and above below and on every side the world was filled with water.

गावस्तु तेन पतता वर्षवातेन वेगिना।।
धूता: प्राणाञ्जहुस्सन्नत्रिकसक्थिशिरोधरा:।। १०।।

The cattle, pelted by the storm, shrank cowering into the smallest size or gave up their breath.

क्रोडेन वत्सानाक्रम्य तस्थुरन्या महामुने।।
गावो विवत्साश्च कृता वारिपूरेण चापरा:।। ११।।

Some covered their calves with flanks and some saw their young onces carried away by the flood.

वत्साश्च दीनवदना वातकंपितकंधरा:।।
त्राहित्राहीत्यल्पशब्दा: कृष्णमूचुरिवातुरा:।। १२।।

Trembling in the wind, the calves cast their piteous looks at their mothers or begged, in low moans, as if, the help of Krṣna.

ततस्तद्गोकुलं सर्वं गोगोपीगोपसंकुलम्।।
अतीवार्त्तं हरिर्दृष्ट्वा मैत्रेयाचिंतयत्तदा।। १३।।

Beholding all Gokula moved with terror and cow-herds and cow-herdesses and cattle stricken with consternations, Hari thus thought—

एतत्कृतं महेंद्रेण मखभंगविरोधिना।।
तदेतदखिलं गोष्ठं त्रातव्यमधुना मया।। १४।।

"This is the work of Mahendara, who has been offended for withholding sacrifices from me; it is therefore my duty to defend this village of herdsmen.

इममद्रिमहं धैर्यादुत्पाट्योरुशिखाघनम्।।
धरायिष्यामि गोष्ठस्य पृथुच्छत्रमिवोपरि।। १५।।

I will uplift this spacious mountain from its snowy base and hold it up as a large umbrella over the cow-pens."

श्रीपराशर उवाच

इति कृत्वा मतिं कृष्णो गोवर्द्धनमहीधरम।।
उत्पाट्यैककरेणैव धारयामास लीलया।। १६।।

गोपांश्चाह हसञ्छौरिस्समुत्पाटितभूधरः।।
विशध्वमत्र त्वरिताः कृतं वर्षनिवारणम्।। १७।।

सुनिवातेषु देशेषु यथा जोषमिहास्यताम्।।
प्रविश्यतां न भेतव्यं गिरिपाताच्च निर्भयैः।। १८।।

Having thus made up his mind, Kṛṣṇa immediately upheld the mountain Govardhana with one hand as if in sport, and said to the cow-herds—"Behold the mountain is on high; enter beneath it speedily, and it will shelter you from the storm; here you will be secure and happy in places defended from the wind; enter speedily and fear not that the mountain will fall."

इत्युक्तास्तेन ते गोपा विविशुर्गोधनैस्सह।।
शकटारोपितैर्भांडैर्गोप्यश्चासारपीडिताः।। १९।।

कृष्णोपि तं दधारैव शैलमत्यंतनिश्चलम्।।
व्रजौकवासिभिर्हर्षविस्मिताक्षैर्निरीक्षितः।। २०।।

Thereupon, all the people with their cattle, waggons, goods, women, afflicted as they were by rain, went to the shelter of the mountain which he held steadily over their heads; and Kṛṣṇa, as he supported the mountain, was contemplated with delight and atonishment by the inhabitants of Vraja.

गोपगोपीजनैर्हृष्टैः प्रीतिविस्तारितेक्षणैः।।
संस्तूयमानचरितः कृष्णश्शैलमधारयत्।। २१।।

As his eyes expanded with joy and wonder, the cow-herds and cow-herdesses sang his glories.

सप्तरात्रं महामेघा ववर्षुर्नंदगोकुले।।
इंद्रेण चोदिता विप्र गोपानां नाशकारिणा।। २२।।

For seven days and nights did the vast clouds, despatched by Indra, pour down showers upon the Gokula of Nanda, to destroy the dwellers, but they were protected by the hight of the mountain.

ततो धृते महाशैले परित्राते च गोकुले।।
मिथ्याप्रतिज्ञो बलभिद्वारयामास तान्घनान्।। २३।।

And being baffled in his purpose, the Indra, the destroyer of Bala, ordered the clouds to cease.

व्यभ्रे नभसि देवेंद्रे वितथात्मवचस्यथ।।
निष्क्रम्य गोकुलं हृष्टं स्वस्थानं पुनरागमत्।। २४।।

The threats of Indra having been fruitless and the sky clear, all the inhabitiants of Gokula came out from the shelter and went back to their respective habitations.

मुमोच कृष्णोपि तदा गोवर्द्धनमहाचलम्।।
स्वस्थाने विस्मितमुखैर्दृष्टस्तैस्तु व्रजौकसैः।। २५।।

Then Kṛṣṇa, in the presence of the inhabitants of the forests filled with surprise, restored the great mountain Govardhana to tis original site.

।। इति श्रीविष्णुमहापुराणे पञ्चमेंशे एकादशोऽध्यायः।। ११।।

अथ पञ्चमेंशे: द्वादशोऽध्याय:

Part V : Section 12

श्रीपराशर उवाच

धृते गोवर्द्धने शैले परित्राते च गोकुले।।
रोचयामास कृष्णस्य दर्शनं पाकशासनः।। १।।

Parāśara said :—After the inhabitants of Gokula had been saved by the upholding of the mountain Govardhana, the chastiser of Pāka (Indra) became desirous of seeing Kṛṣṇa.

सोऽधिरुह्य महानागमैरावतममित्रजित्।।
गोवर्द्धनगिरौ कृष्णं ददर्श त्रिदशेश्वरः।। २।।

चारयंतं महावीर्यं गास्तु गोपवपुधर्मरम्।।
कृत्स्नस्य जगतो गोपं वृतं गोपकुमारकैः।। ३।।

Having mounted his huge elephant Airāvata, that lord of the celestials, the destroyer of enemies, beheld the mighty Kṛṣṇa on the mount Govardhana, tending cattle assuming the person of a cow-boy and encircled by the sons of cow-herds, although the protector of the universe.

गरुडं च ददर्शोच्चैरंतर्द्धानगतं द्विज।।
कृतच्छायं हरेर्मूर्ध्नि पक्षाभ्यां पक्षिपुंगवम्।। ४।।

He saw above his head, Garuḍa, the king of birds, invisible to men, spreading out his wings to shade the head of Hari.

अवरुह्य स नागेंद्रादेकांते मधुसूदनम्।।
शक्रस्सस्मितमाहेदं प्रीतिविस्तारितेक्षणः।। ५।।

Descending from his elephant and taking him at a distance, Śakra, having his eyes expanded with delight, said to the Slayer of Madhu—

इंद्र उवाच

कृष्णकृष्ण शृणुष्वेदं यदर्थमहमागतः।।
त्वत्समीपं महाबाहो नैतच्चिंत्यं त्वयाऽन्यथा।। ६।।

Indra said :—"Hear! hear, O Kṛṣṇa, why I have come here; why I have come to thee; do not think otherwise of it.

भारावतारणार्थाय पृथिव्याः पृथिवीतले।।
अवतीर्णोऽखिलाधार त्वमेव परमेश्वर।। ७।।

Thou, O lord, who art the supporter of the universe, hast descended upon earth to relieve her of her burden.

मखभंगविरोधेन मया गोकुलनाशकाः।।
समादिष्टा महामेघास्तैश्चेदं कदनं कृतम्।। ८।।

Being enraged on account of my rites being obstructed, I sent the clouds to deluge Gokula and they have done this evil deed.

त्रातास्ताश्च त्वया गावस्समुत्पाट्य महीधरम्।।
तेनाऽहं तोषितो वीरकर्मणाऽत्युद्धुतेन ते।। ९।।

By upholding the mountain, thou hast preserved the cattle and really, O hero, I am much pleased with thy wonderous deed.

साधितं कृष्ण देवानामहं मन्ये प्रयोजनम्।।
त्वयायमद्रिप्रवरः करेणैकेन यद्धृतः।। १०।।

The object of the celestials is, now, I think, accomplished, for with thy single hand thou hast uplifted this chief of mountains.

गोभिश्च चोदितः कृष्ण त्वत्सकाशमिहागतः।।
त्वया त्राताभिरत्यर्थं युष्मत्सत्कारकारणात्।। ११।।

Being commissioned by the cattle, O Kṛṣṇa, I have come to thee, to honour thee for thou didst save them.

स त्वां कृष्णाभिषेक्ष्यामि गवां वाक्यप्रचोदितः।।
उपेंद्रत्वे गवामिंद्रो गोविंदस्त्वं भविष्यसि।। १२।।

At their words, I shall install thee as Upendra and as the Indra of the cows thou shalt be called Govinda."

श्रीपराशर उवाच

अथोपवाह्यादादाय घंटामैरावताद्गजात्।।
अभिषेकं तया चक्रे पवित्रजलपूर्णया।। १३।।

क्रियमाणेऽभिषेके तु गावः कृष्णस्य तत्क्षणात्।।
प्रस्नवोद्भूतदुग्धार्द्रां सद्यश्चक्रुर्वसुन्धराम्।। १४।।

Saying this, Mahendra took a ewer from his elephant Airāvata and with the holy water it contained performed the regal ceremony of sprinkling. And as the ceremony was being performed, the cattle deluged the earth with their milk.

अभिषिच्य गवां वाक्यादुपेंद्रं वै जनार्दनम्।।
प्रीत्या सप्रश्रयं वाक्यं पुनराह शचीपतिः।। १५।।

गवामेतत्कृतं वाक्यां तथान्यदपि मे शृणु।।
यद्ब्रवीमि महाभाग भारावतरणेच्छया।। १६।।

Having thus inaugurated Kṛṣṇa, Indra, the husband of Śaci, again affectionately said—"I have done this at the request of the cattle; hear, I shall speak something else to thee, O noble one, being desirous of relieving the earth of her burden.

ममांशः पुरुषव्याघ्र पृथिव्यां पृथिवीधर।।
अवतीर्णोऽर्जुनोनाम संरक्षयो भवता सदा।। १७।।

O foremost of men, a portion of mine, under the name of Arjuna, has descended upon earth—do thou protect him always.

भारावतरणे साह्यं स ते वीरः करिष्यति।।
संरक्षणीयो भवता यथात्मा मधुसूदन।। १८।।

He shall assist thee in relieving the earth of her burden. He should be protected by thee, O Slayer of Madhu, like thy own Self."

श्रीभगवानुवाच

जानामि भारते वंशे जातं पार्थं तवांशतः।।
तमहं पालयिष्यामि यावत्स्थास्यामि भूतले।। १९।।

The Deity Self :—"I know that in the family of Bharata, thy son has been born by Pṛthā. I shall protect him as long as I shall live on this earth.

यावन्महीतले शक्र स्थास्याम्यहमरिंदम।।
न तवादर्जुनं कश्चिद्देवेंद्र युधि जेष्यति।। २०।।

O Śakra, O Slayer of foes, O lord of the celestials, as long I shall be on this earth, no one shall be able to vanquish Arjuna in conflict.

कंसो नाम महाबाहुर्दैत्योऽरिष्टस्तथाऽसुरः।।
केशी कुवलयापीडो नरकाद्यास्तथा परे।। २१।।

हतेषु तेषु देवेंद्र भविष्यति महाहवः।।
तत्र विद्धि सहस्राक्ष भारावतरणं कृतम्।। २२।।

The highly powerful Asura Kansa and Ariṣṭa, Keśi, Nāraka and others being slain, there shall take place a terrible conflict, O king of the celestials; know that, O thousnad-eyed deity, as what will relieve earth of her burden.

स त्वं गच्छ न संतापं पुत्रार्थे कर्त्तुमर्हसि।।
नार्जुनस्य रिपुः कश्चिन्ममाग्रे प्रभविष्यति।। २३।।

Do thou go; it behoves thee not to be anxious for thy son. No enemy of Arjuna shall grow in power before me.

अर्जुनार्थे त्वहं सार्वन्युधिष्ठिरपुरोगमान्।।
निवृत्ते भारते युद्धे कुंत्यै दास्याम्यविक्षतान्।। २४।।

For Arjuna I shall render back Yudhiṣṭhira and his brothers to Kuntī after the great battle of Kurukṣetra."

श्रीपराशर उवाच

इत्युक्तः संपरिष्वज्य देवराजो जनार्दनम्।।
आरुह्यैरावतं नागं पुनरेव दिवं ययौ।। २५।।

Parāśara said :—Being thus addressed, the king of the celestials embraced Janārddana and having mounted the elephant Airāvata again went to the celestial region.

कृष्णो हि सहितो गोभिर्गोपालैश्च पुनर्व्रजम्।।
आजगामाऽथ गोपीनां दृष्टिपूतेन वर्त्मना।। २६।।

Kṛṣṇa too with the cow-herds came back to Vraja by the way sanctified by the looks of the females of the cow-herds.

।। इति श्रीविष्णुमहापुराणे पञ्चमेंशे द्वादशोऽध्यायः ।। १२।।

अथ पञ्चमेंशेः त्रयोदशोऽध्यायः

Part V : Section 13

श्रीपराशर उवाच

गते शक्रे तु गोपालाः कृष्णमक्लिष्टकारिणम्।।
ऊचुः प्रीत्या धृतं दृष्ट्वा तेन गोवर्द्धनाचलम्।। १।।

Parāśara said :—Śakra having departed, the cow-herds, on seeing him uplift the mountain Govardhana, said to Kṛṣṇa of wonderous deeds, delightedly :—

वयमस्मान्महाभाग भगवन्महतो भयात्।।
गावश्च भवता त्राता गिरिधारणकर्मणा।। २।।

"O thou of mighty arms, thou hast saved us from a great fear; by holding up the mountain thou hast protected the cows.

बालक्रीडेयमतुला गोपालत्वं जुगुप्सितम्।।
दिव्यं च भवतः कर्म किमेतत्तात कथ्यताम्।। ३।।

Wonderful are thy childish sports and insignificant is the condition of a herdsman and all thy actions are those of a god. Tell us what is the meanings of all this.

कालीयो दमितस्तोये धेनुको विनिपातितः।।
धृतो गोवर्द्धनश्चायं शंकितानि मनांसि नः।। ४।।

Kālīya has been vanquished in the water; Pralamba has been killed; Govardhana has been lifted up; our minds are filled with surprise.

सत्यं सत्यं हरेः पादौ शपामोऽमित विक्रम।।
यथावद्वीर्यमालोक्य न त्वां मन्यामहे नरम्।। ५।।

We can swear by the feet of Hari, O thou of unbounded might, that beholding thy powers we do not consider thee as man.

प्रीतिस्सस्त्रीकुमारस्य व्रजस्य त्वयि केशव।।
कर्म चेदमशक्यं यत्समस्तैस्त्रिदशैरपि।। ६।।

O Keśava, the woman, the children and the old of Vraja are all pleased with thee—even all the celestials cannot perform the deeds thou hast done.

बालत्वं चातिवीर्यत्वं जन्म चास्मासु शोभनम्।।
चिंत्यमानममेयात्मञ्छंकां कृष्ण प्रयच्छति।। ७।।

Thy boyhood and thy prowess; thy humiliating birth amongest us, are contradictions that fill us with surprise whenever we think of them.

देवो वा दानवो वा त्वं यक्षो गन्धर्व एव वा।।
किमस्माकं विचारेण बांधवोऽसि नमोस्तु ते।। ८।।

Be thou a god, or a demon or a Yakṣa or a Gandharva, or whatever, we may consider thee, we should respect thee for thou art our friend."

श्रीपराशर उवाच

क्षणं भूत्वा त्वसौ तूष्णीं किंचित्प्रणयकोपवान्।।
इत्येवमुक्तस्तैर्गोपैः कृष्णोप्याह महामतिः।। ९।।

When they had finished, Kṛṣṇa remained silent for some time as if hurt and wounded and then said to them.

श्रीभगवानुवाच

मत्संबंधेन वो गोपा यदि लज्जा न जायते।।
श्लाघ्यो वाहं ततः किं वो विचारेण प्रयोजनम्।। १०।।

Herdsmen, if you are not ashamed of my relationship, if I have deserved your praise, then what necessity have you to discuss thus concerning me?

यदि वोऽस्ति मयि प्रीतिः श्लाघ्योऽहं भवतां यदि।।
तदात्मबंधुसदृशी बुद्धिर्वः क्रियतां मयि।। ११।।

If you have any love for me, if I merit your praise, then consider me as your friend.

नाहं देवो न गन्धर्वो न यक्षो न च दानवः।।
अहं वो बांधवो जातो नैतच्चिंत्यमितोऽन्यथा।। १२।।

I am neither a god, nor a Gandharva nor a Yakṣa nor a demon—I am born as thy friend and you should not think otherwise of me."

श्रीपराशर उवाच

इति श्रुत्वा हरेर्वाक्यं बद्धमौनास्ततो वनम्।।
ययुर्गोपा महाभाग तस्मिन्प्रणयकोपिनि।। १३।।

Parāśara said :—Being addressed thus, O

great Muni, the cow-herds remained silent and went into the woods leaving apparently displeased.

कृष्णस्तु विमलं व्योम शरच्चंद्रस्य चंद्रिकाम्।।
तदा कुमुदिनीं फुल्लामामोदितदिगन्तराम्।। १४।।

वनराजीं तथा कूजद्भृंगमालामनोहराम्।।
विलोक्य सह गोपीभिर्मनश्चक्रे रतिं प्रति।। १५।।

Beholding the clear sky with the autumnal moon, and the air perfumed with the fragrance of the wild water-lily in whose buds the culstering bees were murmuring their songs, he felt inclined to join with the females of cow-herds in sport.

विना रामेण मधुरमतीव वनिताप्रियम्।।
जगौ कलपदं शौरिस्तारमंद्रकृतक्रमम्।। १६।।

रम्यं गीतध्वनिं श्रुत्वा संत्यज्यावसथांस्तदा।।
आजग्मुस्त्वरिता गोप्यो यत्रास्ते मधुसूदनः।। १७।।

Thereupon with Rāma he began singing sweet low strains in various measures such as the woman loved; and they, as soon as they heard the music, left their homes and hastened to meet the Slayer of Madhu.

शनैश्शनैर्जगौ गोपी काचित्तस्य लयानुगम्।।
दत्तावधाना काचिच्च तमेव मनसास्मरत्।। १८।।

काचित्कृष्णेतिकृष्णेति प्रोक्त्वा लज्जामुपाययौ।।
ययौ च काचित्प्रेमांधा तत्पार्श्वमविलंबितम्।। १९।।

काचिच्चावसथस्यांते स्थित्वा दृष्ट्वा बहिर्गुरुम्।।
तन्मयत्वेन गोविंदं दध्यौ मीलितलोचना।। २०।।

तच्चित्तविमलाह्लादक्षीणपुण्यचया तथा।।
तदप्राप्तिमहादुःखविलीनाशेषपातका।। २१।।

चिंतयंती जगत्सूतिं परब्रह्मस्वरूपिणम्।।
निरुच्छ्वासतया मुक्तिं गतान्या गोपकन्यका।। २२।।

One damsel gently sang an accompaniment to his song, another attentively listened to his music; one called him by the name and then shrank in bashfulness : whilst another, more bold and prompted by love, pressed close to his side; one, as she came out, saw some of the seniors of her family and dared not venture satisfying herself with meditating on Kṛṣṇa with close eyes and whole-minded devotion by which immediately all acts of merit were effaced by rapture and all sin was expiated by regret at not seeing him : and others again, reflecting upon the cause of the world, in the form of the Supreme Brahmā, obtained, by their sighing, final emancipation.

गोपीपरिवृतो रात्रिं शरच्चंद्रमनोरमाम्।।
मानयामास गोविंदो रासारंभरसोत्सुकः।। २३।।

Thus encircled by the females of cow-herds Kṛṣṇa thought the lovely moon-light night of autumn suited to the Rāsa dance.[1]

गोप्यश्च वृंदशः कृष्णचेष्टास्वायत्तमूर्त्तयः।।
अन्यदेशं गते कृष्णे चेरुर्वृंदावनांतरम्।। २४।।

Many of them so imitated the different actions of Kṛṣṇa that in his absence they wandered through Vṛndāvana representing his person.

कृष्णे निबद्धहृदया इदमूचुः परस्परम्।। २५।।

कृष्णोऽहमेष ललितं व्रजाम्यालोक्यतां गतिः।।
अन्या ब्रवीति कृष्णस्य मम गीतिर्निशम्यताम्।। २६।।

"I am Kṛṣṇa" exclaims one "behold the beauty of my movements." "I am Kṛṣṇa" cries another "Listen to my sing."

दुष्टकालिय तिष्ठात्र कृष्णोहमिति चापरा।।
बाहुमास्फोट्य कृष्णस्य लीलया सर्वमाददे।। २७।।

"Wait! wicked Kālīya, I am Kṛṣṇa" cries out another striking her arms defiantly.

अन्या ब्रवीति भो गोपा निश्शंकैः स्थीयतामिति।।
अलं वृष्टिभयेनात्र धृतो गोवर्द्धनो मया।। २८।।

धेनुकोऽयं मयाक्षिप्तो विचरंतु यथेच्छया।।

A fourth cries out :—"Herdsmen, fear nothing, be steady, there is no danger of the storm any more for I uplift the Govardhana for your protection," and a fifth exclaims—"Now let the cattle graze wherever they will, for I have slain Dhenuka."

1. The Rāsa dance is danced by men and women holding each other's hands and going round in a circle singing the airs to what they dance.

गावो ब्रवीति चैवान्या कृष्णलीलानुसारिणी।। २९।।

एवं नानाप्रकारासु कृष्णचेष्टासु तास्तदा।।
गोप्यो व्यग्रास्समं चेरू रम्यं वृन्दावनांतरम्।। ३०।।

विलोक्यैका भुवं प्राह गोपी गोपवरांगना।।
पुलकांचितसर्वांगी विकासिनयनोत्पला।। ३१।।

ध्वजवज्रांकुशाब्जांकरेखावंत्यालि पश्यत।।

In this wise the females of the cow-herds imitated the various actions of Kṛṣṇa, and in his absence removed their sorrow by mimicking his sports.

One damsel, looking on the earth with the down of her person erect and expanded eyes, exclaims "See here are the impressions of Kṛṣṇa's feet an as he has gone, he has left those marks of the banner, the thunder-bolt and the goad.

पदान्येतानि कृष्णस्य लीलाललितगामिनः।। ३२।।

कापि तेन समायाता कृतपुण्या मदालसा।।
पदानि तस्याश्चैतानि घनान्यल्पतनूनि च।। ३३।।

What fortunate damsel is going with him inebriveate with her passion as her irregular footmarks prove? Here Dāmodara has called flowers from on high, for we see alone the marks of the tips of his feet.

पुष्पापयचमत्रोच्चैश्चके दामोदरे ध्रुवम्।।
येना ग्राक्रांतमात्राणि पदान्यत्र महात्मनः।। ३४।।

Here a nymph has sat down with him bedecked with flowers, fortunate in having propitiated Viṣṇu in a pristime birth.

अत्रोपविश्य वै तेन काचित्पुष्पैरंकृता।।
अन्यजन्मनि सर्वात्मा विष्णुरभ्यर्चितस्तया।। ३५।।

पुष्पबंधनसंमानकृतमानामपास्य ताम्।।
नंदगोपसुतो यातो मार्गेणानेन पश्यत।। ३६।।

अनुयातैनमत्रान्या नितंबभरमंथरा।।
या गंतव्ये दुतं याति निम्नपादाग्रसंस्थितिः।। ३७।।

हस्तन्यस्ताग्रहस्तेयं तेन याति तथा सखी।।
अनायत्तपदन्यासा लक्ष्यते पदपद्धतिः।। ३८।।

Having left her in a haughty mood because he had adored her with flowers, the son of Nanda has gone by this road; for see, unable to follow him with equal steps his companion has here trippled along upon her toes; and that holding his hand, the damsel has passed on is evident from the uneven and intermingled footsteps.

हस्तसंस्पर्शमात्रेण धूर्त्तनैषा विमानिता।।
नैराश्यान्मंदगामिन्या निवृत्तं लक्ष्यते पदम्।। ३९।।

The wicked Kṛṣṇa merely took her by the hand and then left her. The damsel, being disappointed, is returning in faltering steps—for such her foot-marks indicate.

नूनमुक्ता त्वरामीति पुनरेष्यामितेंतिकम्।।
तेन कृष्णेन येनैषा त्वरिता पदपद्धतिः।। ४०।।

Forsooth he proposed to her that he would come back soon, for here are his own footsteps returning with speed.

प्रविष्टो गहनं कृष्णः पदमत्र न लक्ष्यते।।
निवत्ताध्वं शशांकस्य नैतद्दीधितिगोचरे।। ४१।।

Here he has entered the thick forest but as the rays of the moon do not enter here his footsteps can be traced no father."

निवृत्तस्तास्तदा गोप्यो निराशाः कृष्णदर्शने।।
यमुनातीरमासाद्य जगुस्तच्चरितं तथा।। ४२।।

Being hopeless of beholding Kṛṣṇa, the females of the cow-herds came back and arriving at the banks of the Yamunā, they began to sing his songs.

ततो ददृशुरायांतं विकासिमुखपंकजम्।।
गोप्यस्त्रैलोक्यगोप्तारं कृष्णमक्लिष्टचेष्टितम्।। ४३।।

They immediately saw the protector of the three worlds, with a smiling countenance, coming speedily towards them, on which one cried out.

काचिदालोक्य गोविंदमायांतमतिहर्षिता।।
कृष्णकृष्णेति कृष्णेति प्राह नान्यदुदीरयत्।। ४४।।

काचिद्भ्रूभंगुरं कृत्वा ललाटफलकं हरिम्।।
विलोक्य नेत्रभृंगाभ्यां पपौ तन्मुखपंकजम्।। ४५।।

काचिदालोक्य गोविंदं निमीलितविलोचना।।
तस्यैव रूपं ध्यायंती योगारूढेव सा बभौ।। ४६।।

"Kṛṣṇa, Kṛṣṇa being unable to utter any thing else. One liked to contract her forehead with frowns as drinking with the bees of her eyes the lotus of the face of Hari : another, shutting her eyes, meditated, in her mind, upon his form as if being engaged in an act of devotion.

ततः कांचित्प्रियालापैः कांचिद्भ्रूभंगवीक्षितैः।।
निन्येऽनुनयमन्यां च करस्पर्शेन माधवः।।४७।।

ताभिः प्रसन्नचित्ताभिर्गोपीभिस्सह सादरम्।।
ररास रासगोष्ठीभिरुदारचरितो हरिः।।४८।।

Thereupon coming amongst them Mādhava conciliated some with soft words some with gentle looks and some he took by the hand and the illustrious deity sported with them in the stations of the dance, after all the damsels had been propitiated.

रासमंडलबंधोपि कृष्णपार्श्वमनुज्झता।।
गोपीजनेन नैवाभूदेकस्थानस्थिरात्मना।।४९।।

As each of the damsels attempted to remain in one place close to the side of Kṛṣṇa, the circle of the dance could not be constructed.

हस्तेन गृह्य चैकैकां गोपीनां रासमंडले।।
चकार तत्करस्पर्शनिमीलितदृशं हरिः।।५०।।

Thereupon taking each by the hand and when their eye-lids were closed by the effects of such touch Hari formed the circle.

ततः प्रववृते रासश्चलद्वलयनिस्वनः।।
अनुयातशरत्काव्यगेयगीतिरनुक्रमात् ।।५१।।

Then began the dance in accompaniment with the music of their clashing bracelets and songs that celebrated in sweet melody the beauty of the autumnal season.

कृष्णश्शरच्चंद्रमसं कौमुदीं कुमुदाकरम्।।
जगौ गोपीजनस्त्वेकं कृष्णनाम पुनःपुनः।। ५२।।

Kṛṣṇa sang the moon of autumn, a mine of gentle rays but the damsels chanted the praise of Kṛṣṇa only.

परिवृत्तिश्रमेणैका चलद्वलयलापिनीम्।।
ददौ बाहुलतां स्कंधे गोपी मधुनिघातिनः।। ५३।।

काचित्प्रविलसद्बाहुं परिरभ्य चुचुंब तम्।।
गोपीगीतस्तुतिव्याजान्निपुणा मधुसूदनम्।। ५४।।

At times, one of them exhusted by the revolving dance, threw her arms, adorned with the thinking bracelets round the neck of the Slayer of Madhu; another proficient in the art of singing his praises embraced him.

गोपीकपोलसंश्लेषमभिगम्य हरेर्भुजौ।।
पुलकोद्गमसस्याय स्वेदांबुघनतां गतौ।। ५५।।

The drops of perspiration from the arms of Hari were like fertilizing rain which produced a drop of dew upon the temples of the damsels of cow-herds.

रासगेयं जगौ कृष्णौ यावत्तरतरध्वनिः।।
साधु कृष्णेति कृष्णेति तावत्त द्विगुणं जगुः।।५६।।

Kṛṣṇa sang the melody that was suited to the dance." The damsles again and again repeated—"Bravo, Kṛṣṇa," to his song.

गतेनुगमनं चक्रुर्वलनं संमुखं ययुः।।
प्रतिलोमानुलोमाभ्यां भेजुर्गोपांगना हरिम्।। ५७।।

When leading, they followed him, when coming back, they met him and whether he went forwards or backwards they always followed his footsteps.

स तथा सह गोपीभी ररास मधुसूदनः।।
यथाब्दकोटिप्रतिमः क्षणस्तेन विनाऽभवत्।। ५८।।

Whilst sporting thus with the females of the cow-herds, they regarded one moment in his absence, as a myriad of years.

ता वार्यमाणाः पतिभिः पितृभिर्भ्रातृभिस्तथा।।
कृष्णं गोपांगना रात्रौ रमयंति रतिप्रियाः।।५९।।

And although prohibited in vain by their husbands, and brothers, they went out in night to sport with Kṛṣṇa, the idol of their affection.

सोऽपि कैशोरकवयो मानयन्मधुसूदनः।।
रेमे ताभिरमेयात्मा क्षपासु क्षपिताहितः।।६०।।

तद्भर्तृषु तथा तासु सर्वभूतेषु चेश्वरः।।
आत्मस्वरूपरूपोऽसौ व्यापी वायुरिव स्थितः।।६१।।

यथा समस्तभूतेषु नभोग्निः पृथिवी जलम्।।
वायुश्चात्मा तथैवाऽसौ व्याप्य सर्वमवस्थितः।।६२।।

Thus the deity of unbounded prowess, the remover of all imperfections, assumed the character of a youth amongst the damsels of Vraja, pervading their natures and that of their lords, by his own essence all diffusive like the wind, for even as in all creatures the elements of ether, fire, water, and air are comprehended, so also is one everywhere present and in all.

।। इति श्रीविष्णुमहापुराणे पञ्चमेंशे त्रयोदशोऽध्यायः ।। १३ ।।

अथ पञ्चमेंशेः चतुर्दशोऽध्यायः

Part V : Section 14

श्रीपराशर उवाच

प्रदोषाग्रे कदाचित्तु रासासक्ते जनार्दने ।।
त्रासयन्समदो गोष्ठमरिष्टस्समुपागमत् ।। १ ।।

Parāśara said :—One evening whilst Janārddana was engaged in Rāsa, the demon Ariṣtha, disguised as a bull, came there striking terror into the hearts of all.

स तोयतोयदच्छायस्तीक्ष्णशृंगोर्कलोचनः ।।
खुराग्रपातैरत्यर्थं दारयन्धरणीतलम् ।। २ ।।

लेलिहानस्सनिष्पेषं जिह्वयोष्ठौ पुनःपुनः ।।
संरंभाविद्धलांगूलः कठिनस्कंधबंधनः ।। ३ ।।

उदग्रककुदाभोगप्रमाणो दुरतिक्रमः ।।
विण्मूत्रलिप्तपृष्ठांगो गवामुद्वेगकारकः ।। ४ ।।

प्रलंबकंठोऽतिमुखस्तरुखातांकिताननः ।।

His appearance was like a cloud-saturated with waters—his two horns were very sharp and his two eyes were bright like the sun. As he proceeded, he ploughed up the ground with his hoops : his tongue was repeatedly licking his lips; his tail was erect; the sinews of his shoulders were strong and between them rose a hump of encormous proportions; his hunches were soiled with ordour and he was a dread to the herds; his dewlap hung low and his face was marked with scars from butting against the trees.

पातयन्स गवां गर्भान्दैत्यो वृषभरूपधृक् ।। ५ ।।
सदयंस्तापसानुग्रो वनानटति यस्सदा ।। ६ ।।

Terrifying all the kine, and destroying hermits and ascetics that demon, in the guise of a bull, haunts all the forests.

ततस्तमतिघोराक्षमवेक्ष्यातिभयातुराः ।।
गोपा गोपस्त्रियश्चैव कृष्णकृष्णेति चुक्रुशुः ।। ७ ।।

Being greatly stricken with fear on beholding that dreadful bull, the cow-herds and their females cried out "Kṛṣṇa, Kṛṣṇa."

सिंहनादं ततश्चक्रे तलशब्दं च केशवः ।।
तच्छब्दश्रवणाच्चाऽसौ दामोदरमुपाययौ ।। ८ ।।

अग्रन्यस्तविषाणाग्रः कृष्णकुक्षिकृतेक्षणः ।।
अभ्यधावत दुष्टात्मा कृष्णं वृषभदानवः ।। ९ ।।

Kṛṣṇa then shouted and slapped his arms in defiance. When the demon heard the noise, he turned upon his challenger, and fixing his eyes and pointing his horns at the helly of Keśava, he ran furiously upon the youth.

आयांतं दैत्यवृषभं दृष्ट्वा कृष्णो महाबलः ।।
न चचाल तदा स्थानादवज्ञास्मितलीलया ।। १० ।।

आसन्नं चैव जग्राह ग्राहवन्मधुसूदनः ।।
जघान जानुना कुक्षौ विषाणग्रहणाचलम् ।। ११ ।।

Kṛṣṇa did not stir from his place, but smiling in sport and derision, awaited the near approach of the bull, when he siezed him, as an alligator would have done and held him firmly by the horns, whilst he pressed his sides with his knees.

तस्य दर्पबलं भक्त्वा गृहीतस्य विषाणयोः ।।
अपीडयदरिष्टस्य कंठं क्लिन्नमिवांबरम् ।। १२ ।।

उत्पाट्य शृंगमेकं तु तेनैवाताडयत्ततः ।।
ममार स महादैत्यो मुखाच्छोणितमुद्वमन् ।। १३ ।।

Having thus humiliated his pride and held him captive by his horn, he wrung his throat as if it had been a piece of wet cloth; and then tearing off one of the horns, he beat the dreadful demon with it until he died vomitting blood from his mouth.

तुष्टुवुर्निहते तस्मिन्दैत्ये गोपा जनार्दनम्।।
जंभे हते सहस्राक्षं पुरा देवगणा यथा।। १४।।

Seeing him slain the herdsmen glorified Kṛṣṇa as the companies of the celestials of old praised Indra, when he triumphed over the Asura Jambha.

।। इति श्रीविष्णुमहापुराणे पञ्चमेंशे चतुर्दशोध्यायः।। १४।।

अथ पञ्चमेंशेः पञ्चदशोऽध्यायः

Part V : Section 15

श्रीपराशर उवाच

ककुद्मति हतेऽरिष्टे धेनुके विनिपातिते।।
प्रलंबे निधनं नीति धृते गोवर्द्धनाचले।। १।।

Parāśara said :—After these things had happened, Ariṣtha, the bull domon and Dhenuka and Pralamba had been destroyed, Govardhana had been uplifted.

दमिते कालिये नागे भग्ने तुंगदुमद्वये।।
हतायां पूतनायां च शकटे परिवर्त्तिते।। २।।

The serpent Kālīya had been vanquished, the two trees had been broken, the female fiend Pūtanā had been destroyed and the waggon had been overturned.

कंसाय नारदः प्राह यथावृत्तमनुक्रमात्।।
यशोदादेवकीगर्भपरिवृत्ताद्यशेषतः।। ३।।

Nārada went to Kansa and related to him the whole, beginning with the transference of the child from Devakī to Yośadā.

श्रुत्वा तत्सकलं कंसो नारदाद्देवदर्शनात्।।
वसुदेवं प्रति तदा कोपं चक्रे सुदुर्मतिः।। ४।।
सोतिकोपादुपालभ्य सर्वयादवसंसदि।।
जगर्ह यादवांश्चैव कार्यं चैतदचिंतयत्।। ५।।

Hearing this from Nārada, Kansa was greatly enraged with Vasudeva and remonstrated with him hard, and with all the Yādavas in an assembly of the race.

यावन्न बलमारूढौ रामकृष्णौ सुबालकौ।।
तावदेव मया वध्यावसाध्यौ रूढयौवनौ।। ६।।

Then thinking what was to be done he determined to destroy both Kṛṣṇa and Rāma whilist they were yet young and before they had attained to man-hood.

चाणूरोत्र महावीर्यो मुष्टिकश्च महाबलः।।
एताभ्यां मल्लयुद्धेन मारयिष्याम दुर्मती।। ७।।

धनुर्महमहायोगव्याजेनानीय तौ व्रजात्।।
तथा तथा यतिष्यामि यास्येते संक्षयं यथा।। ८।।

Accordingly he made up his mind, to invite them from Vraja under the plea of the solemn rite of the lustration of arms, when he would engage them in a trial of strength with his chief boxers Cāṇūra and Muṣṭika, by whom they would undoubtedly be slain.

श्वफल्कतनयं शूरमक्रूरं यदुपुंगवम्।।
तयोरानयनार्थाय प्रेषयिष्यामि गोकुलम्।। ९।।

"I will send" he said "the noble Akrūra, the son of Swapalka to Gokula to bring them hither.

वृंदा वनचरं घोरमादेक्ष्यामि च केशिनम्।।
तत्रैवासावतिबलस्तावुभौ घातयिष्यति।। १०।।

गजः कुवलायापीडो मत्सकाशमिहागतौ।।
घातयिष्यति वा गोपौ वसुदेवसुतावुभौ।। ११।।

I will order the dreadful Keśin, who frequents the forest of Vṛndāvana, to attack him, and he is of unequalled prowess and will for certain, kill them; or if they come here, my elephant Kuvalayāpīḍa shall trample to death these two cow-boy sons of Vasudeva."

श्रीपराशर उवाच

इत्यालोच्य स दुष्टात्मा कंसौ रामजनार्दनौ।।
हंतुं कृतमतिर्वीरावक्रूरं वाक्यमब्रवीत्।। १२।।

Having thus planned to kill Rāma and Janārdana, the vicious Kansa sent for the heroic Akrūra and said to him,

कंस उवाच

भो भो दानपते वाक्यं क्रियतां प्रीतये मम।।
इतः स्यंदनमारुह्य गम्यतां नंदगोकुलम्।। १३।।

'O master of liberal gifts, hear my words : and out of friendship for me perform my orders. Ascend your chariot and go to the house of the milkman Nanda.

वसुदेव सुतो तत्र विष्णोरंशसमुद्भवौ।।
नाशाय किल संभूतौ मम दुष्टौ प्रवर्द्धतः।। १४।।

The two vicious boys, portions of Viṣṇu, have been born there, for the very object bringing about my destruction.

धनुर्महो ममाप्यत्र चतुर्दश्यां भविष्यति।।
आनेयौ भवता गत्वा मल्लयुद्धाय तत्र तौ।। १५।।

चाणूरमुष्टिकौ मल्लौ नियुद्धकुशलौ मम।।
ताभ्यां सहानयोर्युद्धं सर्वलोकोऽत्र पश्यतु।। १६।।

गजः कुवलयापीडो महामात्रप्रचोदितः।।
स वा हनिष्यते पापौ वसुदेवात्मजौ शिशू।। १७।।

On the fourteenth lunation I intend celebrating the rite of the lustration of arms. I wish them to be brought here by you to take part in the games and that the people may behold them engage in a boxing match with my two skilled boxers Cāṇūra and Muṣṭika; or by chance, my elephant, driven against them by his rider, shall destroy these vicious youngsters—the sons of Vasudava.

तौ हत्वा वसुदेवं च नंदगोपं च दुर्मतिम्।।
हनिष्ये पितरं चैनमुग्रसेनं सुदुर्मतिम्।। १८।।

ततस्समस्तगोपानां गोधनान्यखिलान्यहम्।।
वित्तं चापहरिष्यामि दुष्टानां मद्वधैषिणाम्।। १९।।

When they are out of the way, I shall kill Vasudeva himself, the cow-herds and my foolish father Ugrasena and I will get there by the flocks, herds and all the properties of the rebellious cow-herds who have ever been inimical to me.

त्वामृते यादवाश्चैते द्विषो दानपते मम।।
एतेषां च वधायाहं यतिष्येऽनुक्रमात्ततः।। २०।।

तदा निष्कंटकं सर्वं राज्यमेतदयादवम्।।
प्रसाधिष्ये त्वया तस्मान्मत्प्रीत्यै वीर गम्यताम्।। २१।।

यथा च माहिषं सर्पिर्दधिचाप्युपहार्यं वै।।
गोपास्समानयंत्वाशु तथा वाच्यास्त्वया च ते।। २२।।

Save thou, lord of liberatily, all the Yādavas have been my enemies and I will find out means for their destruction; and I shall then govern my kingdom with thee without any disturbance. If you regard me, do thou go as I direct thee; and thou shalt command the cowherds to bring in speedily their supplies of milk and butter and curds."

श्रीपराशर उवाच

इत्याज्ञप्तस्तदाऽक्रूरो महाभागवतो द्विज।।
प्रीतिमानभवत्कृष्णं श्वोद्रक्ष्यामीति सत्वरः।। २३।।

तथेत्युक्त्वा च राजानं रथमारुह्य शोभनम्।।
निश्चक्राम ततः पुर्य्या मथुराया मधुप्रियः।। २४।।

Being thus advised the illustrious Akrūra the immediately undertook to see Kṛṣṇa and ascending this magnificent chariot he went, out from the city of Mathurā.

।। इति श्रीविष्णुमहापुराणे पञ्चमेंशे पञ्चदशोऽध्यायः।। १५।।

अथ पञ्चमेंशे: षोडशोऽध्याय:

Part V : Section 16

श्रीपराशर उवाच

केशी चापि बलोदग्रः कंसदूतः प्रचोदितः।।
कृष्णस्य निधनाकांक्षी वृंदावनमुपागमत्।। १।।

Parāśara said :—Being commissioned by Kansa's emissary, Keśin, elated with the confidence of his prowess, reached Vṛndāvana, being desrious of bringing about the destruction of Kṛṣṇa.

स खुरक्षतभूपृष्ठस्सटाक्षेपधुतांबुदः।।
दुतविक्रांतचंद्रार्कमार्गो गोपानुपाद्रवत्।। २।।

He assailed the cow-herds, spurning the ground with his hoofs, sacttering the clouds with his mane and obstructing the paths of the sun and the moon.

तस्य हेषितशब्देन गोपाला दैत्यवाजिनः।।
गोप्यश्च भयसंविग्न गोविंदं शरणं ययुः।। ३।।

Being terrfied by the neighings of the demons, assuming the shape of a steed, the cow-herds and their females fled to Govinda for shelter exclaiming,

त्राहित्राहीति गोविंदःश्रुत्वा तेषां ततो वचः।।
सतोयजलदध्वानगंभीरमिदमुक्तवान् ।।४।।

"Save us! Save us!!" Hearing their cries, Govinda replied in a voice deep as the roaring of the thunder cloud.

अलं त्रासेन गोपालाः केशिनः किं भयातुरैः।।
भवद्भिर्गोपजातीयैर्वीरवीर्यं विलोप्यते।। ५।।

Śrīkṛṣṇa said : "Away with the fears of Keśin, O cowherds; being born as Gopālas, why do you destroy my valour and heroism?

किमनेनाल्पसारेण हेषिताटोपकारिणा।।
दैतेयबलवाह्येन वल्गता दुष्टवाजिना।। ६।।

Why are you afraid of one of such little might whose neighings are his only terrors, a galloping and vicious horse who is ridden by the strength of Daityas?

एह्येहि दुष्ट कृष्णोऽहं पूष्णस्त्विव पिनाकधृत्।।
पातयिष्यामि दशनान्वदनादखिलांस्तव।। ७।।

Come on, wretch. I am Kṛṣṇa and I will knock all thy teeth down thy throat, as the weilder of trindent did to Pūṣan."

इत्युक्त्वाऽस्फोट्य गोविंदः केशिनस्संमुखं ययौ।।
विवृतास्यश्च सोप्येनं दैतेयाश्च उपाद्रवत्।। ८।।

Thus defying him, Govinda went to fight with Keśin. The demon with his mouth wide open, ran upon Kṛṣṇa.

बाहुमाभोगिनं कृत्वा मुखे तस्य जनार्दनः।।
प्रवेशयामास तदा केशिनो दुष्टवाजिनः।। ९।।

But Kṛṣṇa, enlarging his arms, thrust it into his mouth and knocked down the teeth which fell from his jaws like fragments of white clouds.

केशिनो वदनं तेन विशता कृष्णबाहुना।।
शातिता दशनाः पेतुः सिताभ्राद्यवा इव।। १०।।

कृष्णस्य ववृधे बाहुः केशिदेहगतो द्विज।।
विनाशाय यथा व्याधिरासंभूतेरुपेक्षितः।। ११।।

Still the arms of Kṛṣṇa in the throat of Kṛṣṇa continued to enlarge, as a disease, neglected in the beginning, increasing till the dissolution.

विपाटितोष्ठो बहुलं सफेनं रुधिरं वमन्।।
सोक्षिणी विवृते चक्रे विशिष्टे मुक्तबंधने।। १२।।

जघान धरणीं पादैश्शकृन्मूत्रं समुत्सृजन्।।
स्वेदार्द्रगात्रश्शांतश्च निर्यत्नस्सोऽभवत्तदा।। १३।।

The torn lips of the demon vomitted forth foam and blood; his eyes rolled in affliction; his joints gave way; he struck the earth with his feet; his body was covered with perspiration and he became incapable of any exertion.

व्यादितास्यमहारंध्रस्सोऽसुरः कृष्णबाहुना।।
निपातितो द्विधा भूमौ वैद्युतेन यथा द्रुमः।। १४।।

Having his mouths rent open by the arm of Kṛṣṇa, that dreadful demon fell down like a tree struck and shattered by lightning, divided into two portions.

द्विपादे पृष्ठपुच्छार्द्धे श्रवणैकाक्षिनासिके।।
केशिनस्ते द्विधा भूते शकले द्वे विरेजतुः।। १५।।

Each of those portions had two legs, half a back, half a tail, one, ear, one eye and one nostril.

हत्वा तु केशिनं कृष्णो गोपालैर्मुदितैर्वृतः।।
अनायस्ततनुस्स्वस्थो हसंस्तत्रैव तस्थिवान्।। १६।।

ततो गोप्यश्च गोपाश्च हते केशिनि विस्मिताः।।
तुष्टुवुः पुंडरीकाक्षमनुरागमनोरमम्।। १७।।

Kṛṣṇa stood, unhurt and smiling after destruction of the demons encircled by the cow-herd, who, together with their females, were filled with surprise at the death of Keśin and glorified the lotus-eyed deity.

अथाहांतर्हितो विप्र नारदो जलदे स्थितः।।
केशिनं निहतं दृष्ट्वा हर्षनिर्भरमानसः।। १८।।

साधुसाधु जगन्नाथ लीलयैव यदच्युत।।
निहतोऽयं त्वया केशी क्लेशदस्त्रिदिवौकसाम्।। १९।।

Beholding the destruction of Keśin, the Brāhmin Nārada, invisible and seated in a cloud, delightedly exclaimed—"Well done, O lord of the universe who has easily destroyed Keśin, the oppresser of the celestials.

युद्धौत्सुकोहमत्यर्थं नरवाजिमहाहवम्।।
अभूतपूर्वमन्यत्र दृष्टुं स्वर्गादिहागतः।। २०।।

I have never heard of such a combat between a man and a horse; being curious to behold it, I have come from heaven.

कर्माण्यऽत्रावतारे तें कृतानि मधुसूदन।।
यानि तैर्विस्मितं चेतस्तोषमेतेन मे गतम्।। २१।।

My heart is filled with joy and surprise, O slayer of Madhu, on beholding the wonderful works thou hast done in thy descent upon earth.

तुरंगस्यास्य शक्रोपि कृष्ण देवाश्च बिभ्यति।।
धुतकेसरजालस्य ह्रेषातोऽभ्रावलोकिनः।। २२।।

O Kṛṣṇa Indra and other celestials lived in fear of this horse, who tossed his mane neighed and looked down upon the clouds.

यस्मात्त्वयैष दुष्टात्मा हतः केशी जनार्दन।।
तस्मात्केशवनाम्ना त्वं लोके ख्यातो भविष्यसि।। २३।।

Because thou hast slain the impious Keśin thou shalt be celebrated in the world by the the name of Keśava. Farewell! I will now go.

स्वस्त्यस्तु ते गमिष्यामि कंसयुद्धेऽधुना पुनः।।
परश्वोऽह समेष्यामि त्वया केशिनिषूदन।। २४।।

I shall meet thee again, O subduer of Keśin, in two days more, when thou shalt be engaged in a conflict with Kansa.

उग्रसेनसुते कंसे सानुगे विनिपातिते।।
भारावतारकर्त्ता त्वं पृथिव्यां पृथिवीधर।। २५।।

When the son of Ugrasena, with his followers shall have been slain, then, O upholder of the earth earth's burden will have been lightened by thee.

तत्रानेक प्रकाराणि युद्धानि पृथिवीक्षिताम्।।
दृष्टव्यानि मया युष्मत्प्रणीतानि जनार्दन।। २६।।

Many are the battles of the kings that have to see, in which thou shalt be renowned; I will now go away, O Govinda.

सोऽहं यास्यामि गोविंद देवकार्यं महत्कृतम्।।
त्वयैव विदितं सर्वं स्वस्ति तेऽस्तु व्रजाम्यहम्।। २७।।

Thou hast accomplished a great deed admired by the celestials, I have been much pleased with thee and take my leave."

नारदे तु गते कृष्णस्सह गोपैस्सभाजितः।।
विवेश गोकुलं गोपीनेत्रपानैकभाजनम्।। २८।।

When Nārada had departed, Kṛṣṇa, who was the cynosure of the eyes of the damsels of Vraja, not the least surprised, went back with the cow-herds to Gokula.

।। इति श्रीविष्णुमहापुराणे पञ्चमेंशे षोडशोऽध्यायः।। १६।।

अथ पञ्चमेंशेः सप्तदशोऽध्यायः
Part V : Section 17

श्रीपराशर उवाच

अक्रूरोऽपि विनिष्क्रम्य स्यंदनेनाशुगामिना।।
कृष्णसंदर्शनाकांक्षी प्रययौ नंदगोकुलम्।। १।।

Parāśara said :—Having issued out of the house of Kansa, Akrūra, being desirous of seeing Kṛṣṇa, proceeded towards the house of Nanda in a swift-coursing car.

चिंतयामास चाक्रूरो नास्ति धन्यतरो मया।।
योहमंशावतीर्णस्य मुखं द्रक्ष्यामि चक्रिणः।। २।।

He thought within himself. "There is none more fourtunate than I, for I shall behold the countenance of a portion of the holder of discus.

अद्य मे सफलं जन्म सुप्रभाताऽभवन्निशा।।
यदुन्निद्राभपत्राक्षं विष्णोर्द्रक्ष्याम्यहं मुखम्।। ३।।

To-day my life has borne fruit, my night is followed by the dawn of day, for I shall behold the countenance of Viṣṇu resembling full-blown lotuses.

पापं हरति यत्पुंसां स्मृतं संकल्प नामयम्।।
तत्पुंडरीकनयनं विष्णोर्द्रक्ष्याम्यहं मुखम्।। ४।।

Blessed are my eyes and blessed are my words, for on beholding Viṣṇu a conversation shall take place between him and me. I shall behold the countenance of Viṣṇu having lotus eyes, which, when seen only in imagination, removes all sins.

विनिर्जग्मुर्यतो वेदा वेदांगान्यखिलानि च।।
द्रक्ष्यामि तत्परं धाम धाम्नां भगवतो मुखम्।। ५।।

I shall behold to-day the mouth of Viṣṇu—the glory of glories, whence proceeded the Vedas and all their divisions.

यज्ञेषु यज्ञपुरुषः पुरुषैः पुरुषोत्तमः।।
इज्यते योऽखिलाधारस्तं द्रक्ष्यामि जगत्पतिम्।। ६।।

I shall behold the lord of the universe by whom the world is sustained, who is worshipped as the best Puruṣa and as the male of sacrifice in sacrificial rites.

इष्ट्वा यमिंद्रो यज्ञा नां शतेनामरराजताम्।।
अवाप तमनंतादिमहं द्रक्ष्यामि केशवम्।। ७।।

I shall behold Keśava, who is without beginning or end, by worshipping whom with a hundred sacrifices, Indra obtained the sovereignty over the celestials.

न ब्रह्मा नेंद्ररुद्राश्विवस्वादित्यमरुद्गणाः।।
यस्य स्वरूपं जानंति प्रत्यक्षं याति मे हरिः।। ८।।

That Hari, whose nature is unknown to Brahmā, Indra, Rudra, the Aśvins, the Vasus, the Ādityas and Maruts, will this day touch my body.

सर्वात्मा सर्ववित्सर्वस्सर्वभूतेष्ववस्थितः।।
योह्यऽचिंत्योऽव्ययो व्यापी स वक्ष्यति मया सह।। ९।।

He, who is the soul of all omniscient, is identical with everything, omnipresent, permanent, undecaying, all-pervading, shall converse with me.

मत्स्यकूर्मवराहाश्वसिंहरूपादिभिः स्थितिम्।।
चकार जगतो योऽजः सोऽद्य मां प्रलपिष्यति।। १०।।

He, the unborn, who has preserved the world in diverse forms of a fish, a tortoise, a boar, a horse, a lion, will this day talk with me.

सांप्रतं च जगत्स्वामी कार्यमात्महृदि स्थितम्।।
कर्तुं मनुष्यतां प्राप्तस्वेच्छादेहधृदव्ययः।। ११।।

The lord of the universe, who assumes shapes at will, has taken upon him the condition of humanity to satisfy some object of his heart.

योनंतः पृथिवीं धत्ते शेखरस्थितिसंस्थिताम्।।
सोऽवतीर्णो जगत्यर्थे माम क्रूरेति वक्ष्यामि।। १२।।

The endless, who holds the earth upon his crest and who has descended upon earth for its protection, will this day call me by my name.

पितृपुत्रसुहृद्भ्रातृमातृबंधुमयीमिमाम्।।
यन्मायां नालमुत्तर्तुं। जगत्तस्मै नमोनमः।। १३।।

Glory to that being, whose deceptive adoption of father, son, brother, friend, mother, and relative, the world is unable to comprehend.

तरत्यविद्यां विवतां हृदि यस्मिन्निवेशिते ।।
योगमायाममेयाय तस्मै विद्यात्मने नमः ।। १४ ।।

Salutation unto him, who is identical with true knowledge, who is inscruptable and through whom, when seated in his heart the ascetic gets over the worldly ignorance and illusion.

यज्वभिर्यज्ञपुरुषो वासुदेवश्च सात्त्वतैः ।।
वेदांतवेदिभिर्विष्णुः प्रोच्यते यो नतोस्मि तम् ।। १५ ।।

I bow to him, who, by the performers of holy rites, is denominated Yajñapuruṣa (the male of a sacrifice), Vāsudeva, by the devotees and Viṣṇu by the adepts in Vedānta philosophy.

यथा यत्र जगद्धाम्नि धातर्येतत्प्रतिष्ठितम् ।।
सदसत्तेन सत्येन मय्यसौ यातु सौम्यताम् ।। १६ ।।

स्मृते सकलकल्याणभाजनं यत्र जायते ।।
पुरुषस्तमजं नित्यं व्रजामि शरणं हरिम् ।। १७ ।।

May he, who comprises in himself cause and effect and the world itself, be pleased with me, through his truth, for I always confide in that unborn and eternal Hari, by meditating on whom man becomes the repository of all auspicious things."

श्रीपराशर उवाच

इत्थं संचिंतयन्विष्णुं भक्तिनम्रात्ममानसः ।।
अक्रूरो गोकुलं प्राप्तः किंचित्सूर्य्ये विराजति ।। १८ ।।

स ददर्श तदा कृष्णमादावादोहने गवाम् ।।
वत्समध्यगतं फुल्लनीलोत्पलदलच्छविम् ।। १९ ।।

प्रफुल्लपद्मपत्राक्षं श्रीवत्सांकितवक्षसम् ।।
प्रलंबबाहुमायामतुंगोरस्थलमुन्नसम् ।। २० ।।

सविलासस्मिताधारं बिभ्राणं मुखपंकजम् ।।
तुंगरक्तनखं पद्भ्यां धरण्यां सुप्रतिष्ठितम् ।। २१ ।।

बिभ्राणं वाससी पीते वन्यपुष्पविभूषितम् ।।
सेंदुनीलाचलाभं तं सितांभोजावतंसकम् ।। २२ ।।

Parāśara said :—Thus meditating upon Viṣṇu, Akrūra, making his mind animated by devot faith, reached Gokula little before sunset; and there he beheld Kṛṣṇa amongst the cattle, dark as the leaf of the full-blown lotus; his eyes of the same colour and his breast adorned with Śrīvatsa mark; long-armed, broad-chested; having a high nose, a graceful countenance with smiles; treading firmly on the ground with feet whose nails were tinted red; dressed in yellow raiments and be-decked with a garland of forest flowers; having a creeper, just collected in his hands, and a chaplet of white lotus-flowers on his head.

हंसकुंदेंदुधवलं नीलांबरधरं द्विज ।।
तस्यानु बलभद्रं च ददर्श यदुनंदनम् ।। २३ ।।

प्रांशुमुत्तुंगबाह्वंसं विकासि मुखपंकजम् ।।
मेघमालापरिवृतं कैलासाद्रिमिवापरम् ।। २४ ।।

Akrūra also saw there Balabhadra, white as a jasmine, a swan or the moon dressed in a blue dress; having large and mighty arms and a countenance as radiant as a blue lotus, like the Kailāśa mountain adorned with a wreath of clouds.

तौ दृष्ट्वा विकसद्वक्त्रसरोजः स महामतिः ।।
पुलकांचितसर्वांगस्तदाऽक्रूरोऽभवन्मुने ।। २५ ।।

When Akrūra, beheld these two youngmen, his countenance expanded with joy and the down of his body stood erect with delight.

तदेतत्परमं धाम तदेतत्परमं पदम् ।।
भगवद्वासुदेवांशो द्विधा योऽयं व्यवस्थितः ।। २६ ।।

साफल्यमक्ष्णोर्युगमेतदत्र दृष्टे जगद्धातरि यातमुच्चैः ।।
अप्यंगमेतद्भगवत्प्रसादात्तदंगसंगे फलवन्मम स्यात् ।। २७ ।।

And he thought—"This is the supreme happiness and repository; this the double manifestation of the divine Vāsudeva; blessed are my eyes for I have seen the protector of the universe and my bodily form shall yield fruit, when by the favour of the deity it shall come in contact with his person.

अप्येष पृष्ठे मम हस्तपद्मं करिष्यति श्रीमदनन्तमूर्त्तिः ।।
यस्यांगुलिस्पर्शहताखिलाचैरवाप्यते सिद्धिरपास्तदोषा ।।
२८ ।।

Shall that assumer of infinite forms place his hand on my back by the touch of whose fingers alone all sins are dispelled and imperishable felicity is secured.

येनाग्निविद्युद्रविरश्मिमालाकरालमत्युग्रमपेत चक्रम्।।
चक्रं घ्नता दैत्यपतेर्हृतानि दैत्यांगनानां नयनाञ्जनानि।। २९।।

And by this hand holding the fierce irresistible discus blazing with all the flames of fire, lightning, and the sun, were slain the Daitya chiefs, and the collyrium from the eyes of their females was washed.

यत्रांबु विन्यस्य बलिर्मनोज्ञानवाप भोगान्वसुधातलस्थः।।
तथामरत्वं त्रिदशाधिपत्वं मन्वंतरं पूर्णमपेतशत्रुम्।। ३०।।

Into this hand Bali poured water and obtained enjoyments in the region under the earth and immortality and dominion over the celestials for a whole Manvantara without danger from any enemy.

अप्येष मां कंसपरिग्रहेण दोषास्पदीभूतमदोषदुष्टम्।।
कर्त्ताऽवमानोपहतं धिगस्तु तज्जन्म यत्साधुबहिष्कृतस्य।।
३१।।

Although I am not sinful, perhaps he will dispise me for my connection with the vicious Kansa. If so, cursed is my birth who is counted amongst the wicked.

ज्ञानात्मकस्यामलसत्त्वराशेरपेतदोषस्य सदा स्फुटस्य।।
किं वा जगत्यत्र समस्तपुंसामज्ञातमस्यास्ति हृदि स्थितस्य।।
३२।।

What is there unknown to him who resides in the hearts of all men, who is ever existent, freed from imperfection, the aggregate of the quality of purity and at one with true knowledge?

तस्मादहं भक्तिविनम्रचेता व्रजामि सर्वेश्वरमीश्वराणाम्।।
अंशावतारं पुरुषोत्तमस्य ह्यनादिमध्यांतमजस्य विष्णोः।।
३३।।

With a heart animated with devout faith I approach the lord of lords, the descended portion of that excellent Puruṣa, Viṣṇu, who is without beginning, middle or end."

।। इति श्रीविष्णुमहापुराणे पञ्चमेंशे सप्तदशोऽध्यायः।। १७।।

अथ पञ्चमेंशे: अष्टादशोऽध्यायः

Part V : Section 18

श्रीपराशर उवाच

चिंतयन्निति गोविंदमुपगम्य स यादवः।।
अक्रूरोस्मीति चरणौ ननाम शिरसा हरेः।। १।।

Parāśara said :—Thus meditating, Akrūra, born in the race of the Yadus, bowed his hand down to the feet of Hari, saying—"I am Akrūra."

सोऽप्येनं ध्वजवज्राब्जकृतचिह्नेन पाणिना।।
संस्पृश्याकृष्य च प्रीत्या सुगाढं परिषस्वजे।। २।।

And Kṛṣṇa placed his hand upon him, which was marked with the flag, the thunderbolt, the lotus, and drew him towards him and affectionately embraced him.

कृतसंवंदनौ तेन यथावद्बलकेशवौ।।
ततः प्रविष्टौ संहृष्टौ तमादायात्ममंदिरम्।। ३।।

Being thus honoured by him, Balarāma and Keśava, delighted, entered with him their own habitation.

सह ताभ्यां तदाऽक्रूरः कृतसंवंदनादिकः।।
भुक्तभोज्यो यथान्याय्यमाचचक्षे ततस्तयोः।। ४।।

यथा निर्भर्त्सितस्तेन कंसेनानकदुंदुभिः।।
यथा च देवकी देवी दानवेन दुरात्मना।। ५।।

उग्रसेने यथा कंसस्य दुरात्मा च वर्त्तते।।
यं चैवार्थं समुद्दिश्य कंसेन तु विसर्जितः।। ६।।

Having entered into conversation with them and been fed, herd lated to them everything duly, how their father Anakadundhubi, the princess Devakī and even his own father had been insulted by the wicked demon Kansa and for what purpose he had been despatched.

तत्सर्वं विस्तराच्छ्रुत्वा भगवान्देवकीसुतः।।
उवाचाखिलमप्येतज्ज्ञातं दानपते मया।। ७।।

करिष्ये तन्महाभाग यदत्रौपयिकं मतम्।।
विचिंत्यं नान्यथैतत्ते विद्धि कंसं हतं मया।। ८।।

Having heard all from him the illustrious slayer of Keśin said—"O thou of liberal gift, I know all thou hast said; O great one, I shall devise proper measures for this—do not think otherwise of this; consider Kansa as already slain.

अहं रामश्च मथुरां श्वो यास्यावस्सह त्वाया।।
गोपवृद्धाश्च यास्यंति ह्यादायोपायनं बहु।। ९।।

निशेयं नीयतां वीर न चिंतां कर्त्तुमर्हसि।।
त्रिरात्राभ्यंतरे कंसं निहनिष्यामि सानुगम्।। १०।।

Rāma and I will go to Mathurā tomorrow along with you. The elders of the cow-herds shall accompany us carrying sufficient offerings. Rest here to night and drive all thy anxiety. Within three nights I will destroy Kansa and all his followers."

श्रीपराशर उवाच

समादिश्य ततो गोपानक्रूरोऽपि च केशवः।।
सुष्वाप बलभद्रश्च नंदगोपगृहे ततः।। ११।।

Parāśara said :—Having thus commanded the cow-herds, Akrūra with Keśava and Rāma retired to rest and slept soundly in the house of Nanda.

ततः प्रभाते विमले कृष्णरामौ महाद्युती।।
अक्रूरेण समं गंतुमुद्यतौ मथुरां पुरीम्।। १२।।

The next morning was clear and the youngmen prepared to proceed to Mathurā with Akrūra.

दृष्ट्वा गोपीजनस्सास्त्रः श्लथद्वलयबाहुकः।।
निशश्वासातिदुःखार्त्तः प्राह चेदं परस्परम्।। १३।।

The females of the cow-herds, on seeing them about to depart, were much afflicted. They wept bitterly—their bracelets were loose upon their arms—and they thus thought within themselves—

मथुरां प्राप्य गोविंदः कथं गोकुलमेष्यति।
नगरस्त्रीकलालापमधु श्रोत्रेण पास्यति।। १४।।

"If Govinda goes to Mathurā, how will he come back to Gokula? His ears will be pleased by the sweet and finished conversation of the damsels of the city.

विलासवाक्यपानेषु नागरीणां कृतास्पदम्।।
चित्तमस्य कथं भूयो ग्राम्यगोपीषु यास्यति।। १५।।

And being used to the language of the graceful females of Mathurā he will never again like the rustic expressions of the Gopīs.

सारं समस्तगोष्ठस्य विधिना हरता हरिम्।।
प्रहृतं गोपयोषित्सु निर्घृणेन दुरात्मना।। १६।।

Hari, the pride of our village is taken away and a fatal blow is laid upon us by inexorable destiny.

भावगर्भस्मितं वाक्यं विलासललिता गतिः।।
नागरीणामतीवैतत्कटाक्षेक्षितमेव च।। १७।।

The women of the city have sweet smiles, graceful language, beautiful air, elegant gait and significant glances.

ग्राम्यो हरिरयं तासां विलासनिगडैर्युतः।।
भवतीनां पुनः पार्श्वं कया युक्त्या समैष्यति।। १८।।

Hari is of rustic breeding, and, captivated by their fascinations, what likelihood is there of his returning to the society of any one amongst us?

एषैष रथमारुह्य मथुरां याति केशवः।।
क्रूरेणाक्रूरकेणात्र निर्घृणेन प्रतारितः।। १९।।

Keśava, who has mounted the car to go to Mathurā, has been deceived by the cruel, vile, and desperate Akrūra.

किं न वेत्ति नृशंसोयमनुरागपरं जनम्।।
येनैवमक्ष्णोराह्लादं नयत्यन्यत्र नो हरिम्।। २०।।

Does not the unfeeling traitor know the affection that we all here feel for our Hari, the joy of our eyes, that he is taking him away?

एष रामेण सहितः प्रयात्यत्यंतनिर्घृणः।।
रथमा रुह्य गोविंदस्त्वर्यतामस्य वारणे।। २१।।

Unkind that he is, Govinda is departing from us, along with Rāma : haste! let us stop him!

गुरूणामग्रतो वक्तुं किं ब्रवीथ न नः क्षमम्।।
गुरवः किं करिष्यंति दग्धानां विरहाग्निना।। २२।।

Why talk of telling our seniors that we cannot bear his loss? What can they do for us, we are consumed by the fires of separation?

नंदगोपमुखा गोपा गंतुमेते समुद्यताः।।
नोद्यमं कुरुते कश्चिद्गोविंदविनिवर्त्तने।। २३।।

The Gopas, with Nanda at their head, are themselves preparing to depart; no one makes any attempt to detain Govinda.

सुप्रभाताद्य रजनी मथुरावासयोषिताम्।।
पास्यंत्यच्युतवक्त्रब्जं यासां नेत्रालिपंक्तयः। २४।।

Bright is the morning that succeeds to this night for the women of Mathurā, for the bees of their eyes will feed upon the lotus face of Acyuta.

धन्यास्ते पथि ये कृष्णमितो यांत्यनिवारिताः।।
उद्वहिष्यंति पश्यंतस्स्वदेहं पुलकांचितम्।। २५।।

Happy are they who may go hence without impediment, and behold, enraptured, Kṛṣṇa on his journey.

मथुरानगरीपौरनयनानां महोत्सवः।।
गोविंदावयवैर्दृष्टैरतीवाद्य भविष्यति।। २६।।

A great festival will delight today the eyes of the inhabitants of Mathurā when they will behold the person of Govinda.

को नु स्वप्नस्सभाग्याभिर्दृष्टस्ताभिरधोक्षजम्।।
विस्तारिकांतिनयना या द्रक्ष्यंत्यनिवारिताः।। २७।।

What pleasureable dream was seen by the happy damsels of the city that their graceful eyes shall behold unobstructed the countenance of Kṛṣṇa!

अहो गोपीजनस्यास्य दर्शयित्वा महानिधिम्।।
उत्कृत्तान्यद्य नेत्राणि विधिनाकरुणात्मना।। २८।।

Alas! the eyes of the females of cow-herds have been deprived of their vision by the relentles Brahmā, after he had shown them this great treasure.

अनुरागेण शैथिल्यमस्मासु व्रजिते हरौः।।
शैथिल्यमुपयांत्याशु करेषु वलयान्यपि।। २९।।

Hari departing with his love for us decayed, the bracelets from our arms slip.

अक्रूरः क्रूरहृदयश्शीघ्र प्रेरयते हयान्।।
एवमार्त्तासु योषित्सु कृपा कस्य न जायते।। ३०।।

The cruel-hearted Akrūra urges on the steeds; who does not feel pity for females like us who are bewailing?

एष कृष्णरथस्योच्चैश्चक्ररेणुर्निरीक्ष्यताम्।।
दूरीभूतो हरिर्येन सोऽपि रेणुर्नलक्ष्यते।। ३१।।

Alas! behold the dust of Kṛṣṇa's chariot-wheels! and now he is distanced from us by that for even that dust is no longer to be seen!"

श्रीपराशर उवाच

इत्येवमतिहार्देन गोपीजननिरीक्षितः।।
तत्याज व्रजभूभागं सह रामेण केशवः।। ३२।।

Thus lamented by the damsels, Keśava and Rāma left the hamlet of Vraja.

गच्छंतो जवनाश्वेन रथेन यमुनातटम्।।
प्राप्तमध्यह्नसमये रामाक्रूरजनार्द्दनाः।। ३३।।

Travelling in a car drawn by quick-coursing steeds they reached, at noon, the banks of the Yamunā when Akrūra requested them to halt a little whilst he performed the usual daily ceremonial in the river.

अथाह कृष्णमक्रूरो भवाभ्यां तावदास्यताम्।।
यावत्करोभि कालिंद्या आह्निकार्हणमंभसि।। ३४।।

श्रीपराशर उवाच

तथेत्युक्तस्ततस्नातस्स्वाचांतस्स महामतिः।।
दध्यौ ब्रह्म परं विप्र प्रविष्टो यमुना जले।। ३५।।

They having agreed to this, the high-minded Akrūra bathed in the water and rinsed his mouth and then entering the stream he stood meditating upon the Supreme Being.

फणासहस्रमालाढ्यं बलभद्रं ददर्श सः।।
कुंदमालांगमुन्निद्रपद्मपत्रायतेक्षणम्।। ३६।।

वृतं वासुकिरंभाद्यैर्महद्भिः पवनाशिभिः।।
संस्तूयमानमुद्गंधिवनमालाविभूषितम्।। ३७।।

दधानमसिते वस्त्रे चारुरूपावतंसकम्।।
चारुकुंडलिनं भांतमंतर्जलतले स्थितम्।। ३८।।

He beheld, in his meditation, Balabhadra, having a thousand-hooded heads, a garland of jasmine flowers, having large-red eyes resembling lotus petals, surrounded by Vāsuki, Rambha and other mighty serpents, praised by Gandharvas, decorated with garlands of wild flowers, clad in dark-coloured raiment, crowned with a chaplet of lotuses, adorned with brilliant ear-rings, drunk and standing at the bottom of the river in the water.

तस्योत्संगे घनश्याममाताम्रायतलोचनम्।।
चतुर्बाहुमुदारांगं चक्राद्यायुधभूषणम्।। ३९।।

पीते वसानं वसने चित्रमाल्योपशोभितम्।।
शक्रचापतडिन्मालाविचित्रमिव तोयदम्।। ४०।।

श्रीवत्सवक्षसं चारु स्फुरन्मकरकुंडलम्।।
ददर्श कृष्णमक्लिष्टं पुंडरीकावतंसकम्।। ४१।।

सनंदनाद्यैर्मुनिभिस्सिद्धयोगैरकल्मषै।।
संचिंत्यमानं तत्रस्थैर्नासाग्रन्यस्तलोचनैः।। ४२।।

He saw on his lap Viṣṇu, having four arms, and holding conch, discus, and mace, having the complexion of cloud, coppery and expansive eyes, excellent ear-rings and an elegant form, clad in yellow clothes, adorned with many coloured flowers and appearing like a cloud adorned with streams of lightnings and the bow of Indra; his breast was marked with celestial sign, four arms were adroned with *keyūras* and head with a brilliant crown : he was attended by Sanandana and; other holy sages, who, fixing their eyes upon the tips of their noses, were absorbed in profound meditation.

बलकृष्णौ तथाक्रूरः प्रत्यभिज्ञाय विस्मितः।।
अचिंतयद्रथाच्छीघ्रं कथमत्रागताविति।। ४३।।

Understanding them as Kṛṣṇa and Balarāma, Akrūra was struck with amazement; and he thought how they could so quickly have got there from the chariot.

विवक्षोस्तंभयामास वाचं तस्य जनार्दनः।।
ततो निष्क्रम्य सलिलाद्रथमभ्यागतः पुनः।। ४४।।

He desired to ask them of this, but Janārddana deprived him of the faculty of speech at that moment.

ददर्श तत्र चैवोभौ रथस्योपरि निष्ठितौ।।
रामकृष्णौ यथापूर्वं मनुष्यवपुषान्वितौ।। ४५।।

Having come out of the waters he then came to the chariot and saw there, like before, Rāma and Kṛṣṇa stationed in their human forms.

निगम्नश्च पुनस्तोये ददर्श च तथैव तौ।।
संस्तूयमानौ गंधर्वैर्मुनिसिद्धमहोरगैः।। ४६।।

And having entered the stream again he saw those two forms praised by Gandharvas, great ascetics, Siddhas and great serpents.

ततो विज्ञातसद्भावस्स तु दानपतिस्तदा।।
तुष्टाव सर्वविज्ञानमयमच्युतमीश्वरम्।। ४७।।

Apprehending then their real nature he enlogized the eternal deity gifted with discriminative knowledge.

अक्रूर उवाच

सन्मात्ररूपिणेचिंत्यमहिम्ने परमात्मने।।
व्यापिने नैकरूपैकस्वरूपाय नमोनमः।। ४८।।

Akrūra said :—"Salutation to thee, who art uniform and manifold, all pervading, Sureme spirit, of inconceivable glory and who art simple existence.

सर्वरूपाय तेऽचिंत्यहविर्भूताय ते नमः।।
नमो विज्ञानपाराय पराय प्रकृतेः प्रभो।। ४९।।

भूतात्मा चेंद्रियात्मा च प्रधानात्मा तथा भवान्।।
आत्मा च परमात्मा च त्वमेकः पञ्चधा स्थितः।। ५०।।

Salutation to thee, O inscrutable, who art truth and the essence of oblations. Salutation to thee, O Lord, whose nature is unknown, who art beyond primeval matter, who existest in five forms, identical with the elements, with the faculties, with matter, with the living soul and with the Supreme spirit.

प्रसीद सर्व सर्वात्मन् क्षराक्षरमयेश्वर।।
ब्रह्मविष्णुशिवाख्याभिः कल्पनाभिरुदीरितः।।५१।।

Be propitiated with me, O soul of the universe, essence of all things, perishable or eternal, whether addressed by the name Brahmā, Viṣṇu, Śiva or like.

अनाख्येयस्वरूपात्मन्ननाख्येयप्रयोजन।।
अनाख्येय भिधानं त्वां नतोस्मि परमेश्वर।। ५२।।

न यत्र नाथ विद्यंते नामाजात्यादिकल्पनाः।।
तद्ब्रह्म परमं नित्यमविकारि भवानजः।। ५३।।

I adore thee, O God, whose nature is indestructible, whose purposes cannot be deciphered, whose name even is unknown; for the attributes of kind or appellation are not applicable to thee, who art that, the supreme Brāhmaṇa, eternal, unchangeable, uncreated.

न कल्पनामृतेर्थस्य सर्वस्याधिगमो यतः।।
ततः कृष्णाच्युतानंतविष्णुसंज्ञाभिरीड्यते।। ५४।।

But as our objects can not be accomplished but through some specific from, thou art termed by us Kṛṣṇa, Acyuta, Ananta or Viṣṇu.

सर्वार्थास्त्वमज विकल्पनाभिरे-
तैर्देवाद्यैर्भवति हि यैरनंतविश्वम्।।
विश्वात्मा त्वमिति विकारहीनमेतत्-
सर्वस्मिन्न हि भवतोस्ति किंचिदन्यत्।। ५५।।

Thou, unborn divinity, art all the objects of these impersonation; thou art the gods and all other beings; thou art the whole world, thou art all. Soul of the universe, thou art free from change and there is nothing except thee in all this existence.

त्वं ब्रह्मा पशुपतिरर्यमा विधाता
धाता त्वं त्रिदशपतिस्समीरणोऽग्निः।।
तोयेशो धनपतिरंतकस्त्वमेको
भिन्नार्थैर्जगदभिपासि शक्तिभेदैः।।५६।।

Thou art Brahmā, Paśupati, Āryaman, Dhātrī and Vidhātrī!; thou art Indra, air, fire, the regent of the waters, the god of wealth and the judge of the dead; and thou, although but one, presidest over the world with various energies directed to various purposes.

विश्वं भवान्सृजति सूर्यगभस्तिरूपो
विश्वेश ते गुणमयोयमतः प्रपञ्चः।।
रूपं परं सदिति वाचकमक्षरं
यज्ज्ञानात्मने सदसते प्रणतोऽस्मि तस्मै।।५७।।

Thou, identical with the solar ray, createst the universe : all elementary substance is composed of thy qualities; and thy supreme form is denoted by the imperishable from *Sat*. I bow to him who is identical with true knowledge and who is and not perceptible.

ॐ नमो वासुदेवाय नमस्संकर्षणाय च ।।
प्रद्युम्नाय नमस्तुभ्यमनिरुद्धाय ते नमः।। ५८।।

Salutation to him the lord Vasudeva, to Saṅkarṣaṇa, to Pradyumna and to Aniruddha.

।। इति श्रीविष्णुमहापुराणे पञ्चमेंशेऽष्टादशोऽध्यायः।।१८।।

अथ पञ्चमेंशेः एकोनविंशोऽध्यायः

Part V : Section 19

श्रीपराशर उवाच

एवमंतर्जले विष्णुमभिष्टूय स यादवः।।
अर्चयामास सर्वेशं धूपपुष्पैर्मनोमयैः।। १।।

Parāśara said :—Having thus praised Viṣṇu, standing in the stream that descendant of the Yadu race worshipped the lord of all with flowers, incense and all other beautiful articles.

परित्यक्तान्यविषयो मनस्तत्र निवेश्य सः।।
ब्रह्मभूते चिरं स्थित्वा विरराम समाधितः।। २।।

Having withdrawn his mind from every

thing else and devoted it to Viṣṇu, he engaged, for some time, in the meditation, "I am Brahman" and then desisted from his abstraction.

कृतकृत्यमिवात्मानं मन्यमानो महामतिः ।।
आजगाम रथं भूयो निर्गम्य यमुनांभसः ।। ३ ।।

Then considering himself as blessed, the high-minded Akrūra got up from the waters of the Yamunā and came to the chariot.

ददर्श रामकृष्णौ च यथापूर्वमवस्थितौ ।।
विस्मिताक्षस्तदाऽक्रूरस्तं च कृष्णोऽभ्यभाषत ।। ४ ।।

Like before, he again saw stationed on the car, Rāma and Kṛṣṇa. Seeing Akrūra thus amazed,—

श्रीकृष्ण उवाच

नूनं ते दृष्टमाश्चर्यमक्रूर यमुनाजले ।।
विस्मयोत्फुल्लनयनो भवान्संलक्ष्यते यतः ।। ५ ।।

Kṛṣṇa said—"Forsooth, O Akrūra your eyes are expanded with surprise. Methinks you have seen something wonderful in the waters of the Yamunā."

अक्रूर उवाच

अंतर्जले यदाश्चर्थं दृष्टं तत्र मयाऽच्युत ।।
तदत्रापि हि पश्यामि मूर्त्तिमत्पुरतः स्थितम् ।। ६ ।।
जगदेतन्महाश्चर्य्यरूपं यस्य महात्मनः ।।
तेनाश्चर्यपरेणाहं भवता कृष्ण संगतः ।। ७ ।।

Akrūra said :—"O Acyuta, the wonder I saw in the waters, I behold here, before me in a bodily shape; I am united with thee, Kṛṣṇa, the marvel I have seen and whose wondrous form is the universe.

तत्किमेतेन मथुरां यास्यामो मधुसूदन ।।
बिभेमि कंसाद्धिग्जन्म परपिंडोपजीविनाम् ।। ८ ।।

No more of this, let us go to Mathurā, O Slayer of Madhu—I am afraid of Kansa. Oh! fie on them who eat the bread of another."

इत्युक्त्वा चोदयामास स हयान् वातरंहसः ।।
संप्राप्तश्चापि सायाह्ने सोऽक्रूरो मथुरां पुरीम् ।। ९ ।।

Saying this he urged on the quick steeds and they arrived, after sunset, at Mathurā.

विलोक्य मथुरां कृष्णं रामं चाह स यादवः ।।
पद्भ्यां यातं महावीरौ रथेनैको विशाम्यहम् ।। १० ।।
गंतव्यं वसुदेवस्य नो भवद्भ्यां तथा गृहम् ।।
युवयोर्हि कृते वृद्धस्स कंसेन निरस्यते ।। ११ ।।

When they came in sight of the city, Akrūra said to Kṛṣṇa and Rāma "You must now go on foot, whilst I proceed alone in the car; and you must not go to the house of Vasudeva for the elder has been banished by Kansa on your account."

श्रीपराशर उवाच

इत्युक्त्वा प्रविवेशाऽथ सोऽक्रूरो मथुरां पुरीम् ।।
प्रविष्टौ रामकृष्णौ च राजमार्गमुपागतौ ।।१२ ।।

Parāśara said :—Having said this Akrūra alone entered the city of Mathurā, Rāma and Kṛṣṇa proceeded thereto following the public road.

स्त्रीभिर्नरैश्च सानंदं लोचनैरभिवीक्षितौ ।।
जग्मतुर्लीलया वीरौ मत्तौ बालगजाविव ।। १३ ।।

All the females and males of Mathurā espied the two brothers with delight. And they went along sportively looking like two young elephants.

भ्रममाणौ ततो दृष्ट्वा रजकं रंगकारकम् ।।
अयाचेतां सुरूपाणि वासांसि रुचिराणि तौ ।। १४ ।।

As they roamed about, they saw a washerman colouring clothes and, with smiling countenances, they went and wanted of him some of his fine linen.

कंसस्य रजकः सोऽथ प्रसादारूढविस्मयः ।।
बहून्याक्षेपवाक्यानि प्राहोच्चै रामकेशवौ ।। १५ ।।

He was a washerman of Kansa and was made insolent by his master's favour, so he remonstrated hard with Rāma and Keśava.

ततस्तलप्रहारेण कृष्णस्तस्य दुरात्मनः ।।
पातयामास रोषेण राजकस्य शिरो भुवि ।। १६ ।।

Thereupon Kṛṣṇa, in rage, struck down the head of that vicious-souled (washerman) on earth.

हत्वाऽऽदाय च वस्त्राणि पीतनीलांबरौ ततः।।
कृष्णरामौ मुदा युक्तौ मालाकारगृहं गतौ।। १७।।

Having thus killed him and taken yellow and blue raiment Kṛṣṇa and Rāma, delightedly came to a flower-seller's shop.

विकासिनेत्रयुगलो मालाकारोतिविस्मितः।।
एतौ कस्य सुतौ यातौ मैत्रेयाचिंतयत्तदा।। १८।।

Seeing them, having expansive eyes, the flower-seller was astonished and thought, O Maitreya, who could they be or whence could they have come.

पीतनीलांबरधरौ तौ दृष्ट्वातिमनोहरौ।।
स तर्कयामास तदा भुवं देवावुपागतौ।। १९।।

Beholding two youths so lovely, dressed in yellow and blue garments, he took them to be divinities descended upon earth.

विकासिमुखपद्माभ्यां ताभ्यां पुष्पाणि याचितः।।
भुवं विष्टभ्य हस्ताभ्यां पस्पर्श शिरसा महीम्।। २०।।

Being asked for some flowers, by them having mouths budding like lotuses he placed his hands upon the ground and touched it with his head, saying—

प्रसादपरमौ नाथौ मम गेहमुपागतौ।।
धन्योऽहमर्चयिष्यामीत्याह तौ माल्यजीवनः।। २१।।

'My lords have shown me great kindness, by coming to my house, fortunate that I am; I will pay them homage."

ततः प्रहृष्टवदनस्तयोः पुष्पाणि कामतः।।
चारूण्येतान्यथैतानि प्रददौ स प्रलोभयन्।। २२।।

Having said this, the flower-seller, with a smiling face, gave them whatever choice flowers they selected, to gain their favour.

पुनःपुनः प्रणम्योभौ मालाकारो नरोत्तमौ।।
ददौ पुष्पाणि चारुणि गंधवंत्यमलानि च।। २३।।

Prostrating himself again and again before them, he presented them again and again with flowers beautiful, fragrant and fresh.

मालाकाराय कृष्णोपि प्रसन्नः प्रददौ वरान्।।
श्रीस्त्वां मत्संश्रया भद्र न कदाचित्यजिष्यति।। २४।।

Being much pleased with him, Kṛṣna gave him the blessing—"Fortune, O good friend, who depends on me, shall never forsake thee.

बलहानिर्न ते सौम्य धनहानिरथापि वा।।
यावद्दिनानि तावच्च न नशिष्यति संततिः।। २५।।

Thou shalt never lose strength or wealth and thy family shall never be extinct.

भुक्त्वा च विपुलान्भोगांस्त्वमंते मत्प्रसादतः।।
ममानुस्मरणं प्राप्य दिव्यं लोकमवाप्स्यसि।। २६।।

Enjoying many things, thou shalt, in the end, remembering me, attain to the region of the celesetials.

धर्मे मनश्च ते भद्र सार्वकालं भविष्यति।।
युष्मत्संततिजातानां दीर्घमायुर्भविष्यति।। २७।।

O good friend, thy mind shall always be in virtue and those, who shall be born in thy race, shall be long-lived.

नोपसर्गादिकं दोषं युष्मत्संततिसंभवः।।
अवाप्स्यपि महाभाग यावत्सूर्यो भविष्यति।। २८।।

O great one, as long as the sun shall exist, none, in thy race, shall be disturbed with famine or other troubles."

श्रीपराशर उवाच

इत्युक्त्वा तद्गृहात्कृष्णो बल देवसहायवान्।।
निर्जगाम मुनिश्रेष्ठ मालाकारेण पूजितः।। २९।।

Parāśara said :—Having said this and been worshipped by the flower-seller, O foremost of Munis, Kṛṣṇa in the company of Balarāma, issued out of his house.

।। इति श्रीविष्णुमहापुराणे पञ्चमेंशे एकोनविंशोऽध्यायः।। १९।।

अथ पञ्चमेंशेः विंशोऽध्यायः
Part V : Section 20

श्रीपराशर उवाच

राजमार्गे ततः कृष्णस्सानुलेपनभाजनाम्।।
दद्दर्श कुब्जामायांतीं नवयौवनगोचराम्।। १।।

Parāśara said :—While thus going along the high road, Kṛṣṇa saw a young girl, who was crooked, carrying a pot of unguent.

तामाह ललितं कष्णः कस्येदमनुलेपनम्।।
भवत्या नीयते सत्यं वदेंदीवरलोचने।। २।।

Kṛṣṇa addressed her in sweet words and said—"For whom are you carrying that unguent? Tell me, lovely maiden, tell me truly."

सकामेनेव सा प्रोक्तासानुरागा हरिं प्रति।।
प्राह सा ललितं कुब्जा तद्दर्शनबलात्कृता।। ३।।

Being thus addressed by him through affection, Kubjā being attracted by his affection and well disposed towards Hari, replied to him also mirthfully :—

कांत कस्मान्न जानासि कंसेन विनियोजिताम्।।
नैकवक्त्रेति विख्यातामनुलेपनकर्मणि।। ४।।

"Do you not know, my lord, that my name is Trivakra, I am the servant of Kansa and appointed to prepare his perfumes.

नान्यपिष्टं हि कंसस्य्प्रीतये ह्यनुलेपनम्।।
भवाम्यहमतीवास्य प्रसादधनभाजनम्।। ५।।

Kansa does not like perfumes prepared by any other female and for this he loves me greatly and shows me favour."

श्रीकृष्ण उवाच

सुगंधमेतद्राजार्हं रुचिरं रुचिरानने।।
आवयोर्गात्र सदृशं दीयतामनुलेपनम्।। ६।।

Kṛṣṇa said :—"O thou having a lovely countenance, give us sufficient unguent used by the king, to rub upon our bodies."

श्रीपराशर उवाच

श्रुत्वैतराह सा कुब्जा गृह्यतामिति सादरम्।।
अनुलेपनं च प्रददौ गात्रयोग्यमथो भयोः।। ७।।

भक्तिच्छेदानुलिप्तांगौ ततस्तौ पुरुषर्षभौ।।
सेंद्रचापौ व्यराजेतां सितकृष्णाविवांबुदौ।। ८।।

"Take it," Kubjā said and she gave them as much of the unguent as was required for their persons and they rubbed it on various parts of their bodies and faces, till they looked like two clouds, one white and one black, decorated by the many-tinted bow of Indra.

ततस्तां चुबुके शौरिरुल्लापन विधानवित्।।
उत्पाट्य तोलयामास दव्यगुनेनाग्रपाणिना।। ९।।
चकर्ष पद्भ्यां च तदा ऋजुत्वं केशवोऽनयत्।।

Then Kṛṣṇa skilled in the curative art, took hold of her under the chin, with the thumb and two fingers and lifted up her head, whilst with his feet he pressed down her feet and in this way he made her straight.

ततस्सा ऋजुतां प्राप्ता योषितामभवद्वरा।। १०।।
विलासललितं प्राह प्रेमगर्भभरालसम्।।
वस्त्रे प्रगृह्य गोविंद. मम गेहं व्रजेति वै।। ११।।

Being thus rendered straight, she became the most beautiful of damsels. Then filled with affection, she took Govinda by the garment and said "Come to my house."

एवमुक्तस्तया शौरी रामस्यालोक्य चाननम्।।
प्रहस्य कुब्जां तामाह नैकवक्रामनिंदिताम्।। १२।।

Hari, smiling, replied—"I shall come to your house some time after."

आयास्ये भवतीगेहमिति तां प्रहसन्हरिः।।
विससर्ज जहासोच्चै रामस्यालोक्य चाननम्।। १३।।

Having thus dismissed her and cast his looks towards Rāma, he laughed aloud.

भक्तिभेदानुलिप्तांगौ नीलपीतांबरौ तु तौ।।
धनुश्शालां ततो यातौ चित्रमाल्योपशोभितौ।। १४।।

Dressed then in blue and yellow raiment and anointed with fragrant unguents and adorned with beautiful garlands, Keśava, and Rāma went to the hall of arms.

आयांगं तद्धनूरत्नं ताभ्यां पृष्टैस्तु रक्षिभिः ।।
आख्याते सहसा कृष्णो गृहीत्वा पूरयद्धनुः ।। १५ ।।

They then inquired of the warder which excellent bow they would take.

ततः पूरयता तेन जभ्यमानं बलाद्धनुः ।।
चकार सुमहच्छब्दं मथुरा येन पूरिता ।। १६ ।।

Being informed, Kṛṣṇa at once took up a bow and bent it; then drawing it with violence he snapped it in two and all Mathurā resounded with the noise made by its fracture.

अनुयुक्तौ ततस्तौ तु भग्ने धनुषि रक्षिभिः ।।
रक्षिसैन्यं निहत्योभौनिष्क्रांतौ कार्मुकालयात् ।। १७ ।।

Abused by the guards for breaking the bow, Kṛṣṇa and Rāma retorted and defied them and left the hall.

अक्रूरागमवृत्तांतमुपलभ्य महद्धनुः ।।
भग्नं श्रुत्वा च कंसोऽपि प्राह चाणूरमुष्टिकौ ।। १८ ।।

When Kansa came to know that Akrūra had returned and Kṛṣṇa had snapped the bow, he then said to Cāṇūra and Muṣṭika :—

कंस उवाच

गोपालदारकौ प्राप्तौ भवभ्द्यां तु ममाग्रतः ।।
मल्लयुद्धेन हंतव्यौ मम प्राणहरौ हि तौ ।। १९ ।।

"Two cow-herd boys have arrived—You must kill them both before me in a trial of strength, for they always try to kill me.

नियुद्धे तद्विनाशेन भवद्भ्यां तोषितो ह्यहम् ।।
दास्याम्यभिमतान्कामान्नान्यथैतौ महाबलौ ।। २० ।।

When you two, gifted with great strength, shall destroy these two cow-herd boys—I shall give you whatever you will desire.

न्यायतोन्यायतो वापि भवद्भ्यां तौ ममाहितौ ।।
हंतव्यौ तद्वधाद्राज्यं सामान्यं वां भविष्यति ।। २१ ।।

These two boys are my enemies; by means, whether foul or fair, you must kill them both.

इत्यादिश्य स तौ मल्लौ ततश्चाहूय हस्तिपम् ।।
प्रोवाचोच्चैस्त्वया मल्लसमाजद्वारि कुञ्जरः ।। २२ ।।

They killed, the kingdom shall be ours in common." Having thus commanded the two wrestlers, he sent for his elephant-driver and said to him loudly —

स्थाप्यः कुवलयापीडस्तेन तौ गोपदारकौ ।।
घयातनीयौ नियुद्धाय रंगद्वारमुपागतौ ।। २३ ।।

"You must place my great elephant Kuvalayāpīḍa who is as huge as a cloud charged with rain, near the gate of the arena and drive him upon the two boys when they shall attempt to enter."

तमप्याज्ञाप्य दृष्ट्वा च सर्वान्मञ्चानुपाकृतान् ।।
आसन्न मरणः कंसः सूर्योदयमुदैक्षतः ।। २४ ।।

Having given these orders, he ascertained that the platforms were all ready and waited for the rising sun, not conscious of his impending death.

ततः समस्तमञ्चेषु नागरस्स तदा जनः ।।
राजमञ्चेषु चारूढास्सह भृत्यैर्नराधिपाः ।। २५ ।।

In the morning the citizens assembled on the platforms set apart for them and the princes with the ministers and courtiers occupied the royal seats.

मल्लप्राश्निकवर्गश्च रंगमध्यसमीपगः ।।
कृतं कंसेन कंसोऽपि तुंगमञ्चे व्यवस्थितः ।। २६ ।।

Kansa made all those sit in front who were judges of the games whilst he himself sat apart, close by, upon a lofty throne.

अंतःपुराणां मञ्चाश्च तथाऽन्ये परिकल्पिताः ।।
अन्ये च वारमुख्यानामन्ये नागरयोषिताम् ।। २७ ।।

Separate platforms were also set up for the ladies of the palace and they sat there.

नंदगोपादयो गोपा मञ्चेष्वन्येष्ववस्थिताः ।।
अक्रूरवसुदेवौ च मञ्चप्रांते व्यवस्थितौ ।। २८ ।।

Nanda and cow-herds had places set apart for them at the end of which sat Akrūra and Vasudeva.

नागरीयोषितां मध्ये देवकीपुत्रगद्धद्धनी ।।
अंतकालेऽपि पुत्रस्य द्रक्ष्यामिति मुखं स्थिता ।। २९ ।।

Amongst the wives of the citizens was

Devakī, mourning for her son, whose lovely countenance she desired to see even in the hour of destruction.

वाद्यमानेषु तूर्येषु चाणूरे चातिवल्गति।।
हाहाकारपरे लोके ह्यास्फोटयति मुष्टिके।। ३०।।

ईषद्धसंतौ तौ वीरौ बलभद्रजनार्दनौ।।
गोपवेषधरौ बालौ रंगद्वारमुपागतौ।। ३१।।

ततः कुवलयापीडो महामात्रप्रचोदितः।।
अभ्यधावत वेगेन हंतुं गोपकुमारकौ।। ३२।।

हाहाकारो महाञ्झज्ञे रंगमध्ये द्विजोत्तम।।
बलदेवोऽनुजं दृष्ट्वा वचनं चेदमब्रवीत्।। ३३।।

हंतव्यो हि महाभाग नागोऽयं शत्रुचोदितः।। ३४।।

इत्युक्तस्सोऽग्रजेनाथ बलदेवेन वै द्विज।।
सिंहनादं ततश्चक्रे माधवः परवीरहा।। ३५।।

करेण करमाकृष्य तस्य केशिनिषूदनः।।
भ्रामयामास तं शैरिरैरावतसमं बले।। ३६।।

ईशोपि सर्वजगतां बाललीलानुसारतः।।
क्रीडित्वा सुचिरं कृष्णः करिदंतपदांतरे।। ३७।।

उत्पाट्य वामदंतं तु दक्षिणेनैव पाणिना।।
ताडयामास यंतारं तस्यासीच्छतधा शिरः।। ३८।।

दक्षिणं दंतमुत्पाट्य बलभद्रोऽपि तत्क्षणात्।।
सरोषस्तेन पार्श्वस्थान् गजपालानपोथयत्।। ३९।।

ततस्तूत्प्लुत्य वेगेन रौहिणेयो महाबलः।।
जघान वामपादेन मस्तके हस्तिनं रुषा।।४०।।

स पपात हतस्तेन बलभद्रेण लीलया।।
सहस्राक्षेण वज्रेण ताडितः पर्वतो यथा।। ४१।।

हत्वा कुवलयापीडं हस्त्यारोहप्रचोदितम्।।
मदासृगनुलिप्तांगौ हस्तिदंतवरायुधौ।।४२।।

मृगमध्ये यथा सिंहौ गर्वलीलावलोकिनौ।।
प्रविष्टौ सुमहारंगं बलभद्रजनार्दनौ।।४३।।

Thereafter the bugles were sounded and Cāṇūra sprang forth and Muṣṭika clapped his arms defiantly and people cried aloud "Alas." Covered with the temporal juice and blood of the elephant, whom they had killed when driven against them by the driver, Balabhadra and Janārddana confidently entered the arena, like two lions amidst a herd of deer, with proud looks towards all.

हाहाकारो महाञ्झज्ञे महारंगे त्वनंतरम्।।
कृष्णोऽयं बलभद्रोयमिति लोकस्य विस्मयः।।४४।।

There arose exclamations of pity and expressions of surprise from all the arena and people said "This is Kṛṣṇa! This is Balabhadra!!

सोऽयं येन हता घोरा पूतना बालघातिनी।।
क्षिप्तं तु शकटं येन भग्नौ तु यमलार्जुनौ।। ४५।।

This is that Kṛṣṇa by whom the she-demon Pūtanā was killed. This that Kṛṣṇna by whom the waggon was upset. This is that Kṛṣṇa who uprooted the two trees.

सोयं यः कालियं नागं ममर्दारुह्य बालकः।।
धृतो गोवर्द्धनो येन सप्तरात्रं महागिरिः।। ४६।।

This is that Kṛṣṇa—the boy who danced upon the hooded fangs of the serpent Kālīya and who for seven days upheld the moutain Govardhana.

अरिष्टो धेनुकः केशी लीलयैव महात्मना।।
निहता येन दुर्वत्ता दृश्यतामेष सोऽच्युतः।। ४७।।

Behold, this is that Kṛṣṇa, who easily destroyed the demons Ariṣṭa, Dhenuka and Keśin. This is that Acyuta.

अयं चास्य महाबाहुर्बलभद्रोऽग्रतोऽग्रजः।।
प्रयाति लीलया योषिन्मनोनयननंदनः।। ४८।।

There is his elder brother Balabhadra, before him, having long arms. He is young, sportively affording delight to the minds and eyes of the damsels.

अयं स कथ्यते प्राज्ञैः पुराणार्थविशारदैः।।
गोपालो यादवं वंशं मग्नमभ्युद्धरिष्यति।। ४९।।

It has been foretold by the wise, skilled in the sense of Purāṇas that he shall, as a cowherd, exalt the depressed Yadu race.

अयं हि सर्वलोकस्य विष्णोरखिलजन्मनः।।
अवतीर्णो महीमंशो नूनं भारहरो भुवः।। ५०।।

This is a portion of the all-existing, all-generating Viṣṇu descended upon earth, who will assuredly lighten her load."

इत्येवं वर्णिते पौरे रामे कृष्णे च तत्क्षणात्।।
उरस्तताप देवक्याः स्नेहस्नुतपयोधरम्।। ५१।।

The citizens having thus described Rāma and Kṛṣṇa, Devakī's heart was filled with compassion and milk oozed out of her breast out of affection.

महोत्सवमिवासाद्य पुत्राननविलोकनात्।।
युवेव वसुदेवोऽभूद्विहायाभ्यागतां जराम्।। ५२।।

And on beholding the faces of his son, Vasudeva forgot his infirmities and felt himself young again.

विस्तारिताक्षियुगलो राजांतःपुरयोषिताम्।।
नागरस्त्रीसमूहश्च द्रष्टुं न विरराम तम्।। ५३।।

सख्यः पश्यत कृष्णस्य मुखमत्यरुणेक्षणम्।।
गजयुद्धकृतायासस्वेदांबुकणिकाचितम्।। ५४।।

The women of the palace, and the females of the city beheld Kṛṣṇa with eyes wide open. "Look friends" said they to their companions "look at the face of Kṛṣṇa; his eyes are reddened by his conflict with the elephant and the drops of perspiration stand upon his cheek outweighing a full-blown lotus in autumn studded with glittering dew.

विकासिशरदंभोजमपश्यामजलोक्षितम्।।
परिभूयं स्थितं जन्म सफलं क्रियतां दृशः।। ५५।।

श्रीवत्सांकं महद्धाम बालस्यैतद्विलोक्यताम्।।
विपक्षक्षपणं वक्षो भुजयुग्मं च भामिनी।। ५६।।

Make your birth blessed and the faculty of vision fruitful, by beholding the breast of the boy, the seat of splendour and marked with the mystic sign Śrīvatsa; and see his arms menacing destruction to the enemies.

किं न पश्यसि दुग्धेंदुमृणालधवलाकृतिम्।।
बलभद्रमिमं नीलपरिधानमुपागतम्।।५७।।

Do you not see Balabhadra coming with him, clad in a blue raiment, having his countenace fair as the jasmine, as the moon and as the fibres of the lotus stem?

वल्गतामुष्टिकेनैव चाणूरेण तथा सखि।।
क्रीडतो बलभद्रस्य हरेर्हास्यं विलोक्यताम्।। ५८।।

See, how he gently smiles at the gestrues of Muṣṭika and Cāṇūra as they spring up.

सख्यः पश्यत चाणूरं नियुद्धार्थमयं हरिः।।
समुपैति न संत्यत्र किं वृद्धा मुक्तकारिणः।। ५९।।

And see Hari is advancing to meet Cāṇūra. Is there no elder present here who will judge rightly?

क्व यौवनोन्मुखीभूतसुकुमारतनुर्हरिः।।
क्व वज्रकठिनाभोगशरीरोऽयं महासुरः।। ६०।।

How can the delicate form of Hari, just in his youth, match the huge and adamantine form of the great demon Cāṇūra?

इमौ सुललितैरंगैर्वर्त्तेते नवयौवनौ।।
दैतेयमल्लाश्चाणूरप्रमुखास्त्वतिदारुणाः।। ६१।।

Two youths of delicate and beautiful forms are on the one side and the athletic friends headed by Cāṇūra on the other. Is this fair?

नियुद्धप्राश्निकानां तु महानेष व्यतिक्रमः।।
यद्बालबलिनोर्युद्धं मध्यस्थैस्समुपेक्ष्यते।। ६२।।

This is a great sin in the umpires to allow a contest between boys and strong men.

श्रीपराशर उवाच

इत्थं पुरस्त्रीलोकस्य वदतश्चालयन्भुवम्।।
ववल्ग बद्धकक्ष्योंतर्जनस्य भगवान्हरिः।। ६३।।

Parāśara said :—The women of the city having thus conversed with one another, Hari tightened his girdle and danced in the ring shaking the ground on which he trod.

बलभद्रोऽपि चास्फोट्य ववल्ग ललितं तथा।।
पदेपदे तथा भूमिर्यन्न शीर्णा तदद्भुतम्।। ६४।।

Balabhadra too, slapping his arms defiantly, danced—and wonder it is that the earth was not riven asunder by his trodding.

चाणूरेण ततः कृष्णो युयुधेऽमितविक्रमः।।
नियुद्धकुशलो दैत्यो बलभद्रेण मुष्टिकः।। ६५।।

The highly powerful Kṛṣṇa engaged with Cāṇūra and the demon Muṣṭika, well-versed in wrestling, began to fight with Balabhadra.

सन्निपातावधूतैस्तु चाणूरेण समं हरिः ।।
प्रक्षेपणैर्मुष्टिभिश्च कीलवज्रनिपातनैः ।। ६६ ।।

पादोद्धूतैः प्रमृष्टैश्च तयोर्युद्धम भून्महत् ।। ६७ ।।

Mutually entwining and pushing and pulling and beating each other with fists, arms and elbows and pressing each other with their knees, interlacing their arms, kicking with their feet, pressing with their whole weight upon another, fought Hari and Cāṇūra.

अशस्त्रमतिघोरं तत्तयोर्युद्धं सुदारुणम् ।।
बलप्राणविनिष्पाद्यं समाजोत्सवसन्निधौ ।। ६८ ।।

And at the time of this national festival, dreadful was the encounter, though without weapons, displaying strength and heroism.

यावद्यावच्च चाणूरो युयुधे हरिणा सह ।।
प्राणहानिमवापाग्र्यां तावत्तावल्लवाल्लवम् ।। ६९ ।।

कृष्णोपि युयुधे तेन लीलयैव जगन्मयः ।।
खेदाच्चालयता कोपान्निजकेसरशेखरम् ।। ७० ।।

And as long as the contest continued, Cāṇūra was gradually losing something of his original vigour and the wreath upon his head trembled from his fury and distress, whilst the world-comprehending Kṛṣṇa wrestled with him but sportively.

बलक्षयं विवृद्धिं च दृष्ट्वा चाणूरकृष्णयोः ।।
वारयामास तूर्याणि कंसः कोपपरायणः ।। ७१ ।।

Seeing Cāṇūra losing and Kṛṣṇa, gaining strength—Kansa, worked up with ire, ordered the music to cease.

मृदंगादिषु तूर्येषु प्रतिषिद्धेषु तत्क्षणात् ।।
खे संगतान्यवाद्यंत देवतूर्याण्यनेकशः ।। ७२ ।।

And as soon as music was stopped by Kansa countless celestial bugles were sounded in the welkin.

जय गोविंद चाणूरं जहि केशव दानवम् ।।
अंतर्द्धानगता देवास्तमूचुरतिहर्षित् ।। ७३ ।।

And the celestials, greatly delighted and invisible, said —"Kṛṣṇa! be thou crowned with success; Keśava, do thou slay that demon Cāṇūra."

चाणूरेण चिरं कालं पीडित्वा मधुसूदनः ।।
उत्पाट्य भ्रामयामास तद्वधाय कृतोद्यमः ।। ७४ ।।

Thereupon sporting for a long time with Cāṇūra, Kṛṣṇa, the slayer of Madhu, at last lifted him up and whirled him with the intention of slaying him.

भ्रामयित्वा शतगुणं दैत्यमल्लममित्रजित् ।।
भूमावास्फोटयामास गगने गतजीवितम् ।। ७५ ।।

Having whirled Cāṇūra round a hundred times until his breath was expended in the sky, he dashed his body on the ground.

भूमावास्फोटितस्तेन चाणूरः शतधाऽभवत् ।।
रक्तस्रावमहापंकां चकार च तदा भुवम् ।। ७६ ।।

As soon as it fell it was sundered into a hundred pieces and the earth was strewn with a hundred pools of glory mire.

बलदेवोऽपि तत्कालं मुष्टिकेन महाबलः ।।
युयुधे दैत्यमल्लेन चाणूरेण यथा हरिः ।। ७७ ।।

Whilst this happened, the powerful Baladeva was engaged likewise with the demon bruser Muṣṭika.

सोऽप्येनं मुष्टिना मूर्ध्नि वक्षस्याहत्य जानुना ।।
पातयित्वा धरापृष्ठे निषिपपेष गतायुषम् ।। ७८ ।।

Striking him on the head with his fists and on the breast with his knees, he stretched him on the ground, and pummelled him there till he was dead.

कृष्ण स्तोशलकं भूयो मल्लराजं महाबलम् ।।
वाममुष्टिप्रहारेण पातयामास भूतले ।। ७९ ।।

Again, Kṛṣṇa encountered the royal bruiser Tomalaka, and felled him to the earth with a blow of his left hand.

चाणूरे निहते मल्ले मुष्टिके विनिपातिते ।।
नीते क्षयं तोशलके सर्वे मल्लाः प्रदुद्रुवः ।। ८० ।।

ववल्गतुस्ततो रंगे कृष्णसंकर्षणावुभौ ।।
समानवयसो गोपान्बलादाकृष्य हर्षितौ ।। ८१ ।।

When the other athlete saw Cāṇūra, Muṣṭika, and Tomalaka killed, they fled from the field; and Kṛṣṇa and Saṅkarṣaṇa danced victorious on the arena, dragging along with them by force the cowherds of their own age.

कंसोऽपि कोपरक्ताक्षः प्राहोच्चैर्व्यायतान्नरान्।।
गोपावेतौ समाजौघान्निष्क्राम्येतां बलादितः।। ८२।।

नंदोऽपि गृह्यतां पापो निर्गलैरायसैरिह।।
अवृद्धार्हेण दंडेन वसुदेवोऽपि वध्यताम्।। ८३।।

वल्गंति गोपाः कृष्णेन ये चेमे सहिताः पुरः।।
गावो निगृह्य तामेषां यच्चास्ति वसु किंचन।। ८४।।

Kansa, his eyes reddening with wrath, called aloud to the surrounding people, "Drive those two cow-boys out of the assembly : seize the villain Nanda, and secure him with chains of iron : put Vasudeva to death with tortures intolerable to his years : and lay hands upon the cattle, and whatever else belongs to those cowherds who are the associates of Kṛṣṇa."

एवमाज्ञापयानं तु प्रहस्य मधुसूदनः।।
उत्प्लुत्यारुह्य तं मञ्चं कंसं जग्राह वेगतः।। ८५।।

केशेष्वा कृष्य विगलत्किरीटमवनीतले।।
स कंसं पातयामास तस्योपरि पपात च।। ८६।।

Upon hearing these orders, the destroyer of Madhu laughed at Kansa, and springing up to the place where he was seated, laid hold of him by the hair of his head, and struck his tiara to the ground : then casting him down upon the earth, Govinda threw himself upon him.

अशेषजगदाधारगुरुणा पततोपरि।।
कृष्णेन त्याजितः प्राणानुग्रसेनात्मजो नृपः।। ८७।।

Crushed by the weight of the upholder of the universe, the son of Ugrasena, Kansa the king, gave up the ghost.

मृतस्य केशेषु तदा गृहीत्वा मधुसूदनः।।
चकर्ष देहं कंसस्य रंगमध्ये महाबलः।। ८८।।

गौरवेणापतिपतता परिघातेन कृष्यता।।
कृता कंसस्य देहेन वेगेनेव महांभसः।। ८९।।

Kṛṣṇa then dragged the dead body, by the hair of the head, into the centre of the arena, and a deep furrow was made by the vast and heavy carcass of Kansa, when it was dragged along the ground by Kṛṣṇa, as if a torrent of water had run through it.

कंसे गृहीते कृष्णेन तद्भ्राताऽभ्यागतो रुषा।।
सुनामा बलभद्रेण लीलयैव निपातितः।। ९०।।

Seeing Kansa thus treated, his brother Sumālin came to his succour; but he was encountered, and easily killed by Balabhadra.

ततो हाहाकृतं सर्वमासीत्तद्रंगमंडलम्।।
अवज्ञया हतं दृष्ट्वा कृष्णेन मथुरेश्वरम्।। ९१।।

Then arose a general cry of grief from the surrounding circle, as they beheld the king of Mathurā thus slain, and treated with such contumely, by Kṛṣṇa.

कृष्णोऽपि वसुदेवस्य पादौ जग्राह सत्वरः।।
देवक्याश्च महाबाहुर्बलदेवसहायवान्।। ९२।।

उत्थाप्य वसुदेवस्तं देवकी च जनार्दनम्।।
स्मृतजन्मोक्तवचनौ तावेव प्रणतौ स्थितौ।। ९३।।

Kṛṣṇa, accompanied by Balabhadra, embraced the feet of Vasudeva and of Devakī; but Vasudeva riased him up; and he and Devakī recalling to recollection what he had said to them at his birth, they bowed to Janārddana, and the former thus addressed him :

श्रीवसुदेव उवाच

प्रसीद सीदतां दत्तो देवानां यो वरः प्रभो।।
तथावयोः प्रसादेन कृतोद्धारस्स केशवः।। ९४।।

Vasudeva said :—"Have compassion upon mortals, O god, benefactor and lord of deities : it is by thy favour to us two, that thou ahst become the (present) upholder of the world.

आराधितो यद्भगवानवतीर्णो गृहे मम।।
दुर्वृत्तनिधनार्थाय तेन नः पावितं कुलम्।। ९५।।

That for the punishment of the rebellious, thou hast descended upon earth in my house, having been propitiated by my prayers, sanctified our race.

त्वमंतः सर्वभूतानां सर्वभूतमयस्थितः।।
प्रवर्त्तेते समस्तात्मंस्त्वत्ते भूतभविष्यती।। ९६।।

Thou art the heart of all creatures; thou abidest in all creatures, and all that has been, or will be, proceeds from thee, O universal spirit!

यज्ञैस्त्वमिज्यसेऽचिंत्य सर्वदेवमयाच्युत।।
त्वमेव यज्ञो यष्टा च यज्वनां परमेश्वरः।। ९७।।
समुद्भवस्समस्तस्य जगतस्त्वं जनार्दन।। ९८।।

Thou, Acyuta, who comprehendest all the gods, art eternally worshipped with sacrifices : thou art sacrifice itself, and the offerer of sacrifices.

सापह्नवं मम मनो यदेतत्त्वयि जायते।।
देवक्याश्चात्मजप्रीत्या तदत्यंतविडंबना।। ९९।।

The affection that inspires my heart and the heart of Devakī towards thee as if thou wast our child, is indeed but error, and a great delusion.

त्वं कर्त्ता सर्वभूतानामनादिनिधनो भवान्।।
त्वां मनुष्यस्य कस्यैषा जिह्वा पुत्रेति वक्ष्यति।।१००।।

How shall the tongue of a mortal such as I am call the creator of all things who is without beginning or end, son?

जगदेतज्जगन्नाथ संभूतमखिलं यतः।।
कया युक्त्या विना मायां सोऽस्मत्तः संभविष्यति।।१०१।।

It is reasonable, that the lord of the world from whom the world proceeds should be born of me, except through illusion?

यस्मिन्प्रतिष्ठितं सर्वं जगत्स्थावरजंगमम्।।
स कोष्ठोत्संगशयनो मानुषो जायते कथम्।।१०२।।

How should he, in whom all mobile and immobile beings exist, be conceived in the womb and born of a mortal being?

स त्वं प्रसीद परमेश्वर पाहि
विश्वमंशावतारकरणैर्न ममासि पुत्रः।।
आब्रह्मपादपमिदं जगदेतदीश त्वत्तो
विमोहयसि किं पुरुषोत्तमास्मान्।। १०३।।

Have pity on me, therefore, O Supreme lord, and being incarnate do thou protect the universe. O god, thou art not my son : thou comprisest the whole universe from Brahmā to a tree. Therefore, O great soul, why dost thou beguile me?

मायाविमोहितदृशा तनयो ममेति
कंसाद्भयं कृतमपास्तभयोऽतितीव्रम्।।
नीतोऽसि गोकुलमरातिभया कुलेन वृद्धिं
गतोऽसि मम नास्ति ममत्वमीश।। १०४।।

Blinded by illusion I considered thee, as my son and hence I was afraid of Kansa. And therefore I did carry thee to Gokula where thou hast grown up; but I no longer consider thee as mine own son.

कर्माणि रुद्रमरुदश्विशतक्रतूनां
साध्यानि यस्य न भवंति निरीक्षितानि।।
त्वं विष्णुरीश जगतामुपकारहेतोः
प्राप्तोसि नः परिगतो विगतोहि मोहः।। १०५।।

Thou Viṣṇu the supreme lord of all, whose actions Rudra, the Maruts, the Aśvins, Indra and the celestials cannot equal although they behold them; thou, who hast descended amongst us for the behoof of the universe, art recognized, and delusion is no more."

।। इति श्रीविष्णुमहापुराणे पञ्चमेंशे विंशोऽध्यायः।। २०।।

अथ पञ्चमेंशेः एकविंशोऽध्यायः

Part V : Section 21

श्रीपराशर उवाच

तौ समुत्पन्नविज्ञानौ भगवत्कर्मदर्शनात्।।
देवकी वसुदेवौ तु दृष्ट्वा मायां पुनर्हरिः।।
मोहाय यदुचक्रस्य विततान स वैष्णवीम्।। १।।

Parāśara said :—Beholding Devakī and Vasudeva obtain true discriminative knowledge on seeing his wonderful feat, Kṛṣṇa, being anxious to beguile them and other descendants of Yadu race, spread again the illusions of Viṣṇu.

उवाच चांब हे तात चिरादुत्कंठितेन मे।।
भवंतौ कंसभीतेन दृष्टौ संकर्षणेन च।। २।।

Thereupon he said to his parents—"O father, O mother, my elder brother Baladeva was all along anxious to behold you. It is out of fear of Kansa he could not do so.

कुर्वतां याति यः कालो मातापित्रोरपूजनम्।।
तत्खंडमायुषो व्यर्थमसाधूनां हि जायते।। ३।।

गुरुदेवाद्विजातीनां मातापित्रोश्च पूजनम्।।
कुर्वतां सफलः कालो देहिनां तात जायते।। ४।।

So long the pious do not serve their parents that portion of their life is spent in vain. O father, blessed is the birth of those men who serve their spiritual preceptors, celestials, Brāhmaṇas and their parents. Thou shouldst therefore forgive us, O father, for the violations committed.

तत्क्षंतव्यमिदं सर्वमतिक्रमकृतं पितः।।
कंसवीर्यप्रतापाभ्यामावयोः परवश्ययोः।। ५।।

For up to this time we were greatly distressed and under the influence of another on account of the prowess and strength of Kansa."

श्रीपराशर उवाच

इत्युक्त्वाऽथ प्रणम्योभौ यदु वृद्धाननुक्रमात्।।
यथावदभिपूज्याथ चक्रतुः पौरमाननम्।। ६।।

Parāśara said :—Saying this Kṛṣṇa bowed unto his parents and other elderly members of the Yadu race and duly honoured the citizens.

कंसपत्न्यस्ततः कंसं परिवार्य हतं भुवि।।
विलेपुर्मातरश्चास्य दुःखशोकपरिप्लुताः।। ७।।

Thereupon Kansa's mothers and wives, being stircken with grief and sorrow, began to lament encircling Kansa lying dead on the ground.

बहुप्रकारमस्वस्थाः पश्चात्तापातुरो हरिः।।
तास्समाश्वासयामास स्वयमस्त्राविलेक्षणाः।। ८।।

Hari then expressed his regret for what had happened, and with eyes saturated with treas he consoled them.

उग्रसेनं ततो बंधान्मुमोच मधुसूदनः।।
अभ्यसिञ्चत्तदैवैनं निजराज्ये हतात्मजम्।। ९।।

The slayer of Madhu then released Ugrasena from prison and placed him on the throne rendered vacant by the death of his son.

राज्येभिषिक्तः कृष्णेन यदुसिंहस्सुतस्य सः।।
चकार प्रेतकार्याणि ये चान्ये तत्र घातितः।। १०।।

Being installed on the throne the Yādava-chief performed the funeral rites of Kansa and of the rest of the slain.

कृतौर्द्धदैहिकं चैनं सिंहासनगतं हरिः।।
उवाचाज्ञापय विभो यत्कार्यमविशंकितः।। ११।।

When the ceremony was finished and Ugrasena had taken his royal seat, Kṛṣṇa addressed him and said :—O Supreme lord, order me freely what else to be done.

ययातिशापाद्वंशोयमपराज्यार्होपि सांप्रतम्।।
मयि भृत्ये स्थिते देवानाज्ञापयतु किं नृपैः।। १२।।

By the curse of Yayāti, our race cannot govern—but having me as your servant you may order even the celestials. How should king disobey them?"

श्रीपराशर उवाच

इत्युक्त्वा सोऽस्मरद्वायुमाजगाम च तत्क्षणात्।।
उवाच चैनं भगवान्केशवः कार्यमानुषः।। १३।।

Parāśara said :—Having said this, Keśava, assuming human shape summoned mentally the deity of the wind, who immediately came there, and said to him—

गच्छेदं ब्रूहि वायो त्वमलं गर्वेण वासव।।
दीयतामुग्रसेनाय सुधर्मा भवता सभा।। १४।।
कृष्णो ब्रवीतिराजार्हमेतद्रत्नमनुत्तमम्।।
सुधर्माख्यसभायुक्तमस्यां यदुभिरासितुम्।। १५।।

"Proceed, Vāyu, to Indra and tell him to lay aside his pomp, and resign to Ugrasena his splendid hall Sudharman : tell him that Kṛṣṇa commands him to send the royal hall, the unrivalled gem of princely courts, for the assemblage of the race of Yadu."

श्रीपराशर उवाच

इत्युक्तः पवनो गत्वा सर्वमाह शचीपतिम्।।
ददौ सोऽपि सुधर्माख्यां सभां वायोः पुरंदरः।। १६।।

वायुना चाहृतां दिव्यां सभां ते यदुपुंगवाः।।
बुभुजुस्सर्वरत्नाढ्यां गोविंदभुजसंश्रयाः।। १७।।

Parāśara said :—Accordingly Vāyu went and delivered the message to the husband of Śaci, who immediately gave up to him the hall Sudharman, and Vāyu conveyed it to the Yādavas, the chiefs of whom thenceforth possessed his celestial court, emblazoned with jewels, and defended by the arms of Govinda.

विदिताऽखिलविज्ञानौ सर्वज्ञानमयावपि।।
शिष्याचार्यक्रमं वीरौ ख्यापयंतौ यदूत्तमौ।। १८।।

The two excellent Yadu youths, versed in all knowledge, and possessed of all wisdom, then submitted to instruction, as the disciples of teachers.

ततस्सांदीपनिं काश्यमवंतीपुरवासिनम्।।
विद्यार्थं जग्मतुर्बालौ कृतोपनयनक्रमौ।। १९।।

वेदाभ्यासकृतप्रीति संकर्षणजनार्दनौ।।
तस्य शिष्यत्वमभ्येत्य गुरुवृत्तिपुरौ हि तौ।।
दर्शयाञ्चक्रतुर्वीरावाचारमखिले जने।। २०।।

सरहस्यं धनुर्वेदं ससंग्रहमधीयताम्।।
अहोरात्रचतुषष्ट्या तदद्भुतमभूद्द्विज।। २१।।

Accordingly they repaired to Sāndīpanī—who, though born in Kāśī, resided at Avanti—to study the science of arms, and, becoming his pupils, were obedient and attentive to their master, exhibiting an example to all men of the observance of instituted rules. In the course of sixty-four days they had gone through the elements of military science, withthe treatises on the use of arms, and directions for the mystic incantations, which secure the aid of supernatural weapons.

सांदीपनिरसंभाव्यं तयोः कर्मातिमानुषम्।।
विचिंत्य तौ तदा मेने प्राप्तौ चंद्रदिवाकरौ।। २२।।

Sāndīpanī, astonished at such proficiency, and knowing that it exceeded human faculties, imagined that the sun and the moon had become his scholars.

सांगांश्च चतुरो वेदान्सर्वशास्त्राणि चैव हि।।
अस्त्रग्राममशेषं च प्रोक्तमात्रमवाप्य तौ।। २३।।
ऊचुतुर्व्रियतां या ते दातव्या गुरुदक्षिणा।। २४।।

They thought that they can teach Sāmas, four Vedas, and education of all weapons etc. When they had acquired all that he could teach, they said to him, "Now say what present shall be given to you, as the preceptor's fee."

सोप्यतींद्रि यमालोक्य तयोः कर्म महामतिः।।
अयाचत मृतं पुत्रं प्रभासे लवणार्णवे।। २५।।

The prudent Sāndīpanī, perceiving that they were endowed with more than mortal powers, requested them to give him his dead son, drowned in the sea of Prabhāsa.

गृहीतास्त्रौ ततस्तौ तु सार्घ्यहस्तो महोदधिः।।
उवाच न मया पुत्रो हृतस्सांदीपनेरिति।। २६।।

दैत्यं पञ्चजनो नाम शंखरूपस्स बालकम्।।
जग्राह योस्ति सलिले ममैवासुरसूदन।। २७।।

Taking up their arms, they marched against the ocean; but the all-comprehending sea said to them, "I have not killed the son of Sāndīpanī; a demon named Pañcajana, who lives in the form of a conch shell, seized the boy : he is still under my waters.

श्रीपराशर उवाच

इत्युक्त्वोंतर्जलं गत्वा हत्वा पञ्चजनं च तम्।।
कृष्णो जग्राह तस्यास्थिप्रभवं शंखमुत्तमम्।। २८।।

यस्य नादेन दैत्यानां बलहानिरजायत।।
देवानां ववृधे तेजो यात्यधर्मश्च संक्षयम्।। २९।।

तं पाञ्चजन्यमापूर्य गत्वा यमपुरं हरिः।।
बल देवश्च बलवाञ्जित्वा वैवस्वतं यमम्।। ३०।।

On hearing this, Kṛṣṇa plunged into the sea; and having slain the vile Pañcajana, he took the conch shell, which was formed of his bones (and bone it as his horn), the sound of which fills the demon hosts with dismay, animates the vigour of the gods, and annihilates unrighteousness.

तं बालं यातनासंस्थं यथापूर्वशरीरिणम्।।
पित्रे प्रदत्तवान्कृष्णो बलश्च बलिनां वरः।। ३१।।

The heroes also recovered the boy from the pains of death, and restored him in his former person to his father.

मथुरा च पुनः प्राप्तावुग्रसेनेन पालिताम्।।
प्रहृष्टपुरुषस्त्रीकामुभौ रामजनार्दनौ।। ३२।।

Rāma and Janārddana then returned to Mathurā, which was well presided over by Ugrasena, and abounded in a happy population both of men and women.

।। इति श्रीविष्णुमहापुराणे पञ्चमेंशे एकविंशोऽध्याय।। २१।।

अथ पञ्चमेंशेः द्वाविंशोऽध्यायः

Part V : Section 22

श्रीपराशर उवाच

जरासंधसुते कंस उपयेमे महाबलः।।
अस्तिं प्राप्तिं च मैत्रेय तयोर्भर्तृहणं हरिम्।। १।।

Parāśara said :—The mighty Kansa had married the two daughters of Jarāsandha, one named Asti, the other Prāpti.

महाबलपरीवारो मगधाधिपतिर्बली।।
हंतुमभ्याययौ कोपाज्जरासंधस्सयादवम्।। २।।

उपेत्य मथुरां सोऽथ रुरोध मगधेश्वरः।।
अक्षौहिणीभि स्सैन्यस्य त्रयोविंशतिभिर्वृतः।। ३।।

Jarāsandha was king of Magadha, and a very powerful prince; who, when he heard that Kṛṣṇa had killed his son-in-law, was much incensed, and, collecting a large force, marched against Mathurā, determined to put the Yādavas and Kṛṣṇa to the sword. Accrodingly he invested the city with three and twenty numerous divisions of his forces.

निष्क्रम्याल्पपरीवारावुभौ रामजनार्दनौ।।
युयुधाते समं तस्य बलिनौ बलिसैनिकैः।। ४।।

Rāma and Janārddana sallied from the town with a slender, but resolute force, and fought bravely with the armies of Māgadha.

ततो रामश्च कृष्णश्च मतिं चक्रतुरञ्जसा।।
आयुधानां पुराणानामादाने मुनिसत्तम।। ५।।

अनंतरं हरेश्शार्ङ्गं तूणी चाक्षयसायकौ।।
आकाशादागतौ विप्र तथा कौमोदकी गदा।। ६।।

हलं च बलभद्रस्य गगनादागतं महत्।।
मनसोऽभिमतं विप्र सानंदं मुसलं तथा।। ७।।

The two youthful leaders prudently resolved to have recourse to their ancient weapons, and accordingly the bow of Hari, with two quivers filled with exhaustless arrows and the mace called Kaumodakī, and the ploughshare of Balabhadra, as well as the club Saunanda, descended at a wish from heaven.

ततो युद्धे पराजित्य ससैन्यं मगधाधिपम्।।
पुरीं विविशतुर्वीरावुभौ रामजनार्दनौ।। ८।।

Armed with these weapons, they speedily discomfited the king of Magadha and his hosts, and re-entered the city in triumph.

जिते तस्मिन्सुदुर्वृत्ते जरासंधे महामुने।।
जीवमाने गते कृष्णस्तेनामन्यत नाजितम्।। ९।।

पुनरप्याजगामाऽथ जरासंधो बलान्वितः।।
जितश्च रामकृष्णाभ्यामपक्रांतो द्विजोत्तम्।। १०।।

Although the wicked king of Magadha, Jarāsandha, was defeated, yet Kṛṣṇa knew that whilst he escaped alive he was not subdued; and in fact, he soon returned with a mighty force, and was again forced by Rāma add Kṛṣṇa to fly.

दश चाष्टौ च संग्रामानेवमत्यंतदुर्मदः।।
यदुभिर्मागधो राजा चक्रे कृष्णपुरोगमैः।। ११।।

सर्वेष्वेतेषु युद्धेषु यादवैस्स पराजितः।।
अपक्रांतो जरासंधस्स्वल्पसैन्यैर्बलाधिकः।। १२।।

Eighteen times did the haughty prince of Māgadha renew his attack upon the Yādavas, headed by Kṛṣṇa; and was as often defeated and put to the rout by them with very inferior numbers.

न तद्बलं यादवानां विजितं यदनेकशः।।
तत्तु सन्निधिमाहात्म्यं विष्णोरंशस्य चक्रिणः।। १३।।

That the Yādavas were not overpowerd by their foes, was owing to the present might of the portion of the discus-armed Viṣṇu.

मनुष्यधर्मशीलस्य लीला सा जगतीपतेः।।
अस्त्राण्यनेकरूपाणि यदरातिषु मुञ्चति।। १४।।

मनसैव जगत्सृष्टिं संहारं च करोति यः।।
तस्यारिपक्षक्षपणे कियानुद्यमविस्तरः।। १५।।

It was the pastime of the lord of the universe, in his capacity of man, to launch various weapons against his enemies; for what effort of power to annihilate his foes could be necessary to him, whose flat creates and destroys the world?

तथाऽपि यो मनुष्याणां धर्मस्तमनुवर्त्तते।।
कुर्वन्बलवता संधिं हीनैर्युद्धं करोत्यसौ।। १६।।

But as subjecting himself to human customs, he formed alliances with the brave, and engaged in hostilities with the base.

साम चोपप्रदानं च तथा भेदं च दर्शयन्।।
करोति दंडपातं च क्वचिदेव पलायनम्।। १७।।

He had recourse to the four devices of policy, or negotiation, presents, sowing dissension, and chastisement; and sometimes even betook himself to flight.

मनुष्यदेहिनां चेष्टामित्येवमनुवर्त्तते।।
लीला जगत्पतेस्तस्य च्छंदतः परिवर्त्तते।। १८।।

Thus imitating the conduct of human beings, the lord of the world pursued at will his sports.

।। इति श्रीविष्णुमहापुराणे पञ्चमेंशे द्वाविंशोऽध्यायः।। २२।।

अथ पञ्चमेंशेः त्रयोविंशोऽध्यायः

Part V : Section 23

श्रीपराशर उवाच

गार्ग्यं गोष्ठ्यां द्विजं। श्यालष्षंड इत्युक्तवान्द्विज।।
यदूनां सन्निधौ सर्वे जहसुर्यादवास्तदा।। १।।

ततः कोपपरीतात्मा दक्षिणापथमेत्य सः।।
सुतमिच्छंस्तपस्तेपे यदुचक्रभयावहम्।। २।।

Parāśara said :—Śyāla having called Gārgya, the Brāhmaṇa, whilst at the cow-pens, impotent, at the cow-pens, impotent, in an assembly of the Yādavas, they all laughed; at which he was highly offended, and repaired to the shores of the western sea, where he engaged in arduous penance to obtain a son, who should be a terror to the tribe of Yadu.

आराधयन्महादेवं लोहचूर्णमभक्षयत्।।
ददौ वरं च तुष्टोऽस्मै वर्षे तु द्वादशे हरः।। ३।।

Propitiating Mahādeva, and living upon iron sand for twelve years, the deity at last was pleased with him, and gave him the desired boon.

संतोषयामास च तं यवनेशो ह्यनात्मजः।।
तद्योषित्संगमाच्चास्य पुत्रोऽभूदलिसन्निभः।। ४।।

The king of the Yādavas, who was childless, became the friend of Gārgya; and the latter begot a son by his wife, who was as black as a bee, and thence called Kālayavana.

तं कालयवनं नाम राये स्वे यवनेश्वरः।।
अभिषिच्य वनं यातो वज्राग्रकठिनोरसम्।। ५।।

The Yavana king having placed his son, whose breast was as hard as the point of the thunderbolt, upon the throne, retired to the woods.

स तु वीर्यमदोन्मत्तः पृथिव्यां बलिनो नृपान्।।
अपृच्छन्नारदस्तस्मै कथयामास यादवान्।। ६।।

Inflated with the conceit of his prowess Kālayavana demanded of Nārada who were the most mighty heroes on earth. To which the sage answered. "The Yādavas."

म्लेच्छकोटिसहस्त्राणां सहस्त्रैस्सोभिसंवृतः।।
गजाश्वरथसंपन्नैश्चकार परमोद्यमम्।। ७।।

प्रययौ स व्यवच्छिन्नं छिन्नयानो दिनेदिने।।
यादवान्प्रति सामर्षो मैत्रेय मथुरां पुरीम्।। ८।।

Accordingly Kālayavana assembled many myriads of Mlecchas and barbarians, with a vast armament of elephants, cavalry, chariots, and foot, advanced impatiently against Mathurā and the Yādavas; wearying every day the animal that carried him, but insensible of fatigue himself.

कृष्णोऽपि चिंतयामास क्षपितं यादवं बलम्।।
यवनेन रणे गम्यं मागधस्य भविष्यति।। ९।।

मागधस्य बलं क्षीणं स कालयवनो बली।।
हंतैतदेवमायातं यदूनां व्यसनं द्विधा।।१०।।

When Kṛṣṇa knew of his approach, he reflected that if the Yādavas encountered the Yavana, they would be so much weakened by the conflict, that they would then be overcome by the king of Māgadha; that their force was much reduced by the war with Māgadha, whilst that of Kālayavana was unbroken; and that the enemy might, therefore, be victorious.

तस्माद्दुर्गं करिष्यामि यदूनामरिदुर्जयम्।।
स्त्रियोऽपि यत्र युद्ध्येयुः किं पुनर्वृष्णिपुंगवाः।।११।।

मयि मत्ते प्रमत्ते वा सुप्ते प्रवसितेऽपि वा।।
यादवाभिभवं दृष्टा मा कुर्वंस्त्वरयोधिकाः।।१२।।

Thus the Yādavas were exposed to a double danger. He resolved therefore to construct a citadel for the Yadu tribe, that should not be easily taken; one that even women might defend, and in which therefore the heroes of the house of Vṛṣṇi should be secure; one in which the male combatants of the Yādavas should dread no peril, though he himself should be drunk or careless, asleep or abroad.

इति संचिंत्य गोविंदो योजनानां महोदधिम्।।
ययाचे द्वादशपुरीं द्वारकां तत्र निर्ममे।। १३।।

महोद्यानां महावप्रां तटाकशतशोभिताम्।।
प्रासादगृहसंबाधामिंद्रस्येवामरावतीम्।।१४।।

Thus reflecting, Kṛṣṇa solicited a space of twelve furlongs from the ocean, and there he built the city of Dwārakā, defended by high ramparts, and beautified with gardens and reservoirs of water, crowded with houses and buildings, and splendid as the capital of Indra, Amarāvati.

मथुरावासिनं लोकं तत्रानीय जनार्दनः।।
आसन्ने कालयवने मथुरां च स्वयं ययौ।। १५।।

Thither Janārddana conducted the inhabitants of Mathurā, and then awaited at that city the approach of Kālayavana.

बहिरावासिते सैन्ये मथुराया निरायुधः।।
निर्जगाम च गोविंदो ददर्श यवनश्च तम्।। १६।।

When the hostile army encamped round Mathurā, Kṛṣṇa, unarmed, went forth, and beheld the Yavana king.

स ज्ञात्वा वासुदेवं तं बाहुप्रहरणं नृपः।।
अनुयातो महायोगी चेतोभिः प्राप्यते न यः।। १७।।

Kālyavana, the strong-armed, recognising Vāsudeva, pursued him; him whom the thought of perfect ascetics cannot overtake.

तेनानुयातः कृष्णोऽपि प्रविवेश महागुहाम्।।
यत्र शेते महावीर्यो मुचुकुंदो नरेश्वरः।। १८।।

सोऽपि प्रविष्टो यवनो दृष्ट्वा शय्यागतं नृपम्।।
पादेन ताडयामास मत्या कृष्णं सुदुर्मतिः।। १९।।

उत्थाय मुचुकुंदोऽपि ददर्श यवनं नृपः।। २०।।

दृष्टमात्रश्च तेनाऽसौ जज्वाल यवनोग्निना।।
तत्क्रोधजेन मैत्रेय भस्मीभूतश्च तत्क्षणात्।। २१।।

Thus pursued, Kṛṣṇa entered a large cavern, where Mucukunda, the king of men, was asleep. The rash Yavana entering the cave and beholding a man lying asleep there, concluded it must be Kṛṣṇa, and kicked him; at which Mucukunda awoke, casting on him an angry glance, the Yavana was instantly consumed, and reduced to ashes.

स हि देवासुरे युद्धे गतो हत्वा महासुरान्।।
निद्रार्त्तस्सुमहाकालं निद्रां वव्रे वरं सुरान्।। २२।।

For, in a battle between the gods and demons, Mucukunda had formerly contributed to the defeat of the latter; and being overcome with sleep, he solicited of the gods as a boon that he should enjoy a long repose.

प्रोक्तश्च देवैस्संसुप्तं यस्त्वामुत्थापयिष्यति।।
देहजेनाग्निना सद्यस्स तु भस्मीभविष्यति।। २३।।

"Sleep long and soundly," said the gods; "whoever disturbs you shall be instantly burnt to ashes by fire emanating from your body."

एवं दग्ध्वा स तं पापं दृष्ट्वा च मधुसूदनम्।।
कस्त्वमित्याह सोऽप्याह जातोहं शशिनः कुले।।
वसुदेवस्य तनयो यदोर्वंशसमुद्भवः।। २४।।

Having burnt up the iniquitous Yavana, and beholding the foe of Madhu, Mucukunda asked him who he was. "I am born," he replied, "in the lunar race, in the tribe of Yadu, and am the son of Vasudeva."

मुचुकुंदोऽपि तत्राऽसौ वृद्धगार्ग्यवचोऽस्मरत्।। २५।।
संस्मृत्य प्रणिपत्यैनं सर्वं सर्वेश्वरं हरिम्।।
प्राह ज्ञातो भवान्विष्णोरंशस्त्वं परमेश्वर।। २६।।

पुरा गार्ग्येण कथितमष्टाविंशतिमे युगे।।
द्वापरांते हरेर्जन्म यदुवंशे भविष्यति।। २७।।

Mucukunda, recollecting the prophecy of old Garga, fell down before the lord of all, Hari, saying. "Thou art known, supreme lord, to be a portion of Viṣṇu; for it was said of old by Garga, that at the end of the twenty-eighth Dwāpara age, Hari would be born in the family of Yadu.

स त्वं प्राप्तो न संदेहो मर्त्यानामुपकारकृत्।। २८।।

तथाहि सुमहत्तेजो नालं सोढुमहं तव।।
तथाहि सजलांभोदनादधीरतरं तव।।
वाक्यं नमति चौवोर्वी युष्मत्पादप्रपीडिता।। २९।।

Thou art he, without doubt, the benefactor of mankind for thy glory I am unable to endure. Thy words are of deepr tone than the muttering of the rain cloud; and earth sinks down beneath the pressure of thy feet.

देवासुरमहायुद्धे दैत्यसैन्यमहाभटाः।।
न सेहुर्मम तेजस्ते त्वत्तेजो न सहाम्यहम्।। ३०।।

संसारपतितस्यैको जंतोस्त्वं शरणं परम्।।
प्रसीद त्वं प्रपन्नार्त्तिहर नाशय मेऽशुभम्।। ३१।।

As in the battle between the gods and demons, the Asuras were unable to sustain my lustre, so even am I incapable of bearing thy radiance. Do thou, who art the alleviator of all distress, show favour upon me, and remove from me all that is evil.

त्वं पयो निधयशैलसरितस्त्वं वनानि च।।
मेदिनी गगनं वायुरापोग्निस्त्वं तथा मनः।। ३२।।

बुद्धिरव्याकृतप्राणाः प्राणेशस्त्वं तथा पुमान्।।
पुंसः परतरं यच्च व्याप्य जन्म विकारवत्।। ३३।।

शब्दादिहीनमजरममेयं क्षयवर्जितम्।।
अवृद्धिनाशं तद्ब्रह्म त्वमाद्यंतविवर्जितम्।। ३४।।

Thou art the oceans, the mountains, the rivers, the forests; thou art earth, sky, air, water, and fire; thou art mind, intelligence, the unevolved principle, vital airs, the lord, life—the soul; all that is beyond the soul; the all-pervading; exempt from the vicissitudes of birth; devoid of sensible properties, sound and the like : undecaying, illimitable, imperishable, subject neither to increase nor diminution; thou art that which is Brahmā, without beginning or end.

त्वत्तोऽमरास्सपितरो यक्षगंधर्वकिन्नराः।।
सिद्धाश्चाप्सरसस्त्वत्तो मनुष्याः पशवाः खगाः।। ३५।।

सरीसृपा मृगास्सर्वे त्वत्तस्सर्वे महीरुहाः।।
यच्च भूतं भविष्यं च किंचिदत्र चराचरम्।। ३६।।

From thee the immortals, the progenitors, the Yakṣas, Gandharvas, and Kinnaras, the Siddhas, the nymphs of heaven, men, animals, birds, deers, reptiles, and all the vegetable world, proceed; and all that has been or will be, or is now movable or fixed.

मूर्त्तामूर्त्तं तथा चापि स्थूलं सूक्ष्मतरं तथा।।
तत्सर्वं त्वं जगत्कर्त्ता नास्ति किंचित्त्वया विना।। ३७।।

All that is amorphous or has form, all that is subtile, gross, satable, or movable, thou art, O creator of the world; and beside thee there is not anything.

मया संसारचक्रेऽस्मिन्भ्रमता भगवंस्तदा।।
तापत्रयाभिभूतेन न प्राप्ता निर्वृतिः क्वचित्।। ३८।।

O lord, I have been whirled round in the

circle of worldly existence for ever, and have suffered the three classes of affliction, and there is no rest whatever.

दुःखान्येव सुखानीति मृगतृष्णाजलाशयाः।।
मया नाथ गृहीतानि तानि तापाय मेऽभवन्।। ३९।।

I have mistaken pains for pleasures, sultry vapours for a pool of water; and their enjoyment has yielded me nothing but sorrow.

राज्यमुर्वी बलं कोशो मित्रपक्षस्तथात्मजाः।।
भार्या भृत्यजनो ये च शब्दाद्या विषयाः प्रभो।।४०।।

सुखबुद्ध्या मया सर्वं गृहीतमिदमव्ययम्।।
परिणामे तदेवेश तापात्मकमभून्मम।।४१।।

The earth, dominion, forces, treasures, friends, children, wife, dependants, all the objects of sense, have I possessed imagining them to be sources of happiness; but I found that in their changeable nature, O lord, they were nothing but vexation.

देव लोकगतिं प्राप्तो नाथ देवगणोऽपि हि।।
मत्तस्साहाय्यकामोभूच्छाश्वती कुत्र निर्वृतिः।। ४२।।

The gods themselves though high in heaven, were in need of my alliance. Where then is everlasting repose?

त्वामनाराध्य जगतां सर्वेषां प्रभवास्पदम्।।
शाश्वती प्राप्यते केन परमेश्वर निर्वृतिः।। ४३।।

Who, without adoring thee, who art the origin of all worlds, shall attain, O supreme deity, that rest which endures for ever?

त्वन्मायामूढमनसो जन्मृत्युजरादिकान्।।
अवाप्य तापान्पश्यंति प्रेतराजमनंतरम्।। ४४।।

ततो निजक्रियासूतिनरकेष्वतिदारुणम्।।
प्राप्नुवंति नरा दुःखमस्वरूपविदस्तव।। ४५।।

Beguiled by thy delusions, and ignorant of thy nature, men, after suffering the various penalties of birth, death, and infirmity, behold the countenance of the king of ghosts, and suffer in hell dreadful tortures, the reward of their own deeds.

अहमत्यंतविषयी मोहितस्तव मायया।।
ममत्वगर्वगर्त्तांतर्भ्रमामि परमेश्वर।। ४६।।

सोऽहं त्वां शरणमपारमप्रमेयं
संप्राप्तः परमपदं यतो न किंचित्।।
संसारभ्रमपरितापतप्तचेता
निर्वाणे परिणतधाम्नि साभिलाषः।। ४७।।

Addicted to sensual objects through thy delusions, I revolve in the whirlpool of selfishness and pride; and hence I come to thee, as my final refuge who art the lord deserving of all homage, than whom there is no other asylum; my mind afflicted with repentance for my trust in the world, and desiring the fulness of felicity, emancipation from all existence."

।। इति श्रीविष्णुमहापुराणे पञ्चमेंशे त्रयोविंशोऽध्यायः।। २३।।

अथ पञ्चमेंशेः चतुर्विंशोऽध्यायः

Part V : Section 24

श्रीपराशर उवाच

इत्थंस्तुतस्तदा तेन मुचुकुन्देन धीमता।।
प्राहेशः सर्वभूतानामनादिनिधनो हरिः।। १।।

Parāśara said :—Thus praised by the wise Mucukunda, the sovereign of all things, the eternal lord, Hari.

श्रीभगवानुवाच

यथाभिवांछितान्दिव्यान्गच्छलोकान्नराधिप।।
अव्याहतपरैश्वर्यो मत्प्रसादोपबृंहितः।। २।।

भुक्त्वा दिव्यान्महाभोगान्भविष्यसि महाकुले।।
जातिस्मरो मत्प्रसादात्ततोमोक्षमवाप्स्यसि।। ३।।

Hari said to him :—"Go to whatever celestial regions you wish, lord of men, possessed of might irresistible, honoured by my favour. When you have fully enjoyed all heavenly pleasures, you shall be born in a distinguished family retaining the recollection your former births; and you shall finally obtain emancipation.

श्रीपराशर उवाच

इत्युक्तः प्रणिपत्येशं जगतामच्युतं नृपः ।।
गुहामुखाद्विनिष्क्रांतस्स ददर्शाल्पकान्नरान् ।। ४ ।।

ततः कलियुगं मत्वा प्राप्तं तप्तुं नृपस्तपः ।।
नरनारायणस्थानां प्रययौ गंधमादनम् ।। ५ ।।

Having heard this promise, and prostrated himself before Acyuta, the lord of the world, Mucukunda, went forth from the cave and beholding men of diminutive stature, now first knew that the Kali age had arrived. The king therefore departed to Gandhamādana, the shrine of Naranārāyaṇa, to perform penance.

कृष्णोपि घातयित्वारिमुपायेन हि तद्बलम् ।।
जग्राह मथुरामेत्य हस्त्यश्वस्यंदनोज्ज्वलम् ।। ६ ।।

आनीय चोग्रसेनाय द्वारवत्यां न्यवेदयत् ।।
पराभिभवनिश्शंकं बभूव च यदोः कुलम् ।। ७ ।।

Kṛṣṇa having by this tratagem destroyed his enemy returned to Mathurā and took captive his army, rich in horses, elephants and cars, which he conducted to Dwārakā, and delivered to Ugrasena, and the Yadu race was relieved from all fear of invasion.

बलदेवोऽपि मैत्रेय प्रशांताखिलाविग्रहः ।।
ज्ञातिदर्शनसोत्कंठः प्रययौ नंदगोकुलम् ।। ८ ।।

ततो गोपाश्च गोप्यश्च यथा पूर्वममित्रजित् ।।
तथैवाभ्यवदत्प्रेम्णा बहुमानपुरस्सरम् ।। ९ ।।

Baladeva, when hostilities had entirely ceased, being desirous of seeing his kinsmen, went to Nanda's cow-pens, and there again conversed with the herdsmen and their females, with affection and respect.

स कैश्चित्संपरिष्वक्तः कांश्चिच्च परिषस्वजे ।।
हास्यं चक्रे समं कैश्चिद्गोपैर्गोपीजनैस्तथा ।। १० ।।

By some, the elders, he was embraced; others, the juniors, he embraced; and with those of his own age, male or female, he talked and laughed.

प्रियाण्यनेकान्यवदन् गोपास्तत्र हलायुधम् ।।
गोप्यश्च प्रेमकुपिताः प्रोचुस्सेर्ष्यमथापराः ।। ११ ।।

गोप्यः पप्रच्छुरपरा नागरीजनवल्लभम् ।।
कच्चिदास्ते सुखं कृष्णश्चलप्रेमलवात्मकः ।। १२ ।।

अस्मचेष्टामपहसन्न कच्चिपुरयोषिताम् ।।
सौभाग्यमानमधिकं करोति क्षणसौहृदः ।। १३ ।।

कच्चित्स्मरति नः कृष्णो गीतानुगमनं कलम् ।।
अप्यसौ मातरं द्रष्टुं सकृदप्यागमिष्यति ।। १४ ।।

The cowherds made many kind speeches to Halāyudha; but some of the Gopīs spoke to him with the affectation of anger, or with feelings of jealousy, as they inquired after the loves of Kṛṣṇa with the women of Mathurā. "Is all well with the fickle and inconstant Kṛṣṇa?" said they : "Does the volatile swain, the friend of an instant amuse the women of the city by laughing at our rustic efforts (to please him)? Does he ever think of us, singing in chorus to his sons? Will he not come here once again to see his mother?

अथ वा किं तदालापैः क्रियंतामपराः कथाः ।।
यस्यास्माभिर्विना तेन विनाऽस्माकं भविष्यति ।। १५ ।।

But why talk of these things? It is a different tale to tell for him without us, and for us without him.

पिता माता तथा भ्राता भर्त्ता बंधुजनश्च किम् ।।
संत्यक्तस्तत्कृतेस्माभिरकृतज्ञध्वजो हि सः ।। १६ ।।

Father, mother, brother, husband, kin, what have we not abandoned for him; but he is a monument of ingratitude.

तथापि कच्चिदालापमिहागमनसंश्रयम् ।।
करोति कृष्णो वक्तव्यं भवता राम नानृतम् ।। १७ ।।

Yet tell us, does not Kṛṣṇa talk of coming here? Falsehood is never, O Kṛṣṇa, to be uttered by thee.

दामोदरोऽसौ गोविंदः पुरस्त्रीसक्तमानसः ।।
अपेतप्रीतिरस्मासु दुर्दर्शः प्रतिभाति नः ।। १८ ।।

Verily this is Dāmodara, this is Govinda, who has given up his heart to the damsels of the city, who has no longer any regard for us, but looks upon us with disdain."

आमंत्रितश्च कृष्णेति पुनर्दामोदरेति च ।।
जहसुस्सस्वरं गोप्यो हरिणा हृतचेतसः ।। १९ ।।

संदेशैस्सामममधुरैः प्रेमगर्भैरगर्वितैः ।।
रामेणाश्वासिता गोप्यः कृष्णस्यातिमनोहरैः ।। २० ।।

So saying, the Gopīs, whose minds were fixed on Kṛṣṇa, addressed Rāma in his place, calling him Dāmodara and Govinda, and laughed and were merry; and Rāma consoled them by communicating to them agreeable, modest affectionate, and gentle messages from Kṛṣṇa.

गोपैश्च पूर्ववद्रामः परिहासमनोहराः ।।
कथाश्चकार रेमे च सह तैर्व्रजभूमिषु ।। २१ ।।

With the cow-herds he talked mirthfully, as he had been wont to do, and rambled along with them over the lands of Vraja.

।। इति श्रीविष्णु महापुराणे पञ्चमेंशे चतुर्विंशोऽध्यायः ।। २४ ।।

अथ पञ्चमेंशे: पञ्चविंशोऽध्यायः

Part V : Section 25

श्रीपराशर उवाच

वने विचरतस्तस्य सह गोपैर्महात्मनः ।।
मानुषच्छद्मरूपस्य शेषस्य धरणीधृतः ।। १ ।।

निष्पादितोरुकार्यस्य कार्येणोर्वीप्रचारिणः ।।
उपभोगार्थमत्यर्थं वरुणः प्राह वारुणीम् ।। २ ।।

Parāśara said :—Whilst the mighty Śeṣa, the upholder of the globe, was thus engaged in wandering amidst the forests with the herdsmen, in the disguise of a mortal—having rendered great services to earth, and still considering what more was to be achieved—Varuṇa, in order to provide for his recreation, said to his wife Vāruṇī (the goddess of wine),

अभीष्टा सर्वदा यस्य मदिरे त्वं महौजसः ।।
अनंतस्योपभोगाय तस्य गच्छ मुदे शुभे ।। ३ ।।

"Thou, Madirā, art, ever acceptable to the powerful Ananta; go therefore, auspicious and kind goddess, and promote his enjoyments."

इत्युक्ता वारुणी तेन सन्निधानमथाकरोत् ।।
वृंदावनसमुत्पन्नकदंबतरुकोटरे ।। ४ ।।

Obeying these commands, Vāruṇī went and established herself in the hollow of a Kadamba tree in the woods of Vṛndāvana.

विचरन् बलदेवोऽपि मदिरागंधमुत्तमम् ।।
आघ्राय मदिरातर्षमवापाथ वराननः ।। ५ ।।

Baladeva, roaming about, came there, and smelling the pleasant fragrance of liquor, resumed his ancient passion for strong drink.

ततः कदंबात्सहसा मद्यधारां स लांगली ।।
पतंतीं वीक्ष्य मैत्रेय प्रययौ परमां मुदम् ।। ६ ।।

पपौ च गोपगोपीभिस्समुपेतो मुदान्वितः ।।
प्रगीयमानो ललितं गीतवाद्यविशारदैः ।। ७ ।।

The holder of the ploughshare observing the vinous drops distilling from the Kadamba tree, was much delighted, and gathered and quaffed them along with the herdsmen and the Gopīs, whilst those who were skilful with voice and lute celebrated him in their songs.

स मत्तोत्यंतघर्मांभःकणिकामौक्तिकोज्ज्वलः ।।
आगच्छ यमुने स्नातुमिच्छामीत्याह विह्वलः ।। ८ ।।

तस्य वाचं नदी सा तु मत्तेक्तामवमत्य वै ।।
नाजगाम ततः क्रुद्धो हलं जग्राह लांगली ।। ९ ।।

Being inebriated with the wine, and the drops of perspiration standing like pearls upon his limbs, he called out, not knowing what he said, "Come hither, Yamunā river, I want to bathe."

गृहीत्वा तां हलांतेन चकर्ष मदविह्वलः ।।
पापे नायासि नायासि गम्यतामिच्छयान्यतः ।। १० ।।

साकृष्टा सहसा तेन मार्गं संत्यज्य निम्नगा ।।
यत्रास्ते बलभद्रोऽसौ प्लावयामास तद्वनम् ।। ११ ।।

शरीरिणी तदाऽभ्येत्य त्रासविह्वललोचना ।।
प्रसीदेत्यब्रवीद्रामं मुञ्च मां मुसलायुध ।। १२ ।।

ततस्तस्याः सुवचनमाकर्ण्य स हलायुधः ।।
सोऽब्रवीदवजानासि मम शौर्यबले नदि ।।
सोऽहं त्वां हलपातेन नयिष्यामि सहस्रधा ।। १३ ।।

The river, disregarding the words of a drunken man came not at his bidding : on which Rāma in a rage took up his ploughshare, which he plunged into her bank, and dragged her to him, calling out, "Will you not come, you jade, will you not come? Now go where you please (if you can)." Thus saying, he compelled the dark river to quit its ordinary course, and follow him whithersoever he wandered through the wood. Assuming a mortal figure, the Yamunā, with distracted looks, approached Balabhadra, and entreated him to pardon her, and let her go : but he replied, "I will drag you with my ploughshare in a thousand directions, since you contemn my prowess and strength."

श्रीपराशर उवाच

इत्युक्तयाति संत्रासात्तया नद्या प्रसादितः।।
भूभागे प्लाविते तस्मिन्मुमोच यमुनां बलः।। १४।।

ततस्नातस्य वै कांतिरजायत महात्मनः।। १५।।

अवसतंसोत्पलं चारु गृहीत्वैकं च कुंडलम्।।
वरुणप्रहितां चास्मै मालामम्लानपंकजाम्।।
समुद्राभे तथा वस्त्रे नीले लक्ष्मीरयच्छत।। १६।।

कृतावतंसस्स तदा चारुकुंडलभूषितः।।
नीलांबरधरस्त्रग्वी शुशुभे कांतिसंयुतः।। १७।।

At last, however, appeased by her reiterated prayers, he let her go, after she had watered all the country. When he had bathed, the goddess of beauty, Lakṣmī, came and gave him a beautiful lotus to place in one ear, and an ear-ring for the other; a fresh necklace of lotus flowers, sent by Varuṇa; and garments of a dark blue colour, as costly as the wealth of the ocean; and thus decorated with a lotus in one ear, a ring in the other, dressed in blue garments, and wearing a garland, Balarāma appeared united with loveliness.

इत्थं विभूषितो रेमे तत्र रामस्तथा व्रजे।।
मासद्वयेन यातश्च स पुनर्द्वारकां पुरीम्।। १८।।

रेवतीं नाम तनयां रैवतस्य महीपतेः।।
उपयेमे बलस्तस्यां जज्ञाते निशितोल्मुकौ।। १९।।

Thus decorated, Rāma sported two months in Vraja, and then returned to Dwārakā, where he married Revatī, the daughter of king Raivata, by whom he had two sons, Niśītha and Ulmuka.

।। इति श्रीविष्णुमहापुराणे पञ्चमेंशे पञ्चविंशोऽध्यायः।। २५।।

अथ पञ्चमेंशेः षड्विंशोऽध्यायः

Part V : Section 26

श्रीपराशर उवाच

भीष्मकः कुंडिने राजा विदर्भविषयेऽभवत्।।
रुक्मी तस्याभवत्पुत्रो रुक्मिणी च वरानना।। १।।

Parāśara said :—Bhīṣmaka was king of Vidarbha, residing at Kuṇḍina. He had a son named Rukmin, and a beautiful daughter termed Rukmiṇī.

रुक्मिणीं चकमे कृष्णस्सा च तं चारुहासिनी।।
न ददौ याचते चैनां रुक्मी द्वेषेण चक्रिणे ।। २।।

Kṛṣṇa fell in love with the latter, and solicited her in marriage : but her brother who hated Kṛṣṇa, would not assent to the espousals.

ददौ च शिशुपालाय जरासंधप्रचोदितः।।
भीष्मको रुक्मिणा सार्द्धं रुक्मिणीमुरुविक्रमः।। ३।।

At the suggestion of Jarāsandha, and with the concurrence of his son, the powerful sovereign Bhīṣmaka affianced Rukmiṇī to Śiśupāla.

विवाहार्थं ततः सर्वे जरासंध मुखा नृपाः।।
भीष्मकस्य पुरं जग्मुश्शिशुपालप्रियैषिणः।। ४।।

कृष्णोऽपि बलभद्राद्यैर्यदुभिः परिवारितः।।
प्रययौ कुंडिनं द्रष्टुं विवाहं चैद्यभूभृतः।। ५।।

In order to celebrate the nuptials, Jarāsandha and other princes, the friends of Śiśupāla, assembled in the capital of Vidarbha;

and Kṛṣṇa, attended by Balabhadra and many other Yādavas, also went to Kuṇḍina to witness the wedding.

श्वो भाविनि विवाहे तु तां कन्यां हृतवान्हरिः ।।
विपक्षभारमासज्य रामादिष्वथ बंधुषु ।। ६ ।।

When there, Hari contrived on the eve of the nuptials, to carry off the princess, leaving Rāma and his kinsmen to sustain the weight of his enemies.

ततश्च पौंड्रकश्श्रीमान्दंतवक्रो विदूरथः ।।
शिशुपालजरासंधशाल्वाद्याश्च महीभृतः ।। ७ ।।

कुपितास्ते हरिं हंतुं चक्रुरुद्योगमुत्तमम् ।।
निर्जिताश्च समागम्य रामाद्यैर्यदुपुंगवैः ।। ८ ।।

Pauṇḍraka, the illustrious Dantavakra, Viduratha, Śiśupāla, Jarāsandha, Śalya, and other kings, indignant at the insult, exerted themselves to kill Kṛṣṇa, but were repelled by Balarāma and the Yādavas.

कुंडिनं न प्रवेक्ष्यामि ह्यहत्सवा युधि केशवम् ।।
कृत्वा प्रतिज्ञां रुक्मी च हंतुं कृष्णमनुद्रुतः ।। ९ ।।

Rukmin, vowing that he would never enter Kuṇḍina again until he had slain Keśava in fight, persued and overtook him.

हत्वा बलं सनागाश्वं पत्तिस्यंदनसंकुलम् ।।
निर्जितः पातितश्चोर्व्यां लीलयैव चक्रिणा ।। १० ।।

निर्जित्य रुक्मिणं सम्यगुपयेमे च रुक्मिणीयम् ।।
राक्षसेन विवाहेन संप्राप्तां मधुसूदनः ।। ११ ।।

तस्यां जज्ञे च प्रद्युम्नो मदनांशस्सवीर्यवान् ।।
जहार शंबरो यं वै यो जघान च शंबरम् ।। १२ ।।

In the combat that ensued, Kṛṣṇa destroyed with his discus, as if in sport the host of Rukmin, with all its horses, and elephants, and foot, and chariots, and overthrew him, and hurled him on the ground, and would have put him to death, but was withheld by the entreaties of Rukmiṇī. "He is my only brother," she exclaimed, "and must not be slain by thee : restrain your wrath, O divine Lord, and give me my brother in charity". Thus addressed by her, Kṛṣṇa, whom no acts affect, spared Rukmin; and he (in pursuance of his vow) founded the city Bhojakāta, and ever afterwards dwelt therein. After the defeat of Rukmin, Kṛṣṇa married Rukmiṇī in due form, having first made her his own by the Rākṣasa ritual. She bore him the gallant Pradyumna, a portion of the deity of love. The demon Śambara carried him off, but he slew the demon.

इति श्रीविष्णुमहापुराणे पञ्चमेंशे षड्विंशोऽध्यायः ।। २६ ।।

अथ पञ्चमेंशेः सप्तविंशोऽध्यायः

Part V : Section 27

श्रीमैत्रेय उवाच

शंबरेण हृतो वीरः प्रद्युम्नः स कथं मुने ।।
शंबरः स महावीर्यः प्रद्युम्नेन कथं हतः ।। १ ।।
यस्तेनापहृतः पूर्वं स कथं विजघान तम् ।।
एतद्विस्तरतः श्रोतुमिच्छामि सकलं गुरो ।। २ ।।

Maitreya said :—How, Muni, happened it that the hero Pradyumna was carried away by Śambara? And in what manner was the mighty Śambara killed by Pradyumna?

श्रीपराशर उवाच

षष्ठेह्नि जातमात्रं तु प्रद्युम्नं सूतिकागृहात् ।।
ममैष हंतेति मुने हृतवान्कालशंबरः ।। ३ ।।

Parāśara said :—When Pradyumna was but six days old, he was stolen from the lying-in chamber by Śambara, terrible as death; for the demon foreknew that Pradyumna, if he lived, would be his destroyer.

हत्वा चिक्षेप चैवैनं ग्राहोग्रे लवणार्णवे ।।
कल्लोलजनितावर्त्ते सुघोरे मकरालये ।। ४ ।।

Taking away the boy, Śambara cast him into the ocean, swarming with monsters, into whirlpool of roaring waves, the haunt of the huge creatures of the deep.

पातितं तत्र चैवैको मत्स्यो जग्राह बालकम् ।।
न ममार च तस्यापि जठराग्निप्रदीपितः ।। ५ ।।

मत्स्यबंधैश्च मत्स्योऽसौ मत्स्यैरन्यैस्सह द्विज।।
घातितोऽसुरवर्याय शंबराय निवेदितः।। ६।।

A large fish swallowed the child, but he died not, and was born anew from its belly : for that fish, with others, was caught by the fishermen, and delivered by them to the great Asura Śambara.

तस्य मायावती नाम पत्नी सर्वगृहेश्वरी।।
कारयामास सूदानामाधिपत्यमनिंदिता।। ७।।

His wife Māyāvatī, the mistress of the household, lorded over the cooks.

दारिते मत्स्यजठरे सा ददर्शातिशोभनम्।।
कुमारं मन्मथतरोर्दग्धस्य प्रथमांकुरम्।। ८।।

And she espied, when the fish was cut open, beautiful child looking like a new shoot of the blighted tree of love.

कोऽयं कथमयं मत्स्यजठरे प्रविवेशितः।।
इत्येवं कौतुकाविष्टां तन्वीं प्राहाथ नारदः।। ९।।

When struck with curiosity she was thinking 'who is this child? How has it come into the womb of the fish?' Nārada came and said to her :—

अयं समस्तजगतः स्थितिसंहारकारिणः।।
शंबरेण हृतो विष्णोस्तनयः सूतिकागृहात्।। १०।।

"This is the son of Kṛṣṇa who creates and destroys the universe. He was stolen away from the nursery room by Śambara.

क्षिप्तस्समुद्रे मत्स्येन निगीर्णस्ते गृहं गतः।।
नररत्नमिदं सुभ्रु विस्त्रब्धा परिपालय।। ११।।

He was devoured by the fish when thrown into the ocean; now he has come under thy control; do thou, O beautiful damsel, tenderly rear this jewel of mankind."

श्रीपराशर उवाच

नारदेनैवमुक्ता सा पालयामास तं शिशुम्।।
बाल्यादेवातिरागेण रूपातिशयमोहिता।। १२।।

Parāśara said :—Thus addressed by Nārada, she took charge of the child and brought it up from boyhood being attracted by the beauty of his person.

स यदा यौवनाभोगभूषितोऽभून्महामते।।
साभिलाषा तदा साऽपि बभूव गजगामिनी।। १३।।

O great saint, when the boy attained to youth, Māyāvatī, moving like a she-elephant, began to cherish desire for him.

मायावती ददौ तस्मै मायास्सर्वा महामुने।।
प्रद्युम्नायानुरागांधा तन्न्यस्तहृदये क्षणा।। १४।।

And fixing her mind and eyes upon the high-minded Pradyumna, Māyāvatī, blinded with lust, gave unto him all her magic powers.

प्रसज्जंतीं तु तां प्राह स कार्ष्णिः कमलेक्षणाम्।।
मातृत्वमपहायाद्य किमेवं वर्त्तसेऽन्यथा।। १५।।

Beholding that lotus-eyed damsel thus passionately attached unto him, Kṛṣṇa's son said to her :—"Why dost thou indulge in feelings which do not become a mother?"

सा तस्मै कथयामास न पुत्रस्त्वं ममेति वै।।
तनयं त्वामयं विष्णोर्हृतवान्कालशंबरः।। १६।।

क्षिप्तः समुद्रे मत्स्यस्य संप्राप्तो जठरान्मया।।
सा हि रोदिति ते माता कांताद्याप्यतिवत्सला।। १७।।

She said to him :—"Thou art not my son; thou art the son of the illustrious Viṣṇu; Kāla Śambara stole thee and threw into the ocean; thou wast swallowed by a fish but rescued by me from its belly cut open. O lord thy loving mother is still weeping for thee."

श्रीपराशर उवाच

इत्युक्तश्शंबरं युद्धे प्रद्युम्नः स समाह्वयत्।।
क्रोधाकुलीकृतमना युयुधे च महाबलः।। १८।।

Parāśara said :—Hearing those words Pradyumna invited Śambara for battle. And worked up with ire that highly powerful one fought with him.

हत्वा सैन्यमशेषं तु तस्य दैत्यस्य यादवः।।
सप्तमाया व्यतिक्रम्य मायां प्रयुयुजेऽष्टमीम्।। १९।।

तया जघान तं दैत्यं मायया कालशंबरम्।।
उत्पत्त्य च तया सार्द्धमाजगाम पितुः पुरम्।। २०।।

In the battle the son of Mādhava killed the entire host of Śambara. Having seven times baffled the delusions and mastered them in the eighth he destroyed that demon Śambara. And having got up into the welkin with her he proceeded to his father's house.

अंतःपुरे निपतितं मायावत्या समन्वितम्।।
तं दृष्ट्वा कृष्ण संकल्पा बभूवुः कृष्णयोषितः।। २१।।

And beholding him descend into the inner apartment with Māyāvatī, Kṛṣṇa's wives considered him as Kṛṣṇa himself.

रुक्मिणी साभवत्प्रेम्णा सास्रदृष्टिरनिंदिता।।
धन्याया खल्वयं पुत्रो वर्त्तते नवयौवने।। २२।।

The highly beautiful Rukmiṇī with her eyes full of tears lovingly said :—"Blessed is the woman who has got such a son in the bloom of youth.

अस्मिन्वयसि पुत्रो मे प्रद्युम्नो यदि जीवति।।
सभाग्या जननी वत्स सा त्वया का विभूषिता।। २३।।

Had he been alive my son Pradyumna would have been of this age. Who is the fortunate mother adorned by thee?

अथ वा यादृशः स्नेहो मम यादृग्वपुस्तव।।
हरेरपत्यं सुव्यक्तं भवान्वत्स भविष्यति।। २४।।

From the affection I feel for thee and from thy appearnace me-thinks thou art assuredly the son of Hari."

श्रीपराशर उवाच

एतस्मिन्नंतरे प्राप्तस्सह कृष्णेन नारदः।।
अंतःपुरचरां देवीं रुक्मिणीं प्राह हर्षयन्।। २५।।

Parāśara said :—At this time Kṛṣṇa arrived there with Nārada; and the latter delightedly said to Rukmiṇī.

एष ते तनयः सुभ्रु हत्वा शंबरमागतः।।
हृतो येनाभवद्बालो भवत्यास्सूतिकागृहात्।। २६।।

"This is thy own son who has come hereafter slaying Śambara, by whom he was carried away when a child from the lying-in chamber.

इयं मायावती भार्या तनयस्यास्य ते सती।।
शंबरस्य न भार्येयं श्रूयतामत्र कारणम्।। २७।

This the pious Māyāvatī, his spouse and not the wife of Śambara.

मन्मथे तु गते नाशं तदुद्भवपरायणा।।
शंबरं मोहयामास मायारूपेण रूपिणी।। २८।।

Hear the reason; when Manmatha had perished, the goddess of beauty, being desirous of effecting his revival, fascinated Śambara by the charms of her delusive form.

विहाराद्युपभोगेषु रूपं मायामयं शुभम्।।
दर्शयामास दैत्यस्य तस्येयं मदिरेक्षणा।। २९।।

And she, having eyes rolling with inerbriction, exhibited herself to him in various illusory enjoyments.

कामोऽवतीर्णः पुत्रस्ते तस्येयं दयिता रतिः।।
विशंका नात्र कर्त्तव्या स्नुषेयं तव शोभने।। ३०।।

This thy son is the incarnation of Kāma and this his spouse is the goddess Rati. Do not doubt the least that she is your daughter-in-law."

ततो हर्षसमाविष्टौ रुक्मिणी केशवौ तदा।।
नगरी च समस्ता सा साधुसाध्वित्यभाषत।। ३१।।

Thereupon Rukmiṇī and Keśava were worked up with delight and the whole city resounded with the exclamations of praise.

चिरं नष्टेन पुत्रेण संगतां प्रेक्ष्य रुक्मिणीम्।।
अवाप विस्मयं सर्वो द्वारवत्यां तदा जनः।। ३२।।

And beholding Rukmiṇī regain a son who had been long lost all the people of Dwārakā were surprised.

।। इति श्रीविष्णुमहापुराणे पञ्चमेंशे सप्तविंशोध्यायः।। २७।।

अथ पञ्चमेंशे: अष्टविंशोऽध्याय:

Part V : Section 28

श्रीपराशर उवाच

चारुदेष्णं सुदेष्णं च चारुदेहं च वीर्यवान्।।
सुषेणं चारुगुप्तं च भद्रचारुं तथा परम्।। १।।

चारुविंदं सुचारुं च चारुं च बलिनां वरम्।।
रुक्मिण्यजनयत्पुत्रान्कन्यां चारुमतीं तथा।। २।।

Parāśara said :—Rukmiṇī bore Kṛṣṇa these other sons Cārudeṣṇa, Sudeṣṇa, Cārudeha, Suṣeṇa, Cārugupta, Bhadracāru, Cāruvinda, Sucāru and the very powerful Cāru; also one daughter Cārumatī.

अन्याश्च भार्याः कृष्णस्य बभूवुः सप्त शोभनाः।।
कालिंदी मित्रविंदा च सत्या चाग्नजिती तथा।। ३।।

देवी जाम्बवती चापि रोहिणी कामरूपिणी।।
मद्रराजसुता चान्या सुशीला शीलमंडना।। ४।।

सत्राजिती सत्यभामा लक्ष्मणा चारुहासिनी।।
षोडशासन् सहस्राणि स्त्रीणामन्यानि चक्रिणः।।५।।

Kṛṣṇa had seven other beautiful wives :—Kālindī, Mitravindā, the pious Nagnajiti, the divine Jambāvatī; the beautiful Rohiṇī; Mādrī, the excellent and lovely daughter of Satrajit and Lakṣmaṇā having lovely smiles. Besides these he had also sixteen thousand other wives.

प्रद्युम्नोऽपि महावीर्यो रुक्मिणस्तनयां शुभाम्।।
स्वयंबरे तां जग्राह सा च तं तनयं हरेः।। ६।।

The highly powerful Pradyumna took the beautiful daughter of Rukmin at her public choice of a husband and she too accepted Hari's son.

तस्यामस्याभवत्पुत्रो महाबलपराक्रमः।।
अनिरुद्धौ रणे रुद्धवीर्योदधिररिंदमः।। ७।।

Of her was born a highly powerful son Aniruddha, fierce in fight on account of prowess and subduer of enemies.

तस्यापि रुक्मिणः पौत्रीं वरयामास केशवः।।
दौहित्राय ददौ रुक्मी तां स्पर्द्धन्नपि चक्रिणा।। ८।।

Keshava demanded in marriage the grand daughter of Rukmin and though the latter was inimical to Kṛṣṇa he gave him his grand daughter.

तस्या विवाहे रामाद्या यादवा हरिणा सह।।
कल्याणार्थं ततस्सर्वे ये चान्ये भूभृतस्तथा।।
रुक्मिणो नगरं जग्मुर्नाम्ना भोजकटं द्विज।। ९।।

On the occasion of his nuptials Rāma and other Yādavas accompanied Kṛṣṇa to Bhojakaṭa, the city of Rukmin.

विवाहे तत्र निर्वृत्ते प्रद्युम्नस्य महात्मनः।।
कलिंगराजप्रमुखा रुक्मिणं वाक्यमब्रुवन्।। १०।।

After the wedding had been finished several of the kings headed by him of Kalinga said to Rukmin :—

अनक्षज्ञो हली द्यूते तथास्य व्यसनं महत्।।
तज्जयामो बलं कस्माद्द्यूतेनैनं महाबलम्।। ११।।

"Although the wielder of plough-share is ignorant of dice he has got a great passion for it: why may not fight with him and beat him in play?"

श्रीपराशर उवाच

तथेति तानाह नृपान्रुक्मी बलमदान्वितः।।
सभायां सह रामेण चक्रे द्यूतं च वै तदा।। १२।।

Parāśara said :—The powerful Rukmin replied to the kings, saying "so be it" and he engaged Balarāma at a game of dice in the palace.

सहस्रमेकं निष्काणां रुक्मिणा विजितो बलः।।
द्वितीयेऽपि पणे चान्यत्सहस्रं रुक्मिणा जितः।। १३।।

Balarāma lost to Rukmin a thousand gold coins; he bated a second time and lost another thousand to Rukmin.

ततो दशसहस्राणि निष्काणां पणमाददे।।
बलभद्रोऽजयत्तनि रुक्मी द्यूतविदां वरः।। १४।।

And the third time he staked ten thousand

Niṣkṣas and this time also won Rukmin the foremost of those expert of gambling.

ततो जहास स्वनवत्कलिंगाधिपतिर्द्विज।।
दंतान्विदर्शयन्मूढो रुक्मी चाह मदोद्धतः।। १५।।

At this time the king of Kaliṅga laughed aloud and the weak and vain Rukmin groaned and said :—

अविद्योऽयं मया द्यूते बलभद्रः पराजितः।।
मुधैवाक्षावलेपांधो योऽवमेनेऽक्षकोविदान्।। १६।।

"By me this Baladava, ignorant of gambling, has been defeated; and blinded by a vain passion for play he think that he understands dice."

दृष्ट्वा कलिंगराजानं प्रकाशदशनाननम्।।
रुक्मिणं चापि दुर्वाक्यं कोपं चक्रे हलायुधः।।१७।।

ततः कोपपरीतात्मा निष्ककोटिं समाददे।।
ग्लहं जग्राह रुक्मी च तदर्थेक्षानपातयत्।। १८।।

Beholding the king of Kaliṅga laugh aloud and hearing the contemptuous words of Rukmin the wielder of plough-share was worked up with ire and increased his stake to ten millions of Niṣkṣas Rukmin accepted the challenge and threw dice.

अजयद्बलदेवस्तं प्राहोच्चैर्विजितं मया।।
मयेति रुक्मी प्राहोच्चैरलीकोक्तेरलं बल।। १९।।

त्वयोक्तोऽयं ग्लहस्सत्यं न मयैषोनुमोदितः।।
एवं त्वया चेद्विजितं विजितं न मया कथम्।। २०।।

This time Baladeva won and cried aloud. "This stake is mine." Rukmin cried loudly and said that he was the winner.

"Tell no lies Bala," cried he, "it is true that the stake is yours, but I did not agree to this—although you have won this, still I am the winner."

श्रीपराशर उवाच

अथांतरिक्षे वागुच्चैः प्राह गंभीरनादिनी।।
बलदेवस्य तं कोपं वर्द्धयंती महात्मनः।। २१।।

Thereupon a deep voice was heard in the welkin increasing the more the ire of the high-minded Baladeva, saying :—

जितं बलेन धर्मेण रुक्मिणा भाषितं मृषा।।
अनुक्त्वापि वचः किंचित्कृत भवति कर्मणा।। २२।।

ततो बलः समुत्थाय कोपसंरक्तलोचनः।।
जघानाष्टापदेनैव रुक्मिणं स महाबलः।। २३।।

"Baladeva has justly won the whole amount; Rukmin speaks lies; although he did not accept the pledge in words he did so by his acts." Thus inflamed and having his eyes reddened with rage, Balarāma got up and struck Rukmin with the board on which the game was played and slew him.

कलिंगराजं चादाय विस्फुरंतं बलाद्बलः।।
बभञ्ज दंतान्कुपितो यैः प्रकाशैर्जहास सः।। २४।।

And holding the trembling king of Kaliṅga, Bala forcibly knocked outthe teeth which he had shown when he laughed.

आकृष्य च महास्तंभं जातरूपमयं बलः।।
जघान तान्ये तत्पक्षे भूभृतः कुपितो भृशम्।। २५।।

And uprooting a huge golden column he, enraged, killed therewith all those princes who had assisted his adversaries.

ततो हाहाकृतं सर्वं पलायन परं द्विज।।
तद्राजमंडलं भीतं बभूव कुपिते बले।। २६।।

Thereupon, O twice-born one, Bala being enraged, the whole circle cried out with fear and fled on all sides from his terror.

बलेन निहतं दृष्ट्व रुक्मिणं मधुसूदनः।।
नोवाच किंचिन्मैत्रेय रुक्मिणी बल योर्भयात्।। २७।।

When the stayer of Madhu heard that Rukmin had been slain by Bala he could not speak anything, being afraid of Rukmin on one hand and Bala on the other.

ततोनिरुद्धमादाय कृतदारं द्विजोत्तम्।।
द्वारकामाजगामाथ यदुचक्रं च केशवः।। २८।।

Thereupon taking with him the newly wedded Aniruddha and the Yadu tribe he returned to Dwārakā.

।। इति श्रीविष्णुमहापुराणे पञ्चमेंशेऽष्टाविंशोऽध्यायः।। २८।।

अथ पञ्चमेंशे: एकोनत्रिंशोऽध्याय:

Part V : Section 29

श्रीपराशर उवाच

द्वारवत्यां स्थिते कृष्णे शक्रस्त्रिभुवनेश्वरः।।
आजगामाथ मैत्रेय मत्तैरावतपृष्ठगः।। १।।

Parāśara said :—Thereupon Śakra, the lord of the three worlds, came mounted on his infuriated elephant Airāvata to visit Śaurī at Dwārakā.

प्रविश्य द्वारकां सोऽथ समेत्य हरिणा ततः।।
कथयामास दैत्यस्य नरकस्य विचेष्टितम्।। २।।

Having entered Dwārakā and been welcomed by Hari he communicated unto him the actions of the demon Nāraka.

त्वया नाथेन देवानां मनुष्यत्वेपि तिष्ठता।।
प्रशमं सर्वदुःखानि नीतानि मधुसूदन।। ३।।

तपस्विव्यसनार्थाय सोरिष्टो धेनुकस्तथा।।
प्रवृत्तो यस्तथा केशी ते सर्वे निहतास्त्वया।। ४।।

(He said) "O slayer of Madhu, by thee, the lord of the deities, although situated in mortal condition, all our afflictions have been soothed; thou hast slain Arishtha, Dhenuka Cāṇūra, Muṣṭika and Keśin—all the demons who were slaying the ascetics.

कंसः कुवलयापीडः पूतना बालघातिनी।।
नाशं नीतास्त्वया सर्वे येऽन्ये जगदुपद्रवाः।। ५।।

Kansa Kavalayāpīḍa and the child-destroying Pūtanā, as well as other oppressors of the world have all been slain by thee.

युष्मद्दोर्दंडसंभूतिपरित्राते जगत्त्रये।।
यज्वयज्ञांशसंप्राप्त्या तृप्तिं यांति दिवौकसः।। ६।।

The three worlds being protected by thy valour and wisdom, the deities, obtaining the share of sacrifices undertaken by the devout, enjoy satisfaction.

सोऽहं सांप्रतमायातो यन्निमित्तं जनार्दन।।
तच्छ्रुत्वा तत्प्रतीकारप्रयत्नं कर्त्तुमर्हसि।। ७।।

Hear, O Janārddana, for what I have come to thee and try to remedy it.

भौमोऽयं नरको नाम प्राग्ज्योतिषपुरेश्वरः।।
करोति सर्वभूतानामुपघातमरिंदम।। ८।।

O slayer of enemies, residing in the city of Prāgyotiṣ, the demon Nāraka, son of Bhūmi, has been inflicting the creatures.

देवसिद्धसुरादीनां नृपाणां च जनार्दन।।
हृत्वा तु सोसुरः कन्या रुरुधे निजमंदिरे।। ९।।

Carrying off the maidens of the celestials, saints, demons and kings he shuts them up in his own palace.

छत्रं यत्सलिलस्त्रावि तज्जहार प्रचेतसः।।
मंदरस्य तथा शृंगं हृतवान्मणिपर्वतम्।। १०।।

अमृतस्त्राविणी दिव्ये मन्मातुः कृष्णकुंडले।।
जहार सोऽसुरोदित्या वांछत्यैरावतं गजम्।। ११।।

He has carried away the umbrella of Varuṇa, always producing water, the jewel mountain crest of Mandara, and the nectar-dropping ear-rings of my mother Aditi; and he now demands my elephant Airāvata.

दुर्नीतमेतद्गोविंद मया तस्य निवेदितम्।।
यदत्र प्रतिकर्त्तव्यं तत्स्वयं परिमृश्यताम्।। १२।।

O Govinda, I have thus related unto thee the oppressions of the demon Naraka—do thou now consider what thou shouldst do in this."

श्रीपराशर उवाच

इति श्रुत्वा स्मितं कृत्वा भगवान्देवकीसुतः।।
गृहीत्वा वासवं हस्ते समुत्तस्थौ वरासनात्।। १३।।

Having heard this, the illustrious son of Devakī gently smiled and taking Vāsava by the hand rose up from the excellent seat.

संचिंत्यागतमारुह्य गरुडं गगनेचरम्।।
सत्यभामां समारोप्य ययौ प्राग्ज्योतिषं पुरम्।। १४।।

Thereupon the lord thinking of the eater of serpents Garuḍa, he immediately appeared there. And having first placed Satyabhāmā on his back he ascended and flew to the city of Prāgjyotiṣ.

आरुह्यैरावतं नागं शक्रोऽपि त्रिदिवं ययौ।।
ततो जगाम कृष्णश्च पश्यतां द्वारकौकसाम्।। १५।।

Having ascended the elephant Airāvata, Indra, the lord of the celestials, set out for his city in the sight of the inhabitants of Dwārakā.

प्राग्ज्योतिषपुरस्यापि समंताच्छतयोजनम्।।
आचिता मौरवैः पाशैः क्षुरांतैर्भूर्द्विजोत्तम।। १६।।

O foremost of twice-born ones, the four sides of the city Prāgjyotiṣ to the extent of a yojana were environed by nooses made by demon Mura, whose edges were as sharp as razors.

तांश्चिच्छेद हरिः पाशान्क्षिप्त्वा चक्रं सुदर्शनम्।।
ततो मुरस्समुत्तस्थौ तं जघान च केशवः।। १७।।

But throwing his discus Sudarśana amongst them Hari sundered them into pieces.

मुरस्य तनयान्सप्त सहस्रांस्तांस्ततो हरिः।।
चक्रधाराग्निनिर्दग्धांश्चकार शलभानिव।। १८।।

Thereupon Mura rose up but Kṛṣṇa killed him and burnt his seven thousand sons like so many moths with the flame of the edge of his discus.

हत्वा मुरं हयग्रीवं तथा पञ्चजनं द्विज।।
प्राग्ज्योतिषपुरं धीमांस्त्वरावान्समुपाद्रवत्।। १९।।

Having slain Mura, Hayagrīva, and Pañcajana the wise Hari soon reached the city of Prāgjyotiṣ.

नरकेणास्य तत्राभून्महासैन्येन संयुगम्।।
कृष्णस्य यत्र गोविंदो जघ्ने दैत्यान्सहस्रशः।। २०।।

There ensued a dreadful conflict with Naraka's army in which Govinda slew thousands of demons.

शस्त्रास्त्रवर्षं मुञ्चंतं तं भौमं नरकं बली।।
क्षिप्त्वा चक्रं द्विधा चक्रे चक्री दैतेयचक्रहा।। २१।।

And the powerful annihilator of the demon tribe cut in two with his discus, Bhūmi's son Naraka who came there showering arrows and weapons upon the celestials.

हते तु नरके भूमिर्गृहीत्वाऽदितिकुंडले।।
उपतस्थे जगन्नाथं वाक्यं चेदमथाब्रवीत्।। २२।।

The demons Naraka being slain, Earth, taking the two ear-rings of Aditi, approached the lord of the world and said :—

पृथ्व्युवाच

यदाहमुद्धृता नाथ त्वयासूकरमूर्त्तिना।।
त्वत्स्पर्शसंभवः पुत्रस्तदाऽयं मय्यजायत।। २३।।

"O lord, when I was upheld by thee in the shape of a boar, then this my son was engendered by thy contact.

सोऽयं त्वैव दत्ते मे त्वयैव विनिपातितः।।
गृहाण कुंडले चेमे पालयास्य च संततिम्।। २४।।

Thou didst confer this son upon me and thou hast slain him now. Do thou now take this pair of ear-rings and protect his progeny.

भारावतरणार्थाय ममैव भगवानिमम्।।
अंशेन लोकमायातः प्रसादसुमुखः प्रभो।। २५।।

Thus, O lord, whose aspect is ever pleasing, hast incarnated on this sphere a portion of thyself to lighten my burden.

त्वं कर्त्ता च विकर्त्ता च संहर्त्ता प्रभवोऽप्ययः।।
जगतां त्वं जगद्रूपस्स्तूयतेऽच्युत किं तव।। २६।।

Thou art the eternal creator, preserver and destroyer of the universe, the origin of all the worlds and identical with the universe; how can we worthily chant thy glories?

व्याप्तिर्व्याप्यं क्रियाकर्त्ता कार्यं च भगवान्यथा।।
सर्वभूतात्मभूतस्य स्तूयते तव किं तथा।। २७।।

Thou art the pervader and that which is pervaded, the act, the agent and the effect—thou art the soul of all creatures and how can we sufficiently chant thy glories?

परमात्मा च भूतात्मा त्वमात्मा चाप्ययो भवान्।।
यथातथा स्तुतिर्नाथ किमर्थं ते प्रवर्त्तते।। २८।।

Thou art the great soul—the sentient and living soul of all beings and imperishable—there is no praise worthy of thee—how can we chant thy glories?

प्रसीद सर्वभूतात्मन्नरकेण तु यत्कृतम्।।
तत्क्षम्यतामदोषाय त्वत्सुतस्त्वन्निपातितः।। २९।।

Have pity, O universal soul and forgive the iniquities which Naraka has committed. Verily it is for his purification that he hath been killed by thee."

श्रीपराशर उवाच

तथेति चोक्त्वा धरणीं भगवान्भूतवानः।।
रत्नानि नरकावासाज्जग्राह मुनिसत्तम्।। ३०।।

Parāśara said :—Having replied to the Earth saying "so be it" the lord, who is the substance of all creatures, took various jewels from Naraka's abode.

कन्यापुरे स कन्यानां षोडशातुलविक्रमः।।
शताधिकानि ददृशे सहस्राणि महामुने।। ३१।।

Having entered the female apartment the highly powerful Kṛṣṇa saw sixteen thousand and one hundred damsels.

चतुर्दंष्ट्रान्गजांश्चाग्र्यान् षट्सहस्त्रांश्च दृष्टवान्।।
कांभोजानां तथाऽश्वानां नियुतान्येकविंशतिम्।। ३२।।

He also found in the palace sixteen thousnd huge elephants each having four tusks, twenty-one lakhs of horses of Kāmboja and other excellent breeds.

ताः कन्यास्तांस्तथा नागांस्तानश्वान् द्वारकां पुरीम्।।
प्रपयामास गोविंदस्सद्यो नरककिंकरैः।। ३३।।

All those Govinda sent to Dwārakā in charge of the servants of Naraka.

ददृशे वारुणं च्छत्रं तथैव मणिपर्वतम्।।
आरोपयामास हरिर्गरुडे पतगेश्वरे।। ३४।।

Thereupon he placed Varuṇa's umbrella and the golden mountain on Garuḍa's back.

आरुह्य च स्वयं कृष्णस्सत्यभामासहायवान्।।
आदित्याः कुंडले दातुं जगाम त्रिदशालयम्।। ३५।।

And having ascended with Satyabhāmā he repaired to the city of celestials to confer upon Aditi her ear-rings.

।। इति श्रीविष्णुमहापुराणे पञ्चमेंशे एकोनत्रिंशोऽध्यायः।। २९।।

अथ पञ्चमेंशेः त्रिंशोऽध्यायः

Part V : Section 30

श्रीपराशर उवाच

गरुडो वारुणं छत्रं तथैव मणिपर्वतम्।।
सभार्यं च हृषीकेशं लीलयैव वहन्ययौ।। १।।

Parāśara said :—Carrying the umbrella of Varuṇa, the jewel mountain and Hṛṣikeśa with his spouse on his back, Garuḍa went along lightly and sportively.

ततश्शंखमुपाध्मासीत्स्वर्ग द्वारगतो हरिः।।
उपतस्थुस्तथा देवतस्सार्घ्यहस्ता जनार्दनम्।। २।।

When Hari arrived at the gate of Swarga he blew his conch on which the celestials came forward to meet him bearing respectful offerings.

स देवैरर्चितः कृष्णो देवमातुर्निवेशनम्।।
शिताभ्रशिखराकारं प्रविश्य ददृशेऽदितिम्।। ३।।

Having received the homage of the celestials he proceeded to the palace of the mother of gods whose turrets resembled the white clouds and found Aditi there.

स तां प्रणम्य शक्रेण सह ते कुंडलोत्तमे।।
ददौ नरकनाशं च शशंसास्यै जनार्दनः।। ४।।

Thereupon having bowed unto her along with the king of celestials he conferred the pair of ear-rings upon her and related unto her the destruction of the demon Naraka.

ततः प्रीता जगन्माता धातारं जगतां हरिम्।।
तुष्टावादितिरव्यग्रा कृत्वा तत्प्रवणं मनः।। ५।।

Well-pleased, Aditi, the mother of Gods with her thoughts wholly devoted unto Hari, the protector of the universe, began to chant his glories :—

अदितिरुवाच

नमस्ते पुंडरीकाक्ष भक्तानामभयंकर।।
सनातनात्मन् सर्वात्मन् भूतात्मन् भूतवभावन।। ६।।

"Salutation unto thee, O thou having lotus eyes, who removest all fear of the devoties, who art eternal, the soul of all creatures, the creator of all and identical with all.

प्रणेतर्मनसो बुद्धेरिंद्रियाणां गुणात्मक।।
त्रिगुणातीत निर्द्वंद्व शुद्धसत्त्व हृदि स्थित।। ७।।

सितदीर्घादिनिश्शेषकल्पनापरिवर्जित।।
जन्मादिभिरसंस्पृष्ट स्वप्नादिपरिवर्जित।। ८।।

Thou art at one with the three qualities and the creator of mind, intellect and senses. Thou art beyond the three qualities, exempt from contraries, pure, residing in the hearts of all; void of colour, extension and every transient modification and uninfluenced by the changes of birth and death and sleep and waking.

संध्यारात्रिरहो भूमिर्गगनं वायुरंबु च।।
हुताशनो मनो बुद्धिर्भूतादिस्त्वं तथाऽच्युत।। ९।।

सर्गस्थितिविनाशानां कर्त्ता कर्त्तृपतिर्भवान्।।
ब्रह्मविष्णुशिवाख्याभिरात्ममूर्त्तिभिरीश्वर।। १०।।

Thou art evening, night and day, earth, sky, air, water and fire, mind, intellect and individuality. Thou art the agent of creation, preservation and destruction and the lord over the agent—thou appearest in various forms which are called Brahmā, Viṣṇu and Śiva—and thou art the master even of all these thy forms.

देवा दैत्यास्तथा यक्षा राक्षसास्सिद्धपन्नगाः।।
कूष्मांडाश्च पिशाचाश्च गंधर्वा मनुजास्तथा।। ११।।

पशवश्च मृगाश्चैव पतंगाश्च सरीसृपाः।।
वृक्षगुल्मलताबह्व्यस्समस्तास्तृणजातयः।। १२।।

स्थूला मध्यास्तथा सूक्ष्मास्सूक्ष्मात्सूक्ष्मतराश्च ये।।
देहभेदा भवान् सर्वे ये केचित्पुर्गलाश्रयाः।। १३।।

Thou art Gods, Yakṣas, Daityas, Rākṣasas, Siddhas, Pannagas, Kūṣmāṇḍas, Piśācas, Gandharvas, men, animals, deer, elephants, reptiles, trees, shrubs, creepers, climbers, and grasses—all things, large, middling, and small, immense or minute; thou art all bodies whatsoever composed of aggregated atoms.

माया तवेयमज्ञातपरमार्थातिमोहिनी।।
अनात्मन्यात्मविज्ञानं यया मूढो निरुद्ध्यते।। १४।।

अस्वे स्वमिति भावोत्र यत्पुंसामुपजायते।।
अहं ममेति भावो यत्प्रायेणैवाभिजायते।।
संसारमातुर्मायायास्तवैतन्नाथ चेष्टितम्।। १५।।

यैस्स्वधर्मपरैर्नाथ नरैराराधितो भवान्।।
ते तरंत्यखिलामेतां मायामात्मविमुक्तये।। १६।।

Those who are ignorant of thy true nature cannot understand thy illusion—the fools (only) follow the illusion and think 'this is mine.' O Lord, thy illusion is the mother of the world—and the notions 'I am, this is mine' are but delusions. O Lord, those men, who attentive to their duties, worship thee, obtain salvation after traversing these illusions.

ब्रह्माद्यास्सकला देवा मनुष्याः पशवस्तथा।।
विष्णुमाया महावर्त्तमोहांधतमसावृताः।। १७।।

Brahmā and all the celestials, men and animals are alike enshrouded by the thick darkness of delusion in the abyss of the illusions of Viṣṇu.

आराध्य त्वामभीप्संते कामानात्मभवक्षयम्।।
यदेते पुरुषा माया सैवेयं भगवंस्तव।। १८।।

This is also thy delusion, O lord, that men having worshipped thee seek the gratification of desires and their own preservation. That people having worshipped thee desire for the total annihilation of themselves is but the outcome of thy delusion.

मया त्वं पुत्रकामिन्या वैरिपक्षजयाय च।।
आराधितो न मोक्षाय मायाविलसितं हि तत्।। १९।।

That I have worshipped thee for son and the destruction of the enemies and not for salvation is also the result of thy fascination.

कौपीनाच्छादनप्राया वांछा कल्पदुमादपि।।
जायते यदपुण्यानां सोपराधः स्वदोषजः।। २०।।

It is the fruit of the iniquitous acts of the impious (to pray for vain things to one who is able to give better things) like asking for a rag to cover nakedness from the tree that confers whatever is solicited from it.

तत्प्रसीदाखिलजगन्मायामोहकराव्यय ।।
अज्ञानं ज्ञानवद्भावभूतं भूतेश नाशय।। २१ ।।

Be propitious with me, O thou imperishable, who hast deceived the whole universe with thy delusion.

नमस्ते चक्रहस्ताय शार्ङ्गहस्ताय ते नमः।।
.... ।।२२ ।।

एतत्पश्यामि ते रूपं स्थूलचिह्नोपलक्षितम्।।
न जानामि परं यत्ते प्रसीद परमेश्वर।। २३ ।।

O lord of creatures, do thou remove this ignorance of mine—the notion that I am wise; salutation unto thee, the holder of discus; salutation unto thee the wielder of bow; salutation unto thee, the holder of a club; salutation unto thee, the holder of a conch. O great god, I do perceive thy perceptible form—buy cannot perceive thy real form; do thou therefore be propitious with me.

श्रीपराशर उवाच

अदित्यैवं स्तुतो विष्णुः प्रहस्याह सुरारणिम्।।
माता देवि त्वमस्माकं प्रसीद वरदा भव।। २४।।

Parāśara said :—Aditi, the mother of gods, having thus chanted the glories of Viṣṇu, he smiling said :—"Thou art our mother, O goddess, be thou propitious and confer upon me a boon."

अदितिरुवाच

एवमस्तु यथेच्छा ते त्वमशेषैस्सुरासुरैः।।
अजेयः पुरुष व्याघ्र मर्त्यलोके भविष्यसि।। २५ ।।

Aditi said :—"So be it, ever as thou wilt; O foremost of men, as long as shalt thou udwell in the land of mortals thou shalt be invincible by celestials and demons."

श्रीपराशर उवाच

ततः कृष्णस्य पत्नी च शक्रेण सहितादितिम्।।
सत्यभामा प्रणम्याह प्रसीदेति पुनःपुनः।। २६ ।।

Thereupon Satyabhāmā, along with Śaci, bowed unto Aditi again and again and said. "Be thou pleased."

अदितिरुवाच

मत्प्रसादान्न ते सुभ्रु जरा वैरूप्यमेव वा।।
भविष्यत्यनवद्यांगि सुस्थिरं नवयौवनम्।। २७ ।।

Whereto Aditi replied saying :—"Fair-browed dame, by my favour thou shalt never experience decrepitude or loss of beauty; thou shalt be of a blameless person and asylum of all graces."

श्रीपराशर उवाच

अदित्या तु कृतानुज्ञो देवराजो जनार्दनम्।।
यथावत्पूजयामास बहुमानपुरस्सरम्।। २८ ।।

Parāśara said :—Being commanded by Aditi, the lord of the celestials duly honoured Janārddana.

शची च सत्यभामायै पारिजातस्य पुष्पकम्।।
न ददौ मानुषीं मत्वा स्वयं पुष्पैरलंकृता।। २९ ।।

Thereupon Kṛṣṇa, accompanied by Satyabhāmā beheld Nandana and other pleasant gardens of the celestials.

ततो ददर्श कृष्णोऽपि सत्यभामासहायवान्।।
देवोद्यानानि हृद्यानि नंदनादीनि सत्तम।। ३० ।।
ददर्श च सुगंधाढ्यं मञ्जरीपुञ्जधारिणम्।।
नित्याह्लादकरं ताम्रबालपल्लवशोभितम्।। ३१ ।।
मथ्यमानेऽमृते जातं जातरूपोपमत्वचम्।।
पारिजातं जगन्नाथः केशवः केशिसूदनः।। ३२ ।।

There Keśava, the lord of the universe and the slayer of Keśi, saw Pārijāta, the favourite of Śaci, having golden bark, young sprouting leaves of a copper colour and bearing numerous fragrant clusters of flowers, and which was produced when the ocean was churned for ambrosia.

तुतोष परमप्रीत्या तरुराजमनुत्तमम्।।
तं दृष्ट्वा प्राह गोविंदं सत्यभामा द्विजोत्तम।।
कस्मान्न द्वारकामेष नीयते कृष्ण पादपः।। ३३ ।।

Beholding that tree, O foremost of twice-born ones, Satyabhāmā said to Govinda. "Why should not this celestial tree be taken to Dwārakā.

यदि चेत्त्वद्वचः सत्यं त्वमत्यर्थं प्रियेति मे।।
मद्गेहनिष्कुटार्थाय तदयं नीयतां तरुः।। ३४।।

If what you always say is true that I am really dear to you then take this tree from here for the gardens of my dwelling.

न मे जांबवती तादृगभीष्टा न च रुक्मिणी।।
सत्ये यथा त्वमित्युक्तं त्वया कृष्णासकृत्प्रियम्।। ३५।।

सत्यं तद्यदि गोविंद नोपचारकृतं मम।।
तदस्तु पारिजातोऽयं मम गेहविभूषणम्।। ३६।।

बिभ्रती पारिजातस्य केशपक्षेणमञ्जरीम्।।
सपत्नीनामहं मध्ये शोभेयमिति कामये।। ३७।।

O Kṛṣṇa, you always say "O Satya, neither Rukmiṇī nor Jāmbavati is beloved unto me like thee," if this is true and not mere flattery then let this Pārijāta be the ornament of my dwelling. Wearing the flowers of this tree in the braids of my hair I wish to appear graceful amidst my fellow queens."

श्रीपराशर उवाच

इत्युक्तस्स प्रहस्यैनां पारिजातं गरुत्मति।।
आरोपयामास हरिस्तमूचुर्वनरक्षिणः।। ३८।।

भो शची देवराजस्य महिषी तत्परिग्रहम्।।
पारिजातं न गोविंद हर्त्तुमर्हसि पादपम्।। ३९।।

उत्पन्नो देवराजाय दत्तस्सोपि ददौ पुनः।।
महिष्यै सुमहाभाग देव्यै शच्यै कुतूहलात्।। ४०।।

Parāśara said :—Thus requested by Satyabhāmā Hari, smiled and taking the Pārijāta plant placed it upon Garuḍa. The guards said :—"O Govinda, this tree belongs to Śaci, the queen of the king of celestials; it is not becoming for thee to remove it.

शचीविभूषणार्थाय देवैरमृतमंथने।।
उत्पादितोऽयं न क्षेमी गृहीत्वैनं गमिष्यसि।। ४१।।

When the ocean was churned by the celestials this tree was produced for providing Śaci with flowery ornaments; thou shalt not go with it uncatched.

देवराजो मुखप्रेक्षी यस्यास्तस्याः परिग्रहम्।।
मौढ्यात्प्रार्थयसे क्षेमी गृहीत्वैनं हि को व्रजेत्।। ४२।।

अवश्यमस्य देवेंद्रो निष्कृतिं कृष्ण यास्यति।।
वज्रोद्यतकरं शक्रमनुयास्यंति चामराः।। ४३।।

तदलं सकलैर्देवैर्विग्रहेण तवाऽच्युतः।।
विपाककटु यत्कर्म तन्न शंसंति पंडिताः।। ४४।।

This is the property of one upon whose countenance the king of the celestials delights to look; it is out of ignorance that thou dost attempt to take it—taking this no one shall be suffered to depart in peace. Forsooth shall the celestial chief punish this audacity; and when he shall take up his thunderbolt all the deities shall follow him. O thou imperishable, it is not proper for thee, to enter into conflict with all the divinities. The wise never undertake a work that terminates fatally."

श्रीपराशर उवाच

इत्युक्ते तैरुवाचैतान् सत्यभामातिकोपिनी।।
का शची पारिजातस्य को वा शक्रस्सुराधिपः।। ४५।।

The guards having said this Satyabhāmā was greatly worked up with ire and said : "How does this Prārijāta belong to Śaci? Who is Śakra, the lord of the celestials?

सामान्यस्सर्वलोकस्य यद्येषोऽमृतमंथने।।
समुत्पन्नस्तरुः कस्मादेको गृह्णाति वासव।। ४६।।

यथा सुरा यथैवेंदुर्यथा श्रीर्वनरक्षिणः।।
सामान्यस्सर्वलोकस्य पारिजातस्तथा द्रुमः।। ४७।।

If this had been produced when the ocean was churned by the celestials then all have equal right over it—why shall Vāsava alone possess it? O ye warders of the garden, ambrosia, the moon and Lakṣmī are the common properties of all; so is this Pārijāta tree.

भर्त्तृबाहुमहागर्वाद्रुणद्ध्येनमथो शची।।
तत्कथ्यतामलं क्षांत्या सत्या हारयति द्रुमम्।। ४८।।

If Śaci has taken possession of it forcibly by the valour of her husband, do ye go and communicate unto her that Satyabhāmā is taking it away and let not Śaci forgive her.

कथ्यतां च दुतं गत्वा पौलोम्या वचनं मम।।
सत्यभामा वदत्येतदितिगर्वोद्धताक्षरम्।। ४९।।

Do ye soon go to her and according to my instructions tell her that Satyabhāmā has given vent to these proud words.

यदि त्वं दयिता भर्तुर्यदि वश्यः पतिस्तव।।
मद्भर्तुर्हरतो वृक्षं तत्कारय निवारणम्।। ५०।।

'If thou art dear unto thy husband, if he is under thine control then let him take back the Pārijāta tree which my husband is taking away.

जानामि ते पतिं शक्रं जानामि त्रिदशेश्वरम्।।
पारिजातं तथाप्येनं मानुषी हारयमि ते।। ५१।।

I know thy husband Śakra is the master of the three worlds. Still being a mortal I take away this Pārijāta tree."

श्रीपराशर उवाच

इत्युक्ता रक्षिणो गत्वा शच्याः प्रोचुर्यथोदितम्।।
श्रुत्वा चोत्साहयामास शची चक्रं सुराधिपम्।।५२।।

Parāśara said :—Being thus accosted, the warders went to Śaci and communicated unto her everything duly. And Śaci excited the lord of the three worlds.

ततस्समस्तदेवानां सैन्यैः परिवृतो हरिम्।।
प्रययौ पारिजातार्थमिंद्रो योद्धुं द्विजोत्तम।। ५३।।

Thereupon accompanied by the army of the celestials, Indra, issued out to fight with Hari, in defence of the Pārijāta tree.

ततः परिघनिस्त्रिंशगदाशूलवरायुधाः।।
बभूवुस्त्रिदशास्सज्जाश्शक्रे वज्रकरे स्थिते।।५४।।

The celestials were armed with clubs, swords, maces and darts and Indra wielded the thunderbolt.

ततो निरीक्ष्य गोविंदो नागराजोपरि स्थितम्।।
शक्रं देवपरीवारं युद्धाय समुपस्थितम्।। ५५।।
चकार शंखनिर्घोषं दिशश्शब्देन पूरयन्।।
मुमोच शरसंघातान्सहस्त्रायुतशशिशतान्।। ५६।।
ततो दिशो नभश्चैव दृष्ट्वा शरशतैश्चितम्।।
मुमुचुस्त्रिदशास्सर्वे ह्यस्त्रशस्त्राण्यनेकशः।। ५७।।
एकैकमस्त्रं शस्त्रं च देवैर्मुक्तं सहस्त्रशः।।
चिच्छेद लीलयैवेशो जगतां मधुसूदनः।। ५८।।
पाशं सलिलराजस्य समाकृष्योरगात्पुनः।।
चकार खंडशश्चंच्वा बालपन्नगदेहवत्।। ५९।।

As soon as Govinda beheld the king of the celestials proceeding against him mounted on his elephant, attended by the immortals he blew his shell so that all the quartes were filled with the sound thereof and he smilingly showered myriods of shafts upon his assailants. When the celestials saw that all the directions and atmosphere were overspread with arrows they also in return hurled numberless missiles. But all these, the slayer of Madhu, and the lord of the three worlds, sundered easily into a thousand pieces with his shafts.

यमेम प्रहितं दंडं गदाविक्षेपखंडितम्।।
पृथिव्यां पातयामास भगवान् देवकीसुतः।। ६०।।
शिबिकां च धनेशस्य चक्रेण तिलशो विभुः।।
चकार शौरिरर्कं च दृष्टदृष्टहतौजसम्।। ६१।।
नीतिग्निश्शीततां बाणैर्द्राविता वसवो दिशः।।
चक्रविच्छिन्नशूलाग्रा रुद्रा भुवि निपातिताः।। ६२।।
साध्या विश्वेऽथ मरुतो गंधर्वाश्चैव सायकैः।।
शार्ङ्गिणा प्रेरितैरस्ता व्योम्नि शाल्मलितूलवत्।। ६३।।

Garuḍa, the devourer of serpants, laid hold of the noose of the king of seas and tore it to pieces with his beak as if it had been a little snake. Devakī's son hurled his mace at the club of Yama and cast it broken upon the ground; he sundered in pieces the litter of the lord of riches with his discus; his eye-looks over-clouded the radiance of the sun; he cut Agni into a hundred parts with his shafts and scattered the Vasus through the realms of the space; he sundered with his discus the points of the tridents of the Rudras and cast themselves upon the earth; and with the arrows shot from his bow he scattered the Sādhyās, Viśvas, Maruts and Gandharvas through the sky, like fleeces of cotton from the pods of the Simal tree.

गरुत्मानपि तुंडेन पक्षाभ्यां च नखांकुरैः।।
भक्षयंस्ताडयन् देवान् दारयंश्च चचार वै।। ६४।।

Garuḍa also diligently plied his beak and wings and bit and bruised and scratched the celestials who opposed his lord.

ततश्शतसहस्रेण देवेंद्रमधुसूदनौ।।
परस्परं ववर्षाते धाराभिरिव तोयदौ।। ६५।।

Like unto two heavy clouds showering raindrops the king of the celestials and the slayer of Madhu overpowered each other with numberless arrows.

ऐरावतेन गरुडो युयुधे तत्र संकुले।।
देवैस्समस्तैर्युयुधे शक्रेण च जनार्दनः।। ६६।।

Garuḍa fought with Airāvata in that conflict and Janārddana engaged with his discus with all the celestials.

भिन्नेष्वशेषबाणेषु शस्त्रेष्वस्त्रेषु च त्वरन्।।
जग्राह वासवो वज्रं कृष्णश्चक्रं सुदर्शनम्।। ६७।।

When all other weapons had been sundered into pieces Indra stood armed with his thunderbolt and Kṛṣṇa with the discus Sudarśana.

ततो हाहाकृतं सर्वं त्रैलोक्यं द्विजसत्तम।।
वज्रचक्रकरौ दृष्ट्वा देवराजजनार्दनौ।। ६८।।

Beholding them thus ready for fight all the inhabitants of the three worlds, cried aloud "Alas! Alas!" In vain did Indra hurl his bolt for Hari caught and arrested it.

क्षिप्तं वज्रमथेंद्रेण जग्राह भगवान्हरिः।।
न मुमोच तदा चक्रं शक्रं तिष्ठेति चाब्रवीत्।। ६९।।

He however, did not hurl his discus, but only called out to Indra to stay.

प्रणष्टवज्रं देवेंद्रं गरुडक्षतवाहनम्।।
सत्यभामाब्रवीद्वीरं पलायनपरायणम्।। ७०।।

Beholding Indra disarmed and his elephant disabled by Garuḍa and the deity about to fly away Satyabhāmā said to him :—

त्रैलोक्येश न ते युक्तं शचीभर्तुः पलायनम्।।
पारिजातस्रगाभोगा त्वामुपस्थास्यते शची।। ७१।।

"O king of the three worlds, it becomes not the husband of Śaci to run away. She will approach you adorned with Pārijāta garlands.

कीदृशं देवराज्यं ते पारिजातस्नगुज्ज्वलाम्।।
अपश्यतो यथापूर्वं प्रणयाभ्यागतां शचीम्।। ७२।।

What shalt thou do with the kingdom of heaven when no longer thou dost behold Śaci approach thee, like before, embellished with Pārijāta garlands?

अलं शक्र प्रयासेन न व्रीडां गंतुमर्हसि।।
नीयतां पारिजातोयं देवास्संतु गतव्यथाः।। ७३।।

Fly not O Śakra; you must suffer shame, take the Pārijāta; let the celestials be no longer annoyed.

पतिगर्वावलेपेन बहुमानपुरस्सरम्।।
न वर्ण्यं गृहं यातामुपचारेण मां शची।। ७४।।

Worked up with the pride of her husband Śaci has not welcomed me to her dwelling with her respectful presents.

स्त्रीत्वादगुरुचित्ताहं स्वभर्तृश्लाघनापरा।।
ततः कृतवती शक्र भवता सह विग्रहम्।। ७५।।

O king of the celestials, I am a woman and therefore of light purpose and am anxious of my husband's fame; for this I have instituted this fight with thee.

तदल पारिजातेन परस्वेन हृतेन मे।।
रूपेण गद्भवता सा तु भर्त्रा का स्त्री न गर्विता।। ७६।।

I do not require the Pārijāta any more. Why shall we steal another's property? What female is not inflated with the pride of her husband? But she is proud of her beauty."

श्रीपराशर उवाच

इत्युक्तो वै निववृते देवराजस्तया द्विज।।
प्राह चैनामलं चंडि सख्युः खे दोक्तिविस्तरैः।। ७७।।

इंद्र उवाच

न चापि सर्गसंहारस्थितिकर्त्ताखिलस्य यः।।
जितस्य तेन मे व्रीडा जायते विश्वरूपिणा।। ७८।।

Parāśara said :—Thus addressed by her the

king of the celestials turned back and said :—"O wrathful dame, thou shouldst not afflict thy friend with further reproaches. I am not ashamed of being defeated by him who is the author of the creation, preservation and destruction of the world, who is the substance of all things, and in whom the universe exists, without beginning or middle, and from whom and by whom at one with all things, it proceeds and will cease to be.

यस्माज्जगत्सकलमेतदनादिमध्या-
द्यस्मिन्यतश्च न भविष्यति सर्वभूतात्।।
तेनोद्भवप्रलयपालनकारणेन व्रीडा
कथं भवति देवि निराकृतस्य।। ७९।।

O goddess, what disgrace it is to any one, to be vanquished by him who is the agent of creation, preservation and destruction?

सकलभुवनसूतिर्मूर्तिरल्पाल्पसूक्ष्मा-
विदितसकलवेद्यैर्ज्ञायते यस्य नान्यैः।।
तमजमकृतमीशं शाश्वतं स्वेच्छयैनं
जगदुपकृतिमर्त्यं को विजेतुं समर्थः।। ८०।।

His form, though infinitely subtle, is the parent of all worlds and is known to those only by whom all that may be known is known; who is capable of defeating the unborn, unconstituted, eternal lord, who has, of his own accord, descended for the behoof of the world?

।। इति श्रीविष्णुमहापुराणे पञ्चमेंशे त्रिंशोऽध्यायः।। ३०।।

अथ पञ्चमेंशेः एकत्रिंशोऽध्यायः

Part V : Section 31

श्रीपराशर उवाच

संस्तुतो भगवानित्थं देवराजेन केशवः।।
प्रहस्य भावगंभीरमुवाचेंद्रं द्विजोत्तम।। १।।

Thus chanted by the king of the celestials, Keśava smiled and replied gravely saying :—

श्रीकृष्ण उवाच

देवराजो भवानिंद्रो वयं मर्त्या जगत्पते।।
क्षंतव्यं भवतैवेदमपराधं कृतं मम।। २।।

"Thou art, O Indra, the king of the celestials : we are mere mortals, O king of the universe : thou must therefore forgive me, for the offence I have committed.

पारिजाततरुश्चायं नीयतामुचितास्पदम्।।
गृहीतोयं मया शक्र सत्यावचनकारणात्।। ३।।

Let this Pārijāta tree be taken to its proper place. I remove it to satisfy Satya's desire.

वज्रं चेदं गृहाण त्वं यदत्र प्रहितं त्वया।।
तवैवैतत्प्रहरणं शक्र वैरिविदारणम्।। ४।।

Take back also this thy thunderbolt which thou didst hurl at me; for this is your proper weapon—O slayer of thy enemies."

इंद्र उवाच

विमोहयसि मामीश मर्त्योहमिति किं वदन्।।
जानीमस्त्वां भगवतो न तु सूक्ष्मविदो वयम्।। ५।।

Whereto Indra replied, saying :—"O lord, thou dost beguile us in calling thyself mortal. We are endowed with subtlety of discernment and therefore know thee as gifted with six qualities.

योऽसि योऽसि जगत्त्राणप्रवृत्तौ नाथ संस्थितः।।
जगतश्शल्यनिष्कर्षे करोष्यसुरसूदन।। ६।।

Whoever thou mayst be, O slayer of thine enemies, thou art engaged in the active preservation of earth and thou removest the thorns implanted in her bossom.

नीयतो पारिजहातोऽयं कृष्ण द्वारवतीं पुरीम्।।
मर्त्यलोके त्वया त्यक्ते नायं संस्थास्यते भुवि।। ७।।

देवदेव जगन्नाथ कृष्ण विष्णो महाभुज।।
शंखचक्रगदापाणे क्षमस्वैतद्व्यतिक्रमम्।। ८।।

O Krsna,thou art god of gods Viṣṇu who had conch-shell, discus, goad in his hand, do thou take this Pārijāta tree to the city of Dwārakā and when thou shalt renounce this land of mortals it shall no longer remain on earth."

श्रीपराशर उवाच

तथेत्युक्त्वा च देवेंद्रमाजगाम भुवं हरिः।।
प्रसक्तैस्सिद्धगंधर्वैस्तूयमानस्सुरर्षिभिः।। ९।।

Parāśara said :—Having agreed to the proposal of the king of the celestials Hari returned to earth eulogised by attendant sages, saints and quiristers of heaven.

ततश्शंखमुपाध्माय द्वारकोपरि संस्थितः।।
हर्षमुत्पादयामास द्वारकावासिनां द्विज।। १०।।

When Kṛṣṇa arrived over the city of Dwārakā he blew his conch and delighted the inhabitants with the sound.

अवतीर्याथ गरुडात्सत्यभामा सहायवान्।।
निष्कुटे स्थापयामास पारिजातं महातरुम्।। ११।।

यमभ्येत्य जनस्सर्वो जातिं स्मरति पौर्विकीम्।।
वास्यते यस्य पुष्पोत्थगंधेनोर्वी त्रियोजनम्।। १२।।

ततस्ते यादवास्सर्वे देहबंधानमानुषान्।।
ददृशुः पादपे तस्मिन् कुर्वंतो मुखदर्शनम्।। १३।।

किंकरैस्समुपानीतं हस्त्यश्वादि ततो धनम्।।
विभज्य प्रददौ कृष्णो बांधवानां महामतिः।। १४।।

कन्याश्च कृष्णो जग्राह नरकस्य परिग्रहान्।। १५।।

ततः काले शुभे प्राप्ते उपयेमे जनार्दनः।।
ताः कन्या नरकेणासन्सर्वतो यास्समाहृताः।। १६।।

एकस्मिन्नेव गोविंदः काले तासां महामुने।।
जग्राह विधिवत्पाणीन्पृथग्गेहेषु धर्मतः।। १७।।

षोडशस्त्रीसहस्राणि शतमेकं ततोधिकम्।।
तावंति चक्रे रूपाणि भगवान् मधुसूदनः।। १८।।

Thereupon alighting from Garuḍa he proceeded with Satyabhāmā to her garden, and there planted the great Pārijāta tree the smell of which extended over the earth for three furlongs and an appraoch to which enabled every one to recollect the events of a pristine existence. And beholding their faces in that tree the Yādavas know themselves in their (original) celestial forms. Then Kṛṣṇa took possession of wealth, elephants, horses and women which he had recovered from Naraka and which had been brought to Dwārakā by the servants of the demon; and at an auspicious hour he married all the maidens whom Naraka had carried off from their friends; and simultaneously at the same time in different mansions he received the hands of all the damsels.

एकैकमेव ताः कन्या मेनिरे मधुसूदनः।।
ममैव पाणिग्रहणं मैत्रेय कृतवानिति।। १९।।

The number of the maidens was sixteen thousand and one hundred and in so many forms did the slayer of Madhu appear, so that every one of them thought that he had wedded her in his single person.

निशासु च जगत्स्रष्टा तासां गेहेषु केशवः।।
उवास विप्र सर्वासां विश्वरूपधरो हरिः।। २०।।

Hari the creator of the world and the assumer of the universal shape lived severally in the mansion of each of these his wives.

।। इति श्रीविष्णुमहापुराणे पञ्चमेंशे एकत्रिंशोऽध्यायः।। ३१।।

अथ पञ्चमेंशे: द्वात्रिंशोऽध्याय:

Part V : Section 32

श्रीपराशर उवाच

प्रद्युम्नाद्या हरेः पुत्रा रुक्मिण्यां कथितास्तव।।
भानुभौमेरिकाद्यांश्च सत्यभामा व्यजायत।। १।।

Parāśara said :—I have enumerated to you Pradyumna and other sons begotten on Rukmiṇī by Kṛṣṇa. Satyabhāmā bore Bhānu and Bhairika.

दीप्तिमत्तम्रपक्षाद्या रोहिण्यां कथिता हरेः।।
बभूवुर्जाम्बवत्यां च सांबाद्या बाहुशालिनः।। २।।

The sons of Rohiṇī were Diptimat, Tāmrepakṣī and others; Jāmbavatī gave birth to the powerful Sāmba and other sons.

तनया भद्रविंदाद्या नाग्नजित्यां महाबलाः।।
संग्रामजित्प्रधानास्तु शैब्यायां च हरेस्सुताः।। ३।।

Bhadravindā and other valiant youths were the sons of Nagnajiti. Saivya bore several sons of whom Saṅgrāmajit was the chief.

वृकाद्याश्च सुता माद्र्यां गात्रवत्प्रमुखान्सुतान्।।
अवाप लक्ष्मणा पुत्रान्कालिंद्याश्च श्रुतादयः।। ४।।

Vṛka and others were begotten by Hari on Mādrī. Lakṣmaṇā gave birth to Gātravat and others; and Śruta and others were the sons of Kālindī.

अन्यासां चैव भार्याणां समुत्पन्नानि चक्रिणः।।
अष्टायुतानि पुत्राणां सहस्राणि शतं तथा।। ५।।

Besides Kṛṣṇa had sons by his other wives in all one hundred and eighty thousand.

प्रद्युम्नः प्रथमस्तेषां सर्वेषां रुक्मिणीसुतः।।
प्रद्युम्नादनिरुद्धोऽभूद्वज्रस्तस्मादजायत ।। ६।।

अनिरुद्धो रणेऽरुद्धो बलेः पौत्रीं महाबलः।।
उषां बाणस्य तनयामुपयेमे द्विजोत्तम।। ७।।

The eldest of the whole was Pradyumna, the son of Rukmiṇī; his son was Aniruddha, whose son was Vraja; his mother was Uṣā, the daughter of Bāṇa the grand daughter of Bāli, whom Aniruddha won in war.

यत्र युद्धमभूद्घोरं हरिशंकरयोर्महत्।।
छिन्नं सहस्रं बाहूनां यत्र बाणस्य चक्रिणा।। ८।।

On that occasion a dreadful onset ensued between Hari and Śaṅkara in which the thousand arms of Bāṇa were cut off by the discus of the former.

मैत्रेय उवाच

कथं युद्धमभूद्ब्रह्मन्नुषार्थे हरकृष्णयोः।।
कथं क्षयं च बाणस्य बाहूनां कृतवान्हरिः।। ९।।

Maitreya said :—How is it, O venerable Brāhmaṇa, that a contest took place, on account of Uṣā, between Śiva and Kṛṣṇa?

एतत्सर्वं महाभाग ममाख्यातुं त्वमर्हसि।।
महत्कौतूहलं जातं कथां श्रोतुमिमां हरेः।। १०।।

And in what manner did Hari cut off the thousand arms of Bāṇa? I am greatly stricken with curiosity to hear this story of Hari—do thou, O venerable Sir, relate this.

श्रीपराशर उवाच

उषा बाणसुता विप्र पार्वतीं सह शंभुना।।
क्रीडंतीमुपलक्ष्योच्चैः स्पृहां चक्रे तदाश्रयाम्।। ११।।

Parāśara said :—Having seen Pārvatī dallying with his lord Śambhu, Uṣā, the daughter of Bāṇa, was inspired with a similar desire.

ततस्सकलचित्तज्ञा गौरी तामाह भामिनीम्।।
अलमत्यर्थतापेन भर्त्रा त्वमपि रंस्यसे।। १२।।

The charming Gaurī, knowing the hearts of all, said to her :—"Do not grieve; you shall have a husband."

इत्युक्ता सा तया चक्रे कदेति मतिमात्मनः।।
को वा भर्त्ता ममेत्याह पुनस्तामाह पार्वती।। १३।।

"But when will this be and who shall be my husband?" thought Uṣā within herself, on which Pārvatī said :—

पार्वत्युवाच

वैशाखशुक्लद्वादश्यां स्वप्ने योभि भवं तव।।
करिष्यति स ते भर्त्ता राजपुत्रि भविष्यति।। १४।।

"He who shall appear to you, princess, in a dream, on the twelfth lunation of the light half of Vaiśākha, shall be your lord."

श्रीपराशर उवाच

तस्यां तिथावुषास्वप्ने यथा देव्या समीरितम्।।
तथैवाभिभवं चक्रे कश्चिद्रागं च तत्र सा।। १५।।

Accordingly, in consonance with the goddess' foretelling a youth appeared in dream to Uṣā on that lunar day, of whom she became enamoured.

ततः प्रबुद्धा पुरुषमपश्यंती समुत्सुका।।
क्व गतोसीति निर्लज्जा मैत्रेयोक्तवती सखीम्।। १६।।

When she got up and no longer saw him she was distressed with grief and not carring for modesty asked of her companion whither he had gone.

बाणस्य मंत्री कुंभांडः चित्रलेखा च तत्सुता।।
तस्यास्सख्यभवत्सा च प्राह कोयं त्वयोच्यते।। १७।।

This companion and friend of the princess was Citralekhā, the daughter of Kubhāṇḍa, the minister of Bāṇa. She said to Uṣā of whom do you speak?"

यदा लज्जाकुला नास्यै कथयामास सा सखी।।
तदा विश्वासमानीय सर्वमेवाभ्यवादयत्।। १८।।

But ashamed she did not reply. However gaining her confidence Citralekhā heard from her everything.

विदितार्थां तु तामाह पुनश्चोषा यथोदितम्।।
देव्या तथैव तत्प्राप्तौ यो ह्युपायः कुरुष्व तम्।। १९।।

चित्रलेखोवाच

दुर्विज्ञेयमिदं वक्तुं प्राप्तुं वाऽपि न शक्यते।।
तथापिं किंचित्कर्त्तव्यमुपकारं प्रिये तव।। २०।।

सप्ताष्टदिनपर्यंतं तावत्कालः प्रतीक्ष्यताम्।।
इत्युक्त्वाभ्यंतर गत्वा उपायं तमथाकरोत्।। २१।।

And again Uṣā requested her who had been informed of all, to devise means by which she might be united with the person whom she had beheld in dream.

श्रीपराशर उवाच

ततः पटे सुरान्दैत्यान्गंधर्वांश्च प्रधानतः।।
मनुष्यांश्च विलिख्यास्यै चित्रलेखा व्यदर्शयत्।। २२।।

Parāśara said :—Thereupon Citralekhā painted the figures of the most eminent celestials, demons, spirits and mortals and showed them to Uṣā.

अपास्य सा तु गंधर्वांस्तथोरगसुरासुरान्।।
मनुष्येषु ददौ दृष्टिं तेष्वप्यंधकवृष्णिणु।। २३।।

Putting aside the likenesses of celestials, spirits, snake-gods and demons, the princess selected those of mortals and amongst them the heroes of the races of Andhaka and Vṛṣṇi.

कृष्णरामौ विलोक्यासीत्सुभ्रूर्लज्जाजडेव सा।।
प्रद्युम्नदर्शने व्रीडादृष्टिं निन्येन्यतो द्विज।। २४।।

दृष्टमात्रे ततः कांते प्रद्युम्नतनये द्विज।।
दृष्ट्वात्यर्थविलासिन्या लज्जा क्वापि निराकृता।। २५।।

सोयंसोयमितीत्युक्ते तया सा योगगामिनी।।
चित्रलेखा ब्रवीदेनामुषां बाणसुतां तदा।। २६।।

चित्रलेखोवाच

अयं कृष्णस्य पौत्रस्ते भर्त्ता देव्या प्रसादितः।।
अनिरुद्ध इति ख्यातः प्रख्यातः प्रियदर्शनः।। २७।।

प्राप्नोषि यदि भर्त्तारमिमं प्राप्तं त्वयाऽखिलम्।।
दुष्प्रवेशा पुरी पूर्वं द्वारका कृष्णपालिता।। २८।।

तथापि यत्नाद्भर्त्तारमानयिष्यामि ते सखि।।
रहस्यमेतद्वक्तव्यं न कस्यचिदपि त्वया।। २९।।

अचिरादागमिष्यामि सहस्व विरहं मम।।
ययौ द्वारवतीं चोषां समाश्वास्य ततः सखीम्।। ३०।।

And when she found the portratis she was bewildered by shame; then she took his eyes away with shame from the portrait of Pradyumna. But as soon as she saw the picture of his son, the object of her passions, she set aside all bashfulness and with wide expanded eyes, cried aloud, "This is he, this is he," Her friend, who was gifed with magic power, requested her to be cheerful and started for Dwārakā through the air.

।। इति श्रीविष्णुमहापुराणे पञ्चमेंशे द्वात्रिंशोऽध्यायः।। ३२।।

अथ पञ्चमेंशे: त्रयत्रिंशोऽध्याय:

Part V : Section 33

श्रीपराशर उवाच

बाणोपि प्रणिपत्याग्रे मैत्रेयाह त्रिलोचनम्।।
देव बाहुसहस्त्रेण निर्विण्णोस्म्याहवं विना।। १।।

कच्चिन्ममैषां बाहूनां साफल्यजनको रण:।।
भविष्यति विना युद्धं भाराय मम किं भुजै:।। २।।

Parāśara said :—Before this, once Bāṇa prayed to the three-eyed diety saying "O lord I am humiliated by the possession of a thousand arms; let some conflict take place in which I may make use of my arms. Without any war what is the use of these arms; they are but a burden to me.

श्रीशंकर उवाच

मयूरध्वजभंगस्ते यदा बाण भविष्यति।।
पिशिताशिजनानंदं प्राप्स्यसे त्वं तदा रणम्।। ३।।

Śaṅkara said :—"When this peacock banner shall be broken thou shalt have war, the delight of the evil spirits that live on human flesh."

श्रीपराशर उवाच

तत: प्रणम्य वरदं शंभुमभ्यागतो गृहम्।।
सभग्नं ध्वजमालोक्य हृष्टो हर्षं पुनर्ययौ।। ४।।

Thereupon pleased and bowing unto Śaṅkara he returned to his house where he found the standard broken which increased his joy.

एतस्मिन्नेव काले तु योगविद्याबलेन तम्।।
अनिरुद्धमथानिन्ये चित्रलेखा वराप्सरा:।। ५।।

At that time the foremost of Apsarās, Citralekhā, came back from Dwārakā and by virtue of her magic powers brought Aniruddha with her.

कन्यांत:पुरमभ्येत्य रममाणं सहोषया।।
विज्ञाय रक्षिणो गत्वा शशंसुर्दैत्यभूपते:।। ६।।

Finding him there with Uṣā, the warders of the inner appartments reported it to the king, who immediately sent a number of his retinue to seize the prince.

व्यादिष्टं किंकराणां तु सैन्यं तेन महात्मना।।
जघान परिघं घोरमादाय परवीरहा।। ७।।

But taking up an iron club the powerful youth killed all his adversaries. Thereat Bāṇa ascended his chariot, proceeded against him and tried to kill him.

हतेषु तेषु बाणोपि रथस्थस्तद्वधोद्यत:।।
युध्यमानो यथाशक्ति यदुवीरेण निर्जित:।। ८।।

मायया युयुधे तेन स तदा मंत्रिचोदित:।।
ततस्तं पन्नगास्त्रेण बबंध यदुनंदनम्।। ९।।

Finding however that Aniruddha was not to be vanquished by power he followed the counsel of his minister and brought his magical faculties into the conflict, by which he succeeded in capturing the Yadu prince and binding him in serpent bonds.

द्वारवत्यां क्व यातोऽसावनिरुद्धेति जल्पताम्।।
यदूनामाचचक्षे तं बद्धं बाणेन नारद:।। १०।।

तं शोणितपुरं नीतं श्रुत्वा विद्याविदग्धया।।
योषिता प्रत्ययं जग्मुर्यादवा नामरैरिति।। ११।।

When Aniruddha was found missing from Dwāravatī and the Yādavas werw equiring of one another whither he had gone, Nārada came and communicated unto them he was a prisoner of Bāṇa, having been taken by a female by virtue of her magical faculties of Śoṇitpura. When they heard that he had ben taken to Śoṇitpura, by a damsel, cenversant with magical powers, thy did not place confidence in his words.

ततो गरुडमारुह्य स्मृतमात्रागतं हरि:।।
बल प्रद्युम्नसहितो बाणस्य प्रययौ पुरम्।। १२।।

Thereupon Kṛṣṇa thought of Garuḍa who immediately arived there. And mounting upon him along with Bala and Pradyumna he started for the city of Bāṇa.

पुरप्रवेशे प्रमथैर्युद्धमासीन्महात्मनः।।
ययौ बाणपुराभ्याशं नीत्वा तान्संक्षयं हरिः।। १३।।

On their appraoch to the city they were opposed by the attendant spirits of Rudra; but they were soon slain by Hari and he and his companions entered the city.

ततस्त्रिपादस्त्रिशिरा ज्वरो माहेश्वरो महान्।।
बाणरक्षार्थमभ्येत्य युयुधे शार्ङ्गधन्वना।। १४।।

Thereupon mighty fever, an emanation of Maheśvara, having three feet and three heads, fought desperately with the holder of conch in defence of Bāṇa.

तद्भस्मस्पर्शसंभूततापः कृष्णांगसंगमात्।।
अवाप बलदेवोपि श्रममामीलितेक्षणः।। १५।।

Baladeva, upon whom his ashes were scattered, was seized with burning heat and his eye-lids trembled—but he obtaiend relief by clinging to the body of Kṛṣṇa.

ततस्स युद्ध्यमानस्तु सह देवेन शार्ङ्गिणा।।
वैष्णवेन ज्वरेणाशु कृष्णदेहान्निराकृतः।। १६।।

Thereupon fighting with the holder of bow, the fever, emanating from Śiva, was soon driven out from Kṛṣṇa's person by the fever engendered by himself.

नारायणभुजाघातपरिपीडनविह्वलम् ।।
तं वीक्ष्य क्षम्यतामस्येत्याह देवः पितामहः।। १७।।

ततश्च क्षांतमेवेति प्रोक्त्वा तं वैष्णवं ज्वरम्।।
आत्मन्येव लयं निन्ये भगवान्मधुसूदनः।। १८।।

Beholding the Śaiva fever bewildered by the strokes of the arms of Kṛṣṇa, Brahmā, the patriarch of the deities, entreated him to desist, upon which the slayer of Madhu refrained and absorbed into himself the fever he had created.

ज्वर उवाच

मम त्वया समं युद्धं ये स्मरिष्यंति मानवाः।।
विज्वरास्ते भविष्यंति त्युक्त्वा चैनं ययौ ज्वरः।।१९।।

The rival fever then went away saying to Kṛṣṇa : "Those men who shall recollect the fight between us shall be freed from febrile disease."

ततोग्नीन्भगवान्पञ्च जित्वा नीत्वा तथा क्षयम्।।
दानवानां बलं कृष्णश्चूर्णयामास लीलया।। २०।।

Thereupon Viṣṇu overcame and destroyed the five fires and with perfect ease slew the Dānavas.

ततस्समस्तसैन्येन दैतेयानां बलेस्सुतः।।
युयुधे शंकरश्चैव कार्त्तिकेयश्च शौरिणा।। २१।।

Then the son of Bali, with the entire Daitya army, aided by Śaṅkara and Kārtikeya fought with Kṛṣṇa. A dreadful battle ensued between.

हरिशंकरयोर्युद्धमतीवासीत्सुदारुणम्।।
चुक्षुभुस्स कला लोकाश्शस्त्रास्त्रांशुप्रतापिताः।। २२।।

प्रलयोयमशेषस्य जगतो नूनमागतः।।
मेनिरे त्रिदशास्तत्र वर्त्तमाने महारणे।। २३।।

Hari and Śaṅkara. Scorched by their burning weapons, all the regions trembled and the celestials thought for certain that the end of the universe was at hand.

जृंभकास्त्रेण गोविंदो जृंभयामास शंकरम्।।
तातः प्रणेमुर्दैतेयाः प्रमथाश्च समंततः।। २४।।

जृंभाभिभूतस्तु हरो रथोपस्थ उपाविशत्।।
न शशाक ततो योद्धुं कृष्णेनाक्लिष्टकर्मणा।। २५।।

With the weapon of Yawning Kṛṣṇa set Śaṅkara agape; then the attendant demons and demi-gods of Śiva were slain on all sides, for Hara, overcome with incessant gaping, sat down in his car and was unable to fight with Kṛṣṇa any longer, who is above the enfluence of all actions.

गरुडक्षतवाहश्च प्रद्युम्नास्त्रेण पीडितः।।
कृष्णहुंकारनिर्धूतशक्तिश्चापययौ गुहः।। २६।।

The deity of war Kārtikeya, wounded in the arm by Garuḍa, struck by the weapons of Pradyumna and disarmed by the shout of Hari, fled away.

जृंभिते शंकरे नष्टे दैत्यसैन्ये गुहे जिते।।
नीते प्रमथसैन्ये च संक्षयं शार्ङ्गधन्वना।। २७।।

नंदिना संगृहीताश्वमधिरूढो महारथम्।।
बाण स्तत्राययौ योद्धुं कृष्णकार्ष्णिबलैस्सह।। २८।।

Beholding Śaṅkara disabled, the demons slain, Guha fled and Śiva's attendants destroyed, Bāṇa proceeded in his huge car, the steeds of which were harnessed by Nandīśa, to fight with Hari and his associates Bala and Pradyumna.

बलभद्रो महावीर्यो बाणसैन्यमनेकधा।।
विव्याध बाणैः प्रभश्य धर्मतश्चापलायत।। २९।।

Attacking the army of Bāṇa, the valliant Balabhadra, wounded them in diverse ways with his shafts and put them to a shameful confusion.

आकृष्य लांगलाग्रेण मुसलेनाशु ताडितम्।।
बलं बलेन ददृशे बाणो बाणैश्च चक्रिणा।। ३०।।
ततः कृष्णेन बाणस्य युद्धमासीत्सुदारुणम्।। ३१।।
समस्यतोरिषून्दीप्तान्कायत्राणविभेदिनः।।
कृष्णश्चिच्छेद बाणैस्तान्बाणेन प्रहिताञ्छितान्।।
विव्याध केशवं बाणो बाणं विव्याध चक्रधृक्।। ३२।।

And their king saw them dragged about by Rāma with his ploughshare or beaten by him with his mace and pierced by Kṛṣṇa with his shafts : he therefore attacked Kṛṣṇa and a fight took place between them; they hurled at each other burning arrows that pierced through their armour; but Kṛṣṇa intercepted with his arrows, those of Bāṇa and sundered them into pieces.

मुमुचाते तथास्त्राणि बाणकृष्णौ जिगीषया।।
परस्परक्षतिकरौ लाघवादनिरशं द्विज।। ३३।।

Bāṇa however, wounded Keśava and the weilder of the discus wounded Bāṇa; and both of them, desirous of victory and endeavouring angrily to bring about the death of his antagonist, hurled diverse missiles at each other.

भिद्यमानेष्वशेषेषु शरेष्वस्त्रे च सीदति।।
प्राचुर्येण ततो बाणं हंतुं चक्रे हरिर्मनः।। ३४।।

When a number of weapons had been sundered into pieces and the weapons began to be exhausted, Kṛṣṇa determined to slay Bāṇa.

ततोर्कशतसंघाततेजसा सदृशद्युति।।
जग्राह दैत्यचक्रारिर्हरिश्चक्रं सुदर्शनम्।। ३५।।

Thereupon the destroyer of the demons took up his discus Sudarśana shining with the radiance of a hundred suns.

मुञ्चतो बाणनाशाय ततश्चक्रं मधुद्विषः।।
नग्ना दैतेयविद्याऽभूत्कोटरी पुरतो हरेः।। ३६।।

As he was about to meet it the mystical goddess of Koṭarī, the magic lore of the demons, stood naked before, him.

तामग्रतो हरिर्दृष्ट्वा मीलिताक्षस्सुदर्शनम्।।
मुमोच बाणमुद्दिश्य च्छेत्तुं बाहुवनं रिपोः।। ३७।।

Beholding her before him, Kṛṣṇa, with open eyes, cast Sudarśana to cut off the arms of Bāṇa.

क्रमेण तत्तु बाहूनां बाणस्याच्युतचोदितम्।।
छेदं चक्रेऽसुरापा स्तशस्त्रौघक्षपणादृतम्।। ३८।।

The discus lopped off successively the numberless arms of Bāṇa against which proved useless the missiles discharged by the celestials.

छिन्ने बाहुवने तत्तु करस्थं मधुसूदनः।।
मुमुक्षुबोणनाशाय विज्ञातस्त्रिपुरद्विषा।। ३९।।

When the slayer of Madhu, aim took in his hand the discus, after ten thousand arms had been sundered, for the total destruction of Bāṇa, the destroyer of the Tripura came to know it.

समुपेत्याह गोविंदं सामपूर्वमुमापतिः।।
विलोक्य बाणं दादडच्छेदासृक्स्त्राववर्षिणम्।। ४०।।

Beholding the blood gushing out from the dissevered arms of Bāṇa, the husband of Umā approached Govinda and requesting to put off his hostilities, said :—

शंकर उवाच

कृष्णकृष्ण जगन्नाथ जाने त्वां पुरुषोत्तमम्।।
परेशं परमात्मानमनादिनिधनं हरिम्।। ४१।।

"O Kṛṣṇa, the lord of the universe, I know thee, the excellent Puruṣa, the supreme lord, the infinite felicity without beginning or end and beyond all things.

देवतिर्यङ्मनुष्येषु शरीरग्रहणात्मिका।।
लीलेयं सर्वभूतस्य तव चेष्टोपलक्षणा।। ४२।।

This sport of universal being in which thou assumest the person of god, animals and men is a subordinate attribute of thy energy.

तत्प्रसीदाभयं दत्तं बाणस्यास्य मया प्रभो।।
तत्त्वया नानृतं कार्यं यन्मया व्याहृतं वचः।। ४३।।

Be propitious, therefore O lord, unto me. I have given Bāṇa assurnce of safety, do not thou falsfy my words.

अस्मत्संश्रयदृप्तोयं नापराधी तवाव्यय।।
मया दत्तवरो दैत्यस्ततस्त्वां क्षमयाम्यहम्।। ४४।।

O thou eternal, this Bāṇa has grown old under my protection, let him not incur thy displeasure.

श्रीपराशर उवाच

इत्युक्तः प्राह गोविंदश्शूलपाणिमुमापतिम्।।
प्रसन्नवदनो भूत्वा गतामर्षोऽसुरं प्रति।। ४५।।

I conferred a boon on this Daitya and therefore I am begging thy forgiveness."

श्रीभगवानुवाच

युष्मद्दत्तवरो बाणो जीवतामेष शंकर।।
त्वद्वाक्यगौरवादेतन्मया चक्रं निवर्त्तितम्।। ४६।।

त्वया यदभयं दत्तं तद्दत्तमखिलं मया।।
मत्तोऽविभिन्नमात्मानं द्रष्टुमर्हसि शंकर।। ४७।।

योहं स त्वं जगच्चेदं सदेवासुरमानुषम्।।
मत्ते नान्यदशेषं यत्तत्वं ज्ञातुमिहार्हसि।। ४८।।

अविद्यामोहितात्मानः पुरुषा भिन्नदर्शिनः।।
वदंति भेदं पश्यंति चावयोरंतरं हर।। ४९।।
प्रसन्नोऽहं गमिष्यामि त्वं गच्छ वृषभध्वज।। ५०।।

Being thus addressed, Govinda, dismissing his resentment against the Asura, smilingly said to Umā's lord, the holder of trident :—"O Śaṅkara, let this Bāṇa, the king of demons draw his breath since thou hast conferred a boon upon him; to honour thy words, I withhold my discus; the assurance of safety given by thee, is also given by me. Do not consider me as distinct from thee. The celestials, Asuras and men and the whole universe are not distnict from us. Those who have been possessed by ignorance consider me as seperate from thee."

श्रीपराशर उवाच

इत्युक्त्वा प्रययौ कृष्णः प्राद्युम्निर्यत्र तिष्ठति।।
तद्वंधफणिनो नेशुर्गरुडानिलपोथिताः।। ५१।।

ततोऽनिरुद्धमारोप्य सपत्नीकं गरुत्मति।।
आजग्मुर्द्वारकां रामकार्ष्णिदामोदराः पुरीम्।। ५२।।

Having said this Kṛṣṇa went to where Aniruddha was; and the snakes that bound him were destroyed by the breath of Govinda.

पुत्रपौत्रैः परिवृतस्तत्र रेमे जनार्दनः।।
देवीभिस्सततं विप्र भूभारतरणेच्छया।। ५३।।

And placing him along with his wife upon the celestials bird, Kṛṣṇa with Pradyumna and Rāma.

।। इति श्रीविष्णुमहापुराणे पञ्चमेंशे त्रयस्त्रिंशोऽध्यायः।। ३३।।

अथ पञ्चमेंशेः चतुस्त्रिंशोऽध्यायः

Part V : Section 34

मैत्रेय उवाच

चक्रे कर्म महच्छौरिर्बिभ्राणो मानुषीं तनुम्।।
जिगाय शक्रं शर्वं च सर्वान्देवांश्च लीलया।। १।।

Maitreya said :—Having assumed a mortal form Śaurī performed mighty achievements, and discomfitted Śakra and Śiva and all other attendant divinities.

यच्चान्यदकरोत्कर्म दिव्यचेष्टाविघात कृत्।।
तत्कथ्यतां महाभाग परं कौतूहलं हि मे।। २।।

O great sir, do thou also describe unto me, his other exploits by which he humiliated the prowess of the celestials; I am desirous to hear them.

श्रीपराशर उवाच

गदतो मम विप्रर्षे श्रूयतामिदमादरात्।।
नरावतारे कृष्णेन दग्धा वाराणसी यथा।। ३।।

Parāśara said :—Hear with respectful attention, O Brāhmaṇa, as described by me of the burning of Vārāṇasī by Kṛṣṇa in the course of his relieving the burden of the earth.

पौंड्रको वासुदेवस्तु वासुदेवोऽभवद्भुवि।।
अवतीर्णस्त्वमित्युक्तो जनैरज्ञानमोहितैः।। ४।।

स मेने वासुदेवोहमवतीर्णो महीतले।।

There was a king of Puṇḍra, who was known as Vāsudeva and flattered by the ignorant people as the descended deity until he thought himself to be the Vāsudeva who had come down upon earth.

नष्टस्मृतिस्ततस्सर्वं विष्णुचिह्नमचीकरत्।। ५।।

दूतं च प्रेषयामास कृष्णाय सुमहात्मने।।

Forgetting his real character he assumed the emblems of Viṣṇu and sent an ambassador to the high-minded Kṛṣṇa with this message.

त्यक्त्वा चक्रादिकं चिह्नं मदीयं नाम चात्मनः।। ६।।

वासुदेवात्मकं मूढ त्यक्त्वा सर्वमशेषतः।।
आत्मनो जीवितार्थाय ततो मे प्रणतिं व्रज।। ७।।

"Give up thy discus, O foolish man, lay aside all my insignia, my name and the character of Vāsudeva and come and do me homage and I shall grant thee, the means of subsistence."

इत्युक्तस्संप्रहस्यैनं दूतं प्राह जनार्दनः।।
निजचिह्नमहं चक्रं समुत्सृक्ष्ये त्वयीति वै।। ८।।

वाच्यश्च पौंड्रको गत्वा त्वया दूत वचो मम।।

Hearing those words and laughing, Janārddana said to the messenger, "Go back, messenger to Pauṇḍraka and tell him in my name 'I shall hand over my emblem, the discus to him.

ज्ञातस्त्वद्वाक्यसद्भावो यत्कार्यं तद्विधीयताम्।। ९।।

गृहीतचिह्नवेषोहमागमिष्यामि ते पुरम्।।
उत्स्रक्ष्यामि च तच्चक्रं निजचिह्नमसंशयम्।। १०।।

Thou wilt properly understand my meaning and consider what is to be done; for I shall come to thy city bringing the discus with me and shall surely give it over to thee.

आज्ञापूर्वं च यदिदमागच्छेति त्वयोदितम्।।
संपादयिष्ये श्वस्तुभ्यं समागम्याविलंबितम्।। ११।।

शरणं ते समभ्येत्य कर्त्तास्मि नृपते तथा।।
यथा त्वत्तो भयं भूयो न मे किंचिद्भविष्यति।। १२।।

If thou dost comand me to come I immediately obey and be with thee tomorrow and shall not delay, and having sought thy protection I shall so manage, O king, that I shall not have to fear anything from thee."

श्रीपराशर उवाच

इत्युक्तेपगते दूते संस्मृत्याभ्यागतं हरिः।।
गरुत्मंतमथारुह्य त्वरितस्तत्पुरं ययौ।। १३।।

So saying he sent away the messenger to communicate these words unto the sovereign, and summoning Garuḍa mounted him and started for the city of Pauṇḍrāka.

ततस्तु केशवोद्योगं श्रुत्वा काशीपतिस्तदा।।
सर्वसैन्यपरीवारः पार्ष्णिग्राह उपाययौ।। १४।।

When the king of Kāśī heard of the preparations of Keśava he sent his army to help Pauṇḍraka himself bringing up the rear.

ततो बलेन महता काशीराजबलेन च।।
पौंड्रको वासुदेवोऽसौ केशवाभिमुखो ययौ।। १५।।

And with the army of the king of Kāśī and his own troops, Pauṇḍraka, the false Vāsudeva marched to meet Kṛṣṇa.

तं ददर्श हरिर्दूरादुदारस्यंदने स्थितम्।।
चक्रहस्तं गदाशार्ङ्गबाहुं पाणिगतांबुजम्।। १६।।

स्नग्धरं पीतवसनं सुपर्णरचितध्वजम्।।
वक्षस्थले कृतं चास्य श्रीवत्सं ददृशे हरिः।। १७।।

किरीटकुंडलधरं नानारत्नोपशोभितम्।।

Hari saw him at a distance standing in his car holding a discus, a club, a mace, a scimitar and a lotus in his hands adorned with a garland of flowers, and bearing a bow; and having his standard made of gold, he had also the mysical mark Śrīvatsa on his brest; he was robed in yellow raiment and embellished with ear rings and a tiara.

तं दृष्ट्वा भावगंभीरं जहास गरुडध्वजः।। १८।।

युयुधे च बलेनास्य हस्त्यश्वबलिना द्विज।।
निस्त्रिंशासिगदाशूलशक्तिकार्मुकशालिना।। १९।।

When the god, whose emblem is Garuḍa, saw him, he laughed aloud and engaged in encounter with the hostile army of cavalry and elephants fighting with swords, scimitars, maces, tridents spears and bows.

क्षेण शार्ङ्गनिर्मुक्तैश्शरैररिविदारणैः।।
गदाचक्रनिपातैश्च सूदयामास तद्बलम्।। २०।।
काशीराजबलं चैवं क्षयं नीत्वा जनार्दनः।।
उवाच पौंड्रकं मूढमात्मचिह्नोपलक्षितम्।। २१।।

Showering upon the enemy the arrows from his Śārańga bow and hurling at them his mace and discus he soon destroyed both the army of Pauṇḍraka and that of the king of Kāśī. He then addressed the former who was foolishly wearing his emblems saying :—

श्रीभगवानुवाच

पौंड्रकोक्तं त्वया यत्तु दूतवक्रेण मां प्रति।।
समुत्सृजेति चिह्नानि तत्ते संपादयाम्यहम्।। २२।।

"Pauṇḍraka, you wanted me through your messenger, to resign to you all my insignia, I now deliver them to you.

चक्रमेतत्समुत्सृष्टं गदेयं ते विसर्जिता।।
गरुत्मानेष चोत्सृष्टस्समारोहतु ते ध्वजम्।। २३।।

Here is my discus; here is my mace; and here is Garuḍa, let him mount upon thy banner."

श्रीपराशर उवाच

इत्युच्चार्य विमुक्तेन चक्रेणाऽसौ विदारितः।।
पातितो गदया भग्नो ध्वजश्चास्य गरुत्मता।। २४।।

Parāśara said :—Saying this he discharged the discus and mace by which Pauṇḍraka was sundered to pieces and cast on the ground; whilst the Garuḍa which was on the banner of Pauṇḍraka was destroyed by the Garuḍa of Viṣṇu.

ततो हाहाकृते लोके काशीपुर्यधिपो बली।।
युयुधे वासुदेवने मित्रस्यापचितौ स्थितः।। २५।।
ततश्शार्ङ्गधनुर्मुक्तैश्छित्त्वा तस्य शिरश्शरैः।।
काशीपुर्यां स चिक्षेप कुर्वंल्लोकस्य विस्मयम्।। २६।।

Beholding this the people cried "alas! alsas"; but the brave king still siding the imposture of his friend carried on the encounter till Śaurī, cut off his head with his arrows and shot into the city of Kāśī to the surprise of all the inhabitants.

हत्वा त पौंड्रकं शौरिः काशीराजं च सानुगम्।।
पुनर्द्वारवतीं प्राप्तो रेमे स्वर्गगतो यथा।। २७।।

Having thus destroyed Pauṇḍraka and the king of Kāśī with all their retinue Śaurī came back to Dwārakā where he resided enjoying heavenly delights.

तच्छिरः पतितं तत्र दृष्ट्वा काशीपतेः पुरे।।
जनः किमेतदित्याह च्छिन्नं केनेति विस्मितः।। २८।।

When the inhabitants of Kāśī beheld the head of their king shot into the city they were much surprised and wondered how it could have been accomplished.

ज्ञात्वां तं वासुदेवेन हतं तस्य सुतस्ततः।।
पुरोहितेन सहितस्तोष यामासशंकरम्।। २९।।

Having come to know that the king had been slain by Kṛṣṇa, the king's son together with the priest of the family propitiated Śańkara.

अविमुक्ते महाक्षेत्रे तोषितस्तेन शंकरः।।
वरं वृणीष्वेति तदा तं प्रोवाच नृपात्मजम्।। ३०।।

Well pleased on account of being worshipped in the sacred place Avimukta the deity asked the prince to pray for a boon, on which he said :—

स वव्रे भगवन्कृत्या पितृहंतुर्वधाय मे।।
समुतिष्ठतु कृष्णस्य त्वत्प्रसादान्महेश्वर।। ३१।।

"O lord, O mighty god through thy favour, let thy mystic spirit slay Kṛṣṇa, the murderer of my father!"

श्रीपराशर उवाच

एवं भविष्यतीत्युक्ते दक्षिणाग्नेरनंतरम्।।
महाकृत्य समुत्तस्थौ तस्यैवाग्नेर्विनाशनी।। ३२।।
ततो ज्वालाकरालास्या ज्वलत्केशकपालिका।।
कृष्णकृष्णेति कुपिता कृत्या द्वारवतीं ययौ।। ३३।।

Parāśara said :—'It shall be so' answered Śaṅkara and from out of the southern fire up sprang a vast and formidable female like flame out of fire, blazing with ruddy light and fiery radiance streaming amidst her hair. Worked up with ire she called upon Kṛṣṇa and departed to Dwārakā.

तामवेक्ष्य जनस्त्रासाद्विचलल्लोचने मुने।।
ययौ शरण्यं जगतां शरणं मधुसूदनम्।। ३४।।

There the people seeing her were struck with terror and fled for protection to the slayer of Madhu the refuge of all worlds.

काशीराजसुतेनेयमाराध्य वृषभध्वजम्।।
उत्पादिता महाकृत्येत्यवगम्याऽथ चक्रिणा।। ३५।।

जहि कृत्यामिमामुग्रां वह्निज्वालाजटालकाम्।।
चक्रमुत्सृष्टमक्षेषु क्रीडासक्तेन लीलया।। ३६।।

Understanding that the friend had been created by the son of the king of Kāśī through his worship of the deity whose emblem is the bull, the wielder of the discus being engaged in sport and playing at dice said to the discus,

तदाग्निमालाजटिलज्वालोद्गारातिभीषणाम्।।
कृत्यामनुजगामाशु विष्णुचक्रं सुदर्शनम्।। ३७।।

"Kill this dreadful creature whose tresses are of plaited flame." Accordingly Sudarśana, the discus of Viṣṇu, attacked the fiend in no time, dreadfully covered with fire and wearing tresses of plaited flame.

चक्रप्रतापनिर्दग्धा कृत्या माहेश्वरी तदा।।
ननाश वेगिनी वेगात्तदप्यनुजगाम ताम्।। ३८।।

कत्या वाराणसीमेव प्रविवेश त्वरान्विता।।
विष्णुचक्रप्रतिहतप्रभावा मुनिसत्तम।। ३९।।

Terrified at the might of Sudarśana, the creation of Maheśvara did no wait for his attack but fled quickly followed by him with equal velocity until she arrived at Vārāṇasī repelled by the superior prowess of the discus of Viṣṇu.

ततः काशीबलं भूमि प्रमथानां तथाबलम्।।
समस्तशस्त्रास्त्रयुतं चक्रस्याभिमुखं ययौ।। ४०।।

The amrs of the king of Kāśī and the whole number of the attendant divinities of Śiva armed with various weapons marched out to oppose the discus.

शस्त्रास्त्रमोक्षचतुरं दग्ध्वा तद्बलमोजसा।।
कृत्या गर्भामशेषां तां तदा वाराणसीं पुरीम्।। ४१।।

But an expert in the use of arms he consumed the whole host by his radiance and then set fire to the city, in which the magic power of Śiva had concealed herself.

सभूभृद्भृत्यपौरां तु साश्वमातंगमानवाम्।।
अशेषगोष्ठकोशां तां दुर्निरीक्ष्यां सुरैरपि।। ४२।।

Thus was Vārāṇasī burnt with all its princes and their followers, its inhabitants, elephants, horses and men, treasures and granaries, houses, palaces and markets.

ज्वालापरिष्कृताशेषगृहप्राका रचत्वराम्।।
ददाह तद्धरेश्चक्रं सकलामेव तां पुरीम्।। ४३।।

The whole of the city that was inaccessible to the celestials was thus covered with flames by the discus of Hari and was totally destroyed.

अक्षीणामर्षमत्युग्रं साध्यसाधनसस्पृहम्।।
तच्चक्रं प्रस्फुरद्दीप्ति विष्णोरभ्याययौ करम्।। ४४।।

The discus, with unsoothed wrath, blazing fiercely and not satisfied with the accomplishment of so easy a task, then returned to the hands of Viṣṇu.

।। इति श्रीविष्णुमहापुराणे पञ्चमेंशे चतुस्त्रिंशोऽध्यायः।। ३४।।

अथ पञ्चमेंशेः पञ्चत्रिंशोऽध्यायः
Part V : Section 35

मैत्रेय उवाच

भूय एवाहमिच्छामि बलभद्रस्य धीमतः।।
श्रोतुं पराक्रमं ब्रह्मन् तन्ममाख्यातुमर्हसि।। १।।

Maitreya said :—O Brāhmaṇa, I have a great desire to listen to some other exploits of Balarāma; to thou describe them unto me.

यमुनाकर्षणादीनि श्रुतानि भगवन्मया।।
तत्कथ्यतां महाभाग यदन्यकृतवान्बलः।। २।।

You have related to me, O reverend Sir, his dragging the Yamunā and other mighty deeds; do thou now recount some other of his acts.

श्रीपराशर उवाच

मैत्रेय श्रूयतां कर्म यद्रामेणाभवत्कृतम्।।
अनंतेनाप्रमेयेन शेषेण धरणीधृता।। ३।।

Parāśara said :—Listen O Maitreya, to the exploits accomplished by Rāma who is the eternal, illimitable Śeṣa, the upholder of the earth.

सुयोधनस्य तनयां स्वयंवरकृतक्षणाम्।।
बलादादत्तवान्वीरस्सांबो जांबवतीसुतः।। ४।।

At the choice of a husband by the daughter of Suyodhana, the princess was taken away by the hero Sāmba, the son of Jāmbavati.

ततः क्रुद्धा महावीर्याः कर्णदुर्योधनादयः।।
भीष्मद्रोणादयश्चैनं बबंधुर्युधि निर्जितम्।। ५।।

Being pursued by Duryodhana, Karṇa, Bhīṣma, Droṇa and other illustrious chiefs who were enraged for his audacity, he was defeated and taken prisoner.

तच्छ्रुत्वा यादवास्सर्वे क्रोधं दुर्योधनादिषु।।
मैत्रेय चक्रुः कृष्णश्च तान्निहंतुं महोद्यमम्।। ६।।

When the Yādavas heard of this event they were greatly enraged with Duryodhana and his companions and addressed themselves to fight with them.

तान्निवार्य बलः प्राह मदलोलकलाक्षरम्।।
मोक्ष्यंति ते मद्वचनाद्यास्याम्येको हि कौरवान्।। ७।।

But Baladeva, in accents suppressed by the effects of inebriety, forbade them and said,

श्रीपराशर उवाच

बलदेवस्ततो दृष्ट्वा नगरं नागसाह्वयम्।।
बाह्योपवनमध्येऽभून्न विवेश च तत्पुरम्।। ८।।

"I will go alone to the sons of Kuru and at my request they will let Sāmba free. Accordingly he went to Hastināpur and took his abode in a grove outside the town which he did not enter.

बलमागतमाज्ञाय भूपा दुर्योधनादयः।।
गामर्घ्यमुदकं चैव रामाय प्रत्यवेदयन्।। ९।।

When Duryodhana and others were informed of his arrival, they sent him a cow, a present of fruits and flowers and water.

गृहीत्वा विधिवत्सर्वं ततस्तानाह कौरवान्।।
आज्ञापयत्युग्रसेनस्सांबमाशु विमुञ्चत।। १०।।

Bala received the offering in the customary form and said to the descendants of Kuru "Ugrasena commands you to liberate Sāmba."

ततस्तद्वचनं श्रुत्वा भीष्मद्रोणादयो नृपाः।।
कर्णदुर्योधनाद्याश्च चुक्षुभुर्द्विजसत्तम।। ११।।
ऊचुश्च कुपितास्सर्वे बाह्लिकाद्याश्च कौरवाः।।
अराज्यार्हं यदोर्वंशमवेक्ष्य मुसलायुध।। १२।।

When Duryodhana, Karṇa, Bhīṣma, Droṇa and others heard this, they were worked up with ire, and Bāhlīka and other friends of the Kauravas who considered the Yadu race as having no claims to regal dignity said to the weilder of the club.

भोभोः किमेतद्भवता बलभद्रेरितं वचः।।
आज्ञां कुरुकुलोत्थानां यादवः कः प्रदास्यति।। १३।।

"What is this, O Balarāma, that thou hast

said? What Yādava shall command the chiefs of the Kuru family?

उग्रसेनोऽपि यद्याज्ञां कौरवाणां प्रदास्यति।।
तदलं पांडुरैश्छत्रैर्नृपयोग्यैर्विडंबनैः।। १४।।

If Ugrasena thus commands the Kuravas, we will take away the white umbrella which he has usurped and which is only fit for the kings.

तद्गच्छ बल मा वा त्वं सांबमन्यायचेष्टितम्।।
विमोक्ष्यामो न भवतश्चोग्रसेनस्य शासनात्।। १५।।

You should go away therefore, Balarāma; you are entitled to our respect; but Sāmba has been guilty of an improper conduct and we shall not let him free either at Ugrasena's commands or yours.

प्रणतिर्या कृतास्माकं मान्यानां कुकुरांधकैः।।
न नाम सा कृता केयमाज्ञा स्वामिनि भृत्यतः।। १६।।

The Kukkura and Andhaka races might not pay the homage due to us, their superiors, but who ever heard of a servant commanding his master?

गर्वमारोपिता यूयं समानासनभोजनैः।।
को दोषो भवतां नितिर्यत्प्रीत्या नावलोकिता।। १७।।

You have been rendered arrogant by our treating you equally with seat and food; we have committed a great mistake in neglecting the policy, for our great friendship for you.

अस्माभिरर्घो भवतो योयं बल निवेदितः।।
प्रेम्णैतन्नैतदस्माकं कुलाद्युष्मत्कुलोचितम्।। १८।।

The present that we sent you today was a sign of personal regard, but it was not fit for us to have offered nor for yours to have expected."

श्रीपराशर उवाच

इत्युक्त्वा कुरवः सांबं मुञ्चामो न हरेस्सुतम्।।
कृतैकनिश्चयास्तूर्णं विविशुर्गजसाह्वयम्।। १९।।

Parāśara said :—Having said this, the Kuru chiefs unanimously refused to liberate Hari's sons and came back to their city.

मत्तः कोपेन चाघूर्णस्ततोधिक्षेपजन्मना।।
उत्थाय पार्ष्ण्या वसुधां जघान स हलायुधः।। २०।।

ततो विदारिता पृथ्वी पार्ष्णिघातान्महात्मनः।।
आस्फोटयामास तदा दिशश्शब्देन पूरयन्।। २१।।

Moving about with intoxication and anger caused by their insolent words, Bala struck the ground furiosusly with his heel so that it burst to pieces with a loud sound that reverberated through the regions of space.

उवाच चातिताम्राक्षो भृकुटीकुटिलाननः।। २२।।

His eyes reddened with rage and his brow curved, with frowns he exclaimed.

अहो मदावलेपोयमसाराणां दुरात्मनाम्।।
कौरवाणां महीपत्वमस्माकं किल कालजम्।।
उग्रसेनस्य येनाज्ञां मन्यंतेऽद्यापि लंघनम्।। २३।।

'What pride is this in such vile and pithless creatures. The sovereignty of Kauravas as well as our own is the work of destiny whose decree it also is that they now disrespect or disobey the commands of Ugrasena.

उग्रसेनः समध्यास्ते सुधर्मां न शचीपतिः।।
धिङ्मानुषशतोच्छिष्टे तुष्टिरेषां नृपासने।। २४।।

पारिजाततरोः पुष्पमञ्जरीर्वनिताजनः।।
बिभर्त्ति यस्य भृत्यानां सोऽप्येषां न महीपतिः।। २५।।

समस्तभूभृतां नाथ उग्रसेनस्स तिष्ठतु।।
अद्य निष्कौरवामुर्वीं कृत्वा यास्यामि तत्पुरीम्।। २६।।

Indra, may, as is his right, command the celestials and Ugrasena exercises equal authority with the lord of Śaci. Fie upon the pride that boasts a throne, the leavings of a hundred mortals. Is not he the sovereign of the earth, the wives of whose servants adorn themselves with the blosssoms of the Pārijāta tree? Ugrasena shall be the undisputed lord of kings; for I will not return to his capital until I have rid the world wholly of the sons of Kuru.

कर्णं दुर्योधनं द्रोणमद्य भीष्मं सबाह्लिकम्।।
दुश्शासनादीन्भूरिं च भूरिश्रवसमेव च।। २७।।

सोमदत्तं शलं चैव भीमार्जुनयुधिष्ठिरान्।।
यमौ च कौरवांश्चान्यान्हत्वा साश्वरथद्विपान्।। २८।।

I will destroy Karṇa, Duryodhana, Droṇa, Bhīṣma, Bhāhlīka, Duśśāsana, Bhūriśravas, Sonavatya, Śalya, Bhīma, Arjuna, Yudhiṣthira, the twins and all the other wretched sons of Kuru with their horses, elephants and chariots.

वीरमादाय तं सांबं सपत्नीकं ततः पुरीम्।।
द्वारकामुग्रसेनादीन्गत्वा द्रक्ष्यामि बांधवान्।। २९।।

I will liberate the hero Sāmba, and carry him along with his wife to Dwārakā where I shall again behold Ugrasena and the rest of my kinsmen.

अथ वा कौरवावासं समस्तैः कुरुभिस्सह।।
भागीरथ्यां क्षिपाम्याशु नगरं नागसाह्वयम्।। ३०।।

Or commanded by the king of celestials, to remove the burden of the earth, I will take this capital of the Kauravas with all the sons of Kuru, and throw Hastināpur into the Bhāgīrathī."

श्रीपराशर उवाच

इत्युक्त्वा मदरक्ताक्षः कर्षणाधोमुखं हलम्।।
प्राकारप्रदुर्गस्य चकर्ष मुसलायुधः।। ३१।।
आघूर्णितं तत्सहसा ततो वै हास्तिनं पुरम्।।
दृष्ट्वा संक्षुब्धहृदयाश्चुक्षुभुस्सर्वकौरवाः।। ३२।।

Saying this with his eyes reddened with ire, Baladeva, the wielder of the club, plunged the blade of his ploughshare downwards beneath the ramparts of the city, and drew them towards him. When the Kauravas beheld Hastināpur tottering, they were much afraid, and called loudly on Rāma, saying,

रामराम महाबाहो क्षम्यतां क्षम्यतां त्वया।।
उपसंह्रियतां कोपः प्रसीद मुसलायुध।। ३३।।
एष सांबस्सपत्नीकस्तव निर्यातितो बलात्।।
अविज्ञातप्रभावाणं क्षम्यतामपराधिनाम्।। ३४।।

"O Rāma! Rāma! hold, hold; supress your anger and have compassion upon us. Here is Sāmba and his wife also delivered up to you. Forgive the sins committed by us ignorant of your wondrous power."

श्रीपराशर उवाच।

ततो निर्यातयामासुस्सांबं पत्नीसमन्वितम्।।
निष्क्रम्य स्वपुरात्तूर्णं कौरवा मुनिपुंगव।। ३५।।
भीष्मद्रोणकृपादीनां प्रणम्य वदतां प्रियम्।।
क्षांतमेव मयेत्याह बलो बलवतां वरः।। ३६।।

Accordingly the Kauravas hurried out of the city and delivered Sāmba and his wife to the mighty Balarāma, who, bowing to Bhīṣma, Droṇa and Kṛpa, who pacified him, said, "I am satisfied," and desisted.

अद्याप्याघूर्णिताकारं लक्ष्यते तत्पुरं द्विज।।
एष प्रभावो रामस्य बलशौर्यपलक्षणः।। ३७।।

The city bears the mark of the shock even to the present day—such was the might of Rāma proving both his strength and power.

ततस्तु कौरवास्सांबं संपूज्य बलिना सह।।
प्रेषयामासुरुद्वाहधनभार्यासमन्वितम् ।। ३८।।

The Kauravas then, offering homage to Sāmba and Bala, sent away the former with his wife and dowry.

।। इति श्रीविष्णुमहापुराणे पञ्चमेंशे पञ्चत्रिंशोऽध्यायः।। ३५।।

अथ पञ्चमेंशेः षट्त्रिंशोऽध्यायः

Part V : Section 36

श्रीपराशर उवाच

मैत्रेयैतद्बलं तस्य बलस्य बलशालिनः।।
कृतं यदन्यत्तेनाऽभूत्तदपि श्रूयतां त्वया।। १।।

Parāśara said :—Listen, O Maitreya, to another achievement accomplished by the powerful Balarāma.

नरकस्यासुरेंद्रस्य देवपक्षविरोधिनः।।
सखाऽभवन्महावीर्यो द्विविदो वनारर्षभः।। २।।
वैरानुबंधं बलवान्स चकार सुरान्प्रति।।
नरकं हतवान्कृष्णो देवराजेन चोदितः।।३।।
करिष्ये सर्वदेवाना तस्मादेतत्प्रतिक्रियाम्।।
यज्ञविध्वंसनं कुर्वन् मर्त्यलोकक्षयं तथा।। ४।।

The great Asura, Naraka, the enemy of the friends of the celestials, had a friend of exceeding might in a monkey named Dwivida, who was worked up with implacable hostility against the celestials, and vowed to revenge on all of them the destruction of Naraka by Kṛṣṇa at the instigation of the king of the celestials, by preventing sacrifices and bringing about the total destruction of the world.

ततो विध्वंसयामास यज्ञानज्ञान मोहितः।।
बिभेद साधुमर्यादां क्षयं चक्रे च देहिनाम्।। ५।।

ददाह सवनान्देशान्पुग्रामंतराणि च।।
क्वचिच्च पर्वताक्षेपैर्ग्रामादीन्समचूर्णयत्।। ६।।

शैलानुत्पाट्य तोयेषु मुमोचांबुनिधौ तथा।।
पुनश्चार्णवमध्यस्थः क्षोभयामास सागरम्।। ७।।

तेन विक्षोभितश्चाब्धिरुद्वेलो द्विज जायते।।
प्लावयंस्तीरजान्ग्रामान्पुरादीनतिवेगवान्।। ८।।

कामरूपी महारूपं कृत्वा सस्यान्यशेषतः।।
लुठन्भ्रमणसम्मर्दैस्सञ्चूर्णयति वानरः।। ९।।

Blinded by ignorance therefore, he interrupted all religious practices, put down all righteous observances, and brought about the death of living creatures; he set fire to forests, to villages and towns : sometimes he deluged cities and villages with a downpour of rocks or lifting up mountains in the waters he cast them into the ocean; then placing himself in the midst of the deep, he agitated the waves until the foaming sea rose above its confines and swept away the villages, and cities situated upon its shores. Dwivida, who was capable of assuming shapes as he liked, enlarged his bulk to an immense proportion, and rolling and tumbling and trampling amidst the corn-fields, he crushed and spoiled the harvest.

तेन विप्रकृतं सर्वं जगदेतदुरात्मना।।
निस्स्वाध्यायवषट्कारं मैत्रेयासीत्सुदुःखितम्।। १०।।

The whole world, disorganised by this vicious monkey, was deprived of sacred study and religious ceremonies, and was greatly afflicted.

एकदा रैवतोद्याने पपौ पानं हलायुधः।।
रेवती च महाभागा तथैवान्या वरस्त्रियः।। ११।।
उद्गीयमानो विलसल्ललनामौलिमध्यगः।।
रेमे यदुकुलश्रेष्ठः कुबेर इव नंदने।। १२।।

Once on a time Halāyudha was drinking in the groves of Raivata along with the illustrious Revatī and other beautiful females; and the celebrated Yadu whose glories were sung and who was pre-eminent amidst graceful and sportive women, resembled Kubera, the god of riches, in his palace.

ततस्स वानरोऽभ्येत्य गृहीत्वा सीरिणो हलम्।।
मुसलं च चकारास्य संमुखं च विडंबनम्।। १३।।

तथैव योषितां तासां जहासाभिमुखं कपिः।।
पानपूर्णांश्च करकाञ्चिक्षेपाहत्य वै तदा।। १४।।

In the meantime, the monkey Dwivida came there and stealing the plough-share and the club of Balarāma, grinned at and mocked him, and laughed at the women and threw over and broke the cups filled with wine.

ततः कोपपरीतात्मा भर्त्सयामास तं हली।।
तथापि तमवज्ञाय चक्रे किलकिलध्वनिम्।। १५।।

Enraged at this, Balarāma threatened the monkey; but the latter disregarded his threates and made a chattering noise.

ततः स्मयित्वा स बलो जग्राह मुसलं रुषा।।
सोऽपि शैलशिलां भीमां जग्राह प्लवगोत्तमः।। १६।।

Thereupon Balarāma started up and seized his club in anger, and the monkey laid hold of a large rock which he hurled at the hero.

चिक्षेप स च तां क्षिप्तां मुसलेन सहस्रधा।।
यादवश्रेष्ठस्सा पपात महीतले।। १७।।

And casting his club at it as it approached him, Bala broke it into a thousand pieces, which together with the club, fell upon the ground.

अथ तन्मुसलं चासौ समुल्लंघ्य प्लवंगमः।।
वेनेनागत्य रोषेण करेणोरस्यताडयत्।। १८।।

Beholding the club thus fallen, the monkey sprang over it and struck the Yādava violently on the breast with his paws.

ततो बलेन कोपेन मुष्टिना मूर्ध्नि ताडितः।।
पपात रुधिरोद्गारी द्विविदः क्षीणजीवितः।। १९।।

Bala returned it with a blow of his fist upon the fore-head of Dwivida which felled him, vomitting blood and lifeless to the earth.

पतता तच्छरीरेण गिरेश्शृंगमशीर्यत।।
मैत्रेय शतधा वज्रिवज्रेणेव विदारितम्।। २०।।

The crest of the mountian on which he fell was sundered into a hundred pieces by the wight of his body, as if the Thunderer had shivered it with his thunder-bolt.

पुष्पवृष्टिं ततो देवा रामस्योपरि चिक्षिपुः।।
प्रश शंसुस्ततोऽभ्येत्य साध्वेतत्ते महत्कृतम्।। २१।।

The celestials threw down a shower of flowers upon Kāma and approached him and praised him for the glorious feat he had performed.

अनेन दुष्टकपिना दैत्यपक्षोपकारिणा।।
जगन्निराकृतं वीर दिष्ट्या स क्षयमागतः।। २२।।

इत्युक्त्वा दिवमाजग्मुर्देवा हृष्टास्सगुह्यकाः।। २३।।

"Well has the world been freed" said they "by thy prowess, O hero, of his vile ape, who was the enemy of the celestials." Then well-pleased, they and their attendant spirits returned to heaven.

श्रीपराशर उवाच

एवंविधान्यनेकानि बलदेवस्य धीमतः।।
कर्माण्यपरिमेयानि शेषस्य धरणीभृतः।। २४।।

Many such inimitable deeds were performed by the illustrious Baladeva, the impersonation of Śeṣa, the supporter of the earth.

।। इति श्रीविष्णुमहापुराणे पञ्चमेंशे षट्त्रिंशोऽध्यायः।। ३६।।

अथ पञ्चमेंशेः सप्तत्रिंशोऽध्यायः

Part V : Section 37

श्रीपराशर उवाच

एवं दैत्यवधं कृष्णो बलदेव सहायवान्।।
चक्रे दुष्टक्षितीशानां तथैव जगतः कृते।। १।।

क्षितेश्च भारं भगवान्फाल्गुनेन समन्वितः।।
अवतारयामास विभुस्समस्ताक्षोहिणी वधात्।। २।।

Parāśara said :—In this way, Krṣṇa, aided by Baladeva, destroyed, for the behoof of the earth, demons and iniquitious kings, and along with Phālguṇa also did he relieve earth of her burden by the death of seven Akṣauhiṇī hosts.

कृत्वा भारावतरणं भुवो हत्वाऽखिलान्नृपान्।।
शापव्याजेन विप्राणामुपसंहृतवान्कुलम्।। ३।।

Having thus relieved the earth of her load and destroyed many impious kings, he exterminated, by the plea of an imprecation denounced by Brāhmaṇas, his own Yādava race.

उत्सृज्य द्वारकां कृष्णस्त्यक्त्वा मानुष्यमात्मनः।।
सांशो विष्णुमयं स्थानं प्रविवेश मुने निजम्।। ४।।

Thereupon quitting Dwārakā and renouncing his mortal frame, the self-born with all his emanations re-entered his own sphere of Viṣṇu.

मैत्रेय उवाच

स विप्रशापव्याजेन सञ्जह्रे स्वकुलं कथम्।।
कथं च मानुषं देहमुत्ससर्ज जनार्दनः।। ५।।

Maitreya said :—Tell me how Janārddana brought about the extermination of his own family under the pretext of a Brāhmaṇical curse and in what manner did he renounce his human body.

श्रीपराशर उवाच

विश्वामित्रस्तथा कण्वो नारदश्च महामुनिः।।
पिंडारके महातीर्थे दृष्ट्वा यदुकुमारकैः।। ६।।

Parāśara said :—At the holy place of Piṇḍārika, Viśvāmitra, Kaṇva and the great sage, Nārada, were seen by some boys of the Yadu family.

ततस्ते यौवनोन्मत्ता भविकार्यप्रचोदिताः।।
सांबं जांबवतीपुत्रं भूषयित्वा स्त्रियं यथा।। ७।।

प्रश्रितास्तान्मुनीनूचुः प्रणिपातपुरस्सरम्।।
इयं स्त्री पुत्रकामा वै ब्रूत किं जनयिष्यति।। ८।।

Inflated with their youths and influenced by predestined results, they dressed and adorned Sāmba, the son of Jāmbavatī, as a female and taking her to the sages, they addressed them with usual reverence, saying :—

श्रीपराशर उवाच

दिव्यज्ञानोपपन्नास्ते विप्रलब्धाः कुमारकैः।।
मुनयः कुपिताः प्रोचुर्मुसलं जनयिष्यति।। ९।।

"What child with this female, the wife of Bābru, who is anxious to have a son, give birth to?"

सर्वयादवसंहारकारणं भुवनोत्तरम्।।
येनाखिलकुलोत्सादो यादवानां भविष्यति।। १०।।

The sages, who were gifted with divine wisdom, enraged at this insult, said :—"She will give birth to a club that will exterminate the entire Yādava race."

इत्युक्तास्ते कुमारास्तु आचचक्षुर्यथातथम्।।
उग्रसेनाय मुसलं जज्ञे सांबस्य चोदरात्।। ११।।

Thus addressed by the sages, the boys went to Ugrasena and related to him what had happened; and after sometime, as foretold, a club was produced from the belly of Sāmba.

तदुग्रसेनो मुसलमयश्चूर्णमकारयत्।।
जज्ञे तदेरकाचूर्णं प्रक्षिप्तं तैर्महोदधौ।। १२।।

Ugrasena had the club, which was made of iron, ground to dust and thrown into the sea, and particles of the dust there became rushes.

मुसलस्याथ लोहस्य चूर्णितस्य तु यादवैः।।
खंडं चूर्णितशेषं तु ततो यत्तोमराकृति।। १३।।

तदप्यंबुनिधौ क्षिप्तं मत्स्यो जग्राह जालिभिः।।
घातितस्योदरात्तस्य लुब्धो जग्राह तज्जराः।। १४।।

There was one part of the iron club which was like the blade of a lance and which the Andhakas could not break; this when thrown into the sea was swallowed by a fish; the fish was caught, the iron spike was extracted from its belly, and was taken by a hunter named Jāra.

विज्ञातपरमार्थोपि भगवान्मधुसूदनः।।
नैच्छत्तदन्यथा कर्तुं विधिना यत्समीहितम्।। १५।।

The all-wise and illustrious slayer of Madhu did not think it proper to counteract the predestination of fate.

देवैश्च प्रहितो वायुः प्रणिपत्याह केशवम्।।
रहस्येवमहं दूतः प्रहितो भगवन्सुरैः।। १६।।

वस्वश्विमरुदादित्यरुद्रसाध्यादिभिस्सह।।
विज्ञापयति शक्रस्त्वां तदिदं श्रूयतां विभो।। १७।।

In the interval an emissary despatched by the celestials came to Kṛṣṇa and said to him in private :—"I am sent to thee, O lord, by the celestials; and do thou hear what Indra together with the Viśvas, Maruts, Ādityas, Sādhyas and Rudras respectfully represent.

भारावतरणार्थाय वर्षाणामधिकं शतम्।।
भगवानवतीर्णोत्र त्रिदशैस्सह चोदितः।। १८।।

More than a century has gone by sinece thou in compliance with the request of the celestials, descended upon earth for the purpose of relieving it of its load.

दुर्वृत्ता निहता दैत्या भुवो भारोऽवतारितः।।
त्वया सनाथास्त्रिदशा भवंतु त्रिदिवे सदा।। १९।।

The demons have been destroyed and the burden of earth has been removed; now let the immortals once again see their king in heaven.

तदतीतं जगन्नाथ वर्षाणामधिकं शतम्।।
इदानीं गम्यतां स्वर्गो भवता यदि रोचते।। २०।।

More than a hundred years have passed, and if thou dost wish, do thou return to heaven. This is the prayer of the celestials.

देवैर्द्धवज्ञाप्यते देव तथात्रैव रतिस्तव।।
तत्स्थीयतां यथाकालमास्थेयमनुजीविभिः।। २१।।

And if this be not thy will, do thou remain here as long as it may be desirable to thy dependants."

श्रीभगवानुवाच

यत्त्वमात्थाखिलं दूत वेद्म्येतदहमप्युत।।
प्रारब्ध एव हि मया यादवानां परिक्षयः।। २२।।

भुवो नाद्यापि भारोऽयं यादवैरनिबर्हितैः।।
अवतार्य करोम्येतत्सप्तरात्रेण सत्वरः।। २३।।

Whereto Kṛṣṇa replied, "I am well aware of all thou hast said. The earth is not relieved of her load until the Yādavas are extirpated. I shall also speedily bring it about in my descent, and it shall take place in seven nights.

यथा गृहीतमंभोधेर्दत्त्वाहं द्वारकाभुवम्।।
यादवानुपसंहृत्य यास्यामि त्रिदशालयम्।। २४।।

Having restored the land of Dwārakā to the ocean and destroyed the race of Jadu, I shall proceed to the region of the celestials.

मनुष्यदेहमुत्सृज्य संकर्षणसहायवान्।।
प्राप्त एवास्मि मंतव्यो देवेंद्रेण तथाऽमरैः।। २५।।

Inform the celestials that having renounced my mortal frame and been accompanied by Saṅkarṣaṇa, I will then return to them.

जरासंधादयो येऽन्ये निहता भारहेतवः।।
क्षितेस्तेभ्यः कुमारोऽपि यदूनां नापचीयते।। २६।।

The tyrants that oppressed the earth, Jarāsandha and the rest, have been slain and a youth even of the race of Yadu is so less than they an incumbrance.

तदेतं सुमहाभारमवतार्य क्षितेरहम्।।
यास्याम्यमरलोकस्य पालनाय ब्रवीहि तान्।। २७।।

Having removed this huge weight of the earth, I will proceed to the mansions of the celestials. Say this to them."

श्रीपराशर उवाच

इत्युक्तो वासुदेवेन देवदूतः प्रणम्य तम्।।
मैत्रेय दिव्यया गत्या देवराजांतिकं ययौ।। २८।।

Parāśara said :—O Maitreya, being thus addressed by Vāsudeva, the messenger of the celestials bowed and took his heavenly course to the king of the deities.

भगवानप्यथोत्पातान्दिव्यभौमांतरिक्षजान्।।
ददर्श द्वारकापुर्यां विनाशाय दिवानिशम्।। २९।।

The illustrious Kṛṣṇa too now espied signs and portents both on earth and in heaven prognosticating day and night the destruction of Dwārakā.

तान्दृष्ट्वा यादवानाह पश्यध्वमतिदारुणान्।।
महोत्पाताञ्छमायैषां प्रभासं याम मा चिरम्।। ३०।।

Beholding those evil omens, he said to the Yādavas; "Behold these dreadful portents; let us hasten to Prabhāsa to avert them."

श्रीपराशर उवाच

एवमुक्ते तु कृष्णेन यादवप्रवरस्ततः।।
महाभागवतः प्राह प्रणिपत्योद्धवो हरिम्।। ३१।।

When he had thus said to the eminent Yādavas, the illustrious Uddhava saluted and said to him :

भगवन्यन्मया कार्यं तदाज्ञापय सांप्रतम्।।
मन्ये कुलमिदं सर्वं भगवान्संहरिष्यति।। ३२।।

"Tell me, O lord, what it is proper that I should do, for it seems to me that thou wilt destroy all this race.

नाशायास्य निमित्तानि कुलस्याच्युत लक्षये।। ३३।।

The signs that are manifest declare nothing less than the annihilation of the race.

श्रीभगवानुवाच

गच्छ त्वं दिव्यया गत्या मत्प्रसादसमुत्थया।।
यद्बदर्याश्रमं पुण्यं गंधमादनपर्वते।।
नरनारायणस्थाने तत्पवित्रं महीतले।। ३४।।

मन्मना मत्प्रसादेन तत्र सिद्धिमवाप्स्यसि।।
अहं स्वर्गं गमिष्यामि ह्युपसंहृत्य वै कुलम्।। ३५।।

द्वारकां च मया त्यक्तां समुद्रः प्लावयिष्यति।।
मद्वेश्म चैकं मुक्त्वा तु भयान्मत्तो जलाशये।।
तत्र सन्निहितश्चाहं भक्तानां हिकाम्यया।। ३६।।

"Thereupon Kṛṣṇa replied :—"Do thou, by my favour proceed, by this celestial course, to the holy place Badrikāśrama in the Gandhamādana mountain, the shrine of Nara Nārāyaṇa; and on that spot sanctified by them, thou, meditating upon me, shalt obtain perfection through my favour. Having extirpated this Yadu race, I shall proceed to Vaikuṇṭha; and after I have quitted Dwārakā; the ocean shall inundate it."

श्रीपराशर उवाच

इत्युक्तः प्रणिपत्यैनं जगामाशु तपोवनम्।।
नरनारायणस्थानं केशवेनानुमोदितः।। ३७।।

Parāśara said :—Being thus addressed by him and commanded by Keśava, Uddhava proceeded to the holy shrine of Nara Nārāyaṇa.

ततस्ते यादवास्सर्वे रथानारुह्य शीघ्रगान्।।
प्रभासं प्रययुस्सार्द्धं कृष्णरामादिभिर्द्विज।। ३८।।

And the Yādavas, with Kṛṣṇa, Balarāma and others, having ascended swift-coursing cars, proceeded to Prabhāsa.

प्रभासं समनुप्राप्ताः कुकुरांधकवृष्णयः।।
चक्रुस्तत्र महापानं वासुदेवेन चोदिताः।। ३९।।

Having reached Prabhāsa, the Kukkuras and Andhakas bathed there and, being excited by Krsna, indulged in liquor.

पिबतां तत्र चैतेषां संघर्षेण परस्परम्।।
अतिवादेंधनो जज्ञे कलहाग्निः क्षयावहः।। ४०।।

As they drank, the destructive fire of dessension was engendered amongst them by mutual collision and fed with the fuel of abuse.

मैत्रेय उवाच

स्वंस्वं वै भुंजतां तेषां कलहः किंनिमित्तकः।।
संघर्षो वा द्विज श्रेष्ठ तन्ममाख्यातुमर्हसि।। ४१।।

श्रीपराशर उवाच

मृष्टं मदीयमन्नं ते न मृष्टमिति जल्पताम्।।
मृष्टामृष्टकथा जज्ञे संघर्षकलहौ ततः।। ४२।।

ततश्चान्योन्यमभ्येत्य क्रोधसंरक्तलोचनाः।।
जघ्नुः परस्परं ते तु शस्त्रैर्दैवबलात्कृताः।। ४३।।

क्षीणशस्त्राश्च जगृहुः प्रत्यासन्नामथैरकाम्।। ४४।।

एरका तु गृहीता वै वज्रभूतेव लक्ष्यते।।
तया परस्परं जघ्नुस्संप्रहारे सुदारुणे।। ४५।।

Worked up with ire by the divine influence, they attacked on another with missile weapons, and when these were finished, they had recourse to the rushes growing nigh. The rushes in their hands became like thunder-bolts, and they assailed one another with them.

प्रद्युम्नसांबप्रमुखाः कृतवर्माथ सात्यकिः।।
अनिरुद्धादयश्चान्ये पृथुर्विपृथुरेव च।। ४६।।

चारुवर्मा चारुकश्च तथाक्रूरादयो द्विज।।
एरकारूपिभिर्वज्रैस्ते निजघ्नुः परस्परम्।। ४७।।

Pradyumna, Sāmba, Kṛtavarman, Sātyaki, Aniruddha, Pṛthu, Vipathu, Cāruvarman, Cāruka, Akrūra, and many others, struck one another with the rushes, which became hard like thunder-bolts.

निवारयामास हरिर्यादवांस्ते च केशवम्।।
सहायं मेनिरेरीणां प्राप्तं जघ्नुः परस्परम्।। ४८।।

Thereupon Kṛṣṇa arriving there prevented them : but they thought that he was taking part with each severally and continued the conflict.

कृष्णोऽपि कुपितस्तेषामेरकामुष्टिमाददे।।
वधाय सोपि मुसलं मुष्टिर्लौहमभूत्तदा।। ४९।।

जघान तेन निश्शेषान्यादवानाततायिनः।।
जघ्नुस्ते सहसाभ्येत्य तथाऽन्येपि परस्परम्।। ५०।।

Thereupon, enraged, Kṛṣṇa took up a handful of rushes to destroy them, which became a club of iron; and with this he killed many of the murderous Yādavas, whilst others fighting fiercely destroyed one another.

ततश्चार्णवमध्येन जैत्रोऽसौ चक्रिणो रथः।।
पश्यतो दारुकस्याथ प्रायादश्वैर्धृतो द्विज।। ५१।।

At this time in the very presence of Kṛṣṇa's charioteer, his swift steeds carried off his *Jaitra* car and entered into the sea.

चक्रं गदा तथा शार्ङ्गं तूणी शंखोसिरेव च।।
प्रदक्षिणं हरिं कृत्वा जग्मुरादित्यवतर्त्मना।। ५२।।

The discus, the club, the bow, the quiver, the shell and the sword of Keśava, having circumambulated their master, flew along the path of the sun.

क्षणेन नाभवत्कश्चिद्यादवानामघातितः।।
ऋते कृष्णं महात्मानं दारुकं च महामुने।। ५३।।

In a short time there was not a single Yādava left alive save the mighty Kṛṣṇa and Dāruka.

चंक्रम्यमाणो तौ रामं वृक्षमूले कृतासनम्।।
ददृशाते मुखाच्चास्य निष्क्रामंतं महोरगम्।। ५४।।

Going towards Rāma, who was sitting at the root of a tree, they saw a huge serpent coming out of his mouth.

निष्क्रम्य स मुखात्तस्य महाभोगो भुजंगमः।।
प्रययावर्णवं सिद्धैः पूज्यमानस्तथोरगैः।। ५५।।

Having issued out of his mouth, the mighty snake proceeded towards the ocean hymned by saints and other great snakes.

ततोर्घ्यमादाय तदा जलधिस्संमुखं ययौ।।
प्रविवेश ततस्तोयं पूजितः पन्नगोत्तमैः।। ५६।।

Bringing an offering of respect, the ocean came to him and then the majestic being worshipped of all the attendant snakes, entered into the waters of the deep.

दृष्ट्वा बलस्य निर्याणं दारुकं प्राह केशवः।।
इदं सर्वं समाचक्ष्व वसुदेवोग्रसेनयोः।। ५७।।

Beholding the departure of the spirit of Baladeva, Keśava said to Dāruka—"Do thou go to Vasudeva and Ugrasena and communicate unto him this.

निर्याणं बलभद्रस्य यादवानां तथा क्षयम्।।
योगे स्थित्वाहमप्येतत्परित्यक्ष्ये कलेवरम्।। ५८।।

Go and inform them of the departure of Balabhadra, and the destruction of the Yādava race, and also that I shall engage in religious meditation and renounce my body.

वाच्यश्च द्वारकावासी जनस्सर्वस्तथाहुकः।।
यथेमां नगरीं सर्वां समुद्रः प्लावयिष्यति।। ५९।।

Do thou also inform Āhuka and the inhabitants of Dwārakā that their city shall be inundated by the ocean.

तस्माद्भवस्सर्वैस्तु प्रतीक्ष्यो ह्यर्जुनागमः।।
न स्थेयं द्वारकामध्ये निष्क्रांते तत्र पांडवे।। ६०।।

तेनैव सह गंतव्यं यत्र याति स कौरवः।। ६१।।

And do ye await the arrival of Arjuna at Dwārakā. When Arjuna, the descendant of Pāṇḍu, shall issue out of the city, none of you should wait there but go whither the descendant of Kuru shall repair.

गत्वा च ब्रूहि कौंतेयमर्जुनं वचनान्मम।।
पालनीयस्त्वया शक्त्या जनोऽयं मत्परिग्रहः।। ६२।।

Do thou also go to the son of Kuntī and tell him that he may at my request protect my family according to his might.

त्वमर्जुनेन सहितो द्वारवत्यां तथा जनम्।।
गृहीत्वा याहि वज्रश्च यदुराजो भविष्यति।। ६३।।

Then go to Hastināpur with Arjuna and all the inhabitants of Dwārakā and, let Vajra be installed king over the race of Yadu."

श्रीपराशर उवाच

इत्युक्तो दारुकः कृष्णं प्रणिपत्य पुनःपुनः।।
प्रदक्षिणं च बहुशः कृत्वा प्रायाद्यथोदितम्।। ६४।।

स च गत्वा तदाचष्ट द्वारकायां तथाऽर्जुनम्।।
आनिनाय महाबुद्धिर्वज्रं चक्रे तथा नृपम्।। ६५।।

Parāśara said :—Thus instructed and having bowed unto and circumambulated Kṛṣṇa again and again, Dāruka departed as he had been desired; and having conducted Arjuna to Dwārāvatī, the intelligent servant of Kṛṣṇa established Vajra as king.

भगवाननि गोविंदो वासुदेवात्मकं परम्।।
ब्रह्मात्मनि समारोप्य सर्वभूतेष्वधारयत्।।
निष्प्रपञ्चे महाभाग संयोज्यात्मानमात्मनि।।
तुर्यावस्थसलीलं च शेतेस्म पुरुषोत्तमः।। ६६।।

Thereupon having concentrated in himself that supreme spirit which is identical with Vāsudeva, the divine Govinda was indentified with all beings.

संमानयन्द्विजवचो दुर्वासा यदुवाच ह।।
योगयुक्तोऽभवत्पादं कृत्वा जानुनि सत्तम।। ६७।।

Respecting the words of the Brāhmaṇa, the curse of Durvāsā, the illustrious Kṛṣṇa sat engaged in meditation, placing his foot upon his knee.

आययौ स जरानाम तदा तत्र स लुब्धकः।।
मुसलावशेषलोहैकसायकन्यस्ततोमरः।। ६८।।

स तत्पादं मृगाकारमवेक्ष्यारादवस्थितः।।
तले विव्याध तेनैव तोमरेण द्विजोत्तम।। ६९।।

Then there came a hunter named Jāra, whose arrow was tipped with a blade made of the iron club, which had not been reduced to powder; and espying from a distance the foot of Kṛṣṇa, he mistook it for a part of a deer, and shooting his arrow, lodged it in the sole.

ततश्च ददृशे तत्र चतुर्बाहुधरं नरम्।।
प्रणिपत्याह चैवैनं प्रसीदेति पुनःपुनः।।७०।।

Approaching his mark, he saw the four-armed king and falling in hiis feet, repeatedly besought his forgiveness, exclaming, "I have done this deed unknowingly, thinking I was aiming at a deer.

अजानता कृतमिदं मया हरिणशंकया।।
क्षम्यतां मम पापेन दग्धं मां त्रातुमर्हसि।।७१।।

Have pity on me who am consumed by my crime; for thou art able to consume me."

श्रीपराशर उवाच

ततस्तं भगवानाह न तेस्तु भयमण्वपि।।
गच्छ त्वं मत्प्रसादेन लुब्ध स्वर्गं सुरास्पदम्।।७२।।

Paraśara said :—Thereupon Bhagavān said : "Thou needst not have the least fear, hunter; by my favour, thou shalt repair to the region of the celestials."

श्रीपराशर उवाच

विमानमागतं सद्यस्तद्वाक्यसमनंतरम्।।
आरुह्य प्रययौ स्वर्गं लुब्धकस्तत्प्रसादतः।।७३।।

As soon as Kṛṣṇa had said this, the celestial car arrived there, ascending which the hunter repaired to the region of the celestials.

गते तस्मिन्सभगवान्संयोज्यात्मानमात्मनि।।
ब्रह्मभूतेऽव्ययेचिंत्ये वासुदेवमयेऽमले।।७४।।
अजन्मन्यमरे विष्णावप्रमेयेऽखिलात्मनि।।
तत्याज मानुषं देहमतीत्य त्रिविधां गतिम्।।७५।।

Thereupon the divine Kṛṣṇa having untied himself with his own pure, spiritual, inexhaustible inconceivable, unborn, undecaying, imperishable, and universal spirit, which is one Vāsudeva, renounced his mortal frame and his connection with the three qualities.

।। इति श्रीविष्णुमहापुराणे पञ्चमेंशे सप्तत्रिंशोऽध्यायः।।३७।।

अथ पञ्चमेंशेः अष्टात्रिंशोऽध्यायः

Part V : Section 38

श्रीपराशर उवाच

अर्जुनोपि तदान्वीक्ष्य राम कृष्णकलेवरे।।
संस्कारं लंभयामास तथान्येषामनुक्रमात्।।१।।

Parāśara said :—Haivng found the bodies of Kṛṣṇa and Rāma, Arjuna performed for them and the rest of the slain the obsequial rites.

अष्टौ महिष्यः कथिता रुक्मिणीप्रमुखास्तु याः।।
उपगुह्य हरेर्देहं विविशुस्ता हुताशनम्।।२।।

The eight queens of Kṛṣṇa, who have been named with Rukmiṇī at the head, embraced Hari and entered the funeral fire.

रेवती चापि रामस्य देहमाश्लिष्य सत्तमा।।
विवेश ज्वलितं वह्निं तत्संगाह्लादशीतलम्।।३।।

O foremost of the pious, embracing the corpse of Rāma, Revatī too entered fire which was cool to her happy heart in contract with her lord.

उग्रसेनस्तु तच्छ्रुत्वा तथैवानकदुंदुभिः।।
देवकी रोहिणी चैव विविशुर्जातवेदसम्।।४।।

Thereupon hearing all this Ugrasena and Vasudeva with Devakī and Rohiṇī entered fire.

ततोर्जुनः प्रेतकार्यं कृत्वा तेषां यथाविधि।।
निश्चक्राम जनं सर्वं गृहीत्वा वज्रमेव च।।५।।

Having performed duly the obsequious rites of the Yādavas, Arjuna, with the inhabitants of Dwārakā and Vajra, issued out of the city.

द्वारवत्या विनिष्क्रांताः कृष्णपत्न्यः सहस्रशः ।।
वज्रं जनं च कौंतेयः पालयञ्छनकैर्ययौ ।। ६ ।।

And Kuntī's son proceeded slowly with thousands of Kṛṣṇa's wives and the residents of Dwārakā.

सभा सुधर्मा कृष्णेन मर्त्यलोके समुज्झिते ।।
स्वर्गं जगाम मैत्रेय पारिजातश्च पादपः ।। ७ ।।

यस्मिन्दिने हरिर्यातो दिवं संत्यज्य मेदिनीम् ।।
तस्मिन्नेवावतीर्णोऽयं कालकायो बली कलिः ।। ८ ।।

With the departure of Kṛṣṇa from the land of mortals both the Sudharman palace and the Pārijāta tree proceeded to heaven; and on the same day that Hari departed from the earth the dark-bodied Kali age set in.

प्लावयामास तां शून्यां द्वारकां च महोदधिः ।।
वासुदेवगृहं त्वेकं न प्लावयति सागरः ।। ९ ।।

The ocean rose an inundated the whole of Dwārakā, except only the dwelling of the deity of the race of Yadu.

नातिक्रांतुमलं ब्रह्मंस्तदद्यापि महोदधिः ।।
नित्यं सन्निहितस्तत्र भगवान्केशवो यतः ।। १० ।।

तदतीव महापुण्यं सर्वपातकनाशनम् ।।
विष्णुश्रियान्वितं स्थानं दृष्ट्वा पामाद्विमुच्यते ।। ११ ।।

पार्थः पञ्चनदे देशे बहुधान्यधनान्विते ।।
चकार वासं सर्वस्य जनस्य मुनिसत्तमः ।। १२ ।।

ततो लोभस्समभवत्पार्थेनैकेन धन्विना ।।
दृष्ट्वा स्त्रियो नीयमाना दस्यूनां निहतेश्वराः ।। १३ ।।

ततस्ते पापकमाणो लोभोपहतचेतसः ।।
आभीरा मंत्रयामासुस्समेत्यात्यंतदुर्मदाः ।। १४ ।।

The sea has not been able to wash away that temple and there even up to the present day Keśava constantly resides; whoever visits that holy shrine where Kṛṣṇa pursued his sports is freed from sins. O foremost of ascetics, one day while proceeding, Arjuna, the son of Pṛthā, halted the people he had brought from Dwārakā in the Pañcanada country; in a rich and fertile spot; the desires of the neighbouring robbers were excited when they saw a number of widowed females and immense riches in the possession of Arjuna alone. Worked up with their cupidity they assembled their villainons herds and said to them :—

अयमेकोऽर्जुनो धन्वी स्त्रीजनं निहतेश्वरम् ।।
नयत्यस्मानतिक्रम्य धिगेतद्भवतां बलम् ।। १५ ।।

This Arjuna, alone with his bow, is passing amongst us having immense riches and numberless women with him, whose husbands have been slain; cursed is thy strength therefore.

हत्वा गर्वसमारूढो भीष्मद्रोणजयद्रथान् ।।
कर्णादींश्च न जानाति बलं ग्रामनिवासिनाम् ।। १६ ।।

His pride hath been increased by the death of Bhīṣma, Droṇa, Jayadratha, Karṇa and others; he is not cognisant of the prowess of the simple villagers.

यष्टिहस्तानवेक्ष्यास्मान्धनुष्पाणिस्स दुर्मतिः ।।
सर्वानेवावजानाति किं वो बाहुभिरुन्नतैः ।। १७ ।।

Up, up, take your long thick staves; this stupid fellow hates us. Why should we not lift up our arms?"

ततो यष्टिप्रहरणादस्यवो लोष्टधारिणः ।।
सहस्रशोभ्यधावंत तं जनं निहतेश्वरम् ।। १८ ।।

Saying this they rushed armed with cudgels and clods of earth, upon the people who were without their lord.

ततो निर्भर्त्स्य कौंतेयः प्राहाभीरान्हसन्निव ।।
निवर्त्तध्वमधर्मज्ञा यदि न स्थ मुमूर्षवः ।। १९ ।।

Arjuna met them and said to them in contempt; "Go away, O ye wretches, ignorant of what is right, if you do not wish to die."

अवज्ञाय वचस्तस्य जगृहुस्ते तदा धनम् ।।
स्त्रीधनं चैव मैत्रेय विष्वक्सेन परिग्रहम् ।। २० ।।

But they neglected his threats and seized his treasures and women, the wives Viśvaksena.

ततोर्जुनो धनुर्दिव्यं गांडीवमजरं युधि ।।
आरोपयितुमारेभे न शशाक च वीर्यवान् ।। २१ ।।

चकार सज्यं कृच्छ्राच्च तच्चाभूच्छिथिलं पुनः ।।
न सस्मार ततोस्त्राणि चिंतयन्नपि पांडवः ।। २२ ।।

Thereupon Arjuna began to brace his celestial bow Gāṇḍīva, irresistible in encounter, but it was in vain, for in spite of his efforts to lighten it, it continued flaccid; neither could he recollect the incantations of superhuman weapons.

शरान्मुमोच चैतेषु पार्थो वैरिष्वमर्षितः ।।
त्वग्भेदं ते परं चक्रुरस्ता गांडीवधन्विना ।। २३ ।।

Losing all patience he discharged, as best as he could, his arrows upon the foes, but they merely scratched the skin.

वह्निा येऽक्षया दत्ताश्शरास्तेपि क्षयं ययुः ।।
युद्ध्यतस्सह गोपालैरर्जुनस्य भवक्षये ।। २४ ।।

The shafts that were given him by Agni for certain destruction, were themselves destroyed and proved fatal to Arjuna in his encounter with herdsmen.

अचिंतयच्च कौंतेयः कृष्णास्यैव हि तद्बलम् ।।
यन्मया शरसंघातैस्सकला भूभृतो हताः ।। २५ ।।

मिषतः पांडुपुत्रस्य ततस्ताः प्रमदोत्तमाः ।।
आभीरैरपकृष्यंत कामं चान्याः प्रदुद्रुवुः ।। २६ ।।

Thereupon he tried to recall the prowess of Kṛṣṇa by the strength where of his shafts had slain many a mighty king; but he tried in vain, for they were either put aside by peasants or they flew at random wide of their marks.

ततश्शरेषु क्षीणेषु धनुष्कोट्या धनञ्जयः ।।
जधान दस्यूंस्ते चास्य प्रहाराञ्जहसुर्मुने ।। २७ ।।

His arrows being all exhausted he beat the robbers with the horn of his bow.

प्रेक्षतस्तस्य पार्थस्य वृष्ण्यंधकवरस्त्रियः ।।
जग्मुरादाय ते म्लेच्छः समस्ता मुनिसत्तम् ।। २८ ।।

They laughed at his blows and in the very sight of Arjuna the barbarians carried off all the women of the Vṛṣṇi and Andhaka tribes and went their way.

ततस्सुदुःखितो जिष्णुः कष्टं कष्टमिति ब्रुवन् ।।
अहो भगवतानेन मुष्टोस्मीति रुरोद वै ।। २९ ।।

Thereupon Jiṣṇu was greatly sorry, and lamented bitterly saying "Alas! Alas! I am deserted by my lord."

तद्धनुस्तानि शस्त्राणि स रथस्ते च वाजिनः ।।
सर्वमेकपदे नष्टं दानमश्रोत्रिये यथा ।। ३० ।।

And immediately the bow, the heavenly arms, his car and steeds perished entirely like a donation to an unlearned Brāhmin.

अहोतिबलवद्दैवं विना तेन महात्मना ।।
यदसामर्थ्ययुक्तेपि नीचवर्गे जयप्रदम् ।। ३१ ।।

"Alas! how powerful is the destiny" said he deprived of my illustrious friend I have been defeated by the base.

तौ बाहू स च मे मुष्टिः स्थानं तस्सोस्मि चार्जुनः ।।
पुण्येनैव विना तेन गतं सर्वमसारताम् ।। ३२ ।।

These two arms are mine; mine is this fist, this is my place; I am Arjuna, but without that righteous help all these are pithless.

ममार्जुनत्वं भीमस्य भीमत्वं तत्कृते ध्रुवम् ।।
विना तेन यदा भीरैर्जितोहं रथिनां वरः ।। ३३ ।।

The bravery of Arjuna, the strength of Bhīma was all his work; without him I am defeated by peasants; it cannot be from any other cause."

श्रीपराशर उवाच

इत्थं वदन्ययो जिष्णुरिंद्रप्रस्थं पुरोत्तमम् ।।
चकार तत्र राजानं वज्रं यादवनंदनम् ।। ३४ ।।

Saying this, Arjuna went to the city of Mathurā and there installed the Yādava prince Vajra as a king.

स ददर्श ततो व्यासं फाल्गुनः काननाश्रयम् ।।
तमुपेत्य महाभागं विनयेनाभ्यवादयत् ।। ३५ ।।

There he saw Vyāsa who was living in a forest and he appraoched the sage and saluted him respectfully.

तं वंदमानं चरणाववलोक्य मुनिश्चिरम् ।।
उवाच वाक्यं विच्छायः कथमद्य त्वमीदृशः ।। ३६ ।।

The ascetic observed him for some time as he lay prostrate at his feet and said to him. "How is it that I see you shorn of lustre?

अवीरजोनुगमनं ब्रह्महत्या कृताथ वा ।।
दृढाशाभंगदुःखीव भ्रष्टच्छयोऽसि सांप्रतम् ।। ३७ ।।

Have you been guilty of an illicit inter-course with a woman or of Brāhmincide? Or have you suffered any previous diappoint-ment that you are so dejected.

सांतानिकादयो वाते याचमाना निराकृताः।।
अगम्यस्त्री रतिर्वा त्वं येनासि विगतप्रभः।। ३८।।

Have your prayers for offspring or other good gifts proved fruitless? Or have you indulged improper passions that your lustre has been clouded?

भुङ्क्तेऽप्रदाय विप्रेभ्यो मृष्टमेकोथ वा भवान्।।
किं वा कृपणवित्तनि हृतानि भवताऽर्जुन।। ३९।।

Or have you devoured the meal given to Brāhmaṇas? Arjuna, say, have you seized upon the property of the poor?

कच्चिन्नु शूर्पवातस्य गोचरत्वं गतोऽर्जुन।।
दुष्टचक्षुर्हतो वासि निश्श्रीकः कथमन्यथा।। ४०।।

Has the wind of a winnowing basket lighted upon you? Or has an evil eye gazed upon you that you look so miserable.

स्पृष्टो नखांभसा वाथ घटवार्युक्षितोपि वा।।
केन त्वं वासि विच्छायो न्यूनैर्वा युधि निजातः।। ४१।।

Have you been touched by the water of a finger nail? Or has the water of a water-jar sprinkled you? Or, what is most probably the case, have you been beaten by your inferiors in battle?"

श्रीपराशर उवाच

ततः पार्थो विनिश्वस्य श्रूयतां भगवन्निति।।
प्रोक्त्वा यथावदाचष्टे व्यासायात्मपराभवम्।। ४२।।

Having sighed deeply Arjuna described to Vyāsa all the circumstances of his defeat, and said :—

अर्जुन उवाच

यद्बलं यच्च मत्तेजो यद्वीर्यं यः पराक्रमः।।
या श्रीश्छाया च नः सोस्मान्परित्यज्य हरिर्गतः।। ४३।।

Hari who was our strength, our heroism, our might, our prowess, our pros-perity and brighteness, has left us and departed.

ईश्वरेणापि महता स्मितपूर्वाभिभाषिणा।।
हीना वयं मुने तेन जातास्तृणमया इव।। ४४।।

Deprived of our illustrious friend who was ever kindly speaking we have become as feeble as if made of straw.

अस्त्राणां सायकानां च गांडीवस्य तथा मम।।
सारता याभवन्मूर्त्तिस्स गतः पुरुषोत्तमः।। ४५।।

Excellent Puruṣa, he, who was the living vigour of my weapon, my arrow, my bow has departed.

यस्यावलोकनादस्माञ्छ्रीर्जयः संपदुन्नतिः।।
न तत्याज स गोविंदस्त्यक्त्वास्मान्भगवान्गतः।। ४६।।

When he looked upon us, fortune, fame, wealth and dignity crowded us; but Govinda has departed from our midst.

भीष्मद्रोणांगराजाद्यास्तथा दुर्योधनादयः।।
यत्प्रभावेन निर्दग्धास्स कृष्णास्त्य मा भुवम्।। ४७।।

That Kṛṣṇa has left earth by whose power Bhīṣma, Droṇa, the king of Aṅga, Duryodhana and the rest were slain.

निर्यौवना गतश्रीका नष्टच्छायेव मेदिनी।।
विभाति तात नैकोहं विरहे तस्य चक्रिणः।। ४८।।

Not I alone but earth has grown old, miserable and lustreless in the absence of the holder of the discus.

यस्य प्रभावाद्भीष्माद्यैर्मय्यग्नौ शलभायतम्।।
विना तेनाद्य कृष्णेन गोपालैरस्मि निर्जितः।। ४९।।

Kṛṣṇa, through devotion to whom Bhīṣma and other powerful men perished like moths in the flame of my valour, has departed and I am now vanquished by cow-herds.

गांडीवस्त्रिषु लोकेषु ख्यातिं यदनुभावतः।।
गतस्तेन विनाऽऽभीरलगुडैस्स तिरस्कृतः।। ५०।।

The bow Gāṇḍīva, that was celebrated all over the three-worlds, has been foiled, on account of his departure, by the sticks of peasants.

स्त्रीसहस्राण्यनेकानि मन्नाथानि महामुने।।
यततो मम नीतानि दस्युभिर्लगुडायुधैः।। ५१।।
आनीयमानमाभीरैः कृष्ण कृष्णावरोधनम्।।
हृतं यष्टिप्रहरणैः परिभूय बलं मम।। ५२।।

The numberless women, over whom I was lord, have been carried off from me by thieves armed only with cudgels; the whole household of Kṛṣṇa, O Kṛṣṇa, has been forcibly carried off by peasants, who with their staves have put my strength to shame.

निश्श्रीकता न मे चित्रं यज्जीवामि तदद्भुतम्।।
नीचावमानपंकांकी निर्लज्जोस्मि पितामह।। ५३।।

I do not wonder that I am shorn of my lustre; it is a marvel that I live. Surely grandsire, I am so shameless that I survive the stain of indignity inflicted by the vile.

व्यास उवाच

अलं ते व्रीडया पार्थ न त्वं शोचितुमर्हसि।।
अवेहि सर्वभूतेषु कालस्य गतिरीदृशी।। ५४।।

Vyāsa replied to Arjuna and said. Think no more my son of the indignity; it does not behold you to grieve. Know that time subjects all beings to similar vicissitude :

कालो भवाय भूतानामभवाय च पांडव।।
कालमूलमिदं ज्ञात्वा भवस्थैर्यपरोऽर्जुन।। ५५।।

Time brings out the production and dissolution of all creatures. All that exists is founded on time. Know this, Arjuna, and preserve thy fortitude.

नद्यः समुद्रा गरयस्सकला च वसुंधरा।।
देवा मनुष्याः पशवस्तरवश्च सरीसृपाः।। ५६।।

सृष्टाः कालेन कालेन पुनर्यास्यंति संक्षयम्।।
कालात्मकमिदं सर्वं ज्ञात्वा शममवाप्नुहि।। ५७।।

Rivers, oceans, mountains, the entire earths, celestials, men, animals, trees, are all created and will all be destroyed by time. Be thou sober, knowing that all that is the effect of time.

कालस्वरूपी भगवान्कृष्णः कमललोचनः।।
यच्चात्थ कृष्णमाहात्म्यं तत्तथैव धनञ्जय।। ५८।।

भारावतारकार्यार्थमवतीर्णस्स मेदिनीम्।।
भाराक्रांता धरा याता देवानां समितिं पुरा।। ५९।।

तदर्थमवतीर्णोऽसौ कालरूपी जनार्दनः।।
तच्च निष्पादितं कार्यमशेषा भूभुजो हताः।। ६०।।

These mighty works of Kṛṣṇa, whatever they have been, have been performed to relieve earth of her load; for this he has come down. Oppressed by her load earth has had recourse to the assembly of the celestials and Janārddana, who is identical with time, has descended on that account.

वृष्ण्यंधककुलं सर्वं तथा पार्थोपसंहृतम्।।
न किंचिदन्यत्कर्त्तव्यं तस्य भूमितले प्रभोः।। ६१।।

This object has now been accomplished : all the kings of the earth have been destroyed; no more remained for him to accomplish.

अतो गतस्स भगवान्कृतकृत्यो यथेच्छया।।
सृष्टिं सर्गे करोत्येष देवदेवः स्थितौ स्थितिम्।।
अंतेंताय समर्थोयं सांप्रतं वै यथा गतः।। ६२।।
तस्मात्पार्थ न संतापस्त्वया कार्यः पराभवे।।
भवंति भावाः कालेषु पुरुषाणां यतः स्तुतिः।। ६३।।

Therefore the lord has departed whither he pleased, his ends being all fulfilled. At the period of creation the god of gods creates; in that of duration he preserves, at the end of all he is the powerful destroyer. Now all is done. Therefore O Arjuna, be not pained by thy defeat; the power of mortals is the gift of time.

त्वयैकेन हता भीष्मद्रोणकर्णादयो रणे।।
तेषामर्जुन कालोत्थः किं न्यूनाभिभवो न सः।। ६४।।
विष्णोस्तस्य प्रभावेण यथा तेषां पराभवः।।
कृतस्तथैव भवतो दस्युभ्यस्स पराभवः।। ६५।।

Bhīṣma, Karṇa and other kings have been slain by this alone; this was the work of time; and why should not therefore thy defeat by those inferior to thee occur? In the same manner as through thy devotion Viṣṇu these were overthrown by thee, so that thy discomfiture by cursed thieves been brought about by time.

स देवेशश्शरीराणि समाविश्य जगत्स्थितिम्।।
करोति सर्वभूतानां नाशमंते जगत्पतिः।। ६६।।

That divinity, assuming various shapes, preserves the world; and in the end the lord of creatures destroys it.

भगोदये ते कौंतेय सहायोऽभूज्जनार्दनः।।
तथांते तद्विपक्षास्ते केशवेन विनाशिताः।। ६७।।

O son of Kuntī, on the occasion of thy good fortune, the illustrious Janārddana was thy help; in thy decline thy enemies have been favoured by Keśava.

कश्श्रद्दध्यात्सगांगेयान्हन्यास्त्वं कौरवानिति ।।
आभीरेभ्यश्च भवतः कः श्रद्दध्यात्पराभवम् ।। ६८ ।।

Who will now believe that thou didst alone defeat Bhīṣma and other Kauravas. Who would believe that peasants have defeated thee?

पार्थैतत्सर्वभूतस्य हरेर्लीलाविचेष्टितम् ।।
त्वया यत्कौरावा ध्वस्ता यदाभीरैर्भवाञ्जितः ।। ६९ ।।

Know it for certain, O son of Pṛthā, that it is but the sport of the Universal Hari that the Kauravas have been slain by thee and thou hast been vanquished by herdsmen.

गृहीता दस्युभिर्याश्च भवाञ्छोचति तास्त्रियः ।।
एतस्याह यथावत्तं कथयामि तवार्जुनः ।। ७० ।।

As regards the women for whom thou dost grieve and who have been carried off by the thieves, hear from me an ancient story that will explain why this has happened.

अष्टावक्रः पुरा विप्रो जलवासरतोऽभवत् ।।
बहून्वर्षगणान्पार्थ गृणन्ब्रह्म सनातनम् ।। ७१ ।।

In ancient time, a Brāhmaṇa, named Aṣṭāvakra, was pursuing his religious penances, standing in water and meditating on the eternal spirit for many years.

जितेष्वसुरसंघेषु मेरुपृष्ठे महोत्सवः ।।
बभूव तत्र गच्छंत्यो ददृशुस्तं सुरस्त्रियः ।। ७२ ।।

रंभातिलोत्तमाद्यास्तु शतशोऽथ सहस्त्रशः ।।
तुष्टुवुस्तं महात्मानं प्रशशसुश्च पांडव ।। ७३ ।।

On account of the overthrow of the Asuras there was a great festival on the summit of Meru; on their way to which Rambhā, Tilottamā and hundreds of other beautiful nymphs praised and hymned him for his devotions.

आकंठमग्नं सलिले जटाभारवहं मुनिम् ।।
विन यावनताश्चैनं प्रणेमुस्तोत्रतत्पराः ।। ७४ ।।

They bowed unto him and eulogised him when he was immersed in water up to his throat, his hair twisted in a braid.

यथायथा प्रसन्नोऽसौ तुष्टुवुस्तं तथातथा ।।
सर्वास्ताः कौरवश्रेष्ठ तं वरिष्ठं द्विजन्मनाम् ।। ७५ ।।

They sang in honour of him whatever they thought would be agreeable to that most emiment of Brāhmaṇas.

अष्टावक्र उवाच

प्रसन्नोऽहं महाभागा भवतीनां यदिष्यते ।।
मत्तस्तद्व्रियतां सर्वं प्रदास्याम्यतिदुर्लभम् ।। ७६ ।।

Aṣṭāvakra at last said to them :—"I am well pleased with you, illustrious damsels; ask of me, whatever you wish and I will give it however difficult it may be of attainment."

रंभातिलोत्तमाद्यास्तं वैदि क्योप्सरसोब्रुवन् ।।
प्रसन्ने त्वय्यपर्याप्तं किमस्माकमिति द्विज ।। ७७ ।।

Thereupon all these nymphs, Rambhā Tilottamā and others mentioned in the Vedas, replied :—"It is enough for us that thou art pleased, what else need we say, O Brāhmaṇa?"

इतरास्त्वब्रुवन्विप्र प्रसन्नो भगवान्यादि ।।
तदिच्छामः पतिं प्राप्तुं विप्रेंद्र पुरुषोत्तमम् ।। ७८ ।।

But some amongst them said :—"If you are indeed pleased with us, O illustrious sire, thou grant us a husband, the best of men and sovereign of Brāhmaṇas."

व्यास उवाच

एवं भविष्यतीत्युक्त्वा ह्युत्ततार जलान्मुनिः ।।
तमुत्तीर्णं च ददृशुर्विरूपं वक्रमष्टधा ।। ७९ ।।

तं दृष्ट्वा गूहमानानां यासां हासः स्फुटोऽभवत् ।।
ताश्शशाप मुनिः कोपमवाप्य कुरुनंदन ।। ८० ।।

Thereupon saying "so be it." Aṣṭāvakra came up from the waters. When the nymphs observed him coming out of the water and saw that he was very ugly and crooked in eight places they could not restrain their merriment and laugh aloud. The Muni was very angry and imprecated them with a curse, saying :—

यस्माद्विकृतरूपं मां मत्वा हासावमानना ।।
भवतीभिः कृता तस्मादेतं शापं ददामि वः ।। ८१ ।।

मत्प्रसादेन भर्त्तारं लब्ध्वा तु पुरुषोत्तमम्।।
मच्छापोपहतास्सर्वा दस्युहस्तं गमिष्यथ।। ८२।।

"Since you have been so impertinent as to laugh at my deformity, I denounce upon you this curse; through the favour I have shown unto you, you shall obtain the first of males for your husband; and on account of my curse, you shall afterwards fall into the hands of thieves.

व्यास उवाच

इत्युदीरितमाकर्ण्य मुनिस्ताभिः प्रसादितः।।
पुनस्सुरेंद्रलोकं वै प्राह भूयो गमिष्यथ।। ८३।।

When the nymphs heard this imprecation they tried to appease the Muni, and they so far succeeded that he told them that they should finally go to the region of the celestials.

एवं तस्य मुनेश्शापादष्टावक्रस्य चक्रिणम्।।
भर्त्तारं प्राप्य ता याता दस्युहस्तं सुरांगनाः।। ८४।।

तत्वया नात्र कर्त्तव्यश्शोकोऽल्पोपि हि पांडव।।
तेनैवाखिलनाथेन सर्वं तदुपसंहृतम्।। ८५।।

भवतां चोपसंहार आसन्नस्तेन पांडव।।
बलं तेजस्तथा वीर्यं माहात्म्यं चोपसंहृतम्।। ८६।।

It is on account of the curse of the asceitc Aṣṭāvakra that these women, who were the wives of Keśava, have fallen into the hands of the barbarians; and there is nothing for you, Arjuna to regret it in the least. All this destruction has been brought about by the lord of all, and your end is also near at hand, since he has withdrawn from your strength, splendour, valour and pre-eminence.

जातस्य नियतो मृत्युः पतनं च तथोन्नतेः।।
विप्रयोगावमानस्तु संयोगः क्षयः।।८७।।

Death is the doom of every one who is born; fall is the end of exhaltation; union terminates in separation and growth tends only to decay.

विज्ञाय न बुधाश्शोकं न हर्षमुपयांति ये।।
तेषामेवेतरे चेष्टां शिक्षंतस्संति तादृशाः।। ८८।।

Knowing all this, wise men are neither subject to grief nor joy; and those who know these ways are equally free from pleasure or joy.

तस्मात्त्वया नरश्रेष्ठ ज्ञात्वैतद्भ्रातृभिस्सह।।
परित्यज्याऽखिलं तंत्रं गंतव्यं तपसे वनम्।। ८९।।

Do you therefore, most excellent prince, unders and this truth and along with your brothers relinquish everything and repair to the holy forest.

तद्गच्छ धर्मराजाय निवेद्यैतद्वचो मम।।
परश्वो भ्रातृभिस्सार्द्धं यथा यासि तथा कुरु।। ९०।।

Go now and say from me to Yudhiṣṭhira that he, to-morrow with his brethren, will tread the path of heroes."

इत्युक्तोभ्येत्य पार्थाभ्यां यमाभ्यां च सहार्जुनः।।
दृष्टं चैवानुभूतं च सर्वमाख्यातवांस्तथा।। ९१।।

Thus instructed by Vyāsa, Arjuna went and described to the other sons of Pṛthā all that he had seen, experienced and heard.

व्यासवाक्यं च ते सर्वे श्रुत्वार्जुनमुखेरितम्।।
राज्ये परीक्षितं कृत्वा ययुः पांडुसुता वनम्।। ९२।।

When he had related unto them the message of Vyāsa, the sons of Pāṇḍu placed Parīkṣit on the throne and went to the forest.

इत्येतत्तव मैत्रेय विस्तरेण मयोदितम्।।
जातस्य यद्यदोर्वंशे वासुदेवस्य चेष्टितम्।। ९३।।

यश्चैतच्चरितं तस्य कृष्णस्य शृणुयात्सदा।।
सर्वपापविनिर्मुक्तो विष्णुलोकं स गच्छति।। ९४।।

I have thus described to you, O Maitreya, in detail the actions of Vāsudeva when he was born in the race of Yadu. And who hears this part will go to Vaikuṇṭha.

।। इति श्रीविष्णुमहापुराणे पञ्चमेंशेऽष्टात्रिंशोऽध्यायः।। ३८।।

।। समाप्तश्चायं विष्णुमहापुराणस्य पञ्चमांशः।।

।। अथ श्रीविष्णुमहापुराणे षष्ठांशः ।।

THE VIṢṆUMAHĀPURĀṆAM, PART - VI

।। श्रीमते रामानुजाय नमः ।।

अथ षष्ठेंशेः प्रथमोऽध्यायः

Part VI : Section 1

मैत्रेय उवाच

व्याख्याता भवता सर्ववंशमन्वंतरस्थितिः ।।
वंशानुचरितं चैव विस्तरेण महामुने ।। १ ।।

Maitreya said :—Thou hast described unto me in detail, O illustrious sage, the creation of the universe, the genealogies of the Patriarchs, the duration of the Manwantaras and the dynasties of the princes.

श्रोतुमिच्छाम्यहं त्वत्तो यथावदुपसंहृतिम् ।।
महाप्रलयसंज्ञां च कल्पांते च महामुने ।। २ ।।

I am willing to hear from you an account of the dissolution of the universe, the time of total destruction and that which occurs at the espiration of a Kalpa.

श्रीपराशर उवाच

मैत्रेय श्रूयतां मत्तो यथावदुपसंहृतिः ।।
कल्पांते प्राकृते चैव प्रलयो जायते यथा ।। ३ ।।

Parāśara said :—Hear from me exactly, O Maitreya, the circumstances attending the dissolution of the world either at the expiration of a Kalpa or that which occurs at the close of the life of Brahmā.

अहोरात्रं पितृणां तु मासोऽब्दस्त्रिदिवौकसाम् ।।
चतुर्युगसहस्रे तु ब्रह्मणो वै द्विजोत्तम ।। ४ ।।

A month of men constitutes a day and night of the progenitors; a year of men is a day and night of the celestials. Twice a thousand aggregates of the four ages is a day and night of Brahmā.

कृतं त्रेता द्वापरं च कलिश्चेति चतुर्युगम् ।।
दिव्यैर्वर्षसहस्रैस्तु तद्द्वादशभिरुच्यते ।। ५ ।।

The four ages are the Kṛta, Tretā, Dwāpara and Kali, comprehending altogether twelve thousand years of the celestials.

चतुर्युगाण्यशेषाणि सदृशानि स्वरूपतः ।।
आद्यं कृतयुगं मुक्त्वा मैत्रेयांत्यं तथा कलिम् ।। ६ ।।

There are infinite successions of those four ages of a similar description, the first of which is always called Kṛta and the last the Kali.

आद्ये कृतयुगे सर्गो ब्रह्मणा क्रियते यथा ।।
क्रियते चोपसंहारस्तथांऽते च कलौ युगे ।। ७ ।।

In the first, the Kṛta is that age which is created by Brahmā; in the last, which is the Kali age, a dissolution of the univese takes place.

मैत्रेय उवाच

कलेस्स्वरूपं भगवन्विस्तराद्वक्तुमर्हसि ।।
धर्मश्चतुष्पाद्भगवान्यस्मिन्विप्लवमृच्छति ।। ८ ।।

Maitreya said :—O venerable Sir, it behoves thee to give a description of the nature of the Kali age in which the four-footed virtue suffers total extinction.

श्रीपराशर उवाच

कलेस्स्वरूपं मैत्रेय यद्भवाञ्छ्रोतुमिच्छति ।।
तन्निबोध समासेन वर्त्तते यन्महामुने ।। ९ ।।

Parāśara said :—Hear, O Maitreya, of the nature of the Kali age, regarding which you have enquired and which is now approaching completion.

वर्णाश्रमाचारवती प्रवृत्तिर्न कलौ नृणाम्।।
न सामऋग्यजुर्धर्मविनिष्पादनहैतुकी।। १०।।

In the Kali age, people will not observe caste, order and institutes, nor the ceremonial enjoined by the Sāma, Ṛk and Yayur Vedas.

विवाहा न कलौ धर्म्या न शिष्यगुरुसंस्थितिः।।
न दांपत्यक्रमो नैव वह्निदेवात्मकः क्रमः।। ११।।

यत्र कुत्र कुले जातो बली सर्वेश्वरः कलौ।।
सर्वेभ्य एव वर्णेभ्यो योग्यः कन्यावरोधने।। १२।।

Marriages in this age, will be celebrated according to the rituals, nor will the rulers that connect the spiritual protector and his disciple will be in force : the laws that regulate the conduct of husband and wife will be neglected and oblations to the celestials with fire no longer be offered. A powerful and rich man, in whatever family he may be born, will have right to marry maidens of every tribe.

येन केन च योगेन द्विजातिर्दीक्षितः कलौ।।
यैव सैव च मैत्रेय प्रायश्चित्तं कलौ क्रिया।। १३।।

In the Kali age, a Brāhmaṇa will be always regarded as such even if he be not initiated properly, and many forms of penance will be prescribed.

सर्वमेव कलौ शास्त्रं यस्य यद्वचनं द्विज।।
देवता च कलौ सर्वा सर्वस्सर्वस्य चाश्रमः।। १४।।

O Maitreya, O twice-born one, all texts will be considered as Śāstras in the Kali age; all celestials will be considered in equal light and all orders of life will be common alike to all persons.

उपवासस्तथाऽऽयासो वित्तोत्सर्गस्तपः कलौः।।
धर्मो यथाभिरुचितैरनुष्ठानैरनुष्ठितः।। १५।।

In this Kali age, fasting, austerity, liberality practised according to the pleasures of those by whom they are observed will constitute piety.

वित्तेन भविता पुंसां स्वल्पेनाढ्य मदः कलौ।।
स्त्रीणां रूपमदश्चैवं केशैरेव भविष्यति।। १६।।

Every trifling property will make men proud of their wealth. Pride of beauty will be inspired by hair.

सुवर्णमणिरत्नादौ वस्त्रे चोपक्षयं गते।।
कलौ स्त्रियो भविष्यंति तदा केशैरलं कृता।। १७।।

Gold, jewels, diamonds, clothes will all have perished, and then hair will be the only ornament with which women can decerate themselves.

परित्यक्ष्यंति भर्त्तारं वित्तहीनं तथा स्त्रियः।।
भर्त्ता भविष्यति कलौ वित्तवानेव योषिताम्।। १८।।

Wives will desert their husbands when they will lose their wealth; and the rich only will be considered by woman as their lords.

यो वै ददाति बहुलं स्वं स स्वामी सदा नृणाम्।।
स्वामित्वहेतुस्संबंधो न चाभिजनता तथा।। १९।।

He who will distribute immense wealth, will be considered as master of men and prestige of birth will no longer be a tittle to supremacy. Accumulated wealth will be spent on ostentatious dwellings.

गृहांता द्रव्यसंघाता द्रव्यांता च तथा मतिः।।
अर्थाश्चात्मोपभोग्यांता भविष्यंति कलौ युगे।। २०।।

The minds of men will be wholly occupied with earning money and that even will be spent on the gratification selfish desires.

स्त्रियः कलौ भविष्यंति स्वैरिण्यो ललितस्पृहाः।।
अन्यायादाप्तवित्तेषु पुरुषाः स्पृहयालवः।। २१।।

Women will follow their own inclinations and be given up to pleasure-seeking. Men will endeavour to acquire riches even dishonestly.

अभ्यर्थितापि सुहृदा स्वार्थमेव निरीक्ष्यते।।
पणार्धार्धार्द्धमात्रेऽपि करिष्यंति तथा स्पृहाम्।। २२।।

No man will part with the smallest fraction of his wealth at his wealth at sacrifice of his own interest even when requested by his friends.

समानपौरुषं चेतो भावि विप्रेषु वै कलौ।।
क्षीरप्रदानसंबंधि भावि गोषु च गौरवम्।। २३।।

In the Kali age all people will consider themselves as equal with the Brāhmaṇas; and cows will be held in reverence only because they supply milk.

अनावृष्टिभयप्रायाः प्रजाः क्षुद्भयकातराः ।।
भविष्यंति तदा सर्वे गगनासक्तदृष्टयः ।। २४ ।।

People will be always in fear of dearth and scarcity and will watch accordingly the appearances of the sky.

कंदमूलफलाहारास्तापसा इव मानवाः ।।
आत्मानं घातयिष्यंति ह्यनावृष्ट्यादिदुःखिताः ।। २५ ।।

They will all live, like anchorets, upon leaves and roots and fruits and put a period to their lives through fear, of famine and want.

दुर्भिक्षमेव सततं तथा क्लेशमनीश्वराः ।।
प्राप्स्यंति व्याहतसुखप्रमोदा मानवाः कलौ ।। २६ ।।

Deprived of wealth, people will be perpetually subject to famine and other afflictions; and they will never enjoy pleasure and happiness.

अस्नानभोजिनो नाग्निदेवतातिथिपूजनम् ।।
करिष्यंति कलौ प्राप्ते न च पिंडोदकक्रियाम् ।। २७ ।।

At the advent of the Kali they will take their food without previous ablutions and without worshipping fire, celestials or guests or offering obsequial libations to their progenitors.

लोलुपा ह्रस्व देहाश्च बह्वन्नादनतत्पराः ।।
बहुप्रजाल्पभाग्यश्च भविष्यंति कलौ स्त्रियः ।। २८ ।।

The women will be fickle, short of stature, gluttonous; they will all have many children and little means.

उभाभ्यामपि पाणिभ्यां शिरःकंडूयनं स्त्रियः ।।
कुर्वंत्यो गुरुभर्तृणामाज्ञां भत्स्यंत्यनादराः ।। २९ ।।

And scratching their heads with both hands they will pay no attention to the commands of their husbands or parents.

स्वपोषणपराः क्षुद्रा देहसंस्कारवर्जिताः ।।
परुषानृतभाषिण्यो भविष्यंति कलौ स्त्रियः ।। ३० ।।

दुःशीला दुष्टशीलेषु कुर्वंत्यस्सततं स्पृहाम् ।।
असद्वृत्ता भविष्यंति पुरुषेषु कुलांगनाः ।। ३१ ।।

They will be selfish, object and slovenly; they will be scolds and liars; they will be indecent and immoral in their conduct and will ever attach themselves to dissolute men.

वेदादानं करिष्यंति बटवश्चाकृतव्रताः ।।
गृहस्थाश्च न होष्यंति न दास्यंत्युचितान्यपि ।। ३२ ।।

And disregarding the rules of studentship youths will study the Vedas. Householders will neither sacrifice nor practise becoming liberality.

वानप्रस्था भविष्यंति ग्राम्याहारपरिग्रहाः ।।
भिक्षवश्चापि मित्रादिस्नेहसंबंधयंत्रणाः ।। ३३ ।।

Anchorets will live upon food accepted from rustics and mendicants will be influenced by regard for friends and associates.

अरक्षितारो हर्त्तारश्शुल्कव्याजेन पार्थिवाः ।।
हारिणो जनवित्तानां संप्राप्ते तु कलौ युगे ।। ३४ ।।

Princes will plunder their subjects instead of protecting them and under the pretext of levying customs they will rob merchants of their property.

योयोऽश्वरथनागाढ्यस्स स राजा भविष्यति ।।
यश्च यश्चाबलस्सर्वस्सस भृत्यः कलौ युगे ।। ३५ ।।

In the Kali Yuga every one, possessing cars and elephants and horses, will be a Rājā; every one who is feeble will be a slave.

वैश्याः कृषिवणिज्यादि संत्यज्य निजकर्म यत् ।।
शूद्रवृत्त्या प्रवर्त्स्यंति कारुकर्मोपजीविनः ।। ३६ ।।

भेक्षव्रतपराः शूद्राः प्रव्रज्यालिंगिनोऽधमाः ।।
पाषंडसेश्रयां वृत्तिमाश्रयिष्यंति सत्कृताः ।। ३७ ।।

Vaiśyas will abandon agriculture and commerce and gain a livelihood by servitude or exercise of mechanical arts; Śūdras, seeking a subsistence by begging and assuming outward marks of religious mendicants, will become the impure followers of impious and heretical doctrines.

दुर्भिक्षकरपीडाभिरतीवोपदुता जनाः ।।
गोधूमान्नयवान्नाढ्यान्देशान्यास्यंति दुःखिताः ।। ३८ ।।

Oppressed by famine and taxation men will desert their native countries and repair to the lands which are fit for coarser grains.

वेदमार्गे प्रलीने च पाषंडाढ्ये ततो जने।।
अधर्मवृद्ध्या लोकानामल्पमायुर्भविष्यति।। ३९।।

The path of the Vedas being obliterated and people having deviated into heresy, iniquity will flourish and the duration of life will therefore decrease.

अशास्त्रविहितं घोरं तप्यमानेषु वै तपः।।
नरेषु नृपदोषेण बाल्ये मृत्युर्भविष्यति।। ४०।।

On account of the horrible penances enjoined by scripture and of the vices of the rulers, children will die in their infancy.

भविता योषितां सूतिः पञ्चषट्सप्तवार्षिकी।।
नवाष्टदशवर्षाणां मनुष्याणां तथा कलौ।। ४१।।

Women will bear children at the age of five, six or seven years and men will beget them, when they are eight, nine or ten.

पलितोद्भवश्च भविता तथा द्वादशवार्षिकः।।
नातिजीवति वै कश्चित्कलौ वर्षाणि विंशतिः।।४२।।

Men will grow old at the age of twelve and no one will live more than twenty years.

अल्पप्रज्ञा वृथालिंगा दुष्टांतःकरणाः कलौ।।
यतस्ततो विनंक्ष्यंति कालेनाल्पेन मानवाः।। ४३।।

Men will possess little sense, vigour virtue and will therefore die in a short time.

यदायदा हि मैत्रेय हानिर्धर्मस्य लक्ष्यते।।
तदातदा कलेर्वृद्धिरनुमेया विचक्षणैः।। ४४।।

O Maitreya, the wise then estimate the approach of Kali when the number of heretics increases.

यदायदा हि पाषंडवृद्धिर्मैत्रेय लक्ष्यते।।
तदातदा कलेर्वृद्धिननुमेया महात्मभिः।। ४५।।

यदायदा सतां हानिर्वेदमार्गानुसारिणाम्।।
तदातदा कलेर्वृद्धिरनुमेया विचक्षणैः।। ४६।।

प्रारंभाश्चावसीदंति यदा धर्मभृतां नृणाम्।।
तदानुमेयं प्राधान्यं कलेर्मैत्रेय पंडितैः।। ४७।।

Whenever, O Maitreya, number of the pious devoted to the lessons of the Vedas, diminishes, the efforts, of the individuals who cultivate virtue, become relax; the first of males becomes no longer the object of sacrifice; respect for the teachers of the Vedas declines and regard is cherished for the dissiminators of declines and regard is cherished for the dissimnators of heresy, the wise estimate the augmented influence of the Kali.

यदायदा न यज्ञानामीश्वरः पुरुषोत्तमः।।
इज्यते पुरुषैर्यज्ञैस्तदा ज्ञेयं कलेर्बलम्।। ४८।।

न प्रीतिर्वेदवादेषु पाषंडेपु यदा रतिः।।
कलेर्वृद्धिस्तदा प्राज्ञैरनुमेया विचक्षणैः।। ४९।।

कलौ जगत्पतिं विष्णुं सर्वस्त्रष्टारमीश्वरम्।।
नार्चयिष्यंति मैत्रेय पाषंडोपहता जनाः।। ५०।।

किं देवैः किं द्विजैर्वेदैः किं शौचेनांबुजन्मना।।
इत्येवं विप्रवक्ष्यंति पाषंडोपहता जनाः।। ५१।।

O Maitreya, in the Kali age corrupted by unbelievers, men will refrain from adoring Viṣṇu, the lord of sacrifice and the creator and sovereign of all and will say "Of what authority are the Vedas? What are the celestials or Brāhmaṇas? What need there is of purification with water?"

स्वल्पांबुवृष्टिः पर्जन्यः सस्यं स्वल्पफलं तथा।।
फलं तथाल्पसारं च विप्र प्राप्ते कलौ युगे।। ५२।।

शाणीप्रायाणि वस्त्राणि शमीप्राया महीरुहाः।।
शूद्रप्रायास्तथा वर्णा भविष्यंति कलौ युगे।। ५३।।

अणुप्रायाणि धान्यानि चाज्यप्रायं तथा पयः।।
भविष्यति कलौ प्राप्ते ह्यौशीरं चानुलेपनम्।। ५४।।

At the approach of the Kali, O Vipra, the clouds will yield scanty rain; the corn will be light in ear and the grain will be poor and of little sap : garments will be mostly made of the fibres of sun : the principal of trees will be the Sami; principal caste will be Śūdra; millet will be the more common grain; the milk in use will be chiefly that of goats; unguents will be made of Uṣira grass.

श्वश्रूश्वशुरभूयिष्ठा गुरवश्च नृणां कलौ।।
श्यालाद्या हारिभार्याश्च सुहृदो मुनिसत्तम।। ५५।।

The mother and father-in-law will be venerated in the place of parents : and a man's friend will be his brother-in-law or one who has a wanton wife.

कस्य माता पिता कस्य यथा कर्मानुगः पुमान्।।
इति चोदाहरिष्यंति श्वशुरानुगता नराः।। ५६।।

Men will say "Who has a father? Who has a mother? Every one is born according to his deeds"; therefore they will regard the wife's or the husband's parents as their own."

वाङ्मनःकायगैर्दोषैरभिभूताः पुनःपुनः।।
नराः पापान्यनुदिनं करिष्यंत्यल्पमेधसः।। ५७।।

And at this place with the least trouble that piety shall be accumulated which could be acquired with the greatest exertions in the Kṛta age.

निस्सत्त्वानामशौचानां निह्रीकाणां तथा नृणाम्।।
यद्यद्दुःखाय तत्सर्वं कलिकाले भविष्यति।। ५८।।

Gifted with little sense they will be subect to all sorts of infirmities of mind, speech and body and will daily commit sins; and every thing that is likely to afflict beings, vicious, impure and wretched will be generated in the Kali Yuga.

निस्स्वाध्यायवषट्कारे स्वधास्वाहाविवर्जिते।।
तदा प्रविरलो धर्मः क्वचिल्लोके निवत्स्यति।।५९।।

Thus, O Brāhmaṇa, when holy study, oblations to fire and convocations of the celestials shall be stopped some few people shall live at a holy place.

तत्राल्पेनैव यत्नेन पुण्यस्कंधमनुत्तमम्।।
करोति यः कृतयुगे क्रियते तपसा हि सः।। ६०।।

And at this place with the least trouble that piety shall be accumulated which could be acquired with the greatest exertions in the age.

।। इति श्रीविष्णुमहापुरोणे षष्ठेंशे प्रथमोऽध्यायः।। १।।

अथ षष्ठेंशेः द्वितीयोऽध्यायः

Part VI : Section 2

श्रीपराशर उवाच

व्यासश्चाह महाबुद्धिर्यदत्रैव हि वस्तुनि।।
तच्छ्रूयतां महाभाग गदतो मम तत्वतः।। १।।

Parāśara said :—Hear, O highly illustrious one, I shall describe fully what the great Vyāsa has related upon the subject.

कस्मिन्कालेऽल्पको धर्मो ददाति सुमहत्फलम्।।
मुनीनां पुण्यवादोऽभूत्कैश्चाऽसौ क्रियते सुखम्।। २।।

Once on a time, the sages assembled and discussed at what season the least morality obtained the greatest reward and by whom it was most easily displayed.

संदेहनिर्णयार्थाय वेदव्यासं महामुनिम्।।
ययुस्ते संशयं प्रष्टुं मैत्रेय मुनिपुंगवाः।। ३।।

In order to terminate the discussion they went to Veda Vyāsa to remove their doubts.

ददृशुस्ते मुनिं तत्र जाह्नवीसलिले द्विज।।
वेदव्यासं महाभागमर्द्धस्नातं सुतं मम।। ४।।
स्नानावसानं ते तस्य प्रतीक्षंतो महर्षयः।।
तस्थुस्तीरे महानद्यास्तरुषंडमुपाश्रिताः।। ५।।

They saw the illustrious sage, my son, immersed in the water of the Ganges, and awaiting the close of his ablutions, the sages remained on the banks of the sacred river under the shelter of a grove of trees.

मग्नोऽथ जाह्नवीतोयादुत्थायाह सुतो मम।।
शूद्रस्साधुः कलिस्साधुरित्येवं शृण्वतां वचः।।
तेषां मुनीनां भूयश्च मभज्ज स नदीजले।। ६।।
साधुसाध्विति चोत्थाय शूद्र धन्योसि चाब्रवीत्।।७।।

As my son plunged into the water and rose up from it the sages heard him exclaim. "Excellent is the Kali age." Again dived he and again did he exclaim in their hearing. "Well done, well done, Śūdra, thou art happy."

निमग्नश्च समुत्थाय पुनः प्राह महामुनिः।।
योषितः साधु धन्यास्तास्ताभ्यो धन्यतरोस्ति कः।। ८।।

Again he sank down and again did they hear him say "Well done, well done, women, they are happy who are more fortunate than they."

ततः स्नात्वा यथान्यायमाचांतं च कृतक्रियम्।।
उपतस्थुर्महाभागं मुनयस्ते सुतं मम।। ९।।

After this my sòn finished his bathing and the sages met him as he approached to welcome them.

कृतसंवंदनांश्चाह कृतासनपरिग्रहान्।।
किमर्थ मागता यूयमिति सत्यवतीसुतः।। १०।।

After they had been seated and offered their respects the son of Satyavatī said to them :—

श्रीपराशर उवाच

तमूचुस्संशयं प्रष्टुं भवंतं वयमागताः।।
अलं तेनास्तु तावन्नः कथ्यतामपरं त्वया।। ११।।

कलिस्साध्विति यत्प्रोक्तं शूद्रः साध्विति योषितः।।
यदाह भगवान्त्साधु धन्याश्चेति पुनःपुनः।। १२।।

"For what you have come here?" The Ṛsis said. "Having entertained some doubts regarding a subject we have come here to consult thee; but let that remain at present; explain to us some thing else. We heard you say "Excellent is the Kali Yuga!"

तत्सर्वं श्रोतुमिच्छामो न चेद्गुह्यं महामुने।।
तत्कथ्यतां ततो हृत्स्थं पृच्छामस्त्वां प्रयोजनम्।। १३।।

We are anxious to learn why this was said and why you repeatedly called them happy. Explain to us the meaning of it if it be not a mystery. We will then place before you the question that engages our thoughts."

श्रीपराशर उवाच

इत्युक्तो मुनिभिर्व्यासः प्रहस्येदमथाब्रवीत्।।
श्रूयतां भो मुनिश्रेष्ठा यदुक्तं साधुसाध्विति।। १४।।

Being thus accosted by the ascetics Vyāsa smiled and said to them "Hear excellent sages, why I said "Well done, Well done!"

व्यास उवाच

यत्कृते दशभिर्वर्षैस्त्रेतायां हायनेन तत्।।
द्वापरे तच्च मासेन ह्यहोरात्रेण तत्कलौ।। १५।।

तपसो ब्रह्मचर्यस्य जपादेश्च फलं द्विजाः।।
प्राप्नोति पुरुषस्तेन कलिस्साध्विति भाषितम्।। १६।।

The fruit of penace of continence, of silent prayer and the like, practised in the Kṛta age for ten years, in the Tretā for one year, in the Dwāpara for a month is obtained in the Kali age in a day and night; therefore I did say "Excellent, excellent is the Kali age."

ध्यायन्कृते यजन्यज्ञैस्त्रेतायां द्वापरेऽर्चयन्।।
यदाप्नोति तदाप्नोति कलौ संकीर्त्य केशवम्।। १७।।

The reward, which a man obtains in the Kṛta age by abstract meditation in the Tretā by sacrifie, in the Dwāpara by adoration, he receives in the Kali Yuga by merely reciting the names of Keśava.

धर्मोत्कर्षमतीवात्र प्राप्नोति पुरुषः कलौ।।
अल्पायासेन धर्मज्ञास्तेन तुष्टोस्म्यहं कलेः।। १८।।

O pious and great ascetics, in the Kali age, by very little exertion men attain to exalted virtue and it is for this reason I speak highly of the Kali Yuga.

व्रत चर्यापरैर्ग्राह्या वेदाः पूर्वं द्विजातिभिः।।
ततस्स धर्मसंप्राप्तैर्यष्टव्यं विधिवद्धनैः।। १९।।

Formerly the Vedas were to be acquired by the twice-born through the diligent observance of self-denial and it was their duty to celebrate sacrifices in accordance with the ritual.

वृथा कथा वृथा भोज्यं वृथेज्या च द्विजन्मनाम्।।
पतनाय ततो भाव्यं तैस्तु संयमिभिस्सदा।। २०।।

असम्यक्करणे दोषस्तेषां सर्वेषु वस्तुषु।।
भोज्यपेयादिकं चैषां नेच्छाप्राप्तिकरं द्विजाः।। २१।।

Thereafter, idle prayers, idle feasts, fruitless ceremonies were performed only to mislead the twice-born; for although observed by them devoutly, yet in consequence of some irregularity in their celebration sin was incurred in all these works and what they ate or what they drank did not bring about this fulfilment of their desires.

पारतंत्र्यं समस्तेषु तेषां कार्येषु वै यतः।।
जयंति ते निजाँल्लोकान्क्लेशेन महता द्विजाः।। २२।।

द्विजशुश्रूषयैवैष पाकयज्ञाधिकारवान्।।
निजाञ्जयति वै लोकाञ्छूद्रो धन्यतरस्ततः।। २३।।

भक्ष्याभक्ष्येञ्षु नास्या स्ति पेयापेयेषु वै यतः।।
नियमो मुनिशार्दूलास्तेनाऽसौ साध्वितीरितः।। २४।।

In all their objects the twice-born enjoyed no independence and attained their respective spheres only with exceeding pain. On the other hand, the Śūdra, more fortunate than they, attains to his assigned station by rendering their service and performing merely the sacrifice of preparing food in which no rules determine what may or may not be eaten, what may or may not be drunk. Therefore, excellent sages, the Śūdra is fortunate.

स्वधर्मस्याविरोधेन नरैर्लब्धं धनं सदा।।
प्रतिपादनीयं पात्रेषु यष्टव्यं च यथाविधि।। २५।।

Men should acquire wealth by means not incompatible with their religious duties and it shoud be given to the worthy and spent upon sacrifices.

तस्यार्जने महाक्लेशः पालने च द्विजोत्तमाः।।
तथासद्विनियोगेन विज्ञातं गहनं नृणाम्।। २६।।

There is great trouble in their acquisition as well as their preservation. And it is equally difficult for them to spend them on pious observances.

एवमन्यैस्तथा क्लेशैः पुरुषा द्विजसत्तमाः।।
निजाञ्जयंति वै लोकान्प्राजापत्यादिकान्क्रमात्।। २७।।

O excellent Brāhmaṇas, by undergoing these troubles and other diverses people attain to the holy region of Prajāpati.

योषिच्छुश्रूषणाद्भर्त्तुः कर्मणा मनसागिरा।।
तद्धिता शुभमाप्नोति तत्सालोक्यं यतो द्विजाः।। २८।।

A woman has only to honour her husband in act, thought and speech to reach the same region to which he is elevated and she thus accomplishes her object without any great exertion.

नातिक्लेशेन महता तानेव पुरुषो यथा।।
तृतीयं व्याहृतं तेन मया साध्विति योषितः।। २९।।

This was the meaning of my exclamation "Well done" the third time. I have thus related to you what you asked.

एतद्वः कथितं विप्रा यन्निमित्तमिहागताः।।
तत्पृच्छतः यथाकामं सव वक्ष्यामि वः स्फुटम्।। ३०।।

Now put to me in any way you please the question for which you came and I will make you a clear reply."

ऋषयस्ते ततः प्रोचुर्यत्प्रष्टव्यं महामुने।।
अस्मिन्नेव च तत्प्रश्ने यथावत्कथितं त्वया।। ३१।।

The ascetics then said to Vyāsa. "The question that we purposed to put to you has already been answered by you in your reply to our subsequent enquiry."

श्रीपराशर उवाच

ततः प्रहस्य तानाह कृष्णद्वैपायनो मुनिः।।
विस्मयोत्फुल्लनयनांस्तापसांस्तानुपागतान्।। ३२।।

Parāśara said :—Hearing this Kṛṣṇa-Dvaipāyana laughed and said to the pious sages who had come to see him whose eyes were wide open with surprise.

मयैष भवतां प्रश्नो ज्ञातो दिव्येन चक्षुषा।।
ततोहं वः प्रसंगेन साधुसाध्विति भाषितम्।। ३३।।

By virtue of my divine knowledge I perceived the question you intended to put to me and in reference to this I uttered the expressions "Well done! Well done!"

स्वल्पेन हि प्रत्यनेन धर्मस्सिध्यति वै कलो।।
नरैरात्मगुणांभोभिः क्षलिताखिलकिल्बिषैः।। ३४।।
शूद्रैश्च द्विजशुश्रूषातत्परैर्द्विजसत्तमाः।।
तथा स्त्रीभिरनाया सात्पतिशुश्रूषयैव हि।। ३५।।

In fact in the Kali age duty is performed by the mortals with very little trouble, whose sins are all washed away by the water of their individual piety—by Śūdras through the diligent service of the twice-born ones and by women through the slight effort of obedience to their husbands.

ततस्त्रितयमप्येतन्मम धन्यतरं मतम्।।
धर्मसंपादने क्लेशो द्विजातीनां कृता दिषु।। ३६।।

It is for this reason O Brāhmaṇas, that I did thrice express my admiration of their happiness; for in the Kṛta and other ages great were the toils of the regenerate to perform their duty.

भवद्भिर्यदभिप्रेतं तदेतत्कथितं मया।।
अपृष्टेनाऽपि धर्मज्ञाः किमन्यत्क्रियतां द्विजाः।। ३७।।

I did not wait for your enquiry but replied at once to the question you wanted to put. Now what do ye, conversant with virtue, wish me to tell you?

श्रीपराशर उवाच

ततस्संपूज्य ते व्यासं प्रशशंसुः पुनःपुनः।।
यथाऽगतं द्विजा जग्मुर्व्यासोक्तिकृतानिश्चयाः।। ३८।।

Parāśara said :—Thereupon the ascetics saluted and praised Vyāsa and freed by him from uncertainty departed as they came. I have also communicated to you.

भवतोऽपि महाभाग रहस्यं कथितं मया।।
अत्यंतदुष्टस्य कलेरयमेको महान्गुणः।। ३९।।

O excellent Maitreya, the secret—this one great virtue of the otherwise vicious Kali age.

यच्चाहं भवता पृष्टो जगतामुपसंहृतिम्।।
प्राकृतामंतरालां च तामप्येष वदामि ते।। ४०।।

I shall now describe to you the dissolution of the world and the aggregation of the elements.

।। इति श्रीविष्णुमहापुराणे षष्ठेंशे द्वितीयोऽध्यायः।। २।।

अथ षष्ठेंशेः तृतीयोऽध्यायः

Part VI : Section 3

श्रीपराशर उवाच

सर्वेषामेव भूतानां त्रिविधः प्रतिसञ्चरः।।
नैमित्तिकः प्राकृतिकः तथैवात्यंतिको लयः।। १।।

Parāśara said :—The dissolution of existing beings is of three kinds, incidental, elemental and absolute.

ब्राह्मो नैमित्तिकस्तेषां कल्पांते प्रतिसञ्चरः।।
आत्यंतिकस्तु मोक्षाख्यः प्राकृतो द्विपरार्द्धकः।। २।।

The incidental is that which relates to Brahmā and takes place at the end of a Kalpa : the elemental is that which occurs after two Parārdhas; the absolute is final liberation from existence.

मैत्रेय उवाच

परार्द्धसंख्यां भगवान्ममाचक्ष्व यया तु सः।।
द्विगुणी कृतया ज्ञेयः प्राकृतः प्रतिसञ्चरः।। ३।।

Maitreya said :—Tell me, O excellent preceptor, what is the enumeration of a Parārdha, the expiration of two of which is the period of elemental disslution.

श्रीपराशर उवाच

स्थानात्स्थानं दशगुणमेकस्माद्गण्यते द्विज।।
ततोष्टादशमे भागे परार्द्धमभिधीयते।। ४।।

Parāśara said :—Parārdha O Maitreya, is that number which takes place in the eighteenth place of figures enumerated according to the rule of decimal notation.

परार्द्धद्विगुणं यत्तु प्राकृतस्स लयो द्विज।।
तदाऽव्यक्तेखिलं व्यक्तं स्वहेतौ लयमेति वै।। ५।।

At the end of twice that period elemental dissolution takes place when all the discrete products of nature are withdrawn into their indiscrete source.

निमेषो मानुषो योऽसौ मात्रामात्रप्रमाणतः।।
तैः पञ्चदशभिः काष्ठा त्रिंशत्काष्ठा कला स्मृता।। ६।।

नाडिका तु प्रमाणेन सा कला दश पञ्च च।। ७।।

The shortest period of time is a Mātrā which is equal to the twinkling of the human eye; fifteen Mātrās make a Kāṣṭhā; thirty Kāṣṭhās one Kalā; fifteen Kalās one Nāḍhikā.

उन्मानेनांभसस्सा तु पलान्यर्द्ध त्रयोदश।।
मागधेन तु मानेन जलप्रस्थस्तु स स्मृतः।।
हेममाषैः कृतच्छिद्रचतुर्भिश्चतुरंगुलैः।। ८।।

A Nāḍhikā is determined by a measure of water with a vessel made of twelve Palas and a half of copper in the bottom of which there is to be a hole made with a tube of gold of the weight of four Māṣas and four inches long. According to the Māgadha measure the vessel should hold a Prastha (or sixteen Palas) of water.

नाडिकाभ्यामथ द्वाभ्यां मुहूर्त्तो द्विजसत्तम।।
अहोरात्रं मुहूर्त्तस्तु त्रिंशन्मासो दिनैस्तथा।। ९।।
मासैर्द्वादशभिर्वर्षमहोरात्रं तु तद्दिवि।।
त्रिभिर्वर्षशतैर्वर्षं षष्ट्या चैवासुरद्विषाम्।। १०।।

Two of these Nāḍis make one Muhūrta; thirty of which make one day and night. Thirty such periods constitute a month; twelve months make a year, or a day and night of the celestials; and three hundred and sixty such days, constitute a year of the celestials.

तैस्तु द्वादशसाहस्त्रैश्चतुर्युगमुदाहृतम्।।
चतुर्युगसहस्त्रं तु कथ्यते ब्रह्मणो दिनम्।। ११।।

An aggregate of four ages consists of twelve thousnad divine years; and a thousand periods of four ages complete a day of Brahmā.

स कल्पस्तत्रमनवश्चतुर्दश महामुने।।
तदंते चैव मैत्रेय ब्राह्मो नैमित्तिको लयः।। १२।।

That period is also termed a Kalpa during which fourteen Munis preside is also termed a Kalpa during which fourteen Munis preside and at the end of it takes place the incidental or Brahmā dissolution.

तस्य स्वरूपमत्युग्रं मैत्रेय गदतो मम।।
शृणुष्व प्राकृतं भूयस्तव वक्ष्याम्यहं लयम्।। १३।।

The nature of this dissolution is very dreadful; hear, I shall describe this as well as that which takes place as the elemental dissolution.

चतुर्युगसहस्त्रांते क्षीणप्राये महीतले।।
अनावृष्टिरतीवोग्रा जायते शतवार्षिकी।। १४।।
ततो यान्यल्पसाराणि तानि सत्वान्यशेषतः।।
क्षयं यांति मुनिश्रेष्ठ पार्थिवान्यनुपीडनात्।। १५।।

At the end of a thousand period of four ages the earth is for the most part exhausted. A total dearth takes place which lasts for a hundred years; and on account of the failure of food all beings become languid and exanimate and at last entirely die.

ततः सभगवान्विष्णू रुद्ररूपधरोऽव्ययः।।
क्षयाय यतते कर्त्तुमात्मस्थास्सकलाः प्रजाः।। १६।।

The eternal Viṣṇu then takes the character of Rudra the destroyer and comes down to reunite all his creatures with himself.

ततस्स भगवान्विष्णुर्भानोस्सप्तसु रश्मिषु।।
स्थितः पिबत्यशेषाणि जलानि मुनिसप्तम।। १७।।

He enters into the seven rays of the sun, drinks up all the waters of the earth and causes all moisture, whatever in living bodies or in the soil to evaporate, thus drying up the whole earth.

पीत्वांभांसि समस्तानि प्राणिभूमिगतान्यपि।।
शोषं नयति मैत्रेय समस्तं पृथिवीतलम्।। १८।।
समुद्रान्सरितः शैलनदीप्रस्त्रवणानि च।।
पातालेषु च यत्तोयं तत्सर्वं नयति क्षयम्।। १९।।

Thus fed with his intervention with profuse moisture, the seven solar rays dilate to seven suns, whose radiance glows above, below and on every side and sets the three worlds and Pātāla on fire.

ततस्तस्यानुभावेन तोयाहारोपबृंहिताः।।
त एव रश्मयस्सप्त जायंते सप्त भास्कराः।। २०।।
अधश्चोर्ध्वं च ते दीप्ता स्ततस्सप्त दिवाकराः।।
दहंत्यशेषं त्रैलोक्यं सपातालतलं द्विज।। २१।।
दह्यमानं तु तैर्दीप्तैस्त्रैलोक्यं द्विज भास्करैः।।
साद्रिनद्यर्णवाभोगं निस्त्रेहमभिजायते।। २२।।

ततो निर्दग्धवृक्षांबुत्रैलोक्यमखिलं द्विज।।
भवत्येषा च वसुधा कूर्मपृष्ठोपमाकृतिः।। २३।।

The three worlds, consumed by these suns, become rugged and deformed all over their mountains, rivers and seas; and the earth bare of verdure, and destitute of moisture alone remains resembling in appearance the back of a tortoise.

ततः कालाग्निरुद्रोऽसौ भूत्वा सर्वहरोऽनलः।।
शेषाहिश्वाससंभूतः पातालानि दहत्यथः।। २४।।

Hari, the destroyer of all things, in the form of Rudra, who is the flame of time, becomes the corching breath of the serpent Śeṣa and thereby reduces Pātāla to ashes.

पातालानि समस्तानि स दग्ध्वा ज्वलनो महान्।।
भूमिमभ्येत्य सकलं बभस्ति वसुधातलम्।। २५।।

The great fire, when it has reduces all the divisions of Pātāla to ashes, proceeds to the earth and consumes it also.

भुवर्लोकं ततस्सर्वं। स्वर्लोकं च सुदारुणः।।
.ज्वालामालामहावर्त्तस्तत्रैव परिवर्त्तते।। २६।।

A vast whirlpool of eddying flame then spreads to the region of the atmosphere and the sphere of the celestials and wraps them in ruin.

अंबरीषमिवाभाति त्रैलोक्यमखिलं तदा।।
ज्वालावर्त्तपरीवारमुपक्षीणचराचरम् ।।२७।।

The three spheres shew like a frying pan amidst the surrounding flames that prey upon all movable and stationary things.

ततस्तापपरीतास्तु लोकद्वयनिवासिनः।।
कृताधिकारा गच्छंति महर्लोकं महामुने।।२८।।

O great saint, the inhabitants of the two upper spheres, having satisfied their respective duties and being assailed by the heat, repair to Maharloka.

तस्मादपि महातापतप्ता लोकात्ततः परम्।।
गच्छंति जनलोकं ते दशावृत्या परैषिणः।।२९।।

When that becomes heated its inhabitants, who after the full period of stay, are desirous of ascending to higher regions depart for the Janaloka.

ततो दग्ध्वा जगत्सर्वं रुद्ररूपी जनार्दनः।।
मुखनिश्वासजान्मेघान्करोति मुनिसत्तम।। ३०।।

ततो गजकुलप्रख्यास्तडित्वंतोऽतिनादिनः।।
उत्तिष्ठंति तथा व्योम्नि घोरास्संवर्त्तका घनाः।। ३१।।

Having consumed the whole universe in the person of Rudra, Janārddana, breathes fourth heavy clouds, and those called Samvartta resembling huge elephants in bulk overspread the sky, roaring and darting lightnings.

केचिन्नीलोत्पलश्यामाः केचित्कुमुदसन्निभाः।।
धूम्रवर्णा घनाः केचित्केचित्पीताः पयोधराः।। ३२।।

केचिद्रासभवर्णाभा लाक्षारसानिभास्तथा।।
केचिद्वैडूर्यसंकाशा इन्द्रनीलनिभाः क्वचित्।। ३३।।

शंखकुंदनिभाश्चान्ये जात्यं जननिभाः परे।।
इंद्रगोपनिभाः केचित्ततशिशिखिनिभास्तथा।। ३४।।

मनशिशलाभाः केचिद्वै हरितालनिभाः परे।।
चाषपत्रनिभाः केचिदुत्तिष्ठंते महाघनाः।। ३५।।

केचित्पुरवराकाराः केचित्पर्वतसन्निभाः।।
कूटागारनिभाश्चान्ये केचत्स्थलनिभा घनाः।। ३६।।

Some are as white as the water-lily, some are dusky like somke; some are yellow; some are of a dun colour, like that of an ass; some like ashes sprinkled on the forehead; some are deep blue, as the *lapis lazuly;* some azure like the sapphire; some are white as the conch or the jasmine; some are black as collyrum; some are like the lady-bird; some are of fierceness of red arsenic and some are like the wing of the painted joy. Such is the colour of these massy clouds; in form some resemble towns, some mountains, some are like houses and hovels and some are like columns.

महारावा मकाकायाः पूरयंति नभःस्थलम्।।
वर्षंतस्ते महासारास्तमग्निमतिभैरवम्।।
शमयंत्यखिलं विप्र त्रैलोक्यांतरधिष्ठितम्।। ३७।।

नष्टे चाग्नौ च सततं वर्षमाणा ह्यहर्निशम्।।
प्लावयंति जगत्सर्वमंभोभिर्मुनिसत्तम।। ३८।।

धाराभिरतिमात्राभिः प्लावयित्वाऽखिलां भुवम्।।
भुवर्लोकं तथैवोर्द्ध्वं प्लावयंति हि ते द्विज।। ३९।।

Huge in size and loud in thunder they fill space. Showering down torrents of water, those clouds quench the dreadful fires which involve the three worlds and then they rain incessantly for a hundred years and deluge the whole universe.

अंधकारीकृते लोके नष्टे स्थावरजंगमे।।
वर्षंति ते महामेघा वर्षाणामधिकं शतम्।। ४०।।

Showering down in drops as large as dice these rains overspread the earth and fill the middle region and inundate the celestials sphere.

एवं भवति कल्पांते समस्तं मुनिसत्तम।।
वासुदेवस्य माहात्म्यान्नित्यस्य परमात्मनः।। ४१।।

The world is now enshrouded in darkness and all things animate and inanimate having perished, the clouds continue to pour down waters for more than a hundred years.

।। इति श्रीविष्णुमहापुराणे षष्ठेंशे तृतीयोऽध्यायः।। ३।।

अथ षष्ठेंशेः चतुर्थोऽध्यायः

Part VI : Section 4

श्रीपराशर उवाच

सप्तर्षिस्थानमाक्रम्य स्थितेंभसि महामुने।।
एकार्णवं भवत्येतत्त्रैलोक्यमखिलं ततः।। १।।

Parāśara said :—O great ascetic, the waters having reached the region of the seven Ṛṣis the whole of three worlds becomes one ocean.

मुखनिश्वासजो विष्णोर्वायुस्ताञ्जलदांस्ततः।।
नाशयन्वाति मैत्रेय वर्षाणामपरं शतम्।। २।।

The breath of Viṣṇu, thereupon, becomes a strong wind, which blows for more than a hundred years until all the clouds are dispersed.

सर्वभूतमयोऽचिंत्यो भगवान्भूतभावनः।।
अनादिरादिर्विश्वस्य पीत्वा वायुमशेषतः।। ३।।
एकार्णवे ततस्तस्मिञ्छेषशय्यागतः प्रभुः।।
ब्रह्मरूपधरश्शेते भगवानादिकृद्धरिः।। ४।।

The wind is then re-absorbed and he, of whom all beings are made, the lord by whom all things exist, he, who is inconceivable, without beginning of the universe, reposes sleeping upon Śeṣa in the midst of the ocean.

जनलोकगतैस्सिद्धैस्सनकाद्यैरभिष्टुतः।।
ब्रह्मलोकगतैश्चैव चिंत्यमानो मुमुक्षुभिः।। ५।।
आत्ममायामयीं दिव्यां योगनिद्रां समास्थितः।।
आत्मानं वासुदेवाख्यं चिंतयन्मधुसूदनः।। ६।।

The creator Hari, sleeps upon the ocean in the form of Brahmā glorified by Sanaka and the saints who had departed to the Janaloka and contemplated by the holy inhabitants of Brahmaloka, anxious for final liberation—involved in mystic slumber, the celestial personification of his own illusions and meditating on his own ineffable spirit which is called Vāsudeva.

एष नैमित्तिको नाम मैत्रेयः प्रतिसञ्चरः।।
निमित्तं तत्र यच्छेते ब्रह्मरूपधरो हरिः।। ७।।

This O Maitreya, is the dissolution called incidental, because, Hari, in the form of Brahmā, sleeps there as its incidental cause.

यदा जागर्त्ति सर्वात्मा स तदा चेष्टते जगत्।।
निमीलत्येतदखिलं मायाशय्यां गतेऽच्युते।। ८।।

When the universal spirit wakes, the world revives : when he clears his eyes all things fall upon the bed of mystic sleep.

पद्मयोनेर्दिनं यत्तु चतुर्युगसहस्त्रवत्।।
एकार्णवीकृते लोके तावती रात्रिरिष्यते।। ९।।

In the same manner a thousand great eyes comprise a day of Brahmā, so his night consists of the same period : during which the world is submerged by a vast ocean.

ततः प्रबुद्धो रात्र्यंते पुनस्सृष्टिं करोत्यजः।।
ब्रह्मस्वरूपधृग्विष्णुर्यथा ते कथितं पुरा।। १०।।

Awaking at the end of his night, the unborn Viṣṇu, in the character of Brahmā, creates the universe anew in the manner formerly described unto you.

इत्येष कल्पसंहारोऽवांतरप्रलयो द्विज।।
नैमित्तिकस्ते कथितः प्राकृतः श्रृण्वतः परम्।। ११।।

I have thus related to you the intermediate dissolution of the world taking place at the end of every Kalpa.

अनावृष्ट्यादिसंपर्कात्कृते संक्षालने मुने।।
समस्तेष्वेव लोकेषु पातालेष्वखिलेषु च।। १२।।

महदादेर्विकारस्य विशेषांतस्य संक्षये।।
कृष्णेच्छाकारिते तस्मिन्प्रवृत्ते प्रतिसञ्चरे।। १३।।

I will now, O Maitreya, describe to you elemental dissolution. When by dearth and fire all the worlds and Pātālas are dried up and the modification of Mahat and other products of nature are by the will of Kṛṣṇa destroyed the progress of elemental dissolution is begun.

आपो ग्रसंति वै पूर्वं भूमेर्गंधात्मकं गुणम्।।
आत्तगंधा ततो भूमिः प्रलयत्वाय कल्पते।। १४।।

At first the water swallow up the property of earth which is the rudiment of smell; and earth, deprived of its property, proceeds to destruction.

प्रणष्टे गंधतन्मात्रे भवत्युर्वी जलात्मिका।।
आपस्तदा प्रवृद्धास्तु वेगवत्यो महास्वानाः।। १५।।

Devoid of the rudiment of odour the earth becomes identical with water. The water then being much increased roaring and rushing along fill up all space whether agitated or still.

सर्वमापूरयंतीदं तिष्ठंति विचरंति च।।
सलिलेनोर्मिमालेन आलोकांतात्समंततः।। १६।।

अपामपि गुणो यस्तु ज्योतिषा पीयते तु सः।।
नश्यंत्यापस्ततस्ताश्च रसतन्मात्रसंक्षयात्।। १७।।

When the universe is thus pervaded by the waves of the watery element its rudimental flavour is licked up by the element of fire and on account of the destruction of these rudimentals the waters themselves are destroyed.

ततश्चापो हृतरसा ज्योतिषं प्राप्नुवंति वै।।
अग्नावस्थे तु सलिले तेजसा सर्वतो वृते।। १८।।

स चाग्निः सर्वतो व्याप्य चादत्ते तज्जलं तथा।।
सर्वमापूर्यतेर्चिर्भिस्तदा जगदिदं शनैः।। १९।।

Devoid of the essential element of flavour they become indentical with fire and the universe is therefore entirely filled with flame which drinks up the water on every side and gradually overspreads the whole of the world.

अर्चिर्भिस्संवृते तस्मिंस्तिर्यगूर्ध्वमधस्तदा।।
ज्योतिषोऽपि परं रूपं वायुरत्ति प्रभाकरम्।। २०।।

प्रलीने च ततस्तस्मिन्वायुभूतेऽखिलात्मनि।।
प्रनष्टे रूपतन्मात्रे हृतरूपो विभावसुः।। २१।।

While space is enveloped in flame above, below and all around the element of the wind siezes upon the rudimental property or form which is the cause of light, and that being withdrawn, all becomes of the nature of air.

प्रशाम्यति तदाज्योतिर्वायुर्दोधूयते महान्।।
निरा लोके तथा लोके वाय्ववस्थे च तेजसि।। २२।।

The rudiment of form being destroyed and fire deprived of its rudiment, air extinguishes fire and spreads resistlessly over space which is deprived of light when fire mages into air.

ततस्तु भूलमासाद्य वायुस्संभवमात्मनः।।
ऊर्ध्वं चाधश्च तिर्यक्च दोधवीति दिशो दश।। २३।।

वायोरपि गुणं स्पर्शमाकाशो ग्रसते ततः।।
प्रशाम्यति ततो वायुः खं तु तिष्ठत्यनावृतम्।। २४।।

अरूपरसमस्पर्शमगंधं न च मूर्त्तिमत्।।
सर्वमापूरयच्चैव सुमहत्तत्प्रकाशते।। २५।।

Air then accompanied by sound which is the source of ether, extends everywhere throughout the ten regions of space until ether seizes upon contact, its rudimental property; by the loss of which air is destroyed and ether remains unchanged : devoid of form, flavour, touch and smell, it exists unembodied and vast and pervades the whole of space.

परिमंडलं च सुषिरमाकाशं शब्दलक्षणम्।।
शब्दमात्रं तदाकाशं सर्वमावृत्य तिष्ठति।। २६।।

Ether, whose characteristic property and rudiment is sound exists alone occupying all the vacuity of space.

ततश्शब्दगुणं तस्य भूतादिर्ग्रसते पुनः।।
भूतेंद्रियेषु युगपद्भूतादौ संस्थितेषु वै।।
अभिमानात्मको ह्येष भूतादिस्तामसस्स्मृतः।। २७।।

भूतांदि ग्रसते चापि महान्वै बुद्धिलक्षणः।। २८।।

उर्वी महांश्च जगतः प्रांतेंतर्बाह्यतस्तथा।। २९।।

But then the radical element egotism devours sound and all the elements and faculties are at once merged into their original. This primary element is conscientiousness combined with the property of darkness and is itself swallowed up by Mahat whose characteristic property is intelligence; and earth and Mahat are the inner and outer boundaries of the universe.

एवं सप्त महाबुद्धे क्रमात्प्रकृतयस्स्मृताः।।
प्रत्याहारे तु तास्सर्वाः प्रविशंति परस्परम्।। ३०।।

येनेदमावृतं सर्वमंडमप्सु प्रलीयते।।
सप्तद्वीपसमुद्रांतं सप्लोकं सपर्वतम्।। ३१।।

उदकावरणं यत्तु ज्योतिषा पीयते तु तम्।।
ज्योतिर्वायौ लयं याति यात्याकाशे समीरणः।। ३२।।

आकाशं चैव भूतादिर्ग्रसते तं तथा महान्।।
महांतमेभिस्सहितं प्रकृतिर्ग्रसते द्विज।। ३३।।

In this manner, as in the creation were the seven forms of nature (Prakṛti) reckoned from Mahat to earth; so at the time of elemental dissolution these seven successively re-enter into each other. The egg of Brahmā, is dissolved in the waters that surround it, with its seven zones, seven oceans, seven regions, and their mountains. The investure of water is drunk up by fire : the stratum of fire is absorbed by that of air : air blends itself with ether; the primary element of egotism devours the ether and is itself taken up by intellect, which, along with all those, is seized upon by nature.

गुणसाम्यमनुद्रिक्तमन्यूनं च महामुने।।
प्रोच्यते प्रकृतिर्हेतुः प्रधानं कारणं परम्।। ३४।।

Equilibrium of the three properties, without excess or deficiency, is called nature (Prakṛti), origin (Hetu), the chief Principle (Pradhāna) cause (Kāraṇa) supreme (Param).

इत्येषा प्रकृतिस्सर्वा व्यक्ताव्यक्तस्वरूपिणी।।
व्यक्तस्वरूपमव्यक्ते तस्मान्मैत्रेय लीयते।। ३५।।

This Prakṛti is essentially the same, whether discrete or indiscrete; only that which is discrete finally is lost or absorbed in the indiscrete.

एकश्शुद्धोऽक्षरो नित्यस्सर्वव्यापी तथा पुमान्।।
सोप्यंशस्सर्वभूतस्य मैत्रेय परमात्मनः।। ३६।।

Spirit also which is one, pure, imperishable, eternal, all-pervading is a portion of that supreme spirit which is all things.

न संति यत्र सर्वेशे नामजात्यादिकल्पनाः।।
सत्तमात्रात्मक ज्ञय ज्ञानात्मन्यात्मनः परे।। ३७।।

तद्ब्रह्म परमं धाम परमात्मा स चेश्वरः।।
स विष्णुस्सर्वमेवेदं यतो नावर्त्तते यतिः।। ३८।।

That spirit which is other than embodied spirit, in which there are no attributes of name, species or the like—which is one with all wisdom and is to be understood as sole existence, that is Brahmā, infinite glory, supreme spirit, supreme power, Viṣṇu, all that is from whence the perfect sage returns no more.

प्रकृतिर्या मयाख्याता व्यक्ताव्यक्तस्वरूपिणी।।
पुरुषश्चाप्युभावेतौ लीयेते परमात्मनि।। ३९।।

परमात्मा च सर्वेषामाधारः परमेश्वरः।।
विष्णुनामा स वेदेषु वेदांतेषु च गीयते।। ४०।।

Prakṛti, which I have described to you as being essentially both discrete and indiscrete and spirit both resolve into supreme spirit, supreme spirit is the upholder of all things and the ruler of all things and is glorified in the Vedas and in the Vedānta by the name of Viṣṇu.

प्रवृत्तं च निवृत्तं च द्विविधं कर्म वैदिकम्।।
ताभ्यामुभाभ्यां पुरुषैस्सर्वमूर्त्तिस्स इज्यते।। ४१।।

Works as sanctioned by the Vedas are of two kinds, active and quiescent; by both of which the universal person is worshipped by mankind.

ऋग्यजुस्सामभिर्मार्गैः प्रवृत्तैरिज्यते ह्यसौ।
यज्ञेश्वरो यज्ञपुमान्पुरुषैः पुरुषोत्तमः।। ४२।।

He, the lord of sacrifice, the male of sacrifice, the most excellent Puruṣa, is worshipped by men in the active mode, by rites enjoined in the Ṛk, Yajur and Sāma Vedas.

ज्ञानात्मा ज्ञानयोगेन ज्ञानमूर्त्तिः स चेज्यते।।
निवृत्ते योगिभिर्मार्गे विष्णुर्मुक्तिफलप्रदः।। ४३।।

The soul of wisdom, the person of wisdom, Viṣṇu, the giver of emancipation is worshipped by the sages in the quiescent form through meditative devotion.

ह्रस्वदीर्घप्लुतैर्यत्तु किंचिद्वस्त्वभिधीयते।।
यच्च वाचामविषयं तत्सर्वं विष्णुरव्ययः।। ४४।।

The exhaustless Viṣṇu is whatever thing that is designated by long, short or prolated syllables or that which is without a name.

व्यक्तस्स एव चाव्यक्तस्स एव पुरुषोत्तमः।।
परमात्मा च विश्वात्मा विश्वरूपधरो हरिः।। ४५।।

He is that which is dissolute or that which is indiscrete : he is exhaustless spirit, supreme spirit, universal spirit, Hari, the assumer of universal forms.

व्यक्ताव्यक्तात्मिका तस्मिन्प्रकृतिस्संप्रलीयते।।
पुरुषश्चापि मैत्रेय व्यापिन्यव्याहतात्मनि।। ४६।।

Nature, discrete or indiscrete is absorbed unto him, and spirit also merges into the all diffusive and unobstructed spirit.

द्विपरार्द्धात्मकः कालः कथितो यो मया तव।।
तदहस्तस्य मैत्रेय विषोरीशस्य कथ्यते।। ४७।।

व्यक्ते च प्रकृतौ लीने प्रकृत्यां पुरुषे तथा।।
तत्र स्थिते निशा चास्य तत्प्रमाणा महामुने।। ४८।।

The period of two Parārdhas, as I have related to you, O Maitreya, constitutes a day of that powerful Viṣṇu, and whilst the products of nature are merged into this source, nature into spirit and that into the supreme, that period is called his night and is of equal duration with his day.

नैवाहस्तस्य न निशा नित्यस्य परमात्मनः।।
उपचारस्तथाप्येष तस्येशस्य द्विजोच्यते।। ४९।।

But in reality, to that supreme spirit there is neither day nor night and these distinctions are only figuratively applied to the Almighty.

इत्येष तव मैत्रेय कथितः प्राकृतो लयः।।
आत्यंतिकमथो ब्रह्मन्निबोध प्रतिसञ्चरम्।। ५०।।

I have thus explained to you the nature of elemental dissolution and will now explain to you which is final.

।। इति श्रीविष्णुमहापुराणे षष्ठेंशे चतुर्थोऽध्यायः।।४।।

अथ षष्ठेंशेः पञ्चमोऽध्यायः

Part VI Section 5

श्रीपराशर उवाच

आध्यात्मिकादि मैत्रेय ज्ञात्वा तापत्रयं बुधः।।
उत्पन्नज्ञानवैराग्यः प्राप्नोत्यात्यंतिकं लयम्।। १।।

Parāśara said :—O Maitreya, having investigated three kinds of worldly pain and having acquired true wisdom and detachment from objects the wise man obtains final liberation.

आध्यात्मिकोपि द्विविधश्शारीरो मानसस्तथा।।
शारीरो बहुभिर्भेदैर्भिद्यते श्रूयतां च सः।। २।।

The first of the three pains, or Ādhyātmika is of two kinds—physical and mental. Bodily pain, as you shall hear, is of many sorts.

शिरोरोगप्रतिश्यायज्वरशूलभगंदरैः ।।
गुल्मार्शःश्वयथुश्वासच्छर्द्यादिभिरनेकधा।। ३।।

तथाक्षिरोगातीसारकुष्ठांगामयसंज्ञितैः ।।
भिद्यते देहजस्तापो मानसं श्रोतुमर्हसि ।। ४ ।।

Affections of the head, catarrh fever, cholic, fistula, spleen, hemorhoids, intumescence, sickness, opthalmia, dysentry, leprosy, and many other diseases constitute physical affliction.

कामक्रोधभयद्वेषलोभमोहविषादजः ।।
शोकासूयावमानेर्ष्यामात्सर्यादिमयस्तथा ।। ५ ।।

Mental pains are love, anger, fear, hate, covetousness, stupefaction, despair, sorrow, malice, disdain, jealousy, envy and many other passions that are created in the mind.

मानसोऽपि द्विजश्रेष्ठ तापो भवति नैकधा ।।
इत्येवमादिभिर्भेदैस्तापो ह्याध्यात्मिकः स्मृतः ।। ६ ।।

These and diverse other afflictions, mental or physical, are comprised under the class of worldly sufferings which is called Ādhyātmika.

मृगपक्षिमनुष्याद्यैः पिशाचोरगराक्षसैः ।।
सरीसृपाद्यैश्च नृणां जायते चाधिभौतिकः ।। ७ ।।

शीतवातोष्णवर्षांबुवैद्युतादिसमुद्भवः ।।
तापो द्विजवरश्रेष्ठैः कथ्यते चाधिदैविकः ।। ८ ।।

The pain Ādhibhautika, O excellent Brāhmaṇa, is every kind of evil that is inflicted upon men by beasts, birds, men, goblins snakes, fiends, or reptiles and the pain that is called Ādhidaivika or suprehuman is the work of cold, heat, wind, rain, lightning and other phenomena.

गर्भजन्मजराज्ञानमृत्युनारकजं तथा ।।
दुःखं सहस्त्रशो भेदैर्भिद्यते मुनिसत्तम् ।। ९ ।।

Affliction, O Maitreya, is multiplied in thousands of shapes in the progress of conception, birth, decay, disease, death and hell.

सुकुमारतनुर्गर्भे जंतुर्बहुमलावृते ।।
उल्वसंवेष्टितो भुग्नपृष्ठग्रीवास्थिसंहतिः ।। १० ।।

अत्यम्लकटुतीक्ष्णोष्णलवणैर्मातृभोजनैः ।।
अत्यंततापैरत्यर्थं वर्द्धमानातिवेदनः ।। ११ ।।

प्रसारणाकुञ्चनादौ नांगानां प्रभुरात्मनः ।।
शकृन्मूत्रमहापंकशायी सर्वत्र पीडितः ।। १२ ।।

निरुच्छ्वास सचैतन्यस्स्मरञ्जन्मशतान्यथ ।।
आस्ते गर्भेऽतिदुःखेन निजकर्मनिबंधनः ।। १३ ।।

The tender animal exists in the embryo surrounded by abundant filth, floating in water and distorted in its back, neck and bones; enduring severe pain even in the course of its development and disordered by the acid, bitter, pungent and saline articles of its mother's food; incapable of extending or contracting its limbs, reposing amidst slime of ordure and urine; every way incommoned with conciousness and calling to memory many hundred previous births. Thus exists the embryo in profound affliction bound to the world by its former works.

जायमानः पुरीषासृङ्मूत्रशुक्राविलाननः ।।
प्राजापत्येन वातेन पीड्यमानास्थिबंधनः ।। १४ ।।

अधोमुखो वै क्रियते प्रबलैस्सूतिमारुतैः ।।
क्लेशान्निष्क्रांतिमाप्नोति जठरान्मातुरातुरः ।। १५ ।।

मूर्च्छामवाप्य महतीं संस्पृष्टो बाह्यवायुना ।।
विज्ञानभ्रंशमाप्नोति जातश्च मुनिसत्तम ।। १६ ।।

When the child is about to be born, its face is besmeared by excrement, urine, blood, mucus, and semen; its attachment to the uterus is ruptured by the Prajāpati wind : it is turned head downwards and violently expelled from the womb by the powerful and painful winds of parturition; and the infant, losing for a time all sensation when brought in contact with the external air, is immediately deprived of its intellectual knowledge.

कंटकैरिव तुन्नांगः क्रकचैरिव दारितः ।।
पूतिव्रणान्निपतितो धरण्यां क्रिमिको यथा ।। १७ ।।

Then born the child is tortured in every limb, as if pierced with thorns or cut to pieces with a saw, and falls from its fetid lodgement as from a sore, like a crawling thing upon the earth.

कंडूयनेऽपि चाशक्तः परिवर्त्तेप्यनीश्वरः ।।
स्त्रानपानादिकाहारमप्याप्नोति परेच्छया ।। १८ ।।

Unable to feel itself, unable to turn itself, it is dependent on the will of others for being bathed and nourished.

अशुचिप्रस्तरे सुप्त कीटदंशादिभिस्तथा ।।
भक्ष्यमाणोऽपि नैवैषां समर्थो विनिवारणे ।। १९ ।।

Laid upon a dirty bed, it is bitten by insects and mosquitoes and has not power to drive them away.

जन्मदुःखान्यनेकानि जन्मनोनंतराणि च ।।
बालभावे यदाप्नोति ह्याधिभौतादिकानि च ।। २० ।।

अज्ञानतमसाच्छन्नो मूढांतःकरणो नरः ।।
न जानाति कुतः कोहं क्वाहं गंता किमात्मनः ।। २१ ।।

केन बंधेन बद्धोहं कारणं किमकारणम् ।।
किं कार्यं किमकार्यं वा किं वाच्यं किं च नोच्यते ।। २२ ।।

को धर्मः कश्च वाऽधर्मः कस्मिन्वर्त्तेऽथ वा कथम् ।।
किं कर्त्तव्यमकर्त्तव्यं किं वा किंगुणदोषवत् ।। २३ ।।

Many are the pangs attending birth and many are those which succeed to birth; and many are the afflictions that are inflicted by elemental and superhuman powers in the state of childhood covered by the gloom of ignorance; and internally bewildered man knows not whence he is, who he is, whither he goeth nor what is his nature; by what bonds he is bound; what is cause and what is not cause; what is to be done and what is to be left undone; what is to be said and what is to be kept silent, what is righteousness and what is iniquity; in what it consists or how; what is right, what is wrong; what is virtue, what is vice.

एवं पशुसमैर्मूढैरज्ञानप्रभवं महत् ।।
अवाप्यते नरैर्दुःखं शिश्नोदरपरायणैः ।। २४ ।।

Thus man, like a brute beast addicted only to animal gratification, suffers the pain that ignorance brings about.

अज्ञानं तामसो भावः कार्यारंभप्रवृत्तयः ।।
अज्ञानिनां प्रवर्त्तंते कर्मलोपास्ततो द्विज ।। २५ ।।

नरकं कर्मणां लोपात्फलमाहुर्मनीषिणः ।।
तस्मादज्ञानिनां दुःखमिह चामुत्र चोत्तमम् ।। २६ ।।

Ignorance, darkness, inactivity influence those devoid of knowledge so that pious works are neglected; but hell is the consequence of neglect of religious acts, according to the great sages, and the ignorant therefore suffer affliction both in this world and in the next.

जराजर्जरदेहश्च शिथिलावयवः पुमान् ।।
विचलच्छीर्णदशनो वलिस्नायुशिरावृतः ।। २७ ।।

दूरप्रनष्टनयनो व्योमांतर्गततारकः ।।
नासाविवरनिर्यातलोमपुञ्जश्चलद्वपुः ।। २८ ।।

प्रकटीभूतसर्वास्थिर्नतपृष्ठास्थिसंहतिः ।।
उत्सन्नजठराग्नित्वादल्पाहारोऽल्पचेष्टितः ।। २९ ।।

कृच्छ्राच्चंक्रमणोत्थानशयनासनचेष्टितः ।।
मंदीभवच्छ्रोत्रनेत्रस्स्रवल्लालाविलाननः ।। ३० ।।

अनायत्तैस्समस्तैश्च करणैर्मरणोन्मुखः ।।
तत्क्षणेप्यनुभूतानामस्मर्ताऽखिलवस्तुनाम् ।। ३१ ।।

When old age comes in, the body is infirm, the limbs are relaxed; the face is emaciate and shrivelled; its skin is wrinkled and scantily covers the veins and sinews; the eyes discern not a far off, and the pupil gazes on vacuity; the nostrils are stuffed with hair; the trunk trembles as it moves; the bones appear beneath the surface; the back is bowed and the joints are bent; the digestive fire is extinct and there is little appetite and little vigour; walking, rising sitting, sleeping are all painful efforts; the ear is dull; the eye is dim; the mouth is disgusting with dribbling saliva; the senses no longer are obedient to the will; and as death approaches, the things that are perceived even are immediately forgotten.

सकृदुच्चारिते वाक्ये समुद्भूत महाश्रमः ।।
श्वासकाशसमुद्भतमहायासप्रजागरः ।। ३२ ।।

The utterance of a single sentence is fatiguing and wakefulness is perpetuated by difficult breathing, coughing and painful exhaustion.

अन्येनोत्थाप्यतेऽन्येन तथा संवेश्यते जरी ।।
भृत्यात्मपुत्रदारणामवमानास्पदी कृतः ।। ३३ ।।

The old man is lifted up by some body else; he is an object of contempt to his servants, his children and his wife.

प्रक्षीणाखिलशौचश्च विहाराहारसस्पृहः।।
हास्यः परिजनस्यापि निर्विण्णाशेषबांधवः।। ३४।।

अनुभूतमिवान्यस्मिञ्जन्मन्यात्म विचेष्टितम्।।
संस्मरन्यौवने दीर्घं निश्वसत्यभितापितः।। ३५।।

Incapable of cleanliness, of amusement, or food, or desire, he is laughed at by his dependents, and disregarded by his kin; and dwelling on the exploits of his youth, as on the actions of a past life, he sighs deeply and is sorely distressed.

एवमादीनि दुःखानि जरायामनुभूय वै।।
मरणे यानि दुःखानि प्राप्नोति शृणु तान्यपि।। ३६।।

Such are some of the pains to which old age is doomed. I will now describe to you the agonies of death.

श्लथद्ग्रवांघ्रिहस्तोऽथ व्याप्तो वेपथुना भृशम्।।
मुहुर्ग्लानिः परवशो मुहुर्ज्ञानलवान्वितः।। ३७।।

हिरण्यधान्यतनय भार्याभृत्यगृहादिषु।।
एते कथं भविष्यंतीत्यतीव ममताकुलः।। ३८।।

मर्मभिद्भिर्भहारोगैः क्रकचैरिव दारुणैः।।
शरैरिवांतकस्योग्रैश्छिद्यमानासुबंधनः।। ३९।।

परिवर्त्तितताराक्षो हस्तपादं मुहुः क्षिपन्।।
संशुष्यमाणताल्वोष्ठपुटो घुरघुरायते।। ४०।।

निरुद्धकंठो दोषौघैरुदानश्वासपीडितः।।
तापेन महता व्याप्तस्तृषा चार्त्तस्तथा क्षुधा।। ४१।।

क्लेशादुत्क्रांतिमाप्नोति यमकिंकरपीडितः।।
ततश्च यातनादेहं क्लेशेन प्रतिपद्यते।। ४२।।

The neck droops, the feet and hands are relaxed; the man is repeatedly exhausted, subdued and visited with interrupted knowledge; the principle of selfishness afflicts him and he thinks what will become of my wealth, my lands, my children, my wife, my servants, my house? The joints of his limbs are tortured with servere pains as if cut by a saw or as if they were pierced by the sharp arrows of the destroyer; he rolls his eyes and tosses about his hands and feet; his lips and palate are prached and dry and his throat obstructed by foul humours and deranged vital airs, emits a rattling sound; he is afflicted with burning heat, thirst and hunger : and he at last passes away tortured by the servants of the judge of the dead, to undergo a renewal of his sufferings in another body.

एतान्यन्यानि चोग्राणि दुःखानि मरणे नृणाम्।।
शृणुष्व नरके यानि प्राप्यंते पुरुषैर्मृतैः।। ४३।।

These are the afflictions to which a man is doomed when he dies. I will now describe to you the tortures which they suffer in hell.

याम्यकिंकरपाशादिग्रहणं दंडताडनम्।।
यमस्य दर्शनं चोग्रमुग्रमार्गविलोकनम्।। ४४।।

Men are bound, when they die, by the servants of the king of Tartarus, with chords, and beaten with their sticks and have then to encounter the fierce aspect of Yama and the horrors of their terrible route.

करंभवालुकावह्नियंत्रशस्त्रासिभीषणे।।
प्रत्येकं नरके याश्च यातना द्विज दुःसहाः।। ४५।।

क्रकचैः पाट्यमानानां मूषायां चापि दह्यताम्।।
कुठारैः कृत्यमानानां भूमौ चापि निखन्यताम्।। ४६।।

शूलेष्वारोप्यमाणानां व्याघ्रवक्त्रे प्रवेश्यताम्।।
गृध्रैस्संभक्ष्यमाणानां द्वीपिभिश्चोपभुज्यताम्।। ४७।।

क्वाथ्यतां तैलमध्ये च क्लिद्यतां क्षारकर्दमे।।
उच्चान्निपात्यमानानां क्षिप्यतां क्षेपयंत्रकैः।। ४८।।

In the different hells there are various intolerable tortures with burning sand, fire, machines, and weapons; some are severed with saws, some roasted in forges, some are chopped with axes, some buried in the ground, some are mounted on stakes, some cast to wild beasts to be devoured, some are gnawed by the vultures, some torn by tigers, some are boiled in oil, some rolled in caustic slime, some are precipitated from great heights, some are tossed upwards by engines.

नरके यानि दुःखानि पापहेतूद्भवानि वै।।
प्राप्यंते नारकैर्विप्र तेषां संख्या न विद्यते।। ४९।।

The number of punishments inflicted in hell, which are the consequences of sin, is infinite.

न केवलं द्विजश्रेष्ठ नरके दुःखपद्धतिः ।।
स्वर्गेपि पातभीतस्य क्षयिष्णोर्नास्ति निर्वृतिः ।।५०।।

पुनश्च गर्भे भवति जायते च पुनः पुनः ।।
गर्भे विलीयते भूया जायमानोऽस्तमेति वै ।।५१।।

जातमात्रश्च म्रियते बालभावेऽथ यौवने ।।
मध्यमं वा वयः प्राप्य वार्द्धके वाथ वा मृतिः ।।५२।।

But not in hell alone do the souls of the deceased undergo pain : there is no cessation even in heaven for its temporary inhabitant is even tormented with the prospect of descending to earth again. He is again liable to conception and to birth; he is merged again into the embryo and repairs to it when about to be born; then he dies, as soon as born, or in infancy, or in youth, or in manhood or in old age. Death sooner or later is inevitable.

यावज्जीवति तावच्च दुःखैर्नानाविधैः प्लुतः ।।
तं तु कारणपक्ष्मौघैरास्ते कार्पासबीजवत् ।। ५३।।

As long as he lives he is immersed in manifold afflictions, like the seed of the cotton amidst the down that is to be spun into thread.

द्रव्यनाशे तथोत्पत्तौ पालने च सदा नृणाम् ।।
भवंत्यनेकदुःखानि तथैवेष्टविपत्तिषु ।।५४।।

In acquiring, losing, and preserving wealth there are many griefs; and so there are in the misfortunes of our friends.

यद्यत्प्रीतिकरं पुंसां वस्तु मैत्रेय जायते ।।
तदेव दुःखवृक्षस्य बीजत्वमुपगच्छति ।। ५५।।

Whatever is produced that is most acceptable to man; that, Maitreya, becomes a seed whence springs the tree of sorrow.

कलत्रपुत्रमित्रार्थगृहक्षेत्रधनादिकैः ।।
क्रियते न तथा भूरि सुखं पुंसां यथा सुखम् ।।५६।।

Wife, children, servants, houses, lands, riches, contribute much more to the misery than to the happiness of mankind.

इति संसारदुःखार्कतापतापितचेतसाम् ।।
विमुक्तिपादपच्छायामृते कुत्र सुखं नृणाम् ।। ५७।।

Where could man, scorched by fires of the sun of this world, look for felicity, were it not for the shade afforded by the tree of emancipation?

तदस्य त्रिविधस्याऽपि दुःखजातस्य वै मम ।।
गर्भजन्मजराद्येषु स्थानेषु प्रभविष्यतः ।। ५८।।

निरस्तातिशयाह्लादसुखभावैकलक्षणा ।।
भेषजं भगवत्प्राप्तिरेकांतात्यंतिकी मता ।। ५९।।

Attainment of the divine being is considered by the wise as the remedy of the three-fold class of ills that beset the different stages of life, conception, ,birth and decay, as characterised by that only happiness which effaces all other kinds of felicity however abundant, and as being absolute and final.

तस्मात्तत्प्राप्तये यत्नः कर्त्तव्यः पंडितैर्नरैः ।।
तत्प्राप्तिहेतुर्ज्ञानं च कर्म चोक्तं महामुने ।। ६०।।

It should therefore be the assiduous endeavour of wise men to attain unto god. The means of such attainment are said, great Muni, to be knowledge and works.

आगमोत्थं विवेकाच्च द्विधा ज्ञानं तदुच्यते ।।
शब्दब्रह्मागममयं परं ब्रह्म विवेकजम् ।। ६१।।

Knowledge is of two kinds, that which is derived from scripture, and that which is derived from reflection. Brahmā that is the word is composed of scripture.

अंधं तम इवाज्ञानं दीपवच्चेंद्रियोद्भवम् ।।
यथा सूर्यस्तथा ज्ञानं यद्विप्रर्षे विवेकजम् ।। ६२।।

Brahmā that is supreme is produced of reflection. Ignorance is utter darkness, in which knowledge, obtained through any sense, shines like a lamp; but the knowledge that is derived from reflection breaks upon the obscurity.

मनुरप्याह वेदार्थं स्मृत्वा यन्मुनिसत्तम ।।
तदेतच्छ्रूयतामत्र संबंधे गदतो मम ।। ६३।।

What has been said by Manu, when appealing to the meaning of the Vedas with respect to this subject. I will repeat to you.

द्वे ब्रह्मणी वेदितव्ये शब्दब्रह्म परं च यत् ।।
शब्दब्रह्मणि निष्णातः परं ब्रह्माधिगच्छति ।। ६४।।

There are two forms of spirit or god, the

spirit, which is word, and spirit, which is supreme. He who is throughly imbued with the word of god obtains supreme spirit.

द्वे वै विद्ये वेदितव्ये इति चाथर्वणी श्रुतिः।।
परया त्वक्षरप्राप्तिर्ऋग्वेदादिमयापरा।। ६५।।

The Atharva Veda also states that there are two kinds of knowledge; by the one, which is the supreme, god is attained : the other is that which consists of the Ṛk and other Vedas.

यत्तदव्यक्तमजरमचिंत्यमजमव्ययम्।।
अनिर्देश्यमरूपं च पाणिपादाद्यसंयुतम्। ६६।।

विभु सर्वगतं नित्यं भूतयोनिरकारणम्।।
व्याप्त व्याप्तं यतः सर्वं यद्वै पश्यंति सूरयः।। ६७।।

तद्ब्रह्म तत्परं धाम तद्ध्येयं मोक्षकांक्षिभिः।।
श्रुतिवाक्योदितं सूक्ष्मं तद्विष्णोः परमं पदम्।। ६८।।

That which is imperceptible, undecaying, inconceivable, unborn, inexhaustible, indescribable; which has neither form, nor hands nor feet; which is almighty, omnipresent, eternal; the casue of all things, and without cause, permeating all, itself unpenetrated, and from which all things proceed, that is the object which the wise behold, that is Brahmā, that is the supreme state, that is the thing spoken of by the Vedas, the infinitely subtle, supreme condition of Viṣṇu.

तदेव भगवद्वाच्यं स्वरूपं परमात्मनः।।
वाचको भगवच्छब्दस्तस्याद्यस्याक्षयात्मनः।। ६९।।

एवं निगदितार्थस्य तत्तत्वं तस्य तत्त्वतः।।
ज्ञायते येन तज्ज्ञानं परमन्यत्त्रयीमयम्।। ७०।।

That essence of the supreme is defined by the term Bhāgavat : the word Bhāgavat is the denomination of that primeval and eternal God : and he who fully understands the meaning of that expression, is possessed of holy wisdom, the sum and substance of the three Vedas.

अशब्दगोचरस्यापि तस्य वै ब्रह्मणो द्विज।।
पूजायां भगवच्छब्दः क्रियते ह्युपचारतः।। ७१।।

शुद्धे महाविभूत्याख्ये परे ब्रह्मणि शब्दिते।।
मैत्रेय भगवच्छब्दस्सर्वकारणकारणे।। ७२।।

The word Bhāgavat is a convenient form to be used in the adoration of that supreme being, to whom no term is applicable; and therefore Bhāgavat expresses that supreme spirit which is individual, almighty, and the cause of causes of all things.

संभर्त्तेति तथा भर्त्ता भकारोर्थद्वयान्वितः।।
नेता गमयता स्त्रष्टा गकारार्थस्तथा मुने।। ७३।।

The letter *Bh* implies the cherisher and supporter of the universe. By *ga* is understood the leader impeller, or creator.

ऐश्वर्यस्य समग्रस्य वीर्यस्य यशसश्श्रियः।।
ज्ञानवैराग्ययोश्चैव षण्णां भग इतीरणा।। ७४।।

The dissyllable *Bhaga* indicate the six properties, dominion, might, glory, splendour, wisdom, and dispassion.

वसंति तत्र भूतानि भूतात्मन्यखिलात्मनि।।
स च भूतेष्वशेषेषु वकारार्थस्ततोऽव्ययः।। ७५।।

The puport of the letter *va* is that elemental spirit in which all beings exist, and which exists in all beings.

एवमेष महाञ्छब्दो मैत्रेय भगवानिति।।
परमब्रह्मभूतस्य वासुदेवस्य नान्यगः।। ७६।।

And thus this Great word Bhagavān is the name of Vāsudeva, who is one with the Supreme Brahmā and of no one else.

तत्र पूज्यपदार्थोक्तिपरिभाषासमन्वितः।।
शब्दोयं नोपचारेण त्वन्यत्र ह्युपचारतः।। ७७।।

This word therefore, which is the general denomination of a adorable object, is not used in reference to the supreme in a general but a special signification.

उत्पत्तिं प्रलयं चैव भूतानामागतिं गतिम्।।
वेत्ति विद्यामविद्यां च स वाच्यो भगवानिति।। ७८।।

ज्ञानशक्तिबलैश्वयवीर्यतेजांस्यशेषतः।।
भगवच्छब्दवाच्यानि विना हेयैर्गुणादिभिः।। ७९।।

When applied to any other thing or person it is used in its customary or general import. In latter case it may purport one who knows the origin and end and revolutions of being and what is wisdom and what ignorance. In the former it denotes wisdom, energy, power, dominion, might, glory, without end and without defect.

सर्वाणि तत्र भूतानि वसंति परमात्मनि।।
भूतेषु च स सर्वात्मा वासुदेवस्ततः स्मृतः।। ८०।।
खांडिक्यजनकायाह पृष्टः केशिध्वजः पुरा।।
नामव्याख्यामनंतस्य वासुदेवस्य तत्त्वतः।। ८१।।

The term Vāsudeva means that all beings abide in that supreme spirit and that he abides in all beings as was formerly explained by Keśīdhvaja to Khāṇḍikya called Janaka when he enquired of him an explanation of the name of the immortal Vāsudeva.

भूतेषु वसते सोंऽतर्वसंत्यत्र च तानि यत्।।
धाता विधाता जगतां वासुदेवस्ततः प्रभुः।। ८२।।

He said "He dwelleth internally in all beings and all things dwell in him; and thence the lord Vāsudeva is the creator and preserver of the world.

स सर्वभूतप्रकृतिं विकारान्गुणादिदोषांश्च मुने व्यतीतः।।
अतीतसर्वावरणोखिलात्मा तेनास्तृतं यद्भुवनांतराले।।८३।।
समस्तकल्याणगुणात्मकको ऽसौ स्वशक्तिलेशावृत-भूतवर्गः।।
इच्छागृहीताभिमतोरुदेहस्संसाधिताशेषजगद्धितो यः।। ८४।।

He though identical with all beings is beyond and separate from material nature, from its products, from properties and from imperfection; he is beyond all investing substance; he is universal soul; all the interstices of the universe are filled up by him; he is one with all good qualities; and all created beings are endowed with but a small portion of his individuality.

तेजोबलैश्वर्यमहावबोध सुवीर्यशक्त्यादिगुणैकराशिः।।
परः पराणां सकला न यत्र क्लेशादयस्संति परावरेशे।। ८५।।

Assuming at with various shapes he bestows benefits on the whole world, which was his work. Glory, might, dominion, wisdom, energy, power and other attributes are collected in him.

स ईश्वरो व्यष्टिसमष्टिरूपो व्यक्तस्वरूपः प्रकटस्वरूपः।।
सर्वेश्वरस्सर्वदृक् सर्वविच्च समस्तशक्तिः परमेश्वराख्यः।। ८६।।

Supreme of the supreme, in whom no imperfections abide, lord over finite and infinite, god in individuals and universals, visible and invisible, omnipotent, omnipresent, omnicient, almighty.

संज्ञायते येन तद स्तदोषं शुद्धं परं निर्मलमेकरूपम्।।
संदृश्यते वाप्यवगम्यते वा तज्ज्ञानमज्ञानमतोन्यदुक्तम्।। ८७।।

The wisdom, perfect, pure, supreme, undefiled and one only by which he is conceived, contemplated and known, that is wisdom; all else is ignorance.

।। इति श्रीविष्णुमहापुराणे षष्ठेंशे पञ्चमोऽध्यायः।।५।।

अथ षष्ठेंशेः षष्ठमोऽध्यायः

Part VI : Section 6

श्रीपराशर उवाच

स्वाध्यायसंयमाभ्यां स दृश्यते पुरुषोत्तमः।।
तत्प्राप्तिकारणं ब्रह्म तदेतदिति पठ्यते।। १।।

Parāśara said :—The Puruṣottama is also known by holy study and devout meditation; and either, as the cause of attaining him, is entitled Brahmā.

स्वाध्यायाद्योगमासीत योगात्स्वाध्यायमावसेत्।।
स्वाध्याययोगसंपत्त्या परमात्मा प्रकाशते।। २।।

From study let a man proceed to meditation

and from meditation to study; by perfection in both supreme spirit becomes manifest.

तदीक्षणाय स्वाध्यायश्चक्षुर्योगस्तथा परम्।।
न मां स चक्षुषा द्रष्टुं ब्रह्मभूतस्स शक्यते।। ३।।

Study is one eye wherewith a behold it and meditation is the other : he who is identical with Brahmā sees not with the eye of flesh.

मैत्रेय उवाच

भगवंस्तमहं योगं ज्ञातुमिच्छामि तं वद।।
ज्ञाते यत्राखिलाधारं पश्येयं परमेश्वरम्।। ४।।

Maitreya said :—Revered preceptor, I am desirous to know what is meant by the term Yoga, by understanding which I may behold the supreme being, the upholder of the universe.

श्रीपराशर उवाच

यथा केशिध्वजः प्राह खांडिक्याय महात्मने।।
जनकाय पुरा योग तमहं कथयामि।। ५।।

Parāśara said :—I will repeat to you, O Maitreya, the explanation formerly given by Keśīdhvaja to the high-minded Khāṇḍikya also called Janaka.

मैत्रेय उवाच

खांडिक्यः कोऽभवद्ब्रह्मन्को वा केशिध्वजः कृती।।
कथं तयोश्च संवादो योगसंबंधकारणात्।। ६।।

Maitreya said :—Tell me, first, Brāhmaṇa, who Khāṇḍikya was and who was Keśīdhvaja; and how it happened that a conversation relating to the practice of Yoga occurred between them.

श्रीपराशर उवाच

धर्मध्वजो वै जनकस्तस्य पुत्रोऽमितध्वजः।।
कृतध्वजश्च नाम्नासीत्सदाध्यात्मरतिर्नृपः।। ७।।

कृतध्वजस्य पुत्रोऽभूत्ख्यातः केशिध्वजो नृपः।।
पुत्रोमितध्वजस्यापि खांडिक्यजनकोऽभवत्।। ८।।

Parāśara said :—There was Janaka named Dharmadhvaja who had two sons Amitadhvaja and Kṛtadhvaja; and the latter was a king ever devoted to the existent supreme spirit; his son was the celebrated Keśīdhvaja. The son of Amitadhvaja was Janaka called Khāṇḍikya.

कर्ममार्गेण खांडिक्यः पृथिव्यामभवत्पतिः।।
केशिध्वजोऽप्यतीवासीदात्मविद्याविशारदः।। ९।।

Khāṇḍikya was diligent and celebrated on earth for pious observances. Keśīdhvaja on the other hand was gifted with spiritual knowledge.

तावुभावपि चैवास्तां विजिगीषू परस्परम्।।
केशिध्वजेन खांडिक्यस्स्वराज्यादवरोपितः।। १०।।

These two were engaged in hostilities and Khāṇḍikya was driven from his principality by Keśīdhvaja.

पुरोधसा मंत्रिभिश्च समवेतोऽल्पसाधनः।।
राज्यान्निराकृतस्सोऽथ दुर्गारण्यचरोऽभवत्।। ११।।

इयाज सोऽपि सुबहून्यज्ञाञ्ज्ञानव्यपाश्रयः।।
ब्रह्मविद्यामधिष्ठाय तर्तुं मृत्युमविद्यया।। १२।।

Expelled from his dominions he wandered with a few followers, his priest and his counsellors, amidst woods and mountains where destitute of true wisdom, he performed many sacrifices expecting thereby to obtain truth and to escape from death by ignorance.

एकदा वर्त्तमानस्य योग योगविदां वर।।
घर्मधेनुं जघानोग्रश्शार्दूलो विजने वने।। १३।।

Once on a time, while Keśīdhvaja, the best of those who are skilled devotion, was engaged in devout practices a fierce tiger slew his milk cow in the lonely forest.

ततो राजा हतां श्रुत्वा धेनुं व्याघ्रेण चर्त्विजः।।
प्रायश्चित्तं स पप्रच्छ किमत्रेति विधीयताम्।। १४।।

When the Rājā heard that the cow had been killed he asked the ministering priests what sort of penance would expatiate the crime.

तेप्यूचुर्न वयं विद्मः कशेरु पृच्छतामिति।।
कशेरुरपि तेनोक्तस्तथैव प्राह भार्गवम्।। १५।।

They said that they did not know and referred him to Kaśeru. And consulted by the king Kaśeru told him that he did not know and Śunaka would be able to tell him.

शुनकं पृच्छ राजेंद्र नाहं वेद्मि स वेत्स्यति।।
स गत्वा तमपृच्छच्च सोप्याह शृणु यन्मुने।। १६।।

न केशरुर्न चैवाहं न चैकस्सांप्रतं भुवि।।
वेत्त्येक एव त्वच्छत्रुः खांडिक्यो यो जितस्त्वया।। १७।।

Accordingly the Rājā went to Śunaka; but he said too. "I am as unable, O great king, to answer your question as Kaśeru has been; there is no one on earth who can give you the information except your enemy Khāṇḍikya, whom you have vanquished."

स चाह तं व्रजाम्येष प्रष्टुमात्मरिपुं मुने।।
प्राप्त एव महायज्ञो यदि मां स हनिष्यति।। १८।।

प्रायश्चित्तमशेषेण स चेत्पृष्टो वदिष्यति।।
ततश्चाविकलो योगो मुनिश्रेष्ठ भविष्यति।। १९।।

Being thus accosted Keśīdhvaja said :—"I will go then and pay a visit to my enemy; no matter; if he kill me, for I shall then obtain the reward that attends being slain in a holy cause; whereas if on the other hand he tells me what penance to perform then my sacrifice will be unimpaired in efficacy."

श्रीपराशर उवाच

इत्युक्त्वा रथमारुह्य कृष्णाजिनधरो नृपः।।
वनं जगाम यत्रास्ते स खांडिक्यो महामतिः।। २०।।

Accordingly he ascended his car, having clothed himself in the deerskin and went to the forest where the wise Khāṇḍikya lived.

तमापतंतमालोक्य खांडिक्यो रिपुमात्मनः।।
प्रोवाच क्रोधताम्राक्षस्समारोपितकार्मुकः।। २१।।

When Khāṇḍikya saw him approach his eyes reddened with ire and he took up his bow and said to him,

खांडिक्य उवाच

कृष्णाजिनं त्वं कवचमाबध्यास्मान्हनिष्यसि।।
कृष्णाजिनधरे वेत्सि न मयि प्रहरिष्यति।। २२।।

मृगाणां वद पृष्ठेषु मूढ कृष्णाजिनं न किम्।।
येषां मया त्वया चोग्राः प्रहिताश्शितसायकाः।। २३।।

"You have armed yourself with deerskin to bring about my destruction thinking that in such a dress you will be safe from me; but fool, the deer upon whose backs thins skin is seen are slain by you and me with sharp arrows, so I will slay you; you shall not go free whilst I am living.

स त्वामहं हनिष्यामि न मे जीवन्विमोक्ष्यसे।।
आततायसि दुर्बुद्धे मम राज्यहरो रिपुः।। २४।।

You are an unprincipled felon, who have robbed me of my kingdom and are deserving of death."

केशिध्वज उवाच

खांडिक्य संशयं प्रष्टुं भवंतमहमागतः।।
न त्वां हंतुं विचार्यैतत्कोपं बाणं विमुञ्च वा।। २५।।

To this Keśīdhvaja replied : "I have come here Khāṇḍikya, to consult you about my doubts and not with any hostile intention; lay aside therefore both your arrow and anger."

श्रीपराशर उवाच

ततस्स मंत्रिभिस्सार्द्धमेकांते सपुरोहितः।।
मंत्रयामास खांडिक्यस्सर्वैरेव महामतिः।। २६।।

Thus addressed Khāṇḍikya retired for a while with his counsellors and his priest and consulted with them what course to adopt.

तमूचुर्मंत्रिणो वध्यो रिपुरेष वशं गतः।।
हतेऽस्मिन्पृथिवी सर्वा तव वश्या भविष्यति।। २७।।

They strongly urged him to slay Keśīdhvaja who was in his grasp and by whose death he would again become the monarch of the whole world.

खांडिक्यश्चाह तान्सर्वानिवमेतन्न संशयः।।
हतेस्मिन्पृथिवी सर्वा मम वश्या भविष्यति।। २८।।

परलोक जयस्तस्य पृथिवी सकला मम।।
न हन्मि चेल्लोकजयो मम तस्य वसुंधरा।। २९।।

Khāṇḍikya replied to them : "It is undoubtedly true that by such an act I would become the monarch of the whole world but he would thereby conquer the next world : whilst the earth would be mine. And if I do not slay him I shall conquer the world to come and leave him this earth.

नाऽहं मन्ये लोकजयादधिका स्याद्वसुंधरा।।
परलोक जयोऽनंतस्स्वल्पकालो महीजयः।। ३०।

तस्मान्नैनं हनिष्यामि यत्पृच्छति वदामि तत्।। ३१।।

It appears to me that this world is not so much valuable as the next : for the subjugation of the next world continues for ever while the conquest over this is but temporary. I will therefore not kill him but tell him what he wishes to know."

श्रीपराशर उवाच

ततस्तमभ्युपेत्याह खांडिक्यजनको रिपुम्।।
प्रष्टव्यं यत्त्वया सर्वं तत्पृच्छस्व वदाम्यहम्।। ३२।।

Parāśara said :—Coming accordingly to Keśīdhvaja, Khāṇḍikya asked him to propose his question which he promised to answer.

श्रीपराशर उवाच

ततस्सर्वं यथावृत्तं घर्मधेनुवधं द्विज।।
कथयित्वा स पप्रच्छ प्रायश्चित्तं हि तद्व्रतम्।। ३३।।

And Keśīdhvaja related to him what had taken place, that death of the cow and desired to know what penance he should perform.

स चाचष्ट यथान्यायं द्विज केशिध्वजाय तत्।।
प्रांयश्चित्तमशेषेण यद्वै तत्र विधीयते।। ३४।।
विदितार्थस्स तेनैव ह्यनुज्ञातो महात्मना।।
यागभूमिमुपागम्य चक्रे सर्वाः क्रियाः क्रमात्।। ३५।।

Keśīdhvaja, in reply, explained to him fully the expiation that was suited to the occasion; and then with his permission Keśīdhvaja returned to the place of sacrifice and regularly fulfilled every necessary act.

क्रमेण विधिवद्यागं नीत्वा सोऽवभृथाप्लुतः।।
कृतकृत्यस्ततो भूत्वा चिंतयामास पार्थिवः।। ३६।।

Having completed the ceremony with its suplementary rites Keśīdhvaja accomplished all his objects : but he then reflected thus,

पूजिताश्च द्विजास्सर्वे सदस्या मानिता मया।।
तथैवार्थिजनोऽप्यर्थैर्योजितोऽभिमतैर्मया।। ३७।।
यथार्हमस्य लोकस्य मया सर्वं विचेष्टितम्।।
अनिष्पन्नक्रियं चेतस्तथापि मम किं यथा।। ३८।।

"The priests whom I invited to attend have all been duly honoured; all those who had any request to make have been pleased with my complying with their desires; all that is proper for this world, has been effected by me; why then my mind should feel as if my duty had been unfulfilled."

इत्थं संचिंतयन्नेव सस्मार स महीपतिः।।
खांडिक्याय न दत्तेति मया वै गुरुदक्षिणा।। ३९।।
स जगाम तदा भूयो रथमारुह्य पार्थिवः।।
मैत्रेय दुर्गगहनं खांडिक्यो यत्र संस्थितः।। ४०।।

Thinking this he remembered that he had not presented to Khāṇḍikya the gift that it is proper to offer to a spiritual preceptor and mounting his chariot he immediately started for the dense forest where the sage resided.

खांडिक्योऽपि पुनर्दृष्ट्वा तमायांतं धृतायुधम्।।
तस्थौ हंतुं कृतमतिस्तमाह स पुनर्नृपः।। ४१।।
भो नाहं तेऽपराधाय प्राप्तः खांडिक्य मा क्रुधाः।।
गुरोर्निक्रयदानाय मामवेहि त्वमागतम्।। ४२।।

Upon his reappearance Khāṇḍikya took up his arms to slay him; but Keśīdhvaja exclaimed "forbear, venerable sage," I have not come hither to injure you; throw off your wrath, Khāṇḍikya, know that I have come here to offer you that present which is due to you as my instructor.

निष्पादितो मया यागः सम्यक्त्वदुपदेशतः।।
सोऽहं ते दातुमिच्छामि वृणीष्व गुरुदक्षिणाम्।। ४३।।

Through your lesson I have fully completed my sacrifice and I am therefore desirous to give you a gift. Demand what it shall be."

श्रीपराशर उवाच

भूयस्य मंत्रिभिस्सार्द्धं मंत्रयामास पार्थिवः।।
गुरुनिष्क्रयकामोऽयं किं मया प्रार्थ्यतामिति।। ४४।।

Having once more consulted his counsellors, Khāṇḍikya told them the purpose of his rival's visit and asked them what he should demand.

तमूचुर्मंत्रिणो राज्यमशेषं प्रार्थ्यतामयम्।।
शत्रुभिः प्रार्थ्यते राज्यमना यासितसैनिकैः।। ४५।।

His friends recommended him to take back

his whole kingdom for prudent men acquire them without conflicting hosts.

प्रहस्य तानाह नृपस्स खांडिक्यो महामतिः।
स्वल्पकालं महीपाल्यं मादृशैः प्रार्थ्यते कथम्।। ४६।।

The king Khāṇḍikya reflecting laughed and said to them "Why should a person like me, be desirous of a temporary earthly kingdom?

एवमेतद्भवंतोऽत्र ह्यर्थसाधनमंत्रिणः।।
परमार्थः कथं कोऽत्र यूयं नात्र विचक्षणाः।। ४७।।

Indeed you are very good advisers as regards the present worldly affairs—but you are undoubtedly ignorant of the life to come."

श्रीपराशर उवाच

इत्युक्त्वा समुपेत्यैनं स तु केशिध्वजं नृपः।।
उवाच किमवश्यं त्वं ददासि गुरुदक्षिणाम्।। ४८।।

Parāśara said :—Saying this he returned to Keśīdhvaja and said to him "It it true that you wish to make me a gift as to your preceptor? "Indeed I do" answered Keśīdhvaja.

बाढमित्येव तेनोक्तः खांडिक्यस्तमथाब्रवीत्।।
भवानध्यात्मविज्ञानपरमार्थविचक्षणः।। ४९।।

यदि चेद्दीयते मह्यं भवता गुरुनिष्क्रयः।।
तत्क्लेशप्रशमायालं यत्कर्म तदुदीरय।। ५०।।

Whereto Khāṇḍikya replied "Then, as it is known tha you are learned in the spiritual learning that teaches the doctrine of the soul, if you will communicate that knowlegde unto me you will have discharged your debt to your preceptor. Communicate unto me what acts are efficacious for the alleviation of human sufferings."

।। इति श्रीविष्णुमहापुराणे षष्ठेंशे षष्ठोऽध्यायः।। ६।।

अथ षष्ठेंशेः सप्तमोऽध्यायः

Part VI : Section 7

केशिध्वज उवाच

न प्रार्थितं त्वया कस्मादस्माद्राज्यमकंटकम्।।
राज्यलाभाद्विना नान्यत्क्षत्रियाणा मतिप्रियम्।। १।।

Keśīdhvaja said :—"But why have you not demanded of me my kingdom free from all troubles; what else save dominion is acceptable to the warrior race?"

खांडिक्य उवाच

केशिध्वज निबोध त्वं मया न प्रार्थितं यतः।।
राज्यमेतदशेषं ते यत्र गृध्नंत्यपंडिताः।। २।।

Whereto Khāṇḍikya replied, "I will tell you why I did not make such a demand nor require that territory which is an object of ignorant ambition.

क्षत्रियाणामयं धर्मो यत्प्रजापरिपालनम्।।
वधश्च धर्मयुद्धेन स्वराज्यपरिपंथिनाम्।। ३।।

It is the duty of the warrior to protect his subjects in peace and to kill in fight the enemies of his way.

तत्राशक्तस्य मे दोषो नैवास्त्यपहृते त्वया।।
बंधायैव भवत्येषा ह्यविद्याप्यक्रमोज्झिता।। ४।।

It is no fault that you should have taken my kingdom from one who was unable to defend it, to whom it was a bondage and who was thus freed from the incumbrance of ignorance.

अल्पोमोपभोगलिप्सार्थमियं राज्यस्पृहा मम।।
अन्येषां दोषजा सैव धर्मं वै नानुरुध्यते।। ५।।

My desire of dominion originated from my being born to possess it : the ambition of others which proceeds from human frailties, is not compatible with virtue.

न याञ्च क्षत्रबंधूनां धर्मायैतत्सतां मतम्।।
अतो न याचितं राज्यमविद्यांतर्गतं तव।। ६।।

To solicit gift is not the duty of a prince and warrior. It is for this reason I have not demanded of you the kingdom, a request which is the outcome of ignorance.

राज्ये गृध्नंत्यविद्वांसो ममत्वाहृतचेतसः।।
अहंमानमहापानमदमत्ता न मादृशाः।। ७।।

Those only, who are ignorant, whose minds are attached to selfishness and who are intoxicated with the liquor of self-sufficiency, desire kingdoms; not such as I am."

श्रीपराशर उवाच

प्रहृष्टस्साध्विति ततः प्राह केशिध्वजो नृपः।।
खांडिक्यजनकं प्रीत्या श्रूयतां वचनं मम।। ८।।

Parāśara said :—Being greatly delighed, the king Keśidhvaja praised Khāṇḍikya and said to him affectionately "Listen to my words.

केशिध्वज उवाच

अहं ह्यविद्यया मृत्युं तर्तुकामः करोमि वै।।
राज्यं यागांश्च विविधान्भोगैः पुण्यक्षयं तथा।। ९।।

Keśidhvaja said :—Through the desire of escaping death by the ignorance of works I exercise the regal power, celebrate various sacrifices and enjoy pleasures subversive of purity.

तदिदं ते मनो दिष्ट्या विवेकैश्वर्यतां गतम्।।
तच्छ्रूयतामविद्यायास्स्वरूपं कुलनंदन।। १०।।

Fortunate it is for you that you mind has attached itself to the dominion of discrimination. Pride of your race! now listen to the real nature of ignorance.

अनात्मन्यात्मबुद्धिर्या चास्वेस्वमिति या मतिः।।
संसारतरुसंभूतिबीजमेतद्द्विधा स्थितम्।। ११।।

The mistaken notion that self consists in what is not self and that property consists in what is not one's own constitute the double seed of the tree of ignorance.

पञ्चभूतात्मके देहे देही मोहतमोवृतः।।
अहं ममैतदित्युच्चैः कुरुते कुमतिर्मतिम्।। १२।।

The ill-judging embodied being, bewildered by the darkness of fascination situated in a body composed of five elements, loudly asserts :—

आकाशवाय्वग्निजलपृथिवीभ्यः पृथक् स्थिते।।
आत्मन्यात्ममयं भावं कः करोति कलेवरे।। १३।।

"This is I" but who would ascribe spiritual individuality to a body in which soil is distinct from ether, air, fire, water and earth.

कलेवरोपभोग्यं हि गृहक्षेत्रादिकं च कः।।
अदेहे ह्यात्मनि प्राज्ञो ममेदमिति मन्यते।। १४।।

What man of understanding assigns to disembadied spirit corporeal fruition or what lands, houses and the like that it should say, "These are mine?"

इत्थं च पुत्रपौत्रेषु तद्देहोत्पादितेषु कः।।
करोति पंडितस्स्वाम्यमनात्मनि कलेवरे।। १५।।

What wise man entertains the idea of property in sons or grandsons begotten of the body after the spirit has abandoned it?

सर्वं देहोपभोगाय कुरुते कर्म मानवः।।
देहश्चान्यो यदा पुंसस्तदा बंधाय तत्परम्।। १६।।

Man performs all acts for the purpose of bodily fruition and the consequence of such acts is another body; so that their result is nothing but confinement to bodliy existence.

मृण्मयं हि यथा गेहं लिप्यते वै मृदंभसा।।
पार्थिवोऽयं तथा देहो मृदंब्वालेपनस्थितः।। १७।।

In the same manner as a mansion of clay is plastered with clay and water, so the body which is of earth is prepetuated by earth and water.

पञ्चभूतात्मकैर्भोगैः पञ्चभूतात्मकं वपुः।।
आप्यायते यदि ततः पुंसो भोगोऽत्र किं कृतः।। १८।।

The body consisting of five elements is nourished by substances equally composed of those elements; but since this is the case, what is there is this life that man should be proud of?

अनेकजन्मसाहस्त्रीं संसारपदवीं व्रजन्।।
मोहश्रमं प्रयातोऽसौ वासनारेणुकुंठितः।। १९।।

Travelling the path of the world for many thousand of births, man attains only the weariness of bewilderment and is smothered by the dust of imagnation.

प्रक्षाल्यते यदा सोस्य रेणुर्ज्ञानोष्णवारिणा।।
तदा संसारपांथस्य याति मोहश्रमश्शमम्।। २०।।

When that dust is washed away by the bland water of real knowledge, then the weariness of bewilderment, sustained by the wayfarer through repeated births, is removed.

मोहश्रमे शमं याते स्वस्थांतःकरणः पुमान्।।
अनन्यातिशयाबाधं परं निर्वाणमृच्छति।। २१।।

When that weariness is relieved the internal man is at peace and he obtains that supreme felicity which is unequalled and undisturbed.

निर्वाणमय एवायमात्मा ज्ञानमयोऽमलः।।
दुःखाज्ञानमया धर्माः प्रकृतेस्ते तु नात्मनः।। २२।।

This soul is pure and composed of wisdom and happiness. The properties of pain, ignorance and impurity are those of nature and not of soul.

जलस्य नाग्निसंसर्गस्थालीसंगात्तथापि हि।।
शब्दोद्रेकादिकान्धर्मांस्तत्करोति यथा नृप।। २३।।

O Muni, there is no affinity between fire and water but when the latter is placed over the former in a caldorn, it bubbles and boils and exhibits the properties of fire.

तथात्मा प्रकृतेस्संगादहंमानादिदूषितः।।
भजते प्राकृतान्धर्मानन्यस्तेभ्यो हि सोऽव्ययः।। २४।।

In the same manner when soul is associated with Prakṛti it is vitiated by egotism and the rest and assumes the qualities of grosser nature although essentially distinct from them and compatible.

तदेतत्कथितं बीजमविद्याया मया तव।।
क्लेशानां च क्षयकरं योगादन्यन्न विद्यते।। २५।।

Such is the seed of ignorance as I have explained it to you : there is but one remedy for earthy sorrows—the practice of devotion; no other is known."

खांडिक्य उवाच

तं ब्रवीहि महाभाग योगं योगविदुत्तम।।
विज्ञातयोगशास्त्रार्थस्त्वम स्यांनिमिसंततौ।। २६।।

Thereupon Khāṇḍikya said :—"Do you then the foremost of those versed in contemplative devotion explain to me what that is, for in the race of the descendants of Nimi you are best acquainted with the sacred writings in which it is taught."

केशिध्वज उवाच

योगस्वरूपं खांडिक्य श्रूयतां गदतो मम।।
यत्र स्थितो न च्यवते प्राप्य ब्रह्मलयं मुनिः।। २७।।

Whereto Keśīdhvaja replied : "Hear the account of the nature of contemplative devotion, which I am imparting to you and by perfection in which the sage attains resolution into Brahmā and never suffers birth again.

मन एव मनुष्याणां कारणं बंधमोक्षयोः।।
बंधाय विषयासंगति मुक्तायै निर्विषयं मनः।। २८।।

The mind of man is the cause both of his bondage and his liberation its addiction to the objects of sense is the means of his bondage; its separation from objects of sense is the means of his liberation.

विषयेभ्यस्समाहृत्य विज्ञानात्मा मनो मुनिः।।
चिंतयेन्मुक्तये तेन ब्रह्मभूतं परमेश्वरम्।। २९।।

आत्मभावं नयत्येनं तद्ब्रह्म ध्यायिनं मुनिम्।।
विकार्यमात्मनश्शक्त्या लोहमाकर्षको यथा।। ३०।।

The sage, who is capable of discriminative knowledge, must therefore restrain his mind from all objects of sense and therewith meditate upon the supreme being, who is identical with spirit, in order to obtain liberation; for that supreme spirit attracts to itself him who meditates upon it, and who is of the same nature, as the loadstone attracts the iron by the virtue which is common to itself and to its products.

आत्मप्रयत्नसापेक्षा विशिष्टा या मनोगतिः।।
तस्या ब्रह्मणि संयोगो योग इत्यभिधीयते।। ३१।।

एवमत्यंतवैशिष्ट्ययुक्तधर्मोपलक्षणः।।
यस्य योगस्स वै योगी मुमुक्षुरभिधीयते।। ३२।।

Contemplative devotion is the union with Brahmā effected by that condition of mind which has attained perfection through those exercises which complete the control of self; and he, whose contemplative devotion is characterised by the property of such absolute perfection, is in truth, O sage, expectant of final liberation from the world.

योगयुक् प्रथमं योगी युञ्जानो ह्यभिधीयते।।
विनिष्पन्नसमाधिस्तु परं ब्रह्मोपलब्धिमान्।। ३३।।

The Yogī, when he first gives himself up to the practice of contemplative devotion, is called the novice or practitioner, when he has attained spiritual union, he is called the adept or he whose meditations are accomplished.

यद्यंतरायदोषेण दूष्यते चास्य मानसम्।।
जन्मांतरैरभ्यसतो मुक्तिः पूर्वस्य जायते।। ३४।।

Should the thoughts of the former be unvitiated by any obstructing imperfection, he will obtain freedom after practising devotion through several lives.

विनिष्पन्नसमाधिस्तु मुक्तिं तत्रैव जन्मनि।।
प्राप्नोति योगी योगाग्निधकर्मचयोऽचिरात्।। ३५।।

The latter speedily obtains liberations in that existence, all his acts being consumed by the fire of contemplative devotion.

ब्रह्मचर्यमहिंसां च सत्यास्तेयापरिग्रहान्।।
सेवेत योगी निष्कामो योग्यतां स्वमनो नयन्।। ३६।।

स्वाध्यायशौचसंतोषतपांसि नियतात्मवान्।।
कुर्वीत ब्रह्मणि तथा परस्मिन्प्रवणं मनः।। ३७।।

The sage, who would bring his mind into a proper state for the performance of devout contemplation, must be devoid of desire and observe invariably continence, compassion, truth, honesty, and disinterestedness; he must fix his mind upon the supreme Brahmā, practising holy study, purification, contentment, penance and self-control.

एते यमास्सनियमाः पञ्च पञ्च च कीर्त्तिताः।।
विशिष्टफलदाः काम्या निष्कामानां विमुक्तिदाः।। ३८।।

These virtues respectively termed the five acts of restraint and five of obligation bestow excellent rewards when practised for the sake of reward and eternal liberation and when they are not prompted by the desire of transient benefits.

एकं भद्रासनादीनां समास्थाय गुणैर्युतः।।
यमाख्यैर्नियमाख्यैश्च युञ्जीत नियतो यतिः।। ३९।।

Endowed with these merits, the sage, self-restrained, should sit in one of the modes termed Bhadrāsana and engage in contemplation.

प्राणाख्यमनिलं वश्यमभ्यासात्कुरुते तु यत्।।
प्राणायामस्स विज्ञेयस्सबीजोऽबीज एव च।। ४०।।

Bringing his vital airs called Prāṇa under subjection, by frequent repetition is thence called Prāṇāyāma which is, as it were, a seed with a seed.

परस्परेणाभिभवं प्राणापानौ यथानिलौ।।
कुरुतस्सद्विधानेन तृतीयस्संयमात्तयोः।। ४१।।

In this, the breath of expiration and that of inspiration are alternately obstructed constituting the act two-fold; and the supression of both modes of breathing produces a third.

तस्य चालंबनवतः स्थूलरूपं द्विजोत्तम।।
आलंबनमनंतस्य योगिनोऽभ्यसतः स्मृतम्।। ४२।।

The exercise, of yogī, whilst endeavouring to bring before his thoughts the gross form of the eternal, is demoninated Alambana.

शब्दादिष्वनुरक्तानि निगृह्याक्षाणि योगवित्।।
कुर्याच्चित्तानुकारीणि प्रत्याहारपरायणः।। ४३।।

He is then to perform Pratyāhāra, which consists in restraining his organs of sense from susceptibility to outward impressions, and directing them entirely to mental perceptions.

वश्यता परमा तेन जायतेति चलात्मनाम्।।
इन्द्रियाणामवश्यैस्तैर्न योगी योगसाधकः।। ४४।।

By these means the entire subjugation of the unsteady senses is effected : and if they are not controlled the sage will not accomplish his devotions.

प्राणयामेंन पवने प्रत्याहारेण चेंद्रिये।।
वशीकृते ततः कुर्यात्स्थितं चेतश्शुभाश्रये।। ४५।।

When by the Prāṇāyāma the vital airs are restrained and the senses are subjugated by Pratyāhāra then the sage will be able to keep his mind steady in its perfect asylum.

खांडिक्य उवाच

कथ्यतां मे महाभाग चेतसो यशशुभाश्रयः।।
यदाधारमेशेषं तद्धंति दोषमलोद्भवम्।। ४६।।

Khāṇḍikya then said to Keśīdhvaja "Illustrious sage, inform me what is that perfect asylum of the mind resting on which it destroys all the products of human infirmity."

केशिध्वज उवाच

आश्रयश्चेतसो ब्रह्म द्विधा तच्च स्वभावतः।।
भूप मूर्त्तममूर्त्तां च परं चापरमेव च।। ४७।।

To this Keśidhvaja replied, "The asylum of mind is Brahmā, which, of its own nature, is two-fold; as being with or without form; and each of these, is supreme and secondary.

त्रिविधा भावना भूप विश्वमेतन्निबोधताम्।।
ब्रह्माख्या कर्मसंज्ञा च तथा चैवोभयात्मिका।। ४८।।
कर्मभावात्मिका ह्येका ब्रह्मभावात्मिका परा।।
उभयात्मिका तथैवान्या त्रिविधा भावभावना।। ४९।।

Apprehension of Brahmā or spirit is again three-fold. I will explain the different kinds to you, they are that which is called Brahmā, that which is named from works, and that which comprehends both is the third. So that mental apprehension is three-fold.

सनंदनादयो ये तु ब्रह्मभावनया युताः।।
कर्मभावनया चान्ये देवाद्याः स्थावरावराः।। ५०।।

Sanandana and other were endowed with the apprehension of the nature of Brahmā. The celestials and others whether animate or inanimate are possessed of that which regards acts.

हिरण्यगर्भादिषु च ब्रह्मकर्मात्मिका द्विधा।।
बोधाधिकारयुक्तेषु विद्यते भावभावना।। ५१।।

The apprehension, that comprehends both works and spirit, exists in Hiraṇyagarbha and others, who are possessed of contemplative knowledge of their own nature and who also exercise certain active functions as creation and the rest.

अक्षीणेषु समस्तेषु विशेषज्ञानकर्मसु।।
विश्वमेतत्परं चान्यद्भेदभिन्नदृशां नृणाम्।। ५२।।
प्रत्यस्तमितभेदं यत्सत्तामात्रमगोचरम्।।
वचसा मात्मसंवेद्यं तज्ज्ञानं ब्रह्मसंज्ञितम्।। ५३।।

Untill all acts, which are the causes of notions of individuality, are discontinued, spirit is one thing and universe is another, to those who contemplate objects as distinct and various; but that is called true knowledge or knowledge of Brahmā which recognises no distinctions, which contemplates only simple existence which is undefinable by words and is to be discovered solely in one's own spirit.

तच्च विष्णोः परं रूपमरूपाख्यमनुत्तमम्।।
विश्वस्वरूपवैरूप्यलक्षणं परमात्मनः।। ५४।।

That is the supreme unborn, imperishable form of Viṣṇu, who is without form and characterised as a condition of the supreme soul, which is variously modified from the condition of universal form.

न तद्योगयुजा शक्यं नृप चिंतयितुं यतः।।
ततस्स्थूलं हरे रूपं चिंतयेद्विश्वगोचरम्।। ५५।।

The sages, in the early stage, cannot perceive this form so they must direct their minds to the gross form of Hari, which is of universal perceptibility.

हिरण्यगर्भो भगवान्वासुदेवः प्रजापतिः।।
मरुतो वसवो रुद्रा भास्करास्तारका ग्रहाः।। ५६।।
गंधर्वयक्षदैत्याद्यास्सकला देवयोनयः।।
मनुष्याः पशवश्शैलास्समुद्रास्सरितो द्रुमाः।। ५७।।
भूप भूतान्यशेषाणि भूतानां ये च हेतवः।।
प्रधानादिविशेषांतं चेतनाचेतनात्मकम्।। ५८।।
एकापदं द्विपादं च बहुपादमपादकम्।।
मूर्त्तमेतद्धरे रूपं भावनात्रितयात्मकम्।। ५९।।

They must meditate upon him as Hiraṇyagarbha, as the glorious Vāsava as Prajāpati, as the winds, the Vasus, the Rudras, the suns, stars, planets, Gandharvas, Yakṣas, Daityas, all the celestials, and their progenitors, men, animals, mountains, oceans, rivers, trees, all beings and all sources of beings, all modifications of natures, and its products, whether sentient of unconscious, one-footed, two-footed, or many-footed; all these are the sensible form of Hari, to be apprehended by three kinds of apprehension.

एतस्सर्वमिदं विश्वं जगदेतच्चराचरम्।।
परब्रह्मस्वरूपस्य विष्णोश्शक्तिसमन्वितम्।। ६०।।

All this universal world, this world of moving and stationary being is bervaded by the energy of Viṣṇu, who is of the nature of supreme Brahmā.

विष्णुशक्तिः परा प्रोक्ता क्षेत्रज्ञाख्या तथाऽपरा।।
अविद्याकर्मसंज्ञान्या तृतीया शक्तिरिष्यते।। ६१।।

यया क्षेत्रज्ञशक्तिस्सा वेष्टिता नृप सर्वगा।।
संसारतापानखिलानवाप्नोत्यतिसंततान्।। ६२।।

This energy is supreme, or when it is that of conscious embodied spirit it is secondary. Ignorance, or that which is denominated from works, is a third energy; by which the omnipresent energy of embodied spirit is ever excited and whence it suffers all the pains of repeated worldly existence.

तया तिरोहितत्वाच्च शक्तिः क्षेत्रज्ञसंज्ञिता।।
सर्वभूतेषु भूपाल तारतम्येन लक्ष्यते।। ६३।।

Obscured by that energy, the energy that is denominated from embodied spirit, is characterised by different degrees of perfection in all created beings.

अप्राणवत्सुस्वल्पा सा स्थावरेषु ततोऽधिका।।
सरीसृपेषु तेभ्योपि ह्यतिशक्त्या पतत्रिषु।। ६४।।

पातत्रिभ्यो मृगास्तेभ्यस्तच्छक्त्या पशवोऽधिकाः।।
पशुभ्यो मनुजाश्चातिशत्ताया पुंसः प्रभाविताः।।६५।।

तेभ्योपि नागगंधर्वयक्षाद्या देवता नृप।। ६६।।

शक्रस्समस्तदेवेभ्यस्ततश्चातिप्रजापतिः।।
हिरण्यगर्भोऽपि ततः पुंसश्शक्त्युपलक्षितः।। ६७।।

एतान्यशेषरूपाणि तस्य रूपाणि पार्थिव।।
यतस्तच्छक्तियोगेन युक्तानि नभसा यथा।। ६८।।

In inanimate things it exists in a very small degree; it is more in things that have life, but are (without motion); in insects it is still more abundant, and still more in birds; it is more in wild animals and in domestic animals the faculty is still greater : men have more of this faculty than animals, and thence arises their authority over them; the faculty exists in a supreme degree in Nāgas, Gandharvas, Yakṣas, celestials, Śakra, Prajāpati and Hiraṇyagarbha; and is above all predominant in that male (Viṣṇu) whom all these various creatures are but the divresified forms, permeated universally by his energy, as all-pervading as the other.

द्वितीयं विष्णुसंज्ञस्य योगिध्येयं महामते।।
अमूर्त्तं ब्रह्मणो रूपं यत्सदित्युच्यते बुधैः।। ६९।।

समस्ताश्शक्तयश्चैता नृप यत्र प्रतिष्ठिताः।।
तद्विश्वरूपवैरूप्यं रूपमन्यद्धरेर्महत्।।७०।।

समस्तशक्तिरूपाणि तत्करोति जनेश्वर।।
देवतिर्यङ्मनुष्यादिचेष्टावंति स्वलीलया।। ७१।।

That state of Viṣṇu, which is without form, is to be meditated upon the sages and this imperceptible and shapeless form of Brahmā is called by the wise "that which is" and in which all the energies, described before, reside. O lord of men, from this state of Viṣṇu and which is formless, proceeds his universal form and other great form and other forms endowed with his diverse energies.

जगतामुपकाराय न सा कर्मनिमित्तजा।।
चेष्टा तस्याप्रमेयस्य व्यापिन्यव्याहतात्मिका।।७२।।

For the behoof of the universe he assumes various forms, that of the celestial, birds and men—but he is never born being influenced by his pristine actions; he is all-comprehending and irresistible.

तद्रूपं विश्वरूपस्य तस्य योगयुजा नृप।।
चिंत्यमात्मविशुद्ध्यर्थं सर्वकिल्बिषनाशनम्।।७३।।

This universal form of his is to be meditated upon by the sage for the purpose of purification for it washes away all sins.

यथाग्निरुद्धतशिखः कक्षं दहति सानिलः।।
तथा चित्तस्थितो विष्णुर्योगिनां सर्वकिल्बिषम्।।७४।।

As the fire, combined with wind, consumes

twigs with its increased flame, so this form of Viṣṇu, when meditated upon by the sage in his heart, destroys all sins.

तस्मात्समस्तशक्तीनामाधारे तत्र चेतसः ।।
कुर्वीत संस्थितिं सा तु विज्ञेया शुद्धधारणा ।। ७५ ।।

शुभाश्रयस्य चित्तस्य सर्वगस्याचलात्मनः ।।
त्रिभावभावनातीतो मुक्तये योगिनो नृप ।। ७६ ।।

Let us therefore fix our mind resolutely upon him who is the asylum of three fold energies and this is the operation of the mind which is called perfect Dhāraṇā; and thus the perfect asylum of individual as well as universal spirit, that which beyond the three modes of apprehension, is attained for the eternal emancipation of the sage.

अन्ये तु पुरुषव्याघ्र चेतसो ये व्यपाश्रयाः ।।
अशुद्धास्ते समस्तास्तु देवाद्याः कर्मयोनयः ।। ७७ ।।

मूर्त्तं भगवतो रूपं सर्वापाश्रयनिस्पृहम् ।।
एषा वै धारणा प्रोक्ता यच्चित्तं तत्र धार्यते ।। ७८ ।।

यच्च मूर्त्तं हरे रूपं यादृक्चिन्त्यं नराधिप ।।
तच्छूयतामनाधारा धारणा नोपपद्यते ।। ७९ ।।

O foremost of men, the gods and others who rest in the minds are impure and spring from acts. The apprehension by the mind of that visible form of Viṣṇu without regard to subsidiary forms is thence called Dhāraṇā and I will now describe to you the perceptible form of Hari which no mental retention will manifest except in a mind that is fit to become the receptacle of the idea.

प्रसन्नवदनं चारुपद्मपत्रोपमेक्षणम् ।।
सुकपोलं सुविस्तीर्णललाटफलकोज्ज्वलम् ।। ८० ।।

समकर्णांतविन्यस्तचारुकुंडलभूषणम् ।।
कंबुग्रीवं सुविस्तीर्णश्रीवत्सांकितवक्षसम् ।। ८१ ।।

वलि त्रिभंगिना मग्ननाभिना ह्युदरेण च ।।
प्रलंबाष्टभुजं विष्णुमथवापि चतुर्भुजम् ।। ८२ ।।

समस्थितोरुजंघं च सुस्थितांघ्रिवरांबुजम् ।।
चिंतये द्ब्रह्मभूतं तं पीतनिर्मलवाससम् । ८३ ।।

किरीटहारकेयूरकटकादिविभूषितम् ।। ८४ ।।

शार्ङ्गशंखगदाखड्गचक्राक्षवलयान्वितम् ।।
वरदाभयहस्तं च मुद्रिकारत्नभूषितम् ।। ८५ ।।

The meditating sage must think of Viṣṇu as having a delightful and lovely countenance with eyes like the leaf of the lotus, smooth cheeks, and a broad and brilliant forehead; ears of equal size, the lobes of which are embellished with splendid pendants, a painted neck and a braod breast on which shines the mystic mark of Śrīvatsa; a belly falling in graceful fold, with a deep-seated navel; eight long arms or else four; and firm and well knit things and legs, with well-formed feet and toes. Let him, with well-goverend thoughts, contemplate, as long as he can persevere with undivided attention, Hari as clad in a yellow raiment, wearing a rich diadem on his head and brilliant armlets and bracelets on his arms and bearing in his hands, the bow, the shell, the mace, the sword, the discus, the rosary, the lotus and the arrow.

चिंतयेत्तन्मयो योगी समाधायात्ममानसम् ।।
तावद्यावद्दृढीभूता तत्रैव नृप धारणा ।। ८६ ।।

व्रजतस्तिष्ठतोन्यद्वा स्वेच्छया कर्म कुर्वतः ।।
नापयाति यदा चित्तत्सिद्धां मन्येत तां तदा ।। ८७ ।।

ततः शंखगदाचक्रशार्ङ्गादिरहितं बुधः ।।
चिंतयेद्भगवद्रूपं प्रशांतं साक्षसूत्रकम् ।। ८८ ।।

The Yogī may believe his retention to be perfect when this image never vanishes from his mind, whether he be going or standing, or be engaged in any other voluntary act. The sage may then meditate upon the form of Viṣṇu without his arms as the shell, mace, discus and bow and as placid and bearing only his rosary.

सा यदा धारणा तद्वदवस्थानवती ततः ।।
किरीटकेयूरमुखैर्भूषणै रहितं स्मरेत् ।। ८९ ।।

When the idea of this image is firmly retained, then he may meditate on Viṣṇu without his diadem, bracelets or other ornaments.

तदेकावयवं देवं चेतसा हि पुनर्बुधः ।।
कुर्यात्ततोऽवयविनि प्रणिधानपरो भवेत् ।। ९० ।।

He may next contemplate him as having but one single limb and may then fix his whole thoughts upon the body to which the limbs belong.

तद्रूपप्रत्यया चैका संततिश्चान्यनिःस्पृहा।।
तद्ध्यानं प्रथमैरंगैः षड्भिर्निष्पाद्यते नृप।। ९१।।
तस्यैव कल्पनाहीनं स्वरूपग्रहणं हि यत्।।
मनसा ध्याननिष्पाद्यं समाधिस्सोऽभिधीयते।। ९२।।

The process of forming a lively image in the mind exclusive of all other objects, consitutes Dhyāna, or meditation, which is perfected by six stages and when an accurate knowledge of self, free from all distinction, is attained by this mental meditation that is termed Samādhi.

विज्ञानं प्रापकं प्राप्ये परे ब्रह्मणि पार्थिव।।
प्रापणीयस्तथैवात्मा प्रक्षीणाशेष भावनः।। ९३।।
क्षत्रज्ञः करणी ज्ञान करण तस्य तेन तत्।।
निष्पाद्य मुक्तिकार्यं वै कृतकृत्यं निवर्त्तते।। ९४।।

After accomplishing this stage the Yogī acquires discriminative knowledge, which is the means of enabling living soul when all the three kinds of apprehension are destroyed to attain the attainable supreme being. Embodied spirit is the user of the instrument, which instrument is true knowledge; and by it that identification of the former is attained. Liberation which is the object to be effected being accomplished discriminative knowledge ceases.

तद्भावभावमापन्नस्ततोऽसौ परमात्मना।।
भवत्यभेदी भेदश्च तस्याज्ञानकृतो भवेत्।। ९५।।

When endowed with the apprehension of the nature of the object of enquiry, then there is no difference between the individual and supreme spirit; difference is the outcome of the absence of true knowledge.

विभेदजनके ज्ञाने नाशमात्यंतिकं गते।।
आत्मनो ब्रह्मणो भेदम संतं कः करिष्यति।। ९६।।

When that ignorance which is the cause of the differnece between the individual and universal spirit is destroyed finally and for ever who shall ever make that distinction between them which does not exist?

इत्युक्तस्ते मया योगः खांडिक्य परिपृच्छतः।।
संक्षेपविस्तराभ्यां तु किमन्यत्क्रियतां तव।। ९७।।

Thus I have, O Khāṇḍikya, in reply to your question, explained to you what is meant by contemplative devotion both fully and summarily. What else do you wish to hear?"

खांडिक्य उवाच

कथिते योगसद्भावे सर्वमेव कृतं मम।।
तवोपदेशेनाशेषो नष्टश्चित्तमलो यतः।। ९८।।

Khāṇḍikya replied to Keśidhvaja and said :—The explanation, that has been given by you of the real nature of contemplative devotion, has satisfied all my wishes and removed all impurity from my mind.

ममेति यन्मया चोक्तमसदेतन्न चान्यथा।।
नरेंद्र गदितुं शक्यमपि विज्ञेयवेदिभिः।। ९९।।

The expression 'mine' that I have been accustomed to use is untruth and cannot be otherwise declared by those who know what is to be known.

अहं ममेत्यविद्येयं व्यवहारस्तथानयोः।।
परमार्थस्त्वसंलापो गोचरे वचसां न यः।। १००।।

The words 'I' and 'mine' constitute ignorance; but practice is influenced by ignorance. Supreme truth cannot be defined for it is not to be explained by words.

तद्गच्छ श्रेयसे सर्वं ममैतद्भवता कृतम्।।
यद्विमुक्तिप्रदो योगः प्रोक्तः केशिध्वजाऽव्ययः।। १०१।।

Depart, therefore, Keśidhvaja; you have done all that is necessary for my real happiness, in teaching me contemplative devotion, the exhaustible bestower of liberation from existence."

श्रीपराशर उवाच

यथार्हं पूजया तेन खांडिक्येन स पूजितः।।
आजगाम पुरं ब्रह्मंस्ततः केशिध्वजो नृपः।। १०२।।

After receiving becoming homage from Khāṇḍikya, Keśidhvaja came back to his capital.

खांडिक्योऽपि सुतं कृत्वा राजानां योगसिद्धये।।
वनं जगाम गोविंदे विनिवेशितमानसः।। १०३।।

And having made his son Rājā he repaired to woods to accomplish his devotions, his whole mind being intent on Govinda.

तत्रैकांतमतिर्भूत्वा यमादिगुणसंयुतः।।
विष्ण्वाख्ये निर्मले ब्रह्मण्यवाप नृपतिर्लयम्।। १०४।।

His whole mind being devoted to one object only and being purified by the practice of self-restraint, self-control and the rest he obtained absorption into the pure and perfect spirit which is termed Viṣṇu.

केशिध्वजो विमुक्त्यर्थं स्वकर्मक्षपणोन्मुखः।।
बुभुजे विषयान्कर्म चक्रे चानभिसंहितम्।। १०५।।

And in order to obtain liberation Keśi-dhvaja became averse from his own perishable works and lived amidst objects of sense and practised religious rites without expecting any benefit thereform.

अकल्याणोपभोगैश्च क्षीणपापोऽमलस्तथा।।
अवाप सिद्धिमत्यंतां तापक्षयफलां द्विज।। १०६।।

Being freed from all sins by pure and auspicious fruition he obtained that perfection which removes all miseries.

।। इति श्रीविष्णुमहापुराणे षष्ठेंशे सप्तमोऽध्यायः।। ७।।

अथ षष्ठेंशेः अष्टमोऽध्यायः

Part VI : Section 8

श्रीपराशर उवाच

इत्येष कथितस्सम्यक् तृतीयः प्रतिसञ्चरः।।
आत्यंतिको विमुक्तिर्या लयो ब्रह्मणि शाश्वते।। १।।

Parāśara said :—I have thus explained to you the third kind of worldly dissolution, that which is absolute and final which is liberation and resolution into eternal spirit.

सर्गश्च प्रतिसर्गश्च वंशमन्वंतराणि च।।
वंशानुचरितं चैव भवतो गदितं मया।। २।।

I have related unto you the primary and secondary creation, the families of patriarchs, the periods of the Manwantaras and the genealogical histories of the kings.

पुराणं वैष्णवं चैतत्सर्वकिल्बिषनाशनम्।।
विशिष्टं सर्वशास्त्रेभ्यः पुरुषार्थोपपादकम्।। ३।।

तुभ्यं यथावन्मैत्रेय प्रोक्तं शुश्रूषवेऽव्ययम्।।
यदन्यदपि वक्तव्यं तत्पृच्छाद्य वदामि ते।। ४।।

I have described briefly to you, who were desirous of hearing it, the imperishable Vaiṣṇava Purāṇa which destroys all sins, the most excellent of all sacred writings and the means of attaining the great end of man. If you have any thing else to ask, put the question and I will answer it.

मैत्रेय उवाच

भगवन्कथितं सर्वं यत्पृष्टोसि मया मुने।।
श्रुतं चैतन्मया भक्त्या नान्यत्प्रष्टयमस्ति मे।। ५।।

Maitreya said :—Holy preceptor, you have indeed said unto me all I wished to know and I listened to it with devoted attention, O great saint, all my doubts have been removed and my heart has been purified.

विच्छिन्नास्सर्वसंदेहा वैमल्यं मनसः कृतम्।।
त्वत्प्रसादान्मया ज्ञाता उत्पत्तिस्थितिसंक्षयाः।। ६।।

By thy favour, I have been acquainted with the account of creation, preservation and destruction.

ज्ञातश्च त्रिविधो राशिश्शक्तिश्च त्रिविधा गुरो।।
विज्ञाता सा च कार्त्स्न्येन त्रिविधा भावभावना।। ७।।

I have also learnt from you of Viṣṇu in his collective four-fold form; his three energies, and the three modes of apprehending the object of contemplation.

त्वत्प्रसादान्मया ज्ञातं ज्ञेयमन्यैरलं द्विज।।
यदेतदखिलं विष्णोर्जगन्न व्यतिरिच्यते।। ८।।

By thy favour I have acquired a thorough knowledge of all this and there is nothing else worthy to be known when it is once understood that Viṣṇu and his world are not mutually distinct.

कृतार्थोहमसंदेहस्त्वत्प्रसादान्महामुने ।।
वर्णधर्मा दयो धर्मा विदिता यदशेषतः ।। ९ ।।

By your kindness, O great Muni, you have removed all my doubts since you have instructed in the duties of the several tribes and in other deities; the nature of active life and discontinuance of action and derivation of all that exists from works.

प्रवृत्तं च निवृत्तं च ज्ञानं कर्ममयाखिलम् ।।
प्रसीद विप्रप्रवर नान्यत्प्रष्टव्यमस्ति मे ।। १० ।।

And I have nothing else to enquire of you, O Venerable Brāhmin; and pardon me, if by answering to my questions you have been fatigued in any way.

यदस्य कथनायासैर्योजितोऽसि मया गुरो ।।
तत्क्षम्यतां विशेषोस्ति न सतां पुत्रशिष्ययोः ।। ११ ।।

Pardon me for the trouble I have given you through that amiable quality of the virtuous which makes no distinction between a disciple and a child.

श्रीपराशर उवाच

एतत्ते यन्मयाख्यातं पुराणं वेदसंमतम् ।।
श्रुतेऽस्मिन्सर्वदोषोत्थः पापराशिः प्रणश्यति ।। १२ ।।

Parāśara said :—I have related to you this Purāṇa which is equally as sacred as the Vedas by hearing which all sins are expatiated.

सर्गश्च प्रतिसर्गश्च वंशमन्वंतराणि च ।।
वंशानुचरितं कृत्स्नं मयाऽत्र तव कीर्त्तितम् ।। १३ ।।

अत्र देवास्तथा दैत्या गंधर्वोरगराक्षसाः ।।
यक्ष विद्याधरास्सिद्धाः कथ्यंतेऽप्सरसस्तथा ।। १४ ।।

मुनयो भावितात्मानः कथ्यंते तपसान्विताः ।।
चातुर्वण्यं तथा पुंसां विशिष्टचरितानि च ।। १५ ।।

पुण्याः प्रदेशा मेदिन्याः पुण्या नद्योऽथ सागराः ।।
पर्वताश्च महापुण्याश्चरितानि च धीमताम् ।। १६ ।।

वर्णधर्मादयो धर्मावेदशास्त्राणि कृत्स्नशः ।।
येषां संस्मरणात्सद्यस्सर्वपापैः प्रमुच्यते ।। १७ ।।

In this, have been described to you the primary and secondary creation, the families of the patriarchs, the Manwantaras, the regal dynasties; the celestials, Daityas, Gandharvas, serpents, Rākṣasas, Yakṣas, Vidyādharas, Siddhas, and heavenly nymphs; ascetics, endowed with spiritual wisdom and practisers of devotion, the distinctions of four castes, and the actions of the most eminent amongst men; holy places on the earth, holy rivers and oceans, sacred mountains, and legends of the truly wise, the deities of the different tribes and observances enjoined in the Vedas.

उत्पत्तिस्थितिनाशानां हेतुर्यो जगतोऽव्ययः ।।
स सर्वभूतस्सर्वात्मा कथ्यते भगवान्हरिः ।। १८ ।।

अवशेनापि यन्नाम्नि कीर्त्तिते सर्वपातकैः ।।
पुमान्विमुच्यते सद्यस्सिंहत्रस्तैर्मृगैरिव ।। १९ ।।

By hearing this, all sins are obliterated. In this also the glorious Hari has been revealed the cause of the creation, preservation and destruction of the world; the soul of all things and himself all things; by the repetition of whose name man is freed from all sins which fly to the wolves that are frightened by a lion.

यन्नामकीर्त्तनं भक्त्या विलायनमनुत्तमम् ।।
मैत्रेयाशेषपापानां धातूनामिव पावकः ।। २० ।।

The repetition of his name with devout faith is the best remover of all sins, destroying them as fire purifies the metal from the dross.

कलिकल्मषमत्युग्रं नरकार्त्तिप्रदं नृणाम् ।।
प्रयाति विलयं सद्यस्सकृद्यत्र च संस्मृते ।। २१ ।।

By the mere recollection of the name of Hari all the stains of Kali Yuga are removed and piety is increased.

हिरण्यगर्भदेवेंद्ररुद्रादित्याश्विवायुभिः ।।
पावकैर्वसुभिस्साध्यैर्विश्वेदेवादिभिस्सुरैः ।। २२ ।।

यक्षरक्षोरगैस्सिद्धैर्दैत्यगंधर्वदानवैः ।।
अप्सरोभिस्तथा तारानक्षत्रैस्सकलैर्ग्रहैः ।। २३ ।।

सप्तर्षिभिस्तथा धिष्ण्यैर्धिष्ण्याधिपतिभिस्तथा ।।
ब्राह्मणाद्यैर्मनुष्यैश्च तथैव पशुभिर्मृगैः ।। २४ ।।

सरीसृपैर्विहंगैश्च पलाशाद्यैर्महीरुहैः ।।
वनाग्निसागरसरित्पातालैस्सुराग्निभिः ।। २५ ।।

शब्दादिभिश्च सहितं ब्रह्मांडमखिलं द्विज ।।
मेरोरिवाणुर्यस्यैतद्यन्मयं च द्विजोत्तम ।। २६ ।।
स सर्वः सर्ववित्सर्वस्वरूपो रूपवर्जितः ।।
भगवान्कीर्त्तितो विष्णुरत्र पापप्रणाशनः ।। २७ ।।

That Hari, who is all existing things, who is Hiraṇyagarbha, Indra, Rudra, the Ādityas, the Aśvins, the winds, the Kinnaras, the Vasus, the Sāddhas, Viśvadevas the celestials, the Yakṣas, serpents, Rākṣasas, the Siddhas, Daityas, Gandharvas, Dānavas, nymphs, the stars asterism, planets, the seven Ṛṣis, the regents and warders of the quarters, men, Brāhmaṇas, and the rest, animals tame and wild, insects; birds, ghosts and goblins, trees, mountains, woods, river, oceans, regions living underneath the earth, the divisions of the earth and all perceptible object—he who is identical with all things, who knoweth all things, who is the form of all things being himself without form and who is everything from the mount Meru to an atom, he the glorious Viṣṇu and the destroyer of all sins, is described in this Purāṇa.

यदश्वमेधावभृथे स्नातः प्राप्नोति वै फलम् ।।
मानवस्तदवाप्नोति श्रुत्वैतन्मुनिसत्तम ।। २८ ।।
प्रयागे पुष्करे चैव कुरुक्षेत्रे तथाऽर्णवे ।।
कृतोपवासः प्राप्नोति तदस्य श्रवणान्नरः ।। २९ ।।

The reward, which one obtains by hearing this Purāṇa, is equal to that obtained by the performance of a horse-sacrifice or by fasting at the holy places of Prayāga, Puṣkara, Kurukṣetra or Arbuda.

यदग्निहोत्रे सुहुते वर्षेणाप्नोति मानवः ।।
महापुण्यफलं विप्र तदस्य श्रवणात्सकृत् ।। ३० ।।

Hearing this Purāṇa once only is as efficacious as offering oblations in a perpetual fire for one year.

यज्ज्येष्ठशुक्लद्वादश्यां स्नात्वा वै यमुनाजले ।।
मथुरायां हरिं दृष्ट्वा प्राप्नोति पुरुषः फलम् ।। ३१ ।।
तदाप्नोत्यखिलं सम्यगध्यायं यश्शृणोति वै ।।
पुराणस्यास्य विप्रर्षे केशवार्पितमानसः ।। ३२ ।।

The man, who having controlled his passions, bathes at Mathurā on the twelfth day of the month of Jyeṣṭha and beholds the image of Hari, obtains a great reward and so does he who with his mind devoted to Keśava, recites this Purāṇa.

यमुनासलिलस्नातः पुरुषो मुनिसत्तम ।।
ज्येष्ठामूले सिते पक्षे द्वादश्यां समुपोषितः ।। ३३ ।।

समभ्यर्च्याच्युतं सम्यङ् मथुरायां समाहितः ।।
अश्वमेधस्य यज्ञस्य प्राप्नोत्यविकलं फलम् ।। ३४ ।।

आलोक्यर्द्धिमथान्येषामुन्नीतानां स्ववंशजैः ।।
एतत्किलोचुरप्येषां पितरः सपितामहाः ।। ३५ ।।

कच्चिदस्मत्कुले जातः कालिंदीसलिलाप्लुतः ।।
अर्चयिष्यति गोविंदं मथुरायामुपोषितः ।। ३६ ।।

ज्येष्ठामूले सिते पक्षे केनैवं वयमप्युत ।।
परामृद्धिमवाप्स्यामस्तारितास्स्वकुलोद्भवैः ।। ३७ ।।

The man, who bathes in the river Yamunā, on the twelfth lunation of the light fortnight of the month in which the moon is in the mansion Jyeṣṭha, and who fasts and worships, Acyuta in the city of Mathurā, receives the recompense of an uninterrupted horse-sacrifice. Beholding the ancestors of some eminent amongst men, attaining prosperity by the pious observances of their descendants, another man's parents and their parents exclaim, 'If any of our descendants, having bathed in the Yamunā and fasted, worships Govinda in Mathurā, in the light fortnight of Jyeṣṭha, he will secure for us an elevated position."

ज्येष्ठामूले सिते पक्षे समभ्यर्च्य जनार्दनम् ।।
धन्यानां कुलजः पिंडान्यमुनायां प्रदास्यति ।। ३८ ।।

Having worshipped Janārddana in the light fortnight of Jyeṣṭha a man of good birth will offer cakes to his fortunate ancestors in the Yamunā.

तस्मिन्काले समभ्यर्च्य तत्र कृष्णं समाहितः ।।
दत्वा पिंडं पितृभ्यश्च यमुनासलिलाप्लुतः ।। ३९ ।।

यदाप्नोति नरः पुण्यं तारयन्स्वपितामहान् ।।
श्रुत्वाध्यायं तदाप्नोति पुराणस्यास्य शक्तितः ।। ४० ।।

एतत्संसारभीरूणां परित्राणमनुत्तमम्।।
श्राव्याणां परमं श्राव्यं पवित्राणामनुत्तमम्।। ४१।।

By reading with devotion one section of this Purāṇa one can acquire the same merit which he will reap by bathing in the Yamunā during the light fortnight of Jyeṣṭha, by giving cakes to the manes and worshipping Janārddana with a devoted merit.

दुःस्वप्ननाशनं नृणां सर्वदुष्टनिबर्हणम्।।
मंगले मंगलानां च पुत्रसंपत्प्रदायकम्।। ४२।।

Those, who have fallen into the ocean of wordliness and been stricken with terror, may be liberated by reading this Purāṇa which frees one from bad dreams and imperfections.

इदमार्षं पुरा प्राह ऋभवे कमलोद्भवः।।
ऋभुः प्रियव्रतायाह स च भागुरयेऽब्रवीत्।। ४३।।

This Purāṇa was originally composed by the Ṛṣi Nārāyaṇa and was communicated by Brahmā to Ṛbhu; he described it to Pryavrata who again related it to Bhāgurī.

भागुरिस्तंभमित्राय दधीचाय स चोक्तवान्।।
सारस्वताय तेनोक्तं भृगुस्सारस्वतेन च।। ४४।।

भृगुणा पुरुकुत्साय नर्मदायै स चोक्तवान्।।
नर्मदा धृतराष्ट्राय नागायापूरणाय च।। ४५।।

ताभ्यां च नागराजाय प्रोक्तं वासुकये द्विज।।
वासुकिः प्राह वत्साय वत्सश्चाश्वतराय वै।। ४६।।

कंबलाय च तेनोक्तमेलापुत्राय तेन वै।। ४७।।
पातलं समनुप्राप्तं ततो वेदशिरा मुनिः।।
प्राप्तवानेतदखिलं स च प्रमतये ददौ।। ४८।।

Bhāgurī recited it to Tambhamitra, and he to Dadhīca, who gave it to Sārasvata. Bhṛgu received it, who imparted it to Purukutsa and he taught it to Narmadā. The goddess gave it to the Nāga King, Dhṛtarāṣtra and to Purāṇa of the same race, by whom it was given to their king Vāsuki. He imparted it to Vatsa and he to Aśavtara from whom it successively proceeded the Kambala and Elāputra. When the ascetic Vedaśirās descended to Pātāla, he there received the whole Purāṇa from the Nāgas and communicated it to Pramati.

दत्तं प्रमतिना चैतज्जातुकर्णाय धीमते।।
जातुकर्णेन चैवोक्तमन्येषां पुण्यकर्मणाम्।। ४९।।

Pramati imparted it to the wise Jātukarṇa and he taught it to many other holy person.

पुलस्त्यवरदानेन ममाप्येतत्स्मृतिं गतम्।।
मयापि तूभ्यं मैत्रेय यथावत्कथितं त्विदम्।। ५०।।

By the blessing of Vasiṣtha I have been acquainted with it and I have faithfully related it to you.

त्वमप्येतच्छिनीकाय कलेरंते वदिष्यसि।। ५१।।

O Maitreya, you will teach it at the end of the Kali age to Samika.

इत्येतत्परमं गुह्यं कलिकल्मषनाशनम्।।
यश्शृणोति नरो भक्त्या सर्वपापैः प्रमुच्यते।। ५२।।

Whoever hears this great mystery which removes the stain of Kali shall be freed from his sins.

समस्ततीर्थस्नानानि समस्तामरसंस्तुतिः।।
कृता तेन भवेदेतद्यश्शृणोति दिनेदिने।। ५३।।

He who hears this every day acquits himself of his obligations to his manes, celestials and men.

कपिलादानजनितं पुण्यमत्यंतदुर्लभम्।।
श्रुत्वैतस्य दशाध्यायानवाप्नोति न संशयः।। ५४।।

Hearing ten chapters of this Purāṇa one obtains the rare and great merit that a man acquires by the gift of a brown cow.

यस्त्वेतत्सकलं शृणोति पुरुषः कृत्वा मनस्यच्युतं
सर्वं सर्वमयं समस्तजगतामाधारमात्माश्रयम्।।
ज्ञानज्ञेयमनादिमंतरहितं सर्वामराणां हितं स प्राप्नोति
न संशयो स्त्यविकलं यद्वाजिमेधे फलम्।।५५।।

He who hears the whole of this Purāṇa meditating on his mind, Acyuta, who is all things and of whom all things are made, who is the stay of the whole universe—the asylum of spirit; who is knowledge and that which is to be known; who is without beginning or end and the benefactor of the celestials—certainly obtains the reward which can be acquired by the uninterrupted celebration of the horse-sacrifice.

यत्रादौ भगवांश्चराचरगुरुर्मध्ये तथांते च स
ब्रह्मज्ञानमयोऽच्युतोऽखिलजगन्मध्यांतसर्गप्रभुः।।
तत्सर्वं पुरुषः पवित्रममलं शृण्वन्पठन्वाचयन्-
प्राप्नोत्यस्ति न तत्फलं त्रिभुवनेष्वेकांतसिद्धिर्हरिः।।५६।।

He who recites and retains with faith this Purāṇa in the beginning, middle and end of which is described the glorious Acyuta, the lord of the universe in every stage—the master of all that is stationary or movable composed of spiritual knowledge acquires such purity as exists not in any world the eternal state of perfection which is Hari.

यस्मिन्न्यस्तमतिर्न याति नरकं स्वर्गोऽपि यच्चिंतने विघ्नो
यत्र निवेशितात्ममनसो ब्राह्मोऽपि लोकोऽल्पकः।।
मुक्तिं चेतसि यस्स्थितो मलधियां पुंसां ददात्यव्ययः
किं चित्रं यदघं प्रयाति विलयं तत्राच्युते कीर्त्तिते।।५७।।

यज्ञैर्यज्ञविदो यजंति सततं यज्ञेश्वरं कर्मिणो
यं वै ब्रह्ममयं परावरमयं ध्यायंति च ज्ञानिनः।।
यं संचिंत्य न जायते न म्रियते नो वर्द्धते हीयते
नैवासन्न च सद्भवत्यति ततः किं वा हरेश्श्रूयताम्।।५८।।

कव्यं यः पितृरूपधृग्विधिहुतं हव्यं च भुंक्ते
विभुर्देवत्वे भगवाननादिनिधनस्स्वाहास्वधासंज्ञिते।।
यस्मिन्ब्रह्मणि सर्वशक्तिनिलये मानानि नो मानिनां
निष्ठायै प्रभवंति हंति कलुषं श्रोत्रं स यातो हरिः।।५९।।

The man who fixes his mind on Acyuta does not go to hell : he who meditates upon him considers even celestial bliss as an impediment; he, in whose mind he abides, thinks little of the region of Brahmā; for when present in the minds of those who are pure, he bestows upon them eternal freedom. What wonder is there that all sins shall be removed by chanting the name of this Viṣṇu? What else should be heard of but that Hari, whom, those devoted to acts worship with sacrifices continually as the god of sacrifice; whom those devoted to meditation contemplate as primary and secondary composed of spirit; by obtaining whom man is not born, nor nourished nor subjected to death; who is both cause and effect; who as the progenitors receives the libations made to them; who, as the gods accepts the offerings addressed to them, the glorious being who is without beginning or end; whose name is both Swāhā and Swadhā; who is the asylum of all spiritual power; in whom the limits of finite, things cannot be measured, and who, when he enters the ear destroys all sin.

नांतोस्ति यस्य न च यस्य समुद्भवोऽस्ति
वृद्धिर्न यस्य परिणामविवर्जितस्य।।
नापक्षयं च समुपैत्यविकारि वस्तु
यस्तं नतोस्मि पुरुषोत्तममीशमीड्यम्।।६०।।

Salutation unto the first of gods, Puruṣottama who is without end and beginning, without growth and decay and death, who is substance that knows no change.

तस्यैव योनु गुणभुग्बहुधैक एव
शुद्धोप्यशुद्ध इव भाति हि मूर्त्तिभेदैः।।
ज्ञानान्वितस्सकलसत्त्वविभूतिकर्त्ता
तस्मै नमोस्तु पुरुषाय सदाव्ययाय।।६१।।

Salutation unto that undecaying Puruṣa, Viṣṇu who assumed sensible qualities, who though pure became as if impure, assuming various shapes, who is gifted with divine wisdom and who is the lord of the preservation of all creatures.

ज्ञानप्रवृत्तिनियमैक्यमयाय पुंसो
भोगप्रदानपटवे त्रिगुणात्मकाय।।
अव्याकृताय भवभावनकारणाय
वंदे स्वरूपभवनाय सदाऽजराय।।६२।।

Salutation unto him who is the instrument of meditative wisdom and active virtue, who confers enjoyments upon human beings; who is identical with three-fold qualities, who is without any change and is the cause of the evolution of the world and who is without any birth or decay.

व्योमानिलाग्निजलभूरचनामयाय
शब्दादिभोग्यविषयोपनयक्षमाय।।
पुंसस्समस्तकरणैरुपकारकाय व्यक्ताय
सूक्ष्मबृहदात्मवते नतोस्मि।। ६३।।

Salutation unto him who is called heaven, air, fire, water, earth and ether who confers all objects that satisfy sense, who benefits mankind, and who is perceptible, subtle, and imperceptible.

इति विविधमजस्य यस्य रूपं
प्रकृतिपरात्ममयं सनातनस्य।।
प्रदिशतु भगवानशेषपुंसां
हरिरपजन्मजरादिकां स सिद्धिम्।। ६४।।

May that unborn eternal Hari, who is seen in manifold forms, whose essence consists of both nature and spirit, confer upon humanity that blessed confidition which is without birth or decay.

।। इति श्रीविष्णुमहापुराणे षष्ठेंशेऽष्टमोऽध्यायः।। ८।।

।। समाप्तोऽयं षष्ठांशः।।

।। इति श्रीविष्णुमहापुराणं समाप्तम्।।